The Museum of
Broadcast Communications

Encyclopedia of
Radio

The Museum of Broadcast Communications

Encyclopedia of Radio

VOLUME 2

F–N

Editor
CHRISTOPHER H. STERLING

Consulting Editor
MICHAEL C. KEITH

FITZROY DEARBORN
AN IMPRINT OF THE TAYLOR & FRANCIS GROUP

NEW YORK • LONDON

Published in 2004 by
Fitzroy Dearborn
An imprint of the Taylor and Francis Group
29 West 35th Street
New York, NY 10001

Published in Great Britain by
Fitzroy Dearborn
An imprint of the Taylor and Francis Group
11 New Fetter Lane
London EC4P 4EE

10 9 8 7 6 5 4 3 2 1

Library of Congress Cataloging-in-Publication Data

The Museum of Broadcast Communications encyclopedia of radio / editor,
Christopher H. Sterling ; consulting editor, Michael Keith.
    p. cm.
 ISBN 1-57958-249-4 (set : alk. paper) -- ISBN 1-57958-431-4 (vol. 1 :
alk. paper) -- ISBN 1-57958-432-2 (vol. 2 : alk. paper) -- ISBN
1-57958-452-7 (vol. 3 : alk. paper)
 1. Radio--Encyclopedias. 2. Radio programs--Encyclopedias. I.
Sterling, Christopher H., 1943- II. Museum of Broadcast Communications.
III. Title.
 TK6544.M84 2004
 384.54'03--dc22
                  2003015683

First published in the USA and UK 2004

Typeset by Andrea Rosenberg
Printed by Edwards Brothers
Cover design by Peter Aristedes, Chicago Advertising and Design, Chicago, Illinois

Cover photos: (from upper left): Guglielmo Marconi; *Let's Pretend*; Aimee Semple McPherson; Casey Kasem; Mary Margaret McBride; A. Atwater Kent; Larry King; Kay Kyser; Rush Limbaugh; Huey Long

CONTENTS

ADVISERS

Stanley R. Alten
Syracuse University

Frank J. Chorba
Washburn University

Lynn A. Christian
International Radio Consultant

Ed Cohen
Clear Channel Broadcasters

Norman Corwin
Radio Playwright

Susan J. Douglas
University of Michigan

James E. Fletcher
University of Georgia

Robert S. Fortner
Calvin College

Stan Freberg
Radio Producer

Donald G. Godfrey
Arizona State University

Marty Halperin
Pacific Pioneer Broadcasters

Gordon H. Hastings
Broadcasters' Foundation

Robert Henabery
Radio Producer

Robert L. Hilliard
Emerson College

Michele Hilmes
University of Wisconsin, Madison

Chuck Howell
Library of American Broadcasting
University of Maryland

Stanley Hubbard
Hubbard Communications

John D. Jackson
Concordia University

Jack Mitchell
University of Wisconsin, Madison

Graham Mytton
BBC World Service (ret.)

Horace Newcomb
Director, Peabody Awards
University of Georgia

Peter B. Orlik
Central Michigan University

Ed Shane
Shane Media Services

Marlin R. Taylor
XM Satellite Radio

CONTRIBUTORS

Michael H. Adams
Alan B. Albarran
Pierre Albert
Craig Allen
Steven D. Anderson
Larry Appelbaum
Edd Applegate
Sousan Arafeh
John S. Armstrong
Philip J. Auter
Robert K. Avery
Glenda R. Balas
Mary Christine Banwart
Warren Bareiss
Ray Barfield
Kyle S. Barnett
Douglas L. Battema
Mary E. Beadle
Christine Becker
Johnny Beerling
Alan Bell
Louise Benjamin
ElDean Bennett
Marvin Bensman
Jerome S. Berg
Rosemary Bergeron
William L. Bird, Jr.
Howard Blue
A. Joseph Borrell
Douglas A. Boyd
John Bradford
L. Clare Bratten
Mark Braun
Jack Brown
Michael Brown
Robert J. Brown
Donald R. Browne
John H. Bryant
Joseph G. Buchman
Karen S. Buzzard
Paul Brian Campbell
Dom Caristi
Ginger Rudeseal Carter
Dixon H. Chandler II
Frank J. Chorba
Lynn A. Christian

Claudia Clark
Kathleen Collins
Jerry Condra
Harold N. Cones
Bryan Cornell
Elizabeth Cox
Steve Craig
Tim Crook
Marie Cusson
Keri Davies
E. Alvin Davis
J.M. Dempsey
Corley Dennison
Neil Denslow
Steven Dick
John D.H. Downing
Pamela K. Doyle
Christina S. Drale
Susan Tyler Eastman
Bob Edwards
Kathryn Smoot Egan
Lyombe Eko
Sandra L. Ellis
Ralph Engelman
Erika Engstrom
Stuart L. Esrock
Charles Feldman
Michel Filion
Howard Fink
Seth Finn
Robert G. Finney
Margaret Finucane
James E. Fletcher
Corey Flintoff
Joe S. Foote
Robert C. Fordan
Robert S. Fortner
James C. Foust
Ralph Frasca
James A. Freeman
Elfriede Fürsich
Charles F. Ganzert
Ronald Garay
Philipp Gassert
Judith Gerber
Norman Gilliland

Donald G. Godfrey
Douglas Gomery
Jim Grubbs
Joanne Gula
Paul F. Gullifor
Linwood A. Hagin
Donna L. Halper
Tona J. Hangen
Margot Hardenbergh
Jeffrey D. Harman
Dorinda Hartmann
Gordon H. Hastings
Joy Elizabeth Hayes
John Allen Hendricks
Alexandra Hendriks
Ariana Hernandez-Reguant
Robert L. Hilliard
Jim Hilliker
Michele Hilmes
John Hochheimer
Jack Holgate
Herbert H. Howard
Chuck Howell
Kevin Howley
W.A. Kelly Huff
Peter E. Hunn
John D. Jackson
Randy Jacobs
Glen M. Johnson
Phylis Johnson
Sara Jones
Lynda Lee Kaid
Stephen A. Kallis, Jr.
Steve Kang
Michael C. Keith
Ari Kelman
Colum Kenny
John Michael Kittross
Frederica P. Kushner
Philip J. Lane
Matthew Lasar
Laurie Thomas Lee
Renée Legris
Frederic A. Leigh
Lawrence W. Lichty
Lucy A. Liggett
Val E. Limburg
Robert Henry Lochte
Jason Loviglio
Gregory Ferrell Lowe
Christopher Lucas

Mike Mashon
Marilyn J. Matelski
Peter E. Mayeux
Dennis W. Mazzocco
Thomas A. McCain
Jeffrey M. McCall
David McCartney
Tom McCourt
Brad McCoy
Allison McCracken
Drew O. McDaniel
Michael A. McGregor
Robert McKenzie
Elizabeth McLeod
Mike Meeske
Fritz Messere
Colin Miller
Toby Miller
Bruce Mims
Jack Minkow
Jack Mitchell
Jason Mittell
Barbara Moore
Matthew Murray
Graham Mytton
Gregory D. Newton
Greg Nielsen
D'Arcy John Oaks
William F. O'Connor
Cary O'Dell
Robert M. Ogles
Ryota Ono
Peter B. Orlik
Pierre-C. Pagé
Brian T. Pauling
Manjunath Pendakur
Douglas K. Penisten
Stephen D. Perry
Patricia Phalen
Steven Phipps
Joseph R. Piasek
Gregory G. Pitts
Mark Poindexter
Tim Pollard
Robert F. Potter
Alf Pratte
Patricia Joyner Priest
Dennis Randolph
Lawrence N. Redd
David E. Reese
Patton B. Reighard

Andre Richte

Edward A. Riedinger

Terry A. Robertson

Melinda B. Robins

América Rodríguez

Eric W. Rothenbuhler

Richard Rudin

Joseph A. Russomanno

Anne Sanderlin

Erica Scharrer

Steven R. Scherer

Karl Schmid

Clair Schulz

Ed Shane

Pam Shane

Mitchell Shapiro

Jason T. Siegel

Ron Simon

B.R. Smith

Ruth Bayard Smith

Lynn Spangler

David R. Spencer

David Spiceland

Laurie R. Squire

Michael Stamm

Christopher H. Sterling

Will Straw

Michael Streissguth

Mary Kay Switzer

Rick Sykes

Marlin R. Taylor

Matt Taylor

Herbert A. Terry

Richard Tiner

Regis Tucci

David E. Tucker

Don Rodney Vaughan

Mary Vipond

Randall Vogt

Ira Wagman

Andrew Walker

Peter Wallace

Jennifer Hyland Wang

Richard Ward

Mary Ann Watson

Brian West

Gilbert A. Williams

Sonja Williams

Wenmouth Williams, Jr.

Roger Wilmut

Stephen M. Winzenburg

Richard Wolff

Roosevelt "Rick" Wright, Jr.

Edgar B. Wycoff

Thimios Zaharopoulos

LIST OF ENTRIES

F

Fadiman, Clifton 1904–1999

U.S. Writer, Editor, and Radio Emcee

Clifton Fadiman came to radio not from newspapers, vaudeville, or Hollywood but from the outwardly quieter world of book and periodical writing, editing, and publishing. As the master of ceremonies of *Information, Please* and other programs between 1938 and the mid-1950s, he used his knowing tone, witty repartee, and fondness for punning to become an appealing advocate of culture, learning, and civilized conversation for the World War II and postwar generations.

Fadiman learned the pleasures of knowledge at an early age. His older brother Edwin taught him to read when he was four, and before his teen years he was absorbing Milton, Homer, Dante, and other classic writers. To support himself during high school and college, he pieced together many jobs, beginning with mixing sodas in his father's Brooklyn drug store and then simultaneously reporting, selling ads, distributing copies, and otherwise helping with his brother's Long Island newspaper. He became a book reviewer for *The Nation* at age 17, and during his Columbia University days he was a ship's chandler, a bookseller, and a paid breaker-in of wealthier students' smoking pipes. By the time he finished his A.B. degree in 1925, he had gained direct experience of popular taste in many fields.

After two years of high school teaching, Fadiman joined Simon and Schuster in 1927, and as general editor there from 1929 to 1935 he made a number of shrewd publication choices that produced best-sellers. At the same time, he lectured at the People's Institute of New York and participated in many public forums, one of which would have a direct bearing on his radio career several years later. In 1934, when he assumed the editorship of *The New Yorker*'s book review page, he also had his first taste of sustained radio work as an on-air book reviewer for WJZ, but that stint lasted only six months. His best radio days were still to come.

In 1938 Dan Golenpaul, a creator of informational radio programs, was brooding over conventional quiz shows, which regularly dragged audience members to the microphone and exposed the shallowness of their knowledge. Golenpaul outlined a fresh approach: invite the public to send in questions to test a panel of experts. In choosing a master of ceremonies, Golenpaul recalled Clifton Fadiman's crisp contribution to a New School for Social Research radio forum on modern literature a few years earlier. Invited to lead the new quiz, Fadiman teasingly framed the questions for a panel gathered to record an audition disc. After some network doubts about public interest, *Information, Please* (titled after telephone operators' then-customary greeting) was first heard on 17 May 1938 on National Broadcasting Company (NBC) Blue. An unexpected hit, it rose to an estimated peak listenership of more than 9 million during its decade on the air and made Clifton Fadiman a popular icon of the intellectual establishment.

While producer Golenpaul battled sponsors' intrusions and brushed aside network directives, Fadiman tweaked the chemistry of the panel, which included newspaper columnist Franklin P. Adams, sportswriter and naturalist John Kiernan, and pianist Oscar Levant. The fourth chair, like the third one when Levant was absent in alternate weeks, was reserved for guest panelists from a wide range of performers, authors, statesmen, and athletes. Fadiman introduced the questions in a tone of mock menace, offering (as a 1941 review put it) an "ingratiating personality, with its intriguing dash of affable arrogance." Seldom missing an opening for a pun, he called Othello's killing of Desdemona an instance of "smother love," and when correspondent John Gunther correctly identified Reza Pahlavi as Iran's head of state, Fadiman pressed the question with "Are you shah?" while Gunther counterpunned, "Sultanly." Years after the program left the air, Fadiman confided that the questions and answers were only "an armature on which to build a sculpture of genuine conversation."

Clifton Fadiman fronted other programs, too. He and composer-conductor Morton Gould led the win-the-war

Clifton Fadiman in 1938
Courtesy AP/Wide World Photos

as a "midcult" peddler of learning to unwashed masses, and more recently critic John Leonard bemoaned Fadiman's "philistine" failure to appreciate William Faulkner's novels. Several generations of readers have been grateful, however, for Fadiman's invitations to learning in *Reading I've Liked* and *The Lifetime Reading Plan,* and listeners to *Information, Please* and *Conversation* discovered that knowledge and wit could be both gratifying and greatly entertaining.

Although the arc of Fadiman's career began and ended in writing and publishing, the middle span made a notable contribution to radio's upward aspirations. In fact, he was most valuable to radio precisely because he was not *from* radio, and for those who wished to condemn broadcasting as merely a noisy, empty-minded enterprise, Clifton Fadiman remained a hard nut to crack.

RAY BARFIELD

Clifton Fadiman. Born in Brooklyn, New York, 15 May 1904. A.B. degree, Columbia University, 1925. Taught at Ethical Culture High School, 1925–27; editor at Simon and Schuster, 1927–35; book editor, *New Yorker* magazine, New York City, 1933–43; debuted on radio doing book reviews, 1934; noted as moderator of *Information, Please,* 1938–48; Book-of-the-Month co-founder and review panelist, 1944–99; member, Board of Editors, Encyclopaedia Britannica, Chicago, 1959–99; Regents Lecturer, University of California, Los Angeles, 1967. Recipient: Award for distinguished service to American literature for radio program, *Information, Please!,* 1940; Clarence Day Award, American Library Association, 1969; Dorothy C. McKenzie Award, Southern California Council on Literature for Children and Young People, 1986; National Book Award for distinguished contribution to American letters, 1993. Died on Sanibel Island, Florida, 20 June 1999.

Radio Series

1938–48   *Information, Please*
1941–42   *Keep 'Em Rolling*
1944–45   *Words at War*
1949   *This is Broadway*
1955   *Monitor*
1954–56   *Conversation*

Television

This Is Show Business, 1949–54, 1956; *Information, Please,* 1952; *First Edition,* 1983–84, 1986

Selected Publications

Reading I've Liked: A Personal Selection, 1941
Party of One, 1955
Any Number Can Play, 1957
The Lifetime Reading Plan, 1960
Enter, Conversing, 1962

entertainment show *Keep 'Em Rolling* on Mutual in 1941–42, and from 1954 to 1956 he hosted NBC's sustaining *Conversation* with author-publisher Bennett Cerf and panel guests. In 1955 he was named a "communicator" for NBC's weekend program *Monitor.* His television contributions included *This Is Show Business* and a short-lived attempt to bring *Information, Please* to the newer medium.

After the mid-1950s, Fadiman largely focused on literary interests. He had been a board member and reviewer for the Book-of-the-Month Club since 1944, and he remained on its board of directors for more than 50 years. Begun in 1949, his "Party of One" column appeared in *Holiday* magazine for a decade. He especially valued his essay on children's literature for the *Encyclopaedia Britannica,* and he continued to assemble anthologies and to write books and essays urging the public to know the pleasures of books, wine, and mathematics.

This man of wit and prodigious memory was genially satirized as the *Duffy's Tavern* habitué Clifton Finnegan, who seemed almost too stupid to breathe. In the intellectually gritty 1950s, Dwight MacDonald more somberly dismissed Fadiman

The New Lifetime Reading Plan (with John S. Major), 4th edition, 1999

Further Reading

Ashley, Sally, *F.P.A.: The Life and Times of Franklin Pierce Adams,* New York: Beaufort Books, 1986

Fadiman, Anne, *Ex Libris: Confessions of a Common Reader,* New York: Farrar Straus and Giroux, 1998; London: Allen Lane, 1999

Kieran, John, *Not under Oath: Recollections and Reflections,* Boston: Houghton Mifflin, 1964

Fairness Doctrine

Controversial Issue Broadcasting Policy

Until 1987 (with related parts lasting until 2000), the Federal Communications Commission (FCC) adhered to a series of policy guidelines collectively called the *fairness doctrine*. These guidelines encouraged stations to cover issues of public controversy, and to provide a variety of points of view on those issues. While they lasted, the policies were among the most controversial of all FCC program regulations.

Origin

A station licensee's duty to present diverse views on public issues was first declared by the Federal Radio Commission in 1928. A dozen years later, however, the FCC reversed direction when it strongly criticized a station for its practice of editorializing. In its 1941 *Mayflower* decision, the FCC concluded that with limited frequencies available for broadcasting, the public interest could not be well served by dedication of a broadcast facility to the support of its own partisan ends. In line with the *Mayflower* decision, broadcasters began to prohibit the sale of commercial time to deal with controversial issues—a policy that also helped them financially since such ads would only serve to anger some listeners and other advertisers.

In 1949 the FCC reversed itself, reconfirming that while stations have an obligation to cover controversial issues of public importance they now could (but did not have to) editorialize. When WHKC in Columbus, Ohio, refused to sell airtime to a labor union, the FCC stated that the station must be sensitive to the problems of public concern in the community and make sufficient time available on a nondiscriminatory basis. The commission concluded that radio stations have the "responsibility for determining the specific program material to be broadcast over their stations." Therefore, they were required to devote broadcast time to "issues of interest in the community served by their stations and [ensure] that such programs be designed so that the public has a reasonable opportunity to

hear different opposing positions on the public issues of interest and importance in the community."

To nail down the proposed new policy on editorializing, the FCC held hearings on the matter. From the hearings came a 1949 statement, *In the Matter of Editorializing by Broadcast Licensees*, which placed two primary obligations on the broadcasters. What would become known later as the "fairness doctrine" required broadcasters (1) to cover controversial issues of public importance, and (2) to provide a reasonable opportunity for the presentation of contrasting viewpoints on those issues.

Development

A decade later, in 1959, Congress entered the fray. Legislators amended Section 315 (the political "equal opportunity" section of the Communications Act) to limit the applicability of the requirement to four types of news programs. At the same time, they made more concrete the broadcaster's responsibility to afford reasonable opportunity for the discussion of conflicting views on issues of public importance. This added phrase would cause considerable legal confusion in the future.

By 1967 the FCC had extended what was now commonly referred to as "the fairness doctrine" to include broadcast advertising of cigarettes, reasoning that because smoking was a controversial health issue, broadcasters were therefore required to provide contrasting viewpoints (This provision lasted until cigarette advertising was removed from the air entirely in the early 1970s.)

Complaining about yet another extension of the fairness doctrine, broadcasters asked what other types of program or advertising might trigger fairness doctrine concerns. To clarify the scope of their doctrine, the FCC instituted a wide-ranging inquiry into the fairness doctrine and its efficacy. As one result, the commission created three "contingent rights of access" policies similar to Section 315: the Zapple rule, the political editorializing rules, and the personal attack rules. The Zapple rule (named for a long-time Senate staff member, Nicholas Zapple, who had been involved with the issue) held that supporters of opposing political candidates must be given approximately the same amount of airtime during election campaigns. In its political editorial rule, the FCC required broadcasters to contact a legally qualified candidate within 24 hours of any station editorial opposing the candidate or endorsing an opponent and to provide a script or tape as well as free time to reply. The political editorial rule pertained only when a station editorial represented the views of the station licensee. Political commentators who were independent of management were subject only to the general fairness doctrine. Finally, the FCC's personal attack rules specified that broadcasters must offer reply time if the honesty, character, or integrity of an identified person or group was attacked during the discussion of a controversial issue of public importance. A person attacked had to be notified within a week of the date, time, and identification of the broadcast. The licensee was required to provide a script, tape, or accurate summary of the attack and offer a reasonable opportunity for the attacked person to respond over the same station at no charge.

The Supreme Court firmly supported the fairness doctrine's constitutionality in its 1969 landmark decision in *Red Lion Broadcasting Co. v FCC*. Broadcasters argued that the number of commercial radio and TV stations in the country was higher than that of newspapers (for which no such "fairness" policy existed because of the First Amendment)—and growing. Therefore, they argued that the fairness doctrine was unnecessary because the public suffered no shortage of opportunities to hear different stations and diverse viewpoints. Broadcasters also contended that the fairness doctrine actually "chilled" or curtailed First Amendment rights of broadcasters by encouraging self-censorship—in other words, that many controversial issues might not be covered at all. The Court rejected both of these contentions, asserting that as long as demand for stations exceeded supply (the high sales price of stations was one such indicator), scarcity of spectrum remained, and thus allowed such FCC policies. In addition, the Court ruled that the doctrine did not violate a broadcaster's First Amendment rights since the right of the viewers and listeners to hear diverse viewpoints was paramount to the right of broadcasters to express their views.

Another Supreme Court case decided five years later, *Tornillo v Miami Herald* (1974), however, concluded that a fairness-type of requirement on newspapers in the state of Florida was clearly unconstitutional. Decided by the same court membership as had decided *Red Lion* five years earlier, the decision showed the stark difference in how the law viewed newspaper and broadcast journalists.

About the same time, the FCC adopted another Fairness Report, which reaffirmed the conclusions of its 1949 decision and upheld the application of a general fairness doctrine requirement for broadcast licensees on both statutory and constitutional grounds.

Demise

Despite the FCC's continuing series of reports and codifications of the fairness doctrine requirements through the 1970s, broadcasters still had problems with the doctrine. They continued to argue that it was too difficult to determine what issues were controversial, which viewpoints should be represented, and suggested that the doctrine was having a "chilling" effect on the flow of ideas: broadcasters would be reluctant to cover controversial issues because according to the doctrine they would be required to report "fairly." IN *FCC v League of Women Voters of California* (1984) the Supreme Court concluded that the scarcity rationale underlying the doctrine might be flawed and that the doctrine might be limiting the breadth of public debate. A footnote suggested that the Court awaited some kind of an indication from the FCC as to whether the conditions that had led to the fairness doctrine (and the *Red Lion* decision) had significantly changed. The doctrine was increasingly difficult to enforce and went against the grain of an increasingly deregulatory commission.

Responding to a complaint brought by a group called the Syracuse Peace Council, on 26 October 1984 the FCC concluded that WTVM-TV (a Syracuse, New York, television station owned by Meredith Corporation), had violated the fairness doctrine in its treatment of a controversy surrounding construction of a nuclear power plant, a conclusion that the Meredith Corporation vigorously contested. A few months later the FCC released another in its series of Fairness Reports to publicly reevaluate the need for the doctrine. The commission concluded that:

> On the basis of voluminous factual record compiled in this proceeding, our experience in administering the doctrine and our general expertise in broadcast regulation, we no longer believe that the Fairness Doctrine, as a matter of policy, serves the public interests. In making this determination, we do not question the interest of the listening and viewing public in obtaining access to diverse and antagonistic sources of information. Rather, we conclude that the Fairness Doctrine is no longer a necessary or appropriate means by which to effectuate this interest. We believe that the interest of the public in viewpoint diversity is fully served by the multiplicity of voices in the marketplace today and that the intrusion by government into the content of programming occasioned by the enforcement of the doctrine unnecessarily

restricts the journalistic freedom of broadcasters. Furthermore, we find that the Fairness Doctrine, in operation actually inhibits the presentation of controversial issues of the public importance to the detriment of the public and in degradation of the editorial prerogative of broadcast journalists (FCC, *Inquiry into Fairness Doctrine Obligations of Broadcast Licensees*, 102 FCC 2d 145, 1985).

The report argued that (1) the doctrine was contrary to the public interest because it "chilled" expression, and, therefore, (2) the doctrine was probably unconstitutional. Despite these conclusions, the FCC retained the doctrine because it doubted that it had the power to abandon it. The FCC's legal advisors concluded that with its 1959 amendments in the 1934 act, Congress had formally incorporated the doctrine into Section 315, and thus the FCC could not remove it. Therefore, the FCC asked Congress to abolish the doctrine; Congress did nothing. Meanwhile, in the *Meredith* case, the FCC was in the awkward position of enforcing a doctrine that it was fervently denouncing. On 19 September 1986 the U.S. Court of Appeals for the District of Columbia (D.C.) Circuit cleared up a legal ambiguity by ruling that the fairness doctrine had never been made a part of the 1934 law but was simply a regulation of the FCC. This meant that the FCC could drop its own regulation.

In the meantime the Meredith Corporation appealed the FCC fairness decision on constitutional grounds. In January 1987 the U.S. Court of Appeals for the D.C. Circuit instructed the FCC to address Meredith's constitutional argument against the fairness doctrine. Faced with this opportunity, on 6 August 1987 the FCC formally announced it would abandon the fairness doctrine on the several bases already argued, chiefly that the doctrine was probably unconstitutional and that it certainly had a chilling effect, exactly opposite from what was intended. The FCC concluded that "the Constitution bars us from enforcing the fairness doctrine," and argued that as the fairness doctrine chilled speech, it could not be construed to be sufficiently narrowly tailored to achieve a substantial government interest—the usual Supreme Court standard for content rules. Therefore, the FCC concluded that the fairness doctrine contravened the public interest.

Shortly after the FCC's decision to drop the fairness doctrine, Congress tried several times to resurrect it by making the doctrine part of federal law. One of the proposed bills stated:

[The fairness doctrine] ha[s] enhanced free speech by securing the paramount right of the broadcast audience to robust debate on issues of public importance; and . . . [it] fairly reflects the statutory obligation of broadcasters under the [Communications] Act to operate in the public interest . . . [The fairness doctrine] strikes a reasonable

balance among the first amendment rights of the public, broadcast licensees, and speakers other than owners of broadcast facilities (H.R. Bill 1934, 100th Congress, 1st Session, proposing new Section 315(a) to the Communications Act, 3 June 1987).

President Reagan vetoed the bill, calling the fairness doctrine a "content-based" regulation and antagonistic to the freedom of expression. In a veto message drafted at least in part by former FCC Chairman Mark Fowler (who had long sought to end the doctrine), Reagan claimed that

S.742 simply cannot be reconciled with the freedom of speech and the press secured by our Constitution. It is, in my judgment, unconstitutional. Well-intentioned as S.742 may be, it would be inconsistent with the First Amendment and with the American tradition of independent journalism. Accordingly, I am compelled to disapprove of this measure (23 *Weekly Compilation of Presidential Documents*, 715–16, 1987).

Congress was unable to override the veto. Attempts to revive the bill in 1989, 1991, and 1993 failed of passage. Such attempts largely ended when Republicans took control of congress in 1994.

The Supreme Court effectively supported the FCC's decision not to continue the doctrine when in 1990 it declined to review a lower court decision upholding the FCC action. Three years later, a federal appeals court decision reaffirmed that the fairness doctrine had been merely a commission policy and not a congressionally mandated law.

Aftermath

After the FCC abandoned the fairness doctrine, it announced it would no longer enforce fairness requirements for broadcast discussions of referenda, initiatives, recall efforts, and bond proposals. However, the commission made clear that its related personal attack, political editorializing, and Zapple rules remained in force. Broadcasters had first asked the FCC to abolish these rules in 1981, following up with at least four more formal requests over the next 16 years; all to no avail.

In December 1998, two leading broadcast trade organizations—the Radio-Television News Directors Association and the National Association of Broadcasters—challenged the constitutionality of the FCC's personal attack and political editorial rules in the U.S. Court of Appeals for the D.C. Circuit. In a series of decisions over the next two years, the FCC was unable to sustain its rules against the Court's firm finding that they appeared to be unconstitutional limits on broadcaster freedom. Angry at the slow moving commission, in October 2000 the court finally ordered that the rules be vacated (dropped) immediately, and the FCC complied. The last vestiges of the long-lasting fairness doctrine were gone.

STEVE KANG

See also Controversial Issues; Editorializing; Federal Communications Commission; Mayflower Decision; Public Interest, Convenience, or Necessity; Red Lion Case

Further Reading

47 USCA section 315 (the "Equal Time" law)
Federal Communications Commission, *Mayflower Broadcasting Corp.*, 8 FCC 333 (1940)
Federal Communications Commission, *In the Matter of Editorializing by Broadcast Licenses*, 13 FCC 1246 (1949)
Federal Communications Commission, *WCBS-TV*, 8 FCC 2d 381 (1967)
Federal Communications Commission, *Letter to Nicholas Zapple*, 23 FCC 2d 707 (1970)
Federal Communications Commission, *Fairness Doctrine and Public Interest Standard* (The Fairness Report), 48 FCC 2d 1 (1974)
Federal Communications Commission, *Memorandum Opinion and Order in Complaint of Syracuse Peace Council against Television Station WTVH*, 2 FCC Rcd 5043 (1987)
President of the United States, Veto Message, 23 Weekly Compilation of Presidential Document 715–16 (1987)
Rowan, Ford, *Broadcast Fairness: Doctrine, Practice, Prospects,* New York: Longman, 1984
Simmons, Steven J., *The Fairness Doctrine and the Media,* Berkeley: University of California Press, 1978
U.S. Congress, United States Senate, Committee on Commerce, *Fairness Doctrine: The FCC's Actions and the Broadcasters' Operations in Connection with the Commission's Fairness Doctrine: Staff Report,* 90th Cong., 2nd Sess., 1968
United States Supreme Court, *Red Lion Broadcasting Co., Inc. v FCC,* 395 US 367 (1969)
United States Supreme Court, *Miami Herald Publishing Co. v Tornillo,* 418 US 241 (1974)
United States Supreme Court, *FCC v League of Women Voters of California,* 468 US 364 (1984)

Family Theater

Radio Drama

Broadcasters have often been criticized for making program decisions based on monetary profit rather than a desire to provide educational and thought-provoking content. But throughout the history of radio broadcasting, some producers have used their talents to create programs designed to educate, enlighten, and assist listeners in coping with the difficult situations that arise in everyday life. *Family Theater,* which became one of the longest running weekly drama anthologies in radio history, was one such program.

On 13 May 1945, the Mutual Broadcasting System broadcast a Mother's Day special with an unusual premise—to unite the country in praying the Holy Rosary. The program featured the Sullivans, a family that had lost five sons in a single naval battle during World War II, and included a guest appearance by Bing Crosby and a message from President Truman. This event was the initiative of Father Patrick Peyton, C.S.C, a priest of the Congregation of the Holy Cross who had immigrated to the U.S. from Ireland in 1928. Inspired by the success of this Mother's Day program, Father Peyton, relying largely on private donations, founded Family Theater Productions in

1947. He enlisted the help of Hollywood stars and other media professionals to produce a weekly half-hour radio drama. The series, called *Family Theater,* premiered as a sustaining program on 13 February 1947 on Mutual. Programs emphasized moral problems, and each installment ended with an encouragement to prayer, using Tennyson's famous words, "More things are wrought by prayer than this world dreams of." Although Father Peyton was a Catholic priest, the dramas, by agreement with the network, were non-sectarian. They emphasized moral themes, but were designed as entertainment programming to appeal to a mass audience. The weekly dramas were supplemented by occasional holiday specials.

One of Mutual's contract provisions was that the series had to include at least one Hollywood star each week. The network's commitment to this series was in airtime alone—Father Peyton promised to pay all production costs. In an effort to help with these costs, stars frequently donated their payment back to the producer.

The first *Family Theater* drama, entitled "Flight From Home," starred Loretta Young, James Stewart, and Don

Ameche, and was written by True Boardman. Subsequent episodes featured Raymond Burr, Bing Crosby, Irene Dunn, Gary Cooper, Gregory Peck, and dozens of other major Hollywood stars. Although the final original production was completed in 1958, *Family Theater* dramas ran for 22 years. When original radio production was halted so that Family Theater Productions could direct its attention to the newer medium of television, the series continued running in repeats on various stations across the country. Many of the programs were rebroadcast as part of a new series called *Marian Theater*. In total, 482 original programs were produced, and, at the height of its popularity, the series ran on 429 stations nationwide. These radio programs were broadcast widely outside of the United States: in Canada, Latin America, Spain, Mozambique, Australia, and the Philippines. *Family Theater* won numerous awards for excellence, from trade associations and private organizations, and from non-Catholic as well as Catholic groups. Its motto became a well-known saying in popular culture, "the family that prays together stays together."

Father Peyton died in 1992, but his work continues in the United States and throughout the world. Family Theater Productions, which is now part of the Holy Cross Family Ministries (www.hcfm.org), has six international offices that produce television and radio programs. As of 2000, a dramatic radio series produced in the United States, called *La Historia*

de Quien Soy (The Story of Who I Am), continues the spirit of *Family Theater*. The Spanish-language drama focuses on the lives of a fictional U.S. Latino family, and explores issues of ethnicity, morality and faith.

PATRICIA PHALEN

See also Drama; Religion on Radio

Announcer
Tony La Frano

Host
Father Patrick Peyton, C.S.C

Producers/Creators
Father Patrick Peyton, C.S.C; Bob Longenecker

Programming History

Mutual Broadcasting Company	13 May 1945 (special Mother's Day Broadcast); 13 February 1947–4 July 1956

Further Reading
Peyton, Patrick J., *All for Her: The Autobiography of Father Patrick Peyton, C.S.C.*, New York: Doubleday, 1967

Fan Magazines

Radio fan magazines serve two popular audiences whose memberships share an intense interest in either the programs and personalities or the technology of radio. The first audience consists of fans who listen to broadcasts, become curious, and seek additional information not provided over the radio. The other group is more concerned with radio's technology, such as amateur and ham radio operators, who are interested in developing and using the technology to both transmit and receive signals using shortwave radio. Both audiences continue to support a number of radio magazines.

Fan magazines enjoyed success because of the large and growing radio audience that was interested in the programs and personalities heard. The magazines were most successful from the mid-1920s through the early 1960s. Fan magazines published a variety of content, including program listings and descriptions. A substantial portion of their content was devoted to radio personalities and included picture stories,

hobbies, home life, and any relevant scandal or gossip. Most of the magazines included reader correspondence. Fan magazines helped audiences keep track of programming and stay interested, and they provided information for interaction among other fans.

The oldest group of radio fans are the amateur and ham radio operators. The American Radio Relay League's (ARRL) monthly magazine, *QST*, started publishing in 1916. *QST* was named for the international signal "QST," which means "attention all stations." Still published by the ARRL, *QST* has for years published product reviews and technical articles. Members share tips and tricks for operating and constructing radios. The difference between *QST* and popular fan magazines is the focus on radio technology rather than content. Because the magazine is published by an organized group, it reports news, legal and regulatory issues, and technical information and performs many of the functions of a trade journal.

Radio News

Cosmopolitan, McClure's, Munsey's, and other general interest magazines provided information about radio in the early 1900s, but it was not until the radio boom of the 1920s that exclusive mass-market radio magazines appeared. The need for a popular publication that served radio audiences was recognized immediately by early broadcasters. For example, KDKA distributed *Radio Broadcasting News* to about 2,000 newspapers. The magazine was developed shortly after the first broadcasts in order to provide background information and program listings that could be published in local newspapers. As radio's popularity increased during the first half of the 1920s, the number of radio magazines grew. By the mid-1920s, there were between 35 and 40 radio magazines serving an audience of nearly 1 million readers. *Radio News* claimed (May 1926) that the top five radio magazines, including *Radio News, Popular Radio, Radio in the Home, Radio Broadcast,* and *Radio Age,* had over half a million readers.

Radio News was one of the first magazines to capitalize on the radio boom and was founded by one of radio's greatest fans, Hugo Gernsback, who was familiar with both publishing and radio. He published a small radio magazine called *Modern Electrics* in New York in the early 1900s as a way to stimulate sales at his radio electronics store. In 1919 Gernsback started *Radio News* as a general interest radio magazine. Like many of the early radio magazines, the content of *Radio News* appealed to a broad audience of radio enthusiasts. Broadcasting was in its developmental stages, but the popular appeal of radio was already evident. *Radio News* was primarily a "booster" for radio, promoting radio to a developing audience of fans. *Radio News* called itself "Radio's Greatest Magazine," and its early content appealed to the amateur operators and listeners who fueled the early 1920s radio craze. Each issue had a Norman Rockwell–like cover with a scene that showed some aspect of radio in modern American life. The magazine was highly illustrated, and the content was diverse. Much of the content targeted amateur operators at a variety of skill levels by providing technical articles on home construction of radios and on the selection of components and equipment. There were regular features offering technical information and articles discussed receiving and transmitting radio signals. *Radio News* also held contests that challenged readers' technical skills with equipment construction and signal reception (DXing). The magazine even offered lessons in Esperanto, promoted as the international language of amateur radio operators.

Radio News promoted radio as a significant social force that served a variety of needs. There were articles about the people who had developed radio and were shaping its future and about the radio celebrities whose voices and sounds were being recognized across the country. The magazine provided station listings and discussed some of the new successful radio stations, including WRNY in New York, where Gernsback delivered a weekly Tuesday night lecture. There were cartoons, poems, and fictional articles in which radio was a central theme. Readers were encouraged to become knowledgeable about radio in a number of ways. Crossword puzzles required readers to know terms and call letters. There were frequent contests, which included submitting drawings of an "ideal" receiving set, composing four-line verses using standard circuit symbols, or identifying errors in the drawings that appeared on the cover of the magazine. *Radio News* sponsored a "radio play" contest and published the works of the winners and finalists.

Radio News also featured a significant amount of advertising. For example, the index of advertisers for the January 1925 issue lists 381 advertisers and includes 180 pages with advertising (out of 240 total). Equipment and services offered by all segments of the emerging radio industry were advertised. There was also a classified advertising section. *Radio News* used product names in some of its construction articles, although it discontinued the practice after Gernsback was accused of selling out to advertisers. In 1926 *Radio News* claimed that it was second only to *Radio Broadcast* (a successful trade magazine) in its volume of advertising.

Radio News enjoyed its greatest success during the chaotic early 1920s. Advertising revenues dropped significantly as the distinction between professionals, amateurs, and listening audiences became more clearly defined. In the early 1930s, *Radio News* narrowed its appeal to the amateur technical audience and continued publishing technical information until in 1959 it became *Electronics World.*

Radio Guide

The successful popular mass-market fan magazines that emerged in the 1930s served the audiences created by broadcasting. There were more than a dozen popular fan magazines published during radio's golden age, including *Movie Radio, Radio Album, Radio Dial, Radio Digest, Radio Guide, Radioland, Radio Mirror,* and *Radio Stars.* These magazines followed the example set by popular movie fan magazines, which focused on personalities, took readers behind the scenes, and always included pictures or portraits of stars on the cover.

Radio Guide is an example of this kind of fan magazine. *Radio Guide* was published weekly by M.L. Annenberg in Chicago beginning in 1932. By 1936 *Radio Guide* was printed in 17 regional editions and was selling 420,000 copies per week, and the content typified the radio fan magazine of the time. Part of the magazine offered stories and pictorials concerning radio personalities. One pictorial feature called the "Radio

Guide Album" included a full-page picture of the cast of a selected network program. There was information and gossip about radio stars and often a short story.

Radio Guide regularly provided short reports about current radio news, shortwave information, and upcoming musical events. Regular features that appeared in the magazine included "Coming Events," "Hits of the Week," "Contests on the Air," "X-word Puzzle," and "Radio Boners." Approximately half of the magazine's content featured a programming guide with day-by-day listings of programs and the stations that aired them. The magazine marked high-quality programs with a star symbol placed next to the listing. Religious programs were identified with a bell symbol. The program section included a log of numerous radio stations, including foreign outlets, and a modest listing of shortwave programs for the week. *Radio Guide* remained an important source of fan support through the early 1940s and laid the groundwork for the same publisher's 1953 creation of the hugely successful *TV Guide*.

Radio Mirror, which started publishing in 1933, changed its name to *TV Radio Mirror* in order to serve the popular interest in television. Fan magazines continued to provide information about radio into the 1960s, but their general content shifted substantially from radio to television. As radio became a medium of music that largely served local markets, the need for mass-market radio fan magazines disappeared.

Web Fan Magazines

The shift from national networks to local programming and the use of syndicated programming have resulted in smaller, more specialized groups of fans for radio programs and fewer opportunities for successful national mass-market fan magazines. A few traditional fan magazines are published in large regional markets, such as the *L.A. Radio Guide* in southern California, but generally the current market for radio fan magazines is limited.

The primary means of reaching fans today is with webpages and *e-zines* (electronic magazines). E-zines are delivered through the internet and presented in formats that resemble traditional fan magazines. Subscriptions are ordered through a webpage. An example is *Krud Radio,* a fan e-zine that offers a humorous look at radio and arrives by e-mail. About.com is accessed through a webpage and offers a "Guide to Radio" that discusses radio news, conducts polls about a variety of radio topics, provides links to internet audio sites, and includes a chat room for discussing radio topics.

Webpages offer fans the same content found in traditional fan magazines but provide a level of interaction not found in traditional magazines. Talk show host Art Bell's webpage logged more than 5.5 million visitors between January 1997 and January 2000, offering program summaries, archives, a chat room, feature articles, links, a studio camera, audio clips, and more.

Fans sometimes establish "unofficial" webpages that target other fans. Howard Stern's show has a number of unofficial webpages. For example, "Heynow's Webpage" offers a collection of Howard Stern RealAudio files. Stern's associate, Fred Norris, known as the King of Mars, has an unofficial fan site that was started because "everyone else on the show has at least one stupid fan page, so why not Fred."

Internet directories of stations and programs are replacing printed directories in fan magazines. Lists of stations and links to internet audio are provided by a number of websites, including RadioLinks.net, Broadcast.com, Macroradio.net, Radio-Stations.net, Netradio.net, Darnell's Black Radio Guide, and the Massachusetts Institute of Technology (MIT) List of Radio Stations.

Amateur and ham radio operators are experiencing a similar change in their fan magazines. There are still a number of specialized periodicals that target amateurs, but the internet is becoming an increasingly important source of information. Most organizations and publishers that produce magazines for this audience also have webpages, including the ARRL. *AntenneX,* a successful magazine that specializes in antennae for amateurs, is now promoting its website, which logged over 2 million visitors between 1997 and early 2003. *Ham Radio Online,* offered by the Virtual Publishing Company, provides technical information, news, opinions, cartoons, on-line discussions, feature stories, up-to-the-minute reports on world disasters, and an on-line newsletter delivered by e-mail.

The internet has revitalized fan interest by providing sites where smaller and more specialized groups of fans can find the content of traditional fan magazines. In addition, the community of fans using the electronic magazines and websites enjoys a level of interaction that traditional magazines could never offer.

MICHAEL BROWN

See also Columnists; DXers/DXing; Ham Radio; Trade Press

Further Reading

Brown, Michael, "Radio Magazines and the Development of Broadcasting: *Radio Broadcast,* and *Radio News,*" *Journal of Radio Studies* 5 (Winter 1998)

Dahlgren, Peter, and Colin Sparks, editors, *Journalism and Popular Culture,* Newbury Park, California: Sage, 1992

Davis, H.P., "American Beginnings," in *Radio and Its Future,* edited by Martin Codel, London: Harper, 1930; reprint, New York: Arno Press, 1971

Douglas, George H., *The Early Days of Radio Broadcasting,* Jefferson, North Carolina: McFarland, 1987

Massie, Keith, and Stephen D. Perry, "Hugo Gernsback and Radio Magazines: An Influential Intersection in Broadcast History," *Journal of Radio Studies* 9 (December 2002)

Maxim, Hiram, "The Radio Amateur," in *Radio and Its Future*, edited by Martin Codel, London: Harper, 1930; reprint, New York: Arno Press, 1971

Peterson, Theodore Bernard, *Magazines in the Twentieth Century*, Urbana: University of Illinois Press, 1968

Rheingold, Howard, *The Virtual Community: Homesteading on the Electronic Frontier*, Reading, Massachusetts: Addison-Wesley 1993

Sova, Harry W., and Patricia L. Sova, editors, *Communication Serials: An International Guide to Periodicals in Communication, Popular Culture, and the Performing Arts*, Virginia Beach, Virginia: Sovacom, 1992

Sterling, Christopher, H., and George Shiers, "Serial Publications," in *History of Telecommunications Technology: An Annotated Bibliography*, Lanham, Maryland: Scarecrow Press, 2000

Wolseley, Roland Edgar, "Digests, Fans, Comics, Sports," in *Understanding Magazines*, by Wolseley, Ames: Iowa State University Press, 1965

Far East Broadcasting Company

U.S.-Based Religious Broadcaster

The Far East Broadcasting Company (FEBC) is an evangelical Christian international radio service that began in Asia and eventually developed stations in much of the world.

Origins

While attending a Bible college in Pasadena in 1934, Robert Bowman became the baritone in a men's quartet that was part of the Haven of Rest radio ministry on KMPC in Los Angeles. The quartet was headed by Paul Myers, known as "First Mate Bob" on the air, and Bowman would often host the program in Myers' absence, thus becoming known as "Second Mate Bobby." He remained with the program for 12 years.

Given his radio experience, Bowman became interested in the potential of radio use by those wishing to reach an international audience with a similar religious message. In 1938 he began initial planning for such an outreach program with John Broger, an actor and producer who was a former classmate of Myers at the Pasadena college. The war intervened and Broger became a communications expert in the Navy. On 20 December 1945, Bowman, Broger, and minister William J. Roberts founded the Far East Broadcasting Company to provide Christian programming in Asia.

After the incorporation of this new venture, Bowman left the Haven of Rest program to become FEBC vice president; Broger was president, Roberts executive secretary. The three agreed that, as Bowman was well known from his years with Haven of Rest, he should head the fund-raising process while Broger sought broadcasting licenses in Asia. As their original aim was to broadcast Christian programs in China, Bowman and Broger worked with the Chicago-based Moody Bible Institute to produce a syndicated radio series, The Call of the Orient. Broger traveled to Shanghai to meet with Christian missionaries, and by June 1946 the China Christian Broadcasting System had been established with plans (never realized) to place stations on the air throughout China. In September Broger was granted a one-year franchise for stations in the Philippines, with the goal of establishing a base for shortwave broadcasting to the rest of Asia.

While Broger was involved in these negotiations, Bowman was raising funds through speaking and singing engagements in churches throughout southern California. He explained that funds were needed for the land, power generators and transmitters, antenna towers, and production equipment needed to put FEBC on the air. In November 1946, FEBC made the final payment for 12.5 acres in Karuhatan (north of Manila) in the Philippines. The next month, the first missionaries traveled to Manila. In April 1947 the first FEBC programs were carried (briefly as it turned out) on local stations in Shanghai, and on 4 July 1948 FEBC's own 1,000-watt station, KZAS (soon changed to DZAS) in Manila was dedicated in what was called Christian Radio City, putting out an AM signal to the metropolitan region. Shortwave capability was added later that year.

Until 1954, Bowman's and Broger's families took 18- to 24-month stints running the station. Bowman's first year was spent attempting to get the one-year franchise extended. With local legal assistance he was able to convince the Philippine Radio Board of Control to grant FEBC its first permanent license.

By July 1949 FEBC had initiated shortwave broadcasts to other parts of Asia from the Philippines, including China and

Russia. (The Shanghai operation had been closed down by the formation of the People's Republic, and listener mail from China disappeared for three decades.) By the end of the year, FEBC was broadcasting in 27 different languages, using station DZH-6 with 10,000 watts.

By the end of 1951, FEBC had five transmitters operating and began broadcasts to Japan that September. Bowman traveled to the U.S. to continue fund-raising efforts to expand the operation, but in 1953 returned to Manila to take over the administration of FEBC. By the end of that year, FEBC had three domestic stations and four more for overseas broadcasts. Broger became an information and education official with the Department of Defense beginning in 1954 and resigned his FEBC post three years later. Bowman became president, a position he held until his 1992 retirement when he became president emeritus.

In 1957 FEBC received licenses to broadcast in Okinawa using two AM stations (these were surrendered in 1972 when the island reverted to Japanese control). In September 1958, FEBC placed its first 50,000-watt transmitter into operation in the Philippines and opened recording studios in Hong Kong, then a British colony. A Tokyo studio followed in the next year. FEBC purchased KGEI in San Francisco in 1960 to initiate broadcasts to Latin America; the station had previously been used by the Office of War Information to broadcast news and information to the Pacific theater during World War II. Becoming known as "The Voice of Friendship," FEBC operated the station (soon placing a second shortwave transmitter on the air) until 1994.

FEBC efforts to broadcast to Asia were expanded in 1968 with the establishment of a British associate company, Far East Broadcasting Associates, to operate shortwave transmitters in the British-controlled (now Commonwealth) Seychelles islands, with the goal of reaching the Middle East, North Africa, and South Asia. Two stations in South Korea and another on the Pacific island of Saipan (1977) replaced the stations lost on Okinawa. Broadcasts to China were expanded with huge transmitters (100 and 250 kilowatts) beaming signals to the mainland from several locations.

By 1979 FEBC was providing some 300 hours of programming per day, in 72 languages from 28 stations. Service was extended to areas of what had been the Soviet Union in the early 1990s. FEBC operated more than 30 transmitters by 1995, with a staff of more than 1,000 (90 percent of whom were non-U.S. citizens) and an annual operating budget of $17 million. In 2000 the Far East Broadcasting Company broadcast its gospel message more than 400 hours a day in 154 languages.

ROBERT S. FORTNER AND CHRISTOPHER H. STERLING

See also Evangelists/Evangelical Radio; International Radio Broadcasting; Religion on Radio

Further Reading

Bowman, Eleanor G., and Susan F. Titus, *Eyes beyond the Horizon*, Nashville, Tennessee: Nelson, 1991

Far East Broadcasting International website, <www.febc.org/history2.html>

Fortner, Robert S., "Saving the World? American Evangelicals and Transnational Broadcasting," in *American Evangelicals and the Mass Media: Perspectives on the Relationship between American Evangelicals and the Mass Media*, edited by Quentin James Schultze, Grand Rapids, Michigan: Academie Books/Zondervan, 1990

Ledyard, Gleason H., *Sky Waves: The Incredible Far East Broadcasting Company Story*, Chicago: Moody Press, 1963

Melton, J. Gordon, Phillip Charles Lucas, and Jon R. Stone, *Prime-Time Religion: An Encyclopedia of Religious Broadcasting*, Phoenix, Arizona: Oryx Press, 1997

Wood, James, *History of International Broadcasting*, vol. 1, London: Peregrinus, 1992, and vol. 2, London: Institute of Electrical Engineers, 2000

Farm/Agricultural Radio

Radio has always had a special place in the lives of farmers and their families. Because of the isolation of rural life, the entertainment and information brought by radio are especially welcome, and up-to-the-minute weather forecasts and agricultural market reports are essential to every modern farmer's business. Even in today's age of television and the internet, farmers still consider radio to be their most important source of agricultural information, and surveys indicate that most of them tune in to farm programs every day.

In 2002, about 75 radio stations, mostly in rural communities, provided what they consider to be a full-time agricultural format, and another 1,000 stations broadcast at least one hour per week of special farm-related programming. In addition, a number of regional and national farm radio networks have evolved to provide stations with specialized programs and advertising.

Federal and state agencies, led by the United States Department of Agriculture (USDA), provide radio reports on topics ranging from the latest research on crop diseases to new agricultural marketing strategies. This information is provided to stations by the USDA in the form of scripts and press releases and as prerecorded audio and video reports that broadcasters can integrate into their own locally produced programs.

On commercial stations, farm programming is generally supported through the sale of advertising. Large corporate producers of agricultural products and services have found radio to be an ideal medium for reaching the widely dispersed farm audience, a group that includes the decision makers of U.S. agribusiness. Farmers who tune in for market reports on these stations are likely also to hear commercials for chemicals, fertilizer, seed, and other agricultural necessities.

Farm programming is also provided by many noncommercial radio stations, especially those associated with land grant colleges and universities with large agricultural research and teaching components. Many of these campuses have strong ties to federal and state farm service offices that provide regionalized agricultural information and programming.

Origins

Radio was just one of several technological innovations in the early part of the 20th century that revolutionized farm life. The telephone, phonograph, automobile, and rural mail delivery all served to greatly reduce the isolation of rural families. But the coming of radio in the 1920s meant that for the first time, farms were instantaneously connected to the outside world. Music, sports, politics, and religion were suddenly available with the twist of a dial. Once-isolated farm families were suddenly a part of the growing national radio audience. In most farm homes, a battery-operated radio became a fixture long before the house was wired for electricity. Perhaps most significant, the radio brought farmers information that had an immediate impact on their livelihoods. Accurate weather reports allowed farmers to time harvests and protect crops from storms, and immediate reports of commodity prices from big-city agricultural markets meant farmers could reap bigger profits and manage operations more efficiently.

In fact, government-produced weather forecasts and agricultural market reports were among radio's first regularly scheduled programs. Initially, these broadcasts were aired experimentally by college and university stations, which were among the first on the air with radio transmitters. As early as 1921 (some sources say earlier) the University of Wisconsin's 9XM (later, WHA) began transmitting agricultural informa-

tion on a regular schedule. Many other stations soon followed suit.

The USDA was especially quick to recognize radio's potential for reaching the far-flung farm audience. By the mid-1920s the agency had begun producing and distributing not only weather and market reports, but also informational programs on crop and livestock problems, agricultural marketing, and home economics. Scripts were distributed free of charge to radio stations through the USDA's vast network of county extension agents. The county agents themselves often worked closely with local radio stations to supplement programming with information on topics of local concern. At least some of the government-produced radio programs also had a distinctly political purpose: since farmers represented an important national voting bloc, the USDA interspersed the more mundane topics with features and talks that explained and promoted the administration's farm policy.

Early on, businesses that catered to rural customers also saw the potential of programming aimed specifically at the farm audience. Although overt radio advertising was still considered inappropriate in the early 1920s, these companies understood the promotional value of having their names on the air. Sears and Roebuck established the Chicago station WLS ("World's Largest Store") in part to promote its booming mail-order business with rural homes. The company was also instrumental in establishing other early stations in the Midwest and South. In Nashville, the National Life and Accident Insurance Company created the station WSM to help promote its products. In this case, "WSM" stood for the company's slogan, "We Shield Millions."

Stations across the country began to realize that the millions of U.S. farm homes constituted a special audience, and many began to produce and carry programs especially tailored for rural listeners, including those aimed at attracting farm women and children. Indeed, the Federal Radio Commission's radio frequency allocation scheme of 1928, with its high-powered clear channel stations designed to serve large rural areas, was very much driven by a concern (some of it admittedly political) for rural audiences. The National Broadcasting Company (NBC)'s *The National Farm and Home Hour*, begun in 1928, became one of the network's longest-running programs.

As radio developed, the government mounted a major campaign to get more farmers to buy receivers. USDA-authored articles in newspapers and farm periodicals told readers that the radio receiver had become an agricultural necessity. Countless anecdotes were reported of how farmers were able to save their crops by radio's advanced warning of bad weather or to increase their income by using radio reports of market price fluctuations.

But despite these efforts, bad economic times meant the adoption rate in rural areas lagged far behind that in cities. In the 1920s and 1930s many farmers barely eked out a subsistence, and hard cash was always in short supply. In addition, farmers generally lived at great distances from stations and needed to buy more expensive receivers to get satisfactory reception. And despite New Deal rural electrification efforts, many regions still lacked electricity, forcing use of battery-powered radios. By the 1940 census, 92 percent of urban U.S. homes reported owning radios, but only 70 percent of rural farm homes did. The situation among rural nonwhites was far worse. The chronic poverty among minority farmers meant that as late as 1940, only 20 percent owned radios.

Farm Radio and Country Music

Early listener response convinced broadcasters that rural and urban audiences differed considerably in their musical tastes. Farmers, it was believed, much preferred what was then called "hillbilly" music. This style was based on the folk songs commonly performed in rural areas, usually by one or two musicians playing simple stringed instruments. As the need grew for more programming to attract and hold the farm audience, several large stations developed live musical variety shows with a distinctly rural flavor. *National Barn Dance,* from Chicago's WLS, and *The Grand Ole Opry,* from WSM in Nashville, were two of the earliest and most successful.

By providing an audience for budding new performers and a ready market for their records, farm radio music shows played an essential role in the development of country music. Record companies began providing free or low-cost performers in exchange for the promotional value of having their stars heard on radio broadcasts. The fact that Nashville was the home of the powerful WSM and its immensely popular *Grand Ole Opry* was a decisive factor in that city's becoming the country music capital of the world.

The National Association of Farm Broadcasters

Radio stations soon recognized the need for specialized broadcast personnel to produce agricultural news and information programming. The position of station "farm director" was generally filled by someone who knew farming well and who could dedicate full attention to researching and reporting on agricultural issues. Often, male farm directors were assisted by women who were delegated the duties of reporting on rural home economics and hosting homemaker-oriented programs of interviews, recipes, and household hints. Today, farm broadcasters are often graduates of specialized university programs in agricultural journalism, and, although men still dominate the field, the role of female broadcasters has broadened considerably.

In the 1940s farm directors from several stations met and formed what would eventually be known as the National Association of Farm Broadcasters (NAFB). Today, the NAFB is farm broadcasting's major trade organization, offering members a news service, sales and marketing assistance, and farm audience research.

Farm Radio in the Television Age

The coming of television meant changes throughout the radio industry. Many of the powerful big-city radio stations no longer found it profitable to target rural audiences, and farm radio programming increasingly became the province of the growing number of lower-powered regional or local stations serving rural areas. At the same time, agricultural news and information programs began to appear on many local television stations that served farm audiences.

Yet for a number of reasons, farm radio has remained a viable medium. The low cost and portability of modern radio receivers means today's farm families can own several sets and listen wherever they happen to be. Radios installed in trucks, tractors, and other farm vehicles can accompany farmers throughout the workday. Timely weather forecasts and market reports remain just as important to farmers today as they were in the early days of radio. At the same time, the relatively low cost of operating a local radio station means that farm broadcasters can stay profitable even while appealing to a relatively narrow audience. In fact, it is just this characteristic that attracts agricultural advertisers, who can zero in on their target audience at a relatively low cost. These characteristics mean that farm radio will continue to flourish.

STEVE CRAIG

See also Trade Associations; WHA and Wisconsin Public Radio

Further Reading

Baker, John Chester, *Farm Broadcasting: The First Sixty Years,* Ames: Iowa State University Press, 1981

Evans, James F., *Prairie Farmer and WLS: The Burridge D. Butler Years,* Urbana: University of Illinois Press, 1969

Frost, S.E., Jr., *Education's Own Stations: The History of Broadcast Licenses Issued to Educational Institutions,* Chicago: University of Chicago Press, 1937

Malone, Bill C., *Country Music, U.S.A.,* Austin: University of Texas Press, 1968; revised edition, 1985

National Association of Farm Broadcasters: About NAFB, "History of NAFB," <www.nafb.com/news.cfm>

Rural Radio Listening: A Study of Program Preferences in Rural Areas of the U.S., New York: Rural Research Institute, 1951

Smulyan, Susan, *Selling Radio: The Commercialization of American Broadcasting, 1920–1934,* Washington, D.C.: Smithsonian Institution Press, 1994

U.S. Department of Agriculture, Bureau of Agricultural Economics, "Attitudes of Rural People Toward Radio Service: A Nation-Wide Service of Farm and Small-Town People," Washington, D.C.: United States Department of Agriculture, January 1946

Wik, Reynold M., "The USDA and the Development of Radio in Rural America," *Agricultural History* 62, no. 2 (1988)

Faulk, John Henry 1913–1990

U.S. Radio Humorist

When his developing radio career was cut short in the mid-1950s because of political blacklisting, Texas-born humorist John Henry Faulk decided to fight back. He undertook a six-year legal battle and eventually beat the right-wing blacklisters who had controlled network assignments of radio and television creative personnel for years.

Early Years

John Henry Faulk (he always used his full name) was born in Austin, Texas, just before World War I. He grew up in a mixed-race neighborhood and was encouraged by his liberal parents to treat everyone alike. His own subsequent liberal politics were partially formed by his parents, both leftist political activists. Working and attending classes part-time, Faulk entered the University of Texas in 1929 but took a decade to earn his bachelor's degree in English. While in school he became fascinated with Texas and American folklore of all kinds. Just over a year later, with a Works Progress Administration research grant, he earned a master's degree with an emphasis in American folklore. He stayed on in Austin to teach English courses at the university for two more years. Despite the military build-up in the early 1940s, the army initially turned him down for health reasons, and Faulk served with the merchant marine and later the Red Cross. The army finally accepted him for stateside service as a medic in 1944.

All through this period, Faulk honed his already impressive storytelling abilities. Overhearing him at a New York party, a Columbia Broadcasting System (CBS) official offered him a program slot of his own. Faulk hosted *Johnny's Front Porch* on the CBS radio network in 1945–46. He moved on to various on air positions with stations WOV and WPAT in New Jersey from 1946 to 1948. He returned to CBS to host the weekday hour-long daily *John Henry Faulk Show* on the network's flagship station, WCBS in New York, starting in 1951. His good-natured Texas humor and characters gathered a growing listening audience and attracted appreciative advertisers.

Blacklisted and a Landmark Suit

By the mid-1950s, as his radio career developed, Faulk had became more concerned about the communist-baiting approach of the officers of the New York local chapter of the American Federation of Radio and Television Artists (AFTRA) performer's union, of which he was a member. For several years union officials had actively cooperated with (and some were officers in) AWARE, Inc., one of the blacklisting organizations that "investigated" the political backgrounds of performers and writers. Along with CBS journalist Charles Collingwood and comedian Orson Bean, Faulk ran for the AFTRA board and was one of 27 "middle of the road slate" members elected to the 35-member board. He was subsequently elected second vice president, taking office in January 1956. The new AFTRA officers promised to cut ties with the blacklisters.

Nursing their wounds, the former union officials used their newsletter to attack Faulk for his own political views and associations, including thinly veiled accusations that, based on his political activity (he had backed Henry Wallace in the 1948 presidential campaign, for example), he at least had strongly communist leanings. In the political climate of the times, with "McCarthyism" in full flower, this was a potentially damning indictment that often cost the accused his or her job. As the attackers expected and as Faulk feared, their classic tactic led to advertiser nervousness about Faulk, and he began to lose commercial advertisers for his program. Although the station initially stood by its employee, diminishing advertiser support and income raised concern, though his contract was renewed in December 1956.

Faced with the loss of his livelihood for a series of false accusations, Faulk decided to take on his tormenters, although

John Henry Faulk
Courtesy AP/Wide World Photos

he knew it would be a difficult and expensive process. With financial support from CBS newsman Edward R. Murrow, among others, Faulk filed a libel suit on 26 June 1956 against AWARE and its officers. But the overall situation turned bad—the "middle of the road slate" lost ground in AFTRA and became a minority again. Though his program continued for a few more months, Faulk was fired by registered letter from CBS while he was on vacation in July 1957.

AWARE managed to delay trial on the libel suit for some five years through a variety of legal maneuvers. In the meantime, Faulk could not obtain work in the broadcast or entertainment fields and had to rely on friends and supporters for the financial means to survive, let alone pay for the ongoing case. The trial of AWARE and its officers finally got under way in the spring of 1962 and lasted for 11 weeks. On 28 June 1962 the New York State jury awarded $3.5 million in damages to Faulk (the largest libel judgment to that point), though this was later reduced to $550,000 by an appeals court. Faulk eventually received about $75,000 for his years of effort and deprivation. Through his lawsuit, he had made an important point about civil liberties that was widely reported, AWARE had declared bankruptcy, and the general public now knew about—and was increasingly appalled by—blacklisting.

Later Life

Faulk returned to Austin in 1968 and lived in Texas for the rest of his life. For a time he operated a small advertising agency. His blacklisting case became known to a new generation in October 1975 when CBS broadcast a two-hour made-for-television docudrama movie based on Faulk's story. William Dev-

ane played Faulk, and George C. Scott played attorney Louis Nizer.

From 1975 to the early 1980s, Faulk played a homespun character on the nationally syndicated *Hee-Haw* television variety program. During the 1980s Faulk wrote and produced two one-man plays. In both *Deep in the Heart* and *Pear Orchard, Texas,* he portrayed characters with the best of human instincts but exhibiting the worst of cultural prejudices. He also lectured widely on college campuses, largely about civil liberties and freedom of expression, drawing on his own case. He died of cancer in Austin in 1990, aged 76.

The central branch of the public library in Austin is named after him, as are the John Henry Faulk Awards given out annually since 1986 by the Texas Storytelling Association for the state's best storyteller. The Center for American History at the University of Texas at Austin (which holds Faulk's professional and legal papers) sponsors an annual John Henry Faulk Conference on the First Amendment.

CHRISTOPHER H. STERLING

See also American Federation of Television and Radio Artists; Blacklisting; Collingwood, Charles; Columbia Broadcasting System; Murrow, Edward R.

John Henry Faulk. Born in Austin, Texas, 21 August 1913. Attended the University of Texas, BA in English, 1939; Masters degree in Folklore, 1940; doctoral work, 1940–42. Served with the Merchant Marine, 1942–43; Red Cross in Cairo, Egypt, 1943–44; U.S. Army, psychiatric social worker, 1944–46. Hosted *Johnny's Front Porch* on CBS radio network, 1945–46; held various on-air positions, WOV, New York City, 1946–47, and WPAT, Paterson, New Jersey, 1948; hosted *The John Henry Faulk Show* on WCBS in New York, 1951–57; elected vice-president, New York local, American Federation of Television and Radio Artists (AFTRA), 1955; filed a libel suit against AWARE, Incorporated, 1956; was fired by CBS and blacklisted for five years; won the largest libel judgment in history, 1962; eventually returned to making motion pictures, wrote a one-man play and acted on television. Died in Austin, Texas, 9 April 1990.

Radio Series
1945–46   *Johnny's Front Porch*
1951–57   *The John Henry Faulk Show*

Television
Leave It to the Girls, 1954; *The Morning Show,* 1955; *Fear on Trial* (writer), 1975; *Hee Haw,* 1975–83; *Adam,* 1983

Film
All the Way Home, 1963; *The Best Man,* 1964; *Texas Chain Saw Massacre,* 1974; *Lovin' Molly,* 1974; *Leadbelly,* 1976

Stage
Pear Orchard, Texas, 1970s

Selected Publications
Fear on Trial, 1964
The Uncensored John Henry Faulk, 1985

Further Reading

Burton, Michael C., *John Henry Faulk: The Making of a Liberated Mind: A Biography*, Austin, Texas: Eakin Press, 1993
Carleton, Don E., *Red Scare! Right-Wing Hysteria, Fifties Fanaticism, and Their Legacy in Texas*, Austin: Texas Monthly Press, 1985
Cogley, John, *Report on Blacklisting*, 2 vols., New York: Fund for the Republic, 1956 (see especially vol. 2, *Radio-Television*)
Foley, Karen Sue, *The Political Blacklist in the Broadcast Industry: The Decade of the 1950s*, New York: Arno Press, 1979
Nizer, Louis, *The Jury Returns*, Garden City, New York: Doubleday, 1966
O'Connor, John J., "TV: CBS Dramatizes John Faulk's 'Fear on Trial,'" *New York Times* (2 October 1975)
Talbot, David, and Barbara Zheutlin, "The Password Is Blacklist: George C. Scott, CBS, and John Henry Faulk: The Way We Really Were," *Crawdaddy* (October 1975)
Wakefield, Dan, "Disc Jockey Fights the Blacklist," *The Nation* (20 December 1958)

Federal Communications Commission

The Federal Communications Commission (FCC) is the federal agency charged with regulating broadcasting and other electronic communications media in the United States; it licenses stations to operate in the "public interest, convenience, and necessity." The FCC was created by Congress in 1934 to succeed the Federal Radio Commission. It is an independent federal agency established by the Communications Act of 1934 to regulate domestic interstate and international electronic communication, both wired and wireless.

Because the FCC was established as an independent federal agency, the "checks and balances" on it are not the same as they would be for administrative agencies (such as the Food and Drug Administration), which answer directly to the U.S. president. Although the president selects the chair and the commissioners (who must be approved by the Senate), the president does not have the authority to remove commissioners during their terms. The FCC is much more beholden to Congress, which controls not only appropriations but also the commission's very existence. Since 1981, the FCC is no longer a permanent agency but instead must be reauthorized by Congress every two years. Therefore, Congress' influence over the FCC has increased significantly during the 1980s and 1990s.

The FCC has a dual role: on the one hand, it makes rules and regulations to carry out the Communications Act, but it also serves as a judicial body, hearing appeals of its decisions. As a quasi-judicial agency, the FCC has the duty of both making rules and also serving as an adjudicator in cases dealing with rules violations and challenges. While the FCC has the responsibility for making, policing, and judging the rules, its decisions are subject to court review. For example, the FCC created a rule requiring regular station identification. It also enforces the rule by asking stations whether they have adhered to it. In cases where stations have been found to violate the rule, the FCC must decide what punishment, if any, to apply. If the offending station challenges the decision, it appeals the judgment to the FCC. In this role, the FCC serves as the equivalent of a federal district court. FCC decisions that are upheld in appeal can then be challenged by appealing directly to the Federal Court of Appeals for the Washington, D.C. Circuit.

Commissioners

The FCC has five commissioners (reduced from seven in 1983), one of whom serves as the chair. Members are appointed by the U.S. president and approved by the Senate. The term of office for commissioners is five years, and they may serve multiple terms. No more than three commissioners from one political party may serve simultaneously.

Although the FCC chair has the same one vote as any of the other four commissioners, the chair has a greater ability to influence the direction of the FCC. The chair's role in selecting issues to pursue sets an agenda for the commission. During the 1970s and 1980s, for example, the FCC adopted a more deregulatory approach, eliminating a number of rules and streamlining the radio license renewal process. Under the leadership of chairmen Richard Wiley, Charles Ferris, and Mark Fowler, the

FCC revisited its responsibilities under the concept of the public interest, adopting the philosophy that the public interest is best served by allowing marketplace forces to function. In the 1990s Chairman Reed Hunt decided to investigate the possibilities of high-definition television and formed a task force to study it. Chairman William Kennard pursued the possibility of adding low-power FM stations to the radio band to provide increased opportunities for disenfranchised members of society to be heard. Although no chair has been successful in pursuing all of his interests, each has had the opportunity to set the commission's, and thus to a certain extent the nation's, communications policy agenda.

The majority of commissioners over the years have been lawyers (the last engineer commissioner retired in 1963). FCC commissioners are creatures of politics and as such are often more versed in politics than in technology. A number of commissioners have had no technological background prior to joining the commission. They count on their staff advisers and employees to provide them with the necessary background information. Fewer than half the commissioners have served their full five-year terms. When they leave the commission, they frequently join communications companies or legal firms providing consulting services. Commission staff members often find themselves dealing with former commissioners.

The personality of the FCC changes over time, based on the various personalities of the commissioners who serve and the political climate of the period. Space does not permit a listing of all former FCC commissioners and their contributions, but a few should be noted. Frieda B. Hennock, the first woman appointed to the commission in 1948, served during the critical period of the television "freeze" (1948–52). During those four years, the FCC stopped licensing new TV stations while it decided the issues of color TV, UHF versus VHF transmission, and channel allocation policies. Benjamin L. Hooks, the first African-American commissioner, was appointed in 1972 and worked diligently for the enforcement of equal employment opportunities. Henry Rivera was the first Hispanic commissioner, appointed in 1981. Robert E. Lee has the distinction of having served longer than any other commissioner to date, from 1953 until 1981. William Kennard was the first African American chairman when appointed in 1993.

FCC commissioners have been perceived alternately as pro- and anti-broadcasting. FCC chairmen James L. Fly (appointed 1939) and Newton N. Minow (appointed 1961) were public interest advocates who raised the ire of many broadcasters during their respective terms. Fly chaired the FCC during the forced sale of the NBC "Blue" Network. Minow is perhaps best remembered for referring to television as a "vast wasteland" in a speech to the National Association of Broadcasters.

On the other hand, James Quello joined the commission in 1974 after retiring from his position as vice president and general manager of station WJR in Detroit. Quello's Senate confirmation hearings lasted longer than any other commissioner's because a number of public interest groups, fearing that he would be too favorable to broadcast interests (Quello replaced public interest advocate Nicholas Johnson), opposed his nomination. In spite of the lengthy process, Quello was overwhelmingly approved by the Senate. While Quello served as interim FCC chair, *Broadcasting* magazine called him "the broadcasters' chairman." In spite of his strong support of broadcast interests, Quello was critical of indecency on radio.

Staff

Although the FCC has only five commissioners, there are nearly 2,000 staff members in dozens of different departments, including a dozen field offices across the U.S. The five FCC commissioners must officially hold a public meeting at least once a month. The business of the commission is largely conducted as items circulate among the commissioners in between meetings, and at the staff level in the operating bureaus. The FCC is divided administratively into a number of offices and bureaus, to which the bulk of the commission's work is delegated. The six major operating FCC bureaus are Consumer and Governmental Affairs, Enforcement, International, Media, Wireless Telecommunications, and Wireline Competition. Most licensing and regulatory activity undertaken in the name of the FCC occurs at this level.

Of greatest concern to broadcasters is the Media Bureau (previously called the Broadcast Bureau), which regulates AM, FM, and television broadcast stations and related facilities. It assigns frequencies and call letters to stations and designates operating power and sign-on and sign-off times. It also assigns stations in each service within the allocated frequency bands with specific locations, frequencies, and powers. It regulates existing stations, ensuring that stations operate in accordance with rules and in accordance with the technical provisions of their authorizations.

The Media Bureau has five divisions: Audio, Video, Policy, Industry Analysis, and Engineering. The Audio Division receives and evaluates approximately 5,500 applications per year for the nation's approximately 14,000 AM, FM commercial, FM noncommercial educational, and FM translator and booster stations. These applications include station modification applications, applications for new stations, assignment or transfer applications, license applications, and renewal applications.

Since the 1996 Telecommunications Act, radio and television stations are licensed for eight years (into the 1980s, the standard term was only three). Licensees are obligated to comply with statutes, rules, and policies relating to program content, such as identifying sponsors of material that is broadcast. The bureau ensures that licensees make available equal opportunities for use of broadcast facilities by political candidates or opposing political candidates, station identification, and identification of recorded programs or program segments. Licensees who have violated FCC rules, and most especially licensees who have "misrepresented" themselves, are subject to such sanctions as forfeitures (fines), short-term renewals, or (rarely) license revocation.

Other FCC offices are established by the commission as organizational tools for handling the tremendous variety of commission tasks. The current FCC offices are Administrative Law Judges, Communication Business Opportunities, Engineering and Technology, General Counsel, Inspector General, Legislative Affairs, Managing Director, Media Relations, Plans and Policy, and Workplace Diversity.

In its attempt to carry out the wishes of Congress as expressed in the Communications Act, the FCC creates or deletes rules. Proposals for new rules come from a variety of sources both within and outside the commission. To begin assessing a new service or proposal on which it has little information, the commission may issue a Notice of Inquiry (NOI) seeking advice and answers to specific questions. If the FCC plans a new rule, it first issues a Notice of Proposed Rule Making (NPRM). The NPRM gives formal notice that the FCC is considering a rule and provides a required length of time during which the commission must allow public comments. After sufficient comment and discussion, new rules are adopted in FCC Reports and Orders and are published in its own official report series, the *FCC Record,* as well as in the government's daily *Federal Register.* The rules are collected annually into Title 47 of the Code of Federal Regulations.

Licensing

Without a doubt, the greatest power of the FCC is its power to license or not license a station. Since its inception, the commission has modified its rules and procedures for determining the manner in which it grants licenses. In keeping with the directive of the Communications Act, the FCC has always licensed stations to operate "in the public interest, convenience, and necessity." The specific manner in which it has made determinations about individual licensees, however, has undergone changes. For decades, the FCC would examine all applicants for a license to determine which would best serve the public interest, considering a range of characteristics, including preferences for local ownership, minority ownership, experienced ownership, and the character of the owners. Even a station that had been in operation for years faced the prospect of losing its license to a superior applicant in a renewal proceeding. The FCC had to conduct time-consuming and expensive comparative hearings whenever two or more applicants sought the same frequency.

The FCC and the broadcast industry have long been critical of the comparative process, which was largely eliminated by the 1996 Telecommunications Act. Now, existing stations have an expectation of license renewal, provided they have not violated important commission rules. The FCC does not allow a new challenger to draw an existing station that has served the public interest into a comparative process. To avoid comparative hearings in the case of new stations, the FCC in 1999 adopted an auction process similar to what it had used earlier for other nonbroadcast frequencies. Rather than spend months (sometimes years) in comparative hearings, the FCC instead determines whether applicants meet minimum eligibility requirements. If they do, the applicants can then bid for new, available stations or purchase existing outlets.

The FCC does not monitor the broadcasts of radio and television stations. It relies on information provided to it by broadcasters, competitors, and audiences. Determinations about whether a station deserves to have its license renewed are based on documents filed by the station, any public comments the commission receives about that station, and challenges to the renewal by interested parties.

The commission is able to enforce regulations primarily through the *threat* of license action. The majority of license renewals are granted with no disciplinary action by the FCC. However, should the commission find rules violations by a licensee, its actions can range from a letter admonishing a station to fines of up to $250,000 and a short-term renewal of the license, and even to the revocation of a license. It is the threat of this action that keeps broadcasters in compliance.

The FCC has the ultimate authority to revoke a station's license or deny its renewal, although that action has rarely been taken. In more than 60 years, the FCC has taken this action only 147 times: an average of fewer than three per year out of thousands of license renewals. More than one-third of those revocations and nonrenewals were due to misrepresentations to the commission. Although such cases have been infrequent, the FCC has acted severely in cases where licensees have intentionally lied.

In 1998, the FCC revoked the license for Bay City, Texas, station KFCC because the owner "engaged in a pattern of outright falsehoods, evasiveness, and deception." Chameleon Radio Corporation had been awarded a license to serve Bay City, but it attempted to move the transmitter closer to Houston, to the extent that Bay City would not even be served by the station. The FCC cited the station for repeated misrepresentations and lack of candor. Chameleon attempted to argue that the merit of its programming should protect it from revocation. The FCC responded that "meritorious programming does not mitigate serious deliberate misconduct such as misrepresentation." Also that year, licenses were revoked for seven stations in Missouri and Indiana that were owned by Michael Rice through three different corporations. Rice was convicted of 12 felonies involving sexual assaults of children. The FCC was prepared to allow the corporations to continue their ownership of the stations after their assertion that Rice would not be involved in station operation. The commission revoked the licenses on a finding that Rice was in fact involved in station operation and that "misrepresentations and lack of candor regarding his role at the stations" was cause for revocation.

Despite all the powers given to the FCC, the 1934 Communications Act specifically states that the commission may not censor the content of broadcasts. According to Section 326, "Nothing in this Act shall be understood or construed to give this Commission the power of censorship over the radio communications or signals transmitted by any radio station." Nevertheless, the FCC's reprimands and fines of stations for broadcasting indecent material at inappropriate times have been upheld by the Supreme Court. The FCC acknowledges its obligation to stay out of content decisions in most areas. The commission has declined to base license decisions on the proposed format of a radio station, and it no longer stipulates the amount of time stations should devote to public service announcements.

Spectrum Management

The FCC also has the important responsibility of managing all users (except the federal government) of the electromagnetic spectrum. This involves two processes. First, the FCC must allocate different uses for different parts of the spectrum in an efficient way that does not create interference. This is followed by the allotment of specific frequencies or channels to particular areas. Licensing of the allotments follows. (AM does not have allotments.) There have been two significant spectrum reallocations affecting radio. In 1945 the FCC moved FM's allocation from 42 to 50 megahertz up to its current location at 88 to 108 megahertz, more than doubling the available channels but rendering the existing FM receivers and transmitters obsolete. In 1979 the upper end of the AM band moved from 1605 kilohertz to 1705 kilohertz to accommodate ten additional AM channels—a change that took years to implement (the first stations shifted to the new higher frequencies only moved in the 1990s).

A second part of maintaining spectrum efficiency is approving equipment that uses the electromagnetic spectrum. The FCC must be certain that all devices emitting electromagnetic signals do so within their prescribed limits. "Type acceptance" is the FCC process of approving equipment that emits electromagnetic radio waves. In most cases, the evidence for type acceptance is provided by the equipment's manufacturer, who provides a written application with a complete technical description of the product and a test report showing compliance with the technical requirements. An FCC identification number can be found on the backs of telephones, walkie-talkies, pagers, and even microwave ovens. The number does not imply that the FCC has inspected that particular unit but rather that the product meets certain FCC minimal standards designed to avoid interference.

Policy is sometimes the result of *in*action by the FCC. For years, the commission was faced with what to do about AM stereo. Rather than choosing a standard from among competing applicants, the FCC adopted in 1982 a marketplace philosophy to allow a winner to emerge from marketplace decisions rather than their own. Many broadcasters believe the introduction of AM stereo was negatively affected by the commission's "decision not to decide." Some stations were reluctant to invest in AM stereo equipment, fearing they might select the losing standard and then lose thousands of dollars. Radio receiver manufacturers had the same concern. The FCC's decision "not to decide" virtually killed any chance for AM stereo.

DOM CARISTI

See also Blue Book; Communications Act of 1934; Deregulation of Radio; Equal Time Rule; Fairness Doctrine; Federal Radio Commission; Frequency Allocation; Licensing; Public Interest, Convenience, or Necessity; Regulation; Stereo; Telecommunications Act of 1996; United States Congress and Radio

Further Reading

Cole, Barry G., and Mal Oettinger, *Reluctant Regulators: The FCC and The Broadcast Audience*, Reading, Massachusetts: Addison-Wesley, 1978

Federal Communications Commission website, <www.fcc.gov>

Flannery, Gerald V., editor, *Commissioners of the FCC 1927–1994*, Lanham, Maryland: University Press of America, 1994

Hilliard, Robert L., *The Federal Communications Commission: A Primer*, Boston: Focal Press, 1991

Kahn, Frank J., editor, *Documents of American Broadcasting*, 4th edition, Englewood Cliffs, New Jersey: Prentice-Hall, 1984

Krasnow, Erwin G., Lawrence D. Longley, and Herbert A. Terry, *The Politics of Broadcast Regulation*, New York: St. Martin's Press, 1973; 3rd edition, 1982

Ray, William B., *FCC: The Ups and Downs of Radio-TV Regulation*, Ames: Iowa State University Press, 1990

Federal Radio Commission

Predecessor to the Federal Communications Commission

The first agency created in the United States specifically to license and regulate radio, the Federal Radio Commission (FRC) existed from 1927 to 1934. During that time, the FRC was responsible not only for licensing radio stations in the United States, but also for laying the regulatory foundation that to some extent still exists today.

Origins

The United States passed the Radio Act in 1912, which provided authorization for licensing of radio stations. It was not until 1920, however, that the secretary of commerce began to exercise this authority. Congress had decided to empower the secretary of commerce because radio was seen as interstate commerce: thus, the Department of Commerce was the logical choice to handle the authorization of these new radio stations.

It did not take long to realize that radio licensing and regulation was a much larger task than could be handled by the secretary of commerce in addition to his regular duties. At the First National Radio Conference in Washington, D.C., in 1922, government officials and amateur and commercial radio operators met to discuss problems facing the infant industry. A technical committee's report resulted in the introduction of legislation in 1923, but it never got out of Senate committee.

At the Second National Radio Conference in 1923, many of the same problems were revisited, most notably concerns about interference. Because interference was greatest in places with the most transmitters (population centers) and less of a problem in remote areas, a recommendation emerged from the conference that the nation be divided into zones and that different rules be established for different zones based on their own specific needs. Again, legislation was introduced into Congress, but it never advanced beyond committee. A third national conference in 1924 produced no legislation either. Finally, the Fourth National Radio Conference in 1925 produced the proposals that would lead to the Radio Act of 1927.

During all this time, the secretary of commerce continued to license radio stations. The difficulty came when secretary Herbert Hoover attempted to *not* license a station. In 1923 Intercity Radio applied for a renewal of its license. The request was denied based on a determination that there was no longer spectrum space available. Intercity appealed the case, and the Federal Circuit Court of Appeals ruled in their favor. According to the court, the 1912 Act authorized the secretary of commerce to grant licenses: it did not grant the authority to deny them. In the court's judgment, the secretary of commerce had to accom-

modate applicants by finding them spectrum space that would cause the least amount of interference.

The secretary's authority was further undermined in a 1926 court decision. Zenith Radio had been operating a station in Denver with a prescribed allocation limiting it to two hours of broadcasts per week. The station challenged the authorization by using other frequencies not specifically allocated to it. When secretary of commerce Herbert Hoover filed suit against Zenith, the court ruled that Zenith was within its rights, citing a section of the Radio Act that allowed stations to use "other sending wave lengths." For all intents and purposes, such a decision authorized any licensed station to operate on virtually any frequency in addition to the one allocated.

The result of the two court cases was devastating to the secretary of commerce's assumed authority to regulate radio stations. Following the decision in the Zenith case, the secretary sent a letter to the U.S. Attorney General requesting an opinion on the authority vested in the secretary of commerce by the Radio Act. The attorney general's response only reinforced what the courts had already decided. The interpretation of the Radio Act of 1912 was that licensed stations could use virtually any frequency they wanted, at whatever times and using whatever transmitting power they wanted. With the secretary's authority eviscerated, President Calvin Coolidge asked Congress to create new legislation. With the president's endorsement, legislation that had been proposed as a result of the 1925 National Radio Conference moved swiftly through Congress, and the Radio Act of 1927 was signed into law by President Coolidge on 23 February 1927.

Initial Tasks

Central to the 1927 Act was the establishment of the FRC. Instead of having one person overseeing licensing and regulation of radio, a commission of five people appointed by the president and approved by the Senate would handle the duties. Perhaps influenced by the thinking that different geographic regions would have different needs, commissioners were to represent those different regions. When it passed the Radio Act of 1927, Congress naively believed that the FRC would need to act for only one year to straighten out all the confusion in radio regulation and licensing. After that, things would be well enough established that the agency could serve only as an appellate board for actions by the secretary of commerce. W. Jefferson Davis wrote in the *Virginia Law Review* that after the first year, "the Secretary of Commerce will handle most of the problems that arise, and the Commission will probably function only occasionally." Clearly, that was not to be the case. The FRC's authority was made permanent in 1930 and was extended until 1934, when it was replaced by the Federal Communications Commission (FCC).

The FRC got off to what was at best a shaky start, as Congress had not financed it. The FRC came into existence without an appropriation from Congress. The original commissioners were required to do their own clerical work, and engineers had to be "borrowed" from other agencies for several years. Furthermore, Congress confirmed only three of the five nominees from President Coolidge in the first year. Two of the five appointees died during the Commission's first year. Only one of the original FRC members, Judge Eugene O. Sykes, was still serving just two years later. In spite of these difficulties, the FRC was able to dramatically advance the nation's radio regulatory policy in its eight years of existence, at a crucial time for the development of commercial radio. Even the publication *Radio News* recognized the enormity of the FRC's task and the efficiency with which it worked. In November 1929, the publication stated,

> Not in the history of federal bureaus has any commission ever been called upon to perform so great a task in so short a span of time. The already overloaded departments of the federal government could not have treated with radio problems on this scale without a great increase in personnel and what would have been tantamount to the setting up of a radio commission within the department to which it might have been assigned. By its segregation and absolute independence, radio has been regulated and its major problems have been solved without handicapping any other federal bureau ("Public Interest, Convenience and Necessity," in *Radio News* [November 1929]).

The Radio Act of 1927 empowered the FRC with the authority and regulatory discretion that the secretary of commerce had lacked under the Radio Act of 1912. The new act specifically granted the FRC authority to license stations for a limited period of time; to designate specific frequencies, power, and times of operation of stations; to conduct hearings and serve as a quasi-judicial body; and to deny a license or to revoke an existing license. All of these powers had been denied the secretary of commerce.

Legal Challenges

It did not take long for the FRC's enforcement authority to be legally challenged. Technical Radio Laboratory sought a license renewal for its station in Midland Park, New Jersey, and was denied by the FRC because there was not adequate spectrum available. Whereas Intercity had successfully challenged denial of its renewal request, Technical Radio Laboratory was not so fortunate, because the courts found that the FRC was within its authority. Dozens of other cases would follow, with similar results. Congress had taken the appropriate steps to provide the FRC with licensing authority.

According to the Radio Act, the FRC's jurisdiction was based on Congress' authority to regulate interstate commerce. Thus, radio stations that did not transmit across a state line might not have to be regulated by them. In theory, at least, radio stations involved only in intrastate commerce rather than interstate commerce were not subject to federal jurisdiction. Just such an assertion was made in the case of *United States v Gregg*. An unlicensed Houston station challenged the FRC's authority, claiming that its signal was not interstate commerce. The court accepted the FRC's argument that it had to have authority over all transmissions, even those that did not cross state lines, because otherwise it could not control the interference that might affect other, regulated stations. Leery of raising questions of states' rights, Congress had avoided the issue in the Radio Act of 1927. In 1933 the court extended FRC authority to cover all radio transmissions.

For the most part, the FRC fared quite well in challenges to its regulatory authority. To be sure, there were cases that the FRC did not win, but it certainly won many more than it lost. The Commission's ability to exercise regulatory authority over the broadcast spectrum became greater with each legal decision. In two highly visible cases, the FRC was able to deny license renewals for stations that had not acted in the public interest. In 1931 the court upheld the FRC in denying a renewal to Dr. John R. Brinkley's station, KFKB (Brinkley had been using his station to prescribe medications). Brinkley claimed that the FRC had no authority to censor him. The court held that the FRC was not engaging in censorship by examining the record to determine if a licensee had acted in the public interest. The following year, Dr. Robert Schuler of Trinity Methodist Church appealed the denial of his station license, KGEF, claiming that his free speech rights had been violated. The court rejected that argument on the premise that the Commission was not preventing Schuler from making his vitriolic comments. As with Brinkley, the FRC could use his past record as an indication of how he would serve the public interest.

Defining the Public Interest

Included in the Radio Act of 1927 was the stipulation that the FRC would act "as public convenience, interest, or necessity requires." Likewise, stations were to be licensed to serve the same public interest, convenience, and necessity. Congress borrowed the language from other legislation regulating public utilities. This vague directive from Congress served as the guiding philosophy for the FRC. In one action in 1928, the FRC denied 62 license renewals and modified the operations of dozens more. A month later, the FRC issued a statement to explain its interpretation of the public interest standard and how it was to be applied. As the FRC pointed out in its statement, "no attempt is made anywhere in the act to define the term 'public interest, convenience, or necessity,' nor is any illustration given of its proper application" (FRC annual report, 166 [1928]). While asserting that a specific definition was neither possible nor desirable, the FRC set forth some general principles regarding the public interest. Perhaps most illustrative of all is the concluding sentence from the FRC's statement: "The emphasis must be first and foremost on the interest, the convenience, and the necessity of the listening public, and not on the interest, convenience, or necessity of the individual broadcaster or the advertiser." The language mirrors the sentiment of Rep. Wallace H. White, cosponsor of the bill that became the Radio Act of 1927, who said:

We have reached the definite conclusion that the right of our people to enjoy this means of communication can be preserved only by the repudiation of the idea underlying the 1912 law that anyone who will may transmit—and by the assertion in its stead of the doctrine that the right of the public to service is superior to the right of any individual to use the ether (67th Cong. Rec. 5479 [1926]).

The FRC determined that the public interest is served by having a "substantial band of frequencies set aside for the exclusive use of broadcasting stations and the radio listening public." It also adopted the general premise that the greatest good is served by minimizing interference. It follows from this that denying licenses in order to prevent interference, detrimental though it may be to some prospective broadcasters, serves the greatest good. The commission stated its intent to use the past record of a licensee to determine whether that station is deserving of a license. The reliability of a station's transmissions were also to be considered. Stations that could not be relied upon to transmit at regularly scheduled, announced times or whose transmission frequencies wandered around the spectrum did not serve the public interest. More than 70 years later, these interpretations of serving the public interest are still considered valid.

Also included in the 1928 statement on the public interest was the principle that stations should operate at different classes of service in order to ensure that there would be some stations serving larger geographic areas, while other stations served only small communities. This coincided with Congress' view, which had been stated earlier that same year when the Radio Act of 1927 was amended by the Davis Amendment in 1928. In addition to extending the FRC's authorization beyond its original year, the amendment directed the FRC to devise a scheme for providing equitable radio services in all zones of the country. One week following the FRC's statement on the public interest, it issued a plan for providing different classes of radio service. Each of the nation's zones would have an equal number of channels assigned as clear channels, regional channels, and local channels. Clear channels were designated to be high-power stations audible at a distance, whereas regional and local channels had decreasing coverage areas. Eight clear channels, seven regional channels, and six local channels were assigned to each of the five zones. The FRC's basic concept of clear, regional, and local channels remained in force more than six decades later.

One of the public-interest principles established by the FRC that did not continue with the FCC was the concept that licenses should not be provided to stations that offer services that duplicate those already available. The FRC stated that simply playing phonograph records on the air does not provide the listening public with anything that it cannot otherwise obtain. The FRC would have maintained a licensing scheme that would compare the programming intentions of the applicants. It can also be inferred that the FRC did not favor licensing stations whose formats mirrored those of stations already in the community. Based on today's radio business, that policy clearly did not survive

DOM CARISTI

See also Brinkley, John R.; Censorship; Clear Channels; Controversial Issues; First Amendment and Radio; Frequency Allocation; Hoover, Herbert; Licensing; Localism in Radio; Public Interest, Convenience, or Necessity; Regulation; United States Congress and Radio; White, Wallace H.; Wireless Acts of 1910 and 1912/Radio Acts of 1912 and 1927

Further Reading

Benjamin, Louise M., "In the Public Interest: The Radio Act and Actions of the Federal Radio Commission," Chapter 5 in *Freedom of the Air and the Public Interest,* Carbondale: Southern Illinois University Press, 2001

Bensman, Marvin R., "Regulation Under the Act of 1927," Chapter 5 in *The Beginning of Broadcast Regulation in the Twentieth Century,* Jefferson, North Carolina: McFarland, 2000

Davis, Stephen Brooks, *The Law of Radio Communication,* New York: McGraw-Hill, 1927

Federal Radio Commission, "Annual Report," Washington, D.C.: Government Printing Office, 1927–33; reprint, New York: Arno Press, 1971

Goodman, Mark, and Mark Gring, "The Ideological Fight Over Creation of the Federal Radio Commission in 1927," *Journalism History* 26 (Autumn 2000)

Schmeckebier, Laurence F., *The Federal Radio Commission: Its History, Activities and Organization,* Washington, D.C.: Brookings Institution, 1932

Slotten, Hugh R., "Radio Engineers, the Federal Radio Commission, and the Social Shaping of Broadcast Technology," chapter 2 in *Radio and Television Regulation:*

Broadcast Technology in the United States, 1920–60, Baltimore, Maryland: Johns Hopkins University Press, 2000

U.S. House of Representatives, Committee on Merchant Marine and Fisheries, *Federal Radio Commission: Hearings,* 70th Cong., 2nd Sess. (January–February 1929)

Female Radio Personalities and Disk Jockeys

Radio's female pioneers, although limited by the social conventions of the times, were quite successful in the early days of radio. Since radio's inception, female personalities have sometimes been limited by legal, economic, and social constraints, as well as by their own perceptions of what is expected of them by listeners and the industry. As radio became more established, women had less formalized input into programming decisions, yet they have had a significant impact on the radio industry. Indeed, a congressional study in the early 1990s concluded that women-owned radio stations were 20 percent more likely to air women's programming than male-owned stations were and 30 percent more likely than non-minority-owned stations were (see Halonen, 1992).

Donna Halper (2001) is one of the few radio historians to track the lives of the early female pioneers: Eunice Randall, Emilie Sturtevant, Marie Zimmerman, Eleanor Poehler, and Halloween Martin. Randall made her radio debut in 1918 and became one of the nation's first female announcers. Sturtevant was one of Boston's first radio programmers in the 1920s. Zimmerman and Poehler were two of the first female radio station managers. The first woman to command Chicago morning radio in the 1920s was Halloween Martin, long before programmers realized the importance of that time slot.

Soap and Sisterhood

By the 1940s, female talk show hosts became popular role models for their female listeners, who sought advice on children, relationships, and detergents, as well as a bit of celebrity gossip and companionship. Television, ironically, seemed to supply an abundant pool of female hosts to the radio networks. While many female listeners tuned to Mary Margaret McBride and Kate Smith, others enjoyed the popular soap operas. The success of female radio personalities was often evaluated in terms of their ability to move merchandise.

By 1954, as the industry's reliance on the radio networks declined, female disc jockeys (although merely a handful across the nation) began to redefine their role in radio. Martha Jean "The Queen" Steinberg was one of the first women in the nation to make the leap from being hostess of a homemaker show to being a rhythm-and-blues disc jockey on Memphis' legendary WDIA-AM. Also across Memphis airwaves, WHER-AM became the first all-girl radio station in the U.S. in 1955. Many of the disc jockeys remained at the station through 1972. WHER was the brainchild of station owner and record producer Sam Phillips. Apart from these exceptions, however, radio disc jockeys were predominantly white and male. With the emergence of rock and roll, these men attempted to out-shock their competitors in the quest for the most listeners, and in the process, they gained power and control over music selection and programming. Women faded behind the scenes for the next decade.

Sexpot Radio

In the mid-1960s, New York's WNEW-FM created "Sexpot Radio," an all-female lineup of disc jockeys. From this experiment, which lasted only 18 months, Alison Steele became known as the "Nightbird." Her legendary sultry voice captivated night audiences as she read poetic and Biblical verses in between music and interviews with rock stars. Steele, who died in 1995, was a member of the Rock and Roll Hall of Fame and the first woman to receive *Billboard Magazine*'s FM Personality of the Year award in 1976. Unlike Steele, many women entered radio in the 1970s as part-time reporters and weekend announcers—after women's groups pressured the Federal Communications Commission (FCC) to revise its affirmative action policies. With free-form FM radio giving way to increasingly segmented formatting, women were often defined, not by their individuality, but within the context of a male-dominated morning show.

Before the turn of the decade, another radio station would once again provide new opportunities for women. Like WHER, it had a female staff and male owner. Connecticut's

WOMN-AM debuted in January 1979. It aired several news stories about women and played numerous female artists throughout the day. The short-lived effort paved the way for less stereotypical advertisements and created a demand for more female artists by radio stations across the nation.

Strong Talk in the 1980s

Music-oriented stations decreased their news and public service commitments and increased the number of songs played per hour. Still, there were signs that "chick" talk would become a valuable commodity in the industry in the years ahead. By the late 1970s, Sally Jessy Raphael had established herself as a popular radio talk show host, broadcasting her advice on love, family, and relationships to a late-night audience at a time when talk radio began to boom. Concurrently, television talk shows began to attract large female audiences away from radio. With every station playing the same songs, personality once again became an integral part of the programming mix.

Strong female personalities, such as Washington, D.C.'s Robin Breedon, soared in their ratings, past their white male competitors. With a decade of television broadcast experience and a degree from Howard University, Breedon became the number-one Arbitron-ranked morning personality in D.C. She proved that many listeners were seeking personalities with compassion and community commitment. *The Washington Post* referred to her as the "Queen of Radio." During her ten-year radio stint, she won seven Emmy nominations and two American Women in Radio and Television National Awards; then-Mayor Sharon Pratt-Kelly even proclaimed a day named in her honor. Breedon left radio in 1998.

By 1988 Howard Stern was on his way to becoming a national icon. Robin Quivers, Stern's articulate sidekick, became a dominant part of what was becoming known as "shock radio." As early as the 1980s, many women entered radio as sidekicks who typically read the morning headlines and provided a laugh track for male-dominated morning shows. In some cases, these women also became the targets of sexist jokes told by male hosts.

The Rise of the Shockette Jock

The real revolution was happening in Rhode Island. Carolyn Fox, Providence's number-one afternoon personality, spouted her liberal views on everything from sex to politics—before Howard Stern even gained national prominence. Fox paved the way for a number of women, such as San Francisco's Darian O'Toole, Austin's Sara Trexler, Denver's Caroline Corley, and Detroit's Kelly Walker, who became the new shock jocks of the 1990s. Many of these women began their careers as sidekicks or night personalities. Trexler, who began her career in 1986,

was selected as *Billboard Magazine*'s Small Market Local Air Personality of the Year in 1999. Emulating their male predecessors, many of these shock jockettes featured the same type of locker-room humor, but from a female perspective.

Karin Begin (a.k.a. Darian O'Toole) has been billed as America's First Shockette. Although Carolyn Fox is her predecessor by more than a decade, the press and the radio industry has portrayed Begin as an American trailblazer for female radio broadcasters. Begin was born and raised in Nova Scotia and worked at a number of small Canadian markets before landing in the United States.

The turning point in her radio career came when she met Program Director Shawn Kelly, a big Howard Stern fan, who encouraged Begin to seek opportunities in the United States. Some of her early gigs included on-air stints in New Jersey, Philadelphia, Baltimore, and Sacramento. In San Francisco, she would become known as Darian O'Toole—the "Caustic Canadian Swamp Witch." Her morning show skyrocketed to number one in San Francisco, climbing from 23rd to 1st place in the market in only three years. She left San Francisco's KBIG in 1997 to take her show to New York. In September 1999 she returned to San Francisco to work at KSAN.

Alternate Models for Female Personalities

The ability to move merchandise, whether soap or soda, will always remain an essential part of commercial radio, for obvious reasons. With every product sold on radio, early female broadcasters knew that their bargaining power would increase tenfold. Some commercial gimmicks to market the female experience, such as the rise and fall of "Sexpot Radio" or the all-women radio station WOMN, have quickly failed within the past 40 years. On the other hand, the Seattle-based syndicated nighttime personality Delilah, a 25-year veteran, is taking a new spin on an old formula—a mix of advice and inspiration to a predominantly female audience, with listeners calling in to her show from more than 200 affiliates around the nation. Reminiscent of Casey Kasem's long-distance dedications, but a bit more personal, she is very much like Mary Margaret McBride in her desire to chat about love, family, and relationships. In October 1998, she announced her pregnancy and promised to share her experience with her listeners. Many American listeners seem comforted by female radio personalities who symbolize traditional family values. Dr. Laura Schlessinger, a controversial conservative talk show host in the 1990s, starts her weekday show by saying "I'm my kid's mom." In the final analysis, there has never been one personality style that has worked for all female broadcasters; rather, the means of success has been their ability to connect to the listeners—both men and women—in some unique way.

PHYLIS JOHNSON

between the investors (who knew virtually nothing about radio technology but understandably sought a return on their funds) and the inventor (who held the technical knowledge but was becoming increasingly difficult to work with). From the beginning, NESCO focused on constantly changing short-term strategies as the partners bickered and fought. There was never an agreed-upon strategic plan for the firm, along the lines that Marconi was so successfully demonstrating at the same period. For example, Fessenden wanted to sell equipment, whereas his backers wanted to develop and market a complete wireless system.

NESCO transmitting stations were built in Washington, New York (Brooklyn), and Philadelphia (in nearby Collingswood, New Jersey) that were designed to provide overland communication in competition with existing wired systems. Despite considerable investment, wireless was still developing and often proved unworkable; not surprisingly, few customers materialized. Under a 1904 contract with GE, NESCO developed further transmitters in Lynn, Massachusetts, and Schenectady, New York, but the contract was cancelled in mid-1905 because of poor performance between transmitters. Faced with this failure, late in 1904, a shift in company priorities saw the partners seeking to develop a transatlantic radio service in competition with Marconi. At the same time, and against Fessenden's advice and pleas, NESCO stopped selling equipment. Transmitting stations were built in Scotland and in Brant Rock, Massachusetts, south of Boston. But they provided only sporadic communications—and almost none in the summer because of atmospheric static. By May 1906 Given and Walker had invested over half a million dollars, with precious little to show for it. That December a storm destroyed the Scottish station, effectively ending NESCO's transatlantic dreams. That, in turn, set the stage for one of Fessenden's most famous accomplishments.

With three days notice to shipowners using Fessenden equipment off the Massachusetts coast, on Christmas Eve of 1906 Fessenden offered what many consider the world's first true radio "broadcast"—a clear (not coded) voice and music transmission intended for widespread reception. Using his new and larger alternator, and with the inventor acting as "announcer," records were played, and Fessenden sang, played the violin, and even made a speech. All of this was repeated a week later on New Year's Eve. Fessenden was not seeking to *broadcast* as we think of the term today, but rather sought an improved means of competition with point-to-point wireline carriers. Unfortunately, his continuing pattern of claiming more for his system than it could in fact accomplish began to hurt. Further, because there was no press coverage (newspapers had not been invited to the experimental transmissions), few knew of the seeming wireless telephony breakthrough.

Radio telephony transmissions required more power and usually did not reach as far as radio telegraphy. But despite this limitation, there seemed to be obvious applications of wireless to the telephone business. In early 1907 Given and Walker made a concerted effort to interest American Telephone and Telegraph (AT&T) in taking over NESCO, and initially their efforts seemed to bear fruit. Both AT&T engineers and top company management were favorably disposed to the idea. However, a financial panic in 1907 led to a change in AT&T management as the J.P. Morgan interests took over, and a major retrenchment took place. Any thoughts of investing in a still largely unproven technology were forgotten. This failure to sell NESCO to AT&T was a major setback and led to increased disagreements between Fessenden and his backers—he again wanted to sell equipment, and they wanted to sell the whole firm.

For a time things looked up with the hiring of Colonel John Firth as the accomplished sales manager NESCO desperately needed. The company resumed equipment sales, thanks to his good relations with navy officials and others, and he also helped to mediate between Fessenden and his two Pittsburgh financial backers. At the same time, however, NESCO scaled down with layoffs and reduced experimental work.

Frustrated with the constant bickering and continued lack of a focused company strategy, Fessenden revived plans to compete with Marconi in transatlantic communication, and toward that end he set up an independent company, Fessenden Wireless Company of Canada, without informing or involving Given and Walker. This led to a break between Fessenden and the backers late in 1910 (because Given and Walker felt they owned the patents in question). In January 1911 Given and Walker dismissed Fessenden from the company. He, in turn, sued for wrongful termination. Some 15 years of litigation followed.

Later Life

NESCO was placed in voluntary receivership to protect it from the inventors' suit (Fessenden eventually won a judgment of several thousand dollars), though research continued with about a dozen engineers. What was most ironic about Fessenden's departure and the demise of NESCO is that by 1911–12, the radio industry had begun to agree on the need to develop continuous-wave equipment for voice transmissions. No longer a part of NESCO, Fessenden was increasingly bypassed, due in no small part to his choleric temper, impatience, and maddening ego.

NESCO entered into a cross-licensing agreement with the Marconi interests after suits for patent violation had been brought. Finally, in 1917, after both Given and Walker had died, NESCO was sold to the International Radio Telegraph Company, which in 1920 fell to Westinghouse (and the patent rights of which were, in turn, transferred to the Radio Corporation of America [RCA] in 1921).

Fessenden's post-NESCO radio work was with the Submarine Signal Company of Boston. Beginning in 1912, he sought to improve underwater signal transmission and reception with what became known as the Fessenden Oscillator, a device also useful in detection of icebergs at sea; a wireless compass; and a fathometer or sonic depth finder. By the time he left Submarine Signal in 1921, however, Fessenden was largely through with radio innovation. In 1921 he received the gold medal of the Institute of Radio Engineers, and later he received the John Scott medal from Philadelphia for his development of continuous-wave wireless. In 1929 he received the Scientific American medal for his inventions concerning safety at sea.

Fessenden was clearly a visionary ("technically farsighted" says historian Susan Douglas, 1987) who sought to pioneer new approaches and systems, often at the margins of practicality of existing electrical capability. But unlike Marconi, Fessenden was totally unfit for marketing and presenting a public persona that would encourage investment. Frustration had helped to make him a very difficult man with whom to deal. He was variously reported as being short-tempered, impatient, intolerant, vain, and a man who rarely listened to others (for example, when he wrongly insisted on a wooden core for the alternator, relenting only when Alexanderson demonstrated the benefit of iron). He drove away many subordinates with his harsh treatment.

As with many radio pioneers, Fessenden proved to be important at pioneering (invention)—in particular at understanding the need for continuous-wave transmission, conceiving the alternator, and defining the heterodyne principal—but a relative failure at developing commercially successful innovations from any of these.

CHRISTOPHER H. STERLING

See also Alexanderson, E.F.W.; De Forest, Lee; Hertz, Heinrich; Marconi, Guglielmo

Reginald A. Fessenden. Born in East Bolton, Canada East (now Quebec), 6 October 1866. Oldest of four sons of Elisha Joseph Fessenden, an Episcopal minister, and Clementina Trenholme; moved to Niagara Falls, Ontario, 1875; attended De Veaux Military College, New York, 1875–77; attended Trinity College School, Port Hope, Ontario, 1877; worked for two years at Imperial Bank, Woodstock, New York; senior classical master, Bishop's College, Lennoxville, Quebec; principal, Whitney Institute, Bermuda, 1883–85; inspecting engineer, Edison Machine Works, New York, 1886; worked in industrial chemistry at Thomas Edison's lab in West Orange, New Jersey, 1887–89; electrical assistant at Westinghouse subsidiary,

United States Company, 1890; electrical assistant at Stanley Company of Pittsfield, Massachusetts, 1891; professor of electrical engineering, Purdue University, 1892; chair of electrical engineering, Western University of Pennsylvania (later University of Pittsburgh), 1893–1900; special agent, U.S. Weather Bureau, 1900–1902; transmitted first speech by wireless and developed high-frequency alternator for wireless transmission, 1900; discovered heterodyne principle, 1901; general manager, National Electric Signaling Company, 1902–11; introduced electrolytic or chemical wireless detector, 1902; established Brant Rock, Massachusetts wireless station, 1905; first broadcast, Christmas Eve 1906; researched submarine signaling systems, 1912–21. Died in Flatts Village, Hamilton, Bermuda, 23 July 1932.

Selected Publications

"The Possibilities of Wireless Telegraphy," *Transactions of the American Institute of Electrical Engineers* 16 (1900)
"Inventions of Reginald A. Fessenden," *Radio News* 6–7 (January–November 1925) (an autobiography)
"Wireless Telephony," in *The Development of Wireless to 1920*, edited by George Shiers, 1977

Further Reading

Aitken, Hugh G.J., *The Continuous Wave: Technology and American Radio, 1900–1932*, Princeton, New Jersey: Princeton University Press, 1985
Douglas, Susan J., *Inventing American Broadcasting, 1899–1922*, Baltimore, Maryland: Johns Hopkins University Press, 1987
Fessenden, Helen May Trott, *Fessenden: Builder of Tomorrows*, New York: Coward-McCann, 1940
Kraeuter, David W., *Radio and Television Pioneers: A Patent Bibliography*, Metuchen, New Jersey: Scarecrow Press, 1992
Kraeuter, David W., "A New Bibliography of Reginald Fessenden," *AWA Review* 8 (1993)
McEvoy, J.F., "Fessenden and the Birth of Radio: Right against the World," *Beaver* (June–July 1990)
Raby, Ormond, *Radio's First Voice: The Story of Reginald Fessenden*, Toronto: Macmillan Canada, 1970
Seitz, Frederick, *The Cosmic Inventor: Reginald Aubrey Fessenden (1866–1932)*, Philadelphia: American Philosophical Society, 1999
Waller, Adrian, "Unsung Genius," *Equinox* (March–April 1989)
Webb, Michael, *Reginald Fessenden: Radio's Forgotten Voice*, Mississauga, Ontario: Copp Clark Pitman, 1991

Fibber McGee and Molly

Radio Comedy Series

For three decades, the consummate comedians Jim Jordan (1896–1988) and his wife Marian Driscoll (1898–1961) imitated and mocked the habits of middle-class American homeowners. They began as musicians and vaudevillians. These theatrical experiences, plus several radio series, prepared them for the initial broadcast of *Fibber McGee and Molly* on Tuesday, 16 April 1935. (The show lasted in various forms until 1959.) The Jordans and their writers, mainly Don Quinn and later Phil Leslie, wisely preserved what worked. During the 1940s, fans always voted it one of their favorite programs. Expressions like "Fibber McGee's closet" percolated into popular speech. So did tag lines like Molly's (Marian) "T'aint funny, McGee," Throckmorton P. Gildersleeve's (Hal Peary) "You're a haaard man, McGee," and the Old Timer's (Bill Thompson) "That's pretty funny, Johnny, but that ain't the way I heerd it." (Fibber McGee's overstuffed closet became an American icon, probably for two reasons: it symbolized the unpredictable fullness of the McGees' world, and its sound of falling hip boots, mandolin, Aunt Sarah's picture, and moose head—a triumph of sound effects—consoled listeners who had a similar storage problem. A replica may be seen at the Museum of Broadcasting in Chicago.)

Their modest home at 79 Wistful Vista attracted visitors from a wide variety of social, economic, and ethnic backgrounds. Such conviviality required explanation because McGee was often uncivil, arguing with bankers and bus drivers and department store managers, a dynamo of precarious amiability. Luckily, Molly moderated his bumptious unconviviality so that their many callers simultaneously experienced the contradictory ideals of defensive homeowner and welcoming hostess.

The perilous balance of discourtesy and diplomacy allowed McGee to insult guests and still retain their friendship. Doc Gamble (Arthur Q. Bryan) often received the master's barbs. One time the doctor looked forward to a vacation he said would leave him "ship shape." Ever the deflator of other people's fantasies, McGee agreed that the doctor already looked like a great big "stern wheeler." In keeping with the American spirit of fair play and the aesthetic rule that helplessness is not funny, Doc returned these insults with agility. Once he scolded McGee for being too cheap to buy a proper suit, dubbing Fibber a "rhinestone Jim Brady" and "our little Lucius Booby in that pin-stripe awning he uses for a sport coat."

Similarly, other drop-ins to their parlor had positions that would ordinarily merit respect but instead received impertinence. Policemen were called "lugans" and "larrigans," told to take off their hats, and given false information (asked his

name, Fibber replied, "Herman Gibbletripe—and this is my wife Clara"). Mayor LaTrivia (Gale Gordon), outside the McGees' home an effective orator, dissolved into babble at the McGees'. He boasted that the City Council had opposed him, but he had "stuck to [his] guns." Both Fibber and Molly confounded him by asking why an elected official needed weapons, suggesting that he might have been more successful if he had not threatened them, and finally warning him that guns should not be tolerated.

Fibber reacted to aristocrats with a peculiar mixture of envy—which prompted get-rich projects to find a substitute for sugar or turn paper back into cloth—and disdain. Despite all the wealth of grand dames like Abigail Uppington (Isabel Randolph) and Millicent Carstairs (Bea Benedaret), Fibber commented that the latter "acts like a coquettish dray horse." He admired clothing store dummies for their "nonchalant, supercilious, haughty" look: "It takes six generations of money in the family to achieve an expression like that." Molly personalized his sociological dictum: "Yes, it's strange how often a vacant face goes with a full pocketbook, which ought to give you a very expressive countenance."

Because he never seemed to work and borrowed tools without returning them, McGee's own income remained ambiguous. He yearned for money so much that he ripped apart their antique sofa to find $20,000 hidden by an ancestor—$20,000 Confederate, that is. The appearance of a maid on some shows, variously called Beulah (played by a man, Marlin Hurt) or Lena (Gene Carroll, also a man), hinted that he was prosperous; the appearance of a renter, Alice Darling (Shirley Mitchell), a gabby factory worker, on other episodes suggested that he needed spare cash. The general impression was of a household relatively secure in the economic parade.

Located in the middle of the middle class, McGee often was bested by those whom snobs would have considered beneath concern. When Ole Swenson (Dick LeGrand), the Swedish janitor at the Elks' Club, said his boy in the submarine service was on a secret mission, McGee paraphrased loftily, "Sub rosa, eh?" Ole calmly torpedoed the hifalutin' Latin with, "No, submarine." Likewise, the recently immigrated Nick DePopoulous (Bill Thompson) steamrolled over "Fizzer," telling his own tales with nonstop, heavily accented malapropisms.

Far from being disturbed by unpredictable standards for social deportment, people in McGee's universe enjoyed the anarchy. Wallace Wimple (Bill Thompson), the hen-pecked victim of "Sweetie Face," his "big, old wife," just wanted to be alone with his bird book. To avoid her abuse, Wallace secretly rented a room under the name "Lancelot Eisenhower

Fibber McGee and Molly
Courtesy Radio Hall of Fame

Dempsey"—a name, he explained dreamily, that "just appealed to me somehow. It's such a *brave* name."

Two final visitors show how the give-and-take of their peculiar hosting rituals eliminated barriers. After Fibber read a bedtime story to Teeny (Marian), the precocious little neighbor girl, she asked, "What's a 'dell'?" Fibber: "Oh, it's a kind of shady nook in the woods where green things grow." Teeny: "You mean like dell pickles." Announcer Harlow Wilcox, ever touting the benefits of Johnson's Wax, delivered his pitches despite McGee's interruptions.

Just as the program democratically blurred social distinctions, the language too evaded rules. McGee frequently delivered such tongue-tangling monologues as:

When I worked in the big mill there, I was quite the dude. 'Mill Dude McGee' I was known as. Mill Dude McGee, a magnificent mass of muscle and manly manners mesmerizing the maidens in the Midwest and mentioned most every month in many of the men's magazines as the mirror and model for male millinery merchants, meticulous material manufacturers, and miscellaneous members of the metropolitan mob, mighty and magnetic from November through May.

Individual words, like manners, evolved into new forms. After getting Mayor LaTrivia's goat, Fibber bragged to Molly, "He sure gets worked up, don't he? He was just liver with rage."

MOLLY: You mean livid, Dearie.
FIBBER: Go on, livid is a girl's name, like Livid De Haviland.
MOLLY: That's Olivia,
FIBBER: Oh, don't kid me, Snookie. Olivia's a country in South America.

During another episode, Fibber skipped from "subtle to subitle to scuttle to shuttle to chateau." Such celebrations of social and linguistic independence during decades of Depression, war, and tumultuous recovery that required national conformity explain the enduring appeal of *Fibber McGee and Molly*.

JAMES A. FREEMAN

See also Gordon, Gale; Situation Comedy; Sound Effects; Vaudeville

Cast

Fibber McGee	Jim Jordan
Molly McGee	Marian Jordan
Teeny	Marian Jordan
Mrs. Abigail Uppington (1936–59)	Isabel Randolph
Nick Depopoulous (1936–59)	Bill Thompson
Widdicomb Blotto	Bill Thompson
Horatio K. Boomer (1936–59)	Bill Thompson
Old Timer (1937–59)	Bill Thompson
Wallace Wimple (1941–59)	Bill Thompson
Wallingford Tuttle Gildersleeve	Cliff Arquette
Throckmorton P. Gildersleeve (1939–59)	Harold Peary
Mayor LaTrivia (1941–59)	Gale Gordon
Foggy Williams	Gale Gordon
Alice Darling (1943–59)	Shirley Mitchell
Beulah (1944–59)	Marlin Hurt
Mrs. Millicent Carstairs	Bea Benaderet
Silly Watson	Hugh Studebaker
Uncle Dennis	Ransom Sherman
Lena	Gene Carroll
Announcer (1935–53)	Harlow Wilcox
Announcer (1953–56)	John Wald

Producers/Directors

Cecil Underwood, Frank Pittman, Max Hutto

Programming History

NBC Blue	April 1935–June 1936
NBC Red	June 1936–1938
NBC	March 1938–September 1959

Further Reading

Griswold, J.B., "Up From Peoria," *The American Magazine* 133 (March, 1942)

Price, Tom, *Fibber McGee's Closet: The Ultimate Log of Performances by Fibber McGee and Molly 1917–1987: A Celebration of the 52nd Anniversary of Fibber McGee and Molly and Jim's 70 Years in Show Business*, 2 volumes, Monterey, California: Thomas A. Price, 1987

Price, Tom, *Performance Logs of Marian + Jim Jordan, #s 1–10, 1917–1980*, Monterey, California: Thomas A. Price, 1980 (Contains logs of *Air Scouts*, 1927–1929; *The Smith Family*, 1927–1932; *Farmer Rusk's Top O'Morning*, 1931–1932; Several Short Series, 1931–1934; *Smackout*, 1931–1935; Appearances and Specials, 1917–1980; *Marquette, The Little French Girl*, 1931–1932; *Mr. Twister, Mind Trickster*, 1932–1933; *Kaltenmayer's Kindergarten*, 1932–1935; *Fibber McGee and Molly*, 1935–1959)

Stumpf, Charles, and Ben Ohmart, *Fibber McGee's Scrapbook*, Boalsburg, Pennsylvania: BearManor Media, 2002

Stumpf, Charles, and Tom Price, *Heavenly Days! The Story of Fibber McGee and Molly*, Waynesville, North Carolina: The World of Yesterday, 1987

Yoder, Robert M, "The McGee's of Wistful Vista," *The Saturday Evening Post* 221 (April 9 and 16, 1949)

Film Depictions of Radio

Radio's depiction in motion pictures initially stemmed from the concurrence of their golden ages, as radio stars were featured in movies, often playing their radio characters. Thereafter, films about radio focused more on radio's producers, dealing with the challenges and ethical issues they faced, or on listeners, depicting the impact radio had on their lives—particularly the medium's ability to unite communities. Mentioned here are many but by no means all of the motion pictures featuring radio-related subjects.

Radio Movies in the Golden Age

Major motion pictures focusing on radio first appeared during the height of Hollywood's studio system in the 1930s and gave fans their first chance to see moving pictures of radio celebrities. Virtually all were comedies or musicals, designed to get the audience's mind off Depression–era realities.

Foremost among these was the series of films beginning with *The Big Broadcast* (1932), which included George Burns, Gracie Allen, and Bing Crosby as employees of a struggling radio station whose survival depends on a group of radio celebrities, including Kate Smith, Cab Calloway, the Boswell Sisters, Arthur Tracy, and The Vincent Lopez Orchestra. This box office success led to a sequel, *The Big Broadcast of 1936* (1935), which finds Burns and Allen with a contraption known as a Radio Eye (what we now call television) on which various stars appear, including Ethel Merman. Still another sequel, *The Big Broadcast of 1937* (1936) followed, wherein Jack Benny is now the radio boss and Martha Raye his secretary; Burns and Allen returned, appearing once again with a host of stars, including Benny Goodman, Benny Fields, and Leopold Stokowski and his orchestra. The final installment, *The Big Broadcast of 1938* (1937), finds W.C. Fields playing twins who race ships that are powered by electricity supplied from radio broadcasts; it starred Raye, as well as Dorothy Lamour, Shirley Ross, and Bob Hope, who sang what became his signature "Thanks for the Memories" for the first time.

Another series of films that tried to mimic the success of the *Big Broadcast* began with *The Hit Parade* (1937), in which a talent search for radio stars turns up a series of celebrities, including Duke Ellington. Sequels included *Hit Parade of 1941* (1940), *Hit Parade of 1943* (1943), *Hit Parade of 1947* (1947), and *Hit Parade of 1951* (1950) and continued the trend of story lines designed to pack in as many acts as possible.

In the same genre of movies about radio stars was *The Great American Broadcast* (1941), which centers on a love triangle between a young woman and two World War I veterans who enter the radio business together, later to become rivals.

The finale hinges on a scheme by one of the men to reunite the woman and his wartime friend after they have parted ways, deciding to step aside and let the true lovers reconcile. His scheme involves organizing the first nationwide radio broadcast, an idea originally conceived by his war buddy, who he knows will surface to take credit and be reunited with his love. The broadcast itself features many top-name acts, including Kate Smith, Eddie Cantor, Rudy Vallee, and Jack Benny.

During this era a number of movies were also produced based upon radio programs themselves, giving audiences a chance to see their favorite radio characters in action. These include a movie version of *Ed Wynn, The Fire Chief* simply titled *The Chief* (1933) and starring Wynn. Several films featured characters of the radio comedy *Fibber McGee and Molly*, featuring the radio stars Jim and Marian Jordan. These films started with featured roles for the Jordans, playing their radio characters, in *This Way Please* (1937), followed by starring roles in *Look Who's Laughing* (1941), co-starring Edgar Bergen and Lucille Ball, *Here We Go Again* (1942), with Bergen, Gale Gordon and radio's *Great Gildersleeve* star Harold Peary, and *Heavenly Days* (1944). Peary enjoyed a string of films based upon *The Great Gildersleeve*, including *Gildersleeve on Broadway* (1943), *Gildersleeve's Bad Day* (1943), and *Gildersleeve's Ghost* (1944). Finally, there is *My Friend Irma* (1949), based on the radio sitcom of the same name and starring the radio show's lead actress Marie Wilson. The film featured the debut pairing of Dean Martin and Jerry Lewis, as did a sequel, *My Friend Irma Goes West* (1950). Band leader and radio star Kay Kyser also appeared in several motion pictures.

What *The Big Broadcast* and its progeny were to 1930s and 1940s radio stars, a series of rock-and-roll radio movies starring renowned disc jockey Alan Freed was to 1950s rock acts. These films included *Rock Around the Clock* (1956), *Don't Knock the Rock* (1956), *Rock, Rock, Rock* (1956), *Mister Rock and Roll* (1957), and *Go, Johnny, Go!* (1959). Showcasing the likes of Bill Haley and the Comets, The Platters, Little Richard, Chuck Berry, and The Moonglows, these movies featured plots that were mainly designed to pack in as many rock performances as possible. Freed's disc jockey career was itself the subject of a later film titled *American Hot Wax* (1978).

Radio Drama on Film

Foremost among films examining challenges facing radio's producers was *FM* (1978). The movie focuses on the successful program director of the number one rock-and-roll station in Los Angeles and his efforts to keep the station's sound from being too influenced by the commercial interests of its corporate owners. The overall theme of the movie is addressed in a pivotal scene, when the new sales manager toasts "to profit, and the quality it brings," to which the program director replies "to quality, and the profit it brings." Highlighting the extreme personalities of the station's air staff, the movie also foregrounds the influence radio has on its community, as the disc jockeys strike rather than give in to over-zealous commercial interests—a move that inspires hundreds of loyal fans to join the protest outside the station.

Director Oliver Stone critically examines the shock jock phenomenon in *Talk Radio* (1988), a film about a late-night talk show host based upon a play by Eric Bogosian. An intense, intelligent examination of hatred, violence, and loneliness in America, all of which are exhibited by callers to a radio program called *Night Talk*, the film is also a study of the host himself, who must suffer the consequences of provoking his late-night listeners to anger. The shock jock is ultimately killed by one of his violent listeners. The film critically examines the capacity of provocative radio talk show hosts to empower society's most troubled members, under the guise of providing entertainment and exploiting radio's First Amendment privileges.

Good Morning Vietnam (1987), perhaps the best known of all the films treated here, was directed by Barry Levinson and tells the partially true story of a wise-cracking, quick-witted disc jockey who joins the staff of Armed Forces Radio Saigon and uses his comic personality to entertain and unite the troops. From presidential impersonations to crass humor, the newcomer (played by Robin Williams) delivers a high-powered series of gags and thinly veiled criticisms of the war, in the process receiving bags-full of fan mail and the contempt of his humorless supervisors. The film also shows a more serious side, as the comic announcer confronts the ethics of army censorship of radio news.

Private Parts (1997) was shock jock Howard Stern's homage to his own rise to power. Based upon his book and starring Stern, the film recounts his career in the radio business, from his first problems with management at a local station, to meeting his long-time on-air companion Robin Quivers, to his network radio days and run-ins with the FCC. A somewhat one-sided retelling of the story, the film presents Stern as a working-class hero who does what he must to entertain the masses, much to the chagrin of his uppity and uptight management counterparts.

Foremost among films focusing on radio's listeners is Woody Allen's *Radio Days* (1987). A nostalgic look at World War II era radio, the film depicts Allen's childhood reminis-

cences of the role radio played in the lives of his Rockaway Beach family. A mock Martian invasion helps an Aunt see the cowardice of her date; the fantasy of a masked avenger allows a boy to imagine a life apart from suburban humdrum, much as exotic South American music allows his cousin to do the same; game shows or a ventriloquist's act provide occasions for family bonding or discussion; news bulletins following rescue efforts to save a young child who fell down a well help the family put their own petty squabbles in perspective; and war reports help a nation define an era. Throughout the film, Allen affords radio a ubiquitous presence, fondly recalling its role in every aspect of his childhood and lamenting that his memories of radio and its era fade more with every passing year.

Radio's influence in uniting communities is depicted even in films not principally focused upon radio. Hence, the cult classic *The Warriors* (1979) depicts a DJ, shown only as a pair of lips speaking into a microphone, as she helps gang members throughout New York City track and hunt members of the Warriors, who are falsely accused of murdering the charismatic leader of the city's most powerful gang; ultimately, she apologizes to the gang for the urbanite community's error. Another inner city set film that highlights radio's role in a community is Spike Lee's *Do the Right Thing* (1989), a drama about the eruption of racial tension on a city street in Brooklyn. The disc jockey of the street's storefront radio station serves as a source of news, reason, and inspiration for the community, helping to calm tension and keep the community apprised of neighborhood happenings. Finally there is George Lucas' classic *American Graffiti* (1973), wherein the omnipresent rock music and hip chatter of archetypal disc jockey Wolfman Jack set the mood of the time and binds together the community of young adults coming of age.

RICHARD WOLFF

See also Fan Magazines; Hollywood and Radio

Further Reading

Beaver, Frank, *Oliver Stone: Wakeup Cinema*, New York: Twayne Publishers, and Toronto, Ontario: Maxwell Macmillan Canada, 1994

Hirshhorn, Clive, *The Hollywood Musical*, New York: Crown Publishers, and London: Octopus, 1981; 2nd edition, New York: Portland House, and London: Pyramid, 1991

Kunz, Don, "Oliver Stone's *Talk Radio*," *Literature-Film Quarterly* 25 (January 1997)

Yacowar, Maurice, "The Religion of *Radio Days*," *Journal of Popular Film and Television* 16 (Summer 1998)

Fireside Chats

President Franklin D. Roosevelt's Use of Radio

The election of Franklin D. Roosevelt to the U.S. presidency in 1932 coincided with the development of radio networks and the growing popularity of radio. Radio was an ideal medium for Roosevelt, whose voice and style of delivery were well suited to the microphone.

Throughout his presidency (1933–45), Roosevelt used radio to talk to Americans about the problems they faced during the Depression and World War II. He inspired listeners to summon their confidence, determination, and courage to combat these threats to the nation's survival. Roosevelt's conversational, informal radio addresses quickly became known as "fireside chats."

As governor of New York, Roosevelt had used radio to appeal directly to the state's voters, and by the time he entered the White House, he was fully aware of the benefits of the medium. Because many newspaper owners were not supporters of his New Deal programs, Roosevelt found an advantage with radio, which allowed him to speak directly and personally with listeners in their own living rooms. Unable to walk without support after 1921 because of polio, Roosevelt found radio to be an ideal way to project an image of active and powerful leadership.

Roosevelt's press secretary, Steve Early, once noted that Roosevelt liked to picture his audience as a small group sitting around a fireside; this image led to a radio introduction that included the phrase "fireside chat." There are varying opinions as to which of Roosevelt's radio addresses should be classified as fireside chats, with the number placed at between 25 and 31 addresses he made during the 12 years of his presidency. Certainly not all of Roosevelt's radio speeches were in this category, as many of his other radio presentations were tied to ceremonial occasions or political events.

The fireside chats tended to be relatively brief, usually less than 30 minutes, and were structured so that the opening generally focused on a recent event. This was followed by a review of government actions and responses, along with an explanation of the likely impact on the country and the lives of listeners, including the roles they could play in helping to solve problems. Roosevelt's informal language included repetitive devices and simple, easily understood terms. He called for forward, progressive action and expressed optimism and faith in the American people and in divine providence.

Most of the fireside chats were scheduled between 9:00 P.M. and 11:00 P.M. and originated from the East Room or the Oval Office of the White House. Frequently, friends or members of the family were in attendance.

Although Roosevelt received assistance with research and preparation, including early drafts, his speeches reflect his own phrasing, personality, and style. Listeners noted that his pleasant and distinctive voice inspired hope and confidence. This played an important part in Roosevelt's ability to communicate ideas and emotions. His relatively slow delivery, clear articulation, and even his Eastern accent contributed to his memorable and successful use of radio.

Early fireside chats described New Deal measures to combat the Depression. Topics included the banking crisis, the National Recovery Administration, the Works Progress Administration, the gold standard, and unemployment. Roosevelt's goal was to assure listeners that his administration was doing everything possible to relieve hardships resulting from economic conditions.

By the late 1930s, although the official U.S. position relative to the war in Europe was one of neutrality, Roosevelt exhibited increasing sympathy for the Allies, and by 1940 the United States was providing nonmilitary support to Britain and France. In a fireside chat during May of that year, Roosevelt urged further American commitment to the Allied cause, and by 19 December, in another radio address, he called on the United States to become the "great arsenal of democracy." Following the Japanese attack on Pearl Harbor, Roosevelt used radio to call on the public for increased industrial production and for the acceptance of necessary restrictions at home during the war effort. During the war, Roosevelt used radio to inform the public, but he also realized that it was important to avoid providing information to the enemy, who could also listen to his broadcasts. Some of the comments in his radio addresses during the war were actually intended for Axis listeners and conveyed the message that the United States was determined and able to persevere to the war's end. The themes of Roosevelt's wartime radio speeches emphasized the nobility of the Allied cause, the inevitability of victory, and the necessity for individual sacrifice. He spoke of the need for more manpower, both military and civilian, and he expressed concern about complacency and overconfidence. Roosevelt used radio to encourage the purchase of war bonds and to describe how everyone could contribute to victory.

Toward the war's end, Roosevelt described the demand for unconditional surrender and plans for a postwar America. In his last fireside chat, delivered 6 January 1945, Roosevelt expressed hope for a United Nations organization, which he described as the best hope for a lasting peace. Franklin D. Roosevelt died 12 April 1945.

U.S. President Franklin D. Roosevelt moments before his fireside chat on 12 March 1933
Courtesy AP/Wide World Photos

Roosevelt was the first president to make extensive and continuous use of modern electronic means to speak directly to his constituents. This capability has contributed to the increased power of the executive branch of government. Roosevelt's use of radio allowed him to influence the national agenda and to counter opposing newspaper editorials. His radio addresses played a major role in his popular image, in his being elected four times to the presidency of the United States, and in the success of his efforts to lead the nation through the years of economic depression and world war.

B.R. SMITH

See also Politics and Radio; United States Presidency and Radio

Further Reading

Becker, Samuel I., "Presidential Power: The Influence of Broadcasting," *Quarterly Journal of Speech* (February 1961)

Braden, Waldo W., and Earnest Brandenburg, "Roosevelt's Fireside Chats," *Speech Monographs* 22, no. 5 (November 1955)

Brandenburg, Earnest, "The Preparation of Franklin D. Roosevelt's Speeches," *Quarterly Journal of Speech* 25 (1949)

Brown, Robert J., "The Radio President," in *Manipulating the Ether: The Power of Broadcast Radio in Thirties America*, by Brown, Jefferson, North Carolina: McFarland, 1998

Chester, Edward W., *Radio, Television, and American Politics*, New York: Sheed and Ward, 1969

Roosevelt, Franklin D., *FDR's Fireside Chats*, edited by Russell D. Buhite and David W. Levy, Norman: University of Oklahoma Press, 1992

Rosenman, Samuel Irving, *Working with Roosevelt*, New York: Harper, 1952

Schlesinger, Arthur Meier, *The Imperial Presidency*, Boston: Houghton Mifflin, 1973

Smith, B.R., "FDR's Use of Radio in the War Years," *Journal of Radio Studies* 4 (1997)

Winfield, Betty, *FDR and the News Media*, Urbana: University of Illinois Press, 1990

First Amendment and Radio

The First Amendment (1791) to the U.S. Constitution provides, in part, that Congress shall make no law abridging the freedom of speech or of the press. Yet in spite of this proscription, there exist a number of regulations that limit free expression on radio. The very fact that stations must be licensed is a restriction that would be considered clearly unconstitutional if it were applied to print media. On the other hand, the courts have stated that radio broadcasting is entitled to First Amendment protection. The amount of protection is less than that enjoyed by print media, but it is still significant.

The fact that the First Amendment protections extend to radio as well as the press was made clear by a 1948 Supreme Court decision, *United States v Paramount Pictures*, which stated, "We have no doubt that moving pictures, like newspapers and radio, are included in the press whose freedom is guaranteed by the First Amendment." In order to best understand what free expression rights are due to radio, one needs to examine the rationale for regulating radio. Courts and legal scholars have provided a variety of arguments for regulation that fit into four general categories: scarcity of broadcast frequencies, the broadcast spectrum as a public resource, the need to alleviate interference, and the pervasiveness and power of the broadcast media.

Scarcity

In a 1984 decision, the Supreme Court stated, "The fundamental distinguishing characteristic of the new medium of broadcasting that, in our view, has required some adjustment in First Amendment analysis is that broadcast frequencies are a scarce resource that must be portioned out among applicants." This scarcity rationale has undergone a number of attacks in recent years with the proliferation of media, but in fact it is still considered a valid regulatory rationale. Although the number of radio stations (as well as the number of most other media outlets) has increased, courts continue to accept a scarcity ratio-

nale. The reason for this is that scarcity does not depend on the number of existing media outlets but rather on the determination of whether a new applicant stands a good chance of entry to the market. A vast number of existing media outlets implies that diversity exists, not that scarcity has been eliminated. If new applicants want to obtain station licenses and are unable to do so, that implies scarcity. Scarcity is a function of the number of people desiring a station to the number of stations available. As long as applicants exceed available frequencies, scarcity exists. As the Supreme Court noted in its *Red Lion* decision in 1969, "When there are substantially more individuals who want to broadcast than there are frequencies to allocate, it is idle to posit an unabridgeable First Amendment right to broadcast comparable to the right of every individual to speak, write, or publish." This is why there will never be scarcity for newspaper publishers, no matter how many newspapers are published in the United States. In theory, at least, any American can start a newspaper (at least there is no legal restriction). The same is not true for starting a radio station.

In 1943 the Supreme Court supported the notion that scarcity entitled the Federal Communications Commission (FCC) to make judgments about who would best serve the public interest. In *National Broadcasting Company v United States*, the Court rejected the argument that chain broadcasting rules were a violation of the First Amendment:

> If that be so, it would follow that every person whose application for a license to operate a station is denied by the Commission is thereby denied his constitutional right of free speech. Freedom of utterance is abridged to many who wish to use the limited facilities of radio. Unlike other modes of expression, radio is not inherently available to all. That is its unique characteristic, and that is why, unlike other modes of expression, it is subject to governmental regulation. Because it cannot be used by all, some who wish to use it must be denied. But Con-

gress did not authorize the Commission to choose among applicants upon the basis of their political, economic or social views, or upon any other capricious basis. . . . The licensing system established by Congress in the Communications Act of 1934 was a proper exercise of its authority over commerce. The standard it provided for the licensing of stations was the "public interest, convenience, or necessity." Denial of a station license on that ground, if valid under the Act, is not a denial of free speech.

Public Resource

In 1962 President John F. Kennedy referred to the broadcast spectrum as a "critical natural resource." The federal government typically regulates the use of natural resources to ensure that they are not damaged and that their use is in the public interest. Viewing the spectrum as a public resource results in a philosophy that views users of the public resource as public trustees, who as such can be expected to act according to the dictates of those allowing them to use the resource. The government could have adopted other models for rationing spectrum, but it didn't. The assumption is that those who use the public resource have some degree of public service obligation.

A good example of this requirement is the demand, found in Section 312 of the Communications Act, that broadcasters provide reasonable access to candidates for federal office. This affirmative obligation on broadcasters, which would be unconstitutional if applied to print media, can only be justified under a public-resource rationale. In the 1981 Supreme Court Decision *Columbia Broadcasting System v Federal Communications Commission*, the Court wrote that such a rule "represents an effort by Congress to assure that an important resource—the airwaves—will be used in the public interest. [The rule] properly balances the First Amendment rights of federal candidates, the public, and broadcasters."

Interference

Undoubtedly the oldest of the regulatory rationales is the assertion that the government must regulate the broadcast spectrum in order to prevent interference. This was provided as rationale for the passage of the Radio Acts in 1912 and 1927. Failure to limit interference would result in a "cacophony" in which no one would be heard. Thus, the government exercises its authority to limit the free speech of some so that others might be heard. Some might contend that interference and scarcity are actually the same rationale, when in fact they are different. Their connection in broadcast contexts is understandable, because the spectrum is subject to both scarcity and interference. It is possible, however, to have interference when there is no physical scarcity. It is interesting to note that the

Supreme Court's 1969 *Red Lion* decision quoted a 1945 print media case involving the Associated Press when it stated "the right of free speech . . . does not embrace a right to snuff out the free speech of others." Clearly, there can be interference without scarcity. In *Red Lion*, the Court stated:

> When two people converse face to face, both should not speak at once if either is to be clearly understood. But the range of the human voice is so limited that there could be meaningful communications if half the people in the United States were talking and the other half listening. Just as clearly, half the people might publish and the other half read. But the reach of radio signals is incomparably greater than the range of human voice and the problem of interference is a massive reality. The lack of know-how and equipment may keep many from the air, but only a tiny fraction of those with resources and intelligence can hope to communicate by radio at the same time if intelligible communication is to be had, even if the entire radio spectrum is utilized in the present state of commercially acceptable technology.

The Supreme Court justified broadcast regulation, in part at least, because of broadcasting's unique physical characteristics.

Pervasiveness and Power

Perhaps most controversial of all the rationales, this claim asserts that broadcast media should be regulated because of the media's unique role in the lives of Americans. In the famous *Pacifica* case (dealing with George Carlin's "Seven Dirty Words" monologue), the Supreme Court stated that "the broadcast media have established a uniquely pervasive presence in the lives of all Americans." Yet no one would attempt to assert that a small-town radio station has more pervasiveness and power than, say, *The New York Times*. Perhaps a more appropriate term for the Court to have used would have been *invasive* rather than *pervasive*. The Court seemed to be influenced by the fact that radio transmissions come into the privacy of one's home and automobile and are instantly available to children, unlike newspapers, which wait outside our homes for us to collect them and are unreadable by children still too young to read. In *Columbia Broadcasting System v Democratic National Committee* in 1973, the Court stated a concern dating back to the 1920s that radio's audience is in a sense "captive" because it cannot simply ignore the messages sent by broadcasters.

It is this rationale that supports limits on broadcast indecency. FCC rules that restrict the use of indecent language during certain hours of the broadcast day (6 A.M. to 10 P.M.) are based on the premise that the audience will consist of a number of minors who should not be subjected to indecent language. Allowing the restriction of indecent material on the air is a recognition of broadcasting's pervasive nature.

First Amendment Protections

In spite of the regulations that do exist, radio is not without First Amendment rights. Section 326 of the Communications Act specifically states:

> Nothing in this Act shall be understood or construed to give the Commission the power of censorship over the radio communications or signals transmitted by any radio station, and no regulation or condition shall be promulgated or fixed by the Commission which shall interfere with the right of free speech by means of radio communication.

Although some might contend that the Section 326 provision is rendered either superfluous by the First Amendment or invalid by rules such as those limiting indecency, the courts have continued to support the general principle that the FCC may not censor broadcasts.

Radio stations also have the right to decide who uses their facilities. The Supreme Court has unequivocally stated that the need to serve the public interest does not require that broadcasters provide access for individuals or organizations. Those who would like to present their positions on public issues have ample opportunity to do so without a government requirement that stations afford them airtime.

The Supreme Court has suggested that the balance between the First Amendment rights of broadcasters and the need for government regulation is not static and that changing conditions might warrant a change in the balance between the two. In the 1973 decision *Columbia Broadcasting System v Democratic National Committee*, the Court stated, "the history of the Communications Act and the activities of the Commission over a period of 40 years reflect a continuing search for means to achieve reasonable regulation compatible with the First Amendment rights of the public and the licensees." Eleven years later, in *Federal Communications Commission v League of Women Voters*, the Supreme Court made it even more clear that regulatory rationales were open to review and revision. In two rather significant footnotes, the Court signaled its willingness to accept a regulatory scheme that was less demanding of broadcasters. In addressing the scarcity rationale, the Court wrote, "We are not prepared, however, to reconsider our longstanding approach *without some signal from Congress or the FCC* that technological developments have advanced so far that some revision of the system of broadcast regulation may be required" (emphasis added). Although the Court was not prepared to lay the fairness doctrine or the scarcity rationale to rest, it opened the door for others to do so. After a series of legal actions, the FCC did in fact eliminate the fairness doctrine.

The entire concept of treating broadcast differently from print media has been challenged for some time, but the practice continues. Modifications have been made, and radio has significantly fewer regulations today than it had prior to the deregulation movement that began in the 1970s. Nonetheless, some would assert that the changing nature of mass media will make it more difficult to have different regulatory schemes based on modes of transmission. With media converging as they are, will regulatory policies that treat media differently based on modes of transmission be able to survive? In an era in which both newspaper and radio messages can reach their audience via the internet, should one be regulated differently from the other? These are questions that have been posed for decades, yet our regulatory policy remains essentially unchanged. Broadcast media are subject to regulation based on the four regulatory rationales stated above, while the print media are largely unregulated. The amount of regulation that will be tolerated is subject to the balancing engaged in by the Supreme Court, but radio (along with television) continues to be subject to regulation.

DOM CARISTI

See also Communications Act of 1934; Federal Communications Commission; Federal Radio Commission; Frequency Allocation; Network Monopoly Probe; Public Interest, Convenience, or Necessity; Red Lion Case; Seven Dirty Words Case; United States Congress and Radio; United States Supreme Court and Radio

Further Reading

Associated Press v United States, 326 U.S. 1 (1945)

Bittner, John R., *Broadcast Law and Regulation*, Englewood Cliffs, New Jersey: Prentice Hall, 1982; 2nd edition, as *Law and Regulation of Electronic Media*, 1994

Caristi, Dom, *Expanding Free Expression in the Marketplace: Broadcasting and the Public Forum*, New York: Quorum Books, 1992

Carter, T. Barton, Marc A. Franklin, and Jay B. Wright, *The First Amendment and the Fifth Estate: Regulation of Electronic Mass Media*, 5th edition, New York: Foundation Press, 1999

Columbia Broadcasting System v Democratic National Committee, 412 U.S. 94 (1973)

Emery, Walter B., *Broadcasting and Government: Responsibilities and Regulations*, East Lansing: Michigan State University Press, 1961; revised edition, 1971

Federal Communications Commission v League of Women Voters of California, 468 U.S. 364 (1984)

Federal Communications Commission v Pacifica Foundation, 438 U.S. 726 (1978)

Ginsburg, Douglas H., *Regulation of Broadcasting: Law and Policy towards Radio, Television, and Cable Communications*, St. Paul, Minnesota: West, 1979; 2nd edition, as *Regulation of the Electronic Mass Media: Law and Policy for Radio, Television, Cable, and the New Video Technologies*, by Ginsburg, Michael Botein, and Mark D. Director, 1991

National Broadcasting Company v United States, 319 U.S. 190 (1943)

Powe, Lucas A. Scot, *American Broadcasting and the First Amendment*, Berkeley: University of California Press, 1987

Red Lion Broadcasting Company v Federal Communications Commission, 395 U.S. 367 (1969)

United States v Paramount Pictures, 334 U.S. 131 (1948)

Fleming, Sir John Ambrose 1849–1945

British Electrical Engineer; Inventor of the Vacuum Tube

Sir John Ambrose Fleming led an active scientific life. His career covered the time from James Clerk Maxwell to the advent of electronic television. Fleming has been described as the scientific and technical link between Maxwell and Guglielmo Marconi. He was an outstanding teacher and highly successful popular scientific lecturer. He published more than 100 important papers on his discoveries. Fleming is best known for the thermionic vacuum tube or valve, the first electron tube that could change alternating current, such as a radio wave, to pulsating, one-way flow direct current. Fleming's diode improved radio reception and was a forerunner of the triode tube developed by Lee de Forest. Although the transistor eventually replaced Fleming's valve, his valve remained an important component of radios for nearly three decades and was used in the early days of computers and television.

Fleming began his study of electricity and mathematics under James Clerk Maxwell in the new Cavendish Laboratory at St. John's College in Cambridge. During his studies there, Fleming worked on improving the Carey Foster Bridge, a method for measuring the difference between two nearly equal resistances in electrical conduction. Fleming's improvement made the measuring device faster and more accurate. Maxwell labeled the device "Fleming's banjo" because of the measuring wire's circular shape.

After receiving his doctor of science degree in 1880, Fleming worked as a consultant for private industry. His consulting work resulted in many new methods and instruments for measuring high-frequency currents and new transformer designs. Fleming was a primary contributor to the development of electrical generator stations and distribution networks for several companies, including the London National Company, the Edison Telephone and Electric Light Companies, and the Swan Lamp Factory. For both the Swan and Edison companies, Fleming lent his expertise to photometry and helped develop the large-bulb incandescent lamp that used an aged filament as the light source.

In 1899 the Marconi Wireless Telegraph Company hired Fleming as a scientific adviser to help design the Poldhu wireless station in Cornwall, England. This was the largest wireless station in England and the source of the first transatlantic wireless telegraph transmission in 1901.

Fleming's most important contribution to electrical engineering was his vacuum tube, widely used in both radiotelegraphy and radiotelephony. In 1888 Thomas Edison announced his "Edison effect," which described how electronic particles were emitted from a hot electric lamp filament. Fleming had repeated Edison's findings in 1899 but had found little practical use for Edison's discovery.

In 1904, however, while searching for a more efficient and reliable detector of weak electrical currents, Fleming was inspired to make a new lamp, or valve, that would have a hot filament and an insulated plate sealed inside a high vacuum tube. When a current was passed through the carbon or metal filament, the rarefied air between the hot filament and the cold plate filled with electrons and became a conductor of electricity. He found that the electrons would travel only when the plate was attached to the positive terminal of a generator and that the plate would attract the negatively charged electrons. Fleming also noticed that this flow of electrons was in only one direction, from the hot filament to the cold metal plate, and not in the reverse direction. Alternating current would enter the device, but direct current would leave. Fleming had converted alternating-current radio signals into weak direct-current signals that could be heard with a telephone receiver. This was a major advance in radio technology. Fleming called his discovery a thermionic valve or tube, because it acted much like a check valve, which allows fluids to flow in only one direction. Eventually, the device was labeled "Fleming's valve." It provided the first truly reliable method to measure high-frequency radio waves. Fleming patented his valve in 1904. This discovery revolutionized radio telegraphy communication technology. The vacuum tube was the foundation of electronics until the 1960s, when solid-state technology was developed, replacing vacuum tubes in most electronic devices.

In 1906 Lee de Forest added a third element to Fleming's diode valve, thus effectively separating the high-frequency circuit from that of the filament, making amplification of radio signals possible. Litigation of the de Forest and Fleming patents continued for years. Court decisions in 1916 tied most companies into knots. As the United States entered World War I, the navy offered to indemnify all manufacturers of radio apparatus for the armed forces against any resulting patent infringement suits. This pooling of all patents enabled manufacturers to produce modern equipment without fear of lawsuits. Patent disputes between de Forest and Fleming were not fully resolved until after American Telephone and Telegraph (AT&T) bought de Forest's Audion patent, the Radio Corporation of America (RCA) acquired rights to the Fleming valve, and AT&T and RCA entered into a cross-licensing agreement in 1920.

Throughout his long career, Fleming lectured often at University College, the Royal Institution, and the Royal Society of Arts. He published extensively and presented several important research papers at learned societies' conferences. After Fleming read a paper on the need for an authoritative body for electrical standards for the burgeoning electric lighting industry, the Board of Trade Laboratory and eventually the National Physical Laboratory were established in Great Britain. Fleming is credited with developing a direct-reading potentiometer, set to read current and potential directly in amperes and volts, and with encouraging R.E.B. Crompton to put it on the market in a practical form.

Fleming placed his long scientific career into perspective when he wrote that in comparing the last half of the 19th century and the first third of the 20th century, there was an enormous increase in practical technical achievement, despite the diminished confidence we now have in the validity of our theoretical explanations of natural phenomena.

His peers regarded Fleming very highly because of his extraordinary devotion to his work. He never lost sight of the potential for wireless. He wrote that

radiotelegraphy has not only given to mankind a superlatively beneficial means of communication, but has also opened up for discussion physical and cosmical problems of profound interest. . . . We are only at the very beginning of this evolution, yet it has already completely revolutionised the practical side of wireless telegraphy, as well as telephony (Fleming, 1921).

PETER E. MAYEUX

See also De Forest, Lee; Early Wireless; Marconi, Guglielmo; Maxwell, James Clerk

John Ambrose Fleming. Born in Lancaster, England, 29 November 1849. Attended University College, London, B.S., 1870; Royal School of Mines, South Kensington, 1872–74; St. John's College, Cambridge, Doctor of Science degree, 1880; worked as clerk in stockbrokerage firm, 1868–70; science master, Rosall School and Cheltenham College, 1872–74; chair of mathematics and physics, University College, Nottingham, 1881; consultant, Edison Telephone and Electric Light Company, Swan Lamp Factory, and London National Company, 1882; elected fellow, St. John's, 1883; professor, electrical technology (engineering), University College, 1885–1926; scientific advisor, Marconi Wireless Telegraph Company, 1899; developed the Fleming valve, 1904; appointed professor emeritus, University College, 1926; president, Television Society of London, 1930–45; received Royal Society fellowship, 1892; Hughes Gold Medal, Royal Society of London, 1910; Albert Medal, Royal Society of Arts, 1921; Faraday Medal, British Institution of Electrical Engineers, 1928; knighthood, 1929; Duddell Medal, Physical Society, 1931; Gold Medal, Institute of Radio Engineers (U.S.), 1933; Franklin Medal, Franklin Institute (U.S.), 1935; Kelvin Medal, 1935; elected honorary fellow, Cambridge, 1927; received honorary degree of D.Eng., Liverpool University, 1928. Died in Sidmouth, Devon, England, 18 April 1945.

Selected Publications

Alternate Current Transformer in Theory and Practice, 1888, 1895
Elementary Manual of Radiotelegraphy and Radiotelephony for Students and Operators, 1908
Principles of Electric Wave Telegraphy and Telephony, 1906
Propagation of Electric Currents in Telephone and Telegraph Conductors, 1911
Thermionic Valve and its Developments in Radiotelegraphy and Telephony, 1919
Wonders of Wireless Telegraphy Explained in Simple Terms for the Non-Technical Reader, 1914, 1919
Fifty Years of Electricity; The Memories of an Electrical Engineer, 1921
Memories of a Scientific Life, 1934

Further Reading

Aitken, Hugh G.J., *Syntony and Spark: The Origins of Radio,* New York: Wiley, 1976
Bondyopadhyay, P.K., "Fleming and Marconi: The Cooperation of the Century," *The Radioscientist and Bulletin* 5 (June 1994)
MacGregor-Morris, John Turner, *The Inventor of the Valve: A Biography of Sir Ambrose Fleming,* London: Television Society, 1954

MacGregor-Morris, John Turner, "Fleming, Sir (John) Ambrose," in *Dictionary of National Biography, 1941–1950*, edited by Leopold George Wickham Legg and Edgar Trevor Williams, London and New York: Oxford University Press, 1959

Sterling, Christopher H., and John M. Kittross, *Stay Tuned: A History of American Broadcasting*, 3rd edition, Mahwah, New Jersey: Lawrence Erlbaum, 2002

Tyne, Gerald F.J., *Saga of the Vacuum Tube*, edited by Diana D. Menkes, Indianapolis, Indiana: Sams, 1977

Flywheel, Shyster, and Flywheel

Radio Comedy Program

Although much of their fame rests on the dozen films they made between 1929 and 1950, the Marx Brothers, working together and as solo performers, enjoyed a measure of success in radio and later television broadcasting. The National Broadcasting Company's (NBC) weekly comedy *Flywheel, Shyster, and Flywheel* was the first network radio program to feature the Marx Brothers. Or, more accurately, it featured two of the four-member comedy team: Groucho and Chico. The remaining brothers—Harpo's silent clown and Zeppo's straight man—were less suitable for radio. Despite the fact that only 26 episodes were produced between November 1932 and May 1933, *Flywheel, Shyster, and Flywheel* opened up new avenues for the Marx Brothers' comic genius.

Flywheel, Shyster, and Flywheel's origins are typical of many programs produced for American radio during the early 1930s. Following on the heels of its rival's success with the *Texaco Fire Chief Program*, the Standard Oil Company sought a vehicle to promote its new product line: Esso gasoline and Essolube motor oil. Working with its advertising agency, McCann-Erickson, Standard Oil agreed to sponsor a weekly variety program called *Five Star Theater*. Every night of the week featured a different program: detective stories, dramas, musicals, and comedies. As Michael Barson notes in the introduction to his edited collection of the program's scripts, "the jewel of the enterprise was Monday night's entry, *Beagle, Shyster, and Beagle, Attorneys at Law*," which featured Groucho as Waldorf T. Beagle, a wisecracking ambulance chaser, and Chico as his incompetent assistant, Emmanuel Ravelli. Indeed, with four successful feature films to their credit—*The Coconuts, Animal Crackers, Monkey Business,* and *Horsefeathers*—landing even half of the Marx Brothers was quite a coup for Standard Oil.

Beagle, Shyster, and Beagle debuted on 28 November 1932 over the NBC Blue network. Although audience reaction is difficult to gauge, at least one listener, a New York attorney named Beagle, was not amused. Anxious to avoid a lawsuit,

the network changed the name of Groucho's character to Flywheel and promptly altered the program's title accordingly. Not surprisingly, the scripts for *Flywheel, Shyster, and Flywheel* are characteristic of the Marx Brothers' penchant for rapid-fire one-liners, puns, putdowns, and malapropisms. And as in their movies, on radio the Marx Brothers had little regard for the rule of law or high society: few cherished American values or institutions were spared a "Marxist" skewering. For example, at the end of one episode, Flywheel (Groucho) advises a would-be philanthropist, "Instead of leaving half of your money to your children and the other half to the orphanage, why not leave your children to the orphanage . . . and the million to me?"

What is most significant about these scripts (the original programs were not recorded, but the majority of the show's transcripts survive in the Library of Congress) is their relationship to the Marx Brothers' film work. In some instances, entire routines from earlier films were reworked for *Flywheel, Shyster, and Flywheel*. For example, some episodes featured plot lines and dialogue taken from the Broadway hit and subsequent film *Animal Crackers*. Even the name of Chico's character, Emmanuel Ravelli, came directly from this film. Several scenes from *Monkey Business* found their way into episodes of the radio program as well. On the other hand, a number of *Flywheel, Shyster, and Flywheel* scripts foreshadowed the Marx Brothers' later film work. Of particular interest are early drafts of now archetypal routines and dialogue from the Marx Brothers' classic *Duck Soup*. The film's infamous trial sequence owes much of its funny business to a *Flywheel, Shyster, and Flywheel* script, as does Chico's hilarious recitation on his difficulties as a spy: "Monday I shadow your wife. Tuesday I go to the ball game—she don't show up. Wednesday she go to the ball game—I don't show up. Thursday was a doubleheader. We both no show up. Friday it rain all day—there'sa no ball game, so I go fishing." The name of Groucho's character, Waldorf T. Flywheel, would be recycled some years later in the 1941 film *The Big Store*.

The need for this recycling of old gags and testing of new material is understandable. Along with their writers, Nat Perrin and Alan Sheekman, Groucho and Chico soon grew tired of traveling cross-country from Hollywood to New York to do a weekly radio program. In fact, in January 1933, *Flywheel, Shyster, and Flywheel* took the then unprecedented step of relocating its broadcast from WJZ in New York to Hollywood for a time. Still, the time constraints facing both writers and performers undoubtedly contributed to their willingness to borrow from established routines while refining others. By the middle of 1933, however, it was a moot point. *Flywheel, Shyster, and Flywheel* was taken off the air. Although its ratings were quite respectable, considering the less-than-desirable airtime of 7:30 P.M., the sponsors were disappointed with the show's performance.

Throughout the 1930s and 1940s, Groucho and Chico returned to the airwaves in various guises. In 1934 they were hired by the Columbia Broadcasting System (CBS) to spoof the latest news in a short-lived program called *The Marx of Time*. Both Groucho and Chico struck out on their own as well. Chico made a number of radio appearances as a musical accompanist and band leader, and Groucho served as host for programs such as *Pabst Blue Ribbon Town*. During the war years, the Marx Brothers, including Harpo, made guest appearances on the Armed Forces Radio Service. Of special note, however, is Groucho's role as the judge in Norman Corwin's fanciful courtroom drama from 1945, *The Undecided Molecule*. Groucho's true calling on radio came in 1947 as a quiz show host on *You Bet Your Life*. Curiously, this popular program shuffled between the radio networks before finding a permanent home on NBC.

In an odd but telling postscript, the British Broadcasting Corporation (BBC) began airing recreations of *Flywheel, Shyster, and Flywheel* in 1990. The programs proved quite popular with British audiences and have subsequently been picked up for broadcast in the United States through National Public Radio (NPR).

KEVIN HOWLEY

See also Comedy; You Bet Your Life

Cast

Waldorf T. Flywheel	Groucho Marx
Emmanuel Ravelli	Chico Marx

BBC Cast

Waldorf T. Flywheel	Michael Roberts
Emmanuel Ravelli	Frank Lazarus

Writers

Nat Perin, Arthur Sheekman, Tom McKnight, and George Oppenheimer

Programming History

NBC Blue	28 November 1932–22 May 1933
BBC	1990–92 (19 Episodes)

Further Reading

Adamson, Joe, *Groucho, Harpo, Chico, and Sometimes Zeppo: A History of the Marx Brothers and a Satire of the Rest of the World*, New York: Simon and Schuster, 1973

Barson, Michael, editor, *Flywheel, Shyster, and Flywheel: The Marx Brothers' Lost Radio Show*, New York: Pantheon, 1988

Marx, Groucho, *Groucho and Me*, New York: Geis, and London: Gollancz, 1959

Mitchell, Glenn, *The Marx Brothers Encyclopedia*, London: Batsford, 1996

FM Radio

Frequency modulation (FM) radio, more usually called VHF radio outside the United States, began with experiments in the 1920s and 1930s, expanded to commercial operation in the 1940s, declined to stagnation in the 1950s in the face of competition from television, resumed growth in the 1960s, and rose to dominance of American radio listening by the late 1970s. This entry focuses first on the basics of FM broadcasting and then explores the development of the service in the United States, where it was first invented and developed; finally, this essay turns to selective brief coverage of FM outside the U.S.

FM Basics

FM transmitters modulate a carrier wave signal's frequency rather than its amplitude. That is, the power output remains the same at all times, but the carrier wave frequency changes in relation to the information (music or talk programs, e.g.)

transmitted. Electronic static (most of which is amplitude modulated) may flow with but cannot attach to FM waves, which allows the desired FM signal information to be separated from most interference by special circuits in the receiver.

Because U.S. FM channels are each 200 kilohertz wide (allowing a wide frequency swing), a high-quality sound image is transmitted (up to 15,000 cycles per second—almost three times the frequency response of AM signals and close to the 20,000-cycle limit of human hearing), usually in multiplexed stereo. The cost for this sound quality is paid for in spectrum— each FM station takes up 20 times the spectrum of a single AM station, although only a portion is used for actual signal transmission, with the remainder serving to protect signals of adjacent stations. FM radio in the United States is allocated to the very high frequencies (VHF), occupying 100 channels of 200 kilohertz each between 88 and 108 megahertz. Each FM channel accommodates hundreds of stations—there are more than 7,000 on the air at the beginning of the 21st century.

VHF transmissions follow line-of-sight paths from antenna to receiver, and thus FM transmitters (or television stations, which use neighboring frequencies) are limited in their coverage to usually not more than 40 to 60 miles, depending on terrain and antenna height. That limitation is balanced by the lack of the medium wave interference that AM radio has, which is caused by signals arriving from ground waves or sky waves at slightly different times because of the distances covered.

Experimental Development (to 1940)

No one person "invented" FM radio—indeed, the man most credited with developing the system, Edwin Howard Armstrong, readily conceded that point. The first patents concerning an FM transmission system were granted to Cornelius Ehret of Philadelphia in 1905, probably the first such patents in the world. Scattered mentions of FM in subsequent years focused on its negative aspects, suggesting that, based on what was then known, FM would not be a useful broadcast medium. Still, technical work continued, and more than two dozen patents had been granted to various inventors and companies by 1928. Much of the impetus behind research into FM work was the search for a solution to the frustrating interference problem with AM radio. By the late 1920s, it was clear that simply using more AM transmitter power would not overcome static, which made AM unlistenable in electrical storms. Something new was needed.

From 1928 to 1933, Edwin Armstrong, a wealthy radio inventor then on Columbia University's physics faculty, focused on trying to utilize FM in a viable broadcast transmission system. Rather than working with narrow bands as had others before him, Armstrong's key breakthrough was to use far wider channels, eventually 20 times wider than those used by AM. The frequency could then modulate over about 150 kilohertz (though it normally used far less), leaving 25-kilohertz sidebands to prevent interference with adjacent channels. This allowed for greatly improved frequency response, or sound quality. Armstrong incorporated various circuits to allow precise tuning of the wide channels while at the same time eliminating most static and interference. Armstrong applied for the first of his four basic FM patents in 1930 and for the last in 1933; all four were granted late in 1933.

From 1934 to 1941, Armstrong further developed and demonstrated FM, working toward Federal Communications Commission (FCC) approval of a commercial system. After a number of long-distance tests (successfully sending signals up to 70 miles with only 2,000 watts of power) in cooperation with the Radio Corporation of America (RCA), Armstrong announced his system to the press early in 1935. A more formal demonstration to a meeting of the Institute of Radio Engineers later that year (and the published paper that resulted) marked the beginning of active FM innovation.

Resistance to the FM idea began to develop at about this time, usually growing out of the competing interests of two other broadcast services. Owners of AM stations, including the major networks, were concerned about the new technology that might totally replace their existing system. And companies already investing heavily in television research, especially RCA, thought that the new video service should receive priority in allocations and industry investment. FM was seen by some as merely a secondary audio service, albeit a far better one technically.

In July 1936 Armstrong obtained permission from the FCC to construct the world's first full-scale FM station in Alpine, New Jersey, across the Hudson River from New York City. After a technical hearing, the FCC provided initial allocations for FM and television (among other services), granting the fledgling FM technology's backers the right to experiment on 13 channels scattered across three widely separated parts of the spectrum—26, 43, and 117 megahertz. Early in 1939 the allocation was expanded to 75 channels located more conveniently between 41 and 44 megahertz. In the meantime, Armstrong's experimental station—the world's first FM transmitter—had gone on the air as W2XMN with low-power tests in April 1938.

Developing further experimentation but also looking toward commercial FM operations, the New England–based Yankee Network began to build two large transmitters in 1938–39. General Electric built two low-power FM transmitters at the same time, and the National Broadcasting Company's (NBC) experimental station began operating in January 1940. The first FM station west of the Alleghenies began transmission tests in Milwaukee just a few days later. Transmitters for most of these operations came from Radio Engineering Laboratories. Receivers were first manufactured by General

Electric in 1939, with other companies joining in the next year; however, most FM sets cost a good deal more than their AM counterparts.

Early Operations (1940–45)

The FCC became the arena for a 1940 battle over whether or not to authorize commercial FM service, and if so, on how many channels and with what relationship to developing television. In March 1940, more than a week of hearings were held to air the industry's conflicting views over the merits of FM and television. On 20 May 1940, the commission released its decision allowing the inception of commercial FM operation as of 1 January 1941; the decision allocated 40 channels on the VHF band (42–50 megahertz), reserving the lowest five channels for noncommercial applicants. Final technical rules were issued a month later. The first 15 commercial station construction permits were issued on 31 October 1940.

As the new year dawned, 18 commercial and 2 educational stations aired (compared to more than 800 AM stations at the time). The first commercial license was granted to W47NV, affiliated with AM station WSM in Nashville. The first West Coast station, a Don Lee network outlet, went on the air in September 1941. FM outlets briefly used unique call signs that combined the letters used with AM stations with numbers indicating the channel used (e.g., W55M in Milwaukee broadcast on 45.5 megahertz). This system was replaced with normal four-letter call signs in mid-1943.

By the end of 1941, and after the United States had entered World War II, the FCC reported 67 commercial station authorizations, with another 43 applications pending. About 30 of the former were actually on the air. Wartime priorities forced the end of further license grants and limited construction material availability after March 1942. By the end of October 1942, 37 stations were in operation, plus an additional 8 outlets still devoted to experiments. But construction materials and replacement parts were increasingly difficult to find, and some owners turned back their authorizations or withdrew their applications pending the end of the war.

The first attempt at an FM network, the American network, never made it on the air, largely because of difficulties in constructing the needed affiliate stations in sufficient markets. Programs offered on FM were of two types—duplicated AM station signals (the most common type) or recorded music. Because of the duplicated content of existing stations, FM stations had little appeal for advertisers. Another problem was FM audiences. There were some 15,000 FM sets in use at the beginning of 1941 and perhaps 400,000 by the time manufacturing was stopped early in 1942, compared to 30 million AM-equipped households. Most observers expected FM to become an important part of the industry after the war.

Frequency Shift and Decline (1945–57)

The next dozen years—from 1945 through 1957—were both exciting and frustrating as the FM service struggled to become established and successful amidst a broadcasting industry increasingly infatuated with television and still investing considerable sums into the expansion of AM. Initial excitement over FM's potential gave way to a slow decline.

Toward the end of the war, potential operators were already concerned that FM's allocation of 40 channels was not sufficient for expected postwar expansion. To further complicate matters, wartime spectrum and related research suggested that the FM allocation of 42–50 megahertz might be subject to cycles of severe sun spot interference. Concerns about television expansion led to demands by some members of the industry for FM's spectrum space to be reallocated to television.

Extensive FCC hearings in mid-1944 aired some of the technical concerns about the FM band, though wartime security limited what could be discussed. Armstrong and his backers argued to retain (or, better yet, to expand) the existing allocation, in part because stations could easily network by picking up each other's signals and passing them on—something that would be impossible were FM to be moved higher in the spectrum (moving lower was out of the question because of existing services). In January 1945 the FCC proposed moving FM to the 84–102 megahertz band to avoid the expected atmospheric interference and to gain more channels, for a total of 90. Subsequent proceedings continued the industry split over what to do and how. Finally, in June 1945, the FCC made its decision, shifting FM "upstairs" to the 88–108 megahertz band with a total of 100 channels that the service occupies today. Continuing the precedent established in 1941, educational users were assigned to channels reserved for them at 88–92 megahertz. The former FM band would be turned over to television and other services after a three-year transition period.

At first it seemed the shift would only disadvantage those stations actually on the air (46 at the time) and those people with FM sets that could not also receive AM signals (perhaps 30,000 old-band FM-only sets in consumer hands). Generally FM's outlook was good. The FCC issued the first postwar grants for new stations in October 1945, and more applications were piling up. Through 1946 there were always at least 200 applications pending, and although the number of stations actually on the air grew fairly slowly, the number of authorized FM stations exceeded 1,000 by 1948—more than all the AM and FM stations on the air just three years earlier. Most applications were coming in from AM stations hedging their bets on the future. Several government agencies issued optimistic publications encouraging still more FM applicants. Two specialized FM trade magazines began to publish. A number of potential FM networks were in the planning stages, and the first, called the Continental network, began operations with four stations early in 1947.

But all was not well. FM's frequency shift was more damaging in the short term than it had seemed. When stations began to transmit on FM's new frequencies, there were few receivers available to pick up the signals. Manufacturers were trying to meet pent-up wartime demand for new AM sets and had little capacity to devote to FM's needs. Thus FM suffered from the lack of a good-sized audience that might appeal to advertisers. Only token numbers of receivers were available until 1950, and by then demand for television sets was threatening capacity devoted to radio. FM's lack of separate programming (after considerable industry argument both ways, the FCC had allowed co-owned AM and FM stations to simulcast or carry the same material) offered little incentive for consumers to invest in one of the rare and expensive FM receivers. A cheap AM set could tune popular local and network radio programs just as well. FM's better sound quality was not enough of a draw. What independent programming did exist was largely classical music and arts material of interest to a relatively small elite. Advertisers saw no reason to invest in FM, especially when FM time was usually given away with AM advertising purchases. Indeed, AM was thriving—more than doubling the number of stations on the air from 1945 to 1950. And the growing concentration on television by broadcasters, advertisers, and the public made FM seem unnecessary.

As these factors combined and intensified, the results soon became apparent. The number of FM new station applications began to drop off, and then overall FM authorizations declined. By 1948 FM stations already on the air, among them some pioneering operations, began to shut down, returning their licenses to the FCC. FM outlets could not be given away, much less sold. The number of stations on the air declined each year. Faced with the seeming failure of his primary invention, Armstrong took his own life in 1954; with the loss of his financial backing, the Continental network had to close down as well.

Rebound (1958–70)

Then, and at first very slowly, FM began to turn around. Reports in several trade magazines late in 1957 picked up the fact that the number of FCC authorizations for FM stations had increased for the first time in nine years. Slowly the pace of new station construction picked up, first in major markets and then in suburban areas. Several factors underlay this dramatic shift.

First, AM had grown increasingly crowded—there were virtually no vacant channels available in the country's major markets. The number of AM stations had doubled from 1948 to 1958, and about 150 more were going on the air annually. However, an increasing proportion of the new outlets were limited to daytime operation in an FCC attempt to reduce nighttime interference. FM, with no need for daytime-only limitations, was now the only means of entering major markets. In addition, the major spurt of television expansion was over, and this eased up pressure on time, money, and personnel, which could now be applied to FM.

But aside from overcrowding in AM and television, FM itself had more to offer. In 1955 the FCC had approved the use of Subsidiary Communications Authorizations, which allowed stations to multiplex (to send more than one signal from their transmitter) such non-broadcast content as background music for retail outlets ("storecasting"). This provided a needed revenue boost. So did the growing number of listeners interested in good music. These "hi-fi" addicts doted on FM operations, and this interest was evident in the increasing availability and sale of FM receivers. A developing high-end audience led advertisers to begin to pay serious attention to the medium.

Another technical innovation gave FM a further boost: the inception of stereo broadcasting. Beginning as early as 1952, some stations, such as New York's WQXR, offered AM/FM stereo using two stations—AM for one channel of sound and an FM outlet for the other. Occasional network two-station stereo broadcasts began in 1958—the same year commercial stereophonic records first went on sale. By 1960, more than 100 stations were providing the two-station system of stereo. But such simulcasting wasted spectrum (two stations with the same content), and the uneven quality of AM and FM provided poor stereo signals. What was needed was a system to provide stereo signals from a single station, and FM's wide channel seemed to offer the means.

In 1959 the National Stereophonic Radio Committee began industry experiments with several competing multiplexed single-station systems. By October 1960 the committee had recommended that the FCC establish FM stereo technical standards combining parts of systems developed by General Electric and Zenith. The FCC issued the standards in April 1961, and the first FM stereo stations began providing service in June. By 1965, a quarter of all commercial stations were offering stereo; by 1970, 38 percent of FM stations had the capability. Though few saw the future clearly, stereo would be a key factor in FM's ultimate success over long-dominant AM stations.

FM's continued expansion led the FCC to establish three classes of FM station in mid-1962. Lower-powered Class A (up to 3,000 watts of power and a service radius of 15 miles) and B stations (up to 50,000 watts of power and a service radius up to 40 miles) would be granted in the crowded northeastern section of the country as well as in southern California. Higher-powered C stations (up to 100,000 watts of power providing a service radius of 65 miles) could be granted elsewhere. A five-year FCC freeze on most new AM station grants beginning in 1968 helped funnel still more industry expansion into FM as the FCC began to see AM and FM as parts of an integrated radio service.

Of even greater importance to FM's continued growth was a series of landmark FCC decisions from 1964 to 1966 requiring separate programming on co-owned AM and FM stations in the largest markets (those with populations over 100,000). Long concerned about the effect of wasting spectrum space by allowing the same programs to run on both AM and FM, the FCC had been persuaded by industry leaders to allow the practice when FM was weak. Indeed, many FM broadcasters expressed great concern about losing their ability to carry popular AM programming. But FM's growth in numbers and economic strength prompted the move—which further accelerated creation of new FM stations. In just a few years the importance of the FCC decisions (which by the late 1960s had been extended to smaller markets) became apparent as FM audiences increased sharply—bringing, in turn, greater advertiser interest and expenditure to make FM economically viable for the first time in its history. By the early 1980s, when the AM-FM non-duplication requirement was eliminated in a deregulatory move, FM stations were dominant in large part because of their unique programming.

That FM had achieved its own identity was exemplified when one of the big-three networks, the American Broadcasting Companies (ABC), initiated a network of FM stations in 1968. Although relatively short-lived, as the industry increasingly began to think of FM as radio rather than something different, the recognition that such a network gave to FM radio was a tremendous boost in the advertising community. Another indicator was Philadelphia's WDVR, which within four months of first airing in 1963 was the number-one FM station in the city, competing for top spot with long-established AM outlets, an inconceivable development just a few years earlier. Five years later, the same station became the first FM outlet to bill more than $1 million in advertising time. The FM business as a whole reported positive operating income in 1968 for the first time (it happened for the second time in 1973, after which the industry as a whole remained profitable).

The key measure of FM's coming of age, of course, is actual audience use of the service. In 1958, for example, FM was available in about one-third of all homes in such major urban markets as Cleveland, Miami, Philadelphia, and Kansas City. By 1961 the receiver penetration figures for major cities were creeping up to about 40 percent, and national FM penetration was estimated at about 10 percent, showing how few FM listeners lived in smaller markets and rural areas, many of which still lacked FM stations. By the mid-1960s, FM household penetration in major markets was hovering at the two-thirds mark, and national FM penetration stood at about half that level. Although stereo and car FM radios were initially expensive, increasing production dropped prices and helped to further expand FM availability.

Dominance (The 1970s and Since)

After the many FM industry and policy changes of the 1960s, the 1970s saw FM becoming increasingly and rapidly important economically. Where FM attracted 25 percent of the national radio audience in 1972, just two years later survey data showed FM accounted for one-third of all national radio listening—although only 14 percent of all radio revenues. By 1979 FM achieved a long-sought goal when for the first time, total national FM listening surpassed that of AM stations. Every major market had at least four FM stations among the top 10 radio outlets. Indeed, FM would never lose that primacy, slowly expanding its role until by the turn of the century, FM listening accounted for nearly 80 percent of all radio listening.

Getting there had not been easy and had taken far longer than early proponents had expected. In part, FM's own success got in the way. After years of promoting FM's upper-scale (though small) audiences, often prejudicially dubbed eggheads and high-fidelity buffs, it was hard to shift gears and promote FM's large and growing audience as being tuned to simply "radio." (Indeed, the number of commercial FM classical music stations had actually declined by half since 1963, to only 30 by 1973.) At the same time, the number of educational FM stations expanded dramatically after 1965, greatly aided by the creation of National Public Radio and the appeal of its programs as well as by the availability of increased funding for station development and operation.

But with success came pressure to keep up. As news and talk formats increasingly defined AM (where the poorer sound quality did not matter), FM flowered with a full cornucopia of musical formats and styles. By the early 1970s, FM stations in the nation's largest markets were developing formats every bit as tight and narrow as those of their AM forebears. Each station and its advertisers were appealing to a specific segment of the once-mass radio audience in an attempt to build listener loyalty in a marketplace often defined by too many stations in most cities. By the late 1980s, FM's primary target market was that defined by its advertisers: listeners aged 26 to 34, followed by those 35 to 44 years of age. Only a relative handful of stations target teens, and fewer than 30 percent are interested in listeners aged 55 or older. As compared with its earlier days, FM has become positively mainstream.

FM's success is also seen in the usual marketplace measure—the price of FM stations being sold on the open market. Where top-market stations could literally not be given away in the early 1950s, by the late 1960s, the first million-dollar prices were being quoted. Three decades later, FM stand-alone stations in top markets sold for tens of millions of dollars, and some have sold for well over $100 million. On the other hand, many miss the old days of FM programs aimed at a small, elitist, sometimes cranky but usually appreciative audience. A

1999 FCC proposal to create scores of low-power FM outlets was intended to bring back some of that spirit, but was severely curtailed by Congress in 2000.

FM Outside the U.S.

FM or VHF radio developed more slowly outside of the United States. In Europe, for example, postwar radio reconstruction in most countries focused first on established medium wave and long wave services and then on television; few countries had economies strong enough to develop FM services at the same time as these other initiatives. And politics played a part, because Europe hoped in the meantime to find a European technical solution to its substantial problems of interference and static.

Given the total destruction of its broadcasting system, Germany had to start over and thus led Europe in beginning FM broadcasting. The first transmitters were on the air by 1949, and most of West Germany was covered with FM signals by 1951. Sale of FM receivers was brisk (some were exported to the United States), partly because television was not a competitor until 1952. By 1955 there were 100 FM transmitters in operation. With a severe shortage of medium wave frequencies, Italy followed suit, providing its first VHF radio services in the early 1950s.

At about the same time, other European nations, working through the European Broadcasting Union (EBU), began to reconsider FM's potential, because they had largely completed the process of repairing or replacing wartime AM radio losses. FM was seen as the only means of reducing serious medium wave overcrowding and resulting interference problems as well as serving regions largely unreached by existing stations, and FM could do so less expensively than could medium wave facilities. Countries also sought additional program channels. Interestingly, the same debate over whether FM should carry the same or different programs (as existing medium wave services) divided industries and governments in Europe as it had in the United States. By the late 1950s, EBU member nations were working together to build a system integrating existing and new VHF radio stations. And, as in the United States, the new services were increasingly programmed independently.

After experimenting with FM in London as early as 1950, the British Broadcasting Company (BBC) began introducing a chain of VHF radio stations in 1955. By 1960, most of the country was reached with the new transmitters, which largely simulcasted the medium wave station signals, though receiver penetration hovered at only about 15 percent, rising to 30 percent five years later. The planned role of the VHF transmitters was to introduce local programming for specific audiences—something that had been lacking in Britain since the early 1920s. By the early 1960s, VHF radio transmitters outnum-

bered medium wave facilities by 160 to 57. A decade later, there were 252 VHF transmitters in Britain. Lower FM receiver prices prompted rapid ownership growth.

Even by the mid-1980s, however, only about 20 countries (most of them in Europe) had extensively developed VHF radio. Despite its potential value to tropical countries, which are plagued by static on their AM or medium wave broadcast stations, few Third World nations had embarked on FM service. They lack the funds and even the need, because they have not fully utilized available medium wave channels. South Africa is an exception, having embarked in 1961 on development of VHF radio to cover the nation. Apartheid politics may have played a role here, because the VHF transmitters made it more difficult for Africans to hear foreign broadcasts, none of which were available on FM. Other African nations only experimented with FM in this period.

In the Far East, Japan experimented with FM for a decade before stations opened in major cities in 1969. The Ministry of Posts and Telecommunications sought to have an FM station in every prefecture and at least two in major cities. All of these are advertising-supported local stations. For a time in the 1970s and 1980s, a raft of mini–FM transmitters called "free radio," which covered a radius of only about 3,000 feet, were very popular, playing music and advertising. Few were licensed, however, and many were closed down in the late 1980s. The service came later to Australia, where what would become FM frequencies had been originally allocated to television. Reallocation of that service made initiation of FM service possible there in the 1980s.

Perhaps the most extreme examples of the FM-based "free radio" movement took place in the 1970s in both France and Italy. A number of unlicensed small local Italian FM stations went on the air in late 1974 and into 1975. When an Italian court held that the state broadcasting authority did not have a monopoly on local radio, hundreds more followed in 1976. By mid-1978, some 2,200 were on the air, providing Italians with the most radio per capita of any nation on earth. Stations programmed music and advertising and often expressed strong political viewpoints on both the right and left. France went through something similar in the late 1970s—by the early 1980s there were more than 100 such stations in Paris alone. Most gave way to a 1982 government decision to provide licenses to many of the stations as well as official permission to advertise.

CHRISTOPHER H. STERLING

See also Armstrong, Edwin Howard; Don Lee Network; Educational Radio to 1967; Federal Communications Commission; FM Trade Organizations; Low-Power Radio/Microradio; Radio Corporation of America; Receivers; Sarnoff, David; Shepard, John; Stereo; Subsidiary Communications Authorization; United States; Yankee Network

Further Reading

Armstrong, Edwin H., "Evolution of Frequency Modulation," *Electrical Engineering* 59 (December 1940)

Besen, Stanley M., "AM versus FM: The Battle of the Bands," *Industrial and Corporate Change* 1 (1992)

Boutwell, William Dow, Ronald Redvers Lowdermilk, and Gertrude G. Broderick, *FM for Education,* Washington, D.C.: United States Government Printing Office, 1944; revised edition, 1948

Codding, George A., "Frequency Modulation Broadcasting," in *Broadcasting without Barriers,* Paris: UNESCO, 1959

Cox Looks at FM Radio: Past, Present, and Future, Atlanta, Georgia: Cox Broadcasting, 1976

Eshelman, David, "The Emergence of Educational FM," *NAEB Journal* 26 (March–April 1967)

"Evolution of FM Radio: Extracts from FCC Annual Reports," *Journal of Broadcasting* 5 (Spring 1961 and Fall 1961), 6 (Summer 1962), 7 (Fall 1963)

Inglis, Andrew F., "FM Broadcasting," in *Behind the Tube: A History of Broadcasting Technology and Business,* Boston: Focal Press, 1990

Lewis, Peter M., and Jerry Booth, *The Invisible Medium: Public, Commercial, and Community Radio,* Washington, D.C.: Howard University Press, and London: Macmillan, 1989

Longley, Lawrence D., "The FM Shift in 1945," *Journal of Broadcasting* 12 (Fall 1968)

Sleeper, Milton B., editor, *FM Radio Handbook,* Great Barrington, Massachusetts: FM Company, 1946

Slotten, Hugh Richard, "Rainbow in the Sky: FM Radio, Technical Superiority, and Regulatory Decision-Making," *Technology and Culture* 37 (October 1996)

"Special Report: FM Sniffs Sweet Smell of Success," *Broadcasting* (31 July 1967)

Sterling, Christopher H., "Second Service: Some Keys to the Development of FM Broadcasting," *Journal of Broadcasting* 15 (Fall 1971)

United States Congress, Senate Special Committee to Study Problems of American Small Business, *Small Business Opportunities in FM Broadcasting,* 79th Congress, 2nd Session, April 10, 1946, Washington, D.C.: GPO, 1946

Wedell, E. George, and Philip Crookes, *Radio 2000: The Opportunities for Public and Private Radio Services in Europe,* Geneva: European Broadcasting Union, 1991

FM Trade Associations

Promoting Radio's Second Service

From the inception of commercial FM radio in 1941, a series of five industry trade organizations appeared—and disappeared—in parallel with the medium's struggles and eventual success. Each was different in its outlook and focus.

The Early Struggle

The first FM group, the National Association of FM Broadcasters Incorporated (FMBI), was created in 1940 to promote the technology as much as the industry. Spearheaded by John Shepherd III of the New England–based Yankee Network and by Walter J. Damm of the *Milwaukee Journal* radio stations (one of which was the first FM station west of the Alleghenies), FMBI published thousands of copies of *Broadcasting's Better Mousetrap* to promote FM's better sound and other qualities. Before and during World War II, a mimeographed newsletter edited by Dick Dorrance appeared regularly to record the slow

initial development of the business. FMBI had 43 members by 1943—most of those either on the air or building new stations—and 137 by September 1944. Among its campaigns was a successful move to persuade the Federal Communications Commission (FCC) to modify FM station call letters from letter and number combinations denoting the channel of the station (e.g., W55M, which was on 45.5 megahertz) to the more familiar all-letter system used with AM stations. The FCC adopted the plan in 1943. Although FMBI fought the shift of FM frequencies that came in 1945, it worked to put the new spectrum into action.

With the end of the war, FMBI voted in 1946 to merge its activities into the FM Department (later Committee) of the National Association of Broadcasters (NAB), a pattern that would be repeated several times. Initially headed by Robert Bartley, later an FCC commissioner, this arm of the main industry trade association sought a place for FM within an industry dominated by rapidly expanding AM stations and developing television.

Believing that the new medium needed the focused attention of a dedicated organization, broadcasters Roy Hofheintz of Houston and Everett Dillard of Washington, D.C., helped form the FM Association (FMA) in 1946. FMA's primary focus was to get AM broadcasters either to build the FM stations they had applied for or to return their construction permits to the FCC. FMA pressure on the FCC led the agency to terminate many "warehoused" but inactive permits, which were an indicator of FM's coming decline. The FMA ended its short existence with a two-year promotional campaign to brighten the medium's future.

All this activity was to no avail, and FM slipped into decline for most of the 1950s as industry attention turned to television.

FM's Revival

Formation of the FM Development Association (FMDA) in 1956 was one early indicator that FM's fortunes were about to take a turn for the better. Larry Gordon of WBUF (FM) in Buffalo, New York, was its president. Made up of about two dozen independent (without a matching AM station) FM station owners, FMDA sought to get broadcasters to place FM stations on the air. It also attempted to combat escalating music licensing fees being charged by the American Society of Composers, Authors, and Publishers (ASCAP).

In January 1959 a group of FMDA members formed the new National Association of FM Broadcasters (NAFMB). The organization decided to hold its first official meeting prior to the forthcoming annual convention of the NAB in Chicago. With the blessing of the NAB, the NAFMB was allowed to hold its first meeting on the Saturday just prior to the NAB FM Day program; at that time Fred Rabell, an independent FM broadcaster and background music franchisee in San Diego, was elected president. This was a nonpaying position, which he volunteered to accept with the help of his wife, and for nearly three years they operated the NAFMB from their FM radio station KITT.

Rabell was followed by another unpaid leader, T. Mitchell Hastings, Jr., owner of the Concert Network FM stations in New York City, Boston, Hartford, Connecticut, and Providence, Rhode Island, and the developer of the Hastings FM tuner, America's first FM car radio. Hastings led the NAFMB for three years. (Prior to his death in the mid-1990s, Hastings was chairman of the Armstrong Foundation, dedicated to the propagation of Edwin Armstrong's name as the father of FM radio through its Armstrong "Major Awards," first presented at the NAFMB conventions.)

Another person who played an important role in making the NAFMB successful was James Schulke, NAFMB's first full-time paid president, who had offices in New York City. Schulke was hired in 1963 after an annual donation of commercial airtime by all National Radio Broadcasters Association member stations; this donated time was subsequently sold to the Magnavox Corporation for $150,000. Special research, programming, and marketing studies were developed by the NAFMB in the 1960s as membership grew from its first 50 stations to nearly 500 by 1969. During those formative years, FM broadcasters volunteered their time and resources to advance public and advertiser awareness of FM radio. Dozens of these FM radio pioneers played major roles in the NAFMB, including Abe Voron of Philadelphia, Robert Herpe of Orlando, and James Gabbert of San Francisco.

The impact of NAFMB activities in the 1960s is reflected in the increase in the number of FM radio stations that went on the air. From just 578 commercial stations in 1959, with the majority duplicating the programming of a co-owned AM facility in the same city, the number of on-air FM stations had grown to more than 1,000 by 1963. The promotion of FM stereo multiplexing following the FCC's adoption of FM stereo radio standards in April 1961, as well as the one-year "Drive with FM" campaign in 1965 and 1966 to motivate consumers and the auto industry to have FM and FM stereo available on their auto and truck radios, also played a role in the accelerated growth of FM.

During the 17-year existence of the NAFMB as an organization that would accept only FM station members, the association was the driving force in promoting, researching, marketing, and expanding the visibility of both FM and FM stereo radio in the United States and Canada.

The NAFMB was both the longest-lived and the most successful of the five FM trade groups. It actively worked with the FCC to develop technical standards for FM stereo in 1960–61. A 1963 Harvard University Graduate School of Business study of FM's potential was sponsored by NAFMB and attracted widespread industry attention. The study's prediction of FM's eventual dominance of AM, seen as a pipe dream by many at the time, was borne out by events in the late 1970s. FM's eventual success was heavily aided by the separation of its programming from colocated AM stations in the late 1960s, something NAFMB lobbied the FCC heavily for. The association issued annual program surveys of FM stations in the late 1960s, which showed the growing variety of formats used by FM outlets. It conducted or supported a variety of other studies of the FM industry in response to growing advertiser interest in the medium. At the same time, the Radio Advertising Bureau focused more on FM's potential, and the NAB published its monthly *Fmphasis* newsletter throughout the 1960s.

Because of pressure by AM and AM/FM station owners and operators who wanted to join the NAFMB, in September 1975, during its annual convention in Atlanta, the NAFMB name and membership criteria were changed. The association became the National Radio Broadcasters Association (NRBA), and AM stations were to be admitted into membership. The new members pushed for the association's dedication to seeking regulatory relief from the FCC. Many stations active with NRBA were dissatisfied with the NAB's efforts for radio deregulation and believed that the older radio/TV association was devoting too much of its resources to television issues. Nine years later, in 1984, the NRBA merged with the NAB.

The success of FM radio in superseding AM radio as the dominant aural medium in America was consistently positioned by the NAFMB with the rationale that "in the long run, a quality product always succeeds with the American consumer." The NAFMB was the leading advocate of FM radio and played an important role in the medium's eventual success.

LYNN A. CHRISTIAN AND CHRISTOPHER H. STERLING

See also Armstrong, Edwin Howard; FM Radio; National Association of Broadcasters; Radio Advertising Bureau; Schulke, James; Stereo; Trade Associations; Trade Press

Further Reading

Advertisers Are Asking Questions about FM, New York: Radio Advertising Bureau, 1961

"And Now FM Will Have the Numbers: Special FM Report," *Broadcasting* (29 July 1963)

"A Dramatic Spurt in FM Development," *Broadcasting* (20 February 1961)

"Identity of Audience Gets Attention of NAFMB," *Advertising Age* (4 April 1966)

Mayberry, Joshua J., *New Dimensions for FM Radio*, Presented before 8th Annual NAFMB Convention (30 March 1968)

Mohr, Donald, "The Potential of FM Radio As an Advertising Medium," Master's thesis, New York University, 1961

"NAFMB Studies Medium's Potential," *Broadcasting* (1 April 1968)

National FM Programming Trends, 1967 and 1968, Washington, D.C.: NAFMB, 1967, 1968

Sterling, Christopher H., "Second Service: A History of Commercial FM Radio to 1969," Ph.D. diss., University of Wisconsin, 1969

Foreign Broadcast Information Service

Monitoring International Radio Broadcasts

The Foreign Broadcast Information (originally Intelligence) Service (FBIS) was created in 1941 as part of the Federal Communications Commission. Operating as part of the Central Intelligence Agency since 1947, FBIS has provided a record of important international radio broadcasts for U.S. government decision makers. In the 1960s it expanded to record other types of foreign media output.

Origins

In 1938, John R. Whitton of Princeton University was heading the Geneva (Switzerland) Research Center, and in conversation with Edward R. Murrow of CBS Whitton became more aware of the growing impact of radio as a propaganda medium. Becoming both concerned about and impressed with the propaganda potential of radio, he hired researcher Thomas Grandin to study developing political uses of radio. In the course of his study, Grandin established a small receiving post in a Paris hotel to better follow selected broadcasts.

On his return to the U.S. in late 1938, Whitton sought funding to set up a continuing radio monitoring service. This led to creation of the Princeton (University) Listening Center in November 1939 with a Rockefeller Foundation grant designed to cover a period of experimentation. In June 1940, Rockefeller extended support for another year. The managing committee included Whitton, sociologist Hadley Cantril (who was co-director of the Office of Radio Research) and William S. Carpenter of Princeton, O.W. Riegel of Washington and Lee University (author of an early book on propaganda), B.R. McCrutcheon (an engineer), and Harold N. Graves (as administrator). Graves recruited a staff of ten to record and transcribe the most important shortwave broadcasts.

From 3:00 P.M. until 11:00 P.M. six days a week, broadcasts were recorded on wax cylinders. Over the 20 months the Center operated, this process produced more than 100 volumes of exact transcripts totaling 8 million words. Broadcasts from Berlin, Rome, Moscow, Paris, and London were included. Some 20 booklets summarizing the detailed findings were widely distributed to American media and researchers between December 1939 and mid-1941.

Early in 1941, the Defense Communications Board asked the Federal Communications Commission (FCC) to develop a more extensive government-supported foreign broadcast monitoring process (as a number of foreign governments had already done). President Roosevelt authorized the transfer of $150,000 (nearly $2 million in 2003 dollars) from war emergency funds for the purpose, and the Foreign Broadcast Monitoring Service (FBMS) was created in late February. Personnel from the Princeton operation were vital to this operation, with Graves acting as director until June 1941. Slowly an organizational structure was established.

Wartime Operation

During the first part of 1942, the FBMS established a number of listening posts to better monitor broadcasts. These were located in Portland, Oregon (the first site, it began operation in October 1941), San Francisco, Kingsville, Texas, Santurce, Puerto Rico, and in London. On 28 July 1942 the FBMS was renamed the Foreign Broadcast Intelligence Service (FBIS). The number of employees and operations reached a peak in March 1943. More listening posts (sometimes dubbed field offices) were established, in Silver Hill, Maryland (just outside of Washington, D.C.), and in Hawaii as well as several other foreign locations.

With teams operating around the clock, recordings were made at each field office. Transcripts and translations were then teletyped, cabled, or mailed to the Washington headquarters. Washington personnel summarized and analyzed the more important broadcasts and distributed them to government offices. The process of analysis soon attracted unwanted attention.

FBIS came under Congressional investigation in the spring of 1943, part of a long and highly critical political review of the FCC. Criticism centered on both FBIS personnel and operations. Partially as a result, most FBIS analysis functions were transferred to the Office of War Information. FBIS continued its basic monitoring and recording functions throughout the war.

In December 1945, the FCC announced plans to close down FBIS. Instead, the War Department took over the operation and in August 1946 it was transferred to the Central Intelligence Group of the National Intelligence Authority. It was renamed the Foreign Broadcast Information Service two months later. The FBIS became a part of the Central Intelligence Agency when the CIA was formed in September 1947.

Postwar Developments

As a "charter member" of the intelligence establishment, FBIS slowly expanded its operation to nearly 20 listening posts in the U.S. and overseas. In 1967 the responsibilities of the FBIS were expanded to include keeping track of foreign newspaper and magazine (and news agency) output, in addition to broadcasts. In 1974 FBIS daily reports came available on a subscription basis to the general public, providing some of what the monitoring service was recording and translating. Some material was restricted for government-only use for six months. Attempts to close down some FBIS functions in the post-Cold War period have occurred at several points, usually in Congressional attempts to save funds.

Television and satellite transmissions were included in the FBIS operation by the 1970s and 1980s, respectively. In the 1990s, technological change had expanded FBIS even further to include commercial and government databases and so-called "gray literature" (where the source and veracity of the material is not always clear). Automatic (unmanned) monitoring by the 1990s expanded FBIS capabilities still further, while fax machines and computer data links allowed faster distribution of time-sensitive material. The agency was dealing with material in more than 60 languages; that number expanded with the end of the Cold War and initiation of media in local languages in many parts of the former USSR.

Because of the FBIS's language capability, its functions have often included translation services for different government needs. While much of what the FBIS records come from "open source" (public) entities such as radio and other media, it also collects information from other sources. The intelligence function of FBIS is best seen in two widely-reported events three decades apart (for which credit is usually shared with its British counterpart, the BBC Monitoring Service)—its recording of Radio Moscow broadcasts that the Soviets were withdrawing their missiles from Cuba in 1962, and the first word (monitored from the TASS news agency) of the short-lived August 1991 coup in Moscow against the government of Mikhail Gorbachev.

CHRISTOPHER H. STERLING

See also BBC Monitoring Service; Cold War Radio; International Radio; Office of Radio Research; Propaganda by Radio

Further Reading

Childs, Harwood L., and John B. Whitton, editors, *Propaganda by Short Wave*, Princeton: Princeton University Press, 1942; reprint, New York: Arno Press, 1972

FBIS "Frequently Asked Questions" website, <http://199.221.15.211/online_faq.html>

Federation of American Scientists, "In Support of FBIS" website, <www.fas.org/irp/fbis/>

George, Alexander L., *Propaganda Analysis: A Study of Inferences Made from Nazi Propaganda in World War II*, Evanston, Illinois: Row and Peterson, 1959

Grandin, Thomas, *The Political Use of the Radio: Geneva Studies X:3*, Geneva, Switzerland: Geneva Research Centre, August 1939; reprint, New York: Arno Press, 1972

Simpson, Christopher, *Science of Coercion: Communication Research and Psychological Warfare, 1945–1960*, New York: Oxford University Press, 1994

Teale, Edward, "America Listens In," *Popular Science Monthly* (June 1941)

Weinstein, Walter W., *Records of the Foreign Broadcast Intelligence Service: Preliminary Inventories No. 115*. Washington: National Archives, 1959

Formats

Defining Radio Programming

A format is the overall programming design of a station or specific program. It is essentially the arrangement of program elements—often musical recordings—into a sequence that will attract and hold the segment of the audience a station is seeking. There are as many as 100 known formats and variations.

Evolution of Formats

Radio formats developed in response to the competitive threat posed by television and the growing number of competing radio stations. For decades, radio stations had been a mass medium, with each outlet trying to be all things to all people. But as television grew in popularity and as more television and radio stations went on the air, audience fragmentation occurred, prompting radio programmers to seek ways to differentiate their programming and attract audiences. By the mid-1950s, radio programmers were willing to try almost anything to preserve the medium.

One lesson was learned from an independent (i.e., non–network-affiliated) radio station in New York, WNEW, which had successfully programmed a music and news format as early as 1935. While other radio network audiences defected to television, WNEW maintained its audience levels, presumably because its music and news format did not demand long-term or high-level attention from listeners, unlike the typical dramatic productions on the networks. The simpler, less demanding programming apparently allowed listeners to tune in for shorter periods of time and while doing other things, such as household chores.

Another lesson was learned from the success of "countdown" programs such as *Your Hit Parade*, a popular radio network program since the 1940s. Countdown programs tended to play the top 40 or so songs, and audience numbers were very strong. Not surprisingly, some programmers working for independent stations tried playing only the top 40 or so most popular records and were successful. In this sense, they were simply attracting an audience by playing what the audience had already proven they wanted to hear. Station owners Todd Storz and Gordon McLendon were among those who turned the concept into a continuous format, creating the hit-oriented playlist.

Many stations quickly adopted the new approach. But as more stations played the same top 40 songs, a further need for differentiation and refinement arose. In 1957 Storz and programmer Bill Stewart are said to have noted the behavior of jukebox users who repeatedly selected their favorite tunes. Taking this observation back to their Omaha station, they refined the playlist to repeat the most popular hits more often than other songs. Other stations followed suit, positioning themselves as stations that guaranteed the top hits.

Eventually various formats evolved as stations sought to differentiate themselves from competing stations with similar formats. Rock, including soft rock and hard rock, was spun off. Adult contemporary (AC) developed as a way to appeal to an older audience demographic by playing current songs, minus the tunes that appealed mostly to teens. As album sales increased, many stations presumed that listeners wanted to hear certain artists, so they switched to playing primarily album cuts, eventually becoming known as album-oriented rock (AOR) stations. Formats were also distinguished simply by the creative names given them, such as "Hot Hits." The names would sometimes be intentionally vague in order to appear distinct to listeners while still seeming inclusive of all listeners to advertisers. AM stations also responded to the competition from FM and its superior frequency response and stereo capability by creating information formats such as news, talk, sports, agriculture, and education. Listener perceptions about AM sound quality became entrenched by the 1980s, forcing most AM stations to switch to non-music formats to survive.

New formats also emerged, partly because of the increasingly sophisticated ratings reports that provided more detailed demographic data. Stations pushed radio ratings companies to provide specific listener demographic data beyond an overall market headcount in order to justify themselves to advertisers. Once sub-audiences could be clearly identified, a symbiotic relationship emerged, with programmers developing formats that appealed to those audiences. Likewise, music trade magazines such as *Billboard* developed specialized charts that coincided with the formats of stations, and vice versa. Some format names, such as rhythm and blues, were in fact coined by *Billboard*.

Format Categories

The increase in artists, particularly crossover artists, has made it difficult for popular music stations to claim a "pure format," that is, one based on agreement by stations nationwide as to what artists are included and excluded. However, today this definition primarily applies only to classical, big band, and similar formats consisting of older music. Many of the originally pure formats, such as AOR, country, and urban, have split into variations of their respective formats. From the standpoint of promotion, advertising, and ratings classification, it is best for a station to identify with a pure format, but the need to be competitive forces stations to adjust to the demands of the audience and industry. In the 1990s the concept of the "microformat" emerged, whereby syndicated and network music and information programming became fine-tuned to a specific audience and market, relying less on a cookie-cutter approach.

Today, each of the major music categories— country, AC, rock, and urban (black)—has several subdivisions. According to Eastman, et al (2002), the country format has three subcategories: traditional country, young (or hot) country, and country gold—each aimed at a specific demographic group. Adult contemporary offers hot AC, mainstream AC, soft AC, and a jazzier version called new adult contemporary/smooth jazz. Urban music is subdivided into urban contemporary, urban adult contemporary, and urban gold. Rock formats include adult album alternative (AAA); contemporary hit radio (CHR); churban (a blend of CHR and urban); active rock (hard/heavy metal); classic rock (popular rock music of the 1960s through the 1980s); and oldies, which is further divided into the decades of the 1960s, 1970s, and 1980s. In addition to these primary formats, there are many distinct formats, such as big band, alternative, contemporary Christian, classical, progressive, and beautiful music/easy listening.

Format Popularity

Country has overwhelmingly reigned in the U.S. as the most popular format among stations, followed by AC, although both of these have slipped in recent years. One of the fastest-growing formats of the 1990s was modern rock, otherwise known as alternative, which capitalized on the mainstream popularization of many "alternative" bands. Because of AM stations and the interests of aging baby boomers, news and talk formats have increased in popularity. Sports and Spanish language formats, including Tejano, have also taken off in the last decade. A relatively new format called adult album alternative (AAA or Triple A) has also emerged, featuring an eclectic choice of music ranging from hard rock to folk music. Christian formats have increased dramatically in recent years.

Broadcasting and Cable Yearbook 2002–03 ranked the U.S. radio formats in terms of the number of stations identifying with each format. The top 20 formats were (in order): country (2,318), AC (1,863), oldies (1,208), news/talk (1,199), religious (889), Christian (869), sports (837), news (769), talk (726), gospel (652), CHR/Top 40 (646), classic rock (606), rock/AOR (601), Spanish (582), classical (529), jazz (426), urban contemporary (350), diversified (321), educational (264), and middle of the road (MOR; 261).

The next most popular formats among stations were (in order): alternative, variety/diverse, progressive, other, nostalgia, black, big band, blues, beautiful music, inspirational, full service, AAA, AOR, agriculture, foreign language/ethnic, public-affairs, Top 40, easy listening, children, new age (soft rock and jazz), Tejano (bicultural Spanish programming), light rock, bluegrass, golden oldies (hits of the 1950s), and folk.

A relative handful of stations identify their format as: polka, Korean, American Indian, reggae, Portuguese, French, Greek, Polish, disco, Chinese, new wave (rock from the United Kingdom, popular in the early 1980s), smooth jazz, comedy, sacred, Native American, Arabic, Russian, Eskimo, Japanese, Vietnamese, or Filipino.

Choosing and Creating a Format

Stations switch formats frequently to pursue more profitable demographic segments and in response to shifting audience tastes. According to Eastman, et al, the steps taken in choosing a format involve an evaluation of (1) the technical facilities of the station (i.e., AM, FM, range), (2) the character of the local market, (3) the delineation of the target audience, (4) the available budget, and (5) the potential revenue.

Stations assemble their formats in several ways. Some simply program recordings in a sequence throughout the schedule, whereas others carry different formats during different dayparts. Still others rely on "Format Syndicators," which provide ready-made formats for a fee via satellite feed or music tapes. The formula for constructing a format goes beyond just music and includes a focus on production, personality, and programming.

Format Audience Characteristics

Certain audience demographics are predictors of format preference. For example, listeners to news are more likely to be married and to have lived in the area for at least two years, whereas AOR listeners are more likely to be single and on the move. Some studies also suggest that urban contemporary fans are the heaviest listeners, country listeners are the most loyal, and AC listeners are less involved in their station.

Formats can also be profiled on the basis of education, income, and age. For example, higher education levels are associated with beautiful music and news. In 1998 the highest household median income numbers were associated with AAA ($62,954), news ($62,722), alternative ($55,298), classical ($55,248), and modern rock ($54,488). The two formats appealing most to older audiences are full-service (60.3 years) and nostalgia (59.3 years). Most formats, however, are showing an increase in the median age of listeners, with one exception: news/talk listeners are getting younger.

Finally, where a listener resides has some effect on format popularity. Country is more popular in the South and Midwest, and news and talk formats are listened to most in the West. Spanish has been the most popular format in Los Angeles.

LAURIE THOMAS LEE

See also individual formats discussed in this essay; Programming Strategies and Processes

Further Reading

Eastman, Susan Tyler, Sydney W. Head, and Lewis Klein, *Broadcast Programming: Strategies for Winning Television and Radio Audiences,* Belmont, California: Wadsworth, 1981; 6th edition, as *Broadcast/Cable/Web Programming: Strategies and Practices,* by Eastman and Douglas A. Ferguson, 2002

Hausman, Carl, Philip Benoit, and Lewis B. O'Donnell, *Modern Radio Production,* Belmont, California: Wadsworth, 1986; 4th edition, 1996

Lynch, Joanna R., and Greg Gillispie, *Process and Practice of Radio Programming,* Lanham, Maryland: University Press of America, 1998

MacFarland, David T., *Contemporary Radio Programming Strategies,* Hillsdale, New Jersey: Erlbaum, 1990; 2nd edition, as *Future Radio Programming Strategies: Cultivating Listenership in the Digital Age,* Mahwah, New Jersey: Erlbaum, 1997

Meril, John, "Listening Down in 98," *Broadcasting and Cable* (29 June 1998)

Routt, Edd, James B. McGrath, and Fredric A. Weiss, *The Radio Format Conundrum,* New York: Hastings House, 1978

France

French radio has passed through several different organizational schemes in its history, slowly expanding its domestic and international service. Radio has always been a primary means of spreading French culture around the world.

Origins

Before 1914, France participated in the development of wireless (telegraphy and telephony) with other industrial nations. World War I stimulated the use of large transmitters: after the one on the Eiffel Tower in Paris (1905) came another at La Doua in Lyon (1914), then one at La Croix d'Hins (1920, meant originally for the use of the U.S. expeditionary force) and one at Sainte-Assise (1922). The war also created thousands of radio specialists, trained in the armed forces, who returned to civilian life in 1919. Furthermore, the war accelerated the formation in 1918 of the Compagnie générale de TSF (CSF), which was one of the four largest broadcast companies in the world (with Marconi in England, Telefunken in Germany, and Radio Corporation of America [RCA] in the United States).

The Mixed System (1922–40)

Considering French capabilities and interests, it is odd that France did not experience the same radio boom as Britain, Germany, or the U.S. However, the educational establishment, the Catholic Church, the press, and most intellectuals had trouble accepting the competition that "vulgar" radio entertainment might represent for other vehicles of culture and information. Successive governments and Parliament were incapable of giving radio a stable status. Left-wing political parties, with their minds on the traditional telegraph monopoly, wanted radio to be exclusively entrusted to the Ministry of

Post, Telephone, and Telegraph (PTT). Right-wing groups reacted rather favorably to the creation of private commercial stations.

After a few experiments in 1921, regular radio transmissions began in February 1922 from the Eiffel Tower station, which the army had handed over to the Post Office. In November 1922 the Radiola station was inaugurated by the CSF, and a third station was created in January 1923 by the École Supérieure (Graduate School) of the PTT. Beginning in 1924, stations appeared in the provinces. After much debate and incoherent legislation, the law of 19 March 1928 established a mixed, highly regionalized radio system.

By 1932 the 13 authorized commercial stations (financed by advertising) had a total transmitting power of 160 kilowatts, whereas the 11 government-operated transmitters had a combined power of 92 kilowatts. In 1938, after an important modernizing effort aided in 1934 by the establishment of an annual fee to be paid by owners of sets (compensated by the abandonment of advertising), the 16 public stations, of which 3 were in Paris (in 1939, the Poste National had its transmitter power raised to 900 kilowatts, making it the strongest in the world), competed against 11 commercial stations, 4 of them in Paris and each associated with a national daily newspaper.

The number of radio receivers increased comparatively slowly: from 600,000 in 1928 to 1.5 million in 1934, 4.7 million in 1938, and 5.2 million in 1940, for a population of 40 million inhabitants. Penetration was about a third less than in Germany or Great Britain. The audience for private stations, whose programs were more popular, was almost equal to that of the PTT network.

The growing European political crisis led the government to increase its control over radio news, and the same newscast was provided on all "public" stations and, from February 1939, on all private stations as well. Just two months before the declaration of war, the management of radio broadcasting was withdrawn from the Post Office and transferred to the office of the Prime Minister. Programs aimed at foreign audiences, especially German and Italian, were increased early in 1938, as were those aimed at French colonies in Africa and Asia.

The Era of Monopoly (1940–81)

From September 1939 to June 1940, radio was mobilized to support the French war effort and the country's morale.

German Occupation (1940–44)

After the armistice of June 1940, the north and west of France were occupied by the Germans, who unified the radio network around Radio Paris as a tool of propaganda in favor of total collaboration with Nazism. In the south, the Vichy regime nationalized radio, and the Radiodiffusion Nationale served the conservative "national revolution" under Marshall Pétain. After the invasion of the southern zone (November 1942), the autonomy of the Vichy radio was gradually diminished. In spite of the prohibition on listening to foreign radios, many French could hear Radio Sottens in French-speaking Switzerland, the British Broadcasting Corporation's (BBC) French Service (Radio Londres), and later the Voice of America, Radio Moscow, or Radio Brazzaville (in the Congo, controlled by General de Gaulle's Free French), and after 1943 Radio Alger in French North Africa. This sad period was crucial for the prestige of radio in France—it continued speaking with different voices. The considerable importance nowadays of radio newscasts for the information of the French, as compared to the printed press or even television, is partly the result of habits formed in those days, when newspapers had lost all credibility.

The Fourth Republic (1944–58)

At the time of liberation, radio remained nationalized and, contrary to the situation between the two world wars, basically centralized. The Radiodiffusion Nationale (renamed Radiotélévision Nationale in 1949) was a public administration that produced three national services on short and medium waves and one service directed to French colonies. The few regional programs did not occupy much space in the schedule. Government control of news programs was very strong, but cultural programs and variety shows often attained remarkable quality. Commercial advertising was banned. Financing came from the annual receiver fee and government subsidies. The number of sets increased rapidly, from 5 million in 1945 to 10.7 million by 1958, by which time practically all households were equipped—even before transistor sets made it possible for a household to own several sets—and there were over 25 million by 1981.

The originality of the French radio landscape was largely due to competing "peripheral" stations, which aired programs made in France and aimed at a French audience but broadcast from transmitters located just beyond the national borders. Thus Radio Luxembourg (1933), Radio Monte-Carlo (1943), and in 1955 Europe 1 from the Saar in Germany all provided the popular sound of U.S. commercial radio, plus newscasts and political columns with content and tone that were far more free than those of the government-run Radio-Télévision Française (RTF). Europe 1 especially managed to innovate successfully by using a conversational and informal style quite different from the more formal and stuffy government radio speakers. The success of radio was also maintained by the late and slow development of television, which in 1958 still operated on only one channel to fewer than 1 million receivers.

The Fifth Republic (Until 1981)

During the administrations of General de Gaulle (1958–69), Georges Pompidou (1969–73), and Giscard d'Estaing (1973–81), the status of the RTF (the ORTF after 1964 with the addition of the word "Office") was modified several times, but the principle of a public monopoly was not questioned even as more management autonomy was granted. Television expanded to three channels and added color, and radio diversified its programs—without, on the whole, giving up their national character. The huge Maison de la Radio (House of Radio) in Paris, inaugurated in 1963, symbolized the centralization of the French broadcasting system, even though by 1980 there were also 34 provincial production centers. In 1959 the annual radio fee was combined with that of television, and it was terminated entirely in 1978, yet radio was not authorized to carry advertising, as television was from 1968.

Although French radio had programs for overseas territories and foreign audiences (which never had the appeal of those of the BBC or the Voice of America), the three national radio programs were dominant: France Inter, France Culture, and France Musique. In 1974 these were gathered under the name Radio France. FM, which made possible the multiplication of local stations, had already been used in Germany to counter the penury of long- and medium-wave frequencies. It could upset the French model of a few AM stations broadcasting at high power. The first French FM station, France Inter Paris (FIP), was created as a local outlet for the Paris region in 1971. Its music, news, and traffic advice format was directed heavily at car radio listeners. Over the next few years, that format spread to the whole country with regional programming.

But it became clear that FM could be used for "illegal" broadcasts: in Italy, beginning in 1973, "free radios," run by radical college students, environmentalists, and labor unions, flouted the broadcasting monopoly of the Radio Audizione Italiana; in 1978 the government had to increase the punishments for such pirates. Faced with the threat of "free radio," Radio France undertook to provide some of the desired programming when in 1980 it started several experimental FM stations, two national—aimed at youth (Radio 7) and older people (Radio Bleue)—and three decentralized outlets: one regional, one at the level of one of the 95 French "départements," and one truly local. They hoped that by applying a policy of multiplying stations, they could keep FM frequencies for the public service.

In spite of its efforts, however, Radio France was gradually losing market shares to the peripheral stations, whose entertainment programs were more popular and whose often caustic news programs sounded less conformist than those of the public service. The situation was all the more paradoxical because it demonstrated how ill-adapted the government "monopoly" was and, mainly, because the French government owned a majority share in the capital of Radio Luxembourg and controlled Europe 1 and Radio Monte-Carlo via SOFIRAD, a company whose capital was owned by the government.

Return to a Mixed System (Since 1981)

The victory of both the Socialist Party and François Mitterrand in the 1981 elections caused a revolution in the radio world (and in television after 1984).

The Mitterrand Revolution

The promises of the social-democratic candidate to allow local "free" FM stations access to the airwaves generated hundreds of them over the next few months. Belatedly, the laws of 9 November 1981 and 29 July 1982 tried to introduce order into the mess. Licenses to broadcast would only be granted to independent stations linked to an association and with a range not greater than 50 kilometers; for their financing, they could only use volunteer work, subscriptions of association members, and government subsidies; and they could not be funded by any local government. In other words, there were to be no municipal radios and no profit-oriented radios. Licenses were delivered by the Haute Autorité de l'Audiovisuel (or HAA, which, after several transformations, became in 1989 the Conseil Supérieur de l'Audiovisuel [CSA]), which is in charge of seeing that laws are respected by all private and public broadcasting companies. That independent body, partly inspired by the American Federal Communications Commission (FCC), was at last to cut the cord that had since the origins of radio linked the French audiovisual system to the government.

The system of association radios was very soon to prove economically inapplicable. In 1985 the HAA had delivered some 1,800 licenses for the whole country. The law of 1 April 1984 authorized stations to set up as commercial companies and use advertising to finance themselves—and also to join into networks, provided that they kept part of their schedule devoted to local programs. The next year, a decree authorized peripheral radios to enter the FM band and thus to build national networks.

After 1985 the revolution in audiovisual communication was spreading to television, but it seemed to have ended for radio: no new institutional reform was going to wreak havoc on that scene. The regulatory body, by gradually settling the many conflicts, managed to more or less stabilize the movement and made it possible to prepare a relatively easy passage into the 21st century and the digital era. In 1995 the CSA set up 16 regional technical bureaus, the better to assume its functions in the provinces. A law (1 February 1994) raised from 25 to 49 percent the share that a given company could own of a station and allowed several networks to gather local station affiliates, provided their cumulative potential audience did not exceed 150 million (the equivalent of three national networks).

To resist the invasion of the airwaves by U.S. audiovisual products, the French government and European Union authorities have promulgated regulations to guarantee a "cultural exception" to the principle of free circulation of goods. Laws of 18 January 1992 and 1 February 1994, applying the European guidelines on "Television without Borders" (30 October 1989 and 1 February 1994), have set a quota of 60 percent European products, including 40 percent French work on all radio and television stations. The CSA finds it very difficult to enforce the quotas, especially regarding pop music.

Modern French Radio

France now enjoys a radio system that is diverse, efficient, dynamic, and modern. It uses both microwave and satellite relays (which are increasing). It is initiating digital audio broadcasting. Most (85 percent) of the French regularly listen to radio; the morning audience for news is particularly high, whereas elsewhere in Europe people turn more often to home-delivered newspapers. The various services of Radio France generally attract a quarter of the French radio audience. Radio France owns two subsidiaries: Radio France Outre-mer, which serves some 2 million inhabitants scattered over the French territories of the Caribbean, the Indian Ocean, and the Pacific, and Radio France Internationale, which provides one service in French plus programs in 18 other languages using a variety of transmitters.

Radio France operates six national services: France-Inter (general interest), France Culture (considered too elitist by some), France Musique, Radio Bleue (for senior citizens), Le Mouv' (for youth), and France-Info (the first all-news station in Europe, begun in 1987 and attracting a large audience). Its 38 regional stations, which cover half the country, are now associated with the France Bleu network. The FIP services still operate in 76 cities. Radio France funds two orchestras and two choirs, produces some 500,000 hours of programming per year, and employs over 3,000 people, including 450 journalists.

Private-sector radio attracts about 70 percent of the audience. It is highly diversified, with some 1,600 stations that often serve several towns on different frequencies. Each of the old "peripheral" stations continues to supply a national general interest schedule, but each is now associated with two or three groups of local private radios and plays a role similar to that of U.S. networks. Radio Luxembourg (called RTL since 1954) is now linked to a vast pan-European holding com-

pany, RTL-UFA. Europe 1 is now associated with the Lagardère (aviation, armament, and publishing) conglomerate. Radio Monte-Carlo is associated with the NRJ network, which now enjoys third place in the French radio hierarchy, behind RTL and Radio France. These networks have extended abroad, where they cooperate with private commercial stations in Germany, Scandinavia, Spain, Eastern Europe, and Russia. The large national networks of local private radios, which have adopted the American music and news format, include 700 stations in all. Then there are some 300 commercial stations that are still independent, sometimes grouped into small regional networks, which thanks to more original programming intend to remain largely local and stay close to their listeners or to serve some religion. Lastly, some 500 fiercely independent "association stations" survive, partly thanks to government subsidies: their audience varies from one place to another and is rather small (2 to 3 percent) but is still a sign of militant protest. The audience of foreign stations is very small.

PIERRE ALBERT

Further Reading

Albert, Pierre, and André Jean Tudesq, *Histoire de la radio-télévision*, Paris: Presses Universitaires de France, 1981; 5th edition, 1996

Bertrand, Claude-Jean, editor, *Médias: Introduction à la presse, la radio et la télévision*, Paris: Ellipses, 1995; 2nd edition, 1999

Brochand, Christian, *Histoire générale de la radio et de la télévision en France*, Paris: La Documentation Française, 1994

Browne, Donald R., "France: From Competition to Monopoly and Back Again," in *Comparing Broadcast Systems: The Experiences of Six Industrialized Nations*, by Browne, Ames: Iowa State University Press, 1989

Duval, René, *Histoire de la radio en France*, Paris: Moreau, 1979

Institut National de l'Audiovisuel (France), *Les chiffres clés de la radio: France, 1996*, Paris: La Documentation Française, 1996

Jeanneney, Jean Noël, and Agnès Chauveau, *L'écho du siècle: Dictionnaire historique de la radio et de la télévision en France*, Paris: Hachette, and Issy-les-Mulineaux: Arte, 1999

Thomas, Ruth, *Broadcasting and Democracy in France*, London: Crosby Lockwood Staples, 1976; Philadelphia, Pennsylvania: Temple University Press, 1977

Freberg, Stan 1926–

U.S. Radio Satirist, Voice Actor, and Recording Artist

The man who rolled a 700-foot mountain of whipped cream into Lake Michigan and topped it with a 10-ton maraschino cherry didn't actually drain the lake and replace the water with hot chocolate. Rather, he did it the easy way by using radio's "theater of the mind."

Stan Freberg's stimulation of the imagination via radio is legendary among people in the radio industry. His series of commercials for radio called "Who Listens to Radio?" was a memorable treatment of situations that could only be achieved in language and sound and visualized in the mind of the listener—the whipped cream, the cherry (dropped by the Royal Canadian Air Force), and the addition of 25,000 cheering extras. In his most sardonic tones, Freberg would end each spot, saying, "Now, you wanna try that on television?" describing radio as a very special medium "because it stretches the imagination." The goal was simple: convince print and TV advertisers to reallocate their budgets to radio.

After the Lake Michigan spots came others: a skit about a pterodactyl taking a bite out of the Superdome; another about a robber who stole nothing but radios. Each was tagged with a jingle called "Who Listens to Radio?" Freberg's lyrics demonstrated his unique brand of humor, including rhyming "in the morning with your toast and marmalade-e-o" with the word "radio." The song was sung by jazz stylist Sarah Vaughn and orchestrated by arranger Quincy Jones. More than 35 years after Freberg first produced "Who Listens to Radio?" the Radio Advertising Bureau received multiple requests each week for copies of the work.

Early Influence

Freberg grew up the son of a Baptist minister in Pasadena, California. His first experience in show business came at age 11 when he was an assistant to his uncle, a magician. In high school, he became enthralled with radio. He wrote, produced, and performed student radio shows and became his high school speech champion, winning a statewide competition. He was awarded a drama scholarship but turned it down to work with Mel Blanc, the actor who created the voices of Bugs Bunny, Porky Pig, and other Warner Brothers cartoon characters.

In the mid-1940s, Freberg became a regular on *The Jack Benny Show* and worked as a voice actor on *The Phil Harris/ Alice Faye Show, The Man Called X,* and *Suspense.* He spent two years in the Army and then joined an orchestra, Red Fox and his Musical Hounds, as comedian and guitarist.

Freberg wrote and performed an early TV show for children called *Time for Beany,* which won an Emmy award. His co-writer and performing partner on the show was Daws Butler, later the voice of TV's Yogi Bear and Huckleberry Hound and a voice actor on many of Freberg's popular skits.

In 1951, Freberg signed with Capitol Records for the release of "John and Marsha," a spoof of soap operas. The only "lyrics" to "John and Marsha" were the two names of the title, repeated throughout the record with a variety of dramatic intonations. "It was an exercise to see if I could run the gamut of emotions and not say anything except the names of the two leading characters," Freberg said.

A friend saw Freberg perform "John and Marsha" as part of a night-club routine and took a tape to Capitol. Freberg re-recorded "John and Marsha" in the Capitol studios with syrupy music in the background, and the single reached #21 on the Billboard chart. Some radio stations refused to play the record, fearing it was too suggestive. Theater of the mind had triumphed again, for the only suggestions were in the tone of Freberg's voice.

Success led to more spoofs on record. Freberg wrote and produced parodies of Cole Porter's "I've Got You Under My Skin" and Johnnie Ray's "Cry." In 1953, Freberg scored a number one single with "St. George and the Dragonet," a parody of the *Dragnet* television series.

The advent of rock and roll gave Freberg new fodder for parody. He satirized hit songs like "Heartbreak Hotel," "Sh-Boom," and "The Great Pretender." In liner notes to a collection of his skits on Capitol Records, Freberg pointed to "The Great Pretender" as one of his favorites because, "In addition to coming out fairly funny it lampoons a musical trend that I personally loathe."

In notes for *A Child's Garden of Freberg,* 1957, Freberg asserted himself as satirist:

> In all my records I have tried to operate not as a record comic but as a satirist. There's a difference between pointless ridicule and earnest satire. A satirist is inherently a critic who seeks to improve society by pointing up its affectations and absurdities through the use of humor. His chief weapon is exaggeration. Satire is healthy.

Satire also creates controversy, as Freberg discovered more than once. His 1958 single "Green Chritma" brilliantly attacked the commercialization of Christmas ("Deck the halls with advertising, what's the use of compromising?"). Many radio stations banned the seven-minute production. In 1960, Freberg irked radio again with his production of "The Old

Stan Freberg
Courtesy CBS Photo Archive

Payola Roll Blues," a satire on the pay-for-play scandals that rocked the industry at the time.

His most successful recording venture was the 1961 album *Stan Freberg Presents the United States of America,* in which Freberg lampooned people and events in American history. At the discovery of the new world, Christopher Columbus and Queen Isabella sang, "It's a Round Round World." George Washington hired an advertising agency to promote the newly formed United States, and Betsy Ross' design for the American flag was celebrated Hollywood-style with "Everybody Wants to Be an Art Director."

On the Air

During the 1950s, Freberg was heard on a variety of radio shows, including *That's Rich* on CBS and a series of programs on New York's WCBS. In 1957, he was signed to *The Stan Freberg Show,* a live radio program on CBS, replacing *The Jack Benny Show,* which had moved to television. Critical response included raves from *Time* magazine about "a fresh, bright new sound that will wrench people away from the TV set." *The New York Daily News* claimed, "Radio's tired blood is being revitalized by Dr. Stan Freberg."

In spite of positive reviews, the series lasted only 15 weeks. In addition to his frequent run-ins with CBS censors, Freberg wanted the show to run with a single, overall sponsor (like Benny's show had), but he would not allow CBS to sell to a cigarette manufacturer. CBS preferred selling individual spot announcements, and Freberg felt that would mean "every three minutes I'd have to drop a commercial in." The program ran without a sponsor. Freberg won no radio awards for the short-lived series, but the collected recordings won a Grammy Award.

Freberg's body of work grew with his Los Angeles-based advertising agency, called "Freberg, Limited" ("but not very" was added as a parenthetical on the letterhead). He produced memorable television commercials for Jeno's Pizza Rolls and Chun King Chinese foods. For radio, he developed more theater of the mind to sell Contadina tomato products ("Who puts eight great tomatoes in that little bitty can?"), tourism in the state of Oregon ("A territory's great, but you've gotta have a state!"), and the California Prune Advisory Board ("Today the pits; tomorrow the wrinkles!").

He took on commercial projects for two of America's biggest advertisers, General Motors and Mellon Bank. Freberg recalled one client, Dupont, asking him, "We know about the prunes and the pizza rolls, have you ever taken on a really serious client?" His answer: "Other than God?" referring to a series of commercials which needled Americans about not attending church regularly. They were used by the Southern Baptist Radio-Television Commission, the Detroit Council of Churches, the National Council of Churches, and the Presbyterian Church of the United States.

Latter Day Freberg

In the 1990s Freberg was heard on radio again with a daily commentary called *Stan Freberg Here*. His subject was anything topical, from learning to use a new computer to his take on the Gulf War. He was signed as host of the weekly radio series *When Radio Was*, a retrospective of old time radio shows.

In 1996, he continued the *United States of America* series by adding a long-awaited Volume 2, which took on subjects such as Morse's first telegram, Custer's Last Stand, and Edison's invention of the light bulb and the phonograph. Freberg coaxed bandleader Billy May out of retirement for orchestration and enlisted actors John Goodman, Tyne Daly, David Ogden Stiers, and Sherman Hemsley for spoken parts.

Freberg was writing Volume 3 of "United States" when, in 1999, Rhino Records asked him to assemble a retrospective box set titled "Tip of the Freberg: The Stan Freberg Collection, 1951-1998." The set includes remastered editions of his early Capitol recordings and a VHS tape of commercials Freberg produced for television.

Throughout the 1990s, Freberg was active as a voice actor, lending his talents to advertising and animation. He was regularly heard as the voice of Junyer Bear in "Bugs Bunny" cartoons and as Bertie in "Cheese Chasers" cartoons. In the feature animated film *Stuart Little*, Freberg was heard as the race announcer.

Freberg noted with pride in a 1999 interview that Paul and Linda McCartney mentioned him in a *Playboy* article when they were asked where the Beatles got their sense of humor. Writer Stephen King said that Freberg's maraschino cherry commercial influenced his imagination, though King misremembered the scene as Puget Sound, not Lake Michigan. Playwright David Mamet referred to the same commercial and remembered the lake correctly, but magnified the cherry to 30 tons and added skyrockets along the shore. Freberg called the mistakes a tribute to the medium of radio that the scenes were remembered as even bigger than they were.

Underscoring his self-description as satirist, Freberg quotes Al Capp, the artist who drew the "Li'l Abner" comic strip: "The fifth freedom is the freedom to laugh at ourselves." To which Freberg adds: "Mr. Capp makes sense. When we stop laughing at ourselves, the decline and fall is not far off."

ED SHANE

See also Comedy; Promotion on Radio

Stanley Victor Freberg. Born in Los Angeles, California, 7 August 1926. Early voice acting with Mel Blanc; regular on *The Jack Benny Show* on radio; wrote and performed for television's *Time for Beany*; signed to Capitol Records, 1951, where he wrote and produced recordings satirizing popular culture; starred in *The Stan Freberg Show*, 1957; record album *Stan Freberg Presents the United States of America*, 1961. Freberg, Limited, advertising agency, produced commercials for Jeno's Pizza Rolls, among many others. *Stan Freberg Here* radio commentaries though the 1990s. Box set *Tip of the Freberg*, Rhino Records, 1999.

Selected Radio Series

1957	*The Stan Freberg Show*
1990–1998	*Stan Freberg Here*
1990–present	*When Radio Was*

Selected Recordings

The Best of The Stan Freberg Show, 1958; *Green Christmas*, 1959; *Stan Freberg Presents the United States of America*, 1961; *Stan Freberg Presents the United States of America, Volume 2: The Middle Years*, 1996; *Tip of the Freberg, 1951–1998: The Ultimate Freberg Box Set*, 1999

Selected Publications

It Only Hurts When I Laugh, 1988

Further Reading

Ken R., "Radio Commercials for . . . Radio!" *Radio World* (14 March 2001)

Frederick, Pauline 1908–1990

U.S. Radio Network Journalist

One of the first female network news correspondents, Pauline Frederick became best known for more than two decades of reporting from the United Nations for National Broadcasting Company (NBC) radio and television. For her first dozen years on network television—until 1960—she remained the only female reporter of lasting duration in the medium.

Frederick grew up in Harrisburg, Pennsylvania, and got her first journalistic experience covering social news for the local paper. She left to earn her bachelor's degree in political science (1929) and a master's degree in international law (1931), both from American University in Washington, D.C. She originally intended to be an attorney but grew more interested in journalism while in school. She worked as a freelance reporter for, among other media, the *Washington Star* on women's issues, and some of her interviews were syndicated by the North American Newspaper Alliance (NANA).

Her first broadcasting work was for NBC Blue, assisting commentator H.R. Baukage by conducting interviews with various newsmakers beginning in 1938 with the wife of the Czech ambassador as Germany occupied that country. She continued at NBC into the 1940s, undertaking scriptwriting and other assignments, few of them on air in an era when female broadcast journalists were almost unheard of. Unable to break that gender barrier, she left the network in 1945 to work full-time for NANA while freelancing occasional "women's news" and other reports for what had become American Broadcasting Company (ABC) radio. This period of intensive international experience included travel to 19 countries in 1945–46; she sent reports from several countries in the Far East, from the Nuremberg trials of Nazi war criminals in Germany, and from Poland.

Frederick returned to broadcasting when, despite being turned down by both the Columbia Broadcasting System (CBS) and NBC (who still felt women's voices were not authoritative enough for news), she obtained a part-time position with fledgling ABC News in 1946, initially focusing (again) on "women's news." Her impressive output—including an exclusive interview with General Eisenhower and later coverage of a foreign ministers' conference—raised her status to full-time employment in 1948. That year she helped anchor ABC's television coverage of the national political conventions, and from August 1948 to March 1949 she hosted the Saturday evening 15-minute *Pauline Frederick's Guest Books* of television news interviews. She was heard on several radio network newscasts, her radio focus becoming international affairs, including the then-new United Nations, on which she quickly became an authority.

In 1954 Frederick returned to NBC and continued covering the United Nations for 21 years until her mandatory retirement (because of her age—she was 65), about which she learned from a story in the *New York Times* in 1974. In this two-decade period she became the voice of the United Nations for many Americans. She was also heard covering political conventions, tensions and wars in the Middle East, the Cuban Missile Crisis and other parts of the Cold War, and the war in Vietnam. At the same time, she continued on NBC radio with *Pauline Frederick Reporting*, a 15-minute daily program.

After retiring from NBC radio and television news, Frederick commented on United Nations affairs for National Public Radio. She also became the first female journalist to moderate a presidential candidates' debate when she presided over one of the 1976 televised forums pitting President Gerald Ford against Governor Jimmy Carter. She retired in 1980.

Frederick received 23 honorary doctorates and was the first woman to win both the Alfred I. DuPont award (for commentary, in 1954 and 1956) and the George Foster Peabody award (1954). She was also the first woman to win the Paul White Award from the Radio-Television News Directors Association (1980). She was a model for many aspiring female journalists and was one of the first to succeed over a long career.

CHRISTOPHER H. STERLING

Pauline Frederick. Born in Gallitzen, Pennsylvania, 13 February 1908. B.A. in political science, 1929 and M.A. in international law, 1931, American University. Performed freelance journalism work, 1920s and 1930s; interviewer, NBC, Washington, D.C., 1938–45; war correspondent, North American Newspaper Alliance, 1945–46; joined ABC radio, 1946–53; returned to NBC, becoming first woman to report serious television news, 1954–74; first woman elected president of the UN Correspondents Association, 1959; international affairs analyst, NPR, 1974–80; first woman to moderate a presidential debate, Jimmy Carter and Gerald Ford, 1976. Recipient: Alfred DuPont Award for meritorious service to the American people, 1953; twenty-three honorary degrees; Headliner Award, Theta Sigma Phi; George Foster Peabody Award, School of Journalism, University of Georgia, 1954; First Pennsylvania Journalism Achievement Award; first woman recipient, Paul White Award, Radio-Television News Directors Association, 1980. Died in Lake Forest, Illinois, 9 May 1990.

Pauline Frederick
Courtesy AP/Wide World Photos

Radio Series
1949–53   *ABC News*
1953–56   *NBC News*
1954–55   *At the UN*

Selected Publications
Ten First Ladies of the World, 1967

Further Reading
Hosley, David H., and Gayle K. Yamada, *Hard News: Women in Broadcast Journalism*, New York: Greenwood Press, 1987

Marzolf, Marion, *Up from the Footnote: A History of Women Journalists*, New York: Hastings House, 1977
Nobile, Philip, "TV News and the Older Woman," *New York Times* (10 August 1981)
Sanders, Marlene, and Marcia Rock, *Waiting for Prime-Time: The Women of Television News*, Urbana: University of Illinois Press, 1988
Talese, Gay, "Perils of Pauline," *The Saturday Evening Post* (26 January 1963)

Freed, Alan 1921–1965

U.S. Disc Jockey

In the 1950s, Alan Freed became the first nationally recognized disc jockey in the U.S. to feature the emerging rhythm and blues and rock musical forms. During a time when many white "platter pilots" were reluctant to play songs by African-American performers, Freed was not; as a result, he helped to advance the careers of a number of artists. He has also been credited with helping to popularize the term *rock and roll*.

Freed, who grew up in Salem, Ohio, began his career in radio as an announcer in New Castle, Pennsylvania, after World War II, and by 1949 he had a popular music request show over WAKR in Akron, Ohio. In 1950 he moved to Cleveland and landed a job at WXEL-TV; however, by June 1951 Freed had returned to radio, hosting a record show over Cleveland's WJMO from 6:00 to 7:00 in the evenings. Less than a month later, he moved over to WJW in Cleveland to host what became a very popular late-evening request show.

Although Freed had started playing rhythm and blues on the air while he was in Akron, the inspiration for his career in rhythm and blues came from Joe Mintz, the owner of a Cleveland record store called the Record Rendezvous. Mintz was convinced that a rhythm and blues show would be popular, because both blacks and whites were buying rhythm and blues records in his store. He convinced Freed to give the music a chance on the air, and the result was *The Moondog Show*, which proved to be a great success.

Freed received wide attention when, in 1952, he took his show on the road. He decided to host a live concert in the Cleveland/Akron area called the Moondog Ball. The show, which featured a variety of acts, drew a crowd of 25,000 people to a 10,000-seat arena, and it was heralded as a successful,

though raucous, event. The near riot created by the ticketless crowd outside the theater attracted press attention to the music Freed was playing.

By 1954 WNJR in New Jersey had begun to air taped copies of Freed's programs, and on 1 May he hosted an Eastern Moondog Coronation Ball at the Sussex Avenue Armory in Newark. Years later, the *New York Times* noted, "Going to one of Alan Freed's rock 'n' roll musicales has always been something like having an aisle seat for the San Francisco earthquake."

Freed moved from Cleveland to New York City in July 1954 after signing with WINS radio for the largest annual salary paid to an independent rhythm and blues jockey up to that point—$75,000. However, blind street musician Louis "Moondog" Hardin objected to Freed's use of the Moondog moniker, and in December of 1954, Hardin won a court injunction against Freed's use of the term. Freed changed the name of his WINS program to *Alan Freed's Rock and Roll Party*, and the age of rock began.

Freed moved to WABC in 1958, but he lost both his prestigious radio program and a television show at WNEW-TV in 1959 as a result of the Congressional quiz-show investigations. The legal action was prompted by accusations that TV networks were rigging popular quiz shows of the day, but the inquiries shifted to radio after Burt Lane, a representative for the American Guild of Authors and Publishers, sent a letter to the Congressional Special Subcommittee on Legislative Oversight citing examples of commercial bribery. Freed and a number of popular disk jockeys were accused of accepting money from record companies in return for playing those companies'

Alan Freed at WABC, June 1958
Courtesy AP/Wide World Photos

songs on the air. Freed pleaded guilty to a charge of taking bribes in 1962 and subsequently left New York City. Freed died in 1965 at 43 years of age in Palm Springs, California.

CHARLES F. GANZERT

Alan Freed. Born Albert James Freed, near Johnstown, Pennsylvania, 21 December 1921. Attended Ohio State University, B.S. in mechanical engineering, 1943; served two years in U.S. Army; disc jockey, WKST, New Castle, Pennsylvania, 1945; radio host, WAKR, Akron, Ohio, 1947; hosted television dance show, WXEL, Cleveland, Ohio, 1950; disc jockey, WJW, Cleveland, Ohio, 1951–54; staged "Big Beat," all-African-American-talent rock and roll shows, 1952–58; hosted *Rock 'n' Roll Party*, CBS-TV, 1957; disc jockey, WINS, New York City, 1954–58; disc jockey, WABC, New York City, 1958; hosted dance party, WNEW -TV, New York City, 1959; disc jockey, KDAY, Los Angeles, California, 1960; worked at WQAM, Miami, Florida, 1962; jazz disc jockey, KNOB, Los Angeles, California, 1964. Elected to the Rock and Roll Hall of Fame, 1986. Died in Palm Springs, California, 20 January 1965.

Radio Series
1947   *Request Review*

1951–54   *The Moon Dog Show*
1954–58   *Alan Freed's Rock 'n' Roll Party*

Films
Rock around the Clock, 1956; *Don't Knock the Rock*, 1956; *Rock, Rock, Rock*, 1957; *Go Johnny Go*, 1959

Further Reading
Fornatale, Peter, and Joshua E. Mills, *Radio in the Television Age*, Woodstock, New York: Overlook Press, 1980
Passman, Arnold, *The Deejays*, New York: Macmillan, 1971
Smith, Wes, *The Pied Pipers of Rock 'n' Roll: Radio Deejays of the 50s and 60s*, Marietta, Georgia: Longstreet Press, 1989
Sterling, Christopher H., and John M. Kittross, *Stay Tuned: A History of American Broadcasting*, 3rd edition, Mahwah, New Jersey: Lawrence Erlbaum, 2002
United States Congress, House Committee on Interstate and Foreign Commerce, *Responsibilities of Broadcasting Licensees and Station Personnel*, 2 vols., Washington, D.C.: GPO, 1960
Ward, Ed, Geoffrey Stokes, and Ken Tucker, *Rock of Ages: The Rolling Stone History of Rock and Roll*, New York: Rolling Stone Press, 1986

Freed, Paul 1918–1996

U.S. Religious Broadcaster

Paul E. Freed founded Trans World Radio in 1952 in Tangiers, Morocco. By 1999 Trans World Radio was broadcasting in 150 languages from 12 locations in the world. Its gospel message is broadcast more than 1,400 hours each week and reaches listeners on three continents.

Freed, the son of missionaries, was born in Detroit, Michigan, in 1918. As a young boy, his family moved to the Middle East, where his parents served with the Christian and Missionary Alliance Church. Freed's early education was sporadic; he attended English and German school in Jerusalem, was home schooled, and worked with tutors. When his parents were home on furlough, he attended Wheaton Academy in Illinois. From the Academy, he matriculated at Wheaton College, where he earned his bachelor's degree. After graduating from Wheaton College, Freed attended Nyack Bible College and graduated from its missions program. Shortly after his mar-

riage to Betty Jane Seawell in 1945, Freed left his employment as pastor of a small church in Greenville, South Carolina. Torrey Johnson, founder of the Youth for Christ movement, recruited Freed as the director of the Greensboro, North Carolina, program.

In 1948 Johnson sent Freed to the Youth for Christ conference in Switzerland. Despite protestations from Freed, Johnson insisted it was God's calling for him. While in Switzerland, Freed was convinced there was a need to transmit the message of God to the evangelical Protestant youth of Franco's Spain. Following a trip to Spain, Freed laid the foundation for a radio organization to bring the gospel message to the people of Spain. The Spanish government refused to sanction such work. Frustrated by his experience, Freed returned to the United States to find a way to fulfill his mission of evangelical radio for the people of Spain.

Rev. Paul E. Freed reports to White House after a visit to Spain, 21 December 1951
Courtesy AP/Wide World Photos

Origins of Trans World Radio

In February 1952 Freed founded International Evangelism (later to be known as Trans World Radio) in the international city of Tangiers, Morocco. Freed acquired a small piece of land directly across the narrow Strait of Gibraltar from Spain. By 1954, at 61 years of age, Freed's father, Ralph Freed, accepted a new ministry to become director of the radio station in Tangiers. Dr. Ralph Freed transmitted the first Christian message from Tangiers, Morocco, on a 2,500-watt transmitter. Working together, by 1956 the Freeds built the Voice of Tangiers into an organization that broadcast the gospel message to 40 countries in over 20 languages. In 1959, when Morocco became a politically independent nation, government officials for the new regime ordered all radio stations to become nationalized. Freed was forced to move his station. Freed was worried that the 80 million listeners of the Voice of Tangiers would be lost, because there were no other full-time gospel radio stations on the air. The tiny Riviera country of Monaco welcomed Trans World Radio and its gospel message.

Freed and Trans World Radio began broadcasting from a transmitter originally built during World War II by the Germans for propaganda purposes.

By 1960 Freed had completed a dissertation at the New York University School of Education. He combined international relations, mass communication, and religious education in preparation for his goal to expand Trans World Radio's broadcast of the gospel message to other areas of Europe. Freed believed that millions of people around the world would be receptive to the gospel message if they could hear it. European radio was not receptive to gospel programs or preachers. Most radio in Europe was controlled by the government, and the few countries that allowed preaching charged extremely high rates for even their lowest-rated times. Other countries that closed their borders to missionaries and the gospel message were also targeted by Freed for radio broadcasts.

The station in Monte Carlo broadcast with 100,000 watts. Freed targeted Spain, Portugal, the British Isles, Scandinavia, the then the Soviet Union, Central Europe, Southern Europe, the Middle East, and North Africa as the primary areas to be reached from Monte Carlo. The first programs aired by Trans World Radio were broadcast in 24 languages. The staff in Monte Carlo received 18,000 letters the first year offering support for their programming efforts. Trans World Radio continued to grow, setting up branch offices in different areas of Europe. Their ministry spread across Europe and into the Middle East.

In August 1964 Trans World Radio added a transmitting station in Bonaire Island, part of the Netherlands Antilles. Through this facility, Trans World Radio programmed 70 hours a week of gospel messages to the Caribbean and the northern part of South America. By 1980 Trans World Radio had established new transmitting stations in Swaziland to reach sub-Saharan Africa and Pakistan, in Cyprus to reach people in 21 countries in the Middle East and North Africa, and in Guam (broadcasting in 35 languages) to reach listeners in Central Asia, South Asia, Southeast Asia, and the Asian Pacific area. In the 1980s Trans World Radio established operations in Uruguay in partnership with "Radio Rural" to carry its gospel message to listeners in Uruguay and northern Argentina.

As Trans World Radio moved into the 1990s, Freed continued to work to expand listenership. Stations were added in Albania, Russia, Johannesburg, and Poland. By 2000 Trans World Radio broadcast 1,400 hours of gospel programs from 12 locations around the world. These programs were broadcast in 150 languages to an estimated 2 billion people. Each year, Trans World Radio receives over 1.4 million letters from listeners in 160 countries. Trans World Radio initially transmitted on AM at 800 kilohertz and has since added shortwave transmissions to reach more listeners. Shortly after Freed's death on 1 December 1996, he was inducted into the National Religious Broadcaster's Hall of Fame.

MARGARET FINUCANE

See also International Radio; Religion on Radio; Shortwave Radio

Paul Ernest Freed. Born in Detroit, Michigan, 29 August 1918. Son of missionaries Ralph and Mildred Freed; attended Wheaton College, B.A.. 1940; graduate of Missions Program, Nyack Bible College, 1944; attended Columbia University, M.A. 1956; New York University, Ph.D. in Mass Communication, 1960; founded Trans World Radio, 1952; awarded "President's silver Medallion for Service to the

Kingdom of God," Toccoa Falls College, 1996; inducted into the National Religious Broadcaster's Hall of Fame, 1997. Died in Cary, North Carolina, 1 December 1996.

Selected Publications

Towers to Eternity, 1968
Let the Earth Hear: The Thrilling Story of How Radio Goes over Barriers to Bring the Gospel of Christ to Unreached Millions, 1980

Further Reading

Melton, J. Gordon, et al., "Paul Freed" and "Trans World Radio," in *Prime-Time Religion: An Encyclopedia of Religious Broadcasting,* Phoenix: Oryx Press, 1997

Free Form Format

During the 1960s, FM was ripe for a new form of radio—radio that burst through established format boundaries, emphasizing wholeness over separation and communal action over atomistic listening. *Free form*—in which imaginative disc jockeys combined many types of recorded and live music, sound effects, poetry, interviews, and calls from listeners—was the aural representation of the counterculture movement. Eschewing the slick professionalism, high-pressure salesmanship, and tight formats of AM radio, free form was—and sometimes still is—distinctly spontaneous, experimental, and challenging. At its best, free form is an exhilarating art form in its own right—a synergistic combination of disparate musical forms and spoken words. At its worst, free form may be pandering and self-indulgent.

Origins

Free form's roots developed in both commercial and noncommercial settings. During the mid-1960s, noncommercial community stations were developing across the country, following the lead established by Pacifica stations in California, New York, and Texas. These stations depended heavily on low-paid (often volunteer) programmers whose anti-establishment agendas rejected the tight structure of most corporate, commercial media. At the same time, commercial FM was still in its infancy, and disc jockeys were encouraged to experiment with longer segments and album cuts. Free form developed amidst

these experimental venues, catching on quickly among community stations and some commercial FM stations—albeit late at night and on weekends.

Free form most likely originated at WBAI in New York City around 1963–64, with three different deejays: Bob Fass (Radio Unnameable), Larry Josephson (In the Beginning), and the following year with Steve Post's the Outside. Soon, it spread to other stations, notably Pacifica stations KPFA in Berkeley and KPFK in Los Angeles, and privately owned KMPX in San Francisco. KMPX's general manager, Tom Donahue, is often credited as being the driving force behind the "underground radio" movement. Although he did not invent free form, Donahue nurtured it and allowed it to grow from a program shift to an entire format (although *anti-format* might be a better term).

Style

Free-form programmers featured everything from cutting-edge musicians such as Bob Dylan and the Grateful Dead to comedy routines from W.C. Fields and Jonathan Winters. Indian ragas and classical music were heard back to back. Shows started late and ran overtime. Guests wandered in and out of control rooms, sometimes speaking on air, at other times just being part of the scene. Disc jockeys pontificated on the day's topics, their delivery styles ranging from chats with listeners and studio guests to rambling, witty monologues—often within the same program. Interviews and announcements regarding the counterculture and antiwar protests peppered broadcasts increasingly as the 1960s wore on.

Free form's deliberately anarchistic and undisciplined sound was, in effect, a form of participatory theater and gained a considerable following within the counterculture. Listeners called in to programs and were often heard on the air, rallies were announced (and broadcast), and listeners met at live remotes and events sponsored by stations (such as WBAI's 1967 "fly in" at Kennedy Airport, organized by WBAI free-form host Bob Foss).

Challenges to Free Form

The popularity of free form reached its peak between 1965 and 1970 and ultimately waned for three primary reasons. Ironically, once established through the success of free form, commercial FM became bound by the same tight formats that defined AM. Also, leaders among free-form disc jockeys, notably WBAI's Larry Josephson, grew weary of underground radio and moved on to other pastures. And the counterculture movement that nurtured free form eventually evolved beyond its communal sentiments. As the movement splintered into subgroups focusing upon sexuality, gender, race, and ethnicity, free form gave way to specialty shows on community radio and to the newer, more professional "public" stations affiliated with National Public Radio (NPR).

The 1980s were particularly difficult for free form, as community stations and NPR affiliates began programming more syndicated programming and professionalizing their sound, especially following NPR's near bankruptcy in 1983. Severe internal battles over station control were sometimes waged, with the fate of free form hanging in the balance. Proponents argued that free form was a unique means of expression that the new professionals simply failed to understand. The latter charged that free form's time had passed and that free form appealed to only a tiny fraction of the potential market. Despite such challenges, free form continued to survive at some stations, albeit most often during the late-night hours where it had originally developed.

Contemporary Free Form

Among the community stations and a dwindling number of public stations that still program it, free form has taken on an air of sanctity, hearkening back to the good old days when community radio was central to the underground movement. Yet without a symbiotic cultural context to fuel and inform it, contemporary free form lacks the immediacy and connection with the public that it once held. As such, free form has become a much more personal medium among disc jockeys, and a successful program is one that has smoothly combined a wide variation of sounds reflective of the programmer's moods and inclinations at the moment. Whereas 1960s free form was jarring and often disturbing in its quirky juxtapositions, contemporary free form is more often about flow and seamless segues.

Besides community and public radio stations, most college radio stations also program free-form music to some extent, although the preferred term is "alternative radio." College radio programmers, however, typically lack a historical awareness of free form and have little concept of its cultural implications. Also, college radio's alternative programming is rarely as diverse as free form heard on community and public stations.

Free form's most recent manifestation is on the internet. Community, public, and college stations increasingly broadcast via the web, and some internet-only stations—often the efforts of individuals working from home—advertise themselves as free-form radio. The internet is also an important meeting place for free form enthusiasts, whose web pages and chat groups provide means of sharing information and ideas.

WARREN BAREISS

See also Internet Radio; KPFA; Pacifica Foundation; WBAI

Further Reading

Armstrong, David, *A Trumpet to Arms: Alternative Media in America,* Los Angeles: Tarcher, 1981

Bareiss, Warren, "Space, Identity, and Public-Access Media: A Case Study of Alternative Radio Station KUNM-Albuquerque," Ph.D. diss., Indiana University, 1997

"Digging FM Rock," *Newsweek* (4 March 1968)

Engelman, Ralph, *Public Radio and Television in America: A Political History,* Thousand Oaks, California: Sage, 1996

Keith, Michael C., *Voices in the Purple Haze: Underground Radio and the Sixties,* Westport, Connecticut: Praeger, 1997

Knopper, Steve, "Free-Form Radio Still on the Dial," *Billboard* (14 January 1995)

Krieger, Susan, *Hip Capitalism,* Beverly Hills, California: Sage, 1979

Land, Jeffrey Richard, *Active Radio: Pacifica's "Brash Experiment,"* Minneapolis: University of Minnesota Press, 1999

Lasar, Matthew, *Pacifica Radio: The Rise of an Alternative Network,* Philadelphia, Pennsylvania: Temple University Press, 1999

Mayor, Alfred, "Accent: Radio Free New York," *Atlantic Monthly* (May 1968)

Frequency Allocation

Providing Spectrum for Broadcasting

Governments allocate bands of frequencies, including radio frequencies, for specific uses. Frequency allocation meshes technical limits and options with political and economic realities to create the compromise solutions behind today's broadcast services.

Three definitions are useful. *Allocation* is the broadest division of the electromagnetic spectrum into designated bands for given services (such as AM radio in the medium waves or FM in the very-high-frequency [VHF] spectrum). *Allotments* fall within allocations—they are given channels that are designated for specific places (only FM and television broadcasting have allotments). Finally, *assignments* are allotments that have actual users operating on them (such as a given station using 98.1 megahertz, for example)—they are virtually the same as a license to operate.

Frequency allocation can be examined under three broad rubrics. First, frequencies are allocated to classes of service. All radio signals that travel through the air use frequencies that are part of the electromagnetic spectrum. By international agreement this natural resource is divided into bands in which certain kinds of broadcasting occur. Medium-wave (or AM) radio occurs in one part of the spectrum, VHF (or FM) radio in another, VHF and ultrahigh-frequency (UHF) television in others, cellular telephony in another, satellite communication in another, and so on.

The frequencies used by different services are a function of three circumstances. First is history. Early experimentation with certain kinds of broadcasting resulted in assumptions that final allocations for that service should occur in the bands, or at the frequencies, originally used. This is because radio and television sets are designed to detect and amplify certain frequencies. Therefore, once such devices begin to be sold, changing the frequency of the service they were designed to use would make them obsolete. This can happen—for instance, in the United States the frequencies used to broadcast VHF/FM were changed in 1945—but the presumption is against such changes if they can be avoided.

Second are the technical needs of a particular service compared to the characteristics of certain portions of the spectrum. For instance, lower frequencies, such as those used for medium-wave/AM radio or shortwave radio, travel farther and propagate in ways that make it possible for them to bypass barriers more effectively than higher frequencies, such as those used for VHF/FM. This makes shortwave an effective means to broadcast transcontinentally or across oceans, medium-wave an effective means to provide national radio services (or international services to contiguous countries), and VHF an effec-

tive means to provide local radio services. Satellite television signals are at such high frequencies that they are effectively blocked by buildings, trees, or other obstacles. Such frequencies would be relatively useless if they were used by terrestrial (or land-based) transmitters, but because the satellite signals travel essentially vertically (from the sky to the earth), they can be used for this service as long as the dishes for receiving them are clear of obstacles. They can be affected by electrical storms or heavy thunderstorms, however, so some disruptions of service are inevitable.

Third are the political compromises made by the signatory administrations (or countries) that sign the allocation agreements under the auspices of the International Telecommunication Union (ITU). Such agreements, for instance, can result in an altered frequency band assignment for a particular service, despite uses of another portion of the spectrum in some countries. This is usually the result of a recognized need to rationalize frequency allocations so that transmission and reception devices can be designed using a worldwide standard. Otherwise the economies of scale may not achieve maximum impact, and the devices made may not be manufactured or sold as inexpensively as they would be otherwise. International broadcasting would be impossible if there were not an international allocation for such services, because the radio sets used to listen to them could not tune the same frequencies from country to country.

Frequencies are also allocated within classes of service to particular countries. Some frequencies assigned are exclusive, and others are shared. The less powerful a station is, the less distance its signals travel. Consequently, it can share its frequency with other stations located at a sufficient distance to avoid interference. This is easier with VHF/FM than with medium-wave/AM, because FM signals travel only by line of sight, whereas the propagation characteristics of amplitude-modulated (AM) signals change at dusk, traveling farther via night-time sky waves, which bounce off a layer of the ionosphere and return many hundreds of miles from their origination point. Countries contiguous to one another must share the total frequency allocation for a particular type of service within its region.

Frequencies are also assigned within particular allocations to particular users (or broadcasters). Different carrier frequencies (the center point of a channel—the frequency that appears on your receiver when you tune a specific station) are assigned to individual stations. In the United States, frequencies are assigned by the Federal Communications Commission (FCC) by means of broadcasting licenses. These licenses stipulate the channel (or band of frequencies centered on the carrier) that a station is to use to broadcast, the power it can use (according to the class of service it is licensed to provide), and its hours of operation. AM stations, for instance, use the 535-to1705-kilohertz band, and FM stations use the 88.1-to107.9-megahertz band. There are 117 AM carrier frequencies that can be assigned and 100 FM frequencies. Because of the propagation characteristics of these two services and the differences in bandwidth (10-kilohertz bandwidths for AM stations and 200-kilohertz bandwidths for FM), there were in 2000 about 4,900 AM stations and more than 6,700 FM stations in the United States. In January 2000 the FCC also began a new class of FM service, allowing both 100-watt and 10-watt stations, which will add many new low-power FM stations to the American broadcast landscape.

The principal exception to these general rules for frequency allocation is the frequencies used for international broadcasting in the shortwave portion of the spectrum. Here, individual stations are not assigned particular frequencies or broadcast power to use. Because the amplitude-modulated carrier waves of shortwave stations have the same propagation characteristics as AM waves generally, shortwave stations must change their frequencies as the seasons change (because the sunspot cycle moves from inactive to active every 17 years) and often as the time of day changes. This is why such stations register their "demands" with the international Frequency Registration Board (FRB), part of the ITU. By registering, they can discover whether they are attempting to use the same frequency as another broadcaster in the same part of the world. Often stations will also collaborate to ensure that their broadcasts will not interfere with one another's.

When radio was just beginning to be used in the early part of the 20th century, scientists believed that there were a limited number of frequencies suitable for broadcasting. When the first stations began to go on the air in about 1919, they used the same few frequencies, and there was significant interference between stations. Shortwave was given its name because people believed that any wavelengths shorter than those first used for radio would be unusable. This was because the shorter the wavelength (and thus the greater the frequency per second with which a wave crosses a particular plane), the more power it takes to move a wave a given distance. In other words, the longer the wave, the farther it will travel with a given transmitter. People thought that if wavelengths became shorter than those used by shortwave, the power required to make them usable would be prohibitively high.

Transmitters have become more efficient, however, and new forms of broadcasting (such as frequency modulation and digital broadcasting) have developed that continue to open up new frequencies for use. At the 1992 World Administrative Radio Conference (WARC), the participants provided new allocations for broadcast satellite service. For audio (or sound) broadcasting, the frequencies 1452–1492 megahertz, 2310–2360 megahertz, and 2535–2655 megahertz were agreed to, and the FCC subsequently allocated the spectrum 2310–2360 megahertz based on the international allocation adopted for the United States by the 1992 WARC for a Digital Audio Radio Service. The 1992 WARC also adopted an even higher set of frequencies for broadcast satellite service for high-definition television, with 17.3–17.8 gigahertz assigned to region 2 and 21.4–22.0 gigahertz for regions 1 and 3. All these new allocations will become effective 1 April 2007.

As seen in Table 1, the ITU has allocated the bands in the electromagnetic spectrum for various uses.

The pattern in these allocations is easy to see. It is useful to note that there are only 20,000 hertz in band 4, 299,970 hertz in band 5, and 2,999,700 hertz in band 6. As the frequencies used for broadcasting rise, the total amount of spectrum available increases not arithmetically (as, for instance, the band numbers do), but exponentially. What this means in practical terms is that the amount of spectrum now available for services has enabled enormously more service, more competition, and more exclusive service allocations at ever-higher frequencies. For broadcasting, this has also meant the opportunity to expand bandwidth as the frequency allocations have risen, thus allowing for higher-fidelity transmissions. Whereas in the AM band, bandwidths of 10 kilohertz only allow stations to broadcast about half of the frequency response that is within human hearing range, with VHF/FM broadcasting two signals (left and right) can be broadcast using the entire 20-kilohertz range and still leave room for sideband broadcasting, guard bands to prevent cross-channel interference, and a broadcasting envelope to prevent atmospheric or manmade interference. Use of even higher frequencies allows the broadcasting of multiple CD-quality digital signals in the same channel, which digital radio delivered by satellite will deliver.

All frequency allocations are based on the use of hertz (or cycles per second) generated by a broadcast transmitter (hertz are named for Heinrich Hertz, whose experiments led to recognition of cycles generated by sound). Human hearing, for instance, can decipher the frequencies from about 20 hertz to 20,000 hertz (or 20 kilohertz). Any vibrating object creates waves at a particular frequency. Large objects (such as kettle drums or tubas) generate mostly low frequencies, whereas smaller ones (such as flutes or piccolos) generate mostly high frequencies. Tuba sounds travel farther than piccolo sounds do. The same principle applies to broadcast transmitters that generate the carrier waves upon or within which sound is carried to radio or television receivers, with some reservations. Low-frequency signals tend to travel along the ground, and much of their power is absorbed by the earth. As the frequencies increase, more of the signal travels through the air than along the ground, and gradually more of it also becomes a sky wave, which travels up and bounces back to earth. These char-

Table 1. International Telecommunication Union Band Allocations

Band Number	Frequencies	Designation	Some Designated Uses
4	10–30 kHz	Very low frequency	Long distance point-to-point broadcasting
5	30–300 kHz	Low frequency	Medium distance point-to-point broadcasting, radio navigation, aeronautical mobile, low-frequency broadcasting
6	300–3000 kHz	Medium frequency	AM broadcasting, short-range communication, international distress
7	3–30 MHz	High frequency	International radio broadcasting; air-to-ground, ship-to-shore, and international point-to-point broadcasting
8	30–300 MHz	Very high frequency	Line-of-sight communication, VHF television broadcasting, FM broadcasting, aeronautical distress
9	300–3000 MHz	Ultrahigh frequency	UHF television broadcasting, space communication, radar, citizens band radio
10	3–30 GHz	Superhigh frequency	Microwave communication, space communication
11	30–300 GHz	Extremely high frequency	Microwave communication, space communication, radar, radio astronomy

acteristics mean that less power will actually move a wave at a higher frequency farther than a wave at very low frequencies, despite the fact that the wavelengths are lower at the higher frequency (wavelength and frequency are in inverse relationship). Therefore, when shortwave propagation was discovered in 1921, it was possible to reach as far with a 1-kilowatt transmitter as organizations had used 200 kilowatts to do before using the ground wave of low-frequency broadcasting.

Frequency allocations thus have to be made with several interrelated factors in mind: (1) the type of propagation that will occur at a given frequency (ground, direct, or sky); (2) the type of service that is to be accomplished with a particular allocation (local, national, or international, via terrestrial or satellite transmission); (3) the fidelity required for the service to be provided (for instance, voice, music, video, or CD quality) and the bandwidth necessary to provide that service; (4) whether the allocations must be exclusive or can be shared with other services; (5) existing experimental or other uses that a particular set of frequencies have been put to (thus providing what are called "squatter's rights"); and (6) the political realities of allocation among the different administrations that seek to employ the frequencies for particular uses.

ROBERT S. FORTNER

See also AM Radio; Clear Channel Stations; Digital Satellite Radio; Federal Communications Commission; FM Radio; Ground Wave; Hertz, Heinrich; International Telecommunication Union; Licensing; North American Regional Broadcasting Agreement; Portable Radio Stations; Shortwave Radio; Subsidiary Communication Authorization; Ten-Watt Stations

Further Reading

Glatzer, Hal, *Who Owns the Rainbow? Conserving the Radio Spectrum*, Indianapolis, Indiana: Sams, 1984

Gosling, William, *Radio Spectrum Conservation*, Oxford and Boston: Newnes, 2000

Jackson, Charles, "The Frequency Spectrum," *Scientific American* (September 1980)

Joint Technical Advisory Committee, *Radio Spectrum Conservation: A Program of Conservation Based on Present Uses and Future Needs*, New York: McGraw-Hill, 1952; revised and expanded edition, as *Radio Spectrum Utilization: A Program for the Administration of the Radio Spectrum*, New York: Institute of Electrical and Electronics Engineers, 1964

Levin, Harvey Joshua, *The Invisible Resource: Use and Regulation of the Radio Spectrum*, Baltimore, Maryland: Johns Hopkins University Press, 1971

Withers, David J., *Radio Spectrum Management: Management of the Spectrum and Regulation of Radio Services*, London: Peregrinus, 1991; 2nd edition, London: Institution of Electrical Engineers, 1999

Fresh Air

Public Radio Arts and Issues Program

Fresh Air host Terry Gross refers to herself and her production team as "culture scouts," seeking the latest in arts, ideas, and issues. The program is one of the most popular on public radio, drawing a weekly audience of more than 4 million listeners on some 435 stations. *Fresh Air*'s Peabody Award citation in 1994 noted that "unlike the cacophony of voices that sometimes obscure and polarize contemporary debate, Ms. Gross asks thoughtful, unexpected questions, and allows her subjects time to frame their answers." *Fresh Air*'s guests have ranged from former First Lady Nancy Reagan to filmmaker Martin Scorsese, from hostage negotiator Terry Waite to novelist Joyce Carol Oates, singer Tony Bennett, playwright David Mamet, and thousands more.

Over the years, *Fresh Air* has evolved from a live, three-hour local program to a highly produced hour-long program that runs nationally. David Karpoff created the show in 1974 when he was program director at WHYY (then WUHY) in Philadelphia; he modeled it on *This Is Radio,* a program he had worked on at WBFO in Buffalo. Karpoff was the first host, interspersing live interviews with classical music. He was followed as host by Judy Blank, and when she moved on, Karpoff in 1975 hired Terry Gross, who had been co-hosting and producing *This Is Radio* in Buffalo.

Gross drew complaints by changing *Fresh Air*'s music to jazz, blues, and rock and roll, but she won listeners over with an interview style that was thoughtful and direct. Gross, who was 24 at the time, had broken into radio just two years earlier when she helped produce and host a feminist program at WBFO.

By 1978, when Bill Siemering arrived as station manager at WHYY, Gross was carrying on the entire three-hour program by herself, "playing records," Siemering recalls, "that were just long enough to show one guest out and lead another one in." As a former station manager at WBFO, Siemering had created *This Is Radio* out of the turmoil of campus protest and had then gone on to develop *All Things Considered* as a program director at National Public Radio (NPR). When he arrived at WHYY (then WUHY), Siemering says the station was in a run-down building in West Philadelphia, where the ladies' room plumbing leaked onto Gross' desk. Siemering got a Corporation for Public Broadcasting grant to upgrade the station and was able to hire intern Danny Miller as an assistant producer for *Fresh Air.*

Miller, who eventually became the program's co-executive producer, says the fact that *Fresh Air* began as a local show is an important source of its strength: "The show had years to mature before it went national." Part of that maturation involved cutting back the amount of time on the air from three hours to two in 1983, because, as Gross says, "Danny and I often felt that in order to fill the airtime, we were forced to focus more on the quantity than the quality of guests." At the same time, Gross and Miller added a weekend "best of" edition of the show that became the seed for the weekly national edition that was to follow.

Gross sees the development of the show as a step-by-step evolution. The next step came in the spring of 1985, when WHYY premiered a weekly 30-minute version of *Fresh Air,* distributed by NPR. It appeared at a time when public radio stations on the East Coast were pressing for an earlier start time for the popular newsmagazine *All Things Considered,* which would enable them to capture more of the drive-time audience. Robert Siegel, then the news director at NPR, resisted the idea, feeling that the show was already stretched to meet a 5 P.M. deadline. Siegel saw *Fresh Air* as an answer to the demand for a 4 P.M. start, because its sensibility matched that of *All Things Considered* without duplicating its news content. "It was a very good program," he says, "and Terry is the best interviewer in public radio."

Gross says the program was reconceived in 1987 as a daily arts-and-culture companion to *All Things Considered.* To integrate it further into the *All Things Considered* sound, the new format included a drop-in newscast. *Fresh Air*'s shorter interviews, reviews, and other features were put in the second half hour so that its pace would match that of the newsmagazine as listeners went from one program to the next. The new *Fresh Air* also featured a recorded interchange between Gross and the hosts of *All Things Considered* in which they discussed what was coming up.

The national version of *Fresh Air* was a hit, both with audiences and with program directors, who liked the show's predictable format because it gave them the flexibility to drop in local material during drive time. However, Gross says she and co-producer Danny Miller grew to feel imprisoned by the rigidity of the format. They were glad, therefore, when the 1991 Gulf War brought new demands on everyone. Even though *Fresh Air* had concentrated on arts and culture, Gross says, "we had to address the war. Everybody was rightly obsessed with it." The producers sought interviews that could supplement the news, looking for what Danny Miller calls "the great explainers," experts on the culture and the history of the region. "Emergencies require change," Gross says, "and emergencies justify change. If an interview ran more than a half hour, we let it." The war coverage restored some of *Fresh Air*'s flexibility and expanded its portfolio to include a full range of contemporary issues.

After nearly three decades on the air, *Fresh Air*'s archives are filled with the voices and thoughts of some of the era's most interesting people, what Gross calls "a scattershot history of American culture."

COREY FLINTOFF

See also National Public Radio; Peabody Awards; Public Radio Since 1967; Siemering, William

Hosts
David Karpoff, 1974
Judy Blank, 1974–75
Terry Gross, 1975–

Producer/Creator
David Karpoff

Co-producers
Terry Gross and Danny Miller

Programming History
WHYY   1974–85
National Public Radio   1985–
(Note: WHYY continued to produce the program after NPR commenced distribution in 1985)

Further Reading
Clark, Kenneth R., "A Talent for Conversation: NPR's Terry Gross Provides Talk Radio with a Breath of Fresh Air," *Chicago Tribune* (19 November 1993)

Dart, Bob, "Fresh and Funky: 'Cultural Scout' for Public Radio Homes In on Truth," *Cox News Service* (January 1994)

Scheib, Rebecca, "Media Diet: Terry Gross," *Utne Reader* (March–April 1997)

White, Edmund, "Talk Radio: Terry Gross," *Vogue* (May 1997)

Terry Gross, host of *Fresh Air*
Courtesy National Public Radio

Regardless of the subject, Gross applies the same demanding preparation for each interview, reading each author's books, viewing the films, and listening to the CDs that she will discuss. Interviews typically last between 20 and 40 minutes, during which Gross gives her guests the opportunity to rethink and rephrase their answers if they feel they can express themselves better. She prides herself on treating guests with respect, but "that doesn't mean I won't challenge you." Gross' critics have complained that she does not ask confrontational questions, but Bill Siemering says her method is much more effective. "If you're on the attack, all you get is their defense. If you're respectful, you get a lot more."

Friendly, Fred 1915–1998

U.S. Broadcast Journalist

Although best known for his work in television journalism and public-affairs programming at the Columbia Broadcasting System (CBS) and at the Public Broadcasting Service (PBS), Fred Friendly's broadcasting roots were in radio. His experience in radio and recording prior to 1950—in Providence, Rhode Island; in the China-Burma-India theater during World War II; and in New York City at the National Broadcasting Company (NBC) and CBS in the late 1940s—provided his entrée into network journalism and influenced his subsequent work in television.

In 1921, Friendly and his father, a jewelry maker, built a radio receiver and listened to the Jack Dempsey–Georges Carpentier championship boxing match broadcast by KDKA in Pittsburgh. Friendly first went on the air in the early 1930s as a high school student on WJAR in Providence, Rhode Island, to perform in a one-act play, *The Valiant*, written by H.E. Porter and R. Middlemass.

Friendly's broadcast career began in earnest in 1936 at WEAN, Rhode Island's first radio station, which was part of the Yankee network and affiliated with the NBC Blue network. At WEAN, Mowry Lowe, a Rhode Island broadcasting pioneer, served as Friendly's mentor. From 1937 to 1941, Friendly produced and broadcast *Footprints in the Sands of Time*, daily five-minute biographies of important historical figures, for which a sponsor paid Friendly $5 per program, in addition to his $35-a-week salary (see Bliss, 1991). Decca Records later purchased the series. Friendly also worked as an announcer at WEAN and appeared on Mowry Lowe's *Sidewalk Backtalk*, a man-in-the-street interview program. During the same period, he operated the Fred Friendly Company, characterized on its letterhead as "A Radio Production Service to Advertising Agencies."

At WEAN, Friendly made occasional news reports. For example, he helped cover the great hurricane of September 1938 in Rhode Island. In July 1941 the Mutual Broadcasting System carried his report on the opening of the naval marine air station in Quonset, Rhode Island. On 1 October 1999, National Public Radio rebroadcast the report on *All Things Considered* as "a piece of radio poetry." The broadcast evoked the verse of Walt Whitman and anticipated the themes of the army wartime film series *Why We Fight*. Friendly celebrated "$30 million worth of cement and steel . . . and mortar and sweat to keep America strong," accomplished by "a melting pot of O'Neils, Murphys, Gustafsons, and Joneses, and Cohens and Marinos."

During World War II, as a result of his radio experience, Friendly served in the Signal Corps and in the Information and Education Section of the army as a master sergeant. In the China-Burma-India theater, he lectured to troops and wrote for the army newspaper, *CBI Roundup*. In addition, Friendly made recordings of bomber runs for the historical archives of the army. He accomplished this by hooking up a wire recorder to a plane's intercom in order to capture the crew's communication, to which he would add his own running account of the mission. He also made recorded combat reports from the front lines of the Eastern Theater for the fledgling Armed Forces Radio Network. In addition, after visiting Europe to cover the Allied victory in the West and the liberation of the Mauthausen concentration camp in Austria, Friendly gave a radio report for Armed Forces Radio from New Delhi.

Following the war, Friendly had an idea for a record album made up of historical figures of the 1930s and 1940s, an extension of the idea behind *Footprints in the Sands of Time*, a project facilitated by the advent of magnetic tape. In 1947, the agent J.P. Gude introduced Friendly to Edward R. Murrow, who provided narration for the 46 voices—from Roosevelt and Churchill to Will Rogers and Lou Gehrig—heard on *I Can Hear It Now*, issued in December 1948 by Columbia Records. Friendly produced five additional records for the *I Can Hear It Now* series. The first album, a spectacular critical and commercial success, initiated the Friendly-Murrow collaboration, which has been called "the most productive, most influential partnership in the whole history of broadcast journalism" (Bliss, 1991).

On 2 July 1948 NBC first aired a radio show, conceived and produced by Friendly, called *Who Said That?* On the show, a panel of journalists and celebrities was given quotations reported during the previous week and tried to identify their sources. Robert Trout served as host, John Cameron Swayze as a regular panelist. In December 1948, Friendly launched a television version of *Who Said That?* on NBC that continued to be carried on radio, one of the first programs to be simulcast. The radio version remained on the air until 1950, the television program until 1955, by which time it had moved to ABC-TV.

In 1950, Friendly produced and directed for NBC *The Quick and the Dead*, a four-part radio dramatization and documentary on the history and future implications of atomic power. Friendly had witnessed the dawn of the nuclear age firsthand, flying in a reconnaissance plane over Hiroshima and Nagasaki several days after their destruction. In the radio documentary, Bob Hope played an average citizen posing questions that were answered by actors playing Albert Einstein and other figures instrumental in the development of the atomic bomb. Friendly collaborated with *New York Times* science

Fred Friendly
Courtesy of Ruth W. Friendly

reporter William Laurence on the program, which included interviews with actual scientists and statesmen as well as with crew members of the plane that dropped the first atomic bomb.

In 1950, as a result of critical acclaim for *The Quick and the Dead,* Sig Mickelson, director of public affairs at CBS, hired Friendly to join the network's radio documentary unit. Friendly immediately teamed up with Murrow to produce *Hear It Now,* a prime-time hour-long radio news magazine carried on 173 stations. The acclaimed program, which combined audiotaped actualities and interviews with newsmakers, prompted imitations at NBC (*Voices and Events*) and at ABC (*Week Around the World*).

Hear It Now lasted only one season before being transformed by the Murrow–Friendly team into the groundbreaking television program *See It Now* (1951–58), with Friendly as its executive producer. Friendly subsequently worked at CBS television as executive director of *CBS Reports* (1959–64) and as president of CBS News (1964–66). After leaving CBS, Friendly served as broadcasting advisor to the Ford Foundation (1966–80), as Edward R. Murrow Professor of Journalism at Columbia University (1968–79), and as originator and director of the Columbia University Seminars on Media and Society (1974–98), which have been broadcast since 1981 on PBS.

A radio sensibility persisted throughout Friendly's television career. Don Hewitt, executive producer of *60 Minutes* and a member of the original *See It Now* team, said that Fred Friendly taught him his most valuable lesson in television: "It is your ear more than your eye that keeps you at the television set. . . . The picture brings you there, and what you hear keeps you there."

RALPH ENGELMAN

See also Hear It Now; Murrow, Edward R.; News; Peabody Awards; World War II and U.S. Radio

Fred W. Friendly. Born Ferdinand Friendly Wachenheimer in New York City, 30 October 1915. Attended Nichols Junior College, 1936; served in U.S. Army, Information and Education Section, Signal Corps instructor, 1941–45; announcer, newscaster, and producer, WEAN-AM, Providence, Rhode Island, 1937–41; correspondent for *CBI Roundup,* U.S. Army, 1941–45; co-creator with Edward R. Murrow, *I Can Hear It Now,* 1948–51; writer and producer of various radio and television shows, 1948–64; president of CBS news, 1964–66; broadcasting advisor, Ford Foundation, 1966–80; Edward R. Murrow Professor of Journalism, Columbia University, 1966–98; director, Columbia University Seminars on Media and Society, 1984–98; director, Michele Clark Program for minority journalists, Columbia University, 1968–75; member, Mayor's Task Force on CATV and Telecommunications, New York City, 1968; visiting professor, Bryn Mawr College, 1981; visiting professor, Yale University, 1984; commissioner,

Charter Revision Committee for City of New York, 1986–90; Montgomery fellow, Dartmouth College, 1986. Received Decorated Legion of Merit and four battle stars; Soldier's Medal for heroism; 35 awards for *See It Now,* including the Overseas Press Club Award, Page One Award, New York Newspaper Guild, and National Headliners Club Award, 1954; 40 awards for *CBS Reports;* Theatre Library Association Award, 1977; 10 George Foster Peabody Broadcasting Awards; honorary degrees from various U.S. universities. Died in New York City, 3 March 1998.

Radio Series

1938–40	*Footprints in the Sands of Time*
1948–50	*Who Said That?*
1950	*The Quick and the Dead*
1950–51	*Hear It Now*

Television Series

See It Now, 1948–55; *CBS Reports,* 1959–64; *Columbia University Seminars on Media and Society* (also known as *The Fred Friendly Seminars),* 1984–98

Selected Publications

See It Now (with Edward R. Murrow), 1955
Due to Circumstances beyond Our Control, 1967
The Good Guys, the Bad Guys, and the First Amendment: Free Speech v. Fairness in Broadcasting, 1976
Minnesota Rag: The Dramatic Story of the Landmark Supreme Court Case That Gave New Meaning to Freedom of the Press, 1981
The Constitution: That Delicate Balance (with Martha J. H. Elliot), 1984

Further Reading

Barnouw, Erik, *A History of Broadcasting in the United States,* 3 vols., New York: Oxford University Press, 1966–70
Bliss, Edward, *Now the News: The Story of Broadcast Journalism,* New York: Columbia University Press, 1991
"A Bloody Test of Wills at CBS," *Broadcasting* (21 February 1966)
Gates, Gary Paul, *Air Time: The Inside Story of CBS News,* New York: Harper and Row, 1978
Halberstam, David, *The Powers That Be,* New York: Knopf, 1979
Mickelson, Sig, *The Decade That Shaped Television News: CBS in the 1950s,* Westport, Connecticut: Praeger, 1998
Pace, Eric, "Fred W. Friendly, CBS Executive," *New York Times* (5 March 1998)
Smith, Sally Bedell, *In All His Glory: The Life of William S. Paley,* New York: Simon and Schuster, 1990
Sperber, Ann M., *Murrow, His Life and Times,* New York: Freundlich Books, 1986

Fritzsche, Hans 1900–1953

German Radio Official and Commentator

Hans Fritzsche is among the more controversial figures in radio history. As Nazi Germany's leading radio commentator, he gained notoriety during World War II. His rise to mass popularity was testimony to the successful efforts of Nazi propaganda to promote a softer, wittier, more popular, and entertaining side of the regime. In addition Fritzsche was a key radio executive within Nazi Germany. He was instrumental in reorganizing German radio to serve the propaganda purposes of Hitler and the Third Reich. During World War II he became the most senior German radio official.

Origins

August Franz Anton Hans Fritzsche was born in Bochum, Germany, on 21 April 1900, the son of a Prussian postal clerk. A volunteer for the Army, he served in Flanders during the final months of World War I. Receiving his high school diploma the following year, he went on to study German, history, and economics at the Universities of Greifswald and Berlin. Without graduating, Fritzsche embarked on a journalistic career in 1923–24, when Germany was just emerging from the dual crisis of inflation and secessionism that had paralyzed the country since the end of the war.

Fritzsche joined several right wing political parties and clubs that served as rallying places of the foes of the newly founded German democracy. In 1923 Fritzsche became first editor of a conservative business journal and later an editor at Telegrafen-Union, a news service controlled by Alfred Hugenberg, a leading German industrialist and an important figure in right-wing and nationalist political circles.

Broadcasting Career

Fritzsche's broadcasting career began in 1932. At the age of 32, he was appointed head of the news section of the German Broadcasting Corporation (Reichsrundfunkgesellschaft or RRG) and was responsible for the coordination of news broadcasts throughout Germany. This astonishing career move to one of the most influential positions in German radio came as part of a right-wing effort to take over the RRG and centralize the loose network of the independently run regional public broadcasting companies. In November 1932 Fritzsche gained recognition beyond professional circles when he started a new program called *Politische Zeitungsschau* (*Political Newspaper Digest*), which was syndicated by several stations throughout Germany.

With his nationalist credentials, Fritzsche was welcomed into the ranks of the Nazi party, which had taken over the German government in January 1933. After Joseph Goebbels had been appointed head of the newly created Reich Ministry of Popular Enlightenment and Propaganda (Reichsministerium für Volksaufklärung und Propaganda, or RMVP), Fritzsche and other staff members of the RRG were incorporated into the press section of the RMVP. Fritzsche continued his work as chief news editor. He was responsible for three daily national news broadcasts in the mornings, afternoons, and evenings. He also organized broadcasts during special events such as the 1936 Berlin Olympics. Because Fritzsche was trusted by Goebbels and enjoyed a good relationship with the population, he was often asked to explain difficult political situations to the public.

In 1938 German propaganda was in disarray after the German occupation of the Czech Sudeten border region, and Fritzsche was appointed first as deputy and then as head of the German press section of the RMVP. In this capacity Fritzsche daily held so-called "press conferences" where journalists were told what to include and exclude in their reporting. Even though Fritzsche was one of Goebbels' close lieutenants, he managed to keep good relations with journalists. He was well liked by the German press corps and knew how to relate to his former colleagues.

Fritzsche's great moment came with the start of World War II. His regular radio broadcast had gained some popularity by that point, but he remained only one of several well-known radio commentators. After September 1939, however, Fritzsche became *the* German broadcaster, someone whose voice was instantly recognized by a majority of the population. To this day, older generations of Germans remember his name and that of his radio show *Es spricht Hans Fritzsche* (This Is Hans Fritzsche). Unlike many German military radio commentators, Fritzsche was a seasoned journalist, an intriguing speaker with a penchant for good formulas, and someone who knew his trade and had a clear grasp of the medium.

The airwave battles between Fritzsche and his British counterparts are legendary. From the Allied point of view, Fritzsche was the most conspicuous German radio commentator, especially during the first phase of the war when his *Politische Zeitungs- und Rundfunkschau* (*Political Newspaper and Radio Digest*) consisted almost exclusively of "replies" to Allied reporting on the war. Wrapped in anti-British propaganda, his broadcasts highlighted the achievements of the Third Reich. As long as Germany was winning, Fritzsche's skirmishes with the Allies were hugely popular among Germans. After the tide had turned, however, his effectiveness as a propaganda weapon diminished. His radio show was scaled back but did continue until the end of World War II.

Later Life

In 1942 Fritzsche was appointed head of the Radio Section of the RMVP, becoming Germany's highest ranking radio official. Loyal to the Nazi regime until the very end, Fritzsche was captured by Russian troops in May 1945 and held in the Lubjanca prison in Moscow. After Goebbels' suicide, Fritzsche, although a comparative junior, was prosecuted among the main war criminals at the Nuremberg International Military Tribunal (IMT) in 1945–46. Acquitted by the IMT, he was subsequently sentenced to nine years in a labor camp by a German denazification court.

Pardoned in 1950, Fritzsche married his second wife, the journalist Hildegard Springer, who published his prison letters and diaries. An unrepentant apologist of the Third Reich, Fritzsche unsuccessfully tried to return to politics. He died in Cologne of cancer in 1953 while working as an advertising executive.

PHILIPP GASSERT

See also Axis Sally; Lord Haw Haw; Propaganda by Radio; World War II and U.S. Radio

August Franz Anton Hans Fritzsche. Born in Bochum, Germany, 21 April 1900. Army service, World War I, 1918. Studied German, history, and economics in Greifswald and Berlin. Editor with Telegrafen-Union, 1924–1932; director of the News Service (Drahtloser Dienst), German Broadcasting Corporation (Reichsrundfunkgesellschaft or RRG) 1932–1938. Nazi party member 1933–1945; Chief Radio News Administrator, Propaganda Ministry, 1933–1938. Government Spokesman and Chief, Press Section, Propaganda Ministry, 1938–1942; Chief, Radio Section, Propaganda Ministry, 1942–1945; radio commentator and host, *Politische Zeitungs- und Runfunkschau* (*Political Newspaper and Radio Digest*), 1937–1945. Defendant, International Military Tribunal, Nuremberg, 1945–46; imprisoned in a Bavarian labor camp 1947–1950. Advertising Executive 1950–1953. Died in Cologne, Germany, 27 September 1953.

Selected Publications

Krieg den Kriegshetzern: Acht Wochen politische Zeitungs- und Rundfunkschau, 1940
Zeugen gegen England: Von Alexander bis Woolton, 1941
Es sprach Hans Fritzsche: Nach, Gesprächen, Briefen und Dokumenten, edited by Hildegard Springer, 1948

Further Reading

Baird, Jay W., *The Mythical World of Nazi War Propaganda, 1939–1945,* Minneapolis: University of Minnesota Press, 1974

Davidson, Eugene, *The Trial of the Germans. An Account of the Twenty-Two Defendants before the International Military Tribunal at Nuremberg,* New York: Macmillan, 1966

Frei, Norbert, and Johannes Schmitz, *Journalismus im Dritten Reich,* Munich: Beck, 1989

Gassert, Philipp, "This is Hans Fritzsche: A Nazi Broadcaster and His Audience," *Journal of Radio Studies* 8, no. 1 (Summer 2001)

Groth, Michael, "Ein Publizist im Dritten Reich: Vorstudien zu einer Biographie von Hans Fritzsche," M.A. thesis, University of Münster, Germany, 1979

Herzstein, Robert E., *The War That Hitler Won: The Most Infamous Propaganda Campaign in History,* New York: Putnam, 1978; London: Hamish Hamilton, 1979

Sington, Derrick, and Arthur Weidenfeld, *The Goebbels Experiment: A Study of the Nazi Propaganda Machine,* London: J. Murray, 1942; New Haven, Connecticut: Yale University Press, 1943

G

Gabel, Martin 1911–1986

U.S. Radio Actor and Narrator

Martin Gabel appeared in some of the most popular American radio programs of the 1930s and 1940s, while also winning critical praise for his work with radio innovator Norman Corwin.

Gabel was born to Jewish immigrant parents in Philadelphia, Pennsylvania. His father supported the family by peddling watches and jewelry on the city's streets. Even as a boy, Gabel recited Shakespeare to himself, preparing for a career in the theater. In 1928, he entered Lehigh University in Bethlehem, Pennsylvania, where he studied English. He left Lehigh in 1931 without a degree and enrolled in the American Academy of Dramatic Arts in New York City, graduating from there in 1933.

Gabel followed a path that was typical for many successful New York actors, combining radio and stage work. In 1935, he starred in the Broadway hit *Dead End*. At the same time, his rich voice and suave, cosmopolitan diction began to win him parts on New York-based radio series. Over the years, he would appear on such programs as *The Columbia Workshop*, *Matinee Theater*, *The Casebook of Gregory Hood*, and *The March of Time*. However, the series that vaulted him to radio celebrity was *Big Sister*. The CBS soap opera, initially sponsored by Rinso Soap Powder, premiered in 1936. Gabel originated the role of Dr. John Wayne, the love interest, and then husband, of the title character. The popular series revolved around "Big Sister" Ruth Evans' selfless devotion to her orphaned brother and sister. John's crises and philandering inspired Ruth to further self-sacrifice. *Big Sister* brought Gabel more than fame among soap-opera fans; it provided him with a handsome income and steady work. In its first years, *Big Sister* aired weekdays from 11:30 to 11:45 A.M., a schedule that left Gabel time to appear in other radio and theater productions.

In 1936, Gabel performed alongside Orson Welles in the Broadway play *Ten Million Ghosts*. The play flopped, but the association with Welles soon would bring Gabel prestigious radio and stage roles. On 23 July 1937, the Mutual network broadcast the first episode of Welles' seven-part radio adaptation of *Les Miserables*, featuring Welles as Jean Valjean and Gabel as his pursuer, Javert. Meanwhile, Welles and John Houseman were forming the Mercury Theater company, with Gabel as a key member. In his memoirs, Houseman describes the young Martin Gabel as an actor of deep sensitivity, insatiable ambition, and furious energy. Houseman also recalls that: "His gravid voice had made him, in his early 20s, one of the country's most successful and sexy radio actors." After creating a sensation with its stage productions, Welles and Houseman's innovative repertory group launched a weekly series on CBS radio. *The Mercury Theater of the Air* debuted on 11 July 1938 with "Dracula." Welles played the vampire and Gabel his nemesis, Van Helsing. Though Gabel appeared in other Mercury radio productions, he was not cast in the "War of the Worlds" broadcast that famously inspired a national panic.

As the 1930s ended, Gabel also began to work with CBS writer-producer-director Norman Corwin. Corwin was already attracting attention for the poetry and aural experimentation of his radio plays. In 1939, Gabel narrated a segment in Corwin's *So This Is Radio* series. A year later, he appeared as the devil in the rebroadcast of Corwin's radio play *The Plot to Overthrow Christmas*. Gabel spent some of the World War II years in the Army, but in 1944 he was again a civilian. That year he appeared in three plays in *Columbia Presents Corwin*: "New York: A Tapestry for Radio"; "A Pitch to Reluctant Buyers"; and "The Long Name None Could Spell," a program about the Nazi occupation of Czechoslovakia.

By the summer of 1944, the collapse of Nazi Germany appeared inevitable. CBS vice-president Douglas Coulter asked Corwin to prepare a special program for VE Day, the moment of Allied victory in Europe. With Corwin working on the West Coast, the program would be broadcast from the

CBS affiliate KNX in Los Angeles. Corwin had tried to use Gabel whenever his radio plays were produced in New York. For such an important project, however, Corwin insisted on flying Gabel to California to serve as narrator. Germany's surrender finally came on 8 May 1945 and *On a Note of Triumph* was broadcast live that evening, with Gabel and a large supporting cast. The program celebrating Allied victory was itself an artistic triumph. *Billboard* editorialized that *On a Note of Triumph* was "the single greatest—and we use greatest in its full meaning—radio program we ever heard." CBS asked Corwin and Gabel to broadcast a live encore performance five nights later.

Corwin thought that Gabel brought the ideal mix of authority, range, and discipline to the two broadcasts. *Triumph* concluded with a prayer to "Lord God of the topcoat and the living wage," a Corwin synthesis of biblical phraseology and American vernacular. According to broadcast historian Erik Barnouw, Gabel gave the prayer a quality that was both Old Testament and Broadway, bringing many to tears. *Variety* praised Gabel's vocal timbre and dramatic restraint and called *On a Note of Triumph* a milestone in radio.

In 1946, Gabel married radio and stage actress Arlene Francis, and the couple had one son. Gabel continued his stage work, as producer and director as well as actor. He also appeared in films and television programs, sometimes teaming with Ms. Francis. Gabel took more radio roles in the postwar years and appeared in two Corwin radio broadcasts for the United Nations. In the 1950s, his radio appearances became less frequent, coinciding with the general decline of radio drama.

Martin Gabel died of a heart attack in 1986. Obituaries stressed his stage and film achievements. However, Norman Corwin believed that Gabel was one of radio's most brilliant and underrated actors, the closest to Orson Welles in range, mellifluousness, and musical power. Upon Gabel's death, Corwin wrote his widow Arlene Francis that: "My work had first found its eloquent expression through Martin."

JOHN S. ARMSTRONG

See also Corwin, Norman; Mercury Theater of the Air; Soap Opera

Martin Gabel. Born in Philadelphia, Pennsylvania, 19 June 1911. Son of Isaac and Rebecca Gabel. Attended Lehigh University, Bethlehem, Pennsylvania, without receiving degree, 1928–31; Associate Degree, American Academy of Dramatic Arts, New York City, 1933. Stage debut in *Man Bites Dog*, 1934; debut as Dr. John Wayne in soap opera *Big Sister*, 1936; joined Mercury Theater stage and radio company, 1937; narrator, *On a Note of Triumph*, 1945. Tony Award, Best Supporting Actor, Drama, for performance in *Big Fish, Little Fish*, 1961. Died in New York City, 22 May 1986.

Further Reading

Barnouw, Erik, *A History of Broadcasting in the United States*, 3 vols., New York: Oxford University Press, 1966–70; see especially volume 2, *The Golden Web, 1933 to 1953*, 1968

"Corwin for Everyone," *Billboard* (19 May 1945)

Corwin, Norman Lewis, *On a Note of Triumph*, New York: Simon and Schuster, 1945

Cox, Jim, *The Great Radio Soap Operas*, Jefferson, North Carolina: McFarland, 1999

Fowler, Glenn, "Martin Gabel, Actor, Director, and Producer Is Dead at 73," *New York Times* (23 May 1983)

Francis, Arlene, and Florence Rome, *Arlene Francis: A Memoir*, New York: Simon and Schuster, 1978

Grams, Martin, Jr., *Radio Drama: A Comprehensive Chronicle of American Network Programs, 1932–1962*, Jefferson, North Carolina: McFarland, 2000

Houseman, John, *Unfinished Business: Memoirs*, London: Chatto and Windus, 1986; New York: Applause Theatre Books, 1989

Leaming, Barbara, *Orson Welles: A Biography*, New York: Viking, and London: Weidenfeld and Nicolson, 1985

"Martin Gabel Obituary," *Variety* (28 May 1986)

Gambling, John B. (1897–1974);
John A. (1930–); and John R. (1950–)

U.S. Radio Show Hosts

The name John Gambling is synonymous with local New York morning radio. From broadcasting's infancy until the end of the 20th century, a dynasty of three John Gamblings greeted wake-up and commuter audiences via its *Rambling with Gambling* show on 50,000-watt WOR (AM).

This radio lineage was sparked by the 1912 *Titanic* sinking. British teenager John B. Gambling felt called to learn wireless telegraphy so that he might help save the lives of passengers aboard subsequent ill-fated vessels. After holding radio operator positions in the Royal Navy and with various commercial lines, John B. opted for the higher-paying American shipping firms. A U.S. citizen and chief wireless operator on a cruise ship by 1924, he fell in love with a young vacationer, proposed, then left the sea in favor of starting married life in New York City. His radio license landed him an engineering job at Newark, New Jersey based WOR, a fledgling 250-watt station that was about to double its power and open a studio in Manhattan.

First Generation

As the newest of the station's tiny technical staff, John B. Gambling was "stuck" with coaxing the transmitter to life for the gruff host of an early-morning New York based exercise show. Two days into this stint, he was told to do some announcing. Morse code had been his preferred stock in trade, but John B. dutifully approached the microphone and introduced the fitness guru. Letters swamped WOR's mailroom. "Who is that beautiful baritone voice?" the predominantly female writers wanted to know. They heard more of him when, a few months later, the calisthenics expert phoned an anxious Gambling to say he wasn't coming in that morning. By mid-1925, the original host (who was also the exercise program's sponsor) quit, leaving John B. Gambling to recite jumping-jack routines, read announcements, and banter with the show's modest musical group, all the while running around the studio and control room flipping switches and checking meters. It was supposed to be a temporary ordeal, but advertisers soon lined up to sponsor the friendly-sounding announcer/host of what was initially called *The Musical Clock*. WOR management lost little time in naming John B. Gambling as permanent host of what would later be affectionately dubbed *Rambling with Gambling*. Transmitter upgrades through the early 1930s eventually set the lighthearted proceedings on a firm 50-kilowatt footing.

The show was never an elaborate affair. Its 1940s incarnation, for example, included tunes from four erstwhile vaude-ville musicians (branded "the world's greatest little orchestra"); 20 canaries (sponsored by a birdseed company) primed for song in front of their own WOR microphone; and Gambling, who did time checks every quarter hour between family-approved jokes that he collected, aired, and then promised not to repeat until the following year. And, not wanting to desert listeners while convalescing from hernia surgery, he went on the air from his hospital bed. Good old-fashioned folksy schlock, always under John B.'s avuncular direction, kept longtime listeners happy at the 710-kilohertz dial position.

Rival Columbia Broadcasting System (CBS) morning man Arthur Godfrey felt *Rambling with Gambling*'s influence, often finding himself leapfrogged in the New York ratings by the WOR staple. Circa 1951, John B. Gambling was producing half of the station's gross advertising revenues. His reported $500,000 annual salary and commissions came to more than the entire WOR operation netted after expenses. In 1955 some 27,000 fans filled Madison Square Garden to witness *Rambling with Gambling*'s 30th anniversary broadcast. Even so, radio insiders studying the younger generation believed the nearly 60-year-old host would eventually have trouble attracting the new audiences needed to keep WOR fresh in big advertisers' minds. They were not alone. Not long after that milestone show, John B. Gambling resolved to find another host for his show. He hoped to turn over the *Rambling with Gambling* microphone to his son, John A. Gambling

Old-time WOR listeners quipped that the John Gambling selected to succeed the venerable John B. should at least display the linear courtesy of having a C for middle initial, rather than an *A*. No matter, on 5 October 1959 John A. Gambling became host of *Rambling with Gambling*. Alongside his father, he had been cohosting the program for about a year, and on that fall morning, the elder broadcaster decided it was time to just stay home. WOR listeners heard no flashy torch-passing announcements.

Second Generation

It was not an automatic ascension for the 29-year-old "newcomer." Some station brass remembered John A. as a toddler warbling Christmas ditties during his Dad's holiday broadcasts and were disinclined to think of him as his own person. They also cited the matter of John A.'s voice. Compared to the original Gambling's more resonant tones, his was quieter, somewhat "barefoot."

New Hampshire stations had provided John A. Gambling with serious steps toward learning his trade. Besides spending free time between Dartmouth classes volunteering at the college's radio station, he paid dues with stints on the Granite State network's outlets in Manchester, Claremont, and Lebanon. Common to most disc jockey starts, Gambling experienced the humble glamour of radio broadcasting in makeshift facilities where one is required to wear many hats . . . and where the plumbing is still something in the station owner's future plans.

Graduation 1951 saw John A., wife Sally, and new son John R. ready for a return to the metropolitan New York area. His father invited him to assist with *Rambling with Gambling* and to participate in other WOR shows, including several aired over the Mutual Broadcasting System. Five years later, the station wanted a test program to determine whether John A. could make the grade as a big-city broadcaster. The station chose the nightly *Music from Studio X,* which was aimed at a sophisticated, young listenership. The show (first offered locally and subsequently via the Mutual network) quickly became a respectably rated easy listening show (on which, for high-fidelity clarity's sake, no record was exposed to the stylus more than once), granting John A. Gambling an outlet for honing the personable, "one-to-one" announcing style he continued to make famous on *Rambling with Gambling* following his father's retirement.

The new host gently massaged his inheritance into a modern 1960s presentation. Most noticeable was a swing away from Sousa marches and Strauss waltz numbers to Broadway show standards and instrumental cover versions of Top 40 hits. Musically, however, John A. drew boundaries around anything that sounded too much like rock and roll. Teens would write to say they "liked *Rambling with Gambling,* but couldn't Mr. Gambling please play a short Beatles single once in a while?"

Record selection became a bit more liberal during the 1970s. By then, though, there was hardly time to spin more than a few each hour. The broadcast's pace had accelerated in order to accommodate the ever-expanding rush-hour commuter crowd, and Gambling shared his show with a helicopter-borne traffic reporter, a weatherman, news commentators, sportscasters, and others. The team exuded a serendipitous brand of good-natured symbiosis not easily fabricated. Without trendy music or questionable humor, *Rambling with Gambling*'s ratings, circa 1975, topped 2 million people weekly, making its formula better received than any other single-station program in America.

As society, as well as morning radio, got edgier, many of Gambling's competitors were mystified at his ongoing success. Instead of sexual innuendo, *Rambling with Gambling* was (and is) sprinkled daily with local public service messages and occasional lost pet announcements. WNBC's Don Imus tried poking fun at the clean-cut WOR host by speculating about the name of a hypothetical game in which housing project tenants wagered on whether or not their commodes ("johns") would function. John Gambling's non-confrontational style stayed the course while many other "gimmicky" New York air personalities, station formats, and call letters took turns in the broadcast business' great revolving door.

Meanwhile, John R., John B.'s grandson and John A.'s son, set his sights on a radio career, but he was unsure about someday hosting *Rambling with Gambling*. A late-1960s summer job at WOR prompted him to get involved in college radio (during the 1970s) at Boston University. After graduation, he served in managerial positions at a number of stations, including some then commonly owned with WOR. Tenure as morning host in the Poughkeepsie, New York, area followed.

During the 1980s, as talk radio spread to many of AM's strongest outlets, WOR was already specializing in the genre. By dropping any remaining music, *Rambling with Gambling*'s helpful informational routine fully qualified as state of the art, opening a spot on the show for a third generation of Gambling. In 1985 John R. began co-hosting with his father, John A. Five years later (just as his dad had done some three decades before), John A. turned over *Rambling with Gambling* to his son.

Third Generation

To stay contemporary without losing a focus on the show's wholesomeness, the youngest of the triumvirate has added more humor, and he feels freer than his predecessors did to express controversial points of view. Even so, the *Rambling with Gambling* audience continued graying without sufficient replacement numbers of younger consumers. Many had been enticed by self-centered talkers offering edgier, decidedly caustic fare.

Not long after Labor Day 2000, WOR's management admitted that its morning show was top-heavy with a largely retirement-age demographic many 21st century advertisers ignore. The station notified Gambling that his contract would be allowed to lapse at the end of the year. John R. responded that he didn't want his listeners to hear him "day after day, dying a slow pathetic [cancellation] death," and then he shocked WOR officials by simply signing off after his 11 September broadcast, some 75 years after his grandfather began the program. Countless calls of disappointment swamped the station's phone system. Among the sympathetic messages were those from New York City's mayor Rudolph Giuliani and the governor of New Jersey, Christine T. Whitman. Each expressed hope that another metropolitan outlet would pick up the long-lived program. These wishes came true shortly thereafter when this third John Gambling showed up on WOR's cross-town rival, WABC.

PETER E. HUNN

See also WOR

John B. Gambling. Born in Norwich, England, 1897. Earned certificate from British School of Telegraphy, 1914; served in the Royal Navy, wireless operator, 1914–19; wireless operator on various commercial vessels, 1919–25; engineer, WOR Radio, New York City, 1925; host, *WOR Musical Clock* (later *Rambling with Gambling*), 1925–59; host of various Mutual Broadcasting System, WOR shows, 1930s–50s, and WOR-TV programs, 1949–50s. Died in Palm Beach, Florida, 21 November 1974.

Radio Series

1925–59   *WOR Musical Clock* (became *Rambling with Gambling*)

John A. Gambling. Born in Teaneck, New Jersey, 5 February 1930. Attended Dartmouth College, B.A. in English drama, 1951; announcer, WKBR, Manchester, New Hampshire, and WTSV Claremont, New Hampshire, 1950; announcer/sales/news, WTSL Lebanon, New Hampshire, 1950–51; host, *Music from Studio X*, WOR, 1956–60; programming assistant (1951–56), co-host (1956–59), and host (1959–90), *Rambling with Gambling*, WOR, New York City. Chairman, JAG Communications, 1983–89. Currently residing in Florida.

Radio Series

1956–60   *Music from Studio X*
1959–90   *Rambling with Gambling*

John R. Gambling. Born in Montclair, New Jersey, 8 April 1950. Attended Boston University, B.A., 1973; promotions director/operations manager, WROR-FM, Boston, Massachusetts, 1973–74; program Director, WAXY-FM, Fort Lauderdale, Florida, 1974–75; operations manager, program director, and morning host, WHPN/WHVW/WHVS FM, Hyde Park, New York, 1975–77; staff announcer and host, *Good Afternoon*, WOR, 1978–85; co-host (1985–90), then host (1990–2000), *Rambling with Gambling*, WOR, New York City. Currently living on Long Island.

Radio Series

1985–2000   *Rambling with Gambling*

Further Reading

"Chronicle: The Radio Gamblings Pass the Torch Again," *New York Times* (15 December 1990)
Gambling, John A., *Rambling with Gambling*, Englewood Cliffs, New Jersey: Prentice Hall, 1972
Rhoads, Eric B, *Blast from the Past: A Pictorial History of Radio's First 75 Years*, West Palm Beach, Florida: Streamline, 1996
Routt, Edd, James B. McGrath, and Fredric A. Weiss, *The Radio Format Conundrum*, New York: Hastings House, 1978

Gangbusters

Detective Drama Series

During the 1920s, the American public lost confidence in law enforcement officers as news of bribery and scandal involving real-life police officers became routine. The onset of the Great Depression in the early 1930s exacerbated this situation, and criminals such as Bonnie Parker and Clyde Barrow, Al Capone, and George "Baby Face" Nelson were often portrayed as folk heroes. Hollywood produced films (e.g., *Public Enemy* with James Cagney and *Little Caesar* starring Edward G. Robinson) that presented gangsters as tragic heroes. *Gangbusters*, the first successful regularly scheduled detective drama on network radio, played a major role in restoring America's confidence in law enforcement officials.

Gangbusters was created by Phillips H. Lord, an actor and producer best known for his portrayal of the title character in the radio series *Seth Parker*. Whereas the earlier series was known for its folksy warm feeling, Lord went in a different direction for his next project. *Gangbusters* was a blend of fact and fiction—dramatizations of actual crimes taken from the case files of local and federal law enforcement offices. The series premiered on the National Broadcasting Company (NBC) in 1935 under the title *G-Men*. After a brief run, the series moved to the Columbia Broadcasting System (CBS) in January 1936, and the title was changed to *Gangbusters*. The series also eventually appeared on the American Broadcasting Companies (ABC) and Mutual during its 22-year run.

The format of *Gangbusters* was simple. Each episode opened with a loud, identifiable opening of marching feet, sirens, and machine-gun fire. The series opening became so

Gangbusters
Courtesy CBS Photo Archive

well known that it led to the phrase "coming on like gang-busters." After the opening sound effects, the narrator would introduce the current episode, followed by an interview with a local law enforcement officer (usually from the locale of the current episode). At the end of each episode was a feature called "Gangbuster Clues," which included information regarding a criminal currently at large. The audience was presented with a detailed description of the wanted person, along with information about how to contact law enforcement officials, and was asked to help bring the suspect to justice. These "clues" led to over 100 arrests during the series' first three years. In subsequent years, many more were brought to justice through this forerunner to several successful television series (e.g., *Unsolved Mysteries* and *America's Most Wanted*).

Lord employed actual law enforcement officials to comment throughout each episode. *Gangbusters'* first narrator was Lewis Valentine, police commissioner of New York City. He was replaced after the first year by Col. Norman Schwartzkopf, former superintendent of the New Jersey State Police (Schwartzkopf's son and namesake would later lead the U.S. troops during the 1991 Persian Gulf War). Schwartzkopf con-

tinued as narrator for most of the next ten years. In 1945, Valentine, now the retired police commissioner of New York City, replaced him.

The first episode was a dramatization of the Federal Bureau of Investigation's (FBI) capture and shooting of John Dillinger. Lord had obtained the cooperation of FBI Director J. Edgar Hoover on the condition that only "closed" cases would be dramatized in the series. Subsequent episodes featured the stories of "Machine Gun" Kelley, "Baby Face" Nelson, "Pretty Boy" Floyd, and Bonnie and Clyde. When the series moved to CBS in 1936, it began to feature the stories of lesser-known criminals.

Gangbusters portrayed detectives as modern-day heroes who led glamorous lives and risked their lives in the service of others. The plots were very simplistic plays in terms of "good versus evil," with good always winning. Rarely was any mention made of the causes of such criminal behavior.

Gangbusters had many imitators, most notably *Dragnet*, which began in 1949 and was arguably the prototype for all crime and detective dramas to follow. Unlike that show, however, *Gangbusters'* television history was short. The format was the same as its radio counterpart. Phillips H. Lord appeared in each episode as the narrator in addition to serving as series writer and creator. As in the radio version, clues regarding at-large criminals were presented, along with photographs. The television version premiered in 1952, alternating each week with *Dragnet*. *Gangbusters* was designed as a temporary series because Jack Webb had trouble producing weekly episodes of *Dragnet* on time. Both were very successful, with *Dragnet* ranking 20th among all network prime-time series and *Gangbusters* ranking 14th. However, as was the initial plan, *Dragnet* was continued the following season, and *Gangbusters,* the fill-in, was canceled.

MITCHELL SHAPIRO

See also Lord, Phillips H.

Cast

Actors

Art Carney, Larry Haines, Frank Lovejoy, Don MacLaughlin, Alice Reinheart, Grant Richards, Julie Stevens, Richard Widmark

Chief Investigator

Lewis J. Valentine

Announcers

Roger Forster, Art Hannes, Charles Stark, Frank Gallop, Don Gardiner, H. Gilbert Martin

Narrators

Phillips H. Lord, Col. Norman H. Schwartzkopf (1938–45); Lewis Valentine (1945–57); John C. Hilley; Dean Carlton

Producer/Creator

Phillips H. Lord

Programming History

NBC (as *G-Men*)	1935
CBS	1936–40; 1949–55
NBC Blue	1940–45
ABC	1945–48
Mutual	1955–57

Gay and Lesbian Radio

A number of attempts, often short-lived, at broadcasting gay and lesbian programs on radio have occurred since the late 1950s. As of 2002 the United States led the way, with more than 100 original gay and lesbian radio shows, which could be heard in large and small cities across the country; however, only a few of these shows are syndicated overseas. Other countries with such radio programs include Australia, Canada, the United Kingdom, Japan, and New Zealand. Gay radio, which targets a multibillion-dollar market, is not represented by a specific format type; rather, its music and talk programming reflects the socio-economic and cultural diversity within the gay and lesbian community. Personal expression through "queer radio" empowered gays, lesbians, bisexuals, and transgender communities to seek new ways to work collectively toward providing information, resources, and fellowship to others in the United States and internationally.

Origins

Five Pacifica radio stations—in Berkeley, California; Los Angeles; New York; Houston; and Washington, D.C.— located in cities with the largest populations of lesbians and gays in the United States, aired the queer perspective in their news, public affairs, and literary discussions, even before the 1969 Stonewall Rebellion—the birth of the modern-day gay movement. Pacifica station KPFA-FM in Berkeley went on the air in 1949 and became the first listener-sponsored radio station in the world. Pacifica's second station, KPFK-FM, began broadcasting in Los Angeles in 1959. The following year, philanthropist Louis Schweitzer donated WBAI-FM, New York, to Pacifica.

The poet Allen Ginsburg would propel gay radio into mainstream debate by challenging the boundaries of American radio in 1956, when he read his controversial poem "Howl" on KPFA. Ginsburg's life of drugs, jazz, and a liberal attitude toward sexuality and morality epitomized the Beatnik rebellion against the status quo of the 1950s. In the late 1950s, San Francisco's KPFA aired what is believed to be the first comprehensive gay-rights radio documentary in the United States. The two-hour documentary brought together a small group of physicians, lawyers, and criminologists with the mother of a gay man and Harold L. Call, an editor for the *Mattachine Review* and a member of The Mattachine Society, America's first gay-rights organization, to discuss the rights of gay men.

Then, in 1962, WBAI aired "The Homosexual in America," a 60-minute program focused on the opinions of a panel of psychiatrists. Protests by Mattachine New York organizer Randolfe Wicker demanded equal time from WBAI management. On 16 July 1962, WBAI aired a radio forum with Wicker and six other gay men, which prompted some listeners to file a complaint with the Federal Communications Commission (FCC). The rejected complaint paved the way for future discussions on homosexuality in the electronic media. In essence, the FCC upheld Pacifica's contention that broadcasts addressing gay issues served the public interest, as long as the topics were handled in good taste.

Radio After the Stonewall Rebellion

Queer broadcasting may be traced back to the people who fought for free expression and civil rights. No event revolutionized and liberalized the gay and lesbian movement more than the Stonewall Rebellion. The decision on what needed to be done to achieve equality, tolerance, and ultimately acceptance by all Americans was made during one fateful Friday night on 27 June 1969 on the streets of New York City. A routine police raid on a Greenwich Village bar that served transvestites, lesbians, and gays turned violent after patrons decided not to run away from the police. What might be perceived as an isolated incident to most Americans sent shock waves throughout the queer community. The riots continued in New York City for three days, and The Gay Liberation Front was formed within weeks.

In 1971 Pacifica's KPFK debuted *imru* ("I am; Are you?"), the first weekly gay radio show in Los Angeles, and perhaps in the United States. Another program, *Amazon Country*, celebrated its 25th anniversary in 1999. That year the show was also the recipient of the 1999 Lambda Award for Outstanding Overall Performance by an Organization/Social-Cultural Group. *Amazon Country* airs on Sunday nights on the University of Pennsylvania's public radio station WXPN-FM, featuring a lesbian/feminist perspective in its music and interviews with artists, authors, and leaders throughout the nation. Since 1974 WXPN has also aired *Q'zine*, a radio magazine show that was originally called *Gaydreams*. It was named partly after a Grateful Dead song and first aired in 1974. Several other queer radio shows were heard mainly on noncommercial college and community radio stations. These programs were almost always volunteer produced, represented the efforts of only a handful of radio collectives, and were limited financially and regionally. The longevity of these shows often depended on the whim of the station manager and program director, and gay and lesbian producers on occasion were forced to compete among themselves for limited time slots.

Repression and Restraint

The 1980s saw a sexual revolution on radio and television—one that prompted public calls for censorship, music labeling, and stronger FCC policies and penalties, as well as for boycotts on stores and stations promoting explicit music. The public outcry against naughty lyrics on the radio seemed stronger than its reaction to Howard Stern's racial and ethnic epithets and verbal gay bashing.

As right-wing conservatism swept the nation during the Reagan era, gay-rights activists were under attack in the mainstream media. The previous victories in civil liberties and free expression were to be challenged once again by the FCC and the religious right. As early as the 1980s, the FCC warned Pacifica that any further broadcast of "Howl" could result in heavy fines or the forfeiture of its license. AIDS would provide the justification and rationale for what would become the widespread abuse of human rights and rise in hate propaganda in the years to follow. It was in this environment that queer broadcasting would push forward and feverishly combat the stereotypical attitudes and hate propaganda that continue to target gays and lesbians.

In 1986 the freedom of queer radio was challenged again by the FCC after Reverend Larry Poland accidentally tuned in to *imru* on KPFK and heard "Jerker," a radio drama about the impact of AIDS on two gay men. The FCC threatened to fine the station "for the patently offensive manner in which the sexual activity was described." The Justice Department declined to take action on the case. In 1991, Pacifica was one of several parties to lead a successful appeal to overturn the 24-hour indecency ban initiated by Congress and put into place by the FCC.

By 1987 the AIDS Coalition to Unleash Power (ACT UP) had attracted mainstream media attention to AIDS issues. "Outing" the famous became "in" among young queers who wanted to end hypocrisy in the media. The sexual revolution of the 1960s was being reinvented by George Michael and Madonna in the electronic media, as both challenged and toyed with gender boundaries in their music and videos. A number of radio stations aired promotional announcements that assured their audiences of "safe" lyrics, and the FCC began to wrestle with "safe harbor" policies designed to protect children from undesirable broadcast content.

The Rise of Queer Music

By the end of the 1980s, Melissa Etheridge and k.d. lang had expanded in popularity beyond college radio and were becoming household words on mainstream radio. The nation seemed ready for something different—and with the rise of alternative radio, a new breed of music was arriving on the scene; its new young audiences embraced the often mystical and mesmerizing video clips of life and love projected across their television screen. For some musicians, it was time for the next step—queer music, in which gays and lesbians would share their experiences about lovers and life partners in their music.

The formation of the National Lesbian and Gay Country Music Association in 1998 was just one example of the trend toward acceptance of queer music in the United States. Other signs toward changing times include the acceptance of country musicians such as Mark Weigle, an independent singer/songwriter who has received regular airplay on Americana shows in Europe. He was nominated (along with Ani DiFranco, Rufus Wainwright, and the B-52's) for two 1999 Gay/Lesbian American Music Awards (GLAMA)—for both Debut Artist and Out Song "If It Wasn't Love." Weigle has been praised by music critics in gay and mainstream music publications such as *Genre, Billboard,* and *Performing Songwriter.* GLAMA is the first and only national music awards program to celebrate and honor the music of queer musicians and songwriters. Its first annual ceremony took place in New York's Webster Hall in October 1996, with about 700 people in attendance. The judges comprised music reviewers from the gay and mainstream media; leaders in radio distribution; executives of major and independent record labels; and those working in performing rights, talent management, and retail. GLAMA's final awards ceremony was held in April 2000; increasing administrative costs were cited as the reason for its demise.

Beyond the Gay Ghetto

In April 1988 Los Angeles radio producer Greg Gordon, a former *imru* producer and host (along with his volunteer staff), created the 30-minute newsmagazine program called *This Way Out,* which began with a weekly distribution to 26 public stations in the United States and Canada. It now airs on more than 125 radio stations—public and commercial—in six countries. The program contains news, author interviews, AIDS updates, humor, poetry, and music recordings by openly gay and lesbian performers rarely heard on commercial radio. The Gay and Lesbian Press Association honored *This Way Out* with its Outstanding Achievement Award in 1988, and the National Federation of Community Broadcasters presented the "Silver Reel" award to its producers in 1991 for their ongoing news and public-affairs commitment to cultural diversity. One affiliate station, Kansas City's KKFI-FM, boasts that more than 500 individuals have presented a myriad of gay, lesbian, and transgender issues across its airwaves. In fact, KKFI is the first and thus far the only station in its market to air a local queer radio program. To some gay media activists, however, the failure to move beyond noncommercial radio and into the mainstream has been a form of "gay ghettoization," or what some queer broadcasters have referred to as "preaching to the choir." For years, noncommercial radio has been the primary vehicle for communicating the queer perspective to the gay community, and increasingly to a straight audience. In 1992 WFNX-FM, a commercial Boston station, debuted *One in Ten,* a three-hour show with a mix of news, entertainment, music, and call-in discussions. In the early 1990s, several other commercial stations experimented, although unsuccessfully, with locally produced programs targeting gay and lesbian audiences.

In 1990 Thomas Davis became the president and general manager of two Amherst commercial stations located in a renowned gay and lesbian community in central Massachusetts. His company's mission was to target listeners outside the gay community, in addition to gays and lesbians themselves. In doing so, the stations would attempt to convey the idea that gays and lesbians function much like any other members of society on a daily basis. As institutional members of the Gay and Lesbian Business Coalition, the stations have been supported on the air by many gay- or lesbian-owned businesses. Programming includes news stories relevant to gays and lesbians, as well as fund-raising efforts for a number of queer community concerns, such as AIDS research and hospice funding.

1992 was the year of the largest commercial venture for gay radio. The KGAY Radio network signed on the air on 28 November 1992 in Denver. KGAY, with its motto "All Gay, All Day," was the inspiration of Clay Henderson and Will Gunthrie. Their previous efforts had included a short-lived 30-minute weekly gay commercial radio show and a weekly gay and lesbian news show called the *Lambda Report,* which first aired on public access cable television in 1989. KGAY Radio was the first attempt to market a 24-hour all gay and lesbian format in America. The KGAY founders planned to use a local Denver station as the headquarters for what they hoped would become a national cable FM operation. The decision to broadcast by satellite from Denver seemed easier and less expensive to the owners than purchasing a commercial radio station in a large or medium market. KGAY's programming was uplinked to satellite dishes in North America, Canada, and the Caribbean. The music and news network was promoted as the first daily media vehicle for the gay and lesbian community in North America. Less than a year after it began, however, the KGAY network, with only a few sponsors and a mostly volunteer staff, failed.

In May 1994 another commercial radio venture was born on adult contemporary WCBR-FM in north Chicago. LesBiGay Radio founder Alan Amberg conversed insightfully every weekday afternoon on America's only drive-time gay radio show, as his signal reached into the Chicago neighborhoods where many gays and lesbians resided. By April 2001, his radio enterprise had logged more than 3,000 hours of programming and had a number of prominent national and local sponsors. Indeed, the show was hailed as the most successful commercial queer radio venture of the 1990s in America, but Amberg was forced to end it in April 2001 because of financial difficulties. The internet is also home to a number of gay radio programs that can only be heard via the web, and this appears to be the trend among gay radio broadcasters who wish to seek a larger audience base to justify commercial sponsorship.

PHYLIS JOHNSON

See also Affirmative Action; Pacifica Foundation; Stereotypes on Radio

Further Reading

Alwood, Edward, *Straight News: Gays, Lesbians, and the News Media*, New York: Columbia University Press, 1996
Gross, Larry, and James D. Woods, editors, *The Columbia Reader on Lesbians and Gay Men in Media, Society, and Politics*, New York: Columbia University Press, 1999
Hendriks, Aart, Rob Tielman, and Evert van der Veen, editors, *The Third Pink Book*, Buffalo, New York: Prometheus Books, 1993
Hogan, Steve, and Lee Hudson, *Completely Queer: The Gay and Lesbian Encyclopedia*, New York: Holt, 1998
Johnson, Phylis, Charles Hoy, and Dhyana Ziegler, "A Case Study of KGAY: The Rise and Fall of the First 'Gay and Lesbian' Radio Network," *Journal of Radio Studies* 3 (1995–96)
Johnson, Phylis, and Michael C. Keith, *Queer Airways: The Story of Gay and Lesbian Broadcasting*, Armonk, New York: M.E. Sharpe, 2001
Lasar, Matthew, *Pacifica Radio: The Rise of an Alternative Network*, Philadelphia, Pennsylvania: Temple University Press, 1999
Schulman, Sarah, *My American History: Lesbian and Gay Life during the Reagan/Bush Years*, New York: Routledge, 1994
"Trends in the Making," *Advertising* (11 August 1998)

General Electric

Manufacturer of Consumer Electronics

General Electric (GE) was instrumental in the shaping of early American radio broadcasting through its creation of the Radio Corporation of America (RCA) in 1919 and its subsequent operation of several pioneering radio stations. GE is a diversified company with holdings in consumer services, technology, and manufacturing. GE operates in more than 100 countries and employs nearly 340,000 people worldwide, including 197,000 in the United States.

Origins

General Electric traces its history to the Edison Electric Light Company, established in 1878 by Thomas Edison, and to the Thomson-Houston Electric Company, established by Elihu Thomson and Edwin Houston in the early 1880s. Both companies grew by the 1890s into leaders in their field and battled over adoption of electrical current standards for the United States. Thomson-Houston promoted alternating current, whereas Edison championed use of direct current. Alternating current was adopted in the United States, and in 1892 the two merged to form GE. GE is the only company that has been listed continuously on the Dow Jones Industrial Index since its inception in 1896.

After the merger, the new company could boast of having some of the best minds in the country. Thomson's financial genius Charles Coffin became GE's first president, and Edison became a director. Thomson helped establish a program of scientific research that led to the creation of GE's Research Laboratory in 1900 under the direction of Dr. Willis R. Whitney. In a career spanning five decades, Thomson was awarded 696 U.S. patents for devices as varied as arc lights, generators, X-ray tubes, and electric welding machines. His successful "recording wattmeter" was a practical method of measuring the amount of electricity used by a home or business. In 1893 a young German, Charles Steinmentz, joined GE, and he designed new methods of designing machinery using alternating current. After the turn of the century, GE expanded its power-generation business by developing the first steam turbine-generator large enough to power cities. In 1903 GE purchased the Stanley Electrical Manufacturing Company of Pittsfield, Massachusetts. William Stanley, the head of that company, joined GE and pioneered electrical line transmission equipment. He is credited with inventing the transformer, which became the heart of the electrical distribution system. In 1910 GE developed ductile tungsten for light bulb filaments; ductile tungsten is still used in virtually every incandescent lamp.

GE and Radio

By the turn of the 20th century, GE began developmental work in wireless radio, and in 1906, E.F.W. Alexanderson developed a practical alternator to produce the high frequencies needed for reliable long-distance transmission. Later, Dr. Irving Langmuir of GE's Research Laboratory designed an amplifier for Alexanderson's alternator, completing the components of a transoceanic radio-transmitting system. This system was the most powerful generator of radio waves then known, and it became the pivotal point for negotiations with American Marconi, the U.S. subsidiary of British Marconi's worldwide wireless enterprise; these negotiations eventually led to the formation of RCA.

During World War I, the navy had operated most radio stations in the United States, including those using GE's Alexanderson alternator. Naval radio experts became convinced that this equipment was vital to U.S. interests, and after the war Admiral W.H.G. Bullard and Captain Stanford Hooper convinced GE executive Owen D. Young not to sell improved vacuum tubes and the exclusive rights to the Alexanderson alternator to the British subsidiary. In a meeting in May 1919, Young told E.J. Nally of American Marconi that GE would not sell the equipment because the U.S. government did not want control of this equipment to pass into foreign hands. Over the summer the two companies' officers negotiated the sale of American Marconi's assets to GE, and the deal they struck resulted in RCA's incorporation on 17 October 1919.

Shortly after its incorporation, RCA and GE entered into patent cross-licensing agreements with American Telephone and Telegraph (AT&T) and Westinghouse. Under these agreements, all signatories shared their patents. With this patent pooling, RCA quickly became one of the leading companies manufacturing and selling wireless radio equipment. By 1922 the company had moved into wireless' newest application—broadcasting. Radio station WGY began broadcasting from Schenectady, New York, with one of the first U.S. radio dramas, *The Wolf.* As this new phenomenon caught on with the American public, GE, with RCA and Westinghouse, became engaged in a series of intercompany battles with AT&T and its manufacturing arm, Western Electric, over who held what rights in broadcasting. To resolve this issue, AT&T sold its radio interests, and RCA created the National Broadcasting Corporation (NBC) in 1926 to oversee network endeavors in broadcasting.

In the early 1930s the Justice Department filed an antitrust suit against General Electric, Westinghouse, and RCA, alleging restraint of trade. In 1932 the companies signed a consent decree, and GE was forced to divest itself of any interest in RCA.

During the Depression years, GE made important improvements and contributions to X rays, electric ship turbines, and the efficiency of electrical light and appliances. In 1940 GE expanded its business by relaying television broadcasts from New York City and by starting FM broadcasts. During World War II, these operations were suspended, as GE turned its efforts to helping win the war. The company supplied much help to the war effort, from aircraft gun turrets and jet engines, to radar and radio equipment, to electrically heated flying suits. GE made propulsion units for nearly 75 percent of the Navy's ships, and from GE laboratories came new systems for the detection of enemy aircraft and ships.

After the war, GE carried out an extensive program of expansion and decentralization. As a result, autonomous product departments developed. Over the years, GE also expanded its research and development divisions as well as its international efforts. Its many manufacturing lines ranged from consumer products such as light bulbs and consumer electronics, to major appliances such as refrigerators and television sets, to industrial and military equipment such as locomotives, aircraft engines, nuclear reactors, and ICBM guidance systems. In addition, GE moved into services such as insurance, consumer credit, and data processing. In 1957 GE opened the world's first licensed nuclear power plant and entered the mainframe computer business, which it sold in 1970 to Honeywell. Two years later GE developed the TIROS 1 weather satellite. During the 1960s and 1970s, the company continued expanding its lighting, aircraft engine, and electrical equipment businesses both domestically and abroad.

Modern GE

In late 1986 GE bought RCA (and NBC) in a $6.28 billion deal that some say ironically came full circle to the 1930s divestiture. The following July, GE sold off the NBC Radio Network to Westwood One for $50 million so that GE/RCA could concentrate on television and newer consumer media. At the same time, the company began selling the NBC-owned-and-operated radio stations. Over the next ten years, GE and RCA combined their consumer electronics businesses and subsequently sold them to Thomson in exchange for its medical equipment business and $800 million in cash. The companies' combined defense business was also sold, to Martin Marietta for $3 billion. GE/RCA retained ownership of the NBC television operations, and during the 1990s these NBC operations became exceedingly profitable for GE.

In 1989, NBC launched the business financial cable television network CNBC, and GE formed a mobile communications joint venture with Ericsson of Sweden. In 1991 NBC acquired the Financial News network (FNN) and sold its interest in the RCA Columbia Home Video joint venture. In 1994 GE created one of the first major industrial websites, \\www.ge.com\\, and two years later NBC and Microsoft joined forces to launch MSNBC, a 24-hour television and internet service. In 1999 GE began e-Business as a key growth initiative. NBC launched NBC Internet (NBCi), a publicly traded internet company that merged the network's interactive properties with XOOM.com and the internet portal Snap.com to form the seventh-largest internet site and the first publicly traded internet company integrated with a major broadcaster. NBCi will use Snap.com as an umbrella consumer brand, integrating broadcast, portal, and e-commerce services. NBC also maintains equity interests in cable channels Arts and Entertainment (A&E) and the History Channel. NBC also has an equity stake in Rainbow Programming Holdings, a leading media company with a wide array of entertainment and sports cable channels. It also holds interests in CNET, Talk City, iVillage, Telescan, Hoover's, and 24/7Media. In partnership with National Geographic and Fox/BskyB, NBC owns and operates the National Geographic Channel in Europe and Asia.

LOUISE BENJAMIN

See also Alexanderson, E.F.W.; National Broadcasting Company; Radio Corporation of America; Westinghouse

Further Reading

Alexander, Charles, "A Reunion of Technological Titans," *Time* (23 December 1985)

Barnum III, Frederick O., *His Master's Voice In America: Ninety Years of Communications Pioneering and Progress: Victor Talking Machine Company, Radio Corporation of America, General Electric Company,* Camden, New Jersey: General Electric Company, 1991

Case, Josephine Young, and Everett Needham Case, *Owen D. Young and American Enterprise: A Biography,* Boston: Godine, 1982

A Century of Progress: The General Electric Story, 1876–1978, Schenectady, New York: GE Hall of History, 1981

GE website, <www.ge.com>

Hammond, John Winthrop, *Men and Volts: The Story of General Electric,* Philadelphia: Lippincott, 1941

Lewis, Tom, *Empire of the Air: The Men Who Made Radio,* New York: Burlingame Books, 1991

Loomis, Carol J., "Ten Years After," *Fortune* (17 February 1997)

Nye, David E., *Image Worlds: Corporate Identities at General Electric, 1890–1930,* Cambridge, Massachusetts: MIT Press, 1985

Reich, Leonard S., *The Making of American Industrial Research: Science and Business and GE and Bell, 1876–1926,* New York: Cambridge University Press, 1985

The George Burns and Gracie Allen Show

Comedy Series

For 17 years, Burns and Allen provided one of radio's most enduring comedy series based on the vaudeville tradition.

Vaudeville Origins

George Burns, born Nathan Birnbaum in New York City on 20 January 1896, left school after fourth grade to sing professionally with the PeeWee Quartet. That move led to his career in vaudeville as a singer, dancer, and monologuist (1910–31). Grace Ethel Cecile Rosalie Allen was born 26 July 1906 in San Francisco. She met George after a 1922 New Jersey vaudeville performance he had done with his partner, Billy Lorraine. Gracie, who began in vaudeville at 14 with her three sisters, wanted to work with Lorraine. She teamed with George instead, and they were married 7 January 1926. They performed together in vaudeville, film, radio, and TV from 1922 until her retirement in 1958.

Gracie played "straight man" until George discovered she was funnier being nice yet dim-witted. George never considered changing Gracie, whom he loved because of her befuddlement and inverted logic. Gracie was a nervous performer, but audiences thought it was an act, part of her giddy, scatterbrained persona. She was uninterested in business, but George enjoyed other responsibilities as script supervisor and manager.

In 1929 Burns and Allen were invited to perform their Vaudeville act in London. After 21 weeks there performing to appreciative audiences at various nightclubs, the duo was asked to go on BBC radio—a successful stint that lasted 26 weeks. The team believed they could experience similar success on American radio.

George Burns and Gracie Allen
Courtesy Radio Hall of Fame

Network Success

In 1930 the National Broadcasting Company (NBC) rejected them because of Gracie's squeaky, high-pitched voice, but she performed on Eddie Cantor's show in 1931 to rave reviews. A week later Burns and Allen played Rudy Vallee's show, which led to their 15 February 1932 debut on the Columbia Broadcasting System's (CBS) *The Robert Burns Panatella Program*. In 1933 their popularity earned them their own show, which lasted 17 years. *The George Burns and Gracie Allen Show*—also known as *Maxwell House Coffee Time, Burns and Allen*, and *The Adventures of Gracie*—presented sketches, music, and vaudeville routines. Among the show's characters was Mel Blanc's Happy Postman, who spoke pleasant and cheerful thoughts but always sounded depressed and near crying.

Originally based in New York, the show made road broadcasts from other cities and military installations throughout the United States. By 1934, the couple began work in film and relocated to Beverly Hills with two adopted children, Sandra Jean and Ronald John. In 1942 ratings dropped temporarily and the sponsor in turn dropped the program. The premise of Burns and Allen as boyfriend and girlfriend no longer worked. George explained: "Everybody knew we were married and had growing children . . . you have to have truth in a joke just the way you do in anything else to make it any good. If it's basically dishonest, it isn't funny." George finally realized the problem was that he and Gracie were too old to do the boyfriend/girlfriend premise. The jokes were stale, so the format was changed to reflect their status as a married couple and the program experienced a renewal of popularity, attracting 45 million listeners per week.

Many promotional strategies featuring Gracie were employed for the program throughout its run. She went on a show-to-show search for her mythical brother. She ran for president in 1940, receiving several hundred votes. In 1942 bandleader Paul Whiteman wrote *Gracie Allen's Concerto for Index Finger*, which Gracie mentioned constantly on the show. Ultimately, she performed the number at Carnegie Hall and with major orchestras, including the Boston Pops.

George and Gracie were not social commentators, prevailing instead with timeless humor and talented performances. In 1950 they successfully moved to TV, and their 239 episodes continue to air in reruns decades later. George explained: "We talked in vaudeville, we talked in radio, we talked in television. It wasn't hard to go from one medium to another." Gracie retired after the final TV episode on 4 June 1958, to be Mrs. George Burns, a mother and a grandmother. Only after her 27 August 1964 death did the public discover she had retired because of heart problems.

In his book *Gracie: A Love Story*, George's first line read: "For forty years my act consisted of one joke. And then she died." George continued in TV as an actor, developer, and producer of *Wendy and Me, No Time for Sergeants, Mona McCluskey*, and *Mr. Ed*. In 1975 he returned to film, replacing his late friend Jack Benny in *The Sunshine Boys*. He also starred in the *Oh, God!* trilogy and a handful of other films. George continued TV guest appearances before being slowed by a 1994 fall. He performed in Las Vegas until his death on 9 March 1996.

W.A. KELLY HUFF

See also Comedy; Vaudeville

Cast

George Burns	Himself
Gracie Allen	Herself
The Happy Postman	Mel Blanc
Tootsie Stagwell	Elvia Allman
Mrs. Billingsley	Margaret Brayton
Muriel	Sara Berner
Waldo	Dick Crenna
Herman, the duck	Clarence Nash
Also featured	Gale Gordon, Hans Conried, Henry Blair
Vocalists	Milton Watson, Tony Martin, Jimmy Cash, Dick Foran
Bandleaders	Jacques Renard, Ray Noble, Paul Whiteman, Meredith Willson
Announcers	Ted Husing, Harry Von Zell, Jimmy Wallington, Bill Goodwin, Toby Reed

Directors

Ralph Levy, Al Kaye, Ed Gardner

Writers

Paul Henning, Keith Fowler, Harmon J. Alexander, Henry Garson, Aaron J. Ruben, Helen Gould Harvey, Hal Block, John P. Medbury

Producer/Creator

George Burns

Programming History

CBS and NBC	15 February 1932–17 May 1950

Further Reading

Blythe, Cheryl, and Susan Sackett, *Say Goodnight, Gracie! The Story of Burns and Allen*, New York: Dutton, 1986

Burns, George, *Gracie: A Love Story*, New York: Putnam, 1988

Burns, George, *All My Best Friends*, New York: Putnam, 1989

Campbell, Robert, *The Golden Years of Broadcasting: A Celebration of the First 50 Years of Radio and TV on NBC*, New York: Scribner, 1976

Finkelstein, Norman H., *Sounds in the Air: The Golden Age of Radio*, New York: Scribner, 1993

Harmon, Jim, *The Great Radio Comedians*, Garden City, New York: Doubleday, 1970

O'Connell, Mary C., *Connections: Reflections on Sixty Years of Broadcasting*, N.p.: National Broadcasting Company, 1986

Wertheim, Arthur Frank, "Scatterbrains," in *Radio Comedy*, New York: Oxford University Press, 1979

German Wireless Pioneers

Arco, Braun, Slaby, and Telefunken

In addition to the seminal figure of Heinrich Hertz, the first experimenter to prove that James Clerk Maxwell's theories concerning the potential of electromagnetic radiation for communication were correct, several later German innovators helped to pioneer the practical introduction of wireless telegraphy at the turn of the 20th century. This entry briefly outlines the lives and contributions of three of them and the early development of the Telefunken company, which in 1903 merged their efforts.

Origins

Born early in 1849, Adolph Slaby spent much of his life as an academic researcher at a succession of prestigious German institutions. Into the early 1890s, he focused his efforts on motors and gas engines, thermodynamics, and some aspects of electricity, and in 1893 he had become the science and technology advisor to Kaiser Wilhelm II, a testimonial to his position in the German academic world. Drawing on the findings of Hertz, Slaby began working in wireless in the mid-1890s, but he was unable to transmit more than about 300 feet (in other words only within the technical high school building where he taught), no matter what changes in his apparatus he tried.

Born in 1850, Ferdinand Braun also became an academic. After earning his Ph.D. at the University of Berlin in 1872, he served as a faculty member at Marburg, the University of Strasbourg, Karlsruhe, and finally again at Strasbourg, becoming the director of the Physical Institute there. Braun applied for his first wireless patent in 1898, for a detector circuit to determine frequency. He would later become best known as the inventor of the cathode-ray oscilloscope, precursor of the modern television tube.

George von Arco, a member of the German nobility, was 20 years Slaby's junior. He would join Slaby as a research assistant and would become an important figure in the early development of Telefunken.

Early Wireless

Thanks to diplomatic channels through William Preece, chief electrician of the British Post Office, Slaby was invited to be present for the important May 1897 Marconi tests across the Bristol Channel from England to Wales that achieved transmission over eight miles. Marconi was unhappy over aiding a possible competitor (as turned out to be the case), but had no choice as the Post Office controlled the experiment.

Slaby returned home impressed with what he had witnessed and determined to improve on the system Marconi had demonstrated. Just two months later he conducted the first German wireless transmissions between suburbs of Berlin where, among others, the Kaiser was in attendance. With the Kaiser's full support in terms of funds and personnel, Slaby made rapid progress, and in the fall of 1897 he initiated wireless experiments up to a distance of about a dozen miles, using aerials held up by captive balloons.

Count von Arco joined Slaby as an assistant in 1898 in the Charlottenburg Technical High School's department of wireless telegraphy. The developing Slaby-Arco system made many improvements. One was to move the signal detector (a coherer) away from the base of the antenna, providing far better results. Soon Germany naval and merchant vessels were experimenting with Slaby-Arco devices. Transmitting stations were established in Austria, Sweden, Norway, Portugal, Russia, Denmark, and Chile in addition to Germany. In 1899, the German General Electric Company (AEG) purchased Slaby-Arco patent rights and provided funding for further experimentation.

By 1897–98, Ferdinand Braun was actively experimenting with wireless systems as well. He focused on four elements, including higher transmitter power and use of an oscillating circuit plus a crude early form of tuning to develop a system, for which he would share the 1909 Nobel Prize in Physics with Marconi. In 1898 he received his first wireless patent for his conduction system that worked for limited distances through water or earth (and was thus sufficiently different from Marconi's work to survive any patent appeal). A short time later, Braun realized what was limiting the range of all wireless experimenters when he added two types of coil to the transmitting circuit and quickly began to achieve greater range, efficiency, and safety in operation.

By 1899 Braun's patents were supported by a commercial syndicate known as Telebraun, which was, in turn, taken over by the Siemens-Halske firm in 1901 with the intention of commercializing the system.

Despite all this innovation, all was not well. Early in 1902, when a brother of the German Kaiser returned from a visit to America, Marconi-equipped ships and shore stations refused to communicate with the Slaby-Arco equipped German passenger liner on which he sailed. Or at least that was the German position—Marconi interests claimed the problem was poor performance and lack of distance achieved by the German radio equipment. At the same time this international rivalry was sharpening, fierce patent litigation developed in German courts between Slaby-Arco (whose patents were held by AEG) and Braun (backed by the Siemens-Halske firm). Concerned that Germany might lose out in the world competition to develop viable wireless systems (and thus would have to rely on Marconi or American wireless equipment), Kaiser Wilhelm II stepped in.

Telefunken

At the Kaiser's insistence, on 27 May 1903 some 30 Slaby-Arco (AEG) and Braun (Siemens-Halske) patents (and as many personnel) were combined to create a new company, Gesellschaft für drahtlose Telegraphie, soon better known as Telefunken. Thanks to substantial government support, the new company soon operated more than 500 stations. Telefunken sold rather than leased (as Marconi did) equipment that initially used coherers as signal detectors but soon transferred to electrolytic detectors and headphones. The quality German equipment and growing number of transmission stations soon created strong competition with Marconi, aided by cooperation among German electrical corporations under the umbrella of government purchases and investment.

In part as a result of the 1902 incident of lack of maritime cooperation, the German government required that all German facilities make use of Slaby-Arco equipment. Imperial Germany also hosted the first international wireless conventions in Berlin in 1903 and 1906 to encourage inter-system communication. These meetings bore testament to the growing importance of German radio efforts in the face of Marconi's attempted maritime radio monopoly.

By 1906 von Arco had conducted wireless-telephony (voice) experiments over distances greater than 20 miles, and Telefunken had developed "singing spark" and "quenched spark"

transmitters, which use shorter aerials and were more efficient than earlier devices. The German army was setting up portable Slaby-Arco wireless telegraphy units for use in the field. The U.S. Navy had relied heavily on Slaby-Arco equipment beginning in 1903 for lack of a reliable American source of wireless equipment and dislike of Marconi policies. The Russian Navy did likewise, though its loss in the Russo-Japanese War of 1904–05 did not help the image of German wireless, especially as the winning Japanese fleet had made better use of its Marconi equipment.

Telefunken began to build a giant wireless transmission station at Nauen, outside of Berlin, to enable faster communication with distant German colonies. By 1910 it had developed into the largest transmitting station in the world, using a von Arco–developed alternator for transmission with antennas covering more than a square mile. By 1914, German wireless stations were communicating regularly with North America and Africa, and stations were being completed to allow regular communication to the Pacific as well. German wireless was certainly equal to anything created by Marconi in Britain or by various competing American companies.

Decline

Compared to the Marconi or American inventors' stories, however, there is comparatively little evident in English-language sources today about these early German innovators and companies.

Slaby died in 1913, and Braun, who had traveled to the U.S. to deal with patent infringement problems, died as an enemy alien in New York five years later. While von Arco continued with Telefunken and lived into the early part of World War II, outside of Germany only Braun is known today, primarily for his pre-television work.

But the end of Germany's growing radio success was due largely to the impact of World War I. Inception of the war in mid-1914 cut off Germany from her own colonies in Africa and elsewhere and isolated her business and industry. Most overseas German radio facilities were destroyed or captured by 1915. When the United States entered the war in April 1917, all German-owned wireless facilities there were taken over as enemy contraband. Losing the war in 1918 left Germany destitute and her industries, including wireless, in disarray. In just four years, Germany had lost her extensive network of international wireless stations and markets while many British and American concerns thrived as radio expanded into the 1920s.

CHRISTOPHER H. STERLING

See also Early Wireless; Hertz, Heinrich; Lodge, Oliver J.; Marconi, Guglielmo; Popov, Alexander

GERMANY 655

George Wilhelm Alexander Hans (Count) von Arco. Born in Grossgorschuetz, Germany, 30 August 1869. Joined Slaby as a research assistant in 1898. Appointed manager of German telegraphs in 1903. Eventually chief engineer of Telefunken. Died in Berlin, 7 May 1940.

Karl Ferdinand Braun. Born in Fulda, Germany, 6 June 1850, sixth of seven children of Johann Conrad Braun, a government official, and Franziska Göhring. Ph.D., University of Berlin, 1872. Associate Professor, Marburg, 1877–79; Associate Professor, University of Strasbourg, 1880–82; Professor, Karlsruhe, 1883–85; Professor of physics, later Director of Physical Institute, Strasbourg, 1895–1918. First wireless patent applied for, 1898. Shared 1909 Nobel Prize in Physics with Marconi. Died in Brooklyn, New York, 20 April 1918.

Adolph Karl Heinrich Slaby. Born in Berlin, 18 April 1849. Studied mechanical engineering and mathematics, Royal Trade School, Potsdam. Appointed to Berlin Trade Academy in 1876. First chair of electrical engineering (1882) and director (1884), Electrotechnical Laboratory of Technical High School at Charlottenburg. Honorary Professor, University of Berlin, 1892. Technical advisor to the German Kaiser, 1893–1912. Died in Charlottenburg, Germany, 6 April 1913.

Further Reading

Blaine, Robert Gordon, "German Systems," in Ætheric or Wireless Telegraphy, by Blaine, London: Biggs, 1905
Fleming, J.A., "The Work of Slaby and Von Arco [and] of Professor F. Braun . . . the Braun-Siemens Practical System . . . the Telefunken System," in The Principles of Electric Wave Telegraphy and Telephony, by Fleming, London and New York: Longmans Green, 1910; 4th edition, 1919; reprint, 1978
Headrick, Daniel R., The Invisible Weapon: Telecommunications and International Politics, 1851–1945, London and New York: Oxford University Press, 1991
Kurylo, Friedrich, Ferdinand Braun: Leben und Wirken des Erfinders der Braunschen Röhre, Nobelpreisträger, 1909, Munich: Moos, 1965; revised edition, as Ferdinand Braun: A Life of the Nobel Prizewinner and Inventor of the Cathode-Ray Oscilloscope, translated and adapted by Charles Susskind, Cambridge, Massachusetts: MIT Press, 1981
Sewall, Charles Henry, "Methods of Dr. Slaby," in Wireless Telegraphy: Its Origins, Development, Inventions, and Apparatus, by Sewall, New York: Van Nostrand Reinhold, 1903; reprint, Waterbury, Connecticut: Brohan Press, 2000
Slaby, Adolph Karl Heinrich, Die Funkentelegraphie, Berlin: Simion, 1897
Slaby, Adolph Karl Heinrich, "The New Telegraphy," Century Magazine (April 1898)

Germany

Despite increasing competition from other electronic media, radio continues to play an important role in Germany. The country's radio system is divided into the long-established network of public service stations—the Association of German Broadcasters (ARD)—and (since 1984) their commercial counterparts. Most stations are FM outlets and have regional or local reach. Although music and entertainment programs are important for German listeners, there are also many niche programs that offer anything from science magazines and minority programs to the renowned Hörspiel (radio drama) experimentations. Moreover, radio still is an information medium; even music stations are expected to offer at least news on the hour and headlines in between.

Over the last two decades, the industry has experienced tremendous change stimulated by deregulation. This has led to an exponential increase of stations and intensified competition resulting in many new radio formats and audience fragmentation. On average, Germans listen to radio for almost three hours per day, which is as much time as they spend watching television.

Origins

On 29 October 1923 the first German radio program was aired from Berlin. As was common in many European countries, the first German radio stations were not privately owned enterprises; instead, they were directly or indirectly controlled by national or regional governments. After World War I, when a nonmilitary radio network became a possibility, several wire services, newspaper publishers, the electrical industry, and other private investors tried to negotiate with the Weimar government to establish commercial radio stations. But ultimately the government prevailed, keeping broadcasts under their control.

A national broadcasting organization and nine regional publicly traded radio organizations were launched. These were controlled by the postal ministry but allowed limited private investments. Two programming organizations produced most of the content. Drahtloser Dienst AG (DRADAG; Wireless Service, Inc.) controlled by the department of internal affairs, produced political information (newscasts). *Deutsche Stunde* (German Hour), controlled by the postal and foreign ministries, was responsible for providing music and cultural programs. The system was financed through a license fee that was added to the price of new radio sets. In the last chaotic years of the Weimar Republic, broadcasting became progressively more centralized; by 1932, the national government took full power over the new medium.

Radio in the Third Reich

After the Nazis seized power in 1933, Joseph Goebbels quickly took control of all cultural and media institutions, restructuring them as part of his propaganda machine. As Minister for Public Enlightenment and Propaganda and head of the Chamber of Culture, he controlled all cultural productions including print, radio, film, theater, literature, and music.

An inexpensively produced radio set called *Volksempfänger* (people's receiver) became one of the Nazis' most successful propaganda instruments because it made tuning other non-German stations almost impossible. Because of these new sets, radio soon reached nearly 100 percent of the population and ensured the almost complete penetration of Third Reich propaganda. Both programming and staffing were monitored by the Chamber of Culture's department for broadcasting. From 1940 on, all German radio stations had to air the same government-created program.

As the war expanded, Allied countries made increasingly effective use of radio in their efforts to counter German propaganda broadcasts. The British Broadcasting Corporation (BBC) and others aired programs in German and other languages of occupied territories. Despite being threatened by a death penalty, an increasing number of listeners turned to these programs as the war continued and Goebbels' propaganda lies became more and more obvious. As the war drew to a close, German radio programs became more limited. Many stations were destroyed until in May 1945 the last intact Nazi-controlled radio station at Flensburg announced Germany's unconditional surrender.

A Divided Postwar System

West Germany

At the end of World War II, the occupying powers (the United States, Britain, and France) established a new broadcasting sys-

tem. In the beginning, all three Western allies tried to establish their respective media systems in their occupied zones. Yet a commercial system such as that in the United States was not viable because war-torn and destroyed Germany could not generate enough advertising support to finance it. On the other hand, the centralized French system resembled too closely the former Weimar system that had allowed an effortless takeover by the Nazis. Therefore, all Western allies at last accepted the British public service system as the basis for the new German radio operation.

It was important to all of the Allies to keep broadcasting away from the influence of the German national government and to decentralize the powerful medium. At first the Allied representatives were directly in charge of programming and station management, but they soon hired German nationals for increasingly responsible positions. The first regional broadcasting organizations were launched right after the war and by the mid-1950s, the now sovereign West Germany had nine regional public broadcasting corporations. They were organized into the Association of German Broadcasters (ARD). Each of the nine independent regional broadcasting corporations covered either one large or several smaller federal states, and each subsequently increased its stations to as many as five that aired different niche programs.

Reflecting Germany's decentralized political structure, each state organized its own media systems. The ARD broadcast corporations were monitored by boards composed of representatives of political parties, unions and industry, youth organizations, religious groups, and other groups that are considered relevant for society. These boards set general programming guidelines and voted on major administrational and editorial staff. Public stations were required to offer a variety of programs that catered to all groups of the public they served. There were also boards that controlled financial matters.

Critics of this system argue that the political parties have too much influence on broadcasting, denying the constitutional freedom of the media. The system is financed by a monthly broadcast fee levied on every household with a radio and by the sales of some limited commercial time. Most ARD organizations had one general station with a broad pop music selection, in addition to news and short features. The other stations were educational and youth talk-based stations, classical and jazz stations (many ARD stations own symphony orchestras and sometimes big band and jazz orchestras), and stations playing traditional music catering to older audiences. More recently, some have added stations with all-news formats. The indirect financing through listener fees allowed the stations to produce programs other than just those with mass appeal, which has made radio an important cultural form. From the 1950s through the 1970s, niche departments (not infrequently headed by Ph.D.s) flourished, producing genres such as *Hörspiel* (radio drama) and other experimental radio work.

Reacting to new technological developments that ended channel scarcity, in the mid-1980s the West German broadcasting system, including radio, was deregulated and allowed commercial competition.

East Germany

The East German media system was organized according to the Soviet-totalitarian model. Following the Marxist-Leninist-Stalinist concepts of media, broadcasting outlets were state-owned and centrally organized and their main purpose was to educate people about communism (usually and rather confusingly termed "socialism" in practice).

The Soviets developed stations in Berlin and other major East German cities—all under a central administration. But by 1952 Soviet forces relinquished control and censorship rights to a state broadcasting committee that was directly monitored by the East German government. East Germany abolished the states as political entities and centralized the media system. After 1955 there were the *Berliner Rundfunk* (Berlin Broadcasting) for East (and potentially West) Berlin; the *Radio DDR* for all East Germans; *Deutschlandsender* (Germany's Station; later *Stimme der DDR* [Voice of German Democratic Republic]) broadcast for West German listeners; and *Radio Berlin International*, which produced programs in German and ten other foreign languages for international listeners. During the height of the Cold War, AM propaganda channels were added: *Freiheitssender 904* (Freedom Station 904) aimed at communists outside the country after 1956; and *Soldatensender 935* (Soldiers' Station 935) geared toward Western soldiers after 1960. They were on the air until a phase of détente in the early 1970s eased the Cold War rhetoric.

A reform in 1987 resulted in a new channel for young people—the soon popular *Jugendradio DT64* (Youth Radio DT64). In addition, the established stations changed to more distinctive formats, under different names. *Radio DDR 1* aired information and music; *Radio DDR 2* aired regional programming in the morning and cultural or educational programming during the day. The *Berliner Rundfunk* focused on Berlin current events. The broadcasting system in East Germany was mainly financed by viewer's fees and state subsidies. All radio and TV sets had to be officially registered.

A special problem for the East German government was that an estimated 80 percent of its people could tune to broadcast signals from the West. Besides the public TV stations, people especially listened to radio stations close to the German border. Although at first the political elite tried to enforce a strict ban on tuning in foreign broadcasts, it later gave in to their popularity. During the first few years of East Germany's existence, members of the state-controlled youth organization were sent out to destroy antennae that were positioned to receive Western broadcasts. Sometimes the government tried to jam (electronically interfere with) transmissions from the West, but that always led to protest from audiences. Under the rule of state council chairman Erich Honecker in the early 1970s, the East German government officially accepted West German broadcasting. Only the most rigid party members then refrained from listening and viewing.

In fact, West German broadcasting became a part of the political agenda. Often East German politicians countered Western news that had not been aired on eastern channels. It has been argued that these years of Western broadcasting had a major impact on destabilizing East Germany, which finally led to the fall of the Berlin Wall in 1989. The constant exposure to unreachable Western consumerism definitely led to a serious level of dissatisfaction among the population. After a phase of several short-lived media reorganizations during the upheaval, with the final German reunification in 1990, the East and West German systems were merged, following the Western model.

Today: A Dual System

In 1984 the West German media system changed to a so-called dual system allowing commercial as well as state governmental radio and television stations. After the reunification, the whole country adopted this system. The new political situation let to the launch of two new ARD organizations in former East Germany and the merger of two Western ones; thus there are now ten regional public service networks under the ARD umbrella. Further deregulation has let to a tremendous growth in the number of commercial radio stations in East and West. Reflecting the decentralized political system, each state has a different setup for commercial radio broadcasting, but most states permit a combination of local and statewide commercial radio stations. Some states only have five or six statewide private stations. Sometimes they are even guaranteed a commercial broadcasting monopoly in their area to guarantee enough advertising support; more competitive systems such as Bavaria have 50 or more private stations. There are some ownership regulations, but they have not stopped many newspaper, magazine, and book publishers from acquiring stations. A number of local newspaper publishers have taken advantage of their existing editorial base to launch radio stations.

The dual system has been redefined repeatedly based on several decisions by the highest constitutional court (*Bundesverfassungsgericht*), state legislation, and joint accords of all states. The latest legislation tries to guarantee survival of public as well as private broadcast entities. Although the German constitution guarantees freedom of the press and independence from government interference, there are several content regulations that apply to public as well as commercial stations. ARD stations are controlled by their boards, but even commercial broadcasters must follow certain rules similar to the former U.S. Fairness Doctrine. These concern the protection of children and young people and balanced coverage of topics of public importance. Each state sets up differently structured boards that license the stations and monitor commercial stations' compliance with these requirements.

Two additional radio organizations do not fit into either the public or the commercial category. *Deutschlandradio* is another result of the reunification. It was launched in 1994 by combining the former national public service AM station *Deutschlandfunk* (Germany Radio) with RIAS (Radio in the American Sector, a station of the U.S. Information Service in Berlin) and a cultural station of former East Germany. Jointly operated by ARD and the German TV network ZDF, it airs two programs from Cologne and Berlin. It is commercial free and governed by its mission to support the reunification of the two Germanys. Its main focus is on political and cultural programs that are broadcast on FM, AM, and shortwave. The second organization, *Deutsche Welle* (*DW*; German Wave), broadcasts programs worldwide via satellite and shortwave radio in 34 languages. Based in Cologne and Berlin, it also broadcasts television programs via satellite. The reunification brought about a new legal situation for *DW*, which was formerly a West German government-controlled station. It is now legally monitored by the ministry of interior affairs and financed by the government, commercials, and sponsoring. In accordance with constitutional broadcasting freedom, however, no government department can directly control its programming.

As of early 2003, every household owning at least one radio paid Euro 5.32 (US$5.60); households with both television and radio paid Euro 16.50 (US$17.30). Twenty-eight percent of the overall collected fees were used to finance radio stations. A committee of representatives from all states decides on changes in fee structure or levels. With commercial competition it has become more difficult for public service broadcasters to defend fee increases. Public service radio stations also air commercials that are by law restricted to Monday-through-Saturday broadcasts at certain times of the day. But commercial local and regional radio broadcasters, which are fully supported by advertising, face almost no advertising regulations.

In 1987 there were only about 44 stations in West Germany, but the 1980s deregulation and German reunification increased that number to about 246 in 1999 in the united Germany. Of those, 59 are public service stations. This number has been fairly stable since the mid-1990s. After a strong growth phase in the first decade after deregulation, Germany seems to have reached a saturation point for its local/regional markets. Recently, new transmission technology has triggered some new national private stations and there are also several internet-only stations in Germany.

Audiences

According to media research in 1999, radio stations reach an average of 82 percent of the German people over age 14, on any given day some time between 5:00 A.M. and 12:00 A.M. Germans listen to the radio an average of 179 minutes a day. These numbers have slowly but steadily been increasing in recent years. Radio has remained popular despite increased competition from other traditional and new media. German listeners seem to be fairly loyal to their stations. When asked how many stations they heard the day before, they name only 1.4, on average, and they name only 2.8 stations heard when asked about their listening habits over the last two-week period. Overall, the public stations in the ARD network are losing listeners to commercial stations; the market share of ARD was 53 percent in 1999, compared to 45 percent for commercial radio. Only seven years earlier, in 1992, the ARD network had a market share of 70 percent, compared to 29 percent for commercial stations.

When asked what they consider to be the most important aspect of radio, 69 percent of women and 65 percent of men name news, 63 percent of women/60 percent of men name music, and 55 percent of women/54 percent of men name services such as weather and traffic reports and time announcements. Other popular genres are general background information on political events and political reporting, as well as regional programs and consumer news. As in the United States, radio listening peaks on Mondays through Fridays during the 7:00 A.M. to 8:00 A.M. "drive time" or commuting period, when almost 40 percent of women and 33 percent of men tune in. Listening slowly declines to another light peak around lunchtime with 22 percent of women and 16 percent of men listening. The afternoon sees another decline, but listening picks up again from 4:00 P.M. to 6:00 P.M., with 21 percent of men and 18 percent of women listening.

Many ARD and commercial stations stream their programs via the internet. There are currently pilot projects in several states testing new digital radio transmission technology (DAB). It is expected that new technology will lead to new stations and might shift radio from local and regional to more national format based stations. Other important factors in the future are the tough competition between public service and commercial broadcasters and the increasing audience fragmentation. German media researchers have discovered a distinctive audience split. Younger, less-educated, less-affluent audiences seem to favor commercial stations, whereas older, better-educated, more-affluent people tend to listen to public radio. The maturation of the "dual" system and new technology will provide more challenges for public and private stations in finding and keeping their audiences.

ELFRIEDE FÜRSICH

See also German Wireless Pioneers; Propaganda by Radio; Radio in the American Sector (Berlin)

Further Reading

Bergmeier, Horst J.P., and Rainer E. Lotz, *Hitler's Airwaves: The Inside Story of Nazi Radio Broadcasting and Propaganda Swing,* New Haven, Connecticut: Yale University Press, 1997

Browne, Donald R., *Electronic Media and Industrialized Nations: A Comparative Study,* Ames: Iowa State University Press, 1999

Hoffmann-Riem, Wolfgang, *Regulating Media: The Licensing and Supervision of Broadcasting in Six Countries,* New York: Guilford Press, 1996

Kuhn, Raymond, editor, *Broadcasting and Politics in Western Europe,* Totowa, New Jersey, and London: Cass, 1985

Noelle-Neumann, Elisabeth, Winfried Schultz, and Jürgen Wilke, editors, *Publizistik, Massenkommunikation,* Frankfurt: Fischer Taschenbuch Verlag, 1989; 6th edition, 2000

Short, Kenneth R.M., editor, *Western Broadcasting over the Iron Curtain,* New York: St. Martin's Press, and London: Croom Helm, 1986

Gillard, Frank 1908–1998

British Correspondent and Executive

Frank Gillard's radio career may be divided into three important phases. He was described as "one of the BBC's most distinguished war correspondents" during World War II. Then during the 1950s and 1960s he was a key management executive determining reforms in British national and local radio. Finally, during his "retirement," he was responsible for acquiring archive interviews and writing the history of the British Broadcasting Corporation (BBC). He was also an adviser and consultant in North America and may have had some influence on the development of U.S. public radio. After his death on 20 October 1998, the then Director-General Sir John Birt described him as having made "an unrivalled contribution to the BBC."

War Correspondent

Following his death, a number of newspaper obituaries praised Gillard as a World War II war correspondent. For example, the London *Times* said, "Gillard's was one of the best known voices on British war time radio . . . his incisive reports kept listeners at home abreast of events from the raid on Dieppe to the Allied entry into Berlin and the final German surrender."

In fact, toward the end of his life Gillard had expressed "shame and disgrace" about the distorted and misleading nature of his BBC report on the ill-fated raid at Dieppe in 1942. This is hardly surprising given the fact that he had broadcast the extraordinary line: "As a combined operation this raid was an all-time model." It can be argued that no amount of censorship required him to express this degree of

enthusiasm for an event regarded as one of the greatest disasters of modern military history. He also regretted that he had followed the army's optimistic line too often in his reports and wished he had been more independent. (He was the only BBC correspondent with the Dieppe force because he had been the regional correspondent closest to Portsmouth.)

Throughout the war, Gillard had to be "on side" and operate in the context of a "white propaganda" role in war reporting. There was strict censorship, and journalistic presence depended on the approval and goodwill of commanding generals. Gillard had been a schoolteacher, not a journalist, before working as a part-time broadcaster and talks assistant for the BBC in western England. His war reports do not, therefore, indicate the instinct of the critical reporter seeking to "tell it as it is" but instead fall into the category of a performer operating as a public relations officer. He replaced Richard Dimbleby in North Africa because Dimbleby had been too closely associated with the failures of General Auchinleck's command. Gillard developed a rapport with Auchinleck's replacement General Bernard Montgomery. But after the Allied victory in North Africa, Gillard fell foul of Supreme Allied Commander General Alexander, who had mistakenly accused him of evading official censorship. But an examination of Gillard's war reports again reveals his role as a broadcast performer rather than a reporter detailing the truth of Allied slaughter in Bocage country between the invasion and break out.

An example of the wartime bias of his journalism is illustrated by this extract from a report broadcast 25 June 1944: "Almost the first words a German says when he is brought in to a British or Canadian headquarters on this front are 'Please don't shoot.' Thousands have been amazed to find that we've no intention or thought of killing them." The fact was that there had been several occasions when Canadian troops did not take prisoners, and instances of prisoners on either side being shot dead or having their throats cut were being covered up by Allied reporting. Gillard and his colleagues failed to report, for example, that German tanks and anti-tank weapons were vastly superior to Allied equipment; that the Nazis had more automatic guns than the Allies; that British and Canadian army tactics in the Bocage were inadequate and contributed to an acceleration of casualties that eventually led to the British Army running out of reserves; that a number of Allied troops were killed by friendly fire; and that the bombing of Caen had been futile, resulting in the deaths of many more French civilians than German combatants. In fact, the Scottish playwright William Douglas-Home was court-martialed for refusing orders in relation to the Caen operation. An attempt to break out with British and Canadian armor in "Operation Goodwood" on 18 July 1944 was an unmitigated disaster and significant German military victory, but this was not even hinted at by any of Gillard's reports.

Management

The second phase of Gillard's career in broadcasting was much more significant. He demonstrated a cunning political ability to lobby for and to effect significant change in structures of BBC institutions and broadcasting. Beginning in 1956, he built up the resources, power, and importance of the BBC West Region and was appointed director of sound broadcasting in 1963.

Gillard went on a tour of the United States in 1954 and there realized that, despite the growing ascendancy of television, he did not meet a single person who thought that radio was dying. He noted that the changes were affecting "big battalion broadcasting" (networks) and "an increasing range of local stations." In particular, Gillard was impressed by the small station WVPO Stroudsburg in the Pocono mountains of Pennsylvania, which operated in daylight hours only and served a community of 15,000 people with a staff of 13. Gillard wrote a special report for the BBC, "Radio in the USA: A Visitor's View," which emphasized that WVPO "spoke to its listeners as a familiar friend and neighbor and the whole operation was conducted with the utmost informality."

His successes included the establishment of a network of BBC local radio stations; the redefining of BBC national networks to incorporate the popular musical format channel *Radio 1*; the introduction of more live, unscripted programming to reflect the changing nature of British popular culture; and the preservation of the BBC monopoly in radio broadcast-

ing long after it had been challenged in television. He could be criticized for axing the radio features department without establishing a context whereby its management could continue with the same force and creativity. He could also be condemned for canceling the *Children's Hour* without finding an alternative method of attracting and developing a new generation of young radio listeners. And his ruthless campaigning against a more democratic distribution of taxation for U.K. public radio and the suppression of commercial radio licensing may have had a negative impact on development and choice in British radio.

Historian

Gillard officially retired from the BBC in 1969, but he remained central to its establishment voice. In the 1970s he became the BBC's archival historian, and according to the *Guardian* journalist Maggie Brown, he was "the custodian of its inner secrets." He originated and managed a project of recording on audiocassette and film the memoirs of BBC personnel, which could only be used "on the BBC's centenary in 2022" when "everyone was safely dead or otherwise." As it has been argued that cultural memory and power are often determined by those who write history, Gillard's influence on historical portrayals/evaluations of the BBC is likely to endure. This is probably why the *Guardian* called him "a BBC Mandarin."

As Leonard Miall noted in his *Independent* newspaper obituary, Gillard, "would have been horrified that BBC News managed to get his age wrong in their announcement of his death." The BBC celebrated his memory by inaugurating awards for local radio broadcasting in his name.

TIM CROOK

See also British Broadcasting Corporation; British Radio Journalists

Frank Gillard. Born in Tiverton, Devon, England, 1 December 1908. Educated at Wellington School, Somerset, and St. Luke's College, Exeter; attended London University, 1929–31: B.S.; schoolmaster and freelance broadcaster, BBC West Region, 1936–40; talks assistant, BBC Bristol, 1941; war correspondent with Southern Command, 1942; accredited to operation on Dieppe, 19 August 1942; war correspondent BBC, accredited to North Africa, Italy, Normandy, Berlin, 1942–45; head of BBC West Regional Programmes, 1945–55; controller, West Region, 1956–63; director and later Managing Director, BBC Radio, 1963–69; consultant to U.S. Corporation of Public Broadcasting and Australian Broadcasting Commission, 1969–70. Officer of the Order of the British Empire, 1946; Commander of the Order of the British Empire, 1961; distinguished fellow of the U.S. Corporation for Public

Broadcasting, 1960–66; honorary LL.D., Exeter, 1987. Died in London, 20 October 1998.

Further Reading

Briggs, Asa, *The History of Broadcasting in the United Kingdom*, 5 vols., Oxford and New York: Oxford University Press, 1961–95 (see especially vols. 3–5)

Crook, Tim, *International Radio Journalism: History, Theory, and Practice*, New York and London: Routledge, 1998

Donovan, Paul, *The Radio Companion*, London: HarperCollins, 1991

Hawkins, Desmond, editor, *War Report, D-Day to VE-Day: Radio Reports from the Western Front, 1944–45*, London: BBC Books, 1946

Hickman, Tom, *What Did You Do in the War, Auntie?* London: BBC Books, 1995

Miall, Leonard, *Inside the BBC: British Broadcasting Characters*, London: Weidenfeld and Nicolson, 1994

Miall, Leonard, "Frank Gillard Obituary" *The Independent* (23 October 1998)

Purser, Philip, "Frank Gillard, Obituary" *The Guardian* (23 October 1998)

Godfrey, Arthur 1903–1983

U.S. Radio Personality

During the years following World War II, Arthur Godfrey was one of the great stars of radio, keeping alive a tradition of variety programming through his simulcast *Talent Scouts* amateur program and also doing a popular morning talk and variety program with a stable of stars. These were Godfrey's radio venues, but he did do other radio programs—particularly during the early 1950s—as Columbia Broadcasting System (CBS) executives sought to take full advantage of his growing appeal. No one challenged the popularity of his other principle venue through the 1950s—a regular Wednesday night television variety program, *Arthur Godfrey and His Friends*.

Radio Origins

The red-haired ukulele player, whose gift for gab was a favorite of radio and television audiences through the post–World War II era, started his radio career in 1930 at WFBR-AM in Baltimore. Later, in the 1930s, he moved to Washington, D.C., first to WMAL-AM and then to CBS affiliate WJSV-AM (later WTOP-AM) for an early-morning program that would begin Godfrey's life-long association with the CBS network. Godfrey remained in Washington, D.C., until 1941, when he moved to New York and CBS's WABC-AM. During this decade and a half, Godfrey perfected what would be his fabled ability to communicate on an almost personal level with his listeners.

Based on his narration for the CBS broadcast of the funeral procession down Pennsylvania Avenue for Franklin Delano Roosevelt in April 1945, CBS executives moved Godfrey to New York to begin a radio daytime series, *Arthur Godfrey Time*. This program would remain his staple for 27 years, frequently changing starting times but always running about an hour, and always ending before the noon CBS news.

In 1946 CBS added *Arthur Godfrey's Talent Scouts*, a copy of the long-running Major Bowes and later Ted Mack programs. *Talent Scouts* was Godfrey's first venture into prime time, and it became a big hit. Indeed, his move into television came in 1948 when he agreed to simulcast *Talent Scouts* on television. This would prove to be his launching pad to national fame.

Although others abandoned radio for television as soon as their popularity made it possible, Godfrey never gave up his morning radio chat fest. He did the morning program and then turned around on Monday nights—with the help of a capable production staff led by Janette Davis—and did *Talent Scouts*. Godfrey was smart enough to know where his comparative advantage lay, and he never gave up the morning radio show. (Indeed, once his popularity inevitably waned, he returned exclusively to radio, continuing his radio career until 1972.)

A Talent Scout

While his morning show touched an audience of housewives and baby boomer children, his fame, fortune, and pioneering activities in prime time brought him to the cover of *Time* magazine. Variety show *Arthur Godfrey's Talent Scouts* proved to be a far greater hit than Major Bowes' or Ted Mack's shows ever were. *Arthur Godfrey's Talent Scouts* ran on both radio and television on Monday nights for a decade and was clearly Godfrey's best prime-time showcase. The show reached number one in the TV ratings in the 1951–52 season but fell behind *I Love Lucy* the next season and thereafter finished behind, but not too far behind, Hollywood-produced shows. It remained a radio staple even as other variety shows switched to TV and abandoned radio altogether.

The formula for *Arthur Godfrey's Talent Scouts* was simple enough, as old as the amateur hour idea from vaudeville, which had been popularized by Major Bowes on radio. For Godfrey's version, "scouts" brought on their "discoveries" to perform live before a national radio and television audience. Most of these "discoveries" were in fact struggling professionals looking for a break, and so the quality of the talent proved quite high, as thousands auditioned with the hope that exposure on Godfrey's show would provide that needed national boost. The winner, chosen by a fabled audience applause meter, often joined Godfrey during the following week on his morning radio show and less frequently as part of his televised *Arthur Godfrey and His Friends*. Some even joined his regular talent pool.

Godfrey and Janette Davis did well with pop and country singers. Through the late 1940s and 1950s, Godfrey significantly assisted the careers of Pat Boone, Tony Bennett, Eddie Fisher, Connie Francis, Leslie Uggams, Lenny Bruce, Steve Lawrence, Connie Francis, Roy Clark, George Hamilton IV, and Patsy Cline. But both Elvis Presley and Buddy Holly never made it past the audition. This Monday night 8:30 P.M. talent search was no place for early rockers, nor for African-Americans. That Godfrey lived in Leesburg, Virginia, and Janette Davis was from Arkansas seemed to enable them to find country talent on the fringes, but they always worked best when mining aspiring stars in the Tin Pan Alley tradition.

The "discovery" of Patsy Cline on 21 January 1957 was typical. Her scout (actually her mother), Hilda Hensley, presented Patsy, who sang a recent recording "Walkin' After Midnight." Though this was a country song, recorded in Nashville, and Cline wanted to wear one of her mother's hand-crafted cowgirl outfits that she wore while appearing on local television in Washington, D.C., Davis forced Cline to wear a cocktail dress. Still, the audience's ovations stopped the meter at its apex, and for a couple of months thereafter Cline appeared regularly on Godfrey's radio program. But despite the fact that Cline had been performing for nearly a decade, had been recording in Nashville since 1954, and had been a regular on local Washington, D.C., radio for more than a year, it is often stated that Godfrey, because of the great ratings and fame of his *Talent Scouts*, discovered Patsy Cline.

For *Arthur Godfrey Time*, Godfrey hosted a straight variety show, employing a resident cast of singers that at times included Julius La Rosa, Frank Parker, Lu Ann Simms, Pat Boone, and the Cordettes. Tony Marvin was both the announcer and Godfrey's "second banana," as he was on *Arthur Godfrey's Talent Scouts*. Although the fame of *Arthur Godfrey Time* never matched that of *Talent Scouts*, the assembled company of singers, all clean-cut young people, remained a 1950s fixture in homes as Godfrey played host and impresario.

Fame and Fortune

By the early 1950s, Godfrey seemed unable to do anything wrong, despite a press that could find little reason for his popularity. During the summer of 1950, Godfrey even appeared twice a week on CBS, in addition to his television and daily radio shows, offering lessons on the ukulele to his television audience on Tuesday and Friday nights. This proved his peak of popularity.

His fall from grace began in October 1953 when he publicly fired the popular Julius La Rosa on the air. Through the mid- and late 1950s Godfrey feuded with newspaper critics who complained of his insensitivity to La Rosa and other employees. Although Godfrey's bout with cancer drew international sympathy, falling TV ratings led to his retreat back to radio.

But he did not give up on television. He flopped on *Candid Camera*. But CBS kept trying, and Godfrey continued to do specials: *Arthur Godfrey in Hollywood* on 11 October 1963, *Arthur Godfrey Loves Animals* on 18 March 1963, and so on once or twice a year. His final television special came on 28 March 1973: *Arthur Godfrey's Portable Electric Medicine Show,* filmed and shown on National Broadcasting Company (NBC) TV, was ironically his only major effort for that network. Radio was where Godfrey started and ended his career—and it was always his best medium.

Despite his critics, many of whom argued that Godfrey had no talent, he was one of the important on-air stars of radio and television for the 15 years after the end of World War II. Indeed, one can credibly argue that through the 1950s, there was no bigger star than this freckle-faced, ukulele-playing variety show host. Through most of the decade of the 1950s, Godfrey appeared in his two top ten prime-time television shows, as well as doing a daily radio program, all for CBS. Despite his fame as a discoverer of talent and as a host, in the end it was something about Godfrey's infectious chuckle, his offbeat sense of humor, and his ability to connect to middle-class Americans that made his fans tune in not one, but two, three, or four times per week, in the morning and during prime time.

To industry insiders, Godfrey's shows were simply vehicles for television's first great pitchman. Godfrey blended a Southern folksiness with enough sophistication to charm a national audience measured in the millions through the 1950s. For CBS in particular, Godfrey was one of the network's most valuable stars, generating millions of dollars in advertising billings each

Arthur Godfrey
Courtesy Radio Hall of Fame

year, with no real talent save being the most congenial of hosts.

On radio and television, Godfrey frequently kidded his sponsors, but he always "sold from the heart," only hawking products he had actually tried or that he regularly used. No listener or viewer during the 1950s doubted that Godfrey really did love what he sold, for Godfrey's rich, warm, resonant timbre made him sound like he was confiding to each audience member. Godfrey delighted in tossing aside prepared scripts and telling his audience: "Aw, who wrote this stuff? Everybody knows Lipton's is the best tea you can buy. So why get fancy about it? Getcha some Lipton's, hot the pot with plain hot water for a few minutes, then put fresh hot water on the tea and let it just sit there." So, despite all his irreverent kidding and the uneven quality of his assembled talent, advertisers loved Godfrey and made him and his various shows a key part of broadcasting during the 1950s.

He did the same magic for Pillsbury, Frigidaire, and Toni (hair) products. Here was a friend recommending the prod-

uct, no snake-oil salesman hawking useless or overpriced merchandise. Godfrey drove CBS network efficiency experts crazy because he refused to simply read his advertising copy in the allocated 60 seconds. Instead, Godfrey talked for as long as he felt was necessary to convince his viewers, frequently running over. CBS chairman William S. Paley detested Godfrey but bowed to his incredible popularity. CBS president (and chief number cruncher) Frank Stanton loved Godfrey because his shows were so cheap to produce yet drew consistently high ratings.

By 1950 Godfrey was making well in excess of a million dollars per year and was among the highest-paid persons in the United States at the time. So popular was Godfrey in his heyday that in 1959, when he underwent one of the first successful operations for the removal of a cancerous lung, it was front-page news across the nation. At one point, in the mid-1950s, he had an estimated audience of 40 million and had more than 80 sponsors for his daily morning show. He received 60,000 letters a week. Because of his homey approach and sometimes sly, off-color wit, radio great Fred Allen dubbed Godfrey "the Huck Finn of radio."

The late 1950s and early 1960s were not kind to Godfrey. He battled cancer and saw his million-dollar yearly salary plunge. Godfrey finally retired from radio in 1972, by then a symbol of another era.

DOUGLAS GOMERY

See also Variety Shows

Arthur Godfrey. Born in New York City, 31 August 1903. Attended Naval Radio School, 1921; Naval Radio Material School, 1929; served in U.S. Navy as radio operator, 1920–24; served in United States Coast Guard, 1927–30; radio announcer and entertainer, WFBR-AM, Baltimore, Maryland, 1930; staff announcer, WRC-AM, Washington, D.C., 1933; worked at other local stations, particularly WJSV-AM (later WTOP-AM), a CBS affiliate in Washington, D.C., 1934–45; joined CBS network, 1945; host of several radio and television programs, 1940s and 1950s; returned exclusively to radio morning show, 1960; retired, 1972. Died in New York City, 16 March 1983.

Radio Series

1945–72   *Arthur Godfrey Time*
1946–56   *Arthur Godfrey's Talent Scouts* (on television until 1958)
1949–59   *Arthur Godfrey and His Friends*

Television Series
Arthur Godfrey and His Friends, 1949–59

Further Reading

"Arthur Godfrey: Oceans of Empathy," *Time* (27 February 1950)
Crosby, John, "Arthur Godfrey: It Doesn't Seem Like Old Times," *Collier's Magazine* (30 September 1955)
Curtis, Joan, editor, *The Arthur Godfrey Nobody Knows* (Famous People Series), New York: Fawcett, 1950
Godfrey, Arthur, "This Is My Story" (as told to Pete Martin), *Saturday Evening Post* (8 parts; 5 November–24 December 1955)
Godfrey, Jean, and Kathy Godfrey, *Genius in the Family*, New York: Putnam, 1962
MacDonald, J. Fred, *Don't Touch That Dial! Radio Programming in American Life, 1920–1960*, Chicago: Nelson-Hall, 1979
Marder, Irving, "The Great Godfrey," *Sponsor* (5 June 1950)
O'Brian, Jack, *Godfrey the Great: The Life Story of Arthur Godfrey*, New York: Cross, 1951
Rhoads, B. Eric, *Blast from the Past: A Pictorial History of Radio's First 75 Years*, West Palm Beach, Florida: Streamline, 1996
Singer, Arthur J., *Arthur Godfrey: The Adventures of an American Broadcaster*, Jefferson, North Carolina: McFarland, 2000
Slocum, William J., "The Arthur Godfrey You Never See," *Coronet* (June 1953)

The Goldbergs

Comedy Serial Program

As early as 1937, just 8 years into its 16-year run on radio, *The Goldbergs* was selected by the industry magazine *Radio Daily* as one of the "Programs that Have Made History." Indeed, *The Goldbergs* was a groundbreaking show that influenced both the form and content of later radio and television programming. Amid early radio fare, such as music variety shows and public talks, *The Goldbergs* (along with *Real Folks* and *Amos 'n' Andy*) was one of the first dramatic serials on network radio and one of the first serials to concentrate on family life. *The Goldbergs* demonstrated the power of serials to attract a loyal audience. Its immediate success in 1929

prompted interest in radio programs that regularly featured familiar domestic situations, recurring characters, and continuing story lines.

The Goldbergs was a hybrid program, part comedy, part drama, and part serial; with its continuing story line and domestic focus, the program was the prototype for both later situation comedies and daytime soap operas. Yet *The Goldbergs* is most fondly remembered for its ethnic content. Among the first urban, ethnic comedies in broadcasting, the program spoke eloquently about the experience of immigrants during the Depression and their struggles to assimilate in their adopted country. *The Goldbergs* remains one of the relatively few programs in the history of radio and television to offer a sustained ethnic perspective on American life.

The stories of the Goldberg family—at 1038 East Tremont Avenue, Apartment 3B, in the Bronx—emerged solely from the creator and writer of the series, Gertrude Berg. As Michele Hilmes (1997) writes, "no other daily serial drama reflected so explicitly its creator's own ethnic background." Gertrude Edelstein Berg (1899–1966) was born in Harlem to Russian Jewish parents. As a teenager at her father's resort in the Poconos, Berg began writing plays to entertain the guests. This hobby continued even after Berg married and gave birth to two children. She soon developed a popular skit featuring a wife and mother named Maltke Talnitsky—modeled after her grandmother, her mother, and herself—her no-good husband, and her children. These characters were the earliest forms of the Goldberg family—Molly Goldberg, a Jewish immigrant mother; Jake Goldberg, a tailor and her sympathetic husband; and her two children, Sammy and Rosalie. Gertrude Berg sent a sample script through a family acquaintance to a New York radio station. Berg was offered jobs writing continuity and translating commercials and recipes into Yiddish on radio.

Although Berg's first network offering, about two working-class salesgirls, *Effie and Laurie,* was picked up by the Columbia Broadcasting System (CBS) in 1929, it was canceled after just one broadcast. After this failure, Berg began to shop around her idea for a family comedy based on her earlier skits. Berg claimed that initially "radio studio big wigs" believed audiences would reject a program about Yiddish life. However, the National Broadcasting Company (NBC) saw the promise of radio's first Jewish comedy and aired *The Rise of the Goldbergs* as a sustaining weekly evening series starting on 20 November 1929. Paid $75 a week to write the series and produce the program, Berg controlled all aspects of the show's development, from scripting the program in longhand to paying the performers. Berg, who voiced the character of Molly Goldberg, assembled a cast of New York stage actors to bring the rest of the Goldberg family to life: James Waters as Jake Goldberg, Alfred Ryder as Sammy, and Roslyn Silber as Rosalie. Berg's importance to the series was recognized by fans; nearly 37,000 letters poured in when Berg became ill and was off the air for a week. NBC acknowledged Berg's role, as well: Berg soon earned more than $7,500 a week for the program. By fans and the industry, Berg was considered one of the most important personalities in broadcasting and one of the greatest women in radio.

By the 1931–32 season, the series, retitled *The Goldbergs,* aired six times a week and had become one of the highest-rated programs on radio. On 13 July 1931, the show was picked up by Pepsodent, who sponsored it for the next three years. Berg ended the serial briefly in 1934 to take the cast and the series on a nationwide promotional tour. When the networks cleared

Gertrude Berg of *The Goldbergs*
Courtesy CBS Photo Archive

serial dramas from the night-time air in 1936, *The Goldbergs* moved to daytime until 1945. In January 1938 Berg was signed to a five-year, million-dollar contract to write and star on *The Goldbergs,* making her one of the highest-paid writers on radio. Oxydol and Procter and Gamble picked up sponsorship of the show until the end of its run.

The Goldbergs was a serial that spoke about the economic and social tensions of the 1930s and 1940s, an assimilationist drama about an immigrant Jewish family living on New York's Lower East Side. Many programs focused on typical domestic situations—report cards, dinner guests, schoolyard loves, and Molly's worries about her family. In the early years of *The Goldbergs,* Berg described life in an urban tenement and the attempts of this immigrant family to achieve economic security during the Depression. But, most important, the serial vividly depicted the clash between old and new, yesterday's traditions and today's values, Old World parents and American-born children.

At the heart of this serial drama was the struggle of an immigrant family to assimilate culturally while still retaining their ethnic identity. Early episodes were marked by generational conflict over how much the family should adapt to life in the United States. The parents, Molly and Jake Goldberg, were ethnic immigrants with "Old World" values. Molly's voice revealed her immigrant background: she spoke with a heavy Yiddish accent and was famous for her "Mollyprops," Yiddish malapropisms that twisted common phrases ("If it's nobody, I'll call back" or "I'm putting on my bathrobe and condescending the stairs"). Their American-born children, Sammy and Rosalie, spoke with relatively little accent and often challenged the traditions of their parents. However, by the end of the serial, the Americanization of Molly's family was nearly complete; like so many other immigrants, the upwardly mobile Goldbergs eventually moved from their New York apartment to the suburbs.

The immigrant experience recounted in *The Goldbergs* clearly resonated in an era characterized by both massive immigration and calls for greater national unity. Although Gertrude Berg moved in more assimilated, upper-middle-class circles, she worked diligently to maintain the "realism" of the ethnic immigrant experience detailed in the series. In 1936, for example, Berg took Dan Wheeler, a writer from the *Radio Mirror*, to the Lower East Side to witness her research. In an article entitled "How the Ghetto Guides *The Goldbergs*," Wheeler recounted Berg's conversations with street vendors and immigrant women and her anonymous participation in a Lower East Side charitable club. Her efforts to represent the ethnic experience were appreciated by contemporary audiences. The program was cited at the time by groups such as the National Conference of Christians and Jews for promoting religious and ethnic tolerance.

The continued popularity of the radio program spawned the 1948 Broadway play *Molly and Me,* a comic strip, several vaudeville skits, and a 1950 film. After the program's demise, *The Goldbergs* was briefly revived in 1949–50 for CBS as a 30-minute weekly radio series, but it endured in American culture as a television situation comedy from 1949 to 1955. *The Goldbergs* became one of the most popular comedies of early television, earning Berg the first Emmy Award for Best Actress in 1950. In 1961–62, Molly Goldberg inspired yet another television series, *Mrs. Goldberg Goes to College* (or *The Gertrude Berg Show*). Because of its acuity in representing a common immigrant experience, the magazine *TV Show* appropriately labeled *The Goldbergs* an "American institution" (Merritt, 1951).

JENNIFER HYLAND WANG

See also Comedy; Jewish Radio; Situation Comedy; Stereotypes on Radio

Cast
Molly Goldberg	Gertrude Berg
Jake Goldberg	James Waters, Phillip Loeb (1949–50)
Sammy Goldberg	Alfred Ryder, Everett Sloane (late 1930s), Larry Robinson (1949–50)
Rosalie Goldberg	Roslyn Silber, Arlene McQuade (1949–50)
Uncle David	Menasha Skulnik, Eli Mintz (1949–50)
Joyce	Anne Teeman
Edna	Helene Dumas
Solly	Sidney Slon
Jane	Joan Tetzel
Seymour Fingerhood	Arnold Stang, Eddie Firestone, Jr.
Sylvia	Zina Provendie
Mr. Fowler	Bruno Wick
Mr. Schneider	Artie Auerback
Esther	Joan Vitez
Mickey Bloom	Howard Merrill
Martha Wilberforce	Carrie Weller
Libby	Jeanette Chinley
Uncle Carlo	Tito Vuolo
Mrs. Bloom	Minerva Pious
Announcer	Clayton "Bud" Collyer, Alan Kent, Art Millet

Creator/Writer
Gertrude Berg

Programming History
NBC   1929–34; 1937 (briefly); 1941 (briefly)
CBS   1935–50

Further Reading
Berg, Gertrude, *The Rise of the Goldbergs,* New York: Barse, 1931
Berg, Gertrude, and Cherney Berg, *Molly and Me,* New York: McGraw Hill, 1961
Hilmes, Michele, *Radio Voices: American Broadcasting, 1922–1952,* Minneapolis: University of Minnesota Press, 1997
Kutner, Nanette, "The Nine Greatest Women in Radio," *Radio Stars* (December 1934)
Merritt, Joan, "Calling: Molly Goldberg," *TV Show* 1, no. 1 (May 1951)
O'Dell, Cary, *Women Pioneers in Television: Biographies of Fifteen Industry Leaders,* Jefferson, North Carolina: McFarland, 1996
"Programs That Have Made History," *Radio Daily* (3 November 1937)
Seldes, Gilbert, "The Great Gertrude," *Saturday Review* (2 June 1956)
Wheeler, Dan, "How the Ghetto Guides the Goldbergs," *Radio Mirror* 6, no. 2 (June 1936)

Goldsmith, Alfred Norton 1888–1974

U.S. Radio Engineer and Inventor

Alfred Norton Goldsmith—teacher, engineer, and inventor—won the admiration of two generations of engineers for his contributions to the field of communication technology.

Goldsmith taught electrical engineering at City College of New York while working as director of research for the American Marconi Company. After World War I, he became the first director of research in the newly organized Radio Corporation of America (RCA), and he ultimately became vice president and general engineer of that company. Though RCA was organized to consolidate the patent rights held by different radio interests, under Goldsmith RCA also began to develop research interests in a number of key wireless technologies. His broad knowledge, both theoretical and practical, served RCA well as the company rapidly expanded.

Goldsmith was a prolific inventor with 134 American patents. He was a consulting engineer after 1930, and he served as editor (1912–54) of the highly influential *Proceedings of the IRE (Institute of Radio Engineers)*.

During a career that spanned more than 50 years, Goldsmith inspired those around him to apply rigorous and thoughtful science to the day-to-day engineering problems encountered by the infant broadcasting industry. The outgrowth of that research significantly influenced modern communications technology. He was responsible for patents related to many fields of communication technology, including radio, television, phonographs, aircraft guidance, and motion pictures. Included among Goldsmith's inventions were the shadow-mask cathode-ray tube used in modern color televisions; interlace scanning, which solved early television flicker problems; the radio diversity-reception system, which reduced signal fading; ultrasonic remote control systems; color facsimile transmission; an instrument landing system for aircraft; and the combination radio-phonograph.

Goldsmith was widely regarded as one of radio's outstanding early engineers. Friends, students, and colleagues described him as brilliant, citing his breadth of knowledge and quick insights, both of which won him the respect of those who worked with him and of the administrators who relied on his expertise. Archer (1939) claims that Goldsmith was responsible for christening RCA's early radios "Radiola," a trade name that became synonymous with RCA products. Later, Goldsmith became a freelance consultant and worked for RCA, Kodak, Radio-Keith-Orpheum (RKO), and other companies, but he remained a friend and trusted adviser to RCA's David Sarnoff.

Goldsmith was also an important voice in the formulation of broadcast policy, serving as a member of the Radio Advisory Committee for the National Bureau of Standards at the four Radio Conferences held from 1922–1925. Later, he led the Board of Consulting Engineers, which helped the Federal Radio Commission develop a policy for international relay broadcasting and television. Goldsmith was able to popularize theoretical problems about early radio problems in language that was easily understood, and he published more than 100 papers and books. He edited several anthologies of technical papers by RCA engineers on facsimile, radio at ultrahigh frequencies, and electron tubes.

Although Goldsmith's engineering capabilities and inventions won him fame, perhaps his greatest contribution to the art of communication was his service to the engineering profession. He served as president of the Institute of Radio Engineers (IRE), an early professional society that he cofounded with Robert Marriot, and he edited the institute's journal, *Proceedings of the IRE,* for 42 years. Goldsmith also served as president of the Society of Motion Picture and Television Engineers. Throughout his career, he continued an active interest in these professional organizations, publishing dozens of technical papers on a remarkably wide range of different communication technologies.

FRITZ MESSERE

Alfred Norton Goldsmith. Born in New York City, 15 September 1888. Attended City College of New York, B.S. 1907; Columbia University, Ph.D., 1911; electrical engineering teacher, City College of New York, 1907–19; consultant, General Electric, 1915–17; Director of Research, American Marconi Wireless Telegraph Company, 1917–19; joined Radio Corporation of America (RCA) as Director of Research; promoted to Vice-President of Research and General Engineer, RCA, 1919–31; became independent consulting engineer for NBC, RCA, and Eastman Kodak, 1931; co-founded Institute of Radio Engineers (IRE; predecessor of IEEE), 1912; edited IRE journal *Proceedings,* 1912–54; served as president of the Society of Motion Picture and Television Engineers, 1932–34, and on Radio Advisory Committee for Bureau of Standards, National Television System Committee (NTSC); held 200 patents related to radio and television, 1919–72, as well as patents in motions pictures, communication technology, and air conditioning. Received Medal of Honor and the Founders Award of the IRE; Modern Pioneer Award, National Association of Manufacturers; Townsend Harris Medal, City College of New York; first recipient of the Haraden Pratt Award. Died in St. Petersburg, Florida, 2 July 1974.

Selected Publications
Radio Telephony, 1918
This Thing Called Broadcasting: A Simple Tale of an Idea, an Experiment, a Mighty Industry, a Daily Habit, and a Basic Influence in Our Modern Civilization (with Austin C. Lescarboura), 1930

Further Reading
"Alfred N. Goldsmith, Biographical Notes," *Journal of the SMPTE* 81 (November 1972)

Archer, Gleason Leonard, *Big Business and Radio,* New York: American Historical Society, 1939; reprint, New York: Arno Press, 1971

Dreher, Carl, "His Colleagues Remember 'The Doctor'" *IEEE Spectrum* (August 1974)

Dunlap, Orrin Elmer, Jr., *Radio's 100 Men of Science: Biographical Narratives of Pathfinders in Electronics and Television,* New York: Harper, 1944

Kraeuter, David W., "Alfred N. Goldsmith," in *Radio and Television Pioneers: A Patent Bibliography,* edited by Kraeuter, Metuchen, New Jersey: Scarecrow Press, 1992

The Goon Show

BBC Comedy Program

British radio comedy reached its peak in the 1950s, before television took over as the dominant medium around 1960. Of all the varied series, *The Goon Show* was the most outrageous, the most inventive, and the most demanding in its use of the medium. Rooted in off-the-wall humor such as Lewis Carroll, the Marx Brothers, and Hollywood cartoons, it became a cult item—loved by schoolboys and jazz musicians and hated by schoolmasters and the British Broadcasting Corporation (BBC) establishment.

It was the creation of four young performers, all of whom had been in the Armed Forces during World War II and had been involved with troop entertainments to some degree—Michael Bentine, Spike Milligan, Harry Secombe, and Peter Sellers. In the postwar period they performed in theatrical variety and made occasional radio appearances; Milligan made contributions to radio comedy scripts through his friendship with Jimmy Grafton, who ran a public house, Grafton's, in London's Victoria area and who wrote scripts for the conventional *Derek Roy Show*.

From meetings and experimental performances in Grafton's, the four put together a comedy show that they suggested to the BBC. After a pilot recording and some false starts, the first season began on 28 May 1951. The four had wanted to call it *The Goon Show,* borrowing from the Goons in the Popeye comic strip, but the BBC, not understanding the name (one official asked, "What is this *Go On Show?*") insisted that it be called *Crazy People*.

There were 17 shows in the first season and 25 in the second, which started on 22 January 1952. The format of the program included short sketches, very cartoonish in nature and

gradually building up the use of idiot logic and outlandish sound effects. After the second season, Michael Bentine left to follow his own slightly different comedy style, and the three others formed the basic cast for the rest of the show's life.

The third season, now at last called *The Goon Show,* offered 25 shows starting on 11 November 1952. It continued in the sketch format, with two straight musical items from mouth organist Max Geldray and Ray Ellingon's jazz-style quartet. With the fourth season (30 shows from 2 October 1953), the shows took on the format that would become the standard, telling a single story that was interspersed with the two musical items. Plots included sending the Albert Memorial to the moon and chasing the Kippered Herring Gang.

From the beginning of the fifth season (26 shows) on 28 September 1954, the series gained a worldwide audience through recordings sold to overseas radio stations by the BBC's Transcription Services; the show's overseas popularity outlasted the series itself by many years through repeats. The style had by now settled down, through the use not only of strong, daft plots but also of strongly drawn characters, created by scriptwriter Milligan both alone and in collaboration with Eric Sykes and Larry Stephens.

The main character, around whom all the plots revolved, was Neddie Seagoon (Secombe)—short, fat, stupid, noisy, patriotic, and well-meaning but gullible. In most cases, he was deceived into carrying out some ridiculous task—such as ferrying snow to the Sahara in cardboard boxes—for apparently patriotic reasons but in fact at the behest of the two master criminals, Hercules Grytpype-Thynne (Sellers), a smooth George Sanders type, and Count Jim Moriarty (Milligan), who degenerated over the series into a cringing, starving wreck who dragged Grytpype-Thynne down with him ("Keep still, Moriarty—do you want us both out of this suit?").

In the course of his adventures Seagoon would meet up with other eccentric couples. The senile Minnie Bannister (Milligan) ("We'll all be murdered in our beds!") and Henry Crun (Sellers) ("You can't get the wood, you know") were based, Milligan later claimed, on his parents: their dithering and bickering marked every appearance.

Another couple, usually cast as Seagoon's helpers, were Eccles (Milligan) and Bluebottle (Sellers). Eccles was a combination of Walt Disney's Goofy and the village idiot, and Bluebottle was the eternally hopeful Boy Scout, who almost always got blown up.

The main remaining character, Major Dennis Bloodok (Sellers), was a loose-boweled, lecherous, and greedy army officer of dubious morals. There were also many minor characters, including the baby Little Jim (Milligan), whose only line, whenever appropriate, was "He's fallen in the water!" and the excitable Indians Lalkaka and Bannerjee.

In most radio series, the actors played characters who took part in the plot, but in *The Goon Show* it was the characters themselves who performed the plot, often making asides that showed they were indeed "only acting," which gave an odd extra dimension to the comedy.

Apart from an occasional special show, the remaining seasons were the sixth (10 shows from 20 September 1955), the seventh (25 from 4 October 1956), the eighth (26 from 30 September 1957), a special season of reworked repeats for Transcription Services (14, recorded in 1957–58), the ninth (17 from 3 November 1958), and the final short season of 6 episodes beginning 24 December 1959. By this time the strain of writing and performing the shows had caused Milligan a nervous breakdown and a good deal of subsequent strain—which was showing in the writing—and the series came to an end on 28 January 1960.

Subsequently there were a few special appearances by the trio and a strange television series, *The Telegoons*, reworking old scripts with new recordings of the performers (without an audience) and puppets for the visuals: it was not successful.

The final appearance of the Goons was in the special show *The Last Goon Show of All*, recorded on 30 April 1972 for radio and also televised. The subsequent death of Sellers in 1980 made further reunions impossible.

The Goon Show had a lasting effect on British comedy. It took radio to the boundaries of what was possible through the use of detailed production and complex sound effects, and its irreverent and wildly illogical look at British life influenced many subsequent shows and performers—most famously television's *Monty Python* team. The shows have continued to be extremely popular for many years through repeats and issues on records, tapes, and CDs.

ROGER WILMUT

See also British Broadcasting Corporation; British Radio Formats

Cast

Neddie Seagoon (in various guises)	Harry Secombe
Eccles	Spike Milligan
Miss Minnie Bannister	Spike Milligan
Count Jim Moriarty	Spike Milligan
Bluebottle	Peter Sellers
Mr. Henry Crun	Peter Sellers
Major Denis Bloodnok	Peter Sellers
Hercules Grytpype-Thynne	Peter Sellers

Creators

Spike Milligan, Jimmy Grafton, Peter Sellers, Harry Secombe, Michael Bentine, Eric Sykes, Larry Stephens

Programming History

BBC   1951–60

Further Reading

Milligan, Spike, *The Goon Show Scripts,* London: Woburn Press, and New York: St. Martin's Press, 1972

Milligan, Spike, *More Goon Show Scripts,* London: Woburn Press, 1973; New York: St. Martin's Press, 1974

Milligan, Spike, *The Book of the Goons,* London: Robson, and New York: St. Martin's Press, 1974

Took, Barry, *Laughter in the Air: An Informal History of British Radio Comedy,* London: Robson, 1976; 2nd edition, 1981

Wilmut, Roger, *The Goon Show Companion: A History and Goonography,* London: Robson, 1976

Gordon, Gale 1905–1995

U.S. Radio, Film, and Television Actor

Gale Gordon, a hard-working radio (and, later, television) actor, may never have been a household name, but his voice and face were known to millions. Born into a theatrical family, he spent the first five years of his life in England. His father, Charles Aldrich, was a quick-change artist and his mother was actress Gloria Gordon, best known for her portrayal of Mrs. O'Reilly on radio's *My Friend Irma*.

Born with a cleft palate, Gordon endured two painful operations to correct the problem, and his parents pushed him into show business to help him perfect his speech. By the time he was 17, Gordon's voice was so richly developed that it became his trademark. "His voice was colorful and powerful so he could bend and shape the dialogue he was given," according to Lucie Arnaz. "He also used his whole body for effect, not just his voice," Arnaz added.

While still a teenager, Gordon made his Broadway debut with Richard Bennett in *The Dancers* in the 1920s. He then moved over to try the new medium of radio. Radio offered something new for actors: steady work. Gordon soon became one of the busiest actors in radio, sometimes appearing in 20 to 30 shows per week. In 1929, he moved to the West Coast for the role of Judas in *The Pilgrimage Play*. After a year of touring, he returned to Hollywood where he worked as a freelance actor and announcer. No role daunted him—he supplied the voices of villains, Tarzan, and Flash Gordon, in addition to playing straight dramatic roles in syndicated shows such as *The Adventures of Fu Manchu* and *English Coronets*.

Hy Averback, noted television and movie producer, described Gordon as a combination of Laurence Olivier and Charley Chaplin. Called the master of the slow burn and stack blowing, Gordon found his true forte in comedy. He became everyone's idea of the perfect stuffed shirt and comic foil. His bellowing voice proved to be indispensable and assured gainful employment in dozens of character roles on radio, including his well-known long-running radio roles as Mayor LaTrivia on *Fibber McGee and Molly*, the harried sponsor on *The Phil Harris and Alice Faye Show,* and the apoplectic banker Attenbury on Lucille Ball's *My Favorite Husband.*

Gordon was Lucille Ball's first choice for next-door neighbor and landlord Fred Mertz when *I Love Lucy* was brought to television in 1951. "My mother could always depend on Gale and trusted his acting choices on the radio show," Lucie Arnaz said. "And my mother wasn't fond of change; just for change's sake she would have gladly given Gale the part of Fred Mertz. But Gale was under exclusive contract with CBS Radio so William Frawley got the part."

Gordon worked with many notable actors in radio, including Jimmy Durante, Doris Singleton, Eve Arden, George Burns and Gracie Allen, Richard Crenna, Claire Trevor, Edward G. Robinson, Bea Benaderet, Jack Webb, Mary Pickford, Jack Haley, and Dennis Day. The only actor with whom he seemed to conflict was Mel Blanc, creator of the voice of Bugs Bunny and many other Warner Brothers cartoon characters; the two were constantly in competition for the same parts.

In October 1941, Gordon began playing the role of Mayor LaTrivia on *Fibber McGee and Molly*. (Mayor LaTrivia would arrive at the McGee house, start an argument, become tongue-tied, and blow his stack.) Gordon's only break from the show during 15 seasons was his service in the U.S. Coast Guard, where he served as chief gunner's mate during World War II.

In 1948 Gordon was given the role of Osgood Conklin in *Our Miss Brooks*, a situation comedy about a high-school English teacher forced to endure the supervision of this stuffy, by-the-rules, pain-in-the-rear school principal. Gordon's Conklin was dry, cynical, blustery, and explosive, all at once. It was to be his last role in radio; the show moved to television in 1952 and ran until 1956, with most of the original radio cast, including Gale Gordon, making a successful transition to the new visual medium.

Gordon met his wife, Virginia Curley, while working on the *Death Valley Days* radio program. They married in 1937 and later played together as Mr. and Mrs. Osgood Conklin in both the radio and television versions of *Our Miss Brooks*; they remained together until their deaths a few weeks apart in 1995.

ANNE SANDERLIN

See also Fibber McGee and Molly; Our Miss Brooks

Gale Gordon. Born Charles T. Aldrich in New York City, 2 February 1906. Made Broadway debut in "The Dancers," 1920s; radio debut, *The Church Mouse*, 1934; featured on *Michael and Mary, Flash Gordon*, and many other shows; served in the U.S. Coast Guard during World War II; returned to radio, 1945. Died in Escondido, California, 30 June 1995.

Radio Series

1934	*The Church Mouse*
1934	*Michael and Mary*
1938–40	*Irene Rich*
1940	*Those Who Love; Crossroads*
1942	*Maxwell House Coffee Time*
1941–42, 1945–56	*Fibber McGee and Molly*
1946–47	*The Fabulous Dr. Tweedy*

1947	*The Irene Show*
1947–50	*The Phil Harris and Alice Faye Show*
1948–51	*The Judy Canova Show*
1948–51	*My Favorite Husband*
1948–57	*Our Miss Brooks*
1950	*The Penny Singleton Show*
1950–53	*Fibber McGee and Molly*

Films

Here We Go Again, 1942; *A Woman of Distinction,* 1950; *Here Come the Nelsons,* 1952; *Francis Covers the Big Town,* 1953; *Our Miss Brooks,* 1956; *Rally 'Round the Flag, Boys!* 1959; *The 30 Foot Bride of Candy Rock,* 1959; *Visit to a Small Planet,* 1960; *Give Up the Ship,* 1961; *All Hands on Deck,* 1961; *Dondi,* 1961; *All in a Nights Work,* 1961; *Sergeant Deadhead,* 1965; *Speedway,* 1968; *The Burbs,* 1989

Television

Our Miss Brooks, 1952–56; *The Brothers,* 1956–57; *Sally Bascomb Bleacher,* 1958; *Pete and Gladys,* 1960–62; *Dennis the Menace,* 1962–63; *The Lucy Show,* 1963–68; *Here's Lucy,* 1968–74; *Life with Lucy,* 1986

Further Reading

Brooks, Tim, *The Complete Directory of Primetime Television Stars, 1946–Present,* New York: Ballantine, 1987

DeLong, Thomas A., *Radio Stars: An Illustrated Biographical Dictionary of 953 Performers, 1920 through 1960,* Jefferson, North Carolina: McFarland, 1996

Fidelman, Geoffrey Mark, *The Lucy Book: A Complete Guide to Her Five Decades on Television,* Los Angeles: Renaissance Books, 1999

Gospel Music Format

The gospel music format is a popular genre of radio programming that features generally upbeat music with a Christian message.

Gospel music has long been a staple of radio, particularly in the Bible Belt, and it was featured on several early radio stations, including WFOR in Hattiesburg, Mississippi; KWKH in Shreveport, Louisiana; WSM in Nashville, Tennessee; WVOK in Birmingham, Alabama; and WKOZ in Kosciusko, Mississippi.

Today's gospel music format originated with and grew out of special programming. As local radio stations began to dot the landscape of the United States, many of them featured gospel music on Sundays, or perhaps 30 minutes to an hour each day. Typically, this special programming featured either white Southern quartets, groups, and soloists (including the Statesmen Quartet, the Blackwood Brothers, the Chuck Wagon Gang, and Tennessee Ernie Ford), or black groups and soloists (such as the Jackson Southernaires, Edwin Hawkins Singers, or Mahalia Jackson).

During the 1980s, some radio stations began to program gospel music exclusively, billing themselves as "all gospel all the time." With deregulation of the broadcasting industry in the 1980s, the number of radio stations significantly increased, and program directors created specialized music formats to target specific audiences. The gospel music format began to burgeon; a number of stations chose it as the only type music they featured, complete with the "clock hour," which delineates and specifies every element of programming during each hour. The clock hour, also known as the "format wheel" or "programming wheel," could be compared to a pie cut into approximately 25 parts. For example, the top of the hour on the format wheel might include five minutes of national news from a network (not a few gospel stations are affiliated with the *USA Radio Network* because its content and style of reporting correlate with issues with which some Christians are concerned). At five minutes past the hour, a number-one song from yesteryear might be featured, followed by a top-ten gospel hit, followed by a totally new selection that might prompt the disc jockey to remark, "And you heard it first right here." In this way, the gospel music format is similar to the structure of a Top-40 station, with on-air personalities using their names, throwing in some pleasantries, and striving to create an image appealing to the target audience—in the case of gospel, a bright, happy, encouraging sound.

Top radio groups such as Jacor, Clear Channel, and Infinity see gospel as a viable format. Capitalizing on audience loyalty to the music, a number of stations have improved their ratings after switching to the gospel format, increasing their average quarter hour listening shares and paving the way for advertising acceptance. The gospel music format is typically appealing to advertisers, although gospel music stations decline to advertise certain products or services, such as alcoholic beverages or night clubs. If a gospel music station is airing a sporting event, typically the operator at the station has been instructed to block any network advertisements which pertain to alcohol or tobacco products.

Radio stations have increasingly subscribed to gospel music programming via satellite services. Listeners to such services may well feel that the syndicated announcers are actually present at the local station playing the music and making the comments, even though these DJs are merely part of the download. One of the most popular formats is called *The Light*, which features a mix of black urban gospel artists and includes cross-over collaborations by mainstream artists such as Cheryl "Salt" James of *Salt-n-Pepa* and Stevie Wonder.

Some stations have recently begun to feature specific gospel subgenres, such as southern, African American, country, jazz, contemporary, bluegrass, and even rap.

DON RODNEY VAUGHAN

See also Christian Contemporary Music Format; Evangelists/ Evangelical Radio; National Religious Broadcasters; Religion on Radio

Further Reading

Collins, Lisa, "Urban Radio Sees the Light," *Billboard Magazine* (2 August 1997)
Schwirtz, Mira, "No Longer up in the Air," *Media Week* (11 May 1998)

Goulding, Ray. *See* Bob and Ray

Grand Ole Opry

Country Music Variety Program

As the 20th century ended, the *Grand Ole Opry* was the most famous and longest-running live radio broadcast still on the air. A traditional radio barn dance, originating on WSM radio from Nashville, Tennessee, the *Opry* has reached homes across the eastern half of the United States. Although it started as a local show and later reverted to that status, through the 1940s and most of the 1950s the *Grand Ole Opry* was a staple on Saturday nights on the National Broadcasting Company (NBC). To most Americans, the *Opry* defined what a radio barn dance was and is. Because of its triumph over all major rivals, exemplified by the centralization of the country music industry in Nashville, the *Grand Ole Opry* occupies an important place in both radio and recording industry history.

The *Grand Ole Opry* made its debut on 28 November 1925 on WSM-AM's Studio B to an audience of 200 people. C.A. Craig, one of the founders of the National Accident Insurance Company of Nashville, Tennessee, owned a radio station during the early 1920s (later called WSM for "We Shield Millions"); in 1925 he hired George D. Hay away from WLS-AM in Chicago to develop a barn dance show for WSM, as Hay had done for WLS with the *National Barn Dance*. Hay

began in November 1925, and within a month the new show was a two-hour-long Saturday night staple.

By 1927, as an NBC affiliate, this two-hour local country hoedown followed the network broadcast of the National Symphony Orchestra, which aired Saturday nights from 8:00 to 9:00 P.M. One night, probably 8 December 1928, Hay reportedly stated, "For the past hour you have heard music largely taken from grand opera; now we will present the *Grand Ole Opry.*" True or not, the title is now world famous.

Regional success can be measured by the show's need within a few years to move to a new studio, Studio C, which held 500 persons; later, after a series of temporary moves, the show made its permanent home in the 2,000-seat Ryman Auditorium at Fourth and Broadway in downtown Nashville in 1943. The show remained at that location throughout its network radio days and then, in 1974, moved to a new auditorium as part of the opening of the Opryland theme park in suburban Nashville.

The show had started informally as what scholar Charles Wolfe calls "a good natured riot." But although the program seems informal, getting on was always a struggle for the new

Marty Robbins on stage at the Grand Ole Opry at the Ryman Auditorium
Courtesy Radio Hall of Fame

artist, and many argued that it became more and more commercialized. By the 1930s "hillbilly" stars had been developed, and some dead singers were immortalized. The music was spread thanks to the diffusion and growth of the population, and even greater stars emerged during the post–World War II era. The Opry management, particularly James Denny, took advantage of this interest, and the network (and many clear channel stations) carrying *Grand Ole Opry* enabled the broadcast to become one of the most popular radio programs in the country. Denny and his colleagues also worked with leading record labels to make Nashville the center of the "country and western" universe.

The *National Barn Dance*, from Chicago's WLS, was already an NBC fixture when a half-hour segment of the *Grand Ole Opry* was added to a number of NBC's regional broadcasts, including 26 stations in the Tennessee area. In 1939 NBC began to carry the *Opry* regularly on a regional basis. Two years later the *Opry* went out all across the NBC network.

The coming of TV and format country radio signaled the end of the barn dance radio show. Yet WSM-AM stuck with the *Grand Ole Opry,* and Nashville became not just one center for the making of country music but the leading one. Indeed, many of the early Nashville recordings were done in WSM studios, until Owen Bradley and others began to fashion "Music Row" several miles west of the Ryman Auditorium. And by the time that Bradley at Decca and Chet Atkins at the Radio Corporation of America (RCA) began to remake "hillbilly" music into crossover country music with stars such as Hank Williams and Patsy Cline, the "Athens of the South" had become "Music City."

DOUGLAS GOMERY

See also Country Music Format; National Barn Dance; WSM

Cast

Announcers
George Dewey Hay, Grant Turner

Comedienne
Cousin Minnie Pearl

Singers (partial listing)
Roy Acuff, Hank Williams, Bill Monroe, Patsy Cline, Kitty Wells, Red Foley, George Morgan, Ernest Tubb, Grandpa Jones, DeFord Bailey, Uncle Dave Macon, Eddy Arnold, Loretta Lynn, Hank Snow, Little Jimmy Dickens, Lorrie Morgan, Trisha Yearwood, Vince Gill, Garth Brooks, Emmylou Harris, Ricky Skaggs

Programming History

WSM (and other local Tennessee stations at various times)	1925–present
NBC	1939–57

Further Reading

Eiland, William U., *Nashville's Mother Church: The History of the Ryman Auditorium*, Nashville, Tennessee: Opryland USA, 1992

Hagan, Chet, *Grand Ole Opry*, New York: Holt, 1989

Hickerson, Jay, *The Ultimate History of Network Radio Programming and Guide to All Circulating Shows*, Hamden, Connecticut: Hickerson, 1992; 3rd edition, as *The New, Revised, Ultimate History of Network Radio Programming and Guide to All Circulating Shows*, 1996

Kingsbury, Paul, *The Grand Ole Opry History of Country Music: 70 Years of the Songs, the Stars, and the Stories*, New York: Villard Books, 1995

Malone, Bill C., *Country Music U.S.A.*, Austin: University of Texas Press, 1968; revised edition, 1985

Wolfe, Charles K., *A Good-Natured Riot: The Birth of the Grand Ole Opry*, Nashville, Tennessee: Country Music Foundation Press and Vanderbilt University Press, 1999

The Great Gildersleeve

Situation Comedy

"Great" is the perfect epithet for the character Throckmorton P. Gildersleeve. First a foil on *Fibber McGee and Molly*, then star of his own program, he was a large man in the tradition of Shakespeare's pleasure-loving Falstaff. Loud but never mean, he began sparring with Fibber, the archetypal windbag, in 1937. His character was honed as the bumptious, explosive Gildersleeve, who typically ended a duel with his exasperated phrase, "You're a harrrd man, McGee!" His very name, coined by script writer Don Quinn, combined dignity (Basil Gildersleeve was a famous Victorian classicist) and inside joke (the actor playing Gildersleeve lived on Throckmorton Place). The character left *McGee*, taking the train from the National Broadcasting Company's (NBC) Wistful Vista to Summerfield on 31 August 1941, thus becoming radio's first successful spin-off. The program would last 16 years, until March 1957. Gildersleeve, or "Gildy" to some, was played by actor Hal Peary to 1950 and by Willard Waterman from 1950 to 1957.

In his new town, Gildy's abrasive personality mellowed as he embraced home, work, and social life. Each contact in Summerville deflated his grandiosity and humanized him. Once he planned to attend a costume ball dressed as an ancestor. He daydreamed about possible relatives—a romantic castaway on a tropical island, a dashing pirate, a Gilded Age tycoon—only to learn that he was descended from Goldslob the Pennsylvania butcher (24 March 1948). His appetites kept housekeeper Birdie Lee Coggins busy. More feisty than most of radio's black domestics, Birdie moderated his pomposity by repeating herself ("You know what I said? That's right! That's what I said"). Birdie often mirrored her employer. Both belonged to fraternal groups (she to "The Mysterious and Bewildering Order of the Daughters of Cleopatra," he to "The Jolly Boys"); both sang well. Her talents and industriousness silently rebuked Gildy's natural sloth. Her chocolate cake won a prize, and when she went on vacation, no one could prepare a suitable dinner. She also provided a mother surrogate for Gildy's wards, niece Marjorie Forrester and nephew Leroy.

In an era when single-parent families usually implied a widow with children, Gildy was unusual. Like other unmarried guardians (Donald Duck, Sky King), he coped with the younger generation by combining bossiness, wheedling, and exasperation. Marjorie usually abided by his rules, but she began dating a series of boys who fell short of Gildy's expectations. After wedding Bronco Thompson on 10 May 1950 and bearing twins (21 February 1951), she set up her own household next door. Although she dutifully catered to Gildy's whims, double dating with him before the marriage and asking him to babysit after the kids arrived, her in-laws tried his patience. Used to dominating her husband, Mrs. Thompson openly defied Gildy until they bonded on a picnic. But everyone else had become accustomed to their bickering, so they obligingly pretended to spat (22 March 1950).

Leroy gave little promise of accepting maturity: he reacted to his "Unk's" apparently foolish directions with an exasperated "Oh, for corn sakes." Gildy tried patience but often resorted to the ultimate threat, a menacingly drawn-out "Leeeroy." Certainly Leroy needed direction. His academic work would have embarrassed anyone, but it particularly discomfited Gildy, who courted the school principal, Eve Goodwin. Leroy's troubles with bullies, jobs, attractive girls, stolen lumber, and toothaches often defied logical advice, yet they somehow solved themselves.

Gildy seemed to be an unlikely source of practical wisdom. He loitered through his job as water commissioner, sometimes aided by his simple secretary Bessie. His campaign for mayor in 1944 floundered when he lost his temper on a political broadcast. When he discovered that no one in the city knew him or his job, he hatched a publicity stunt: to dive into the reservoir (23 April 1952). The bungled descent temporarily dampened his quest for recognition. Romance, at any rate, interested him more. Various women with descriptive names like Eve Goodwin and Adeline Fairchild prompted him to buy perfumes and candy from the crusty druggist, Peavey. Gildy should have imitated Peavey's famous tag line, "Well, now, I wouldn't say that," because his amorous crusades never led to the altar. His closest approach, with Leila Ransom, a flirtatious Southern widow, ended when her supposedly dead spouse Beauregard turned out to be alive (27 June 1948).

Gildy's male friends provided enough excitement to compensate for these losses. Judge Horace Hooker, the "old goat" who monitored Gildy's care of Marjorie and Leroy, diminished his ego by staying when Gildy wished to court a lady friend or by demanding vegetarian food when he came for dinner. So did Rumson Bullard, Gildy's wealthy and insulting neighbor, who drove a big car and disdained to invite him to a neighborhood party. The "Jolly Boys"—Peavey, Hooker, Floyd Munson the barber, and police chief Gates—met to gossip and sing. The bonding sometimes frayed, inspiring Chief Gates to plead, "Aw, fellows; let's be Jolly Boys!"

Network politics might have caused disaster, because the original Gildy, Hal Peary, launched his own short-lived Columbia Broadcasting System (CBS) show, *Honest Harold*, in 1950. Luckily, Willard Waterman, a friend of Peary's who often teamed with him on other shows, sounded like him and took over the lead until the show ended in 1957. Both men had fine singing voices and incorporated easy listening songs into the plot.

The two prolonged Gildy's life in movies and television. Peary appeared briefly in four amusing films (*Comin' Round the Mountain*, 1940; *Look Who's Laughing*, 1941; *Country Fair*, 1941; *Unusual Occupations*, 1944) and starred in four others (*The Great Gildersleeve*, 1942; *Gildersleeve's Bad Day*, 1943; *Gildersleeve on Broadway*, 1943; *Gildersleeve's Ghost*, 1944). Waterman was featured in 39 TV episodes (September 1955–September 1956). Radio writers Paul West, John Elliotte, and Andy White followed, sometimes recycling story lines (Gildy's aforementioned dive into the reservoir; his attraction to Bullard's sister from 19 September 1951). However, they overemphasized Gildy's womanizing tendencies for the first 26 programs. Other shows toned down Leroy's mischief, substituted new actors (only three originals remained), and lost a major sponsor. Still, both films and TV communicated some of the great man's foibles and successes familiar to radio fans.

JAMES A. FREEMAN

See also Comedy; Fibber McGee and Molly

Cast

Throckmorton P. Gildersleeve	Hal Peary (1941–50), Willard Waterman (1950–57)
Leroy Forrester	Walter Tetley
Marjorie Forrester	Lorene Tuttle (1941–44), Louise Erickson (mid 1940s), Mary Lee Robb (mid 1940s–56)
Judge Horace Hooker	Earle Ross
Birdie Lee Coggins	Lillian Randolph
Mr. Peavey	Richard Legrand, Forrest Lewis
Floyd Munson	Arthur Q. Bryan
Police Chief Gates	Ken Christy
Leila Ransom	Shirley Mitchell
Adeline Fairchild	Una Merkel
Eve Goodwin	Bea Benaderet (1944)
Nurse Kathryn Milford	Cathy Lewis (1950s)
Bashful Ben	Ben Alexander (mid 1940s)
Bronco Thompson	Richard Crenna
Rumson Bullard	Gale Gordon, Jim Backus (1952)
Craig Bullard	Tommy Bernard
Bessie	Pauline Drake, Gloria Holliday
Announcer	Jim Bannon (1941–42), Ken Carpenter (1942–45), John Laing (1945–47), John Wald (1947–49), Jay Stewart (1949–50), Jim Doyle, John Hiestand

Producers/Directors

Cecil Underwood, Frank Pittman, Fran Van Hartesveldt, Virgil Reimer, and Karl Gruener

Programming History
NBC   1941–57

Further Reading

Harmon, Jim, *The Great Radio Comedians*, Garden City, New
    York: Doubleday, 1970
"Helpful Hints to Husbands," *Tune In* 4 (July 1946)

Salomonson, Terry, *The Great Gildersleeve: A Radio
    Broadcast Log of the Comedy Program*, Howell, Michigan:
    Salomonson, 1997
Stumpf, Charles, and Ben Ohmart, *The Great Gildersleeve*,
    Boalsburg, Pennsylvania: BearManor Media, 2002
Thomsen, Elizabeth B., The Great Gildersleeve,
    <www.ethomsen.com/gildy>
"Throckmorton P," *Newsweek* (13 December 1943)

Greece

Radio began in Greece later than in most other European nations, and the country was one of the last to develop an official government station. In a radio industry characterized by its state of constant flux, private stations and others controlled by the armed forces have existed alongside government outlets. Advertising has been accepted on some outlets, not on others.

Origins

Experimental radio stations were operated in Greece in the 1920s, but the first station offering a regular program schedule was established in Thessaloniki in 1928 as a private operation. Greek radio listeners relied primarily on stations in other nations, and considerable confusion and change was evident as the ministry in charge of radio kept switching. Despite several attempts, no other regularly operated stations existed in the country until the 1930s. In 1936 the government decided to develop a national broadcasting system that could educate Greek society. In 1938, Greece became one of the last European nations to develop a state-run radio station. The Ethnikon Idryma Radiophonias (EIR), or National Radio Foundation, provided programs consisting largely of music by the station's orchestra, choirs, and news.

At the beginning of World War II, the station helped boost the morale of the soldiers and the public. Eventually, the occupying German forces sealed radio receivers in Athens to receive only the national station, which they controlled. In the countryside people were ordered to turn in their radios or face severe punishment.

In 1945, EIR closed down the private station after an unsuccessful attempt to force it to broadcast the national signal. In the late 1940s, additional stations were built by EIR, as well as by private interests and the Armed Forces. Armed Forces stations were established to "enlighten" the people of Northern Greece about the dangers of communism. The United States,

which had taken a major role in the Greek Civil War, built two radio stations that transmitted Voice of America programs part of the day and state programming the rest of the day.

The Armed Forces stations were financed through army funds and advertising. In 1952, as Armed Forces stations gained popularity, EIR established a Second Program. This service carried commercials and more popular music, unlike the original station's (First Program) more serious orientation. That service carried news, information, and fine arts programming, but no commercials. In 1954, EIR established the Third Program that primarily provided classical music broadcasts. All stations from 1946 to 1953 were under strict government censorship, while some form of censorship continued until 1975.

A new Greek constitution drafted after the fall of the military junta (1967–1974) placed radio and television "under the immediate control of the state." A new state organization, Hellenic Radio-Television (ERT), heavily controlled by the government, was created to operate the public stations.

Structure

According to a 1975 law, and subsequent broadcast laws, the purpose of ERT is to provide "information, education, and recreation for the Greek people (through) the organization, operation and development of radio and television." In addition, the act states that "ERT programs must be imbued with democratic spirit, awareness of cultural responsibility, humanitarianism and objectivity, and must take into account the local situation." Finally, this law stated: "The transmission of sound or pictures of any kind by radio or television by any natural person or legal entity other than ERT and the Armed Forces Information Service (YENED) shall be prohibited" ("Greek Radio-TV Law," 1976). This brought an end to any legal private broadcasting in Greece.

In 1982, the socialist governing party, PASOK, placed all YENED stations under civilian government control. Nevertheless, there was a great reluctance to open the airwaves to private citizens. No political party was willing to part with control of broadcasting, which they could use for self-promotion when in power.

In 1987, a new legal structure for broadcasting created one company, Hellenic Radio-Television S.A. (ERT), now a corporation owned by the state, to control all public service broadcasting in Greece. One of its entities is Hellenic Radio (ERA), made up of the four domestic radio services (ERA-1, ERA-2, ERA-3, ERA-4) and the Voice of Greece shortwave radio service (ERA-5).

Nevertheless, the major importance of the 1987 law was that, despite initial opposition from the government, it provided for the establishment of private stations. The impetus for this change came from political pressure brought on by opposition political parties that wanted a piece of the airwaves. Candidates running for local elections pledged to build municipal radio stations. Eventually, opposition candidates won the mayoral races in Greece's three largest cities and the breakdown of the state broadcasting monopoly was imminent.

The new mayor of Athens insisted that if a legal structure for "free" radio was not created by the end of March 1987, he would build a municipal radio station anyway. On May 31, 1987, municipal station "Athens 98.4 FM" went on the air without a license.

A major problem with the 1987 law, and relevant decrees that followed, was that it did not deal with the issue of the number of frequencies available. Nevertheless, the first nonstate radio station licenses were approved in May 1988, most going to municipalities and publishing companies (Roumeliotis, 1991). However, the Licensing Commission never announced the criteria used in allocating these licenses and did not tie them to specific frequencies.

Following the initial allocation of licenses, which had to be renewed in two years, the government failed to implement legislation regulating private broadcasting. Related laws and decrees were passed, but since no action ever took place, all radio station licenses expired at the end of the initial two-year period. Thus, technically some 1000 radio stations in Greece were operating illegally.

Current Scene

It was not until May 2001 that the first "permanent" radio station licenses were allocated for the Athens area. This license approval process is to continue for the rest of the country. However, given its history, Greek radio likely will not stabilize for some time to come. The radio environment in Greece, despite some maturation that forced many stations to go out of business, remains in a state of anarchy. In addition to hundreds

of illegal stations, there are stations that never even requested licenses and others that hold more than one frequency, while most do not pay the relevant taxes as required by the broadcast laws (Zaharopoulos, 1993).

State radio broadcasting has dramatically diminished in importance as its audiences have dwindled. Nevertheless, ERA still has 19 local and regional stations on AM, two AM relay stations, and 40 FM transmitters throughout the country. The ERA networks have also undergone certain changes. In 2002 the First Program was renamed NET Radio—NET (New Hellenic Television) being the name of Greek television's second channel, which has a serious orientation. The Second Program (ERA-2) carries more popular music and a few magazine and public affairs programs. One of the Second Program's frequencies in Athens was used to create ERA's fifth domestic service called "Kosmos" radio in 2002, carrying primarily world music. ERA-4 became ERA Sport, carrying mostly sports programming.

Municipal stations have also diminished in importance. Many have closed down, as their audiences were won over by commercial stations, and as cities could no longer afford to subsidize municipal radio.

Private stations built by former pirates have generally not succeeded either. Many of them either went out of business, were sold to larger corporations, or still broadcast as "mom and pop" operations. The real winners in the Greek radio scene have been the large media corporations or other industrial companies with their own stations. Most Greek industrialists who went into broadcasting did so in order to use their media voices to gain government contracts for their other businesses. Thus, even if most of these stations today lose money, their owners still view them as valuable sources of revenue.

Despite the trend toward program specialization resulting from a great number of stations, the two most popular stations in Athens (Sky, Antenna) feature variety formats with emphasis on news, political talk, and music entertainment. Another successful station is Flash, which is a news and information station. Generally, on the Greek airwaves today one can find any radio format imaginable. At the same time, public service broadcasting struggles to survive, while municipal public service broadcasting, with a few exceptions, is nearly dead. The next wave in Greek radio is expected to see foreign conglomerates entering the Greek market by buying existing stations.

THIMIOS ZAHAROPOULOS

Further Reading

Emery, Walter B., "Greece: Anxiety and Instability," in *National and International Systems of Broadcasting: Their History, Operation, and Control,* by Emery, East Lansing: Michigan State University Press, 1969

Keshishoglou, John E., "The Development of Broadcasting in Greece," Master's thesis, University of Iowa, 1962

Roumeliotis, A., *Imaste ston aera* [We're on the Air], Thessaloniki: Paratiritis, 1991

Zaharopoulos, Thimios, and Manny E. Paraschos, *Mass Media in Greece: Power, Politics, and Privatization,* Westport, Connecticut: Praeger, 1993

The Green Hornet

Juvenile Drama Series

Joining a number of American fictional superheroes already entertaining the large radio audience from the late 1930s through the war and into the 1950s, *The Green Hornet* debuted over Detroit station WXYZ on 31 January 1936. The series began simply as *The Hornet* (the descriptive color was added later in order to copyright the title, according to radio historian Jim Harmon). Another brainchild of Detroit station operator George W. Trendle, who also created *The Lone Ranger,* the two half-hour action dramas shared more than classical music themes (for which no copyright fees needed to be paid) and the same creator. In this case, the famous sound of a buzzing hornet was made by a musical instrument called the theremin, while the music was Rimsky-Korsakov's "The Flight of the Bumblebee."

Russo (2001) reports that the first 260 episodes of the series lacked individual titles (they were simply numbered), but those broadcast after 9 August 1938 carried episode names as well. Most if not all of the early scripts (perhaps the first five years) were written by Fran Striker (who also authored *The Lone Ranger*), but they increasingly became a WXYZ team effort for the remainder of the 16-year run. At different times the half-hour drama appeared weekly or twice-weekly.

The protagonist was Britt Reid (also the Green Hornet), who served as a wealthy young newspaper publisher of *The Daily Sentinel* during the day and transformed into evil's arch enemy after sunset. The Green Hornet's mission, according to the opening narration, was to protect us (the law-abiding American citizen) from those "who sought to destroy our way of life." If one listened carefully, one of the series' conceits was made clear—the familial connection of the Green Hornet with his great uncle, the Lone Ranger. References to the earlier legendary figure were abundant. Young Reid was seen as carrying on the family tradition of fighting for justice and the American way. Against the backdrop of an uncertain world, the Green Hornet reassured listeners that the forces of good would always triumph over the forces of darkness. Only three charac-ters knew that Reid was also the Hornet—his father (who appeared rarely), his secretary (who never lets on until late in the series), and Kato.

Kato served as the Green Hornet's faithful valet and partner in crime fighting. Kato also drove the Hornet's famous high-speed car, Black Beauty, during countless breathtaking chases in pursuit of the bad guys. A famous radio legend has it that Kato, who had been described for five years as Japanese, became a Filipino overnight after the 1941 Pearl Harbor attack. Harmon and other sources say, however, that Kato had been described as a Filipino of Japanese ancestry well before the war began. The role partially reflected a continuing American fascination with things oriental.

Unlike most crime fighters, the Green Hornet did not use lethal weaponry; his gun fired a knockout gas instead of bullets. And in contrast with most other radio superheroes, the Green Hornet often assumed a bad guy persona in order to capture criminals, and this frequently confused law enforcement officials, richly adding to the plot line. He and Kato would always escape the crime scene just before law enforcement officers (and reporters from Reid's own paper) arrived. The final scene would usually feature a newspaper boy hawking the latest headlines of the Hornet's ventures as featured in *The Daily Sentinel*, noting that the Hornet was "still at large" and being sought by police. They never did catch him.

Like other superhero programs of the day, *The Green Hornet* adventure series had its genesis in the pulp detective novels of the 1920s, and the characters also appeared in comic books during and well after the radio broadcasts. The series was resurrected for one season on ABC television in the mid-1960s, riding on the coattails of the tremendously popular *Batman* series.

MICHAEL C. KEITH AND CHRISTOPHER H. STERLING

See also Lone Ranger; Striker, Fran; WXYZ

Cast

Britt Reid (The Green Hornet)	Al Hodge (to 1943); Donovan Faust (1943); Bob Hall (1944–51); Jack McCarthy (1951–52)
Kato	Tokutaro Hayashi, Rollon Parker, Michael Tolan
Lenore Casey Case	Leonore Allman
Michael Axford	Jim Irwin (to 1938), Gil Shea
Ed Lowery	Jack Petruzzi
Dan Reid	John Todd
Newsboy	Rollon Parker

Announcers

Charles Woods, Mike Wallace, Fielden Farrington, Bob Hite, Hal Neal

Director

James Jewell

Writer

Fran Striker and several others

Programming History

WXYZ, Detroit	January 1936–April 1938
Mutual	April 1938–November 1939
Blue Network/ABC	November 1939–December 1952
ABC (Television)	September 1966–July 1967

Further Reading

Bickel, Mary, *George W. Trendle*, New York: Exposition, 1973

Harmon, Jim, "From the Studios of WXYZ-III (*The Green Hornet*)," in *The Great Radio Heroes*, Garden City, New York: Doubleday, 1967; revised edition, Jefferson, North Carolina: McFarland, 2001

Osgood, Dick, *WYXIE Wonderland: An Unauthorized 50-Year Diary of WXYZ Detroit*, Bowling Green, Ohio: Bowling Green University Popular Press, 1981

Russo, Alexander, "A Dark(ened) Figure on the Airwaves: Race, Nation, and *The Green Hornet*," in *Radio Reader: Essays in the Cultural History of Radio*, edited by Michele Hilmes and Jason Loviglio, New York: Routledge, 2001

Striker, Fran, Jr., *His Typewriter Grew Spurs: A Biography of Fran Striker—Writer*, Lansdale, Pennsylvania: Questco, 1983

Van Hise, James, *The Green Hornet Book*, Las Vegas, Nevada: Pioneer, 1989

Greenwald, James L. 1927–

U.S. Radio Marketing Executive

James L. Greenwald was one of the most important leaders of the station representative business. He was also an early proponent of the commercial value of FM radio.

Early Career

Greenwald began his career as a songwriter. In 1955 he determined that it might be more profitable to sell "air." Thus began a career in the national media sales business that spanned 41 years at the Katz Agency, Katz Communications, and Katz Media Corporation, where he served as chairman and chief executive officer until 1995. When Greenwald joined Katz Radio as a salesman, the firm represented only 25 stations. When he retired, the firm represented over 2,500 stations.

He was named assistant manager of the radio division in 1963 and president in 1970. With a company that by then had 65 clients, he began building an organization that launched many innovative sales and marketing concepts. Greenwald was among the first national radio sales executives to foresee the emergence of FM radio. In a speech before the West Virginia Broadcasters Association, he said: "The days of FM stations being looked upon as supplements to AM stations are over. FM is radio."

In 1972 one of his first major steps as president of Katz Radio was to begin selling FM radio audience. Until then, most FM stations, if they were sold to national advertisers at all, were coupled with sister AM stations. Nearly all FM stations, except those that programmed classical music, simulcast programming with their AM counterparts, and Katz Radio was particularly steeped in the history of selling large AM stations only.

Greenwald visited with the owners of the major Katz AM stations that also had FM stations and first convinced them to sell their fledgling FM stations in combination with their AM stations. In many instances the additional audience, which was essentially sold for the same price as the AM-only audience, resulted in higher rates and larger shares of budgets for the AM station. The Katz clients responded favorably. When the Federal Communications Commission (FCC) in 1965 passed the rule limiting simulcasting to 50 percent of the program day, Greenwald formed an in-house programming consulting unit within the Radio Division that urged the owners of FM stations to aggressively program their FM properties independently. Greenwald foresaw a national sales market rapidly developing that was willing to spend large sums to reach the emerging FM audience. By 1976, national sales on Katz-represented FM stations had grown to represent over 20 percent of the company's total volume. By 1980 it had eclipsed 35 percent, and by 1990, 70 percent.

Greenwald was an early believer in packaging audiences for advertisers. He recognized that with the represented FM stations emerging with strong audience, there was an opportunity to package stations for a larger share of market dollars. He created a concept called the Katz AID Plan, which provided an advertiser a substantial discount based on the share of budget placed exclusively on the Katz-represented stations.

During the early 1970s, the only network selling of national radio was being done by the traditional wired networks. Greenwald, having expanded the list of Katz Radio–represented stations to over 200, developed the non-wired radio network and formally organized the Katz Radio Network. This sales unit combined the Katz-represented stations on a customized basis to fit a particular advertiser's audience and demographic needs. Furthermore, the advertiser was offered the convenience of one invoice and could thus avoid dealing with hundreds of stations individually. It was part of Greenwald's marketing plan to make radio advertising easier to plan and buy.

Radio audience research was another Katz Radio innovation fostered by Greenwald. He strongly believed that radio should not sell against newspapers and other media but rather with them. Under his leadership, the Katz Radio Probe Research System was developed in 1975 using early computer technology; the system demonstrated how a radio schedule could enhance the reach of a newspaper buy by utilizing a relatively small portion of the newspaper budget. Later, the same concept was enhanced to include the combination of radio with television and outdoor, and the name Katz Probe Media Mix was created.

By the end of the 1970s, Greenwald had been promoted to executive vice president of the corporate entity, Katz Communications. His responsibilities were expanded to include the Katz Television representation. However, he never removed himself from close contact with and oversight of the radio division.

In 1976 Katz Radio, with Greenwald's support, took the bold step of representing more than one station in a single market when it simultaneously served WRNG and WGST in Atlanta and later WAIT-AM and WLAK-FM in Chicago. Greenwald reasoned that two weak stations had a better chance of getting larger budgets if they combined their sales pitch. The concept of dual representation quickly spread within Katz markets, because even though exclusive representation was considered desirable by many owners, the huge advantages of the research, network sales operations, and the expansion of sales offices into regional territories was compelling to the stations. They understood that having a representative who could partner them with compatible stations would allow them to gain larger shares of budgets. This concept was the beginning of the consolidation of the representation industry and later of the radio industry in general.

Greenwald was instrumental in establishing an employee stock ownership plan at Katz that made the purchase of the firm from the Katz family possible, and Katz became the first employee-owned station representative firm in the industry.

The next giant step for Katz under Greenwald's leadership came in 1984, when Katz Communications purchased Christal Radio Sales from Robert Duffy. Katz-owned representation companies now competed directly against one another in nearly all of the top 100 radio markets. Katz also purchased the Jack Masla Company, Eastman Radio, Blair Radio, RKO Radio Sales, and Metro Radio Sales. These purchases set in motion the total consolidation of the radio representation industry. By 1992 there were only three major national representatives, Katz Radio Group, Interep, and Columbia Broadcasting System (CBS) Radio Spot Sales. CBS Radio Spot Sales was sold to Interep in 1995, leaving just two.

From his position as executive vice president of Katz Communications, Greenwald went on to become chairman, president, and chief executive officer of the newly named Katz Media Corporation. During Greenwald's tenure as the leader of the company, Katz entered broadcast ownership for the first time in its 100-year history when it purchased Park City Communications from Richard Ferguson in 1982. Katz sold the radio group in 1986. During his leadership of Katz Media Corporation, Greenwald expanded Katz Television into dual-ownership representation within a single market; purchased Seltel, a competing television representation firm; and instituted many of the innovative selling and research strategies created during his tenure at Katz Radio. Greenwald retired in 1995 and remains chairman emeritus of Katz Media Corporation.

GORDON H. HASTINGS

See also FM Radio; Station Rep Firms

James L. Greenwald. Born in New York City, 2 April 1927. Began career as songwriter; salesman, Katz Communications and Katz Media Corporation, 1955, assistant manager, radio division, 1963; formally organized Katz Radio Network;

executive vice president of corporate entity and assumed responsibility for Katz Television representation, 1970–75; president, 1975–82; chairman of the board of directors and chief executive officer, 1975–95; sold radio group of Katz Media Corporation, 1986; director, Granite Broadcasting Company, Paxson Communications Corporation and the Young Adult Institute; honorary trustee, Foundation of American Women in Radio and Television; past president, International Radio and Television Foundation; past president, Station Representatives Association; chairman emeritus, Katz Media Corporation, 1995–; director, Source Media, 1996–.

Ground Wave

A ground wave is a radio signal that propagates along the surface of the earth. It is one of two basic types of AM signal propagation, the other being the sky wave, which travels skyward from the transmitting antenna and then may be refracted back toward earth by the atmosphere. The behavioral characteristics of both types of wave are important both to frequency allocation and to the nature of various radio services.

The term *ground wave* includes three different types of waves: surface waves, direct waves, and ground-reflected waves. Surface waves travel directly along the surface of the earth, following terrain features such as hills and valleys. Direct waves follow a "line-of-sight" path directly from the transmitting antenna to the receiving antenna, and ground-reflected waves actually bounce off the surface of the earth.

Both ground-wave and sky-wave signals can be used to provide radio communication. The distance each type of signal can travel is determined by a number of factors, among them frequency, power, atmospheric conditions, time, and—in the case of ground waves—terrain and soil conductivity.

The principal determinant of which type of signal provides the communication is transmitting frequency. At very low frequencies (below 300 kilohertz), signal propagation takes place mostly by surface ground waves, which at these frequencies may provide a reliable signal for several thousand miles. At medium frequencies (300 kilohertz to 3 megahertz), surface ground waves may propagate hundreds of miles, and sky waves may travel thousands of miles. At high frequencies (3 to 30 megahertz), sky waves provide the principal means of signal propagation, and they may provide usable signals for many thousands of miles. At very high frequencies (30 megahertz and above), propagation is largely by ground-reflected and direct ground waves, although at these frequencies the waves generally travel less than 100 miles.

The standard broadcast (AM) band (535–1705 kilohertz) is a medium-frequency band and is thus characterized by both ground-wave and sky-wave signals. During the day, AM propagation takes place mainly by ground-wave signals; sky-wave signals generally travel through the atmosphere and into space. However, during night-time hours, changes in a portion of the ionosphere known as the Kennelly–Heavyside layer cause the sky waves to be reflected back toward the earth's surface. These refracted sky waves can then provide usable service over many hundreds—or even thousands—of miles, although sky waves are generally more susceptible to interference and fading than are ground waves. A certain amount of AM sky-wave propagation also takes place in the hours immediately before sunset and immediately after sunrise. In contrast, propagation in the FM band (88–108 megahertz) takes place by line-of-sight or near–line-of-sight direct and ground-reflected ground waves only.

The complexities of signal propagation in the AM band have presented significant challenges for the allocation of frequencies since the inception of broadcasting in the 1920s. Primary among these, of course, is the presence of both ground-wave and sky-wave signals at various times of the day. The Federal Communications Commission (FCC) has established three service area categories for AM stations: (1) primary service area, in which the ground-wave signal is not subject to objectionable interference or fading; (2) intermittent service area, in which the ground-wave signal may be subject to some interference or fading; and (3) secondary service area, in which the sky-wave signal is not subject to objectionable interference.

Another significant factor is that AM signals—both ground-wave and sky-wave signals—can cause objectionable interference over a much wider area than that for which they can provide usable service. For example, although a given station may not be able to provide a listenable signal more than 50 miles from its transmitter, that station's signal can still create objectionable interference to other stations on the same frequency over a much wider area. Signals in the FM band do not create this type of wide-area interference, and thus FM stations can be placed geographically closer together on the same frequency.

Perhaps the best illustration of the problems of allocation in the AM band is the dispute over clear channel stations, which began in the 1930s and was not completely resolved until 1980. Clear channel stations were originally created to provide wide-area service to rural audiences through their vast secondary service areas; other stations that were assigned to clear channel frequencies had to sign off at sunset in order to avoid interfering with the dominant stations' sky-wave signals. Clear channel stations sought to maintain and enhance their status by seeking power increases and the maintenance of their clear night-time frequencies. Other classes of stations called for the "breakdown" of clear channels by adding more stations to clear frequencies and by allowing daytime-only stations to broadcast full-time. At the heart of this dispute was an engineering argument over the best way to provide radio service to isolated areas: Clear channel stations maintained that the only way to provide effective rural service was by increasing the power of clear channel stations so that their secondary service areas would expand. On the other hand, other classes of stations called for more stations, located in close geographic proximity to the isolated rural areas, to provide ground-wave service to those areas.

Ultimately, the FCC decided to assign additional full-time stations to use clear channel frequencies, but the FCC protected a substantial portion of the clear channel stations' existing secondary service areas (a roughly 700- to 750-mile radius). Only clear channel stations (now called "Class A" stations) receive protection from interference in their secondary service areas.

The characteristics of ground waves and sky waves are in many cases the determining factors in the purposes for which radio services at various frequencies are used. AM broadcast service can provide reliable ground-wave communication at all times of the day and somewhat less reliable sky-wave communication at night. FM broadcast service can provide reliable line-of-sight service over shorter distances, with less blanketing of interference. Broadcasters in high-frequency bands (shortwave) can provide international sky-wave service.

JAMES C. FOUST

See also AM Radio; Antenna; Clear Channel Stations; DXers/DXing; Federal Communications Commission; FM Radio; Frequency Allocation; Shortwave Radio

Further Reading

Federal Communications Commission, *Radio Broadcast Services,* part 73, 47 CFR 73 (2001)
Foust, James C., *Big Voices of the Air: The Battle over Clear Channel Radio,* Ames: Iowa State University Press, 2000
Jordan, Edward C., editor, *Reference Data for Engineers: Radio, Electronics, Computer, and Communications,* Indianapolis, Indiana: Sams, 1985; 7th edition, 1999
Orr, William Ittner, *Radio Handbook,* Indianapolis, Indiana: Sams, 1972; 23rd edition, 1992
Smith, Albert A., Jr., *Radio Frequency Principles and Applications: The Generation, Propagation, and Reception of Signals and Noise,* New York: IEEE Press, 1998

Group W

Westinghouse Radio Stations

Westinghouse Broadcasting (Group W after 1963) remained active in radio broadcasting longer than any other company—beginning with the initial airing of Pittsburgh's KDKA in November 1920 and lasting into the late 1990s. Thanks to constant retelling of the KDKA story, the earliest years of Westinghouse Broadcasting are well known, but throughout the history of broadcasting the company was an important owner of both radio and later television stations, eventually merging into the once-independent Columbia Broadcasting System (CBS) network.

Getting into Radio (to 1931)

A Westinghouse engineer, Frank Conrad, had been experimenting with wireless for a number of years, and in 1919–20 he operated amateur station 8XK, playing recorded music one or two nights a week. A September 1920 newspaper advertisement by a local department store seeking to sell receivers to people who wanted to hear Conrad's broadcasts caught the eye of Harry Phillips Davis, a Westinghouse vice president in charge of radio work. Davis perceived that making receivers for a possible new radio service could be the answer to West-inghouse's predicament. He urged Conrad to develop his hobby station into something bigger, and the inauguration of station KDKA on 2 November 1920 was the result.

The success of that initial operation led Davis to the development of a second station, WJZ, at the company meter plant in Newark, New Jersey, in September 1921 (the station was sold to the Radio Corporation of America [RCA] a year later). In the same month, station WBZ took to the air in Springfield, Massachusetts, followed by station KYW in Chicago in December and by WBZA in Boston in 1924. These pioneering outlets made Westinghouse an important early station operator that pioneered many types of program service.

Westinghouse stations were initially located at the factories, which meant that early performers had to learn to entertain in a room filled with electronic equipment, with only an engineer as their audience. Ultimately, the studios were moved to more aesthetically pleasing locations, such as hotels or office buildings.

Experimenting with the potential of shortwave technology, Westinghouse placed KFKX on the air in Hastings, Nebraska, in 1923 to make KDKA's signal more widely available. Another experimental shortwave station, W8XK, was established in Pittsburgh and was soon broadcasting 18 hours per day including a "far north" service to the Arctic. It was joined in 1930 by yet a third station, W1XAZ, in East Springfield, Massachusetts. By the late 1920s, Westinghouse was also pioneering in television research.

Evans Years (1931–55)

On Davis' death in 1931, Walter Evans became the next Westinghouse radio chief. He had joined the company as chief of operations in 1929 and would serve for more than two decades. Evans took a different approach to managing the company's stations and in 1933 signed a contract with the National Broadcasting Company (NBC) network to manage them all, including provision of all local and national programs selling advertising time. The agreement lasted until 1940, when it ended as part of the Federal Communications Commission's (FCC) investigation of national networks, and Westinghouse took over day-to-day operations itself.

Westinghouse operations expanded in the prewar years. Station KYW was moved from Chicago to Philadelphia in late 1934 as part of a deal with the FCC to provide service in underserved areas. Two years later, Westinghouse purchased its first station (it had built its previous operations), WOWO in Fort Wayne, Indiana, along with WGL in the same city, both of which were licensed to a new entity, Westinghouse Radio Stations (WRS). In 1940, WRS took control of all Westinghouse stations, separating the broadcast operations from other company functions.

Westinghouse shortwave (international) stations consolidated operations in Pittsburgh (8XS, which became WPIT in 1939 but closed a year later) and Boston (WIXT, which became WBOS). Westinghouse's international broadcasting was a multilingual operation that by late 1941 was providing 12 hours of programming a day: 5 hours to Europe and 7 to Latin America. Government programs expanded that total to 16 hours just a few months later. Early in 1942, the Boston station was taken over by the government's Office of War Information.

Westinghouse was an early player in FM radio: by 1943 the company owned five FM stations in cities where it also operated AM outlets. Original programming was provided on those FM facilities, but they had all reverted to simulcasting by the end of 1948. That same year, Westinghouse placed its first television station, WBZ-TV in Boston, on the air. As the operation continued to grow, the broadcast subsidiary's headquarters moved several times, finally ending up in New York in 1953, when it became known as Westinghouse Broadcasting Company (WBC), in part because of the addition of television.

McGannon Years (1955–81)

The man who served longest as head of the Westinghouse stations was Donald H. McGannon, who ran the operation from 1955 (after a few interim leaders) until 1981. McGannon soon earned a reputation as a man concerned about public service and program quality as well as profit. He brought Westinghouse back to Chicago with the 1956 purchase of WIND for $5.3 million—at that point the highest price paid for a station. He also began a Washington news bureau to serve his stations in 1957. That same year WBC initiated an arts and classical music format from 4 P.M. to midnight on the four FM stations it still owned. But FM was then a weak service, and by 1970 Westinghouse was down to just two FM outlets, one in Boston and the other in Philadelphia, both programming classical music and suffering from a lack of promotion or advertising.

McGannon faced three serious policy crises early in his tenure. The first concerned Philadelphia's KYW AM and TV. Under at least an implied threat of losing NBC network affiliations for its Philadelphia and Boston television stations, Westinghouse agreed to "trade" its Philadelphia radio and television stations (KYW) for NBC outlets in smaller Cleveland in 1955. Over the next decade various business, FCC, and Congressional investigations brought to light the network threats that had created the deal, and it was undone in 1965, with the KYW stations returning to Philadelphia.

Two other problems briefly threatened Westinghouse licenses. Its Cleveland and Boston radio stations were implicated in the national payola scandal of the late 1950s, and several disc jockeys were fired. Their activities figured in widely covered Congressional investigations. In 1961 antitrust price-fixing convictions against Westinghouse threatened the company's ownership of broadcast stations. Because of the independence of WBC from the parent manufacturing company, its licenses were renewed after several months of threatened FCC hearings. In mid-1963, WBC was renamed Group W.

Because the Westinghouse stations were situated in major cities, they produced sufficient revenue to allow for further acquisitions. In 1962, for example, Westinghouse shut down WBZA in Springfield (which had mainly been simulcasting the much more successful WBZ in Boston for years), making it possible to buy another station, KFWB in Los Angeles and by 1965 was offering an all-news format on WINS in New York. By the early 1960s, Westinghouse had begun using the term "Group W" to make its owned radio and TV stations more memorable.

A contemporary move was the successful implementation of all-news operations at three major-market radio stations. The conversion began with station WINS in New York, purchased in 1962, which suffered from a weak rock music format. Likewise, KYW had returned to Philadelphia to follow a weak decade of NBC station operation in its place. Westinghouse stations became known for a commitment to news and public affairs (Group W had operated its own news bureau in Washington, D.C., since 1957). All-news operations began KYW and WINS in 1965. KFWB in Los Angeles was purchased in 1966, and two years later it was also converted from rock music to an all-news format. Although not first with the format, Group W was the first to make it a lasting success in major markets.

Only toward the end of McGannon's tenure as Group W chief did the company begin to reconsider FM radio, which by 1980 was dominating national radio listening for the first time. That year Group W purchased two major-market Texas FM stations, KOAX (FM) in Dallas, which soon was renamed KQZY (FM), and KODA-FM in Houston. But although there were adjustments in station lineup, Group W's overall size and contribution to the Westinghouse bottom line (roughly 15 to 20 percent of annual revenues) remained remarkably stable.

Final Decades (1981–2000)

On McGannon's retirement, Daniel L. Ritchie became Group W's leader and served into the late 1980s, to be succeeded in turn by Burton B. Staniar. The expansion into FM continued with the purchase of KJQY (FM) in San Diego and KOSI (FM) in Denver in 1981. A San Antonio FM station, KQXT, was purchased in 1984; KMEO AM and FM in Phoenix were bought a year later; and WNEW-FM in New York was added to the Group W stable in 1989. Although some outlets were

spun off, the overall effect was to slowly grow the company—and to increase the proportion of FM to AM stations.

Group W switched AM outlets in Chicago as well. In the aftermath of Martin Luther King, Jr.'s 1968 assassination, WIND suspended popular on-air figure Howard Miller, whose statements about race and the police were becoming more strident. A breach of contract suit was settled out of court, but the station lost audience steadily for years thereafter and was sold in 1985 to a Spanish language broadcaster. Three years later, Group W purchased WMAQ, the one-time NBC outlet, thus resuming a role in Chicago radio.

In the late 1990s, Group W underwent a series of mergers and acquisitions that changed the face of the company and eventually caused it to disappear into other entities. The process began with the 1995 purchase by Westinghouse Electric of the weakened CBS network from Lawrence Tisch for $5.4 billion dollars. The deal needed and received several cross-ownership waivers from the FCC, as the radio and television stations of Group W and the network were located in many of the same cities. The new entity controlled 39 radio stations, worth $1.4–1.7 billion, and became the largest group owner in terms of revenues. In buying CBS, Westinghouse purchased a radio division that provided two services Westinghouse had been paying other companies to provide—network news and national sales representation.

In late 1996 CBS/Westinghouse merged with Infinity Broadcasting, combining under the CBS Radio Group name 83 stations, for a time the largest single ownership block in the industry. Over the next couple of years, Westinghouse sold off its traditional manufacturing base (power systems, which had been losing money, and electronic and environmental systems) and its original name to concentrate on the development of its radio and television holdings under the CBS name. The Group W trademark was briefly retained to identify technical support for television distribution and sports marketing, and as owner of record of six AM radio stations, the original KDKA (Pittsburgh), WBZ (Boston), and KYW (Philadelphia), as well as the later-acquired outlets WNEW (New York), WMAQ (Chicago), and KTWV (Houston).

By the turn of the 21st century, however, the radio group was operating under the Infinity name and the one-time Westinghouse (or Group W) stations were merely one integrated part of what had become the country's third largest group owner of radio stations.

MARY E. BEADLE, DONNA L. HALPER,
AND CHRISTOPHER H. STERLING

See also Columbia Broadcasting System; Conrad, Frank; FM radio; KDKA; KYW; McGannon, Don; National Broadcasting Company; Network Monopoly Probe; Radio Corporation of America; Westinghouse; WBZ; WINS; WMAQ; WNEW

Further Reading

Broadcasting Yearbook (1935)

Davis, H.P., "The Early History of Broadcasting in the United States," in *The Radio Industry: The Story of Its Development*, Chicago and New York: Shaw, and London: Shaw Limited, 1928; reprint, New York: Arno Press, 1974

Douglas, George H., *The Early Days of Radio Broadcasting*, Jefferson, North Carolina: McFarland, 1987

Westinghouse Electric Corporation, *The History of Radio Broadcasting and KDKA*, East Pittsburgh, Pennsylvania: Westinghouse Electric Corporation, 1940

Gunsmoke

Western Series

Gunsmoke, a western on the CBS Radio Network, was introduced at a time when most radio drama was disappearing. It not only lasted nearly a decade but also spawned television's longest-running drama series. *Gunsmoke*'s devoted fans, who have praised its historical accuracy and realism, would likely attribute the program's longevity to its brilliant writing and acting. Others would say, "it's just a good story."

The stories on *Gunsmoke* provided the groundwork for the so-called adult western, a dominant TV genre for nearly 20 years. There were many radio westerns before *Gunsmoke*, particularly as daytime serials or evening programs, but most of them, such as the even longer-running *Lone Ranger*, were aimed primarily at a young audience.

Origins

Gunsmoke was the result of a collaboration between several writers and producers (all "urban oriented," according to William N. Robeson), including John Meston and producer Norman Macdonnell, who worked together at CBS from 1947 on *Escape* and other radio dramas. Robeson, who created *Escape*, admitted that that program was "pretty darned close to *Suspense*." Macdonnell was an assistant director with Robeson, and William Conrad was the announcer on *Escape*. With writer John Meston, several experimental western stories were tried between 1947 and 1950. In 1949 the team also produced two pilots of what they conceived of as an "adult western" with a hero named Mark Dillon.

The first *Gunsmoke* program came about when another program was abruptly canceled. Norman Macdonnell and writer Walter Brown Newman used elements from several of Macdonnell's earlier western stories to create "Billy the Kid," the first episode, which ran on 26 April 1952. Although unforeseen at the time, after "Billy the Kid" there would be 412 more episodes of *Gunsmoke*; the final show aired 18 June 1961.

Raymond Burr and Robert Stack (both of whom later became famous TV actors) were considered for the lead role, but at the last moment the job went to William Conrad. While he was the announcer on *Escape* and a veteran radio actor (he would also later star in several TV series), Conrad had just finished the movie *The Killers* and was considered a "heavy." In the pilot, the hero had to narrate much of the story in voice-over. Chester, his assistant, appeared in the first episode, but the part quickly grew larger, and the important characters of Doc and Miss Kitty evolved. From the first show to the last, *Gunsmoke* kept its cast of William Conrad as Marshal Matt Dillon, Georgia Ellis as Kitty Russell, Howard McNear as Doctor Charles Adams, and Parley Baer as Chester Wesley Proudfoot. While the relations between the four characters held the program together, it was the deep, booming voice of Conrad that provided the program's unmistakable signature. In addition to these regulars, veteran radio actors appeared in episode after episode.

Among fans of radio drama, *Gunsmoke* is considered the best western ever made. The series was marked by high-caliber writing and used only a score of authors during its entire run. Meston wrote 183 stories, and there were three years in which he wrote more than 45 episodes per year. His scripts often concerned the difficulties of frontier life, particularly for women.

After a light Christmastime show in 1952, Meston wrote "The Cabin," broadcast on 27 December, to assure the audience that *Gunsmoke* had not "gone soft." The episode concerned a young woman named Belle who had been raped. By the end of the program the marshal has killed the men who raped her (though this is not acted out explicitly) and is asked by the woman if he is married. "Too chancy," he replies. Matt tells Belle, "Don't let all this make you bitter, there are lot of good men in the world," and she replies, "So they say." As he heads back to Dodge, Matt ends by noting that the blizzard

Gunsmoke soundman Bill James beside William Conrad, who plays Marshall Dillon
Courtesy CBS Photo Archive

was gone but it was still bitter cold, "like riding through a vast tomb."

Most of the episodes end violently and tragically, usually with Matt being forced to kill someone. Meston said that violence was rampant in the Old West; there was no medicine, no sanitation, no heat, just sand, little water, and not much food. Meston's view may not be entirely accurate as history, but his shows appealed to an audience raised on the myths of the American West. Meston's scripts were also marked by their mostly factual treatment of Native Americans (called Indians in the shows). The stories often noted that Indians intermarried with whites, suffered as the buffalo were wiped out, were forced into virtual concentration camps, and that federal policy toward the Native Americans was to wipe them out. In "Sunday Supplement" (24 June 1956), a citizen of Dodge says to Matt, "Marshal, you're not standing up for a redskin are you?" Of course he was.

The 19 July 1954 episode, "The Queue," by Meston, is about a Chinese man who has come to Dodge. When others ridicule him and make nasty remarks about foreigners, Matt says, "Except for the Indians we're all foreigners here." Matt learns that the man speaks good English but feigns a Chinese accent because he knows it is expected of him. Kitty also talks of "darn few jobs that a woman couldn't do [she pauses] anywhere." Later the Chinese man is murdered (choked to death by his own pig tail, which is cut off) and robbed of a small box he always carries. Matt tracks down and kills the robbers. The box contains a faded paper indicating that the Chinese man had been honored for his service in the Army of the Potomac in the Civil War, and thus was awarded citizenship. Marshal Dillon suggests that the man be buried at a nearby army fort, whereas they just "plant" the two robbers he has just killed in "Boot Hill." The story was also produced as a first-season TV episode on 3 December 1955.

Although Meston was the principal writer, there were also many scripts by Les Crutchfield and Katherine Hite (Hite was one of the first women writers to work regularly on a western). The program frequently used three technicians creating sound effects. The sound patterns and music were often used to carry a program when the dialogue was sparse. Macdonnell noted that people who are working just don't talk all the time.

Within two years of its start, the program was a big hit for radio, which was losing programs, stars, and especially advertisers to television. *Gunsmoke* was sponsored by a cigarette company, and soon several other radio westerns appeared on the air. By 1957, however, most weeks' shows had no sponsor but only public service announcements and promotions for other CBS programs, and Meston was spending most of his time writing for the television version. A number of the early radio episodes were adapted for the TV program, which began on 10 September 1955. When it finished its run 20 years later, the TV series boasted 233 half-hour and 402 one-hour episodes. Later four made-for-TV movies were also produced. The final radio broadcast—a repeat—aired in June 1961 as the CBS announcer said matter-of-factly, "This concludes the series of *Gunsmoke*."

LAWRENCE W. LICHTY

See also Conrad, William; Westerns

Cast

Marshal Matt Dillon	William Conrad
Miss Kitty	Georgia Ellis
Doctor Charles Adams	Howard McNear
Chester Wesley Proudfoot	Parley Baer

Producer

Norman Macdonnell

Programming History

CBS   1952–61

Further Reading

Barabas, SuzAnne, and Gabor Barabas, *Gunsmoke: A Complete History and Analysis of the Legendary Broadcast Series with a Comprehensive Episode-by-Episode Guide to Both the Radio and Television Programs*, Jefferson, North Carolina: McFarland, 1990

Hickman, John, producer, "The Story of Gunsmoke," Washington, D.C.: WAMU, 1976 (an audio history with interviews and excerpts of about 5 hours which is available for purchase in a number of old radio and cassette catalogs)

H

Ham Radio

Hobbyist or Amateur Radio Operators

The Federal Communications Commission (FCC) defines amateur radio operators as "qualified persons of any age who are interested in radio technique solely with a personal aim and without pecuniary interest." Amateur operators are an international phenomenon. Since 1925, the International Amateur Radio Union (IARU) has championed their cause with governments around the world. In the United States, an early amateur radio pioneer named Hiram Percy Maxim organized the American Radio Relay League (ARRL) in 1914. The ARRL is a member of the IARU. There are currently more than 700,000 licensed amateur stations in the United States alone.

Since their beginnings in the early 1900s, amateur radio enthusiasts have also been known as "ham" radio operators. Historians are unsure of how the name came into common usage, but there is strong evidence that the term was bestowed by commercial telegraphers, who considered amateurs to be "ham-fisted"—that is, they sent Morse code very poorly. For many years, operators were also known in official circles as "Citizen Operators"—not to be confused with today's Citizens Band (CB) radio operators.

Although he clearly had commercial interests in mind, the first amateur radio operator was arguably Guglielmo Marconi himself. Until about 1908, all radio experimenters hoped to capitalize on wireless communication. When Marconi successfully sent a wireless signal across the Atlantic in 1901, he used equipment of the same type used by radio hobbyists.

Origins

The history of amateur radio is in essence the history of all wireless communication. Amateurs developed many of the processes key to electronic communication and refined others. In 1909, when the first radio clubs were formed, radio frequency energy was generated by allowing a spark to jump across a wide gap. The frequencies used at the time were in the range of today's commercial AM broadcast band and below (300–6,000 meters).

With the onset of U.S. participation in World War I in early 1917, amateurs in the United States were ordered to dismantle their facilities for the duration of the conflict. Technical developments during the war included the replacement of spark-gap transmission with continuous-wave (vacuum-tube powered) transmission. The bandwidth of such emissions is much narrower, is not as prone to interference, and allows clear voice operation. The celebrated November 1920 broadcasts of pioneer station KDKA in Pittsburgh, Pennsylvania, began as experimental amateur programs under the call sign 8XK. The radio transmission of the Dempsey–Carpenter boxing match in 1921, another milestone in early radio, was organized by the National Amateur Wireless Association.

During this period, the issue of who controlled the airwaves was very unclear. In 1926 a federal court declared the only existing law, the Radio Act of 1912, to be essentially unenforceable. The Radio Act of 1927 created the Federal Radio Commission and federal statutes using the word *amateur* for the first time. The Communications Act of 1934 (which later created the Federal Communications Commission) continued many of the FRC's policies and precedents, including licensing of amateurs.

All amateur activity was again suspended when the United States entered World War II in late 1941; amateurs were only allowed back on the air on 15 November 1945. Within those four years, wartime research opened up new communication options. Single sideband (SSB)—a mode of voice transmission in which the carrier and one of the duplicate sidebands are suppressed—was described in *QST* magazine in 1948. (*QST*, defined as a signal meaning "Calling All Radio Amateurs," is the official house organ of the ARRL.) The popularity and advantages of SSB transmissions were well established by 1960. While most amateur equipment was still powered by vacuum tubes, transistor technology was beginning to appear in both commercial and self-built equipment.

Amateur radio has always been attractive not only to the general citizenry, but also to the rich and famous. Howard Hughes was a licensed amateur radio operator. Senator Barry Goldwater (K7UGA/K3UIG) tried to become the first ham in the White House. Heads of state include the late King Hussein of Jordan (JY1), who encouraged amateur radio as a means of providing technical education for the citizens in his country. Noted radio broadcaster Jean Shepherd (K2ORS) was a very active amateur radio operator. The son of President Herbert Hoover was eventually elected as the president of the ARRL. Marlon Brando operated on the amateur bands from his South Sea compound for many years. Owen Garriott (W5LFL) became the first amateur to operate on board a space shuttle in 1983.

Licensing

With the pressure on the U.S. government to cut costs, in 1984 the FCC created the Volunteer Examiner Program. Tests for all classes of amateur licenses (which were once handled by the FCC) are now administered by approved volunteer examiner programs. In 1991 the privileged place of Morse code, long a tradition and requirement for an amateur license, finally yielded to the first code-free amateur radio license. The FCC administers six classes of operator license, each authorizing varying levels of privileges. The higher classes still require knowledge of Morse code.

In the United States, amateur call signs once consisted of the letter "W" and a numeral from 1 to 0, followed by two or three alphabetic characters. (The numerals 1 through 9 are used and roughly translate to geographical regions. For example, the ninth call area includes Illinois, Indiana, and Wisconsin. The numeral 0 [zero] is also used for the tenth call area.) These replaced the earliest call signs, which consisted of only the numeral and the following letters—often the operator's initials. Prior to World War II, the United States agreed to begin all call signs with prefix letters assigned by international agreement. By 1953, all possible W call signs had been issued, and the K prefix came into use. Today, prefixes include combinations of the letters W and K, followed by other letters in the alphabet as demand requires. The N prefix is also in use, as well as A.

New Directions

In 1961, through the efforts of a group of amateur operators collectively known as Project OSCAR (Orbiting Satellite Carrying Amateur Radio), thousands of amateur operators around the world listened in on the 50-milliwatt Morse code beacon of OSCAR I as it sent its "HI" message. The relative speed of the code transmitted rudimentary telemetry and told of the condition of the satellite.

The OSCAR satellite rode into space in place of "ballast" on a regularly scheduled rocket launch. Current OSCAR satellites rival early commercial communication satellites (such as Telstar and others) in that they have the capability to relay both voice and data transmissions over half the planet simultaneously. OSCAR satellite experiments in the 1970s served as a prototype for the Global Positioning Satellite Service. Amateurs have also pioneered communication by bouncing signals off of the Earth's moon, off the tails of comets, and via reflection from the aurora borealis. Schoolchildren participate in direct communication with the space shuttle via amateur radio stations.

Morse code, the basis of all early wireless communication, is a very rudimentary form of digital communication. With an abundance of surplus equipment available after World War II, amateur operators adapted teleprinter systems to work via their stations. Later, radioteletype transmissions switched from the five-bit Baudot code to standard ASCII code.

By the early 1980s, with the interest in computers and the availability of components at hobbyist prices, a group of both Canadian and U.S. amateur operators began experimenting with advanced forms of digital communication. Their efforts would eventually lead to the creation of the AX.25 packet protocol—a wireless version of the X.25 protocol that underpinned much of the data communication through the end of the 20th century. Some OSCAR satellites (known as PACSATs or Packet Satellites) are even capable of relaying packet transmissions. Amateurs also experiment with spread-spectrum technologies. This system spreads the information in a transmitted signal over a wide frequency range. While it is not an efficient use of radio spectrum, its attraction is that it can co-exist with narrowband signals using the same frequency range. To narrowband users, the spread spectrum signal appears only as a slight increase in noise level.

The Future

In spite of dire predictions during the 1980s that amateur radio was dying, the number of amateurs in the United States alone by the end of the 1990s stood at 710,000, nearly triple the number of amateurs in 1970. The code-free license, in combination with the popularity of low-cost very-high-frequency (VHF) and UHF portable transceivers and repeater stations, fueled much of the expansion. Growth of the internet, low-cost cellular phone communication, and other new technologies serve as a formidable detractor to future growth, but many amateurs have learned unique ways to marry the two forms of communication. Amateurs have developed shortwave radios and scanners that can be controlled remotely over the worldwide web. Another group provides a real-time experimental navigational service that locates participating amateurs and displays the results on a graphical web interface. Messages move freely from the internet to amateur satellites to amateur packet repeaters. Amateur radio will likely continue to adapt and endure for many years to come.

JIM GRUBBS

See also Armstrong, Edwin Howard; Shepard, John; Shortwave Radio

Further Reading

The ARRL Handbook for Radio Amateurs, Newington, Connecticut: American Radio Relay League, 79th edition, 2002 (updated annually)

Berg, Jerome S., *On the Short Wave, 1923–45: Broadcast Listening in the Pioneer Days of Radio*, Jefferson, North Carolina: McFarland, 1999

Carron, L. Peter, *Morse Code: The Essential Language*, Newington, Connecticut: American Radio Relay League, 1986; 2nd edition, 1991

Davidoff, Martin R., *The Radio Amateur's Satellite Handbook*, Newington, Connecticut: American Radio Relay League, 1998

DeSoto, Clinton, *Two Hundred Meters and Down: The Story of Amateur Radio*, West Hartford, Connecticut: American Radio Relay League, 1936

Douglas, Susan J., *Listening In: Radio and the American Imagination*, New York: Times Books, 1999

Fifty Years of A.R.R.L., Newington, Connecticut: American Radio Relay League, 1965

Grubbs, Jim, *The Digital Novice*, Springfield, Illinois: QSky, 1986

Helms, Harry L., *All about Ham Radio*, San Diego, California: HighText Publications, 1992

Jahnke, Debra, and Katharine A. Fay, editors, *From Spark to Space: A Pictorial Journey Through 75 Years of Amateur Radio*, Newington, Connecticut: American Radio Relay League, 1989

Laster, Clay, *The Beginner's Handbook of Amateur Radio*, Indianapolis, Indiana: Sams, 1979; 4th edition, New York and London: McGraw-Hill, 2000

Harvey, Paul 1918–

U.S. Radio Personality

Six days a week, some 1,300 radio stations across the United States air Paul Harvey's *News and Comment* and *The Rest of the Story* radio programs. Twenty-four million listeners tune in to hear his combination of news and views.

Harvey was born Paul Harvey Aurandt in Tulsa, Oklahoma, in September 1918. Harvey and his sister were raised by his mother after his police officer father was killed in action when the boy was three years old. His interest in radio first emerged when he built his own crystal radio sets as a boy. Harvey was a high school student and champion orator when an English teacher encouraged him to go into broadcasting. Like others enamored of radio, he hung around and did odd jobs at a local station, KVOO-AM in Tulsa, until he was eventually hired. Harvey attended Tulsa University while still a staff announcer at KVOO, but a radio career proved more enticing than an academic degree.

In the mid-1930s and early 1940s Harvey worked at KFBI (Abilene, Kansas), KOMA (Oklahoma City), KXOK (St. Louis), and WKZO (Kalamazoo, Michigan), learning about radio news, management, and programming. KXOK was the most memorable stop, as it was there that Harvey met his wife-to-be, a young student teacher named Lynne Cooper. He proposed to "Angel" (his pet name for Lynne) on their first date, and they married on 4 June 1940. Angel would become an energetic business partner as both producer of Paul Harvey's *News and Comment* and president of Paulynne Productions.

In late 1943 Harvey enlisted in the U.S. Army Air Corps, but he was given an honorable medical discharge just a few months later, after an obstacle course injury ended his military service. Heading back into broadcasting by 1944, Harvey was attracted to Chicago because it was home to several famous broadcasters and was the originating city for many national radio programs. Harvey hoped to move into "major market" broadcasting with his news reporting and radio drama skills. While he was in Chicago, two important events took place. First, he dropped his last name to become the more radio-friendly "Paul Harvey." Second, on the advice of his wife, he no longer did radio plays and concentrated on radio news. He

Paul Harvey
Courtesy of Paul Harvey News

was given a 10 P.M. news slot on WENR-AM and within a year was at the top of the ratings in Chicago.

Depending on which source is used, Harvey was propelled into network broadcasting either by Joseph P. Kennedy or by Harvey's wife, Lynne. One story suggests that the elder Kennedy befriended Harvey and urged the new ABC network to use him as a substitute broadcaster. His newscasts were so well liked by the affiliate stations that he was put on the network schedule by popular demand. The other story indicates that Harvey's wife persuaded an advertising agency to sponsor his broadcasts on the same network. In either case, 1951 marked the beginning of Paul Harvey's *News and Comment* on network radio.

Harvey's program is a blend of news of the day, trivia, amusing small-town yarns, and inspirational narratives. Some of the appeal of his program comes from the entertaining stories that Harvey composes. He has said that he applies the "Aunt Betty" test to his radio copy. Aunt Betty (based on Harvey's sister-in-law) is your typical old-fashioned, Middle American housewife, and if his story content is perplexing for Aunt Betty, then he rewrites it using simpler words or throws it out entirely.

Perhaps more than skillful writing, it is the unmistakable, resonant voice and inimitable delivery style that draw his huge radio audience. Harvey has a rhythmic reading style that features a mastery of changing inflection, pace, and use of the dramatic pause. Each news program begins with the familiar, "Hello, Americans. This is Paul Harvey. Stand by . . . [pause] . . . for news!" According to Harvey, that pause came about by accident when he allowed "dead air" while waiting for the clock to be where it should be before beginning his actual newscast. That dramatic halt often shows up during the news to deliver the punch line to a story, and Harvey uses it again at the end of the newscast in his stock close, "Paul Harvey . . . [pause] . . . Good Day!"

In 1976, with the help of his son, Paul Jr., Harvey expanded a segment from his news program into a new program, *The Rest of the Story*. In *The Rest of the Story*, Harvey uses the patented Harvey delivery style to spin a human-interest tale about the life of a famous person or little-known facts about a well-known event. Presented as a mini-mystery, amusing anecdotes and facts tell the story, with the identity of the individual or event revealed only at the end. Two collections of these stories have made their way into print: *Paul Harvey's The Rest of the Story* and *More of Paul Harvey's The Rest of the Story*.

Radio has always been Harvey's mainstay, but he has also had a syndicated TV series, a newspaper column syndicated by *The Los Angeles Times*, and a weekly commentary on *Good Morning America*. He also still maintains an extensive speaking schedule at conventions and college campuses across the country.

Over the years, Harvey has not only reached millions of listeners, but he has been frequently recognized by the radio industry. He has won the prestigious Marconi Award four times as "Network Personality of the Year." The National Association of Broadcasters and the Museum of Broadcasting have both inducted him into their Halls of Fame. The National Radio Broadcasters Association and the International Radio and Television Society gave him the Golden Radio Award and the Gold Medal Award, respectively. Paul Harvey earned a Peabody Award in 1993 and, in 1998, was included by *George* magazine as one of "The Twentieth Century's Most Significant Americans."

DAVID E. REESE

See also Commentators; News

Paul Harvey. Born in Tulsa, Oklahoma, 4 September 1918. Attended Tulsa University; announcer, KVOO, Tulsa, Oklahoma, 1941; station manager, KFBI, Abilene, Kansas; special events director, KXOK, St. Louis, Missouri, 1933–40; married Lynne Cooper, 1940; newscaster, KOMA, Oklahoma City; program director, WKZO, Kalamazoo, 1941–43; news director, Office of War Information, 1941–43; served in U.S. Army Air Force, 1943–44; news broadcasts, radio drama, and eventually 10 P.M newscast at WENR, Chicago, 1944–51; started *Paul Harvey News*, ABC radio network, 1951; added radio program, *The Rest of the Story*, 1976. Received American Legion Radio Award, 1952; elected to Oklahoma Hall of Fame, 1955; Top Commentator of the Year award, *Radio-TV Daily*, 1962; Illinois Broadcaster award, 1974; named to National Association Broadcasters Hall of Fame, 1979; Marconi Award for Network Personality of the Year, 1989, 1991, 1996, and 1998; Museum of Broadcast Communications Radio Hall of Fame, 1990; Broadcasting & Cable Magazine Hall of Fame, 1995; George Foster Peabody Award, 1993. Currently resides in River Forest, Illinois, and on a ranch in Missouri.

Radio Series

1951–	*Paul Harvey's News and Comment*
1976–	*The Rest of the Story*

Television Series

Paul Harvey Comments, 1968–88

Selected Publications

Paul Harvey's For What It's Worth, 1991

Further Reading

Aufderheide, Pat, "Paul Harvey, Good Day!" *The Progressive* 50 (July 1986)

Fang, Irving E., *Those Radio Commentators!* Ames: Iowa State University Press, 1977

Fisher, Marc, "Good Days for Paul Harvey," *Broadcasting* (14 October 1985)

Fisher, Marc, "Still Going," *American Journalism Review* (1 October 1998)

Gunlock, James R., "An Analysis of the Speaking of Paul Harvey," Master's thesis, Bowling Green State University, 1970

Ragan, Mark Lawrence, "Stand by for . . . This Quirky Newsman," *Insight on the News* (5 August 1991)

Hate Radio

Extremist Views on the Air

The messages of extremists are no strangers to radio. From the medium's inception there have been those who have exploited the airwaves to promote their agendas of prejudice and hatred. Despite the obligation of broadcasters to operate as public trustees, programs featuring blatant contempt and unvarnished loathing for different racial, ethnic, religious, political, and lifestyle groups have long been aired. Malevolent and inhumane attitudes and beliefs have unfortunately comprised the core of thousands of radio broadcasts.

Early Rancor on the Air

Beginning in the early 1920s, a number of radio programs were promoting ideological, philosophical, and political rancor. The first nationally successful (and what many consider one of the most influential) use of the airwaves to spread political and social invective were the broadcasts of a Catholic priest, Father Charles E. Coughlin. Coughlin began his radio career in Detroit in 1926 and moved to the Columbia Broadcasting System (CBS) in 1930, where he established the format and approach that right-wing media personalities over the decades have emulated.

Similar to some televangelists today, Coughlin's approach was to target certain groups in order to obtain the support of others and to garner, through his radio talks, millions of dollars in donations. He railed against Jews, labor unions, immigrants, and racial minorities, stirring and reinforcing resentment and hate against these competitors for jobs and social status in pre–World War II, Depression-ridden America. He called for a nation of Christians who would rule politics and the economy. This type of language anticipated the rhetoric that would be employed by far-right radio personalities of the 1990s. Indeed, Coughlin was the forerunner of the Holocaust-deniers and neo-Nazis of today.

Many people think of Walter Winchell, arguably the best-known radio commentator of the 1930s–1950s era, as a precursor to modern radio's Rush Limbaughs. His radio show, begun in 1932, was ostensibly a gossip program, but it expanded into right-wing political commentary. His shows had a huge, loyal audience, and he could affect national policy and make or break an individual's career with a few seconds of on-air commentary. He spread rumors, set styles, waged feuds, and excoriated some politicians while promoting the programs of others; he articulated the public's moods, fears, and prejudices.

The differences between the so-called left and right radio commentators became more pronounced in the late 1940s, when Senator Joseph R. McCarthy (R-Wisconsin) began to exploit Cold War fears and exercised great influence on American thought and action, throwing fear and obeisance not only into the media industries—principally film, radio, and television—but also into leaders and opinion makers of the country. Almost all commentators either supported McCarthyism or, out of fear of being blacklisted, were afraid to criticize him or his methods.

Most commentators in the pre- through postwar era were similar to Fulton Lewis, Jr., who is considered by some as the predominant right-wing commentator of that time and to whom Rush Limbaugh is often compared. Lewis supported McCarthy's contention that the U.S. government was infiltrated by communists and that secret plots were being hatched by communist secret agents throughout the country. This view helped fuel the later witch-hunts that often resulted in the professional, if not mental and physical, destruction of those accused—nearly always without foundation—of being communist sympathizers or fellow travelers.

After McCarthyistic suppression and punishment were no longer a concern to the media and the counterculture of the

1960s began to emerge, the media reinstated some elements of free speech, including several news and public-affairs shows that dealt with controversial issues, and more talk shows. It was not until after full-service radio networks disappeared in the early 1950s and specialized limited-time networks consisting mostly of music took their place—along with community-targeted narrowcasting, also mostly music, on local stations—that talk show hosts with set opinions emerged in force.

The far right seemed to understand more fully than the middle or the left the power of talk radio and quickly deluged stations with calls and opinions and stimulated a demand for, as some put it, loud-mouthed right-wing talk show hosts. One such host was Joe Pyne, who became one of the most popular talk personalities in the country with glib, biting, and unabashedly opinionated comments. A number of hosts, such as Bob Grant, later became famous for using Pyne's caustic approach. Grant often referred to African-Americans as "savages" and used expletives about other targets freely. Grant attributed his reputation to show business techniques, not bigotry. Ira Blue, who hosted a talk show in San Francisco in the 1960s, openly admitted during his on-air reign that the radio talker succeeds most when he is brazenly opinionated.

As the 1950s and 1960s progressed, many right-wing talk show programs and hosts became more subtle, using twisted logic rather than blatant vituperation to persuade their audiences. Meanwhile, right-wing rancor on talk shows went in two distinct directions during the decades that followed. As the number of stations increased, more on-air opportunities existed for fringe advocators. Ranters and ravers, some affiliated with organizations dedicated to violence, found microphones available to them. At the same time, soft-spoken intellectuals dispensing the same bottom line also had their access.

Late Millennium Waves of Rancor

The 1990s saw the greatest rise in the use of radio by far-right extremist groups, among them white supremacists, armed militias, survivalists, conspiracy theorists, and neo-Nazis. Many of these groups had effectively used the shortwave radio medium to promote their dark agendas in the 1980s, and they sought to go more mainstream with their messages by utilizing the AM and FM bands in the 1990s. Dozens of broadcast stations around the country gave airtime to organizations and individuals intent on denigrating people of color as well as those with non-Christian religious orientations. The bulk of these stations were smaller AM outlets, many of which were battling for their economic survival in the face of vastly declining audiences and shrinking revenues. Far-right programs were a source of income.

Today, far-right hate groups still promote their ideologies over radio stations, but not to the degree that they did prior to the Oklahoma City federal building bombing in 1995. This tragic extremist deed prompted the president to issue an antiterrorism bill making it clear that anyone employing the airwaves to promote violence and hatred would be hunted down and prosecuted. Technology, however, provided right-wing radicals with yet another way to propagate their racist and antigovernment views. The internet soon became the new home and the preferred medium for hate groups, which relished the freedom and lack of censorship that cyberspace afforded them.

In 1996 a white supremacist organization calling itself Stormfront launched what is considered the first extremist website. A former grand dragon of the Ku Klux Klan, Don Black, operates the internet site, which also features a link for children—"Stormfront for Kids"—run by his 11-year-old son. Within four years, a nearly incalculable number of radical-right websites, replete with sophisticated graphics and chat rooms, were in full operation, and many claimed thousands of hits each week. Several watchdog groups, among them the Simon Weisenthal Center, the Anti-Defamation League, Political Research Associates, and the Southern Poverty Law Center, reported that many of the same organizations and individuals, once so dependent on the airwaves to get their messages out to the public, now download their proclamations of hatred to thousands of websites, thus relegating radio to a secondary medium for their egregious purposes. One cannot help but note an ironic analogy in this migration of radio users to another medium. However, one suspects that the impact of this conversion will be far less traumatic for radio than the one brought on by the rise of television.

MICHAEL C. KEITH AND ROBERT L. HILLIARD

See also Controversial Issues; Coughlin, Father Charles; Pyne, Joe; Winchell, Walter

Further Reading

Berlet, Chip, editor, *Eyes Right! Challenging the Right Wing Backlash,* Boston: South End Press, 1995
Hilliard, Robert L., and Michael C. Keith, *Waves of Rancor: Tuning In the Radical Right,* Armonk, New York: Sharpe, 1999
Kurtz, Howard, *Hot Air,* New York: Basic Books, 1996
Laufer, Peter, *Inside Talk Radio: America's Voice or Just Hot Air?* Secaucus, New Jersey: Carol Group, 1995

Hear It Now

CBS Documentary Program

Hosted by esteemed newsman Edward R. Murrow, *Hear It Now* was more important in broadcasting's history that its mere six-month run on the Columbia Broadcasting System (CBS) radio network would suggest. The program developed from a series of successful documentary record albums and helped to pave the way for the even more important television documentary series *See It Now*, which presented some of Murrow's finest work.

The Recordings

The idea of making record albums featuring the actual sounds of historical events originated with Fred Friendly, a World War II veteran working as a producer for the National Broadcasting Company (NBC). Friendly saw that the relatively new medium of magnetic tape would make editing sounds recorded during historical events far easier. When Friendly realized that he needed a narrator for his recordings, CBS producer Jap Gude introduced him to newsman Edward R. Murrow and a team was born. Sometime around 1947, Friendly and Murrow approached Decca Records, but that firm was not interested in "talking" records, which were usually money losers. On the other hand, Columbia Records (a subsidiary of CBS) had available capacity as well as interest: a "scrapbook for the ear" they called it.

The initial recording, *I Can Hear It Now, 1933–1945,* was released in the winter of 1948 as a boxed set of five 78-rpm records (10 sides, about 45 minutes total). Murrow provided the historical context and narrated the many sound bites. There was no music or sound other than those of the actual events. To the surprise of virtually everyone involved in the project, the set sold 250,000 copies in the first year, highly unusual for talking records. It was said to be the first financially successful non-musical album.

A second album covering the postwar years (1945–48), with sound bites drawn largely from the extensive archives of the British Broadcasting Corporation (BBC), came out a year later, and a third, *I Can Hear It Now: 1919–32* (which did use actors for some events when recordings were not available), appeared in 1950. Although the reasons are no longer clear, plans for a forth album were abandoned. All were issued as 78-rpm albums originally, but some were later reissued in long-playing (LP) format. The title was resurrected in the 1990s for *I Can Hear It Now: The Sixties,* a two-compact-disc set narrated by Walter Cronkite.

The Broadcasts

The idea of broadcasting recorded sounds of historical or present-day events was anything but new. It had been done for *The March of Time* series beginning in 1931, and was often used during World War II. But there had been limited use of such material in part due to the networks' long-standing ban on use of recordings on the air. Something of a pilot program existed in CBS files—a 1948 proposed "Sunday with Murrow" documentary that had never aired for lack of advertiser support. Murrow and Gude now proposed a new program, called simply *Hear It Now* to stress its current-events emphasis, for a half-hour time slot. CBS Chairman William S. Paley so liked the idea, however, that he urged them to make it an hour-long program. Part of the difference in acceptance from the 1948 attempt to 1950 was a change in world events: the Korean War had begun and people once again were interested in world events.

When CBS began to look for a producer for the series, Gude suggested Friendly and CBS hired him away from NBC while the second *I Can Hear It Now* record album was being made. It was an easy choice, given Friendly's role as producer for the recordings and with several radio documentaries for the senior network. The series also provided a vehicle for Murrow upon his return from reporting from the Korean War battlefront.

As it aired, *Hear It Now* included "columnists" covering different subjects: CBS correspondent Don Hollenbeck discussed the media, Abe Burrows dealt with entertainment, and sportscaster Red Barber covered professional teams in several sports. The program had an original musical score by U.S. composer Virgil Thomson. Murrow decided which topics would be included and the order in which they were presented, but he and Friendly wrote the program together. Friendly was the key editor of essential sound bites. The result was a "magazine of sorts, covering the news events of the previous six days in the voices of the newsmakers themselves, by transcription and hot live microphones" in an era before recordings of actual events were common in radio news (quoted in Dunning, 1998). *Show Business Weekly* said the program, which won a Peabody Award, was "almost breath-taking in scope and concept." It was carried on 173 CBS affiliates. Other networks quickly caught on to the idea and imitated it. NBC's *Voices and Events* and ABC's *Week Around the World* provided essentially the same sort of content, but without Murrow and Friendly.

Fred Friendly (left) and Edward R. Murrow on *Hear It Now,* 1950
Courtesy CBS Photo Archive

In many ways, the program was a radio vehicle for Murrow, who was then little interested in (and indeed, uneasy about) television. But as the realization became clear that pictures would add considerably to the *Hear It Now* idea, the audio version left the air while video preparations began. *See it Now* premiered on 18 November 1951 and ran until 1955.

CHRISTOPHER H. STERLING

See also Columbia Broadcasting System; Documentary Programs; Friendly, Fred; March of Time; Murrow, Edward R.; News

Commentators
Edward R. Murrow, Red Barber, Abe Burrows, Don Hollenbeck

Writer/Producer
Fred Friendly

Programming History
CBS   15 December 1950–15 June 1951

Further Reading
Bliss, Edward, Jr., *Now the News: The Story of Broadcast Journalism,* New York: Columbia University Press, 1991
Dunning, John, *On the Air: The Encyclopedia of Old-Time Radio,* New York: Oxford University Press, 1998
Kendrick, Alexander, *Prime Time: The Life of Edward R. Murrow,* Boston: Little Brown, 1969
Sperber, Ann M., *Murrow: His Life and Times,* New York: Freundlich Books, 1986

Heavy Metal/Active Rock Format

The "Heavy Metal/Active Rock" format encompasses a musical genre that has played a marginal role in commercial radio programming, while the medium of radio has at times played crucial roles in the acceptance, rejection, and content of the music itself. The moniker is the radio industry's term for a category that has gone in and out of style while maintaining a core fan subculture since heavy metal's emergence in the early 1970s. The music in this format is characterized by a distorted guitar sound, a heavy bass-and-drums rhythm section, and a vocal approach that eschews traditional melodic conventions in favor of an aggressive, emotionally raw sound. The name "heavy metal" was at first uncomfortably accepted by first-generation rock bands such as Led Zeppelin, Deep Purple, and Black Sabbath and later happily adopted by second-generation acts such as AC/DC, Kiss, Blue Öyster Cult, Motörhead, and others.

Initially, few heavy metal bands found a place on commercial radio. Commercial rock radio itself was only then taking shape on the FM dial, as progressive/free-form stations (such as WOR in New York and KMPX in San Francisco) gave way to the new album-oriented rock (AOR) format, at stations such as WNEW in New York and WMMS in Cleveland, designed to reach a larger listening and buying public. Thus, heavy metal was not welcome in the earlier progressive rock format that grew out of the late-1960s counterculture, whose ideology did not complement the nihilism of groups like Black Sabbath. A few bands, however, did find their place on the FM dial in the early 1970s. One band, Led Zeppelin, in fact became central to AOR playlists through much of the decade.

If radio largely ignored heavy metal during the 1970s, in the 1980s the format would find new popularity. By the late 1970s, music on the radio was still functioning much as it had earlier in the decade, due to the continuing influence of AOR, which increasingly programmed the most benign rock music to appeal to the largest audience possible. The heavy metal music that did find its way onto the airwaves was limited to a few songs played endlessly in a station's rotation. The effect was that a few songs on AOR radio came to stand in for heavy metal as a musical genre and in the process became emblematic of the genre's perceived creative bankruptcy by the end of the decade.

In the late 1970s, competition from new genres such as disco and punk had some influence on American radio formats, but both musical styles returned to the level of subculture within a few years. Meanwhile, heavy metal was being reinvigorated, first by British bands such as Def Leppard, Iron Maiden, and Judas Priest, and then by U.S. bands such as Quiet Riot and Guns N' Roses. By the mid-1980s, heavy metal from bands like Scorpions and Mötley Crüe could regularly be heard on American radio. Still, some saw a certain sacrifice in the newfound popularity of the genre on the airwaves. The anticommercial heavy metal of the 1970s gave way, slowly but surely, to a new style sometimes derisively called "lite metal," which meant less emphasis on long instrumental breaks featuring virtuosic guitar solos and greater emphasis on radio-friendly melodies and more traditional pop song structures.

In recent years, the heavy metal format has struggled amidst the relative fragmentation of radio into new formats that have eroded a once-loyal listenership. The format has become one choice in a sea of others, and stations carrying the format increasingly find themselves fighting for audiences in an ever-smaller market share. The emergence of the classic rock format in the mid-1980s and the alternative rock format in the 1990s has meant the loss of both older listeners alienated by newer bands and younger listeners with little allegiance to older heavy metal. Interestingly, the classic rock format has largely not designated earlier heavy metal music as classic. Heavy metal radio was slow to incorporate the music of alternative rock formats after the "grunge" explosion of the 1990s, headed by bands such as Nirvana, Pearl Jam, and Soundgarden. While grunge had stylistic links to the heavy metal bands of the 1970s, it also embraced the punk aesthetic.

The music played on heavy metal radio in the late 1980s and early 1990s, in comparison, largely catered to the mainstream music industry. Alternative rock formats encroached on both heavy metal and classic rock listeners with the success of stations such as KNDD in Seattle and WHTZ in New York, both of which made significant gains in their respective radio markets. Later in the decade, newer bands stylistically associated with heavy metal, such as Limp Bizkit and Rage against the Machine, developed. These groups owed much to the emergence of hip-hop music as a predominant popular style in the 1990s. The heavy metal/active rock format has embraced these groups in order to garner younger listeners, while the format expands and absorbs influences in a confusing radio market environment.

As the radio industry continues to change and programmers again return to once-outmoded formats, it will be interesting to see whether the heavy metal/active rock format will thrive in the new fragmented format environment. Other new venues for radio, including both internet and low-power radio initiatives, may serve heavy metal music fans in ways that commercial radio cannot.

KYLE S. BARNETT

See also Album-Oriented Rock Format; Alternative Rock Format; Classic Rock Format; Contemporary Hit Radio Format/Top 40; Music; Progressive Rock Format

Further Reading

Keith, Michael C., *Radio Programming: Consultancy and Formatics,* Boston and London: Focal Press, 1987

O'Donnell, Lewis B., Philip Benoit, and Carl Hausman, *Modern Radio Production,* Belmont, California: Wadsworth, 1986

Ross, Sean, "Music Radio—The Fickleness of Fragmentation," in *Radio: The Forgotten Medium,* edited by Edward C.

Pease and Everette E. Dennis, London and New Brunswick, New Jersey: Transaction, 1995

Walser, Robert, *Running with the Devil: Power, Gender, and Madness in Heavy Metal Music,* Hanover, New Hampshire: University Press of New England, 1993

Weinstein, Deena, *Heavy Metal: A Cultural Sociology,* New York: Lexington Books, and Toronto: Macmillan Canada, 1991

Herrold, Charles D. 1875–1948

U.S. Broadcasting Pioneer

Charles Herrold is a relatively little-known broadcasting pioneer whose most significant work took place between 1912 and 1917. Although today most historians believe Herrold's claim that he was the first to broadcast radio entertainment and information for an audience on a regularly scheduled, preannounced basis, he is dismissed as a minor figure because he failed to have a long-lasting impact on the radio industry. Nevertheless, his early broadcasts show innovation and originality and are of interest because Herrold is symbolic of many of the early broadcast pioneers: unknown, underfinanced, and overshadowed by the major corporations that would control broadcasting beginning in 1920.

Herrold was born in 1875 in the Midwest and grew up in San Jose, California. In high school he was recognized by his teachers and classmates for his superior grasp of mechanical and scientific subjects. After graduation, he attended Stanford University in nearby Palo Alto, but he dropped out for health reasons. In 1900 Herrold set up an electrical manufacturing company in San Francisco, but when the Great Earthquake of 1906 destroyed his residence, he moved to Stockton, California, to teach at a technical college. Building on his work as an inventor and his experience with students, Herrold returned in 1909 to San Jose and opened a vocational school. The Herrold College of Wireless was a way to provide an income and at the same time to allow him access to the laboratory environment necessary to continue his research.

Like Lee de Forest, Reginald Fessenden, and others, Herrold was most interested in inventing a radiotelephone system that would make him rich and famous. His contributions to the technology of the radiotelephone were lacking in scientific originality, although his device did allow him to broadcast. As the inventor of an arc transmitting system, he spent years attempting to differentiate his system from that of Danish inventor Valdemar Poulsen. Herrold received six U.S. patents for his devices, patents that certainly would have been challenged by the Poulsen people were it not for the fact that by 1917 the perfection of the vacuum tube as the basis of all future radiotelephones made such arc-based devices obsolete.

Early notice of Herrold's use of the radiotelephone to "broadcast" to an audience is a notarized statement by Herrold, published in an ad for wireless equipment in the 1910 catalog of the Electro-Importing Company: "We have been giving wireless phonograph concerts to amateur men in the Santa Clara Valley," a statement prophetic of what broadcasting was to become. And although his 1910 listeners were amateurs and hobbyists, he did broadcast to public audiences daily during the 1915 San Francisco World's Fair. But Herrold's most significant contribution was that between 1912 and 1917 he operated a radio station providing programs of information and entertainment for an audience on a regular schedule, many of them announced previously in the newspapers. That he accidentally stumbled onto what was to become radio broadcasting may have been a function of his role as the headmaster of a wireless trade school. Because Herrold had the responsibility of providing daily technical activities for hundreds of eager young boys, it is likely that the broadcasting of the popular music of the day by his students to an audience of friends, families, and possible future students was the cauldron from which broadcasting emerged, Charles Herrold style.

Interviews with former students indicate that Herrold was broadcasting to a sizable audience: "It was a religion for 'Prof' Herrold to have his equipment ready every Wednesday night at nine o'clock. He would have his records ready, all laid out, and what he wanted to say. And the public or listeners, it became a habit for them to wait for it," according to Herrold's assistant, Ray Newby. Recalled Newby in an interview with Gordon

Greb, "We even had a San Jose music store that supplied us records, of course free of charge, and I think we played them all. We would take the *Mercury-Herald* in San Jose, and we would read headlines and discuss them a little bit, just something to yak about and make it interesting at the same time, to develop an audience, I would say." A local news story of a typical Herrold broadcast illustrates the method:

> For more than two hours they conducted a concert in Mr. Herrold's office, which was heard for many miles around. The music was played on a phonograph furnished by the Wiley B. Allen Music company. Immediately after the first record was played numerous amateurs from various points in the valley notified (the announcer) that they had heard the music distinctly. He gave the names of the records he had on hand and asked those listening to signify their choice (San Jose *Mercury-Herald*, 22 July 1912).

The question remains: if Herrold's was the first broadcasting station, why do not more people know about it? Some of the misunderstanding surrounding the "who was first" broadcasting claims can be traced to an early historian, George Clark. In 1921 Clark, RCA's in-house historian, dismissed the claims of all who broadcast before KDKA, because, as he wrote, "ordinary citizens" could not buy radios until KDKA, and therefore men like Herrold and de Forest were not really broadcasters, because their audiences were engineers or amateurs, not "citizens." Still, Herrold was the first to use radio to broadcast entertainment programs to an audience on a regular basis. He was not the first to broadcast pre-announced to an audience—that was Fessenden in 1906; he was not the first to broadcast election returns—that was de Forest in 1916; he was not the first to get a broadcast license—that was Conrad in 1920. Herrold returned to the air in 1921 licensed as KQW, ran the station until 1925, and later specialized in radio adver-

tising. During World War II, he worked as a janitor at the Oakland shipyards. He died in 1948. Until 1958, when his story was uncovered by San Jose journalism professor Gordon Greb, almost no one outside of northern California had ever heard of Charles Herrold.

MICHAEL H. ADAMS

See also De Forest, Lee; Fessenden, Reginald; KCBS/KQW

Charles D. Herrold. Born in Fulton, Illinois, 16 November 1875. Studied astronomy, Stanford University (no degree), 1895; head of technical department, Heald's College, Stockton, California, 1906–08; started Herrold College of Wireless and Engineering, San Jose, California, 1909; began a regularly scheduled, pre-announced broadcast operation, 1912–17; invented a wireless radiotelephone and developed other new products in various fields; broadcast operation licensed as KQW, 1921; sold airtime for several Bay area radio station, 1925–30; worked at Oakland Public Schools as media technician, 1932; worked as janitor at Oakland shipyards during World War II. Died in Hayward, California, 1 July 1948.

Further Reading

Adams, Michael H., "The Race for Radiotelephone: 1900–1920," *AWA Review* 10 (1996)

Adams, Michael H., et al., *Broadcasting's Forgotten Father: The Charles Herrold Story* (videorecording), Los Altos, California: Electronics Museum of the Perham Foundation, 1994

Barnouw, Erik, *A History of Broadcasting in the United States*, 3 vols., New York: Oxford University Press, 1966–70; see especially vol. 1, *A Tower in Babel: To 1933*, 1966

Greb, Gordon, "The Golden Anniversary of Broadcasting," *Journal of Broadcasting* 3, no. 1 (Winter 1958–59)

The Charles Herrold Historic Site, <www.charlesherrold.org>

Hertz, Heinrich 1857–1894

German Physicist

In a series of laboratory experiments in 1887–88, Heinrich Hertz verified James Clerk Maxwell's theory that electromagnetic waves, or wireless transmissions, existed, and that these invisible forms of radiant energy traveled at the speed of light. Hertz paved the way for the development of wireless radio communications by notables such as Edouard Branly, Sir Oliver

Lodge, Guglielmo Marconi, Reginald Fessenden, Sir John Ambrose Fleming, E.F.W. Alexanderson, and Lee de Forest.

Hertz's research placed the field of electrodynamics on a firm footing, sparked enormous activity among scientists, and laid the foundations for the development of wireless telegraphy. He showed that electricity could be propagated or transmitted as electromagnetic waves through space (without wire connections) and could be detected at a point distant from the transmitting source. The discoveries that he described in his May 1888 paper "Electromagnetic Waves in Air and Their Reflection" would later move the scientific community to call these waves "Hertzian" in his honor.

Hertz began wireless research in 1879 just as mathematical physics began to be recognized as a separate subdiscipline in Germany. Hermann von Helmholtz was a pre-eminent figure in the 19th-century scientific renaissance in Germany and was Hertz's lifelong mentor in Munich. Helmholtz encouraged Hertz to participate in a competition designed to solve a problem posed by James Clerk Maxwell's theories. Hertz's active wireless experimentation began in 1886 while he was a faculty member at the Technische Hochschule (Technical High School) in Karlsruhe. His discoveries began as he was conducting a class demonstration in electricity.

Hertz experimented with gaps in a wire coil connected to a Leyden jar to generate waves at various frequencies. The inner and outer foils of the Leyden jar became the two arms of a dipole or two-part transmitting antenna. Hertz tuned two flat coils of wire or metal strips to the same frequency so that the waves generated and received were identical. The Leyden jar stored the electrical charges while an induction coil magnified them as the spark gap and metal plate radiated the charges into the ether (or across the metal-laden laboratory). Thus, Hertz demonstrated the transfer of energy that Maxwell had predicted.

Hertz conducted his experiments in less-than-ideal laboratory conditions: steel and lead in the lab affected his measurements. His scientific apparatus (use of a spark gap) was crude. He used simple laboratory devices and often built his own devices to confirm Maxwell's prediction that electromagnetic waves existed, both as light and radio waves. The physically confined space Hertz used for his experiments required him to work with fast laboratory oscillations and short wavelengths. Eventually, Hertz showed that, like light waves, electromagnetic waves were reflected and refracted and, most important, that they traveled at the speed of light but had a much longer wavelength.

European scientists were reluctant to accept the results of Hertz's experiments. Researchers were slow to see the significance of Hertzian waves and to accept his conclusion that such waves traveled at the speed of light. They tended to cling to older, more familiar concepts, such as the corpuscular theory of light, which implied that light traveled in the form of material particles. However, Hertz's mentor, Helmholtz, never wavered in his support for his protégé.

Hertz did influence several scientific studies and research efforts around the world. He was generally regarded not as an innovator but as an uncommonly critical and lucid intelligence who addressed the conceptual problems of physics. Hertz helped connect the traditional study of mechanics and the evolving study of electrodynamics.

Other scientists credited Hertz for their achievements. Albert Einstein, in an 1899 letter to his fiancée, indicated that Hertz's *Electric Waves* stimulated his interest in the electrodynamics of moving bodies; this interest would ultimately lead to his special theory of relativity. Hertz's work on the photoelectric effect (although the existence of electrons was unknown at the time) helped to verify Einstein's quantum equation for the photoelectric effect and identified certain phenomena as being clearly associated with the ultraviolet portion of the spectrum. Hertz also influenced Max Planck's development of quantum physics by providing equations for the emission and absorption of energy by oscillators. Wilhelm Conrad Roentgen credits his discovery of X rays in late 1895 to Hertz and Lenard's cathode-ray experiments.

Hertz did not extend his work to include potential applications of his discoveries. He was not interested in going beyond the theoretical stage of study. His experimental work on electromagnetic waves, however, led directly to radio telegraphy and to later innovations. The material he read about Hertzian waves influenced Guglielmo Marconi significantly. Marconi became the practical inventor and took Hertz's studies further.

Hertz helped move wireless theories and experiments to practical reality and refinement. He helped formulate suggestions on the proper approach theoretical physicists should take toward the physical universe. He suggested future research to build on his discoveries. His fusion of theory and experiment with a creative interest in philosophical and logical foundations is unique among scientists. Hertz succeeded in delineating central concepts and pointing the way to fruitful future research initiatives, and his achievements were lauded in science publications, the popular press, and in public speeches. He was a model for many future generations of physicists.

Leading physicists of the day had profound respect for Hertz both as a physicist and as a man. John Ambrose Fleming, who would use Hertz's discoveries for his own experiments, noted that Hertz's work marked a fresh epoch in electrical discovery. Hertz's name is used internationally to indicate a unit of frequency (what had been called a cycle, as in kilocycle, is now hertz or kilohertz) in his honor.

Hertz's final years were devoted almost entirely to exploring the theoretical implications of Maxwell's electrodynamics for the rest of physics. While at the peak of his productivity, Hertz died tragically at age 37 of chronic blood poisoning. At his funeral in Hamburg, Hertz was praised for his noble simplicity and genuine modesty.

Heinrich Hertz was one of the last classical physicists. Had he lived longer, he would doubtless have been a major participant in the development of modern physics.

PETER E. MAYEUX

Heinrich Rudolf Hertz. Born in Hamburg, Germany, 22 February 1857. Attended private school of Richard Lange, 1863 and 1872–74; admitted to upper class of *Johanneum Gymnasium*, Hamburg, 1874; began engineering studies at Dresden Polytechnic, 1876; switched from engineering to physics at University of Munich, 1877–78; attended Friedrich-Wilhelm University, Berlin, doctoral degree *magna cum laude*, 1880; Master builder intern, Frankfurt Public Works Department, 1875–76; military service with railway regiment, Berlin, 1876–77; assistantship with Hermann von Helmholtz, Berlin Physics Institute, 1880–83; lecturer, mathematical physics, Kiel, 1883; appointed professor of physics, Technische Hochschule in Karlsruhe, 1885; appointed professor of physics, Friedrich-Wilhelm University, Bonn, 1888. Received Philosophical Faculty prize, 1879 (leading to the discovery of electromagnetic waves); Matteucci Medal, Italian Scientific Society, 1888; Baumgartner Prize, Vienna Academy of Sciences, 1889; La Caze Prize, Paris Academy of Sciences, 1889; Rumford Medal, British Royal Society, 1890; Bressa Prize, Turin Royal Academy, 1891; elected corresponding member of several major scientific societies, including the Berlin Academy of Sciences, the Manchester Literary and Philosophical Society, the Cambridge Philosophical Society, and the Accademia dei Lincei; official adoption by the International Electrotechnical Commission of the name *hertz* as a unit of frequency, 1933. Died in Bonn, Germany, 1 January 1894.

Selected Publications

Erinnerungen Briefe Tagebucher, 1927; *Memoirs, Letters, Diaries,* 2nd (German-English) enlarged edition, edited by Mathilde Hertz and Charles Susskind, 1977

Collected Works, edited by Philipp Werke, 1896–99

Further Reading

Aitken, Hugh G.J., *Syntony and Spark: The Origins of Radio,* New York: Wiley, 1976

Baird, Davis, R.I.G. Hughes, and Alfred Nordmann, editors, *Heinrich Hertz: Classical Physicist, Modern Philosopher,* Boston: Kluwer Academic, 1998

Bryant, John H., *Heinrich Hertz, The Beginning of Microwaves,* New York: Institute of Electrical and Electronics Engineers, 1988

Cichon, D.J., and W. Wiesbeck, "Heinrich Hertz, Wireless Experiments at Karlsruhe in the View of Modern Communication," in *International Conference on 100 Years of Radio,* London: Institution of Electrical Engineers, 1995

Kniestedt, J., "Heinrich Hertz: The Discovery of Electromagnetic Waves 100 Years Ago," *Archiv für das Post- und Fernmeldewesen* 41 (February 1989)

Lodge, Oliver, *Signalling across Space without Wires: Being a Description of the Work of Hertz and His Successors,* London: The Electrician, 1894; 4th edition, 1911

Mulligan, Joseph F., "Heinrich Hertz and the Development of Physics," *Physics Today* 42 (March 1989)

O'Hara, James.G., and Willibald Pricha, *Hertz and the Maxwellians: A Study and Documentation of Electromagnetic Wave Radiation, 1873–1894,* London: Peregrinus, 1987

Plank, M., "Gedächtnisrede auf Heinrich Hertz," *Verhandlungen der Physikalischen Gesellschaft zu Berlin* 13 (1894)

Hicks, Tom 1946–

U.S. Broadcast Executive

Thomas O. "Tom" Hicks is the president and chief executive officer (CEO) of Hicks, Muse, Tate, and Furst, a Dallas-based leveraged-buyout firm. At one point during the late 1990s, Hicks and his investment firm held ownership interests in more radio stations in the United States than any other company or individual. Hicks, Muse, Tate, and Furst came into existence in 1989 when Hicks and three partners formed the private investment firm after several successful industry buyouts. Today, the portfolio of companies controlled by the firm includes real estate, consumer products, movie theaters, sports franchises, and broadcast stations.

Hicks became a common name in the radio industry during the 1990s, when he served as CEO for AMFM Incorporated, formerly Chancellor Media Company. Under Hicks, Chancellor invested heavily in radio prior to the passage of the 1996 Telecommunications Act. With the elimination of ownership limits under the new legislation, Chancellor was well positioned to take advantage of further consolidation in radio.

Within a few months, Chancellor became one of the largest radio operators in the United States, at one point owning more than 400 radio stations.

Thomas O. Hicks was born in 1946 in Houston, Texas. One of four sons of a Dallas media representative, Hicks grew up with a strong understanding of and appreciation for the radio business. His father became an owner of a few radio stations in a number of small Texas markets, including Beaumont, Bryan, Port Arthur, Laredo, and Big Springs. As a teenager, Hicks worked as a radio announcer at his father's station in Port Arthur. Following high school, Hicks graduated from the University of Texas with a business degree in 1968. He then moved west, completing a master's of business administration degree at the University of Southern California.

Hicks and his partner, Bobby Haas, established a strong reputation for putting together profitable deals for investors, acquiring companies such as Dr. Pepper, Sybron Corporation, 7-Up, Thermadyne Industries, and Spectradyne. In 1989 Hicks formed Hicks, Muse, Tate, and Furst, as a venture capital firm with a buy-and-build philosophy.

Hicks began acquiring radio stations in earnest in 1993, with Chancellor Broadcasting and CapStar Broadcasting forming the cornerstones of the radio group as part of Hicks, Muse, Tate, and Furst's overall investment strategy. Acquisitions continued in 1996 and 1997 as Chancellor was renamed Chancellor Media. The company acquired several existing radio group holdings, including Evergreen, SFX, and Viacom.

The firm also ventured into television with the purchase of stations owned by LIN Television, as well as several outdoor advertising companies. In July 1999 shareholders approved the merger of the former Chancellor Media and CapStar into a new company known as AMFM Incorporated to reflect the emphasis on radio as well as to match the name of the company's national radio network. Early in 1999, AMFM owned 460 radio stations.

Aside from being one of the largest radio owners in the country, Hicks established a new type of entrepreneurial spirit in the radio industry. By clustering stations in geographical areas and appealing to different target audiences, Hicks capitalized on the changing economics of radio and the resultant cash flow that would come with streamlined operations. In an interview published in *Broadcasting and Cable* in 1997, Hicks called radio "one of the all-time great businesses for pre-cash flows." Hicks understood that by clustering operations, fixed costs could be lowered, while profit margins would increase.

Hicks' business philosophy toward radio spurred other groups to consolidation in order to maintain a national presence in the radio industry. Hicks demonstrated to other investors that radio was still a profitable investment. Although the consolidation movement in radio was not without controversy, there is no doubt that the radio industry experienced renewed interest among the investment community and higher valuation as an industry group with Hicks as one of its leading advocates.

Throughout 1999, the stock value of AMFM remained flat amid investor concerns that the company was carrying too much debt. The company surprised the radio industry by disclosing in March 1999 that it would consider a possible sale or merger. In October 1999, a dramatic $23.5 billion merger was announced between Clear Channel Communications and AMFM, creating the world's largest radio company. Once the merger was finalized in 2000, Clear Channel owned a total of 830 radio stations, capable of reaching an audience of more than 100 million listeners.

With the merger, Tom Hicks moved into a new role as the vice chairman of Clear Channel, working closely with Chairman L. Lowry Mays. Hicks remains one of the company's largest stockholders. Although he maintains less of a public role in his new position, he will continue to influence the radio industry with his presence on Clear Channel's board of directors.

ALAN B. ALBARRAN

See also Clear Channel Communications; Ownership, Mergers and Acquisitions; Telecommunications Act of 1996

Thomas O. Hicks. Born in Houston, Texas, 7 February 1946. Attended University of Texas, B.A. in business administration, 1968; University of Southern California, M.B.A. 1970; became disc jockey at father's radio station at age 15; worked at Continental Illinois; investment officer, Morgan Guaranty Trust Company; president of venture capital affiliate, National Bank of Dallas, First Dallas Capital Corporation; first leveraged buyout with Louis Marx, Jr., 1977; co-managing partner, Summit Partners, LBO; co-chairman and CEO, Hicks and Haas, 1980s; formed buyout firm Hicks, Muse, Tate and Furst, 1989; owns Southwest Sports Group; chairman, University of Texas Investment Management Company.

Further Reading

Albarran, Alan B., and Gregory G. Pitts, *The Radio Broadcasting Industry,* Boston: Allyn and Bacon, 2000

Hurt, Harry, "Texas-Tall Buyouts: Dallas-Based Hicks, Muse Outguns Wall Street Firms," *U.S. News and World Report* (26 January 1998)

Michaels, James, "Tuning in with Tom Hicks," *Forbes* (1 June 1998)

Rathburn, Elizabeth, "Count 'em: 830," *Broadcasting and Cable* (11 October 1999)

"Thomas Hicks Follows the Radio-TV Muse," *Broadcasting and Cable* (23 June 1997)

Whitley, Glenna, "The Player," *Texas Monthly* 19 (March 1994)

High Fidelity

High fidelity is a term used to mean the highly accurate reproduction of sounds within the spectrum of human hearing, usually considered to be between 20 hertz and 20,000 hertz. English engineer Harold Hartley first applied the term in 1926. Much of today's understanding of what constitutes high fidelity reproduction stems from pioneering research into the way humans hear and interpret sound done by Harry Olsen for the Radio Corporation of America (RCA) and Harvey Fletcher at the American Telephone and Telegraph Company's (AT&T) Bell Laboratories.

Origins

Early sound reproduction devices such as Edison's cylindrical phonograph (1877) and Emile Berliner's Gramophone disk developed a decade later demonstrated the feasibility of recording, but they produced tinny sound with significant distortion and limited reproduction of voice and music. The near-simultaneous developments of radio broadcasting and sound motion pictures led engineers to search for ways to improve sound quality.

E.C. Wente's invention of the condenser microphone (1916) and improvements in loudspeaker technology by Rice and Kellogg at General Electric, Peter Jensen and others (1925) greatly improved the ability to record and reproduce audio. In the 1920s Edwin Armstrong's development of the heterodyne circuit improved the sensitivity and selectivity of radio receivers, and Harold Black's discovery of negative feedback provided improved audio reproduction, but several obstacles still prevented accurate reproduction of sound. The surface noise associated with records, coupled with their limited audio range and short playing time, sharply curtailed improvements in mechanical sound reproduction. AM radio transmissions were subject to significant noise and static interference. Engineers thought that reducing the audio bandwidth would reduce annoying whistles and associated distortions.

Simultaneous research into improved audio occurred in Britain, Germany, and the United States, but it was AT&T that spearheaded high-quality audio development. AT&T's Bell Laboratories undertook long-term development of sound reproduction in conjunction with high-quality long-distance telephone service. With the 1922 construction of WEAF, AT&T's flagship New York City radio station, the telephone company carried out research to improve broadcasting microphones, consoles, and transmitters. Bell Labs also developed the transcription turntable using a slower speed (33 1/3 revolutions per minute) to increase playing time to 30 minutes to meet the needs of broadcasters and motion picture engineers.

By 1929 the introduction of the matched-impedance recorder, coupled with development of gold master records, increased the attainable frequency response to 10,000 Hz and greatly reduced surface noise for records.

By 1930 both RCA and Bell Labs were experimenting with various means of improving audio quality for records. One year later Leopold Stokowski, the famed conductor of the Philadelphia Orchestra, enlisted Bell Labs' help in setting up an audio test room at the Academy of Music. The first disk recordings capable of accurate sonic reproduction were cut with Stokowski's help, and Bell Labs made more than 125 high-quality recordings of the 1931–32 Philadelphia musical season. During this time Stokowski recorded the first binaural recording using AT&T's new two-styli cutter, developed by Arthur C. Keller, and in 1933 the first U.S. stereophonic transmission over telephone lines occurred when Bell Labs demonstrated a three-channel audio system in Constitution Hall in Washington, D.C. In 1938 Keller received a patent for a single-groove stereophonic disk record system.

Improving Radio

Although various advancements in the technology allowed AM radio to improve substantially, the narrow channel bandwidth adopted by the Federal Radio Commission and static interference problems created technical limitations to full high fidelity transmission. By 1935 radio stations that specialized in quality music were eager to adopt improved technology. The Federal Communications Commission (FCC) licensed four stations on three channels at the high end of the AM frequencies (in the 1500–1600 kHz region) to experiment with high fidelity broadcasting using a wider channel bandwidth. WHAM, a clear channel station that originated Rochester Philharmonic Orchestra broadcasts on the National Broadcasting Company's Blue Network, and WQXR in New York were among the early pioneers of high fidelity AM broadcasting. These stations used new Western Electric transmitters boasting better frequency response with a wider dynamic range. Improved radio receivers capable of better fidelity were manufactured by WHAM's parent company, Stromberg-Carlson, E.H. Scott, and others.

Regularly scheduled high fidelity FM broadcasts began on 18 July 1939 as Edwin Armstrong's station retransmitted classical music programs from New York's WQXR via special telephone lines. That same year, the Yankee radio network began high fidelity FM broadcasting, soon followed by General Electric and others. In 1944 Britain's Decca records introduced full fidelity recordings capable of reproducing most of the audio spectrum.

Hi-Fi Era

After World War II, rapid improvements in recording and playback technology accelerated the development of true high fidelity sound reproduction. Crosby Research and Ampex (1948) introduced high fidelity tape recorders. The broadcasting and recording industries quickly adopted these new machines. Columbia Records (1948) and RCA Victor (1949) revolutionized the record industry with their respective introduction of the 33 1/3 rpm long play album (LP) and the 45 rpm record. The new records used small microgrooves and a vinyl medium to reduce surface noise and improve fidelity. With the introduction of the LP, entire symphonic movements could be played at home without having to change records. Quality three-speed record changers developed by Webster-Chicago (Webcor), Voice of Music, and Garrard could play stacks of records without interruption. These innovations substantially improved the sound quality of recorded music, making affordable record players available to the general listening public. In 1950 Seeburg introduced its soon-legendary 100 series jukebox, boasting high fidelity amplifiers and large speakers and capable of playing 100 different 45 rpm selections. These jukeboxes were immediate hits with teens and helped usher in the era of the 45 hit single.

By the early 1950s all of the components necessary for accurate sound reproduction were available to consumers and the "high fidelity era" industry began. Fairchild and General Electric introduced magnetic phonograph cartridges, while Rek-O-Kut, Thorens, and Grado introduced specialized turntables and tone arms for audiophiles. Webcor's famous model 210 high fidelity tape recorder was introduced and specialized radio manufacturers such as Fisher, H.H. Scott, Macintosh, and Sherwood Labs began selling limited production high fidelity amplifiers and FM tuners. Speaker manufacturers improved the quality of home loudspeaker systems. Jensen's development of the SG-300 triaxial speaker (1949) and bass-reflex enclosure made it possible for enthusiasts to build their own high-quality systems, whereas AR introduced the acoustic suspension system (1954), capable of reproducing powerful bass with small bookshelf enclosures. Altec Lansing and JBL speakers became popular with audiophiles. Specialized magazines such as *High Fidelity* and *Audio* catered to the "hi-fi" enthusiast by reviewing the latest in audio equipment.

Commercial development of stereophonic sound continued throughout the 1950s, culminating with RCA Victor's introduction of the stereophonic LP in 1958 and the FCC's approval of FM stereophonic broadcasting in early 1961. Combination AM/FM phonograph consoles gained popularity throughout the early 1960s, but with the introduction of transistorized equipment and new smaller sound formats such as the audio cassette (1963) and the 8-track (1966), compact stereophonic equipment eventually replaced larger console systems. Although four-channel record systems were introduced in the 1970s, they never received wide acceptance. By 1988 audio cassettes and compact discs were outselling LP records more than three to one.

The introduction of the compact disc player by Sony and Phillips ushered in the beginning of the digital audio era in 1982. Various digital recording formats, including digital audio tape systems (1986), recordable compact discs (1990), and minidiscs (1992) currently provide the capability to make high fidelity recordings that are virtually indistinguishable from the original sound sources. Today, new broadcasting technologies such as satellite-based and in-band digital audio broadcasting and computer data compression advances suggest that even higher-quality broadcast distribution of music is on the horizon.

FRITZ MESSERE

See also Dolby Noise Reduction; Receivers; Recordings and the Radio Industry; Stereo

Further Reading

Aldred, John, *100 Years of Cinema Loudspeakers*, <www.filmsound.org/articles/amps/loudspeakers.htm>

Grado, Joseph, "Audio Milestones: 50 Years and More of Record Playing," *Audio* 81, no. 5 (May 1997)

Jordan, Robert Oakes, and James Cunningham, *The Sound of High Fidelity*, Chicago: Windsor Press, 1958

Long, John J., Jr., "High Fidelity Broadcasting: Details of the Newly Installed System at WHAM, Rochester," *Communication and Broadcast Engineering* (February 1935)

McGinn, Robert E., "Stokowski and the Bell Telephone Laboratories: Collaboration in the Development of High-Fidelity Sound Reproduction," *Technology and Culture* 24, no. 1 (1983)

Schoenherr, Steven E., "Sound Recording Research at Bell Labs," <history.acusd.edu/gen/recording/bell-labs.html>

Hill, George Washington 1884–1946

U.S. Innovator in Radio Advertising

One of the key figures in the development of early radio advertising, George Washington Hill was a strong believer in using repetitive slogans to hammer home his products' benefits. His singular devotion to selling Lucky Strike cigarettes helped to underpin several popular network radio programs.

Hill was one of those larger than life figures who helped to shape both the tobacco industry and the advertising business. He grew up in the former as his father took on increasingly senior roles in the American Tobacco Company after it had been broken into 14 parts by a 1911 Supreme Court decision. In 1911, Hill became the vice president in charge of merchandising the company's products while his father served as president. On the senior Hill's death in 1925, G.W. Hill began two decades of company leadership.

He was singularly devoted to the company and its products. Concerned about the sales of the competing "Camels" brand of cigarettes, he initiated the "Lucky Strike" brand in 1917 and appeared to devote his every waking hour to its success. Working with such publicity experts as Edward Bernays and advertising genius Albert Lasker of the Lord and Thomas advertising agency, Hill sought out new and innovative ways to sell his brand of cigarettes, including widespread use of billboards and print advertising. He was also an early user of fledgling network radio.

From all reports, Hill was not an easy man to work for. His blustery personality and single-mindedness (other than fishing, he seemed to have few hobbies) gave him a focus few could—or wanted to—match. Hill was the model for the unlikable Even Llewelyn Evans, the protagonist in Federick Wakeman's 1946 (the year Hill died) best-selling novel *The Hucksters,* which was made into a successful 1947 motion picture. Wakeman was a former Lord and Thomas employee and wrote from his own experience as well as that of others.

Hill's Radio Role

Hill was an early if initially somewhat hesitant advertiser on network radio. Perhaps noting William Paley's success in selling La Palina cigars on the struggling Columbia Broadcasting System (CBS) network, Hill decided to see what the new medium could do for his Lucky Strike brand. He sponsored the *Lucky Strike Dance Hour* on the National Broadcasting Company (NBC; 1928–31). "Hill dictated the format, chose the announcer and orchestra, and approved all the tunes before broadcast" (Fox, 1984). He wanted loud, lively, and syncopated music that people would remember. To test the new medium's ability to attract buyers, in November and December 1928 he stopped all other Lucky Strike advertising, and sales rose 47 percent on the basis of radio advertising alone. With that, he was sold on radio. He went on selling cigarettes even when he got into trouble, as he did with the "Reach for a Lucky instead of a sweet" campaign, designed to get women to smoke. Candy manufacturers took him on, and he had to modify the sales approach. The program featured popular music, and Hill played a central role:

> George Washington Hill—a churlish, canny fellow who even in his office wore a titled sombrero adorned with fishhooks, and who rode down Fifth Avenue in an open Cadillac manned by a bodyguard and decorated on the windshield with Lucky Strike packages—lived and breathed to increase Lucky Strike sales. All his waking hours were apparently spent in devising new schemes to that end. At Lord & Thomas, he found willing lieutenants. On Saturday mornings, Hill insisted that Lord & Thomas and NBC executives, male and female, join him at rehearsals of the Lucky Strike orchestra to foxtrot to music and test its danceability. America should defeat the Depression by dancing its way out, said Hill. Therefore such dignitaries as John Royal, NBC vice president in charge of programs, and Bertha Brainard, his stylish program manager, had to dance at the Saturday morning command performances. Meanwhile the commercials got longer and more strident. NBC acquiesced, dancing to Hill's tune (Barnouw, 1968).

Long-time New York radio critic Ben Gross repeated virtually the same story in his memoirs, as told to him by NBC President Deac Aylesworth, another occasional dancer.

On this and subsequent programs he sponsored, Hill sought a "loud, hard-hitting style of performance" (Barnouw, 1968), making use of repeated slogans and often inflated claims. Sometimes it was shock value—"There is no spit in Cremo," cried the announcer in some cigar advertising on the CBS network in 1930–31.

His focus remained on his beloved Lucky Strike brand, and Hill is credited with some of the best-known and most-remembered slogans of radio advertising, such as "Lucky Strike green has gone to war" (the material used in making the package color was needed in some wartime product); "LS/MFT," which was first heard in 1942 and stood for "Lucky Strike Means Fine Tobacco," a statement both spoken and sometimes tapped out with Morse code keys; and another claim for the cigarettes as being "so round, so firm, so fully packed." Hill

George Washington Hill, 1935
Courtesy AP/Wide World Photos

retained two auctioneers (L.A. "Speed" Riggs and F.E. Boone) at $25,000 per year just to open and close programs he sponsored with rapid-fire tobacco auction sounds ending with a very clear "sold American."

Hill supported several later programs, including *Your Hit Parade,* which he "ran with an iron hand" (Dunning, 1998), meaning he controlled the songs played, the voices used, and, of course, the advertising that supported the program. One of the ad phrases promoting the show was "The best tunes of all go to Carnegie Hall," when the program moved to the New York concert hall normally known for classical music.

The *Information Please* quiz show cost American Tobacco some $11,500 a week in production and advertising costs—not including the network time—in early 1946. The company spent even more for the top-rated *Jack Benny* program, which cost the company $22,500 a week—the highest price of any show then on the air, again exclusive of airtime charges. American Tobacco remained a big radio sponsor for years after Hill's death.

CHRISTOPHER H. STERLING

George Washington Hill. Born in Philadelphia, Pennsylvania, 22 October 1884. Graduated from Horace Mann school, 1902; attended Williams College; entered tobacco business working for American Tobacco in North Carolina factories and leaf market operation, 1904; purchased tobacco company, Butler and Butler, with his father, Percival Hill, and headed merchandising, 1907; after American Tobacco trust was reorganized, became vice president and sales manager of cigarette division, 1911–12; inaugurated Lucky Strike brand, 1917; president, American Tobacco, 1925. Died near Matapedia, Quebec, 13 September 1946.

Further Reading

"The American Tobacco Company . . . ," *Fortune* (December 1936)

American Tobacco Company, *"Sold American!" The First Fifty Years,* New York: American Tobacco Company, 1954

Barnouw, Erik, *A History of Broadcasting in the United States, 1933–1953,* 3 vols., New York: Oxford University Press, 1966–70; see especially vol. 2, *The Golden Web, 1933 to 1953,* 1968

Bernays, Edward L., *Biography of an Idea: Memoirs of a Public Relation Counsel,* New York: Simon and Schuster, 1965

Dunning, John, *Tune in Yesterday: The Ultimate Encyclopedia of Old-Time Radio, 1925–1976,* Englewood Cliffs, New Jersey: Prentice-Hall, 1976; revised edition, as *On the Air: The Encyclopedia of Old-Time Radio,* New York: Oxford University Press, 1998

Fox, Stephen, *The Mirror Makers: A History of American Advertising and Its Creators,* New York: Morrow, 1984

Gross, Ben, *I Looked and I Listened: Informal Recollections of Radio and TV,* New York: Random House, 1954

Wagner, Philip, "Cigarettes vs. Candy," *The New Republic* (13 February 1929)

Hill, Lewis 1919–1957

U.S. Founder of KPFA-FM and Pacifica Foundation

Lewis Hill was the founder of the world's longest-running listener-sponsored, noncommercial radio station, KPFA-FM in Berkeley, California, and its parent organization, the Pacifica Foundation. In his writings in the 1950s, Hill articulated the first general outline of listener-supported broadcasting.

Early Years

Hill was born in 1919 in Kansas City, Missouri. His father was an attorney and his mother an heir to the Phillips petroleum fortune. Hill's father, who also owned interests in oil, later became speaker of the Oklahoma state legislature. The Hills sent Lewis to a military academy. As a teenager he rebelled against this decision by enrolling at Stanford University. There he majored in philosophy and poetry, studying with the noted poet and scholar Yvor Winters.

At Stanford, Hill fell in with the pacifist student movement and filed as a conscientious objector (CO) during World War II. After a short stay at a CO camp in Coleville, California, he served in Washington as the American Civil Liberties Union's advocate for pacifists in CO camps and prison. Possessing an excellent voice, he also worked as a radio news announcer for the National Broadcasting Company (NBC) Blue network. When asked in 1945 to read a newswire story about an incident at a Japanese internment camp in California that he believed to be false, Hill refused to do so and quit his job. Shortly afterward, he relocated to San Francisco.

Hill came out of these experiences convinced that the pacifist movement, with its emphasis on dissent against an overwhelmingly popular war, had marginalized itself. He felt that pacifism's task should now be to build institutions that both demonstrated and advocated the possibility of what he called "a pacific world in our time." With his background in poetry, he convinced a number of people associated with San Francisco's literary scene, especially poet Kenneth Rexroth, to endorse his pilot project, the construction of a pacifist-controlled radio station supported by listeners. In 1946 he and a small group of pacifists filed articles of incorporation with the state of California for the Pacifica Foundation. The organization would "carry a radical war resistance program into a mass medium," explained a 1948 circular written by Hill, "to make possible a more and more intensive cultivation of the interests of common people in resisting war." Hill warned in an early fundraising prospectus against "ivory-towerism" in the Foundation's approach to broadcasting. The Foundation's first project, KPFA-FM in Berkeley, went on the air on 15 April 1949.

KPFA and Pacifica

Between Pacifica's incorporation and KPFA's inauguration, however, the overall goals of the organization underwent significant change. Although the Foundation had originally planned an AM station in the working-class city of Richmond, the Federal Communications Commission denied Hill's application for an AM license in 1947. The foundation was forced to file for an FM license in Berkeley at a time when FM service was marginal. This adjustment transformed the social character of KPFA from a venue designed to attract "common people" to a mecca for those few, primarily university-educated individuals who owned FM receivers in the late 1940s.

When KPFA temporarily went silent in 1950 because of a lack of subscriptions, Hill felt he had no choice but to return to the ivory tower strategy. Accordingly, he created a praxis for listener-sponsored broadcasting designed to attract support from the wealthy benefactors Pacifica was to rely on for its first two difficult decades. This philosophy first surfaced in a 1952 article on KPFA in the *Quarterly of Film, Radio and Television*. "The survival of this station is based upon the necessity of voluntary subscriptions from 2 percent of the total FM audience in the area in which it operates" (Hill, 1952). This percentage most likely had its origins in pacifist dogma rather than in statistics and math. Since the early 1930s, war resisters such as Albert Einstein had argued that if 2 percent of the populace of most nations would refuse to cooperate with the draft, wars would become extinct. Now Hill used such logic to appeal to a sense of noblesse oblige in potential benefactors. The 2 percent the-

ory, Hill wrote in *Voluntary Listener Sponsorship,* his final report to the Ford Foundation, represents *"a way of extending the legitimate functions of social and cultural leadership.* Obviously, to earn systematic support from the community's intellectual leadership, the listener-sponsored station must give the values and concerns of that leadership an accurate reflection at their highest level" (emphasis in original).

Hill's KPFA tended to reflect these values; for example, the station broadcast the sermons of Zen scholar Alan Watts, the film commentary of Pauline Kael, and the book reviews of Kenneth Rexroth. A "highbrow's delight," *Time* magazine called KPFA in the 1950s. In 1953 a small faction of ex-COs within KPFA, many of them resentful of Hill's leadership, staged a bureaucratic coup and expelled him from his position as general manager at KPFA. After a long and draining struggle, Hill used his leverage with the Ford Foundation to restore himself to even greater formal authority than he had enjoyed before the quarrel.

But, probably because of the bitterness of the conflict, by the mid-1950s Hill became increasingly distant from Pacifica's affairs. He spent more time on a Rockefeller grant that, with assistance from Rexroth, he had received to produce radio programs about poetry and the famous poets of his time. This project enabled Hill to travel about the United States and Europe, corresponding with Marianne Moore, T.S. Eliot, and Wallace Stevens, the last of whom was probably Hill's favorite writer. Hill himself was a published poet, his verse appearing in *Poetry* magazine in the early 1950s. One of Hill's last surviving programs on KPFA consists of a 1957 panel discussion on Allen Ginsberg's *Howl,* copies of which had just been confiscated by the San Francisco police department at the City Lights bookshop.

By that year, Hill's health had significantly deteriorated. He had long suffered from painful arthritis of the spine and had been taking harmful amounts of cortisone for the malady. In August of 1957 Hill took his own life, leaving a mysterious suicide note: "Not for anger or despair/but for peace and a kind of home." He was survived by his wife and three children. The Pacifica Foundation went on to acquire the licenses for four more radio stations, in Los Angeles, New York City, Houston, and Washington, D.C.

MATTHEW LASAR

See also Community Radio; Educational Radio to 1967; KPFA; Pacifica Foundation; Public Affairs Programming

Lewis Kimball Hill. Born in Kansas City, Missouri, 1 May 1919. Interned as conscientious objector, 1942–43; lobbyist for ACLU National Committee on Conscientious Objectors, 1943–45; concurrent service as announcer at WINX (Washington, D.C.), 1944–45. Moved to San Francisco, early 1946, and took position as announcer, station KYA. Studied philosophy and poetry, Stanford University, 1939–41; filed Articles of Incorporation with California, forming Pacifica Foundation, 1946; launched KPFA-FM, Berkeley, 15 April 1949. Died (suicide) 1 August 1957, in San Francisco.

Selected Publications

"The Theory of Listener-Sponsored Radio," *Quarterly of Film, Radio, and Television* 7 (1952)
Voluntary Listener Sponsorship: A Report to Educational Broadcasters on the Experiment at KPFA, 1958

Further Reading

Land, Jeff, *Active Radio: Pacifica's Brash Experiment,* Minneapolis: University of Minnesota Press, 1999
Lasar, Matthew, *Pacifica Radio: The Rise of an Alternative Network,* Philadelphia, Pennsylvania: Temple University Press, 1999
Lewis, Peter M., and Jerry Booth, *The Invisible Medium: Public, Commercial, and Community Radio,* Washington, D.C.: Howard University Press, and London: Macmillan Education, 1989

Hindenburg Disaster

The broadcast of a recording of the 1937 explosion, crash, and incineration of the German zeppelin *Hindenburg* marked the first time NBC played a recording of a news event over its networks. Because the original of that recording was slightly off speed, and because in subsequent years only short excerpts have been broadcast, many people have an incomplete understanding of the reporting of the event.

The Original Recording

On 6 May 1937, at about 6:30 P.M., Herbert Morrison, an announcer and program host from WLS, Chicago, began: "How do you do everyone. We're greeting you now from the Naval Air Base at Lakehurst [New Jersey]." His words were preserved on an experimental portable Presto phonograph disc being made by WLS engineer Charles Nehlsen. Announcer Morrison and engineer Nehlsen had flown to New York on American Airlines, which had DC-3 airliners standing by for connecting flights for passengers bound to many American cities. The broadcast was intended to be good publicity for American Airlines.

Morrison told his listeners that the giant airship had been due that morning, but adverse winds over Newfoundland had slowed the trip. The *Hindenburg* had appeared over New York at noon but had to wait till dusk, when there was less wind, to dock. The ship had left Frankfurt, Germany, two and a half days earlier. This was the first crossing of the season, and also the first anniversary of this air service across the Atlantic.

For about eight minutes Morrison described the hovering *Hindenburg,* its crew, the trip, and carefully related the setting and the preparations for what everyone assumed would be a routine landing. He planned to interview several Chicago-bound passengers. Here is part of his description:

The ship is riding majestically toward us like some great feather, riding as though it was mighty, mighty proud of the place it's playing in the world's aviation. The ship is no doubt bustling with activities, as we can see, orders are shouted to the crew, the passengers probably lining the windows looking down [at] the field ahead of them, [voice in background over a loudspeaker: ". . . mooring now"] getting their glimpse of the mooring mast. And these giant flagships standing here, the American Airlines flagships waiting to rush them to all points in the United States when they get the ship moored. There are a number of important persons on board and no doubt new commander Captain Max Pruitt is thrilled too, for this is his great moment. The first time he commanded the *Hindenburg,* for on previous flights he acted as the chief officer under Captain Leyman. It's practically standing still now, they lowered ropes out of the nose of the ship, and uh, it's been taken ahold of down on the field by a number of men. It's starting to rain again, the rain had slacked up a little bit. The back motors of the ship are just holding it uh, just enough to keep it from. [A shout is heard, from some one apparently standing nearby.]

It burst into flame! [There is a click, as the arm with the needle is knocked off the recording machine. It is replaced by the engineer and Morrison is heard again.]

Get out of the way. Get out of the way. Get this Charlie. Get this Charlie. And it's crashing, it's crashing terrible. Oh my, get out of the way please. It's burning, bursting into flame and it's falling on the mooring mast, and all the folks between it. This is terrible. This is one of the worst catastrophes in the world. Oh, it was four or five hundred feet in the sky. It's a terrific crash ladies and gentlemen, the smoke and the flames now. And the frame is crashing to the ground, not quite to the mooring mast. [His voice is cracking, and he almost seems to cry.] Oh, the humanity and all the passengers screaming around here.

Morrison tells Nehlsen to stop the recording so he can catch his breath. (The recording was stopped five or more times.) He reports that he has "raced down to the burning ship" and met a dazed man who was burned but had survived. Morrison says the man told him that a number of passengers had jumped clear of the ship and were safe.

Until approximately 8:30 P.M., over a span of about two hours, Morrison and Nehlsen recorded some 40 minutes on several discs, including Morrison's accounts of helping with the wounded and his interviews with survivors. Although he first reported that it would not be possible for anyone to survive, he soon corrected himself. Amazingly, 61 people did survive, but 35 passengers, crewmen, and one ground handler were killed in the fire that lasted just over half a minute.

The first news bulletin describing the tragedy was reported on NBC's Red and Blue networks at about 7:45 P.M. EST. There were later bulletins, and a live report from an NBC mobile unit at about 2:50 A.M.

Morrison hid the four 16-inch discs under his coat and said they had to avoid people—maybe American Airline officials and other reporters—in Newark, Buffalo, and Detroit on their trip back, fearing someone might try to confiscate the recordings. In Chicago they came into the WLS studios through a back freight elevator.

Impact of the Recordings

That next day NBC broke a long-standing rule prohibiting recordings on the networks and presented parts of Morrison's recording and interviewed him live from a Chicago studio to which he and Nehlsen had returned. An announcer on NBC Blue said, "we present now one of the most unique broadcasts we have ever presented." Morrison set the scene and a recording was played. WLS later made commemorative copies of the recordings. Most radio, television, and phonograph documentaries, however, use only the most sensational first few seconds, beginning with "It burst into flame."

Broadcast historians long suspected that the original discs (or later copies) were recorded too slowly, so that when they were played back they pitched Morrison's voice too high, making him sounding rushed and hysterical. Sixty years later another recording of Morrison at a band remote in May 1938

was found that could be used for reference. Chuck Schaden of the Museum of Broadcast Communication in Chicago produced a restored, speed-corrected version of the original *Hindenburg* broadcast and played it on his program on WNIB 3 May 1997.

Repeated presentations of the slightly off-speed version and the selective use of only a small part of the recordings have given an incorrect impression. While Morrison was naturally horrified by the explosion and erroneously assumed that all on board had died, he quickly corrected himself as new information became available. Listening to the entire set of recordings reveals that he was generally calm. Despite very difficult operating conditions, his reporting was mostly clear and accurate.

John Houseman, speaking of the Mercury Theater and Orson Welles' production of "War of the Worlds," has recalled that the actor portraying a radio news reporter at the Martian ship in a New Jersey field listened repeatedly to the disc of the *Hindenburg* report, and one of his lines is: "This is the most terrifying thing I've ever witnessed." (Morrison at the *Hindenburg* had said: "Listen folks I'm going to have to stop for a few minutes because I've lost my voice, this is the worst thing I've ever witnessed.")

Morrison, a native of Pennsylvania, had begun his radio career at WMMN in Fairmont, West Virginia. His stint at WLS in Chicago was followed by work at stations in New York, and for many years in Pittsburgh. In the 1960s he returned to West Virginia to help West Virginia University develop a radio-television program. After Morrison retired from the university, he lived in Morgantown until his death in 1989.

The crash of the *Hindenburg* was a tragic beginning for on-the-spot recording of broadcast news. The original recordings were presented by WLS to the National Archives in January 1938.

LAWRENCE W. LICHTY

See also Documentary Programs; News; Recording and Studio Equipment; WLS

Further Reading

Chuck Shaden's restored, correct-speed recording of the *Hindenburg* broadcast, including a discussion of his research and his method of correcting the speed, is available from the Museum of Broadcast Communications in Chicago.

"Hindenburg Disaster: Herb Morrison Reporting" website, <www.otr.com/hindenburg.htmlhtml>
"WLS Scoops the World," *Broadcasting* (15 May 1937)

Hispanic Radio

U.S. Spanish-Language Broadcasting

Whether described as *Spanish language* or *bilingual,* programming that targets people of Latin American descent has been among the fastest-growing segments of the U.S. radio industry. From its inception in the 1920s to the present, its development has been closely tied to the character of Latin American immigration to the United States.

Early U.S. Spanish Language Radio

U.S. Spanish language radio differed significantly from the Spanish language press on the key question of ownership. Unlike newspapers, which were largely owned by members of the immigrant community, radio stations that broadcast Spanish language programming were almost never owned by Hispanics. There were no immigrant-oriented radio stations in the 1930s—only immigrant-brokered foreign language radio *programs.* The principal reason for this was cost. Compared to a small newspaper, the initial capital outlay for radio stations was seen as prohibitively high.

In the first decades of the broadcasting industry, radio station owners found that some hours of the day were less viable commercially. Owners sold these "off hours" for nominal fees to Spanish (and, in other parts of the country, to other minority) language radio programmers, who were responsible for acquiring their own sponsors. In this early period, radio station owners and advertisers did not think of the Spanish-speaking audience as consumers. This can be attributed to the relative isolation of Mexican and Mexican-American communities—the largest Latino immigrant group then and now—from the rest of society. Spanish speakers were occupationally and residentially segregated from the merchant and business classes, including radio station owners. Until Spanish speakers were conceptualized as a product that could be sold profitably to advertisers, the importance of Spanish language programming to station owners remained negligible.

However, for immigrant radio producers in the late 1920s and early 1930s, the audience was not in any sense an abstract one. Rather, programming was shaped within the immigrant enclave: face-to-face communication was key. For example, in Los Angeles, broker/programmer Rodolfo Hoyos spent much of his time walking through the commercial district of his southern California *barrio* (neighborhood) making personal calls on potential sponsors of his one-hour daily live music and talk program. During these sales calls on bakeries and *bodegas* (shops), that day's musical selections, or a recent community event that might be mentioned on the air, would also be discussed.

Emblematic of these early Spanish language radio broadcasters was Mexican musician and radio producer Pedro González. His radio program, *Los Madrugadores,* (The Early Risers) began broadcasting from KELW, Burbank, California (just north of Los Angeles) in 1927. The program mixed live performances by Mexican musicians with information about jobs and community services and was extremely popular with the city's Mexican immigrant community. González was, by training and predilection, a musician and performing artist. His response to social and political circumstances of the late 1920s and 1930s transformed him into one of the best-known Mexican-American political figures of his generation, a man *The New York Times* described in an obituary as a "folk hero and social advocate."

Following on the heels of World War I and growing isolationist feelings, and again at the onset of the Great Depression in the late 1920s, the U.S. government deported tens of thousands of Mexican immigrants. González was arrested in 1934 and was subsequently convicted on trumped-up rape charges. He was sentenced to 50 years in prison, all the while protesting his innocence. After sustained protests from the Los Angeles Mexican community, he was released from jail and deported in 1940.

González translated and broadcast advertisements from general market advertisers, such as Folger's Coffee, who were discovering the Spanish-speaking consumer market. Nonetheless, under political pressure after González's arrest, the radio station discontinued all Spanish language programming. During the early 1930s, other broadcasters in Texas and throughout the Southwest also curtailed their foreign language programming in response to harassment directed at ethnic broadcasters and the imposition of more stringent radio licensing rules. These rules from the Federal Communications Commission closely examined ownership of stations (one had to be a U.S. citizen) and required that station management be fully aware of the English meaning of all material broadcast.

The reaction of American political and commercial sectors to the emerging Spanish-speaking audience was contradictory. On the one hand, advertisers had begun to recognize the potential profitability of this audience, and radio station owners discovered that by selling blocks of formerly "dead" airtime to immigrant brokers, they could generate increased revenue. At the same time businesses were courting this community, however, politicians, labor unions, and other community leaders were characterizing Mexican immigrants as a threat.

As a cultural complement to mass deportations, in the mid-1930s the Los Angeles district attorney and other government authorities campaigned to ban Spanish from the airwaves. Although many stations continued to program Spanish language blocks, others wishing to reach Mexican-Americans moved their operations to the Mexican side of the border out of the reach of U.S. authorities. The tension created by the contradictory responses of the Anglo establishment to the Mexican community—commercially welcoming, but politically and culturally rejecting—would continue to shape the development of a Hispanic audience.

The Early Transnational Hispanic Audience

Emilio Azcárraga, patriarch of the Mexican entertainment conglomerate today known as *Televisa*, began his broadcasting empire with radio stations in the 1930s. Shortly thereafter, he began transmitting music from his Mexico City station XEW, *La Voz de América Latina* (The Voice of Latin America), to a radio station in Los Angeles, which then relayed it to other U.S. stations. In addition, Azcárraga owned five radio stations along the United States–Mexico border that transmitted directly into the United States. For Azcárraga and his fledgling broadcasting empire, the border that separates the United States from Mexico was little more than a bureaucratic nuisance. Mexicans who listened to radio lived on both sides of the official separation of the two countries.

By the 1940s U.S. broadcasters were discovering that the emotional impact of an advertising message delivered in a listener's first language and suggestively enfolded in a program of music or drama, evoking the most nostalgic memories of a listener's far-away birthplace, was infinitely greater than the same message in English. These Spanish language radio programs were broadcast weekly, not daily, in four states: New York, Arizona, Texas, and California, most of them in the off hours.

The early Spanish language radio audience in the United States was defined by its "otherness," particularly its continuing close ties to Mexico. When the commercial establishment began to imagine Spanish speakers as members of *their* marketplace, they began to mold Spanish language radio for an imagined audience more commensurate with that of the dominant, majority society. Immigrant program hosts were urged to shorten their commentary and pick up their pace, so as to better match the quick tempo of the new advertisements they were reading. The length of the music selections was also shortened to make room for more advertising breaks.

Changing the Immigrant Paradigm

In the postwar period outside the Southwest, Spanish language radio shared off-hour time slots with other foreign language radio. By the 1950s, German, Polish, Scandinavian, and other foreign language radio broadcasting began a steady decline. This was largely attributable to the assimilation of European immigrants into the dominant culture. As these peoples were recognized as predominantly English monolingual, the commercial appeal of foreign language radio programs declined; these consumers could be reached with general radio programming and advertising. As such, foreign language broadcasting was not as attractive to advertisers and thus not as appealing to radio station owners.

During this period, the number of weekly hours of U.S. Spanish language radio doubled. Two-thirds originated in the Southwest, the region most heavily populated with Spanish speakers. By 1960 Spanish language radio accounted for more than 60 percent of all U.S. foreign language radio. Spanish was the only foreign language to command entire stations and entire broadcast days. Because of continuing immigration, U.S. Spanish language radio was growing at a time when other foreign language broadcasting was dying.

Radio station owners and their advertisers were among the first to notice (in commercial terms) that the European paradigm of immigration to the United States was not identical to that of Latin American immigration. Most European immigrants, within a generation or two of their arrival, were socially and economically integrated into the majority culture, losing their European "mother tongue" in favor of English monolingualism. In addition, European immigration to the United States was discontinuous, disrupted by two world wars and the vastness of the Atlantic Ocean. Once new German immigrants, for example, stopped arriving, a generation or so later all but a few reduced their use of German or stopped speaking German completely. Consequently, the market for German language radio dropped off precipitously.

In contrast, immigrants from Latin American countries, primarily Mexico, have arrived in a steady stream (of varying size) to the United States for most of this century. Monolingual Spanish speakers settling in the United States renew the life of the language and provide a core audience for Spanish language radio programming. Today, the Spanish-speaking audience is in many ways the ideal specialized audience. Language, race, and continued close association with Latin America made it an easily identifiable audience. Between 1960 and 1974, spurred by immigration from Cuba and Puerto Rico, the number of radio stations carrying Spanish language programming doubled.

In the next quarter century, that number doubled again as immigration from Mexico and Central America increased and, in equal measure, the United States born Latino population grew. At the same time, the Hispanic audience was "discovered" by Madison Avenue and the narrowcasting broadcasting industry to be "targetable," that is, definable in market terms, and therefore a potentially profitable "niche market."

Today there are more than 400 Spanish language radio stations in the United States. Like general market U.S. radio, it is shaped by ownership chains, with the Spanish Broadcasting System being the largest. Spanish language radio formats vary from news/talk to different kinds of music—*salsa*, *norteña*, and *rock en español*. In Los Angeles and Miami, the two U.S. cities with the highest concentrations of Latinos, Spanish language radio has been consistently rated first by audience measurement firms such as Arbitron throughout the 1990s.

Reflecting the permanence and diversity of Latino communities, radio programmers have begun experimenting with bilingual radio. Youth-oriented music dominates this format, with the disc jockeys' patter and the advertisements in Spanish *and* English, as well as in Spanglish.

AMÉRICA RODRÍGUEZ

See also Border Radio; Mexico; South America

Further Reading

Fowler, Gene, and Bill Crawford, *Border Radio: Quacks, Yodelers, Pitchmen, Psychics, and Other Amazing Broadcasters of the American Airwaves,* Austin: Texas Monthly Press, 1987

Gutiérrez, Félix, and Jorge Reina Schement, *Spanish Language Radio in the Southwestern United States,* Austin: Center for Mexican-American Studies, University of Texas, 1979

Rodriguez, América, "Objectivity and Ethnicity in the Production of the *Noticiero Univisión,*" *Critical Studies in Mass Communication* 13, no. 1 (1996)

Rodriguez, América, *Making Latino News: Race, Language, Class,* Thousand Oaks, California: Sage, 1999

Rodriguez, América, "Creating an Audience and Remapping a Nation: A Brief History of U.S. Spanish-Language Broadcasting, 1930–1980," *Quarterly Review of Film and Video* 16, nos. 3–4 (2000)

Hoaxes

Pranks, Policies, and FCC Rulings

Until the early 1990s the Federal Communications Commission (FCC) had taken a relatively laissez-faire attitude toward radio hoaxes, admonishing offenders but avoiding several penalties. From 1975 to 1985 the Commission threw out a number of programming content policies initiated a decade earlier. In 1985 the FCC, under Chairman Mark Fowler's leadership, voted to eliminate its policy of restricting "scare" announcements as part of its deregulation initiatives during the Reagan administration. When the public became subject to a number of hoax abuses, however, in May 1992 the FCC issued a ruling prohibiting pranks that cause immediate public harm or divert resources from law enforcement.

War of the Worlds

Orson Welles perpetrated the first hoax in radio history in his 1938 radio play, "War of the Worlds." The national public panic over a well-crafted imaginary Martian invasion of the east coast of the United States was the ultimate demonstration of radio's impact on an audience. Subsequently, after the Welles broadcast, the FCC warned broadcasters not to use the words *bulletin* or news *flash* in entertainment programs and to provide adequate cautionary language in the airing of dramatizations.

Beginning in the 1950s legendary deejays such as Dick Biondi and Wolfman Jack attempted to shock their audiences with crazy stunts and wild antics. Radio stations across the nation undertook many pranks and trickery, such as turkeys thrown out of airplanes and a scavenger hunt for a $1,000 bill hidden in a public library, in the name of fun and higher market ratings. In the 1960s the FCC began a new era of regulation, in part because of what it perceived to be the public's vulnerability to deceptive programming and promotions. In 1960 it issued a policy statement that addressed intentional distortion or falsification of programming (i.e., news staging). In 1966 the FCC issued a stronger policy, which warned against airing "scare" announcements. The 1966 policy was a reaction to specific complaints about radio contests that disrupted traffic, caused property damage, diverted law enforcement, alarmed listeners with imaginary dangers, and threatened life. The FCC stand slowed down the occurrence of hoaxes over the next several years.

Then, in 1974, Rhode Island's WPRO-FM recreated "War of the Worlds." The program had been promoted as a spoof throughout the day. During the actual broadcast, however, 45 minutes elapsed before the station aired a public disclaimer. One hundred and forty listeners called the radio station. While station personnel had warned the local police department of its intent to air the program, the FCC admonished WPRO on the basis of its 1966 statement concerning broadcast of scare announcements.

In another instance, that same year a Tucson, Arizona radio personality, with the help of the news director, faked his own kidnapping. The commission failed to renew the license of KIKX-AM, specifically based on its violation of FCC policies related to the "fake kidnapping" (i.e., news staging, false newscasts, and licensee failure to exercise adequate control over station operations) and to a lesser extent on its technical violations on several station program logs and its Equal Employment Opportunity record. The commission affirmed its position in 1980, and two years later the District of Columbia Circuit Court upheld the decision.

Serious Radio Hoaxes

After the FCC eliminated its scare announcement policy, between 1989 and 1991 a number of serious radio hoaxes popped up across the United States; at least five are documented in the commission's ruling "Regarding Broadcast Hoaxes." Four of these incidents resulted in admonishment by the FCC, although only one resulted in a $25,000 fine. On 2 October 1989 the FCC admonished KSLX-FM in Scottsdale, Arizona, for a stunt that faked the station being taken hostage by terrorist activity. In July 1990 the commission admonished WCCC-AM/FM in Hartford, Connecticut, for reporting a nearby volcanic eruption.

In 1991 three other serious hoaxes were perpetrated by St. Louis' KSHE, Los Angeles' KROQ, and Rhode Island's WALE. On 29 January 1991 KSHE morning personality John Ulett staged a mock nuclear alert during the morning drive time, complete with a simulated Emergency Broadcast System (EBS) tone and an authentic-sounding civil defense warning that announced that the nation was under nuclear attack. There was no disclaimer until two hours after the broadcast. Four hundred listeners called the station. The FCC fined KSHE $25,000 based on the false use of EBS during the hoax. The KROQ morning team staged a false confession from an anonymous caller who claimed to have brutally murdered his girlfriend. Police spent nearly 150 hours investigating the case and the incident was featured twice on the syndicated TV program *Unsolved Mysteries*. On 9 July 1991 the WALE news director in Rhode Island announced that the overnight on-air personality had been shot in the head. Police and media rushed to investigate the incident. Upon hearing the broadcast, the program director called the station and told the producer to cease the hoax. When the producer failed to do so, the program director shut off the transmitter. The station went back on the air one minute later, with a disclaimer that aired every 30 minutes for the following 30 hours. Although the program director terminated the news director, the talk show host, and the pro-

ducer, the FCC admonished WALE for broadcasting false and misleading information and stated that the licensee was not excused by subsequent remedial action.

Anti-Hoax Ruling

The Commission's 1992 anti-hoax rule (Section 73.1217) did not discourage the morning crew at WNOR-FM in Norfolk, Virginia, from staging a series of news reports that the city park built over a landfill was about to explode. Local police, overwhelmed with concerned calls from listeners, filed complaints with the FCC. A month after the WNOR-FM incident, the FCC issued its anti-hoax ruling in an effort to target those incidents involving a false report of a crime or catastrophe. The FCC was eager to clear its docket of what appeared to be a stream of hoax violations and to enact a middle range of enforcement. The commission said that its ruling would provide enforcement flexibility by allowing fines that could range up to $25,000 a day. In the ruling the commission states:

> No licensee or permittee of any broadcast station shall broadcast false information concerning a crime or catastrophe if (a) the licensee knows this information is false, (b) it is foreseeable that broadcasting the information will cause substantial public harm. Any programming accompanied by a disclaimer will be presumed not to pose foreseeable harm if the disclaimer clearly characterizes the program as fiction and is presented in a way that is reasonable under the circumstances (amendment to Part 73 Regarding Broadcast Hoaxes, Communications Act, Report and Order, 7FCCRcd4106 [1992]).

This ruling clearly demonstrated the FCC's desire to manage promotional content abuses on the airwaves by assigning specific monetary punitive actions for serious hoaxes that posed a substantial threat to the public safety and welfare.

PHYLIS JOHNSON

See also War of the Worlds

Further Reading

Cantril, Hadley, *The Invasion of Mars: A Study in the Psychology of Panic*, Princeton, New Jersey: Princeton University Press, 1940
Cobo, Lucia, "False Radio Broadcast Evokes FCC Investigation," *Broadcasting* (4 February 1991)
"FCC Admonishes Station for Airing Hoaxes," *The News, Media, and the Law* 16, no. 1 (Winter 1992)
"FCC Moves to Revamp EBS," *Radio and Records* (25 September 1992)
Fedler, Fred, *Media Hoaxes*, Ames: Iowa State University Press, 1989

Jessell, Harry A., "FCC Picks up Pace on Indecency Enforcement," *Broadcasting* (31 August 1992)

Johnson, Phylis, and Joe S. Foote, "Pranks and Policy: Martians, Nuclear Bombs, and the 1992 Ruling on Broadcast Hoaxes," *Journal of Radio Studies* 2 (1993–94)

"KROQ Team Suspended after Murder Hoaxes," *Radio and Records* (19 April 1991)

"KSHE Radio Jolts Listeners with Fake Nuclear Bomb News," *St. Louis Post-Dispatch* (30 January 1991)

Ray, William B., *FCC: The Ups and Downs of Radio-TV Regulation,* Ames: Iowa State University Press, 1990

Tunstall, Jeremy, *Communications Deregulation: The Unleashing of America's Communications Industry,* New York and Oxford: Blackwell, 1986

Hogan, John V.L. "Jack" 1890–1960

U.S. Radio Inventor and Engineer

Jack Hogan was a key figure in early American wireless and radio broadcast development, combining invention with practical innovation. He developed the single-dial radio tuner, the first high-fidelity radio station, and later turned to mechanical television and then facsimile.

Origins

Hogan was born in Bayonne, New Jersey, in 1890. He built his first amateur radio station in 1902 at age 12, using a coherer as a detector. (A coherer was a device in which iron fillings cohered in the presence of an electrical signal, making it a useful "detector" of those signals.) Just four years later he was working as a laboratory assistant with Lee de Forest. Hogan attended the Sheffield Scientific School at Yale University, as had de Forest, specializing in physics, mathematics, and electric waves. In 1910 he went to work for Reginald Fessenden's National Electric Signaling Company (NESCO) at its Brant Rock, Massachusetts, station, as a telegraph operator. Fessenden was so impressed with Hogan that he assigned him to supervise erection of a terminal station in Brooklyn, New York. There he developed perhaps the first ink tape siphon (a method for permanently recording on a paper tape) for recording transatlantic radio signals, using an Audion amplifier. Hogan remained with Fessenden until 1914.

Radio

Hogan was a cofounder of the Institute of Radio Engineers in 1912 (he served as IRE president in 1920). In 1913 he directed acceptance tests of the U.S. Navy's first high-power station at Arlington and served as the Navy's chief research engineer until 1917, focusing on high-speed recorders for long-distance wireless. In 1917 he became commercial manager of the Inter-national Radio Signal Company. He was placed in charge of operations and manufacturing with emphasis on radio for what were then called submarine chasers (destroyers) and aircraft. In 1918 he was made manager of the International Telegraph Company.

Hogan established his own consulting practice in 1921 (founding Radio Inventions, Inc. in 1929), where he specialized in broadcast apparatus and radio regulations. During this period he also wrote *The Outline of Radio* (1923), a guide for the general public about how radio worked; the book was so well received that several subsequent editions appeared. Always interested in tonal quality, Hogan built the first high-fidelity experimental radio station, licensed as W2XR, in 1929. Hogan and Elliott Sanger converted it to become commercial classical music station WQXR in New York City in 1936.

Graphic Communication

In the 1930s Hogan began to work on television technology, and then on facsimile systems. Since his television efforts had concentrated on what turned out to be outmoded mechanical scanning systems, Hogan soon dropped television to concentrate on the more promising field of facsimile transmission, which he worked on well into the 1940s. His system was said to be both faster and to provide more fidelity of reproduction than the crude systems that preceded his. He demonstrated his system to industry observers in New York and Milwaukee in the late 1930s, using experimental radio transmitters licensed by the Federal Communications Commission (FCC). The Radio Corporation of America (RCA) nearly adopted the Hogan system, but World War II intervened.

Hogan wrote a number of articles in the 1940s, for both specialist and lay readers, on what facsimile systems could do. During World War II, he acted as advisor to several government agencies on radar, guidance systems, and missiles. He also chaired Panel 7 of the radio industry's Radio Technical Planning Board during World War II, which concerned itself with spectrum needs and technical standards for facsimile and made recommendations about these topics to the FCC.

After the war, Hogan returned to his facsimile work (resigning from WQXR in 1949 to focus his efforts further), but the systems then being touted did not develop commercially and are unrelated to facsimile as we use it today. Today Hogan is perhaps most remembered for his invention of single-dial tuning and as one of three cofounders of the Institute for Radio Engineers, the predecessor of today's Institute of Electrical and Electronic Engineers (IEEE).

CHRISTOPHER H. STERLING

See also De Forest, Lee; Fessenden, Reginald; Technical Unions; WQXR

John Vincent Lawless ("Jack") Hogan. Born in Bayonne, New Jersey, 14 February 1890. Son of John Lawless Hogan, salesperson, and Louise Eleanor Shimer, writer and musician; worked with Lee de Forest, 1906; attended Sheffield School, Yale University, 1908–10; telegraph operator with Fessenden's NESCO, 1910–14; patented single-dial radio tuning system, 1912; co-founder, Institute of Radio Engineers, 1912; chief research engineer, U.S. Navy, 1914–17; commercial manager, International Signal Company, 1917; manager, International Radio Telegraph Company, 1918–21; consultant, 1921; formed Radio Inventions, 1929; founded station W2XR (later WQXR) in New York, 1929; worked with government agencies during World War II, including Office of Scientific Research and Development; chaired Panel 7 of Radio Technical Planning Board, 1943–45; resigned as president of WQXR, 1949. Died in Forest Hills, Queens, New York, 29 December 1960.

Selected Publications

The Outline of Radio, 1923

Further Reading

Dunlap, Orrin Elmer, Jr., *Radio's 100 Men of Science: Biographical Narratives,* New York and London: Harper, 1944
Kraeuter, David W., *Radio and Television Pioneers: A Patent Bibliography,* Metuchen, New Jersey: Scarecrow Press, 1992

Hollywood and Radio

In this era of studio-owned television networks, it is difficult to remember that only a few years ago, accounts of the history of television and broadcasting cast their relationship in terms of a bitter bicoastal rivalry. Hollywood hated and resisted television as it had radio, these historians said: they turned their back on it and refused to let their stars appear on it, and one studio even forbade television sets from appearing in its films.

If we take a closer look at history, however, nothing could be further from the truth. From the earliest years of radio, Hollywood studios regarded the upstart sound-only medium with a great deal of interest—despite the fact that in those days movies had no voice at all. After a period of experimentation with movie/radio cross-promotion, a few studios attempted to enter the network business. Thwarted by both economics and regulation, the film industry turned to steady and profitable production for radio, to the point that in the mid-1930s both major networks, the National Broadcasting Company (NBC) and the Columbia Broadcasting System (CBS), constructed major studios of their own in the heart of filmland. This pro-

ductive relationship continued through the early years of television, and although radio lost its importance in the Hollywood scheme of things as television quickly took over the production of dramatic programs, film companies still maintained a presence in radio station ownership and also in the production of recorded music, so vital to radio's new format mode. The merger mania of the 1980s and 1990s consolidated these cross-ownership positions, as radio, television, film, music, and new media became interlocking parts of the same communications conglomerates.

Origins

One of the earliest instances of film/radio cooperation took place not in Hollywood but on the stage of the Capitol Theater in New York City, part of the Loews/Metro Goldwyn Mayer (MGM) chain. In 1923 theater manager Samuel L. Rothafel entered into an agreement with American Telephone and Telegraph (AT&T) to broadcast his prefilm stage show over their new station, WEAF. The results were so positive that the show quickly became a regular feature, called *Roxy and His Gang,* one of the earliest hits of radio broadcasting. Soon other theaters jumped on the bandwagon.

Movies might not have been able to talk, but that didn't mean there wasn't a lot of musical entertainment in the theaters. Many big-city theaters featured elaborate stage shows and enormous theater organs, whose musical accompaniments animated their film showings. Concerts by theater organists were broadcast over WMAC, WGN, and KWY in Chicago and in many other cities starting in 1925. That year, Harry Warner of Warner Brothers Studios proposed that the film industry as a whole should start a radio network to publicize their pictures. He began by opening a Warner Brothers radio station, KFWB in Los Angeles, and in 1926 a second one, WBPI in New York City. Other studios took note. Pathe, producers of newsreels, announced that they would begin distributing a script version of their news films for delivery over local stations. By 1927 Universal chief Carl Laemmle inaugurated the *Carl Laemmle Hour* over WOR-New York, presenting vaudeville and film stars and giving previews of upcoming pictures. MGM experimented with the world's first "telemovie": a dramatic, blow-by-blow narration of MGM's new release, *Love,* starring Greta Garbo and John Gilbert, delivered on the air by WPAP's announcer Ted Husing (usually known for his sports coverage) as it unreeled before his eyes in the Embassy Theater in New York.

That same year, MGM announced an ambitious project with the Loews theater chain: a planned network based on movie materials and promotion that would link over 60 stations in more than 40 cities. This proposal followed a more detailed one announced the previous spring by Paramount Pictures Corporation. Paramount, in conjunction with the Postal Telegraph Company, planned to start up the Keystone network "for dramatizing and advertising first-run motion pictures." Because AT&T had a lock on the land lines vitally needed to link stations together into a network, and because AT&T had an exclusive contract with the existing radio networks, Paramount needed Postal Telegraph to provide its lines. Despite much excitement in the industry, neither the Keystone Chain nor the MGM/Loews network reached fruition. A combination of regulatory discouragement, exhibitor opposition, and competition from other sources diverted studios' radio ideas in other directions. Paramount shortly thereafter purchased a 49 percent interest in the CBS network, still struggling to compete with its deep-pocketed competitor. Meanwhile, NBC's parent company, the Radio Corporation of America (RCA), acquired its own film studio, Radio-Keith-Orpheum (RKO), in 1929. Though this was intended more as a way to capitalize on RCA's new sound-on-film system than as a radio venture, the era of "talking pictures" would facilitate a renewed interest in the potential of film/radio cooperation.

Depression Years

By 1932 America had been hard hit by the Depression. Film industry profits suffered, as theaters went out of business and box office receipts slowed to a trickle. Radio, however, continued to thrive. As advertising agencies began to take the broadcast medium seriously as an outlet for their customers' campaigns, a new and influential partnership was about to emerge. Dissatisfied with CBS's and NBC's staid approach to programming, several aggressive advertising firms turned their attention to Hollywood's untapped potential for radio-based product promotion. One of the most influential in this Hollywood/agency alliance was John U. Reber of the J. Walter Thompson Company (JWT), whose plan for radio advertising envisioned big-budget, star-studded productions sponsored by JWT clients over the major radio networks. He determined to form a working relationship with the proven entertainment producers in Hollywood, and by the mid-1930s JWT was producing at least five shows out of each year's top ten, most of them featuring Hollywood talent. Other major agencies included Young and Rubicam, Blackett-Sample-Hummert, and Dancer Fitzgerald. When in 1936 AT&T, as a result of an investigation by the Federal Communications Commission, reduced their land line rates to the West Coast, a "rush to Hollywood" resulted, and most major agencies, along with the two national networks, opened up studios in Los Angeles. Radio had gone Hollywood.

This productive and profitable association would have great impact on both the radio and film industries. A variety of radio programs developed that centered on movie industry stars, properties, and Hollywood celebrities. The most prestigious was the movie adaptation format pioneered by JWT's *Lux Radio Theater.* Hosted by celebrity director Cecil B. DeMille, *Lux* presented hour-long radio adaptations of recent Hollywood film releases, introduced and narrated by DeMille and featuring well-known film stars. It started on NBC in 1934 but jumped in 1935 to CBS, where it ran until 1954. From 1936 on, the program was produced in Hollywood. Others in this format, often referred to at the time as "prestige drama," included *Screen Guild Theater, Hollywood Premiere, Academy Award Theater, Dreft Star Playhouse, Hollywood Startime,* and *Screen Directors' Playhouse.* A popular feature of these programs was the intimate, casual interviews with famous stars; DeMille, for instance, would chat at the end of each show with that night's leading actors, often casually working in a mention of the sponsor's product.

The second major venue for Hollywood stars and film promotion was radio's leading genre, the big-name variety show. Starting with the *Rudy Vallee Show* in 1929, almost all of the top-rated programs on the major networks in the 1930s belonged to this genre: the *Kate Smith Hour, Maxwell House Showboat, Shell Chateau* (Al Jolson), the *Chase and Sanborn*

Hour (Bergen and McCarthy), the *Jack Benny Program, Kraft Music Hall* (Bing Crosby), *Texaco Star Theater*, the *Eddie Cantor Show, Burns and Allen, Town Hall Tonight* (Fred Allen), and many more. All featured regular guest appearances from Hollywood's best and brightest, often promoting their latest pictures or acting out skits related to film properties. Many stars eventually began hosting such programs themselves, especially in the late 1930s and early 1940s. Adolph Menjou and John Barrymore served as hosts for *Texaco Star Theater;* Al Jolson appeared on radio almost exclusively after 1935; and William Powell and Herbert Marshall hosted *Hollywood Hotel* at various times. Some directors also got into the act: Orson Welles was a frequent variety show guest and often guest-hosted for Fred Allen, and Alfred Hitchcock established a reputation on radio before becoming a television personality. Furthermore, a whole set of Hollywood's secondary ladies became more famous via radio performances than their film careers had permitted: Lucille Ball, Dinah Shore, Joan Davis, Hattie McDaniel, Ann Sothern, and many others began as frequent guest stars, then headlined their own continuing programs on radio and later television.

Dramatic series programs also featured Hollywood talent. Most were the anthology-style programs that would also become early television's most prestigious fare. *First Nighter, Cavalcade of America, Hollywood Playhouse, Grand Central Station, Four Star Playhouse, Ford Theater, Everyman's Theater,* and many others brought film stars to radio in a wide range of stand-alone drama and comedy pieces. During the war years, Hollywood generously donated its talent to morale-boosting programs, sometimes on the regular networks and sometimes for the Armed Forces Radio Service only, such as *Command Performance, Free World Theater, Everything for the Boys, The Doctor Fights,* and many more. Hollywood stars moved freely between film and radio, and they would host and perform just as frequently on television's early dramas. Only in the mid- to late 1940s, however, did film stars begin turning up as leading actors in series comedies and dramas. The situation comedy form, pioneered by radio programs such as *Amos 'n' Andy, The Goldbergs, Fibber McGee and Molly,* and *Vic and Sade,* would be given a new gloss and prestige as Hollywood luminaries, particularly the comediennes mentioned above, moved into regular series production in shows such as *Joan Davis Time, My Favorite Husband, My Friend Irma, Maisie, Our Miss Brooks,* and *Beulah.*

Finally, mention should be made of the ever-popular genre of Hollywood gossip and talk. Many leading figures built their reputations on film industry chitchat, including the print divas Louella Parsons and Hedda Hopper. Walter Winchell also started in print but achieved full status on radio, combining gossip with news-related material. Ed Sullivan, Earl Wilson, and Jimmy Fidler all trafficked in celebrity news and views. A late-developing genre, the so-called breakfast program, presaged the television morning show *Today* with a combination of host chatter, celebrity guest interviews, and light news. Journalist Mary Margaret McBride pioneered the talk show format on radio in her long-running program of the same name. Another writer, Pegeen Fitzgerald, tried out McBride's formula in an early-morning show called *Pegeen Prefers;* she and her husband Ed would develop the first of the big-time breakfast shows, *The Fitzgeralds.* Others in this genre were *Tex and Jinx* (Tex McCrary and Jinx Falkeberg) and *Breakfast with Dorothy and Dick* (Dorothy Kilgallen and Richard Kollmar).

The film industry came increasingly to rely on the star-producing capabilities of radio as well. Radio personalities starred in many popular Hollywood films, from Freeman Gosden and Charles Correll ("Amos" and "Andy") in *Check and Double Check* in 1929, to special "radio" movies such as *The Big Broadcast of 1936* (and *1937* and *1938*), to the Bing Crosby/Bob Hope/Dorothy Lamour "Road" movies in the 1940s (*Road to Morocco, Road to Zanzibar, Road to Rio,* etc.). Rudy Vallee, Eddie Cantor, and Jack Benny all met with box-office success. Orson Welles' flamboyant production of *War of the Worlds* for the CBS *Mercury Theater of the Air* won him the contract to make *Citizen Kane* in Hollywood.

Radio and Television

As television loomed on the horizon after World War II, movie studios stood in a strong position to move into television production. A combination of network economics, the emphasis on "live" programming during television's early days, and royalty disputes within the film industry would delay the Hollywood/television alliance until the late 1950s. Though the nature of radio changed dramatically once television came onto the scene, some studios did maintain a persistent presence in radio ownership and production. Warner Brothers, Paramount, RKO, and MGM all owned radio stations, and they were to get in on television station ownership early on as well. MGM went into syndicated radio program production and distribution in the late 1940s with such programs as *MGM Theater of the Air* and *Maisie*, starring Ann Sothern. As attention and dollars shifted to television in the late 1940s and early 1950s, and as radio became once again primarily a musical medium, Hollywood stars and on-air production would migrate to the newer medium as well. Soon film studios would dominate prime-time television programming, though this would not translate into network power until passage of the FCC's financial interest and syndication rules broke up the networks' tight vertical integration in the 1970s. However, just as film companies diversified into television, they also began to acquire interests in the music industry, the new backbone of radio, with frequent cross-promotion between music and film.

Merger Mania

As the 1980s wave of mergers and acquisitions continued into the 1990s, the film majors of yore became part of diversified media conglomerates. Warner became part of the Time/Warner/Turner empire, with more than 50 labels under its imprint, including Warner Music International, Atlantic, Elektra, Rhino, Sire, and Warner Brothers. The conglomerate also has interests in music publishing, record clubs, recording technology, and music distribution. Time Warner accounted for 21 percent of U.S. music sales in 1997. Columbia Pictures was acquired by the Sony Corporation, owner of Columbia Records (acquired from CBS) and associated labels, the Columbia House music club, and other manufacturing and distribution arms, all of which accounted for 15 percent of U.S. music revenues. Universal became a part of the Music Corporation of America (MCA), which was later acquired by Seagram. MCA has long been a major presence in the music industry, with 11 percent of the U.S. market. Its labels include A&M, Decca, Def Jam, Deutsche Grammophon, Interscope, Geffen, MCA, MCA Nashville, Motown, Island, Phillips, Polydor, Universal, and Verve.

In 1995 Paramount was acquired by Viacom, owner of MTV and related cable music channels (M2, VH1), a considerable power in the music business. MTV produces radio programming as well, including radio versions of *MTV Unplugged, MTV News,* and *Weekend Revolution.* In 1995 Viacom announced a partnership with radio's largest program syndicator and station groups, Westwood One, to launch a new MTV Radio network featuring music-related material. The Disney Corporation also holds extensive interests in music recording, and with its merger with American Broadcasting Company (ABC) in 1995, it now owns radio stations that reach 24 percent of U.S. households. Twentieth Century Fox was purchased by Rupert Murdoch's News Corporation in the 1980s and is now linked with satellite music channels worldwide. News Corporation also owns the Australian Mushroom and Festival record labels. And in this age of synergy, the tie between movies and music has become tighter than ever before, with movie sound tracks used to promote artists and recordings, and sound track releases often achieving billions of dollars in sales.

In the era of new media, where the lines between film, radio, television, music, recordings, and the internet seem to be growing more blurry every day, the integrated entertainment corporations formerly designated by the term *Hollywood* have fingers in nearly every form of media that reaches into the home—or that reaches the viewer anywhere she or he might be. Now internet radio technology gives companies the ability to go on-line with their own "radio" services. DisneyRadio.com already provides a schedule of music and features from its films and artists, oriented toward children. Television shows on studio-owned networks promote recordings distributed by the company's record arm, which become hits on pop radio. Recording stars launch film careers; even radio personalities such as Howard Stern might receive a moment of celluloid fame. Though in the United States the days of radio drama and comedy faded, transferring their stars and audiences to television, the film industry continues to play a vital behind-the-scenes role linking radio to a host of other media. Without Hollywood, American radio could never have risen to the heights of creativity and popularity it achieved in its heyday. That the older medium bequeathed this tradition to a newer medium might be radio's loss, but it was television's gain.

MICHELE HILMES

See also Film Depictions of Radio; Television Depictions of Radio

Further Reading

Anderson, Christopher, *Hollywood TV: The Studio System in the Fifties,* Austin: University of Texas Press, 1994

Balio, Tino, editor, *Hollywood in the Age of Television,* Boston: Unwin Hyman, 1990

Hilmes, Michele, *Hollywood and Broadcasting: From Radio to Cable,* Urbana: University of Illinois Press, 1990

Jewell, Richard B., "Hollywood and Radio: Competition and Partnership in the 1930s," *Historical Journal of Film, Radio, and Television* 4, no. 2 (1984)

Lucich, Bernard, "The Lux Radio Theatre," in *American Broadcasting: A Source Book on the History of Radio and Television,* compiled by Lawrence Wilson Lichty and Malachi C. Topping, New York: Hastings House, 1975

Rothafel, Samuel Lionel, *Broadcasting, Its New Day,* New York and London: Century, 1925

Smoodin, Eric, "Motion Pictures and Television, 1930–1945," *Journal of the University Film and Video Association* 34, no. 3 (Summer 1982)

Watt, Kenneth, "One Minute to Go," *Saturday Evening Post* (2 April 1938 and 9 April 1938)

Hooperatings

Radio Ratings Service

Hooperatings was radio's best known and most widely quoted rating service in radio broadcasting during its heyday from 1934 to 1950. C.E. Hooper (1898–1955) pioneered a technique, the coincidental telephone call, that became an industry standard. Hooper sold subscriptions to his ratings information, making his service the first commercial venture in the field of radio ratings. C.E. Hooper, known as "Hoop," was imbued with a mission, and through his salesmanship he made his ratings service famous not just to the broadcasting industry but also to the public.

Origins

Hooper began his business career by selling aluminum utensils from door to door. He went on to earn an MBA (1923) from Harvard Graduate School of Business Administration. He took a job in Yakima, Washington, as assistant manager of the Liberty Savings and Loan Company. Between 1924 and 1926, he was advertising manager at the *Harvard Business Review*. He then took a similar job at *Scribner's Magazine*. He switched from selling space to buying space in 1929 as an account executive for Doremus and Company. After two years, at age 33, he entered the market research field as a member of the Daniel Starch organization.

Daniel Starch had taught business psychology at Harvard when Hooper was a student there. Starch conducted pioneering radio audience research for the new NBC network in 1928 and 1930, and in 1931 established the first continuous service for measuring the readerships of magazine and newspaper advertisements.

Since March 1930, Archibald Crossley had been "rating" broadcasts to estimate audience size for advertisers and for agencies that supported the Cooperative Analysis of Broadcasting (CAB). Crossley used a telephone recall method to ask listeners about their previous day's listening. He limited his surveys to areas of equal network opportunity, the 32 cities where all four networks (National Broadcasting Company [NBC] Red and Blue, Columbia Broadcasting System [CBS], and, after 1934, Mutual) could be heard with equal ease.

Hooperatings Begin

In 1934 Hooper left Starch to go into business as president of Clark–Hooper, a service that measured magazine and newspaper effectiveness. He also entered the field of radio audience measurement that same year using telephone *coincidental* calling when the audience was still listening, a method suggested to him by George Gallup. The team of Clark–Hooper, Inc. was encouraged by a group of magazine publishers who wanted to set up a more valid measure of radio's advertising effectiveness. These publishers were convinced that Crossley's ratings overstated the actual number of radio homes. More popular programs under Crossley's rating system would achieve ratings as high as 40 to 60 percent of the radio audience. To make matters worse, despite the fact that Crossley merely provided a rating index, many broadcasters persisted in projecting CAB ratings to total radio homes, resulting in an astronomical number of radio homes. The reason for this rating inflation was that Crossley initially used only the "identified listening audience," or what is now called the "share" (proportion of people tuned to a given channel based on all those using radio receivers at that time), as the base for his ratings. All of these factors hurt magazines and were factors that Clark–Hooper, Inc. undertook to correct.

Hooper's first important publicity came when, in collaboration with CBS, he estimated the number of adult listeners to President Roosevelt's fireside chat of 10 June 1936 in time for the next day's newspapers.

By 1938 the team of Clark–Hooper, Inc. had disbanded, and Hooper continued alone in the field of radio measurement. Although magazine publishers encouraged Hooper's service, they did not underwrite it. Hooper's method allowed him to innovate such features as the available audience base, resulting in ratings half the size of Crossley's. (The available audience included those not listening as well as those listening, whereas Crossley used only those listening.) Hooper also supplied an average audience rating, rather than give the total program listeners as CAB had done. An average audience rating was a program's total audience divided by the time intervals. Crossley's method, by comparison, presented only the total listeners to a given program in a sample or only the program's total audience. Furthermore, the coincidental technique eliminated what Hooper considered another major flaw with the recall method: the memory factor.

Hooper managed to make his name a household word. CAB reports had been primarily available to the buyers of advertising time, and consequently reports were guarded. Hooper, on the other hand, openly courted the press, making himself and his ratings newsworthy. His name began to appear in a vast assortment of trade magazines. In addition, he was written up in daily newspapers and even garnered a feature article in the *Saturday Evening Post* in 1947. Publicity surrounding Hooperatings rode such a crest during this period that Crossley was later to remark wryly that his defeat could be traced to the fact that his name did not rhyme with anything. (A genius at promotion, Hooper had a field day attaching his name to such derivatives as Hooperuppers, Hooperdowners, Hoopermania, and Hooperhappy.)

Whereas Crossley's reports aided the advertising community, Hooper courted the other side of the street, the networks and the stations. In particular, he did this by introducing services specifically designed to aid stations and networks. Hooper's next move, in the early 1940s, was to introduce his "Stations Listening Area Reports" for local radio markets, quickly signing up 205 local markets to CAB's none. Stations were quick to assume 44.5 percent of the cost of Hooper's operation. Hooper was, of course, weakest in advertising clients, the community sponsoring CAB. This move to local market reports, together with Hooper's open press policy, made a major impact on CAB's clients—the advertising community.

By 1944 the CAB had lost ground to Hooper's coincidental method, and over time, Crossley also switched his service to the telephone coincidental method. With both services using the coincidental method, with growing costs, and with increasing numbers of interviews yet different results, industry executives began to argue that having two services was repetitive and wasteful. CAB was considered superfluous and was forced out of business in 1946.

In 1945 Hooper made his reports available to advertisers, agencies, and networks. This strategy, which included local stations as a vital part of his service, resulted in both economic and methodological advantages. The economic results were to increase the scope of Hooper's service without excessive financial burden to any one subscriber. In this sense, Hooper operated the first radio pool made up of the commercial interests in radio, a precedent that became an industry norm.

As Frank Nye points out in *"Hoop" of Hooperatings,* the odds had been against Hooper, an unknown selling a deflationary method to those who wanted optimal figures; furthermore, his service was based on a technique one-third more costly and was pitted against a service backed by three powerful associations. Whereas CAB had been developed to serve the advertising community, Hooper had worked the other side of the street, serving stations in 60 cities and their rep firms.

Through Hooper's showmanship, the Hooperatings became increasingly important. Although Hooper took great pains to emphasize in his writings that radio program ratings are measures of quantity, not quality, many critics complained that the ratings took on the sinister quality of being an absolute artistic standard for radio programming.

Although the industry had attacked CAB in particular, telephone-based methods were coming under closer scrutiny in general. In 1929 there were 10.25 million radio homes in the U.S. (approximately 35 percent of all homes), compared to 12.4 million telephone homes (42 percent of all homes). However, the situation changed rapidly when the number of radio homes began to grow substantially faster than the number of telephone homes, raising the question of the representativeness of a telephone-based sample to measure radio. As radio went into World War II, radio homes were approaching saturation and were estimated to reach a national average of 85 percent of all homes, growing at twice the rate of telephone homes. The radio industry was beginning to grumble about the exclusion of listeners on farms, in small towns, and in areas remote from transmitters.

Coming Up on the Outside: Competition from A.C. Nielsen

Hooperatings did not survive the challenge of a new competitor, A.C. Nielsen. Its defeat lay, oddly enough, in the method it had championed, the telephone coincidental, as it attempted to measure the rise of a new advertising medium, television. The year was 1948, a year that brought attacks on two key fronts of the established Hooperatings by the up-and-coming A.C. Nielsen. These two fronts were projectable ratings (ratings projectable to a true national cross section) and TV ratings.

It became increasingly apparent that Hooper's telephone-based service was doomed if it could not develop a national sample. Hooper's Program Hooperatings measured only urban areas and were not projectable to a national audience. Because projectable ratings required a sample representative of national radio homes, Hooper's key challenge was to develop a representative sample. In April 1948 Hooper launched U.S. Hooperatings, his first projectable service of radio's listening audience. U.S. Hooperatings were an attempt to achieve this national cross section by adding a diary method to the coincidental method, in order to measure non-telephone homes. Hooper's projectable ratings were not an entity of their own but took the coincidental measurements as a base and projected them to a national total through information collected from diaries. Hooper planned to charge a separate fee to subsidize this new service, and he planned to operate it on a regular basis if enough subscriptions could be found. His primary client for such a service would be the networks.

However, Nielsen had begun integrating projectable ratings as a feature of his service with no extra charge. In addition, by March 1948 Nielsen had expanded his sample to a national basis. The bottom line was that, until ratings could be projected, they were merely indices of arbitrary value: the numbers were comparable one to another within urban areas but not representative of a national population. Nielsen thus offered a significant product innovation through the development of projectable ratings. Nielsen's projectable ratings offered both a pricing advantage and a superior method. Both strategies resulted in an eventual defeat of Hooperatings. U.S. Hooperatings failed to achieve enough subscriptions to launch the projectable rating service as a regular feature.

A second critical factor in Hooper's defeat by Nielsen was the rise of television. The Hooper network service covered only the larger urban areas with telephone homes. This coverage, however, represented only 20 percent of the population. Television had hit these urban areas the hardest and had made the most impact in cities where Hooper had based his radio rating service. In other words, although radio use was falling in the areas measured by Hooper's network service, it was not falling in 80 percent of the nation's homes. Thus, according to Nielsen, it was utterly unrealistic for Hooper to ignore TV's impact in his network radio cities.

Hooper had based his network program ratings wholly on telephone homes in the urban areas where television had made the greatest inroads. Thus, his sample was attacked for overweighing the influence of TV on radio listenership. To make matters worse, telephone subscribers were found to own a disproportionate number of TVs, when compared to nonsubscribers. Hooper consequently was accused of shortchanging and deflating radio.

In February 1950 Hooper sold his national ratings services (national radio and national TV ratings) to A.C. Nielsen, Inc. Hooper cited three factors in his decision. First, the number of sponsored network radio programs on the air had dropped 40 percent in three years. Thus, his radio network service had declined because of the flight of advertisers to network TV. Second, Hooper noted the increased competition from Nielsen. According to Hooper, without Nielsen competition, he would have continued his network Hooperatings, "riding the radio curve down and the television curve up." With the growing revenue split between Hooper and Nielsen, even the network TV rating business did not bring the total network ratings to a profitable level. Revenue had dropped from $40,000 annually in January 1949 to $25,000 by January 1950. Third, Hooper stated that television had so changed listening habits in cities with TV service that the averaging of listeners in cities with and without TV was no longer plausible.

The 36-city–based network Hooperatings assumed that "conditions" under which measurements were taken remained relatively constant and that consequently the change in the rating index or rank was a valid indication of change in popularity. Because television came first to the big cities, where Hooper had based his samples, his reports indicated that radio audiences were moving in large numbers to TV. However, this was not true in most of the country. In not being representative, National Hooperatings indices had become essentially meaningless.

Although Hooper quit the national rating business, he planned to continue at the local level with city Hooperatings, city teleratings, area coverage indices, and sales impact ratings. These local markets were now where Hooper was getting two-thirds of his profits. In a prophetic statement, Hooper argued that the shift in their packaging was away from one average index to analytic reports of individual markets and of differences between markets. Hooper left the national rating field for TV and radio to A.C. Nielsen, Inc., and his Audimeter. Though he planned to continue his local market services, Hooper's untimely death in a boating accident prevented these plans from reaching fruition. The American Research Bureau (later Arbitron) purchased Hooper's remaining local service in 1955.

KAREN S. BUZZARD

See also A.C. Nielsen Company; Arbitron; Audience Research Methods; Cooperative Analysis of Broadcasting; Diary

Further Reading

Beville, Hugh Malcom, *Audience Ratings: Radio, TV, Cable,* Hillsdale, New Jersey: Erlbaum, 1985; 2nd edition, 1988

Buzzard, Karen S., *Chains of Gold: Marketing the Ratings and Rating the Markets,* Metuchen, New Jersey: Scarecrow Press, 1990

Buzzard, Karen S., "Radio Ratings Pioneers: The Development of a Standardized Ratings Vocabulary," *Journal of Radio Studies* 6, no. 2 (Autumn 1999)

Chappell, Matthew Napoleon, and Claude Ernest Hooper, *Radio Audience Measurement,* New York: Daye, 1944

Nye, Frank Wilson, *"Hoop" of Hooperatings: The Man and His Work,* Norwalk, Connecticut: n.p., 1957

Small, C.E., "Biggest Man in Radio: C.E. Hooper," *Saturday Evening Post* (22 November 1947)

Hoover, Herbert 1874–1964

United States Secretary of Commerce (1921–1928) and President (1929–1933)

Although he later became President (1929–33), Herbert Hoover's importance to radio broadcasting lies in his service as the medium's first federal regulator. Hoover's cabinet department licensed and regulated radio stations while he served as Secretary of Commerce (1921–28). Managing the largest department of government at that time, Hoover attempted to influence the fledgling radio industry through speeches and called four national radio conferences in an effort to develop support for legislation that he eventually achieved with the Radio Act of 1927.

Among Hoover's vast array of concerns as Secretary of Commerce was the growth of radio broadcasting. When broadcasting burst onto the scene in the early 1920s, Hoover defined, explained, and advocated certain fundamental principles of public policy that today remain the accepted foundation upon which U.S. broadcasting rests.

Almost immediately after becoming Secretary of Commerce, Hoover was made aware of the challenges plaguing broadcasting. Because of the limited use of wireless prior to the advent of radio broadcasting, there had been no pressing need for spectrum planning, let alone further legislation. Hoover had to make policy decisions using the expertise of his staff, who supplied him with an array of recommendations on the direction radio regulation should take. The staff perceived the primary difficulties to be the determination of who was to broadcast, what was to be broadcast, and under what conditions.

From his experience in public life, Herbert Hoover had developed a strong philosophy of the proper relationship between government, business, and the individual. Facing a rising storm of listener protest over growing signal interference from the flood of stations taking to the air on a limited number of frequencies, Hoover undertook three approaches to resolving the policy impasse. From 1922 through 1925 he called four national radio conferences in Washington to poll industry figures for a consensus on what should be done. The first was attended by about 30 engineers and attorneys; the fourth attracted the attendance and participation of several hundred people from all parts of the growing industry. Department staff drafted agendas for the meetings, made recommendations, and supported conference results that paralleled their own thinking, often ignoring those that did not. Each conference concluded with ever stronger pleas to Congress to replace the obsolete and limited Radio Act of 1912 with something specifically designed for broadcasting.

At the same time, Hoover's department slowly expanded the number of frequencies available for broadcast station use—from only one in 1920 to three channels by August 1922

and the beginnings of a band of continuous frequencies in mid-1923. By April 1927, most of the present AM band had been so allocated. But Hoover and the department were doing this largely on their own initiative, as the Radio Act of 1912 provided little guidance and gave the secretary no discretion.

That lack of regulatory discretion eventually halted his activity, laudable though everyone agreed that it was. When Hoover sought to rein in what he saw as renegade stations that changed frequency, power, or location, thus adding to interference problems, he lost. A 1926 Chicago case held that he lacked the authority to issue such orders—the Radio Act merely allowed the department to issue licenses. Adding to the bleak picture, the U.S. Attorney General issued an advisory opinion that Hoover had largely exceeded his authority under the 1912 Act. It was clear that Congress would have to take action on new legislation.

Hoover often used the term "public interest" in reference to radio. He asserted that radio had become a "public concern impressed with the public trust" and that its use should be considered primarily "from the standpoint of the public interest to the same extent and on the same basis of the same general principles as our other public utilities." Use of this language by Hoover and his staff helped Congress to settle on the phrase "public interest, convenience, or necessity" in the 1927 Radio Act. Hoover stated often and consistently that broadcast regulation must: (1) establish service to the public as its paramount characteristic; (2) avoid monopoly in the control of facilities but not restrict necessary growth; (3) prohibit censorship by either private parties or groups or the government; (4) sustain broadcasting as an area for free and full development by private enterprise; and (5) be subject only to the degree of regulation necessary to protect the public against abuses.

Through trial and error, the essential ingredients of the regulatory scheme embodied in the Act of 1927 were refined during the daily operations of the Bureaus of Navigation and Standards of the Department of Commerce. The new legislation that finally passed was greatly influenced by the philosophy expressed and promoted by Secretary Hoover and was a reflection of his general influence in government and of the respect with which he was viewed.

MARVIN BENSMAN

See also Dill, Clarence C.; Frequency Allocation; Public Interest, Convenience, or Necessity; Regulation; United States Congress and Radio; White, Wallace H.; Wireless Acts of 1910 and 1912/Radio Acts of 1912 and 1927

Herbert Hoover (left), 1939
Courtesy CBS Photo Archive

Herbert Clark Hoover. Born in West Branch, Iowa, 10 August 1874. Graduate of first four-year class of Stanford University, 1895; organized assistance for U.S. citizens stranded in London at start of World War I, 1914; organized Commission for Relief of Belgium, 1914–17; appointed Food Administrator by President Wilson, 1917; organized European Children's Relief Agency and campaigned for League of Nations, 1921; became Secretary of Commerce, 1921; served as 31st President of the United States, 1928–32; lost presidential election to Franklin D. Roosevelt, 1932; active in public service as leader of Commission on the Organization of the Executive Branch of Government under Presidents Truman and Eisenhower, 1947–49 and 1952–55; received numerous honors from broadcast industry for his role in the development of the U.S. system of broadcasting. Died in New York City, 20 October 1964.

Selected Publications

Address upon the American Road, 1922
American Individualism, 1922
American Ideals versus the New Deal, 1936
Memoirs; Volumes I and II, 1951–52

Further Reading

Archer, Gleason Leonard, *History of Radio to 1926,* New
    York: American Historical Society, 1938; reprint, New
    York: Arno Press, 1971

Bensman, Marvin R., *The Beginning of Broadcast Regulation in the 20th Century,* Jefferson, North Carolina: McFarland, 2000

Bernstein, Marver H., *Regulating Business by Independent Commission,* Princeton, New Jersey: Princeton University Press, 1966

Brandes, Joseph, *Herbert Hoover and Economic Diplomacy: Department of Commerce Policy, 1921–1928,* Pittsburgh, Pennsylvania: University of Pittsburgh Press, 1962

Cochrane, Rexmond Canning, *Measures for Progress: A History of the National Bureau of Standards,* Washington, D.C.: Department of Commerce, National Bureau of Standards, 1966

Irwin, Will, *Herbert Hoover: A Reminiscent Biography,* New York: Century, and Grosset and Dunlap, 1928

Lyons, Eugene, *The Herbert Hoover Story,* Washington, D.C.: Human Events, 1959

Wilbur, Ray Lyman, and Arthur Mastick Hyde, *The Hoover Policies,* New York: Scribner, 1937

Wolfe, Harold, *Herbert Hoover, Public Servant and Leader of the Loyal Opposition: A Study of His Life and Career,* New York: Exposition Press, 1956

Hope, Bob 1903–2003

U.S. Comedian and Actor

Recognized for his versatility in vaudeville, on Broadway, in films, and on television, and for his USO performances for military troops around the world, Bob Hope is also remembered for his contributions to radio, where he starred in variety programs for a decade. In company with comedian Jack Benny and ventriloquist Edgar Bergen, Hope was consistently listed among the top ten network radio shows during World War II, perhaps because such programs helped audiences to forget the serious world outside.

Although Hope initially rejected radio because he thought it "would never amount to anything," Henderson (1988) remarks that Hope's "crackling, one-liner patter suited radio and he soon became one of the most popular performers on the air." His radio appearances on Columbia Broadcasting System (CBS) and National Broadcasting Company (NBC) radio were memorable because of his non-sequiturs and barbed monologues that he had honed in vaudeville and on Broadway.

In May 1937 Hope signed a 26-week contract for the *Woodbury Soap Show,* broadcast from New York. Later that same year, when he traveled to Hollywood to film *The Big Broadcast,* he continued the show on a transcontinental hookup. After the Woodbury program, he was signed to *Your Hollywood Parade,* which originated in California. By the time he signed to work with Paramount, the show blended with his plans, enabling him to fulfill the demands of both film and radio. It was during this period that he developed his trademark topical joke and monologue. Morella (1973) says the tone for the radio shows would be set by the breezy, irreverent monologue, heavily spiced with pointed allusions to current affairs. During the airing of one show, Hope was clocked at seven jokes per minute. To help maintain the frenetic radio pace, he had as many as a dozen writers producing about 150 jokes a week just to fill his three-minute monologue and four-minute guest spot. *The Bob Hope Pepsodent Show* was the top-rated radio program of 1944.

Among the many techniques Hope used to become a major radio entertainer was his arranging for an ongoing feud with singer Bing Crosby. They pretended dislike for one another over Hope's envy of Crosby's wealth, singing ability, and status as leading man. Thompson (1981) says that the early radio broadcasts of the Pepsodent Show from 1938–1948 established a pattern to the Hope-Crosby relationship: Crosby was the archetypal city slicker and Hope the brash country bumpkin who was always being used but somehow managed to come out right in the end. Hope's efforts at ridicule sometimes backfired, however. For instance, in an episode in which Hope pretended to kill his sidekick Jerry Colonna (who was playing the part of Santa Claus), the level of negative reaction was so intense that for a short time the sponsoring Pepsodent company considered canceling the show. Colonna was an important part of Hope's radio broadcasts that audiences associated with the show, in addition to orchestra leader Skinnay Ennis and the vocal group Six Hits and a Miss.

When World War II began, Hope tried to enlist but was told he could better serve as an entertainer. With his USO troupe he made trips to Sicily, Britain, Alaska, North Africa, and the South Pacific. He was the mainstay of the Armed Forces Radio Service (AFRS), the network of stations the army and navy set up in the European and Pacific war theaters, and he performed regularly on such AFRS programs heard only by military personnel, such as *Command Performance, Mail Call,* and *GI Journal.*

Bob Hope
Courtesy of NBC

After the war, both the critics and the public began to desert Hope and his new sponsor, Lever Brothers. Some criticism was directed at the sameness of Hope's material; "the old zing was missing," writes Morella. In 1948 Hope dropped two of his best-known associates, Colonna and Vera Vague. However, in 1953 a move to morning radio and new sponsor General Foods landed Hope a $2 million contract, the biggest single-season deal in radio history to that date. Morella explains that, although Hope's experiment with daytime radio was successful and his show lasted for five years, he eventually decided to stop bucking the tide. Radio listeners preferred music and talk shows; radio comedy had lost its appeal.

With the decline of network radio, Hope was one of a number of CBS stars (others included Groucho Marx, Kate Smith, and Ed Wynn) who were lured to NBC television in 1948–49. After doing stand-up humor and slapstick sketches on several programs, Hope was able to add a visual dimension to his established radio format and his own *Bob Hope Show* made its debut in 1952.

Unlike Hope's *Pepsodent Show,* his television work was confined mostly to monthly specials, particularly his Christmas shows for service personnel in remote areas. Schulman and Youman (1966) note that his popularity and acceptance were such that whoops of laughter greeted his barbed comments on social and political problems—comments that, from another comedian, might have been considered a breach of taste and manners.

The basic format of Hope's comedy shows—a monologue followed by sketches with other guest stars—remained unchanged since his radio days in the 1930s. The passing years diminished neither the polish nor the exuberance of his performance. When he was honored by the Kennedy Center in 1985 for his mastery of television, film, and radio, it was estimated that, during seven decades in show business, he had been seen and heard by more people than any other entertainer on earth. A resolution passed by the U.S. Congress in October 1997 declared Hope "a part of American folklore."

ALF PRATTE

See also Comedy; Crosby, Bing; Hollywood and Radio

Bob Hope. Born Leslie Townes Hope in Eltham, England, 29 May 1903. Moved to United States, 1907; raised in Cleveland, Ohio; fought briefly as amateur boxer; worked in vaudeville, and theaters across country; appeared in first Broadway show, 1927; first radio appearance on *Capital Family Hour,* 1932; first movie appearance in *The Big Broadcast of 1938;* first TV show, *The Bob Hope Show,* 1952; appeared in over 50 films; president, American Guild of Variety Artists, 1953. Received Oscars for humanitarian work, Academy of Motion Picture Arts and Sciences, 1940, 1944, 1952, 1959, 1965; Peabody Award for three decades of broadcasting, 1968; Presidential Medal of Freedom, 1969. Died in Toluca Lake, California, 27 July 2003.

Radio Series

1937	*Woodbury Soap Show*
1938	*Your Hollywood Parade*
1938–48	*The Bob Hope Pepsodent Show*

Television Series

The Bob Hope Special, 1950–51; *The Colgate Comedy Hour,* 1952–53; *The Bob Hope Show,* 1952–56; *The Bob Hope Christmas Special,* 1954–74; *Academy Awards* (master of ceremonies), 1960–75; *Bob Hope Presents the Chrysler Hour,* 1963–67

Selected Films

The Big Broadcast, 1938; *Thanks for the Memory,* 1938; *Road to Singapore,* 1940; *Caught in the Draft,* 1941; *Road to Zanzibar,* 1941; *Road to Morocco,* 1942; *On the Road to Utopia,* 1945; *Monsier Beaucaire,* 1946; *Road to Rio,* 1947; *The Paleface,* 1948; *The Great Lover,* 1949; *Fancy Pants,* 1950; *On the Road to Bali,* 1952; *The Seven Little Foys,* 1955; *Beau James,* 1957; *Road to Hong Kong,* 1962; *Critic's Choice,* 1963; *Cancel My Reservations,* 1972

Selected Publications

They Got Me Covered, 1941
I Never Left Home, 1944
So This Is Peace, 1946
Have Tux Will Travel, 1954
I Owe Russia $1200, 1963
Five Women I Love: Bob Hope's Vietnam Story, 1966
The Last Christmas Show, 1974
The Road to Hollywood: My 40-Year Love Affair with the Movies (with Bob Thomas), 1977
Bob Hope's Confessions of a Hooker: My Lifelong Love Affair with Golf, 1985

Further Reading

Henderson, Amy, *On the Air: Pioneers of American Broadcasting,* Washington, D.C.: Smithsonian Institution Press, 1988

Morella, Joe, Edward Z. Epstein, and Eleanor Clark, *The Amazing Careers of Bob Hope: From Gags to Riches,* New Rochelle, New York: Arlington House, 1973

Shulman, Arthur, and Roger Youman, *How Sweet It Was: Television: A Pictorial Commentary,* New York: Bonanza Books, 1966; as *The Golden Age of Television: How Sweet It Was,* New York: Bonanza Books, 1979

Thompson, Charles, *Bob Hope: Portrait of a Superstar,* New York: St. Martin's Press, 1981

Horror Programs

Horror programs occasionally featured classic monsters like vampires and werewolves, but more often were home to the walking dead, disembodied spirits, or unique creations. In the 1940s, *Inner Sanctum*'s no-holds-barred formula set the standard, and its "creaking door" is one of radio's best-remembered icons. Listeners never knew what would happen on *Inner Sanctum* or who would be the next victim. In many cases, the episode's narrator turned out to be the murderer! As John Dunning observes, "without benefit of the guilty knowledge, the listener was recruited as the killer's sidekick."

Origins

The real origins of radio horror can be found in the 1930s, but like all popular phenomena, the trend did not occur in isolation. Dime novels had been popular since before the turn of the century, and their direct descendants, the pulp magazines, had become increasingly lurid throughout the 1920s and early 1930s.

Pulps like *Weird Tales* displayed fantastic, horrific, and just plain odd cover images. The March 1923 *Weird Tales* cover, illustrating the story "Ooze," depicts a tentacled, shadowy figure. Horned devils (October 1925), fiendish dwarves (March 1926), wolf-women (September 1927), treacherous druids (October 1930), and monstrous gorillas (September 1929) were common. Stories included Carl Jacobi's "Mive" (January 1932), about carnivorous butterflies, and H.P. Lovecraft's stories of unnamable, lurking monstrosities and rats inside walls. Horror was certainly in the air when Universal Studios inaugurated its series of "monster movies" with 1931's *Dracula* and *Frankenstein*.

Radio's *Collier Hour* serialized stories of Fu Manchu in 1929, complete with menacing fungus and poisonous green mist. "The Shadow" first appeared as a nameless narrator on the *Street & Smith Detective Story Magazine Hour* but would reincarnate in his own program, as an adventurer "with the power to cloud men's minds." Research is now uncovering isolated references to early 1930s horror programs, but the first significant horror program was *The Witch's Tale*, which began on New York's WOR on 28 May 1931.

Written by Alonzo Deen Cole, the series derived from the folk tale tradition. "Old Nancy, the witch of Salem," began by gathering listeners around her fire. "A hunnert and fifteen year old" (her age changed frequently), she sat with "Satan, her wise black cat," inviting listeners to "turn out them lights" and "gaze into the embers" as she wove her tales. Old Nancy's dialect and stories are "straight from the Middle Ages," as Dunning notes. The supernatural dominates, as ghosts seek vengeance, tombs are defiled, and curses are cast. Caucasians laugh at "silly native superstitions" in "Spirits of the Lake" and "The Boa Goddess," only to die horribly. Cole adapted legends like "The Flying Dutchman" and even tackled Mary Shelly's *Frankenstein*. In "The Bronze Venus," a man dies in the arms of a living bronze statue, and in "The Troth of Death," a man betrays his lover, only to be doomed to spend eternity chained to a cemetery.

Nationally syndicated in 1934, the program survived at least half a dozen incarnations. (Ironically, one of the best and most popular surviving *Witch's Tale* episodes, "Four Fingers and a Thumb," originated in Australia.) Adelaide Fitz-Allen, Martha Wentworth, and 13-year-old Miriam Wolfe provided Old Nancy's voice.

In 1934, Wyllis Cooper created *Lights Out* for Chicago's WENR, drastically changing the tone of radio horror. Creative sound effects embellished imaginative nightmares, like people turned inside out, or the "Chicken Heart," which grows to monstrous size. In "Murder Castle," a killer suffocates. "Snake Woman" gains revenge with trained serpents. A chemist discovers "Oxychloride X," a chemical that eats through anything. By 1939, writer Arch Oboler turned to more mainstream fare, claiming that he couldn't keep on topping his own horror stories.

The Hermit's Cave originated in 1935 on Detroit's WJR. It was syndicated nationally by the 1940s, with a later West Coast version. The Hermit (played variously by John Kent, Klock Ryder, Toby Gremmer, and Charles Penman, who also directed) was a cackling counterpart to Old Nancy. He spoke over howling winds, promising "Ghost stories! Weirrrrrd stories! And murders, too! The hermit knows of them all!" Detroit acting troupe "The Mummers" produced ghost stories like "A Haunted House," witchcraft tales like "The Red Mark," and grisly fare like "The Vampire's Desire."

By the mid 1930s, local stations were anxious to cash in with programs like WKY's *Dark Fantasy*, which broadcast from Oklahoma City. Network "Creepy hosts" like Ted Osborne can be heard on two surviving episodes of *The Black Chapel*, while Charles Penman hosted *The Devil's Scrapbook* in 1938. Others like *The Devil's Roost* and *The Witching Hour* no longer exist.

Inner Sanctum Mysteries began on 7 January 1941. "Raymond" was a new model for the "creepy host," and *Inner Sanctum* incorporated both strands of previous horror programming—Old Nancy's melodramatic supernatural tales and *Lights Out*'s explicit detail—and added its own unique flavor. Shamelessly theatrical, *Inner Sanctum* resorted to any melodramatic device to engage the listener. Background screams and sudden appearances of characters thought dead were common. Best of all, Raymond relished puns. He professed to keep a "happy medium around to keep in the right . . . spirit." Raymond's moral of an ax murderer story was "Knife can be beautiful . . . if you look out for people with an ax to grind. They may be trying to get a HEAD of you."

Many non-horror series contained occasional genre trappings during their run. Orson Welles had famously adapted *Dracula* in 1938, and his *War of the Worlds* adaptation frightened thousands. The high profile *Suspense* adapted H.P. Lovecraft's *The Dunwich Horror,* and in "The Diary of Sophronia Winters," Agnes Moorehead's character wallops Ray Collins in the head with an axe. A werewolf stalks "The House in Cypress Canyon."

The Shadow fought monsters like "The Gibbering Things" and "The Weird Sisters" (both written by Alonzo Deen Cole), and *The Hound of the Baskervilles* was periodically reincarnated in *The New Adventures of Sherlock Holmes.* Beginning in 1939, the best-remembered serial adventure, *I Love a Mystery,* depicted gruesome murders and (apparently) supernatural menaces. Jack, Doc, and Reggie often encountered weird horrors like "Temple of the Vampires" or the "Monster in the Mansion," which involved an arm amputation and a headless black cat. A slasher roams the halls as a ghostly baby cries in "The Thing That Cries in the Night."

Still, *Inner Sanctum*'s influence dominated, as new narrator/hosts appeared on other programs. *Suspense* was introduced by "The Man in Black," and by 1942 even a crime melodrama like *The Whistler* featured a nameless host. *The Mysterious Traveler* (Maurice Tarplin) rode a ghostly train, inviting listeners to join "another journey into the strange and terrifying." The Traveler told science fiction (insects seek revenge), ghost stories (haunted honeymoon cottage), and originals like "Behind the Locked Door." In this gem, trapped archaeologists discover sightless, horribly mutated descendants of a lost wagon train. *The Strange Dr. Weird,* who lived "on the other side of the cemetery," was a 15-minute version of *The Mysterious Traveler* and was also voiced by Maurice Tarplin.

A 1942 *Lights Out* revival had new narration, droned by Arch Oboler: "It-is-later-than-you-think." (The original *Lights Out* Chicago series began more effectively with "This is the witching hour. An hour when dogs howl, and evil is let loose on a sleeping world.") *The Haunting Hour*'s opening was similar to the *Lights Out* original, with "Stay where you are! Do not break the stillness of this moment!" but the scripts were *Inner Sanctum* rewrites. *The Sealed Book* from 1945 sounded like *The Hermit's Cave,* as Philip Clarke, "The Keeper of the Book," unlocked "the great padlock," revealing "all the secrets and mysteries of mankind through the ages." Astonishingly, Don Douglas provided *all* the voices on *The Black Castle.*

Mystery in the Air, a 1947 summer replacement series with oily-voiced Peter Lorre, adapted classics like "The Tell-tale Heart," "The Black Cat," and "The Horla." Lorre's effective performances usually ended with his screaming insanely. Willis Cooper returned with one of the finest horror/fantasy programs in 1947. *Quiet, Please* was surrealistic, lyrical and subdued. In "Let the Lillies Consider," Cooper asked, "What if plant life could think . . . and plot against us?" A resurrected god appears in "Whence Came You?" and something perches atop an oil rig in "The Thing on the Fourble Board." Each week, the *Quiet, Please* host signed off with, "I'm quietly yours, Ernest Chappell."

The Hall of Fantasy, originally broadcast from Salt Lake City's KALL, was revived by producer/director/writer Richard Thorne for Chicago's WGN in 1949. The show began with sounds of footsteps on wet concrete and featured unusually excellent production values, adapting Poe's "The Cask of Amontillado" and J. Sheridan LeFanu's "Green Tea." Thorne also contributed originals like "The Hand of Botar," in which a man develops intelligence in his right hand, and "The Jewels of Kali," in which a bizarre four-armed body searches the world for four mystical rubies.

Himan Brown's *CBS Radio Mystery Theater* adapted Poe and Shelly in the 1970s and 1980s, and similar radio programming continues today. Recreations are popular at conventions, and amateur groups often mix horror programs and science fiction productions. Still, as Hollywood movies feature increasingly realistic digital effects, it remains for new talents to harness the imagination with the aural medium and convincingly recreate the horror genre on radio.

DIXON H. CHANDLER II

See also Brown, Himan; I Love a Mystery; Inner Sanctum Mysteries; Lights Out; Oboler, Arch; The Shadow; Suspense; War of the Worlds

Further Reading

Cole, Alonzo Deen, *The Witch's Tale: Stories of Gothic Horror from the Golden Age of Radio,* edited by David S. Siegel, Yorktown Heights, New York: Dunwich Press, 1998

Dunning, John, *Tune in Yesterday: The Ultimate Encyclopedia of Old-Time Radio, 1925–1976,* Englewood Cliffs, New Jersey: Prentice-Hall, 1976; revised edition, as *On the Air: The Encyclopedia of Old-Time Radio,* New York: Oxford University Press, 1998

Gibson, Walter Brown, *The Shadow Scrapbook,* edited by Anthony Tollin, New York: Harcourt Brace Jovanovich, 1979

Goodstone, Tony, editor, *The Pulps: Fifty Years of American Pop Culture,* New York: Bonanza Books, 1970

Hickerson, Jay, *The Ultimate History of Network Radio Programming and Guide to All Circulating Shows,* Hamden, Connecticut: Hickerson, 1992

Server, Lee, *Danger Is My Business: An Illustrated History of the Fabulous Pulp Magazines*, San Francisco: Chronicle Books, 1993

Swartz, Jon David, and Robert C. Reinehr, *Handbook of Old-Time Radio: A Comprehensive Guide to Golden Age Radio Listening and Collecting*, Metuchen, New Jersey: Scarecrow Press, 1993

Hottelet, Richard C. 1917–

U.S. News Correspondent

One of the legendary "Murrow boys," Richard Curt Hottelet served as a radio correspondent for Columbia Broadcasting System (CBS) News during World War II. Edward R. Murrow hired the 26-year-old Hottelet in January 1944. He worked for CBS from 1944 until 1985, as both a radio and a television reporter.

Of German descent, Hottelet was born on 22 September 1917 in New York. During the Depression, his father lost his import-export business, and his family moved around frequently. After Hottelet graduated with a B.A. degree in philosophy from Brooklyn College in 1937, he had no clear-cut career ambitions, so his father suggested that he go to Berlin to study and live with a family relative. After he saw his philosophy professor at the University of Berlin greeting students with the Nazi salute, Hottelet tried out several other classes before dropping out altogether. Though he held no real interest in becoming a journalist, the United Press hired him as a stringer, and eventually he became a full-time correspondent. Along with another future "Murrow boy," Howard K. Smith, Hottelet worked at the United Press' Berlin bureau from the late 1930s until 1941.

Hottelet became a seasoned reporter in his early 20s. He covered Germany's marches into the Sudetenland and later into Belgium and France by the time he was 22; he also witnessed the Dunkerque evacuation. His penchant for investigating the aftermaths of British bombing raids in Berlin and his "unconcealed abhorrence of Nazism" caught the attention and ire of the Gestapo (Bliss, 1991). He already had been taken into custody and questioned after phoning in a story on the deporting of Jews. Hottelet's girlfriend, Ann Delafield (whom he later married), worked at the British passport control office in Spain, and she had formerly worked at the British embassy in Berlin. The Gestapo arrested Hottelet for espionage and charged him with sending German secrets to his girlfriend in Spain (Cloud and Olson, 1996).

The only American reporter arrested by the Gestapo, Hottelet spent four months in jail in 1941, in Alexanderplatz and Moabit prisons, where he was threatened with execution. His arrest became a *cause célèbre* back in the United States. He was finally released in July 1941, along with another reporter, in exchange for the U.S. release of two German spies. After returning to the United States, Hottelet worked at the United Press' Washington bureau and then for the Office of War Information (OWI) in London. Hottelet's duties at the OWI included making broadcasts in German and writing propaganda leaflets that were dropped over Germany.

Hottelet resigned from the OWI in December 1943. He later described his decision: "I felt that government service was not for me and asked Ed Murrow for a job. He was thinking about building up the staff for the events of 1944, and in January I joined CBS" (quoted in Bliss, 1991). Murrow had already known him by that time. Hottelet was the youngest of the Murrow boys, and the most conservative in his personal views (Cloud and Olson, 1996).

As the newest of Murrow's crack reporting team, Hottelet covered the D-Day landing from a B-26 Marauder bomber while reporting on the Ninth Air Force. His was the first news report made at the beginning of the Battle of the Bulge in December 1944; he covered the U.S. First Division, popularly known as the Big Red One. In March 1945, Hottelet covered Operation Varsity from an unarmed B-17 bomber with other reporters, photographers, and observers and had to bail out after the plane was hit.

As did other war correspondents, Hottelet saw firsthand the Nazi death camps in 1945. In April of that year, he was the first to report on the monumental meeting of the U.S. and Russian armies at the Elbe River. Among his other exploits, Hottelet went into Berlin on 4 May 1945, against military regulations; Russian soldiers detained him for a short time.

After the war's end, Hottelet's reporting assignments took him to Moscow, New York, and Philadelphia. In 1951, he went back to Europe, with an assignment in Bonn. When CBS decided to combine its radio and television divisions into one

Richard Hottelet
Courtesy CBS Photo Archive

news department in 1954, Hottelet became a television correspondent. Starting in 1957, Hottelet anchored *The CBS Morning News;* his stint lasted four years before CBS changed the program's format. Hottelet became well known for his expertise in reporting international stories; he was assigned to the United Nations in 1960 and anchored a special report on the 1967 war in the Middle East. He served as editor of the volume on the United Nations in *The Dynamics of World Power* series.

Just as he was the last of the Murrow boys hired, Hottelet was also the last to leave CBS. He retired from the network in October 1985, around the time of the cutbacks that occurred at CBS in the mid-1980s. However, Hottelet has remained active in the world of international affairs. In addition to having served as the spokesperson for the U.S. ambassador to the United Nations, he returned to radio in 1993 as moderator of *America and the World*, an interview show sponsored by the Council on Foreign Relations that aired on National Public Radio (NPR). In 1995 Hottelet served as the NPR representative on a panel program concerning President Franklin D. Roosevelt and radio, which aired on C-SPAN. His expertise in analyzing foreign affairs found several media outlets well into the end of the century; during the 1990s he narrated a series of audiobooks on political hot spots around the world and continued to write on foreign affairs for the *Christian Science Monitor* into the early 2000s.

ERIKA ENGSTROM

See also Murrow, Edward R.; National Public Radio; News; Office of War Information; World War II and U.S. Radio

Richard Curt Hottelet. Born in New York City, 22 September 1917. Attended Brooklyn College, B.A. in philosophy, 1937. Started as stringer and then became United Press correspondent, Berlin, Germany, 1938–41; only U.S. reporter arrested by the Gestapo, 1941; worked in UP Washington bureau, 1942; U.S. Office of War Information, London, England, 1941–43; radio and television correspondent, originally hired by Edward R. Murrow, CBS TV and radio, 1944–85; host, *America and the World*, National Public Radio, 1993; foreign affairs columnist, *Christian Science Monitor*, late1990s and as of late 2002.

Selected Publications

The United Nations, vol. 5 in *The Dynamics of World Power* series, general editor Arthur M. Schlesinger, Jr., 1973
World's Political Hot Spots (audiobook series), 1994
Kosovo, Serbia, Bosnia: All You Want to Know: The History Behind the Conflict in Central Europe (audio cassette), 1999

Further Reading

Auster, Albert, "Richard C. Hottelet," in *Encyclopedia of Television News*, edited by Michael D. Murray, Phoenix, Arizona: Oryx Press, 1999
Bliss, Edward, Jr., *Now the News: The Story of Broadcast Journalism*, New York: Columbia University Press, 1991
Cloud, Stanley, and Lynne Olson, *The Murrow Boys*, Boston: Houghton Mifflin, 1996
Mickelson, Sig, *The Decade That Shaped Television News: CBS in the 1950s*, New York: Praeger, 1998

Howe, Quincy 1900–1977

U.S. Radio Commentator

In 1939 Quincy Howe began broadcasting news and commentary on radio station WQXR in New York. In 1942 he moved to the Columbia Broadcasting System (CBS), where he helped make analysis an accepted part of news reporting. He was one of the first radio journalists to bring the news of World War II into American homes.

Howe was born on 17 August 1900 in Boston, Massachusetts, to Fanny Howe and Mark Howe, who worked as an editor and a writer at the Atlantic Monthly Company. Howe attended St. George's School in Newport, Rhode Island, and then matriculated to Harvard University, from which he graduated *magna cum laude* in 1921. Howe then studied for a year at Christ's Church, Cambridge University, in England. When he returned to Boston in 1922, he became an editor for *Living Age*, a magazine published by the Atlantic Monthly Company. *Living Age* was sold in 1928, however, and Howe soon moved to New York. Archibald Watson, who had purchased the mag-azine, hired Howe as editor in chief in 1929. Howe selected articles that were topical and also contributed a regular column about world affairs.

Howe, a Boston liberal, married Mary L. Post, with whom he had two children. He helped get food to striking miners in Harlan County, Kentucky, in 1932. Later that year, he became the director of the American Civil Liberties Union (ACLU), which, under his guidance, opposed censorship. Howe served as director of the ACLU until 1940.

In 1934 Howe published *World Diary: 1929–1934*, an arresting study about the causes of the Great Depression as well as a prediction about the growth of nationalism. A year later he became editor in chief of Simon and Schuster. Under Howe's leadership, the company published more topical nonfiction. In 1937 he published his controversial book *England Expects Every American to Do His Duty*, in which he proposed isolationism for the United States. Howe argued that the

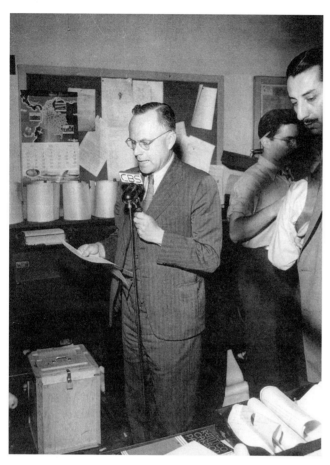

Quincy Howe
Courtesy CBS Photo Archive

United States should not get involved in another war merely to protect Britain's empire. Politicians on both sides of the Atlantic discussed his ideas. Two years later, he published *Blood Is Cheaper than Water: The Prudent American's Guide to Peace and War,* which examined the differences between isolationists and interventionists.

Howe gained experience on radio in 1938, when he provided analysis of the Munich Agreement for the Mutual Broadcasting System. Then, beginning in 1939, he provided three 15-minute news commentaries a week for WQXR, a radio station in New York. Howe's New England twang and educated opinions were well suited for radio, and his voice became one of the most recognizable for listeners almost immediately. Howe maintained his isolationist views until the United States entered World War II in December 1941.

Howe moved to CBS in 1942. He was hired to do news commentary, and he helped to make commentary an important ingredient of broadcast journalism. Like other notable commentators at the time, Howe wrote his own scripts, each containing about 1,500 words. These scripts contained informed

opinion about newsworthy events, especially about the war in Europe. Howe was able to accomplish the task because he was a professional writer as well as an excellent speaker. He usually opened his analysis with several maxims about world affairs to make his commentaries interesting and coherent. He became known for his insightful analysis. Others who worked in radio viewed him as one of the most authoritative news analysts around, primarily because of his vast knowledge about world affairs. Howe did more than read the news: he informed his listeners as to how national and international events would affect their lives.

Under H.V. Kaltenborn's leadership, Howe and 30 other commentators based in New York helped organize the Association of Radio News Analysts in 1942. The guild advocated that commentators be permitted to comment when presenting news. In 1943 Howe wrote about the power of those who advertised on radio in "Policing the Commentator: A News Analysis," published in the November *Atlantic Monthly.* He warned that advertisers could cause news and commentary to become slanted.

When World War II ended, Howe attempted to enter television. He worked as a commentator on the CBS evening news until the network was urged by an advertiser to let him go because he was too bombastic and too liberal. Howe was dropped from the evening news, but he continued to work as a reporter and narrator of documentaries for the network. In 1948, for instance, he covered the Republican and Democratic national conventions.

In 1949 he published the first volume of his three-volume history of the 20th century, *A World History of Our Times* (the last volume appeared in 1972). Later that year he left CBS and taught journalism at the University of Illinois until 1954; he left when the American Broadcasting Companies (ABC) hired him. At ABC Howe covered world affairs. In addition, he moderated the last presidential debate between John F. Kennedy and Richard M. Nixon in 1960 as well as the trial of Adolf Eichmann in Israel a year later. He received several awards, including the George Foster Peabody Award and the Overseas Press Club Award, for his work in broadcast journalism.

In addition to his work for ABC, Howe contributed articles to the *Saturday Review of Literature* and other magazines. In 1961 he became the editor of *Atlas: The Magazine of the World Press,* a monthly that featured articles from the foreign press. He served as editor until 1965. Howe died in 1977.

EDD APPLEGATE

See also Commentators; News; Peabody Awards

Quincy Howe. Born in Boston, Massachusetts, 17 August 1900. Served in U.S. Marine Corps, SATC, Harvard Unit, 1918; attended Harvard University, A.B. degree (magna cum laude), 1921; studied at Christ's College, Cambridge University, England, 1921–22; staff member, *Atlantic Monthly*, 1922–29; editor, *Living Age*, 1929–35; editor-in-chief, Simon and Schuster, 1935–42; news commentator, WQXR, New York, 1939–42; news commentator, Columbia Broadcasting System radio and television, 1942–50; associate professor of journalism and news analyst for WILL, University of Illinois, Urbana, 1950–54; news analyst, ABC, 1954–63; editor, *Atlas: The Magazine of the World Press*, New York, 1961–65; news analyst, Radio New York Worldwide, 1966–70; commentator, WTFM, New York, 1973–74; contributing editor, *Atlas World Press Review*, New York, 1974–77. Received George Foster Peabody award, 1955; Overseas Press Club award, 1959; Columbia-Catherwood award, 1962. Died in New York City, 17 February 1977.

Selected Publications

World Diary: 1929–1934, 1934
England Expects Every American to Do His Duty, 1937
Blood Is Cheaper than Water: The Prudent American's Guide to Peace and War, 1939
The News and How to Understand It, in Spite of the Newspapers, in Spite of the Magazines and in Spite of the Radio, 1940, 1968
A World History of Our Times, 3 vols., 1949–72

Further Reading

DeLong, Thomas A., *Radio Stars: An Illustrated Biographical Dictionary of 953 Performers, 1920 through 1960*, Jefferson, North Carolina: McFarland, 1996
Fang, Irving E., *Those Radio Commentators!* Ames: Iowa State University Press, 1977
Howe, Quincy, "Policing the Commentator: A News Analysis," *Atlantic Monthly* 172, no. 5 (November 1943)
Sperber, Ann M., *Murrow: His Life and Times*, New York: Freundlich Books, 1986
Tebbel, John William, *Between Covers: The Rise and Transformation of Book Publishing in America*, New York: Oxford University Press, 1987

Hulbert, Maurice "Hot Rod" Jr. 1916–1996

U.S. Disc Jockey

Maurice "Hot Rod" Hulbert Jr. was one of the most popular black disc jockeys in radio during the 1950s and 1960s. For a period during his heyday, he could be heard hosting different programs on radio stations in Baltimore, Philadelphia, and New York. His fluid and at times nonsensical on-air patter and high profile in the black broadcasting world helped him inspire a generation of black disc jockeys who came of age in the late 1950s and the 1960s.

Hulbert was also one of America's pioneering black disc jockeys, joining WDIA in Memphis, Tennessee, as it was evolving into the nation's first all-black-oriented radio station. Before arriving at WDIA in 1949, Hulbert had worked as a dancer, comedian, bandleader, and emcee in various mid-South nightclubs and traveling tent shows. Hulbert also helped produce musicals with black students in the Memphis school system, and it was while working on one such production that WDIA's general manager, Bert Ferguson, approached him about working at the station. The meeting led to a job, and soon Hulbert was hosting three shows for WDIA: *The Sepia Swing Club*, an afternoon blues and jazz show; *The Delta Melodies*, an early-morning program of spiritual music; and *Moods by Maurice*, a midmorning program tailored to housewives.

At WDIA Hulbert became increasingly adept at switching personas as each show required. On his *Sepia Swing Club*, he became "Hot Rod," describing for listeners his rocket ship on which they would be flown through a solar system of hot music. Listeners to the *Sepia Swing Club* responded enthusiastically, as did those who where charmed by the suave "Maurice the Mood Man" on the *Moods by Maurice* program. By 1951 Hot Rod prepared to board his rocket ship for a galaxy in a larger market called Baltimore.

The management of WITH in Baltimore had cast its net for a popular established black disc jockey to pull in black listeners, and after a national search, they had located Hulbert, whose high ratings in Memphis confirmed his popularity. WITH hired him in 1951, making him the first full-time black disc jockey in Baltimore history. The Hot Rod–rocket man persona followed Hulbert to Baltimore, and almost immediately the rhythm and blues music shows he hosted became popular among young blacks and whites. Listeners enjoyed Hot Rod's outer-space persona as well as the tongue twisters and slick shtick that he rained on Baltimore. They had never heard such on-air wildness before. With good-natured bravado, he might greet the city with, "Not the flower, not the root, but the seed, sometimes called the herb, not the imitator but the originator, the innovator, the true living legend—The Rod!" In addition, he peppered his on-air patter with extra, nonsensical sounds, for example, *ee-us*, as in "This is Hee-us-ot Ree-us-od." This jive complemented the music he played and tickled the ears of his listeners. He ended many programs and pronouncements by proclaiming "VOSA," which meant the "Voice of Sound Advice."

By the late 1950s, Hot Rod moved on to WHAT in Philadelphia where, in his morning time slot, he repeated his Baltimore success. It was in Philadelphia that he became a three-market personality. WWRL in New York, hoping to grab some of Hulbert's luster, paid him to commute to Manhattan for an afternoon show, and then WWIN in Baltimore asked him to tape a program for broadcast there. Few, if any, black disc jockeys enjoyed such exposure in the 1950s and 1960s.

Hot Rod was back in Baltimore exclusively by the late 1960s, hosting a popular live show, first on his old home station WITH and then on WWIN. Hulbert's popularity, particularly among Baltimore's black audiences, was never more evident than during the riots that plagued the city in the wake of Martin Luther King Jr.'s 1968 assassination. Government officials asked the popular local figure to go on television to help calm the violence and tension. "I could get through," he told author Gilbert Williams in 1991, "and I talked to the people, trying to sober them up because people had gone mad. . . . I think many jocks did that all over the country." Hulbert frequently spoke out in advocacy of civil rights for blacks, marching in the streets and discussing related issues on the air.

In the 1970s, Hulbert switched to the sales and management side of radio, working for various Baltimore radio stations. By the time of his retirement in 1993 he was the general manager of WBGR/WEBB. He died in 1996 after a battle with throat cancer.

MICHAEL STREISSGUTH

See also Black-Oriented Radio; Disk Jockeys; WDIA

Maurice Hulbert, Jr. Born in Helena, Arkansas, 30 July 1916. Senior disc jockey on several radio stations, including WDIA, Memphis, Tennessee, 1949–51; became first full-time African-American disc jockey, WITH, Baltimore, Maryland, 1951–late 50s; simultaneous disc jockey positions, WWIN (Baltimore, Maryland), WHAT (Philadelphia, Pennsylvania), WWRL (New York City), 1950s–60s; disc jockey, WITH, then WWIN, Baltimore, Maryland, late 1960s; worked in sales and management for various Baltimore radio stations, including WKTK, WWIN, and WBGR\WEBB, 1974–93; became general manager of WGBR/WEBB, Baltimore, Maryland, 1993. Died in Towson, Maryland, 24 December 1996.

Further Reading

Cantor, Louis J., *Wheelin' on Beale: How WDIA-Memphis Became the Nation's First All-Black Radio Station and Created the Sound That Changed America*, New York: Pharos Books, 1992

Dates, Jannette Lake, and William Barlow, editors, *Split Image: African Americans in the Mass Media*, Washington, D.C.: Howard University Press, 1990; 2nd edition, 1993

Newman, Mark, *Entrepreneurs of Profit and Pride: From Black-Appeal to Radio Soul*, New York: Praeger, 1988; London: Praeger, 1989

Streissguth, Michael James, "WDIA and the Rise of Blues and Rhythm-and-Blues Music," Master's thesis, Purdue University, 1990

Williams, Gilbert Anthony, *Legendary Pioneers of Black Radio*, Westport, Connecticut: Praeger, 1998

Hummert, Anne 1905–1996
Hummert, Frank 1885–1966

U.S. Writers and Producers, Creators of Soap Operas

Anne and Frank Hummert nearly monopolized the creation of radio daytime serials—soap operas—in the 1930s and 1940s. Working within an advertising agency, they took advantage of the advertiser's interest, the new medium, the available audience, and the era. The Hummerts were not the creators of the first soap opera, a form that evolved over a few years, but they were responsible for molding the genre and moving soap operas from evening to daytime, convincing advertisers that women could listen to radio while they were doing their housework. The Hummerts provided programming that included advertising and propaganda (the latter including messages supporting government policies during World War II) plus entertainment for as much as half of daytime network; they also originated sponsored children's programming and many other programs.

Despite speaking to so many people for decades, the Hummerts maintained a very private, secluded life, leaving few biographical details. Frank is reputed to have been a Texas Ranger, a reporter on the *St. Louis Dispatch,* a manager of a writing school, and then a highly regarded copywriter in New York City. He is credited with coming up with the idea of writing advertising as feature news, having written the slogan "Bonds or Bondage" during World War I and Camay's slogan, "For the skin you love to touch." Blackett and Sample lured Frank Hummert away from the Lord and Thomas agency in New York to Chicago with the opportunity to set up his own radio production unit in 1927. Although Hummert was not a partner in the agency, his name was put on the masthead and he retained ownership of all the programs he produced. Hill Blackett and John Glen Sample were interested in attracting clients by providing programming for women during the day, and to get their desired audience's perspective they encouraged Frank Hummert to hire a woman. Anne S. Ashenhurst had just come from a newspaper job with the Paris *Herald,* had a young son, and was looking for a job. Frank reluctantly hired her in 1927. Anne was a very deft writer and was able to communicate with Frank. They married after seven years, and were partners in producing serials for three decades.

After Pepsodent's success with the daily 15-minute program *Amos 'n' Andy,* other writers attempted to produce popular evening serials. As advertisers, Frank and Anne Hummert had program ideas for their clients and hired their writers. It was one way both to control the content and also to produce many hours. In 1931 Anne Ashenhurst and Frank Hummert hired Charles Andrews to write *The Stolen Husband,* a very simple program that was then adapted to become *Betty and Bob.* Their first success was *Just Plain Bill* in 1932, also written by Andrews, and Anne convinced the sponsors to move it to daytime in 1933, arguing that women would be able to listen while doing their chores. Within a few years the Hummerts had as many as 18 daytime serial dramas on the air at the same time, bringing in as much as one-half of network daytime revenues.

The Hummerts used a technique that many have called a soap opera factory to produce the programs. By 1935 the Hummerts had moved their agency to New York City and had a staff of about 20 writers, 6 editors, and 60 clerical workers. Anne and Frank worked out of their house in Connecticut, first creating the title and the rough summary for each show. The staff in the office expanded this, and then the Hummerts created the story line, a sketch of the action for five to six episodes. The Hummerts then sent the theme and story line to five writers, called dialoguers, who would produce sample scripts, with the best script winning the writing job. The writer would then have to stay at least three weeks ahead at all times. The Hummerts would relay any ideas they had for character and plot development to the writer through one of the six editors—all in writing. By 1938 more than 5 million words were being written annually for the Hummert serials alone, the equivalent of 50 full-length novels.

Their control is documented by noting the copy on the first page of all scripts, written in lavender ink: the title followed by the notation that this is a Hummert Radio Feature. The Hummerts gave themselves the credits for the title, original story line, the general supervision of script and production, and ownership. They had a set of rules that covered every eventuality. Nothing could be added in production that was not in the script: no extra sound effects, lest the dialogue not be heard; no overlapping of speeches; and the actors had to have the clearest enunciation—a trait Anne Hummert had herself.

Most of the 36 daytime serials produced by the Hummerts were melodramas about domestic life that moved very slowly and included lengthy advertisements. The Hummerts described them as "successful dramas about unsuccessful people, people who were not wealthy but had successful family lives and were able to help others have good relationships." The themes were often based on relationships of people from different backgrounds, worried about their future happiness. As Anne later said, "Worry, for women, is entertainment. . . . Nobody can understand the phenomenal success of the soaps without knowing when they were born. It was during the Depression. The housewife was at home worrying about everything. Would her husband lose his job? Where was the family's next meal coming from? They found escape in the lives of the people on the soaps."

The format for most of their daytime serials started with a lead-in delivered by the announcer; for example, for *Our Gal Sunday,* the lead-in was, "Can a girl from a little mining town in the West find happiness as the wife of England's richest, most handsome lord?" with "Red River Valley" as theme music. Then the announcer read a chatty commercial for a minute and a half and gave background for this particular program, followed by nine minutes of dialogue, a few leading questions for the next day's show, and a closing commercial. The commercials were written in the problem-solution formula—for example, try new improved Oxydol to make washing easier. Premium promotions were also written in as a means of proving there were large audiences for the advertisers. The offer of a Love Bird Pin just like Helen Trent's with "real simulated-gold flashing," a lavaliere designed by Mary Noble, or a can opener said to have been invented by Lorenzo Jones were written into the scripts months ahead. The audience was asked to send in a dime with a box top or some other proof of purchase of one of the advertised products to receive

Anne and Frank Hummert
Courtesy CBS Photo Archive

the premium. During World War II, at the request of the Office of War Information, the Hummerts wrote their dramas to help overcome the white soldier's fear of the black soldier and to help the war effort in general. After the war, the Hummerts were two of the few writers who never flinched during the McCarthy Era, continuing their work without any concern about the blacklist.

Some say that the reason the Hummerts led such a secretive life was that they were aware of the disdain held by much of the public for their work. Anne did admit that her son disapproved of her work and told a reporter, "As a matter of fact I sit behind my desk with two black eyes." But they did feel they were writing for audiences all over the country. The Hummerts also produced musical programs and crime dramas and were the first to convince advertisers to sponsor children's programming.

When the networks cut back on programming and the soaps were taken off the air in the early 1950s, the Hummerts retired to travel rather than taking their soaps to television.

MARGOT HARDENBERGH

See also Ma Perkins; Premiums; Soap Opera

Anne Hummert. Born in 1905. Graduated from Goucher College, Baltimore, Maryland, 1925; married John Ashenhurst, 1926–27; writer, Paris *Herald*, 1926; writer, Blackett, Sample and Hummert advertising agency, 1927; married Frank Hummert, 1934; co-producer of 36 radio serials. Died in New York City, 5 July 1996.

Frank Hummert. Born circa 1885. Reporter, *St. Louis Dispatch*; copywriter, Chicago, 1920s; worked in New York

City for Lord and Thomas agency; writer for Blackett and Sample when he hired Anne as his assistant; firm became Blackett-Sample-Hummert, although Hummert had no interest in the firm; married Anne Ashenhurst, 1934; started Air Features, a radio production company, where he and Anne produced more than 35 different radio series. Died in New York City, 1966.

Radio Series

1931–51	*American Album of Familiar Music*
1932	*The Stolen Husband*
1932–35	*Skippy*
1932–40	*Betty and Bob*
1932–49	*Manhattan Merry-Go-Round*
1932–55	*Just Plain Bill; Judy and Jane*
1933–48	*Waltz Time*
1933–60	*Ma Perkins; The Romance of Helen Trent*
1934–36	*Lavender and Old Lace*
1935–38	*Mrs. Wiggs of the Cabbage Patch*
1935–59	*Backstage Wife*
1936–37	*Rich Man's Darling*
1936–41	*John's Other Wife*
1936–51	*David Harum*
1937–42	*Arnold Grimm's Daughter*
1937–46	*Second Husband*
1937–55	*Lorenzo Jones; Mr. Keen, Tracer of Lost Persons; Stella Dallas*
1937–59	*Our Gal Sunday*
1938–39	*Alias Jimmy Valentine; Central City; Those Happy Gilmans*
1938–56	*Young Widder Brown*
1939–42	*Orphans of Divorce*
1940–46	*Amanda of Honey Moon Hill*
1941–44	*Helpmate*
1941–48	*American Melody Hour*
1941–54	*Front Page Farrell*
1943–50	*Lora Lawton*
1944–48	*The Strange Romance of Evelyn Winters*
1948–51	*Molle Mystery Theater* (also produced as *Mystery Theater,* with spin offs known as *Mark Sabre* and *Hearthstone of the Death Squad*)
1950–51	*Nona from Nowhere*

Further Reading

Cox, Jim, *Frank and Anne Hummert's Radio Factory: The Programs and Personalities of Broadcasting's Most Prolific Producers,* Jefferson, North Carolina: McFarland, 2003

Edmondson, Madeleine, and David Rounds, *From Mary Noble to Mary Hartman: The Complete Soap Opera Book,* New York: Stein and Day, 1976

Meyers, Cynthia B., "Frank and Anne Hummert's Soap Opera Empire: 'Reason-Why' Advertising Strategies in Early Radio Programming," *Quarterly Review of Film and Video* 16, no. 2 (1997)

Nachman, Gerald, *Raised on Radio: In Quest of the Lone Ranger, Jack Benny . . . ,* New York: Pantheon, 1998

Stedman, Raymond William, *The Serials: Suspense and Drama by Installment,* Norman: University of Oklahoma Press, 1971; 2nd edition, 1977

Thurber, James, "Soapland," in *The Beast in Me and Other Animals,* by Thurber, New York: Harcourt Brace, 1948; London: Hamish Hamilton, 1949

I

I Love a Mystery

Adventure/Mystery Thriller Series

Though relatively short-lived (five years in its original run with a three-year revival based on the original scripts), *I Love a Mystery* (*ILAM*) continued its hold on radio aficionados for several decades after it aired. This was due in part to its creator and writer—Carleton E. Morse—but also to the wide-ranging nature of the adventures of the three key characters.

The Radio Serial

A serial with dozens of continuing stories that were usually presented in three-week units for a total of 1,784 episodes, the program varied from 15-minute to half-hour segments depending on the network carrying it. The program was more of an adventure/thriller than a classic detective story, despite its detective agency basis. *ILAM* originated in Hollywood for its original five-year run, moving to New York when the Mutual Broadcast System reused all but five of the original scripts (and added one new script) with a new cast. Adding to later collector confusion, the Mutual series often used different story titles. Though audition tapes were made in 1954 for a revival on CBS, that series never materialized.

In the program, Jack Packard, a one-time medical student, is head of the Triple A-1 Detective Agency, located "just off Hollywood Boulevard and one flight up," whose motto is "no job too tough, no mystery too baffling." At 37, he is older than the other staff members and is clearly the most cool-headed and clear thinking under pressure. His fellow-adventurers include the Texas-born roughneck "Doc" Long, who loves women and adventure in about that order. The third member of the original trio is Britisher Reggie Yorke, who is refined but also serves as the group's muscle. These original protagonists met in China while fighting the Japanese, and they took over an abandoned detective agency on returning to the Untied States.

Yorke was written out of the series in 1942 when the actor portraying him took his own life. His character was replaced

with distaff interest in the form of handsome secretary Jerry Booker. When she joins the WACs during World War II, her secretarial role is taken on by Mary Kay Brown.

Carlton E. Morse, writer-producer of *I Love A Mystery,* working with soundperson
Courtesy CBS Photo Archive

The programs concerned exotic adventures, and while they sometimes had far-fetched aspects, the resolution of the stories was always rational and realistic. Each segment ended with a cliff-hanger situation designed to bring listeners back regularly. Unlike many serials, a given ILAM story ended before another began.

ILAM in Other Media

Three movies (only the first with a script by Morse) were developed from the series, and a 1967 television pilot film, *I Love a Mystery*, was made though not shown until 1973. No series resulted. An earlier (1956) attempt to develop a television series had also failed.

Don Sherwood created a short-lived 1960s comic strip based on the stories and characters of the radio series. *ILAM* creator Carleton E. Morse wrote one related novel and published it before his death; others were planned but did not appear.

CHRISTOPHER H. STERLING

See also One Man's Family

Programming History

NBC West Coast network	January 1939–September 1939
NBC	1939–40
Blue Network	1940–42
CBS	1943–44
Mutual	1949–52

Cast

Jack Packard	Michael Raffetto (1939–44), Russell Thorson (1949–52), Robert Dryden (1952)
Doc Long	Barton Yarborough (1939–44), Jim Bowles (1949–52)
Reggie Yorke	Walter Paterson (to 1942), Tony Randall (1949–52)
Jerry Booker	Gloria Blondell (after 1942), Athena Lord (1949–52)
Mary Kay Brown	Athena Lord (1949–52)

Creator-Writer-Producer-Director
Carleton E. Morse

Films Based on the Series
I Love a Mystery (1945)
The Devil's Mask (1946)
The Unknown (1946)

Further Reading

Grams, Martin, Jr., "Episode Listing of *I Love a Mystery*," in *Radio Drama: A Comprehensive Chronicle of American Network Programs, 1932–1962*, by Grams, Jefferson, North Carolina: McFarland, 2000

Harmon, Jim, "Jack, Doc, and Reggie," in *The Great Radio Heroes*, by Harmon, Garden City, New York: Doubleday, 1967

Morse, Carleton E., *Stuff the Lady's Hatbox*, Woodside, California: Seven Stones Press, 1988

Packard, Jack, Doc Long, and Reggie York, *I Love a Mystery: The Further Adventures of Jack, Doc, and Reggie*, <www.lofcom.com/nostalgia/ilam>

Unofficial I Love a Mystery Page, <www.angelfire.com/on/ilam>

Imus, Don 1940–

U.S. Radio Disc Jockey and Host

Don Imus moved to WNBC New York in 1971 after just three years in radio. After working at stations in California (Palmdale, Stockton, Sacramento), as well as in Cleveland, Ohio, Imus came to the largest market in the U.S. and to the station with the best combination of a low frequency and high power—arguably the biggest station in the United States. Thirty years later, Imus is still at WNBC.

Origins and Early Radio Years

John Donald Imus, Jr., was born 23 July 1940 in Riverside, California, and lived with his family in the nearby town of Perris. While in high school, he lived briefly in Scottsdale and then Prescott, Arizona. Imus wanted to be a popular singer and participated in theater, but he joined the Marine Corps before his last year of high school. After two years in the military and the failure of a rock band formed with his brother Fred, he worked as a miner in Arizona and for a railroad in California. Using money from an injury lawsuit (and/or the GI bill), he attended the Don Martin School of Broadcasting in Hollywood—then a well-established trade school known for turning out a number of announcers and disc jockeys.

Before graduation, and apparently still owing the school tuition money—which he says he has never paid—Imus got a job at a Palmdale station in the high desert north of Los Angeles. Like most morning DJs, he got attention with stunts like saying he was running for congress in 1968 and holding a press conference—"Put Don Imus on the gravy train." He quickly moved to KJOI in Stockton, where he apparently completed one course in political science at San Joaquin Delta College. Then he moved to KXOA in Sacramento, began calling his show *Imus in the Morning,* and created outrageous characters such as "Judge Hanging," "The Reverend Billy Sol Hargis," and "Crazy Bob," who presented his own suggestive versions of fairy tales. Imus often used phone calls in his stunts—such as calling a local McDonald's one morning, identifying himself as a sergeant in the Air National Guard and ordering 1,200 hamburgers to go. Then he confused the manager by specifying, "on 300 hold the mustard but put on plenty of mayonnaise and lettuce."

Imus began broadcasting in Cleveland in September 1970 and was named by *Billboard* as "the major market DJ of the year." For many of his more memorable bits, he called people on the phone: asking to buy silver bullets as the Lone Ranger, trying to order a rental car to race in the Indianapolis 500, and saying that he had left his clothes in a hotel phone booth after changing from Clark Kent to Superman and asking that they be returned. Often he talked with women whom he told to "get naked."

One character, The Reverend Billy Sol Hargis, who sounded much like Billy Graham, was from "The First Church of the Gooey Death and Discount House of Worship, right here in Del Rio, Texas," and sang "I don't care if it rain or freezes, long as I've got my plastic Jesus riding on the dash board of my car, I can go a 100 miles an hour as long as I got the almighty dollar glued up there by my pair of fuzzy dice."

Imitating President Lyndon Johnson, Imus explained "Why shouldn't the Viet Nam war costs 150 billion dollars?" with: "Let Judge Hanging remind you, my fellow Americans, that you pay for what you get. You don't run down to Sak's Fifth Avenue and pick up some slick suit for $29.95 and you don't wage war for 15 cents. It cost money to dress well and it cost money to kill people."

An Imus character called "Tricky Dick" sold used cars from 1600 Pennsylvania Avenue. Like many other radio comedians, Imus crafted characters that sounded a bit like real life radio

Don Imus
Courtesy of Don Imus

personalities of his youth. Certainly anyone hearing Rev. Hargis was instantly reminded of various paid religious programs from stations across the Mexican border that Imus had heard as a young man in Arizona or while in the Marines at Camp Pendelton.

Cleveland newspaper reviews called Imus "gross, tasteless, vulgar, and nauseating." But in just a few months the station ranked number one in ratings. In December 1971, Imus was hired by WNBC in New York, which then was an adult contemporary to middle-of-the-road music station.

New York Radio

The transition was not easy. Imus missed many days of work—an average of two days a week in 1973—and later admitted to problems with alcohol and cocaine. Later he said: "I was drunk and coked up for 20 years, it's a wonder I'm even alive." In a 1976 interview Imus explained, "I have an aversion to authority, some kind of immaturity . . . it's just the way I am." His appeal, he assumed, was to those many people who rose each morning thinking that they would like to "take their job and shove it," as a song of the time put it.

While insisting that he had 19 lawyers to protect him against his employers, Imus said that he thought he could find a job in radio anywhere. But he was fired from WNBC at the end of August 1977 and remained out of work for some time, eventually ending up back in Cleveland. The shooting star seemed to have fizzled.

Imus did return to WNBC in 1979, but there was more drinking and drugs. In 1985 he was one of the first video jockeys on the cable program service VH1. In 1988 WNBC, with the new call letters of WFAN, adopted a sports talk format, and Imus continued to produce about one half of the station's revenues during his morning shift. He adopted a more mature tone, which better fit with the station's new format and with the fact that fewer AM stations were playing music, but his trend to more serious topics, he says, was accelerated by the Gulf War controversy beginning in the fall of 1990. Now more and more of his phone conversations were with journalists and politicians, the latter particularly during campaigns.

Beginning in July 1993 the program was also syndicated, and by 2001 it was carried on about 55 stations. Since 3 September 1996, it has also been carried on MSNBC and was said at times to be the highest-rated program on the cable channel. While MSNBC uses multiple cameras and adds many graphics and tape clips, Imus insists that he is still doing a radio show and usually ignores or disparages the video coverage.

In 1981 Imus and Charles McCord, the newsman on his program, published a novel, *God's Other Son*, but it did not sell well. Reissued in 1994, it became a best seller. In 1997 Imus also published, with his brother Fred, a book of photographs of the American Southwest.

Yet another controversy involved remarks he made 21 March 1996, at the Radio and Television Correspondents dinner in Washington. Beforehand he had apparently told Bill Clinton it would be a little "rough" and the President said that would be "fine." The President also said that appearing on the Imus show might have helped him get elected. However, as Imus spoke of Clinton's legal problems, his family, and other matters, it was clear from the telecast and from later news reports that the President was angry.

In 1997 *Time* magazine named Imus one of its "most influential" people, and *Newsweek* did a cover story on him in December 1998. Since 1997, he has also operated a ranch in New Mexico for children with cancer. His program is frequently broadcast from the ranch, especially during the summer when the children visit, and fund raising for the ranch is often discussed.

Since the beginning of his radio career in 1968, Imus' strong opinions and remarks about people in public life have been the main attraction for his listeners. Here is a recent sampling:

Bill Clinton: "is a dirt bag and a low rent weasel."
Al Gore: "phoniest person on the planet, disgraceful human being."
George W. Bush: "we're going to be stuck with that moron George Bush [and] Cheney and a bunch of old people will run the country."
Chris Matthews (who is also on MSNBC): "a blow hard and the most annoying person on television."
XFL football (carried on channels owned by Viacom which also owns WFAN): "The fans are neanderthal morons. It is lame. It really sucks."

"I'm trying to be entertaining, I'm trying to show a different side of these people. We are not trying to hurt people. We are trying to make people laugh."

LAWRENCE W. LICHTY

John Donald Imus, Jr. Born in Riverside, California, 23 July 1940. Quit high school, but later earned GED. U.S. Marine Corps 1957–1959. Worked at radio stations in California before moving to Cleveland, Ohio, 1970; on-air host at WNBC (later WFAN), New York, 1971–77, 1979–present.

Radio Series
1971–77; 1979–present   *Imus in the Morning*

Selected Publications
God's Other Son: The Life and Times of the Rev. Billy Sol Hargus, 1981
Two Guys, Four Corners: Great Photographs, Great Times, and a Million Laughs (with Fred Imus), 1997

Further Reading
Tracy, Kathleen, *Imus: America's Cowboy*, New York: Carroll and Graf, 1999

Indecency. *See* Obscenity/Indecency on Radio

India. *See* All India Radio

Infinity Broadcasting Corporation

Infinity Broadcasting Corporation, a subsidiary of media giant Viacom, is one of the largest radio broadcasting companies in the U.S. Infinity is focused on the "out-of-home" media business, which includes operations in radio broadcasting through Infinity Radio and outdoor advertising through Viacom Outdoor. Infinity's self characterization of being an "out-of-home" media business comes from the fact that the majority of radio listening and practically all viewing of outdoor advertising occurs outside the consumer's home, from places such as automobiles and public transportation systems. The majority of Infinity's revenue, therefore, is generated from the sale of advertising. Infinity Radio consists of more than 180 radio stations serving over 40 markets. Approximately 94 percent of Infinity's radio stations are located in the 50 largest U.S. radio markets. Infinity also manages and holds an equity position in Westwood One, Inc.

The original Infinity Broadcasting Corporation is not the same as the Infinity currently in existence. The original Infinity was formed by two former Metromedia Communications Corporation executives, Gerald Carrus and Michael A. Weiner, in 1972 and acquired its first radio station in May 1973. Carrus and Weiner planned to emulate Metromedia president John W. Kluge's strategy of acquiring unsuccessful radio stations in the country's largest media markets, where the greatest amount of radio advertising dollars are spent, and developing them.

Seeking someone to run the original Infinity, Carrus and Weiner turned to Mel Karmazin in 1981. Karmazin had spent the previous 11 years working for Metromedia, where he managed the company's AM and FM outlets and gained a reputation for paying substantial amounts of money for on-air talent while exercising the tightfistedness he had learned from Kluge to keep operating costs down. When Karmazin requested the opportunity to manage one of Metromedia's TV properties, Kluge turned him down, and Karmazin began to consider other options. By offering him a lucrative salary and equity in the original Infinity, Carrus and Weiner were able to lure Karmazin to the company.

The original Infinity, under Karmazin's leadership, substantially increased its acquisitions by paying record prices for top radio stations in large cities. The success of the original Infinity was also based on its ability to acquire the radio broadcast rights to a number of professional sports teams and to seek out high-profile radio personalities for its stations.

One of those high-profile personalities was "shock jock" Howard Stern, who signed on with the original Infinity in 1985 after being fired from WNBC. The original Infinity provided Stern with a national platform. As a result of Stern's bold activities on the airwaves, the company received numerous warnings from the Federal Communications Commission (FCC) that the *Howard Stern Show* was dangerously close to violating indecency standards. The warnings brought substantial publicity to the original Infinity, and the show's ratings soared, to the dismay of the many national and community watchdog groups working to have the show taken off the air. In 1995, as the fines from the FCC escalated, the original Infinity agreed to put the controversy to rest by paying $1.7 million in exchange for the FCC's dismissal of all pending complaints against the company's stations.

Despite the controversy, the original Infinity became popular not only with the listening audience, but also with Wall Street. The original Infinity went public in 1986 and was then bought back in a leveraged buyout in 1988. The original Infinity was again taken public in 1992. Shares issued in 1992 for $17.50 each were worth $170 when the company was eventually purchased in 1996.

In November 1995 Westinghouse Electric Corporation acquired the Columbia Broadcasting System (CBS), creating the nation's largest TV and radio station group. After Congress passed the Telecommunications Act in February 1996, which permitted the expansion of TV and radio station holdings, Westinghouse began considering its options for growth and, recognizing the potential of the radio industry, purchased the original Infinity in December 1996 for $4.7 billion. After acquiring the original Infinity, Westinghouse decided to sell its industrial businesses and reinvent itself solely as a media company. In December 1997 the new media company was launched as the CBS Corporation, the largest radio and television entity in history, with Karmazin as its president and chief operating officer.

In September 1998 CBS formed the currently existing Infinity Broadcasting Corporation in the largest initial public offering in media history. The "new" Infinity was created as a wholly owned subsidiary to own and operate CBS's radio and outdoor-advertising business. In addition to his duties at CBS, Karmazin was named president and chief executive officer of Infinity. The name of the original Infinity had been changed to Infinity Media Corporation in anticipation of the creation of the new corporation with the same name.

In May 2000 CBS was merged with and into Viacom, Inc. with Farid Suleman becoming Infinity's Chief Executive Officer. In March 2002 John Sykes replaced Suleman as Chief Executive Officer. The company is headquartered in New York City. Among its stations are WFAN-AM in New York (sports format), which is the nation's top-billing station in terms of advertising dollars, and KDKA-AM in Pittsburgh (news/talk format), the oldest regular radio broadcaster in America. In addition to Stern, notable personalities at Infinity include Don Imus, Casey Kasem, Larry King, Charles Osgood, and Tom Snyder.

KARL SCHMID

See also Columbia Broadcasting System; Karmazin, Mel; Westinghouse

Further Reading

Douglas, Susan Jeanne, *Listening In: Radio and the American Imagination: From Amos 'n' Andy and Edward R. Murrow to Wolfman Jack and Howard Stern,* New York: Times Books, 1999

Quaal, Ward L., and Leo A. Martin, *Broadcast Management: Radio, Television,* New York: Hastings House, 1968; revised 2nd edition, by Quaal and James Anthony Brown, 1976; 3rd edition, as *Radio-Television-Cable Management,* by Quaal and Brown, New York: McGraw Hill, 1998

Smith, F. Leslie, *Perspectives on Radio and Television: An Introduction to Broadcasting in the United States,* New York: Harper and Row, 1979; 4th edition, as *Perspectives on Radio and Television: Telecommunication in the United States,* by Smith, John W. Wright II, and David H. Ostroff, Mahwah, New Jersey: Erlbaum, 1998

Inner Sanctum Mysteries

Horror Series

Squeeeeeaakkkk!!!!!! "Good Evening, friends of the inner sanctum. This is your host, Raymond, to welcome you through the squeaking door. Been shopping around for a nice case of murder? Of course you have. And you have come to the right place because the characters on this program simply *kill* themselves to keep you amused. Why only the other day we were accused of making murder our business. But we wouldn't do that friends, oh no, because that would be mixing business with pleasure, and we consider it a *pleasure* to give some stiff the *business* . . . heh heh heh."

So began one of the most famous openings in radio history. The squeaking door and host Raymond's gallows humor marked *Inner Sanctum Mysteries* as a distinctively campy horror series that reveled in its grisly subject matter. It was one of the first and most successful of radio thriller dramas, a genre that peaked in popularity during the 1940s. *Inner Sanctum* was created, produced, and directed throughout its entire run from 1941 to 1952 by Himan Brown, one of radio's most prolific showmen. Brown balanced the program's macabre humor with carefully chosen organ sounds, blood-curdling screams,

and other effects, creating some of the most unsettling soundscapes ever heard on radio. Brown used the organ to heighten the listener's fear, incorporating sharp stings to spark terror and creating suspense by using what John Dunning has called "doom chords" to signal approaching trouble. Murders were conveyed in the most disturbing manner possible through sound effects: Jim Harmon notes that when Brown wanted to produce the sound of a head being bashed in, he "devised a special bludgeon with which he would strike a small melon" (1967).

Inner Sanctum took its name from a line of Simon and Schuster mystery novels, but its scripts were generally original (although Edgar Allen Poe's work was a favorite of Brown's and was frequently adapted). Like other programs of the genre, *Inner Sanctum* relied on realism to heighten the listener's fear that "this could happen to me!" Ghostly behavior was commonly explained by the presence of a mad relative or an actual dead body that refused to stay quiet. As critics and even the show's own writers have noted, however, *Inner Sanctum*'s plots were driven by contrivances and coincidences that were highly implausible. The nurse hired by the judge's wife happens to be the girlfriend of the murderer the judge just sent to the gallows (and she's not happy with him!). The wailing of a man's dead wife that haunts him for 40 years is actually caused by a hole in the wall in which he entombed her body (and which he, so terrified, had never thought to investigate earlier). Frequently, the program employed the device of an insane narrator to throw listeners off track and increase their horror at identifying with a murderer. The violence and gore of the program occasionally got Brown into trouble with parents and with the Federal Communications Commission, who were particularly concerned that youth, especially, might be unduly traumatized and might even pick up a thing or two about how to carry out a murder. Brown himself was proud of the fact that "[s]hrinks said [the program] was scaring people out of their wits."

Like other programs in the genre, *Inner Sanctum* stories were a counterpoint (some might even say an antidote) to the suburban ideal of the postwar period. Husbands and wives did not get along well in *Inner Sanctum* stories, which were replete with film noir-type characters (including a healthy number of femme fatales) who murdered each other at terrific rates. Titles such as "Til Death Do Us Part," "Til the Day I Kill You," "Last Time I Killed Her," and "Honeymoon with Death" give some sense of the program's portrayal of marriage. Host Raymond took great glee in the violent disintegration of the postwar family and the impossibility of happy coupling; his closing puns or rhymes commented approvingly on the evening's grim outcome: "He hid her body in a bell, and that's where he made his mistake because she *tolled* on him." "Never tangle with a girl with red hair," he would chuckle, "A man is safer in the electric chair" (which, of course, is where this particular man ended up). The trademark tongue-in-rotting-cheek humor of the program is perhaps best conveyed by some of its more amusing titles, including "Hell Is Where You Find it," "The Dead Want Company," "Death Has a Vacancy," "The Meek Die Slowly," "The Girl and the Gallows," "Death Is a Double-Crosser," "The Long Wait Is Over," "The Man on the Slab," "Ring Around the Morgue," "Corpse on the Town," "Corpse without a Conscience," "The Corpse Who Came to Dinner," "Blood Relative," "One Coffin Too Many," and "The Corpse Nobody Loved."

Screen horror great Boris Karloff was the program's regular star for much of its first season, appearing in the Poe classics "The Tell-Tale Heart" and "The Fall of the House of Usher." According to radio program historian John Dunning, Karloff wanted more gore than the networks would allow, and he appeared much less frequently thereafter. *Inner Sanctum* devel-oped its own stable of stars, which included Larry Haines, Mason Adams, Alice Rhinehart, Everett Sloane, Santos Ortega, Lawson Zerbe, and Elspeth Eric. In addition, up-and-coming film stars such as Mercedes McCambridge and Richard Widmark made frequent guest appearances. Although the programs emphasized plot over character, the alternately haunted and psychotic characters gave the actors a chance to stretch their range; women especially got the rare opportunity to narrate stories and play some very unladylike people.

Paul McGrath replaced Raymond Edward Johnson as host in 1945; he set a lighter tone than his predecessor, but the substance of the programs remained the same. Himan Brown attempted to revive the program in other forms in 1959 (as the *NBC Radio Theatre*) and 1974 (as the *CBS Radio Mystery Theatre*), but neither version proved as successful as the original. Of the more than 500 programs that were produced of *Inner Sanctum Mysteries*, more than 100 are available on tape, providing a unique and still entertaining radio legacy.

ALLISON MCCRACKEN

See also Brown, Himan; Horror Programs

Hosts
Raymond Edward Johnson (1941–45), Paul McGrath (1945–52)

Producer/Creator/Director
Himan Brown

Programming History
January 1941–October 1952 (528 episodes)

Further Reading
DeLong, Thomas A., *Radio Stars: An Illustrated Biographical Dictionary of 953 Performers, 1920 through 1960*, Jefferson, North Carolina: McFarland, 1996

Dunning, John, *Tune in Yesterday: The Ultimate Encyclopedia of Old-Time Radio, 1925–1976*, Englewood Cliffs, New Jersey: Prentice-Hall, 1976; revised edition, as *On the Air: The Encyclopedia of Old-Time Radio*, New York: Oxford University Press, 1998

Harmon, Jim, "And Here Is Your Host," chapter 4 of *The Great Radio Heroes*, New York: Ace, 1967; revised and expanded edition, Jefferson, North Carolina: McFarland, 2000

Intercollegiate Broadcasting System

The Intercollegiate Broadcasting System (IBS) was founded in 1940 by the originators of AM carrier-current college campus radio. Initially, college radio's primary interest concerned exchanging technical information among colleges via this new avenue of transmission. As more college stations were established, the interest evolved to include station management, programming, funding, recruiting, and industry training. Today, IBS is a nonprofit association of student-staffed radio stations located at schools and colleges throughout the United States. Approximately 600 IBS stations operate various types of radio facilities, including closed-circuit, AM carrier-current, cable radio, and Federal Communications Commission (FCC)–licensed FM and AM stations.

The majority of the early college radio stations in the United States were operated under the auspices of campus academic departments of electrical engineering; the primary objectives of these stations focused on the technical aspects of radio broadcasting rather than the public service potential. In 1925, 171 such stations were on the air, but by 1937, only 38 remained in operation. The decline in stations is credited to a general loss of campus interest or funding after the novelty of radio wore off. The few stations that sought to continue as AM broadcasters lost their licenses to commercial interests through comparative hearings before the FCC.

Lobbying in favor of college-based stations led to the FCC's 1938 decision to preserve such stations and to its 1941 and 1945 decisions to reserve FM channels designated for educational use. From the 1960s into the 1980s, the FM stations licensed to colleges and universities in the United States continued to provide leadership for the nation's public radio movement. By the mid-1990s, the majority of the 1,800 noncommercial so-called public radio licenses were granted to colleges and universities.

The formation of IBS was crucial to the preservation of college radio. IBS actively campaigned for reserved FM channels for college radio use. The result was the 1945 continuation of a reserved band of FM frequencies (this time at 88.1 to 91.9 MHz) where most noncommercial stations are now located. IBS was also active in convincing the FCC to establish the category of Class D (10-watt) noncommercial FM stations as an entry-level training ground for college radio. The Class D decision permitted hundreds of fledgling stations to get started; most of these gained momentum and graduated to the increased power of a Class A facility, 100 watts.

Increasingly throughout the years, IBS has taken on the fight for the protection of college radio. In 1978, when copyright laws changed to allow performing rights associations to collect fees for noncommercial broadcast performances, IBS presented testimony that resulted in lower rates being applied to college radio than to other classes of broadcast stations. IBS also filed objections against FCC on a proposal governing underwriting announcements. The IBS favored changes, which were adopted, and gave stations unprecedented latitude in the frequency and content of broadcast announcements, thus encouraging new interest from potential underwriters. Additionally, IBS was the first industry organization to file an FCC Petition for Reconsideration, which resulted in the FCC ruling exempting noncommercial operators from the $35 application permit fee.

IBS is a centralized information source by which college radio remains informed about industry politics, problems, and solutions. IBS lobbies for educational radio through an aggressive campaign of printed materials, e-mail, ground mail, telephone and fax communication, and regional and national seminars and workshops. Beyond addressing the needs of individual member stations, IBS acts as college radio's primary representation before the FCC and other governmental and industry agencies. IBS directors comprise a cross section of professionals representing a broad range of industry-experienced people who contribute their expertise on a voluntary basis.

The volunteer efforts of IBS personnel make sponsorship of new stations possible. IBS assists in launching new stations through a plan of action that includes advisory tips on conducting a frequency search; purchasing an existing station; and implementation of legal alternatives, such as utilizing on-campus carrier-current AM or cable FM piped into existing cable systems. Additionally, IBS offers basic advice regarding the complicated paperwork involved in filing for FCC permits.

IBS also provides helpful tips to member stations on increasing a station's coverage. IBS advises conducting frequency research to see if expansion is possible. They will assist in discussing the pros and cons of increased power versus increased height. For example, maintaining the same power but increasing the antenna height could give the increased coverage desired.

ELIZABETH COX

See also College Radio; Educational Radio to 1967; Low-Power Radio/Microradio; Public Radio Since 1967; Ten-Watt Stations; WHA and Wisconsin Public Radio

Further Reading

Bloch, Louis M., Jr., *The Gas Pipe Networks: A History of College Radio 1936–45*, Cleveland: Bloch and Company, 1980

Engleman, Ralph, *Public Radio and Television in America: A Political History*, Thousand Oaks, California: Sage, 1996

Frost, S.E., Jr., *Education's Own Stations*, Chicago: University of Chicago Press, 1937

Intercollegiate Broadcasting System (IBS) <www.ibsradio.org>

McCluskey, James, J., *Starting a Student Non-Commercial Radio Station*, Boston: Pearson Custom, 1998

International Radio Broadcasting

International radio broadcasting is usually associated with national governments, which certainly do make great use of it to communicate their viewpoints to listeners in other nations. Yet that is only one of many uses by one of many agencies: religious groups, commercial firms, and numerous others have also employed it. By the end of the 20th century, more than half of the world's sovereign nations were or had at one time been hosts to such services, which continued to attract many listeners despite the ending of the Cold War and the rising worldwide popularity of television.

Origins

Although radio amateurs often communicated across national borders, it was not until 1926 that any nation made even occasional use of radio to reach listeners in other nations. The Soviet Union broadcast to the then-Romanian (but formerly Russian) province of Bessarabia in an attempt to intimidate Romania into relinquishing its control of the province. The broadcasts lasted for several days and had no immediate effect. The Soviets also broadcast to miners in Great Britain for a few days during the General Strike of 1926, encouraging their dissatisfaction with the government, but again without visible effect. Both ventures were early examples of short-term tactical uses of the medium, but in 1927 the Netherlands launched the first long-term international broadcasting service when the Phillips electronics company's shortwave radio station PCJ began to broadcast to Dutch citizens living overseas. Over the next five years, Great Britain, France, and Germany launched similar services for their present and former citizens living abroad; the Soviet Union joined their ranks, but mainly for the purpose of reaching communists and gaining converts to communism from around the world.

It is doubtful that any of those services attracted large numbers of listeners since they broadcast almost exclusively over shortwave transmitters, and the shortwave radio sets needed to receive the signals were expensive. France and Great Britain ruled large colonial empires and used the newly created international radio services to keep overseas citizens in touch with their homelands; in those cases, the investment in receivers probably seemed little enough to pay in order to have a touch of "home away from home." However, as fascism began to spread through Europe in the 1930s, Germany, Italy, and Spain began to use mediumwave transmissions to reach nearby nations (in the case of Spain, reaching the opposition during the Spanish Civil War was at least as important as reaching foreign listeners), intimidating some with threats, reassuring others of their good intentions, and even attempting to persuade a few to join them. Because most of Europe was in the midst of an economic depression at the time, the relative economic strength of Germany and Italy provided their international radio services with potentially attractive success stories, and workers in other European nations were a frequent target of those services. Whether the messages were persuasive is an open question, because survey research was still in its infancy.

The increasing level of activity in international radio wasn't limited to politically motivated services. Radio Vaticana had come on the air in 1931, thanks in part to a generous financial donation by Italy's "father of radio," Guglielmo Marconi. Radio Vaticana brought a Catholic message to much of the world, in many languages. It also had company before the end of the year: a Protestant service to Latin America, HCJB, operated from Quito, Ecuador, but received financial and administrative support largely from the United States. HCJB was far more interested in converting its listeners to its version of Protestantism, whereas Radio Vaticana hoped to sustain its listeners in their Catholic faith. A commercially oriented service also appeared during the early 1930s: Radio Luxembourg, taking advantage of its location amid several European nations with little or no commercial broadcasting of their own, began to provide these nations with services in their own languages, heavily laden with popular music and ads.

But it was the politically motivated services that dominated, a domination that only increased as World War II drew nearer. The Soviet service, Radio Moscow, and the German *Weltrundfunk-sender* had been exchanging condemnations of each other's governments since the early 1930s. Italy's Radio Bari began to foment discord in British-ruled Palestine starting in 1934; four years later, the British Broadcasting Corporation (BBC) began its first foreign language service with its Arabic language broadcasts to listeners in the Middle East, largely to defend Great Britain against the continuing attacks of Radio Bari. Japan's Radio Tokyo became active in broadcasting intimidating messages to China in the late 1930s, as the Japanese army moved to occupy parts of the country. Some broadcasters began to make use of a more personality-oriented approach, with conversational styles breaking the pattern of highly formal speech that had predominated on most stations. Some also made use of clandestine (concealed or false identity) stations in hopes of deceiving listeners into believing that broadcasts came from within the listeners' own nations.

World War II

Once World War II had begun, international radio moved into high gear, with most of the major combatants—Great Britain, the United States, Germany, Italy, and Japan—rapidly adding language services, increasing their broadcast hours, and strengthening their transmitter power. The Nazis also attempted to ensure that German citizens would not have access to German language broadcasts from the Western allies by using jamming (electronic interference), by exacting severe penalties for such listening, and by making available only inexpensive radio receivers incapable of picking up the more distant incoming signals. Nevertheless, the Allied services developed an array of specialized programs designed to reach German officers, frontline soldiers, U-boat (submarine) crews, and others; these programs featured fake Germans in roles such as "Der Chef," a German "officer" who spread rumors about misconduct and luxurious lifestyles among high-level German civilians in his broadcasts over Great Britain's Soldatensender—a clandestine radio service for German military personnel. However, the success of any of the broadcasts was difficult to determine. Survey research was not well developed at the time, and conducting surveys in areas governed by the enemy was not an option.

The Cold War

When the war ended in August 1945, there was considerable sentiment in Great Britain and the United States favoring sharp reductions and even elimination of the international radio services. The Voice of America (VOA) was nearly disbanded in 1945–46, and BBC external services were considerably reduced. Radio Moscow at first reduced its services slightly but then expanded them, even as it worked with the Central and Eastern European nations now under Soviet influence to create miniature Radio Moscows in Poland, Hungary, and elsewhere. Influential legislators returning from trips to those nations reported hearing strong anti-Western messages over Radio Moscow, Radio Warsaw, and other stations in the region. This fact, coupled with the virtual disappearance of cooperation

between the Western allies and the Soviet Union, helped lead to dramatic reversals of fortune for VOA and BBC, which soon had sizable Czech, Romanian, Russian, and other language services appropriate for the situation.

The United States went even further. The British had operated more clandestine stations during the war, but now the United States took the lead on a grand scale with the creation of Radio Free Europe (RFE) and Radio Liberation from Bolshevism (later Radio Liberty [RL]). The U.S. authorities considered these to be "the sorts of services the captive peoples of eastern Europe and the Soviet Union would want if they had a free choice." Although their broadcast messages did not call for the overthrow of communist governments, RFE and RL at times suggested work slowdowns and other actions that might help weaken those governments and eventually lead to liberation from communism. The stations spent far more time pointing out the rapid economic growth of the West, comparing that growth with the allegedly poor economic progress of the East. The communist international stations reported on strikes and other signs of the "inevitable decline of capitalism," contrasting that decline with what they claimed was the generally robust performance of the communist economies. Increases in broadcasts from the West were met by increases in jamming in the East. However, surveys taken among refugees from Eastern Europe indicated that some of the signals were getting through and that they seemed particularly effective in causing those who heard them to be more and more skeptical of communist media claims that life under communism was far superior to life under capitalism and that the gap between the two was steadily growing.

When China joined the ranks of communist nations in 1949, it soon added its own international broadcast voice, causing the United States to create an Asian equivalent of RFE/RL in the form of Radio Free Asia (RFA, 1951–55; a new Radio Free Asia came on-air in 1996). The small numbers of radio receivers in North Korea and in China, the difficulty of recruiting suitable Asian language speaking talent, and heavy jamming of RFA caused the United States to drop the service, even as China's newly founded Radio Peking (later Beijing) grew to become one of the largest of all international broadcast services, with North Korea's Radio Pyongyang not far behind. In each case, the Soviet Union assisted both materially and ideologically; the Soviet Union played a similar role with respect to Radio Havana Cuba starting in the early 1960s.

The Third World Speaks and Listens

The Soviet Union had become increasingly active in broadcasting to the Third World (industrially developing nations) during the late 1950s, as African, Asian, and Latin American nations emerged from their colonial status. The Chinese, North Korean, and Cuban international services added their voices to Radio Moscow's in denouncing colonialism where it still existed while praising the efforts of the newly independent nations to stake out their own ideological positions in the Cold War. Two of those nations—Egypt and India—were already operating international radio services by the mid-1950s, with Africa and the Islamic nations as prime targets of the former and South and Southeast Asia the targets of the latter. Although they too denounced colonialism, and therefore Western nations such as France and Great Britain, they were not necessarily sympathetic to communism, either. Thus, they constituted yet another international radio voice with yet another cultural and political perspective. As more newly independent nations emerged, some of them also developed international services; Radio Ghana was broadcasting in several West African and European languages by the end of the 1950s. But no single nation among them ever set out to coordinate their efforts into a unified anticolonial voice, as the Soviet Union managed to do to some degree with the other communist international services during the 1950s.

That coordination began to crumble as China increased in strength and in prestige. By the late 1950s, China had begun to part ways with the Soviet Union over the correct interpretation of Marxism–Leninism. The disagreement gave rise to the broadcast of many verbal duels between the two communist powers, generally of little or no interest to anyone but committed Marxist–Leninists. The United States and Great Britain were beginning to see that, as the old colonial system broke apart, they faced both an opportunity and a challenge in reaching African, Asian, and Latin American audiences. It took a few years for each to realize that a new message would have to speak to a new relationship—one that respected the independence of what were now sovereign nations. BBC's World Services and VOA were sufficiently alert to recognize, as Radio Moscow often had not (although it made an effort to do so through Radio Peace and Progress, founded in 1964), that programs dealing with African, Asian, and Latin American events, cultures, and personalities were likely to prove far more attractive than had the one-worldwide-size-fits-all approach generally taken by Moscow. (Radio Peking was generally more sensitive to Third World cultural aspirations and often portrayed the People's Republic of China as a Third World nation.)

By the late 1960s, both VOA and BBC had developed African, Asian, and Latin American services with a variety of cultural and informational programs tailored for those regions. VOA also had introduced a limited-vocabulary/slow-rate "Special English" newscast in 1959; because it was well suited to English language learners, of which there were many in the Third World, the newscast was able to attract listeners. Surveys taken by or for VOA and BBC during the 1960s showed increasing numbers of Third World listeners for both and minuscule numbers for the communist services, with the notable exception of Radio Havana in Latin America. Cuban President Fidel Castro enjoyed considerable popularity among Latinos for his willingness to stand up to the United States, and Radio Havana blended programs featuring Cuban and other Latin American cultures with informational programs that generally avoided the heavy ideological jargon of many such programs broadcast over Radios Moscow, Peking, Pyongyang, and other communist stations.

Religious Voices

There was yet another major entrant in the post–World War II international radio lists, although it grew more slowly than had the communist or Western sectors. Religious stations, few in number in the 1930s, began to multiply in the late 1940s and early 1950s, in part as a reaction to the spread of "godless communism," in part in recognition of the beneficial effects for fund-raising of broadcasting international religious programs for non-Christians and for religion-deprived listeners in communist nations around the world. Most of the new services were financed by U.S. religious groups, most were evangelical, and virtually all were Protestant. They established stations and relay transmitters in Africa (Morocco, Liberia, Ethiopia; in the 1960s, Burundi and Swaziland); Asia (Sri Lanka, the Philippines, Korea); Latin America (Netherlands Antilles); and also in the United States and Europe. Many of the English language programs were rebroadcasts of U.S. evangelical preachers, many of whom had heavy southern accents and made references to people and places that would be unfamiliar to foreign listeners, so it was not surprising that religious stations on the whole did poorly in listener surveys. The exceptions were HCJB in Quito, Ecuador, and FEBC in the Philippines, both of which provided a widely varied assortment of information and entertainment and were careful to show respect to other religious denominations and faiths.

Clandestine Services

Clandestine stations generally flourished in the unstable atmosphere of the Cold War. Not only were they prominent in the conflict between East and West, but they also played roles in the many regional conflicts taking place in Asia, Africa, and the Middle East. Their programs generally were political and often featured exceptionally strong language, including calls for the assassination of political leaders. They also served as channels through which politicians in exile could reach their former homelands with messages criticizing government officials and even encouraging uprisings.

The Cold War Ends

With the collapse of communism in Eastern Europe and in the Soviet Union by the early 1990s, the Cold War came to an end. That also brought radical changes for international radio, which had been so heavily involved in the struggle between communism and capitalism. No longer did many of the governments that had financed the stations see the need for so many language services, so many hours of transmission, and so many foreign transmitter bases, and annual financial appropriations began to decline. Most of the communist countries either cut their international services to the bone or dropped them altogether. The clandestine stations also felt the pinch, since many of them had been partially or wholly financed by the East and the West so that they could play roles in Cold War politics in addition to serving the more narrowly focused ends of some of the groups operating them. Their places were taken to a limited extent by Islamic fundamentalist and paramilitary group operations, and political exile groups continued to use them in Africa and Asia.

Still, there were some bright spots for the international stations during the 1990s. The spread of the internet made it possible for them to begin to provide interference-free service through websites, and by the end of the decade virtually all of the major stations were doing so. There was also the prospect of direct transmission via satellite to individual receivers (the use of satellites to relay signals to foreign transmitter bases had been around since the early 1980s), although the cost of such receivers was discouragingly high. A U.S.-based commercial firm, WorldSpace, launched a satellite-delivered multichannel radio service to Africa in October 1999, but economic data suggested that few African listeners could afford the specialized receivers needed to bring in its transmissions.

As the new millennium dawned, there was every indication that international radio would continue to be viable, even if on a reduced scale. Some of the international commercial radio services from France—Radio Monte Carlo Middle East, Radio Méditerranée Internationale, Afrique Numéro Une (Africa No. 1; for sub-Saharan Africa)—still enjoyed financial success, largely because they provided their audiences with more "worldly" entertainment (largely Western or Western-flavored pop music) and broader and less-biased perspectives on regional and world events than did domestic stations in those areas. Instability in parts of southeast Asia, Africa, the Balkans, and the former Soviet Union helped to ensure that the comprehensive and generally reliable informational broadcasts of the BBC World Service, the Voice of America and Radio Free Europe/Radio Liberty, Germany's Deutsche Welle, and smaller-scale services such as Radio Netherlands, Radio Canada International, Radio Australia, and Radio Japan would have audiences, especially in the areas of conflict themselves.

The Voice of Russia (formerly Radio Moscow), Radio Beijing, Radio Pyongyang, and certainly Radio Havana Cuba also continued to provide their versions of current events to listeners who appreciated Russian, Chinese, North Korean, and Cuban perspectives, even if those perspectives might have become less meaningful with the ending of the Cold War. Reli-gious stations seemed no more or less popular than they had been in earlier decades, but the chief reason for the existence of many of them—to help stimulate contributions from those anxious to bring the gospel message to nonbelievers—remained viable. Increases in the efficiency of distribution of television broadcasts on an international basis, especially when coupled with the invention of modestly priced television sets capable of receiving signals directly from satellites, almost certainly would reduce the attraction of international radio. So would the provision by domestic broadcast services in presently autocratic nations of more balanced and detailed coverage of events at home and abroad. Neither of those changes seems an immediate prospect.

DONALD R. BROWNE

See also Africa No. 1; Axis Sally; BBC World Service; Clandestine Radio; Cold War Radio; Developing Nations; Far East Broadcasting Company; Jamming; Lord Haw-Haw; Propaganda by Radio; Radio Free Asia; Radio Free Europe/Radio Liberty; Radio Luxembourg; Radio Martí; Radio Moscow; Radio Sawa/Middle East Radio Network; Religion on Radio; Tokyo Rose; Vatican Radio; Voice of America; World War II and U.S. Radio

Further Reading

Benhalla, Fouad, *La guerre radiophonique*, Paris: Collection de la Revue Politique et Parlementaire, 1983

Boelcke, Willi A., *Die Macht des Radios: Weltpolitik und Auslandsrundfunk, 1924–1976*, Frankfurt: Ullstein, 1977

Bookmiller, Kirsten Nakjavani, "The War of Words without the War: Radio Moscow, the British Broadcasting Corporation World Service, and the Voice of America in the Old and New International Order," Ph.D. diss., University of Virginia, 1992

Browne, Donald R., *International Radio Broadcasting: The Limits of the Limitless Medium*, New York: Praeger, 1982

Fortner, Robert, *Public Diplomacy and International Politics: The Symbolic Constructs of Summits and International Radio News*, Westport, Connecticut: Praeger, 1994

Hale, Julian, *Radio Power: Propaganda and International Broadcasting*, Philadelphia, Pennsylvania: Temple University Press, and London: Elek, 1975

Krugler, David F., *The Voice of America and the Domestic Propaganda Battles 1945–53*, Columbia: University of Missouri Press, 2000

Mytton, Graham, *Global Audiences: Research for Worldwide Broadcasting, 1993*, London: Libbey, 1993

Nelson, Michael, *War of the Black Heavens: The Battles of Western Broadcasting in the Cold War*, Syracuse, New York: Syracuse University Press, 1997

Rawnsley, Gary, *Radio Diplomacy and Propaganda: The BBC and VOA in International Politics, 1956–64*, New York: St. Martin's Press, and London: Macmillan, 1996

Sémelin, Jacques, *La liberté au bout des ondes: Du coup de Prague à la chute du mur de Berlin*, Paris: Belfond, 1997

Soley, Lawrence C., and John Spicer Nichols, *Clandestine Radio Broadcasting: A Study of Revolutionary and Counterrevolutionary Electronic Communication*, New York: Praeger, 1987

Soley, Lawrence C., *Radio Warfare: OSS and CIA Subversive Propaganda*, New York: Praeger, 1989

Tyson, James L., *U.S. International Broadcasting and National Security*, New York: Ramapo Press, 1983

Wettig, Gerhard, *Broadcasting and Detente: Eastern Policies and Their Implication for East-West Relations*, London: Hurst, and New York: St. Martin's Press, 1977

Wood, James, *History of International Broadcasting*, vol. 1, London: Peregrinus, 1992; vol. 2, London: Institute of Electrical Engineers, 2000

International Telecommunication Union

The International Telecommunication Union (ITU) is a specialized agency operating under the auspices of the United Nations. It attempts to assist in the development of broadcasting and point-to-point communication by providing fora for the discussion of, and adoption of agreements on, issues common to all countries' communications activities, including tariffs, technical standards for interconnection across frontiers, the sharing of broadcasting frequencies, the allocation of geosynchronous satellite locations, and the permissible uses for international communication. It also registers countries' use of shortwave frequencies to provide the basis for frequency coordination among the different users of this broadcasting medium.

Origins

Originally called the International Telegraph Union, the ITU was formed on 17 May 1865 by 20 European countries that desired to facilitate international telegraph communication. Until the convention that established the ITU was signed, telegraph activities occurred entirely within individual countries: messages had to be transcribed at each border, translated into the language of the neighboring country, and then carried across the frontier where they would be rekeyed for further transmission. Each country also used its own telegraph code to safeguard its military and political messages. This made international telegraphy cumbersome at best and prevented the new technology from having a significant positive impact on the relations of the suspicious European powers.

Linking up the different domestic telegraph systems required that three issues be resolved. First, the electrical transmission systems used had to be standardized. Different wire gauges, signal voltages, and wire connection systems had to be standardized so that there would be no technical breaks in lines traveling across frontiers. Otherwise, communication would be impossible. Second, the allocation of revenues had to be agreed on, so that if a message traveled, say, between London and Berlin, the British, French or Belgian, and German telegraph companies (usually state-owned) would each receive an equitable portion of the tariff. Otherwise, there would be no financial inducement to connect the lines. Messages often traveled through a country's system without actually being delivered to anyone within it. (As in the above example, in which the message must travel across France to Germany for delivery.) So a system was devised that compensated different telegraph authorities according to the miles of line used for a message to reach its destination, regardless of origination or destination point. Third, a common language had to be used for messages so that their meaning could be accurately transcribed regardless of the language of the telegraph operator. Morse code, which represented all the letters of the alphabet with a combination of short and long pulses, was adopted as this common language. Also, agreements forbade private codes that shortened messages (such as FYI for "for your information") to assure that those who used the telegraph system were paying their fair share of its costs.

The original Telegraph Convention (or treaty) established the basic rules that the ITU was to administer on behalf of the signatory states and provided the foundation for subsequent agreements as new technologies developed. The ITU was not granted, and still does not have, any enforcement powers to use against states (called administrations) that break the conventions, so it functions as technical advisor, facilitator of new conventions as required, and administrator of agreements between signatory nations.

Since that first convention adopted to coordinate telegraphy, new technologies have called for new agreements and expansion of the ITU's activities. The submarine cable, which connected countries under the sea, began to be widely used in the 1850s, and the first transatlantic cable was successfully laid in 1866. This new form of telegraphy, as well as wired telephony, invented in 1876, both required essentially the same type of agreements between states that the overland telegraph had.

The ITU and Radio

Wireless telegraphy, however, required a different set of agreements. Wireless crossed international frontiers whether a country objected or not. And although wireless operators did not require the use of facilities within every country whose territory they crossed, signals were subject to interference from other transmitters using the same frequency. Furthermore, wireless signals were important as a means to communicate with ships that were not on any country's actual territory. Two issues emerged beyond the earlier concerns. First, should all ships, regardless of country of registry, be required to have both wireless apparatus and trained operators on duty 24 hours per day? Second, were the private monopolies that were being pursued by private companies (such as British Marconi) to take precedence over safety at sea? Marconi, for instance, forbade its operators from communicating with ships using wireless apparatus manufactured by its competitors. This policy was not successfully broken until the *Titanic* disaster (1912) demonstrated the necessity of doing so. The development of wireless telegraphy resulted in the convening of a preliminary radiocommunication conference at Berlin in 1903 and a Radiotelegraph Conference in 1906 that resulted in the first International Radiotelegraph Convention. Three principles emerged from these radiotelegraph meetings. These were (1) that frequencies should be reserved for specific services; (2) that all administrations should take the steps necessary to avoid interference with other users; and (3) that all use of frequencies should be registered.

During the 1920s, three consultative committees were established under the auspices of the ITU to draw up international standards for the telegraph, telephone, and radio. The International Telephone Consultative Committee was set up in 1924, the International Telegraphy Consultative Committee in 1925, and the International Radio Consultative Committee (CCIR) in 1927. These committees all coordinated the technical studies undertaken to develop new standards, developed means to conduct tests and measurements, and made recommendations to conferences convened to adopt new regulations. The telephone and telegraph committees were combined in 1956 into the International Telephone and Telegraph Committee (CCITT).

In 1927 the ITU allocated frequencies to the different radio services that were in operation at that time. These included fixed services (point-to-point wireless radiotelegraphy), maritime and aeronautical mobile services (for ships and airplanes), radio broadcasting, and amateur and experimental services.

The Modern International Telecommunication Union

On 1 January 1934, the old ITU officially became the International Telecommunication Union. This was a result of a decision made at the 1932 Madrid plenipotentiary conference to combine the two original agreements (the International Telegraph Convention of 1865 and the International Radiotelegraph Convention of 1906) into a single International Telecommunication Convention. The ITU became a specialized agency of the United Nations on 15 October 1947.

In the same year, the table of frequency allocations that had been established in 1912, which allocated to each type of radio service specific frequency bands to use so as to avoid interference with other types of uses, was made mandatory. The International Frequency Registration Board (IFRB) was set up to manage the radio frequency spectrum under the auspices of the ITU.

In 1959 the CCIR established a study group to look into space communications as a result of the launch of the Soviet *Sputnik* in 1956. In 1963 the first administrative conference on space communications was held to allocate frequencies to space services.

The ITU has divided the world into three regions for purposes of dealing with frequency allocation issues and technical standards. These regions, roughly, are Region 1, Europe and Africa; Region 2, Asia; and Region 3, the Americas. Some differences in technical standards may exist among these regions, although within each area technical standards are consistent. For instance, in Europe medium wave (or what Americans call AM) bands are 9-kilohertz wide, whereas in the Americas they are 10-kilohertz wide. This small difference allows the larger number of countries in Europe to have additional frequencies for this service that are not needed in the Americas, which are dominated by large countries (especially Brazil, Canada, Mexico, and the United States).

The ITU has a complicated organizational structure. Its permanent staff is included in the General Secretariat headed by the Secretary-General of the United Nations. Since a 1990s reorganization, there are three bureaus in this secretariat, including the Radiocommunication Bureau, the Telecommunication Standardization Bureau, and the Telecommunication Development Bureau. The members of the ITU elect a Council that oversees the secretariat between their plenipotentiary conferences, which is where major policy changes are made and regulations or resolutions are adopted concerning either radiocommunication or telecommunication. Specialized conferences are also held to deal with specific issues, such as World or Regional Administrative Radio Conferences (WARCs and RARCs), World Telecommunication Standardization Assemblies, and World or Regional Telecommunication Development Conferences. Each of these three types of conferences also has advisory and study groups that survey world practice in their subject concern, commission studies, or distill technical information that is used as the basis for determining new regulations or standards in the different areas. In addition, the WARC/RARC conferences have a Radio Regulations Board because of the more difficult matter of administrations coming to agreements and enforcing them when the communications activity in question is wireless (whether terrestrial or satellite point-to-point or terrestrial or satellite broadcasting). This is because such radiocommunication activities (including the assignment of geosynchronous satellite "parking spaces") either cross frontiers or operate in the "air space" above countries that may not derive any benefit from them.

ITU Functions

The ITU's responsibilities under this organizational structure can be grouped into three main activities. First, it coordinates radio frequency assignments, including band assignments for services and the use of the geostationary orbit for satellites, including orbital slots. Second, it recommends technical standards for international communications, including those for wired connections, bandwidths, and other technical parameters. Third, it regulates international common carrier services, including telegraphy, telephony, and data communication.

The globalization of communication that has occurred in the satellite age—including intercontinental distribution of radio and television programs, satellite-based telephony, the development of Global Positioning System (GPS) receivers and maritime communication; the explosive growth of the internet; and the need to allocate the limited number of "parking spaces" for geosynchronous satellites serving countries that are, themselves, not on the equator above which these satellites "park"—has involved the ITU in an increasing number of sovereignty-based technical issues. For instance, developed countries have argued that the allocation of orbit slots should be based on need, whereas developing countries have contended that, despite their inability to use satellites at a given time, slots should be reserved for their future use. So the question of whether technological change will enable more satellites, or more powerful satellites, to be deployed in time to meet future needs has had to be considered alongside the demands for access made by those over whose territory the satellites orbit. And because all geosynchronous satellites must orbit above the equator to maintain their positions relative to the Earth's surface (and thus appear to be stationary), the application of sovereignty arguments has had to be considered alongside the

technical or economic arguments of more advanced countries. It is under the auspices of the ITU and its various technical committees, study groups, conferences, and plenipotentiaries that such issues are ultimately resolved.

One significant issue that the ITU has had to confront concerning radio has been the use and abuse of shortwave frequencies. Shortwave is the one radio service for which individual stations are not assigned particular frequencies. There are a variety of technical reasons for this, but the bottom line is that, depending on various factors, shortwave radio stations have to change their frequencies periodically. Keeping track of the use of stations' use of these frequencies is thus a major activity of the IFRB. Also, shortwave radio has historically been used for international broadcasting, and stations have purposely broadcast in multiple languages to the people of other countries. Two contentious issues developed. The first was the question of whether stations were engaged in propaganda. The second, related issue was whether a country was deliberately interfering (or jamming) the signals of a station originating outside its borders to stop the station's propaganda. Purposely interfering with another station's signal is against ITU radio regulations, so even countries that are widely known to jam others' signals have steadfastly denied that they engage in such practices. The IFRB could only register use, however, since it had no enforcement power to use in such cases.

ROBERT S. FORTNER

See also Digital Audio Broadcasting; Frequency Allocation; International Radio Broadcasting; North American Regional Broadcasting Agreement; Shortwave Radio

Further Reading

Codding, George A., Jr., *The International Telecommunication Union: An Experiment in International Cooperation*, Leiden, The Netherlands: Brill, 1952

Codding, George A., Jr., and Anthony M. Rutkowski, *The International Telecommunication Union in a Changing World*, Dedham, Massachusetts: Artech House, 1982

Fortner, Robert S., *International Communication: History, Conflict, and Control of the Global Metropolis*, Belmont, California: Wadsworth, 1993

Michaelis, Anthony R., *From Semaphore to Satellite,* Geneva: International Telecommunication Union, 1965

Tomlinson, John D., *The International Control of Radiocommunications*, Ann Arbor, Michigan: Edwards, 1945; reprint, New York: Arno Press, 1979

Internet Radio

Delivering Radio Programs Online

Internet radio involves the delivery of audio programming via digital means from one computer to other computers over the internet. It involves both simulcasts of existing over-the-air radio stations and content from internet-only stations. Internet radio was made possible by the 1995 arrival of streaming. Previously, users had to download an entire audio file before being able to listen to it. Even audio clips of short duration could take hours to download. Streaming allows the user to listen to the audio programming as it arrives in real time. This means users do not have to wait for a complete audio file to download before listening to it. Internet radio streaming can involve both live material and archived clips of audio content recorded earlier. In either case, the user must have special software that matches the software used by the station to encode and transmit the data.

Internet radio was a booming enterprise into the late 1990s, but legal decisions and a downturn in internet advertising have effectively shut down many stations today. In 2002, a dispute between internet broadcasters and the music industry came to a head when a copyright appeals board required internet radio stations to pay a per-song, per-listener fee that was prohibitively expensive for many stations. The fee was an especially great hardship for small operations, such as religious broadcasters and college radio stations, and amounted to thousands of dollars more than they made. This led to hundreds of internet-based radio stations shutting down.

By late 2002, a compromise was worked out whereby internet broadcasters could pay royalty fees on a percentage of their revenue instead of on a per-song, per-listener basis. The *Small Webcaster Settlement Act of 2002* was seen as a big victory by small webcasters and by early 2003 many small internet broadcasters were beginning to reappear.

The three leading technologies for delivering internet radio are the RealOne Player, Microsoft Windows Media, and MP3 streaming. Internet radio stations will often select one of the technologies for the delivery of their content. In some cases, stations choose to make their audio stream available in more than one of these formats, allowing listeners to choose the way they want to listen.

Streaming generally sacrifices audio quality because of the need to compress the data for delivery via narrowband (56k) telephone line modems still used by most households. Early internet radio quality was very poor, and many listeners became discouraged by the poor audio quality and problems maintaining a continuous stream. The stream would often stop and buffer (download data before it was used), inhibiting continuous delivery of the program.

Today, technological improvements and new broadband connections allow better streams and near-CD-quality sound. Listeners with cable modems or telephone DSL (digital subscriber line) services are the biggest beneficiaries. The adoption of these faster broadband connections is rising sharply. In an 18-month period between January 2001 and July 2002, the percentage of Americans with residential broadband internet access surged from 13 percent to 28 percent. As that number continues to grow, the audience for internet radio services will build as well.

Radio Stations on the Internet

Studies show that internet usage is cutting into time people would otherwise spend listening to broadcast radio. For traditional broadcast stations, delivery of programming on the internet may help recapture some of these listeners and may even generate new listeners in distant locations. Even small-market radio stations can reach the same international audiences as stations in larger markets. The concept of signal strength does not apply in the on-line world, and all stations start out on equal footing. Location is no barrier, either. It costs no more to send an internet radio program 1,000 miles than it does to send it 10 miles. On-line radio listeners say they listen more to radio stations outside their local market than they do to stations in their own locale.

One Arbitron and Edison Media Research study showed that by the middle of 2002, 35 percent of Americans had listened to internet radio, compared with 19 percent in 1998. This growth has given traditional radio broadcasters cause for concern because radio listeners now have a much greater number of listening choices on-line than they do on the radio dial.

Internet radio listeners are sometimes referred to as "streamies." As a group, streamies represent a very desirable demographic for advertisers. Streamies are among the most active group of internet users, spending more time on-line than the average internet user. Streamies are twice as likely to click on web ads and to make on-line purchases and are very interested in new devices to enable even more convenient listening. Internet radio listeners tend to be better educated and come from homes with higher incomes than regular internet users.

Capturing the internet audience and persuading listeners to revisit, however, is made more difficult with such a range of choices. Developing content worthy of repeat visits is one of the biggest challenges for internet broadcasters. Merely having a web presence to promote a station's broadcast operation is not enough. Internet broadcasters are using interactive features such as contests and live chat rooms to gain and hold on to the elusive internet audience. Concert information, celebrity interviews, and fashion information are also important content categories for the young internet radio audience.

Broadcast radio stations have traditionally had strong local identities. On the internet, some stations may decide to adopt a more national identity. Far-flung listeners with ties to a community can stay up to date with "local" news, sports, and community events from anywhere in the world.

Stations looking for a national audience may develop niche programming such as specific music genres or sports. Certain music formats may be more popular than others in the on-line world. A 1999 Arbitron and Edison Media Research study showed that 91 percent of radio listeners who have internet access prefer alternative rock. The next highest categories were Top 40 (68 percent), classical (68 percent), religious (54 percent), adult contemporary (52 percent), and news/talk (50 percent). The top-rated internet radio stations tend to be eclectic and unique-sounding outlets not commonly found on the air.

Some broadcasters remain unconvinced of the value of internet radio. For one thing, there are far fewer internet-connected computers than there are available radio sets. Internet radio also lacks the portability of broadcast radio and is not generally available in cars, at the beach, a picnic, or other gathering places outside the home or workplace. Sound quality of internet radio varies greatly, and listeners with low-speed modem connections or slow computers are often disappointed with the overall quality. Furthermore, studies have shown that many people sample on-line stations but don't return regularly. Many broadcasters are still waiting to see a return on their investment in internet radio.

Making Money on Internet Radio

Although broadcast radio is an audio-only medium, internet radio stations are free to offer interactive programming and can include images, animation, and even video. Whereas broadcast radio relies on estimating the size of audiences via ratings, internet radio can measure each time a user accesses a particular page or program and in many cases can provide detailed demographic data about the people visiting their sites.

There are three ways for internet radio stations to make money on-line; advertising, transactions, and subscriptions. Advertising is the model broadcast stations have adopted and used for decades. The ability of internet radio to reach a global audience means not only the potential for a greater number of listeners, but also that stations may be able to attract national, as well as local, advertisers. Internet radio listeners represent a desirable demographic of technology-savvy young people to advertisers as well.

Besides the standard audio-only commercials so familiar on the radio, internet radio allows stations to generate revenue through graphic advertising banners and pop-up ads as well. The "banner ad" is an easy and effective way to display advertising on a station's website. Stations charge different amounts, depending on banner size, placement, and duration on a page. The banner ad may be placed on the same page listeners go to when they want to listen to the station on-line. A greater amount can be charged for what are called "click-throughs" (money earned when users click the banner ad and go to the advertiser's site).

Other sources of revenue can be generated through classified ads and direct sales or transactions. For example, many internet radio listeners say that they would like to be able to buy music on a station's site. Advertising on internet radio stations can be tied directly to transactions conducted on-line. Whereas broadcast radio commercials depend on delayed gratification (listeners hear a commercial and will ideally buy something later), internet radio is more interactive and allows the user to go immediately from the desire to buy directly to a page where a purchase can take place. This immediacy in the on-line world changes the very nature and approach of advertising for the new medium.

Many internet radio stations have moved away from being a free service and are now charging a subscription fee. KPIG in California was the first commercial broadcaster to use the internet back in 1995. Because of copyright fees and dwindling advertising revenue, KPIG is now charging a per month fee for listeners to access their content.

Internet-Only Radio Stations

In many cases, internet radio stations exist only on the internet. Often referred to as music "channels," these ventures often play lesser-known groups and alternative music formats. In many cases, internet-only sites are providing original content, multiple channels, and fewer commercials. For artists and labels finding it difficult to get playtime on traditional stations, internet radio provides a viable option for exposure of new music.

The cost for starting up an internet radio station is far less than the cost of building or buying a broadcast station. An internet radio station can be established for less than $10,000 and does not require a license from the Federal Communications Commission.

One of the major targets of internet-only stations is the workplace. There tend to be more computers in use around offices than radio and television receivers. Internet-only stations hope to attract workers disenfranchised by traditional radio by offering more finely niched music choices, fewer commercials, and the opportunity to buy on-line. However, since internet radio uses a tremendous amount of bandwidth, workers listening to it could put a strain on a company's network and the ability to handle e-mail and other work-related applications.

Personal Internet Radio Stations

New technology and software allow anyone to become an internet radio broadcaster. Individuals can start their own stations and operate them from their homes. All it takes is a computer, an internet connection, and some free software. Users can create and customize their own radio stations on-line without the trouble of acquiring and setting up a server. Some on-line sites allow users to create their own playlists of genres and artists and to actually specify how often each is heard. The sites have large archives of music available. Once users have built their stations based on their music preferences, they can go to a webpage and listen to their own personalized station. The web address can be given to others so they can listen to the station as well.

One of the most successful audio technologies on the internet is the MP3 format. MP3 (MPEG Audio Layer 3) is a highly compressed audio format that delivers near-CD-quality sound with very small file sizes. Users can download high-quality MP3 music files even on low-bandwidth connections. On-line MP3 sites offer a great deal of free downloadable music, and one is often able to listen to new artists who promote and distribute their music on these sites. MP3 player software is available free on-line.

STEVEN D. ANDERSON

See also Audio Streaming; Digital Audio Broadcasting

Web Sites

SaveInternetRadio, <www.saveinternetradio.org>
SoundExchange, <www.soundexchange.com>
BRS Web-Radio, <www.web-radio.fm>

Further Reading

Bachman, Katy, "Not Streaming Profits," *Mediaweek* (6 September 1999)
Cherry, Steven M., "Web Radio: Time to Sign Off?" *IEEE Spectrum* (August 2002)
Graven, Matthew, "Web Radio Days," *PC Magazine* (14 December 1999)
"Internet 9: The Media and Entertainment World of Online Consumers," *Arbitron/Edison Media Research* (5 September 2002)
Kerschbaumer, Ken, "Radio Next for RealNetworks," *Broadcasting & Cable* (26 August 2002)
Kuchinskas, Susan, "Tune It to Internet Radio," *Mediaweek* (19 April 1999)
"New Media Eyes Radio's Audience," *Billboard* (23 October 1999)
Rathbun, Elizabeth A., "Clash of the 'Casters," *Broadcasting and Cable* (6 September 1999)
Shiver, Jube, Jr., "Internet Adds Dimension to Radio," *Providence Business News* (30 August 1999)
"Small Webcasters Get Break on License Fees for Transmissions of Music Recordings, as Authorized by Small Webcaster Settlement Act," *Entertainment Law Reporter* (December 2002)
"Small Webcasters, RIAA Formally Unveil Royalty Accord," *Communications Daily* (17 December 2002)
"Streaming Media Sites Expand: Downloadable Tunes Help Build Audience," *Computerworld* (19 July 1999)
Taylor, Chuck, "Webcasters Reshape Radio Landscape," *Billboard* (5 June 1999)

Ireland

Radio enjoys a special place in Irish public discourse. Ireland is a society of strong literary and verbal traditions, out of which have emerged writers such as William Butler Yeats, James Joyce, Kate O'Brien, and Samuel Beckett. The words spoken on Ireland's airwaves likewise have had considerable significance and power. From 1926, following the formation of an Irish state independent of the United Kingdom, radio came to play an important role in creating a new sense of nationalist identity. Extensive radio coverage of the Eucharistic Congress of 1932 greatly helped to consolidate close connections between the Roman Catholic Church and Irish politicians, connections that remained until recently a characteristic feature of the state.

Before 1988, the single state-owned broadcaster (Radio Eireann, later Radio Telefis Eireann [RTE]) enjoyed a monopoly of all broadcasting in the Republic of Ireland. Eamon de Valera, the predominant Irish prime minister (*Taoiseach*) of the mid-20th century, used radio effectively to disseminate his protectionist vision of an Ireland that was not only politically neutral but that he thought might also stand apart culturally from the modern world.

Listening to radio in the Republic of Ireland has often been a community experience, and people have consistently shared their relationship with the medium. In the 1950s and 1960s, men regularly gathered around a radio set on Sunday afternoons to listen to the distinctive commentaries of Michael O'Hehir on "Gaelic" football, a sport with its own special rules designed to distinguish it from "foreign" games. Today the contents of particular radio programs frequently provide a principal topic of conversation at home and in the pubs or restaurants.

Notwithstanding the fact that most householders in the Republic of Ireland now receive directly from the United Kingdom many English language television services of high quality, in addition to the four national Irish television channels, radio still has a wide listenership during the daytime and significantly influences political and media agendas. The Irish have for many years spent more time tuned to the radio than have their British neighbors.

In particular, Radio 1, the main radio service of the state-owned RTE, has provided coverage that emulates the best of the tradition of public broadcasting in Europe. During the daytime, Radio 1 creates a public space within which current and sometimes sensitive or controversial issues are discussed in a participatory fashion by well-known presenters; their guests; and members of the public, who are encouraged to phone in. During the 1990s, a wide variety of privately owned county and local radio services developed rapidly and have attracted many listeners away from RTE. Yet the main characteristic of most of these services is their local speech content. The most critically acclaimed programs on the privately owned national radio service, Today FM, are also speech centered, as opposed to music centered.

The perceived power of the spoken word in Ireland is reflected in special legislative provisions, known as Section 31, that have allowed the government to prohibit from time to time the broadcasting of interviews or reports of interviews with spokespeople for organizations that are deemed by the government to be involved in violent and undemocratic political activity, especially that relating to the conflict in Northern Ireland (the broadcasting of visual images of such organizations has never been banned).

The Republic of Ireland's transition from being a postcolonial and economically underdeveloped country to its status as the thriving "Celtic Tiger" of Europe has been reflected in part by the emergence of populist music-driven radio. Perhaps the most anomalous example of this phenomenon was Atlantic 252 (also known as Radio Tara), a long-wave station owned ultimately by RTE but managed in practice by CLT (Luxembourg). This station's diet of pop music and Americanized disc jockey patter was targeted principally at audiences across the Irish Sea and was created in 1989 to derive revenue from British advertisers, who were eager to sell their products to young English audiences. As the U.K. gradually licensed new national stations aimed at the same audience, Atlantic 252 ceased to be viable and finally went off the air on 31 December 2001.

Development

The history of Irish radio enjoys associations with several "firsts" in broadcasting. Most Irish histories of wireless point to the early radio broadcast from leaders of the Irish uprising that occurred during Easter week, 1916, when leaders of the uprising transmitted Morse code messages from their headquarters in the General Post Office on what is now Dublin's O'Connell Street. Many of the early experiments in wireless conducted by Marconi emanated from Ireland (RTE's headquarters in Dublin's Donnybrook area, the home of Marconi's Irish mother, Annie Jameson). The development of Irish radio can be seen as emerging in five phases.

Beginnings of Irish Broadcasting 1926–1945

Irish broadcasting had a modest beginning. Broadcasting began with a 1-kilowatt transmitter and an aerial system mounted on wooden sailing masts in the center of Dublin. The first broadcast was a speech by the soon to be first President of the Republic, Douglas Hyde, in January 1926. The radio service reported to the minister for post and telegraphs, and by the early 1930s the service had transmitters in Dublin, Cork, and Athlone, allowing for national coverage. Sponsored programs were part of Irish radio from the beginnings, and news coverage was provided by Irish radio reporters, rather than relying on news services. In 1937, the year that the Irish Constitution was adopted, the service became known as Radio Eireann; it held that name into the 1960s.

Quest for Independence 1945–1953

This period saw Irish radio attempt to forge a model of broadcasting that was different from that of the British Broadcasting Corporation (BBC) and one that was not mired in the bureaucracy of government. With the government of Eamon DeValera firmly in place, the radio service continued to develop in order to serve the political and economic goals of the new Free State.

Ireland did not participate in World War II, officially referring to this time period as "The Emergency." Radio Eireann featured a professional repertory company, symphony orchestra, light orchestra, news service, staff scriptwriters, outside broadcast officers, and engineers. Broadcasting during The Emergency and maintaining neutrality put a strain on what could be reported. All programming was required to be cleared by the director, and often this spilled into the Dail (parliament) debates and became a matter of public debate. Mentions of the weather, for example, were prohibited from all broadcasts, as was the coverage of sporting events. As Gorham noted, "the Government was not going to let Radio Eireann be used as an advanced weather station in the Atlantic for the belligerents of either side" (Gorham, 1967).

It was from this "emergency" situation that Radio Eireann sought independence in the years immediately following the Allied victory in Europe. The postwar move toward freedom of expression for broadcasting included the establishment of an advisory panel in 1952 that laid the groundwork for the establishment of an independent authority to oversee broadcasting that was not directly under the control of the government.

Rise and Fall of Comhairle Radio Eireann 1953–1960

The deficiencies of Irish radio were the subject of much public and government debate during this period. Some favored the continuation of direct government control, whereas others advocated following the European ethos of public service broadcasting with oversight by an independent authority. A compromise established an advisory committee, Comhairle Radio Eireann.

Comhairle Eireann's five-member council provided oversight for the radio service, subject to the approval of the minister for post and telegraphs, until the 1960 establishment of Radio Eireann. The director of broadcasting was Maurice Gorham. There was continual disagreement over the scope and function of Irish broadcasting because of lack of public funds, the need to make a decision about television, and the British electronic "invasion." There were nearly 500,000 licensed listeners for Irish radio during this period, though not all areas of the country could receive a signal. The government subsidy was augmented with the sale of program sponsorships. There were 380 employees of the radio operation, including actors, writers, and engineers, as well as the Irish Symphony Orchestra.

Radio Telefis Eireann, the "Pirates," and the Coming of Television 1960–1984

Irish radio in this period found a new regulatory environment, new sources of revenue from advertising, expanded coverage throughout the day, a Gaelic language station, authoritative news coverage, FM stations, and radio pirates. It was during this era that building a television service appeared foremost in the minds of government officials. Radio Eireann was established as an autonomous entity to be the authority over both radio and television. The first director general of the authority was an American, Edward Roth, who had been a consultant to the National Broadcasting Company (NBC) and had experience in starting up stations in Mexico and Peru. His attention, and that of others at Radio Eireann, was on television. There

was a grand exodus from the radio service to the television side of "The House," which moved to new quarters in Donnybrook. Radio Telefis Eireann (RTE) was adopted by the authority as the official name of the public service broadcaster.

The rise of rock and roll and pirate radio stations had a tremendous impact on Irish broadcasting. In 1978 alone, more than two dozen pirate stations went on the air. There were numerous raids to shut them down in the early years, but these proved to be ineffective. There was little direction from the government regarding these popular broadcasters, and this, coupled with the lure of advertising dollars, allowed illegal radio operators to play popular music to the delight of their audiences. RTE's response was to launch its own music station (RTE 2) directed toward the under-25-year-olds, who represented more than half of the population. By 1984 there were more than 70 illegal radio stations operating and gaining increasing numbers of listeners and advertising dollars.

Pirate radio became a part of Irish life, it was commercially successful, the announcers had "star" status, and the government appeared helpless to do anything about it. Raids to shut down Radio Nova and Sunshine Radio in Dublin in 1983 resulted in large public demonstrations in support of these highly popular stations.

Rise of Independent Broadcasting since 1984

Ireland entered the local and private broadcasting arena at a different time and under different circumstances than most countries. The procedures and means for silencing the pirates and bringing on board replacements suitable for the audience was to be no small feat. The Irish audience had grown to depend on the illegal broadcasters during their raid on the island. The Radio and Television Act of 1988 created Ireland's independent broadcast operators and silenced the illegal operators. The Independent Radio and Television Commission (IRTC) was formed, and by the summer of 1990, new radio licenses had been awarded to 24 different ownership groups serving all counties. By 2000, 12 community radio stations, 21 independents, and a new national radio service (Today FM) were serving Irish listeners—with several new licensees set to go on the air as well. RTE introduced Lyric FM as a new service specializing in classical music and extended coverage for its Gaelic language stations.

Organizations and Stations

There are three major types of radio in Ireland, all of them claiming some allegiance to the public service broadcasting ideals that are associated with European radio generally: the state-owned RTE radio network stations, independent local commercial radio, and community radio. In addition, there are five hospital/institutional radio stations.

RTE radio channels that provide national coverage on a variety of frequencies throughout the country include RTE Radio 1; 2FM; Lyric FM; and the Irish language station, Raidio Na Gaeltachta. One local RTE radio service, Radio Cork, operates a limited schedule.

There is one independent national radio channel that provides national coverage on a variety of frequencies throughout the country, called Today FM. By 2000, there were 21 independent local commercial stations: CKR FM, East Coast Radio, Radio Kilkenny, South East Radio, WLR, Radio Kerry, Galway Bay FM, Clare FM, FM 104, LMFM, Tipp FM, Shannon-side 104 FM, Highland Radio, Cork 96 FM/County Sound, 98 FM, North West Radio, Midlands Radio 3, Tipperary Mid West Radio, Northern Sound Radio, Limerick 95FM, and Mid West Radio. Ten of these stations serve the Dublin metro area, and the others serve listening areas across the countryside.

The newest radio stations on the air are the community and community of interest radio stations. Community radio stations are owned and controlled by not-for-profit organizations whose structure provides for membership, management, operation, and programming primarily by members of the community at large. These include Community Radio Castlebar, Wired FM, Dublin South Community Radio, West Dublin Community Radio, FLIRT FM, Phoenix FM, South West Clare Community Radio, Cork Campus Radio, Connemara Community Radio, NEAR FM, Community Radio Youghal, Tallaght Community Radio, Radio na Life, and the special interest station Anna Livia FM.

There are three hospital/institutional stations in Dublin, one in Waterford, and one in Cork city.

Programming

Radio programming in Ireland was long associated with extensive sports coverage of the "national" games of Gaelic football and hurling and in particular with the voice of Radio Eireann's best-known sports commentator, Michael O'Hehir. The broadcasting of popular music from outside Ireland was for decades restrained, although an antijazz campaign led by a Catholic priest in the 1930s was not entirely successful. In the 1970s young people in large numbers began to tune into foreign and domestic pirate (unlicensed) radio stations. Since 1988, local independent broadcasting has steadily grown in size and stature.

During the last quarter of the 20th century, the most influential programs on Irish radio were broadcast by RTE Radio 1 and included *Women Today,* which was feminist in concept and execution, and *Morning Ireland,* which still enjoys a very large breakfast and drive-time listenership. The main presenters associated with the great success of daytime speech programming on RTE Radio 1 during this period included David Hanly; Marian Finucane; Pat Kenny; John Bowman; Colm Keane; Myles Dungan; and Ireland's best-known broadcaster,

Gay Byrne. Other well-known RTE radio personalities who present lighter programs on 2FM include Gerry Ryan, Dave Fanning, and Larry Gogan. The abiding influence and popularity of speech programming in Ireland is underlined by the fact that the most critically acclaimed program on Ireland's only privately owned national radio service, Today FM, has been *The Last Word,* which is presented in the early evening (5:00 P.M. to 7:00 P.M.) and whose establishing presenter Eamon Dunphy developed a distinctive style of in-depth discussion of controversial issues.

The programming of the independent and community radio stations reflects local content and in some cases local music. They have captured the listening ears of the contemporary audience with personalities and recorded music. Both RTE major radio services (2FM and RTE 1) and the majority of the independent stations also have digital signals that allow Irish programming to be heard worldwide via the internet.

Financial Support

Most revenue for radio comes from advertising, although RTE does receive a subsidy from a broadcast license fee, which in 2000 was 70.00 Irish punts (approximately U.S. $100) per subscribing household. In addition to RTE stations, the license fee also subsidizes the National Orchestra and three television services, among other entities. Traditionally, two-thirds of RTE's revenue has come from advertising.

The advertising and sponsorship revenue for the independent radio sector has seen steady growth, with increases of 14 to 17 percent in the years 1997 and 1998. The total radio advertising revenue in 1998 for independent stations was £32.87 million ($45 million U.S.).

Policy and Regulation

Irish radio was first established under the aegis of the Wireless Telegraphy Act of 1926, four years after a bitter civil war and six years after Ireland won its independence from Great Britain. The act defined "wireless telegraphy," in a prophetic manner, as "any system of communicating messages, spoken words, music, images, pictures, prints or other communications, sounds, signs or signals by means of radiated electromagnetic waves." Radio in Ireland operated under the portfolio of the minister for posts and telegraphs until the Broadcasting Authority Act was passed in April 1960. Under terms of this law, the Radio Eireann Authority regulated radio broadcasting; it became the Radio Telefis Eireann Authority in 1966 and is most commonly referred to as RTE. The Radio and Television Act of 1988 created Ireland's independent broadcast operators.

The Irish Constitution and its regulations regarding broadcasting pose several restrictions on freedom of expression. Irish radio, like other broadcasting, operates with a "fairness doctrine." There is an affirmative obligation on the part of all broadcasters, RTE, private, and community stations to be fair, objective, and impartial. The legacy of public service broadcasting includes statutory restrictions on several content areas, including an absolute prohibition on editorializing, the requirement that private radio broadcasting services devote a minimum of 20 percent of their airtime to news and public-affairs programming, and the absolute prohibition on broadcast advertising of religious or political advocacy.

The amount of advertising is statutorily limited to 5 percent for RTE stations and 10 percent for independents. The Broadcasting Authority Act of 1993 amended the Broadcasting Act of 1990 (passed in order to implement the European Communities Directive on Television Broadcasting) and liberalized the amount of revenue that RTE could make from advertising. A 1995 Green Paper on broadcasting examined philosophical and strategic issues for Irish radio and other electronic media.

Two separate oversight committees govern regulation of Irish radio. The Broadcasting Commission of Ireland (BCI, known as the Independent Radio and Television Commission from its foundation in 1988 until 2001) provides oversight and licensing for the independent broadcasters, and the RTE Authority sets policy and oversight for the government-owned broadcasters. Members of both these autonomous policy-guiding bodies are government appointees.

Audience Research

The Joint National Listenership Research Committee (JNLR), comprising all broadcasting organizations, the advertising agencies, and the major advertisers, conducts audience research in the Republic of Ireland. Control of the comprehensive twice-yearly survey is handled by a JNLR Technical Committee consisting of representatives of RTE (the state-owned broadcaster), Today FM (the only privately owned national radio station), the BCI (the regulator), and the Institute of Advertising Practitioners in Ireland (the agencies). The JNLR data provide very specific information on audiences and their preferences, including a detailed analysis of the social class, age, and gender of listeners over the age of 15 for each quarter hour of the day. A JNLR software package is available to permit media buyers to plan their advertising campaigns.

JNLR findings are based on personal interviews, conducted in the home, with a sample of 6,660 people over the age of 15 in the Republic of Ireland. Special adjustments are made to ensure a minimum sample of 200 for each local radio franchise area. Results of the JNLR research are divided into "listenership" and "market share." The "listenership" figures total more than 100 percent because they give equal weighting to any stations heard by the respondents on the day before the survey date, regardless of the duration of listening in each particular case. The "market share" information does total 100 percent and requests that respondents state how long they tuned in to any particular station on the day before the survey date. The latter figure is a better indicator of overall performance than is the former.

During 1999, for the first time, the combined market share of privately owned radio stations edged ahead of the combined market share of the radio services operated by the state-owned RTE. However, Radio 1, which is RTE's flagship radio service and which broadcasts mainly speech programming, continues to surpass by far any other single service, either public or private, with a national audience share around 33 percent.

As the state-owned RTE is dually funded, both from public monies and from advertising, the JNLR results are important to both RTE and the private sector in their competition for revenue.

Radio Audience and Irish Emigration

In the United States, some 30 to 35 million Americans claim Irish ancestry, quite a feat for a country of 3.5 million people. Since the beginning of Irish radio, broadcasters have considered ways and means to reach the millions of people who are connected via ancestors or interest. In 1946 the Irish Government initiated a plan to develop a high-power shortwave station that could broadcast to the United States. The project was aborted before its first broadcast, but not before a 100-kilowatt transmitter and a directional antenna that stretched over 40 miles were constructed. Today's satellite feeds and digital radio on the internet finally allow Irish broadcasters to serve their extended world audience. Irish radio stations are electronically connected via e-mail; all of the national networks and most of the local independent stations have websites; and many are "streaming" their programming, making it available to listeners worldwide. A metamorphosis of Irish radio policy and practice from an insular, nationalistic, and pastoral focus to one that includes international, local, and national constituencies has occurred over four decades. The 21st century promises continued transformations for Irish radio. The voices of Irish radio have always had something to say. They have said it with style. Today they have an expanding world audience tuning in.

COLUM KENNY AND THOMAS A. MCCAIN

Further Reading

Boyle, Raymond, "From Our Gaelic Fields: Radio, Sport, and Nation in Post-Partition Ireland," *Media, Culture, and Society* 14 (1992)
Broadcasting Commission of Ireland, <www.bci.ie>

Broadcast Ireland: Streaming Radio Stations, <www.broadcastireland.com/radio.html>

Cathcart, Rex, *The Most Contrary Region: The BBC in Northern Ireland 1924–84*, Belfast: Blackstaff Press, 1984

Clark, Paddy, *Dublin Calling: 2RN and the Birth of Irish Radio*, Dublin: Radio Telefís Éireann, 1986

Fisher, Desmond, *Broadcasting in Ireland*, London and Boston: Routledge and Kegan Paul, 1978

Gorham, Maurice Anthony Coneys, *Forty Years of Irish Broadcasting*, Dublin: Talbot Press, 1967

Hall, Eamonn G., *The Electronic Age: Telecommunication in Ireland*, Dublin: Oak Tree Press, 1993

Ireland Department of Arts, Culture, and the Gaeltacht, *Gníomhach nó Fulangach? Fáthmheas ar an Réimse Craolacháin; Active or Passive? Broadcasting in the Future Tense* (bilingual Irish-English edition), Baile Átha Cliath, Ireland: Oifig an tSoláthair, 1995

Ireland's National Broadcasting Organisation (RTÉ),

Kelly, Mary, and Wolfgang Truetzschler, "Ireland," in *The Media in Western Europe: The Euromedia Handbook*, edited by Bernt Stubbe Østergaard, London and Newbury Park, California: Sage, 1992; 2nd edition, London and Thousand Oaks, California: Sage, 1997

Kenny, Colum, "Section 31 and the Censorship of Programs," *Irish Law Times and Solicitor's Journal* 12, no. 3 (March 1994)

Kenny, Colum, "The Politicians, the Promises, and the Mystery Surrounding Radio Bonanza," *Sunday Independent* (21 June 1998)

McCain, Thomas A., "Radio's Oscillating Policies Jolt New Zealand and Ireland—An Applied Research Example," in *Applied Communication in the 21st Century*, edited by Kenneth N. Cissna, Mahwah, New Jersey: Erlbaum, 1995

McCain, Thomas A., and G. Ferrell Lowe, "Localism in Western European Radio Broadcasting: Untangling the Wireless," *Journal of Communication* 40, no. 1 (1990)

Mulryan, Peter, *Radio Radio*, Dublin: Borderline, 1988 (on independent, local, community, and pirate radio in Ireland)

Isay, David 1965–

U.S. Radio Producer

Independent producer David Isay's acclaimed documentaries and features, broadcast on National Public Radio (NPR), beginning in the 1990s served as the benchmark for aurally lush, compelling, and socially responsible radio. Isay, the first radio producer awarded a Guggenheim Fellowship, received a MacArthur Fellowship in 2000.

In an era in which marginalized group members are often depicted as freakish or dangerous, Isay's work paints sensitive portrayals of people living in poverty (*Charlie's Story*, among others), people with all-consuming passions, or people caught up in social struggles (*Remembering Stonewall*). Many pieces investigate spirituality; others highlight vanishing professions or fading historical icons, such as Coney Island, roadside dinosaur museums, and Jewish synagogues in the South.

Isay attended a Jewish elementary school and then a prep school in Connecticut before moving to Manhattan, where he attended high school at Friends Seminary. He graduated from New York University in 1987 and planned to start medical school, a path chosen because many of his family members are physicians. Meanwhile, however, he received grant money to produce a small documentary film about drug addiction. He notified local media about a story he felt merited attention when he met two former addicts planning to open an addiction museum. Only Pacifica station WBAI was interested, and they asked him to report the story. WBAI provided equipment and later helped edit the piece. NPR editor Gary Covino heard the broadcast and lightly re-edited it for airing on NPR; Isay earned $250 for this five-minute debut. Covino has edited most of Isay's projects since then, and Isay set aside plans for medical school to take up a brilliant career as an independent producer. He found that working in audio neatly drew together his abilities and interests.

Isay's mother, Jane, served as an early mentor; her work as a book editor influenced his finely honed editing style. From his father, Richard, a psychoanalyst, he developed an interest in people on the margins of society.

Though based in New York City, Isay has interviewed individuals across America: he has stalked poisonous reptiles with snake handlers in West Virginia and has spent time with men serving life terms in Louisiana's Angola Prison. This latter piece, *Tossing away the Keys*, resulted in the release of an inmate who had unfairly served more than 40 years in Angola.

His concerns about capital punishment earned him his third Peabody Award, one shared with longtime collaborator Stacy Abramson. The 2000 piece, *Witness to an Execution*, provided an insider's glimpse into the Texas death chamber as experienced by the narrator, Warden Jim Willet, and others who work on death row. The program generated more correspondence than any NPR had ever broadcast.

Isay's best work springs from collaborations in which he guides people as they provide accounts of their own lives. His most celebrated pieces, *Ghetto Life 101* and *Remorse*, resulted from a collaboration with African-American teenagers LeAlan Jones and Lloyd Newman, who reported on life in and around a Chicago housing project. *Our America*, a book compiled from transcripts from these collaborations, has sold 50,000 copies. In 1999 Miami University required freshmen to read the book, and companion materials for high schools have been prepared. Because the teens' forthright on-air conversations encompassed revelations of criminality by the boys and others in their neighborhood, *Ghetto Life 101* infuriated some African-American staff members at NPR, who argued that it propagated racist stereotypes. Isay, devastated by the criticism, feared that the network might bar all future work, but the piece then won several prestigious awards.

NPR occasionally turns down Isay's pieces, claiming that materials are too raw or exhibit a lack of balance. Documentaries about a Mormon town and about a former prostitute dying of AIDS were rejected, as was one about a hospital for the criminally insane, a piece later commended by the American Psychological Association.

Most of Isay's work, however, is virtually guaranteed distribution, and many of his works are reviewed in the *New York Times* and elsewhere. Isay feels this acclaim from outside NPR has been crucial to his success at the network and with grantors.

Although Isay is known for his meticulous editing and strong story sense, his writing is also superb. Drawing from conversations with collaborators, he writes a highly natural-sounding script. His use of outsider narrators is often copied; he himself is rarely heard in his pieces.

Isay's style is richly symphonic. Such intricately edited surround sound results from painstaking work and deep on-site immersions. Isay and colleague Stacy Abramson spent 14 months working on *Sunshine Hotel*, an award-winning project recorded at a New York City flophouse.

The Corporation for Public Broadcasting underwrites most of Isay's productions, but this support and NPR's fees cover only a portion of production costs. Because few foundations provide grants to individuals, Isay established his nonprofit Sound Portraits Productions in 1994. Support comes from a wide array of large and small foundations. Grant monies are supplemented with outside projects, such as a Showtime movie deal about his relationship with the Chicago teens; monthly transcripts, newly collected, for the *New York Times Sunday Magazine;* and a deal with audible.com to lend his name and some of his work to their enterprise. He allots just $50,000 for his salary. His business model and high-quality work provide inspiration for other independent producers.

Isay's website, soundportraits.org, is often mentioned in the press as a "cool site." The site, which receives about 1,000 hits weekly, posts soundfiles and updates about people profiled in previous pieces.

Isay shares his fees and prize money with collaborators and develops long-lasting, supportive friendships. He hopes to expand his organization to include a social worker and an education coordinator.

Isay has also collaborated with mainstream writers to produce features. Isay sometimes finds such work frustrating because of pressures from marketing departments. He now prefers to collaborate only if the writer is obscure. He believes his mission is to broadcast voices from the margins; he aspires to draw attention to poverty and other social ills.

Sound Portrait's productions have been translated into many languages and broadcast in Europe. A 1999 work, *The Jewish Giant*, debuted at a Jewish museum, an unusual way to draw audiences to radio fare. Working with all-but-forgotten Yiddish-language programming miraculously salvaged by ethnomusicologist Henry Sapoznik, Isay showcased "The Yiddish Radio Project" on NPR and in a multimedia presentation that toured major cities in 2002.

In 2003, Isay began a long-term initiative called Story-Corps, a network of public kiosks where families can work with facilitators to record intergenerational interviews. A related Sound Portrait project includes training for high school students in conducting and editing oral histories.

PATRICIA JOYNER PRIEST

See also Documentary Programs; Jewish Radio; National Public Radio

David Isay. Born in New Haven, Connecticut, 5 December 1965. Attended New York University, B.A. in psychology and chemistry 1987; produced *The Museum of Addiction* as freelancer for WBAI, New York, 1988; produced *Remembering Stonewall*, his first documentary to air on NPR, 1989; produced, with two Chicago teenagers, the award-winning *Ghetto Life 101*, 1993, and *Remorse*, 1996; founded not-for-profit company Sound Portraits, 1994; produced acclaimed *Sunshine Hotel*, 1998; honored with ten-year retrospective by WNYC, 1998. Received Livingston Award for Young Journalists for *Tossing Away the Keys*, 1990; American Psychological Association recognition for *Ward 2-West*, 1991; Peabody Award for *American Folklife Radio Project*, 1992; Livingston Award and Prix Italia for *Ghetto Life 101*, 1993;

Guggenheim Fellowship, 1994; Robert F. Kennedy Journalism Award for Reporting of the Disadvantaged, *All the Way Broken*, 1995; Peabody Award and Robert F. Kennedy Journalism Award Grand Prize and Radio Winner for *Remorse: The 14 Stories of Eric Morse*, 1996; Prix Italia and Society of Professional Journalists Award for *Sunshine Hotel*, 1999; MacArthur Fellowship, 2000; Peabody Award for *Witness to an Execution*, 2000.

Radio Documentaries

1988	*The Museum of Addiction; Pledge of Allegiance and Jehovah's Witnesses*
1989	*Remembering Stonewall; Statue of Liberty's Flame Keeper; Rat Patrol; Workman's Circle Rest Home; Obituary Writing; Harlem Youth Write about Inner-City Life; Russian Baths in New York City's Lower East Side; Underground NYC: Shocking Aging System; Harlem Renaissance and Black Physicians; Telephone References at NY Public Library; WWI and WWII Black Veterans Overlooked for Medals*
1990	*Dan Field, Marriage Broker; Bedford-Stuyvesant Volunteer Ambulance; "Angolite": Louisiana Prison Magazine; Tossing Away the Keys; Brooklyn Black Opinion of FAMA Conviction; Brooklyn Elite Checker Club; Prison Radio Station in Angola Louisiana; Coney Island; Cynical Santa*
1991	*Passover Hangover at US's Oldest Winery; Automat's Last Day in New York City; Airplane Ashes; Ward 2-West; Joe Franklin, Longest Daytime TV Talk Show Host; Mississippi Jews*
1992–94	*American Folklife Radio Project*
1992	*Jefferson County Gospel Quartets; Hunan Chef; Riverside Hotel; "Steam Train" Maury Graham, Hobo; They Shall Take Up Serpents; Brewer Bell Museum*
1993	*Dinosaur Gardens; Foxhunters; American Talkers; Ghetto Life 101; Kipperman's Pawnshop; Woolworth's Closes Famous North Carolina Location*
1994	*Robert Shields World's Longest Diary; The Gods of Times Square; Slaves in the Family*
1995	*All the Way Broken*
1995–96	*Julius Knipl: The Radio Cartoon*
1996	*Jim Bishop, Castle Builder; Remorse: The 14 Stories of Eric Morse; Lindy Hop Step Creator; Museum of Jurassic Technology; A Letter to Butchie; Looking for Mary*
1998	*Charlie's Story; My Grandmother Was a Slave; The Sunshine Hotel; 1953 Polygamy Arrests*
1999	*Death Row Diaries; The Jewish Giant*
2000	*Summer Triptych; Weegee; Witness to an Execution*
2001	*The Execution Tapes*
2002	*Youth Portrait Series; Yiddish Radio Project*

Selected Publications

Holding On: Dreamers, Visionaries, Eccentrics, and Other American Heroes (with pictures by Harvey Wang), 1996

Our America: Life and Death on the South Side of Chicago (with LeAlan Jones and Lloyd Newman and pictures by John Anthony Brooks), 1997

A Guide to Ghetto Life 101, 1998

New York Times Magazine monthly pieces, 1999–

Flophouse: Life on the Bowery (with Stacy Abramson and pictures by Harvey Wang), 2000

Further Reading

Chaplin, Heather, "Vox Populi," *salon.com* (12 October 1999) <www.salon.com/ent/feature/1999/10/12/isay/index.html>

Fisher, Marc, "The Ashcan School of Storytelling," *Washington Post* (8 September 1998)

Freedman, Samuel G., "David Isay: A Microphone on the Margins," *New York Times* (8 November 1998)

Janssen, Mike, "'Execution Tapes' Bypasses Pubradio's Main Gatekeeper," *Current* (14 May 2001)

Kurtz, Howard, "NPR Staff Split over *Ghetto Life 101*," *Washington Post* (1 July 1993)

Osborne, D.M., "Radio on the Margins," *Brill's Content* 1, no. 5 (December 1998–January 1999)

Stewart, David, "Isay's People: Survivors Holding on with Dignity," *Current* (23 April 2001)

Israel

It is not uncommon to observe parallels between a nation's political events and the development of its media. Because of the ability of the media to influence opinion, governments recognize the value of using those media to propagate political points of view. At the same time, citizens in free societies recognize the value of media that are not under the control of governments, and those citizens often exert great and passionate effort to contend for free media. Such has been the case with the history of radio in Israel, a history that can be divided into three periods corresponding to diverse political and historical circumstances.

Three Historical Eras

Israel's radio history begins with the Palestine Broadcasting Service (PBS) era, which began in 1936 when the British Mandate Authority introduced radio to the Middle East. Not surprisingly, PBS was modeled after the British Broadcasting Corporation (BBC) domestic service. Programming was produced in Hebrew, Arabic, and English by broadcasters who were given some degree of autonomy. But ultimate authority remained with the government, first as part of the British Post Office and then as a department of the colonial government of Palestine. A number of clandestine radio services were also in operation. Although the British attempted to stop the illegal broadcasts, various Jewish and Arab political organizations were engaged in a discreet electronic battle, voicing their respective views on underground stations while the Palestinian conflict ensued.

The second period might be referred to as the Voice of Israel era, which began in 1948 when the State of Israel was established. With the organization of the new independent government, broadcasting was first placed under the control of the Ministry of Interior and was later transferred to the prime minister's office and given the name *Kol Yisrael* (the Voice of Israel). During this time, the government exercised great control over the medium in an effort to maintain security and to protect Israelis from potential negative influences by immigrants of diverse backgrounds. An official Israeli military station was also established.

The third period of Israel's radio history is the Israeli Broadcasting Authority (IBA) era, which began in 1965 and has continued into the 21st century. The IBA was established when the Israeli government yielded to public pressure to create a public authority to manage broadcasting. Radio in Israel had come full circle and again resembled the British model. Like the BBC, its existence was created by legislation, its economy funded in part by taxation, and its function mandated by law.

Israeli Broadcasting Authority

Under the Broadcasting Authority Law, the IBA serves five functions: information and entertainment; the promotion of Israeli creative efforts; Arabic language broadcasts promoting peace and understanding with Israel's Arabic-speaking population; broadcasts targeting the Diaspora (dispersed Jews); and broadcasts to foreign countries. Within the scope of that mandate, the IBA formulates policy related to programming, management, and operations.

The organizational structure of the IBA is three-tiered. A 31-member *Plenum* (council) is appointed by the government. The *Plenum* is responsible for general broadcasting policy, including a range of matters from budget oversight to program schedule approval. It is helpful to note that because the council's membership politically reflects the membership of the *Knesset*, or legislature, consensus can sometimes be elusive. From the *Plenum*, the government selects seven members to serve as the Managing Committee, which has responsibility for broadcast operations, including budget preparation. Finally, a director general is appointed to implement the policies and procedures put in place by the *Plenum* and the Managing Committee.

In addition to the three-tiered structure of the IBA, there is the potential for further governmental involvement with radio in Israel. The Ministry of Telecommunications is responsible for the technical operation and transmission facilities. The Ministry of Defense and the military both have censorship authority when it is deemed to be in the national interest. The Ministry of Finance has significant control over budget matters, at least on the revenue side of the ledger, because of the methods used for funding broadcasting in Israel.

The IBA—and consequently radio in Israel—receives its funding from several sources. Like the British model, it is funded by a hybrid of public and private revenues. Israeli citizens pay a license fee each year for television sets in the household and an additional fee for radios in automobiles. These license fees are a major part of funding for the IBA. In addition, radio advertising is a growing source of revenue, and some funds also come from the Jewish Agency (specifically for broadcasts targeting the Diaspora) and the Ministry of Foreign Affairs.

Although advertising has become a significant source of revenue for radio in Israel, it should be noted that there are restrictions and guidelines on advertising, mostly related to the religious aspects of Jewish law. For example, until recently radio advertising by physicians, dentists, lawyers, psychologists, and many other professionals was banned. There are stringent controls on advertising copy and commercial content.

Commercial scheduling is limited or forbidden on the Sabbath and on religious holidays.

Radio programming in Israel is quite varied, owing in part to the diverse mix of cultures and languages within the population. Additionally, some programming targets audiences beyond the geographic boundaries of the state. Programs are broadcast in Hebrew, Arabic, English, French, Hungarian, Romanian, Russian, and Spanish, as well as in several Jewish dialects. Domestic radio service includes music and entertainment, variety, news and public affairs, drama, children's programming, and religious features. An Arabic channel programs music, talk, and news to Arabic-speaking citizens of Israel, as well as to the Arabic-speaking populations of neighboring states. An external radio service broadcasts news programs and features on Israeli culture in various languages to nations around the world by shortwave.

Beyond standard entertainment and information, radio in Israel is involved in the media battle of ideologies being waged by the different participants in the Middle East conflict. On one hand, Israel presents the issues from its perspective using its terrestrial media system. At the same time, the United States beams its Radio Sawa ("together") signal into Israel, targeting young Arabs by mixing popular music with Western ideology in Arabic. On the other hand, the Palestinian "intifada"— using the internet—attempts to counter the Israeli message with its own take on the issues, while Syria, Egypt, and Iran transmit messages into Israel (in Hebrew) that oppose Israel's governmental policies.

RICHARD TINER

See also Radio Sawa/Middle East Radio Network

Further Reading
Boyd, Douglas A., "Hebrew-Language Clandestine Radio Broadcast and the End of the British Palestine Mandate," *Journal of Radio Studies* 6, no. 2 (Autumn 1999)
Browne, Donald R., *International Radio Broadcasting: The Limits of the Limitless Medium*, New York: Praeger, 1982
Head, Sydney W., *World Broadcasting Systems: A Comparative Analysis*, Belmont, California: Wadsworth, 1985
Hilliard, Robert L., and Michael C. Keith, *Global Broadcasting Systems*, Boston: Focal Press, 1996
Katz, Elihu, and George Wedell, *Broadcasting in the Third World: Promise and Performance*, Cambridge, Massachusetts: Harvard University Press, 1977
Shinar, Dov, and Akiba A. Cohen, "Israel," in *International Handbook of Broadcasting Systems*, edited by Philip T. Rosen, New York: Greenwood Press, 1988

Italy

Italy, the country where radio was invented, is home to one of the most advanced and diversified of the world's radio systems. The distinguishing feature of Italian radio is its 3,000 different stations, a figure that places Italy second only to the United States in the total number of signals available. With an average of one radio set for each of its 60 million people, Italy has one of the world's highest levels of radio penetration. Generating more than $400 million in annual revenues, Italy's commercial radio sector is the seventh largest in the world.

Developments

In few other countries does radio have a more colorful history. The home of Guglielmo Marconi, the Italian city of Bologna was where, in 1895, a practical system of wireless communication was first demonstrated. Patents for radio that Marconi subsequently obtained in Great Britain led to the formation of Compagnia Marconi, a multinational radio manufacturing enterprise that in the 1920s and 1930s helped advance the growth of radio in Europe.

State control of the Italian radio system began shortly after the country's first regular radio broadcasts in October 1924. Although a private company called URI (Union Radio Italiana) had transmitted the first broadcasts, from a facility located in the Corrodi Palace in Rome, radio was soon nationalized when URI was compelled to enter into a licensing compact with Italy's Fascist government. In 1927 Fascist leaders gained full control of URI and transformed the operation into the state-owned monopoly that became RAI.

Italian radio grew steadily during the 1930s and 1940s. Although most of its facilities were destroyed during World War II, RAI was rapidly rebuilt. Second and third RAI channels had been added by 1950. In 1952 RAI launched Italy's first TV service. The first attempt to privatize and expand Italian radio ended unsuccessfully in 1960 when the country's Constitutional Court upheld RAI's monopoly status.

In the early 1970s, however, a public protest movement directed at the management of RAI and at the system's close ties to the Christian Democratic Party erupted throughout Italy. The result was sweeping reforms. Beginning in 1974, a series of rulings by the Constitutional Court not only rescinded the RAI monopoly but expedited the rapid proliferation of privately owned local stations. Italy's terrestrial, cable, and satellite TV systems were similarly deregulated.

Contemporary Italian Radio

Contemporary Italian radio was shaped during a significant period of deregulation and privatization that began in the mid-1970s and culminated in the early 1990s. Ten to 15 years before Great Britain, France, Germany, and other European countries took similar steps, Italy was the first country in the region to abandon a system that had begun as a state-run public broadcasting monopoly. In Italy, this public broadcast unit is known as RAI (Radiotelevisione Italiana). Operating several channels, RAI remains one of the most widely used Italian radio services. Yet Italy's vast number of additional stations—all propelled by privatization—now define radio throughout the country.

In structure, Italian radio is similar to that in the United States. Regulation defers to a radio-television governing board that is active mainly in the licensing of stations and in spearheading a strict policy of local operations. In a country no larger in area than the state of Arizona, more than 150 cities, towns, and communities have licensed local radio stations. In major cities such as Rome, Milan, Naples, and Turin, upward of 100 stations can be heard. Roughly 60 percent of the stations operate on an FM band nearly identical to that in the United States. The remainder are medium wave stations with frequencies analogous to those of the American AM band.

One of the main outcomes of privatization has been the conversion of Italian radio from a taxpayer-supported public system into a system supported mainly by commercial advertising. Virtually all of Italy's 3,000 stations depend on advertising. Although RAI, the public unit, still relies on tax support, it, too, has developed commercial revenue streams. No country (including the United States) surpasses Italy in levels of commercial competition.

Radio stations in Italy narrowcast to niches in the broadcast audience. The culture of Italy has generally led to a preponderance of music and personality-driven entertainment formats. Music, ranging from symphonies and operas to popular fare, has been a mainstay of programming on RAI. The many newer stations have dramatically increased the number of offerings and, in many cases, have imported musical formats—from country and western music to Top 40 and blues—that were developed in the United States.

Two of Italy's most popular radio stations are Radio Deejay and Radio Sunshine. Both specialize in popular music and high-profile announcers, and both are available in Rome and Milan, the country's two largest cities. Another leader is the Milan-based progressive music outlet Radio Planet FM. Other well-known Italian radio stations, all with music and entertainment formats, are RClub (Naples), Musica (Milan), Dimensione Suano (Rome), Radio Babboleo (Genoa), and Radio Base Popolare (Venice).

Although Italian radio has not traditionally been a showcase for news and public-affairs broadcasting, a series of political scandals in the 1990s, which resulted in the removal of Italy's long-dominant Catholic-oriented Christian Democratic Party, helped inspire several news-and-information ventures. RAI, traditionally the main source of news in Italy, is now challenged by the country's first all-news broadcast station, the Rome-based Radionews, which has correspondents and outlets in most major Italian cities. Another all-news station is Radio Reporter. In addition, talk and discussion stations are widely available. Although most news and talk stations broadcast in Italian, several cater to French, German, and Slovenian audiences in and around the country's northern border regions.

Although Italian radio thrives, the country's general lack of a public service philosophy, its assimilation of new technologies, and its collaboration with other European Union countries are issues. Another concern is the consolidation of Italy's leading radio properties into corporations such as those owned by Italian media magnates Silvio Berlusconi and Callisto Tanzi, who dominate the country's television industry.

Besides its domestic operations, Italy is identified with two important international radio services. One of these is Vatican Radio, initiated under the leadership of Marconi in 1931 and today available in 34 languages on shortwave, medium wave, and FM radio. Like Vatican Radio, Radio Roma, a shortwave service operated under the auspices of RAI, has a global audience.

CRAIG ALLEN

See also Marconi, Guglielmo; Vatican Radio

Further Reading

Barendt, Eric M., *Broadcasting Law: A Comparative Study*, Oxford: Clarendon Press, and New York: Oxford University Press, 1993

Emery, Walter B., "Italy: State Supremacy in Broadcasting," in *National and International Systems of Broadcasting: Their History, Operation, and Control*, by Emery, East Lansing: Michigan State University Press, 1969

Grandi, Roberto, "Italy," in *International Handbook of Broadcasting Systems*, edited by Philip T. Rosen, New York: Greenwood Press, 1988

Mazzoleni, Gianpietro, "Broadcasting in Italy," in *Broadcasting Finance in Transition: A Handbook*, edited by Jay G. Blumler and T.J. Nossiter, New York: Oxford University Press, 1991

Mazzoleni, Gianpietro, "Italy," in *The Media in Western Europe: The Euromedia Handbook*, edited by Bernt Stubbe Ostergaard, London and Newbury Park, California: Sage, 1992; 2nd edition, London and Thousand Oaks, California: Sage, 1997

Noam, Eli M., *Television in Europe*, New York: Oxford University Press, 1991

Sassoon, Don, "Italy: The Inception of Private Broadcasting," in *The Politics of Broadcasting*, edited by Raymond Kuhn, New York: St. Martin's Press, 1985

J

Jack Armstrong, the All-American Boy

Children's Adventure Series

Even before World War II, Jack Armstrong of *Jack Armstrong, the All-American Boy* (a sort of *Johnny Quest* of the radio airwaves) was the image of the patriot, the great white hope, the upstanding citizen. The creation of former journalist Robert Hardy Andres, *Jack Armstrong, the All-American Boy* was a daily adventure series whose core audience skewed just slightly older (and, we can assume, more male) than its closest radio rival, *Little Orphan Annie*. It ran on various networks from 1933–51.

Jack, a perpetual teenager despite his nearly 30 years on the air, was a student and star athlete at Hudson High, where the school fight song (which doubled as the series theme) frequently cheered him on to end-of-the-game saves. But young Jack's real role was as globe-trotting adventurer with his Uncle Jim Fairfield and cousins Billy and Betty. Only barely into the first year of the program, the pep rallies and classrooms of Hudson High were abandoned by Jack and his program's writers in favor of death-defying, hair-raising adventures played out at the four corners of the world. From mountain climbing and airplane flying (Uncle Jim owned a hydroplane) to undersea diving and chasing down evildoers and pirates, from the Arctic Circle and the Philippines to other "wild," "exotic," and "untamed" locales, Armstrong's adventures ran daily in late-afternoon, 15-minute episodes. In true serial format, similar to the Saturday afternoon matinee escapades of *The Crimson Ghost* and its ilk, each story had a cliff-hanger ending that encouraged listeners to tune in the next day. And millions of kids and preteens did so with near-religious devotion.

This being radio, the producers were free to create outrageous situations and transport their audience to any number of "real-life" places—Jack and company traveled from the Amazon jungle to the Far East via only a few carefully chosen sound effects. A foghorn simulated a ship, and conga drums conjured up images of the darkest places of the dark continent. Meanwhile, the actors never had to leave the comfort of a Chicago radio studio.

Though Jack Armstrong was not technically an orphan, he was one at least symbolically, for in his traipsing around the world with his uncle and cousins, little mention was ever made of Mom and Dad back home.

Though Uncle Jim, with his authoritative voice, was along on all the adventures as a parental role model (a catchall character to represent the entire world of adulthood), it was not unusual to find him missing in action or conveniently at a distance when the real events began, thereby leaving the three youngsters on their own. However, the adultless world that Jack, Bill, and Betty inhabited never devolved into a *Lord of the Flies*-like scenario. Instead, the trio, like a modern-day Tom Sawyer, Huck Finn, and Becky Thatcher with Jack acting as ad hoc leader, proved themselves smart, resourceful, and empowered enough to save the world, a message they no doubt imparted to their youthful audience. As the program ran during the entire duration of World War II, Jack and company did their bit for the war effort, encouraging listeners to plant victory gardens and to write letters to overseas servicemen.

As with Jack's streamlined family situation, his growing-up years were equally simplified. For Jack (and Betty and Billy, for that matter), there was no mention of such staples of adolescence as self-doubt, acne, and romantic yearnings—and no youthful rebellion. Such sentiment and realism would serve not only to turn off most of the young listeners but would surely also get in the way of all the exciting action. There was no time for planning for the prom in the world of Jack Armstrong!

Not to say that Jack's freewheeling lifestyle did not come under scrutiny during the program's long run. Several sources report that enough mothers (and perhaps fathers, too) wrote to criticize the program for Jack's never being in school that, in response, a few references to homework were eventually dropped into scripts, as was a later character who acted as the children's traveling tutor.

Charles Flynn as Jack Armstrong, the All American Boy
Courtesy of Mrs. Charles Flynn

Although child psychologist Martin Reymert was engaged to scrutinize each script to make sure it contained no torture or excessive violence, such restraint did not extend to protecting children from heavy-handed consumerism. For *Jack*'s entire run, the show was sponsored by Wheaties, and the show's ongoing celebration of athletics, clear good-versus-evil storytelling, and basic American values worked well for the "breakfast of champions." In addition, *Jack Armstrong* was the airwaves' perhaps most aggressive pitchman for product tie-ins. For the right number of Wheaties box tops, youthful listeners could send in for secret decoders or "hike-o-meters." Girls could send away for a bracelet "just like Betty's."

During its run, the broadcast went through many cast changes, including five different Jacks (the longest-playing one was Charles Flynn, whose voice sounded youthful enough that in his 30s, he was still playing the teen). Eventually, in the program's last years, it dropped Uncle Jim (played for the entire run by Jim Goss) and the others altogether. And Jack, who had become too old to be considered a "boy," became an adult agent for justice in the retitled series *Armstrong of the SBI*.

An entertaining, fun, quaint relic now, *Jack Armstrong, the All-American Boy*—the all-American kid from an all-American town—despite its wild, world-traveling adventures, always had a certain air of innocence about it, portraying a world of honesty and virtue, where the good guys always won.

CARY O'DELL

See also Premiums

Cast

Jack Armstrong	St. John Terrell (1933), Jim Ameche (1933–38), Stanley Harris (1938–39), Frank Behrens (1939), Charles Flynn (1939–43; 1944–51), Michael Rye (Rye Billsbury) (1943)
Billy Fairfield	Murray McLean (during war years), John Gannon (1933–43), Roland Butterfield, Milton Guion, Dick York (postwar years)
Betty Fairfield	Scheindel Kalish (Ann Shephard) (1933), Sarajane Wells (1933–41), Loretta Poynton (1941–43), Naomi May (1943), Patricia Dunlap (postwar years)
Uncle Jim Fairfield	James Goss
Gwendolyn Duval	Sarajane Wells, Naomi May
Coach Hardy	Arthur Van Slyke, Olan Soulé, Ed Davison
Vic Hardy	Ken Griffin (1950–51), Carlton KaDell (1950–51)
Captain Hughes	Don Ameche, Jack Doty, Frank Dane
Babu	Frank Behrens
Blackbeard Flint	Robert Barron
Sullivan Lodge	Kenneth Christy
Talia-San	Kenneth Christy
Lal Singh	Michael Romano
Pete	Art McConnell
Dickie	Dick York
Michael	Frank Behrens
Weissoul	Herb Butterfield
Lorenzo	Herb Butterfield
Announcers	David Owen (1930s), Tom Shirley (1930s), Truman Bradley (1930s), Paul Douglas (1930s), Franklyn MacCormack (1940s), Bob McKee (postwar years), Ed Prentiss (1950–51), Ken Nordine (1950–51), Norman Kraft (postwar years)

Creator/Writer
Robert Hardy Andrews

Producer
James Jewel

Programming History
CBS   July 1933–April 1936
NBC   August 1936–September 1941
Mutual   September 1941–July 1942
NBC-Blue   August 1942–August 1947
ABC   September 1947–June 1951

Further Reading
Harmon, Jim, *The Great Radio Heroes*, Garden City, New York: Doubleday, 1967; revised edition, Jefferson, North Carolina: McFarland, 2001
Harmon, Jim, *Radio Mystery and Adventure: And Its Appearances in Film, Television, and Other Media*, Jefferson, North Carolina: McFarland, 1992
Nachman, Gerald, *Raised on Radio: In Quest of the Lone Ranger . . .* , New York: Pantheon, 1998

Jamming

Jamming is the deliberate interference of one radio transmission by another. As long as there have been two or more radio transmitters on the air at the same time, there has been some form of jamming. A somewhat more technical definition describes jamming as an activity *designed* to interfere with someone else's effective use of the electromagnetic spectrum. The Voice of America (VOA) defines *jamming* as intentional interference created through the transmission of broadcasting noises or programming on the same frequency as a signal that some entity (often a political body) does not want others to hear.

More recently, jamming has been referred to as "electromagnetic countermeasures" to reflect more accurately the broad range of electronically based communication systems targeted. The most recent literature refers to jamming as "electronic attack." No matter what you call it, jammers actually target receivers—not transmitters.

Origins

Before the inception of regular broadcasting in the United States, radio hobbyists and experimenters shared the radio spectrum primarily with government stations. Communication was restricted to signals using Morse code. By their nature, the spark-gap transmitters commonly used created very broad signals. Early detectors or receivers did not help the situation. Most were unable to discriminate between two signals of widely different carrier frequencies, much less between those in close proximity. What government operators often took to be deliberate jamming was really just hobbyists using equipment unable to detect the other signal.

By the 1920s, as broadcasting began to gain popularity, the number of stations grew while the frequency range made available was limited. Interference was inevitable, but some of it was intentional, because competing broadcasters jammed rival radio programs; still, much of the suspected jamming was really unintentional interference.

History generally attributes the first organized jamming to Germany's use of it during World War I. Jamming was used as a political weapon beginning in the 1930s. With the onset of World War II, sophisticated jamming networks were aimed at disabling military communication and radio-guided weapons systems. All sides participated in jamming.

Jamming of Shortwave Broadcasts

At the end of World War II, a massive jamming campaign became part of the Cold War. In 1948 the Soviet Union committed perhaps a dozen jammers to operate against Russian language broadcasts of the VOA. By 1956 the number of jammers in this service was estimated at 3,000—all aimed at Western broadcasters in a variety of languages—from approximately 200 different sites. It is estimated that more than 600,000 kilowatts of transmitting power was used to block shortwave broadcasts. According to estimates by the British Broadcasting Corporation (BBC) monitoring service, the equivalent of up to $918 million was spent annually by the Soviet Union on jamming.

According to Rimantas Pleikys, author of *Jamming*, on 3 February 1948, one year after the VOA began broadcasting in Russian, jamming started to become a part of international shortwave broadcasting. This jamming effort continued for the next 40 years. On 29 November 1988, much of the jamming against Western broadcasters ceased. Soviet leadership stopped the activity without an announcement but apparently in response to the easing of East-West tensions.

Despite the reduction in jammers in Eastern Europe, other countries maintain active jamming operations. In addition to operations in Cuba, many jammers still operate from Asia and the Middle East. Radio Martí's AM-band transmissions from Marathon, Florida, have been jammed by Cuba since the service first went on the air.

Interestingly, some former jammers have found new life as local, regional, and international broadcasting outlets. George Jacobs, who spent nearly 40 years in government service, is credited with pioneering and developing the worldwide broadcasting system of the VOA and the post-1974 modernization of Radio Free Europe and Radio Liberty broadcasting facilities. Jacobs was involved in transforming the OPEN RADIO in Moscow from a Soviet jamming station into a successful Russian broadcasting operation; Jacobs also markets the leasing of shortwave facilities at a former Soviet jamming center in Tbilisi, Georgia.

Characteristics of Jamming

In order to effectively block international shortwave broadcasts, two different techniques can be used. *Skywave* jamming blocks shortwave reception in targeted areas by sending signals from one part of the world to another. The distance from the jammer to the area to be blocked needs to be the same as the distance from the broadcaster being targeted to the intended audience. In metropolitan areas, *groundwave* jamming simply overpowers signals by operating in close proximity to the targeted audience. In addition to these two basic forms of jamming, which are based on two different types of radio propagation, a variety of techniques are used to enhance the effectiveness of jamming.

Cochanneling involves operating a jamming transmitter on or very near the same frequency as the signal being jammed. The signal may be well modulated and carry a standard program from the host country. But the intent is not to reach the audience with this outlet; rather, blocking out or interfering with the unwanted signal is the goal. A variation on this technique is called *Mayak* jamming. A country's home broadcasting service is used to overmodulate the jamming transmitter, making it very unpleasant to listen to. This technique was commonly used against Radio Liberty and some VOA programs prior to 1987. So-called growling or grinding noise is likely a Mayak jammer when it is not being modulated by a program.

During the Gulf War and afterward throughout the Middle East, a bubble or warble sound had been used for jamming. *Wobbler, warble,* or *bubble* jammers modulate a single frequency with a slowly varying tone that is low in pitch. Howling noise is the result. Synthetic radio noise can be transmitted with random variations in amplitude and frequency. Because of the similarity to background noise, these warbling methods are often difficult to detect as jamming.

By using a series of tones that increase and decrease in pitch, stepped tones can be used against AM or FM voice circuits. The result often sounds like bagpipes. Another technique electronically imitates the sound of sea gulls, and yet another technique creates the electronic equivalent of grunting. Even the venerable spark signal remains a very effective jamming technique.

Jamming systems may be relatively simple or highly sophisticated. International broadcasters often employ a worldwide monitoring system to determine the effectiveness of their broadcasts to allow adjustments in order to reach the target audience. These operations, sometimes known as control and correction facilities, can also be used to target stations for jamming and can be used to determine the relative effectiveness of the jamming efforts. Some jamming stations transmit an identification in Morse code, making it possible to coordinate efforts throughout a jamming network.

Countermeasures

Countermeasures are often used in order to overcome jamming. For example, during the 1960s, prior to the availability of communication satellites, Armed Forces Radio (AFRS) routinely used its shortwave facilities to deliver major events, especially professional sports, to its international outlets. Although the programming sounded just like that heard on advertised frequencies, these feeds were made on multiple shortwave frequencies determined just before the broadcast. On the receiving end, affiliates would choose the frequency with the least interference, often trying to stay one step ahead of the jammers.

In spite of the number of jamming stations available worldwide, often only a single jamming site would be assigned to such a broadcast, making it possible to try to stay a step ahead of the interfering signal. From a vantage point in Tokyo, Japan, for example—where one of the AFRS shortwave facilities used to feed stations in Vietnam was located—it was possible to monitor several of these frequencies and listen to the jamming follow as the control operator for AFRS in Tokyo switched between frequencies.

Using electronic spectrum analyzers, jamming operations can automatically detect a change in a targeted frequency range when a new carrier appears, automatically assigning a jamming signal to the new carrier. Some broadcasters appear to try to counter this technique by randomly popping up silent carriers to attract the jamming transmitters before beginning their scheduled broadcasts.

Jamming Across the Spectrum

Jammers target more than just AM, FM, and shortwave broadcast operations. A 1999 report released by the Federal Communications Commission (FCC) reports that the commission handled more than 1,200 interference complaints from federal, state, and local public safety and emergency officials during 1998. Jammers targeted police communication and interfered with communication between dispatchers and officers. Some pretended to be dispatchers or other police officials.

During 1998, the Federal Aviation Administration requested assistance from the FCC 75 times, including instances involving interference on air traffic control frequencies. Several cases of intentional jamming were discovered.

In late 1999 the FCC's Office of Engineering and Technology and the FCC's Compliance and Information Bureau warned against the "manufacture, importation, marketing or operation of transmitters designed to prevent or otherwise interfere with Cellular Radio Communication."

Entrepreneurs interested in addressing a perceived market for devices designed to prevent or jam the operation of cellular telephones in hospitals, theaters, and other locations asked for the FCC's position on such devices. According to the Communications Act of 1934 and the commission's rules, these devices are not allowed in the United States.

The history of jamming begins with the taming of the electromagnetic spectrum for communication and continues to this day. The basic techniques have changed little over the medium's 100-year development.

JIM GRUBBS

See also Armed Forces Radio Service; Cold War Radio; International Radio; Propaganda by Radio; Radio Free Europe/Radio Liberty; Radio Martí; Shortwave Radio; Voice of America

Further Reading

Enders, Thomas O., *Radio Marti and Cuban Interference: May 10, 1982*, Washington, D.C.: U.S. Dept. of State, Bureau of Public Affairs, Office of Public Communication, Editorial Division, 1982

Frederick Research Corporation, *Handbook on Radio Frequency Interference*, 4 vols., Wheaton, Maryland: Frederick Research, 1962

Levitt, Barry K., *FH/MFSK Performance in Multitone Jamming* (microform), Pasadena, California: National Aeronautics and Space Administration, Jet Propulsion Laboratory, California Institute of Technology, 1985

Mertel, Herbert K., *International and National Radio Frequency Interference Regulations*, Gaithersburg, Maryland: Don White Consultants, 1978

Pleikys, Rimantas, *Jamming*, Vilnius, Lithuania: n.p., 1998

Sowers, Mary W., and Gregory R. Hand, *Monitoring of Harmful Interference to the HF Broadcasting Service: Summary of Monitoring Programs Held between 1984 and 1989*, Boulder, Colorado: U.S. Dept. of Commerce, National Telecommunications and Information Administration, 1990

Wood, James, "Jamming on the Shortwaves," in *History of International Broadcasting*, by Wood, London: P. Peregrinus and the Science Museum, 1992

Japan

Japanese radio broadcasting was initiated by commercial corporations, transformed into a government corporation, used as an effective tool of government propaganda in World War II, and shaped by the democracy brought in by the Occupation after the war. Radio broadcasting has been an important medium for disseminating information, education, and entertainment to the people in Japan.

Origins

The Ministry of Communications—called *Teishinshou*—and various individuals had conducted wireless experiments after Marconi's initial research in Italy. By 1920 the ministry began to consider establishing radio broadcasting stations in Japan, particularly when they heard about station KDKA in the United States. Responding to the call for radio broadcasters, a total of 64 applications were submitted to the ministry. Many applications came from manufacturers of wireless equipment, newspaper companies, or news agencies. The ministry encouraged them to consolidate among themselves and to form nonprofit public corporations to establish stations. After the consolidation process, stations in Tokyo, Nagoya, and Osaka each received a license and started broadcasting in 1925.

The successful deployment of radio broadcasting service by the three stations soon caught the attention of the government, which then proposed to incorporate them into one public corporation under government supervision. The government argued that such operation was necessary to spread the service across the whole nation. Some critics observed that the government could not leave broadcasting to the private sector after seeing the potential of its great influence.

Despite their strong resistance, the three stations were forced to merge, and *Nippon Hoso Kyokai* (NHK) was established in 1926 as a nonprofit legal entity under the supervision of the Ministry of Communications. NHK completed the construction of most of its nationwide broadcasting network by 1929. Two years later, it launched a second radio service called NHK Radio 2 to broadcast mostly educational programs.

NHK started broadcasting a national baseball tournament played by high school teams in 1927; *Radio Taiso* (an instruction for physical stretching with a special music) began in 1928; and NHK broadcast games of the 1932 Olympics from Los Angeles. *Radio Taiso* is still broadcast every morning and is the oldest radio program in the world.

Radio Before 1945

In the late 1920s, Japan began to experience turmoil, which was exacerbated by the deepening economic recession, the slump in the stock market, increasing unemployment, and the acceleration of antigovernment activity by right-wing groups. Under these circumstances, the government gradually tightened its control of NHK. In 1934 NHK's regional branches were dissolved and placed under the control of headquarters in Tokyo. Later, even NHK's program planning was to be largely dictated by government officials.

On 26 February 1936, a group of 1,400 military officers and soldiers attempted a coup d'état, which lasted three days. The government had little success in persuading them to surrender until a message was broadcast through NHK radio that led to the surrender of the group. This single incident made the government and the military realize the power of radio and encouraged both to use it as a propaganda tool.

On 8 December 1941, Japan began war with the United States (war in China had been underway for five years). NHK was placed under the direct control of military authorities. All programs were designed, produced, and broadcast to make the people understand government policy, to guide thinking favorable to the military, and to create patriotism among the people. Widespread broadcasting of false information about how well the Japanese military had been fighting ended when atomic bombs were dropped in Hiroshima and Nagasaki. On 15 August 1945, the emperor announced the nation's defeat over NHK radio facilities—the first time most Japanese had heard his voice.

Postwar Transition

The restructuring of Japan's radio broadcasting was set out by Supreme Commander Allied Powers (SCAP), headed by General Douglas MacArthur. SCAP aimed at democratizing radio broadcasting by removing all government and military controls over NHK. SCAP submitted a memorandum on 11 December 1945 delineating its plans to democratize NHK's organization. SCAP also instructed NHK to modify its programming by introducing continuous broadcasting from early morning to late evening without any break in between, changing the minimum length of a program from 20 minutes to 15 minutes, and establishing a weekly program. It also encouraged NHK to produce programs that would involve audience participation in various ways. *Nodojiman Shirouto Ongakukai* (Amateur Song Contest) was the first entertainment program in which non–media-related people appeared in a radio program. The program has been broadcast since 1946. Entertainment programs including games, quizzes, and soap operas (the concept for these having been brought from the United States) increased in number.

On 16 October 1947, the Civil Communications Section of SCAP presented to NHK and the government its view about the desirable nature of broadcasting in Japan. The four principles pushed forward were freedom of broadcasting, impartiality, a public service obligation, and conformance with technical standards. They also instructed that an autonomous regulatory organization be established, which would be completely separate from any ministry of the government as well as from any interest groups such as political parties and private corporations. In addition, they suggested that privately owned broadcasting companies be developed to compete with NHK in the future.

The then–Ministry of Telecommunications, called *Denkitsushinshou*, which had replaced Teishinshou in 1949 following SCAP's recommendation, soon began to prepare necessary bills to establish these principles, and three bills were passed by the Japanese Diet in 1950: the Radio Law, the Broadcast Law, and the Radio Regulatory Commission Establishment Law. The Broadcast Law changed the characteristics of NHK from a monopoly public corporation financially supported by the government as well as by private media-related corporations to an independent public corporation of which income was mostly in the form of receiving fees collected from the audience. The Radio Regulatory Commission was made responsible for allocation of broadcasting frequencies and the granting of broadcasting licenses. On 21 April 1951, 16 preliminary licenses were given, and soon *Chubu Nihon Hoso* in Nagoya and *Shin Nihon Hoso* in Osaka aired programs as the first commercial radio broadcasting stations in Japan. Their financial source was advertising revenue. The Radio Regulatory Commission itself was dissolved in 1952, and its functions were transferred to the Ministry of Posts and Telecommunications, called "*Yuseishou*," which was established by combining the Ministry of Telecommunications and the Ministry of Posts in the same year.

After World War II, NHK produced many popular radio programs influenced by similar American shows, and radio broadcasting played an important role in comforting people during the often difficult transition period after the war. Some of those NHK programs included a song program, *Nodojiman Shirouto Ongakukai* (Amateur Song Contest); radio dramas such as *Mukou Sangen Ryoudonari* (My Neighbors) and *Kaneno Naru Oka* (The Hill with a Bell); and quiz programs such as *Kiminonawa* (What Is Your Name?), *Watashiwa Daredeshou* (Who Am I?), and *Tonchi Kyoushitsu* (The Wit Class). Commercial broadcasting stations also aired many entertainment programs.

Radio and Television

Following the postwar reestablishment of radio broadcasting, the first TV service was begun by both NHK and a commercial company, Nihon Television (NTV), in 1953. Because people were quite satisfied with radio broadcasting and enjoyed many favorite programs, initial deployment of the TV service was slow. However, a 1959 live broadcast triggered an increase in the sale of receivers—the wedding ceremony of Prince Akihito and Miss Michiko Shouda, who was the first ordinary citizen to become the bride of an imperial prince. Many advertisers shifted their messages from radio to television, and as a result, the radio services began to lose their major revenue.

Commercial radio stations came up with several strategies to rebuild the popularity of radio listening. They extended broadcasting hours after midnight to target individual audiences; marketed their disc jockeys' unique and interesting personalities as the appeal of a program; and reduced the number of dramas and quiz programs, which were more expensive to produce. Audience segmentation was introduced, meaning that a certain audience group, such as family, housewives, or young people, was targeted as the major audience sought during a certain time period in a day. Another strategy most commercial broadcasters began to use in 1964 was to air night games of professional baseball, especially those played by the *Yomiuri Giants*. Because of the necessity to broadcast those games across the country, commercial radio stations formed two networks, Japan Radio Network (JRN) and National Radio Network (NRN). As of December 2001, JRN had 34 affiliated stations, and NRN had 40. The networks are still mainly used to relay professional baseball games.

These strategies proved successful, and the popularity of radio broadcasting resumed by 1965. Midnight broadcasting was geared toward teenagers. Many disc jockeys played the roles of big brothers and sisters and became national celebrities among younger listeners. In addition, as the number of automobiles in Japan increased significantly in the 1960s and 1970s, radio stations succeeded in demonstrating their importance by providing timely news and information in drive time.

Although there had been strong demand for a license for FM radio broadcasting since the mid-1950s, the ministry had been worried about the commercial feasibility of FM stations. In the meantime, the ministry encouraged NHK to try to explore FM broadcasting by granting it a license as an experimental station. By 1968, NHK's FM broadcasting network covered almost 80 percent of the country. People had begun to realize the high quality of FM reception, and FM radio receivers were becoming widely diffused. Because of that circumstance, Japan's first licensed FM radio broadcasting was started by FM NHK and FM Aichi Music in 1969, and by FM Osaka Music, FM Tokyo, and FM Fukuoka Music a year later.

NHK

A 1950 Broadcast Law reestablished NHK as an independent public corporation responsible for public broadcasting service. NHK neither receives direct funding from the government nor is responsible for any governmental work. Article 7 of the law states that NHK's goal is to broadcast for the public welfare throughout the country. In order to meet this goal, Article 9 requires that NHK be responsible for domestic and international broadcasting, plus research and development to improve broadcasting in general.

NHK has a Board of 12 governors as its supreme decision-making body. Each governor represents a geographical district, and governors are chosen from various fields such as education, culture, science, and industry. Governors are appointed with a term of three years by the prime minister with the approval of the Parliament, and they are expected to operate NHK for the benefit of the people. The board is responsible for an annual budget, operating plans, and master plans for program production. A board of directors runs NHK on a day-to-day basis and consists of a president appointed by the board and a vice president and three directors who are appointed by the president with the approval of the board. In contrast with many other public corporations in Japan, in which finance, management, and personnel matters are subject to strong government influence, NHK possesses complete autonomy.

NHK is financed by fees collected from the audience. The basis of the receiving fees is included in Article 32 of the Broadcast Law, which requires that those able to tune to NHK "have to agree on a receiving contract with NHK." What this means in practice is that listeners have to pay fees to NHK regardless of whether they listen to NHK programs. Because NHK is the sole public broadcasting station independent from any government organization, receiving fees are regarded as the price necessary for its operation. In 2000 such receiving fees accounted for almost 99 percent of NHK's total operating income. A budget that includes projections of the amount of the receiving fees for the coming year, an operational report, and a settlement of accounts of the past year is annually prepared by NHK, submitted to the Minister of Posts and Telecommunications, endorsed by the Cabinet, and approved by the Parliament. Although the minister can add some comments to the budget plan, he or she is not allowed to change it.

NHK has several missions to achieve, as delineated in Article 44 of the Broadcast Law. They are (1) to broadcast quality programs in order to meet a variety of needs of the public and to contribute to the elevation of cultural standards through the broadcasting of quality programs; (2) to support the traditional culture as well as to foster new culture; (3) to provide a nationwide broadcasting network so that programs can be received at any place in the country; (4) to produce programs not only geared toward the whole country but also tailored to individual regions; (5) to conduct research and development and to disseminate the results as widely as possible; and (6) to broadcast NHK programs in foreign countries to contribute to better international understanding. Because of the public nature of NHK (and its past involvement in the government/military propaganda), the Japanese people expect NHK to produce programs that are accurate, fair, politically impartial, and neutral, with the presentation of the widest possible range of viewpoints.

NHK operates three radio services: Radio 1, Radio 2, and FM. According to 2000 statistics, Radio 1 devoted about half its time to news, about a quarter to cultural programs, and the final quarter to entertainment (a minimal amount of time, about 2 percent, went to education). On Radio 2, 66 percent was educational programs, followed by cultural programs with 20 percent and news with 14 percent. For the FM service, 41 percent was devoted to cultural programs, 37 percent to entertainment, 18 percent to news, and 4 percent to education. These data show that the primary focuses of Radio 1, Radio 2, and FM are news, education, and culture, respectively. In international broadcasting, 66 percent of the programs were news, and 32 percent dealt with various types of information. As of July 2001, Radio 1 had 214 stations, Radio 2 had 140 stations, and FM NHK had 520 stations in the country. These stations effectively cover all of Japan.

Present Radio System

All radio stations in Japan today are categorized as either general (i.e., they must air news, and more than 30 percent of programs must be education and culture related) or specialized. The latter are further divided into education or music. For an education station, more than 50 percent of programs must be educational, and more than 30 percent must be cultural. NHK Radio 2 fits into this category.

As of December 2001, there were 47 commercial radio companies, holding among them 252 AM stations; 35 of these companies were also operating TV broadcasting stations. There were 53 companies holding altogether 242 FM stations. All FM stations (except for nine outlets) were music stations and belonged to either Japan FM Network (JFN: 37 stations) or Japan FM League (JFL: five stations). Other stations included one short-wave station, one BS analog station, 10 BS digital stations, one CS analog station, six CS digital stations, and 140 FM community stations.

Sixty-eight percent of all radio programs in both NHK stations and commercial stations focused on entertainment, 14 percent was related to culture, 13 percent was news, and 3 percent was education. Advertising expenses in radio in 2000 amounted to $1.73 billion in U.S. dollars and accounted for 3.4 percent of the total advertising expenses in Japan.

RYOTA ONO

Further Reading

20 seiki housou shi [Broadcasting History in the 20th Century], Tokyo: NHK, 2001

2002 NHK Nenkan [NHK Radio and Television Yearbook 2002], Tokyo: NHK, 2002

Housou Handbook: Bunka o Ninau Minpou no Gyoumu Chishiki [Broadcasting Handbook], Tokyo: Toyo Keizaishinpo, 1997

Inada, Taneteru, *Housou media nyumon* [Introduction to Broadcasting Media], Tokyo: Shakai Hyouronsha, 1996

Ito, Masami, et al., *Broadcasting in Japan,* London: Routledge, 1979

Kataoka, Toshio, *Housou gairon: Seidono haikei o saguru* [An Introduction to the Broadcasting System in Japan], Tokyo: Nihon Housou Shuppan Kyokai, 1988

NHK Data Book Sekaino Housou 2002 [NHK Data Book of World Broadcasting 2002], Tokyo: NHK Housou Bunka Kenkyujo, 2002

NHK Sogo Housou Bunka Kenkyujo, *50 Years of Japanese Broadcasting,* Tokyo: NHK, 1977

NHK Sogo Hoso Bunka Kenkyujo, *The History of Broadcasting in Japan,* edited by the History Compilation Room, Radio & TV Culture Research Institute, Tokyo: NHK, 1967

Nishi, Tadashi, *Zukai housou gyokai handbook* [A Diagrammed Guide to the Broadcasting Industry], Tokyo: Toyo Keizaishinpo, 1998

Tracey, Michael, "Japan: Broadcasting in a New Democracy," in *The Politics of Broadcasting,* edited by Raymond Kuhn, New York: St. Martin's Press, 1985

Tracey, Michael, *The Decline and Fall of Public Service Broadcasting,* Oxford and New York: Oxford University Press, 1998

Jazz Format

The growth of television in the early 1950s gradually replaced commercial radio as the primary family entertainment medium in the home. Radio adapted to a new role by establishing radio formats. Individual stations targeted narrow audience segments by specializing in news, talk, or any of a variety of music genres.

Although jazz music traces its roots to the formative years of the United States, it did not evolve into a bona fide radio music format until the 1950s. During the 1920s and 1930s, mainstream society viewed jazz music in the same way that rock and roll was viewed in the late 1950s: it was considered decadent. Because jazz was closely identified with black culture and affected by the racism that prevailed nationwide during that time, many of the greatest black jazz artists fled to Europe, some permanently, where they and their music were accepted openly. Paris became a cultural center of American jazz music, and the jazz music genre remains very popular there to this day in clubs and on radio. In fact, jazz radio is probably more popular in Europe than it is in the United States.

What is jazz radio? Jazz fans sometimes refer to it as music by musicians, not electricians. It includes blues, swing, bebop, fusion, Latin, and a number of other subcategories within its overall definition. Music that includes flat line piano, boring guitar, and braying saxophone is sometimes associated with jazz, but not legitimately so. New-wave music is not jazz.

Jazz grew out of blues, ragtime, and Dixieland music during the early 20th century. Following the swing era of the 1930s and 1940s, the style evolved into bebop, modern, cool, and other straight-ahead sounds by the 1960s. By this time, jazz had also been accepted as a legitimate popular art form throughout the United States. American audiences embraced the music as much as the Europeans had a decade earlier.

Jazz radio on the East Coast most likely had its roots in "Symphony Sid" Torin's live WJZ-AM radio broadcasts from the Royal Roost in New York City. Trumpeter Rex Stewart and critic and composer Leonard Feather had their own shows on AM in the early 1950s, as did Felix Grant and Ed Beech. These jazz disc jockeys are important, because early jazz formats were very much personality driven and involved a lot of talk in addition to the music.

"Sleepy" Stein, who was doing all-nighters in Chicago, moved his show to KNOB-FM in Los Angeles in 1956, and West Coast jazz radio was established. KJAZ in San Francisco had Pat Henry. KNOB and KJAZ had similar formats: one- and two-hour programs that were oriented totally toward personalities, with disc jockeys involved in lengthy announcements preceding and following each song played, which included mentioning every player or sideman, the composer, and even the record label. There were not that many jazz recordings at the time, and talkative disc jockey personalities

could play virtually every current jazz record release over a 24-hour period. Other jazz radio personalities included Dick Buckley, Howard LaCroft, Frank Evans, Bob Young, Al Fox, Al "Jazzbo" Collins, Jim Gosa, Pete Smith, Dick McGarvin, and Chuck Niles. Niles, probably the "dean" of active jocks, was still doing a regular show on KLON-FM, Long Beach, as the new millennium began.

The growth of FM radio and the intrusion of album-oriented rock and underground radio during the 1970s resulted in the erosion of commercial jazz formats. For example, KKGO in Los Angeles converted to a classical music format, and KZJZ in St. Louis simply went off the air. By the mid-1990s, only a few jazz formats remained on commercial radio stations in the United States. Noncommercial radio filled the void, however, with jazz being adopted as a format at several large public radio stations and at many college stations. In 1977 National Public Radio (NPR) initiated *Jazz Alive*, a public radio network show that almost all NPR stations carried. Today, the two stations with the largest international audiences are both noncommercial: WBGO-FM in Newark, New Jersey, and KLON-FM in Long Beach, California. Both of these large public radio stations are carried on numerous cable systems and are relayed via satellite to the far corners of the globe. KLON has a special program titled *Euro Jazz* that is relayed via satellite throughout the European continent.

The format itself has changed as well. Research into audience behavior has demonstrated that most listeners want less talk and more music. This "modal music research" calls for serving a greater number of people, replacing talk with 30-second breaks, limiting the number of announcements, and not airing anything squeaky or long. The jazz format of the future will involve less talk, sharpen the focus of the music, and include memorable moments in jazz history. In all likelihood, the music will be based in the jazz styles made popular in the 1950s and 1960s (i.e., bebop, cool, straight-ahead). The big band era is blending with early rock and roll popular music into a successful commercial format.

New developments in electronic technology, such as digital audio via satellite and multiple stream audio on demand via the internet, provide new venues for jazz radio formats. For example, DirecTV carries jazz programming in Japan, and the number of internet radio stations is growing rapidly. XM Radio and Sirius are two commercial satellite radio services that offer more than 100 channels each, several of which are devoted to various forms of jazz music. These mobile services are provided to subscribers for a monthly fee and are not likely to supplant FM radio as a mainstream jazz music format. Given the fact that mainstream jazz music will always target a narrow niche, the new multi channel environment provides an ideal conduit for delivering jazz to a growing number of fans all over the world. The music itself is established as a truly American music genre; it is taught in schools and clinics and performed by prestigious musical groups throughout the world, much as classical music has been for centuries. Accordingly, the music will continue to evolve but will also remain a viable radio format for years to come.

ROBERT G. FINNEY

See also FM Radio; National Public Radio

Further Reading

Eberly, Philip K., *Music in the Air: America's Changing Tastes in Popular Music, 1920–1980,* New York: Hastings House, 1982

Gioia, Ted, *The History of Jazz,* New York: Oxford University Press, 1997

Harris, Rex, *Jazz,* London: Penguin, 1952

Kenney, William Howland, *Recorded Music in American Life: The Phonograph and Popular Memory, 1890–1945,* New York: Oxford University Press, 1999

Jehovah's Witnesses and Radio

The religious group that took the name Jehovah's Witnesses in 1931 (prior to that date the group preferred the name Bible Students) owned and operated several radio stations in the United States and Canada beginning in 1924 and used syndicated recordings on hundreds of commercial stations to supplement its broadcast outreach between 1931 and 1937. The controversial and often confrontational views of the sect involved it in frequent conflicts with other denominations and with broadcasting regulators.

The story of the Bible Students'/Jehovah's Witnesses' involvement in radio is largely the story of their second president, Judge Joseph Franklin Rutherford—a former Missouri lawyer and substitute judge with a commanding personality and a booming orator's voice. Born in 1869, Rutherford took control of the Watch Tower Society and its associated groups in 1916, following the death of the sect's founder, Pastor Charles Taze Russell. In 1917 Rutherford and several associates were convicted of sedition for their public opposition to the World War I draft; their convictions were overturned in 1919. Upon his release from prison, Rutherford took steps to revive the struggling movement, implementing a renewed program of publishing and public speaking.

As part of this effort Judge Rutherford delivered his first radio address over station WGL in Philadelphia on 16 April 1922. Soon afterward, the Bible Students acquired a plot of land on Staten Island, New York, and began construction of their own broadcasting station.

On 24 February 1924 the Bible Students inaugurated station WBBR. The noncommercial station featured classical music and hymns performed by Bible Student musicians, talks on home economics and other practical subjects, and lectures on the group's complex interpretations of Bible prophecy and chronology by Rutherford and others. The success of WBBR led to the operation of additional Bible Student stations over the next several years, including WORD in Batavia, Illinois (later WCHI), KFWM in Oakland, California, CYFC in Vancouver, British Columbia, CHCY in Edmonton, Alberta, CHUC in Saskatoon, Saskatchewan, and CKCX in Toronto, Ontario.

During 1927 and 1928 the broadcasting activities of the Bible Students began to attract the attention of government regulators. In June 1927 Rutherford testified before the Federal Radio Commission (FRC) to protest a decision denying WBBR's application to share the frequency of station WJZ, owned by the Radio Corporation of America and the flagship of the newly formed National Broadcasting Company's (NBC) Blue network, alleging that NBC was part of a religious/commercial conspiracy seeking to deny his group fair access to the radio audience. Although the FRC dismissed Rutherford's complaint, NBC offered the Bible Students free air time for the broadcast of a talk by Rutherford. The speech, entitled "Freedom for the Peoples," was delivered on 24 July 1927 and in it Rutherford denounced all other religions, the clergy, big business, and all human governments as agents of Satan. A barrage of complaints received in the wake of this address led NBC to deny Rutherford and the Bible Students any further access to its stations.

The following year the Bible Students ran afoul of broadcasting authorities in Canada. Protests from clergymen over the broadcasts of Bible Student stations in Canada were followed by allegations that the group had on two occasions sold time over its Saskatoon outlet to the Ku Klux Klan. On the strength of these complaints the licenses for the Canadian stations were revoked in March 1928.

Unable to secure time on any established network, the Bible Students turned to a network of their own—buying time on over a hundred stations from 1928 through 1930 for "The Watchtower Hour." Anchored by WBBR, and connected by American Telephone and Telegraph (AT&T) circuits, the "Watchtower Network" functioned for an hour each week, presenting talks by Rutherford and hymns performed by Bible Student musicians.

Increased costs led the organization to discontinue the live network at the end of 1930, replacing it with transcribed syndication. The Watch Tower Society purchased time on local stations and the lectures of Judge Rutherford were distributed on 16-inch shellac transcriptions manufactured by the Columbia Phonograph Company. By 1933 over 400 stations around the world were broadcasting these 12-minute talks. This "wax chain" would be supplemented by occasional live hookups from the organization's annual conventions.

As the Depression deepened, the Witnesses (adopting that name in July 1931) became increasingly combative in their attacks on organized religion, politicians, and big business and this, in turn, brought them into further conflict with station owners and the FRC. Catholic authorities, especially, took offense at Rutherford's statements and pressured station owners to discontinue the broadcasts. In 1933 the Witnesses began a nationwide petition drive for "freedom of broadcasting" and presented more than 2 million signatures to the FRC in early 1934. Allegations were immediately made that many of the signatures were forged, but the petition led Representative Louis McFadden (R-Pennsylvania) to introduce a bill that would require broadcasters to guarantee free and equal use of air time to all nonprofit organizations. Several Watch Tower Society representatives were among those testifying for this bill in March 1934. Buried under an avalanche of opposition from the National Association of Broadcasters, the established networks, and the Federal Council of Churches of Christ, the bill died quietly in committee.

Opposition to the Witnesses' broadcasts mounted steadily during the mid-1930s, culminating in Philadelphia in 1936 when Catholic leaders urged a boycott of Gimbels Department Store, owners of station WIP, which had carried the Rutherford programs for several years. Stations became increasingly reluctant to sell time to the Watch Tower Society and finally, in October 1937, the organization announced its withdrawal from commercial broadcasting, although it used special hookups for convention broadcasts until 1941.

Rutherford died in 1942 and his successors have moved away from his aggressive stances, ignoring the broadcast media in favor of direct house-to-house canvassing. Station WBBR remained in operation until 15 April 1957, when it was quietly sold. The call letters were changed to WPOW and the once-combative voice of the Watch Tower Society became a commercial station specializing in recorded music.

ELIZABETH MCLEOD

See also Religion on Radio

Futher Reading

1975 Year Book of Jehovah's Witnesses

"Bible Students Protest," *Broadcasting* (1 February 1934)

Duffy, Dennis J., *Imagine Please: Early Radio Broadcasting in British Columbia,* Victoria, British Columbia: Sound and Moving Image Division, Province of British Columbia, Ministry of Provincial Secretary and Government Services, Provincial Archive, 1983

Jehovah's Witnesses in the Divine Purpose, New York: Watch Tower Bible and Tract Society, 1959

"McFadden's Religious Time Bill Believed Defeated at Hearings," *Broadcasting* (1 April 1934)

Penton, M. James, *Apocalypse Delayed: The Story of Jehovah's Witnesses,* Toronto and Buffalo, New York: University of Toronto Press, 1985; 2nd edition, 1997

Rutherford, Joseph Franklin, *Freedom for the Peoples,* New York: Watch Tower Bible and Tract Society, 1927

Rutherford, Joseph Franklin, *Government: Speech of World-Wide Interest, Broadcast to All Continents: Hiding the Truth, Why?* Brooklyn, New York: Watch Tower Bible and Tract Society, 1935

Rutherford, Joseph Franklin, *Enemies: The Proof That Definitely Identifies All Enemies, Exposes Their Methods of Operation, and Points Out the Way of Complete Protection for Those Who Love Righteousness,* Brooklyn, New York: Watch Tower Bible and Tract Society, 1937

"Rutherford Protests to Radio Commission," *New York Times* (15 June 1927)

"Under Constant Duress," *Broadcasting* (1 April 1934)

Jepko, Herb 1931–1995

U.S. Radio Talk Show Host

Herb Jepko began what would later become the Nitecap Radio Network on KSL, Salt Lake City, Utah, on 11 February 1964 and is acknowledged by many to be the father of network talk radio.

Origins

Born in Colorado and adopted as an infant by his stepparents in Prescott, Arizona, Jepko was the only child in his family. His adoptive mother left before he was four years old and his adoptive father, Metro, was forced into Veteran's Administration hospitals on and off for the next ten years for injuries he sustained in World War I. During those times Jepko was raised by a series of foster parents until he and his father were reunited for most of his late teenage years. At age 18 Jepko entered the U.S. Army, where he learned the crafts of film production and radio broadcasting.

In the late 1950s and early 1960s Jepko pursued a series of radio jobs along the California coast, in Idaho, and eventually in Utah. He was hired by KDYL in Salt Lake City to play late-night jazz, but he soon grew bored playing music. Working a late-night shift, he began talking to his listeners about the mountains, the weather, and non-controversial news of the day. Since there were no facilities for broadcasting calls over the air, Jepko would talk to his listeners over the phone off the air while music was playing. Mail began arriving from all over the Rocky Mountain area, and it was not long before the managers of Mormon-owned 50,000 watt KSL took note of the new, talented air personality across town. While KSL had a history of hiring only Latter Day Saints (Mormons), exceptions were sometimes made for on-air talent. Jepko's nominal Catholicism and occasional drinking would later create significant tensions.

In 1962 Jepko was hired to host KSL's midday program *Crossroads*. He quickly realized that this was a different audience than the one he had been connecting with in his late-night shift at KDYL. Perhaps in part because of his unstable childhood, it was this late-night audience of the lonely, fearful, sickly, or disaffected for whom he felt the greatest affinity. Despite being a 50,000-watt clear channel, KSL was off the air from 1 A.M. to 5 A.M., and Jepko was anxious to use that time period. KSL management felt no good could come from giving listeners a reason to be awake at that hour and no advertisers would pay to reach those listeners who were awake all night. Jepko had so much confidence in his ability to make the time period work, however, that he accepted a 50 percent cut in pay, resigned from his midday job, and agreed to a six-week deadline to prove he could make the show work, or be fired.

Nitecaps Program

Just after midnight on 11 February 1964, Jepko began what would become the most successful program in KSL's history. For the first few weeks of the program, station engineers had rigged only one phone line that could be put on the air. Even on that first night, however, Jepko was seldom at a loss for callers. One of the first advertisers was for a venison cookbook, and Jepko's wife Patsy, who supported him in this late-night experiment, found herself filling orders on the kitchen table while listening to the show at night. After a night on the air, Jepko would return at 7 A.M. to shower, change, and begin making sales calls while Patsy took care of the kids. For the first year of the show, they subsisted on two or three hours of sleep each weeknight.

The program's unprecedented success was almost immediate. Within a year, local chapters of *Nitecaps*, as they became known following an on-air contest to choose a name, were meeting in five states. As the only workable method for responding to the thousands of letters received each day, Jepko began publishing *The Wick,* a monthly magazine, in June 1965. Conventions were held that drew thousands of listeners from over 30 states. KSL managers and Latter Day Saints church officials belatedly realized they had a perfect platform from which to reach those in need with proselytizing messages, but Jepko fought to keep the program away from issues of controversy and denominational religion. Some within the station expressed concerns that such a successful program was being run on church-owned facilities by a nonmember. Eventually Arch Madsen, president of KSL, would side with Jepko, allowing him to buy time from the station and operate as an independent contractor, but tensions between other KSL personnel and Jepko continued to intensify.

In January 1968 KXIV Phoenix signed on as the first Nitecap Radio Network affiliate, and network talk radio was born. The 50,000-watt clear channel KVOO, Tulsa, Oklahoma, carried the show from October 1969 to September 1971. In January 1973 WHAS Louisville, Kentucky, another 50,000-watt clear channel station, picked up the show, giving Jepko the first-ever coast-to-coast coverage for a talk show. By mid-1974, more than 80 "Nitestands" were active, with members meeting for socializing and to organize service to the elderly in their areas. While the core of the *Nitecap* audience was retired, Arbitron estimates showed a surprising number of 18–24 year olds in the midnight-to-1 A.M. hour (the only overnight hour measured by Arbitron at the time). Outside of Salt Lake City (KSL) and Louisville, Kentucky (WHAS), the audience was largely rural, because of the difficulties of receiving, in a dense metropolitan area, a clear signal from a distant AM station.

Almost all revenues from the show were derived from direct-response advertising, and Jepko insisted that *Nitecap* staff handle all order fulfillment. Too often he had seen listeners of other programs robbed by direct-response advertisers who went bankrupt without fulfilling paid orders. So Jepko required Nitecap Radio Network advertisers to ship sufficient product to his Salt Lake City offices before allowing the commercials to air. Other revenue streams included commissions earned by a travel agency and insurance company franchise operated by Nitecaps International. At its peak, a staff of 15 full-time employees handled order fulfillment, insurance policies, Nitecap tours, membership cards, and publishing of *The Wick*.

In November 1974 WBAL Baltimore affiliated with the Nitecap Radio Network, providing a clear signal into Washington, D.C., Philadelphia, and New York. This provided the first exposure to the program for many media executives living on the East Coast. On 4 November 1975, the Mutual Broadcasting System (MBS) began carrying the *Nitecap* program nationally. Thanks to the dozens of new affiliates, membership in the Nitecaps International Association (NIA) soared to over 300,000. Within a year, Arbitron estimated 10 million listeners were tuned in to the program nightly. NIA memberships likewise soared as new "Nitestands" were established across the nation. Following the affiliation with MBS, Jepko distanced himself further from KSL by building separate studios and offices for the show.

Unfortunately, as part of the agreement for MBS to carry the show, Jepko had to relinquish control over order fulfillment and sales strategy to the network. MBS sales executives attempted to sell the program on a cost-per-thousand (CPM) basis to national advertisers, but the reputation of the show as appealing primarily to an older, less-affluent, rural audience made this a difficult sale. MBS account executives quickly moved on to more profitable dayparts, and Jepko, while still enjoying the largest audience in the history of the program, began to suffer extraordinary financial losses. The combination of the increased expenses of operating his own studios and the decrease in revenue from the shift in sales strategy away from proven direct-response advertising would ultimately prove fatal.

By the fall of 1976 Jepko was under intense pressure from MBS to change the program to attract a younger audience. MBS felt more controversy and conflict would serve to attract the younger demographics, which would be easier to sell on a CPM basis to national advertisers. Jepko in turn pressured MBS to continue to serve the existing audience, to whom he

Herb Jepko
Courtesy Radio Hall of Fame

felt a strong commitment. With MBS account executives unwilling, or unable, to work deals for sufficient direct-response advertising, the show began to fail. On 28 May 1977 MBS replaced the *Nitecap* program with Long John Neble and Candy Jones. When Long John died less than a year later, MBS gave Larry King his first shot at a national audience. (Others later mistakenly cite King's program as the first network radio talk show.)

In June 1977 the Nitecap Radio Network was reborn with 10 affiliates, including KSL, but without WHAS. By 1977 14 more affiliates had joined the network, but most used low power at night and the vast majority of the core audience was unable to receive the program. Network radio, in an era before satellite distribution, required expensive American Telephone and Telegraph (AT&T) landlines, which were feasible only with the economies of scale offered by scores of stations sharing the cost. Larry King, other all-night radio programs, 24-hour broadcast television, and cable TV had fractionalized the late-night radio audience. As renewal of *Wick* subscriptions dropped, Nitestands disbanded, and orders from direct-response appeals declined, old tensions between KSL management and Jepko resurfaced, aggravated by his increased drinking. In August 1978 KSL, without advance notice to listeners or to Jepko, dropped the *Nitecap* program.

The show continued for about a year before going off the air in August 1979. Jepko made several attempts to resurrect the program in the 1980s, with the most successful involving purchasing time on WOAI, a 50,000-watt clear channel in San Antonio, Texas, which lasted for several months. The last attempt to restart the program over was made at KTKK in Salt Lake City in 1990 with Randy Jepko, Jepko's son from Patsy's first marriage, serving as co-host, but the show lasted only a few months. When Jepko's son Herb Junior died in 1992, it proved to be the final tragedy from which Jepko could not recover. He died in Salt Lake City of complications from drinking on 31 March 1995.

JOSEPH G. BUCHMAN

See also All Night Radio; KSL; Mutual Broadcasting System

Herbert Earl Jepko. Born in Hayden, Colorado, 20 March 1931. Adopted by Metro and Nellie A. Jepko of Prescott, Arizona; completed two years of college and enlisted in U.S. Army as broadcast specialist, 1953–55; worked odd jobs in radio in California and Idaho; landed late-night shift at KDYL, Salt Lake City, 1961; joined KSL, Salt Lake City, as host of midday *Crossroads*; launched *The Other Side of the Day*, midnight to 6:00 A.M., 11 February 1964, later renamed the *Nitecaps*; first network talk radio program, 1 January 1968;

operated as *Nitecap Radio Network* through 4 November 1975. Died in Salt Lake City, Utah, 31 March 1995.

Radio Series

1964–77   *The Other Side of the Day* (became *Nitecaps*)

Further Reading

Bick, Jane Horowitz, "The Development of Two-Way Talk Radio in America," Ph.D. diss., University of Massachusetts, 1987

Broder, Mitch, "Small-Talk Show Is Big Draw in Wee Hours," *The New York Times* (23 February 1975)

Denton, Craig L., "Revamping the Wick Magazine," Master's thesis, University of Utah, 1976

Rose, Hilly, "The Talkers," in *But That's Not What I Called About,* by Rose, Chicago: Contemporary Books, 1978

Jewish Radio Programs in the United States

Religious broadcasts usually connote church services and evangelists. Although it is true that most radio religious programs have been directed at a Christian audience, a number of Jewish programs have been on the air since radio's earliest years.

Origins

In March 1922 New York station WJZ's radio listing announced a "radio chapel service," featuring a talk by Rabbi Solomon Foster and music by cantor Maurice Cowan. Although it had been customary for radio stations to offer short inspirational messages (usually in the morning), these were usually provided by well-known Christian clergy. In some cities with large Jewish populations, however, a rabbi was occasionally asked to speak. To the listener in 1922–23, this was something of a social revolution. Most Christians had never met or heard a rabbi before.

Rabbi Harry Levi of Temple Israel, a Reform congregation, was invited to take a turn on a daily religious program that was broadcast over Boston's WNAC in mid-1923. He got such a positive response that he was invited back. By January 1924 WNAC made arrangements to broadcast Temple Israel's services twice a month, certainly the first time most non-Jews had encountered what a Jewish worship service was like. (In March 1926 listeners could also hear a Jewish wedding, as New York's WRNY made Winnie Gordon and Julius Goldberg,

along with Rabbi Josef Hoffman, radio stars for a day.) Boston's "Radio Rabbi" Harry Levi became so popular during 16 years on the air that two books of his sermons were issued, and numerous non-Jews who heard him on WNAC wrote him fan letters or came to his temple to ask for his autograph.

Radio in the early 1920s provided its audience with the chance to hear some of Judaism's biggest names, including New York's Rabbi Stephen S. Wise, long regarded by the print media as a spokesman for liberal Jews: both the *New York Times* and *Time* magazine often quoted him. As early as March 1922, Rabbi Wise gave a radio talk to encourage donations to help European Jewish refugees. On a fairly regular basis throughout the 1920s, his speaking engagements were broadcast from a number of cities; Rabbi Wise's sermons were often about the dangers of intolerance, such as a 1924 speech to protest the growing popularity of the Ku Klux Klan. A dynamic orator, Rabbi Wise developed such a following that the radio editors at major newspapers often used a bold headline and a photo to let the audience know that he was about to give another radio sermon.

Radio produced a sort of ecumenism; one listing for New York's WEAF in December 1923 featured Christmas songs for children at 6 P.M. followed by Hanukkah songs at 7. Seeing the possibilities in radio as a vehicle to promote understanding, Dr. Cyrus Adler, a scholar and president of Dropsie College in Philadelphia, helped to create a weekly program that would not be limited to sermons. In cooperation with the United Synagogues of America, an organization of Conservative Jews, the Wednesday night program went on the air in late August 1923 on WEAF, after first offering an experimental broadcast in May to see if the response would be positive. It was. This weekly Jewish program featured Jewish folk and liturgical music (sometimes sung in Yiddish, sometimes in Hebrew), discussions of Jewish holidays, and a number of famous speakers from all over the United States.

Entertainment

Jewish programming in the 1920s was not only religious in nature. Thanks to radio, listeners were able to hear two famous Cantors—the great cantor Josef (Yossele) Rosenblatt, along with the popular Jewish comedian Eddie Cantor; both appeared at a 1924 banquet to honor the Young Men's Hebrew Association's 50th anniversary. There were also programs of popular music to benefit Jewish causes; Jewish bandleaders and performers such as Irving Berlin, Leo Reisman, and Eddie Cantor were among those who participated. And by the late 1920s, most cities from the East Coast to the West Coast had rabbis on the air, usually around the major Jewish holidays. In addition to rabbis and scholars discussing Jewish customs, there was at least one popular radio show with a Jewish immigrant family as the protagonists— Gertrude Berg had created a comedy-drama called *The Goldbergs*, which began a successful run on the National Broadcasting Company (NBC) in November 1929. It was an era when many performers with ethnic names changed them to sound more "American," yet Gertrude Berg did not hide the ethnicity of her characters, nor did she hide her own ethnicity. She wrote a syndicated advice column for the Jewish press and did speaking engagements on behalf of Jewish charities. And unlike some comedy routines such as "Cohen on the Telephone," a hit record that made fun of a Jewish immigrant who was losing his battle with the English language, the Goldbergs were portrayed sympathetically, and anyone of any religion could identify with their problems. (There were also a number of popular singers and comedians on radio who were Jewish, such as Jack Benny, Fanny Brice, and Al Jolson, but at a time when anti-Semitism still flourished, most Jewish entertainers did not make overt mention of their religion.)

By the 1930s, some network programs featured Jewish themes. One of the earliest was *Message of Israel*, first heard on NBC Blue in late 1934 and hosted by Lazar Weiner, the music director of New York's Central Synagogue. Boston's Harry Levi was invited to speak on this program, which featured some of America's best-known Reform rabbis, in 1937 and again in 1938.

There were also a number of charitable and philanthropic organizations that provided radio programs, such as Hadassah, the Federation of Jewish Charities, and the American Jewish Joint Distribution Committee. Also, when a special occasion took place, such as the 50th anniversary of the Jewish Theological Seminary in March 1937, highlights from the event were broadcast. At a time when Federal Communications Commission (FCC) guidelines called for a certain amount of religion and public service, such programs served a useful purpose for the station while providing the Jewish organizations far-reaching exposure they would not otherwise have received.

And then there was the rabbi who decided to leave the pulpit to become a radio singer. Rabbi Abraham Feinburg took the air name "Anthony Frome"; known as the "Poet Prince of the Airwaves," he could be heard singing love songs on several New York stations from 1932 to 1935, at which time he gave it all up and went back to being a rabbi again. On the other hand, there was a famous opera singer who also became a cantor; his radio concerts were critically acclaimed whether he was doing Hebrew prayers or portraying the lead tenor role in "La Traviata." Jan Peerce was discovered by the famous impresario Samuel Rothafel (better known as Roxy) while singing at a hotel banquet in 1932. Soon, he was singing on NBC Blue's *Radio City Music Hall of the Air*, and by 1941 at the Metropolitan Opera, where he performed for 27 years. But throughout his life, as he had done in his neighborhood synagogue before he became famous, Peerce would chant the Jewish liturgical prayers at the High Holy days. He also made a number of recordings of sacred Jewish music, some of which have been reissued.

During the 1930s a few radio stations were airing mainly ethnic and foreign language programs, brokering out segments of the day to particular groups. One of the best known ethnic stations was New York's WEVD, where some long-running Yiddish programs made their home; thanks to WEVD, it was possible to hear anything from folk songs to entire Yiddish plays. And because WEVD had a working agreement with a Jewish newspaper called the *Forverts* ("Forward"), there were always commentators and critics who discussed the news from a Jewish perspective. WEVD also had Moses Asch, who would go on to found Folkways Records, but who in the mid-1930s hired and recorded many of the performers whose music was played on WEVD. America in the 1930s still had many immigrants who missed the culture of the old country, and radio helped to provide it. One program, *Yiddish Melodies in Swing*, went on the air on New York's WHN in 1939, and in 1941 fans were still waiting in line to get tickets to be in the studio audience.

Speaking Out

However, the 1930s became a more serious time for Jewish broadcasters as the situation in Europe worsened. As news of Hitler and the Nazis dominated newspapers, some Jewish radio programs began providing news and information that the network newscasts were hesitant to mention. Nazi military conquests were front-page news, but it was not until the 1940s that newspapers such as the *New York Times* finally decided the extermination of Jewish people was a major story. Thus, it was up to the Jewish press, and the news commentators on Jewish programs (along with a few non-Jewish commentators who spoke out, most notably NBC's Dorothy Thompson), to make sure the story was told. Rabbi Stephen Wise took to the airwaves to condemn fascism overseas while also condemning bigotry in America, as personified by Father Charles Coughlin, the anti-Semitic radio priest. The chairmen and women of many Jewish organizations, such as the American Jewish Committee and the Jewish Labor Committee, decried the persecution of Jews in Europe and tried to raise funds to help them. But Jewish public affairs programs were usually short and were seldom on the air more than once a week. Although they did call attention to the problems Jews faced, they could not compensate for the lack of coverage the rest of the week.

Ethics and Culture

The next major network program with a Jewish theme came from the Jewish Theological Seminary. Developed by seminary president Louis Finkelstein, *The Eternal Light* first aired on NBC in October 1944, featuring radio dramas about biblical personalities and famous Jewish men and women past and present. It often presented thought-provoking stories with ethical dimensions, and it was still on the air (having moved to television) in the 1980s, celebrating its 40th anniversary in 1985. Among the famous performers who were heard on this award-winning program over the years were Ed Asner, Gene Wilder, and E.G. Marshall. At the height of its popularity, this program was heard on more than 100 stations, and it won a Peabody Award for excellence.

Some Jewish celebrities began to offer their own radio shows, making use of Jewish or Yiddish culture. From 1951 through 1955, parodist and comedian Mickey Katz starred in his own radio show on KABC in Los Angeles, and in the 1960s, actor and folksinger Theodore Bikel starred in *Thedore Bikel at Home,* which aired on FM stations in New York, Chicago, and Los Angeles. Some announcers who began their careers doing Jewish-oriented programming in the 1930s or 1940s could still be heard many years later. Zvee Scooler, who had originally been an actor in Yiddish theater, did commentary on WEVD for four decades. Max Reznick, whose show *The Jewish Hour* included everything from parodies to cantorial records to the popular style of Jewish jazz known as "klezmer," was on the air on several Washington, D.C., stations from the 1940s until he retired in 1986. Ben Gailing's Jewish program *Fraylekher Kabtsen* (The Happy Poor Man)

was on the air in Boston for more than 50 years. And in Chicago, Bernie Finkel's *Jewish Community Hour* celebrated its 37th anniversary in the summer of 2000.

Jewish Programs Today

Jewish music or commentary was readily available on radio as the new century began. There were radio talk shows with Jewish themes, such as *Talkline with Zev Brenner,* heard on stations in New York and New Jersey. (Brenner had even started an all-Jewish radio station, WLIR, Long Island, NY, in May 1993, and after that venture, he resumed his job as a radio and cable television talk host.) Another popular radio program with a loyal following combined requests and dedications with a wide range of Jewish music, plus commentary from an Orthodox point of view—*JM in the AM* ("Jewish Moments in the Morning") with Nachum Segal had been on the air since 1983 on WFMU in Jersey City, New Jersey. The growth of the internet enabled Jewish programs from foreign countries (including Israel) to be heard in America. The internet was also helpful to those Jewish programs that at one time were heard on small AM stations; they could now broadcast on the world wide web and gain a much larger potential audience. Newspaper owner Phil Blazer was among those who took advantage of the new technology; the *Phil Blazer Show* has been on radio in Los Angeles since 1965, but it began webcasting in 2000. Talk show host Zev Brenner also began doing webcasting, and Boston radio host Mark David, whose show *Yiddish Voice* aired on WUNR in Brookline, MA, also made his program available over the internet. National Public Radio has aired holiday concerts of Jewish music at Hanukkah (including one concert featuring Theodore Bikel), and a number of Jewish recording artists are making their music available to be heard or downloaded.

Unlike the Jewish radio programs of the early days, there are not as many radio sermons or famous radio cantors, although there certainly are Jewish programs that have a moral or ethical dimension and shows that stress Jewish theology. There are even internet programs that teach Torah (Jewish Bible) on-line and play sound files to help with singing and pronunciation.

Although much of Jewish radio programming today is oriented toward music, there are also shows about Israel and current events. And even though tolerance is much more a part of American life than it was during radio's early years, myths and stereotypes still exist; when a celebrity utters an anti-Jewish remark, or when there are questions about Jewish beliefs (such as in 2000 when U.S. Senator Joseph Lieberman, an Orthodox Jew, was the Democratic candidate for vice president), agencies such as the Anti-Defamation League or the American Jewish Congress send spokespeople to address the issue on radio and television talk shows.

One continuing controversy is the presence on the air of so-called Messianic Jewish programs, such as Sid Roth's syndicated *Messianic Vision* or *Zola Levitt Presents,* which is now heard over the internet in addition to its long run on television. Messianic programs are broadcast by Christian stations, but their intention is to convert Jews. Hosts claim they are still Jewish even though they have accepted Christianity; they use Hebrew words and Jewish terminology to disguise evangelical Christian concepts, such as referring to Jesus as "Yeshua HaMoshiah," with the hope that Jewish listeners will be less threatened by a show that says one can convert to Christianity without leaving Judaism. These shows have evoked some vehement protest from leaders of the organized Jewish community, who object to what they feel is a distortion of Jewish teachings and accuse the hosts of using deceptive tactics.

Now that there is no longer an FCC guideline encouraging religious programming, few stations are willing to give free time to a religious show. As a result, the majority of religious programs on the air are sponsored by Christian denominations or individual preachers. With the radio networks no longer providing free time, and with production costs so expensive, there are few if any religious shows of the caliber of *The Eternal Light* on radio anymore. In fact, most of the popular music stations air no religious programs at all, and yet there are still Jewish programs on radio, just as there were in the 1920s. The shows offer a wide range of styles: some are traditional, with old-timers who play the great cantorial music of the past and reminisce about the old days, but others are quite modern and exemplify the interests of the younger audience. One such show is heard on WSIA, Staten Island, New York; it features Jewish women's music and is hosted by Michele Garner, who calls herself the "Rockin' Rebbetzin" (the Yiddish word for a woman who is married to a rabbi is *rebbetzin,* and not only is her husband Eliezer a rabbi, but he too does a show on WSIA, playing Jewish rock music). Thanks to Jewish radio shows and the performers who love European Jewish culture, the Yiddish language is being kept alive; klezmer music has enjoyed a rebirth and newfound popularity with a younger demographic. Jewish radio shows are also proving helpful to Jews-by-choice, people who have converted to Judaism on their own and now want to learn more about Judaism's various customs and musical traditions.

Although it is certainly true that most religious programs on radio are done by and for Christians, there continues to be a consistent Jewish presence on the air, with shows that help to create a sense of community and a sense of identity.

Another interesting trend is the resurgence of Yiddish radio programs. Although only a few American Jews speak the language, there has been great interest in reviving it, especially given its impact on Jewish music and theater in the Golden Age of Radio. Leading this effort is the Yiddish Radio Project, which, beginning in March 2002 (some excerpts appearing in late 2001), could be heard on National Public Radio. Much of the work restoring the recordings and doing the historical research was done by a New York author and musician, Henry Sapoznik. A two-volume compact disc has been issued by the Yiddish Radio Project containing the first ten episodes of the NPR program, and the Project has a website with updated information (see below).

DONNA L. HALPER

See also Cantor, Eddie; The Goldbergs; Israel; Religion on Radio; Stereotypes on Radio; WEVD

Further Reading
Fine, Joyce, "American Radio Coverage of the Holocaust," <www.motlc.wiesenthal.com/resources.books/annual5/chap08.html>

Goldman, Ari, "For Orthodox Jews, a Gathering Place on the Air," *New York Times* (24 September 2000)

Kun, Josh, "The Yiddish Are Coming: Mickey Katz, Anti-Semitism, and the Sound of Jewish Difference," *American Jewish History* 87, no. 4 (1999)

Leff, Laurel, "A Tragic Fight in the Family: The New York Times, Reform Judaism, and the Holocaust," *American Jewish History* 88, no. 1 (2000)

Shandler, Jeffrey, and Elihu Katz, "Broadcasting American Judaism," in *Tradition Renewed: A History of the Jewish Theological Seminary,* edited by Jack Wertheimer, vol. 2, New York: Jewish Theological Seminary, 1997

Wishengrad, Morton, *The Eternal Light: Twenty-Six Radio Plays from the Eternal Light Program,* New York: Crown, 1947

Yiddish Radio Project website, <www.yiddishradioproject.org>

Jingles

Station identification jingles—catchy musical motifs often accompanied by vocals—are a basic ingredient of the sound of radio stations in most regions of the world. Although they are most associated with pop and rock music commercial radio services, jingles are also common in speech-based stations and even in publicly funded radio services.

Jingles are principally used by stations to insinuate their names and slogans into the minds of listeners. In so doing, jingles help ensure that, when questioned by audience researchers, listeners will recall particular stations over their rivals. This is especially vital for commercial stations, whose advertising rates are largely dictated by the results of such surveys.

In addition to this near-brainwashing technique of implanting the station names in the minds of listeners, radio jingles can be regarded as having the following attributes:

- They provide a positive, confident, "station sound" and a general "feel-good" factor.
- They promote the most important programming elements, for example, the style and quantity of music, contests, and local information.
- They "announce" different program elements, such as news, weather, sports, and disc jockey names.
- They serve as a way of "changing gears" between different program elements, for example, between news, commercial stop-sets, and travel information.
- They serve as a way of making musical transitions, for example, between slow- and fast-paced music.

Origins

The first known singing radio jingle was done in the mid-1920s, when Ernie Hare and Billy Jones, known as "The Happiness Boys," sang songs for a number of consumer products. By the late 1930s, advertising jingles had developed to a sophisticated level of production, often involving singing choirs and full big band orchestras. The station identification jingle developed naturally from this by the 1940s: WNEW in New York, for example, asked recording artists to sing short ditties incorporating the station's call letters.

By the mid-1950s radio station management saw the jingle as part of the battle for audience ratings success in a marketplace that was becoming ever more competitive—not just with other radio stations but with the new medium of television. In this period, radio stations were rapidly moving away from the "full-service" network model with a variety of programs and toward local operations, with most adopting one of three or four basic formats, and managements had to convince listeners that their stations were in fact better than and different from the opposition. They therefore marketed and promoted in ways similar to those of any consumer product. The fact that the station jingles sounded very similar to the advertising jingles of products and services was no coincidence: they were often written, performed, and produced by the same companies.

The "founding fathers" of station jingles as a distinct entity were Bill Meeks and Gordon McLendon. The latter bought KLIF in Dallas in 1947 and appointed Meeks as his music director with a specific brief to put together live music shows. As with so many other innovations, the modern station jingle happened by accident: the jingles were used as a way of bridging the time needed in live broadcasting to set up each new vocal group.

Meeks left KLIF to start his own company, Production Advertising Marketing Service (PAMS), in Dallas in 1951. By the mid-1950s he was compiling individual station jingles into "packages"—whole series of jingles using variations of the same musical structure and slogans—to different stations across the country. By the end of 1964 the primary business of PAMS had become station jingles, and the company became the world leader in a new stratum of services to the radio industry. Meanwhile, McLendon hired another musical director, Tom Merriman, who developed and elaborated on the station identification jingles at KLIF; other stations in different parts of the United States heard these and asked for customized sets of their own. Merriman also left KLIF and in 1955 formed the Commercial Recording Corporation; his company produced some of the first jingles specifically for Top 40 radio, which was rapidly emerging as the number-one radio format.

There was a good deal of creativity and innovation in this period. PAMS is credited with being the first company to use the Moog synthesizer and the Sonovox—a device originally developed to enable people who had lost the use of their vocal chords to make intelligible speech—to create an extraordinary electronic "singing" voice. The "variable station logo" technique meant that many disparate programming elements could be linked and blended using variations on the same musical motif, often with lyrical variations of the same slogan or "positioning statement."

Despite this, the overall style of these jingles—close vocal harmonies and lush orchestrations common in the pre–rock and roll period—was outdated even by the late 1950s, and yet, curiously, the style persisted for at least another 20 years. It appears that for many years, the radio jingle was accepted by the listening public as being a musical genre of its own, with no need to bow to changes in popular music.

Occasionally, though, attempts were made to overcome this anachronism by somewhat cheekily adopting more contemporary styles: one of the PAMS jingle sets adopted the Beatles' sound, even using the group's trademark "yeah yeah." Even here, though, the jingles outlasted the creations of the form on which they were based. Stations playing more contemporary formats belatedly moved away from the traditional close harmonies and lush orchestrations, seeing these techniques as distinctly "uncool" and embarrassingly old-fashioned (U.S. FM rock stations had always taken this view of jingles and had consequently eschewed them from the start).

In 1974 former PAMS employee Jonathan Wolfert and his wife Mary Lyn set up a new company, JAM (Jon and Mary)—also based in Dallas, the world's center for station jingles—which quickly established itself as one of the leading companies in the jingles field. In 1976 they secured the contract for the most famous and imitated Top 40 radio station in the world—WABC in New York—which used PAMS jingles from 1962 to 1974. Probably the most-played jingle in the world was recorded for this station in the spring of 1976—lasting just two and a half seconds. In 1990 Wolfert bought up the rights to the jingles from PAMS (which had suspended operations in 1978 after a series of financial crises). These jingles were still in demand in many radio markets throughout the world—especially on golden oldies stations, which had their own station names and slogans sung over the original music tracks, often using many of the same singers.

Modern Era

The length of station jingles varies greatly, although most average between five and seven seconds. JAM also claims to have recorded the longest known jingle—for WYNY in the fall of 1979—which lasted three and a half minutes. "The New York 97 Song" is a vocal and musical narrative of a day in the life of a listener in New York, with repeated use of the station location, frequency, and call letters—"New York 97, WYNY."

The international ubiquity of the station identification jingle cannot simply be explained as the result of the competitiveness of the U.S. commercial radio system. Jingles are used in radio services in very different types of economic and media systems. For example, the British public service broadcaster, the British Broadcasting Corporation (BBC), which held a monopoly on domestic radio in the United Kingdom until 1973, began using PAMS jingles in 1967 on its new rock and pop network, Radio 1. This service was set up on instructions from the government after it had produced legislation outlawing the "pop pirates" of the mid-1960s—many of which had copied U.S. Top 40 and beautiful music formats and used jingles from PAMS in Dallas. Radio 1 ordered the same series of jingles that had been used by the most commercially successful

of the offshore pirates, the Texan-backed Radio London. Even though the BBC carried no commercials and had no authorized competition during the late 1960s and early 1970s, its managers thought that station jingles had become an essential part of pop music programming and youth culture. Many other state broadcasters have also felt the need to invest in the "Dallas Sound" of jingles, as have the publicly funded armed forces radio networks of both the United States and the United Kingdom. The jingles have also been sung in languages other than English: the U.S. radio jingle can be fairly regarded as a form of cultural imperialism, albeit one of a benign nature.

By the mid-1980s, a new vogue for electronically produced "Sweepers," with a spoken rather than sung vocal track, became the vogue on many contemporary hit radio and adult contemporary stations. As with all commercial operations, the jingles business—dominated in the world market by JAM and TM Century—had to adapt to these new demands or face extinction. In the late 1990s, there was some indication that the fashion had moved, if not full circle, then perhaps 180 degrees, when many stations—especially those targeted to the baby boom generation, which had grown up with the Dallas Sound—began investing in the more traditional type of jingle production, albeit with a more contemporary edge.

Although fashions in station jingles will no doubt evolve still further, the one constant need for stations faced with ever more competition for listeners' loyalty is to ensure that they promote themselves on the air in the most attractive and distinctive audio fashion possible.

RICHARD RUDIN

See also McClendon, Gordon; Promotion on Radio

Further Reading

Chapman, Robert, *Selling the Sixties: The Pirates and Pop Music Radio*, London and New York: Routledge, 1992

Douglas, Susan J., *Listening In: Radio and the American Imagination*, New York: Times Books, 1999

Fong-Torres, Ben, *The Hits Just Keep on Coming: The History of Top 40 Radio*, San Francisco: Miller Freeman Books, 1998

Garay, Ronald, *Gordon McLendon: The Maverick of Radio*, New York: Greenwood Press, 1992

Hilmes, Michele, *Radio Voices: American Broadcasting, 1922–1952*, Minneapolis: University of Minnesota Press, 1997

Keith, Michael C., *Voices in The Purple Haze: Underground Radio and the Sixties*, Westport, Connecticut: Praeger, 1997

MacFarland, David, T., *The Development of the Top 40 Radio Format*, New York: Arno Press, 1979

Joyce, William. *See* Lord Haw-Haw

Joyner, Tom 1942–

U.S. Radio Disc Jockey

Tom Joyner's daily round-trip airline commute of 1,600 miles between Chicago and Dallas earned him the moniker "The Fly Jock." Beginning in 1985, Joyner continued this daily commute for eight years. It was one of several accomplishments that transformed a once small-town disc jockey into one of America's most well known on-air personalities. Another well-deserved nickname would come later, one that was just as fitting and appropriate as the earlier one—"The Hardest-Working Man in Radio."

Early Career and Life

The Tuskegee, Alabama, native started announcing during college. He had at first sung with Lionel Ritchie and the Commodores, a rhythm and blues group, but he was discouraged by his father in this pursuit. So Joyner tried announcing instead. He first worked as a local announcer at Tuskegee Institute, where he attended college, playing records in the university cafeteria and announcing at sporting events. Upon graduation, he landed an on-air position at WMRA-AM in nearby Montgomery, Alabama.

He left that job for other on-air positions in successively larger markets. For example, after WMRA, Joyner worked at Memphis' WLOK-AM. From Memphis, he moved up the river to St. Louis, where he found an announcing job at KWK-AM. From there, Joyner was hired as an announcer at Chicago's WJPC-AM. While there, he worked as a morning air personality and program director (1978–83). Moreover, he was also producer and host of the *Ebony/Jet Celebrity Showcase*, a television show. While at WJPC-AM, the station's owner and Joyner's mentor, John H. Johnson, publisher of *Ebony* and *Jet* magazines, gave Joyner his first big break. Johnson put Joyner's picture in *Jet* magazine each week as part of the promotion for the television program, and Johnson featured him in a television commercial with boxing great Muhammad Ali. In addition to his work at WJPC-AM, Joyner also worked as a disc jockey at several other Chicago radio stations, including WVON-AM, WBMX-FM, and WGCI-FM.

The Fly Jock

Joyner left WGCI-FM for a morning air personality position at Dallas' KKDA-AM. By the time his contract at the Dallas station was nearing its end, WGCI-FM management wanted him back. Joyner listened to both offers and decided to take both because neither contract had an exclusivity clause that would prevent him from working at another radio station. Joyner said "greed" got the best of him, and he signed two concurrent $1 million-plus contracts, running six years (Dallas) and five years (Chicago). Thus began the odyssey of the Fly Jock.

From 1985 to 1993, Joyner accrued 7 million frequent-flier miles, as he made the round-trip commute three days each week between Dallas and Chicago. Joyner did a morning show in Dallas at KKDA-FM (the station had acquired the license for an FM facility) from 5:30 to 9:00 A.M. In the afternoons, from 2:00 to 6:00 P.M., he did an afternoon show at WGCI in Chicago. Joyner paid $30,000 to reserve a guaranteed round-trip seat on an airline over five years.

The Hardest-Working Man in Radio

In 1994 the American Broadcasting Companies (ABC) Radio network approached Joyner with the idea of developing his radio program for national distribution and syndication. With its debut in 1994, the *Tom Joyner Morning Show* became the first live syndicated program produced by an African-American performer on radio. It is broadcast from 5:00 to 9:00 A.M. central time to a nationwide audience, Monday through Friday. Joyner's Dallas-based show combines, in more or less equal parts, rhythm and blues music, comedy, and politics. Although based primarily in Dallas, the *Tom Joyner Morning Show* is often broadcast from remote studios in various cities around the United States. It is the number-one-rated urban morning radio show in the country. Joyner's show is heard on 95 stations, reaching 5 million listeners. The show targets the 25–54 demographic group, an attractive group for advertisers. Joyner's show, when broadcast on other outlets, has catapulted many of these radio stations to number one in their respective

Tom Joyner
Courtesy ABC Radio Networks

markets. Critics complain, however, that Joyner's success has come at the expense of local disc jockeys, who are fired because they are no longer needed. Joyner, on the other hand, sees his success as an opportunity for low-rated radio stations to increase listeners and advertising revenues and to provide national programming that comes with his syndicated show.

Joyner also produces a weekend program. The *Tom Joyner Movin' on Weekend Show* can also be heard nationally and is distributed by the ABC Radio network.

Community Service

Joyner's sustained support of community service activities has endeared him to the African-American community. Among the issues he has supported include a 1980s campaign called "Drop a Dime on the Man," which identified speed traps targeting African-Americans in Dallas. In 1999 Joyner, along with political commentator and fellow team member Tavis

Smiley, started a crusade to persuade retailers such as Comp-USA, for example, to expand their advertising in black-owned media.

In addition, he has started the Tom Joyner Foundation, a nonprofit organization that assists college students in completing their college education at historically black colleges and universities. The foundation accepts donations from many sources, but Joyner's "Dollars for Scholars" campaign has raised more than $40,000 for students at historically black colleges, which is made available to them through his Foundation.

GILBERT A. WILLIAMS

See also Black-Oriented Radio; Disk Jockeys

Tom Joyner. Born in Tuskegee, Alabama, 1942. Bachelor's degree in Sociology, Tuskegee Institute, 1964; after graduation worked at radio stations WRMA-AM, Montgomery, Alabama; WLOK-AM, Memphis, Tennessee; KWK-AM, St. Louis, Missouri; worked at WJPC-FM (on-air personality and program director, 1978–83), WVON-AM, WGCI-FM, WBMX-FM, Chicago, Illinois; worked simultaneously at KKDA-AM, Dallas, Texas and WGCI-FM, Chicago, Illinois, earning him nickname "Fly Jock"; worked at KKDA-FM, Dallas, Texas; television producer and host, Ebony/Jet Showcase, 1982–83; host of ABC-syndicated radio show *Tom Joyner Morning Show,* 1994–; established Tom Joyner Foundation, 1998. Received four *Billboard Magazine* "Best Urban Contemporary Air Personality" awards; *Impact Magazine's* Joe Loris award for "Excellence in Broadcasting"; Mickey Leland Humanitarian Award, Congressional Black Caucus; named "Man of the Year", 100 Black Men; President's Award, NAACP; elected to the Radio Hall of Fame, 1998.

Radio Series
1980s	*On the Move*
1994–	*The Tom Joyner Morning Show*

Further Reading
Barlow, William, *Voice Over: The Making of Black Radio,* Philadelphia, Pennsylvania: Temple University Press, 1999

Newman, Mark, *Entrepreneurs of Profit and Pride: From Black-Appeal to Radio Soul,* Westport, Connecticut: Praeger, 1988; London: Praeger, 1989

Sherrell, Rick, "Tom Joyner, Playa Jock and King of the Hill," *Upscale Magazine* 9 (September/October 1998)

Sturgis, Ingrid, "Tom Joyner," *BET Weekend* (July/August 1998)

Williams, Gilbert Anthony, *Legendary Pioneers of Black Radio,* Westport, Connecticut: Praeger, 1998

Judis, Bernice 1900–1983

U.S. Station Manager

In the midst of network radio's golden age and on through television's first wave of success, Bernice Judis developed an inexpensive music-oriented radio program style that survived big-budget competition. Her implementation and massaging of the format over WNEW New York was analyzed and often imitated by countless media insiders from Los Angeles to Luxembourg.

Judis enjoyed admitting that she loved radio the way most men love fine cars. Reportedly, every room in her home, as well as a compartment in her handbag, was equipped with a receiver. She was always listening, or so it seemed: none of her announcers was exempt from an instructive studio hotline call, sometimes well past midnight. They affectionately nicknamed Judis "La Mama," though they never called into question their teacher's talent to motivate. Each remembered her as an executive with an instinct for hiring good people and then challenging them to be great. Even the disc jockey she fired for violating WNEW's "fashion code" by wearing red socks considered his strict boss a valued mentor.

Her entrance into broadcasting resulted from a friendship with a woman whose husband had recently purchased part interest in a radio station. In 1934 the well-heeled Judis had just returned from a European tour when her friend casually suggested that she help out the new enterprise. Within a year of Judis' agreeing to the request, her programming acumen was so evident that she graduated to general manager of fledgling WNEW.

The independent station had inadequate funding to stage the types of celebrity-oriented comedy, music, drama, or soap opera fare that was typically the province of network outlets. That never mattered, though, because Judis considered such offerings boring. She preferred a steady diet of positive pop tunes, and she maintained that others (especially young women, who often controlled the family radio dial) would share her tastes. One of her specialties was an instinct for hiring announcers who possessed the voice and ability to create a descriptive picture in the listener's mind. Judis looked for radio people ready to bloom into true "air personalities." Paramount was their potential to sell WNEW audiences the products offered by the station's growing list of advertisers.

Martin Block had a smooth spark in his delivery that Judis believed represented star quality. Her direction of the erstwhile $20-per-week announcer rocketed him to disc jockey stardom and, for years, propelled Block's *Make Believe Ballroom* program to highly salable ratings. Judis instructed him to work closer than normal to the microphone in order to generate an air of gentle romantic authority.

When authoritative columnist Walter Winchell wished (in print) for a radio station that would keep metropolitan New York's all-night work force company during the wee hours, Judis introduced the *Milkman's Matinee*. In 1936 the decision made WNEW a pioneer in 24-hour broadcasting. Although she scheduled some shows with live musicians, most of her format (including *Milkman's Matinee* and *Make Believe Ballroom*) was built around disc jockeys skillfully ad-libbing between recorded tunes. Prior to the late 1940s, most other big-city programmers considered transcriptions (in place of live bands and singers) the stuff of minor-league presentation. WNEW's shrewd manager used her sizable record library to offer people an anticipated radio staple: consistency in repeated elements. Such is the stuff that turns an ordinary song into a familiar hit recording. Literally hundreds of daily record requests flooded WNEW's switchboard. Some listeners sought to hear again and again obviously goofy selections the airstaff had spun purely as gags.

Judis is also known for adding non-musical content to what would be subsequently dubbed the "modern radio format." In the mid-1930s, Americans were gripped by the kidnapping of the infant son of transatlantic flight hero Charles Lindbergh. During the ensuing trial, the then novice WNEW official ordered her station's remote news crew to report proceedings directly from the New Jersey courthouse. Since their microphones were barred from courtroom use, Judis had her staff headquartered in the venue's nearest lavatory. Although at risk of transmitting indelicate sounds, these bathroom broadcasts were the sole electronic media offerings from inside the judicial building. Between reports, disc jockeys in the main studio played popular music. Listeners were captivated.

When the Japanese bombed Pearl Harbor, Judis was convinced that people would want more news. She scheduled round-the-clock, hourly (initially, on the half hour) newscasts by 1942—something no one else was doing. Judis' hunch quickly made "WNEW—Your station for music and news" an even more important companion for increasingly busy audiences. She rightly speculated that regular bites of pertinent information sandwiched between friendly disc jockeys conveying uplifting pop would yield a compelling soundtrack. At World War II's end, the Judis-directed WNEW targeted a young, urbane demographic, and her approach received high marks for successfully standing up to radio's postwar enemy: television.

When many radio veterans were moving to the expanding visual medium, Judis, along with her husband Ira Herbert, Rhode Island broadcaster William Cherry, and several others paid more than $2 million for WNEW. The savvy general manager and new part owner wagered that the spread of suburbs and concomitant commute of workers into cities would strengthen radio's influence, even in the face of television's quickly growing popularity. Judis met TV's evening primetime dominance by further tweaking her various 6 A.M. to 8 P.M. slots. Fourteen hours daily of popular music favorites, news briefs, and chatty disc jockeys gave ample opportunity for reaching the increasingly mobile and sophisticated thirty-something audience that corporate America's advertising agencies desperately sought to influence around the clock. People not glued to nighttime TV caught Judis' unique early-1950s counter-programming experiments. For example, she had disc jockeys spin spoken-word records, hired Milton Berle to do a serious Shakespeare performance, and tried a game show spoof in which contestants were eligible to lose their personal effects.

An attractive offer for WNEW led its owners to sell in 1954. With their share of the proceeds, Judis and her husband bought an interest in a Southern broadcast group. She oversaw the firm's Birmingham, Alabama, AM outlet. By the late 1960s, the couple had left the radio business. Judis died in Fort Lauderdale, Florida, in 1983.

PETER E. HUNN

See also Block, Martin; WNEW; Women in Radio

Bernice Judis. Born 1900. Only daughter of New York–area real estate tycoon; socialite activities and European travel, 1920s–early 1930s; New Jersey Women's Golf Champion, early 1930s, program director, WNEW New York, 1934; general manager, WNEW New York, 1935–54; part owner, WNEW New York, 1950–54; part owner of Basic Communications Stations, 1960s. Died in Fort Lauderdale, Florida, 24 May 1983.

Further Reading

Gordon, Nightingale, *WNEW: Where the Melody Lingers On*, New York: Nightingale Gordon, 1984

Passman, Arnold, *The DeeJays*, New York: Macmillan, 1971

"Radio Splits over Strategy against TV," *Business Week* (31 May 1952)

"Station WNEW Sold by Bulova and Biow for Substantially More than $2,000,000," *New York Times* (18 November 1949)

K

Kaltenborn, H.V. (Hans von) 1878–1965

U.S. Radio Commentator

Hans von Kaltenborn was radio's first news commentator and a pioneer in radio news for three decades. Prior to his broadcasting career, Kaltenborn engaged in newspaper reporting and editing and in public lecturing on current events. He is best remembered for his live broadcasts of battles during the Spanish Civil War, his marathon broadcasts of the 1938 Munich Crisis, and for President Harry S. Truman's mimicking of his 1948 election reports.

Origins

Kaltenborn was born in Milwaukee, Wisconsin, in 1878. His father, Baron Rudolph von Kaltenborn, was a former officer in the Hessian Army who came to the United States to protest the absorption of Hesse by Prussia. His mother, an American schoolteacher, Betty Wessels, died soon after Hans was born, and he was raised by a stepmother.

The family moved to Merrill, Wisconsin, when Hans was 14 years old. After only a year in high school, he ran away to work in a lumber camp. Then, for five years he worked for his father in the building material business and did odd jobs for the local newspaper, the *Merrill (Wis.) Advocate*. Later, while serving in the army during the Spanish-American War, young Hans sent articles about army life back to the *Merrill Advocate* and to the *Milwaukee Journal*. Although he did not leave the United States during the war, young Kaltenborn, who was athletic and nearly six feet tall, developed a desire for travel and adventure. After a short time as city editor of the *Merrill Advocate*, he worked his way to Europe in 1900 and spent the next two years in Germany and France. He attended the Paris International Exposition of 1900 and continued sending freelance news material back to newspapers in the United States. When he returned to the United States in 1902, he worked as a reporter and editor for the *Brooklyn Eagle*, a newspaper with which he would be associated, on and off, for about 27 years.

Lacking a high school diploma, Kaltenborn entered a special one-year program for journalists at Harvard College in 1903. After completing high school equivalency exams—he had great difficulty with the mathematics section—Kaltenborn was admitted as a regular student, majoring in political science. In 1909 he received his B.A. degree cum laude and was elected to the prestigious Phi Beta Kappa honor society. At Harvard, he debated, studied speech, won oratorical contests, ran cross country, organized a dramatic club, and perfected his distinctive German accent.

Following college, Kaltenborn traveled around the world on shipboard as a tutor to Vincent Astor. In 1910 he married Olga von Nordenflycht, a German baroness, and returned to the *Brooklyn Eagle*, for which he served as a Washington, and later, a Paris correspondent before being named the *Eagle's* war editor. With his growing reputation as a geopolitical expert, Kaltenborn delivered, as an *Eagle* editor, a series of weekly public talks about current events in the newspaper's auditorium.

On to Radio

In 1922 Kaltenborn delivered his first radio commentary from station WYCB on Bedloe's Island in New York Harbor. The following year, he became the first regularly scheduled radio commentator when the *Eagle* sponsored Kaltenborn's regular weekly news commentaries over WEAF in New York. He remained with the *Brooklyn Eagle* until 1930, when he joined the Columbia Broadcasting System (CBS) to devote himself full-time to radio news.

During the early 1930s, when wire service reports were seldom available to radio stations, CBS and the National Broadcasting Company (NBC) employed a number of experienced newsmen to comment on the day's events. Although Kaltenborn had the advantage of being the first radio

Paul White and H.V. Kaltenborn
Courtesy CBS Photo Archive

commentator, he also benefited from his speech training, his lecturing experience, and several other unique abilities, all of which kept him in the forefront of news commentary. His spoken delivery was distinctive—clipped, precise, and easy to understand even when he spoke at a rapid pace. Among his special attributes were a firsthand knowledge of many world leaders, whom he interviewed during frequent travels abroad; fluency in the French, German, and English languages; and training in world politics. Kaltenborn also had the advantage of being able to speak without a script. For many years he delivered his radio commentaries extemporaneously with only a few notes. He also extemporaneously described political conventions, international conferences, wars, and other crises.

One of Kaltenborn's early broadcast triumphs was his live description of a 1936 Spanish Civil War battle. Perched on a haystack on high ground in France overlooking a besieged Spanish town, the commentator, wearing a steel helmet, described the battle to CBS listeners in the United States. His report was accompanied by live sounds of machine-gun fire in the background. Radio's first on-air battle report, though physically risky for 58-year-old Kaltenborn and his engineer, added greatly to his stature as a radio newsman.

Two years later, Kaltenborn was called upon by CBS to coordinate and anchor a series of radio broadcasts during the Munich Crisis in 1938. At stake was the future of the Sudetenland, as Germany's dictator Adolph Hitler, British Prime Minister Neville Chamberlain, and other European leaders met to seek a solution to the conflict in Czechoslovakia. Kaltenborn's role was to interpret and analyze the wire dispatches, short-wave reports from CBS newsmen on the scene, and speeches by the participants. Relying on his ability to understand German and French, Kaltenborn translated and provided instantaneous commentary on the speeches of various government officials received in New York by shortwave. A *Time* reporter noted that without pause, Hans von Kaltenborn translated and distilled a 73-minute speech and then for 15 minutes proceeded extempore to explain its significance and to correctly predict its consequences. Kaltenborn remained at his post at CBS in New York for some 18 days, giving about 100 separate broadcasts. He subsisted mainly on soup brought to him by his wife and napped on a couch in the studio between the frequent broadcasts.

Because of a tendency for outspokenness on controversial issues, Kaltenborn had some difficulty keeping a sponsor during the 1930s. However, by the end of the decade the Pure Oil Company became Kaltenborn's regular sponsor on CBS. In 1940 the sponsor moved Kaltenborn's commentaries to NBC to get a better time on the evening schedule. Soon Kaltenborn's keen insight into geopolitical developments was evident in his warnings about Japanese aggression, including a warning only a few days before Pearl Harbor. During World War II, Kaltenborn was exempted from the Office of War Information's requirement that commentators not deviate from scripts submitted in advance of their broadcasts. Also during the war, Kaltenborn began using the initials *H.V.* to minimize his German ancestry.

In covering the 1948 presidential election while at NBC, Kaltenborn assured listeners that even though President Truman was running a million votes ahead in the early popular vote, when the rural votes came in, the winner would certainly be Thomas E. Dewey, the governor of New York. In probably the best-known instance of presidential mimicry of a news commentator, President Truman, at a post–election dinner, told the audience that he had heard Mr. Kaltenborn's broadcast. Then the president imitated the crisp Kaltenborn's remarks and said he just went back to sleep undisturbed. The next morning, the nation learned that, as Mr. Truman had never doubted, the president was reelected to serve a full four-year term.

Kaltenborn continued to broadcast his regular commentaries until 1953. Afterward, he did occasional broadcasts on a semi-retired basis until 1958. For 33 years, H.V. Kaltenborn had covered practically all of the world's major news events and had given the public his views on the meaning of the news. He also contributed to many magazines and was the author of several books. He spent his retirement years living in Florida and died in New York City in 1965 while visiting his son.

HERBERT H. HOWARD

Hans von Kaltenborn. Born in Milwaukee, Wisconsin, 9 July 1878. Served in U.S. Army, Spanish American War; worked as city editor, *Advocate*, Merrill, Wisconsin, 1899–1900; traveled in Europe, 1901–02; reporter, *Eagle*, Brooklyn, New York, 1902; attended Harvard University, B.A. in political science, 1909; returned to *Eagle*, 1910, correspondent in Washington and Paris, later served as *Eagle's* war editor; delivered first radio commentary from experimental station on Bedloe's Island, 1922; first regularly scheduled news commentator on WEAF, for *Eagle*, 1923; hired as full-time radio commentator by CBS, 1930; broadcast battle descriptions of Spanish Civil War live on CBS, 1936; broadcast 18-day coverage of Munich Conference from CBS in New York, 1938; moved to NBC, 1940; predicted Dewey victory in presidential election, 1948. Received Phi Beta Kappa, Harvard University, 1909; DuPont Foundation Award, 1945; honorary doctorates from University of Wisconsin and Hamilton College. Died in New York City, 14 June 1965.

Selected Publications

I Broadcast the Crisis, 1938
Fifty Fabulous Years, 1950
It Seems Like Yesterday, 1956

Further Reading

Culbert, David Holbrook, *News from Everyman: Radio and Foreign Affairs in Thirties America*, Westport, Connecticut: Greenwood Press, 1976

Downs, Robert Bingham, and Jane B. Downs, *Journalists of the United States*, Jefferson, North Carolina: McFarland, 1991

Fang, Irving E., *Those Radio Commentators!* Ames: Iowa State University Press, 1977

McKerns, Joseph P., editor, *Biographical Dictionary of American Journalism*, New York and London: Greenwood Press, 1989

Taft, William Howard, *Encyclopedia of Twentieth-Century Journalists*, New York: Garland, 1986

Karmazin, Mel 1943–

U.S. Radio Executive

There was no more powerful executive in radio in the last two decades of the 20th century than Mel Karmazin. After gaining a decade of experience in radio sales and management, Karmazin formed and ran Infinity's profitable group of radio stations during the 1980s. He then merged Infinity with the Columbia Broadcasting System (CBS) in the 1990s and moved to "Black Rock," the Eero Saarinen-designed headquarters building for CBS on 6th Ave in New York City, first to run its radio operation and then to head the entire company as it merged with media conglomerate Viacom. Karmazin brought effective consolidation and cost cutting to radio station and group operation as he headed CBS's second most lucrative division and radio's top revenue-producing chain as the 20th century ended.

Born and raised in Long Island City, New York, across the East River from Manhattan, Mel (never Melvin, his given name) worked days as an account executive at the Ziowe Advertising Agency in the city while attending Pace University at night. Upon graduation, he took a position in sales, rising quickly to manager at WCBS-AM, an all-news radio powerhouse located in the heart of Manhattan. During the 1970s, Karmazin worked for Metromedia, eventually rising to general manager of its WNEW-AM and FM combination. It was from this position that he launched Infinity Broadcasting and became his own boss at the age of 37.

As a manager, Karmazin became most famous for his relentless cost cutting and format switching. Yet he was willing to try any technique to raise profits. In 1993, for example, as others were selling radio networks, Karmazin purchased Westwood One; three years later, with the merger with CBS (for $5 billion), Karmazin lorded over all the major radio networks—save American Broadcasting Companies (ABC). These networks could and did feed programming cheaply not only to stations owned by Infinity and later CBS, but also to thousands of other stations across the United States.

Karmazin never sought to own all radio stations; instead, he aimed to group stations in nearly every major city—led by stations in the top four markets of New York City, Los Angeles, Chicago, and San Francisco. Under Karmazin, CBS owned far fewer radio stations than 1999 top dog Clear Channel Communications, yet its more than 160 radio stations earned just as much in revenues, as advertisers looked to radio in major markets to couple with television and newspapers to complete their advertising plans.

Thus, through radio station operation, Karmazin was able to quietly generate about half of CBS's profits in the late 1990s. Karmazin aimed to be either number one or two in every major radio market where CBS had stations. When Mel Karmazin succeeded Michael Jordan in 1998 in CBS's top executive position, he had already formulated this plan, and thereafter he always counted on squeezing significant profits from the CBS radio group while the world looked at the ups and downs of the far more famous television network. As the 1990s ended, Karmazin operated not only flagship WCBS-AM in New York City but dozens of other stations in the country's top-twenty media market cities, including eight stations in Los Angeles (the #2 media market) and seven in Chicago (#3).

Just after Labor Day 1999, a Hollywood company most people had never heard of—Viacom—took over CBS. Although the deal was announced by Sumner Redstone, chairman and chief executive officer of Viacom, Mel Karmazin was named president and chief executive officer of the new colossus. Redstone would step aside, and Karmazin would run the day-to-day operations. This made Karmazin one of mass media's top executives, with radio now only a part of his overall responsibilities.

Redstone and Karmazin's goal in the 21st century would be to make Viacom a media conglomerate the equal of Disney, Time Warner, or the News Corporation. Redstone retained his ownership majority and thus control of the new Viacom, and Karmazin took over day-to-day operations of a corporation able to produce, promote, distribute, and present all forms of mass entertainment, from radio and television to movies and music. With a portfolio of some of the world's most recogniz-

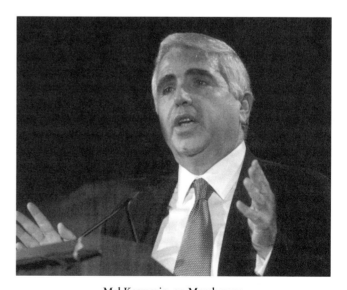

Mel Karmazin, 25 March 1999
Courtesy AP/Wide World Photos

able brands, Karmazin and Redstone boldly proclaimed global superiority for an operation conservatively estimated as worth $35 billion.

The union of CBS and Viacom promised to test the economic theory that owning significant stakes in many mass media can provide a synergy by which the parts together can produce more profits than if they operated individually. Could CBS's radio division cross-promote and make more profitable Viacom's cable music channels (MTV, VH1, and TNN)—and vice versa? Karmazin will test his management skills in an arena wider than radio, encompassing all of mass entertainment. Owner Sumner Redstone has passed the torch, because the fine print in the merger obligates him to stick with Karmazin until 2003.

DOUGLAS GOMERY

See also Columbia Broadcasting System; Infinity Broadcasting; Ownership, Mergers, and Acquisitions; Westinghouse

Mel Karmazin. Born in New York City, 24 August 1943. Grew up in Long Island City, Queens, New York; attended Pace University, B.A. in business administration, 1965; account executive for Ziowe Advertising Agency, 1966; sales manager, WCBS, New York, 1967–70; vice president and general manager, WNEW-AM and WNEW-FM, Metromedia, 1970–81; president of Infinity Broadcasting, 1981–96; CEO of CBS Station Group, 1996–98; president and CEO, CBS, 1999–present.

Further Reading

Compaine, Benjamin M., and Douglas Gomery, *Who Owns the Media?* 3rd edition, Mahwah, New Jersey: Erlbaum, 2000

Duncan, James H., Jr., "A Second Generation Enters the Radio Industry," *Duncan's Radio Comments* 16 (June 1996)

Fahri, Paul, "Justice Department Clears Westinghouse Purchase of Infinity," *Washington Post* (13 November 1996)

Rathbun, Elizabeth A., "CBS, ABC: Two Roads to Radio," *Broadcasting and Cable* (15 September 1997)

Siklos, Richard, "Reinventing CBS," *Business Week* (5 April 1999)

Kasem, Casey 1932–

U.S. Radio Personality

For many rock and roll fans, the name Casey Kasem is synonymous with the American Top 40 Countdown, a weekly radio program of the most popular songs in the United States. It was the first nationally syndicated countdown program, and as its host and one of its founders, Kasem's impact on the landscape of American popular music is undeniable. His voice is among the most recognizable in rock and roll, joining the likes of Wolfman Jack as both a disc jockey and a celebrity.

The son of Lebanese immigrants, Kemal Amen Kasem was born in 1932 in Detroit, Michigan. Upon graduating from Northwestern High School, Kemal became an intern at WDTR, Detroit Public School's radio station. From there, he attended Wayne State University, where he landed the lead role as "Scoop Ryan, Cub Reporter," the most popular show on the campus station. As a result of his success there, he earned his own 15-minute Saturday morning show on WJR, a 50,000-watt Detroit station. He also took a position as a full-time actor on WXYZ, an American Broadcasting Companies (ABC) affiliate.

In April 1952, Kasem was drafted for army service in Korea. Because of his broadcast experience, he was assigned to Radio Station Kilroy, an Armed Forces Radio Network Affiliate in Taegu, Korea, where he started his own production team. After the war, he returned to Detroit and took a job as a newsman at WJBK, where he adopted the moniker "Casey at the Mike." After a successful stint of substituting for a disc jockey, Kasem became the station's primary disc jockey. That same year he became Krogo the Clown, hosting a children's TV program on WJBK-TV. He then left television to assist at his family's grocery store and finally relocated to Cleveland in 1959, where he took a job as a radio host at WJW.

The most prominent Cleveland disc jockey at this time was Mad Daddy (Pete Meyers), whose fast-talking, slang-laden, rhyming radio patter influenced Kasem's on-air personality. Kasem again used the nickname *Casey at the Mike*. In Cleveland, Kasem also hosted the television show *Cleveland Bandstand*, while working at WJW. The program was canceled after

Casey Kasem
Courtesy of Casey Kasem

a few months, and WJW switched formats, so he began looking for other work.

Kasem worked at WBNY in Buffalo and KEWB in Oakland before arriving at KRLA in Los Angeles in 1963. During the process, Kasem shed his comic routines and fast talk, and became a more serious, informative disc jockey following his chance discovery of a 1962 copy of "Who's Who in Pop Music," which he used thereafter to provide his listeners with information on bands and singers.

In Los Angeles, Kasem began calling himself simply *Casey Kasem*, a simpler and more serious name than *Casey at the Mike*, and he was hired by Dick Clark to host an *American Bandstand*–type program called *Shebang*, which ran on KTLA from 1965 to 1968. Kasem made his mark on the program by improvising his introductions rather than reading the prewritten cue cards. Mike Curb, a producer for Tower Records, introduced Kasem to the world of commercial voice-overs, which eventually led to his two biggest roles off the radio dial: providing the voice of Robin on the cartoon series *Batman and Robin* and also the voice of Shaggy on *Scooby Doo, Where Are You?* In addition, he provided voices for countless other cartoon shows and promotions for the National Broadcasting Company (NBC) network.

In late 1968, Kasem reunited with his old friend Don Bustany and created Kasem-Bustany productions, which they operated from Kasem's Hollywood apartment. In the summer of 1969, Kasem and Bustany met with Tom Rounds, an executive at Charlatan Productions, and Ron Jacobs, a respected program director in Los Angeles. Rounds and Jacobs had earlier formed Watermark Productions, a Los Angeles radio production company. With the financial backing of Tom Driscoll, heir to a strawberry-growing fortune, Kasem, Bustany, Rounds and Jacobs laid the groundwork for *American Top 40 (AT40)*, which would change Casey Kasem from a local disc jockey to a household name. *Casey's Coast to Coast*, in partnership with *Billboard Magazine*, was launched on 3 July 1970, a Friday night, at 7:00 P.M., by KDEO in El Cajon, a suburb of San Diego.

In order to increase its exposure, *AT40*'s creators bartered with stations; for instance, they would provide a three-hour *AT40* program, and the station would receive airtime for two advertisements in exchange. However, in late 1971 Rounds decided to begin selling *AT40* for varying amounts depending on the size of the market. (The show lost approximately $600,000 before it began to turn a profit.) In 1973 Kasem produced a special episode called "The Top 40 Disappearing Acts," a show based on one-hit wonders. This show highlighted his talent with human-interest storytelling and helped to put *AT40* on the map.

During the 1970s, musicians began to record much longer songs, which made the three-hour format difficult to maintain. So in 1978, *AT40* expanded to four hours, and Kasem introduced two other signature features of the program. First, he would begin each program by playing the top three songs from the past week's countdown. This served as a teaser for the listening audience. Second, he would introduce the "long-distance dedication," *AT40*'s most popular feature. On 26 August 1978, Kasem played Neil Diamond's "Desiree."

Kasem's work on the program was publicly recognized on 26 April 1981, when he received a star on Hollywood's Walk of Fame. His charm, storytelling ability, and embracing voice made *AT40* the most popular radio program in history, with an audience stretching from coast to coast. In 1988, he left *AT40* to begin *Casey's Top 40* for the Westwood One Radio Network, which he broadcast until March 1998, when he made a triumphant return to *AT40*. Kasem and Bustany bought the program, and revived it 38 months after it had been taken off the air.

Kasem's return to his countdown roots and the rebirth of his signature program seem to exemplify the phrase with which he ended each program: "Keep your feet on the ground and keep reaching for the stars."

ARI KELMAN

See also American Top 40; KRLA

Casey Kasem. Born Kemal Amen Kasem in Detroit, Michigan, 27 April 1932. Son of Amin and Helen Kasem, Lebanese immigrants; attended Wayne State University, 1948–52; worked at WJR and WXYZ Detroit, 1950–52; served in Korean War as broadcaster on Radio Station Kilroy, Taegu, Korea, 1952–56; host, *Krogo the Clown*, WJBK-TV Detroit, 1956; disc jockey, WJW, Cleveland, 1959; disc jockey, KRLA, Los Angeles 1963–69; host, *Shebang*, KTLA-TV, Los Angeles, 1965–68; host, *American Top 40*, 1970–88, 1998–present.

Radio Series

1970–88, 1998–present	*American Top 40*
1988–98	*Casey's Top 40*

Selected Television Series

Krogo the Clown, 1956; *Shebang*, 1965–68

Films

The Girls from Thunder Strip, 1966; *The Glory Stompers*, 1967; *The Doomsday Machine*, 1967; *Wild Wheels*, 1969; *55,2000 Years Later*, 1969; *The Cycle Savages*, 1969; *Scream Free!* 1969; *The Transplant*, 1971; *The Incredible 2-Headed Transplant*, 1971; *The Night that Panicked America*, 1975; *The Day the Lord Got Busted*, 1976; *The Gumball Rally*, 1976; *New York, New York*, 1977; *Disco Fever*, 1978; *The Flintstones Meet Rockula and Frankenstone*, 1979; *Ghostbusters*, 1984; *The Transformers: The Movie*, 1986; *Wild Wheels*, 1992; *Mr. Wrong*, 1996; *Undercover Angel*, 1999

Further Reading

Durkee, Rob, *American Top 40: The Countdown of the Century*, New York: Schirmer Books, 1999

Fong-Torres, Ben, *The Hits Just Keep on Coming: The History of Top 40 Radio*, San Francisco: Miller Freeman Books, 1998

"Top 40 Rock Show Aims for 150 U.S. Cities," *Billboard* (11 July 1970)

KCBS/KQW

San Jose, California (Later San Francisco) Station

KQW, San Jose, was one of the pioneering radio stations in the United States, the eighth to receive a Department of Commerce license, which was granted on 9 December 1921. But the major significance of KQW was that its owner, Charles Herrold, was the first person to operate a broadcast station. And although being one of the earliest stations to go on the air is important, it is the story of how Herrold got there, beginning in 1909, that makes KQW important. Today KQW is the 50,000-watt all-news KCBS in San Francisco.

Charles Herrold, after dropping out of Stanford University in 1899 and spending a decade as a freelance inventor and college instructor, decided to go into business for himself. He borrowed money from his father and in 1909 opened the Herrold College of Wireless and Engineering in a downtown San Jose bank building. The purpose of the college was to prepare young men for what was becoming a lucrative profession: wireless operator. Herrold also had a vision of inventing a new technology for a radiotelephone. Wireless was primarily Morse code based, but several inventors were just beginning to find ways to make the wireless talk. Herrold had invented and patented a system based on an oscillating DC arc, a device with its roots in the bright arc lighting of the day. His patents were for a water-cooled carbon microphone, an array of arcs burning under liquid, and a unique antenna system.

Between 1912 and 1917 Herrold, his wife Sybil, and his assistants and students at the school began a broadcasting station, regular in schedule and announced in the newspapers, with programming consisting of phonograph music and news read from the local papers. It was new, it was popular, it attracted students to the college, and it allowed Herrold to have audio content for his radiotelephone inventing. Prior to 1912, the students on the air identified the station by saying, "This is the Herrold college station broadcasting from the Garden City bank in San Jose." Later, Herrold used the call sign FN, and in 1916 he received an experimental radiotelephone license, 6XE. The evidence indicates that Herrold's small audi-ences began to look forward to the broadcasts, and he would have continued them were it not for the United States' entry into World War I. In April 1917, all amateurs and experimenters were ordered to cease all radio activities.

When the ban on radio activity was lifted in 1919, the arc technology once used successfully by Herrold was obsolete. So in 1919, Herrold opened a store in San Jose and built radios as a source of income. He wanted to return to the air and broadcast as before, but he lacked money for the equipment. By December 1921, Herrold had applied for and received a license as KQW, and a new transmitter using vacuum tubes was put on the air.

Like many broadcasters in the early 1920s, Herrold did not have a way to support his station. Advertising was in its infancy, and local stations had to share dial space, making it difficult for listeners to separate stations amid the interference. Many stations were sold or just went off the air, their operators giving up. In 1925 Herrold turned over his KQW license to the First Baptist Church of San Jose. In exchange for the license, the church agreed to retain and pay Herrold as its chief engineer. After a year, his contract apparently up, the church, citing financial problems of its own, fired Herrold. A headline in the San Jose paper read, "Father of Broadcasting Fired!"

In 1926 Fred Hart approached the church and offered to run KQW and make a profit with agricultural programming. In return, Hart promised the Baptists that KQW would air their Sunday morning services. The station made money as an agricultural news outlet, and Hart soon bought the station. By the end of the 1920s, broadcasting was a fully formed business, but Fred Hart still had his eye on the historical significance of his station. Contacting Charles Herrold, then a freelance sales representative for several Bay Area stations, Hart asked Herrold to try to resurrect some of the early 1909 to 1917 history and bring in materials and photos of the early station, and a promotion was developed around this information.

In 1934 Hart sold KQW to Ralph Burton and Charles McCarthy of San Francisco, and its power was soon raised to 5,000 watts. In 1942 KQW began its affiliation with the Columbia Broadcasting System (CBS). The main studios were moved to the Palace Hotel in San Francisco, although legally KQW was still licensed to San Jose, so its transmitter had to remain there. KQW was an important station during World War II, acting as a relay for shortwave transmissions for the Pacific Coast, along with airing well-known CBS network personalities. In 1945 KQW attempted one final time to publicize its pioneer history. An engineer was sent with a disc recorder to the local rest home where the aging Charles Herrold was spending his final days. A one-hour historical documentary was written, produced, and aired, with Herrold's recorded voice used at the end of the show. The actor hired to portray Herrold was Jack Webb.

After the end of World War II, KQW and CBS fought a long Federal Communications Commission battle with another station over the rights to relocate to 740 kilohertz and to increase power to 50,000 watts. In 1949 the call letters were changed from KQW to KCBS, and the transmitter was relicensed and legally moved to San Francisco; a 50,000-watt transmitter went into operation in 1951. Throughout the 1950s KCBS operated as a "full-service" station, airing a combination of news, personality, music, and CBS network offerings.

It was not until the late 1950s that CBS rediscovered that KCBS might have some status as a pioneer station. Research leading to this celebration began in 1958, when San Jose State University professor Gordon Greb discovered the Herrold history in a private local museum. The curator had pieces of the early Herrold arc transmitter technology and strong evidence that the long-forgotten broadcasts took place. Greb located the still-living witnesses to the events, including Herrold's first wife and son and former students and teachers at the Herrold school. Greb located a collection of Herrold correspondence, patents, and photographs from the important pre-1920 period. In 1959, 50 years after Herrold's 1909 beginning, a "50th Anniversary of Broadcasting" was staged by KCBS and San Jose State University's journalism department. A Herrold arc transmitter was reassembled from parts found in a local museum, and dignitaries and personalities from CBS in New York were brought to San Jose, where dinners and a parade highlighted a week of celebration. Several historical audio documentaries were aired, and a congressional resolution pro-

claiming KCBS the first radio station was read into the public record in Washington, D.C.

Then the most important event in the Herrold/KQW/KCBS story took place: the publication in 1959 of Greb's article in the *Journal of Broadcasting*. This story of Charles Herrold not only became the scholarly basis for the KCBS claim but also provided the historical community with evidence of Herrold's work, which has found its way into subsequent broadcast history texts.

What about the KCBS claim of "first station?" The most significant study on first broadcaster claims was published in the *Journal of Broadcasting* in 1977. In a study of four claimants by two respected historians, it was determined that KDKA in Pittsburgh could claim the title of "oldest station," because that station began on the air in 1920 and has continued, uninterrupted, to broadcast up until the present. KCBS, because of the lapse between when Herrold left the air during World War I and his return as KQW in 1921, was deemed not to be the oldest, but it could legitimately claim to be the "first station." In an ironic twist, the two large station owners, Westinghouse with KDKA and CBS with KCBS, who battled for years in the court of public opinion for the title of first broadcaster, are today owned by the same company—Viacom.

MICHAEL H. ADAMS

See also CBS; Herrold, Charles D.; KDKA

Further Reading

Adams, Mike, producer, writer, and director, *Broadcasting's Forgotten Father: The Charles Herrold Story* (videorecording), <www.kteh.org/productions/docs/docherrold.html>

Baudino, J.E., and John M. Kittross, "Broadcasting's Oldest Stations: An Examination of Four Claimants," *Journal of Broadcasting* 21 (Winter 1977)

The Broadcast Archive: Radio History on the Web, <www.oldradio.com>

The Charles Herrold Historical Site, <www.charlesherrold.org>

Greb, Gordon, "The Golden Anniversary of Broadcasting," *Journal of Broadcasting* 3, no. 1 (Winter 1958–59)

Schneider John F., "The History of KQW/KCBS," Master's thesis, San Francisco State University, 1990

KCMO

Kansas City, Missouri Station

KCMO-AM is known both regionally and nationally for two reasons: (1) it was once a high-power, 50,000 watt station that could be received across a large portion of the Midwest; and (2) because the station once employed Walter Cronkite, who has mentioned it often in discussing his early career. Originally based in Kansas City, Missouri, its studios are now located in a nearby Kansas suburb. It now operates on 10,000 watts during the day and 5,000 watts at night.

The KCMO call was first used in 1936 for a station formerly known as KWKC (which had been on the air since the 1920s) that was taken over by investors Lester E. Cox and Thomas L. Evans. By the mid-1930s, the station suffered from low power (100 watts) and no network affiliation.

Walter Cronkite, who worked for the station at that time, recalled in his biography that KCMO did not subscribe to a news wire. Cronkite, who was assigned the air name "Walter Wilcox" while at KCMO, recalls announcing sports play by play (from Western Union telegraph wire dispatches), covering news, and eventually leaving the station (but not before meeting his wife-to-be Betsy Maxwell, another station employee) when he had a dispute with management over how to react to reports of a fire at City Hall. Cronkite's version of the story is that he wanted to verify the seriousness of the fire—which turned out to be minor—with the fire department, but the station's program manager wanted to go on the air with false reports of people jumping from the building. Cronkite says that he was fired for "daring to question management's authority" and that his KCMO experience "cooled any thought I had that radio might be an interesting medium in which to practice journalism" (*A Reporter's Life*, 1996).

KCMO made major advances in solving its coverage problems by increasing to 1,000 watts in 1939 (the same year it received National Broadcasting Company [NBC] network affiliation), to 5,000 watts in 1940, and to 50,000 watts (daytime, with reduced power at night) in 1947, at which time it was assigned the frequency of 810 AM, which it occupied until the late 1990s.

The station's most stable period (and its longest continuity of ownership) began not in the golden age of radio, but as radio was being surpassed by television in 1953, when the Meredith Corporation purchased KCMO at a cost of $2 million. Under Meredith, the station heavily promoted the range and quality of signal that its 50,000 watts gave it, allowing it to reach listeners across western Missouri, much of Kansas, and parts of Iowa and Nebraska. Despite its strong daytime signal, however, its reduced power and especially its directional pattern at night often resulted in poor reception after dark in the Kansas suburbs.

Under Meredith, the station built a strong news department, and from the 1950s through the 1970s KCMO offered popular and country music formats (at one time referring to its air sound as a combination of the two). After serious losses in ratings in the late 1970s, Meredith invested heavily in a news format in 1980, at one point employing well over a dozen people in news-related capacities alone. The hoped-for surge in audience never came, however, and the news format evolved to a less expensive talk format, which also failed to move the station to a dominant position in the market. In 1983 Meredith sold KCMO to Fairbanks Communications, beginning a string of ownership changes with subsequent sales to Summit (1983), Gannett (1986), Bonneville (1993), Entercom (1997), and Susquehanna (2000).

MARK POINDEXTER

KDKA

Pittsburgh, Pennsylvania Station

KDKA in Pittsburgh began operation in 1920 and is often called the oldest regular broadcast station in the United States. The station, still owned by Westinghouse (now merged with Columbia Broadcasting System [CBS]), pioneered in many areas during its initial years on the air. Within months of its debut, the station broadcast the first regularly scheduled church services; the first program broadcast from a theater; the first on-air appearance by a Cabinet member (the Secretary of

War); and the first sporting event, a 10-round boxing match, soon followed by regularly broadcast baseball scores. KDKA developed the first orchestra exclusively used on radio, another precedent soon adopted by many other stations. The station had by then hired the first full-time radio announcer, Harold W. Arlin, a Westinghouse engineer. And a regular farm program was begun in mid 1921.

Westinghouse experimented with different means of extending and improving KDKA's signal. A shortwave station, KFKX, was placed on the air in Hastings, Nebraska, in 1923 and another followed in Pittsburgh. These and others lasted into World War II, eventually under government operation. They were one means of providing KDKA's "Far North Service" that sent the sounds of home to explorers and pioneers in northern Canada in the 1920s and early 1930s, often their only connection with the outside world.

Origins

KDKA radio began as experimental radio station 8XK in the Wilkinsburg, Pennsylvania, garage of Frank Conrad, an electrical engineer employed by the Westinghouse Corporation's East Pittsburgh plant. Conrad's experimental station was established as a point-to-point operation to test radio equipment manufactured by Westinghouse for U.S. military use in World War I. In 1919 the U.S. government canceled Westinghouse's remaining military contracts and the corporation was facing idle factories. Conrad was among the first to put his 8XK back on the air as an amateur radio telephone station and in contact with ham (amateur) radio operators. Conrad's main concerns were with the quality of his signal and the distance it would travel. He would read from newspapers and then await reports from listening posts commenting on the quality of the reception.

The people operating the listening posts soon tired of hearing news they had already seen in the newspapers and they grew weary of hearing Conrad's voice. One of them suggested that Conrad play a phonograph record. Conrad did so and soon the Westinghouse headquarters received a flood of mail requesting newer music and specific song titles. Frank Conrad had become the world's first disc jockey.

The news of Conrad's airborne music reached a department manager at Pittsburgh's Joseph Horne Department Store, who realized that people who wanted to listen to Conrad might want to purchase assembled radios. An ad was placed in the *Pittsburgh Sun*'s 29 September 1920 issue, featuring wireless sets for $10.00. That ad was seen by Harry P. Davis, a Westinghouse vice president who realized that a vast potential market could be developed for home wireless sets and that Westinghouse already had the ideal product: the SCR-70, a radio receiver made for the U.S. military in the recently concluded world war.

Decisions were made to move Conrad's station to the roof of the East Pittsburgh plant's administration building, to install a stronger transmitter, and to redesign the station for public entertainment. All was to be ready by early November 1920, a presidential election year. On 2 November, the Harding-Cox election results were broadcast by KDKA, the newly assigned call letters on its Department of Commerce license. The success of KDKA was rapidly assured, and soon many newspapers across the country were publishing the station's program schedule (usually an hour of music and talk in the evening).

According to Baudino and Kittross (1977), KDKA is the oldest U.S. station still in operation, as reckoned by the following standards: KDKA (1) used radio waves (2) to send out noncoded signals (3) in a continuous, scheduled program service (4) intended for the general public and (5) was licensed by the government to provide such a service.

Later Developments

The station's frequency shifted several times in the 1920s, between 950 and 980 kilohertz, and one final time in March 1941 (due to the North American Regional Broadcasting Agreement) to 1020 kilohertz, which it still uses. KDKA became a 50,000-watt clear channel operation by the late 1920s. In 1933, Westinghouse turned over daily management of KDKA and its other radio stations to the National Broadcasting Company (NBC) network, an arrangement that lasted until 1940.

Beginning in 1927, engineers experimented with FM transmission, using that mode for KDKA signals several hours a day. A Westinghouse commercial FM outlet was on the air in Pittsburgh by April 1942, initially programmed separately but simulcasting the AM outlet by 1948. Likewise, KDKA personnel experimented with a crude system of television in the late 1920s. However, a regular television operation appeared only when Westinghouse purchased DuMont's Channel 2 (then the only television station in Pittsburgh), dubbing it KDKA-TV, in January 1955.

As it did to most other stations, the decline of network programming brought hard times to KDKA for several years as management attempted a host of middle-of-the-road format ideas in the struggle to maintain listener loyalty, a challenge shared by other major market stations. In 1954 disc jockey Rege Cordic was hired from competing station WWSW and his huge morning drive-time popularity (in part because of his zany characters and fake commercials) helped propel KDKA up the ratings ladder over the next decade, until he left for Los Angeles. A decision in 1955 to resume broadcasts of Pittsburgh Pirates baseball games also contributed to KDKA's renewed popularity. Station newscasts expanded from several years of rip-and-read wire service-based summaries to a full news staff with substantial local presence.

The station celebrated its half-century anniversary in 1970 with considerable promotion and again laying claim to being the oldest radio station in the country. At that time it was the ratings leader in its market, reaching 50 percent more homes than its nearest competitor. In July 1982 KDKA became one of the first AM outlets to provide stereo service. A decade later the station switched from its long-time "full service" or "middle of the road" programming to take on a news/talk format that continued into the new century.

REGIS TUCCI AND CHRISTOPHER H. STERLING

See also Conrad, Frank; Group W.; Westinghouse

Further Reading

Baudino, Joseph E., and John M. Kittross, "Broadcasting's Oldest Stations: An Examination of Four Claimants," *Journal of Broadcasting* 21 (Winter 1977)

Davis, H.P., "The Early History of Broadcasting in the United States," Chapter 7, *The Radio Industry: The Story of Its Development,* Chicago: A.W. Shaw, 1928

Douglas, George H., "KDKA," *The Early Days of Radio Broadcasting,* Jefferson, North Carolina: McFarland, 1987

It Started Hear: The History of KDKA Radio and Broadcasting, Pittsburgh: Westinghouse, 1970

KDKA website, <www.kdkaradio.com>

Kintner, S.M., "Pittsburgh's Contributions to Radio," *Proceedings of the Institute of Radio Engineers* 20: 1849–1862 (December 1932)

Myer, Dwight A., "Up from a Bread-Board—KDKA's Tale," *Broadcasting,* 24 November 1941

Saudek, Robert, "Program Coming in Fine. Please Play 'Japanese Sandman'," *American Heritage: The Twenties* (August 1965)

Keillor, Garrison 1942–

U.S. Radio Humorist

Garrison Keillor is a public radio personality and writer best known for his variety program *A Prairie Home Companion,* which is produced live on Saturday evenings by Minnesota Public Radio (MPR) and distributed by Public Radio International (PRI). The program features a weekly monologue from Lake Wobegon, Keillor's fictitious hometown, where "all the women are strong, all the men are good looking, and all the children are above average." Keillor's main contribution to modern radio was to reintroduce the variety-show format. A *Time* magazine cover story called Keillor "a radio bard" and noted that his "storytelling approaches the quality of Mark Twain's."

Keillor was raised Gary Edward Keillor in a rural area eight miles outside of his hometown of Anoka, Minnesota. His family belonged to a conservative religious sect called the Plymouth Brethren, which shunned television and motion pictures but found enjoyment in a "strictly monitored" Zenith radio set. Keillor's early radio idol was Cedric Adams, star of Minneapolis Columbia Broadcasting System (CBS) station WCCO, which also carried variety shows such as *The Red River Valley Gang* and *The Murphy Barn Dance.* As a boy, Keillor would also pull in clear channel radio station signals carrying exotic rhythm and blues from far-away cities. At age 14 he discovered *The New Yorker* and dreamed of being a literary figure. In

1966 he graduated with a BA in English from the University of Minnesota, where he performed on radio station KUOM and edited the campus literary magazine.

He went to work for Minnesota Public Radio in 1969 at KSJR in the central Minnesota town of Collegeville. There he developed a three-hour morning program that evolved from classical music into an eclectic mix of musical styles that included folk, rock, and bluegrass. It was on this show that Keillor began referring on the air to the fictitious town of "Lake Wobegon." He published his first *New Yorker* fiction piece in 1970. Entitled "Local Family Keeps Son Happy," it was a short parody of small-town journalism about parents who hire a live-in prostitute to keep their teenager off the streets at night. Keillor quit radio in 1971 to concentrate on writing, but after six months he joined the staff at KSJN, MPR's St. Paul flagship station. In 1973 he again quit in order to write full-time.

During the summer of 1973, Keillor spent time listening to tapes of his boyhood WCCO radio favorites, including *The Red River Valley Gang,* which featured a regular monologue about the banjo player's visits to an uncle in North Dakota. That summer he also listened to tapes of Gene Autry programs from the "Melody Ranch" studio and to recordings of Smilin' Ed McConnell's vintage radio program, which also featured a

Garrison Keillor
Courtesy Radio Hall of Fame

story in the middle of the broadcast. When he returned to KSJN in 1974, Keillor called his morning program *A Prairie Home Companion*, its name taken from the Prairie Home cemetery in Moorhead, Minnesota. In April of 1974 he traveled to Nashville to cover the *Grand Ole Opry*'s last broadcast from the old Ryman Auditorium for *The New Yorker*. During and shortly after this trip, an idea crystallized in his mind. Keillor pitched to MPR his concept for a weekly, live, old-fashioned musical variety show revolving around a monologue about Lake Wobegon. On 6 July 1974 he hosted the first broadcast of the program, which, like his KSJN morning show, was called *A Prairie Home Companion*.

Despite the growing popularity of the program, National Public Radio (NPR) declined to distribute the show nationally because it felt the show was too regional, contributing to Minnesota Public Radio's decision to set up its own network, American Public Radio (APR; today called Public Radio International). National syndication on APR began in May 1980. The program won the George Foster Peabody Award for broadcast excellence in 1981. In 1985 Keillor married Ulla Skaerved, who had been a Danish exchange student at Anoka High School and with whom Keillor became reacquainted at their 25th class reunion. Two years later, as the Twin Cities newspapers ran front-page coverage of what Keillor considered his private affairs, he abandoned *A Prairie Home Companion* and moved to Denmark, and later New York. In 1989 he began a new radio show in New York called *The American Radio Company of the Air*, which was similar in format to his earlier program. In 1992 he moved the program's production site to St. Paul, and in 1993 he reclaimed the concept and the title of *A Prairie Home Companion*, which at the beginning of 2003 was heard by some 5 million listeners weekly on more than 450 public radio stations. Keillor continues to publish works of fiction and keeps a rural Wisconsin home outside of the Twin Cities, as well as a residence in New York City.

MARK BRAUN

See also Comedy; Minnesota Public Radio; Prairie Home Companion; Public Radio Since 1967

Garrison Keillor. Born Gary Edward Keillor in Anoka, Minnesota, 7 August 1942. Married Mary Guntzel, 1965; attended University of Minnesota, Minneapolis, B.A. in English, 1966; worked for Minnesota Public Radio, Collegeville station, KSJR, 1969–71; MPR's Saint Paul flagship KSJN, 1971–73, 1974–82; broadcast *A Prairie Home Companion* on Minnesota Public Radio, 1974–87; hosted *American Radio Company* (similar to *Prairie Home Companion*), New York, 1989–92; revived *A Prairie Home Companion*, 1993–present; hosts daily five-minute radio program, *The Writer's Almanac*, 1993–present; writes biweekly

romance advice column for online magazine *Salon*. Received National Humanities Medal, National Endowment for the Humanities, 1999; inducted into Radio Hall of Fame, Museum of Broadcast Communications, Chicago, 1994; George Foster Peabody Award, 1981; Edward R. Murrow Award, 1985; two ACE Awards for work in cable television, 1988; Grammy Award for recording of *Lake Wobegon Days*, 1985.

Radio Series

1974–87, 1993–present	*A Prairie Home Companion*
1989–92	*The America Radio Company of the Air*
1993–present	*The Writer's Almanac*

Selected Publications

Happy to Be Here, 1982
Lake Wobegon Days, 1985
Leaving Home: A Collection of Lake Wobegon Stories, 1987
Don: The True Story of a Young Person, 1987
We Are Still Married, 1989
WLT: A Radio Romance, 1991
The Book of Guys, 1993
Cat, You Better Come Home, 1995
The Old Man Who Loved Cheese, 1996
The Sandy Bottom Orchestra (with Jenny Lind Nilsson), 1996
Wobegon Boy, 1997
The Best American Short Stories (coedited with Katrina Kenison), 1998
Me: By Jimmy "Big Boy" Valente as Told to Garrison Keillor, 1999
Lake Wobegon Summer 1956, 2001
Good Poems (editor), 2002

Recordings

A Prairie Home Album, 1972; *The Family Radio*, 1982; *Gospel Birds and Other Stories of Lake Wobegon*, 1985; *Lake Wobegon Days*, 1986; *A Prairie Home Companion: The Final Performance*, 1987; *A Prairie Home Companion: The 2nd Annual Farewell Performance*, 1988; *More News from Lake Wobegon*, 1989; *Garrison Keillor's American Radio Company: The First Season*, 1990; *Local Man Moves to the City*, 1991; *Songs of the Cat*, 1991; *A Visit to Mark Twain's House with Garrison Keillor*, 1992; *The Young Lutheran's Guide to the Orchestra*, 1993; *A Prairie Home Companion 20th Anniversary Collection*, 1994; *A Prairie Home Christmas*, 1995; *The Hopeful Gospel Quartet: Climbing Up on the Rough Side*, 1997; *Garrison Keillor's Comedy Theater*, 1997; *Mother, Father, Uncle, Aunt: Stories from Lake Wobegon*, 1997; *The Best American Short Stories 1988* (coedited with Katrina Kenison), 1998; *Life These Days: Stories from Lake Wobegon, Vol. 2*, 1997; *A Prairie Home Companion*, 1999; *Me: By Jimmy "Big Boy" Valente As told to Garrison Keillor*,

1999; *A Prairie Home Commonplace Book: 25 Years on the Air with Garrison Keillor,* 1999; *A Prairie Home Companion: Pretty Good Joke Book,* 2000; *Definitely Above Average: Stories and Comedy for You and Your Poor Old Parents,* 2000; *Lake Wobegon Summer 1956,* 2001; *Good Poems,* 2002; *A Few More Pretty Good Jokes,* 2002

Further Reading

Baenen, Jeff, "Books and Authors: Garrison Keillor Spins More Tales from Lake Wobegon," *New York Times* (16 May 1990)

Fedo, Michael, *The Man from Lake Wobegon,* New York: St. Martin's Press, 1987

Karlen, Neal, "A Prodigal Son Makes His Way Home," *New York Times* (27 March 1994)

Lee, Judith Yaross, *Garrison Keillor: A Voice of America,* Jackson: University Press of Mississippi, 1991

Minnesota Public Radio: A Prairie Home Companion: Garrison Keillor, <www.prairiehome.org/cast/garrison_keillor.shtml>

Scholl, Peter A., *Garrison Keillor,* New York: Twayne, and Toronto, Ontario: Macmillan Canada, 1993

Kent, A. Atwater 1873–1949

U.S. Radio Inventor and Manufacturer

From 1921 to 1935 A. Atwater Kent's company was one of the most important U.S. manufacturers of radio receivers.

Early Years

Born in New England of an upper-middle-class family, A. Atwater Kent (he never used his first name) attended the private Wooster Polytechnic Institute from 1895 to 1897 but left before graduating to enter business. (Three decades later, he was awarded an honorary doctorate by the institution, whose laboratory he endowed in his will.) His father had been a part-time inventor and machinist before becoming a doctor, and his handiwork may have been the son's first exposure to mechanical devices. Kent's first foray into the working world came with the Kent Electric Manufacturing Company, which he formed in about 1895, with financial support from his father, and which made small electric motors, fans, and even "Amperia," a battery-powered electrical game. Although this foretold his future, it may not have been financially successful, because in about 1900 he sold his firm to Kendrick and Davis of Lebanon, New Hampshire, and briefly worked for that company.

The central part of his career came with his formation of the Atwater Kent Manufacturing Works in downtown Philadelphia in 1902. The new company made telephones, small voltmeters, and other small electrical devices. Three years later the product line was expanded to include automobile devices, including the 1906 Kent-invented spark generator ignition system, later dubbed the "Unisparker," that remained widely used into the 1970s. By the end of his life, Kent would hold 93 patents granted from 1901 to 1943.

During World War I the Kent company, by now located on Stenton Avenue in Germantown just north of center-city Philadelphia, manufactured military equipment for the U.S. Army, including a panoramic gun sight, fuse-setting equipment, a gun-training (aiming) theodolite, and a device to precisely incline a rifle. Using his trained staff, which in 1919 numbered about 125, and the manufacturing facilities developed during the war (which after wartime contracts were completed or terminated would otherwise become largely redundant), Kent's company joined the postwar bandwagon to radio receiver manufacturing. Though other firms were also entering the radio market, Kent's company enjoyed the benefits of extensive manufacturing expertise and facilities as well as an existing chain of dealerships for his automobile and electrical devices.

Radio Years

The Atwater Kent firm began selling radio receiver components in late 1921, trading on its reputation and network of dealers. Just a year later Atwater Kent radio advertising depicted fully assembled receivers in response to the growing demand for sets. The several initial models were dubbed "breadboards" because they lacked an external case and arranged their components along a wooden base. Over several years more than 120,000 steadily improved breadboard models were sold. Though successful, the radio market was changing and demanded furniture-like devices rather than experimental-looking breadboards. The company needed more space and was unable to expand in Germantown, so a new 20-acre site on Wissahickon Avenue was purchased and a

Atwater Kent, 24 November 1942
Courtesy AP/Wide World Photos

new factory begun, the first part of which began turning out radios in 1923.

The first fully enclosed Atwater Kent receivers, the Model 20, appeared in April 1924. By the end of 1926 the company had manufactured 1 million radio receivers and was making them at the rate of more than 5,000 a day, or 11 sets per minute. The factory had been enlarged twice so that the roof covered 15 acres, a feature often noted in company advertising featuring the plant. By then virtually all radios were offering single-dial tuning, which was far easier to operate than the multiple dials required before. By late 1927 the company offered metal-encased AC-powered receivers that plugged into a wall socket, dispensing with heavy and messy batteries. The trend to ever-bigger and fancier radios worked well through the late 1920s. A 16.5-acre addition to the manufacturing plant opened in 1929; together all the buildings presented a half-mile frontage on Wissahickon Avenue.

The Atwater Kent company sponsored the popular *Atwater Kent Hour* of concert and opera music, which first aired in 1925 on New York station WEAF and its hookup of stations. The program was continued on the new National Broadcasting Company (NBC) network from 1926 to 1931 and again briefly as a half-hour program on the Columbia Broadcasting System (CBS) in the fall of 1934. As a pioneering radio manufacturer, Kent was one of several hundred delegates to the 1924 and 1925 National Radio Conferences called by Secretary of Commerce Herbert Hoover, which called for a stronger governmental role in the licensing of stations.

The coming of the Great Depression in 1929 brought tighter competition from a number of small-radio manufacturers seeking to meet growing demand for less-expensive receivers. But the Atwater Kent firm had moved to manufacturing larger console radio models with higher profit margins—a classic case of poor timing. Atwater Kent models only belatedly met the demand for smaller sets as factory production peaked in about 1931. From that point on, however, production slipped, and little new research or improvement on receiver models took place. Parts of the newly enlarged factory lay idle. The added competition and lower profit margins from smaller receivers caused Kent to lose interest in the business.

Final Years

The company ceased operations in 1936, and Kent destroyed the firm's remaining records. Through his foundation he endowed the Atwater Kent Museum (1938), which focuses on social history and everyday life in Philadelphia, and purchased and refurbished the Betsy Ross Home in the same city. Kent retired to Hollywood, California, and lived a lavish retirement until his death there in 1949. An Atwater Kent Manufacturing Company (Wilmington, Delaware) still exists; now an investment entity, it is controlled by the family and retains some family papers.

CHRISTOPHER H. STERLING

See also Receivers

Arthur Atwater Kent. Born in Burlington, Vermont, 3 December 1873. Son of Prentiss J. Kent, physician, and Mary Elizabeth Atwater; formed Kent Electric Manufacturing Company, 1895; attended Wooster Polytechnic Institute, 1895–97; formed Atwater Kent Manufacturing Works, 1902–36; awarded John Scott Legacy Medal from Franklin Institute, 1914; delegate to National Radio Conferences, 1924; received honorary degree, Wooster Polytechnic Institute; endowed Atwater Kent Museum, Philadelphia, 1938. Died in Hollywood, California, 4 March 1949.

Further Reading

A.W.A. Review 12 (1999) (special issue edited by Ralph O. Williams entitled "The Atwater Kent Radios")

Douglas, Alan, "Atwater Kent," in *Radio Manufacturers of the 1920s*, by Alan Douglas, vol. 1, Vestal, New York: Vestal Press, 1988

Kraeuter, David W. "A. Atwater Kent (1873–1949)," in *Radio and Television Pioneers: A Patent Bibliography*, by Kraeuter, Metuchen, New Jersey: Scarecrow Press, 1992

Williams, Ralph O., "Atwater Kent Early Radio Development," *The A.W.A. Review* 1 (1986)

Williams, Ralph O., "Atwater Kent: Master of Marketing," *The A.W.A. Review* 10 (1996)

Kesten, Paul 1898–1956

U.S. Radio Network Executive

Paul Kesten served as a key Columbia Broadcasting System (CBS) executive who helped to shape the network through the end of World War II. Before retiring because of ill health, he was the likeliest heir-apparent to network chief William Paley, having run CBS during the latter's wartime service.

Early Years

Born in Milwaukee in 1898, Kesten was the son of George Henry Keston (a pharmacist and optometrist) and Lucy (Davies) Keston. He attended high school in Milwaukee and briefly attended but did not graduate from the University of Wisconsin, Madison. He joined the U.S. Marine Corps in 1918 but was released a few months later at the war's conclusion.

For the next dozen years, he held a number of advertising positions, first in Milwaukee, then Chicago, and finally New York. He began as the assistant advertising manager for the Gimbels' Department Store in Milwaukee late in 1918, becoming manager in 1919. The next year he moved to the McJunkin Advertising Agency in Milwaukee and remained there as vice president and advertising manager until 1922. He returned to the retail clothing business as vice president and advertising manager for Foreman and Clark, a clothing store chain, for four years. In 1926–27, he took a year off and studied abroad at the Sorbonne, Oxford, and Heidelberg, among other places, before returning to Foreman and Clark. Kesten moved to New York as a copywriter for the Lennon and Mitchell agency in 1929.

Radio and CBS

Kesten moved into radio when Edward Klauber of CBS hired him as the first director of sales promotion for the network in 1930. As network founder William Paley later noted, Kesten "just bubbled from the start with ideas and strategies for promoting the network." But perhaps more important—and a key to Kesten's rapid career growth from that point—was how closely he "clicked" with the boss. Paley relates:

Kesten and I were so compatible that we understood each other in a kind of mental shorthand. We could cover a lot of ground in a few minutes of conversation. We saw eye to eye from the start on the importance of design and good taste. In those early days it was necessary to persuade some advertisers about what was tasteful and effective in the spoken advertisement on radio. Kesten had a feeling for elegance and taste along with a

touch of majesty, with which he presented the image of CBS to certain advertisers. We proved to be able to work together as a unique and effective team (Paley, 1979).

Kesten's interest in fine arts, literature, and the theater paralleled Paley's and contributed to their good working relationship—and to Kesten's work for the network. This is especially evident, even today, in the host of research and promotion publications issued by the network, nearly all under Kesten's direct supervision, in the early 1930s. Each assessed some aspect of radio and featured CBS. They were handsomely designed and printed efforts—many in hardcover formats—far above the normal throwaway material issued by most companies of the time. Some featured strikingly handsome art deco photography and multicolor graphics. Most of them dealt with aspects of radio's audience and how that audience might best be reached (through CBS, of course) by advertisers. To many, Kesten was the father of the network's image.

Kesten also made his mark in his decisions to hire others. In 1935 he brought on Frank Stanton to work on audience research (Stanton would eventually succeed him as senior network officer under Paley in 1946), and he hired engineer Peter Goldmark in 1936. Encouraging the work of the latter, Kesten committed CBS to a strong television developmental effort. By 1940 he strongly backed Goldmark's system of semi-mechanical color transmission, which was designed to operate on UHF frequencies. Kesten was soon dubbed the "vice president in charge of the future" around CBS headquarters. Kesten persuaded Paley to bet much of the network's future on Goldmark's color system, a decision that would cost CBS heavily by the early 1950s, long after Kesten had left, when the network belatedly had to develop its own stations and operations in black and white.

As Kesten rose in the hierarchy of the expanding network—becoming a network vice president in 1934 and a member of the board of directors three years later—he increasingly clashed with his chief rival, ironically the man who had originally hired him, Edward Klauber. Men of very different character and personalities, both were featured as key network executives in a warm *Fortune* essay in the middle of the decade.

For a variety of reasons, chief among them Klauber's difficult personality, Kesten won out in 1942, becoming general manager of the network when his senior colleague left in 1942. For all practical purposes, Kesten was already running CBS when Paley left for war work in Europe. Kesten became executive vice president and chief executive officer for two years in Paley's absence, 1943–45. At the same time, he served as a director of the National Association of Broadcasters (1942–44) representing CBS and as director of the War Advertising Council. Kesten was one of the industry's leading figures.

Final Years

During this period, he formed firm ideas about how best to develop CBS in the face of fierce competition from the National Broadcasting Company (NBC). On Paley's return in 1945, Kesten gave him a 15-page design for the network's future, arguing that CBS should concentrate on educated and cultivated listeners rather than on mass-appeal programs. He felt strongly that the network should play up what both Kesten and Paley had often discussed before the war—radio's proven ability to bring culture and elite-appeal programs into discerning homes. For perhaps the first time in their working relationship, Paley was appalled. He saw Kesten's plan as a surrender to NBC's hegemony, and he was having none of it. In many discussions, the two sharply disagreed over the future direction of the network.

Yet at the same time, Paley could see what Kesten had done for CBS. And being unsure of his own future plans, Paley offered Kesten a continuing top role, essentially working as in partnership. He was genuinely shocked when Kesten turned him down, first in 1945 and more finally a year later. Pleading ill health (Kesten had suffered serious arthritis for years), but also no longer comfortable working for Paley, both because of their divergent visions of CBS's future and because of Paley's increasingly autocratic ways, Kesten moved up to be vice chairman of the CBS board before his final retirement from the network in August 1946.

Kesten lived for another decade, but he played no further role in broadcasting save for occasional consulting work with CBS. He became vice chairman of the fledgling company Cinerama, working to develop a wide-screen system for theatrical films. Foreseeing television's impact on motion pictures, he worked to help the film industry develop one of the means of holding audiences in the face of the electronic box in the living room. He married late in life and spent more time on the arts that he had always enjoyed. But his health continued to deteriorate, and he died at age 58 in late 1956.

CHRISTOPHER H. STERLING

See also Columbia Broadcasting System; Klauber, Edward; Paley, William S.; Stanton, Frank N.

Paul W. Kesten. Born in Milwaukee, Wisconsin, 30 August 1898. Son of George Henry, pharmacist and optometrist, and Lucy (Davies) Klauber; attended University of Wisconsin; joined U.S. Marine Corps, 1918; assistant advertising manager, Gimbels' Department Store, Milwaukee, 1918, manager, 1919; vice president and advertising manager for McJunkin Advertising Agency, Milwaukee, 1920–22; vice president and advertising manager for Foreman and Clark, a clothing store chain, 1922–26; studied at University of Sorbonne, University of Oxford, and University of Heidelberg, 1926–27; copywriter, Lennon and Mitchell agency, New York City, 1929; joined CBS as director of sales promotion, 1930, became vice president, 1934, Class A Director (Board of Directors), 1937, general manager, 1942–43, executive vice president and CEO, 1943–45; concurrent service as director of War Advertising Council; resigned as vice chairman of the board, becoming executive consultant, 1946; vice-chairman, Cinerama Inc., 1946. Died in Great Barrington, Massachusetts, 5 December 1956.

Selected Publications
"Merchandizing a Radio Program," in *Radio and Education 1932*, edited by Josephine H. MacLatchey, 1932

Further Reading
"And All Because They're Smart," *Fortune* 11 (June 1935)
Columbia Broadcasting System, "Publications of the Columbia Broadcasting System," in *Radio and Television Bibliography*, New York: CBS, 1942
Paley, William S., *As It Happened: A Memoir*, Garden City, New York: Doubleday, 1979
Slater, Robert, *This . . . Is CBS: A Chronicle of 60 Years*, Englewood Cliffs, New Jersey: Prentice-Hall, 1988

KFFA

Helena, Arkansas Station

Starting in the 1940s, KFFA played an important role in disseminating blues music to black listeners throughout the upper Mississippi Delta region of the mid-South. The primary showcase for the station's blues offerings was the *King Biscuit Time*, a program that gave valuable exposure to blues performers and that inspired various young black listeners to pursue careers in blues music. The station's black-appeal programming also served as an example to other stations in the region that would later target the black audience.

Sam W. Anderson, a former superintendent of schools in Dyess, Arkansas, conceived the idea of establishing KFFA and recruited John Thomas Franklin and J.Q. Floyd to join him in the investment. Operating as the Helena Broadcasting Company, the men put the station on the air on 19 November 1941. Within a few months, KFFA was carrying a regularly scheduled blues music program.

At the time of KFFA's inception, blacks in the Mississippi Delta region had begun enjoying a measure of increased prosperity, in part because wage labor in farming had replaced the sharecropping system. As a result, businesses had begun marketing more frequently to blacks. Max Moore, who distributed flour through his Interstate Grocer Company, was seeking to market a high-quality flour to blacks and approached KFFA about sponsoring a program that would reach his target population. The new station, ready to try anything that might succeed, inaugurated *King Biscuit Time*, which aired blues music from 12:15 to 12:30 P.M. Monday through Friday. Named for Moore's high-grade flour, the show featured bluesman Rice Miller (also known as Sonny Boy Williamson II), a harmonica player who attracted a large number of listeners who, in turn, began to spend their dollars on the sponsor's product. The show became so popular that Moore began marketing to blacks a cornmeal dubbed "Sonny Boy Meal" after *King Biscuit Time*'s star.

Although KFFA and Max Moore paid Rice Miller very little, the musician could advertise his gigs, which helped fill the venues he played. Club owners, therefore, were more likely to book Miller and to pay him more because of his radio-fueled prominence. Shortly after *King Biscuit Time* debuted, Miller, who had initially performed solo, began recruiting a band for the broadcast. First came Robert Lockwood Jr. on guitar, and then James "Peck" Curtis on drums and Robert "Dudlow" Taylor on piano. Exposure on KFFA helped promote these men's careers. Furthermore, throughout the 1940s and 1950s bluesmen such as Muddy Waters, Little Walter Jacobs, Houston Stackhouse, Robert Nighthawk, Joe Willie "Pintop" Perkins, and Willie Love appeared on KFFA, reaching audiences that otherwise would never have heard their music; each would go on to enjoy influential careers in the world of blues music.

As KFFA became an important amplifier for blues music in the 1940s, it was inevitable that aspiring blues performers would be influenced by the music and musicians they heard on the station. James Cotton, a well-known harmonica player, was so inspired by the sounds he heard as a child on *King Biscuit Time* that he traveled to Helena to learn from Rice Miller. America's foremost blues performer, B.B. King, also paid close attention to the sounds of *King Biscuit Time* during his boyhood in the Mississippi Delta. "We'd come in from the fields for our noon meal and relax by listening to Sonny Boy," wrote King in his 1996 autobiography. "He had him some famous songs like 'Fattening Frogs for Snakes,' but nothing made him as famous as this show, sponsored by King Biscuit Flour. I'd been listening to it so long, I felt like I knew Sonny Boy personally."

In the immediate wake of *King Biscuit Time*'s burgeoning success, other blues music shows joined the KFFA schedule as advertisers saw the value of reaching the black audience. By the mid-1950s, more than 30 hours of KFFA's weekly programming was black oriented. The station's success with the black-appeal programming that began in the early 1940s served as a significant model for other stations. The station helped fuel a small groundswell of black-oriented programming in the mid-South and was a major impetus in the rapidly growing number of black voices that actually appeared behind the microphones on mid-South radio in the 1940s. The growth of black-oriented programming on mid-South stations like KFFA culminated in the all-black format that debuted on Memphis radio station WDIA in 1949. Just as KFFA promoted the dissemination of blues music, it also promoted black-appeal programming.

Except for a few years in the 1980s, KFFA's *King Biscuit Time* has continued to broadcast on weekdays around noontime, but now disc jockey Sonny Payne provides the music. Payne, who was working at KFFA on the day Rice Miller debuted on *King Biscuit Time*, has carried on the blues tradition at the station, featuring plenty of Rice Miller's recordings and helping to coordinate Helena's annual King Biscuit Blues Festival. KFFA is currently owned by Delta Broadcasting, which bought the station from the Helena Broadcasting Company in 1980.

MICHAEL STREISSGUTH

See also Black-Oriented Radio; Blues Format; King Biscuit Flower Hour

Further Reading

Cantor, Louis, *Wheelin' on Beale: How WDIA-Memphis Became the Nation's First All-Black Radio Station and Created the Sound That Changed America,* New York: Pharos Books, 1992

Dates, Jannette Lake, and William Barlow, editors, *Split Image: African Americans in the Mass Media,* Washington, D.C.: Howard University Press, 1990

George, Nelson, *The Death of Rhythm and Blues,* New York: Pantheon Books, 1988

Hoffman, Larry, "Interview with Robert Lockwood, Jr.," *Living Blues* 26, no. 3 (June 1995)

Khatchadourian, Sonia, "A Ray of Sunshine in the Blues," *Living Blues* 22, no. 3 (May/June 1991)

King, B.B., and David Ritz, *Blues All around Me: The Autobiography of B.B. King,* New York: Avon Books, and London: Sceptre, 1996

Newman, Mark, *Entrepreneurs of Profit and Pride: From Black-Appeal to Radio Soul,* New York: Praeger, 1988; London: Praeger, 1989

Palmer, Robert, *Deep Blues,* New York: Viking Press, 1981; London: Penguin, 1982

Poindexter, Ray, *Arkansas Airwaves,* N.p., 1974

KFI

Los Angeles, California Station

KFI radio was one of three Los Angeles radio stations to emerge from 1922's early broadcasting confusion and survives today as one of the top radio stations in the United States.

Origins

The story of KFI begins with California's leading Packard automobile distributor, Earle C. Anthony. He became one of the most important early radio station owners, not only on the West coast, but also in the entire nation. An article in the *Saturday Evening Post* gave Anthony the idea to use radio to communicate between his Packard auto dealerships. He built a 50-watt transmitter on his kitchen table and on 16 April 1922 began broadcasting in Los Angeles as KFI radio.

The KFI studios were on the roof of his Packard dealership at 1000 South Hope Street, at the corner of 10th (now Olympic) and Hope in downtown Los Angeles. The station started out with only two employees, who put the station on for a few hours per day. They would then take KFI off the air for a dinner break and return to the air for the evening program. One man booked talent for programs, announced them on the air, played musical accompaniments, and, when necessary, filled in program gaps with music. The other man's job was to take care of the technical aspects of putting the programs on the air. In 1923 KFI presented the "June Bride Contest of 1923." The winner had her wedding broadcast over KFI. The bride and groom also received $1000 worth of electrical appliances (a tidy sum in those days).

With radio becoming the new national fad, KFI did its part to help new listeners. People who bought a crystal set or a more complicated radio could call KFI for help. The station would then send out a technician to help them set up their radio and antenna. KFI is also one of four stations that claim to have used musical chimes between programs before the National Broadcasting Company (NBC) began using them. The chimes were also used when KFI signed on the air each evening in the early 1920s. By the time KFI celebrated its fourth anniversary in 1926, the station boasted a staff of 20 people in the program, technical, and office departments.

Anthony soon realized that KFI could attract new customers into his car dealership. Programs were carefully tailored to the tastes of listeners that Anthony believed would buy Packards. High-class musical and educational programs were featured. The Los Angeles *Herald* and *Examiner* newspapers cooperated with KFI to provide news coverage in the early years. To promote both the station and his car business further, Anthony made sure that the station identification announcements always included the words "This is KFI, Los Angeles. The Radio Central Super Station of Earle C. Anthony, Incorporated, California Packard Distributors." The words "KFI-PACKARD" were also placed on the transmitter towers atop the Packard dealership to keep KFI radio in the public's mind as they traveled through that section of Los Angeles. Program listings in magazines and newspapers during the mid-1920s show that Anthony advertised Packard cars on KFI through such programs as the *Packard Six Orchestra, Packard Ballad Hour,* and *Packard Radio Club.*

Development

KFI soon initiated a policy of cooperating with schools, government agencies, and civic groups. In 1924 the first broadcast of a symphony orchestra in the West was presented over KFI; it also sponsored the first remote broadcast of a complete opera from the stage. That same year the first West coast network was set up when KFI exchanged programs with KPO in San Francisco. Over 500 miles of telephone lines connected the two stations. Another "first" was a broadcast of the Hollywood Bowl Summer Concert Season. As the station gained a reputation for its good programming and public service, nearly every important person who visited Southern California made it a point to be heard over KFI's microphone. A mid-1920s favorite of KFI listeners was real-life detective Nick Harris, a forerunner of the "who-done-it" shows. Harris would tell stories proving the folly of committing crime. The Nick Harris program remained a KFI feature through the 1930s.

KFI started a steady growth in popularity and began increasing its output power: from 50 to 500 watts in early 1923, to 5,000 watts by 1927, and finally to 50,000 watts in 1931, all on 640 kHz (since May 1923). The station's signal had already been heard coast to coast on cold winter nights, and radio fans in England and Australia sent in letters in 1924 and 1925 reporting reception of KFI—this owing to occasional sky wave reception. In 1927 KFI supplied the remote equipment for NBC to provide the first national radio coverage of the Rose Bowl football game from Pasadena. KFI's slogan, "A National Institution," made sense when readers of *Radio Listeners Guide* magazine voted KFI as the only West coast station among the 10 most-popular radio stations in the United States. KFI's program schedule was listed regularly in the *New York Times* and other Eastern newspapers.

KFI had several talented announcers on its staff over the years, including two of the most popular men heard on network radio throughout the 1930s and 1940s. Don Wilson was KFI's chief announcer from 1929 to 1933. He later gained fame as Jack Benny's longtime announcer on radio and TV. Ken Carpenter also served as chief announcer at KFI, was later heard on many network radio shows, and was chiefly identified with Bing Crosby's *Kraft Music Hall.* Roger Krupp was another network announcer who did local work on KFI. Chet Huntley was a newscaster from 1937–39 at KFI, years before he became a household name on NBC television's *Huntley Brinkley Report* in the 1950s and 1960s.

As an original NBC affiliate, KFI brought music, comedy, and dramatic programs from New York and Hollywood into Southern California homes, along with the daytime soap operas. The long-time NBC favorites included shows such as Jack Benny, Burns and Allen, *Fibber McGee and Molly,* Fred Allen, Abbott and Costello, and many others. KFI continued to carry its share of local programming, such as *Packard Fiesta* and *Great Moments in History.* One longtime KFI feature that started in 1938, *Art Baker's Notebook,* was heard on the station for two decades.

By December 1939 KFI (and co-owned station KECA) had grown so much that it moved to new studios and offices at 141 North Vermont Avenue. The building included the latest broadcasting equipment and a 250-seat theater for audiences to see local KFI shows on the air.

During World War II, KFI was the station Southern Californians tuned to each night at 10 P.M. to hear the latest war news from reporter John Wahl, sponsored by Richfield gasoline. The 15-minute newscast was followed by *Inside the News,* with Jose Rodriguez and Sid Sutherland and later John Burton. Because the area surrounding Los Angeles was mostly agricultural at the time, KFI presented daily farm news reports and had a full-time farm director. Farmers were also served by KFI with nightly fruit frost warnings in the winter, at 8 P.M. each night. These were heard on KFI into the early 1970s.

Postwar Development

In the 1950s KFI's all-night talk show, *Ben Hunter's Nite Owls,* became quite popular. During the 1960s the station changed from block programming to middle of the road music with local disc jockeys, local and NBC news on the hour, and Los Angeles Dodgers baseball. Later, morning personalities Al Lohman and Roger Barkley tickled listeners' funny bones on KFI from 1969 until 1986.

KFI founder Earle C. Anthony died in 1961. His corporation held the KFI license until the station was sold to Cox Broadcasting in 1973 for $15.1 million. The music on KFI gradually changed to a more contemporary Top 40 format, with several air personalities over the years, including Dave Hull, Bob Hudson, Dave Diamond, and Sonny Melendrez. The station also moved from the more than 30 year old studios on Vermont to a new facility at 610 South Ardmore Avenue in late 1975.

Since the late 1980s KFI has turned from broadcasting music and become one of the most listened to talk radio stations in the United States, using the slogan "More Stimulating Talk Radio." KFI's program director, David G. Hall, is behind much of that success. The station has been the flagship for such talk hosts as Dr. Laura Schlessigner and Phil Hendrie. KFI also has an award-winning local news staff of 16, which has won many Golden Mike and Associated Press awards. As of early 2001, KFI was owned by Clear Channel Communications.

JIM HILLIKER

See also Clear Channel Communications; National Broadcasting Company; Wilson, Don

Further Reading

"A Baby Earle Anthony Wouldn't Give Up," *Broadcasting* (18 October 1971)

Blanton, Parke, *Crystal Set to Satellite: The Story of California Broadcasting, the First 80 Years*, Los Angeles: California Broadcasters Association, 1987

Blond, Stuart R., *Earle C. Anthony*, Oakland, California: Packard Club, 1985

Carr, Marc, "When 500 Watts Was a Super Station," *Radio Life Weekly* (16 January 1944)

Higby, Mary Jane, *Tune In Tomorrow; or, How I Found the Right to Happiness with Our Gal Sunday, Stella Dallas, John's Other Wife, and Other Sudsy Radio Serials*, New York: Cowles, 1968

Poindexter, Ray, *Golden Throats and Silver Tongues: The Radio Announcers*, Conway, Arkansas: River Road Press, 1978

KGO

San Francisco, California Station

When West Coast residents first tuned to KGO on 8 January 1924, the station was an innovative business experiment. The General Electric Company (GE) wanted to sell radio sets by attracting consumers to the new medium. During the next 75 years, KGO would symbolize the powerful "key stations" of radio's golden age, develop and name a major new radio format, and be recognized as one of the nation's most successful radio stations.

Early Years

KGO's first studios and transmitter were built at a GE factory in Oakland. This mid-coast tower site reached listeners up and down the West Coast. Its power of 1,500 watts at 790 kHz made it one of the five most powerful stations in the nation. It switched to 810 kHz in 1941. KGO's first program schedule totaled six hours weekly: 8-10 P.M. on Tuesday, Thursday, and Saturday. Most radio shows of this era were produced live in the station's studios. San Francisco's enormous wealth of musical, dramatic, and educational talent provided the station with an unlimited supply of performers. Adding studios in the St. Francis Hotel in May 1924 encouraged participation by world famous touring artists.

When radio drama was born on the networks in the late 1920s, KGO reacted by producing local plays. The station employed a full-time dramatic director for the *KGO Players*, a weekly drama. These shows broke new ground by fully enhancing the spoken word with music and sound effects. Top orchestras and community events were also broadcast live. But as broadcast hours expanded, all programming could not remain local. In 1927 both KGO and KPO became San Francisco affiliates of the National Broadcasting Company (NBC).

KGO was affiliated with NBC's Red Network and KPO was affiliated with NBC's Blue Network. KPO later became KNBC, then KNBR.

A momentous turning point in KGO's history occurred in 1929, when NBC assumed management of the station, named it the key station for the Blue and Gold networks on the West Coast, and moved it into NBC's studios with KPO. This placed KGO in the creative environment where nationally broadcast network programs such as *One Man's Family* were being produced. (It was the first network radio serial to originate in San Francisco, became the longest-running serial drama in U.S. radio history, and paralleled the golden age of radio from 1932 to 1959.)

In 1942 NBC, KGO, and KPO moved to a $1 million state of the art studio then called the most perfect plant of its kind ever designed. Ten air-conditioned studios were mounted on springs with suspended walls and ceilings for perfect sound-proofing and acoustics. One studio seated an audience of 500 people. NBC was ordered by the Federal Communications Commission (FCC) to sell the Blue Network in 1943 for anti-trust reasons. The change gave KGO a new owner, the American Broadcasting Company, and a network re-named ABC (in 1945).

When the FCC authorized an increase to 50,000 watts in 1947, a new three-tower transmitting facility was built near the Dumbarton Bridge. This facility included the first multi-tower directional antenna system in San Francisco. Three 300-foot towers were anchored in salt water and guided KGO's signal in a north-south direction. The station was then billed as "The Sunset Station" because of its powerful nighttime coverage of the Pacific Coast region from Alaska to Mexico. The new transmitting facilities also doubled KGO's daytime coverage area. One of the towers partially collapsed during the 17 October 1989 Loma Prieta earthquake, but the station returned to the air in less than five minutes.

The explosive growth of television in the 1950s captured radio listeners and marked an end to the so-called golden age of radio. As KGO's network shows such as *Don McNeill's Breakfast Club* suffered declining ratings, the station turned to personality disk jockeys. Innovative programs such as *Coyle and Sharpe* (a combination of *Bob and Ray* and *Candid Camera*) and broadcasts by *Les Crane Live from the Hungry I* were featured. But by 1962 the ratings placed "The Sunset Station" eighth in the San Francisco market.

Introducing Talk

The most significant transformation in KGO's history came in 1964 when station manager Don Curran engineered a dramatic change in format by introducing an all-day talk format and leading a team that invented the terms *newstalk* and *infotainment*. The success of this experiment proved the viability of talk radio and eventually led to its expansion into a major new radio format; by 1998 talk radio was being offered by more than 1,000 stations and earned a national audience share of 10 percent. By 1978 KGO had become the most popular radio station in the Bay Area among persons 12 and over.

In October 2000 KGO celebrated its 75th anniversary by continuing its dominance of the nation's fourth-largest market for more than 20 consecutive years. The station's 6.3 share among persons 12 and over captured the number one slot for the 90th consecutive San Francisco Arbitron Ratings book. *Radio Ink* wrote, "This is something that has never occurred in a major market in America before." About 850,000 different listeners tuned in to KGO each week at that time.

A long list of "firsts" contributed to these impressive ratings. KGO was the first Bay Area station with helicopter traffic reports. Its 27-member news department was the first to send a local radio reporter to cover national and international news. In 1997 KGO ranked as the 14th highest-billing station in the nation with revenues of more than $30 million. In 1994 Duncan's *Radio Market Guide* called NewsTalk 810 "the most admired station in the nation." KGO's strengths lay in hiring and keeping enormously talented people and in understanding, serving, and relating to the people and issues of the Bay Area to an extraordinary degree.

In 2000 NewsTalk 810 was one of the first stations in the nation to add a "Push to Talk" feature to its website (www.kgo.com). This allowed visitors to the website to participate in talk shows via the internet with one click of the mouse. And the industry trend to ownership of multiple stations in a single market brought KGO's management team a fresh challenge from owner ABC/Disney—to duplicate their success at sister newstalk station KSFO-FM.

JERRY CONDRA

Further Reading

Broadcast History Website: Schneider, John, "Voices out of the Fog: A History of Broadcasting in the San Francisco Bay Area" <www.adams.net/~jfs>

Duncan, James H., Jr., editor, *Duncan's Radio Market Guide,* Kalamazoo, Michigan: Duncan Media Enterprises, 1984

Fracchia, Charles A., *Fire and Gold: The San Francisco Story,* Encinitas, California:

Heritage Media, and San Antonio, Texas: Lammert, 1994

McKinsey and Company, et al., *Radio in Search of Excellence: Lessons from America's Best-Run Radio Stations,* Washington, D.C.: National Association of Broadcasters, 1985

Rhoads, Eric, "Mirror, Mirror on the Radio," *Radio Ink* 8 (November 2000)

Talkers Magazine Online, <www.talkers.com>

KHJ

Los Angeles, California Station

The second oldest station in Los Angeles, KHJ was a broadcast pioneer and prominent originator of network programming during radio's golden age. In the late 1960s, KHJ became the most-imitated radio station in North America following a dramatic ratings turnaround by means of a variant of the basic Storz Top 40 formula.

KHJ began broadcasting with 5 watts at 760 kilohertz on 13 April 1922 from a 10- by 12-foot room atop the Los Angeles *Times* building. Although the *Times* operated the station, C.R. Kierulff, an electrical pioneer, founded it. The first program included "The Star Spangled Banner," an address by *Times* publisher Harry Chandler, vocal selections, a comedy routine, news bulletins, and children's bedtime stories. Three days later the station aired Easter services. The *Times* purchased the KHJ call letters (kindness, health, joy) from Kierulff in November 1922 and increased power to 500 watts. During its earliest years, KHJ stopped broadcasting for 3 minutes out of each 15-minute period in order to clear the air for distress calls. On 31 December 1922, KHJ broadcast throughout New Year's Eve, reported to be an unprecedented event.

As radio entered its golden age, KHJ became the principal West Coast affiliate of Mutual and the flagship of the regional Don Lee network, which was named for its owner, an automobile sales tycoon. The station originated numerous network programs, including the Columbia Broadcasting System (CBS) show *Hollywood Hotel,* hosted by Louella Parsons (during the years before CBS acquired station KNX). Other programming included Raymond Paige and a 50-piece staff orchestra, *Chandu the Magician,* Eddie Cantor, Burns and Allen, *Queen for a Day,* and *Hopalong Cassidy.*

Some prominent figures in mass communication passed through KHJ during its early years. Sylvester (Pat) Weaver, later president of the National Broadcasting Company (NBC), was an announcer in 1934. Helen Gurley Brown, later responsible for revamping Hearst's *Cosmopolitan,* answered listeners' letters while she was a student.

In 1950 RKO General (Tire) purchased the Don Lee broadcast properties, which included KHJ, KHJ-FM, and KHJ-TV. As music and news began to dominate local radio programming in the 1950s, KHJ featured disc jockeys and popular records. In the early 1960s, the station featured the talk personality format that had been successful at RKO General's WOR in New York. Nevertheless, by the end of 1964 KHJ had not developed a niche in the competitive Los Angeles market. In the ratings, the regional facility—on 930 kilohertz with 5 kilowatts of power and a directional antenna at night—was a lusterless 17th from the top.

The management of RKO General's radio division announced that KHJ would undergo a complete change of programming by May 1965. Although initially opposed to rock and roll or country and western, management chose to pursue an around-the-clock contemporary music format that would draw the bulk of young listeners without offending any other segment of the potential audience. That decision set in motion a chain of events that ultimately brought KHJ from virtual obscurity to legendary status.

In early 1965 RKO General retained "two men who had previously taken 'average' stations and transformed them into number one ranking in areas similar to our own." Those specialists were Gene Chenault and Bill Drake. Chenault was licensee of KYNO in Fresno, the original Top 40 station in the central valley of California. Drake had worked for Gerald Bartell's WAKE in Atlanta and KYA in San Francisco prior to joining Chenault as program director of KYNO. Drake's programming had led KYNO to victory in a tough ratings battle with KMAK, Chenault's tough Fresno competitor.

After Drake's success with KYNO, he and Chenault formed a consulting service. Their first client was KGB in San Diego, which rose from lowest to first in ratings on the 63rd day of Drake-Chenault programming. The success of KGB brought Drake-Chenault to the attention of RKO General management.

Drake and Chenault brought in Ron Jacobs, who had been program director of their Fresno opponent, KMAK, to be the new program director at KHJ. Drake and Jacobs crafted a streamlined version of Top 40 for KHJ centered on a very limited playlist of contemporary favorites aired, when possible, in sweeps of two or three songs. Most sound effects associated with Top 40 (e.g., horns, tones, beepers) were eliminated. A cappella jingles by Johnny Mann were short. Commercial loads were cut to 12 to 13 minutes per hour and clustered in strategically scheduled stop sets. News aired at 20 minutes past the hour or 20 minutes before the hour to counterprogram competitors' newscasts on the hour or at five minutes before the hour. The mix was given an on-air slogan, "Boss Radio."

Jacobs premiered a "sneak preview" of the Boss Radio format in late April 1965. Compared with other Los Angeles Top 40 stations (KFWB, KRLA in Pasadena), KHJ was noticeably uncluttered. KHJ rose to lead Los Angeles ratings during the first six months with Drake-Chenault as consultants. At the height of its popularity in the late 1960s, KHJ attracted one out of four Los Angeles radio listeners. After KHJ's phenomenal success, RKO General signed Drake and Chenault as consultants for KFRC in San Francisco, CKLW in Windsor (Detroit), WOR-FM in New York, WRKO in Boston, and WHBQ in Memphis.

By 1968 stations paid Drake-Chenault up to $100,000 annually for Bill Drake's services. Although Drake-Chenault consulted a total of only nine stations (including KAKC in Tulsa), the influence of their 1965 win in the tough Los Angeles market diffused throughout the radio broadcasting industry as managers across the nation copied the KHJ format and conservative playlist. Drake-Chenault also attracted critics who blamed the widespread imitation of the KHJ playlist for constrained promotional efforts for innovative music during the late 1960s.

The turnaround of KHJ is a classic business success story of personalities, competition, performance, and impact. In 2000, KHJ continued to thrive with a successful Spanish language format, and the Drake-Chenault sound remained popular in Los Angeles via KRTH's (formerly KHJ-FM) oldies format, which is reminiscent of KHJ during the late 1960s.

ROBERT M. OGLES

See also Chenault, Gene; Contemporary Hit Radio Format/ Top 40; Don Lee Broadcasting System; Drake, Bill; Mutual Broadcasting System; Weaver, Sylvester

Further Reading

"Adviser Becomes Boss: Drake Signs with RKO," *Broadcasting* (16 October 1972)

Fornatale, Peter, and Joshua E. Mills, *Radio in the Television Age*, Woodstock, New York: Overlook Press, 1980

"A History of Rockin' Times: A *Radionow!* Interview with Gene Chenault," *Radionow!* 2, no. 2 (1992)

Jacobs, Ron, *KHJ: Inside Boss Radio,* Stafford, Texas: Zapoleon, 2002

MacFarland, David T., *The Development of the Top 40 Radio Format,* New York: Arno Press, 1979

Puig, C., "Back When Jocks Were Boss," *Los Angeles Times* (25 April 1993)

"Rock and Roll Muzak," *Newsweek* (9 March 1970)

King Biscuit Flower Hour

Syndicated Showcase for Rock Artists

During the 1970s and 1980s, the *King Biscuit Flower Hour* presented recorded concert performances by more than a thousand artists, including the Rolling Stones, the Who, Eric Clapton, Elton John, U2, John Lennon, Elvis Costello, Aerosmith, the Beach Boys, the Fixx, Led Zeppelin, and many current and future members of the Rock and Roll Hall of Fame. It was the first live performance radio show to offer a glimpse into the daily lives of rock bands on tour. At its peak of popularity, more than 300 U.S. radio stations carried the *King Biscuit Flower Hour,* and the syndicators estimated that the weekly audience surpassed 5 million listeners.

The program's name pays homage to *King Biscuit Time* (later called *King Biscuit Flour Hour*), a famous radio program that originated in 1941 on KFFA, Helena, Arkansas. Sponsored by the makers of King Biscuit Flour and hosted by Sonny Boy Williamson and Robert Lockwood Jr., *King Biscuit Time* showcased the country blues music of the Mississippi Delta region, one of the important roots of rock and roll. Every important performer who played the honky tonks and juke joints along the "Chittlin' Circuit" from New Orleans to St. Louis appeared on the show until it left the air in 1967. Helena is now the site of the annual King Biscuit Blues Festival, which keeps the musical tradition alive.

Bob Meyrowitz and Peter Kauff were the first producers for the *King Biscuit Flower Hour.* Their company, DIR Broadcasting, began syndicating the program in 1973. The first show featured John McLaughlin's Mahavishnu Orchestra, a popular jazz-fusion band; Blood, Sweat and Tears; and an unknown group named Bruce Springsteen and the E Street band. For the next 17 years, the format remained the same. Live performances were interspersed with backstage interviews and minimal intrusion from the hosts for continuity. Venues ranged from stadiums to large auditoriums to small clubs. Every hour featured 50 minutes of music heard just as it had been performed before the live crowd.

Later, the company began a similar weekly series featuring country music artists. Production of the original *King Biscuit Flower Hour* ceased in 1990, with a library of more than 24,000 master tapes of classic rock and roll live performances. Soon thereafter, King Biscuit Entertainment bought the series and began syndication of reruns in the United States and Great Britain.

In 1996 King Biscuit Entertainment started releasing a limited number of *King Biscuit Flower Hour* performances on tapes and compact discs, using the syndicated program as a promotional vehicle. Although the classic rock radio format suffered from declining audience shares in the mid-1990s, *King Biscuit Flower Hour* retained its syndication base because its library contained material from other genres such as new wave, modern rock, blues, and alternative.

For the 25th anniversary of *King Biscuit Flower Hour* in 1998, the syndicator produced a two-hour special retrospective program, released a commemorative double compact disc, and made an important announcement. Production had begun on a new series of live performances for future *King Biscuit Flower Hour* programs. King Biscuit Entertainment also added a streaming media website (king-biscuit.com) to promote the radio series and sale of recordings and related merchandise. At the turn of the millennium, the *King Biscuit Flower Hour* could be heard weekly on nearly 200 radio stations in the United States as well as on BBC-2 in Great Britain.

ROBERT HENRY LOCHTE

See also KFFA; Rock and Roll Format

Programming History
Nationally Syndicated   18 February 1973–present

Further Reading

Cohodas, Nadine, "The King Biscuit Blues Festival: The Sonny Boy Legacy in Helena," *Blues Access* 31 (Fall 1997) <www.bluesaccess.com/No_31/kbbf.html>

King Biscuit Radio: The Legendary King Biscuit Flower Hour Radio Show, <www.king-biscuit.com/right_about3.html#kingbiscuit>
Taylor, Chuck, "King Biscuit to Observe Its 25th," *Billboard* (11 July 1998)

King, Larry 1933–

U.S. Radio and Television Talk Show Host

Larry King, who estimates he has conducted more than 35,000 interviews during his 40-year career, revitalized the possibilities of the radio and television talk show for a national as well as worldwide audience during the cable era. Although King has crafted a laid-back persona in his signature suspenders, the *Guinness Book of World Records* recognizes the indefatigable King as having logged more hours on national radio than any other talk personality in broadcasting history. From the 1980s on, King's omnipresence on radio and television and in print made him the interviewer of choice for many celebrities and politicians.

King's agreeable style and "everyman" appeal refashioned the talk show format into an international town meeting. His first interview series, on Mutual Radio, pioneered the concept of the nationwide talk show. His television series on CNN, also simulcast on Westwood One radio stations since 1994, created the first international arena for talk, reaching more than 230 million households in well over 200 countries. King credits his innate curiosity as the main ingredient for this far-reaching popularity and commercial success.

Throughout King's career, critics have questioned his ability to ask insightful and tough questions of his guests. Howard Kurtz of the *Washington Post* labeled him "a great schmoozer who makes no pretense to being a newsman." King readily admits that he never covered a news event and that, in fact, he does little research or preparation for any interview. His technique is to ask short, conversational questions, hoping to connect with his guests on a friendly level. For King, who detests confrontation, the best guest is "anyone passionately involved in what he does."

Like many broadcasters of his generation, King grew up listening to network radio, which would disappear because of television as he came of age. Born Lawrence Zieger in Brooklyn, the young King was an indifferent student, enthralled only with everything related to radio, from the escapism of *Captain Midnight* to the quiet satire of Bob Elliott and Ray Goulding. Aspiring to be the next Red Barber, the colorful sports announcer of the Brooklyn Dodgers, or Arthur Godfrey, whose on-air folksiness King would adopt with an urban twist, the frequent studio visitor was told to seek his broadcasting fortune in a smaller market. In 1957 King journeyed to Miami and got his first job, as a handyman at WAHR, a 250-watt AM station. He took over for the late-morning disc jockey and, at the station manager's suggestion, changed his name from the ethnic Zieger to King.

King was quickly noticed by larger Miami stations, and in 1958 he was hired by WKAT to anchor the valuable early-morning broadcasts. Encouraged to stand out among other drive-time disc jockeys, King created offbeat characters in the style of his comic heroes, Bob and Ray. The popularity of one such character, Captain Wainright of the Miami State Police, a *Highway Patrol* takeoff, led to his first talk show. Pumpernik's restaurant hired the entertaining upstart to host a four-hour show, live from the eatery. King discovered his talents in the ad-lib interview, first talking with waitresses and garrulous patrons, then with anyone who came by. Celebrities began to drop by the restaurant, and King flourished in the freewheeling atmosphere of the spontaneous interview. King's ability to draw people out was on display with such young performers as Don Rickles, Lenny Bruce, and Bobby Darin.

King's horizons began to expand when he was hired by WIOD in 1962. Management recognized his potential and moved his Pumpernik's show to the houseboat that served as the luxurious setting for the American Broadcasting Companies (ABC) television series *Surfside Six* for nightly broadcasts of interviews and phone calls. He realized his dream to be a sportscaster when WIOD offered him Sunday duty as color

Larry King
Courtesy Radio Hall of Fame

commentator for the Miami Dolphins. His fame opened other media doors. King began writing columns, first for the *Miami Beach Sun-Reporter,* followed by stints at the *Miami Herald* and the *Miami News*. He hosted a local talk show on Sunday nights with no time limits on WLBW in 1963, and a year later he switched to WTVJ-TV with a weekend show.

King has said he felt as if he "owned Miami" and piled up outrageous debts. Embroiled in a larceny scandal, King's career was shattered by his high-living notoriety. By 1972 he lost every media position he had accrued. During the mid-1970s King accepted any job he was offered, working as a public relations official with a horse-racing track in Shreveport, Louisiana, and as a radio commentator for the Shreveport Steamers of the World Football League. The freelance phase of his career ended when a new general of WIOD listened to archival tapes of King's best work. He was rehired to host an evening talk show, and soon the newspaper and television assignments returned. King still could not control his spending and eventually declared bankruptcy in 1978.

While getting his finances in order, King was hired to do a late-night program on the Mutual radio network. The *Larry King Show,* running from midnight to 5:30 A.M. (EST), debuted on 30 January 1978 in 28 cities and legitimized the format of the nationwide talk radio show. There had been other national talk hosts, including Herb Jebco from Salt Lake City and Long John Nebel from New York, but King demonstrated that the talk format was not a local phenomenon. Although King reveled in an uncontrolled environment, there was a distinct tripartite structure to most broadcasts. Most programs featured an hour-long interview with a guest; two hours of call-in questions for that guest; and the final hour, "Open Phone America," in which King's assorted group of "insomniacs and graveyard-shift workers" would call and chat about anything. Unlike most hosts, King did not screen calls, and he described this formula as "talk show democracy."

For the first two months, King's radio series was broadcast from Miami, and then the show was relocated to Arlington, Virginia, so that government officials could appear as guests.

The coverage grew exponentially; by the time the broadcast switched to daytime in 1992, more than 430 stations were carrying King's brand of talk. In 1982 he received the coveted George Foster Peabody Award. As he did in Miami, King used his radio fame as a calling card for other pursuits, such as writing a weekly column for *USA Today* and working for Ted Turner's CNN.

In 1985 he adapted his mostly single-guest and call-in format for cable television. *Larry King Live* has consistently been CNN's highest-rated show, emerging as a national forum on topical issues. In 1992 the major presidential candidates courted King's viewers, including H. Ross Perot, who declared his availability if "drafted" by the people. King also made headlines by arranging a debate on the North American Free Trade Agreement (NAFTA) between Perot and vice president Al Gore. Guests have ranged from world leaders and newsmakers (Mikhail Gorbachev, Margaret Thatcher, Norman Schwarzkopf, and the Dalai Lama) to entertainment and sports luminaries (Frank Sinatra, Marlon Brando, Barbra Streisand, and Arthur Ashe).

Larry King emerged as one of the dominant figures from radio's post-network era. His agreeable interviewing style attracted a wide audience across diverse demographic lines. King demonstrated that radio still has possibilities as a national medium. When music programming held sway on the FM band in the 1970s, King was one of the pioneers to conceive of the AM band as a nationwide vehicle for talk radio. The self-described "street kid from Brooklyn" helped to revive the tradition of network radio that had inspired him as a youngster.

RON SIMON

See also Mutual Broadcasting System; Peabody Awards; Talk Radio

Larry King. Born Lawrence Harvey Zeiger in Brooklyn, New York, 19 November 1933. Educated at Lafayette High School; disc jockey and interviewer at various Miami stations, 1957–71; columnist, various Miami newspapers, 1965–71; freelance writer and broadcaster, 1972–75; radio talk-show host, WIOD, Miami, 1975–78; host, Mutual Broadcasting System's *Larry King Show*, 1978–94; host, CNN's *Larry King Live*, 1978–present; host, the Goodwill Games, 1990; columnist, *USA Today* and *The Sporting News*. Received George Foster Peabody Award, 1982; National Association of Broadcasters' Radio Award, 1985; founded Larry King Cardiac Foundation, 1988; International Radio and TV Society's Broadcaster of the Year, 1989; named to Broadcaster's Hall of Fame, 1992; Scopus Award from American Friends of Hebrew University, 1994; Emmy Award, Outstanding Interviewer, 1999.

Radio Series
1978–94   *The Larry King Show*

Films
Ghostbusters, 1984; *Lost in America*, 1985; *Contact*, 1997; *Primary Colors*, 1998

Television Series
Larry King Live, 1978–present (CNN); cameos on *Murphy Brown*, *Frasier*, and *Murder One*

Selected Publications
Larry King (with Emily Yoffe), 1982
Tell It to the King (with Peter Occhiogrosso), 1990
When You're from Brooklyn, Everywhere Else Is Tokyo (with Marty Appel), 1992
On the Line: The Road to the White House (with Mark Stencel), 1993
The Best of Larry King Live: His Greatest Interviews, 1995
Future Talk: Conversations About Tomorrow with Today's Most Provocative Personalities, 1998
Anything Goes! 2000

Further Reading
Laufer, Peter, *Inside Talk Radio: America's Voice or Just Hot Air?* Secaucus, New Jersey: Carol, 1995
Munson, Wayne, *All Talk: The Talkshow in Media Culture*, Philadelphia, Pennsylvania: Temple University Press, 1993
Timberg, Bernard, *TV Talk: The History of the TV Talk Show*, Austin: University of Texas Press, 2002

King, Nelson 1914–1974

U.S. Country Music Disc Jockey

Historians have rated Nelson King among the disc jockeys who exerted the greatest influence on the commercialization of country music in the years following World War II. For almost 15 years, King served up country music to millions of listeners on his *Hillbilly Jamboree*, broadcast from 50,000-watt radio station WCKY in Cincinnati, Ohio. King's *Jamboree* transmitted strongly into the eastern United States, proving that his show could garner large audiences for country music from that populous region. He belongs to a class of early pioneering country music disc jockeys that includes Randy Blake (WJJD, Chicago, Illinois) and Rosalie Allen (WOV, New York).

After graduation from Portsmouth (Ohio) High School in 1932, King worked briefly as a stock boy at Woolworth's, but soon joined a small band, serving as its master of ceremonies. His resonant speaking voice, exhibited on various Ohio bandstands, helped him land his first radio job at WPAY in Portsmouth, where he was a staff announcer. Two years later, he became the chief announcer and musical director at radio station WSAZ in Huntington, West Virginia. At WSAZ, King's tenure included his role as part of an announcing team that covered the devastating West Virginia floods of 1937 for 381 continuous hours.

Departing soggy Huntington for Cincinnati in 1938, King began hosting a recorded music program over radio station WCPO; his *Jam for Supper* showcased the swing music of Benny Goodman, Tommy Dorsey, Artie Shaw, and others. After subsequent brief stays at radio stations WGRC in Louisville, Kentucky, and WKRC in Cincinnati, he joined WCKY in January of 1946.

It was at WCKY that management asked the new employee (then known as Charles Schroeder) to find a radio name. He was handed a Cincinnati phone book and plucked from it the pseudonym Nelson King (a change he later legalized). Soon after his arrival, he took the helm of WCKY's *Birthday Club*, *Man in the Street*, *Keep Happy Club*, and *Hillbilly Jamboree*; however, it would be *Hillbilly Jamboree*, the latter program carrying his name to national prominence.

WCKY and King had introduced the *Jamboree* in 1946, riding the growing popularity of country music during that time. King and the *Jamboree* would fuel that popularity. On the nightly show, King featured popular country music recording artists Eddy Arnold, Ernest Tubb, Red Foley, and others who were helping to establish country music as a commercial force in the late 1940s. The music of Arnold and others enjoyed burgeoning record sales and exposure on Saturday night music programs such as WSM radio's *Grand Ole Opry* and WLS radio's *National Barn Dance*. Their following would

increase even more on the airwaves of the four-and-a-half hour *Jamboree*, one of the few nightly country music disc jockey programs to reach a national audience during the mid-to-late 1940s. The show also streamed into Canada, Mexico, and parts of South America.

From early in the *Jamboree*'s run, it was evident that King was attracting a significant audience during the nighttime hours. When WCKY offered to send listeners promotional pictures of the hillbilly jockey, more than 76,000 letters deluged the station over a two-week period. Products that King hawked on the air—everything from baby chicks to "genuine imitation granite" tombstones to Last Supper tablecloths that glowed in the dark—sold briskly.

King's ability to reel in a vast audience greatly impressed record companies. In an interview with the present writer, Bob McCluskey, a promotional representative for RCA Victor Records, recalled that King's show influenced tastes: "Nelson's program really controlled [the East] late at night. The people that listened to the station were very, very record conscious at that time because what was played, they bought" (see Streissguth, 1997). In light of King's influence, record companies worked diligently to court his favor. Major stars such as Gene Autry and Eddy Arnold regularly called on the powerful disc jockey, and the record companies rained refrigerators, color television sets, and crates of liquor on him. "One of the things I did . . . was I bought time on the station," said McCluskey. "In doing so, I involved Nelson . . . with a promise to play the records that I asked [him] to play." The record company practice of buying influence with popular disc jockeys was widespread during the 1940s and 1950s. However unethical the record companies' gifts and King's acceptance of them, the exchanges served to illustrate King's immense sway with listeners as well as his country music ambassadorship.

Nelson King also proved to be a boon to bluegrass music, the acoustic sub-genre of country music popularized by Bill Monroe, Lester Flatt and Earl Scruggs, and others. King loved the dynamic bluegrass sound, sitting mesmerized for hours at bluegrass performances and featuring a liberal helping of the music on his broadcasts. A major retailer of bluegrass records, Jimmie Skinner's Music Center of Cincinnati, advertised regularly on King's show and saw remarkable sales in part because of it.

Throughout the 1950s King continued to distinguish himself as an important conduit for country music. He became active in the Country Music Disc Jockey Association (which would evolve into the Country Music Association, an important trade group), and he collected *Billboard* magazine's top disc jockey award for eight consecutive years. Not even the growth of rock and roll music could wrench him from his disc jockey slot.

In the end, it would take alcoholism to mute King. Years of alcohol abuse caught up with him in 1961, when the station fired him for going on the air inebriated. He worked outside radio until 1968 when he assumed the morning disc jockey shift at radio station WCLU in Cincinnati. But his continuing alcoholism and the onset of lung cancer ended his radio career in 1970. Although he eventually gave up alcohol, he succumbed to the cancer in 1974.

Nelson King was elected posthumously to the Country Music Disc Jockey Hall of Fame in 1975, recognized as one of country music's foremost emissaries.

MICHAEL STREISSGUTH

See also Country Music Format; Disk Jockeys; Grand Ole Opry; Perryman, Tom; WSM

Nelson Charles King. Born Charles Edward Schroeder in Portsmouth, Ohio, 1 April 1914. One of three children born to Stanley and Sue Schroeder; announcer, WPAY, Portsmouth, Ohio, 1934–36; chief announcer and musical director, WSAZ, Huntington, West Virginia, 1936–38; disc jockey, WCPO, Cincinnati, Ohio, 1938–45; announcer, WGRC, Louisville, Kentucky, 1945; announcer, WKRC, Cincinnati, Ohio, 1945–46; host of *Hillbilly Jamboree,* WCKY, Cincinnati, Ohio, 1946–61; disc jockey, WCLU, Cincinnati, Ohio, 1968–70. Inducted posthumously into Country Music Disc Jockey Hall of Fame, 1975. Died in Cincinnati, Ohio, 16 March 1974.

Radio Series

1946–61   *Hillbilly Jamboree*

Further Reading

Cherry, Hugh, "Country DJs Carry Music to the People," *Music City News* (October 1980)
Friedman, Joel, "Radio, Country Music, Like Twins, Grow Big Together," *Billboard* (22 May 1954)
Kingsbury, Paul, editor, *The Encyclopedia of Country Music: The Ultimate Guide to the Music,* New York: Oxford University Press, 1998
Malone, Bill C., *Country Music U.S.A.,* Austin: University of Texas Press, 1968; revised edition, 1985
Streissguth, Michael, *Eddy Arnold: Pioneer of the Nashville Sound,* New York: Schirmer, and London: Prentice Hall, 1997

Kirby, Edward M. 1906–1974

U.S. Broadcast and Advertising Executive

Edward Kirby had a long and successful career in broadcasting, advertising, and public relations. His most important contributions to radio, however, were made while wearing his nation's uniform, working for the biggest sponsor of them all, the U.S. government.

Origins

Born in Brooklyn, New York, on 6 June 1906, Kirby was the son of a coal merchant. Sent off to boarding school at a young age, he returned to New York for a time in his high school years before going to a private military academy in upstate New York. He was later accepted at the Virginia Military Institute (VMI), where he wrote for various humor and literary magazines. Kirby received his bachelor's degree from VMI in 1926.

After graduation, Kirby worked as a reporter for the *Baltimore Sun* and later undertook economic, statistical, and market analysis for several investment banks. He eventually worked his way into advertising and public relations with C.P. Clark, Inc., of Nashville in 1929. For that firm, he directed national advertising campaigns for several important clients, including the General Shoe Corporation. He also got his first radio experience, producing nationally distributed programs for General Shoe and others.

While with C.P. Clark, Kirby came to the attention of Edwin Craig, vice president of the National Life and Accident Insurance Company of Nashville, owner of radio station WSM. Craig hired Kirby in 1933, and soon the company had increased its insurance in force by 57 percent (to $525 million) owing largely to Kirby's use of WSM as a sales tool. In 1936 Kirby married Marjorie Arnold, daughter of the dean of the

Vanderbilt Law School and a staff actress at WSM; in time they had two daughters, Patricia and Kip.

Toward the end of his tenure at WSM, Kirby gained valuable experience in working under duress during the disastrous 1937 floods. Radio's response proved exemplary and gave Kirby hints of what the medium was capable of in times of national emergency. Later that year Kirby became the National Association of Broadcasters' first full-time director of public relations, helping set up what later became the Broadcast Advertising Bureau. He initiated a campaign to make "radio as free as the press" and also participated in the creation of Broadcast Music Incorporated.

Wartime Service

In December 1940 Kirby was loaned to Secretary of War Henry L. Stimson as a "Dollar a Year" civilian adviser for radio, eventually becoming the de facto head of the army's radio branch. In that capacity, he successfully lobbied for the continued independence of radio in the face of the increasing inevitability of the United States' entry into World War II. Shortly after the U.S. entered the war, work began under Kirby's direction on two radio programs: the *Army Hour,* for listeners on the home front, and *Command Performance,* for all those in uniform. The *Army Hour* was an attempt to bring the war home to the American people through the power and immediacy of radio. As Kirby saw it, the show would "let the Army drop the stuffed-shirt approach . . . instead, go directly to the people with its own radio program, supplied by the men who were doing the fighting." The program was heard on the National Broadcasting Company (NBC), and highlights included interviews with top brass and returning combat veterans, as well as some of the most descriptive battlefield reporting of the war. The program did not sugarcoat the war: it showed the army at its darkest moments as well as in victory. An early broadcast featuring the terse translation of the last Morse code message from the besieged defenders of Corregidor in May 1942 had no equal for drama on the airwaves.

Command Performance was the brainchild of Louis Cowan, the creative force behind such hit programs as *Quiz Kids,* who was asked by Kirby to come up with a show to entertain the troops overseas. As Kirby later wrote, "The GI who was trained to obey commands in the line of duty could *now command* anything he wanted from the radio world in the way of entertainment. . . . It was unique, it was democratic, it was American." The requests ranged from the sentimental to the bizarre. A corporal who had never met his infant son reported that the "little guy is teething" and asked "to hear him yowl!" Soldiers from New York City asked to hear the hubbub of Times Square on New Year's Eve. Stars from Bob Hope and Bing Crosby to Judy Garland and Merle Oberon appeared gratis in response to soldiers' letters. The single most

famous request involved film star Carole Landis, who was commanded to "step up to the microphone and sigh. That's all brother, just sigh!"

In May 1942 Kirby became a lieutenant colonel in the army with substantially the same duties he had had as a civilian. In 1944 he was attached to General Eisenhower's staff to carry out perhaps the most important broadcasting-related assignment of the war: coordinating all radio coverage of D Day and the subsequent invasion, as well as establishing an Allied radio network to serve all the troops involved in the operation. For his efforts, he was promoted to full colonel and was awarded the Legion of Merit and the Order of the British Empire. In 1944 he was honored with a Peabody Radio Award for "Yankee Ingenuity on a global scale."

Later Years

After the war, Kirby did freelance public relations work for a time, gathering an impressive list of clients that included Paramount Pictures. He also wrote a book (with Jack Harris) chronicling radio's part in World War II. Called *Star-Spangled Radio,* it remains an excellent eyewitness description of the tremendous role played by radio during that period.

After Kirby made an abortive attempt at radio station ownership, the army recalled him during the Korean conflict for an emergency tour of duty as chief of the army's Radio-TV Branch. Col. Kirby reactivated the army's public information activities and effectively launched its use of television, creating the program *The Big Picture,* a fixture on American television for the next two decades. Kirby left the army in March 1953. Work with the Washington, D.C., Board of Trade (where he originated the Christmas "Pageant of Peace") and the People-to-People Foundation kept Kirby busy until 1957, when he accepted the position of director of public relations for the United Service Organizations (USO). He worked tirelessly to raise funds and established strong ties with the Advertising Council to facilitate national exposure for USO radio, television, and print campaigns. Col. Kirby resigned from the USO in 1970, and he and wife Marjorie returned to Washington, D.C., where he died in 1974.

CHUCK HOWELL

Edward M. Kirby. Born in Brooklyn, New York, 6 June 1906. Attended Virginia Military Institute, A.B. 1926; reporter and feature writer, *Baltimore Evening Sun* 1926–28; statistician, newsletter writer for investment banks, 1928–29; vice president and account executive, C.P. Clark Advertising Agency, Nashville, Tennessee, 1930–33; advertising manager, National Life and Accident Insurance, Nashville; Public Relations Chief for station WSM-AM, 1933–37; director of public relations, National Association of Broadcasters, 1937–40; civilian advisor to Secretary of War for Radio, 1940–42;

commissioned lieutenant colonel, U.S. Army, 1942; chief, Radio Branch, War Department, Bureau of Public Relations, 1942–44; produced *Army Hour* and *Command Performance;* attached to staff of General Eisenhower; coordinated D-Day radio coverage, acted as allied radio liaison for SHAEF (supreme headquarters, allied expeditionary forces), 1944–45; promoted to full colonel, 1945; public relations consultant, 1945–50; co-author *Star-Spangled Radio*, 1948; recalled to active duty as Chief, U.S. Army Radio-TV Branch, 1950–53; public relations work with Washington, D.C. Board of Trade, People-to-People Foundation, 1953–57; director of public relations, USO, 1957–70. Peabody Radio Award, 1944; awarded Legion of Merit and Order of the British Empire, 1945. Died in Washington, D.C., 1974.

Selected Publications

Star-Spangled Radio (with Jack W. Harris), 1948

Further Reading

Barnouw, Erik, *A History of Broadcasting in the United States, 1933–1953*, 3 vols., New York: Oxford University Press, 1966–70; see especially vol. 2, *The Golden Web, 1933 to 1953*, 1968

Christman, Trent, *Brass Button Broadcasters*, Paducah, Kentucky: Turner, 1992

"Kirby Takes Military Control of Radio Branch in the Army," *Broadcasting* (4 May 1942)

"We Pay Our Respects to—Edward Montague Kirby," *Broadcasting* (1 February 1937)

Klauber, Edward A. 1887–1954

U.S. Radio Network Executive

Edward Klauber, a key Columbia Broadcasting System (CBS) executive through the 1930s, helped to formulate what would become CBS News, defining many basic policies for all of radio journalism.

Early Years

Born in Louisville, Kentucky, in 1887, Klauber graduated from high school in 1903. Intending to study medicine, he briefly attended the University of Louisville and the University of Pennsylvania. He did not earn a degree from either institution, having in the meantime become far more interested in journalism. His uncle, Adolph Klauber, was then drama critic for the *New York Times* and may have had something to do with Klauber's direction. In any case, his uncle helped Klauber obtain his first news job, as a copy editor for the *New York World* in 1912.

After four years in this post, Klauber moved uptown as a reporter for the *Times* in 1916, covering a variety of stories around the city. He became especially well known for his coverage of the September 1920 anarchist bombing of Wall Street, in which 30 were killed and 100 injured. By the late 1920s, he had become the *Times'* night city editor, although he was anything but popular to those who worked for him. In a pattern that would later become familiar at CBS, Klauber became a hated boss—taciturn in mood, quick to criticize (often in front of others), and slow to give compliments.

CBS Executive

In 1928 Klauber left the news business for public relations, joining the Lenman and Mitchell advertising agency in New York as director for that area. He served for a year, moving on to join the offices of Edward L. Bernays, already the guru of the growing field. But his sometimes abrasive personality did not work well in a small office, and Bernays suggested Klauber to William Paley, president of CBS, as a good organizational manager, knowing that Paley needed such a person. Klauber joined the network in 1930 as assistant to the president. Years later, Paley noted that Klauber was "an indefatigable day-and-night worker, always keeping in touch with me, providing me with written reports and eventually becoming my advisor on all sorts of things" (Paley, 1979). Indeed, he became the virtual gatekeeper controlling access to Paley and something of the network hatchet man (early on, he terminated the network's contract with his old boss Bernays, saying that CBS didn't need two public relations experts on salary). Klauber was also the oldest member of the management team.

Although he was given wide credit for imposing discipline and organization on Paley as he firmly streamlined CBS operations, Klauber's personality got in the way time and again. "Charmless and utterly lacking in humor, Klauber seemed the antithesis of everything Paley valued in a man" (Smith, 1990). Klauber was already uncomfortable with Paul Kesten, the promotion and advertising expert he had hired in 1930, who in

Ed Klauber
Courtesy CBS Photo Archive

many ways was closer to Paley—the two increasingly became rivals for Paley's attention and affection, which was somewhat evidenced in the *Fortune* profile of the network's leadership that was published in 1935.

Radio Journalism

Where Klauber made a lasting difference in radio was in the rise of broadcast news. As Paley described him, he was an "advisor, guide and mentor on how CBS should handle news." Faced with the cutoff of press association news during the 1933 press-radio "war," Klauber persuaded General Mills to put up half of the cost to develop a Columbia News Service (the immediate predecessor to CBS News), hiring Paul White as his chief news aide. The two men added CBS news bureaus in Chicago and Los Angeles and contracted with many news stringers elsewhere. They hired the men (and virtually all were men at that point) who, in turn, provided the base for what CBS News became during World War II. In August 1939

Klauber persuaded respected journalist Elmer Davis (whose best man he had been) to join CBS as a commentator.

Behind all of this were Klauber's strongly held views, growing out of his decade and a half in New York newspaper journalism, of just what radio news should be and thus could become. He knew and disseminated the importance of presenting news fully and fairly, in accurate form and without bias. He helped to shield news people and content from advertiser demands as needed. He was a perfectionist in his own work and required the same level of achievement by others. He enforced the network's policy of not espousing editorial views when he wrote in 1939:

> Columbia's announced policy of having no editorial views of its own and not seeking to maintain or advance the views of others will be rigidly continued. In being fair and factual, those who present the news for Columbia must not only refrain from personal opinions, but must refrain from microphone manner designed to cast doubt, suspicion, sarcasm, ridicule, or anything of that sort on the matter they are presenting (quoted in White, 1947).

But Klauber also grew increasingly tyrannical as he assumed greater day-to-day responsibilities. By 1936 he was making $71,000 per year (worth more than ten times that amount today), second only to Paley. This was a clear indication of his value to the network. But at the same time, Paley noted that "Klauber developed a strong sense of possessiveness toward me, which . . . caused management problems."

The many complaints about Klauber's working relationships with his subordinates began to wear. At the same time, as the network faced substantial wartime pressures in news and elsewhere, Klauber faced his own personal hell. His first wife was dying of cancer, and, torn between caring for her and his network duties, he had two heart attacks in a short span of time. Sometime in 1941 or early 1942, Paley made a decision on the network's leadership future. To clear the way for Paul Kesten, Paley appears to have eased the way for Klauber to resign from CBS in March 1942.

Klauber moved to the Office of War Information (OWI), where he worked as associate director for Elmer Davis, OWI's director, until 1945. While at OWI, he played much the same hatchet man and organizational role for Davis as he had fulfilled for Paley. After the war, many of his ideals for broadcasting showed up in the National Association of Broadcasters Code of Good Practices, which he helped to revise and update in 1948. Klauber died in New York in 1954 at age 67.

CHRISTOPHER H. STERLING

See also Columbia Broadcasting System; Davis, Elmer; Kesten, Paul; Office of War Information; Paley, William S.; White, Paul

Edward A. Klauber. Born in Louisville, Kentucky, 24 February 1887. Son of Morris and Ray (Forst) Klauber; attended but did not graduate from Universities of Louisville and Pennsylvania; reporter, *New York World*, 1912–16; reporter, *New York Times*, 1916–27; night city editor for the *Times*, 1927–28; public relations director, Lenman and Mitchell advertising agency, New York City, 1928–29, with Edward L. Bernays, 1929; assistant to president, CBS, 1930; vice president, CBS, 1931; executive vice president, CBS, 1931–42; named to board of directors, 1937; chaired executive committee,1942; retired, 1942; associate director, Office of War Information, 1943–45. Died in New York City, 23 September 1954.

Further Reading

"And All Because They're Smart," *Fortune* (June 1935)

Metz, Robert, "The Father of Broadcast Journalism," in *CBS: Reflections in a Bloodshot Eye*, by Metz, Chicago: Playboy Press, 1975

Paley, William S., *As It Happened: A Memoir*, Garden City, New York: Doubleday, 1979

Smith, Sally Bedell, *In All His Glory: The Life of William S. Paley: The Legendary Tycoon and His Brilliant Circle*, New York: Simon and Schuster, 1990

White, Paul Welrose, *News on the Air*, New York: Harcourt Brace, 1947

Kling, William 1942–

U.S. Public Radio Executive and Entrepreneur

William (Bill) Kling enjoys several distinctions in the field of public radio. His tenure of more than 30 years as head of Minnesota Public Radio (MPR) and its predecessors easily surpasses that of any of his peers heading major U.S. public radio services. The sheer scope of the enterprise that he has been largely instrumental in creating is unmatched in the field of public radio. And his particular devotion to local and regional broadcast journalism has helped the MPR news department to become the largest (more than 70 staff members as of 2003) and by some accounts the most prestigious local radio newsroom in the country.

Origins

Kling's background before public radio gives relatively little indication that he would excel along those lines. Born in St. Paul, Minnesota, in 1942, he attended grade and high school there (and also built radio sets), then went to nearby St. Johns University (SJU) in Collegeville. He began a liberal arts degree with an emphasis in physics but ended up majoring in economics. He worked briefly with the SJU student radio station but did not care for its pop music format. Following graduation, he enrolled in the master's program at Boston University's School of Public Communication, and returned to Minnesota early in 1966. His fellow students at various levels recall him as being bright, congenial, well organized, and very persistent in reaching his goals. He was devoted to a seemingly chimerical goal of creating a high-quality, non-commercial radio service based in central Minnesota that would

provide a balanced mix of classical music with local and regional news.

That devotion may be part of a world outlook nurtured by Kling's high school and college teachers, some of them Jesuit or Benedictine monks and priests. Broadly speaking, Jesuits stress the need to question, Benedictines the need to serve and the importance of the fine arts. Kling's brief experience with student radio, as well as his development of a self-operated "alternative" radio service while at SJU, showed him that radio can serve society and that it can do a better job of that by questioning existing models. Two non-commercial stations then operated in Minnesota: KUOM at the University of Minnesota in Minneapolis/St. Paul and WCAL at St. Olaf College in Northfield. Neither service impressed Kling in its presentation of classical music; both seemed inadequate in providing daily coverage of local and statewide news.

In 1965 Kling created the opportunity to realize his goal by convincing SJU professor (soon to be SJU president) Father Colman Barry that the school could further distinguish itself by supporting a public service-oriented radio station that would reach listeners throughout Minnesota. Barry agreed, but financial support would be modest. Kling recruited a staff that was willing to work for low wages, as he did, and to produce a classical music service that would improve upon what KUOM and WCAL were providing. There also would be a small-scale news service that would concentrate on Minnesota news, but its development would be slower. KSJR-FM came on the air from Collegeville in January 1967 under the title of Minnesota Educational Radio (MER).

The classical music service began to attract the attention of newspapers in the Twin Cities, as Kling had hoped it would. Listeners in the northwest suburbs could pick up the signal, and owners of lake cottages in central Minnesota found that they had a new and very different voice to add to the chorus of mosquitoes and the few stations readily available to them as they vacationed. Twin Cities residents began to write to the station, expressing the hope that there would be an increase in signal strength or perhaps even a Twin Cities version of KSJR in the near future. Kling secured additional financial backing, applied for a non-commercial license, and KSJN-FM came on air from makeshift St. Paul studios in September 1967. By the following year, it was providing a Talking Book Service over a subchannel—another idea of Kling's and a service of particular pride to him.

The expansion to St. Paul was not without risk. Operating costs would be higher than they had been in Collegeville, especially as more of the KSJR staff moved. Although the U.S. Congress had passed the Public Broadcasting Act of 1967, stations such as KSJN and KSJR were realizing little financial benefit from that source. St. John's had provided as much as it could, but that stretched only so far, and some people in the SJR administration found it difficult to argue for increased support as the service became more and more of a Twin Cities operation. In 1971 Kling reached an agreement with SJU that KSJR and KSJN would become independent public service radio stations affiliated with National Public Radio (NPR), although St. John's would remain a sponsoring organization.

By the early 1970s, NPR was establishing itself as a major journalistic presence. Kling applied for a Corporation for Public Broadcasting grant to develop a full-fledged newsroom, and in 1972 KSJN began to provide daily coverage of Minnesota news. While operating costs increased, revenue did not keep pace, and Kling arrived at work one day to find a bank overdraft notice on his door. A bank loan resolved the crisis, but Kling realized that the financial situation needed major attention if the stations were even to survive, let alone expand. Yet, as he said in a 1999 interview with *Current,* he was determined to press on with expansion of the existing levels of service while at the same time redoubling efforts to attract corporate and individual sponsors.

Rather than emphasize MER's precarious financial state, Kling indicated how far it had come in such a short time and how much more public service it could provide if financial support were to increase. Several institutions of higher education signed on as sponsors; so did some of the state's larger businesses, foundations, and private donors. Listener pledge drives, which had been around since 1968, were expanded and made more attractive through the offering of premiums donated by individuals and businesses. The outpouring of support attested to Kling's skills as a fund-raiser and also convinced him that one more aspect of his goal—a truly statewide service with transmitters and studios in cities throughout Minnesota—might be attainable. So might a still more ambitious plan: separate frequencies throughout the state for a classical music service and a news and public affairs service.

Minnesota Public Radio

The statewide service proved easier to realize than did the dual service concept. Several institutions of higher education found it economical to affiliate with the renamed (in 1974) Minnesota Public Radio (MPR), to set up relay transmitters, and in some cases to create small studios. By 1980 most parts of Minnesota were served by at least one MPR signal. However, a few independent public radio ventures, notably in the Twin Cities (KFAI-FM), at St. Cloud State (KSCU-FM), and in Grand Rapids (KAXE-FM), found Kling to be an obstacle to their efforts to come on air or to increase their transmitter power. While reasons for the creation of a statewide service varied, a recurrent theme ran through them all: why put money into a host of small public radio stations when one large service could do the job so much better? A Governor's Task Force on the future of public radio in Minnesota recommended in 1975 that steps be taken to develop a statewide dual-service public radio system and praised MPR for its efforts along those lines but stopped short of saying that MPR should necessarily be the parent organization for both. Kling had no doubts that it should.

Kling knew that he would have to obtain a second FM frequency in the Twin Cities if MPR were to function effectively as a dual service. However, all the reserved frequencies for non-commercial services were taken, and the commercial frequencies had long since been claimed. Purchase of an existing station seemed to be the only option, but the expense would be great. He secured pledges of financial support from business and industry, but the only stations available at a reasonable price were on the AM band. In 1979 the MPR board approved purchase of KRSI-AM (St. Louis Park, a first-tier Minneapolis suburb), which allowed MPR to shift the bulk of its news and public affairs programming over to 1330 AM and to make KSJN-FM into a largely classical music service. It wasn't until 1990 that MPR was able to acquire a Twin Cities FM frequency (99.5) by purchasing WLOL-FM. The Minnesota Broadcasters Association objected on the grounds that the action deprived listeners of a commercial radio service and that the purchase itself probably involved state funding. (MPR and other public radio stations have received state support since the late 1970s.)

During the 1980s, Kling continued to develop "second channel" services throughout Minnesota (as of 2000, there were ten of them, plus an eleventh in Decorah, Iowa), aided by the money being generated through two further MPR initiatives in which he played a leading role: American Public Radio (APR), later named Public Radio International (PRI), and Rivertown Trading Company. APR was created in 1983, after Kling and four other managers of major public radio stations were unable to convince NPR to syndicate some of its leading programs—in MPR's case, Garrison Keillor's *A Prairie Home Companion*. They leased satellite time, and soon had a sizeable lineup of public radio stations as paying subscribers. (PRI's revenues in 1999 were $19.7 million.)

The popularity of Keillor's various fictional creations, especially Powdermilk Biscuits, led Kling to propose to the MPR Board of Directors that T-shirts and other paraphernalia associated with *A Prairie Home Companion* be marketed through a catalog. The board approved. The venture proved highly successful and led to the creation in 1981 of the Rivertown Trading Company but also drew criticism from commercial broadcasters as yet another example of MPR having its noncommercial cake and eating it, too. In the mid-1990s, a few state legislators pressed MPR for full disclosure of Kling's salary and called for details on the nature of the relationship between non-commercial MPR and the for-profit Greenspring Company (which by then included the MNN Radio Network, the MPR magazine *Minnesota Monthly* and other periodicals, and Rivertown). Kling and a number of MPR Board members defended their action by pointing out that this was just what the U.S. Congress and the Reagan administration had encouraged public broadcasting stations to do: become less dependent on government appropriations.

The Minnesota legislature eventually found nothing illegal in the MPR-Rivertown arrangement. However, Rivertown was sold to the Dayton-Hudson Corporation (now the Target Corporation) in 1998, by which time it had annual sales of about $195 million. MPR's "parent" company, the Minnesota Communications Group (MCG), reported a gain on the Rivertown sale of about $94 million, of which $85.6 million was set aside as a permanent endowment for MPR. As Robert Unmacht (publisher of the radio industry newsletters *M Street Journal* and *M Street Daily*) observed of Kling, "He's figured out how to provide a service to the public and make a lot of money."

The "Klingon Empire," as some of Kling's critics and supporters alike have dubbed it, continues to grow. In May 2000, the public radio program service *Marketplace* was sold to MPR. This again raised speculation regarding Kling's motives. Was he bidding to compete directly with NPR? He dismissed that possibility and could point to a May 2000 agreement with NPR to develop an internet service. However, he clearly was delighted with the acquisition of Southern California Public Radio (KPCC-FM, in Pasadena), which would provide MPR with the opportunity to show listeners in the Los Ange-

les area what a *real* news and public affairs service was like: as Kling said in a May 1999 interview with *Current*, "I think we need a model in a tough city, a big city, the second largest city."

Kling's goal remains the same as it was more than 30 years ago: service. He has not exercised editorial control over MPR's news and public affairs programs, although he did stop a few stories (abortion, politics, feminist perspectives on violence) from appearing in *Minnesota Monthly* in the mid 1970s. Rather, it is the capacity of public radio to provide a reflection of the social, political, and cultural life of the community and the region that seems to continually excite him—and to drive him to seek the resources necessary to maintain excellence in that realm, whether he pleases or angers people in the process.

DONALD R. BROWNE

See also Minnesota Public Radio; National Public Radio; Public Radio International; Public Radio Since 1967

William H. Kling. Born in St. Paul, Minnesota, 29 April 1942. Attended St. Johns University, B.A. in economics, 1966; operated own radio station while at St. Johns University, 1963–64; attended Boston University School of Public Communication M.A. program, 1964–66. Founding member and manager of KSJN-FM, Collegeville, Minnesota, 1967–69; manager, Minnesota Educational Radio, 1969–70; Assistant Director of Radio Activities, Corporation for Public Broadcasting, 1970–71; President, Minnesota Educational Radio, 1971–74; President and CEO, Minnesota Public Radio, from 1974. Cofounder and Vice Chairman, American Public Radio, 1983–93; President, Minnesota Communications Group, from 1987; President, Greenspring Company (for-profit arm of Minnesota Public Radio), from 1987; President, Rivertown Trading Company (direct marketing division of Greenspring until 1998), 1981–98; Vice Chairman of Southern California Public Radio, from 1999.

Further Reading

Conciatorre, Jacqueline, "'We're a Player' in Minnesota, Kling Says," *Current* (10 May 1999)

Gilyard, Burl, "All Unquiet on the Western Front," *City Pages* (Minneapolis/St. Paul) (26 April 2000)

Holston, Noel, "Not So Nonprofit," *Minneapolis Star Tribune* (22 September 1996)

"MPR: An Idea That Grew," *Minnesota Monthly* 11, no. 1 (1977)

KMOX

St. Louis, Missouri Station

KMOX (1120 kilohertz) is a 50,000-watt clear channel AM radio station in St. Louis, Missouri. The station is best known for the talk-centered format it introduced in 1960, which for many years gave it the largest market share of listeners of any radio station in the top 50 U.S. markets. KMOX was put on the air on Christmas eve (the origin of the X in the station's call letters) in 1925 by a group of investors called "the Voice of St. Louis." In 1927 it began carrying programs from United Independent Broadcasters, which later became the Columbia Broadcasting System (CBS), initially receiving $50.00 per hour of broadcast time. CBS has owned and operated the station since 1932.

KMOX was a fairly typical network station until February 1960 when, faced with erosion of audience to television and with competition from new radio stations that had joined the market in the postwar period, KMOX initiated a radical change in format and became one of the first stations in the United States to offer a talk-centered format. Although a number of stations pioneered the talk format in the 1960s (including KABC in Los Angeles), KMOX was unusual both in the success it achieved with the format (moving rapidly to first in the market) and in the amount of influence that was exerted over the station for decades by a single individual—Robert F. Hyland Jr., who became general manager of KMOX in 1955 and CBS vice president in 1959 and who continued in both those roles until his death at the age of 71 in 1992.

A number of characteristics set KMOX's air sound apart from that of other stations. In an industry where the norm is short stints for on-air talent, under Hyland's direction the station developed a reputation for just the opposite—talent stayed for decades. From the 1960s through the early 1990s, KMOX's style and content were often closer to those of the British Broadcasting Corporation (BBC) or public radio in the United States than to those of other commercial stations. The style was slightly formal, sometimes described as "dignified," and placed emphasis on both breadth and depth of information. Talk often consisted of a brief interview with a public figure or an expert on topics ranging from medicine to plumbing, followed by telephone calls from listeners. Although he eventually allowed some pure "open line" discussion in which the on-air talent simply chatted with callers, Hyland demanded even then that information of substance be a part of the presentation. If callers were kept on the line too long, Hyland would often reprimand hosts for "back fencing" or engaging in "therapy" with a listener, rather than keeping the discussion on topic. Hyland said in 1960 that one of the

purposes of the new talk-oriented format was to educate in addition to entertain.

One of the puzzling paradoxes of KMOX was how it could sound so much like noncommercial, public service radio and yet achieve ratings so much higher than such stations usually do. In 1976 KMOX had a 26 share of the audience in its market, with its nearest competitor holding less than a 9 share. The best clue to understanding this success may be found in a common saying that had developed among journalists and politicians in Missouri by the 1970s: "KMOX is more like a newspaper than a radio station." It was sometimes called St. Louis' "third newspaper" (when the *Globe Democrat* and the *Post-Dispatch* were the other two) and then the "second newspaper" after the *Globe-Democrat* ceased publication. It was idiosyncratic (running marches and prayers as part of a morning ritual) and involved in its community, much like some of the famous editor-dominated newspapers of the 19th century, such as Horace Greeley's *New York Tribune* and Joseph Pulitzer's *St. Louis Post-Dispatch*. The approach Hyland used to advance his radio station was indeed similar to what Pulitzer had tried successfully in the same city almost a century earlier: heavy community involvement (Hyland was reputed to have belonged to approximately 100 different organizations), aggressive investigative reporting, and a combination of entertainment (Hyland tied up all the major professional sports teams for KMOX and carried play-by-play broadcasts of important college games as well) and serious reporting, all seasoned with heavy self-promotion and one editorial campaign after another. Shortly after he became general manager, Hyland made KMOX the first CBS-owned station to carry editorials (the first was in advocacy of fluoridation of St. Louis county water and accused the county government of cowardice for refusing to take a stand). Hyland also followed the lead of newspapers and had KMOX endorse specific candidates for office.

The format that gave KMOX dominance and made it one of the most valuable properties owned by CBS (chairman William Paley once called it "the jewel in the CBS crown") was expensive. At its peak, the station employed more than 100 people, more than 70 of them full-time, and kept a number of "retainers" on the payroll, especially in sports, so that the station would have access to them and so that they would not sell their on-air services elsewhere (a practice that was abandoned as too expensive not long after Hyland's death). The station was intensely local, so much so that when President John F. Kennedy was assassinated in 1963, Hyland ordered the staff to break away from the CBS network feed and to focus on reaction to the assassination in the St. Louis area.

KMOX's similarity to a newspaper illustrates its strengths as well as its vulnerability. The station's high costs required continued high ratings in order to remain profitable, and it could not maintain those ratings as younger people turned away from KMOX's type of serious talk, much as they had also turned away from newspapers. In 1989 a headline in the *Post-Dispatch* read "How Long Will KMOX Be No. 1?" and the accompanying article reported that the station (although still strong overall and especially among the older population) held only a 9.2 percent share of the audience aged 18 to 34. In the 1990s the share in that critical age group would drop even more, to less than 5.0. Even more important, by 2002 the station's overall share had dropped to below 10, which, although still enough to make it number one in the market, was down dramatically from what it had been a decade earlier. The shift from AM to FM listening and the aging of its audience had finally caught up with KMOX.

Robert Hyland maintained until his death in March of 1992 that KMOX should not trivialize or tabloidize its programming, asserting in a 1990 speech to the St. Louis Press Club:

> The fact that we live in a fast-paced, entertainment-oriented age does not relieve us of the responsibility to live up to the sacred trusts inherent in our profession. . . . Virtually everyone reads newspapers, hears radio and views television. It must be our sacred mission that what they read, hear and view shall have meaning and import beyond filling space and killing time.

Hyland argued that as long as the station maintained its stronghold on major-league play-by-play sports, young listeners would learn its dial position and would eventually turn to KMOX as they got older and became more interested in being informed than in the latest music trends.

Following Hyland's death, a number of changes took place at the station and at CBS that would change KMOX's sound. Much of the station's long-standing on-air staff left. Bob Hardy, who had been on the air for more than 30 years, died, and Jim White and Anne Keefe, also on the air for decades, retired. Jim Wilkerson left for a competing station in a 1996 talent raid that also grabbed two other established voices at KMOX (Wendy Wiese and Kevin Horrigan), transplanting the station's morning sound almost intact to the competing station. But the most drastic change to come to KMOX in the wake of Hyland's death took place in 1994, when a key daytime slot once used for local interviews was turned over to Rush Limbaugh's nationally syndicated show. The decision to put Limbaugh on the air appears to have been primarily defen-

sive—Limbaugh had begun running on a competing station, and the choice was either to have him on KMOX or to compete against him. Limbaugh went on the air from 11 A.M. to 2 P.M. in April 1994, and late in 1999 he was still scheduled in that period. The decision to put Limbaugh on the air may or may not have saved KMOX from further ratings erosion, but it definitely changed the station's sound in three significant ways: (1) where KMOX had long been intensely local, Limbaugh's show has no sense of a particular place; (2) Limbaugh uses various news vignettes and excerpts to support discussion centering on a conservative political point of view; and (3) his sometimes frenetic delivery style is quite different from the calm, public service radio tone that even the younger, post-Hyland KMOX hosts employ.

In 1996 major cutbacks, including reductions in staff, were ordered by Westinghouse, the new owner of CBS. When one irate program host, Kevin Horrigan, walked out and took a job with a competing station, he charged that KMOX was in "chaos," that "part-timers and college kids are writing news and producing shows," and that "everything is being done on the cheap." The cause of the problem, according to the *Post-Dispatch*, was that Westinghouse was demanding a 40 percent profit margin, meaning that the station would have to produce a profit of about $9 million on total advertising sales of about $22.5 million per year, or about double what its past profits had been.

In November 2002 another program host, former CNN correspondent Charles Jaco, was fired (for reasons KMOX management never publicly revealed), and as he left Jaco blasted station management for "dumbing down" its program content in an attempt to raise ratings. The controversy over Jaco's firing (which was covered extensively by St. Louis news media) came on the heels of a number of setbacks, including the erosion of the station's dominance in professional sports play by play. By 2001, KMOX no longer had broadcast rights for the games of the St. Louis hockey and football teams, although it did still provide play by play for Cardinal baseball games. In the first years of the 21st century, KMOX could be viewed as embattled, owing to its decline in ratings and to increasingly negative coverage by other media, including the *St. Louis Post-Dispatch* (a 2002 headline proclaimed the station was "losing its grip on listeners") and the *St. Louis Journalism Review* (which in its December 2002/January 2003 issue carried an article on what it referred to as the "unsavory underside" of KMOX in which allegations of right-wing bias and anti-union policies appeared). However, the station could also be viewed as a survivor: in 2002, more than a decade after a newspaper article questioned how long it could remain in the top position, KMOX was still the number one station in St. Louis in total audience.

MARK POINDEXTER

See also Columbia Broadcasting System; Talk Radio

Further Reading

Chin, Sandra Hardy, *At Your Service: KMOX and Bob Hardy, Pioneers of Talk Radio,* St Louis, Missouri: Virginia Publishing, 1997

Gallagher, Jim, "How Long Will KMOX Be No. 1?" *St. Louis Post-Dispatch* (4 December 1989)

Rains, Sally, and Bob Rains, *The Mighty 'Mox: The 75th Anniversary History of the People, Stories, and Events that Made KMOX a Radio Giant,* South Bend, Indiana: Diamond Communications, 2002

KNX

Los Angeles, California Station

From its beginnings in a small bedroom of a Hollywood residence more than 80 years ago, KNX has grown to become one of the nation's most substantial all-news radio stations. KNX is the oldest radio station operating in Los Angeles and one of the oldest stations in the United States.

Origins

What eventually became KNX started as a 5-watt amateur radio station, with the call sign of 6ADZ. The station was built and operated in a back bedroom of his Hollywood home by Fred Christian, a former shipboard wireless operator. KNX historical records indicate that on 20 September 1920 Christian began broadcasting records he had borrowed from music stores, in return for plugs on the air. It is not known how often Christian provided such broadcasts at 200 meters/1500 kilohertz, and he had to leave the air quite often so other amateur radio operators could take their turns at their common hobby.

Christian's main occupation was running the Electric Lighting Supply Company on West Third Street in Los Angeles, selling parts for people to build their own receivers and broadcasting music for them to enjoy. By late 1921 the U.S. Department of Commerce decided to license radio stations that could broadcast music and entertainment to the public, thus removing congestion from amateur radio bands. On 8 December 1921 Christian was granted a license for 360 meters (833 kilohertz), with the call letters KGC.

Christian soon grew tired of broadcasting only recorded music. He moved KGC to the top of the California Theatre Building in downtown Los Angeles. His plans were to broadcast "live" music from the theater. KGC took up the new call sign of KNX when it moved on 1 May 1922. Christian built a new 50-watt transmitter to send its signal to more listeners. (The station was briefly off the air a year later while a new 100 watt transmitter was installed.) The station was also known as

the "California Theatre Radiophone" between 1922 and 1924. Because there were so few available frequencies and no viable government regulation, stations during that period had to share air time. KNX negotiated with about 15 active radio stations in the Los Angeles area to determine each month the hours the stations would go on the air. KNX usually featured Carli Elinor's California Theatre Concert Orchestra of 50 to 60 musicians during an afternoon or evening broadcast four days a week, along with music from the theater's organ. The orchestra often performed musical scores from movies playing at the theater, to draw KNX listeners to see the films. Several early Hollywood film celebrities were heard over KNX, including Conrad Nagel, Wallace Reid, Harry Langdon, and Lon Chaney.

Radio magazines of the day that printed KNX program schedules also showed ads for the Electric Lighting Supply Company. Christian sold radios and radio parts to help defray the cost of running the station, because advertising on radio was not common yet. He sold KNX to the Los Angeles *Evening Express* newspaper on 14 October 1924, and the station shifted from 833 to 890 kilohertz and increased power from 100 watts to 500 watts. Under the leadership of owner-publisher Guy C. Earl, KNX soon promoted itself to radio fans as "The Voice of Hollywood" and used that slogan for many years. Earl had used KNX before to promote his newspaper and soon sold advertising regularly on the station. When KNX showed a profit of $25,000 in 1925, Earl focused more of his time on the radio side, and other Los Angeles stations took notice of what selling advertising could do for them. In the mid- and late 1920s, KNX offered a daily schedule from early morning to late night. One regular feature was music from Ray West's Cocoanut Grove Orchestra from the Hotel Ambassador. KNX also offered listeners sports and a variety of informational talks, plus drama from the KNX players. From its earliest days, news was an important part of KNX's broadcast day.

In late 1928 KNX shifted from 890 to 1050 kilohertz and moved to the Paramount Pictures lot in Hollywood. The station increased transmitter power to 5,000 watts in 1929 and doubled that in 1932. Earl sold the Los Angeles *Evening Express* but stayed in radio, running KNX under the ownership of the Western Broadcasting Company. When KNX moved its offices and studios again in 1933, to the corner of Vine Street and Selma Avenue, station power was boosted to 25,000 watts and finally to 50,000 watts in 1934. In 1936 KNX moved to Sunset Boulevard.

CBS Ownership

KNX was sold to the Columbia Broadcasting System (CBS) for $1.25 million in 1936, then the highest price ever paid for a radio station. New KNX/CBS studios were constructed and opened on 30 April 1938 at 6121 Sunset Boulevard. The Hollywood landmark station remains there today. Known as Columbia Square, the studios were home to several top-rated radio shows through the 1940s, including *Silver Theater, Melody Ranch* with Gene Autry, *Lucky Strike Hit Parade*, Jack Benny, Burns and Allen, Edgar Bergen and Charlie McCarthy, and Red Skelton. The long-running *Lux Radio Theatre* originated from the Vine Street Playhouse nearby. During World War II, *GE Radio News* with Frazier Hunt was heard. Local shows such as *The Housewives Protective League, Hollywood*

Melody Shop, and *Hollywood Barn Dance* were favorites with southern California listeners. On 29 March 1941 KNX shifted its frequency one last time, to 1070 kilohertz.

In the late 1940s comedian Steve Allen worked at KNX as a disc jockey, but he soon turned his airtime into a very popular late-night interview and comedy show. The program got Allen noticed by CBS executives and was a springboard to his highly successful subsequent TV career. Bob Crane, who gained fame on TV's *Hogan's Heroes*, was a very funny morning personality on KNX from 1956 to 1965. During this time KNX had become mostly a music station with news and sports features.

In April 1968 KNX initiated an all-news format and soon operated the largest radio news department in the western United States. KNX claims to have won more awards for broadcast journalism than any other radio station in the United States. These honors include Best Newscast Award from the Associated Press and Best Newscast Award from the Radio-TV News Association (RTNA) 27 times in the past 30 years. KNX has also won more than 150 Golden Mikes from the RTNA.

JIM HILLIKER

Further Reading

Blanton, Parke, *Crystal Set to Satellite: The Story of California Broadcasting, the First 80 Years*, Los Angeles: California Broadcasters Association, 1987

KOA

Denver, Colorado Station

As a 50,000-watt clear channel station, KOA is said to stand for "Klear Over America." One of the first radio stations in Denver, KOA later became one of the West's most popular stations. KOA's powerful signal is capable of reaching 38 states in the evening hours, and the station has been heard in Canada, Mexico, and nearly every state in the United States under the right atmospheric conditions.

Changing Hands

KOA went on the air on 15 December 1924 and was authorized for 1,000 watts at 930 kilohertz. Built and operated by the General Electric Company, the station underwent many changes in operating power and dial position before settling at 50,000 watts in 1934 and at 850 kilohertz in 1941.

KOA underwent many ownership changes over the years. The station became affiliated with the National Broadcasting Company (NBC) in 1928. In 1929 NBC took over operation of KOA from General Electric, and the license was officially assigned to NBC in 1930. However, the actual change of ownership did not occur until NBC bought the transmitter from General Electric in 1934. NBC added a sister station, KOA-FM (later KOAQ-FM, now KRFX-FM), in 1948. The stations were sold to the Metropolitan Television Company (MTC) in 1952. One of MTC's principal stockholders was legendary radio, television, and motion picture entertainer Bob Hope. This group added a television station in 1953, channel 4 KOA-TV (now KCNC-TV). Bob Hope sold his interest in 1964, and General Electric repurchased the station in 1968. In 1983 General Electric sold KOA-AM and sister station KOAQ-FM to

Belo Broadcasting. In 1987 KOA was sold to Jacor Broadcasting, which merged with Clear Channel Communications in 1999.

Programming

The opening broadcast in 1924 was launched with much fanfare. With colorful prose, the station avowed its purpose "to serve with special intimacy the states that lie in the great plain—from the Dakotas and Minnesota to Texas—to the Mississippi and beyond; to spread knowledge that will be of use to them in their vast business—to further their peoples' cultural ambitions—to give wider play to their imaginations, and make melody in their ears—to bid them lift up their eyes unto these western hills whence comes new strength" (cited in *Colorado Mac News*, 1984)

In the early days, a large number of KOA radio listeners were farmers, and the station had a heavy emphasis on farm, weather, and agriculture market–related programming. *Farm Question Box* and *Mile High Farmer* were two of the longest-running and most popular agriculture-related programs on the station.

KOA claims a number of historical "firsts" in broadcasting. On 18 February 1927 KOA did a remote broadcast of the "hole-ing through" of the Moffatt Tunnel, which was at the time the longest railroad tunnel in the world. Using the railroad's telegraph circuit, which ran to the entrance of the tunnel, KOA engineers ran lines more than three and one-half miles into the tunnel to broadcast the event. On 15 November 1928 KOA engineers lugged a transmitter to the top of Pikes Peak near Colorado Springs to become the first station to originate from atop a 14,000-foot peak in the Rockies. On 6 May 1936 KOA successfully broadcast a concert nationwide from a specially equipped Radio Corporation of America (RCA) Victor train heading into Denver. Leopold Stokowski conducted Stravinsky's *The Firebird* with a portion of the Philadelphia Symphony Orchestra on board. On 27 February 1937, a ski official involved in a ski race at Berthoud Pass in Colorado was set up with one of NBC's first "pack sets" on his back and a catcher's mask with a microphone mounted inside. The idea was for him to describe what he saw and felt as he sped down the mountain. The nation waited to hear how it felt to ski down a challenging mountain course. The technical apparatus worked perfectly, but the skier forgot to talk, and all the nation heard was several minutes of heavy breathing and the rush of air.

For a number of years, the KOA Staff Orchestra, an all-string ensemble, was featured on the NBC network as a sustaining program. Such programs as *Golden Memories, Rhapsody of the Rockies,* and *Sketches in Melody* spread the fame of the KOA Staff Orchestra across the country.

The 1960s and 1970s saw the development of KOA as a news powerhouse. The station built a reputation as a leading source of news and information throughout the Rocky Mountain West.

On 18 June 1984 outspoken KOA talk show host Alan Berg was murdered in front of his condominium in Denver. The slaying, which had political and religious overtones, generated a tremendous amount of national media coverage because of the circumstances. Berg took on many groups on his high-rated talk show, including right-wing Christians, knee-jerk liberals, and the Ku Klux Klan. There were connections between Berg's death and a group called "The Order," a white supremacist group in Colorado and the Pacific Northwest. The murder weapon was later found in the home of Gary Lee Yarbrough of Sandpoint, Idaho, a member of The Order.

Today, KOA concentrates its efforts as a news/talk/sports station. The station has the largest news-gathering staff in the market and carries play-by-play coverage of the Denver Broncos National Football League team, the Colorado Rockies baseball team, and the University of Colorado football games. The station's internet address is www.koaradio.com, which includes the KOA broadcast signal.

STEVEN D. ANDERSON

Further Reading

"A Brief History of the 50,000 Watt 'Voice of the West,'" *Colorado Mac News* (3 December 1984)

KOA website, <www.koaradio.com>

Singular, Stephen, *Talked to Death: The Life and Murder of Alan Berg,* New York: Beach Tree Books, 1987

KOB

Las Cruces/Albuquerque, New Mexico Station

KOB was a pioneering noncommercial, educational radio station established in Las Cruces, New Mexico, in the years after World War I. Affiliated with the New Mexico College of Agriculture and Mechanic Arts (NMA&MA)—now New Mexico State University—and supported by the college's engineering department, KOB began as an experimental student project using equipment salvaged from the U.S. Army. Ralph W. Goddard, a professor of engineering at NMA&MA, organized the school's Radio Club on 11 October 1919. The campus organization soon acquired not only a 500-watt Marconi standard Navy spark transmitter and 60-foot tower, but also three experimental radio licenses—5CX, 5FY, and 5FZ. License 5XD, which would become KOB, was granted on 3 June 1920.

In 1922, 500 new stations began broadcasting and KOB was one of them, going on the air on 5 April. Programming included market and stock reports, live performances, recorded music, weather reports, and news accounts provided by two El Paso newspapers, the *Times* and *Herald-Post*. The college's Agricultural Extension Service was an early ally for KOB and provided ongoing support for the radio project's contributions to rural life in southern New Mexico.

Goddard, who was eventually named Dean of Engineering at NMA&MA, was a key figure in the growth and development of KOB. He was responsible for guiding the station from its beginning as a project of the Radio Club—which was largely interested in amateur and relay work—to its status a few years later as a station broadcasting to all of New Mexico. He led efforts to expand the station's programming, facilities, and wattage, negotiating for clear channel status and a power allotment of 5,000 watts with the Federal Radio Commission (FRC); both were granted on 11 November 1928. By March of the following year, the station had been approved for an allotment of 10,000 watts, making it the most powerful college radio station in the United States and the country's 13th most powerful station of any type. In the fall of 1929, Goddard applied for FRC permission to double the station's power again, which would increase its power to 20,000 watts.

Ironically, even as KOB developed as one of the country's premier radio stations, its support from the university community decreased. In spite of continuing interest in and contributions to the station by the Agricultural Extension Service, local civic groups, and segments of NMA&MA, the college administration began suggesting in late 1928 that Goddard should start looking for a buyer for the station. This diminished administrative support for KOB would ultimately prove fatal. Goddard's dream of building an educational radio station that would broadcast throughout most of the Southwest dissolved

with his tragic death on New Year's Eve, 1929. While attempting to shut the station down for the afternoon, Goddard—whose shoes were soaked from a walk in the rain—was electrocuted. Although another NMA&MA professor was named station director and the application for 20,000-watt status was approved, KOB never recovered from the loss of its founder and most ardent supporter. Lacking his hands-on leadership and personal drive, station staff could muster neither adequate management expertise nor local support to keep KOB on the air. When the FRC began sending off-frequency reports and complaints that the station was not modulating, the college decided to accept a lease-purchase offer from T.M. Pepperday, owner of the *Albuquerque Journal*.

The station's assets were subsequently leased to the *Journal* in the fall of 1931; all equipment was transferred by truck more than 200 miles to Albuquerque in September 1932; and KOB's first broadcast from Albuquerque aired on 5 October 1932. The station's disposition was completed in August 1936, when NMA&MA sold KOB to the *Journal*'s newly-formed subsidiary, the Albuquerque Broadcasting Company. KOB affiliated with the National Broadcasting Company (NBC) the following year.

KOB is one example of the way in which a number of noncommercial, educational radio stations were transferred from public to private ownership in the 1930s. Lacking financial resources, institutional support, and strong leadership, this flagship western station could not endure as a publicly owned, noncommercial entity. Like many college stations, KOB's purchase and network affiliation helped to facilitate the development of a network-dominated broadcasting system in the United States. Many local listeners in Las Cruces were grieved by the station's departure, and the New Mexico State Legislature conducted an extensive debate about the station's sale to a private company. Governor Floyd Tingley, a New Dealer with close ties to Franklin D. Roosevelt, suggested that KOB become a state owned and operated public station, an idea that would be echoed in later discussions of state public networks elsewhere.

The North American Regional Broadcasting Agreement (1941) forced KOB (and many other U.S. stations) to change frequencies. In 1941 KOB moved to 1030 kilohertz, the same channel used by a Boston clear channel outlet. Later that year, just before U.S. entry into World War II, KOB moved again, this time thanks to a Federal Communications Commission (FCC) temporary permit, to 770 kilohertz, a clear channel frequency then used by what is now WABC in New York. The potential for mutual interference between the stations led to the longest legal battle in FCC history. Attorneys for each station inundated the commission with legal attempts to force the other outlet off the shared frequency. KOB was allowed to raise its power to 50,000 watts in the daytime but was required to drop back to 25,000 watts at night in an attempt to protect the New York station. In 1956 KOB was also required to install a directional antenna to reduce interference with WABC. By 1962 it had FCC permission to raise its nighttime power to 50,000 watts. Legal filings from both outlets continued to plague the FCC into the early 1980s, when KOB's final appeal to overcome WABC's primary status on the channel was turned down. Both stations remain on 770 kilohertz today, with KOB continuing to shield the New York outlet by means of directional antenna patterns.

A KOB television station was added in 1948, and in 1967 an affiliated FM outlet was added in Albuquerque. The station changed hands several times; it was purchased by Hubbard Broadcasting in 1957, which operated KOB for three decades before selling it in 1986. It changed hands again several times

in the 1990s, by which time its call letters had been changed to KKOB. On 15 October 1994 the station was purchased by Citadel Communications, and by 2000 it was programmed as news/talk.

In the meantime, the university that had first supported the radio outlet lost its right to free airtime in 1951, although for a number of years that arrangement continued informally. Ralph Goddard's important role in its early years was remembered when the Las Cruces university again became a licensee in 1964 and placed KRWG (Goddard's initials) on the air as the first college/university FM station in the New Mexico. It, too, was joined by a television outlet with the same call letters eight years later.

GLENDA R. BALAS

Further Reading

Velia, Ann M., *KOB, Goddard's Magic Mast: Fifty Years of Pioneer Broadcasting*, Las Cruces: New Mexico State University Press, 1972

KPFA

Berkeley, California Station

KPFA-FM in Berkeley, California, is the first station of the Pacifica radio network and the first listener-sponsored station in the United States. Poet, philosopher, and conscientious objector Lewis Hill created the station as a means to "help prevent warfare through the free and uncensored interchange of ideas in politics, philosophy and the arts."

KPFA first went on the air 15 April 1949, and controversy dogged the non-commercial station from the start. In a postwar America known for Cold War conformity and rampant consumerism, KPFA brought many non-mainstream voices to its microphones, including African-American actor and activist Paul Robeson, Zen philosopher Alan Watts, leftist commentator William Mandel, Beat poet Lawrence Ferlinghetti, political theorist Herbert Marcuse, film critic Pauline Kael, and voices from the Bay Area's academic, pacifist, and anarchist communities.

Hill created the idea of listener sponsorship in order to fund the station's operation without having to sell commercials. This freed the station of corporate control and gave it the chance to promote political alternatives. The operating funds,

Hill theorized, would come if 2 percent of the potential audience paid $10 a year to support the station.

Listener sponsorship was not the only unusual aspect of the station's operations. In the beginning, despite a bureaucratic hierarchy, everyone on staff at KPFA was paid the same salary, and decisions were made collectively. Also, clocks were removed from on-air studios so that programs could run to their natural conclusions.

Despite such innovations, financial problems and internal tensions among the staff, the volunteers, and the station's advisory board quickly came to the fore. In 1950 the station went off the air for nine months because of lack of funds. The following year, Pacifica received a $150,000 grant from the Ford Foundation, which allowed it to resume broadcasting.

In June 1953 Lewis Hill resigned because of internal political struggles at the station. A new group felt constrained under his leadership. Despite the internecine problems, KPFA continued to make history with its innovative and intellectually challenging programming. Throughout the 1950s, the station's public-affairs programs regularly addressed such hot-button issues as racial segregation, economic disparity, and McCarthyism. In April 1954 a pre-recorded radio program that advocated the decriminalization of marijuana created an uproar and led to the tape's impoundment by California's attorney general.

In August 1954 founder Lewis Hill returned to run the station. But three years later, in late July of 1957, the 38-year-old Hill, suffering from crippling rheumatoid arthritis and depression, committed suicide. He left the following note: "Not for anger or despair/but for peace and a kind of home."

KPFA and Pacifica won numerous broadcast awards for children's programming and for special programs on the First Amendment by legal scholar Alexander Meiklejohn. KPFA's public-affairs director, Elsa Knight Thompson, continued pushing the broadcast envelope despite attempts to censor the station. The Federal Communications Commission (FCC), for example, questioned KPFA's broadcasts of poets Allen Ginsberg and Lawrence Ferlinghetti, broadcasts that the government found to be "vulgar, obscene, and in bad taste."

In 1960 KPFA broadcast a three-hour documentary on the riots following House Committee on Un-American Activities (popularly known as HUAC) hearings in San Francisco. It subsequently broadcast programs on homosexuality, the blacklist, and the FBI. HUAC reacted by investigating Pacifica for "subversion," and the FCC investigated "communist affiliations" at the station, but the Commission ultimately renewed KPFA's license after a 3-year delay. KPFA later gave extensive coverage to the Berkeley Free Speech Movement, and many University of California, Berkeley, faculty members were heard regularly.

Though the public-affairs programs often stirred controversy, the station's arts programming had a significant impact on the Bay Area's cultural scene. KPFA's first music director, Americo Chiarito, boldly mixed jazz, classical, folk, and other forms of noncommercial music throughout the broadcast day. Over a 25-year period, subsequent music director Charles Amirkanian interviewed and gave exposure to the work of nearly every living composer of importance in the West, including Terry Riley, LaMonte Young, Steve Reich, Lou Harrison, Pauline Oliveros, and John Cage. Philip Elwood, later the jazz critic for the San Francisco *Examiner*, hosted various on-air jazz programs for nearly 40 years. Sandy Miranda's *Music of the World* program featured live music, interviews, and rare recordings that drew a large and devoted following that made significant financial contributions to the station. For nearly a quarter of a century, the station devoted considerable airtime to contemporary poetry and literature under the direction of Erik Bauersfeld.

Through the 1970s and 1980s there was a gradual, if fundamental, shift in how KPFA and the Pacifica network (which by then included stations in New York, Los Angeles, Houston, and Washington, D.C.) defined themselves and their target audience. Unlike the early days in Berkeley, when the audience was presumed to be an elite, educated, intellectual minority, KPFA gradually became known as a "community" radio station. Its audience, and even many on-air programmers, became increasingly defined not by ideas but by gender, ethnicity, race, and class. Third-World and women's departments were eventually created at the station. As these and other groups in the community demanded a place on the broadcast schedule, bitter arguments ensued over ideology and over questions about who speaks for whom and which groups deserve access to the microphone.

In 1999 many of these questions came to a head when the Pacifica network attempted to make programming and staff changes at KPFA, removing the station's popular general manager. The network defended the changes as an attempt to increase audience numbers and diversity. Many of the staff and volunteers, as well as activist members of the community, charged that the network was engaging in strong-arm tactics in an attempt to consolidate power and avoid accountability. What started as a personnel matter soon mushroomed into a widely publicized struggle over the station's future, prompting walkouts, strikes, and demonstrations.

Although such controversies have occurred periodically at a number of the Pacifica stations over the years, it was especially ironic that an organization that that has done so much to protect the broadcast of free speech would resort to censorship when its newscasters attempted to cover the story. When KPFA's investigative reporter Dennis Bernstein defied a network gag order by covering the crisis at the station, he was suspended from his job, then arrested along with 51 KPFA staff and activists who refused to leave the building. A live, open microphone caught the entire drama. Pacifica officials then cancelled regular programming and boarded up the station for much of July and September.

But faced with a demonstration of 10,000 angry KPFA supporters, Pacifica relented and permitted KPFA staff to go back to work. This and subsequent controversies at all five Pacifica stations sparked a grassroots campaign to democratize the network. By December of 2001 a new Board of Directors had been assigned the task of revising the foundation's by-laws to give the network's listener-sponsors more say over governance.

LARRY APPELBAUM AND MATTHEW LASAR

See also Community Radio; Hill, Lewis; Pacifica Foundation; Public Radio Since 1967

Further Reading

Hill, Lewis, *Voluntary Listener-Sponsorship: A Report to Educational Broadcasters on the Experiment at KPFA, Berkeley, California*, Berkeley, California: Pacifica Foundation, 1958
KPFA website, <www.kpfa.org>

Land, Jeff, *Active Radio: Pacifica's Brash Experiment*, Minneapolis: University of Minnesota Press, 1999

Lasar, Matthew, *Pacifica Radio: The Rise of an Alternative Network*, Philadelphia, Pennsylvania: Temple University Press, 2000

Thompson, Chris, "War and Peace: The Battle for KPFA and the Soul of Pacifica Is Over: Now the Damage Assessment Begins" (*East Bay Express*, 9 January 2002; http://www.eastbayexpress.com/issues/2002-01-09/feature.html/1/index.html)

KQW. *See* KCBS/KQW

KRLA

Los Angeles, California Station

KRLA (1110 kilohertz) is a 50,000-watt AM station serving the Los Angeles market. It was a popular Top 40 station in the 1960s, featuring stand-out radio personalities such as Casey Kasem, Bob Eubanks, Dave Hull, and Bob Hudson. KRLA associated itself strongly with the Beatles at that time, sponsoring several Beatles concerts in Los Angeles. It became the number one station in that market in 1964 and held that distinction for several years. Ironically, it was during KRLA's ratings heyday that its long legal struggle with the Federal Communications Commission (FCC) began. In 1962 the FCC denied a license renewal to station owner Donald Cooke and his company, Eleven Ten Broadcasting, over questionable on-air practices. This set off a 17-year battle, during which KRLA was operated by a nonprofit interim company. The license renewal case for KRLA is a rare instance of FCC license denial based on content and behavior rather than technical considerations.

Origins

The station's history began in 1940 when J.R. Frank Burke and other investors formed the Pacific Coast Broadcasting Company in order to apply for a broadcasting license in Pasadena, California. Burke was a fund-raiser for the Democratic Party and publisher of the *Santa Ana Register*. The FCC issued a construction permit in September 1941, just months before the United States entered World War II and placed a moratorium on all new radio construction. The new station would have the call letters KPAS and operate at 10,000 watts on 1110 kilohertz. By February 1942 an operating license was issued and KPAS went on the air as an unaffiliated station with block pro-

gramming typical of the time period. Burke's accountant, Loyal King, became the station manager. In addition to music, news, and religious programs, KPAS featured dramatic sketches performed by the Pasadena Playhouse actors. Local programming and public service were hallmarks of the station in the 1940s.

In 1945, Burke sold his interest to religious broadcaster William Dumm, who in turn sold his share in the station to Loyal King two years later. The license was retained by Pacific Coast Broadcasting. The station's call letters were changed to KXLA in 1945 to suggest a more metropolitan target audience. In 1948 King began to run a popular syndicated program called *Country Crystals* and by the early 1950s, KXLA had become a country western station. Most commercial radio stations in the United States were switching to musical formats at this time, as radio talent and network financing were migrating to television.

In 1958 a major change for the station occurred when New York businessman Donald Cooke signed an agreement to purchase KXLA from Pacific Coast Broadcasting. Cooke's brother, Jack Kent Cooke, was the true interested party, but as a Canadian citizen, he was prohibited by the Communications Act of 1934 from owning a U.S. radio station. In order to help his brother finance the purchase, Jack Kent Cooke would buy the station facilities through his newly formed company, Broadcast Equipment Corporation (BEC). Don Cooke's company, Eleven Ten Broadcasting, would file for the license transfer and lease the facilities from BEC.

In March 1959, the FCC approved the transfer with the understanding that Jack Kent Cooke would have no role in managing the station. In fact, he had already been heavily involved, and in the months to come he would play a significant role in station management by making personnel decisions and planning on-air contests and promotions. The Cookes' intention was to change the format to Top 40 rock and roll and to concentrate on the teenage demographic throughout the Los Angeles market. At midnight on 1 September 1959, the station officially switched over. Nineteen-year-old disk jockey Jimmy O'Neill announced, "You have been listening to KXLA. You are now listening to KRLA-Radio for the young at heart."

Fifteen Years of "Interim" Owner Operation

In August 1959, all southern California stations were required to submit applications for license renewal according to the regular FCC schedule of renewals. KRLA did so, but in July of 1960, the FCC notified Donald Cooke that there would be a hearing for KRLA's license renewal. The FCC was concerned about several problems, including programming promises not being met, falsified logs, fraudulent contests, and the involvement of a non-citizen in station management. Although the hearing examiner recommended a one-year probationary renewal, the FCC denied renewal in 1962. The decision was upheld on appeal and the FCC ordered KRLA off the air. Comparative hearings would be held to determine the new licensee, but the FCC was concerned about leaving the frequency vacant in the meantime, as that meant the Mexican station XERB would be allowed to increase its power under provisions of an international treaty.

Oak Knoll Broadcasting, a nonprofit company, was selected to be the interim owner and licensee of KRLA. Eighty percent of their profits were to go to KCET, an educational TV station, and the other 20 percent would be distributed to other charities. Oak Knoll took possession of the station in 1964 and continued to operate it until 1979, when a new company, KRLA Incorporated, was finally selected to take over the license, ending the interim period. Oak Knoll's long period in control stemmed from the protracted FCC proceedings required to choose between more than a dozen applicants for the station license.

The early Oak Knoll years were KRLA's strongest in terms of its position in the market. In 1964, KRLA sought to distinguish itself from KFWB, its primary competitor, by focusing on a single band, the Beatles. The station played all of the cuts from Beatles LPs rather than just the hits and provided information about the music and the band members, promoting itself as "Beatle Radio." KRLA also sponsored three Beatles concerts in Los Angeles from 1964 to 1966. This strategy enabled KRLA to become a contender in the competitive and saturated Los Angeles AM market.

During the 1970s KRLA's format changed several times. In 1971 the station switched to album-oriented progressive rock in an attempt to appeal to young people in the counterculture. This move proved unsuccessful, as FM radio was already offering that format with better sound quality. In 1973 KRLA moved to soft rock, which was more successful, but not enough so to make the station profitable. In 1976, under the direction of Art Laboe, KRLA changed to an Oldies format in a successful move to recapture a segment of the dwindling AM audience.

KRLA Incorporated was actually a merger of five of the companies that had applied for the KRLA license in 1964. It operated the station until 1985, when it was purchased by Greater Los Angeles Radio, Inc. Greater Los Angeles Radio moved the studios from the Huntington Hotel in Pasadena, where they had been since 1942, to Wilshire Boulevard in Los Angeles. The transmitter was moved to Irwindale the following year. In 1997 KRLA was acquired by Infinity Broadcasting, a subsidiary of Viacom, and its format was changed to talk radio. Infinity sold KRLA to Disney-owned ABC Radio in 2001. The format was changed to sports programming with an ESPN affiliation and the acquisition of Anaheim Angels baseball games. ABC Radio relaunched the station under the new call letters KSPN and as of January 2003 had swapped frequencies with KDIS-AM (Disney Radio) on 710 kilohertz. KDIS, now on the 1110 frequency, is formatted for children with Disney product. The KRLA call letters were acquired by Salem Communications for its talk station KIEV-AM at 870 kilohertz.

CHRISTINA S. DRALE

See also Contemporary Hit Radio Format/Top 40; Kasem, Casey; Licensing; Oldies Format

Further Reading

Beem, Donald C., "Standard Broadcast Station KRLA: A Case Study," Masters thesis, California State University at Fullerton, 1980
Earl, Bill, *Dream-House*, Valencia, California: Delta, 1989; 2nd edition, 1991

KSL

Salt Lake City, Utah Station

In the early days of radio, one of the key groups of licensees was composed of churches. As is the case with many such stations, it is difficult to discuss the vision and role of KSL without considering its church affiliation and the dream to proselytize. The Church of Jesus Christ of Latter-day Saints (LDS; Mormon) acquired a radio station to broadcast general conferences of the LDS Church to people throughout the area without their having to come to the tabernacle on the city's Temple Square. Although the functions and operations of the station's mission have changed dramatically over the years, the religious influence can still be found.

KSL's predecessor, KZN, went on the air on 6 May 1922 and was among the first in the Western United States. It broadcast on 1160 kilohertz, and was designated a class A (clear channel) station in 1925. The station is still located at 1160 AM. At 8 P.M. on the first day of its broadcast, from atop the building housing the LDS-operated *Deseret News* newspaper, the station broadcast LDS Church President Heber J. Grant, who spoke of the church's mission and doctrine, quoting from the church's scriptures. Some observers felt that President Grant's remarks were the beginning of the fulfillment of a dream voiced earlier that the president of the church could deliver his sermons "and be heard by congregations assembled in every settlement of the Church from Canada to Mexico, and from California to Colorado" (see Anderson, 1922).

During its first years of operation, the station carried the voices of several famous figures. In addition to church authorities, other noted speakers used this new, fascinating, and promising medium. William Jennings Bryan delivered a ten-minute address on 25 October 1922. In 1923 President Warren G. Harding spoke over the station in a broadcast originating from the church's tabernacle. It was the first known instance of a U.S. President speaking over radio in that area.

In June 1924 *The Deseret News* sold KZN to John and F.W. Cope, who planned to overcome some of the station's engineering problems. The call letters were changed to KFPT. Later that year, in October, the station broadcast the general conferences of the LDS Church, an event that was to occur semiannually through the rest of the century. Listeners could sit at home in their own living rooms next to their radio receivers and attend to the business and spiritual matters of that faith.

In June 1923 the Mormon Tabernacle Choir began its first formal broadcast on KZN (whose call letters were changed to KFPT in 1924, then to KSL in 1925) with the program *Music and the Spoken Word*, a program that continues in the early 21st century. A few years later, when KSL joined the National Broadcasting Company (NBC) as an affiliate, it began a regular Sunday broadcast of the choir. The program continued when, in 1932, KSL moved its affiliation to the Columbia Broadcasting System (CBS). (The radio station is still a CBS affiliate, although KSL-TV is now affiliated with NBC.) It continues as the oldest continuous sustained radio program in America. The program brought fame to the station and the church, as well as a wider audience for the choir and for the tabernacle organ, from their rich acoustical setting in the century-old tabernacle.

As radio developed into a commercial medium, troubles loomed for the Mormon-owned station. Although church leaders saw nothing wrong with the business operation in conjunction with its function as "a factor in the spread of the gospel of Jesus Christ across the world" (see Hinckley, 1947), the church's standards came into conflict with some commercial practices. For example, the church advocated against the use of alcohol and tobacco. Yet network programs carried by KSL contained commercials selling beer and cigarettes, and programs contained themes or characters using these products. Not to carry such programs with their commercials could mean severance from network feeds and a drastic reduction in profits and income. Continuing to carry the programs appeared hypocritical in light of the church's teachings of abstinence from these products. With CBS's position of hard business practices guiding the decision-making process, the church was poised to lose the network affiliation and become a secondary, perhaps insignificant influence in radio in the intermountain area. Policy was established not to accept spot advertising (contracted individually with the station) for beer, wine, or tobacco, but the national network ads would continue to be carried as a necessary evil. KSL would not try to restrict network advertising or interfere with network contracts. KSL-FM was Utah's first FM station, beginning operation on 26 December 1946. Its programming was different and separate from its AM outlet.

Becoming successful as a business, KSL became the flagship station in the church's broadcast ownership, Bonneville International, established in 1964. The group owned radio and television stations in Seattle, Washington, then acquired FM outlets in New York City, Chicago, San Francisco, Los Angeles, Dallas, and Kansas City. As of 2003, Bonneville had 15 stations. From the mid-1960s to 1975, Bonneville operated an international shortwave radio station reaching various countries.

KSL quickly realized that its clear channel signal of 50,000 watts AM served more than just Salt Lake City, extending to the entire Western region of the United States. It also tried to reflect a sense of commitment to serve this extended community, as mandated by church president David O. McKay in the mid-1960s. The station moved from broadcasting high school and church basketball tournaments in the 1950s to political broadcasts of substance. Bonneville's production arm created the "Home Front" public-service messages, which sent nondenominational messages about families and values to listeners who might not otherwise tune in to religious programming. These "Home Front" features were distributed to stations throughout the country to air in a variety of programs.

The church influence in KSL's programming has brought occasional criticism of censorship and biased influence. Yet the wide range of political viewpoints, the representations of other religious denominations, and the respect garnished from its news reporting seem to quell such criticism for many observers. One KSL news director disavows any meddling in the news agenda or its coverage of stories, including those local stories critical of church policies. Although some complaints have gone to the Federal Communications Commission, none has been taken seriously enough to limit the church's operation of its stations.

Broadcast management has indicated that today KSL is a station intent to make a profit, "not to evangelize." It is a commercial broadcast enterprise owned by a religious organization "operated strictly as a business and seeking no special treatment" (see Brady, 1994). Although the station started with a dream to evangelize, the realities of commercial broadcasting make its mission for community good more general in nature.

VAL E. LIMBURG

See also Mormon Tabernacle Choir

Further Reading

Anderson, Edward H., "The Vacuum Tube Amplifier," *The Improvement Era* 25, no.3 (March 1922)

Avant, Gerry, "Major Events, 1920–1929," *Church News* (13 March 1999)

Brady, Rodney H., *Bonneville at Thirty: A Value-Driven Company of Values-Driven People*, New York: Newcomen Society, 1994

Donigan, Robert W., "An Outline History of Broadcasting in the Church of Jesus Christ of Latter-Day Saints, 1922–1963," master's thesis, Brigham Young University, 1963

Godfrey, Donald G., Val E. Limburg, and Heber G. Wolsey, "KSL, Salt Lake City: 'At the Crossroads of the West,'" in *Television in America: Local Station History from across the Nation*, edited by Michael D. Murray and Donald G. Godfrey, Ames: Iowa State University Press, 1997

Hinckley, Gordon B., "Twenty-Five Years of Radio Ministry," *Deseret News* (26 April 1947)

Lichty, Lawrence, and Malachi Topping, *American Broadcasting: A Source Book on the History of Radio and Television*, New York: Hastings House, 1975

Limburg, Val E., "An Analysis of Relationships between Religious Programming Objectives and Methods of Presentation Used by Selected Major Religious Program Producers as Compared to the Church of Jesus Christ of Latter-Day Saints," Master's thesis, Brigham Young University, 1964

Wolsey, Heber Grant, "The History of Radio Station KSL, from 1922 to Television," Ph.D. diss., Michigan State University, 1967

Zobell, Albert L., Jr., "Twenty Magnificent Years on the Air," *Improvement Era* 52, no. 9 (September 1949)

KTRH

Houston, Texas Station

A longtime news, talk, and information station, KTRH was the starting point for the careers of several national celebrities, including the two best-known anchors on Columbia Broadcasting System (CBS) television.

The history of KTRH meshes with the history of modern Houston. KTRH was a relative latecomer when it signed on the air 5 March 1930. The city had boasted an experimental radio station as early as 1919. Several commercial stations were on the air in the early 1920s, although none lasted longer than a few years. Only rival KPRC, launched by the *Houston Post-Dispatch* during a newspaper convention in the city in 1925, hinted at the promise radio would hold in the city.

The opportunity to build KTRH came as a result of the Great Depression. The economic downturn caused the regents of the University of Texas to decide against supporting their experimental station in Austin, KUT. Houston real estate magnate Jesse H. Jones, builder of Houston's emerging skyline and owner of the *Houston Chronicle*, purchased KUT and had the station's equipment boxed and transported the 165 miles to Houston.

Jones hoped to house his new station at the *Chronicle,* but the paper's editor dismissed the idea. The manager of Jones's Rice Hotel, on the other hand, was enthusiastic about a station's broadcasting from his facility and wanted the station to be "irretrievably tied to the hotel," according to Jesse Jones's nephew, John T. Jones, who would ultimately inherit KTRH from his uncle. The *TRH* in the new station's call letters stood for "The Rice Hotel."

When Ross Sterling, owner of KPRC and the *Houston Post-Dispatch,* suffered financial reverses in 1931, Jesse Jones came to the rescue and briefly controlled the *Post-Dispatch,* the *Chronicle,* and KTRH and KPRC radio stations. Jones gained such power that when he secured the Democratic Party's national convention for Houston in 1928, he also won the hearts of Texas Democrats: all 40 of Texas's electors cast their ballots for Jones's nomination for president, even though New York Governor Al Smith would ultimately win the nomination.

In 1947 the *Chronicle* established the first FM station in Houston and called it KTRH-FM. For its first two years, it simulcast the programming of KTRH-AM, and then it launched a "fine music" program of light classics. After a few years, the station returned to simulcasting. The popularity of album rock music in the late 1960s and early 1970s prompted a change of format and call letters for KTRH-FM. The letters KLOL were chosen because they resembled the 101 dial position.

On the death of Jesse Jones in 1956, the ownership of KTRH, sister station KLOL, and the *Chronicle* passed to Jones's nephew, John T. Jones, who operated the stations under the corporate name "The Rusk Corporation" (named for the downtown street where Jones's offices were located). The *Chronicle* was operated by a private foundation, Houston Endowment, that was established by the elder Jones for charitable purposes.

A graduate of Houston's San Jacinto High School, Walter Cronkite worked part-time at KTRH on his way to a journalism degree at the University of Texas in Austin. During the early 1930s Cronkite worked for the University of Texas newspaper, *The Daily Texan;* at United Press International (UPI); and at several state capital news bureaus at the same time. Dan Rather began working at KTRH in 1950, shortly after his graduation from Sam Houston State University in nearby Huntsville, Texas, where he had been a reporter for both the Associated Press and UPI. Rather's early KTRH broadcasts originated in the newsroom of the *Houston Chronicle* with the clack of wire service teletype machines in the background. "We got (the) bright idea that it would give the news program more authenticity," said John T. Jones. The younger Jones told the story of a *Chronicle* religious editor whose desk was next to

Rather's broadcast desk. At the end of each newscast, said Jones, the editor would correct Rather's grammar. In 1956 Rather became the station's news director.

CBS-TV sports anchor Jim Nantz also began his career at KTRH, in 1981. While studying on a golf scholarship at the University of Houston, Nantz was an intern at the station and later host of the *Sportsbeat* call-in program.

KTRH is credited with originating the *Dr. IQ* radio quiz show during the 1930s. Ted Nabors, then KTRH program director, performed as the Doctor, and announcer Babe Fritsch took a roving microphone into the audience to choose contestants who won silver dollars when they answered questions correctly. Fritsch was the first to say, "I have a lady in the balcony, Doctor!" *Dr. IQ* was developed for national broadcast on the National Broadcasting Company (NBC) network beginning in 1939, with Lew Valentine performing as the Doctor and Allan C. Anthony as the announcer.

In the mid-1960s, KTRH began a move to the talk format under General Manager Frank Stewart. Although KTRH was not the first station to adopt the new format, it was an early entry into the talk arena. Texas farm and ranch industries prompted KTRH to establish a strong presence in agribusiness reporting, at first with information for area ranchers and later with lawn and garden programs.

In 1981 the station broadcast two live talk shows from the People's Republic of China, a first for U.S. broadcasters. Talk host Ben Baldwin and KTRH Vice President and General Manager Hal Kemp answered listener questions and described events of their travels, including a rare firepower demonstration by the People's Army Infantry. "They literally blew up a mountain for us," Baldwin reported. The station staged subsequent live broadcasts from China during the early 1980s and aired weekend features prepared by the English language staff of Radio Beijing.

Because KTRH had affiliated with the CBS Radio network in the first year of its operation, one of the stories the Houston radio rumor mill circulated in the 1970s and 1980s was that CBS had a blank check ready if John T. Jones ever decided to sell KTRH. He didn't—and the stories were never confirmed. At Jones's retirement, his son Jesse Jones III, known as "Jay," assumed operation of the stations and acquired properties in San Antonio and Austin, expanding Rusk Corporation holdings.

In 1989 Jacor Communications made a $60 million offer for KTRH and KLOL, but the deal was never consummated. Ultimately, the two stations were sold in 1993 to Evergreen Media for $51 million. Evergreen became Chancellor and later AMFM after mergers made possible by the Telecommunications Act of 1996. KTRH moved to the Clear Channel Communications roster after that company's merger with AMFM.

ED SHANE

Further Reading

Boudreaux, Phillip H., "Houston Radio: The First Sixty Years," Senior thesis, University of St. Thomas, 1982

"KTRH Stages First Live Talk Show from China," *Radio and Records* (6 March 1981)

"KTRH's Zak to Be Honored on and off the Air," *Houston Post* (5 January 1981)

"Radio Peking: The Red Rose of Texas," *Earshot* (25 October 1982)

Writers' Program, *Houston: A History and Guide*, Houston, Texas: Anson Jones Press, 1942

Kuralt, Charles 1934–1997

U.S. Broadcast Journalist

One of the most beloved of journalists, Charles Kuralt was a traveler. Most of his life was spent "on the road," a phrase that became the title of his best-known television series. But he began his career in radio, first at WUNC, the student-run station at the University of North Carolina, Chapel Hill, and later at Columbia Broadcasting System (CBS) Radio. Accompanied by a few years' newspaper experience at *The Charlotte News*, where he won a prestigious 1956 Ernie Pyle Memorial Award for his writing skills, Kuralt showed great promise as he began work at CBS Radio.

Kuralt began as a radio writer in 1957, becoming the youngest ever network correspondent just two years later at age 24 and quickly winning a reputation as a hard-news reporter. At the time he was hired by CBS, network radio's viability was uncertain. As at the other major networks, news head Dick Salant was dealing with the sweeping loss of audiences and advertisers to the upstart television medium. After dropping all its soaps and traditional programs in favor of an all-news format, CBS Radio needed unique programming to hold on to affiliated stations, and Salant's solution was a series of very short, horizontally scheduled features—"programlets" that ran four minutes or so and were embedded in commercials. The network would repeat these features as many as eight times each day, returning with fresh stories on successive weekdays. Salant picked Kuralt to do the feature series called *To Your Health*, which quickly became a popular element of CBS's successful Dimension Radio and established Kuralt as a top-notch writer and on-air reporter. After gaining television experience as host of *Eyewitness to History*, Kuralt was expected to step rapidly into the nightly network newscast—a prestigious position on the Tiffany network with the most lauded news of the day. Salant and others had tremendous expectations, touting the young Kuralt as perhaps "the next Edward R. Murrow!" Those were very big shoes for anyone to fill, but in typical fashion, Kuralt dismissed the comparison as "ridiculous."

Because Kuralt preferred the adventure of travel to the stability of a daily news job, he moved from radio to television, covering the war in Vietnam for four tours and reporting on other world trouble spots. He became CBS's chief correspondent in Latin America and later on the West Coast, but he eventually left the hard-news side of television and radio in 1967, when he found his ideal vehicle in the famed *On the Road* series. For more than two decades, Kuralt roamed America's small towns and back roads in a CBS camper, reporting on heartwarming events in ordinary people's lives. Often called the Walt Whitman (or the Norman Rockwell) of American television, he did offbeat Americana stories, telling viewers about, for example, a school for unicyclists, a gas station/poetry factory, and a 104-year-old entertainer who performed in nursing homes. He talked to lumberjacks, cooks, poets, and farmers. He told of the Franciscan Sisters of Perpetual Adoration in Wisconsin, who have been continuously praying—in shifts—for the last 100 years. Finding everyman poetry in everyday life, his offbeat human-interest stories enchanted, delighted, and touched millions of television viewers and radio listeners. These reports became part of the *CBS Evening News*, *CBS Sunday Morning*, and the weekday *Morning* program; they also aired on the CBS Radio Network. Kuralt is said to have logged more than a million miles on the road. He is quoted as saying about CBS Radio: "Going wherever I wanted to go and doing whatever I wanted to do, CBS didn't even know where I was; didn't care much where I was. I just wandered. And that was probably the best job in journalism." After more than a decade as host of the television program *CBS Sunday Morning*, he retired, only to come back as host of *An American Moment*, a 90-second series that harked back to his radio days. He also hosted for a short time the CBS Cable show *I Remember*, a weekly reexamination of significant news stories from the historical past. After a brief illness, Charles Kuralt died in 1997 of complications arising from lupus.

During his career at CBS, Kuralt wrote several best-selling books, won 11 Emmy Awards, three Peabody Awards, and numerous other prestigious broadcasting awards. At his death, Walter Cronkite called him "one of the true, greatly talented people in television." A month later, the North Carolina legislature passed a resolution honoring him, observing that "Charles Kuralt possessed a peculiar insight that enabled him to contribute substantially and effectively to the improvement and betterment of the world around him, enriching the lives of those with whom he was associated and came in contact." He was a truly great storyteller.

SUSAN TYLER EASTMAN

Charles Kuralt. Born in Wilmington, North Carolina, 10 September 1934. Son of Wallace Hamilton Kuralt and Ina Bishop Kuralt; attended University of North Carolina at Chapel Hill, B.A. in journalism, 1955; WUNC radio dramatist, 1953; editor, *Daily Tar Heel*; reporter for *Charlotte News*, 1955–57, received Ernie Pyle Memorial Award for writing, 1956; joined CBS as writer, 1957, news correspondent, 1959–94. Received 11 Emmy Awards, three Peabody Awards, George Polk Memorial Award, 1981; inducted into North Carolina Journalism Hall of Fame, 1981; International Radio and Television Society (IRTS) Broadcaster of the Year, 1985; John Tyler Caldwell Award for the

Humanities, 1997 (posthumous). Died in New York City, 4 July 1997.

Television Series (many also carried on CBS Radio)
To Your Health, 1957–59; *Eyewitness to History* (later, *Eyewitness*), 1960–61; *On the Road*, 1967–80; *Who's Who*, 1977; *CBS Sunday Morning*, 1979–94; *CBS Morning News* (later, *Morning with Charles Kuralt*), 1980–82; *I Remember*, 1997; *An American Moment*, 1997

Selected Publications
To the Top of the World, 1968
Dateline America, 1979
On the Road with Charles Kuralt, 1985
North Carolina Is My Home, 1986
Southerners, 1986
A Life on the Road, 1990
Charles Kuralt's America, 1995

Further Reading
Gates, Gary Paul, *Air Time: The Inside Story of CBS News*, New York: Harper and Row, 1978
Joyce, Ed, *Prime Times, Bad Times*, New York: Doubleday, 1988
Matusow, Barbara, *The Evening Stars: The Making of the Network News Anchor*, Boston: Houghton Mifflin, 1983
McCabe, Peter, *Bad News at Black Rock: The Sell-Out of CBS News*, New York: Arbor House, 1987

KWKH

Shreveport, Louisiana Station

KWKH, a 50,000-watt clear channel station, played an important role in the commercialization of country music and rock and roll music during the 1940s and 1950s. In addition, as one of the first radio stations in Louisiana, it helped pioneer radio broadcasting in the state.

The station that KWKH would become first crackled on the air in early 1922. Engineer William E. Antony built the physical operations under the auspices of the Elliott Electric Company; in 1923 a team of investors led by a retailer of radio sets purchased the station, dubbing it WGAQ. One of the investors bought out his partners in 1925 and rechristened the station with his initials. William Kennon Henderson, who owned and operated the Henderson Iron Works and Supply in Shreveport,

promptly turned KWKH into his own soapbox. At arbitrary moments during the broadcast day, he often burst into his studios and grabbed the microphone from his announcer. "Hello world, doggone you! This is KWKH at Shreveport, Lou—ee—siana, and it's W.K. Henderson talkin' to you." He railed against the national debt and chain retail stores and ridiculed over the air anybody who dared to disagree with him. He condemned the Radio Act of 1927 and sparred with both the U.S. Department of Commerce and the Federal Radio Commission, claiming that both favored chain (network) stations over independent outlets.

In the late 1920s, when Henderson applied for a power boost to 10,000 watts, federal regulators turned him down, claiming that KWKH was nothing more than a broadcaster of phonograph records. But Henderson argued that his format—which in actuality encompassed more than just record playing—satisfied his listeners' wishes. The rejection only incited the maverick's ranting resolve, and by 1930 Washington conceded to him and granted the increase in power.

As eccentric and egotistical as Henderson was, his desire to see KWKH prosper and expand its signal range helped consolidate radio's presence in Louisiana. His on-air tirades forced people to note the presence of radio, and entrepreneurs looked to the growth of KWKH as an example when they invested their own dollars in radio stations. Furthermore, it was probably Henderson's distaste for the uniformity of chain stations that led KWKH to recruit local talent to perform on its airwaves. The use of local talent, most of whom performed hillbilly music (as country music was known in the 1920s and 1930s), planted the seeds that would grow into KWKH's *Louisiana Hayride*.

In 1932 Henderson sold KWKH to the International Broadcasting Corporation, and the station changed hands again in 1935 when the *Shreveport Times*, owned by oilman John D. Ewing, took control. Under Ewing, KWKH continued the growth that Henderson had initiated, moving to modern facilities in downtown Shreveport's Commercial Building in 1936 and receiving permission to operate at 50,000 watts in 1939. (In 1934, probably much to the former owner's ire, KWKH had established a network affiliation with the Columbia Broadcasting System [CBS].) Carrying on Henderson's tradition of hiring local talent, station manager Henry B. Clay, who was Ewing's son-law; program director Horace Logan; and commercial manager Dean Upson established the *Louisiana Hayride*, which would become KWKH's most lasting mark on country music history and, indeed, on radio history.

KWKH's *Louisiana Hayride* was a country and western stage show that played weekly on the station from 1948 to 1960. Dubbed "the Cradle of the Stars," the program aired on Saturday nights from Shreveport's Municipal Auditorium and boasted among its cast members musical performers who would be the primary shapers of post–World War II country music. Important country music figures such as Hank Williams, Jim Reeves, and Johnny Cash appeared as regulars on the *Hayride* early in their careers; each used the program as a springboard to broader acceptance. In addition to providing a stage for important country music performers, KWKH and the *Hayride* would leave a lasting mark on the history of rock and roll in the mid-1950s, when singer Elvis Presley became a regular cast member on the show; the exposure he received as a cast member from 1954 to 1956 helped fuel his rise to national prominence.

KWKH's 50,000 watts of power gave the *Louisiana Hayride* its muscle. The station's signal stretched like a fan across the southwestern and northwestern regions of the United States and clipped across national borders to reach countries as near as Mexico and as far as Australia. A regular spot on KWKH's Saturday night hoedown, any aspiring country act knew, could attract recording contracts and generate bookings. The *Hayride*'s influence grew mightier in the early 1950s with its insertion into the schedule of a CBS regional network.

However, the *Hayride* would never be as mighty as the *Grand Ole Opry* on WSM in Nashville, Tennessee, and because of that, KWKH failed to hold on to its rising stars. As *Hayride* personalities gained momentum, they inevitably shifted their eyes toward the *Opry* and Nashville, where a colony that included booking agents and music publishers awaited to capitalize on the artists' successes. KWKH and Shreveport lacked such ancillary components of the music industry and therefore could not keep name artists on the show very long. The *Louisiana Hayride* became known as an "*Opry* farm club," and, largely because of the constant talent drain, it ceased regular broadcasting in 1960. The program has been reincarnated in various forms over the years, but it has never achieved the influence it enjoyed in the late 1940s and 1950s.

Today, KWKH is owned by Clear Channel Communications, which acquired the station in 1999. Although the *Louisiana Hayride* disappeared long ago from its airwaves, the station still recalls former glories with its "country gold" format, which features vintage country music from as early as the 1940s.

MICHAEL STREISSGUTH

See also Clear Channel Stations; Country Music Format; Grand Ole Oprey; WWL

Further Reading

Escott, Colin, George Merritt, and William MacEwen, *Hank Williams: The Biography*, Boston: Little Brown, 1994
Guralnick, Peter, *Last Train to Memphis: The Rise of Elvis Presley*, Boston: Little Brown, 1994
Hall, Lillian Jones, "A Historical Study of Programming Techniques and Practices of Radio Station KWKH, Shreveport, Louisiana, 1922–1950," Ph.D. diss., Louisiana State University, 1959
Logan, Horace, and Bill Sloan, *Elvis, Hank, and Me: Making Musical History on the Louisiana Hayride*, New York: St. Martin's Press, 1998
Streissguth, Michael, *Like a Moth to a Flame: The Jim Reeves Story*, Nashville, Tennessee: Rutledge Hill Press, 1998

Kyser, Kay 1905–1985

U.S. Big Band Leader and Radio Host

Largely forgotten today, Kay Kyser's band scored 11 No. 1 records and 35 top 10 hits. Kyser hosted a top-rated radio show for 11 years on the National Broadcasting Company (NBC), and he and his band starred in seven motion pictures. He has two stars set into the sidewalk on Hollywood Boulevard in Los Angeles, one for radio and another for film work. Although best known as a musical figure, in fact Kyser could not sing, read music, or play any instrument.

Origins

Kay Kyser's roots and much of his life are based in North Carolina. Born there, he originally intended to study law while attending the state university. Instead, at the suggestion of bandleader Hal Kemp, Kyser (then a university cheerleader) formed his first small band in 1926, the group consisting of six fellow students. With this initial group, Kyser soon established his role as an energetic MC, rather than as a musician. Over the next several years, the band added some professional musicians and slowly improved, but life on the road was a series of relatively short performance gigs in Depression America.

In the mid-1930s, appearances at venues in Santa Monica and then in Chicago (at the Blackhawk restaurant and club) propelled the band to national recognition and appeal. In part this was due to the music played, but much of the band's particular appeal was built around the light-hearted humor and antics of Kyser as its energetic leader. The band was something of an extension of Kyser's outgoing personality.

Radio Years

Sometime in 1937, the "college" concept was first developed to attract more customers on otherwise slow Monday evenings at the Blackhawk. Originally called "Kay's Klass," it was a kind of amateur performers night, supplemented with questions from Kyser to the musical contestants to both relax them and amuse the audience. The classroom notion may have been the idea of Kyser's young agent, Lew Wasserman. Chicago station WGN began to broadcast the band's performances as *Kay Kyser's Kampus Class*. By this point the Kyser band had developed another unique feature that would remain for many years: the "singing song title," in which a band vocalist would sing the title's words at the beginning before a full performance of the song.

In February 1938, the Mutual Broadcasting System began an eight-week series of programs carrying the Blackhawk-based band program regionally. The American Tobacco Company took up sponsorship of the show for its Lucky Strike cigarette brand and brought it to New York City and the NBC network, with the first program airing on 30 March 1938. Now known as *Kay Kyser's College of Musical Knowledge* (sometimes *College* is rendered *Kollege*) with Kyser cast as "The Old Professor," the program was an almost instant hit.

The *College* program's format was classic radio variety, built around the band's music but adding the related quiz feature along with comedy routines. Each broadcast began with Kyser's warm North Carolina–accented "Evenin' folks, how y'all?" "Diplomas" were mailed to listeners sending in music quiz questions used on the air.

Among the many instrumentalists and singers in Kyser's band, several stood out over the years. Perhaps best known was "Ish Kabibble" (Merwyn Bogue), who got his odd show business name from his comedy version of an old Yiddish song, "Isch Ga Bibble" (loosely translated, "I should worry?"), which he first performed after joining the band in 1931. He played the cornet but thrived on developing the rural "Ish" character with a "pudding bowl" hair cut, who constantly interrupted the show to recite nonsensical poems to a seemingly frustrated Kyser, becoming his onstage comedy foil. As is often the case with such performers, he was no dummy offstage, and he handled the program's payroll. He stayed with the band until the program wrapped up its television series in 1951. Among the many singers heard over the years were tenor Harry Babbitt, San Antonio native Ginny Simms, who was the band's first permanent female voice and often sang duets with Babbitt, and Mike Douglas, who would go on to become a famous variety and talk show host for television.

Kyser recorded no fewer than 11 number one songs in the space of seven years. These were "The Umbrella Man" and "Three Little Fishies" (1939); "(Lights Out) Til Reveille" and "(There'll Be Bluebirds) Over the White Cliffs of Dover" (1941); "Who Wouldn't Love You," "Jingle, Jangle, Jingle," "He Wears a Pair of Silver Wings," "Strip Polka," and "Praise the Lord and Pass the Ammunition" (1942); and "Old Buttermilk Sky" and the "Woody Woodpecker" song (1946). Overall, the band recorded some 400 songs beginning in 1935, mostly on the Brunswick, Columbia (parent of Brunswick), and Victor labels.

Kyser's band became one of the first to perform at military bases even before World War II. The first such performance took place at the San Diego marine base on 26 February 1941. Kyser became a highly successful wartime bond salesman with these and other appearances—a total of more than 500 shows at military camps and bases by the time the war ended. These

Kay Kyser
Courtesy Radio Hall of Fame

mance, had earned more than enough money, and wanted to return to North Carolina to do other things. There was also a medical reason: Kyser had begun to have serious trouble with his feet due to an arthritic-type condition in his toes, perhaps exacerbated by his years of energetic performance. Not finding help in traditional medicine, he turned to Christian Science to find relief. He became very active in the church, managing its film and broadcast department in Boston for five years in the 1970s.

He also undertook many altruistic projects, including highway safety campaigns, a health-related campaign in North Carolina, funding scholarships and providing other support for his university alma mater, and helping to establish an educational TV station for Chapel Hill, North Carolina.

CHRISTOPHER H. STERLING

James King Kern ("Kay") Kyser. Born in Rocky Mount, North Carolina, 18 June 1905. Graduated from the University of North Carolina at Chapel Hill in Commerce, 1928. Formed first orchestra, 1926; toured with orchestra, 1926–34; played Blackhawk Club, Chicago, Illinois, 1934; made radio debut in a band remote, 1937; known as host of *Kay Kyser's College [or Kollege] of Musical Knowledge,* 1938–49; retired from broadcasting, 1951; managed radio and television broadcast department, Christian Science Church, Boston, 1974–79. Died in Chapel Hill, North Carolina, 23 July 1985.

Radio Series
1937   *Kay Kyser Band Remote*
1938–49   *Kay Kyser's College of Musical Knowledge*

Television
Kay Kyser's Kollege of Musical Knowledge, 1949–50, 1954

Film
That's Right, You're Wrong, 1939; *You'll Find Out,* 1940; *Playmates,* 1941; *My Favorite Spy,* 1942; *Around the World,* 1943; *Swing Fever,* 1943; *Carolina Blues,* 1944

Further Reading
A Tribute to Kay Kyser, <http://www.ibiblio.org/kaykyser/>
Kay Kyser: A Documentary in Progress, <http://www.kaykyser.net/>
Simon, George, *The Big Bands,* New York: Macmillan, 1967; 4th edition, New York: Schirmer, and London: Collier-Macmillan, 1981

"road shows" had a somewhat different sound from the earlier broadcasts. A band bus fire in April 1942 destroyed 15 years' worth of musical arrangements, prompting a hiatus for the act. When the band reappeared, the singing song titles were gone and a newer, updated musical style became evident. Because of the pressure of the wartime appearances, the band undertook no commercial gigs (except those booked previously) for the duration, concentrating on the continuing radio show, military service shows, and the seven movies that featured Kyser and the band, all of them made within a five-year period.

Later Years

Kyser and the band moved to television with their own series, debuting in 1949. With the end of the TV series in 1951, Kyser retired at the top of his form and with nary an announcement that he was going. He was tired after years of relentless perfor-

KYW

Chicago, Cleveland, and Philadelphia Station

One of Westinghouse's original outlets, KYW has been described as "the wandering radio station." Though it has served the Philadelphia area for most of its life, the call letters were also found on stations in Chicago and Cleveland. KYW's wanderlust is a result of the federal government's intermittent efforts to manage how much control large broadcasters had over America's most important cities. In the end, these labors produced voluminous litigation but little in the way of permanent results.

KYW had a Chicago address for only a dozen years, but its early start earned it a place in radio history as a pioneer radio station. In fact, it was Chicago's first radio station. Legend has it that the call letters stood for "Young Warriors."

The station first broadcast from the Commonwealth Edison office in Chicago on 11 November 1921. KYW was originally started as a partnership. Westinghouse provided the transmitter and Commonwealth Edison the broadcast location. For its part, Westinghouse rushed KYW and sister stations WBZ in Massachusetts and WJZ in Newark, New Jersey, to the air as a direct result of the success of KDKA in Pittsburgh. Westinghouse's motivation was to stimulate sales of the crystal radio sets the company manufactured. For five years, KYW was operated as a joint venture, although Westinghouse dominated the partnership. In 1926 the working relationship ended, and Commonwealth Edison eventually became associated with crosstown radio station WENR.

Three notable early programming experiments punctuate KYW's Chicago history. The first broadcast by KYW featured opera, and regular weekly opera broadcasts on the station proved an immediate success. At one point, the opera broadcasts were credited with selling nearly 2,000 radio receivers a week in the Chicago area. Second, KYW featured an early version of children's programming. Early radio personality Uncle Bob (Walter Wilson) broadcast children's stories each night, being sure to finish by 7 P.M. so as not to disturb his listeners' bedtimes. KYW also featured breaking news supplied by the *Chicago Tribune*. Seeing potential in the new medium, the Tribune Company decided to get in on the business itself and launched WGN in 1924.

The Federal Radio Commission soon grew concerned about the large number of stations in Chicago. Westinghouse offered to shift KYW out of Chicago and moved the station on 3 December 1934 to Philadelphia. Then the nation's third-largest media market, Philadelphia would prove less lucrative to Westinghouse than broadcasting from Chicago, then the nation's second most important city.

In its new hometown, KYW continued its tradition of reporting breaking news. For example, KYW covered the June 1937 *Hindenburg* disaster in nearby Lakehurst, New Jersey. From a telephone booth, a KYW reporter described to the radio audience the horrific fire, and the on-the-spot report was broadcast over both National Broadcasting Company (NBC) networks.

The association with NBC would eventually set the stage for KYW's third move—to Cleveland, Ohio. On 22 January 1956, Westinghouse, under great pressure from NBC, which wanted to upgrade its own facilities to a larger market, exchanged its Philadelphia broadcast operations for NBC's Cleveland stations. In consideration for Westinghouse receiving the smaller and less profitable Cleveland outlets, NBC also paid Westinghouse $3 million.

Later, as a result of federal investigation into NBC's actions, it was demonstrated that NBC had forced Westinghouse into the exchange. Had Westinghouse not complied, it would have lost its valuable NBC network affiliation for its budding television operations. The Federal Communications Commission (FCC) ordered the swap undone in 1964 and found NBC culpable of abusing its network power. KYW's call letters were shifted from Cleveland, and the AM, FM, and television stations to which they were attached returned again to Philadelphia in June 1965 (the Cleveland AM station is now known as WTAM, formerly WWWE).

In October 1965, KYW became one of the first radio stations to adopt an all-news format. The format change did not bring immediate ratings success, and, reportedly, the station lost money for several years. The first decade was particularly difficult, given the popularity of crosstown AM contemporary music outlets such as WFIL and WIBG.

Today, KYW's competition comes mostly from FM stations, because KYW has long been the market's leading AM station. Like other historic AM broadcasters, KYW found that information-based spoken-word programming can be effective against music-based FM competitors. In programming its all-news format, the station uses a 30-minute news wheel and features traffic reports every ten minutes. The station does particularly well in the winter season, when the station issues snow-related closing notices for schools in eastern Pennsylvania, southern New Jersey, and northern Delaware. Arbitron reports that KYW, in addition to regularly being one of the top-three radio stations in the market, has a weekly cumulative audience of well over 1 million listeners.

Though technically the radio station is not on a full clear channel frequency, the 50,000-watt signal produced from the station's directional antenna can regularly be heard across the northeastern United States, far outside the station's primary Delaware Valley coverage area. The station has been located at 1060 kilohertz since 1941. The studios of KYW radio are housed on Independence Mall within sight of the Liberty Bell. It shares the same building as its sister television station, KYW-TV 3, now a Columbia Broadcasting System (CBS) television affiliate. The television station was Philadelphia's first when it began experimental operations just as W3XE in 1932

Despite Westinghouse's historic attempts to keep its network-owning rivals at arm's length, the company, disappointed by its prospects in manufacturing, eventually decided to concentrate on broadcast programming and merged with the CBS network in 1995. Subsequently, the Westinghouse identity disappeared. Today, the license to KYW radio is owned by Infinity Broadcasting, the radio company closely associated with CBS.

A. JOSEPH BORRELL

See also Hindenburg Disaster

Further Reading

Samuels, Rich, "It All Began with an Oath and an Opera: Behind the Scenes at Chicago's First Broadcast," *Chicago Tribune* (8 November 1993)

Shanahan, Eileen, "FCC Orders NBC to Return Station," *New York Times* (30 July 1964)

L

Landell de Moura, Father Roberto 1861–1928

Brazilian Wireless Pioneer

In the 1890s and early 1900s, Father Roberto Landell de Moura produced a series of wireless communication devices that were as original in their day as they were unrecognized.

Origins

Roberto Landell de Moura was born in Porto Alegre, the capital of Rio Grande do Sul, on 21 January 1861. Graduating as a distinguished student from a local Jesuit high school, he moved to Rio de Janeiro to study at the Polytechnic Institute. Unable to pay tuition, however, he took a job as a store clerk.

In 1881 his brother, on his way to Rome to study for the priesthood, visited him; Roberto decided to accompany him and also become a priest. He studied theology at the seminary in Rome for students from the Americas and physics and chemistry at the Gregorian University. He also became aware of scientific developments in Italy and Europe. Ordained in 1885, he returned to Rio de Janeiro and for a brief period was a temporary chaplain in the Brazilian imperial court, occasionally conversing with Emperor Dom Pedro II, who had met Alexander Graham Bell and later introduced the telephone to Brazil.

From 1887 through the 1890s Landell de Moura had a series of parish assignments in Rio Grande do Sul and then in São Paulo. He had a difficult temperament and had to be transferred several times to different parishes.

Wireless Inventions

It was during the 1890s, while posted in Campinas, São Paulo, that he formulated theories about controlled, wireless conduction of vibratory movements and light beams, believing that any sound, including the human voice, could be transmitted over land, through the air, and under the water.

During 1893 and 1894 he demonstrated these ideas in the center of the city of São Paulo. He transmitted sound without wires between two of the highest points in the city, over five miles apart, using a type of three-electrode conductor lamp. These demonstrations occurred in the presence of the British Consul and years before similar demonstrations were made by Marconi and de Forest.

Despite presenting his inventions before a representative of one of the most inventive and commercial countries in the world, however, he failed to attract interest or investment. Worse, word about his strange, "diabolical" inventions aroused the suspicions of his parishioners. They invaded his rectory and destroyed his machines.

Undismayed, he rebuilt and refined them, by 1900 obtaining Brazilian patent 3,279 for a machine transmitting sound with or without wires via space, land, or water. Continuing to find no local interest, however, he moved to the United States. Taking up residence in New York City in 1901 and surviving on a subsistence income, he remade his inventions and obtained U.S. patents 771,917 (11 October 1904), 775,337 (22 November 1904), and 775,846 (22 November 1904) for a sound wave transmitter, a wireless phone, and a wireless telegraph, respectively. The wave transmitter produced electrical oscillations of light from sound vibrations generated by the human voice or other source. The sound waves passed through a receptor with induction coils and condensers that changed them into electric or light waves, allowing their wireless transmission to a receptor that could convert them to voice or sound or light signals. His wireless phone transmitted and received voice via light waves. The wireless telegraph transmitted and received signals via various types of sound waves.

EDWARD A. RIEDINGER

See also Early Wireless

Father Landell de Moura. Born in Porto Alegre, Rio Grande do Sul, Brazil, 21 January 1861. Fourth of twelve children of Inácio José Ferreira de Moura and Sara Mariana Landell de Moura; honors graduate of Jesuit high school in São Leopoldo, Rio Grande do Sul; moved to Rio de Janeiro to study, ca. 1879; accompanied brother to study for priesthood in Rome, 1881, specialized in theology, physics, and chemistry; ordained priest, 1885; returned to Brazil, became seminary instructor in Porto Alegre, 1887–91; parish priest, Uruguaiana, Rio Grande do Sul, 1891; parish priest, Santos, Campinas, and Sant'Ana, São Paulo, 1892–99; formulated theories on and built devices for wireless sound communication; public demonstrations of inventions in capital of São Paulo, 1893–94, equipment destroyed by parishioners; received Brazilian patent for machine transmitting sound with or without wires via space, land, or water, 1900; moved to New York City, 1901–04; rebuilt his inventions and received U.S. patents, 1904; returned to Brazil, 1905; desisted from inventing; returned to parish work in São Paulo and then Rio Grande do Sul, ca. 1906. Died in Rio Grande do Sul, Brazil, 30 June 1928.

Further Reading

Almeida, B. Hamilton, *O outro lado das comunicações: A saga do Padre Landell de Moura*, Porto Alegre, Brazil: Sulina, 1983
Cauduro, Fernando, *O homem que apertou o botão da comunicação*, Porto Alegre, Brazil: FEPLAM, 1977
Fornari, Ernani, *O "incrível" Padre Landell de Moura: História triste de um inventor brasileiro*, Rio de Janeiro: Globo, 1960; 2nd edition, Rio de Janeiro: Biblioteca do Exército, 1984
"Talking Over a Gap of Miles along a Ray of Light," *New York Herald* (12 October 1902)

Lazarsfeld, Paul F. 1901–1976

U.S. (Austrian-Born) Sociologist and Radio Research Innovator

"Paul Lazarsfeld," writes one media historian, "was undoubtedly the most important intellectual influence in shaping modern communication research" (Rogers, 1994). His pioneering radio research in the late 1930s and early 1940s helped to shape our understanding of the medium's effects and made applied radio industry research more respectable in the eyes of many academics.

Origins

Born at the beginning of the 20th century in Vienna, Austria, Lazarsfeld came of age in the lively intellectual climate of that city in the years between the world wars. Brilliant in mathematics, he earned a Ph.D. at the age of 24. But with academic jobs scarce in the mid-1920s, he taught at a Vienna high school and served as a part-time instructor at the University of Vienna while seeking a more permanent university post. He established a Research Center for Economic Psychology at the University of Vienna (where he served as an adjunct faculty member) in 1925. It became a model that Lazarsfeld would follow with later research groups in the United States. With the help of students, he directed a landmark study of unemployment in the small town of Marienthal, Austria, in 1931–32 that brought him wide attention. But because of the difficult economic times, his socialist background, and his Jewish heritage, Lazarsfeld was facing limited opportunities in Austria.

Thanks to the Marienthal study, Lazarsfeld's work reached the notice of the Rockefeller Foundation, which sponsored him for two years of research-related traveling in the United States in 1933–35. He visited many universities and research academics. When a political coup in Austria made his return to academic life there even more unlikely, he accepted a post as acting director at the University of Newark's research center in 1936. It was a tiny operation—so much so that some of his published papers appeared under a pseudonym ("Elias Smith") to disguise the fact that he was the only full-time research person working there.

Radio Research

Lazarsfeld's active importance in radio research spanned nearly two decades. This research began without him—with a proposal to the Rockefeller Foundation of a study of "The Essential Value of Radio to All Type of Listeners," proposed by Hadley Cantril of Princeton University and Frank Stanton of the Columbia Broadcasting System (CBS), to undertake experimental work about radio's audiences. Cantril, busy with his own work (as was Stanton, who by then had more than

100 research people under his direction at CBS), recommended Lazarsfeld to direct the new effort. With that change, Princeton's Office of Radio Research undertook a broader approach, with survey and secondary data analysis.

Becoming very much a creature of its director's wide interests, the office combined quantitative and qualitative research approaches, including content analyses, panel studies, focused interviews, and some secondary data analysis to attack radio research questions from a variety of viewpoints and methodological angles. The office published Hugh Beville's important 1939 study of radio ratings methodologies. Lazarsfeld's first book on radio resulted from the Rockefeller Foundation's demand for product before it would extend the funding of the office beyond the initially agreed-upon two years. Building on a 1939 issue of the *Journal of Applied Psychology* that Lazarsfeld had edited to summarize two years of the office's efforts, the result was *Radio and the Printed Page* (1940), an important early comparison of the varied impacts of the newspaper and radio.

This was followed by what was intended to be a research annual, but which in fact resulted in three volumes, all co-edited by Lazarsfeld and Stanton. *Radio Research 1941* included studies of foreign-language broadcasts over local stations (most such broadcasts would disappear when the United States entered the war), the popular music industry, Theodor Adorno's initial study of classical music on radio, the use of radio and the press by young people, and the role of radio for the farmer. The second volume, *Radio Research 1942–1943*, began with Herta Herzog's important study of radio serials, discussed radio during wartime, and offered a number of studies of radio in operation and the radio audience. *Mass Communication Research 1948–49* demonstrated in its title the broader concerns of the research team; it was the final volume to appear.

One important research device came out of the office projects, based on previous work done by both Lazarsfeld and Stanton. Beginning in 1937, the two men and their assistants developed the "program analyzer" (or "little Annie," as it was soon called), which measured audience likes and dislikes of what they were hearing:

> The Program Analyzer was a wooden box, two feet long, one foot wide, and one foot high, that contained a constant-speed electric meter driving a six-inch wide roll of white recording paper, which moved at the rate of one-fifth of an inch per second. . . . Mounted just above the roll of paper were ten ink pens, each connected to an electromagnet attached to a six-foot-long cord with an off-on switch at the other end. The Program Analyzer was placed on a table, with up to ten respondents sitting around the table, each with an off-on switch marked green for "like" and red for "dislike." When the dislike (on) switch was pressed, it lifted the corresponding pen slightly off the recording paper. It thus fixed a point in time when a respondent changed his or her reaction to the radio message (Rogers, 1994).

The device and variations of it were used for years afterwards. A later "big Annie" could accommodate up to 50 respondents and was, in modified form, used to test new television programs and commercials. CBS eliminated its "Annie"-based research office in 1986.

Later Years

During and after the war, Lazarsfeld undertook research for several government agencies, including the military and the Department of State, becoming interested in the role and impact of propaganda, among other subjects. He worked closely with his Columbia University sociology colleague Robert K. Merton for more than three decades, and the two collaborated on a variety of studies over that time.

Although it had moved beyond its initial radio focus by the late 1940s, Columbia's Bureau of Applied Social Research would thrive in the 1950s and 1960s (it lasted until 1977), undertaking a variety of both academic and corporate-sponsored research. The bureau set a model of combining network and advertiser financial support with academic research.

The vast majority of its funding was external—Columbia University merely provided space (and in later years a small annual stipend). The Bureau produced dozens of books and hundreds of research articles and book chapters. Two, one co-authored by Lazarsfeld and the other by a former student, became landmark media studies: Elihu Katz and Lazarsfeld's *Personal Influence* (1955) and Joseph Klapper's *Effects of Mass Communication* (1960). Their findings of minimal media impact had begun with *The People's Choice* (1944), a Lazarsfeld co-authored study of 1940 Ohio voting behavior suggesting that media played a small role in voting decisions.

But Lazarsfeld, who stepped down as bureau director (becoming associate director) on taking the chairmanship of the sociology department at Columbia in 1949, began to lose interest in mass communications research in the 1950s. He became deeply involved in debates within the field of sociology as to what the field was about and the degree to which it should accept industry support for applied research. He became the president of the American Sociological Association in 1960, but only after two prior attempts at the office. He took an endowed chair at Columbia in 1962, retiring seven years later. The last years of his life saw him commuting from New York to teach at the University of Pittsburgh.

As Rogers (1994) makes clear, Lazarsfeld was "an academic entrepreneur spanning the boundary between the university's scholarly focus on theory and research versus the applied interests of government and private industry. . . . more than any other individual, Paul F. Lazarsfeld directed communication research toward the study of effects."

CHRISTOPHER H. STERLING

See also Audience; Audience Research Methods; Education About Radio; Office of Radio Research; Stanton, Frank

Paul F. Lazarsfeld. Born in Vienna, Austria, 13 February 1901. Attended University of Vienna, Ph.D. in applied mathematics, 1925; taught math and physics in Vienna high school; instructor, University of Vienna; established Research Center for Economic Psychology, 1925; acting director, University of Newark Research Center, 1936; director, Office of Radio Research, Princeton University, 1937–40; office moved to Columbia University, 1939, renamed Bureau of Applied Social Research, 1944; served as director until 1950; associate professor of sociology, 1941; became U.S. citizen during World War II and served as consultant to Office of War Information, War Production Board, and War Department; chair of department of sociology, Columbia University, 1948; president, American Sociological Association, 1960; Quetelet Professor of Social Science, Columbia University, 1962; retired from Columbia University, 1969; distinguished professor, University of Pittsburgh, 1970. Died in New York City, 30 August 1976.

Selected Publications

"Radio Research and Applied Psychology," *Journal of Applied Psychology* 23, no. 1 (special issue edited by Lazarsfeld, February 1939)

Radio and the Printed Page: An Introduction to the Study of Radio and Its Role in the Communication of Ideas, 1940

Radio Research 1941 (with Frank Stanton), 1941
Radio Research 1942–43 (with Frank Stanton), 1944
The People's Choice: How the Voter Makes Up His Mind in a Presidential Campaign, 1944
The People Look at Radio (with Harry Field), 1946
Radio Listening in America: The People Look at Radio—Again (with Patricia Kendall), 1948
Mass Communication Research 1948–49 (with Frank Stanton), 1949
Personal Influence (with Elihu Katz), 1955

Further Reading

Coleman, James S., "Paul F. Lazarsfeld: The Substance and Style of His Work," in *Sociological Traditions from Generation to Generation: Glimpses of the American Experience,* edited by Robert K. Merton and Matilda White Riley, Norwood, New Jersey: Ablex, 1980

Glander, Timothy, *Origins of Mass Communications Research during the American Cold War: Educational Effects and Contemporary Implications,* Mahwah, New Jersey: Erlbaum, 2000

Merton, Robert K., James S. Coleman, and Peter H. Rossi, editors, *Qualitative and Quantitative Social Research: Papers in Honor of Paul F. Lazarsfeld,* New York: Free Press, 1979

Pasanella, Ann K., *The Mind Traveller: A Guide to Paul F. Lazarsfeld's Communication Research Papers,* New York: Freedom Forum Media Studies Center, 1994

Rogers, Everett M., "Paul F. Lazarsfeld and Mass Communication Effects," in *A History of Communication Study: A Biographical Approach,* New York: Free Press, 1994

Sills, David, editor, *International Encyclopedia of the Social Sciences,* 19 vols., New York: Free Press, 1979; see especially vol. 18

Lesbian Radio. *See* Gay and Lesbian Radio

Let's Pretend

Children's Program

The theme song sounded each Saturday morning to the delight of children listening to this Columbia Broadcasting System (CBS) program:

Hello, hello,
Come on let's go!
It's time for *Let's Pretend.*
The gang's all here and standing near
Is Uncle Bill, your friend.
The story is so exciting from the start right to the end.
So everyone, come join the fun.
Come on and let's pretend!

Let's Pretend was so popular that it became the prototype of children's programming, and its creator, Nila Mack, became the director of children's programming for the CBS network.

Let's Pretend was a half-hour children's radio program heard on CBS during the late-Saturday-morning time slot. Its forerunner was *The Adventures of Helen and Mary,* which began on 7 September 1929 and ran until 17 March 1934, with writer Yolanda Langworthy and director Nila Mack.

One week after the end of *Helen and Mary, Let's Pretend* began. Using her background as a Broadway actress and vaudevillian, Nila Mack wrote and directed this children's program for most of its 20-year run. Drawing on her own childhood memories, Mack based the program on variations of familiar children's tales from the Grimm brothers, *The Arabian Nights,* Andrew Lang, and Hans Christian Andersen. She freely adapted each story to emphasize human virtues. For example, her annual Christmas show, *House of the World,* promoted the themes of brotherhood and tolerance.

Mack felt that children should tell the stories and be the voices of the characters. She established an ensemble of versatile juvenile talent with members who could easily shift from being a young princess one week to an aging witch the next. She chose her cast from auditions open to any child interested in being considered. She tested each one for the ability to be versatile and to ad lib easily—especially to cover up any production mishaps that might occur during the actual broadcast.

Many of these young performers went on to stage and screen careers. For example, Nancy Kelly scored a major hit on Broadway and in film as the mother in *The Bad Seed,* and Dick Van Patten went on to television fame in *I Remember Mama* and *Eight Is Enough.*

Salaries began at $3.50 per show—less than half the going rate for many long-running shows. However, being on the program was considered an honor and a serious undertaking.

Arthur Anderson, an 18-year veteran of the show, wrote of this theatrical experience in glowing terms. Anderson's book, *Let's Pretend: A History of Radio's Best Loved Children's Show by a Longtime Cast Member* details the cast members' view that this was an opportunity to learn a craft while actually doing a radio program live over the airways. Other actors, such as Arnold Stang and Jimmy Lydon, have recounted the rigors of maintaining Mack's standard of excellence.

Musical conductor Maurice Brown's theme became one of the hallmarks of juvenile radio—especially in 1943, when he used the newly allowed sole program sponsor as the subject for the violin-backed lyrics:

Cream of Wheat is so good to eat.
Yes, we have it every day.
We sing this song; it will make us strong.
And it makes us shout HOORAY.
It's good for growing babies.
And grown-ups too to eat.
For all the family's breakfast,
You can't beat Cream of Wheat!

Having a sponsored children's program was a departure from the norm for CBS. The broadcast company felt that it was not prestigious to permit commercials to air on *Let's Pretend.* However, economic considerations must have won out, because Cream of Wheat became the long-time sponsor in the 1940s.

In addition to the musical commercial program introduction, the show also added an "Uncle Bill" played by Bill Adams, who greeted children with his "Hellooo, Pretenders!" The children in the studio audience would respond, "Hellooo, Uncle Bill." Then Bill would call out, "How do we travel to *Let's Pretend*?" Some child would suggest a mode of transportation—such as a magic carpet.

Imaginative sound effects were the mainstay for building effective theater of the mind for all the children tuned in each Saturday. In her article "Writing for Children," published in *Off Mike,* Mack paid tribute to sound department head Walter Pierson:

Fortunately for me, he is an imaginative person, for when I spoke of needing the effect of "moon beams shimmering," a "flying trunk," a "magic carpet," he didn't blink an eye. . . . I even had a flying trunk (on the secondhand side) that flew and zoomed, when it finally landed and bumped its way to a stop, it made the audience laugh.

Let's Pretend
Courtesy CBS Photo Archive

After Mack died of a heart attack on 20 January 1953, Jean Hight replaced her as director. Johanna Johnston became the show's writer. The last broadcast of *Let's Pretend* was on 23 October 1954.

Mack was lauded as "the fairy godmother of radio." As a tribute to her genius during the final two years of the show, the Nila Mack Award was bestowed on the actors who gave the best performances.

MARY KAY SWITZER

See also Children's Programs

Cast

Host	"Uncle" Bill Adams
Helen	Estelle Levy (Gwen Davies)
Mary	Patricia Ryan

Announcers	George Bryan, Jackson Wheeler, Warren Sweeney

Producers/Creators/Directors
Yolanda Langworthy, Nila Mack, Jean Hight

Programming History

CBS	March 1934–October 1954

Further Reading

Anderson, Arthur, *Let's Pretend: A History of Radio's Best Loved Children's Show by a Longtime Cast Member*, Jefferson, North Carolina: McFarland, 1994

Boemer, Marilyn Lawrence, "Let's Pretend," in *The Children's Hour: Radio Programs for Children, 1929–1956*, Metuchen, New Jersey: Scarecrow Press, 1989

Lewis, William B. 1904–1975

U.S. Network Executive

There were few more influential radio executives in the late 1930s than William Bennett Lewis. With no producing experience, Lewis seemed innately to recognize and foster talent and encourage new ideas. Though not a particularly creative radio figure himself, Lewis made it possible for the likes of Norman Corwin and Orson Welles to establish landmarks in radio history. Lewis—with William S. Paley's support—put the Columbia Broadcasting System (CBS) on the map as the locus for original, innovative programming such as *The Mercury Theater* and *Words without Music.*

After passage of the Communications Act of 1934, William Paley promised the Federal Communications Commission (FCC) that CBS would use its sustaining time for more than simply airing cheap lectures or concerts. By accident he found William B. Lewis, who had little direct radio experience, but who impressed Paley at his interview. Lewis knew radio from his experience at the J. Walter Thompson advertising agency and in 1935 signed up with CBS. Within a year Paley elevated Lewis to head all CBS radio programming.

Lewis proved to be the right man for the job. Irving Reis, a CBS studio engineer, suggested an experimental radio series with the title *Columbia Workshop.* Although previous executives had rebuffed Reis, in July 1936 Lewis took up his suggestion. In time many prominent actors, producers, directors, and writers, ranging from Archibald MacLeish to William Saroyan, Orson Welles, and Norman Corwin came to the workshop.

As such, Lewis was the corporate supporter behind such works as MacLeish's *The Fall of the City,* a fascist allegory about inhabitants of a nameless city waiting for the arrival of their conqueror. The program was broadcast 4 March 1937, not from the CBS studio, but from the Seventh Regimental Armory in New York City with a vast crowd made up of students and faculty from the City College of New York. The leads included Burgess Meredith and, as the "Radio Announcer," Orson Welles in one of his first credited roles. Scheduled for Sunday at 7 P.M. against Jack Benny's highly popular program, *The Fall of the City* did not achieve high ratings, but it did demonstrate what radio could do with a network's financial muscle. *The Fall of the City* was later printed in an edition wherein MacLeish called on poets to recognize radio as a legitimate means of expression.

Almost immediately after *The Fall of the City* was broadcast, a stream of verse plays started arriving in Lewis' office as poets of the stature of W. H. Auden, Stephen Vincent Benet, Maxwell Anderson, and Edna St. Vincent Millay gave radio a shot. According to Eric Barnouw, Lewis personally obtained huge satisfaction from this recognition, and Paley, his boss,

glowed in the fame that rival National Broadcasting Company (NBC) was *not* achieving. Emboldened by the prestige of literary programming, in the summer of 1937 Lewis announced an unprecedented Shakespeare series for CBS radio, to be directed by Brewster Morgan, starring the likes of Burgess Meredith as Hamlet, Walter Huston as Henry IV, and Brian Aherne as Henry V.

Early in 1938 Lewis announced the *Mercury Theater of the Air,* under the creative directorship of Orson Welles and John Houseman, to run on Sunday nights on CBS at 8 P.M. opposite another NBC mega-hit, the comedy of Edgar Bergen and Charlie McCarthy. *The Mercury Theater of the Air* started in the summer of 1938, with Welles producing, directing, and starring in many of the productions. On Sunday evening, 30 October 1938, *The Mercury Theater* presented, as a Halloween stunt, Howard Koch's adaptation of H.G. Wells' "The War of the Worlds," and caused a panic. But the series also performed a six-episode dramatization of Victor Hugo's "Les Miserables," and many other prestigious and experimental dramas.

Later in 1938 Lewis authorized Norman Corwin's *Words without Music* for Sunday afternoons—typically a dead network radio airtime. This half hour was for poetry production and experimentation that was unlike anything radio had tried before. Corwin had been trying to enter radio for many years, and it was Lewis who gave him his network break. Corwin is now part of radio's legacy.

World War II ended this period of network-sponsored creativity, but not before Lewis sent a young Edward R. Murrow to London where Murrow established radio's vital importance in war reporting. At about this time, Archibald MacLeish—at the request of President Franklin D. Roosevelt—created a new government agency, the Office of Facts and Figures, to help the public understand the government's war activities. MacLeish named Lewis as head of its radio activities. Lewis in turn recruited Norman Corwin for his first radio project, celebrating the 150th anniversary of the adoption of the Bill of Rights. MacLeish, with FDR's enthusiastic backing, sought to make this anniversary a symbol for the U.S. way of life, and the 15 December 1941 production starred Orson Welles, Lionel Barrymore, Walter Brennen, Walter Huston, Marjorie Main, Edward G. Robinson, Rudy Valle, and Jimmy Stewart.

Lewis would go on to produce *This Is War,* with scripts by Maxwell Anderson, Stephen Vincent Benet, Philip Wylie, and Norman Corwin. All sides praised this morale boosting. In July 1942 the Lewis unit became the radio bureau of the Office of War Information domestic branch and the principal voice of the government on radio during World War II.

After the war, Lewis did not return to CBS, but joined the Kenyon & Eckhardt advertising agency. There he produced more radio, and later TV, programs. His most famous effort—for television—was undoubtedly the "Ford Fiftieth Anniversary Show," starring Ethel Merman and Mary Martin, in 1953.

DOUGLAS GOMERY

See also Columbia Broadcasting System; Corwin, Norman; Murrow, Edward R.; Paley, William S.

William B. Lewis. Born in Lakewood, Ohio, 12 August 1904. Attended the University of Missouri, 1922–24. Started as an advertising apprentice, J. Walter Thompson Company, 1924; worked for various agencies as an advertising copy writer, 1925–35; hired by CBS as director of programs, 1936–37; vice-president for programming, CBS, 1937–41; moved to Washington, D.C. as coordinator of government radio, Office of Facts and Figures, 1941; chief, Domestic Radio Bureau, Office of War Information, 1942–43; assistant director, Domestic Radio Bureau, Office of War Information, 1943; vice president, Kenyon & Eckhardt Inc., 1944–51; president, Kenyon & Eckhardt Inc., 1951–60; chairman of the board of directors, American Cancer Society. Died in Sarasota, Florida, 24 February 1975.

Further Reading
Bannerman, R. LeRoy, *Norman Corwin and Radio: The Golden Years*, University: University of Alabama Press, 1986
Barnouw, Erik, *A History of Broadcasting in the United States, 1933–1953*, 3 vols., New York: Oxford University Press, 1966–70; see especially vol. 2, *The Golden Web*, 1968
Hilmes, Michele, *Radio Voices: American Broadcasting, 1922–1952*, Minneapolis: University of Minnesota Press, 1997
Houseman, John, *Run-through: A Memoir*, New York: Simon and Schuster, 1972; London: Allen Lane, 1973
Smith, Sally Bedell, *In All His Glory: The Life of William S. Paley, the Legendary Tycoon and His Brilliant Circle*, New York: Simon and Schuster, 1990
Sperber, Ann M., *Murrow: His Life and Times*, New York: Freundlich Books, 1986; London: Joseph, 1987

Liberty Broadcasting System

The Liberty Broadcasting System (LBS) was created by broadcaster Gordon McLendon in 1948. Headquartered in Dallas, the network grew quickly from a state, to a regional, and finally to a full-fledged national network within three years. By then, the 458-affiliate LBS was the second-biggest radio network in America.

LBS's popularity among station affiliates and listeners centered on its heavy schedule of sports programming. LBS flagship station KLIF in Dallas had become well known for its broadcasts of major-league baseball games, most of which were expertly re-created in the KLIF studios by Gordon McLendon. Radio station owners in nearby communities reached by KLIF's signal found many of their listeners attracted to McLendon's baseball games. The owners were soon inquiring about carrying the games, and before long enough of them had signed on as KLIF affiliates for McLendon to decide to formally launch LBS.

The McLendon success with baseball game re-creations resulted from a peculiar scarcity of "live" game coverage on the established radio networks. Major-league teams during the 1930s and 1940s held tight reins over broadcast rights to their baseball games. Radio stations that broadcast these games reached fans within a well-defined and limited coverage area. And because most major-league teams of the period were located in the Northeast and Midwest, baseball fans outside these areas had only the World Series broadcasts to satisfy their interest in major-league games. LBS stepped in to fill the void. An audience ranging in size between 60 and 90 million listeners proved that the network fulfilled a need that major-league club owners had either failed to recognize or ignored.

Although Gordon McLendon's re-created baseball games were popular, he decided in 1949 to challenge the major-league baseball establishment's prohibition of LBS live coverage from the ballparks. A complaint filed with the U.S. Justice Department, suggesting that major-league team owners were violating antitrust laws, finally opened the door for LBS to begin live game coverage. During the 1950 season alone, McLendon signed contracts to carry a minimum of 210 major-league baseball games. The games, numbering about eight per week, were split between American League and National League teams. Besides its baseball games, LBS carried a full slate of weekend college and professional football games during the fall. Noted sportscaster Lindsey Nelson was hired to announce many of these games.

McLendon expanded LBS programming beyond baseball in 1950. Expansion came when McLendon saw his network as now fully in competition with the older, more established National Broadcasting Company (NBC), Columbia Broadcasting System (CBS), American Broadcasting Companies (ABC), and Mutual networks. The traditional program fare that had made these networks popular was copied by LBS with varying degrees of success. Thus, the LBS daily broadcast hours were lengthened and filled with variety shows, musical shows, quiz shows, and soap operas. A number of these were produced in LBS studio facilities in Dallas, and a few were produced and aired from remote facilities in New York and Hollywood. An LBS repertory company supplied the talent for the soap operas; an in-house orchestra supplied live music; and a team of reporters located in Washington, D.C., supplied six daily newscasts for the fledgling network.

The early success enjoyed by LBS was described as phenomenal, especially given the network's youth and the inexperience of Gordon McLendon in running a radio network. Equally phenomenal was the network's success in competing with television's popularity at a time when NBC, CBS, and ABC were de-emphasizing their roles in network radio. What set LBS apart for the moment was McLendon's decision to concentrate his network's most popular programming during daytime hours, which had not yet been heavily infiltrated by television.

Any optimism for the network's future, however, disintegrated in 1951 when the major LBS advertiser, Falstaff Brewing Company, moved its advertising from LBS to Mutual. Loss of Falstaff's income revealed how few national advertisers—and the revenue that such advertisers provided—LBS had attracted. Too much effort had been placed in developing and programming the network, and too little effort had gone toward creating an effective and productive commercial sales apparatus.

In need of an immediate source of cash to keep LBS afloat, McLendon turned to Houston oilman and multimillionaire Hugh Roy Cullen. Cullen agreed to invest $400,000 in LBS and to loan the network an additional $600,000. In return, Cullen received 50 percent ownership of the network. Critics later charged that strings attached to the deal meant that Cullen would have a radio network platform by which to broadcast his ultraconservative political views. Little evidence exists to suggest that Cullen took such advantage of his LBS co-ownership.

The political issue became moot in 1952, when major-league baseball owners decided that broadcasters henceforth would have to negotiate coverage rights with individual baseball clubs rather than collectively with the National and American Leagues. The costs of coverage rights had escalated significantly over the previous year; now they were likely to rise to even greater heights. Added to Gordon McLendon's financial predicament at this point was the refusal of several major-league teams to negotiate any LBS coverage rights whatsoever. A much-reduced baseball schedule meant that LBS affiliates began departing the network. McLendon reacted by filing a $12 million antitrust suit against major-league baseball. The suit never went to trial, however. In January 1955 major-league owners offered Gordon McLendon $200,000 to settle the suit. McLendon had little choice but to accept, since LBS was by then in bankruptcy.

The end for LBS came quickly. Gordon McLendon announced to LBS affiliates on 6 May 1952 that LBS programming would be cut immediately from 16 hours to 8 hours daily. One week later, on 15 May, McLendon announced to affiliates that LBS was suspending operation at 10:45 P.M. on that date. The network filed for bankruptcy two weeks later.

Gordon McLendon continued in radio with great success, but he never again ventured into network broadcasting. McLendon gained much fame in later years as a radio program innovator, but he always regarded his days as an LBS play-by-play baseball announcer as the most memorable of his career.

RONALD GARAY

See also McLendon, Gordon; Recreations; Sports on Radio; Sportscasters

Further Reading

Garay, Ronald, *Gordon McLendon: The Maverick of Radio*, New York: Greenwood Press, 1992

Glick, Edwin, "The Life and Death of the Liberty Broadcasting System," *Journal of Broadcasting* 23 (Spring 1979)

Harper, Jim, "Gordon McLendon: Pioneer Baseball Broadcaster," *Baseball History* (Spring 1986)

Nelson, Lindsey, *Hello Everybody, I'm Lindsey Nelson*, New York: Beech Tree Books, 1985

Schroeder, Richard, *Texas Signs On: The Early Days of Radio and Television*, College Station: Texas A & M University Press, 1998

Licensing

Authorizing U.S. Stations to Broadcast

Because they must use frequencies on the electromagnetic spectrum, and to avoid as much interference as possible, no transmitter (broadcasting or otherwise) may operate without a federal license. In the United States, such licenses have been required since 1912, although many of the details of both procedure and substance have changed since then. Since 1934, the Federal Communications Commission (FCC) has been the source of federal licenses for all who would broadcast.

Origins

The Radio Act of 1912 vested the Secretary of Commerce and Labor with the authority to license radio transmitters in the United States. Administration of this provision before World War I presented no serious problems, as there was far more spectrum available than people wanting to use it. After the war, however, the demand for frequencies increased dramatically, especially after the 1920 inception of broadcasting. By 1925 there were many more would-be broadcasters than available frequencies, and Secretary of Commerce Herbert Hoover attempted to accommodate all applicants by limiting operating power levels and permissible hours of operation. In 1926 the courts ruled that Hoover had no power to place such conditions on operations, and the situation deteriorated into chaos. In response, Congress passed the Radio Act of 1927, giving the newly created Federal Radio Commission the power to license and regulate radio broadcasting. Those powers were transferred in 1934 to the FCC.

The Communications Act of 1934, as amended, requires the FCC to license radio broadcasters in the public interest, convenience, and necessity. Originally, broadcast licenses lasted no longer than three years, but various changes in the act lengthened the license period, until with the 1996 amendments all broadcast licenses were extended to run for eight years. During the license term, the licensee has exclusive use of a particular frequency in a specific location. However, licensees do not "own" the frequencies they use; they are considered trustees of the spectrum, which is owned by the public. As public trustees, licensees must operate their stations to serve the public's interest.

Qualifications

In order to receive a broadcast license, applicants must be legally, technically, and financially qualified, as specified in the Communications Act and in FCC rules. To be legally qualified, applicants must be citizens of the United States or corporations with no more than 20 percent foreign ownership. Parent companies of corporate licensees must have no more than 25 percent foreign ownership. Applicants must not be in violation of FCC media ownership rules (that is, they cannot already own the maximum number of radio stations in a market) and must meet certain "character" guidelines. Character qualifications relate to certain kinds of criminal convictions and antitrust violations. Lying to the commission is considered a serious character defect—one that almost certainly would disqualify an applicant.

Applicants demonstrate financial qualifications in many ways. If the applicant is applying for a new station, financial qualification is shown by certifying that the applicant has enough money to build the station and operate it for three months without significant advertising revenues. To be technically qualified, applicants must demonstrate the technical proficiency to build and operate the station and to comply with the commission's technical regulations. In most situations, applicants hire engineering consultants to meet their technical needs.

Getting on the Air

If an applicant is seeking a license for a new radio station, the applicant must first find an unused frequency that can be used in or near the community to be served. For AM stations, finding a frequency requires a complex engineering study to determine which frequency could be used in the proposed service area without causing harmful interference to other stations. For FM, the process of finding a usable frequency is often easier, because FM channels are allotted (positioned before licensing) across the country based on specified mileage separation requirements rather than signal interference contours.

Once a frequency has been located, the applicant files an application for a construction permit (CP) with the commission. If the applicant meets the basic qualifications for licensing and the application is not otherwise contested, the commission will grant the CP application. Once the CP is granted, a permittee typically has one year to build a station and begin technical and program testing. Assuming the testing is successful and no other problems arise, the permittee applies for the actual broadcast license, which is then routinely granted by the commission.

Complications in licensing typically arise when more than one party applies for the same frequency in the same market. These are known as mutually exclusive applications, because only one license can be granted for use of the frequency. Prior to 1994, when confronted with mutually exclusive radio applications, the FCC decided which applicant would best serve the public interest (and thereby be awarded the license) through an often lengthy and costly "comparative hearing." These trial-like hearings, presided over by a special FCC employee known as an administrative law judge (ALJ), involved the presentation of evidence, witnesses, and cross-examination. After the hearing, the ALJ would consider all the evidence and pick a winner based on the commission's comparative criteria. Several levels of appeal within the commission were then available to the losing applicants.

The commission's comparative criteria were twofold: diversification of media ownership and best practicable service to the public. The diversification of ownership criterion favored applicants with little or no existing media ownership: the commission at that time favored new owners in an attempt to diversify media ownership. The second criterion, best practicable service to the public, considered issues such as broadcast experience, efficient use of the frequency, and the extent to which the owners would also be integrated into the management of the station. In 1994 the District of Columbia Court of Appeals struck down the FCC's comparative licensing criteria, finding no nexus between the criteria and applicant qualifications. The FCC now settles mutually exclusive application situations through lotteries and spectrum auctions.

Most radio station owners today do not receive their licenses by applying for a new frequency but instead purchase the licenses from other licensees. License transfers must also be approved by the commission in order for the FCC to determine whether the transferee meets the basic qualifications of a radio licensee.

Renewals

The most common licensing situation in the United States today involves the renewal of an existing license. Upon the expiration of a radio license, the licensee must apply to the commission for a renewal. At that time, FCC personnel review the application to determine whether the licensee has performed in the public interest during the previous license term. If the licensee has a good record and no one objects, the renewal application is routinely granted. The vast majority of licenses are renewed in this way—more than a thousand of them each year.

Non-renewal of a license, though rare, might be based on any number of factors. The commission might not renew a license if it finds that the licensee has engaged in willful or repeated violations of the act or the commission's rules, has changed its ownership without informing the commission, or has in some way lied to the commission. If the violations are not severe enough to warrant non-renewal, the commission

has the power to issue a short-term renewal or to order special reporting requirements during the license term.

Until 1996, any time a station's license came up for renewal other applicants could also apply for the frequency. This led to what the commission referred to as a "comparative renewal," in which the past performance of the incumbent licensee was compared to the paper promises of the challenging applicant. As with other mutually exclusive licensing situations, comparative renewal cases were decided in a trial-like hearing. In 1996 Congress amended the Communications Act to disallow competing applications at renewal time. According to the revised law, existing broadcasters are judged as to their fitness to continue as licensees. If they continue to be qualified, their licenses are renewed. New applications for the frequency are allowed only when the incumbent licensee is judged unfit and the license renewal is denied.

In all licensing situations, interested parties, including members of the public who live in a station's listening area, have the opportunity to challenge the grant of a license by filing a "petition to deny" the application. If the petition alleges a "substantial and material question of fact," that is, an allegation so serious that if true it would call into question the basic qualifications of the applicant, the commission must hold a hearing on the application.

Section 312 of the Communications Act lists the actions that would justify revocation of a license during the license term. Such actions include willful and repeated violations of the Act, falsifying information, violation of relevant provisions in the U.S. criminal code (e.g., broadcasting lottery information or obscene material), and failure to provide reasonable access to airtime to candidates for federal political office.

MICHAEL A. MCGREGOR

See also Communications Act of 1934; Federal Communications Commission; Federal Radio Commission; Frequency Allocation; Hoover, Herbert; Localism in Radio; Public Interest, Convenience or Necessity; Telecommunications Act of 1996; Wireless Acts of 1910 and 1912/Radio Acts of 1912 and 1927

Further Reading

Browne, Donald R., *Electronic Media and Industrialized Nations: A Comparative Study*, Ames: Iowa State University Press, 1999

Carter, T. Barton, Marc A. Franklin, and Jay B. Wright, "Broadcast Licensing," in *The First Amendment and the Fifth Estate: Regulation of Electronic Mass Media*, 5th edition, New York: Foundation Press, 1999

Cole, Barry G., and Mal Oettinger, *Reluctant Regulators: The FCC and The Broadcast Audience*, Reading, Massachusetts: Addison Wesley, 1978

Edelman, Murray, *The Licensing of Radio Services in the United States, 1927–1947*, Urbana: University of Illinois Press, 1950

Emery, Walter B., *Broadcasting and Government: Responsibilities and Regulations*, East Lansing: Michigan State University Press, 1961; 2nd edition, 1971

Krasnow, Erwin G., Lawrence D. Longley, and Herbert A. Terry, *The Politics of Broadcast Regulation*, New York: St. Martin's Press, 1973; 3rd edition, 1982

Sterling, Christopher H., "Billions in Licenses, Millions in Fees: Comparative Renewal and the RKO Mess," *Gannett Center Journal* 2 (Winter 1988)

Lights Out

Horror Series

The first radio horror serial to attract a large following was the National Broadcasting Company's (NBC) *Lights Out,* a Chicago-produced serial that began in 1934 and was broadcast nationwide by the spring of 1935. The brainchild of first Wyllis Cooper and then Arch Oboler, *Lights Out* pioneered many of the horror sound effects and stream-of-consciousness storytelling techniques that would be widely imitated by later programs. Its graphic content was new to radio, and the program's success proved to the industry that listeners' imaginations could be effectively tapped through the skillful combination of sound effects and narrative suggestion. As radio program historian John Dunning has commented, "Never before had such sounds been heard on the air. Heads rolled, bones were crushed, people fell from great heights and splattered wetly on the pavement. There were garrotings, chokings, heads split by cleavers, and, to a critic at *Radio Guide,* 'the most monstrous sound of all sounds, human flesh being eaten'" (Dunning, 1998). Audiences were indeed horrified, some even calling the police. But they were also riveted to their radios.

Lights Out aired late at night throughout its 1930s run. The opening of the show dared the audience to tune in: 12 chimes were followed by a voice announcing, "This is the witching hour! . . . it is the hour when dogs howl and evil is let loose on the sleeping world. Want to hear about it? Then turn out your lights!" The show's original creator/producer was Wyllis Cooper, a staffer for Chicago's NBC studios. Although his work on the show has been largely overshadowed by that of his successor Arch Oboler, Cooper established *Lights Out*'s basic tone and structure. He combined fantasy and the supernatural with stream-of-consciousness narration to help involve the audience in the reality of its horrors. In particular, Cooper pushed the envelope on gruesome special effects, creating a sort of "can you top this" tradition that was continued by Arch Oboler when he took over the show in 1936 (Cooper moved to Hollywood for a screenwriting career). Real bones (spareribs) were broken on the show to simulate limbs snapping, cabbages were cut in half by meat cleavers to convey heads being bashed in, and wet noodles were crushed with a bathroom plunger to create the sound of human flesh being eaten. One of the program's most famous effects was that of a person being turned inside out, which was accomplished by stripping off a wet rubber glove while crushing a berry basket to simulate broken bones.

Oboler became one of the most famous of radio's auteurs, and his years on *Lights Out* helped establish his reputation as one of the most prolific and imaginative radio writers. Between May 1936 and July 1938, he penned more than 100 *Lights Out* scripts. Oboler continued the *Lights Out* tradition of making the supernatural and science fiction believably scary for the listener, and he has often been compared to Rod Serling and Ray Bradbury in this regard. "I didn't write about little green men," he told media critic Leonard Maltin, "monsters with dripping talons from the special effects department . . . I wrote about the terrors and monsters within each of us" (Maltin, 1997). Oboler's first play, "Burial Services," hit too close to home for many listeners. He told the story of a paralyzed girl being buried alive, and NBC received thousands of horrified letters. Although he never again touched so personal a nerve, Oboler's stream-of-consciousness style, sharp dialogue, and apt metaphors helped pull listeners in by giving his stories a psychological reality. In "Cat Wife," one of Oboler's most famous plays for *Lights Out,* Boris Karloff's duplicitous wife is transformed into an actual human-sized feline, reflecting both her monstrousness to him and his inability to cope with her.

Oboler's plays often contained messages or morals that critiqued greed or man's inhumanity to man. "The Ugliest Man in the World," for example, is not ugly to the woman who loves him. "State Executioner" suggests the horrors of capital punishment and the dangers of greed by having a state executioner execute a man he knows is innocent because he wants the payment; the horror multiplies when he finds out the man was his own son. "The Word" tells of a couple who descend from the Empire State Building to discover that everyone else in the world has disappeared; they conclude that God "got tired of the way [people] were doing things and destroyed them." This couple survived, to make Oboler's point that "plain ordinary people" could make the world a new and better place. Although occasionally heavy-handed, Oboler never hesitated to tackle weighty subjects within the framework of a mass horror genre, winning a new respect for the form.

As the 1930s progressed and the threat of war became clearer, Oboler left *Lights Out* and turned his writing skills to patriotic material. He revived the program for the 1942–43 season, broadcasting from New York over NBC. Oboler hosted the program himself, and its famous beginning became the one that has been most associated with the show since. To the chimes of a gong, Oboler spoke the words "It . . . is . . . later . . . than . . . you . . . think." As John Dunning (1998) has noted, the earlier hour of this series (all the broadcasts were at 8:00 P.M.), made it more accessible to people, and this became the best-remembered year of the series. Scripts were largely recycled from Oboler's previous shows, however, because he was busy doing war work. Its successful 1940s run also owes much to the sudden popularity and growth of the thriller/horror/suspense genre during the war period; *Lights Out* was the granddaddy—and model—of many of the more than 40 such programs that took to the airwaves during that time, most famously *Inner Sanctum* and *Suspense*.

The reputation and influence of the program remained strong long after television supplanted radio. This is due in part to Oboler's status as a celebrated auteur (most of Oboler's shows, unlike Cooper's, are available on tape). But *Lights Out* also stands as pivotal to radio history because it demonstrated the way in which radio programs could push listeners' imaginations to horrifying limits beyond those of reasoned vision. Radio, as horror author (and Oboler admirer) Stephen King has noted, has the ability to "unlock the door of evil without letting the monster out" (quoted in Nachman, 1998). *Lights Out* was the first program to demonstrate and exploit this aspect of radio, to the delight of its terror-stricken fans.

ALLISON MCCRACKEN

See also Horror Programs; Oboler, Arch; Sound Effects

Host
Arch Oboler

Narrator
Boris Aplon (1946)

Actors
Boris Karloff, Harold Peary, Betty Winkler, Mercedes McCambridge, Willard Waterman, Arthur Peterson, Betty Caine, Ed Carey, Sidney Ellstrom, Murray Forbes, Robert Griffin, Robert Guilbert, Rupert LaBelle, Philip Lord, Raymond Edward Johnson, and others

Writers/Producers/Directors
Wyllis Cooper, Arch Oboler, Albert Crews, and Bill Lawrence

Programming History

WENR, Chicago	January 1934–April 1935
NBC	April 1935–August 1946
CBS	October 1942–September 1943
ABC	July 1947–August 1947

Further Reading

DeLong, Thomas A., *Radio Stars: An Illustrated Biographical Dictionary of 953 Performers, 1920 through 1960*, Jefferson, North Carolina: McFarland, 1996

Dunning, John, *Tune in Yesterday: The Ultimate Encyclopedia of Old-Time Radio, 1925–1976*, Englewood Cliffs, New Jersey: Prentice-Hall, 1976; revised edition, as *On the Air: The Encyclopedia of Old-Time Radio*, New York: Oxford University Press, 1998

Harmon, Jim, *The Great Radio Heroes*, New York: Doubleday, 1967; 2nd edition, Jefferson, North Carolina: McFarland, 2001

Maltin, Leonard, *The Great American Broadcast: A Celebration of Radio's Golden Age*, New York: Dutton, 1997

Nachman, Gerald, *Raised on Radio: In Quest of the Lone Ranger, Jack Benny . . .* , New York: Pantheon, 1998

Stedman, Raymond William, *The Serials: Suspense and Drama by Installment*, Norman: University of Oklahoma Press, 1971; 2nd edition, 1977

Limbaugh, Rush 1951–

U.S. Talk Show Host

Media critic Howard Kurtz says that it is not much of an exaggeration to say that Rush Limbaugh single-handedly revived AM radio beginning in the mid-1980s and led the stampede of conservative talk show hosts that followed. By the beginning of the 1990s, Limbaugh was heard on more than 650 stations, reaching an estimated 20 million people each week. He continued to achieve similar numbers in the early 21st century. Kurtz claims that Limbaugh is more influential than other talk show hosts and commentators, even TV network giants Dan Rather, Tom Brokaw, and Peter Jennings, because he defined talk radio in a way that no one ever had before.

In addition to developing a new public forum, Limbaugh's influence has been felt in a number of other areas. His radio programs are the foundation of a multimillion-dollar empire that includes everything from conservative books to T-shirts to a monthly newsletter. In a tradition similar to that in the era of *Amos 'n' Andy,* dozens of restaurants around the country reserve "Rush Rooms" for his followers (who call themselves "dittoheads") to eat and listen to his three-hour weekday broadcasts.

In 1994 Limbaugh was credited with being the most important grassroots voice for conservative Republicans, who took control of the House of Representatives after decades of Democratic control. A *National Review* magazine cover story named Limbaugh "the leader of the opposition." His drumbeat criticism of the Clinton White House and of Hillary Rodham Clinton finally prompted the president to attack talk radio in general and Limbaugh in particular (to Limbaugh's delight). The increase in one-sided attacks over the airwaves also triggered a movement to restore the Fairness Doctrine killed by the FCC in 1987. *The Wall Street Journal* described the movement as the "Hush Rush Bill."

Tom Lewis, author of *Empire of the Air: The Men Who Made Radio* (1991), argues that Limbaugh's success speaks more to the power of radio and Limbaugh's ability to use the medium in which he has worked since he was a teen. "Better than most liberals or conservatives," says Lewis, Limbaugh is "a consummate showman who understands radio and sound, especially their ability to create a picture in the minds of listeners and their potential to capture imaginations."

To bring this about, Limbaugh borrows from the word-making skills of gossip columnist and 1930s broadcaster Walter Winchell, who coined words that not only distorted reality but evoked a wild form of humor. Limbaugh's terms, such as "feminazis" (to describe those in the women's movement) and "environmental wackos," are typical of his confrontational but engaging manner, which attracts primarily older white males. But Limbaugh also uses satire, thumping, popular recordings, and a variety of sound effects. When he talks about abortion, for example, the sound of a vacuum cleaner is heard in the background. He offers trading cards and rock songs mocking political figures.

Lewis says that Limbaugh draws from the tradition of radio humorists such as Jack Benny, Fred Allen, and even the Great Gildersleeve. "A man, a legend, a way of life," Limbaugh repeats over his Excellence in Broadcasting (EIB) radio network as well as in books, pamphlets, and newsletters. "I am Rush Limbaugh from the Limbaugh Institute for Advanced Conservative Studies. Yes, my friends, the Doctor of Democracy is on the air." According to Limbaugh, the reason for his popularity is that he's "the epitome of morality and virtue . . . with talent on loan from God."

Limbaugh's format includes lengthy monologues that sometimes meander and consist of incomplete sentences and muddled paragraphs. Along with other conservative talk show hosts, he helps to create an almost conspiratorial approach against big government and liberals in politics and the media; at the same time he celebrates the common sense of other Americans—particularly himself. Although he does not usually have guests on his program, Limbaugh is generally polite to his callers. Larry King, a talk show host who depends on guests, says Limbaugh comes to his broadcast with an agenda. "Agenda broadcasters will do anything. They'll lie. They'll fabricate, to keep the agenda going," King says.

A self-described nerd, Limbaugh got his start in broadcasting in 1967 as a disc jockey for the radio station partially owned by his father in Cape Girardeau, Missouri, where he was born and raised. After dropping out of Southeastern Missouri State University, he worked for and was fired from radio stations in McKeesport (Pennsylvania), Pittsburgh, and Kansas City, where he was also a publicist for the Kansas City Royals and announcer for its station. Because of his controversial nature, Limbaugh was also dismissed from the Kansas City station. He went to Sacramento, California, in the fall of 1984, where he replaced Morton Downey, who had been fired for telling an ethnic joke.

In California, Limbaugh found his radio audience by attacking communism, feminism, and environmentalists, developing a style that he admits is more entertainment than news or even debate. He has repeatedly said that his principal job is not so much to champion causes and proselytize but to hold an audience. After nearly tripling his California audience in four years, in July 1988 he moved to New York City's

Times credits Limbaugh not only with the NAFTA victory but with helping sweep Republicans to Congressional victory in 1996 and with destroying the crime and lobbying bills of President Clinton. In his own words, he continues to serve as "a man, a legend, a way of life" and the "Doctor of Democracy."

ALF PRATTE

See also Commentators; Controversial Issues; Fairness Doctrine; Talk Radio

Rush Limbaugh. Born Rush Hudson Limbaugh III in Cape Giradeau, Missouri, 12 January 1951. Attended Southeast Missouri University but did not graduate; worked for radio station WIXZ, McKeesport, Pennsylvania, KQV in Pittsburgh, and KUDL, KFIX, and KMBZ, all in Kansas City, where he was also a publicist and announcer for the Kansas City Royals; hired by KFBK, Sacramento, California, 1984; signed a two-year contract with EMF Media Management, New York City, 1988; nationally-syndicated talk radio show broadcast to more than 600 stations, 2003.

Radio Series

1988–present   *The Rush Limbaugh Show*

Television Series

The Rush Limbaugh Show, 1992–1996

Selected Publications

The Way Things Ought to Be, 1992
See, I Told You So, 1993

Further Reading

Franken, Al, *Rush Limbaugh Is a Big Fat Idiot, and Other Observations,* New York: Delacorte Press, 1996
Kurtz, Howard, *Hot Air: All Talk All the Time,* New York: Times Books, 1996
Laufer, Peter, *Inside Talk Radio: America's Voice or Just Hot Air?* Secaucus, New Jersey: Carol, 1995
Rendall, Steve, Jim Naureckas, and Jeff Cohen, *The Way Things Aren't: Rush Limbaugh's Reign of Error: Over 100 Outrageously False and Foolish Statements from America's Most Powerful Radio and TV Commentator,* New York: New Press, 1995
Rutenberg, Jim, "Despite Other Voices, Limbaugh's Is Still Strong, *New York Times* (24 April 2000)
Seib, Philip M., *Rush Hour: Talk Radio, Politics, and the Rise of Rush Limbaugh,* Fort Worth, Texas: Summit Group, 1993

Rush Limbaugh
Copyright 1998 Brad Trent/Premiere Radio Networks

WABC, where his program was syndicated and his loyal following multiplied and mobilized. A nationally syndicated one-half hour television program begun in 1992 was not as successful as his radio program and was dropped.

In his programs and books, Limbaugh describes and mocks various liberal movements and the effects of their agendas on society. "I believe that in order to combat the misinformation that is so prevalent on our political landscape today we have to remain informed and alert to the things that are occurring," he writes in *The Way Things Ought To Be* (1992). "The best way to do that is to read, listen to, or watch me."

An ardent admirer of Ronald Reagan and supporter of George Bush and Robert Dole, Limbaugh provided a great service for the Clinton administration when he endorsed the North American Free Trade Agreement (NAFTA) and attacked Ross Perot's anti-NAFTA crusade. However, the *New York*

Little Orphan Annie

Children's Serial Drama

A pioneer of the children's serial genre, *Little Orphan Annie* first bowed—or curtsied—in 1930 on Chicago station WGN. On 6 April 1931 it premiered nationally on the NBC Blue Network, later moving to Mutual Broadcasting System. Shirley Bell and Janice Gilbert portrayed Annie during the series' 11-year run; Bell from the beginning until 1940, Gilbert from 1940 to 1942.

Based on Harold Gray's popular comic strip, *Annie* featured 15 minutes of action and high adventure every weekday afternoon or early evening, initially based primarily in her adopted hometown of Tompkins Corners, and later in more exotic, faraway places. She fought all forces of evil, including gangsters and criminals, reminding her faithful listeners at the end of the show to "be sure to drink your Ovaltine." Indeed, the premium toys offered by *Little Orphan Annie* and its longtime sponsor seemed at times to compete with the stories themselves, taking up four to six minutes of the 15-minute broadcast. Children who tuned in were urged to get their own "swell Ovaltine shake-up drinking mug" by sending ten cents and the proof of purchase from an Ovaltine can.

In addition to Bell and Gilbert, other cast members included Allan Baruck and Mel Torme (Joe Corntassel, Annie's best friend), Henry Saxe, Boris Aplon, and Stanley Andrews (Oliver "Daddy" Warbucks), Henrietta Tedro and Jerry O'Mera (Ma and Pa Silo, the farm couple who cared for Annie when Daddy Warbucks was away on business), and Pierre Andre (Uncle Andy, the announcer). The voice of Sandy, Annie's dog, was provided by Brad Barker. Among Annie's favorite expressions were "Leapin' lizards" and "Jumpin' grasshoppers."

The program's writers employed a simple but very effective technique to keep listeners, especially young children, returning to hear the next installment of Annie's adventures: the cliffhanger. Episodes seldom ended with finality or resolution. Instead, story lines "flowed" from one episode to the next, occasionally reaching a conclusion but never without the development of a new story line to take its place. Beginning with *Annie*, this open-ended approach—leaving listeners in suspense at the end of each daily broadcast—was particularly evident for decades to come in children's radio and television programming and motion picture serials. In addition, Annie's radio adventures appealed to youngsters because the episodes often articulated childhood dreams of experiencing the glamour of the adult world.

NBC's radio network connections were not completed for regular U.S. coast-to-coast broadcasting until 1933, two years after *Little Orphan Annie*'s network premiere. As a consequence, *Annie* in its infancy was actually two different programs—one originating in Chicago, the other in San Francisco. Listeners in the eastern and central areas of the U.S. heard Shirley Bell in the lead role, while listeners in the far west heard Floy Hughes. Identical scripts ensured some consistency between the two productions, but west coast listeners were no doubt startled to suddenly hear different actors after the program's operations were consolidated in Chicago in 1933.

For over five years *Little Orphan Annie* aired six times a week, going to five times weekly beginning in 1936. The series moved from NBC to Mutual in 1940, at which time Ovaltine, the show's original sponsor, decided instead to put its advertising dollars in *Captain Midnight*, a new children's suspense show. Taking the chocolate drink mix's place as *Annie*'s sponsor was the breakfast cereal Puffed Wheat Sparkies, but by this time other adventure shows were outgunning Annie at her own game. Faced with declining ratings, *Little Orphan Annie*'s last broadcast was on 26 January 1942.

DAVID MCCARTNEY

Cast

Little Orphan Annie	Shirley Bell, Floy Hughes, Bobbe Deane, Janice Gilbert
Joe Corntassel	Allan Baruck, Mel Torme
Oliver "Daddy" Warbucks	Henry Saxe, Stanley Andrews, Boris Aplon
Mrs. Mary Silo	Henrietta Tedro
Mr. Byron Silo	Jerry O'Mera
Uncle Andy (announcer)	Pierre Andre
Sandy (Annie's dog)	Brad Barker
Aha	Olan Soule
Clay	Hoyt Allen

Producer/Creator

Based on the comic strip by Harold Gray

Programming History

WGN Chicago	1930
NBC Blue	1931–October 1936
NBC	November 1936–January 1940
Mutual	1940–42

Further Reading

Boemer, Marilyn Lawrence, *The Children's Hour: Radio Programs for Children, 1929–1956*, Metuchen, New Jersey: Scarecrow Press, 1989

Dunning, John, *Tune in Yesterday: The Ultimate Encyclopedia of Old-Time Radio, 1925–1976*, Englewood Cliffs, New Jersey: Prentice-Hall, 1976; revised edition, as *On the Air: The Encyclopedia of Old-Time Radio*, New York: Oxford University Press, 1998

Swartz, Jon D., and Robert C. Reinehr, *Handbook of Old-Time Radio*, Metuchen, New Jersey: Scarecrow Press, 1993
Terrace, Vincent, *Radio Programs, 1924–1984: A Catalogue of over 1800 Shows*, Jefferson, North Carolina: McFarland, 1999

Localism in Radio

U.S. Regulatory Approach

The concept of "localism," or serving a specific community, has always been central to the practice of radio programming and to government policies concerning broadcasting in the United States. In contrast to most of the rest of the world, American radio stations were allocated to local communities and licensed to serve audiences defined by the boundaries of those communities. The Federal Communications Commission (FCC) has described its radio allocation priorities as (1) providing a usable signal from at least one station to everyone and diversified service to as many persons as possible, and (2) creating sufficient outlets for local expression addressing each community's needs and interests. That system of license allocation remains the foundation of American broadcasting. As for programming, local service has frequently been a key element in a station's ability to survive and prosper. Research and experience have consistently demonstrated that local content is one of the things listeners value most highly.

However, economic realities have usually impelled broadcasters toward centralized program distribution. Networks began developing in broadcasting's earliest days, and although the traditional radio networks have long been reduced to providing news and sports for radio, a new generation of networks offering full-time formats appeared as the increased availability of satellite service in the 1980s made such a service viable. By 2000, the emergence of distribution technologies that no longer rely exclusively on nearby transmitters to reach individual audience members—such as direct-to-home satellites and the internet—and the ability of large radio groups to program clusters of stations from a central location led some to suggest that localism is an idea destined to be little more than a quaint relic of a bygone age. Larry Irving (then head of the National Telecommunications and Information Administration) told the 1999 National Association of Broadcasters convention in Las Vegas that localism has "gone the way of the buffalo." Yet other industry observers continue to argue forcefully that the most successful radio stations are those that do the best job of connecting with the localized needs and interests of their audiences. This view holds that localism will be even more important in a future of ever-greater competition from sources such as the satellite-based Digital Audio Radio Services (DARS), offered nationwide since November 2001 by XM Satellite Radio and since 2002 by Sirius.

These contradictory assertions may all, in fact, be accurate, depending on one's vantage point. Much like the phrase "The public interest," the meaning of localism has always been in the eye of the beholder—typically either the FCC or a station licensee. The very vagueness of the term has enabled a variety of regulators, industry spokespersons, and public service advocates to laud the importance of localism in different situations.

Localism in U.S. Broadcast Regulation

As a matter of policy, localism is closely tied to a number of regulatory goals. These are generally expressed as the need to limit centralized (program) power or authority in order to create more diverse content—the robust and varied "marketplace of ideas" central to the American understanding of free speech. For several decades, the FCC has pointed to the importance of localism as a means of providing diverse program content for the furtherance of the public interest. Some policy makers also argue for the need to protect local communities and smaller interests from being overwhelmed by programs developed by (and for) larger national interests. The desire to diffuse political power has been a running theme throughout American history (the federal system of government is perhaps the most obvious result). Added to the widely accepted notion that the media are capable of exerting great influence on society, the decision to dilute the power of a single broadcast entity—station or especially network—seems an obvious choice.

The commission has a specific charge in the Communications Act to "encourage the larger and more effective use of radio in the public interest." The FCC has generally interpreted this to mean that it should try to allocate the maximum technically feasible number of stations around the country. Thus, structural definitions of localism (in a geographic or spatial sense) have most often guided policy makers. This understanding of localism assumes that stations licensed to transmit to a geographically restricted area will focus their programming on the specific needs and interests of the citizens residing in that area. In this context, localism as policy has been put into regulations affecting the distribution of licenses to various communities. Localism is also seen in the bedrock obligation of all broadcast licensees to serve the needs and interests of their community of license (which at one time involved an elaborate process to ascertain the needs of that community) and in the preference that was granted to active local ownership when, prior to 1996, the comparative hearing process was used to choose a licensee from among mutually exclusive competing applicants.

In one of the earliest examples of localism, the Radio Act of 1927 divided the country into five "zones" and, in the case of competing license applications, directed the Federal Radio Commission (FRC) to distribute stations among the zones according to frequency, power, and time of operation, with concern for fairness, equity, and efficiency. The Davis Amendment, added one year later, required the FRC to provide *equality* of service, in terms of both transmission and reception, in each of the five zones. These sections, with slight modification, passed into the Communications Act of 1934. Although the zone system was repealed in 1936 and the law was modified to require once again that the FCC simply provide a fair, efficient, and equitable distribution of radio service to each state and community, localism was (and is) undeniably a powerful concern in Congress.

Another significant, and more recent, example of the FCC's structural concern with localism was the decision to drastically restructure the system of FM station allocation in order to increase the number of available stations in the early 1980s. Generally referred to by its FCC docket number (80-90), this order authorized three new classes of stations and modified the interference and operational rules with the goal of allowing first (and sometimes second) FM stations in communities where none had been possible before under the original 1962 Table of Assignments. As a result, the number of FM stations in the United States grew from around 3,000 in 1980 to slightly under 6,000 by the end of 1990 and continued to climb to more than 8,500 by 2003.

Localism and the Business of Radio

However, the growth was not solely good news for the industry or the audience. Many observers lamented the increase in interference in the FM band. The rise in the number of stations combined with the simultaneous deregulation of radio to rapidly escalate station values. Many owners found themselves too far in debt, particularly during the economic downturn in the late 1980s and early 1990s. Sometimes as a result of the significant economic hardships resulting from the combination of increased competition and debt load, sometimes in response to a perceived change in the desires of the audience, stations cut back or eliminated local air staffs and news operations. If the goal of the FCC's restructuring was to create more local content for more communities, the result could best be described as mixed. Although many stations continue to thrive by providing their audience a programming diet heavy with local content and involvement, satellite-provided formats, other syndicated product, and the ever-increasing ease of automating a station combine to create a significant economic incentive for many licensees to reduce localism to commercials and weather forecasts.

This illustrates the inherent conflict between policy rhetoric and the changing economic realities facing licensees. Though frequently lauding localism in policy pronouncements, the FCC has seldom promulgated, and even more infrequently enforced, local program guidelines or requirements. Nearly all of those that ever existed, such as the fairness doctrine, the ascertainment primer, commercial guidelines, and news and public-affairs guidelines, disappeared by the mid-1980s. The reasons behind this deregulatory trend (critics would term it failure) have been hotly debated because they are so complex. The regulatory problem is one of accommodating the various interests—licensees, program producers, audiences, networks, regulators, advertisers—in a rule that comports with common understanding of the First Amendment. Although this task was difficult under the public trustee model of regulation that guided broadcasting's first 50 years, it is practically impossible to set firm local content guidelines under the current regulatory philosophy, which moves much of the control from government policy to marketplace competition.

A further complicating factor is the constant evolution of the media environment. From the system envisioned at the time of the Communications Act in 1934, rigidly structured along relatively narrow geographic lines, radio in the United States moved almost immediately to a distribution system with a wider geographic frame (regional and national sources feeding the majority of programming on "local" stations). From a few hundred local stations linked with relatively new networks at the time the Communications Act of 1934 was written, radio grew decades later to a business of thousands of "local" outlets providing a relatively few national music or talk program formats. Development of internet and satellite distribution has merely enhanced the trend to national program types provided through local outlets. The degree to which any one of those outlets wishes to be truly local (reflecting and projecting its own community) is left to the discretion of the licensee.

The vague nature of localism itself is a final complication. One's understanding of concepts such as "local" or "community" colors any practical application of localism. The term *can* mean full-scale involvement of a station with its community, or (as is more usually the case) it can mean mere mention of local weather (and local commercials) within a syndicated music format heard on hundreds of stations across the country. As traditionally viewed by the FCC, real localism is probably somewhere in the middle, but much closer to the former—and many argue that it's also good business. In his book *Radio Programming: Tactics and Strategy*, programmer and consultant Eric Norberg asserts that localism and human contact are the elements that listeners value most in a station and that therefore the core of what makes a station successful is the relatable local person on the air. This viewpoint takes on the air of common wisdom in the industry trade press, particularly in advice given to programmers and air talent. Researchers repeatedly find that local information (weather forecasts, traffic information, event news) is one of the top reasons people tune in to radio.

Localism as a Social Construct

Critics, and occasionally even the FCC, have suggested that the goals of localism can be addressed in a different fashion, recognizing that communities frequently form around shared tastes, interests, and ideals without specific reference to a geographic boundary. For example, in the rulemaking that eliminated many of the radio programming guidelines, the commission noted that

> communities of common interests need not have geographic bounds. . . . The economics of radio . . . allowed that medium to be far more sensitive to the diversity within a community and the attendant specialized community needs. Increased competition in large urban markets has forced stations to choose programming strategies very carefully. (FCC, "Deregulation of Radio," *Notice of Inquiry and Proposed Rulemaking,* 73 F.C.C.2d 457 [1979], at 489)

This alternative view of community can also be seen in the FCC's decision to approve satellite-delivered DARS. Despite the diversity of programming alluded to above, many program interests go unfulfilled by traditional terrestrial radio because the audience for a particular type of music or information is simply too small within the service area of a single station or is otherwise unattractive to advertisers. Beginning in late 2001, however, satellite radio services included program channels

that would not be economically viable on a single station in a given market (e.g., five separate jazz channels). The technology can aggregate widely separated audiences in a fashion that does not serve traditional localism but surely adds to content diversity.

Trials of Modern Localism

Sometimes, competing concerns such as spectrum efficiency have prevailed over localism. Prior to 1978, the FCC issued Class D FM licenses to college and community stations, permitting low-power operation (a maximum of 10 watts, with a tower height less than 100 feet) in the noncommercial part of the FM band. These stations represented a variety of operational styles, from student-run stations at colleges or high schools to stations licensed to civic groups and generally run by a largely volunteer or all-volunteer staff. By their very nature, these operations were strongly committed to their community and would appear to personify the localism ideal, often featuring material not available through full-power stations.

In 1972 the Corporation for Public Broadcasting (CPB) petitioned the FCC to explore several issues related to more efficient use of the FM channels set aside for noncommercial educational stations. In comments to the commission, they argued (with the support of others, including the National Federation of Community Broadcasters) that the 10-watt broadcasters were effectively blocking more efficient use of the spectrum. Essentially, CPB and its supporters were arguing for more stations that met their qualifying guidelines for size and professionalism, at the expense of smaller operations. Supporters of Class D stations, primarily the licensees themselves, countered with various arguments for retaining the service as it was, including the point most relevant here—the truly local nature of the service.

The FCC recognized that the Class D stations were indeed meeting discrete local needs. But in this case, the commission put the emphasis on the efficiency argument put forth by CPB, announcing new rules that effectively forced existing Class D stations to upgrade their facilities to Class A minimums or else become a secondary service, facing interference or being bumped from their assignments. In the FCC's view at that time, there was not sufficient spectrum available for both full-power, larger coverage area stations and low-power operations (although the commission has long accepted the need for low-powered translator and booster stations that extend the coverage of existing FM and TV stations but are prohibited from originating any programming themselves).

It is somewhat ironic that the FCC issued rules in 2000 that will create a new class of low-powered FM or microradio stations. The rulemaking comes in response to petitions arguing that, in the wake of industry consolidation following the 1996

Telecommunications Act, radio ownership and content are insufficiently diverse, and that current stations often fail to address local needs. Although congressional intervention curtailed the number of LPFM stations that could be licensed, the FCC had issued more than 400 construction permits by the end of 2002, and 73 LPFM stations were on the air in January 2003

GREGORY D. NEWTON

See also Australian Aboriginal Radio; Canadian Radio and Multiculturalism; College Radio; Community Radio; Deregulation; Licensing; Low-Power Radio/Microradio; Pacifica Foundation; Ten-Watt Stations

Further Reading

Barrett, Andrew C., "Public Policy and Radio—A Regulator's View," *Media Studies Journal* 7 (1993)
Collins, Tom A., "The Local Service Concept in Broadcasting: An Evaluation and Recommendation for Change," *Iowa Law Review* 65 (1980)
Federal Communications Commission, *Commission en banc Programming Inquiry, Report and Statement of Policy,* 44 FCC 2303 (1960)
Federal Communications Commission, *Deregulation of Radio, Notice of Inquiry and Proposed Rulemaking,* 73 FCC 2d 457 (1979)
Federal Communications Commission, *The Suburban Community Policy, the Berwick Doctrine, and the De Facto Reallocation Policy, Report and Order,* 93 FCC 2d 436 (1983)
Jones, Steven G., "Understanding Community in the Information Age," in *CyberSociety: Computer-Mediated Communication and Community,* edited by Steven G. Jones, Thousand Oaks, California: Sage, 1995
Kelley, E.W., *Policy and Politics in the United States: The Limits of Localism,* Philadelphia: Temple University Press, 1987
Kemmis, Daniel, *Community and the Politics of Place,* Norman: University of Oklahoma Press, 1990
McCain, Thomas A., and G. Ferrell Lowe, "Localism in Western European Radio Broadcasting: Untangling the Wireless," *Journal of Communication* (Winter 1990)
Milam, Lorenzo W., *Sex and Broadcasting: A Handbook on Starting a Radio Station for the Community,* 2nd edition, Saratoga, California: Dildo Press, 1972; 4th edition, as *The Original Sex and Broadcasting,* San Diego, California: MHO and MHO, 1988
Norberg, Eric G., *Radio Programming: Tactics and Strategy,* Boston: Focal Press, 1996
Stavitsky, Alan G., "The Changing Conception of Localism in U.S. Public Radio," *Journal of Broadcasting and Electronic Media* 38 (1994)

Local Marketing Agreements

Brokered Agreements among Stations

As part of the deregulation of radio ownership initiated by the Federal Communications Commission (FCC) during the late 1970s and early 1980s, radio station owners and operators began to sign program service and/or marketing agreements, known in the industry as local marketing agreements. In 1992 the FCC formally approved this form of ownership and operations agreements, and they became commonplace, particularly in the four years leading to the easing of ownership rules in the 1996 Telecommunications Act.

Alliances for local marketing agreements may be located in the same market, in the same region, or in the same service (AM or FM). The allied owners and operators draw up and sign legal agreements defining financial control over their allied properties, but the owners still maintain their separate licenses and studios. After 1996, it often became simpler to simply purchase a station, but local marketing agreements were still used to make transitions to new owners cheaper, easier, and more cost-effective.

A local marketing agreement thus has become a time-brokering agreement between stations that can address either programming or advertising time. Basically, the originating or principal station in the local marketing agreement pays the "affiliate" a monthly fee either to partially simulcast programming or to air original satellite-delivered programming. This type of agreement differs from a satellite format network affiliation arrangement, wherein the affiliate pays for programming. The originating station in a local marketing agreement can strike an arrangement with the leased station for either handling or sharing advertising sales.

The benefits of local marketing agreements to the originating station include expanded coverage area and thus the potential for increased sales of advertising. For example, during the early 1990s, owners of many struggling AM stations signed local marketing agreements to stabilize their flow of profits rather than take on the risks and costs involved in trying to establish a new format.

By 2000, although the number of stations and formats seems endless in major markets, in fact, local marketing agreements allowed two separate radio stations to operate jointly, and so the number of operators (or voices) was actually far fewer than the number of stations (or outlets). Usually the financially strong station reaches a combined operation and sales agreement with a financially troubled station in the same community to oversee programming and advertising time sales for a percentage of the advertising sales. Although the parties exercising a local marketing agreement are not required to file the agreement with the FCC, the licensee of the weaker partner station is still required to meet the station's maintenance and community standards (although in practice these requirements have become so minimal during the 1990s that this threat of losing a licensee over such a deal offers no risk).

The local marketing agreement policy helped redefine the institutional relationship that had formerly been restricted to affiliation. Indeed, once the FCC in 1992 formally relaxed regulations to allow local radio owners to own and control more than one station in the same service market, a wave of deals took place. One scholar calculated that over 50 percent of the commercial radio stations became involved in some aspect of consolidation between 1992 and 1996, including local marketing agreements. The pace of consolidation has increased tremendously since the Telecommunications Act of 1996 became law, with local marketing agreements used to make the transition to combinations of radio stations.

Local marketing agreements permit the parties to take advantage of cost and organizational structural efficiencies; to dominate a market with variations of one format; to eliminate redundant jobs; to develop broader marketing plans and solutions for advertisers; and, in the end, to increase profits for stockholders and investors. One can simply buy a station, or, to be more flexible in the short run, one can set up a local marketing agreement to test whether a formal alliance might work better. Some owners delay formal merger decisions until they figure out how to consolidate personnel and facilities.

There have been, therefore, numerous examples of different uses of local marketing agreements, as owners have utilized combinations of acquiring stations to form new and, they hope, more profitable alliances. Consider a top 50 market, Charlotte, North Carolina, where in spring 1992 the market was being served by ten radio owners and operators, who owned 3 AM and 12 FM stations. Two years later, those ten had dwindled to six owners and operators. By fall 1996, Charlotte had consolidated to the point of having only four viable radio owners and operators controlling the same 15 stations. Local marketing agreements created much, though not all, of this consolidation.

DOUGLAS GOMERY

See also Licensing; Ownership, Mergers, and Acquisitions

Further Reading

Albarran, Alan B., *Management of Electronic Media*, Belmont, California: Wadsworth, 1997

Chan-Olmsted, Sylvia M., "A Chance for Survival or Status Quo? The Economic Implications of the Radio Duopoly Ownership Rules," *The Journal of Radio Studies* 3 (1994)

Compaine, Benjamin M., and Douglas Gomery, *Who Owns the Media?* White Plains, New York: Knowledge Industry, 1979; 3rd edition, Mahwah, New Jersey: Erlbaum, 2000

Ditingo, Vincent M., *The Remaking of Radio*, Boston: Focal Press, 1995

Federal Communications Commission, Mass Media Bureau, Policy and Rules Division, *Review of the Radio Industry, 1997*, MM Docket No. 98-35 (13 March 1998, as part of 1998 Biennial Regulatory Review)

Lodge, Oliver J. 1851–1940

British Wireless Pioneer

An important British physicist and mathematician of the late 19th and early 20th centuries, Oliver Lodge was one of the first people to experiment with wireless transmission, and he disseminated the pioneering work of Heinrich Hertz and his contemporaries. Because of his scientific reputation, a crucial invention, and his position in British higher education, Lodge helped to promote wireless as a practical proposition.

Early Years

Oliver Lodge was born into a comfortable middle class English family and endured four years of a hard Victorian boarding school education. In 1865, at age 14, he went to work for his father in the family's successful clay and glaze business called "Potteries." But he was attracted to science at an early age and decided to continue his education in the field of chemistry. He returned to school in 1872 seeking a university education.

At the University of London, his interest focused more on mathematics, and he earned his bachelor's degree in 1875. That same year he published his first scientific article, and four years later he wrote his first book (on elementary mechanics). These publications were but the beginning of a prolific writing career. Lodge was able to clearly explain scientific or mathematical principles to those lacking formal scientific training, and thus his published writings demonstrated both academic research and popular journalism.

For the last two decades of the 19th century, University College, Liverpool (later the University of Liverpool) became his academic base for teaching and scientific research, including his important wireless work. At this time, Lodge also demonstrated his growing interest in psychic research, which would fully occupy his final years. His university duties included considerable teaching, research, and writing, as well as extensive academic administration.

Wireless Research

In the early 1870s, while still a student, Lodge had first read James Clerk Maxwell's two-volume theoretical work that contained a complicated early concept of wireless. He worked to perfect the Branly "coherer" device used to detect electromagnetic signals, and gave it its name. Lodge followed research in this and other arms of physics, and on holiday travel in Europe he met and compared research ideas with German physicist Heinrich Hertz, who in 1888 had preceded him to publication with experiments proving the "wireless" theories of Maxwell. When Hertz died prematurely in 1894, Lodge delivered and

published a memorial lecture that would eventually go through four ever-larger editions and help introduce the world to the theory of wireless and its potential application. The lecture included a general description of Lodge's own system for wireless transmission and detection.

Three months later, on 14 August 1894, Lodge demonstrated his transmitting system by sending electromagnetic waves in the form of Morse Code signals 150 yards between buildings at Oxford during a meeting of the British Association. This was the first public demonstration of what would become known as wireless or radio telegraphy, though the eventual importance of the technology was not yet recognized by Lodge or anyone else. Lodge was merely seeking scientific parallels between the transmission of light and electrical signals. Despite his breakthrough (which was presented with little fanfare), Lodge did not immediately focus on furthering his wireless effort.

With Marconi's 1896 arrival in Britain and his soon widely publicized experiments with wireless at ever-greater distances, however, Lodge's ambitions were stoked. He was understandably jealous over the public acclaim accruing to Marconi for work that paralleled efforts Lodge had undertaken several years earlier. In an attempt to pick up his earlier wireless theorizing, Lodge began to work with electrical engineer Dr. Alexander Muirhead (1848–1920), who with his brother manufactured telegraph instruments. Lodge and Muirhead had met at the former's 1894 lecture. To Lodge's theoretical physics, Muirhead added practical technology and a clear vision of what wireless telegraphy could accomplish.

In the course of his long life, Lodge would accumulate 29 patents (some shared with others, including 11 with Muirhead) from 1883 to 1931. By far the most important two were granted in 1897 for what Lodge termed "syntony," or a telegraphy system that allowed a receiving device to select among competing transmitted signals. This innovation was an outgrowth of his recognition of the need for detectors of wireless signals to be able to differentiate among a growing number of available signals. This patent, along with several others (in 1898 Lodge also took out a patent on a rudimentary loudspeaker) was central to what would become the "Lodge-Muirhead" system that would briefly compete with Marconi, who only belatedly perceived the need to tune signal detectors. At the same time, Lodge was one of several authorities who reported to British postal authorities and the Admiralty that there were ways of operating an effective wireless system without relying upon Marconi's patents. Lodge stated several times that he was unhappy primarily with those around Marconi, not the Italian inventor himself. Along with many other critics, Lodge felt that Marconi tried to take on too much and overestimated what the crude technology of the period could provide.

Lodge and Muirhead established a syndicate (a limited company) in 1901 to develop and manufacture equipment based on their jointly developed patents in wireless telegraphy. After considerable testing of improved detectors at growing distances, early in 1903 the Lodge-Muirhead Syndicate announced its system of wireless telegraphy, said to be effective at distances up to 60 to 80 miles. The system was tested (though not adopted) by the British Army and was actually put into practical use in 1904 by the colonial Indian government to communicate several hundred miles to some off-shore islands. Steady improvements were made. But other than a few experimental stations, the Lodge-Muirhead Syndicate never became an active operating entity as did Marconi, its chief competitor. The need after 1904 to obtain a license from the British Post Office (which utilized Marconi equipment) for any transmitting station was one stumbling block to expansion, as was the entrenched market position of the Marconi interests.

Lodge's vital syntony or tuning patent expired in 1911, although under British law and after a patent trial (in which the judge found in favor of Lodge's priority over Marconi in the basic tuning principle) it was extended to 1918. Because they were vital to its own expanding Empire wireless operations, however, rights to the Lodge patent were then purchased by the Marconi company. As a part of the deal, the Lodge-Muirhead Syndicate was closed down. Despite having lost the legal case, Marconi had managed to buy out its chief potential British competition.

The lack of lasting success with wireless was disappointing but not central in Lodge's life. He had been approached at the turn of the century to help found a new university in Birmingham, and after having turned down the offer twice, he finally accepted it. As he later wrote, "I was too busy with teaching work to take up telegraphic or any other development nor had I the insight to perceive what has turned out to be its extraordinary importance to the navy, the merchant service, and indeed, land and war services too." Further, he felt strongly it was not the role of a scientist to pursue commercial ends. That innovative role he left to others, chiefly Marconi, as it turned out.

Later Years

Lodge was deeply involved in helping to develop the new university after 1900. He remained active on many research and writing fronts in addition to his wireless work, demonstrating a growing interest in and concern over such social issues as poverty. After 1910 he focused increasingly on his psychic research and writing, especially after the 1916 death of his youngest son Raymond in World War I. His efforts to communicate with his dead son were widely reported and were the focus of one of his better-known books. His interests extended to the relationship of science and religion, extensive work with mediums, and spiritualism. In these areas, however, he was more a philosopher than a practical investigator.

Lodge "retired" in 1920, although over the next few years he turned out a dozen books, including a 1931 autobiography, and considerable magazine journalism, some dealing with the expanding radio business. He also presented many broadcasts over the BBC about radio, among other subjects. A related area of concentrated interest and research was his theorizing about the behavior of the "aether" or atmosphere.

CHRISTOPHER H. STERLING

See also Early Wireless; German Wireless Pioneers; Hertz, Heinrich; Marconi, Guglielmo; Maxwell, James Clerk; Popov, Alexander

Oliver Joseph Lodge. Born in Penkhull, England, 12 June 1851, first of eight children of Oliver Lodge (a successful businessman) and Grace Heath. Boarding school, 1859. BS 1875, DcS. 1877, University of London. Lyon James Professor of Experimental Physics and Mathematics, University College, Liverpool, 1881–1900. Principal of Birmingham University, 1900–1919. Elected Fellow of the Royal Society, 1887; Rumford Medal of the Royal Society, 1898; knighted, 1902; Albert Medal of the Royal Society of Arts, 1919; Faraday Medal of the Institution of Electrical Engineers, 1932. Died in Amesbury, England, 22 August 1940.

Selected Publications

Signalling across Space without Wires: Being a Description of the Work of Hertz and His Successors, 1894; 3rd edition, 1900; reprint, 1974
The Ether of Space, 1909
Talks about Radio, with Some Pioneering History and Some Hints and Calculations for Radio Amateurs, 1925
Past Years: An Autobiography, 1931

Further Reading

Aitken, Hugh G.J., "Lodge," in *Syntony and Spark: The Origins of Radio,* by Aitken, New York and London: Wiley, 1976
Besterman, Theodore, compiler, *A Bibliography of Sir Oliver Lodge, F.R.S.,* London: Oxford University Press, and Milford, 1935
Hunt, Bruce J., *The Maxwellians,* Ithaca, New York: Cornell University Press, 1991

Jolly, W.P., *Sir Oliver Lodge*, London: Constable, and Rutherford, New Jersey: Fairleigh Dickinson University Press, 1974

Kraeuter, David W., "Oliver Lodge," in *British Radio and Television Pioneers: A Patent Bibliography,* by Kraeuter, Metuchen, New Jersey: Scarecrow Press, 1993

O'Hara, J.C., and W. Pricha, "Hertz and Oliver J. Lodge," in *Hertz and the Maxwellians: A Study and Documentation of the Discovery of Electromagnetic Wave Radiation, 1873–1894,* by O'Hara and Pricha, London: Peregrinus, 1987

Rowlands, Peter, and J.P. Wilson, editors, *Oliver Lodge and the Invention of Radio,* Liverpool: PD, 1994

London Broadcasting Company

First British Commercial Radio Station

In early 1973 LBC—the London Broadcasting Company, largely owned by Canadian-backed Selkirk Communications—was awarded the United Kingdom's first independent local radio franchise, with a contract from the Independent Broadcasting Authority to provide a news, talk, and information service for the greater London area. It was also to be the home of Independent Radio News—a wholly owned LBC subsidiary—the monopoly provider of international and national news for an expected chain of some 60 local radio stations. This service was financed by a subscription levied on the size of the audience to each station.

LBC—the first authorized commercial radio station in the United Kingdom after more than 50 years of British Broadcasting Corporation (BBC) monopoly—went on the air at 6 A.M. on 8 October 1973 from studios in London's Gough Square, just off the famous Fleet Street, then home to most of the United Kingdom's national newspapers. The station was awarded the "speech" franchise in contrast to the "general and entertainment" franchise that was awarded to Capital Radio. Like Capital and the other franchises offered in the 1970s, the station was allocated both AM and FM frequencies. By U.S. standards, the programming was a hybrid format—a mixture of rolling news, current affairs features, celebrity interviews, sports, personality-led talk, and magazine programs, including a weekly round-up of London's arts scene.

Unfortunately, it was launched at about the worst possible time for a new media enterprise relying on advertising income. The Middle East war, which led to a quadrupling of oil prices, had just begun, and Prime Minister Edward Heath launched his controversial Phase Three prices and incomes policy. Shortly afterward, a miners' strike led to widespread power blackouts and to the country's being put on a three-day working week. In addition, the station was credited with disappointing audience figures, and within a month of its launch Labour Member of Parliament Gerald Kaufman called for the station "to be put out of its misery." In the first three months of 1975, union disputes over staff cutbacks temporarily put the station off the air five times.

The station was relaunched in 1978. It gradually settled down and built a loyal audience base, with much-praised coverage of major news stories, including Irish Republican Army terrorism, the siege at London's Iranian embassy, and political developments such as the sudden resignation of Prime Minister Harold Wilson in March 1976 and the turbulent life of the Greater London Council. However, it was probably the station's coverage of the 1982 Falklands War that, above all, ensured that the station was reawarded the London "speech" franchise in September that year.

In 1988 Crown Communications bought out Selkirk, and the new management made the fateful decision to end simulcasting on its AM and FM frequencies and to drop the now well-established name of LBC. In October 1989 the FM service was named Crown FM; it was to be in direct competition with the BBC's network speech service, Radio 4. The AM service was renamed London Talkback Radio and was aimed at a more downmarket audience with a populist talk-back format. The first audience figures for the new services, published four months later, showed a drastic drop in overall listening. In June that year, a number of Australians from Crown Communications were drafted in; the AM and FM services were simulcast over the weekend, and the FM service's name was changed to LBC News Talk 97.3 FM. The financial hemorrhage continued unabated, however, with losses for 1992 posted at £2.5 million, and in January the following year Crown went into receivership. Chelverton Investments took over, chaired by Dame Shirley Porter—a controversial figure in Conservative local politics and heiress to the Tesco supermarket company.

Just two months later the new regulator, the Radio Authority, announced that LBC had lost its license to London News Radio (LNR), although LNR would not take over until the following year. LNR planned a rolling news service on FM and a phone-in format on AM. Meanwhile, LBC said it would bid for the new national commercial speech service. In March 1994 it failed to win this license, Dame Shirley resigned, and two weeks later LBC went into receivership, although the station stayed on the air. In April 1994 LBC and LNR struck a deal so that the services could continue until the formal handover, and in May Reuters made a bid for LNR's two licenses, before the new services had even gone on the air. The Radio Authority agreed to this change of ownership, provided that the new owners kept to the program promises made by LNR when it was awarded the licenses. In August 1994 the new managing director announced that the channels were to be rebranded yet again, to London News 97.3 FM and London News Talk 1152 AM. Further changes in share ownership and a failed management buyout eventually led, by April 1996, to the Great Western Radio (GWR) group and Independent Television News' gaining control, with the *Daily Mail* and General Trust and Reuters owning 20 percent each. In July that year the much-loved name LBC reemerged as the AM service, and in October 1998 the station celebrated 25 years on the air.

In the Fall of 2002 both stations were bought from GWR by the Chrysalis group, and the new owner soon announced that, after agreeing a "frequency swap" with the Radio Authority, it would reformat both services. It believed that the stations were on the "wrong" frequencies—a rolling news service more "naturally" belonging to AM and the more general talk and lifestyle service on FM, which it intended to pitch against national commercial station TalkSport and the BBC network Radio 5 Live. Consequently, in January 2003, the two stations were relaunched as LBC 97.3 FM and LBC News 1152 AM. The management hoped to return the overall LBC brand to its 1980s heyday when 2.4 million listeners tuned in each week. In 1989 revenues had stood at £11 million; by the end of 2002 they were just £4million. However, although there had undoubtedly been some major mistakes in both financing and programming in those 13 years, with a consequent disillusionment on the part of staff, investors, and audience, the period had also seen greatly increased competition in the London radio market, both in the overall number of services and specifically those offering talk and news. In addition, the arrival of rolling TV news channels, as well as the general expansion of media and the consequent fragmentation of audiences, must make the return to former audience and revenue levels questionable.

Throughout this turbulent history, the station has been host to some of the best-known names in British broadcasting, including Frank Bough, Douglas Cameron, Anne Diamond, Brian Hayes, Bob Holness, Pete Murray, Michael Parkinson, and Janet Street-Porter. In addition to its basic fare of news and news-talk programming, the station has been one of the last bastions in U.K. commercial radio for drama productions, which have won international awards. However, its major influence has been in the editorial and production practices of radio news—adapted from U.S., Canadian, and Australian commercial services—providing a new model of informality for the commercial sector that the BBC was to learn from and incorporate in its own networks, particularly Radio 5 Live and its news bulletins on the youth network, Radio 1. Specifically, the use of shorter, "crisper" reports, greater use of "actuality" (clips of interviewees, including eyewitnesses) contrasted with the BBC's then more ponderous, formal approach. Indeed, the whole notion of and demand for "rolling news" in the United Kingdom was pioneered by LBC, which was able to broadcast events as they happened and to stay with the story with live reports, interviews, and audience reaction, rather than having to return to regular programs. Many of what are now commonplace conventions on both radio and television in the United Kingdom were pioneered and developed by LBC.

RICHARD RUDIN

See also British Commercial Radio; Radio Authority

Further Reading

Crisell, Andrew, *An Introductory History of British Broadcasting*, London and New York: Routledge, 1997
Crook, Tim, *International Radio Journalism: History, Theory, and Practice*, London and New York: Routledge, 1998
Franklin, Bob, *Newszak and News Media*, London and New York: Arnold, 1997
LBC website, <www.lbc.co.uk>
Shingler, Martin, and Cindy Wieringa, *On Air: Methods and Meanings of Radio*, London and New York: Arnold, 1998

The Lone Ranger

Western Adventure Program

The Lone Ranger originated at WXYZ in Detroit, Michigan, in 1933. The program gained in popularity with both child and adult listeners and reached a national audience when it played an instrumental role in the creation of the Mutual Broadcasting System in 1934. In the early 1940s, The Lone Ranger moved to the National Broadcasting Company (NBC) Blue Network, which became the American Broadcasting Companies (ABC) in 1945. The Ranger evolved into a variety of media forms, becoming the subject of comic strips, comic books, books for children, novels for adults, films, and television.

In 1932 George W. Trendle, one of the owners of WXYZ, decided that the station could increase its profitability by breaking ties with the Columbia Broadcasting System (CBS) network and locally producing its own programs, including dramatic shows. Trendle called station manager Harold True, dramatic director James Jewell, and other station personnel together to outline the concept for programs to be developed. One concept that emerged from this conference was a show to be aimed at children. Trendle specified several characteristics he felt were essential. The program should be a western and should feature a leading character who would exemplify model behavior for young listeners. This hero should be mature and possess some of the qualities of Zorro and Robin Hood. In subsequent meetings, details were further developed. The hero was to be a lone operator, perhaps a former Texas Ranger. Finally a name emerged—the Lone Ranger.

With this basic format in mind, Trendle turned to Fran Striker, a script writer in Buffalo, New York, to bring a fully developed Ranger to the radio audience. Striker's scripts for the Warner Lester, Manhunter series had gained national attention. Striker had also created his own radio western for WEBR in Buffalo, and elements of this series, Covered Wagon Days, may have influenced the content and tone of The Lone Ranger. For many years, however, George Trendle countered implications that anyone besides himself could be considered the creator of The Lone Ranger, and he insisted that Striker, as well as other WXYZ personnel, sign over legal ownership of the program.

Trial airings of The Lone Ranger on WXYZ received limited publicity, and sources disagree as to the exact date of the first actual broadcast of a complete and polished program, with some specifying 30 or 31 January and others 2 February 1933. As the program evolved, the Ranger was given a white horse named Silver and a "faithful Indian companion," Tonto, who addressed the Ranger as "kemo sabe." This gave the Ranger someone to talk to, lessening the need for an announcer's narration of action for the radio audience. Rossini's "William Tell" Overture became the theme music for the show, another example of using classical music in the public domain in order to avoid royalty payments. The music was accompanied by the announcer's enthusiastic and authoritative description of "the daring and resourceful masked rider of the plains who led the fight for law and order in the early western United States." Listeners were invited to "return with us now to those thrilling days of yesteryear. . . . From out of the past came the thundering hoofbeats of the great horse Silver! The Lone Ranger rides again!"

The fame of the Ranger spread beyond Detroit as WXYZ fed the show to the Michigan Radio network. The program was the most important attraction to WLW Cincinnati, WGN Chicago, and WOR New York when they joined WXYZ in creating the Mutual Broadcasting System in 1934. When more distant stations signed up with Mutual, the Ranger's popularity reached a national level.

The show had already gained a huge following before the Ranger's background and the reason why he wore the mask were fully developed. These questions were answered in a 1938 Republic film serial portraying an ambush on a group of five Texas Rangers. They were all believed dead, but one survived. When this lone surviving Ranger recovered, he wore a mask to protect his identity and anonymity. This version of the Ranger's origin was also reflected in the radio program by 1941. The Lone Ranger's secret silver mine provided the means for supporting himself and was the source of his silver bullets.

A basic skeleton plot that was reflected in many scripts featured the development of a complication or problem and a failed attempt at its solution by a character in the story before the Ranger came onto the scene. When the Ranger did appear and successfully resolved the difficulty by the end of the program, someone would ask, "Who was that masked man?" Another would explain, "That was the Lone Ranger!" He was also a master of other disguises, further confounding villainous attempts at revealing his true identity.

Fran Striker, the show's chief writer, involved the Lone Ranger in getting telegraph lines strung across the West, in helping build the Union Pacific Railroad, and in carrying out special assignments for President Lincoln. The Ranger also assisted Buffalo Bill and Wild Bill Hickok. Furthermore, he provided advice to Billy the Kid, General Custer, and Sitting Bull.

One memorable plot concerned the Lone Ranger's discovery of his nephew, Dan Reid, who had been saved from an Indian attack on a wagon train. Reid had been brought up by a pioneer woman who, with her dying breaths, described his family, revealing that the boy's father was the Lone Ranger's brother. Dan Reid's son, Britt, became the Green Hornet, another masked man in a later radio show that was also scripted by Fran Striker.

For much of its radio existence, *The Lone Ranger* was broadcast live on the NBC Blue network (later ABC) on Mondays, Wednesdays, and Fridays. Because of time zone differences, this schedule required three separate live feeds, the first beginning at 7:30 Eastern time. The second feed was produced for the Mountain zone, and the third for the West Coast.

B.R. SMITH

See also Children's Programs; Striker, Fran; Westerns; WXYZ

Cast
Lone Ranger	George Stenius (George Seaton) (1933), Jack Deeds, James Jewell, Earle Graser (1933–41), Brace Beemer (1941–54)
Tonto	John Todd
Thunder Martin	Paul Hughes
Dan Reid	Ernie Winstanley, Dick Beals, James Lipton
Butch Cavendish	Jay Michael
Various characters	Paul Hughes, John Hodiak, Rollon Parker, Bob Maxwell, Frank Russell, Ted Johnstone, Jack Petruzzi, Herschel Mayall, Elaine Alpert, Mel Palmer, Fred Rito, Bertha Forman, Ruth Dean Rickaby, Malcolm McCoy, Jack McCarthy, Bill Saunders, Beatrice Leiblee, Harry Goldstein, Lee Allman
Announcer	Harold True, Brace Beemer, Harry Golder, Charles Wood, Bob Hite, Fred Foy

Creator
George W. Trendle

Directors
James Jewell, Charles D. Livingstone

Programming History
Michigan Radio Network	January 1933–34
Mutual	February 1934–May 1942
NBC-Blue	May 1942–44
ABC	1944–54

Further Reading
Bickel, Mary E., *Geo. W. Trendle, Creator and Producer of: The Lone Ranger, The Green Hornet, Sgt. Preston of the Yukon, The American Agent, and Other Successes*, New York: Exposition Press, 1971

Boemer, Marilyn Lawrence, *The Children's Hour: Radio Programs for Children, 1929–1956*, Metuchen, New Jersey: Scarecrow Press, 1989

Bryan, J., "Hi-Yo, Silver!" *The Saturday Evening Post* (14 October 1939)

Harmon, Jim, *Radio Mystery and Adventure: And Its Appearances in Film, Television, and Other Media*, Jefferson, North Carolina: McFarland, 1992

Jones, Reginald M., Jr., *The Mystery of the Masked Man's Music: A Search for the Music on The Lone Ranger Radio Program, 1933–1954*, Metuchen, New Jersey: Scarecrow Press, 1987

Osgood, Dick, *Wyxie Wonderland: An Unauthorized 50-Year Diary of WXYZ Detroit*, Bowling Green, Ohio: Bowling Green University Popular Press, 1981

Rothel, David, *Who Was That Masked Man? The Story of the Lone Ranger*, South Brunswick, New Jersey: Barnes, 1976

Long, Huey 1893–1935

U.S. Senator and Radio Speaker

Huey Pierce Long, one-time Louisiana governor and U.S. senator, was one of America's most colorful and controversial political figures. He was one of the first American politicians to master the young medium of radio and to artfully manipulate and exploit radio's potential as a political tool.

Huey Long ran unsuccessfully for Louisiana governor in 1924 but parlayed his support among rural voters into winning election to that office in 1928. As governor, Long worked rapidly to take control of political patronage and to develop populist programs to shore up his political base. Powerful

Senator Huey Long of Louisiana at the Democratic National Convention in Chicago, 28 June 1932
Courtesy AP/Wide World Photos

opponents in the state legislature impeached but failed to convict Governor Long in 1929.

Huey Long launched his second gubernatorial campaign in a 3 August 1927 speech carried over radio station KWKH in Shreveport. The station, owned by Long's friend William K. Henderson, played a major role in many of Huey Long's future radio addresses, all of which—like his 3 August speech—were carried free of charge and for unlimited time.

Huey Long's radio skills were honed to perfection during his years as governor. His unique oratorical style fit perfectly with the expectations of his listeners. Long often spoke effortlessly and without notes for two or three hours at a time. His rapid-fire monologues freely moved from quoting Bible verses, to joking, to harsh name calling of political foes. He even resorted to deliberately mispronouncing words and ignoring accepted rules of grammar in order to identify himself more closely with his audience.

Many of Huey Long's radio addresses were broadcast over KWKH by remote control from the Governor's Mansion in Baton Rouge or from a hotel room. He often began his remarks by telling listeners that Huey Long (or the "Kingfish"—a sobriquet that he began using in the late 1920s that came from a character's name on the popular *Amos 'n' Andy* radio show) was going to be talking and that they should phone a friend who also might tune in. He then would spend several minutes in small talk while calls were made and listeners gathered.

Huey Long was elected to the U.S. Senate in 1930 while serving as Louisiana governor. He retained the governorship for another year and was finally sworn in to the U.S. Senate in January 1932. Soon after his arrival in Washington, Long made waves by proposing what he called his "Share-Our-Wealth" plan as a means of redistributing wealth in America. He told a Depression-weary America of his plan during a 30-minute February 1934 nationwide radio broadcast on the National Broadcasting Company (NBC) network. Time for the broadcast was donated, following the practice of both NBC and the Columbia Broadcasting System (CBS) to supply such time to members of the U.S. Congress. The enormous number of letters that flowed into Senator Long's office following his radio address required some 48 secretaries and typists to answer, and by 1935 Long had a bigger office and more employees than any other U.S. Senator. Although economists berated his "Share-Our-Wealth" plan as unworkable, the noto-

riety that Long was gaining nevertheless persuaded the radio networks to allow the senator more airtime.

Network radio proved to be more than just an excellent forum to push his economic plan, though, when in August 1935 Senator Long announced his break with President Roosevelt over policy issues and his plans to run for the presidency himself. His chances of defeating Roosevelt seemed good, according to knowledgeable observers who placed Huey Long's political strength as second only to the president's. Long departed from his short-lived campaign in September 1935 to be present during a special session of the Louisiana legislature. While hurrying through a hallway of the state capitol on 8 September, he was gunned down by an assassin, a Baton Rouge physician named Carl Weiss. Other than a presumed dislike for Long's dictatorial politics, no definite reason for the assassination has ever been determined. Huey Long remained conscious for two days after the shooting but died on 10 September at age 42.

RONALD GARAY

See also Controversial Issues; KWKH; U.S. Congress and Radio

Huey Long. Born in Winnfield, Louisiana, 30 August 1893. One of ten children of Huey Pierce and Caledonia (Tison) Long. Studied law at Oklahoma School of Law (1912–13) and Tulane University (1914–15); admitted to bar and began practicing law, Winnfield and Shreveport, Louisiana, 1915; member of Louisiana State Railroad Commission, 1918–28; governor of Louisiana, 1928–32; U.S. Senator, 1932–35; announced candidacy for U.S. President, 1935. Died (assassination) in Baton Rouge, Louisiana, 10 September 1935

Further Reading
Bormann, Ernest, "A Rhetorical Analysis of the National Radio Broadcasts of Senator Huey Pierce Long," *Speech Monographs* 24 (November 1957)
Bormann, Ernest, "This Is Huey P. Long Talking," *Journal of Broadcasting* 2 (Spring 1958)
Brinkley, Alan, *Voices of Protest: Huey Long, Father Coughlin, and the Great Depression,* New York: Knopf, 1982
Hair, William Ivy, *The Kingfish and His Realm: The Life and Times of Huey P. Long,* Baton Rouge: Louisiana State University Press, 1991
Williams, T. Harry, *Huey Long,* New York: Knopf, 1969

Lord Haw-Haw (William Joyce) 1906–1946

World War II Propaganda Broadcaster

During World War II, William Joyce, known to his British listeners as "Lord Haw-Haw," was one of the most famous expatriate radio propagandists for the Axis powers (others included "Axis Sally," Ezra Pound, and "Tokyo Rose"). After the war, Joyce was found guilty of treason and executed by the British.

Origins

William Joyce was born in 1906 in New York City to Irish parents who were naturalized American citizens; he was thus a citizen himself, an issue of import at the end of his life. When he was three, his family returned to Ireland, eventually settling in Salthill, Galway.

Joyce was educated at the College of St. Ignatius Loyola in Galway, but his education was interrupted by the bitter struggle for Irish independence. By his own later admission, Joyce worked as a spy for the British "Black and Tans" in 1920–22. This was a despised military force sent to Ireland in the summer of 1920 to reinforce the Royal Irish Constabulary. Joyce's support of and cooperation with such an intensely despised organization was enough to force the Anglophile family to move to England after the Irish achieved independence in 1922. There Joyce first attended Battersea Polytechnic and later Birkbeck College of University of London, from which he received a first class honors degree in English in 1927.

While in college, Joyce became politically active in conservative and then far-right circles. He eventually dropped out of graduate study and in 1933 joined Sir Oswald Mosley's British Union of Fascists, rising to be director of propaganda and later deputy leader. He later fell out with Mosley and was dropped from the party. In 1933 he made what became a fatal mistake: declaring he was a British citizen (and one born in Galway when Ireland was part of Britain) to obtain a British passport to ease his ability to travel as political tensions rose. He renewed the passport (and in essence, the citizenship vow) in August 1939. The fraudulently acquired passport was later a central element in the post-war charge of treason.

Broadcasting for Germany

In August 1939, Joyce and his second wife, fearing arrest as avowed fascists while war loomed, fled England and went to Germany. He soon found a position with German radio, broadcasting anti-British propaganda beginning on 18 September 1939. In 1940 he became a naturalized German citizen. Both he and his wife worked for the Nazi regime for the rest of the war.

His voice was beamed to Britain on a program called *Views on the News*. Broadcasts featured war-related news and ad hominem attacks on Allied leaders, Jews, and communists. His signature opening, "Germany calling, Germany calling," became well known to the British public. The "Lord Haw-Haw" appellation came first from a *Daily Express* correspondent who referred to his "speaking English of the haw-haw, dammit-get-out-of-my-way variety." British listeners were at first amused at his somewhat affected high-class and sneering tone as he attacked Jews and other enemies of Germany.

Through 1942, as the Third Reich enjoyed a number of military successes, Joyce related events to his overseas listeners with considerable candor. As war-related news was then being censored by the British government and the BBC, many Britons turned to Joyce to ascertain the facts. As the war turned against Germany, however, Joyce's broadcasts—nearly always made from studios in Berlin—grew more pointed and shrill, and the declining number of British listeners no longer trusted what they heard.

Joyce's final and arguably most dramatic broadcast was recorded at a transmitter near the Danish border in April 1945 after Hitler's suicide. Though never broadcast, in it Joyce railed yet again against the dangers of Bolshevism and reflected upon Germany's role in the war. He was quite clearly agitated and may have been intoxicated. A few weeks after the war ended in May, he was captured by British troops as he tried to flee Germany.

Trial and Execution

Joyce was returned to England and tried for treason in a three-day London jury trial in September 1945. He was quickly found guilty and sentenced to death. The trial and appeals of the judgment were widely followed, and transcripts were published in two contemporaneous books. The tricky citizenship issue was over-ridden by arguments that in fraudulently seeking a British passport before the war, he had placed himself under the protection of—and thus in a position of loyalty to—the British crown. After all appeals were exhausted, in January 1946 Joyce was hanged at London's Wandsworth prison.

Joyce's propaganda role is significant. For one thing, his broadcasts served as something of a radio role model for Ezra Pound, who later performed analogous services for Italy. Second, Joyce's broadcasts (and those of both "Axis Sally" and "Tokyo Rose," who were Americans and were also tried for treason) raise the question of whether broadcast polemics and editorializing necessarily constitute treason. Joyce's execution poses a third question: is it possible for the victors in any given struggle to try the vanquished in such a way as to ensure fair treatment for the defeated?

WILLIAM F. O'CONNOR AND CHRISTOPHER H. STERLING

See also Axis Sally; Fritzsche, Hans; Propaganda; Tokyo Rose; World War II and U.S. Radio

William Brooke Joyce. Born in Brooklyn, New York, 24 April 1906, son of Michael Joyce, an Irish-born naturalized American citizen, and Gertrude Emily Brooke. Moved to Galway, Ireland, 1909. Attended College of St. Ignatius Loyola, Galway, Ireland; family moved to England, 1922; attended Battersea Polytechnic, London, England, 1922–23; Birkbeck College of University of London, B.A. 1927; Deputy Leader, British Union of Fascists, 1933–37; broadcast Nazi propaganda, Berlin, 1939–45. Executed at Wandsworth prison, London, England, 3 January 1946.

Selected Publications
Twilight over England, 1940

Further Reading
Cole, John Alfred, *Lord Haw-Haw and William Joyce: The Full Story,* London: Faber, 1964; New York: Farrarr Straus and Giroux, 1965
Doherty, M.A., *Nazi Wireless Propaganda: Lord Law-Haw and British Public Opinion in the Second World War,* Edinburgh: Edinburgh University Press, 2000
Hall, J.W., editor, *Trial of William Joyce,* London: William Hodge, 1946
Roberts, Carl E. Bechhofer, editor, *The Trial of William Joyce,* London: Jarrolds, 1946
Selwyn, Francis, *Hitler's Englishman: The Crime of Lord Haw-Haw,* London: Routledge and Kegan Paul, 1987
West, Rebecca, "The Revolutionary," in *The New Meaning of Treason,* by West, New York: Viking Press, 1964

Lord, Phillips H. 1902–1975

U.S. Radio Actor, Writer, Producer

SOUND EFFECTS: [Marching feet, machine-gun fire, siren wail.]
VOICE: Calling the police! Calling the G-Men! Calling all Americans to war on the underworld!
ANNOUNCER: *Gangbusters!* With the cooperation of leading law-enforcement officials of the United States, *Gangbusters* presents facts in the relentless war of the police on the underworld.

Loud and urgent openings such as this signaled another episode of the radio program *Gangbusters,* which aired for more than 20 years. This fast-paced drama was renowned for snappy dialogue and realistic sound effects, particularly at the show's beginning. (These features gave rise to the expression "coming on like gangbusters" to describe anything with a rapid start.) The creator of *Gangbusters* was Phillips H. Lord, a radio actor, writer, producer, and developer who was one of the industry's most successful artists during the "Golden Age" of radio in the 1930s and 1940s.

As Lord explained when the show (called *G-Men* for its first year) debuted on 16 September 1935, the series was based on actual FBI cases provided by Director J. Edgar Hoover. Lord and his assistant Helen Sioussat had an office in the

Department of Justice next to Hoover, who allowed them unprecedented access to FBI case files. "I went to Washington, was graciously received by Mr. Hoover, and all of these scripts are written in the department building," Lord told listeners during the inaugural program, which was about the killing of John Dillinger. "Tonight's program was submitted to Mr. Hoover, who checked every statement, and made some very valuable suggestions."

However, Hoover almost backed out of the project after the first broadcast, in the wake of scattered criticism about this new style of radio entertainment. Lord hastily wrote Hoover to mollify him, vowing "There is NOTHING that I won't do to win your respect and confidence." What Hoover required Lord to do was to use only the material provided by the FBI and nothing more. Moreover, all scripts had to be approved by Hoover or one of his aides, and all had to show that every criminal was punished, either with death or a long jail sentence.

Lord endured these stringent guidelines because he recognized the importance of the new show—as a new genre of radio entertainment and a legacy for his career. "This series, Mr. Hoover, means more to me than anything else in the world," Lord explained in private correspondence. "My whole future will be based on the success of this program, and there isn't a stone I'll leave unturned toward making it the finest thing in radio."

Before he created this crime drama, Lord's future had seemed secure in a different broadcast format. He was one of the brightest stars on radio with a loyal nationwide audience for *Sunday Evening at Seth Parker's*. Lord played the elderly preacher from Jonesport, Maine, who discussed local happenings with his family and neighbors in the parlor. The *Seth Parker* broadcasts conjured up images of white, steepled churches, modest cape-style homes, and vessels plying the harbor, as the friendly folks prayed, sang, and discussed morality. The dialogue and plots hearkened to a simple, old-fashioned way of life during the uncertainty of the Depression. Lord created and wrote the series, and even wrote some of the hymns. It spawned a 1931 movie, *Way Back Home*, which starred a 29-year-old Lord in heavy makeup.

Lord based *Sunday Evening at Seth Parker's* on his own experiences. The son of a Connecticut Congregational minister, Lord developed his narrative skills from his grandfather, Hosea Phillips, a traveling salesman "whom none could beat in story telling, witticisms, and good common sense," Lord later wrote. After education at Bowdoin College and stints as a high school principal and candy maker, Lord got his break when the National Broadcasting Company (NBC) approved his proposal for a radio show about small-town life. "An old-fashioned cottage gathering of friends and neighbors coming together to sing hymns and discuss news of the town," Lord described it. The show became a huge success, as ten million listeners tuned in weekly to the cottage by the sea.

After five years Lord decided to have the Parkers and their Jonesport neighbors take an around-the-world cruise while Lord and his cast did so in real life. They departed on 8 December 1934, in the four-masted schooner *Seth Parker*, with sophisticated shortwave broadcasting equipment aboard that enabled them to continue their weekly broadcasts. This remarkable and highly publicized voyage was cut short two months later when a hurricane disabled the boat in the South Seas, 300 miles from Tahiti. The schooner's passengers were rescued by the Australian heavy cruiser *HMS Australia*, which carried one of King George's sons. Convinced that the ship's SOS calls were a publicity stunt, Australian officials demanded that Lord be brought up on charges. He was exonerated after the cruiser's captain asserted that Lord's maritime distress was real.

Embarrassed by this international incident, Lord abandoned the *Seth Parker* show and changed career paths. He developed the fast and violent action show *G-Men* in 1935 as a sharp contrast to the leisurely and gentle *Seth Parker*. After renaming the show *Gangbusters*, Lord and his production company, Phillips H. Lord Inc., developed other programs. The factual human-interest show *We the People* debuted in 1936 and aired for three seasons. It was soon followed by the

serial drama *By Kathleen Norris*, the aviation adventure *Sky Blazers*, and the crime dramas *Treasury Agent* and *Counterspy*. Lord even revived *Seth Parker*. Before he turned 40, Lord had become one of the most successful writers, actors, and producers in radio.

Amid the flurry of development, Lord produced a new courtroom drama set in New York, entitled *Mr. District Attorney*. Horror-fiction writer Alonzo Deen Cole sued Lord for appropriation of literary property, claiming that he had submitted the idea to Lord but was never compensated or acknowledged. Lord won in trial court, but the verdict was overturned on appeal. The New York Court of Appeals ruled that Lord had indeed stolen the idea from Cole.

Lord tried to make the transition to television as a producer, but after two failed series he retired to coastal Maine, where he found contentment promoting community dances and sing-alongs. ("I'm exceedingly ambitious," he once told a reporter, but then added, "I'd swap all I have for contentment.") After suffering from myasthenia gravis, he died on 19 October 1975 in Ellsworth, Maine, just a short drive from Jonesport.

RALPH FRASCA

See also Gangbusters

Phillips H. Lord. Born in Hartford, Connecticut, 13 July 1902. Played title role on *Sunday Evening at Seth Parker's*, 1929–36, 1938–39; embarked on around-the-world cruise, broadcasting from the ship *Seth Parker*, 1934; shipwrecked near Tahiti, 1935; creator, producer, narrator for *Gangbusters*, 1935–57. Died in Ellsworth, Maine, 19 October 1975.

Radio Series

1929–36, 1938–39	*Sunday Evening at Seth Parker's*
1932–33	*The Country Doctor*
1934–45, 1951–52	*The Story of Mary Marlin*
1935–57	*Gangbusters* (*G-Men* during first year)
1936–39	*We, the People*
1941	*Great Gunns*

Films
Way Back Home, 1931

Selected Publications
Seth Parker and His Jonesport Folks: Way Back Home, 1932

Further Reading
Cole v Phillips H. Lord Inc., 28 New York State Supp. 2nd series 404 (1st Dept.) (1941)
DeLong, Thomas A., *Radio Stars: An Illustrated Biographical Dictionary of 953 Performers, 1920 through 1960*, Jefferson, North Carolina: McFarland, 1996

Helen J. Sioussat Papers, Library of American Broadcasting, University of Maryland, <www.lib.umd.edu/LAB/ COLLECTIONS/sioussat.html>

Menken, Harriet, "Radio Personalities," *New York American* (9 February 1936)

"Radio Writer and Producer Phillips H. Lord Dies," *Ellsworth American* (23 October 1975)

Low-Power Radio/Microradio

Small Community Radio Stations

Microradio is a political movement with the goal of putting low-power FM transmitters into the hands of community activists, minority groups, and those with no hope of getting a traditional Federal Communications Commission (FCC) license to broadcast. Under the leadership of Free Radio Berkeley (FRB) founder Stephen Dunifer, instructions are readily available to anyone who wants a low-cost transmitter kit, programming help, and legal representation. Microradio broadcasters are often students and street people without property, and when ordered by the FCC to cease operations, they simply move to another location. FCC enforcement is uneven and has been complicated by recent court rulings. In *United States v Dunifer* (July 2000), the court ruled against Dunifer's right to broadcast without a license. That decision led activists to pressure the FCC more strongly for a licensed low-power FM service.

Origins

The history of unlicensed radio goes back to the early radio-telephone experimenters who simply went on the air without asking anybody's permission. By the end of the 1920s, the radio spectrum had been divided between commercial, amateur, and experimental users. All were required to have licenses, first from the Federal Radio Commission and after 1934 from the FCC. But there have always been scofflaws, mostly referred to as "pirate broadcasters." From ships anchored offshore with powerful transmitters to radio hobbyists broadcasting entertainment on amateur radio frequencies, there is a long history of unlicensed broadcasting. The most blatant of those illegal operators were usually caught and fined, and their equipment was confiscated. Unlike the modern microradio movement, most such "pirates" were not political activists.

For a time, however, small radio stations were not only allowed, they were actively encouraged. With the inception of FM radio, the FCC encouraged noncommercial operations.

When frequencies went begging, the FCC in 1948 initiated a low-power category of stations, the so-called Class D outlets, that might use as little as ten watts of power and cover a very small area with a usable signal. But they were broadcast outlets, often held by nonprofit groups unable to afford anything larger. By the 1970s there were several hundred such stations on the air.

Low-power stations were increasingly resented by the FM radio business, which was rapidly expanding in the 1970s and 1980s. Tiny stations took up valuable frequencies that full-power outlets coveted. In 1978 the FCC began to reverse course, requiring these stations to use at least 100 (and more likely 1,000) watts or give way to full-power stations that would provide more services to more listeners. By the mid-1990s, only a handful of the old Class D stations remained, and most of those were preparing to use the required higher amounts of power.

A model for what could develop with radio was borrowed from television. As a result of experiments originating in Canada in the 1970s, the FCC became interested in and eventually approved a class of low-power television stations in the early 1980s. These were to use very low power on VHF channels or up to about 1,000 watts on UHF channels that would be "dropped in" among already allotted full-power channels in such a way as to keep interference at a minimum. After years of legal wrangling over how best to handle the mountain of conflicting applications, the FCC was granted the right to hold lotteries among mutually exclusive applications. By 2000 there were hundreds of low-power television outlets on the air, some providing original programs but many connected by satellite and offering typical entertainment programs otherwise not receivable in isolated rural areas.

Ted Coopman (1999) tells of the beginning of the modern microradio movement:

The modern micro broadcasting movement began on November 25, 1986 in a public housing development in

Springfield, IL. Put on the air for about $600, the one-watt station broadcast openly on 107.1 FM as Black Liberation Radio (now Human Rights Radio). The operator, Mbanna Kantako, a legally blind African-American in his mid-thirties, started the station because he felt that the African-American community in Springfield was not being served by the local media. Kantako felt that because the African-American community had a high illiteracy rate, radio would be the best way to reach this community.

According to FRB founder Dunifer, the goal of the microradio movement was to have so many transmitters in use across the country that the FCC would be overwhelmed, finding itself in a situation similar to one it faced in the early 1970s, when the FCC was unable to control the widely popular citizens band radio service. Licensing for that service was eventually dropped. Unlike the "pirates" of the past, who hid from the FCC, microradio proponents act in open defiance of the law, challenging the government to arrest them, to shut them down. They believe that they are entitled to the airwaves; that they are shut out of the current allocation of FM licenses; and that, because of scarcity and resulting high cost, licenses are available only to the wealthy.

Dunifer was successful in convincing the National Lawyers Guild that the right to broadcast was a civil rights issue, one of giving access to all people, especially those disenfranchised by licensed media. In 1993 Dunifer's ten-watt radio station started operation at 104.1 FM, offering music and political commentary while actively challenging the FCC. In June 1993, the FCC issued a *Notice of Apparent Liability* to Dunifer for unlicensed broadcasting and fined him $20,000. Dunifer was represented by the Lawyers Guild, and in 1995 a U.S. district court in Oakland, California, heard arguments on constitutional issues in Dunifer's case, arguments stating that the FCC had not proved that his broadcasts caused harm to licensed broadcasters. The FCC responded, saying that siding with Dunifer would cause thousands more to go on the air, and the resulting interference would be chaotic.

The attorney arguing the case for Dunifer raised other issues in the hearing that would eventually cause the FCC to study the possibility of a licensed low-power FM service. One such issue was that the 1978 elimination of the Class D ten-watt educational license in favor of licenses for stations over 100 watts was overly restrictive and violated Dunifer's First Amendment right to free speech. It was argued that the commission's failure to provide a low-power service did not provide for the public interest, convenience, and necessity required under the Communications Act of 1934. It was further argued that the financial qualifications required for an FM station license violated the equal protection clause of the Constitution. The FCC disagreed on all counts.

In November 1997 Federal District Judge Claudia Wilken ruled in favor of Dunifer, saying the FCC had failed to prove Dunifer had done harm to existing broadcasters. Buoyed by this victory, Dunifer continued to help others get on the air and to promote the creation of a low-power service. But in June 1998 the FCC prevailed in court, and Dunifer was taken off the air, based on the fact that he had applied for neither a license nor a waiver to broadcast and therefore lacked standing to challenge the FCC. In July 1999 Dunifer's attorneys appealed, arguing that the FCC had not acted in good faith when dealing with microradio, citing as evidence a San Francisco applicant's request for such a license, which had been ignored by the FCC.

Development of the microradio movement has been based on a common belief that stations very low in power escape the jurisdiction of the FCC. This misconception is based on Part 15, Subpart D of the FCC rules, which permits unlicensed operation of very low power transmitters. This rule only allows, however, for an effective service range of 35 to 100 feet in the FM band. On AM frequencies, unlicensed transmitters cannot cover a radius larger than about 200 to 250 feet. The FCC argues that if microradio stations are able to reach listeners, they are almost certainly operating illegally.

Low-Power FM

As the number of microradio stations grew and complaints from the National Association of Broadcasters (NAB) increased, the FCC closed a number of unlicensed microradio operations. Both the protests and the microbroadcasting movement continued to grow, however. Media reports suggested that between 500 and 1,000 microradio stations were on the air in 1998, although five years earlier only a handful existed.

In spite of NAB protests, FCC Chair William E. Kennard suggested that proposals to establish a legal microbroadcasting service were worthy of consideration. The FCC issued a *Notice of Proposed Rulemaking* on 28 January 1999 to authorize an LPFM broadcast service. The FCC's *Notice* cited concern about the increasing concentration of ownership of media properties, with concomitant loss of diversity, in addition to suggesting that smaller communities outside metropolitan areas were often deprived of local focus in programming.

In response to its *Notice*, the FCC received thousands of comments representing the views of community groups, labor unions, religious organizations, state and local government, and others. The commission announced that response to the petition had indicated a broad interest throughout the country in the LPFM proposal. Further, the commission's webpage on "Low Power Broadcast Radio Stations" was accessed more than 15,000 times in 1998 alone. The FCC received thousands of additional phone and mail inquiries each year regarding the legality of low-power broadcasting.

The commission's decision was released 20 January 2000 with the announcement that such a service would, in fact, be established. In spite of aggressive protest and threatened legal action by the NAB, the FCC voted to create an entirely new type of radio station, with the intention of enhancing service to underrepresented groups and local communities. The FCC's restrictions were as follows:

These (LPFM) stations are authorized for noncommercial educational broadcasting only (no commercial operation) and operate with an effective radiated power (ERP) of 100 watts (0.1 kilowatts) or less, with maximum facilities of 100 watts ERP at 30 meters (100 feet) antenna height above average terrain (HAAT). The approximate service range of a 100 watt LPFM station is 5.6 kilometers (3.5 miles radius). LPFM stations are not protected from interference that may be received from other classes of FM stations (www.fcc.org).

Several years after the initial announcement of the Low Power (LPFM) service, the FCC had received several thousand applications. Most of the applicants have been from religious organizations, the rest from community foundations and educational entities. A current list is on the FCC database (<www.fcc.gov/fcc-bin/fmq?state=&serv=FL&vac=&list=2>). Approximately 200 Construction Permits (CP) had been issued and 40 applicants had received actual licenses. Most of these were in the L1 category, 100 watts or less. Only a few have been under the L2 designation, 10 watts or less. As of the beginning of 2003, the FCC was not taking any additional applications.

While at least some of the original impetus for the LPFM service was to either legitimize or remove from the air the so-called pirates or micro broadcasters, based on the list of applicants, CPs and licenses issued, many observers suggest that the following will likely happen: former big city pirate/micro broadcasters will not receive licenses due to interference concerns in crowded FM markets; most licensees will be religious organizations, schools, and community foundations. And if the experience from the educational FM "boom" of the 1970s is repeated, most of these LPFM broadcasters will eventually lose interest and funding and abandon their licenses, many of which will be taken over by larger NPR broadcasters and well-funded networks and religious organizations.

MICHAEL H. ADAMS AND STEVEN PHIPPS

See also British Pirate Radio; College Radio; Community Radio; FM Radio; Licensing; Localism in Radio; Ten-Watt Stations

Further Reading

Coopman, Ted M., "FCC Enforcement Difficulties with Unlicensed Micro Radio," *Journal of Broadcasting and Electronic Media* 43, no. 4 (Fall 1999)

The Free Radio Network: Pirate Radio Top 20 Links of All Time <www.frn.net/links>

New York Free Media Alliance Microradio Documents <artcon.rutgers.edu/papertiger/nyfma/str/links.html>

Rogue Radio Research: Research and Resources on Micro Radio/Low Power FM <www.rougecom.com/rougeradio/>

Sakolsky, Ron, "Anarchy on the Airwaves: A Brief History of the Micro Radio Movement in the USA," *Social Anarchism* 17 (July 1992)

Sakolsky, Ron, and Stephen Dunifer, *Seizing the Airwaves: A Free Radio Handbook*, Edinburgh and San Francisco: AK Press, 1998

Soley, Lawrence, *Free Radio*, Denver, Colorado: Westview, 1999

Yoder, Andrew R., *Pirate Radio Stations: Tuning In to Underground Broadcasts*, New York: McGraw Hill Professional, 1990

Lum 'n' Abner

Comedy Show

A party line rings, two "backwoods" voices respond ("I-grannies, Abner, I believe that's our ring." "I-doggies, Lum, I believe you're right."), and the announcer gently brings us up to date with the latest events here in Pine Ridge, Arkansas, home of the "Jot 'Em Down Store" run by Columbus "Lum" Edwards and Abner Peabody. On *Lum 'n' Abner*, Chester Lauck (Lum) and Norris "Tuffy" Goff (Abner) performed their homespun country characters for more than 20 years, starting on a local Arkansas station and eventually airing for a time on every major radio network.

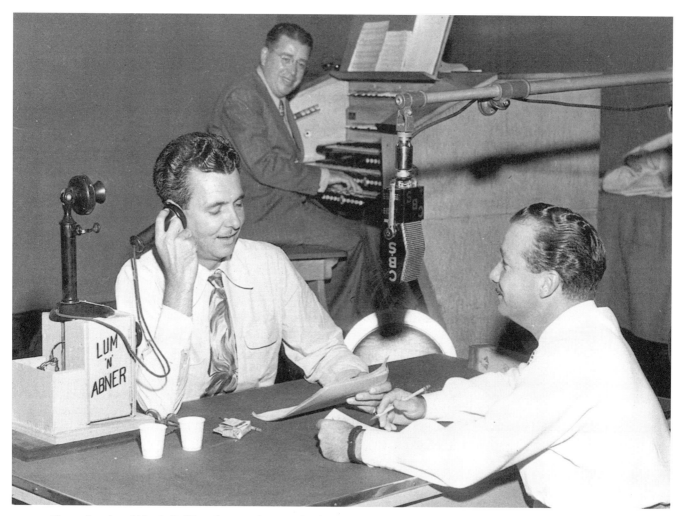

Chester Lauck and Norris Goff broadcast another episode of *Lum 'n' Abner* in 1947–48 as organist Ralph Emerson awaits his cue
Courtesy National Lum & Abner Society

Lauck and Goff met as boys in a Mena, Arkansas, grade school, and they were performing impressions and blackface comedy together by the early 1920s. In 1931 an Arkansas radio station invited locals to perform for a flood-relief benefit, and Lauck and Goff planned to do their blackface act. Seeing the station overrun with other blackface teams, they instead performed an "Ozarkian humor" routine to great listener response. They were signed to a weekly 15-minute program on KTHS in Hot Springs, Arkansas, and by late summer of that year they had both a sponsor (Quaker Oats) and a foothold on a regional National Broadcasting Company (NBC) station, Chicago's WMAQ. From then on, *Lum 'n' Abner* became an increasingly hot property; whenever Lauck and Goff were not pleased with their time slot, pay, or sponsor, another network gladly wooed them away.

The show's style was wry and folksy, deriving much of its humor from a combination of misfiring schemes and "countri-

fied" misunderstandings of aspects of the everyday lives of their listeners, as when Lum and Abner try to do their taxes or when the town blacksmith, Cedric Weehunt (Lauck), tries to become a ventriloquist without realizing that ventriloquists are supposed to change the dummy's voice and try not to move their lips. The characters were not stooges, though (despite Abner's regular catchphrase—"Huh?"—often uttered after Lum's long and involved explanation of his latest plan): the folks of Pine Ridge always ended up on top. There was a gentle tone to the humor and a relaxed pace to the steadily rolling plot arcs that made the program a long-lived and reliable performer in the ratings.

Some plotlines were self-contained in a single episode, as when Lum and Abner struggle to do their 1942 taxes, first concluding that they owe "the givverment" 8,912 sacks of sugar, then realizing that the government actually owes them (though they decide instead to send along the extra cash in the till to help the war effort). However, more often the plots wove their way onward for weeks, as when the town's richest man, Diogenes Smith, holds a campaign to discover and reward the kindest person in town, which begins a complex train of events in which Lum eventually becomes an unwitting courier of counterfeit money.

Lauck and Goff performed the voices of most of the program's major characters. In fact, for the first six years they performed all of the characters, and those they did not perform (the female characters in particular) were only talked about in the store and never actually appeared on the show. NBC executives were continually pushing to broaden the program's scope; one 1933 memo read, "I have impressed upon the boys the necessity of more action and other characters. Their scripts from now on will have both. They are afraid of women characters, for they feel they can't write the dialogue. However, we will work hard to accomplish this." In the late 1930s female characters did begin to appear occasionally, most often voiced by Lurene Tuttle.

The program was particularly popular in its home setting, rural Arkansas. In 1936, to celebrate *Lum 'n' Abner*'s fifth anniversary on the air, the unincorporated Arkansas town of Waters officially changed its name to Pine Ridge at a ceremony attended most notably by the governor of Arkansas, Lauck, Goff, and town resident Dick Huddleston, a fictionalized version of whom was voiced by Goff on the program. To this day one can visit the "Jot 'Em Down Store" in Pine Ridge, which serves as a *Lum 'n' Abner* museum and which is where the National Lum and Abner Society holds conventions for aficionados. There is also a country store in Kentucky's Fayette County that styles itself the "Jot 'Em Down Store"; it dates back to a 1937 visit by Lauck and Goff on their way through the area to buy some horses.

The show's popularity was parlayed over the years into a series of seven feature films starring Lauck and Goff (with appearances by performers such as Zasu Pitts, Grady Sutton, Franklin Pangborn, and Barbara Hale) and produced by RKO, beginning with *Dreaming Out Loud* in 1940 and ending with *Partners in Time* in 1946. One additional film was released by "Howco Productions" much later, in 1956, an odd installment that found Lum and Abner out of the familiar territory of Pine Ridge, traveling to Paris and Monte Carlo. It was actually an edited-together version of three *Lum 'n' Abner* television pilots that the Columbia Broadcasting System (CBS) had originally produced in 1949 to no great acclaim.

In late 1948, during its second stint on CBS, *Lum 'n' Abner* changed from its 15-minute serial-comedy format to a half-hour comedy variety program, including for the first time such trappings as an orchestra and a studio audience. This was how the program seemed to end its days, going off the air in the spring of 1950. But three years later it reappeared once more in its traditional 15-minute format, first for a limited 13-week series and then for a final six-month run.

Lum 'n' Abner is one of the radio programs for which many recordings and scripts still survive. Some tapes are available from commercial sources, but there are also thriving collections circulating in the hands of ordinary fans. *Lum 'n' Abner* may not have the instant modern name recognition of programs such as *Amos 'n' Andy*, but it has made its mark—not only among radio fans, but also on the map of the United States.

DORINDA HARTMANN

Cast

Columbus "Lum" Edwards, Cedric Weehunt, Grandpappy Spears, Snake Hogan	Chester Lauck
Abner Peabody, Squire Skimp, Dick Huddleston, Mousey Gray, Doc Miller	Norris Goff
Ellie Conners, Sgt. V.W. Hartford, Nurse Lunsford	Lurene Tuttle
Diogenes Smith, B.J. Webster, Mr. Sutton	Frank Graham
Detective Wilson, Dr. Roller, Pest Controller, Mr. Talbert, FCC Man	Howard McNear
Duncan Hines, W.J. Chancellor	Francis X. Bushman
Ira Hodgekins, Caleb Weehunt	Horace Murphy
The Baby, J.W. Tiffin	Jerry Hausner
Mr. Talbert's Father	Ken Christy
Dr. Samuel Snide (dentist)	Eddie Holden
Doc Ben Withers (veterinarian)	Clarence Hartzell
Lady Brilton	Edna Best
Rowena	Isabel Randolph
Otis Bagley	Dink Trout

Announcers

Tom Nobles (1931), Charles Lyon (1931), Del Sharbutt (1931–33), Gene Hamilton (1933–34), Carlton Brickert (1934–38), Lou Crosby (1938–44), Gene Baker (1944–45), Forrest Owen (1945–48), Wynden Niles (1948–50), Bill Ewing (1953–54)

Producer

Larry Berns

Directors

Bill Gay, Robert McInnes, Forrest Owen

Writers

Betty Boyle, Norris Goff, Chester Lauck, Roz Rogers, Jay Sommers, Howard Snyder, Hugh Wedlock, Jr.

Programming History
26 April 1931–7 May 1954 (many changes in network and
time slots)

Further Reading
"Amid the Native Corn," *Newsweek* (6 October 1947)
Crawford, Byron, "Setting Store by a Name,"*Courier-Journal*
(Louisville, Kentucky, 24 May 1991)

Lum 'n' Abner: Frigidaire Announces Sponsorship," *New
York Times* (18 August 1948)
"*Lum 'n' Abner* to End," *New York Times* (30 June
1948)
Salomonson, Terry G.G., *The Lum 'n' Abner Program: A
Radio Broadcast Log of the Comedy Drama Program*,
Howell, Michigan: Salomonson, 1997

Lux Radio Theater

Anthology Drama

One of the most popular and prestigious radio programs for
two decades, *Lux Radio Theater* was a dramatic anthology
that mainly presented movie adaptations with big-name Hollywood stars.

Lever Brothers had been using celebrities to endorse its Lux
Toilet Soap in magazine ads throughout the 1920s, and in
1934 the J. Walter Thompson Advertising Agency proposed to
Lever Brothers an extension of this promotional tactic, the
sponsorship of a radio drama presenting stars of the stage and
screen. The resulting program, *Lux Radio Theater,* aired on
the National Broadcasting Company (NBC) and originated
from downtown Manhattan, premiering on 14 October 1934.
Given its New York locale, the program presented mostly
Broadway talent and properties in this early period. During the
first season, the show's host was a fictitious character named
Douglass Garrick, played by John Anthony and billed as the
show's producer. Peggy Winthrop, another fictional character
played by Doris Dagmar, supplied commercials. In addition to
commercials, the show's framework included a scripted chat
session between Garrick and each particular episode's stars.

By the end of its first season, *Lux Radio Theater* was a critical success, but given their sizable investment in the show,
Lever Brothers had hoped for higher listener ratings. When the
Columbia Broadcasting System (CBS) offered them the advan-
tageous 9 P.M. Monday night slot, *Lux* made the switch to that
network and time. The second season brought a few other
changes: a new actor, Albert Hayes, played Douglass Garrick;
Art Millett was added as announcer; and the Peggy Winthrop
character was eliminated.

By the end of the 1935–36 season, ratings still were not
where Lever Brothers wanted them. Under the assumption that
film stars would draw larger national audiences than Broadway stars, in 1936 *Lux* moved to Hollywood, specifically to

the Music Box Theater on Hollywood Boulevard. Producers
also hoped to bring in a famous Hollywood name to replace
the Douglass Garrick figure as host. They settled on famed
movie director Cecil B. DeMille, who, although he was
assigned the title of producer, was simply a host figure and
often appeared only for dress rehearsals and the actual recordings. It was hoped that DeMille's famed persona as creative
tour de force would help lend a prestigious, glamorous image
to the show. Additionally, by specifically presenting him as a
producer, essentially an authorial voice, *Lux Radio Theater*
posed the show as a first-rate cultural experience on par with
DeMille's epic film productions. Equally important, framing
DeMille as a creative force helped to elide the fact that the
show was really created by an ad agency concerned mainly
with advertising revenue, rather than solely a culturally beneficial endeavor.

As a result of these changes, the 1936–37 season brought a
plethora of stars in movie adaptations, such as Errol Flynn and
Olivia de Havilland in "Captain Blood," Irene Dunne and
Robert Taylor in "Magnificent Obsession," and Fredric March
and Jean Arthur in "The Plainsman." Cooperation between J.
Walter Thompson and the Hollywood studios made this possible. The studios would offer the broadcast rights to film properties for a fee (usually no more than $1,000), though
sometimes the rights would be offered for free in exchange for
publicity on the air. The show's most substantial expense came
from talent costs. DeMille made $2,000 per show in this
period, and each headlining star received $5,000. (The average
yearly salary in the U.S. in 1937 was $1,327.00) Given that a
minimum of two headliners per episode was the general rule,
talent costs could reach as high as $20,000 per episode.

In 1940 *Lux Radio Theater* changed recording facilities to
the Vine Street Playhouse. This venue offered a more spacious

Lux Radio Theater, Spencer Tracy, Fay Wray, and Cecil B. DeMille
Courtesy CBS Photo Archive

stage, and the actors would thus all stand on the stage throughout the whole program, even if their parts were completed in the first act. DeMille sat off to the side at a card table, and an offstage mike provided sound effects and some commercials. The New York version of the show had not been presented in front of an audience, and a change in this policy upon the move to Hollywood resulted in a furious weekly demand for tickets.

The next period of upheaval for *Lux Radio Theater* came in 1944, when DeMille left the show. His departure stemmed from a dispute with the American Federation of Radio Artists (AFRA). A proposition on that year's state election ballot would have allowed a Californian the right to obtain employment without first gaining union affiliation. AFRA strongly opposed this measure and charged all members one dollar to fund a battle against its passage. The right-wing DeMille resolutely objected both to AFRA's stance and to their demand that members fund it, and he refused to pay his dollar. This resulted in a suspension of his AFRA membership, meaning he was also barred from any radio work. *Lux* first turned to guest hosts in the interim, including Brian Aherne and Lionel Barrymore, but when it became clear that neither AFRA nor DeMille would relent, the producers settled on a permanent host in William Keighley, a lesser-known Hollywood director. Keighley took on DeMille's role as host and faux-producer; however, he could never match the famed director's prestigious presence and vaunted image.

Keighley retired in 1952 and was replaced by Irving Cummings, a fellow Hollywood director. However, *Lux Radio Theater*'s ratings began a precipitous slide, particularly into 1954, as Lever Brothers and J. Walter Thompson were giving more attention and money to the television version of the program, *Lux Video Theater* (1950–57). In 1954, NBC reclaimed *Lux Radio Theater* and tried to resurrect the show's stately image with a marketing campaign and presentation of "twenty of the greatest Hollywood pictures" during the 1954–55 season. However, this did little to stem the show's decline, and the show aired its final broadcast on 7 June 1955. The television version carried on until 1957, but it never reached the popularity of the radio version, particularly because it could not offer the caliber of stars the radio show had. Only the radio version could tout a history of 926 episodes starring the most famous talent of the era.

CHRISTINE BECKER

Cast

Host "Douglass Garrick"	John Anthony (1934–35)
Other Hosts	Cecil B. DeMille (1936–45), William Keighley (1945–52), Irving Cummings (1952–55), Lionel Barrymore (1945), Walter Huston (1945), Mark Hellinger (1945), Brian Aherne (1945), Irving Pichel (1945)
Announcers	Melville Ruick (1936–40), John Milton Kennedy (1940s), Ken Carpenter (later years)

Directors

Antony Stanford (1934–36), Frank Woodruff (1943), Fred MacKaye (1944–51), Earl Ebi (1951–55)

Programming History

NBC Blue	October 1934–June 1935
CBS	July 1935–June 1954
NBC	September 1954–June 1955

Further Reading

Billips, Connie J., and Arthur Pierce, *Lux Presents Hollywood: A Show-by-Show History of the Lux Radio Theater and the Lux Video Theater, 1934–1957*, Jefferson, North Carolina: McFarland, 1995

DeMille, Cecil B., *The Autobiography of Cecil B. DeMille*, edited by Donald Hayne, Englewood Cliffs, New Jersey: Prentice-Hall, 1959; London: Allen, 1960

Hilmes, Michele, *Radio Voices: American Broadcasting, 1922–1952*, Minneapolis: University of Minnesota Press, 1997

Jewell, Richard B., "Hollywood and Radio: Competition and Partnership in the 1930s," *Historical Journal of Film, Radio, and Television* 4, no. 2 (1984)

M

Magazines. *See* Fan Magazines; Trade Press

Make Believe Ballroom. *See* Block, Martin

Mankiewicz, Frank 1924–

U.S. Broadcast Executive, President of National Public Radio

Frank Mankiewicz, the third president of National Public Radio (NPR), led the organization from obscurity to national significance. Mankiewicz took over leadership of the seven-year-old NPR in August 1977.

Public radio, as represented by NPR and the Association of Public Radio Stations, had just emerged from two years of internal strife by merging to create a "new," more powerful National Public Radio to provide political, promotional, technical, and programming leadership. The fresh start required a new president, someone who was "somebody," preferably a politician, a journalist, a showman, a promoter, and a celebrity whose phone calls would be returned. The new NPR board found that individual in Frank Mankiewicz, scion of the Hollywood family, press secretary to the late Senator Robert Kennedy, director of George McGovern's 1972 campaign for president, and a syndicated columnist and author. Along the way, Mankiewicz had spent six years as a Hollywood lawyer, had directed Peace Corps operations in Latin America, and had run unsuccessfully for the California state legislature and the U.S. Congress from Maryland. His name was also to be

found on the enemies list of President Richard Nixon, about whom Mankiewicz had written two books.

Mankiewicz did not disappoint. He transformed public radio in four critical areas: publicity, programming, politics, and satellite delivery.

Publicity

The news media finally discovered NPR after having virtually ignored it for its first seven years. Much of the publicity centered on Mankiewicz as a personality. He was good copy, always ready with the quick quip and the memorable sound bite. More fundamentally, his programming and political exploits gave the media something interesting to write about.

Programming

Mankiewicz persuaded President Jimmy Carter to participate in a two-hour national call-in program from the White House on a Saturday afternoon, 13 October 1979. For those two

Frank Mankiewicz
Courtesy AP/Wide World Photos

hours, all media focused on the previously unknown NPR. In addition to publicity, the president's exclusive appearance gave the obscure network much-needed credibility. Similarly, Mankiewicz persuaded the Senate leadership to allow NPR to broadcast live its debate on the Panama Canal Treaty. Although the Senate had always excluded cameras and microphones from its chambers, Mankiewicz broke that barrier, creating what he described to the press as a historic broadcast of a historic event.

In entertainment, Mankiewicz reached back to his boyhood, when his father, Herman Mankiewicz, teamed with Orson Welles on the *Mercury Radio Theater* and its most famous production, "War of the Worlds." NPR would collab-

orate with George Lucas on a radio adaptation of the *Star Wars* film trilogy. The series brought new attention and new listeners to NPR.

Of most lasting consequence, however, was Mankiewicz's decision to move NPR news into radio's prime time, morning drive. *Morning Edition*'s debut in November 1979 more than doubled NPR's news output, its budget, and its staff, and it focused those resources where they could reach the most potential listeners. *Morning Edition* indirectly transformed both NPR and the programming on its member stations. NPR became a competitive 24-hour news organization for the first time, changing its public image and its internal psychology from that of an ancillary alternative service to that of a primary source of breaking news. To make room for *Morning Edition* in prime morning hours, stations were forced to rethink and refocus their entire approach to programming. For the most part, they eliminated their weakest program elements and concentrated on their strongest. A combination of these changes doubled public radio's cumulative audience from 4 million to 8 million a week between 1979 and 1982.

Politics

After almost a decade of struggle between public radio and public television over the division of federal funds between the two media, Mankiewicz boldly persuaded Congress to earmark 25 percent of its funding for public radio. Public television had argued that radio should receive only 10 percent; prior to Mankiewicz, public radio had felt victorious when it won 17 percent. The extra money made possible *Morning Edition* and other dramatic improvements in the public radio service.

Satellite Delivery

Congress also agreed in 1979 to fund a satellite delivery system for public radio, the first radio network to use that technology for network distribution of programs. The satellite not only improved the technical quality of NPR programming but also provided the flexibility to produce programming from a variety of locations around the country, making possible such important innovations as the live broadcasts of Garrison Keillor's *A Prairie Home Companion* from Minnesota each Saturday night.

Despite all his success, the Mankiewicz presidency did not end happily. The election of Ronald Reagan in 1980 resulted in a 25 percent reduction in federal funding for public broadcasting in 1983. With typical brashness, Mankiewicz proposed to meet that challenge not by reducing service but by expanding it. He planned to raise the necessary money from the private sector, through increased "underwriting" of programming and through business ventures that would utilize NPR's satellite capacity to provide a variety of commercial services to the public. The concepts had merit, but Mankiewicz did not have the time or the money to realize them. None would produce significant revenue for several years, and all required significant investments right away.

By early 1983 NPR found itself running a $3 million deficit, which increased to $6 million and threatened to reach $9 million if drastic action were not taken. NPR was insolvent. Ulti-

mately, member stations and the Corporation for Public Broadcasting bailed NPR out of its difficulties, but a condition of that bailout was the firing of Frank Mankiewicz in April 1983. Although he had hoped to leave NPR to become commissioner of baseball, Frank Mankiewicz instead formed an alliance with Republican political operative Robert Gray to spend the rest of his career in one of Washington's most influential lobbying organizations.

JACK MITCHELL

See also National Public Radio

Frank Mankiewicz. Born in New York City, 16 May 1924. Son of Herman J. and Sara (Aaronson) Mankiewicz; attended University of California, Los Angeles, A.B., 1947, Columbia University, M.S., 1948, and University of California, Berkeley, LL.B, 1955; served in U.S. Army Infantry, 1943–46; journalist, Washington, D.C. and Los Angeles, 1948–1952; admitted to Bar of California, 1955; practiced law in Beverly Hills, 1955–61; director, U.S. Peace Corps, Lima, Peru, 1962–64, and Latin America regional director, 1964–66; press secretary for Senator Robert F. Kennedy, 1966–68; syndicated columnist with Tom Braden, 1968–71; national presidential campaign director for Senator George Mc Govern, 1971–72; author and journalist, 1973–77; president, National Public Radio, 1977–83; public relations executive and consultant, Hill and Knowlton, 1983–present.

Selected Publications

Perfectly Clear, Nixon from Whittier to Watergate, 1973
U.S. v Richard M. Nixon: The Final Crisis, 1975
With Fidel: A Portrait of Castro and Cuba (editor, with Kirby Jones), 1975
Remote Control: Television and the Manipulation of American Life (with Joel Swerdlow), 1978

Further Reading

Collins, Mary, *National Public Radio: The Cast of Characters,* Washington, D.C.: Seven Locks Press, 1993
Engelman, Ralph, *Public Radio and Television in America: A Political History,* Thousand Oaks, California: Sage, 1996
Looker, Thomas, *The Sound and the Story: NPR and the Art of Radio,* Boston: Houghton Mifflin, 1995
McDougal, Dennis, "The Public Radio Wars," *Los Angeles Times* (8–11 October 1985) (four-part series)
Zuckerman, Lawrence, "Has Success Spoiled NPR?" *Mother Jones* 12, no. 5 (June–July 1987)

Ma Perkins

Serial Drama/Soap Opera

A widow whose homespun wisdom guided her family, friends, and neighbors in the fictitious rural community of Rushville Center, *Ma Perkins* was also one of radio's most enduring soap operas, captivating American and, at times, overseas audiences for 27 years, from 1933 to 1960. Throughout its entire run of 7,065 episodes, Virginia Payne portrayed the leading character.

A 15-minute daytime serial drama, *Ma Perkins* premiered on NBC radio on 4 December 1933, three months after its local debut on WLW in Cincinnati, Ohio. Cincinnati-based Procter and Gamble Company, makers of Oxydol soap flakes, initially sponsored the broadcast. The drama was so popular it was picked up by competing networks, CBS and Mutual, at various times, while continuing its broadcasts on NBC as well. CBS acquired exclusive rights to the show in 1949, where it remained until its final broadcast in 1960.

Ma had three children, John, Fay and Evey, whose husband Willie Fitz (portrayed by Murray Forbes, also for all 27 years of the broadcast) managed Ma's lumber yard business. Shuffle Shober, Ma's business partner, was portrayed by Charles Egleston for 25 years, until his death in 1958. Edwin Wolfe succeeded him for the remaining run of the show. Writer Orin Tovrov wrote the scripts for more than 20 years.

Ma Perkins' roots can be traced not only to Cincinnati, but also to Chicago, where advertising executives Frank and Anne Hummert created the program. It was in Chicago that the Hummerts also originated other popular daytime drama serials in the early 1930s, including *The Romance of Helen Trent* and *Just Plain Bill.* Though each of the serials offered different characters with different story lines, they were all products of the Hummerts' desire to present familiar themes that had proven popular with Depression-era listeners seeking some measure of assurance and security in an unstable world. According to Marilyn Matelski, the Hummert approach was a simple formula. "[It] combined fantasies of exotic romance, pathos and suspense with a familiar environment of everyday life in a small-town or rural setting. Combined with an identifiable hero or heroine, this formula produced an overwhelming audience response" (see Matelski, 1988).

The story lines for *Ma Perkins* often reflected the turbulence of the times. In one broadcast during World War II, for example, Ma learns that her son John was killed in combat in Europe. The "news" prompted a flood of letters from devoted listeners expressing their sympathy. Throughout its run, *Ma Perkins* conveyed the vulnerability of life in ways not depicted before on radio. It did so while reaffirming the belief that people could solve their problems so long as they believed in one

another. In 1938, Ma offered this observation: "Anyone of this earth who's done wrong, and then goes so far as to right that wrong, I can tell you that they're well on their way to erasing the harm they did in the eyes of anyone decent."

Virginia Payne was only 23 years old when the serial drama premiered, and, remarkably, she never missed a performance in its 27-year run. A Cincinnati native and graduate of the University of Cincinnati, she faithfully dressed the part at countless public appearances and even personally answered many of her listeners' letters. Her down-home language included such expressions as "I ain't sure I understand it" and "Land sakes!"

U.S. audience interest in radio soap operas declined during the 1950s because of the growth of television, and *Ma Perkins* was no exception. By 1960 CBS radio cut three of its ten serials, and NBC dropped its last surviving soap opera; ABC had ended all of its daytime serials the year before. The sponsors that owned the programs abandoned radio in favor of television because of its increasing audience appeal. The transition to television created a vacuum in radio advertising sales, and by 1960 only one quarter of network radio advertising time was being sold. Local radio, meanwhile, was blossoming: disc jockeys replaced radio network programs in large numbers by the end of the 1950s, and radio station managers discovered that the locally hosted music program proved cheaper for advertisers and more popular to listeners as well. By the 1955–56 season, *Ma Perkins'* radio audience share had fallen to one quarter of its all-time high in 1944–45. On 25 November 1960, the show's final broadcast featured the family at its traditional Thanksgiving meal:

"I look around the table at my loved ones and to me the table stretches on and on. Over beyond the other end past Shuffle I see faces somehow familiar and yet unborn, except in the mind of God... Someday, Fay will be sitting here where I'm sitting, or Evey, or Paulette... They'll move up into my place and I'll be gone, but I find right and peace in that knowledge... I give thanks that I've been given this gift of life, this gift of time to play my little part in it," Ma said at the table.

Virginia Payne was only 50 years old when *Ma Perkins* ended. During the 1960s and 1970s she remained active in show business, appearing in radio commercials and touring in such productions as *Life With Father, Becket,* and *Oklahoma!* Shortly before her death in Cincinnati on 10 February 1977, she appeared on radio one last time on *The CBS Radio Mystery Theater.*

DAVID MCCARTNEY

See also Hummert, Frank and Anne; Soap Opera

Cast

Ma Perkins	Virginia Payne
Fay Perkins Henderson	Rita Ascot; Marjorie Hannan; Cheer Brentson; Laurette Fillbrandt; Margaret Draper
Evey Perkins Fitz	Dora Johnson; Laurette Fillbrandt; Kay Campbell
John Perkins	Gilbert Faust
Shuffle Shober	Charles Egleston (1933–58); Edwin Wolfe (1958–60)
Willie Fitz	Murray Forbes
Junior Fitz	Cecil Roy; Arthur Young; Bobby Ellis
Paulette Henderson	Nannette Sargent; Judith Lockser
Augustus Pendleton	Maurice Copeland
Mathilda Pendleton	Beverly Younger
Gladys Pendleton	Patricia Dunlap; Helen Lewis
Paul Henderson	Jonathan Holoe
Gregory Ivanoff	McKay Morris
Gary Curtis	Rye Billsbury
Charley Brown	Ray Suber
Tom Wells	John Larkin; Casey Allen

Announcers

Bob Brown, Jack Brinkley, Dick Wells, Marvin Miller, Dan Donaldson

Producers/Creators

Frank and Anne Hummert; Robert Hardy Andrews

Writers

Robert Hardy Andrews, Lee Gebhart, Lester Huntley, Natalie Johnson, and Orin Tovrov

Programming History

WLW, Cincinnati, Ohio	August 1933–December 1933
NBC	1933–49
NBC Blue	February 1937–December 1937; June 1938–November 1938
CBS	January 1938–May 1938; September 1942–November 1960
Mutual	1935–36

Further Reading

Allen, Robert Clyde, *Speaking of Soap Operas*, Chapel Hill: University of North Carolina Press, 1985

Cox, Jim, *The Great Radio Soap Operas*, Jefferson, North Carolina: McFarland, 1999

Edmondson, Madeleine, and David Rounds, *The Soaps: Daytime Serials of Radio and TV*, New York: Stein and Day, 1973

LaGuardia, Robert, *From Ma Perkins to Mary Hartman: The Illustrated History of Soap Operas*, New York: Ballantine Books, 1977

Matelski, Marilyn J., *The Soap Opera Evolution: America's Enduring Romance with Daytime Drama*, Jefferson, North Carolina: McFarland, 1988

Stedman, Raymond William, *The Serials: Suspense and Drama by Installment*, Norman: University of Oklahoma Press, 1971; 2nd edition, 1977

Stumpf, Charles K., *Ma Perkins, Little Orphan Annie, and Heigh-Ho Silver*, New York: Carlton Press, 1971

The March of Time

Network Docudrama Series

The *March of Time*, a radio forerunner of today's television "docudramas," was a widely heard and imitated news dramatization program—a "radio newsreel"—that lasted 14 seasons on network radio (1931–45) and led to a famous motion picture documentary series of the same name. *The March of Time* is best remembered by the words of the title spoken by the mellifluous narrator Westbrook Van Voorhis, who also spoke on the newsreel version and ended both by saying "Time marches on."

Origins

The idea for a digest of the news for radio broadcast originated with Fred Smith, the first station director at WLW in Cincinnati. Smith wrote and directed dramas for WLW and introduced many program ideas at the station. In 1925 he hit upon the novel idea of reading various items taken (without permission) from newspapers and magazines. Smith called the program *Musical News;* after each story, a brief musical piece was played by the staff organist.

About the same time, a similar idea was put into print in a new kind of weekly magazine. Henry R. Luce and Briton Hadden, friends since prep school and Yale, quit their jobs at the *Baltimore News* in 1922 to found a magazine that summarized the week's news—an idea they had discussed since their days in boot camp during World War I. The magazine was *Time,* and its first issue appeared 3 March 1923. (Luce ran *Time* alone after the death of Briton Hadden in 1929.)

In 1928, Fred Smith at WLW got permission from *Time* to use an advance, or "makeready," copy of the magazine sent to him by airmail (then just begun) so that he could rewrite items for a weekly news summary on WLW. Soon Smith was hired by Time Incorporated and traveling the Midwest, signing up stations for a daily news summary the magazine would syndicate to radio stations. Beginning on 3 September 1928, 10-minute scripts were delivered by airmail to be read by local announcers on more than 60 stations. In New York, WOR called the program *NewsCasting* and broadcast it from 5:50 P.M. to 6:00 P.M., Monday through Friday. Smith himself was WOR's reader for the first year.

The radio program's title was apparently the first use of the word *newscast,* and it was listed in the *New York Times* radio logs by that title. While at WLW, Smith had coined *radarios,* after *radio* and *scenario,* for original radio plays he wrote and produced. (*Time* was even better known for its neologisms, coining *cinemaddict, newsmagazine,* and *socialite,* among others.) By the spring of 1929, the ten-minute summaries were being carried on as many as 90 stations (up from 60 stations just a half-year earlier)—the first large-scale regular daily news broadcast carried in the United States—but it was never a true network program because each station developed its own script.

Fred Smith next conceived of dramatizing the news. In September 1929 he produced a five-minute "news drama" in cooperation with *Time* and submitted his audition program to a number of stations with the title *NewsActing.* Although *newsacting* did not become a household word, the program idea caught on. By December 1929 Smith and a crew of six to eight actors were producing a weekly five-minute drama for distribution by electrical transcription. These programs were not full-scale dramatic productions, but they included sound effects, occasional music, and the portrayal of the voices of actual people involved in the news stories. Within a few months the *NewsActing* records were being broadcast over more than 100 stations nationwide. At the time, other network programs were dramatizing history, but none had tried a weekly presentation of current news.

Henry Luce wanted to advertise *Time* on the radio networks, and on 6 February 1931, an experimental program was sent via telephone wires to the home of a Time Inc. executive where a small group was gathered that included CBS president William S. Paley. Exactly a month later, on Friday, 6 March 1931, *The March of Time* was fed from CBS's New York studios and carried on 20 of the network's affiliates (there were then about 80) at 10:30 P.M. EST. (The program's title was taken from a Broadway show tune of the same name.) After a five-second fanfare, the announcer said:

> The March of Time. On a thousand fronts the events of the world move swiftly forward. Tonight the editors of *Time,* the weekly newsmagazine, attempt a new kind of reporting of the news, the re-enacting as clearly and dramatically as the medium of radio will permit some themes from the news of the week.

Network Years

This first program dramatized the reelection of William "Big Bill" Thompson as mayor of Chicago, the sudden death of the *New York World* by merging with the *New York Telegram,* and shorter segments on French prisoners sent to Devil's Island, revolution in Spain, prison reform in Romania, a roundup of news of royalty, an auction of Czarist possessions in New York, and the closing of the 71st United States Congress.

During the first season the program ran 13 weeks. It returned on 8 September 1932, but as a sustaining feature because *Time* executives had decided that they could not afford advertising, which they said the magazine no longer needed. In the magazine the editors justified the radio show's cancellation by asking, "should a few (400,000 *Time* subscribers) pay for the entertainment of many (9,000,000 radiowners)?" In the 29 February 1932 issue, *Time* also argued, "For all its blatant claims to being a medium of education, radio contributes little of its own beyond the considerable service of bringing good music to millions." In November 1932 the magazine resumed its sponsorship. *The March of Time* did its part to promote magazine sales: at the end of each program, listeners were reminded that they could find more details in the issue of *Time* magazine soon to be on newsstands.

On 1 February 1935, the *March of Time* newsreel began as a monthly film series in movie theaters. It began as a typical newsreel with several items in each issue, but the January 1938 issue focused on a single topic, "Inside Nazi Germany." After October 1938, single subjects were being treated exclusively as the series became a documentary rather than strictly a news series. The documentary series ran until 1951. Time Inc. also produced historical television documentary series, such as *Crusade in Europe,* based on the book by General Dwight D. Eisenhower (1948). The title *March of Time* was also used for a syndicated series of television documentaries produced by David Wolper.

Broadcast of *The March of Time*
Courtesy CBS Photo Archive

During the 1933–34 season, *March of Time* was sponsored by Remington-Rand, and Westbrook Van Voorhis became the voice of the program. In 1935 there was a variety of sponsors when a daily 15-minute version was tried for one season. In 1938 the program was sponsored by Time Inc.'s *Life* magazine (purchased by Luce in 1936), and the announcer worked that title in to the opening of the program: "Life! The life of the world, its conflicts and achievements, its news and fun, its leaders and its common people." The program was not aired during the 1939–40 and 1940–41 seasons. After seven years on CBS, it moved to the NBC Blue network. In July 1942 the format was changed to only one or two dramatized segments and many more live, on-the-spot news reports. By the 1944–45 season, *March of Time*'s last, listeners were hearing the actual voices of newsmakers on many network programs.

At the century's end much was being made of the "synergy" of cross-media ties, the idea being that the interaction of a media corporation's units (say, a magazine division feeding story ideas to a film company) would encourage the making of products and profits greater than the sum of the corporation's parts could make by acting alone. *The March of Time* was one of the first examples of synergy. Fred Smith's idea of reading a few news items accompanied by musical selections that became *Musical News*, *NewsCasting*, *NewsActing*, and *March of Time* led to the many "dramatized news" programs—documentaries and docudramas—on television today.

LAWRENCE W. LICHTY

See also Documentary Programs; News

Narrators
Ted Husing, Westbrook Van Voorhis, Harry Von Zell

Programming History
CBS   1931–39
NBC Blue   1941–45

Further Reading
Bohn, Thomas W., and Lawrence W. Lichty, "The March of Time: News As Drama," *Journal of Popular Film* 2, no. 4 (Fall 1973)

Fielding, Raymond, *The American Newsreel, 1911–1967*, Norman: University of Oklahoma Press, 1972
Fielding, Raymond, *The March of Time, 1935–1951*, New York: Oxford University Press, 1978
Lichty, Lawrence W., and Thomas W. Bohn, "Radio's March of Time: Dramatized News," *Journalism Quarterly* 51, no. 3 (Autumn 1974)

Marconi, Guglielmo 1874–1937

Italian Wireless Inventor

Marconi's daughter Degna Marconi published an account of the prophetic revelation given at the future inventor's birth: as the household servants joined family members in crowding into the birth room, a servant tactlessly commented, "What big ears he has!" Guglielmo's mother, Annie, although spent from a difficult labor, is said to have defended her newborn by saying, "He will be able to hear the still, small voice of the air." Little did she know that 21 years later, he would be sending messages across distances of more than a mile with no wires, but only air between the transmitter and receiver.

Youth

Marconi's early years afforded little formal education. He was born in the Italian countryside to an Italian father and an Irish mother. Although he attended an occasional school, he rarely got along well in such settings. Most of his education was gained either under his mother's tutelage, lessons that included readings from the Bible and English language instruction, or from books in his father's library. In the library, he was introduced not only to Greek mythology and history, but also to heroes of electricity such as Benjamin Franklin and Michael Faraday.

Marconi's father was impatient with his son's excessive interest in electricity and his constant tinkering with mechanical apparatuses. While constructing experiments based on Franklin's writings about electricity, the young Marconi succeeded in getting high-voltage electricity to vibrate a series of dinner plates to the point of destruction. Thereafter, his father began to systematically ruin Guglielmo's experimental equipment whenever he found it. It was his mother who worked to nurture her son's interest in exploring science. She helped him protect and hide the scientific devices he built.

The First Wireless Transmissions

At about the age of 20 Marconi was given the attic in the family's house as a private workspace where he could dabble in his hobby. He spent many secluded hours there working on experiments inspired by an article about the electromagnetic wave experiments of Heinrich Hertz. Marconi realized the possibilities for wireless communication if he could improve on Hertz's work. Although Hertz had showed that an alternating electric current in a closed electrical system could cause sparks to result in a totally separate loop of wire a few feet away, he had not conceived of the communication possibilities. However, others were making a communication connection. Even before Marconi had read about Hertz's experiment, others were building more powerful electromagnetic demonstrations and showing that the waves traveled for many feet without wires. None of the other experimenters, however, actually created anything practical in a communication sense.

Marconi began by duplicating Hertz's experiments in his attic. One night in 1894 he woke his mother and led her to the attic. There he tapped a telegraph key on one side of the attic. From the far end of the attic came the sound of a bell ringing every time the telegraph key was struck. While Marconi was said to lack the theoretical capacity of others experimenting with electromagnetic waves, his persistence and his ability to make his mechanical apparatuses do what he wanted them to do made him successful where others were not.

A neighbor, Professor Augusto Righi of the University of Bologna, provided informal tutelage on electromagnetic waves and gave suggestions for improving Marconi's early experiments. But Righi was also one of those who discouraged Marconi, suggesting that he would not succeed in making wireless communication practical. Such discouragement served to

Guglielmo Marconi
Courtesy Marconi International Fellowship Foundation

solidify Marconi's resolve to find a solution. Marconi's signals soon began to reach from the attic to the lowest corner of the home's interior. By the spring of 1895, Marconi began to experiment with communicating over longer and longer distances outdoors. By summer, he could send signals several hundred yards.

Much of the ability to advance the distance at which signals could be received was based simply on increasing the electrical power used by the transmitter, a very inefficient mode of sending signals over distances. It was at this point that Marconi made one of his most important early breakthroughs. In an attempt to transmit radio waves over greater distances, he used two large sheets of iron, placing one on the ground and holding the other in the air. Suddenly the distances the waves traveled were vastly multiplied. Marconi realized that placing part of the transmitter in the ground reduced the electrical resis-

tance, allowing the signal to travel up to a mile and a half. He had invented the grounded antenna. Soon he was sending signals more than two miles, even over and around hills and other obstacles.

Selling the Wireless Idea

Because Marconi did not have the high-level connections that a formally educated scientist would have developed, he and his mother relied on the advice of the parish priest and the family physician to decide how to pursue promoting his new invention. They chose to send a detailed document describing the invention to the Italian Minister of Post and Telegraph in early 1896. The invention, however, was rejected, and Marconi took this as a rejection by his country. (He may have fared better had he submitted the invention to the Italian Navy, which may well have recognized the invention's tremendous potential for ship-to-shore communication.) Based on that initial rejection, and probably also at the urging of his Irish mother, they decided that England, the greatest maritime power of that time, was most likely to be interested in the invention.

After applying for a patent in London, Marconi presented his invention to William Preece, an official of the British postal system. Preece arranged for Marconi to present his invention to many prominent scientists, who were impressed with his achievements. As the commercial possibilities began to be realized, Marconi was asked to sell his invention, but instead he formed his own company, the Marconi Wireless Company, and sold only a minority interest to investors. He achieved a wireless link across the 8.5 miles of the Bristol Channel in 1897 and began to install radio towers on the coast to warn ships in dangerous waters.

Marconi was also invited to demonstrate his invention to the Italian Navy, a right that he had reserved for his invention when his patent was filed. In his demonstrations and tests in Italy, he first proved that his signals could pass beyond the horizon through, it would seem, a wall of ocean. This finding would prove crucial in forecasting his eventual transatlantic communication.

Marconi was not only an inventor, but also a shrewd businessman. When asked to set up a transmitting station on a ship off the coast of England to transmit reports on a yacht race, he was quick to take up the challenge. Although this move did little to advance his scientific knowledge, he knew it would provide immense publicity for his invention. Queen Victoria picked up on the idea of ship-to-shore communication and adopted its use for the royal family between Osborne House on the Isle of Wight and the royal yacht.

In 1899 Marconi established a wireless link across the 32 miles of the English Channel. But simply conquering greater and greater distances became somewhat less important for Marconi, who had realized that the nature of wireless communication allowed only one transmitter at a time to operate in an area without interference. If two stations operated simultaneously, they would cancel each other out. Therefore, Marconi began to fix his attention on both focusing the direction of the signal and tuning the signal. Shortly after his Channel link was established, he wrote to Preece that he had made some advances in tuning the radio signal. He received a patent for this tuning invention a few years later.

While Marconi was in the process of experimenting with tuning in 1899, he took his first trip to the United States at the invitation of American businessmen who encouraged him to set up wireless systems for the America's Cup yachting races. In addition to these publicity-oriented transmissions, Marconi also met with the U.S. Navy and Army for demonstrations.

During these tests, Marconi experimented with the tuning components of his system but refused to let navy personnel in on the full details, because he had not yet applied for a patent. The navy, although only mildly enthusiastic, ordered several ships to be outfitted with wireless devices, but a deal with the Marconi company later fell through because of the high cost—ten cents per word—for using the devices. Shortly after his departure after his two months in America, an associate filed papers to charter the American Marconi Company.

On the return voyage from the United States, Marconi established a couple of other firsts in wireless transmission. The *St. Paul*, on which he sailed, was outfitted with a wireless to contact the English coast upon their approach. From 66 nautical miles away, the wireless connection was made. This allowed enough time for news of the South African War to be telegraphed to the ship, copies of the *Transatlantic Times* printed with the news, and the copies sold to passengers so that they could catch up on the news hours before they reached port.

Crossing the Atlantic

Marconi continued to focus for the next couple of years on developing his tuning device, but he was also aiming toward his next major target, transatlantic communication. Many great minds in the scientific community had determined that transatlantic wireless would be impossible because of the inability of radio signals to follow the curvature of the Earth. Marconi had of course already demonstrated to himself that he was sending signals that would bend around the Earth over bodies of water. To make this transatlantic leap, he first built a transmitting station at Poldhu, on the coast of southwestern England. He then tried to build a receiver on Cape Cod, Massachusetts, in early 1901, but he was beset by storms that destroyed his stations.

He then took a shortcut to prove his theory correct. He sailed to Newfoundland and, using a kite, hoisted a wire 400 feet in the air. At 12:30 P.M. on 12 December 1901, Marconi and one assistant heard the three distinct clicks of the letter *S* telegraphed according to a preset schedule from Poldhu to St. Johns, Newfoundland, a distance of more than 2,100 miles. The transmission was received repeatedly that afternoon. Two days later, Marconi released his results to the press, results that were heralded by some and belittled by others (critics credited static electricity as the cause of the signals).

Though Marconi initially planned to build a permanent receiving station in St. Johns, threats from transatlantic cable companies to institute legal action persuaded him to move south to Nova Scotia. There, the Canadian government worked to help him build a permanent receiving station. The funding they provided also helped finish the facility being completed on Cape Cod. Still, there were many unknowns in the technical aspects of transatlantic signals. In 1902, on a trip from England back to North America, Marconi discovered that signals traveled better at night than during a clear day. This was an important, if misunderstood, discovery. Try as he might, Marconi could not overcome the daytime impediment to his long-distance transmissions for several years, because he did not understand the impact of various frequencies on the propagation of electromagnetic waves.

Later Life

The Marconi companies faced considerable financial pressures through these years because the promise of transatlantic wireless seemed uncertain owing to problems with dependability in the system. To make these transmissions commercially viable, they had to be available on demand at any time. It was 1907 before commercial transmissions began in earnest between Glace Bay in Nova Scotia and a new station in Clifden on the west coast of Ireland. The Marconi company continued to concentrate on wireless telegraph service, with all ships required to have telegraph service by 1911.

All his work on creating a practical wireless method of international communication earned Marconi the Nobel Prize for physics in 1909. When the liner *Republic* went down after a midocean collision that same year, all passengers were saved thanks to wireless distress calls. The *Titanic* similarly used its wireless in 1912 to summon help that saved one-third of the passengers. Marconi sought further developments, including a portable wireless that could be used from lifeboats at sea, automatic warning alarms for untended wireless equipment, and triangulation techniques that would pinpoint a ship's position more accurately.

The early 1910s were filled with patent fights and business battles, but they were also largely profitable ones for the Marconi companies. Incorporating the inventions of others, Marconi's companies even began sending some wireless telephony messages of voice and music, a practice becoming known as "radio." After Italy entered World War I in 1915, Marconi was made an officer on the engineering staff responsible for wireless. Because of the need for secrecy in communication, he worked on developing shortwave communication and direction finders for the Italians and secured funding to update and expand the insufficient quantity of wireless equipment.

After the war, in 1920, the British rescinded a Marconi experimental license for broadcasting an opera performance, saying that it interfered with legitimate services. Thus, the U.S. got a two-year head start on Britain in regular radio broadcasting and the mass production of receivers. In 1922 Marconi was again allowed to begin limited broadcast service. By this time he was performing many of his radio experiments on his yacht, *Elettra*, which he had purchased in 1919.

Marconi's personal experiments continued to improve on his wireless inventions. He was eventually able to send directional signals and could make them circle the globe using shortwave technology. He capitalized on this achievement by establishing permanent communication links between territories of the British Empire. He also helped to establish Vatican Radio on shortwave so that the pope could speak to the whole world at once.

By 1927 Marconi's health began to fail. He continued to work on experiments in radar and with microwaves. He again overcame the doubts of theoreticians about the ability of microwaves to travel long distances, and he set up the first microwave communications link at the Vatican. Marconi died in 1937.

STEPHEN D. PERRY

See also Early Wireless; Fleming, John Ambrose; Hertz, Heinrich; Vatican Radio

Guglielmo Marconi. Born in Bologna, Italy, 25 April 1874. Self-educated and tutored by scientist Augusto Righi; invented methods of propagating electromagnetic waves over short distances, 1895, eventually reaching across Atlantic ocean, 1901, and around the world, 1922; invented method of tuning signals to avoid interference, 1904; worked on developing radar and microwave systems, advancing shortwave systems, and implementing permanent wireless communication between British colonies; set up Vatican radio service enabling Pope to speak to world, 1931. Received Nobel Prize in physics, 1909. Died in Rome, Italy, 20 July 1937.

Selected Publications

Wireless Telegraphy, 1899
Signals Across the Atlantic, 1901
The Progress of Electric Space Telegraphy, 1902
Recent Advances in Wireless Telegraphy, 1906
Wireless Telegraphic Communication, 1909
Radiotelegraphy, 1911

Further Reading

Baker, W.J., *A History of the Marconi Company,* New York: St. Martin's Press, 1971
Carter, Alden R., *Radio: From Marconi to the Space Age,* New York: Watts, 1987
Dunlap, Orrin Elmer, Jr., *Marconi: The Man and His Wireless,* New York: Macmillan, 1937; reprint, New York: Arno Press, 1971
Gunston, David, *Marconi: Father of Radio,* New York: Crowell-Collier Press, 1965; as *Guglielmo Marconi: Father of Radio,* London: Weidenfeld and Nicolson, 1965
Ivall, Tom, and Peter Willis, "Making Continuous Waves," *Electronics World* 103, no. 2 (February 1997)
Jolly, W.P., *Marconi,* New York: Stein and Day, and London: Constable, 1972

Kreuzer, James H., and Felicia A. Kreuzer, "Marconi—The Man and His Apparatus," *The A.W.A. Review* 9 (1995)

Marconi, Degna, *My Father, Marconi,* New York: McGraw Hill, and London: Muller, 1962

Masini, Giancarlo, *Marconi,* New York: Marsilio Publishers, 1995

Simons, R.W., "Guglielmo Marconi and Early Systems of Wireless Communication," *GEC Review* 11, no. 1 (1996)

Market

Radio markets are defined in geographic, demographic, and psychographic terms. Often, the definition of a radio market involves all three factors.

The primary definition of a market for radio is geographic—the area served by the transmitter's coverage, whether one city, a group of counties, or an entire region. Within that "market," the station establishes its listener base and sells advertising to attract those listeners to area retailers.

The second definition for radio derives from the medium's ability to target individual audience segments. Demographically drawn markets allow stations to focus programming on specific age groups: young adult women, for example, or teenagers. National radio programs define their markets using demographics.

Some markets defy geography and demography and consist of people of similar interests and tastes—psychographics. These similarities are often referred to as "lifestyle characteristics." However, consultant George A. Burns cautions radio marketers to understand the differences: "A group of nude skydivers may have only that in common. Their radio tastes can vary widely. While there may be broad commonalities among listeners to an individual radio station, it seems almost impossible to define them." Burns (1980) suggested that lifestyle characteristics of a particular group "*converge* at an individual radio station, *as far as radio listening is concerned.*"

As radio emerged in the 1930s as a viable—and valuable—medium for advertisers, geographic divisions were the most effective and most often used because of network radio's national reach. A 1939 promotional flyer from the National Broadcasting Company (NBC) showed the percentage of radio ownership in each of nine regions of the United States. The same flyer divided radio families by each of the four standard time zones, by size of city, and by whether listeners were in rural or urban locations.

Geography

The specific geographical definition of a market begins with guidelines set by the U.S. government's Office of Management and Budget (OMB). Radio's ratings services base their market areas on OMB's "Metropolitan Statistical Area" (MSA), "Primary Metropolitan Statistical Area" (PMSA), and "Consolidated Metropolitan Statistical Area" (CMSA). The government assigns each county surrounding a major population area to a specific MSA, PMSA, or CMSA.

For purposes of radio and television ratings, the definitions are modified by the Arbitron Company for radio and Nielsen Media Research for television, based on the needs and desires of their subscribers. Stations subscribing to the ratings service vote on which counties are included in a ratings report and which are excluded or assigned to another market area. Modern media markets are typically defined in three ways: for radio, the Metro Survey Area ("Metro") and the Total Survey Area (TSA); for television, the Designated Market Area (DMA).

As an example, the San Francisco, California, Arbitron ratings report contains data from Sonoma County listeners, and Sonoma County is considered part of the San Francisco Metro in Arbitron ratings reports. Sonoma County radio station operators, however, elected to define their county as a radio market, too. The result was a ratings report for San Francisco and an additional report for Santa Rosa (the largest city in Sonoma County). The ratings for Santa Rosa are duplicated in the San Francisco report, creating what is called an "imbedded market."

In contrast, Philadelphia and Wilmington, Delaware, are similar in that they are geographically side by side. Just as Sonoma County listeners hear San Francisco stations as easily as local outlets, Wilmington listeners can hear Philadelphia stations. However, the two are separate and distinct radio markets, as elected by Arbitron's subscribers in each area. The Philadelphia report and the Wilmington report have no duplication.

The Federal Communications Commission (FCC) generally defines a market area based on the signal contours of individual stations and overlapping signals. The FCC definition thus often differs from the Arbitron definition.

Targeting

Targeting was first found in advertising texts of the early 20th century. There was clear awareness of the use of different periodicals to target various populations: children, farmers, college students, and religious people, for instance. There were "trade" or "class" magazines such as those aimed at plumbers or Masons. Small-town newspapers targeted their audiences specifically, giving local influence to the advertisements. In 1915 Ernest Elmo Calkins suggested "canvassing consumers" in different cities around the country in order to gather information for an ad campaign. Calkins was a pioneer of targeting specific types of people as audiences and creating non-geographic markets.

General Motors advertising was an early example of targeting and segmentation. Trying to work out of a sales slump in the 1920s, the company reorganized its strategy based on price segments. Chevrolet, Pontiac, Buick, and Cadillac automobiles were priced differently and advertised to different markets based on socio-economic criteria.

This led manufacturers to support magazines and radio stations that reached the consumer segments they wanted for their products. Radio at the time was more mass than segmented; however, it became an ideal demographic and segmentation medium, creating communities of like-minded listeners. Writing in *American Demographics* magazine, Joseph Turow recognized the benefit of targeting to specific communities: "Target-minded media help advertisers [target a specific audience] by building primary media communities formed when viewers or readers feel that a magazine, radio station, or other medium resonates with their personal beliefs, and helps them chart their position in the larger world."

Just as media has changed since targeting and segmentation began, so has research. The statistical tools available to the researcher have grown tremendously over the years. The plunging cost of computation makes it both economically and logistically feasible to merge large databases and create new analyses. Researchers are now able to uncover relationships among demographic, attitudinal, behavioral, and geographic elements of the population. Those relationships are called "clusters."

Clusters

The saying "birds of a feather flock together" represents the idea of clustering. By combining demographic data, a market can be grouped into clusters, also known as "geodemographic segmentation systems."

Cluster systems take many demographic variables and create profiles of different individual or household characteristics, purchase behaviors, and media preferences. Most clusters used in media sales and analysis have catchy, descriptive names in an attempt to make them easier to remember. Examples are "Elite Suburbs," "2nd City Society," "Heart Landers," and "Rustic Living"—all from Claritas' PRIZM cluster system.

Marketing Tools magazine claims that cluster systems

are especially powerful when used in conjunction with business mapping. Sophisticated mapping software programs easily link demographics to any level of geography (a process called "geocoding"). Some software can pinpoint specific households with neighborhoods from . . . customer data and then create schematic maps of neighborhoods by cluster concentrations.

The geographic element distinguishes clusters from psychographic segments. Another difference is that cluster categories are based on socio-economic and consumer data, not attitudinal data.

When mapping and media mix, Zip codes are often used as a targeting tool. Radio stations tend to use Zip codes to target potential Arbitron diary keepers, but this is not an exact science. In *The Clustering of America* (1988), Michael Weiss introduced the use of Zip codes as a clustering device. His work introduced marketers to age, education, and buying segments originally developed by Claritas Corporation for their PRIZM database. As effective as Weiss was in describing clustering, the net result among media sellers was his Zip code analyses.

With more than 36,000 Zip codes in the United States, precise segmentation is difficult. A Zip code does not constitute a segmented market, even though a single Zip code can contain 35,000 addresses or more. In New York City, because of the density of the population, Zip codes are somewhat cohesive in terms of ethnic and socio-economic mix. In the smallest towns, there may be only one Zip code, thus defying segmentation. That is why the cluster systems were developed.

Lifestyles

Cluster analysis is often confused with psychographics, and the words *psychographics* and *lifestyles* tend to be used interchangeably. There is a difference, though: *psychographics* usually refers to a formal classification system that categorizes people into specific types based largely on psychological characteristics; *lifestyle* is more vague and generally refers to organizing people by attitudes or consumer behavior—"politically conservative," for example, or "avid golfer." Cluster systems are based on purchase behavior (i.e., "owns a cell phone") and demographics (age, sex, income, and education).

According to researcher James Fletcher, qualitative information about lifestyle includes data collected in one or more of the following categories: (1) activities: work, hobbies, social events, vacations, entertainment, club and community activity, shopping, sports; (2) interests: family, home, recreation, fashion, food and wine, media, personal achievement; (3) media behavior: light, medium, or heavy users of electronic media; local newspaper readership; magazine subscriptions; (4) recreation: sports fans, sports participants, travel for recreational purposes, live theater, concerts, movies; (5) social activity: joiners who frequent the social scene or participate in clubs and organizations, house bodies who concentrate on do-it-yourself projects and gardening; (6) purchase patterns: recent purchases, intention to purchase, likely choices when the purchase time arrives; (7) opinion: social issues, politics, business, education, products, culture, the future; (8) demographics: age, sex, education, income, occupation, family size, rent or own housing, geography.

In radio, demographics are often equated with age and sex. In general use, however, the additional elements listed above are all part of demographics. Given radio's ability to create communities of people with similar tastes and attitudes, it can be said that the medium not only serves markets, but also creates them.

ED SHANE

See also Audience Research Methods; Station Rep Firms

Further Reading

Beville, Hugh Malcolm, Jr., *Audience Ratings: Radio, Television, and Cable,* Hillsdale, New Jersey: Erlbaum, 1985; revised edition, 1988

Burns, George A., *Radio Imagery: Strategies in Station Positioning,* Studio City, California: Burns, 1980

Burns, George A., *Playing the Positioning Game: Aiming at the Core,* Studio City, California: Burns, 1981

Dygert, Warren B., *Radio As an Advertising Medium,* New York and London: McGraw-Hill, 1939

Fletcher, James E., *Handbook of Radio and Television Broadcasting: Research Procedures in Audience, Program, and Revenues,* New York: Van Nostrand Reinhold, 1981

Fletcher, James E., and Mark E. Dorming, *Profiting from Radio Ratings: A Manual for Radio Managers, Sales Managers, and Programmers,* Washington, D.C.: National Association of Broadcasters, 1989

Miller, Berna, "A Beginner's Guide to Demographics," *Marketing Tools* (October 1995)

Shane, Ed, *Selling Electronic Media,* Boston and Oxford: Focal Press, 1999

Turow, Joseph, "Breaking Up America: The Dark Side of Target Marketing," *American Demographics* 19, no. 11 (November 1997)

Weiss, Michael, *The Clustering of America,* New York: Harper and Row, 1988

Marketplace

U.S. Public Radio Program

Marketplace: *The International Magazine of Business and Finance* is a daily program on U.S. public radio billed as the "first truly global program using business and economics as its prism to understand the world." The program's trademark is its non–Wall Street approach, designed, in the words of program originator Jim Russell, "for normal human beings, not CEOs." It is known for its hip and sometimes irreverent reporting; it is short on statistical market data and long on feature reporting and analysis. *Marketplace* went on the air on 2 January 1989 and quickly became the fastest-growing national program on public radio, entering 2003 with nearly 6 million

listeners per week. *Marketplace* airs five days per week, with a 30-minute evening program and five 9-minute reports in the morning. It is carried on more than 355 stations throughout the United States and is also heard in Europe on the public radio satellite channel America One and worldwide on the Armed Forces Radio Network. The program is hosted by David Brancaccio and produced by J.J. Yore. *Marketplace* originates in Los Angeles and is distributed by Public Radio International of Minneapolis. In April 2000, Marketplace Productions was acquired by Minnesota Public Radio, which built a new program production center in downtown Los Angeles.

Origins

Marketplace was born at a time when public radio programmers were looking for a business program suitable specifically for public radio. During the summer of 1988, officials at Public Radio International (then the American Public Radio Network [APR]) approached former *All Things Considered* producer Tim Russell with a request that he provide a critique of its daily business program, *Business Update*, which was being produced for public radio by Columbia Broadcasting System (CBS) Radio. Russell's report concluded that, although the program featured solid reporting and was well produced, it had an unquestionably "CBS sound" that did not match the style that listeners had come to expect on public radio. Russell outlined in his report an alternative vision of a public radio business program that was slightly more witty and smart. This type of program, Russell felt, would not necessarily appeal to business professionals, but it could be targeted to a much broader, but still well-educated, audience.

In the fall of 1988, APR officials gathered a group of public radio programmers together at its Minnesota headquarters to discuss Russell's report and his idea for this new kind of business program. The concept won the group's endorsement, though it was agreed that, in order to avoid domination by the media establishment, the program would be produced neither in the Twin Cities nor on the East Coast. Instead, the new show would be produced in California so that it might develop its own voice and foster access to the Pacific Rim business markets. It thus became the first, and only, national daily news program to originate on the West Coast. The name *Marketplace* was selected as the main title specifically because it did not carry the strong Wall Street connotations of the words *business* or *finance*, which were relegated to the subtitle of the program. Russell was hired as the new program's executive producer and general manager, and within three months a staff was hired and the program went on the air, debuting 2 January 1989 from Long Beach, California. The program nearly went off the air after just a few months, but in 1990 USC Radio at the University of Southern California stepped in, offering money, new studios, and help in finding corporate underwriters. The program's original host, Jim Angle, left for a job at ABC in 1993 and was replaced by David Brancaccio, a former KQED public radio reporter (and a San Francisco rock disc jockey before that) who had opened the show's London bureau.

Covering Business

Marketplace draws from international bureaus in Tokyo, London, Beijing, and in South Africa; it has five domestic bureaus. The program features a number of key elements: it defines business as "*anything* having to do with money." It takes an international perspective on the assumption that business shapes world events. The program producers avoid statistics, operating on the maxim of "no data without context." Instead, the show uses an "op ed" approach for background and analysis by featuring a roster of about 75 commentators from a spectrum of cultures, political backgrounds, and ethnicities. It also maintains unique editorial relationships with such traditional sources as the *Economist Magazine,* London's *Financial Times,* and Reuters.

The fact that it is a "business program for the rest of us" is typified by reporting that shows the human side of economics and that attempts to demystify the world of finance (both general manager Russell and morning host Glaser promote their barely passing grades in college economics classes). Host David Brancaccio brags about not having an MBA, and on-air mentions of his home on USC's Fraternity Row and his daily commute to work on a bicycle add to the hip, quirky approach. The program's trademark irreverence is typified by the background music played when its hosts "Do the Numbers" each day: the song "Stormy Weather" is used when the Dow Jones Industrial Average is down, and "We're in the Money" is played when the Dow is up. It features a variety of non-economic feature stories on the assumption that every topic has some financial or business angle.

Forty-one percent of *Marketplace* listeners are women, and its audience is relatively young: almost 20 percent of its listeners are in the 25–34 age demographic, and nearly 30 percent are 35–44 years old. Its weekly audience, approaching 6 million listeners, is said to be the second-largest audience in the United States for a TV, cable, or radio business program, behind PBS's *Nightly Business Report.* In 1998 *Marketplace* won a Silver Baton award for broadcast journalism from Columbia University. In 2000, general manager Jim Russell received a Missouri Honor Medal from the University of Missouri's School of Journalism. In 2001 the program won the prestigious Peabody Award.

MARK BRAUN

Cast

Hosts   David Brancaccio
Morning Hosts Kai Ryssdal, Tess Vigeland

Producer

J.J. Yore

Programming History

Public Radio International   January 1989–present

Further Reading

Ahrens, Frank, "Funny Business: 'Marketplace' Keeps It Light with Humor and Music," *Washington Post* (12 January 1999)

Baxter, Kevin, "Popular 'Marketplace' Brings Business World to Street Level: Radio Program Focuses on Effects of High Finance, Commerce, and Industry on the Average Person," *Los Angeles Times* (1 January 1999)

Marketplace Radio Business News, <www.marketplace.org>

Puig, Claudia, "They're Putting a Friendly Face on Financial News Radio: For Six Years, 'Marketplace' Has Reached a Literate, Curious Audience, but Not One Necessarily Knowledgeable about Business," *Los Angeles Times* (1 June 1995)

Sarsfield, AnnMarie, "Program Appeals to Novice Investors," *Tampa Tribune* (17 October 1999)

Simon, Clea, "PRI's 'Marketplace' Means Business," *Boston Globe* (7 January 1999)

Markle, Fletcher 1921–1991

Canadian Writer, Producer, and Director

Fletcher Markle was a leading producer/writer/director (and sometime actor) during commercial radio's "second wave" in the 1940s. Inspired by the protean hyphenate Orson Welles, who later became a friend, Markle sustained the tradition of dramatic adventure exemplified by the *Mercury Theater*. When network radio died in the early 1950s, Markle was able to shift his dramatic vision to television and film.

Markle was one of the pioneering Canadian broadcasters who journeyed across the border to make a major impact on American entertainment. Born in Winnipeg and raised in Vancouver, the young Markle had a speech impediment, which was corrected by constant listening to and imitation of the narrator of the *March of Time,* Westbrook Van Voorhis. The adolescent also paid attention to the speech patterns of the entire program's cast and was especially entranced by the resonant tones of Orson Welles. Soon he was speaking and writing in the Wellesian style. He began writing, directing, and acting for a local program on Sunday afternoons, *Imagine, Please.* Impressing the radio community in Vancouver, he again emulated his distant mentor and sold adaptations of *Jane Eyre* and *Treasure Island* to the regional dramatic series *From the Bookshelf.*

One of the leading producers in Canadian radio, Andrew Allen, took notice, and Markle was hired to write radio plays for the Canadian Broadcasting Corporation (CBC) series *Baker's Dozen.* Writing for an ensemble, Markle also based scripts on his own life, including "There Was a Young Man," which was influenced by "lost generation" literary lions F. Scott Fitzgerald and Ernest Hemingway. In 1942 he enlisted in the Canadian Royal Air Force and wrote scripts for the documentary series *Comrade in Arms.* Replacing Edward R. Murrow, he wrote narration for a British Broadcasting Corporation (BBC) short film about German air attacks, *The V-1: Story of the Robot Bomb,* which was nominated for an Academy Award in 1944.

After the war, Markle continued his work for Allen, writing and directing for an anthology series, *Radio Folio.* His words captured the ear of legendary writer Norman Corwin, and he was invited to write and direct shows for the Columbia Broadcasting System's (CBS) experimental series *Columbia Workshop.* While in New York, he first met his hero, Orson Welles, and played for him transcription discs of a Canadian production, *Life with Adam,* a fictionalized account of Welles' radio and Broadway exploits. Welles hired Markle to produce and direct the satire for his *Mercury Summer Theater of the Air,* with regulars including conductor Bernard Hermann and actress Mercedes McCambridge, whom Markle would later marry. Over the years, he assisted Welles in numerous projects, including writing scenes for *The Lady from Shanghai* and researching two television pilots.

In 1947 CBS programmer Davidson Taylor contracted Markle to produce and direct the most ambitious anthology series in postwar radio, *Studio One.* Again with Wellesian flair, Markle assembled his own repertory company of solid radio professionals, including Everett Sloane, Anne Burr, Hester Sondergaard, and Robert Dryden. Markle was given complete freedom in the selection of scripts, and he opened the series with an adaptation of Malcolm Lowry's autobiographical *Under the Volcano.* He took a chance on novices, hiring Agnes Eckhardt, for example, to adapt novels of Sinclair Lewis. Eckhardt, who would later use her married name Nixon, became one of daytime television's legendary creators. Markle received the George Foster Peabody Award for his production of Robert Ardrey's *Thunder Rock.*

Markle resisted casting stars on the New York–based *Studio One*. When Ford began sponsoring the show in October 1948, the automobile manufacturer demanded big names, and production was shifted to Los Angeles under the new series title *Ford Theater*. The inaugural broadcast, an adaptation of *Madame Bovary*, featured Marlene Dietrich, Van Heflin, and Claude Rains. No longer an ensemble, the main attraction was star power: Burt Lancaster (*Double Indemnity*), Lucille Ball and James Garfield (*The Big Street*), Ingrid Bergman (*Camille*), Gene Kelly (*The Gentle People*), and Montgomery Clift (*Wuthering Heights*). Markle returned to acting, appearing opposite Helen Hayes in *A Farewell to Arms*. He also developed a friendship with Jack Benny because of their successful radio adaptation of Benny's notorious movie, *The Horn Blows at Midnight*. Even with movie luminaries and familiar plots, *Ford Theater* lasted less than a year; radio drama was doomed because of the invasion of television.

Markle switched to directing motion pictures and employed many of the actors he had worked with on the *Ford* series. He directed the caper movie *Jigsaw* (1949) for United Artists and the social drama *Night into Mourning* (1951) for Metro Goldwyn Mayer. In 1952 he returned to CBS and New York, having been hired to produce the fourth season of the television anthology series *Studio One*. Working with directors Franklin Schaffner and Paul Nickell, he produced approximately 40 live telecasts. For the production of the romantic teleplay "Rendezvous," he gave fellow Canadian Lorne Greene his first starring role in the United States.

Markle's success with *Studio One* led to his directing the first live color series from Hollywood, the nostalgic *Life with Father* (1953–55), in which Markle showed his directorial versatility by supervising this comedy starring Leon Ames and Lurene Tuttle. Throughout the 1950s he was hired to direct a wide array of genres: Broadway adaptations for *Front Row Center* (1955), suspenseful episodes of the *George Sanders Mystery Theater* (1957), police action on Lee Marvin's *M-Squad* (1957), and epic adventures on *Tales of the Vikings* (1959). In the early 1960s he produced a pilot for Boris Karloff's *Thriller* and directed the situation comedy *Father of the Bride*, with Robert Maxwell. During this period Markle directed one of Disney's most popular animal films of all time, *The Incredible Journey* (1963)

In the early 1960s, the onset of diabetes prevented Markle from undertaking demanding productions, and he returned to Canada. He created and hosted the long-running interview series *Telescope*. He conducted over 300 filmed interviews, including rare talks with Buster Keaton and Walt Disney. In the early 1970s, he was appointed head of the television drama department of the CBC. In 1976 he produced four specials for the CBC on the history of the Olympics, narrated by Christopher Plummer.

In 1979 Markle and Elliott Lewis tried to revive radio drama by producing and directing *Sears Radio Theater* on CBS. Broadcast every night from Los Angeles and divided into such theme nights as "The Western," "Love-and-Hate," and "Adventure," this hour-long series featured such established names as Howard Duff, Eve Arden, Daws Butler, and Hans Conried. After a year Sears and CBS withdrew support, and the series switched networks, continuing for nearly two years as *Mutual Radio Theater*. Again, Markle and his generation learned the sad fact that there is a small audience for any type of drama on radio.

Fletcher Markle was one of those creative individuals whose sensibility was formed by radio. He was able to revive the tradition of national drama on radio for several years after World War II. When the possibilities for creative expression became limited, Markle showed that directing techniques learned in radio could be transferred to film and television. To the end though, his heart belonged to his first medium; he was very active in the Society to Preserve and Encourage Radio, Drama, Variety, and Comedy (SPERDVAC) before his death in 1991.

RON SIMON

See also Canadian Radio Drama; Mercury Theater of the Air; Playwrights on Radio

Fletcher Markle. Born in Winnipeg, Manitoba, Canada, 27 March 1921. Actor and writer for local Vancouver programs, 1940–41; hired to write scripts for CBC series, *Baker's Dozen*, 1941; enlisted in Royal Canadian Air Force, 1942; appeared *in Journey Together*, 1942–45; writer and director, *Radio Folio*, 1946; producer and director, CBS, 1947–48; directed films for United Artists and MGM, 1949–51; producer, CBS television version of *Studio One*, 1952–53; directed television comedy, *Life with Father*, 1953–55; freelance television director, 1955–59; producer of *Thriller* with Boris Karloff, 1960; returned to Canada and created *Telescope*, oversaw CBC's television drama department; produced and directed *Sears Radio Theater* and *Mutual Radio Theater*, 1979–82; adapted *The Short Happy Life of Francis Macomber* and Edith Wharton's *Summer*, 1983–84. Received George Foster Peabody Award, 1947; member of Society to Preserve and Encourage Radio Drama, Variety, and Comedy. Died in Pasadena, California, 23 May 1991.

Radio Series

1940	*Imagine, Please; Theatre Time; From the Bookshelf*
1941	*Baker's Dozen*
1944	*Stage 44*
1946	*Columbia Workshop*
1947	*Mercury Summer Theatre of the Air; Studio One*
1948	*Ford Theater*

1979–80 *Sears Radio Theater*
1980–81 *Mutual Radio Theater*

Television Series

Studio One, 1952–53; *Life with Father*, 1953–55; *Front Row Center*, 1955; *The Ford Theatre*, 1955; *Panic*, 1957; *Without Warning*, 1957; *The George Sanders Mystery Theater*, 1957; *M-Squad*, 1957; *Colgate Theatre:* "Tonight in Havana," 1958; *Buckskin*, 1958; *Tales of the Vikings*, 1959; *Hong Kong*; *Thriller*, 1960; *Telescope*, 1960s; *Father of the Bride*, 1961–62; *The Olympics: A Television History of the Golden Games*, 1976

Films

The V-1: Story of the Robot Bomb, 1944; *Journey Together*, 1945; *Jigsaw*, 1949; *Night into Mourning* (a.k.a *People in Love*), 1951; *The Man with the Cloak*, 1951; *The Incredible Journey*, 1963

Further Reading

Skutch, Ira, editor, *Five Directors: The Golden Years of Radio: Based on Interviews with Himan Brown, Axel Gruenberg, Fletcher Markle, Arch Oboler, Robert Lewis Shayon*, Lanham, Maryland: Scarecrow Press, and Los Angeles: Directors Guild of America, 1998

Maxwell, James Clerk 1831–1879

Scottish Physicist and Theorizer of Radio Waves

James Clerk Maxwell was a physicist best known for his contributions to electromagnetic theory, including predictions of electromagnetic radiation that Heinrich Hertz later demonstrated in the laboratory and that Guglielmo Marconi and others applied in developing wireless communication systems. The influence of his experimental and theoretical work reached beyond these applications, paving the way for Einstein's theory of relativity and for theories about the structure of atoms and molecules.

Origins

James Clerk Maxwell was born on 13 June 1831 in Edinburgh, Scotland. His father, John Clerk, assumed the name Maxwell in legal proceedings after inheriting land not far from Edinburgh in southwestern Scotland. A house was built there and the estate named Glenlair. From time to time throughout his life, Maxwell returned to the quiet country life at Glenlair and did much of his writing there.

Maxwell's mother, Frances Cay, who supervised his early education, died when he was eight years old. After spending two years with an unsatisfactory tutor, in 1841 Maxwell was sent to Edinburgh Academy, where he took honors in English, English verse, and mathematics. Maxwell's father, a lawyer and fellow of the Royal Society of Edinburgh, took an active interest in his son's progress, taking him to meetings of the Royal Society. When Maxwell was 14, his father showed the boy's paper describing a new method for drawing ovals to J.D.

Forbes, professor of natural philosophy at Edinburgh University. The paper was read at a meeting of the Royal Society and printed in the April 1846 proceedings.

In 1847 Maxwell entered the University of Edinburgh. In October 1850 he went to Cambridge (Peterhouse College for one term, then Trinity College). During this time, his experiments in geometrical optics led to the discovery of the "fish-eye" lens. In 1854 he graduated second wrangler (awarded for excellence in mathematics) and first Smith's prizeman (for an essay incorporating original research). He then became a fellow at Trinity and a lecturer in hydrostatics and optics. In a paper read to the Cambridge Philosophical Society in 1855, Maxwell provided a method of approaching electrical problems by using mathematical language to discuss the lines of force surrounding the electrical and magnetic fields Michael Faraday had demonstrated. In *On Faraday's Lines of Force* (1855–56), Maxwell used an analogy of space as filled with a medium or with an imaginary, massless fluid. Electric and magnetic fields could then be understood as analogous to motion in this incompressible fluid. He worked out a series of equations to account for the continuum that the lines of force seemed to create within that medium. In an essay that won the fourth Adams prize at Cambridge, Maxwell used mathematical proofs to demonstrate that Saturn's rings could not be solid but must be composed of a multitude of small satellites.

In 1856 Maxwell accepted a professorship of natural philosophy at Marischal College in Aberdeen and in 1858 married the principal's daughter, Katherine Mary Dewar. When a reorganization of the college eliminated his position at Aberdeen in 1860, Maxwell became a professor of natural philosophy at King's College. There, in London, he renewed an earlier interest in color mixing, set up a laboratory in the attic, and with his wife's help began a series of experiments in color vision. Using what he called his "colour-box" he investigated variations in color sensitivity across the retina. In a lecture to the Royal Institution on the theory of three primary colors, he demonstrated the first color photograph. His wife also assisted in his experiments to measure the viscosity of gases.

Electromagnetic Theory

Maxwell continued his work on electromagnetic theory, producing two more significant papers. *On Physical Lines of Force* (1861–62) was the result of his attempts to illustrate Faraday's law of induction. Maxwell constructed a mechanical model and attempted to demonstrate that there is in principle a physical mechanism in space that carries transverse waves and accounts for what was known about electromagnetism. Calculating the speed at which these waves travel, he found that it was very close to the speed of light and concluded that what we perceive as light is actually another phenomenon of electromagnetism. In *A Dynamical Theory of the Electromagnetic Field* (1864), Maxwell departed from the idea of a physical medium and instead advanced the concept of field as an energy-bearing continuum. To describe the electrical field, he developed a group of equations. In their final form, Maxwell's Equations provided a method to predict the behavior of electricity and magnetism under given conditions.

In 1865, following an illness, Maxwell retired to Glenlair. Although he took periodic trips to London to serve as external examiner for mathematical exams at Cambridge, he devoted much of his time to scientific writing, including *Theory of Heat* (1870) and *Treatise on Electricity and Magnetism* (1873). In 1871 he was appointed Chair of Experimental Physics at Cambridge University. There he designed and oversaw the creation of the Cavendish Laboratory, where experimental work done under his direction emphasized precision in measurements.

Maxwell died of abdominal cancer at the age of 48 on 5 November 1879 and was buried in a small churchyard in Parton, Scotland.

Although some of his contemporaries received more public recognition during his lifetime, James Clerk Maxwell's influence on 20th-century physics has been more far-reaching. Those who had corresponded with him and would carry on his work and keep his memory and research alive became known as the "Maxwellians." His theories predicting electromagnetic radiation led directly to the experimental and applied work underlying our entire system of radio communication. He speculated about the effect of the motion of the emitter of light

on the velocity of light, and his theories paved the way for Einstein's special theory of relativity. He made significant advances in the kinetic theory of gases, contributed to the development of quantum theory, and conducted innovative studies in several other scientific fields. On the 100th anniversary of Maxwell's birth in 1931, the importance of his work was described in a tribute by Einstein as the most profound and fruitful change in the conception of reality in physics since the time of Newton.

LUCY A. LIGGETT

See also Early Wireless; Hertz, Heinrich

James Clerk Maxwell. Born in Edinburgh, Scotland, 13 June 1831. Only child of John Clerk Maxwell and Frances Cay; attended University of Edinburgh, 1847–50, Cambridge University, 1850–54; graduated second wrangler and first Smith's prizeman, Trinity College, 1854; fellow and lecturer, Trinity College, England, 1854–56; professor, Marischal College, Aberdeen, Scotland, 1856–60; professor, King's College, London, England, 1860–65; elected to Royal Society, 1861; appointed chair of experimental physics, Cambridge University, 1871; appointed to British Association for the Advancement of Science committee to develop international electrical standards, 1862. Died in Cambridge, England, 5 November 1879.

Selected Publications

On Faraday's Lines of Force, 1855–56
On Physical Lines of Force, 1861–62
A Dynamical Theory of the Electromagnetic Field, 1864; edited by Thomas F. Torrance, 1982
Theory of Heat, 1870
Treatise on Electricity and Magnetism, 2 vols., 1873
Matter and Motion, 1876
Electrical Researches of Hon. Henry Cavendish, 1879
Elementary Treatise on Electricity, edited by W. Garnett, 1881
Scientific Papers of James Clerk Maxwell, 2 vols., edited by W.D. Niven, 1890

Further Reading

Campbell, Lewis, and William Garnett, *The Life of James Clerk Maxwell, with Selections from His Correspondence and Occasional Writings and a Sketch of His Contributions to Science,* London, 1882; reprint, New York: Johnson Reprint, 1969
Domb, Cyril, "James Clerk Maxwell—100 Years Later," *Nature* (15 November 1979)
Everitt, C.W.F., *James Clerk Maxwell: Physicist and Natural Philosopher,* New York: Scribner, 1975
Hendry, John, *James Clerk Maxwell and the Theory of the Electromagnetic Field,* Boston and Bristol: Hilger, 1986

Simpson, Thomas K., *Maxwell on the Electromagnetic Field: A Guided Study*, New Brunswick, New Jersey: Rutgers University Press, 1997

Tricker, R.A.R., *The Contributions of Faraday and Maxwell to Electrical Science*, Oxford and New York: Pergamon Press, 1966

Mayflower Decision

FCC Radio License Renewal Decision, 1941

The *Mayflower* decision, issued by the Federal Communications Commission (FCC) in 1941, is most noted for its conclusion that, as public trustees, broadcasters could not use their stations to advocate their own causes. In other words, broadcasters should not editorialize.

In 1939 the Yankee Network filed an application to renew the license of its Boston radio station, WAAB. At the same time, the Mayflower Broadcasting Corporation filed an application with the FCC to operate a radio station on the same frequency used by WAAB, thus challenging the renewal of WAAB. In its challenge, Mayflower claimed that WAAB was violating federal law by broadcasting editorials that endorsed certain political candidates for public office.

WAAB did not deny broadcasting the editorials in 1937 and 1938, but the station had discontinued the practice after being questioned by the FCC. As a result of this change in station policy and because Mayflower was found not to be financially qualified, WAAB's license was renewed. But the *Mayflower* decision sent a signal to broadcasters that station editorials were not considered to be in the public interest.

In writing the *Mayflower* decision, the FCC pointed out that the broadcaster has the initial responsibility for the conduct of the station. But because radio frequencies are limited, the interests of the public must be paramount over those of the licensee. Therefore, according to the FCC: "[T]he broadcaster cannot be an advocate. A truly free radio cannot be used to advocate the causes of the licensee. It cannot be used to support the candidacies of his friends. It cannot be devoted to the support of principles he happens to regard most favorably."

In the language of the *Mayflower* decision, the FCC was expressing its interpretation of the Communications Act of 1934 and the phrase "public interest, convenience or necessity." Broadcasters are public trustees who have the privilege of using public property—frequency space on the electromagnetic spectrum. Therefore, they are licensed to operate their stations in the "public interest" (as the phrase has been shortened over the years). In *Mayflower*, the FCC stated: "Indeed, as one

licensed to operate in a public domain the licensee has assumed the obligation of presenting all sides of important public questions, fairly, objectively and without bias." This was the basis for the FCC policy prohibiting radio editorials.

But that policy was to be challenged when the FCC encountered more station renewal petitions involving coverage of public issues. In the 1945 *WHKC* case, a station license renewal was challenged on the basis of a policy prohibiting the sale of commercial time for programs that discuss controversial subjects. In resolving the case, the FCC accepted an agreement between the station and the labor-union petitioner. The station agreed to change its policy and consider each request for commercial time on an individual basis. The commission noted that "the operation of any station under the extreme principles that no time shall be sold for the discussion of controversial public issues . . . is inconsistent with the concept of public interest established by the Communications Act."

In the 1946 *Scott* decision, the FCC was petitioned to revoke a station's license based on its refusal to make program time available for the discussion of atheism. The licensee of the station defended the refusal based on its "firm belief that it would not be in the public interest to lend our facilities to Mr. Scott for the dissemination and propagation of atheism." The commission stated that the station could not have a policy that denied views "which may have a high degree of unpopularity." Again, balanced coverage of controversial issues became the central point of the petition.

By the late 1940s, the FCC had decided to hold hearings to clear up confusion about its policies in this area. In 1949 the commission issued what came to be known as the "fairness doctrine." The doctrine established the policy that "broadcast licensees have an affirmative duty generally to encourage and implement the broadcast of all sides of controversial public issues over their facilities, over and beyond their obligation to make available on demand opportunities for the expression of opposing views." Ironically, the fairness doctrine also reversed FCC policy banning station editorials.

As a result of broadcaster complaints, the National Association of Broadcasters asked the commission to reconsider its policy on station editorials. After reviewing its policies on coverage of public issues, the FCC concluded that "overt licensee editorialization, within reasonable limits and subject to the general requirements of fairness detailed above, is not contrary to the public interest. . . . Licensee editorialization is but one aspect of freedom of expression by means of radio."

FREDERIC A. LEIGH

See also Controversial Issues; Editorializing; Fairness Doctrine

Further Reading

Federal Communications Commission, *In the Matter of The Mayflower Broadcasting Corporation and the Yankee Network Inc. (WAAB)* 8 FCC 323 (1941)

Federal Communications Commission, *In Re United Broadcasting Co. (WHKC)*, 10 FCC 515 (1945)

Federal Communications Commission, *In Re Petition of Robert Harold Scott for Revocation of Licenses of Radio Stations KQW, KPO, and KFRC*, 11 FCC 372 (1946)

Federal Communications Commission, *In the Matter of Editorializing by Broadcast Licenses*, 13 FCC 1246 (1949) [later known as the Fairness Doctrine]

Franklin, Marc A., *The First Amendment and the Fourth Estate: Communications Law for Undergraduates*, Mineola, New York: The Foundation Press, 1977; 7th edition, 1997

Gillmor, Donald M., and Jerome A. Barron, *Mass Communication Law: Cases and Comment*, St. Paul, Minnesota: West Publishing, 1969; 3rd edition, 1979

Horwitz, Robert Britt, *The Irony of Regulatory Reform*, New York: Oxford University Press, 1989

Kahn, Frank J., editor, *Documents of American Broadcasting*, New York: Appleton-Century-Crofts, 1968; 4th edition, Englewood Cliffs, New Jersey: Prentice Hall, 1984

Nelson, Harold L., and Dwight L. Teeter, Jr., *Law of Mass Communications*, Mineola, New York: The Foundation Press, 1982; 9th edition, 1998

Pember, Don R., *Mass Media Law*, Dubuque, Iowa: Brown, 1977; 9th edition, Boston, Massachusetts: McGraw Hill, 1998

McBride, Mary Margaret 1899–1976

U.S. Radio Journalist and Program Host

A broadcast journalist and what would today be called a talk show host, Mary Margaret McBride projected a warm, down-home personality on her highly popular, long-running radio programs. For some 20 years she was the best-known woman in radio, although today she is almost forgotten.

Origins

McBride was born at the very end of the 19th century in Missouri. As a child, she moved frequently from farm to farm with her family. She entered William Woods College (then a preparatory school) in 1906. In 1916 she entered the University of Missouri, from which she graduated with a degree in journalism in 1919.

After a year as a reporter for the *Cleveland Press* (Ohio), she worked as a reporter for the *New York Evening Mail* until 1924. She then turned to freelance magazine writing, soon becoming very successful, with her work appearing in *The Saturday Evening Post*, *Cosmopolitan*, and *Good Housekeeping*, among others. McBride also edited the woman's page of the Newspaper Enterprise Association syndicate from 1934 to 1935. She became one of the best-paid women of her time, but the Depression cut into her income, as it did many others', and opened up another option.

Radio Career

McBride's radio career began in 1934 with a competition among 50 women to host an advice and interview program on New York City radio station WOR. Successful in the competition, she appeared as "Martha Deane" (a name owned by the station), playing the role of a grandmother with several children and grandchildren. After three weeks she gave it all away on the air and admitted that she was no grandmother, merely "a reporter who would like to come here every day and tell you about places I go, people I meet." This did not seem to hurt her rising popularity one bit.

Paralleling much of her magazine journalism (which continued), the program offered daily advice directed largely at women. Her advice was readily accepted by listeners due to the

Mary Margaret McBride
Courtesy CBS Photo Archive

combination of her clear knowledge about the matters discussed, her homey Missouri accent, and her ability to project (even as a young woman) a kind of grandmotherly kindness combined with wit. And she could think rapidly, making a new art of the ad-lib interview and program (none were scripted). As radio historian Erik Barnouw put it, her career "was built on a unique ability to draw others out."

McBride's program began to appear three times a week on the Columbia Broadcasting System (CBS) network in 1937 as a 45-minute amalgam of ad-lib commentary and interviews that soon drew an audience in the millions. (She continued daily on WOR until 1940 when other women took over the Martha Deane role.) It also allowed her a greater degree of freedom from network oversight than most program hosts enjoyed. Celebrities from all walks of life appeared (or sought to appear) on McBride's program, and her own folksy and plain-

talking commentary made her an excellent saleswoman for sponsors' products. Although advertisers eagerly sought to have their products touted on her program, she would not promote any product that she had not personally tried and liked. And Mary Margaret (as she was known to her listeners) refused to advertise tobacco or alcohol.

McBride's daily radio program was carried on NBC from 1941 to 1950. In 1948 NBC attempted to transfer her radio popularity to television by placing her talk and interview program right after Milton Berle's hotly popular *Texaco Star Theatre*. But as a conversationalist, her program was all interviews and discussion—"talking heads" primarily—decades before such talk programs became a staple of television. McBride never left her seat for the entire 50-minute program, after first telling her TV viewers that she looked "better from the table up." The program was canceled after three months, and

McBride became one of the first of many radio stars who failed to make a successful transition to television. But she had staying power on radio—her tenth anniversary program was held at Madison Square Garden, and her 15th anniversary show in 1949 was broadcast from Yankee stadium, "the only facility large enough to hold the 75,000 people who filled every seat and formed huge crowds outside" (Hilmes).

In 1950 McBride left NBC—taking many of her sponsors with her—and went to the struggling American Broadcasting Company (ABC) network. She finally retired from network radio in 1954 after the death of her longtime business manager and partner, Stella Karn. From 1953 to 1956 McBride wrote a syndicated newspaper column for the Associated Press. After 1960 she was heard on a syndicated program of the *New York Herald Tribune* radio operation. In her last years she conducted a thrice-weekly radio show from her own upstate New York home. She died in early 1976.

CHRISTOPHER H. STERLING

See also Women in Radio

Mary Margaret McBride. Born in Paris, Missouri, 16 November 1899. Studied journalism at University of Missouri, 1916–19; reporter, *Cleveland Press*, 1919–20, *New York Evening Mail*, 1920–24; freelance magazine journalism, 1920s and 1930s; on WOR, New York City, as "Martha Deane," 1934–40; host of own national interview program, CBS, 1937–41, NBC, 1941–50, and ABC, 1950–54; television program, 1948; authored syndicated column for Associated Press, 1953–56. Awarded medal for "greatest contribution to radio" by Women's National Exposition of the Arts and Industries, 1936. Died in West Shokan, New York, 7 April 1976.

Radio Series

1934–40   *Martha Deane*
1937–54   *Mary Margaret McBride*

Television Series

Mary Margaret McBride Show, 1948

Selected Publications

Jazz (with Paul Whiteman), 1926
Charm: A Book about It and Those Who Have It, for Those Who Want It (With Alexander Williams), 1927
Paris Is a Woman's Town (with Helen Josephy), 1929
London Is a Man's Town, but Women Go There (with Helen Josephy), 1930
Story of Dwight W. Morrow, 1930
New York Is Everybody's Town (with Helen Josephy), 1931
Beer and Skittles—A Friendly Modern Guide to Germany (with Helen Josephy), 1932
Here's Martha Deane, 1936
How Dear to My Heart, 1940
America for Me, 1941
Tune In for Elizabeth: Career Story of a Radio Interviewer, 1945
How to Be a Successful Advertising Woman, 1948
Mary Margaret McBride's Harvest of American Cooking, 1957
Mary Margaret McBride's Encyclopedia of Cooking, 1958
Growing Up of Mary Elizabeth, 1966
Long Way from Missouri, 1959
Out of the Air: The Most Radio-Active Woman in America–Her Own Story of the Golden Decades of Broadcasting, 1960

Further Reading

Cerf, Bennett, "Here Comes McBride," *Saturday Review of Literature* (1 March 1947)
Churchill, Allen, "Mary Margaret McBride," *American Mercury* (January 1949)
Heggie, Barbara, "Mary Margaret McBride: A Profile," *The New Yorker* (19 December 1942)
Hilmes, Michele, "Origins of the Magazine Format," in *Radio Voices: American Broadcasting, 1922–1952*, by Hilmes, Minneapolis: University of Minnesota Press, 1997
St. John, Jacqueline D., "Sex Role Stereotyping in Early Broadcast History: The Career of Mary Margaret McBride," *Frontiers* 3 (1978)

McDonald, Eugene F., Jr. 1886–1958

U.S. Radio Manufacturer and Broadcaster

One of the founding fathers of the broadcasting and consumer electronics industries, "Commander" Eugene F. McDonald, Jr., guided Zenith Radio Corporation for almost 40 years as its founding president. McDonald also played a significant personal role in the adoption of the shortwave spectrum for long-distance communications, the formation of the National Association of Broadcasters (NAB), and the creation of the Federal Communications Commission (FCC).

Born in Syracuse, New York, 11 March 1886, McDonald was fascinated as a child with electrical and mechanical devices and in high school had a business repairing electric doorbells. In 1912 McDonald organized a company to finance car purchases on time payments, a first in the auto industry. He enlisted in the navy during World War I and held the rank of Lieutenant in Naval Intelligence.

In 1921 McDonald joined two young radio amateurs, Karl Hassel and R.H.G. Mathews, who had formed the Chicago Radio Laboratory and were manufacturing and selling radio receivers. In 1923 they formed the Zenith Radio Corporation with McDonald as president. In the same year, McDonald founded pioneer Chicago station WJAZ to broadcast music and to communicate with the 1923–24 Arctic expedition of his close friend, Donald B. MacMillan. WJAZ broadcast messages and entertainment programming to the expedition during the long Arctic night, and these programs also became wildly popular to a national radio audience. The national exposure from the expedition was invaluable in McDonald's drive to develop Zenith as a national brand. Also in 1923, McDonald formed and became the first president of NAB.

McDonald, then a Lieutenant Commander in the Naval Reserve Force, played a seminal role in the development of shortwave radio for long-distance communications when Zenith developed shortwave receivers and transmitters for the 1925 MacMillan Arctic Expedition. He also persuaded navy communications chief Admiral Ridley McLean to send a radio amateur equipped with similar gear on the fleet's 1925 Pacific cruise. The communications over the 12,000 miles between the MacMillan expedition in northern Greenland and the fleet in New Zealand waters had much to do with the adoption of the shortwave spectrum for global communications. The 1925 MacMillan Arctic Expedition, with McDonald as both cosponsor and the second in command, also marked the first use of ship-to-ship shortwave telephonic communications, the first use of aircraft in major geographic exploration, and the first successful use of shortwave communications in polar regions; furthermore, the expedition served as a training ground for American polar explorer Richard Evelyn Byrd.

At the same time, McDonald became concerned about the seemingly dictatorial powers of the Secretary of Commerce over the radio industry and was upset that WJAZ was forced to share airtime with a station in Denver. Hoping to force legal action that would lead to a different approach to the government regulation of the emerging radio industry, McDonald intentionally shifted the frequency of WJAZ to a channel reserved for Canadian broadcasters. Secretary of Commerce Herbert Hoover responded by taking McDonald to court, where McDonald's view of the limited powers of the federal government, based on the 1912 Radio Act, prevailed. In the congressional hearings that followed, McDonald was one of several people who suggested the formation of a federal commission to regulate the radio industry. In his testimony, McDonald was the first person to use the name "Federal Communications Commission." Following the hearings, Congress formed the Federal Radio Commission in 1927, which in 1934 became the Federal Communications Commission (FCC).

McDonald's genius for leadership, coupled with the financial and managerial acumen of Zenith executive Hugh Robertson, enabled Zenith to withstand the crash of 1929 and the early years of the Depression with much more resilience than most of their competitors. Zenith emerged from the Depression as a major force in the consumer electronics industry. The company prospered in the latter part of the Depression, producing the famous Big Black Dial radios.

McDonald's private life was as flamboyant and public as was his effect on the radio and broadcasting industries. Long one of the wealthiest and most attractive bachelors of his generation, McDonald lived aboard a series of ever-larger yachts, culminating in his 1928 purchase of the 185 foot long *Mizpah*. McDonald's fascination with the entertainment industry, and not incidentally with showgirls and singers, led to lifelong friendships with many of the nation's leading entertainers, who were regular guests aboard the *Mizpah*. At the beginning of World War II, McDonald contributed the ship to the U.S. Navy, where she served as an armed convoy escort and command vessel throughout the war. McDonald married rather late in life and had two children.

McDonald's personal interest in world affairs combined with the gathering clouds of war to lead the Zenith Corporation to develop the Zenith Trans-Oceanic radio line, which was introduced almost simultaneously with Pearl Harbor. In the early months of World War II, the ever-patriotic McDonald led most radio manufacturers to contribute their patent holdings to the government for the duration of the war. Unlike

Zenith invented the first wireless television remote control in 1956, named Space Commander in McDonald's honor (later Space Command).

From his earliest days in radio, McDonald's close associates remarked on his uncanny ability to predict the future of this very innovative and volatile industry. McDonald was inducted posthumously into the Broadcast Pioneers Hall of Fame on 4 April 1967, nine years after his death. Among the accomplishments listed in the citation were his roles as founder, president, and first chairman of the board of Zenith Radio Corporation; his dynamic merchandising strategies; his inventions (29 patents) and innovations; his role as explorer; and his role as the first president of NAB. He was also cited for having established one of the nation's pioneer radio stations (WJAZ) and for fostering the development of shortwave radio, international communication, ship-to-shore, FM, VHF and UHF television, radar, and subscription television. In 2000 the Commander was an inaugural inductee into the Consumer Electronics Hall of Fame by the Consumer Electronics Association.

HAROLD N. CONES AND JOHN H. BRYANT

See also National Association of Broadcasters; Zenith Radio

Eugene F. McDonald. Born in Syracuse, New York, 11 March 1886. Served as Lieutenant in World War I; formed and became president of Zenith Radio Corporation with Karl Hassel and R.H.G. Mathews, 1923; founded WJAZ radio station, Chicago, 1923; formed and became president of National Association of Broadcasters (NAB), 1923; developed shortwave radio receivers, 1925; pioneered early television with Zenith's W9XZV, 1939; helped create Zenith's FM radio station, WEFM, 1940; posthumously inducted into Broadcast Pioneers Hall of Fame, 1967; posthumously inducted into Consumer Electronics Hall of Fame, 2000. Died in Chicago, Illinois, 15 May 1958.

Selected Publications

Youth Must Fly: Gliding and Soaring For America, 1942

Further Reading

Bensman, Marvin, "The Zenith-WJAZ Case and the Chaos of 1926–27," *Journal of Broadcasting* 4 (Fall 1970)
Bryant, John H., and Harold N. Cones, *The Zenith Trans-Oceanic: The Royalty of Radios,* Atglen, Pennsylvania: Schiffer, 1995
Bryant, John H., and Harold N. Cones, *Dangerous Crossings: The First Modern Polar Expedition, 1925,* Annapolis, Maryland: Naval Institute Press, 2000
"Commander McDonald of Zenith," *Fortune* (June 1945)

Eugene F. McDonald, Jr.
Courtesy of Zenith

many of his competitors, McDonald also established a design and planning unit early in the war to design the initial postwar commercial lines. This planning unit also allowed Zenith to maintain employment for a number of engineers who had families in occupied Europe and thus could not qualify for war production work. This kind of generosity coupled with enlightened self-interest was typical of McDonald's approach to life.

Commander McDonald's lifelong passion for television began in 1933. Zenith went on the air with W9XZV in 1939, and in 1941, the first color broadcast was transmitted. Because of McDonald's interest in FM radio and his friendship with Edwin Howard Armstrong, Zenith's FM station went on the air on 2 February 1940, operating under the call letters W9XEN (later W51C and WEFM). McDonald is probably best remembered today as the first and most vocal advocate of what was to become cable and pay-per-view television. Thanks to his personal persistence and political acumen, Zenith received permission to conduct a limited commercial test of "Phonevision" in 1951. Also under his direction and guidance,

Cones, Harold N., and John H. Bryant, *Eugene F. McDonald, Jr.: Communications Pioneer Lost to History*, Record of Proceedings, 3rd International Symposium on Telecommunications History, Washington, D.C.: Independent Telephone Historical Foundation, 1995

Cones, Harold N., and John H. Bryant, *Zenith Radio: The Early Years: 1919–1935*, Atglen, Pensylvania: Schiffer, 1997

Cones, Harold N., and John H. Bryant, "The Car Salesman and the Accordion Designer: Contributions of Eugene F. McDonald, Jr., and Robert Davol Budlong to Radio," *Journal of Radio Studies* 8, no. 1 (Spring 2001)

Zenith Radio Corporation, *The Zenith Story: A History from 1919*, Chicago: Zenith Radio Corporation, 1955

McGannon, Don 1921–1984

U.S. Broadcasting Executive

Don McGannon was the long-time head of Westinghouse Broadcasting (Group W) and a respected member of the industry's leadership in the 1960s and 1970s. He sought quality programs and public service as well as profits. He is best known for Group W's successful introduction of the all-news format to radio and for developing a stronger commitment to public affairs by the Group W stations. He was a strong believer that broadcasters should serve in the public interest.

Origins

Donald McGannon was born in New York City in 1921. One of four children, he attended Fordham University (which would decades later name a communications research center after him), earning a B.A. in 1940. As with many others of his generation, he served in the U.S. Army during the war (becoming a major), returning to Fordham to earn a law degree in 1947. Admitted to the Bar in both New York and Connecticut, McGannon became a practicing attorney for several years. He worked briefly for a Connecticut democratic congressman, but when the politician suffered a fatal heart attack, McGannon was out of work. Here family ties helped out. McGannon's dentist brother had a patient who was a DuMont television executive, seeking some help. On learning of the out-of-work attorney, he agreed to interview McGannon and hired him.

Thus McGannon's broadcasting management career began in 1951 when he became the assistant director and then general manager of the several owned-and-operated television stations for the struggling DuMont Television Network. Just months before that network closed operations in 1955, he moved to Westinghouse Broadcasting Company as vice president and general executive, and he was elected president later that year.

Developing Public Service

One of McGannon's first major actions at Westinghouse—masterminding the retrieval of former Westinghouse property KYW-AM-TV (then in Cleveland, Ohio) from the National Broadcasting Company (NBC)—was indicative of the confrontational stance he would take with the titans of the industry. The Federal Communications Commission (FCC) found that Radio Corporation of America (RCA) Chairman David Sarnoff, who had been quoted in print threatening to withdraw his network's affiliation with Westinghouse, had coerced the company into swapping for NBC facilities in the smaller market of Cleveland; the FCC ordered the trade undone.

In 1956 McGannon took the bold step of severing the network affiliations of all Westinghouse radio stations and beginning to build an independent news-gathering operation. A well-staffed Washington bureau was soon established. Facilities for foreign operations began building in 1961.

Under McGannon, Westinghouse Broadcasting Company (by 1963 known as "Group W") was both admired and disliked in the industry. It was admired because the company was a leader in public service. To many it was the model of what a broadcasting group should be. The company was disliked because this willingness to do more than the law required put the company at odds with most of the industry and with the National Association of Broadcasters (NAB), which fought the FCC on every rule it imposed. McGannon had a keen awareness of Westinghouse's historic role in the birth of commercial radio (KDKA), and he imbued his employees with a sense of mission and social responsibility. As a corporation, Westinghouse believed that the right of the federal government to regulate the airwaves was legitimate. The broadcast spectrum was indeed a public resource to be managed for the good of all, and McGannon cast himself as the "good steward" who obeyed all

Donald H. McGannon
Courtesy AP/Wide World Photos

the rules—who in fact did more than the rules required—and yet managed to give an enviable return to his stockholders. This undercut the argument propagated by the NAB, *Broadcasting* magazine, and others that the fairness doctrine, license renewal requirements, "equal time" regulations, and other government stipulations were onerous and financially burdensome.

McGannon's position was simple. The station licenses were what made Westinghouse broadcasting possible, so they must be protected. If the FCC wanted half an hour of community-oriented programming per week, then McGannon would give them two as insurance. McGannon often stated that the more public service his company did, the more money it made. It was almost embarrassing, he joked.

In keeping with this approach, McGannon also instituted something called the Public Service Conferences. These were held regularly beginning in 1956 in cities where Westinghouse owned stations. Multi-day events, the conferences brought together radio and television personnel, scholars, and politicians from around the country to discuss the role broadcasting should play in dealing with issues of concern to the nation. The first conference was held in Boston and featured addresses by Senator John F. Kennedy and Vice President Richard Nixon. These conferences were important in their own right and enhanced the reputation of Westinghouse immeasurably.

Instituting All-News Radio

In July 1962 Westinghouse Broadcasting Company purchased WINS-AM for a reported $10 million. Westinghouse at first experimented with various music formats in an unsuccessful

effort to top market leader WABC-AM. Then, on Monday, 19 April 1965, WINS-AM went to an all-news format, becoming one of the first stations to make what was then considered a radical format transition. Importantly, WINS-AM pioneered the all-news format in the largest media market in the United States.

WINS-AM became the place on the dial where New Yorkers tuned to learn about breaking news. In November 1965, when a major blackout darkened northeastern cities, WINS-AM kept millions informed during the crisis as they listened on battery-powered portable radios. Eventually, three of Group W's radio stations adopted the format. WINS-AM continued to broadcast "all news, all the time" in 2000.

McClendon's all-news radio stations broadcast mostly hard news in 15-minute blocks. Each block featured its own reporter, who compiled and edited wire-service copy and read it on the air. McGannon's version of the all-news format differed in that it made extensive use of Westinghouse's growing news-gathering capabilities, which included Washington and foreign bureaus as well as news staff in the large cities where Westinghouse owned outlets. An established network of stringers was also available when needed. Because of this, Westinghouse presented a much more varied slate of material, including local, national, and international features; sports; education; religion; finance; and "actualities." The Westinghouse/Group W approach to the all-news format was an immediate success.

Impact

During his long tenure heading Westinghouse, McGannon developed and refined the broadcasting group as a recognized entity within the industry. Previously, the two main organizing principles of radio and especially of television were the network and the individual station, which was almost always a network affiliate. Westinghouse Broadcasting Company was neither fish nor fowl. Although its television stations were network affiliates, they were first and foremost Westinghouse stations. This group identity was even more pronounced in Westinghouse's radio properties, which dropped all network ties in 1956. The previously mentioned Public Service Conferences were actually seen as a way of establishing the "Group" concept in the mind of the industry and the public.

McGannon's Westinghouse was ahead of its time on several issues. In a mostly white male world of button-down shirts and blue suits, McGannon sought diversity. To this end, he founded a job-training program to help minority workers get a start in the industry. Called the Broadcast Skills Bank, its name was later changed to the Employment Clearinghouse. McGannon also ordered all Westinghouse properties to drop cigarette advertising several years before legally required to do so.

McGannon resigned the position of president in 1978 and stepped down as chairman of Group W in December 1981. He consulted for the company for a time before declining health forced a permanent reduction in his activities. Donald McGannon died on 23 May 1984 at the age of 63, of Alzheimer's disease.

CHUCK HOWELL AND DOUGLAS GOMERY

See also All News Format; Group W; KYW; Westinghouse; WINS

Donald Henry McGannon. Born in South Bronx, New York City, 1921. One of four children of Robert E. McGannon; attended Fordham University, B.A. 1940; served in U.S. Army, 1941–46; returned to Fordham and received law degree, 1947; admitted to Bar in New York and Connecticut; practicing attorney, 1947–51; assistant director and general manager of stations in Dumont Television Network, 1951–55; vice president and general executive, Westinghouse Broadcasting Company, 1955, and elected president later that year. Received *Printer's Ink* Gold Medal; PULSE "Man of the Year" award; NAB Distinguished Service award; New York University Department of Journalism's "Kappa Tau Alpha" award (the first non-working journalist so honored), 1978; honorary degrees from Fordham and nine other institutions. Died in Chester, Connecticut, 23 May 1984.

Further Reading

Brown, Les, *Television: The Business behind the Box*, New York: Harcourt Brace Jovanovich, 1971
"Donald Henry McGannon," *Broadcasting* (28 May 1984)
"Donald McGannon," *Washington Post* (25 May 1984)
"Donald McGannon: A Former Chairman of Broadcast Group," *New York Times* (24 May 1984)
"An Original," *Broadcasting* (9 November 1981)
"WINS New York Going to an All-News Format," *Broadcasting* (22 March 1965)

McLaughlin, Edward F. 1926–

U.S. Radio Network and Station Executive

Edward F. McLaughlin is a recognized leader and innovator in the radio industry who played a crucial role in redefining network radio from the 1970s to the 1990s. He developed a new program distribution system and began a revival of long-form network programming that changed the face of the industry.

A native of San Francisco, McLaughlin attended San Francisco State University, then went to work at radio station KTIM in San Rafael, California. He later joined national radio sales firm Peters, Griffin and Woodward in San Francisco, and then went to station KGBS in Los Angeles. He returned to San Francisco in 1964 as sales manager of KGO Radio and was promoted to the position of general manager.

McLaughlin was instrumental in establishing the talk format that moved KGO into profitability and ultimately to the number one rank in the market. His background in talk radio would come into play again at the American Broadcasting Companies (ABC) Radio Networks and later at EFM (for "Edward F. McLaughlin") Media. In 1972 he was named president of the ABC Radio Networks and moved to New York City. McLaughlin served as ABC Radio Networks president from 1972 to 1986. He was well known for building relationships with affiliates that became fundamental links in his success at ABC and later in establishing the nationally syndicated *Rush Limbaugh Show*.

McLaughlin's first major innovation during his tenure as a network executive was to change the method of network program distribution from telephone lines to digital satellite. McLaughlin secured readily available space on satellite Satcom 1-R, created a digital distribution system called Advanced Digital Distribution System (ADDS), and set in motion a timetable for all ABC affiliates to install satellite dishes to receive ABC programming. Later all radio networks adopted the ADDS system, abandoning analog technology.

Having created a revolutionary distribution system, McLaughlin sought ways to reestablish long-form network radio programming as a means of expanding sales inventory. He formed the ABC Radio Network's Special Programming Department and named Richard A. Foreman as vice president in charge of producing long-form network specials. These shows included *Elvis Memories*, *The Barbra Streisand Special*, *The Neil Diamond Special*, *Country Greats in Concert*, and *The Silver Eagle*. Simultaneously, McLaughlin negotiated the purchase of Watermark Inc. by ABC and acquired long-form programming distribution. McLaughlin was chosen to become the first chairman of the newly created Radio Network Association, an organization designed to advance network radio's marketing image.

McLaughlin left ABC in 1986 when it was purchased by Capital Cities and in 1987, with his wife Patricia, formed EFM Media. Their initial product was the syndication of the *Dr. Dean Edell Show*. McLaughlin contracted with ABC for both studio and satellite distribution facilities and began a search for additional talent for EFM Media.

Rush Limbaugh was brought to McLaughlin's attention in 1987 by Bruce Marr, a radio consultant based in Reno, Nevada. Limbaugh was hosting a highly successful conservative local radio show on KFBK in Sacramento, California. In April of 1988 McLaughlin signed an options contract with Limbaugh stipulating that EFM Media deliver either a New York or Los Angeles outlet for Limbaugh, who was first brought to New York by McLaughlin in July 1988 to host a local two-hour show on WABC radio. A national two-hour show was added a month later. After a year, the national show was expanded to three hours, and WABC agreed to carry the national program, thus ending the local show. A year later the *Rush Limbaugh Show* was being aired in 100 markets, which grew to 500 markets by 1991. When McLaughlin was presented with the National Radio Award by the National Association of Broadcasters in 1996, he was cited for his many innovations, including the tremendous success that the *Rush Limbaugh Show* and EFM Media had made in reversing AM radio's long slide in audience share and reestablishing national personalities in radio broadcasting.

In 1997 the assets of the *Rush Limbaugh Show*, the *Dr. Dean Edell Show*, and the *Limbaugh Letter* were sold by McLaughlin to Jacor Communications.

GORDON H. HASTINGS

See also American Broadcasting Company; American Top 40; Limbaugh, Rush

Edward F. McLaughlin. Born 12 October 1926, in San Francisco. Attended San Francisco State University, B.A. 1958; promoted to general manager, KGO Radio, 1964; president of ABC Radio Networks, 1972–86; introduced return of live radio sports broadcasts with Mohammed Ali versus Leon Spinks fight, 1978; negotiated exclusive live radio network rights to Olympic Games, Lake Placid, New York, 1980, and Los Angeles, California, 1984; formed EFM Media with wife Patricia, 1987; signed contract with Rush Limbaugh, 1988. Received National Radio Award from National Association of Broadcasters, 1996.

Edward F. McLaughlin
Courtesy Radio Hall of Fame

programs *American Top 40* with Casey Kasem and *American Country Countdown* with Bob Kingsley. He also brought Dr. Dean Edell from KGO to network radio and expanded the Paul Harvey news broadcasts to include the program series known as *The Rest of the Story*.

McLaughlin's network programming innovations also included the return of live sports broadcasts. In 1978 the ABC Information Network broadcast the Mohammed Ali–Leon Spinks rematch live from New Orleans, Louisiana. It was the first live sporting event broadcast by ABC in over 18 years. He also negotiated the first exclusive live radio network rights to the 1980 Winter Olympics in Lake Placid, New York, and the 1984 Summer Olympic Games in Los Angeles. In addition McLaughlin acquired for ABC the radio broadcast rights to the Triple Crown of horse racing, the Kentucky Derby, The Preakness, and The Belmont. During this period of expansion other networks quickly followed ABC's lead in satellite digital

McLendon, Gordon 1921–1986

U.S. Radio Programming Innovator

Gordon McLendon is considered one of the greatest radio program innovators. His major contributions to radio, coming at a time when the older medium was struggling to compete with the brash new medium of television, are credited with renewing radio's vitality and with popularizing program formats that remained staples of the radio industry for the latter half of the 20th century.

Early Radio Career

McLendon became interested in radio as a youth in Atlanta, Texas, listening to his idol, sportscaster Ted Husing. McLendon decided that he too wanted to be a sportscaster, and he spent the better part of his youth preparing himself for such a career. His first real chance to work in radio came as a student at Yale University in the late 1930s. There he spent time as a sportscaster and reporter for Yale's radio station WOCD. McLendon's stint in the U.S. Navy during World War II allowed him to polish his radio skills as an announcer in the South Pacific. A one-year postwar stint at Harvard Law School convinced McLendon that radio was his true calling, and so he returned to his native Texas to enter the radio business full-time.

McLendon's first venture into radio station ownership occurred in Palestine, Texas, where he became part owner (by way of a loan from his father) of KNET in 1946. McLendon's father, Barton R. (B.R.) McLendon, continued a partnership with his son for the rest of Gordon's career. B.R.'s name was rarely mentioned when Gordon was lauded for one of his many successes in the radio business, but B.R. McLendon was a silent partner in these successes. It was the father's financial expertise and support that made possible much of what the son accomplished.

Gordon McLendon's stay in Palestine was short-lived. Within one year he sold his part ownership of KNET and moved to Dallas, Texas. Before leaving, however, McLendon had begun developing a skill that in a short time would make him famous—that of re-creating major-league baseball games. Reading a game summary supplied by Western Union teletype and utilizing sound effects that approximated a baseball game, McLendon became adept at re-creating baseball games that sounded nearly identical to live coverage of the real thing.

McLendon arrived in the Oak Cliff section of Dallas in 1948 and immediately acquired a license to construct radio station KLIF. McLendon's baseball game re-creations quickly became the station's most popular programming—so popular, in fact, that radio station owners in nearby towns began requesting permission to carry them. An informal network soon developed that carried the KLIF baseball games to states bordering Texas, then to the entire Southwest and Southeast, and within a year to most of the United States. McLendon formalized the upstart network by naming it the Liberty Broadcasting System (LBS), a patriotic name suggested by B.R. McLendon.

The LBS appeal centered on McLendon's baseball game re-creations. Because major-league team owners prohibited radio stations beyond a limited distance from their ballparks from carrying live broadcasts of ball games, re-creations were the only means by which most radio listeners could hear major-league games. McLendon was happy to oblige listeners, but his interest in broadcasting live from the major-league ballparks led him to file a complaint with the U.S. Justice Department in 1949, charging major-league owners with violation of federal antitrust laws. The antitrust implications convinced team owners to open their ballparks to LBS for live game coverage. McLendon's optimism about the network's future was dashed in 1951, when LBS suffered the loss of its major advertiser and the major-league baseball establishment agreed to allow each team to independently negotiate broadcast coverage rights to its baseball games instead of allowing the American League or National League to negotiate coverage rights collectively. This meant that LBS could ill afford to pay for programming vital to the network's livelihood. LBS had little choice but to cease operations and file for bankruptcy.

Fate had dealt McLendon a more beneficial blow than he realized. Within a few years television's popularity had forced national radio networks into a much-diminished media role. And besides, McLendon now could turn full attention to running KLIF.

Development of the Top 40 Radio Format

McLendon's idea for KLIF was to determine what listeners wanted to hear and then to program the station accordingly. Rather than relying on programs that by chance might appeal to listeners, McLendon approached the process much as a scientist approaches an experiment. His tinkering with program elements was McLendon's initial foray into what came to be called "formula" or "format" radio. McLendon soon became an expert at crafting radio formats, but the first that he is credited with helping to create—Top 40—remained his most important.

Todd Storz and his assistant Bill Stewart are credited with inventing the concept of Top 40. The idea came to them, so the

Gordon McLendon
Courtesy of Bart McLendon

story goes, as they observed bar patrons repeatedly playing their favorite tunes on a 40-record jukebox. Storz and Stewart transferred the idea to radio, where a program director would prepare a 40-record playlist from which a disc jockey would choose selections to play during a four-hour "board" shift. The Top 40 idea was tried initially on Storz's Omaha, Nebraska, station KOWH at some point in 1952. The station quickly zoomed to first place in the market by 1953.

Gordon McLendon picked up on the Top 40 idea and hired Bill Stewart away from Storz to install the format at KLIF. Working together, McLendon and Stewart meticulously developed Top 40 in such a way that KLIF soon became the home of what many in the radio industry regarded as the format's most popular and successful version. To the playlist idea was added a fast pace, carried along by a cadre of outstanding disc jockeys who provided patter between records, read commercials and public service announcements themselves, and participated in KLIF promotions. McLendon also incorporated specially produced jingles throughout the program day to remind listeners that they were tuned to KLIF.

The McLendon brand of Top 40 was identified most easily by the stunts and station contests that KLIF constantly promoted and by KLIF's unique concept of Top 40 news. KLIF promotions were notorious for stirring up interest and excitement. A money-filled balloon drop from a downtown Dallas hotel that tied up traffic for hours and a treasure hunt contest that had thousands of Dallas residents digging up property in search of buried money are two examples of promotional stunts that kept KLIF in the public eye. KLIF news was no less attractive to listeners. Newscasts were localized, prepared by a well-trained staff of writers, and delivered at the same rapid clip as used by KLIF disc jockeys. McLendon was also the first to build a fleet of mobile units that allowed KLIF reporters to drive to news events around Dallas and to report live from their remote locations.

McLendon periodically wrote and delivered editorials that were inserted into KLIF newscasts. The editorials allowed the well-read and opinionated McLendon an opportunity to address important local and national issues. From the 1950s into the 1960s, he delivered approximately 5,000 editorials. McLendon did not shy from controversial subjects, and he did not hesitate to tell listeners he was wrong whenever subsequent thought and investigation proved to him that an initial opinion could no longer be supported. McLendon's editorials often created a stir among his listeners, which, of course, served his intent to promote KLIF.

KLIF began broadcasting the Top 40 format in late 1954. Within 60 days KLIF was the number-one radio station in Dallas. The station's prominence as one of the highest-rated stations in the United States continued for years and attracted station owners and program directors alike, who traveled to Dallas to learn how they too could implement Top 40 in their own markets. They were assisted by a growing collection of McLendon policy manuals that contained explicit details on every facet of KLIF's operation.

The McLendon brand of Top 40 radio began appearing throughout America, and many of the most successful Top 40 stations belonged to Gordon and B.R. McLendon. The McLendons bought and sold some 25 radio and television stations during their two decades in broadcasting. Gordon's insistence on creating policies to direct his program decisions applied as well to the manner in which he and his father acquired radio stations. B.R. McLendon handled the financial side of all transactions, and Gordon handled the programming and management side. Gordon's policy was to find a station with mediocre ratings in a market where he wished to expand and then to make an offer to purchase the station. Once the station was purchased and the license transfer approved, Gordon directed his staff to rebuild the station according to the McLendon plan, often changed the station's call letters to a more attention-grabbing combination, fired practically the entire existing staff, and replaced them with veteran McLendon employees. The most important station acquisition step, however, was to install the new Top 40 format and to launch a promotional blitz to introduce market listeners to the McLendon sound. Time after time McLendon used this method to turn moribund radio stations into market leaders.

Other Radio Ventures

Gordon McLendon made radio history of an offbeat nature in 1961 when he decided to provide citizens of Sweden with commercial Top 40 radio. An earlier visit to the country had convinced McLendon that the government-operated radio service there was not providing listeners with the programming they wanted to hear. McLendon subsequently purchased an old herring boat, equipped it with a radio studio, transmitter, and personnel, and positioned it in international waters off the Swedish coast where its signal reached Stockholm. McLendon's objective to make money with this "pirate" operation proved successful. The station, called Radio Nord, was a huge programming as well as commercial success, but the Swedish government was not amused. Failing to find any particular violation of international law, the government finally passed laws that prohibited Swedish merchants from associating with the pirate operation. Thus deprived of any means to resupply Radio Nord, McLendon closed his operation and set sail for friendlier waters in 1962.

McLendon's Radio Nord venture was indicative of his creativity and willingness to push new ideas to their limit. McLendon's innovative nature led to experiments with a number of new radio formats—some of which succeeded and some of which failed miserably. One of the most successful was the beautiful music format introduced on San Francisco's KABL in

1959. The format was a blend of Top 40 and easy listening music especially designed for the sophisticated West Coast audience. The format was tried with equal success at WWWW in Detroit and WNUS in Chicago. However, when the beautiful music format was imported into the Buffalo, New York, market via WYSL, it fell flat. An effort to replace the format with the telephone discussion format proved equally unsuccessful. The idea of the new format was to allow listeners to engage in on-air discussion by phone. The format, which was nearly identical to the later talk radio format, proved Gordon McLendon's prescience for program ideas.

One of the most successful McLendon formats was all-news radio. He did not invent the format, but he perfected it at station XTRA in the Los Angeles area. XTRA was physically located near Rosarita, Mexico, just across the border from San Diego, California. From there its signal reached Los Angeles with enough clarity to make listeners think that XTRA was broadcasting from their midst. And McLendon made certain that XTRA station identifications were muffled in such ways as to disguise the station's Mexican origins. Despite its distant location, XTRA served Los Angeles reasonably well with news provided by several wire services. The XTRA operation allowed experimentation with the all-news format to the extent that the all-news format became a fixture at McLendon's WNUS in Chicago by 1964.

One of Gordon McLendon's biggest failures was the all-want-ad format he introduced in 1966 at KADS in Los Angeles. The format required that listeners call the station to advertise items they wished to sell. In true classified ad fashion, KADS clustered its time segments for specific product or service categories. The format lasted for little more than a year, failing primarily because its success depended on listeners' ability to recall information from memory or from hurriedly scribbled notes in order to respond to the ads. Radio could not supply a handy reference tool comparable to the newspaper's classified ad section. This design flaw doomed the all-want-ads format.

Departure from Radio

A major player in the radio industry by the 1960s, McLendon chose that decade to begin his departure from the medium. He and B.R. McLendon actually started divesting their radio station properties in the early 1960s, and by 1967 the McLendons announced plans to sell their prize possession, KLIF. The station was sold to Fairchild Industries in 1971 for $10.5 million. Gordon McLendon gave several reasons for his departure from radio. First, he felt he had achieved all that he had wanted in radio and had few challenges remaining in the industry. Second, he was tired of the many struggles he had endured with the Federal Communications Commission (FCC). Being a radio maverick had required that he push FCC rules to their limit and

occasionally beyond, and the results had been several prolonged clashes with the Commission. McLendon felt that he no longer wanted to cope with federal regulators, for whom he had a very low regard. A third reason was McLendon's wish to explore opportunities outside of radio.

Gordon McLendon's extra-radio interests were apparent by the early 1960s. He and B.R. McLendon had developed a small group of East Texas outdoor movie theaters into one of the country's biggest chains of outdoor/indoor theaters. As an outgrowth of that business, Gordon McLendon produced hundreds of movie promotion spots for major motion picture studios. McLendon also tried his hand at movie production in the late 1950s, turning out such forgettable titles as *The Killer Shrews, The Giant Gila Monster,* and *My Dog Buddy.* All were set at McLendon's ranch Cielo, and all were packed with characters played by KLIF employees, including Gordon himself. McLendon also tried his hand at politics, running unsuccessfully for the U.S. Senate in 1964 and for Texas governor in 1968. These and other assorted ventures as well as money accumulated during his years in radio combined to put Gordon McLendon on the *Forbes* magazine list of the wealthiest Americans in 1984.

Gordon McLendon was proud of his accomplishments, but he admitted near the end of his life that his achievements in radio meant more to him than anything else. McLendon was diagnosed with esophageal cancer in 1985 and died from the disease at his ranch in September 1986. One year later, the National Association of Broadcasters bestowed its highest honor on Gordon McLendon by naming him to its Hall of Fame. And in 1999, *Broadcasting and Cable* magazine placed McLendon on its list of the "100 individuals who made signal contributions to the Fifth Estate during the 20th Century."

RONALD GARAY

See also All News Format; Contemporary Hit Radio Format/ Top 40; Liberty Broadcasting System; Recreations; Sportscasters; Storz, Todd

Gordon McLendon. Born in Paris, Texas, 8 June 1921. One of two children of Barton Robert and Jeannette Eyster McLendon; inducted into U.S. Navy during senior year at Yale University, 1942; served in U.S. Navy Intelligence, 1942–45; attended Harvard Law School, 1945; co-owner of KNET, Palestine, Texas, 1946; co-owner, with father, of KLIF, Dallas, Texas, 1948–71, and McLendon Station Group, 1950s and 1960s; promoter, United Artists, 1963–66; unsuccessful candidate for U.S. Senate, 1964, and for Texas governor, 1968; included on *Forbes* magazine list of wealthiest Americans, 1984. Inducted posthumously into National Association of Broadcasters Hall of Fame, 1987. Died in Denton, Texas, 14 September 1986.

Further Reading

Eberly, Philip K., *Music in the Air: America's Changing Tastes in Popular Music, 1920–1980*, New York: Hastings House, 1982

Fornatale, Peter, and Joshua E. Mills, *Radio in the Television Age*, Woodstock, New York: Overlook Press, 1980

Fowler, Gene, and Bill Crawford, *Border Radio*, Austin: Texas Monthly Press, 1987; 2nd edition, Austin: University of Texas Press, 2002

Garay, Ronald, *Gordon McLendon: The Maverick of Radio*, New York: Greenwood Press, 1992

Hall, Claude, and Barbara Hall, *This Business of Radio Programming: A Comprehensive Look at Modern Programming Techniques Used throughout the World*, New York: Billboard, 1977

Harper, Jim, "Gordon McLendon: Pioneer Baseball Broadcaster," *Baseball History* 1 (Spring 1986)

MacFarland, David T., *The Development of the Top 40 Radio Format*, New York: Arno Press, 1979

Passman, Arnold, *The Deejays*, New York: Macmillan, 1971

Patoski, Joe Nick, "Rock 'n' Roll's Wizard of Oz," *Texas Monthly* 8 (February 1980)

Routt, Edd, *Dimensions of Broadcast Editorializing*, Blue Ridge Summit, Pennsylvania: G/L TAB Books, 1974

Routt, Edd, James B. McGrath, and Fredric A. Weiss, *The Radio Format Conundrum*, New York: Hastings House, 1978

Schroeder, Richard, *Texas Signs On: The Early Days of Radio and Television*, College Station: Texas A&M University Press, 1998

McNamee, Graham 1888–1942

U.S. Announcer and Sportscaster

Announcer and sportscaster for two decades beginning in the 1920s, Graham McNamee has been called the "father of sportscasting." He was the first network sportscaster and, of necessity, one of the inventors of play-by-play and color sports announcing ("color announcing" being everything aside from the play-by-play, nowadays often provided by a retired player to give the sportscast an "inside" perspective). Trained as a baritone singer, McNamee's voice commanded attention, aroused emotion and excitement, and inspired great affection. Indeed, his announcing of the first broadcast of a World Series, in 1923, generated more than 1,700 enthusiastic letters to WEAF in New York (then owned by American Telephone and Telegraph [AT&T] and later flagship station of the National Broadcasting Company's [NBC] Red network). His announcing of the 1925 World Series brought in an astonishing 50,000 letters (Gorman, Calhoun, and Rozen, 1994). His signature sign-on, "Good evening, ladies and gentlemen of the radio audience," and sign-off, "This is Graham McNamee saying good night, all" became widely recognized.

McNamee was active in sports in school, but at the urging of his mother, he turned to piano and then to singing. He sang in church choirs, in a Broadway show, and for an opera company, and he gave his own concert at New York's Aeolian Hall. At the beginning of the 1920s he undertook a multi-city concert tour.

In May 1923 McNamee visited the WEAF radio studios on a break from jury duty nearby, bearing an introduction from the music supervisor of the New York public schools. He was given an audition and, after a decade in a professional singing career, he was hired as a utility announcer and singer. Deciding he would try the new medium for a few summer months when music bookings were limited, he soon captured the affection of thousands of sports fans with his mellifluous voice. Within months he became the "color" or background announcer for the first broadcast of a World Series and astounded listeners with his play-by-play of the 1923 middleweight championship match between boxers Harry Greb and Johnny Wilson at the Polo Grounds. His particular talent was his remarkable ability to capture the ups and downs of tension in a game or match, speeding and slowing to match the rise and fall of intensity in action. He became the model for many of the next generation of sportscasters, including such Hall of Fame luminaries as Red Barber, Mel Allen, and Lindsey Nelson. Sports historian Curt Smith rated McNamee as being as influential to his generation as Curt Gowdy was in the 1960s and 1970s (see Smith, 1987, revised 1992).

McNamee was equally versatile in live news reporting. He became NBC's chief announcer when it was formed in 1926 and he covered national political conventions and important live news events of the day. He covered Calvin Coolidge's 1923 address to Congress and both political conventions in 1924, including the 14 days of Democratic balloting. A 1925 WEAF recording by the Victor Talking Machine Company of Chief

Graham McNamee (right) seated with Phillips Carlin
Courtesy Library of American Broadcasting

Justice William Howard Taft's oath of office and inaugural address has McNamee's voice in the background, saying "We are ready." Another classic recording includes McNamee's breathless description of Charles Lindbergh's return to U.S. soil after his historic 1927 solo flight across the Atlantic.

It was as a sportscaster, though, that McNamee was most widely known. He covered World Series games from 1923 to 1935, major college football games (including the first Rose Bowl broadcast in 1927, which was also NBC's first coast-to-coast broadcast), significant tennis matches, and momentous prize fights, including the second "fight of the century" between Gene Tunney and Jack Dempsey in 1927. His colorful broadcast of that match for the 73-station NBC Red network reached an estimated 50 million people, a staggering number given the relatively few radio sets then in use.

As was common for early journalists, McNamee tended to embellish the moment to create emotional impact, but his style fit with the times and made the announcer as much a star as the athletes he covered. His mere presence conveyed to listeners that an event had importance. In describing the players, he cultivated heroic images that outshone many athletes' actual achievements. The mythic aura around such legendary giants as Babe Ruth and Jack Dempsey was largely the creation of a generation of sportscasters known for their hyperbole. McNamee and his contemporaries spun a web of adulation for sports heroes that endures among fans today.

After covering a dozen World Series between 1923 and 1935, as well as hundreds of boxing and tennis matches and football games, McNamee's sports announcing ended with the rise of a new group of radio announcers. The times demanded terse and factual reporting of sports in the style of such greats as Red Barber and Lindsey Nelson, and NBC pulled him from covering the 1935 World Series and moved him to other tasks. McNamee had become dated and controversial because he talked so much and because many sportswriters and fans found his vivid game dramatizations unwarranted. At the same time, subsequent sportscasters idolized him for his great voice, his historic sportscasts, and his ongoing achievements in developing play-by-play and color sports announcing. McNamee's role in creating the celebrity sportscaster and building the national fan base for major sports has not been forgotten.

His final years at NBC were largely given over to announcing for Rudy Vallee's variety program and appearing as a straight man for Ed Wynn. He occasionally did spot news reporting, as with the maiden voyage arrival in New York of the *Queen Mary* in 1936 and a pier-side description of the burning of the French liner *Normandie* in February 1942. On 24 April 1942 he announced *Elsa Maxwell's Party Line*—his final broadcast. He died shortly thereafter of an embolism of the brain, just two months before his 53rd birthday. Obituaries and editorials on his death appeared across the country; "Mr. Radio is Dead" is how the *Cleveland Plain Dealer* headlined its story.

McNamee was one of the first celebrities of the new medium, touted as "The World's Most Popular Announcer" on a cup from *Radio Digest* in 1925 after winning a national competition over 132 other announcers (listeners were fickle: two years later he was ranked ninth in another poll; in 1931 he was ranked fourth, but second among sports announcers, after Ted Husing). Long after his death, McNamee was recognized with the first group of notables inducted (in 1977) into the National Association of Broadcasters Hall of Fame. A national award in his honor was established for a sportscaster who achieved success in a second field of endeavor, just as he had gone from singing to announcing. The Graham McNamee award has gone to such noted individuals as President Ronald Reagan, Walter Cronkite, Bryant Gumbel, and Larry King, all of whom were sportscasters at some point in their careers. Heywood Hale Broun wrote that "McNamee justified the whole activity of broadcasting," adding that he "has been able to take a new medium of expression and through it transmit himself—to give it vividly a sense of movement and of feeling. Of such is the kingdom of art" (cited in Smith, 1987, 1992).

SUSAN TYLER EASTMAN

See also National Broadcasting Company; Sportscasters; WEAF

Graham McNamee. Born in Washington, D.C., 10 July 1888. Trained as baritone, New York City, 1907–21; made professional debut, 1921; radio announcer, WEAF, 1923–26; color announcer for first broadcast of World Series, 1923; chief announcer for live news and sports, NBC Radio Red Network, 1926–34. Inducted posthumously into National Association of Broadcasters Hall of Fame, 1977. Died in New York City, 9 May 1942.

Selected Publications

You're on the Air, 1926

Further Reading

Gorman, Jerry, Kirk Calhoun, and Skip Rozen, *The Name of the Game: The Business of Sports,* New York: Wiley, 1994
Harwell, Ernie, *Tuned to Baseball,* South Bend, Indiana: Diamond Communications, 1985
Rader, Benjamin G., *American Sports: From the Age of Folk Games to the Age of Televised Sports,* Englewood Cliffs, New Jersey: Prentice Hall, 1983; 2nd edition, 1990
Smith, Curt, *Voices of the Game: The First Full-Scale Overview of Baseball Broadcasting, 1921 to the Present,* South Bend, Indiana: Diamond, 1987; revised edition, as *Voices of the Game: The Acclaimed Chronicle of Baseball Radio and Television Broadcasting—From 1921 to the Present,* New York: Simon and Schuster, 1992

McNeill, Don 1907–1996

U.S. Radio Morning Show Host

For 35 years, many Americans woke up to the easygoing banter of Don McNeill, the genial host of the Chicago-based *Breakfast Club* program. To a considerable degree, he created the morning radio format that became widely popular throughout the industry.

Origins

Born in Illinois in 1907 and raised in Wisconsin, McNeill moved around to a number of radio stations in the Midwest, San Francisco, and New York for several years. He struck it

Don McNeill
Courtesy of family of Don McNeill

big (though that was anything but clear at the time) when NBC-Blue asked him to take over *The Pepper Pot*, a struggling morning show in Chicago that had no advertisers and precious few listeners. Starting at $50 a week, McNeill began hosting the program on 23 June 1933 and renamed it *The Breakfast Club* a few months later.

Breakfast Club Years

Right from the start, McNeill made changes that greatly helped turn the program into a huge success. For its hour-long slot, he fairly quickly developed what he called the "four calls to breakfast," which divided the program into quarter-hour segments, each of which emphasized something different. It started with an opening song that usually began:

> *Good morning, Breakfast Clubbers, we're glad to see ya!*
> *We wake up bright and early just to howdy-do ya*

The first segment offered interviews with the studio audience (added in 1938); the second featured "memory time" with sentimental poetry and prayer time (added in 1944 and retained after the war, along with hymns provided in a nonsectarian fashion); the third was "march time"; and the fourth and last was dubbed "inspiration time" and also often included more sentimental poetry. Although the audience never knew it, no breakfast was ever consumed on the program.

After the first few years, McNeill sought and was granted permission to move from a scripted program to a variety program that was both unrehearsed and spontaneous. *Breakfast Club* took on greater charm at that point, as McNeill's ability to ad-lib in almost any situation came through. So did his genial nature and easygoing tone, along with that of the rest of the regular cast, which sometimes included his wife and young sons. One singer on the program, Charlotte Reid (known on the air as Annette King), later became a member of the Federal Communications Commission and of the U.S. Congress. Other regulars at one time or another included Fran Allison and singers Patti Page, Johnny Desmond, and Anita Bryant. Some cast or orchestra members stayed around for decades. While the jokes were often bad and the program corny, it was appealing for its ability to seemingly speak to each listener individually. Many of the segments were enlightened by listener mail that amounted to thousands of weekly letters by the 1940s. And on occasion, the program left Chicago to go on tour, broadcasting from other cities.

The show's huge popularity became very evident with a 1944 promotional offer. As John Dunning writes: "When the sponsor offered *Breakfast Club* membership cards, 850,000 people wrote in. No more than 15,000 were expected, and McNeill had to go on the air and beg out of the promotion. It still cost the sponsor $50,000 to retreat" (see Dunning, 1998).

Luckily by then there *were* sponsors. Through the 1930s the program lacked advertising support. During most of the war years, only about a quarter of the program was sponsored. Indeed, it was not fully supported by advertising until 1946—13 years after McNeill had taken it over and demonstrated he could build big and loyal audiences. Saturday broadcasts were dropped in 1945, by which time McNeill was making $1,000 a week.

The show was clearly aimed at middle America, just as it was broadcast *from* middle America. The program was first broadcast (until 1948) from the 19th-floor NBC studios in Chicago's huge Merchandise Mart building, then for five years from the Little Theater in the Civic Opera Building. In 1953 it moved to the Terrace Casino of the Morrison Hotel and two years later to the College Inn at the Sherman House, and finally in 1963 to specially rebuilt Clouds Room on the 23rd floor of the Allerton Hotel, all in downtown Chicago. But its heart and content were clearly not in the city, but rather in rural America. And the do-good nature of the program came through in constant appeals to visit those in retirement homes or hospitals, to collect food for the starving refugees in postwar Europe, and to help the poor at holiday time at home. Listeners and often studio audiences came through every time.

Final Years

In 1950, by then making $100,000 a year, McNeill signed a 20-year contract with the network to continue the program, one that gave him two months of vacation per year. *Don McNeill's TV Club* aired on ABC-TV in 1950–51 and a brief attempt to simulcast the successful radio program on television as *The Breakfast Club* failed after just one season on ABC in 1954–55. In 1957, the program began to be tape recorded a day before broadcast. Toward the end of the program's run, McNeill was receiving upwards of 10,000 letters each month. The program was still being carried on more than 220 stations when it ended its 35 year run on 27 December 1968, the last regularly scheduled network radio broadcast originating in Chicago. The old-fashioned sound of *The Breakfast Club* no longer fit a radio industry largely devoted to popular music formats, or a country facing the height of the Vietnam War and political assassinations.

CHRISTOPHER H. STERLING

See also American Broadcasting Corporation; Godfrey, Arthur; Morning Shows

Donald Thomas McNeill. Born in Galena, Illinois, 23 December 1907. Graduated from Marquette University, 1930: B.Phil. Entered radio with work at WISN, Milwaukee, 1928; WTMJ, Milwaukee, 1929; WHAS, Louisville, 1930. NBC *Breakfast Club* host, 1933–68. Taught communications at

Marquette and Notre Dame Universities, 1970–72. Spokesperson for Deltona Corporation, 1970–80. Inducted into Broadcaster's Hall of Fame, 1979; Radio Hall of Fame, 1989. Died in Evanston, Illinois, 7 May 1996.

Radio Series

1933–68   *The Breakfast Club*

Television

Don McNeill's TV Club, 1950–51; *The Breakfast Club*, 1954–55 (simulcast)

Selected Publications

20 Years of Memory Time; The Most Popular Selections since 1933, 1953

Mr. Don McNeill, esq. Presents his Breakfast Club Family Album, 1942

Further Reading

The Don McNeill Collection is housed at Marquette University's Memorial Library.

"'Breakfast Club' Ending its 35-Year Stay on Radio," *New York Times* (27 December 1968)

Doolittle, John, *Don McNeill and His Breakfast Club*, Notre Dame, Indiana: University of Notre Dame Press, 2001

Dunning, John, "The Breakfast Club," in *On the Air: The Encyclopedia of Old-Time Radio*, New York: Oxford University Press, 1998

Froman, B., "The Man Who Came to Breakfast," *Colliers* (13 May 1950)

McPherson, Aimee Semple 1890–1944

U.S. (Canadian Born) Radio Evangelist

The Pentecostal evangelist Aimee Semple McPherson, known as "Sister Aimee" to her followers, was an early celebrity of mass media religion. She was the first woman both to preach by radio (1922) and to hold a station license (1924). She founded the third radio station in Los Angeles, the still-extant KFSG, as the mouthpiece for her new denomination, the International Church of the Foursquare Gospel. At the time of her death in 1944 she had made plans for the United States' first televangelist network.

For this extraordinary career as one of the first modern media-savvy evangelists, her early preparation seems rather unremarkable. She was a dutiful missionary wife and later was a little-known itinerant preacher. Born Aimee Elizabeth Kennedy in 1890 in rural Ingersoll, Ontario, she was converted to Pentecostalism by her future husband, Robert Semple, during a 1907 revival. The Semples set off in 1910 to evangelize China, but Robert died shortly after their arrival and just weeks before the birth of their first child, Roberta Star Semple. Aimee Semple then left the ministry for about five years, during which time she went to the United States, married again, and had a second child, Rolf. By 1915, however, she was back on the road working full-time as an itinerant preacher on the Pentecostal tent circuit. Her travels and spreading fame eventually took her to Los Angeles in 1918, which remained her home for the rest of her life.

By 1921, when McPherson broke ground for Angelus Temple on West Sunset Boulevard, she was already famous for her faith-healing meetings ("stretcher days," as she called them), which packed stadium-sized crowds in San Diego, San Jose, and Denver. Her fast-growing organization, now called the International Church of the Foursquare Gospel, was the largest private relief charity in Los Angeles during the Depression years (and has since become a thriving worldwide church). At Angelus, to the accompaniment of a huge organ, a 14-piece orchestra, a brass band, and a 100-voice choir, she performed "illustrated sermons" every Sunday night for 20 years. These illustrated sermons were stage spectacles and Biblical dramas with elaborate costumes rented from Hollywood studios and with huge sets and special effects.

McPherson had first preached on Oakland's Rockridge radio station (now KNEW) in April 1922. She preached occasional services over *Los Angeles Times* station KHJ while raising $75,000 to construct a 500-watt broadcasting facility inside Angelus Temple. Her own radio station, KFSG, began broadcasting on 6 February 1924. A Class A 500-watt transmitting station, with unlimited broadcast time, the station could be heard over much of the western United States and the Pacific, even as far away as Hawaii. Like other early radio pioneers in the 1920s, McPherson occasionally "wandered" the airwaves in search of a clearer broadcast frequency. In reply to Secretary

Aimee Semple McPherson, 21 August 1930
Courtesy AP/Wide World Photos

of Commerce Herbert Hoover's 1927 directive to keep to her assigned frequency, she fired off an infamous telegram that read, "PLEASE ORDER YOUR MINIONS OF SATAN TO LEAVE MY STATION ALONE. YOU CANNOT EXPECT THE ALMIGHTY TO ABIDE BY YOUR WAVELENGTH NONSENSE. WHEN I OFFER MY PRAYERS TO HIM I MUST FIT INTO HIS WAVE RECEPTION. OPEN THIS STATION AT ONCE." Eventually Sister Aimee learned to be more diplomatic in her dealings with the federal regulators; renewal of Sister Aimee's license to operate KFSG was never denied.

KFSG featured nearly round-the-clock programming: there were Sunday devotional and revival services simulcast in their entirety from the main auditorium, programs of sacred music, programs designed for children, a "family altar call," civic talks, and weekly divine healing and baptismal services. Later, McPherson added travel shows, a religious news program, and even live studio serials patterned after popular radio dramas of the time, with titles such as *Jim Trask: Lone Evangelist*. Perhaps more so than any other fundamentalist media preacher, she duplicated the genres of commercial radio. But faith healing, in particular, set McPherson apart as a radio phenomenon. Listeners were invited to kneel by their radios, touching the speakers to receive cures for their ailments. Prayers for healing were a regular part of the programming of KFSG and brought heavy mail response claiming cures for every known disease. Speaking in tongues was also a regular feature of KFSG programming, except during World War II, when McPherson stopped airing speaking in tongues because of wartime prohibitions against coded messages.

Sister Aimee's regional following was numbered at 30,000 by 1930, and her radio audience was certainly much larger. In 1937, on her license renewal application, McPherson claimed that KFSG constituted a "church of the air" with a registered membership exceeding 50,000. Most of her adherents and regular listeners came from the ranks of the lower middle class, including many recent migrants to the West Coast. As Sister Aimee herself put it, perhaps slightly tongue in cheek, "I bring spiritual consolation to the middle class, leaving those above to themselves and those below to the Salvation Army." Fundamentalist churches in the area drew close to 80 percent of their membership from people who had lived in Los Angeles for less than ten years. Eager for the familiar and positive message Sister Aimee radiated, these recent arrivals were nonetheless embedded in the emerging consumer and entertainment culture of the time, and radio was a natural way for her growing denomination to tap a huge potential audience.

The latter half of her ministry was dogged by controversy, although McPherson's media outlets and her rigorous schedule of services and appearances did not falter. During the lean Depression years, when many smaller religious radio stations and programs went off the air for lack of funds, KFSG continued to broadcast (although with a shared-time arrangement

with KRKD Los Angeles), and McPherson opened additional branches of her church in dozens of cities. She died in Oakland, California, just before her 54th birthday. Her son Rolf continued the ministry until 1988. After her death, the Church operated one of Los Angeles' early FM stations, KKLA FM (97.1) until the early 1950s and later assumed control of KRKD's AM and FM outlets.

McPherson's radio career permanently linked religious broadcasting with show business and successfully bridged old-time revivalism and modern mass communication. Her imprint remains not just on Pentecostalism itself, but on the exuberant, colorful, and sometimes all-too-human face of media evangelism throughout the century.

TONA J. HANGEN

See also Evangelists/Evangelical Radio; Religion on Radio

Aimee Semple McPherson. Born in Ingersoll, Ontario, Canada, 9 October 1890. Only daughter of James Kennedy and Mildred Ona Pearce; married Irish Pentecostal itinerant preacher Robert Semple, 1908; widowed in Hong Kong, 1910, their daughter born later that year; married Harold McPherson, 1912; became Pentecostal itinerant, 1915, often traveling with her mother and two children; settled in Los Angeles, 1918; established Angelus Temple in Hollywood, 1923; founded radio station KFSG, 1924; established the International Church of the Foursquare Gospel, early 1920s (name incorporated 1927); married David Hutton, 1931; broadcast at least weekly over KFSG for 20 years. Died in Oakland, California, 27 September 1944.

Selected Publications
Bridal Call, 1917–1934
This Is That: Personal Experiences, Sermons and Writings of Aimee Semple McPherson, Evangelist, 1923
Aimee Semple McPherson: The Story of My Life, 1973

Further Reading
Blumhofer, Edith Waldvogel, *Aimee Semple McPherson: Everybody's Sister*, Grand Rapids, Michigan: Eerdmans, 1993
Epstein, Daniel Mark, *Sister Aimee: The Life of Aimee Semple McPherson*, New York: Harcourt Brace Jovanovich, 1993
Mavity, Nancy Barr, *Sister Aimee*, Garden City, New York: Doubleday Doran, 1931
McLoughlin, William, "Aimee Semple McPherson: Your Sister in the King's Glad Service," *Journal of Popular Culture* 1 (Winter 1967)
McWilliams, Carey, "Aimee Semple McPherson: 'Sunlight in My Soul,'" in *The Aspirin Age: 1919–1941*, edited by Isabel Leighton, New York: Simon and Schuster, 1949; London: Bodley Head, 1950

Media Rating Council

Industry Self-Regulatory Group

Originally known as the Broadcast Rating Council (BRC) and then as the Electronic Media Rating Council (EMRC), the official sanctioning body for ratings services now goes by the name Media Rating Council (MRC). The MRC works to maintain confidence and credibility in ratings through its self-stated goal of setting standards that ensure that surveys of media audiences are conducted in a manner that encourages quality, integrity, and accurate disclosure of the research process. A nonprofit agency sanctioned by the U.S. Justice Department, the MRC consists of 70 members from broadcast and cable trade associations, media owners, advertising agencies, cable networks, print and internet companies, and national networks.

The MRC is a nonprofit industry organization that is run on its membership fees. Each member organization provides one person to serve on the MRC board of directors, which makes the final decision as to whether reports that have been audited will receive accreditation from the council. Among the members of the New York–based MRC are the National Association of Broadcasters, the Television Bureau of Advertising, the Radio Advertising Bureau, and the Cable Advertising Bureau.

The MRC was established in 1964, when it was known as the BRC. A self-regulatory agency, the BRC was formed in response to an investigation by the House Subcommittee on Communications of the Interstate and Foreign Commerce Committee, under the chairmanship of Oren Harris. The Harris Committee, as it was known, held hearings in 1963 to investigate ratings and audience research. The hearings arose both from an increased focus on television ratings after the quiz show scandals of 1961 and from complaints by advertisers that they couldn't obtain upfront information about research methodology from the Nielsen Company. Essentially, the Harris Committee was concerned that if ratings were defective or deceptive, they would affect programming selections by stations and work in a manner that was not in the public interest.

The credibility and validity of ratings became a growing industry concern as U.S. representatives questioned executives from broadcast-measurement companies about the quality of their research. Faced with the possibility of government interference in the ratings business, broadcast industry leaders obtained permission from the U.S. Justice Department (to avoid any perception of antitrust violations) to set up the BRC, thereby ensuring a means of self-regulation.

The BRC changed its name to the Electronic Media Rating Council in 1982 to include all electronic media, such as radio, television, and cable. The "Electronic" in the council's name was dropped in 1997 when the council started performing audits on print services as well as broadcast services. On 4 September 1996 the *Study of Media and Markets* (a national survey of over 20,000 adults performed by Simmons Market Research Bureau) became the first multimedia research study with a primary focus on print media to receive accreditation from the council. Today the MRC audits organizations such as Mediamark Research (which provides research to all forms of advertising media collected from a single sample) and J.D. Power and Associates (which publishes the annual *Car and Truck Media Studies* to assist with marketing and media strategies).

Audience measurement services voluntarily submit their studies to the MRC for review and possible accreditation. The MRC then commissions audits by an independent accounting firm (currently the Ernst and Young Corporation) to review the data. The ratings services pay the cost of the audit to the MRC, which in turn pays the auditors. This system allows for some separation between the parties and establishes that the MRC, not the ratings service, is supervising the audit.

Even though the auditing process is voluntary, many organizations still seek accreditation so that they will be considered legitimate in the industry and will therefore be better able to sell their ratings. Organizations seeking accreditation must agree to conduct their service as represented to users and subscribers, undergo MRC audits, and pay for the costs of the audits. The results of the audits are reviewed by the council's board of directors to determine if the ratings service will receive accreditation. Should a report receive accreditation, the organization submitting the report still must re-apply the following year and have the report reviewed on an annual basis. The MRC accredits syndicated services and individual reports, not entire companies. Accredited services and reports carry the MRC double-check logo.

In 1993 the council made an unprecedented move when it voted to suspend its accreditation of the spring Atlanta Arbitron survey, citing an on-air promotional campaign by Atlanta broadcasters that "hyped" (aimed to increase response rates) the survey by urging listeners to cooperate with Arbitron's diary-based system. The council decided that the effort could have an adverse effect on methodology and thus distort the survey results. The move to suspend accreditation met with sharp criticism from the Radio Advertising Bureau (RAB), which was upset with what it believed was an unfair bias toward television. Despite the controversy, the RAB currently holds membership in the MRC.

The MRC has expanded its role over the years but still functions primarily in an effort to maintain rating confidence and credibility. Melvin A. Goldberg, then EMRC executive director, explained in 1989 that obtaining accreditation required adherence to specific minimum standards that outlined basic objectives of reliable and useful electronic media audience measurement research. Acceptance of those standards was voluntary and was one of the conditions of EMRC membership.

According to Goldberg, the minimum standards fell into two groupings: (1) "Ethical and Operations Standards," and (2) "Disclosure Standards." The Ethical and Operations Standards governed the quality and integrity of the overall process of producing ratings. Meanwhile, the Disclosure Standards specified which information a ratings service had to make available to users, to the EMRC, and to its auditing agent. The overall effect of the standards was to assure anyone using EMRC-accredited ratings that the ratings actually measured what they said they did.

Thus, the minimum standards established professional codes of conduct that ratings services had to agree to in order to gain accreditation. For example, a ratings service was required to submit complete information on its survey methodology, including sampling techniques, recruiting procedures, weighing, tabulations, coding and computer software, and the eventual ratings. The standards that Goldberg referred to are still in effect today. However, the MRC has also added electronic delivery requirements that govern the proper way for ratings services to deliver data to a third party electronically. The MRC has also incorporated internet ratings reports into its auditing processes.

MATT TAYLOR

See also A.C. Nielsen Company; Arbitron

Further Reading

Beville, Hugh Malcolm, *Audience Ratings: Radio, Television, and Cable,* Hillsdale, New Jersey: Erlbaum, 1985; 2nd edition, 1988
Goldberg, Melvin A., "Broadcast Ratings and Ethics," *Review of Business* (Summer 1989)

Mergers. *See* Ownership, Mergers, and Acquisitions

Mercury Theater of the Air

Anthology Radio Drama Series

Mercury Theater of the Air was an offshoot of Orson Welles' successful theater company that had catapulted him to Broadway fame. Using many of the same actors, he put on a series of radio plays in 1938 under the title *First Person Singular,* although the *Mercury Theater* name was better known. At first the show had no sponsor and few listeners, but the success of the legendary "War of the Worlds" episode in 1938 persuaded Campbell's Soup to back it. The radio plays gave Welles national fame and allowed him to branch into films with his seminal *Citizen Kane* in 1941. The originality and technical flair that marked that film applied equally to Welles' radio productions.

By 1938 Welles, an accomplished Shakespearean actor, was becoming a noted radio performer, having worked on *March of Time;* adapted, directed, and starred in the seven-part *Les misérables;* and, most notably, by becoming the voice of *The Shadow.* He was approached by William Lewis, head of programming at Columbia Broadcasting System (CBS), to make nine one-hour adaptations of famous books. Welles' budget of $50,000 for the nine shows was not much, given that he had been earning $1,000 per week, and the shows were slated for an unpromising timeslot against the popular *Edgar Bergen and Charlie McCarthy.* However, the deal did offer Welles creative carte blanche; he did not need to worry about pleasing a sponsor or appealing to any target audience. (CBS made the offer at a time when Congress was threatening legislation aimed at raising radio standards, so owner William S. Paley wanted programs that could turn CBS into a veritable patron of the arts.)

Broadcasts began on 11 July 1938 on the WABC network with "Dracula." Like subsequent performances, it followed Welles' view that "the less a radio drama resembles a play the better it is likely to be." This represented a major departure from many previous programs that had tried to recreate live theater down to the last detail, even including intermissions and chatting patrons. Instead, Welles introduced an omnipresent narrator, himself, who played several roles. This not only allowed Welles to take center stage but also changed the narrator into a storyteller, all the other characters effectively becoming projections of himself. Welles was equally innovative in his use of music. He asked Bernard Herrmann (head of music for CBS) for an unprecedented amount of musical scoring for each drama: up to 40 minutes in 57-minute-long performances. Similar demands were made with regard to sound effects, which overlapped the dialogue instead of occurring at the end of a speech as had been the practice. Welles demanded that even the faintest rustle of leaves be reproduced, despite the fact that very few listeners would have been able to hear these effects on their crackling AM radios. (They can now be appreciated on compact disc recordings, however.)

Nearly all of the dramas performed by the Mercury Players, which included "Treasure Island," "The Thirty-Nine Steps," and "The Count of Monte Cristo," were classics with family appeal. Their tone was not patronizing, but neither were they too advanced for children to appreciate. Welles decided which story to perform each week, but despite opening credits saying that each play was "produced, directed, and performed by Orson Welles," his participation was strictly limited to reviewing the script, making last minute changes, and performing. His long-time collaborator John Houseman and experienced radio man Paul Stewart oversaw the script writing and rehearsals. For the cast, Welles was able to call upon members of the Mercury stage theater such as George Coulouris, as well as other experienced radio actors including Ray Collins, Agnes Moorehead, and Martin Gabel.

Despite this range of talents, the programs rarely attracted more than four percent of the national radio audience until "War of the Worlds" greatly increased Welles' fame. The resulting sponsorship by Campbell's Soup caused the title of the series to be changed to *The Campbell Playhouse Series* in midseason 1939. This new name also reflected the demise of the Mercury Theater, which had fallen apart following a number of unsuccessful theater productions.

Ostensibly, *The Campbell Playhouse Series* was the same program as the *Mercury Theater of the Air*, and the dramas continued to be hour-long adaptations. However, the new and bigger budget allowed Welles to cast star names, including Katharine Hepburn ("A Farewell to Arms"), Laurence Olivier ("Beau Geste"), Gertrude Lawrence ("Private Lives"), and Walter Huston ("Les misérables"), as his co-stars. Former members of the Mercury stage theater continued to work on the show, but they were now reduced to supporting roles. The presence of a star also affected the show's format, as the play would now be sandwiched between segments of talk show style patter as Welles chatted with his guest star. This would invariably include some banal reference to the joys of Campbell's soup. Campbell's also inserted commercial breaks for soup ads into the plays themselves. The *Mercury* broadcasts had been uninterrupted, but now cliff-hangers had to be created to insure that listeners did not tune in a different program during the commercials.

The *Campbell's* plays were also based upon noticeably different books. The *Mercury's* eclectic mix of classics was forsaken in favor of more populist and more modern works, primarily bestsellers from the previous decade. There were also reworkings of previous Welles productions, which were an indicator of the extent to which the program lost much of the *Mercury's* originality and innovation. Welles' contribution also dropped off considerably as he began to concentrate more on theater before relocating to Hollywood. During this period, he would fly to New York on the day of the performance, make the broadcast, and then fly back to Hollywood. The production of the plays was thus left to Houseman and Stewart, with almost no input from Welles at all. However, *Campbell Playhouse* was one of the most popular shows on radio until Welles finally pulled the plug in March 1940 to fully concentrate on cinema. He had considered moving the show to Los Angeles so that his actors could be employed while he worked in films, but Campbell's refused to give up the Broadway panache that the show's New York connection provided. The *Mercury* name did make some sporadic returns to radio whenever Welles needed to raise some quick cash, but these later programs were mainly rehashes of previous performances that added little to the originals.

NEIL DENSLOW

See also Drama; Playwrights on Radio; War of the Worlds.

Cast

The "Mercury Players"	Orson Welles, Ray Collins, Agnes Moorehead, George Coulouris, Frank Readick, Georgia Backus, Bea Benaderet, Everett Sloane, Edgar Barrier

Producers/Creators

Orson Welles and John Houseman

Programming History

WABC (CBS)

First Person Singular/Mercury Theater of the Air	July 1938–December 1938
Campbell's Playhouse Series	December 1938–March 1940; 1946

Further Reading

Brady, Frank, *Citizen Welles: A Biography of Orson Welles,* New York: Scribner, 1989; London: Hodder and Stoughton, 1990

Callow, Simon, *Orson Welles: The Road to Xanadu,* London: Jonathan Cape, 1995; New York: Viking, 1996

Houseman, John, *Run-through: A Memoir,* New York: Simon and Schuster, 1972; London: Allen Lane, 1973

Leaming, Barbara, *Orson Welles,* New York: Viking, and London: Weidenfeld and Nicholson, 1985

Naremore, James, *The Magic World of Orson Welles,* New York: Oxford University Press, 1978

Thomas, François, "Dossier: La radio d'Orson Welles," *Positif* (October 1988)

Metromedia

Group Owner of Radio Stations

Corporate executive John Kluge made his mark as the founder of Metromedia, a media conglomerate that operated through the 1960s and 1970s both with independent television stations in major U.S. cities and with owned and operated major-market radio stations as well. Although not well known to the general public, Kluge emerged in this period as one of the most powerful media moguls. Kluge proved that independent television stations and big-city radio stations could make millions of dollars in profits by counterprogramming. In 1985, when Australian Rupert Murdoch offered Kluge nearly $2 billion for Metromedia's seven television stations, he sold out and began to reinvent Metromedia. He was out of big-city radio during the late 1980s.

John Werner Kluge surely represents the American success story. Kluge grew up poor in Detroit, but in 1933 he won a scholarship to Columbia University, where he earned a degree in economics. Serving U.S. Army Intelligence during World War II, he returned with little taste for resuming a career in the employ of others. He looked for ways to make money, including buying and selling radio stations.

After World War II, Kluge came to radio (and television) for its advertising power in the growing market of Washington, D.C., where he had served in World War II. Kluge bought and sold radio stations; his first was WGAY-FM in Silver Spring, Maryland, a Washington, D.C., suburb. As radio reinvented itself as a format medium, Kluge bought and sold stations across the United States, with early investments in radio groups including the St. Louis Broadcasting Corporation, Pittsburgh Broadcasting Company, Capitol Broadcasting Company (Nashville), Associated Broadcasters (Fort Worth–Dallas), Western New York Broadcasting Company (Buffalo), and the Mid-Florida Radio Corporation (Orlando).

Kluge became aware of television as an investment possibility when he ran into an acquaintance on a street in Washington, D.C.; the acquaintance casually mentioned that the failed Dumont television network was going up for sale. In January 1959 Kluge acquired Paramount Pictures' share of what remained of DuMont, the television stations of Metropolitan Broadcasting, for $4 million. He then consolidated his radio and television holdings and later bought and sold interests in restaurants, outdoor and direct-mail advertising, and magazines.

Indeed, Kluge never stopped trading radio—if he figured he could make a profit. So in 1982, for example, he sold WMET-FM (Chicago) and KSAN-FM (San Francisco) and acquired KHOW-AM and WWBA-FM in Tampa, Florida. Yet with Federal Communications Commission rules permitting Metromedia to own only seven AM and seven FM radio stations, Kluge held on to stations in top markets because they made the most money. Metromedia held WNEW-AM and -FM in New York City, KLAC-AM in Los Angeles (acquired in 1963), and WIP-AM in Philadelphia (acquired in 1960) for the longest amount of time. Once a station was acquired, Kluge assigned managers to squeeze maximum profits, not caring what format was used. His stations employed all formats: adult contemporary, beautiful music, all-news—any format that worked in that particular major market.

In his heyday, Kluge grew famous for cutting costs and maximizing revenues; indeed, once he had assembled Metromedia, he moved the operation's headquarters out of expensive Manhattan across the Hudson River to Secaucus, New Jersey, where rents were lower. He secured the cheapest possible programming, and then, even with small audience shares, Metromedia could, with bare-bones costs, make a profit. But not every well struck oil. One disastrous misstep was Kluge's purchase of the niche magazine *Diplomat*. Another was his vision of forming a fourth television network, a venture in which Kluge only lost millions of dollars.

In April 1984 Kluge took Metromedia private, and so he possessed three-quarters of Metromedia stock when he sold the seven television stations to Rupert Murdoch a year later. The eventual sale of the radio stations in the late 1980s would make Kluge more than $100 million, a great deal of money, but little compared to the billions made from the sale of the television stations.

But by the 1990s Kluge was again at work building a new corporate empire. He again took a qualified risk by sinking his fortune into paging devices such as beepers and mobile telephones. He bought licenses for operation in major markets, waited as the market evolved, and then sold out at a profit. He also went global, forming Metromedia International Telecommunications to bring wireless cable and communications businesses to the emerging markets of Eastern Europe and the former Soviet republics. In 1994 Kluge began to break into the radio broadcasting business once again by acquiring Radio Juventus in Hungary. By 1999 Metromedia International was a leading operator of radio stations in Eastern Europe and the former Soviet Union, with 15 stations in ten markets.

DOUGLAS GOMERY

Further Reading

Compaine, Benjamin M., and Douglas Gomery, *Who Owns the Media?* New York: Harmony Books, 1979; 3rd edition, Mahwah, New Jersey: Erlbaum, 2000

Gelman, Morris J., "John Kluge: The Man with the Midas Touch," *Television Magazine* (July 1964)

Gomery, Douglas, "Vertical Integration, Horizontal Regulation—The Growth of Rupert Murdoch's Media Empire," *Screen* 27, nos. 3–4 (May–August 1986)

Kluge, John W., *The Metromedia Story*, New York: Newcomen Society in North America, 1974

Metropolitan Opera Broadcasts

Bringing Opera into the Home

Performances of New York's Metropolitan Opera have been broadcast regularly on radio since 1931 and occasionally on television since 1977. Milton Cross was the voice of these broadcasts for more than four decades. The continuous support of Texaco (ChevronTexaco after 2000) from 1940 to 2004 formed what was probably the world's longest-running commercial broadcast sponsorship.

Origins

New York's Metropolitan Opera Association was formed in October 1883, and soon the city was presented with an annual season of fine opera performances by top-drawer orchestras and singers. But for decades the only way to hear and see a "Met" performance was to purchase an expensive ticket and attend a program in New York.

The first hint of an alternative means of delivering opera came on 13 January 1910. With the permission of the Opera's assistant director, wireless inventor (and opera lover) Lee de Forest set up one of his transmitters high in the attic above the stage with a temporary bamboo antenna on the roof. Several microphones were placed on the stage. That first transmission included scenes from *Cavalleria Rusticana* and Enrico Caruso singing in *Pagliacci* and was heard primarily by other radio operators and some reporters. And what they heard was anything but a clear signal, given the crude equipment of the time. The poor results did not endear the company's management to the rising medium of radio.

Despite radio's later development, opera director Giulio Gatti-Casazza resisted further experimentation with radio microphones for two decades out of a fear of lost ticket sales. He also felt mere *listeners* would lose the visual aspect of opera. Public reasons given for the lack of radio coverage included technical problems with placement of microphones and contracts with lead singers that forbade such transmission. Yet the Met was being bypassed by others.

The Chicago Civic Opera went on the air in 1922 when station KYW debuted with a focus on opera broadcasts. And other performing companies were heard in other cities. So were some performances by the Manhattan Opera Company that then competed with the Metropolitan Opera. The fan magazine *Radio Digest* began an editorial campaign to get the Met to change its mind that same year. Station WEAF wasn't waiting—they formed their own in-studio opera companies, one for grand and one for light opera—and broadcast their performances for several years. The original language of the composer was used, but performances were cut to fit one-hour time slots. And they took place in a studio, not on an opera stage, limiting what could be accomplished. Broadcasts of opera from Europe could occasionally be picked up by U.S. listeners tuning shortwave. The broadcast sound quality left much to be desired, but at least the operas were being heard.

What finally turned the tide was the Met's need for new sources of operating funds during the depression. NBC secured the broadcast rights for $120,000 for the first season, outbidding rival CBS. Broadcasts began with *Hansel and Gretel* on Christmas Day of 1931 with Deems Taylor providing the initial commentary. He received howls of protest when he timed his comments to appear over the music and soon changed his approach. The first broadcasts also featured announcer Milton Cross, who would remain as host until 1975, doing more than 800 broadcasts and missing only two in all those years.

Metropolitan Opera Auditions of the Air was developed as a separate program (1935–58; on NBC until 1937, then Blue/ABC) and also featured commentary by Milton Cross with Edward Johnson, managing director of the Met, as host. Each week aspiring operatic performers would do their best to earn audience support and a contract from the Met.

Despite the interest of a small but vocal audience, sponsorship for the broadcasts was difficult to arrange and harder to perpetuate. Several backers (American Tobacco, RCA, and Lambert drugs) came and went, and by the late 1930s, opera broadcasts from New York were threatened by a lack of continuing advertiser support.

Texaco Sponsorship

Beginning on 7 December 1940, the Texaco oil company took up sponsorship of the weekly broadcasts. Though at first this seemed merely the latest in a changing parade of financial backers, Texaco stuck with the program, pleased with the highbrow audience it attracted. More than six decades later, ChevronTexaco continued to support the Metropolitan Opera broadcasts, forming what was probably the longest continuing relationship of an advertiser and a program in radio history. The broadcasts under Texaco at first continued on NBC, then moved to Blue (which became ABC) until 1958, at which point CBS carried on the series for two years. But Texaco became unhappy with declining network interest and decided to create its own specialized network of stations to carry the Saturday matinees. So in 1960 the Texaco-Metropolitan Opera Radio Network was created, with Texaco arranging for the AT&T connecting lines to link the slowly growing number of stations carrying the broadcasts.

As microphone and other radio technologies improved, so did the sound of the opera on the air. By the late 1940s a more complex multiple microphone technique was being used. The opera company understandably insisted that no microphone be placed where it could be seen, so broadcasts utilized four microphones placed near the stage footlights. These were aimed at the floor to receive a more equal (reflected) sound of the varied singing voices and spoken lines and were supplemented by two more microphones suspended above the orchestra. Stereo transmissions were added in the 1960s. The entire radio operation was upgraded with the move of the Met into its new opera house in New York's Lincoln Center in 1966. The opera network was connected by satellite in the 1980s.

Over the years the opera broadcasts were supplemented with the "Texaco Opera Quiz" and "Opera News on the Air," features that became very popular. On Milton Cross' death in 1975, Peter Allen took over the host role and continued it into the 21st century. In 1977 several operas were televised on the Public Broadcasting Service, which still does three or four such performances each season (with English subtitles). Texaco also supported formation of a Media Center to archive past broadcasts.

Over the years the audience for the programs grew, first in the United States and then beyond. The 20-week (November–April) season of Saturday matinees has long been transmitted throughout the United States and Canada (more than 325 stations across North America), and beginning in 1990, to 27 European countries. Australia and New Zealand joined the network in 1997, and in 2000 the Texaco network welcomed Brazil and Mexico. By the end of the 2000–2001 season, Texaco had sponsored 1,212 Metropolitan Opera broadcasts of 144 different operas.

In May 2003 ChevronTexaco (as the sponsor had become after a 2000 merger) announced that the 2003–04 season of matinee broadcasts would be the last they would sponsor, ending a nearly 65-year run, the longest continuous sponsorship in radio history. The Metropolitan Opera said it would continue the broadcasts and seek new sponsors. ChevronTexaco said the series had been costing about $7 million a year, reaching some 10 million listeners in 42 countries. Their announcement to terminate sponsorship came after the oil company saw a drop in both profits and stock price.

CHRISTOPHER H. STERLING

See also Classical Music Format; Cross, Milton; De Forest, Lee; KYW; Music; Taylor, Deems

Programming History

NBC Red or Blue (sometimes both)	1931–40
NBC Red	1940–43
Blue Network/ABC	1943–58
CBS	1958–60

Texaco-Metropolitan Opera Radio 1960–2000
 Network

ChevronTexaco-Metropolitan 2000–2004
 Opera Radio Network

Further Reading

De Forest, Lee, *Father of Radio: The Autobiography of Lee De Forest*, Chicago: Wilcox and Follett, 1950

DeLong, Thomas A., *The Mighty Music Box: The Golden Age of Musical Radio*, Los Angeles: Amber Crest Books, 1980

Jackson, Paul J., *Saturday Afternoons at the Old Met: The Metropolitan Opera Broadcasts, 1931–1950*, Portland, Oregon: Amadeus Press, and London: Duckworth, 1992

Jackson, Paul J., *Sign-Off for the Old Met: The Metropolitan Opera Broadcasts, 1950–1966*, Portland, Oregon: Amadeus Press, and London: Duckworth, 1997

LaPrade, Ernest, *Broadcasting Music*, New York: Rinehart, 1956

Metmaniac Opera Archive Online <www.metmaniac.com>

Pogrebin, Robin, "Chevron Texaco to Stop Sponsoring Met's Broadcasts," *New York Times* (21 May 2003)

Mexico

Radio reaches more people in Mexico than any other electronic medium of communication. Despite the broad reach of television and the growing role of cable and the internet, radio broadcasting continues to be a central arena of commerce, culture, education, and politics. Beginning in the 1920s and 1930s, radio's dynamic sound format made it an ideal medium for Mexico's orally based popular cultures, including music, verbal humor, and melodrama. Despite the strong influence of the U.S. commercial broadcasting model, radio practices in Mexico reflect the interaction of a variety of social forces: local popular cultures, the national state, transnational commercial interests, and civic groups.

Broadcasting Begins: The 1920s and 1930s

Beginning with Mexico's first radio transmission in 1908, radio was the domain of amateur operators who used the medium primarily for point-to-point communication. With the authorization of the first non-experimental broadcasting stations in 1923, however, state and commercial interests began to develop radio as a broadcast medium. State-sponsored stations were operated by specific branches of government (e.g., the Navy, the Ministry of Education) with limited public funding. Commercial stations were financed by entrepreneurs who drew on both transnational capital and domestic capital accumulated in ancillary fields (e.g., newspaper publishing, electronics, retail sales). The first commercial station, CYL, was launched by Luis and Raul Azcárraga, distributors of U.S. radio parts and receivers, in partnership with the Mexico City newspaper *El Universal*. Another early station, CYB (later XEB), was started by a cigarette company, El Buen Tono, with

French financial backing. Sixteen stations were broadcasting by 1926, and nineteen by 1929, the year Mexican stations received the "XE" and "XH" call letter designations.

Beginning in the early 1920s, the U.S. government and U.S. media interests made a concerted effort to open broadcasting markets in Mexico and Latin America to U.S. commercial interests. At the 1924 Inter-American Conference on Electrical Communications held in Mexico City, however, Latin American delegates resisted this offensive and argued that a strong governmental role in radio was essential to economic self-determination. Although they conceded to the principle of commercial competition where feasible, Latin American delegates resolved that electronic communication media were public services over which national governments held direct control. These resolutions became the basis for Mexico's first radio law of 1926, the Law of Electrical Communications (LCE) and the subsequent Law of General Means of Communication (LVGC).

Despite considerable U.S. pressure, Mexico's radio regulations were strongly influenced by state activism and economic nationalism. The 1926 LCE declared the airwaves to be a national resource, allowed only Mexican citizens to own or operate radio stations, and prohibited any transmissions that attacked state security, public order, or the established government. The LVGC established a system of 50-year concessions for commercial broadcasters. Concessionaires were prohibited from making political or religious broadcasts and were required to carry government transmissions free of charge. Further regulations prohibited radio studios from being located on foreign soil and required broadcasting in Spanish. In practice, this regulatory framework ensured the rapid development of commercial broadcasting while giving the state a privileged position of access and control within a highly nationalistic broadcasting system.

Commercial broadcasting grew enormously during the 1930s with an infusion of advertising revenue from transnational companies like Colgate-Palmolive and Proctor and Gamble. Although many prominent regional stations started in the early 1930s, Mexico City became the undisputed power center of commercial broadcasting. The centerpiece of Mexico City broadcasting was XEW, "La Voz de América Latina desde México" ("The Voice of Latin America from Mexico"), founded by Emilio Azcárraga in 1930. XEW soon became the most powerful and most popular radio station in the country. By the late 1930s Azcárraga had organized two national radio networks anchored at stations XEW and XEQ in Mexico City. Along with the rise of the Azcárraga group, the late 1930s witnessed the consolidation of the commercial broadcasting industry and the formation of a powerful industry group that became the Radio Industry Chamber (the CIR, later CIRT) in 1942.

As commercial broadcasting advanced, the central state also expanded its efforts to harness the new medium. The number of government-operated radio stations reached a peak of 14 during these years. Important stations were operated by the National Revolutionary Party (PNR, later the PRI), the Ministry of Public Education, and the Autonomous Department of Press and Publicity. Beginning in 1937 the government produced a "National Hour" program of official information and national culture that all stations were required to broadcast weekly. At the same time, radio regulations promoted national culture by requiring all broadcasters to include 25 percent "typical" Mexican music in their broadcasts. The 1930s also saw the beginning of state-sponsored radio education projects, which included the distribution of radio sets to rural schools and working class neighborhoods.

Whereas comedies and drama serials dominated U.S. broadcasting during the 1930s, music was the mainstay of Mexican radio. This was due, in part, to an explosion in the production and circulation of popular music in Mexico and Latin America beginning in the 1920s. Musical programs included boleros, mambos, and rancheras performed by orchestras, bands, and soloists, often interspersed with comedy interludes in a "musical variety" format. In addition, radio regulations created a climate that promoted national musical forms over the radio medium. Commercial broadcasters found that Mexican singers and musicians performing popular Mexican tunes provided the ideal radio content to satisfy state nationalism and capture the national broadcasting market. Mexican orchestras featuring performers like Agustín Lara and Toña la Negra dominated the XEW network schedule.

Although dramatic series were less prominent than music during the 1930s, broadcasters developed a number of dramatic and nonfiction program formats by modifying and adapting U.S. soap operas, game shows, and news and sports programs. Radionovelas, for example, combined the techniques and formats of U.S. soap opera production with the melodrama of Latin American music, film, and theater.

Radio listening grew considerably over this period as the number of stations grew, the quality and consistency of programming improved, and the price of radio sets dropped. Listeners had been scarce in the 1920s, but between 1930 and 1935 the number of radio receivers grew to an estimated 200,000 sets and reached an estimated 600,000 sets by the end of the decade. Surveys from Mexico City indicate that well over half of the urban population had regular access to the medium by the late 1930s, although radios were still rare in rural areas and smaller regional cities.

A Golden Age: The 1940s and 1950s

The 1940s and 1950s were characterized by steady growth and consolidation in the radio industry and the increasing popularity of the radio medium. Between 1941 and 1950 the number of radio sets grew from more than 600,000 to almost 2 million. Assuming approximately six listeners for every radio receiver, a 1943 survey indicates that over 90 percent of the populations of Monterrey and Torreón had regular access to radios, compared to 79 percent in Guadalajara, 68 percent in Mexico City, and only 33 percent in Puebla and Morelia. In 1941 Azcárraga and his partner Clemente Serna Martínez consolidated their radio holdings into a single company, Radio Programs of Mexico (RPM). By the mid-1940s RPM networks encompassed nearly half the stations in Mexico and included more than 30 affiliates in Central America, the Caribbean, and the northern rim of South America. Several other national networks emerged in the 1940s, including networks anchored by stations XEB and XEOY-Radio Mil.

Mexican broadcasters' regional power became evident in 1946 when the chief organ of the radio industry, the CIR, organized the Inter-American Association of Radiobroadcasters (AIR) to promote commercial broadcasting throughout Latin America. In 1948 AIR delegates drew up the *Bases of the AIR*—a set of principles to guide broadcasting legislation in the region. These principles declared broadcasting to be a fundamentally private activity undertaken in the public interest. The document argued that government regulations should be limited to the technical aspects of broadcasting and that the state should be prohibited from competing with private broadcasters for advertising dollars. The unstated goal of the AIR was to ensure that the commercial model of broadcasting would guide television development in the region.

World War II had a significant impact on the consolidation and expansion of the Mexican radio industry. During the war the U.S. government sponsored a massive propaganda campaign through the Office of the Coordinator of Inter-American Affairs (CIAA). Headed by Nelson Rockefeller, the CIAA aimed to counter Nazi propaganda in Latin America by increasing the dependency of Latin American broadcasters on U.S. corporate advertising, strengthening oligopolies (especially Azcárraga's), and blacklisting uncooperative broadcasters. The CIAA ultimately discovered that the best way to convey its propaganda was to incorporate it into Azcárraga's popular Mexican commercial content. As a result, the Azcárraga group benefited from CIAA funding without losing significant control over radio content.

Indeed, the era of the CIAA has been described as a "golden age" of radio in Mexico and Latin America as a whole. Mexican performers such as Jorge Negrete and Agustín Lara became international stars through the synergy of radio, records, and cinema. Musical variety programs and radionovelas of a distinctly Mexican pitch became the institutional and economic mainstay of commercial radio. Of the most popular radionovelas first produced during this period, *El derecho de nacer* (The Right to be Born) and *Simplemente María* (Simply Maria) later became classics of the telenovela genre.

While television entered the majority of U.S. homes by the late 1950s, it was adopted much more slowly in Mexico. Although a small number of television and FM stations were launched at this time, their audiences remained extremely limited due to the expense of television sets and FM-compatible receivers. Instead, AM radio continued to grow and expand during the 1950s and remained the primary broadcasting medium until well into the 1960s and 1970s. Radio Cadena Nacional was one of several new networks that emerged in the 1950s. Azcárraga's RPM organization, however, remained dominant and increased its national broadcasting coverage by buying two independent networks. Expansion abroad also increased during this period as Azcárraga's Latin American network grew to 80 affiliates and RPM began exporting programs to Spain. At the same time, the AIR expanded its international activities and opposed government broadcasting initiatives in several countries. The postwar period also witnessed the formation of labor and professional organizations in Mexican broadcasting, including the Union of Radio and Television Industry Workers (STIRT) and the National Association of Mexican Announcers (ANLM).

Growth and Competition: The 1960s and 1970s

The 1960s and 1970s were decades of tremendous growth for the radio industry. The radio audience exploded from almost 3 million to more than 14 million between 1960 and 1970 and reached 20 million by the end of the 1970s. The structure of the industry remained highly centralized despite the Azcárraga group's increasing shift to television. Important new radio

chains developed during this period, including Sociedad Mexicana de Radio, S.A., Asociacion de Concesionarios Independientes de Radio, Organización Impulsadora de Radio, and Organización Estrellas de Oro. In the early 1970s Clemente Serna Alvear (son of Serna Martínez) purchased Radio Cadena Nacional and formed Radio Red, a network devoted to talk and news programming.

Despite robust growth in radio, however, television began to siphon off both talent and advertising revenue. Although radionovelas continued to draw vast audiences during the early 1960s, by the end of the decade live radio production was increasingly replaced by less expensive recorded programs (mostly music). Polls indicate that the percent of stations airing radionovelas declined to 27 percent in 1977 and less than 7 percent by 1981. Television competition also led radio broadcasters to explore new technologies as a means of increasing their markets. Beginning in 1970 the Mexican Association of FM Broadcasters began to promote commercial FM broadcasting and encourage the manufacture of FM radios. By 1980, the number of FM stations had more than doubled (from 65 to 174) and the commercial model of FM radio was firmly in place.

The 1960s and 1970s also witnessed important developments in broadcast regulation. The 1960 Federal Law of Radio and Television (LFRT) established a regulatory structure that would remain in place through the year 2000. The LFRT followed many of the recommendations made by the AIR and CIRT and declared broadcasting to be an activity undertaken "in the public interest," rather than a "public service." At the same time, the LFRT continued to assert a national interest in broadcasting with regulations that promoted national morality and culture.

Social change and state activism in broadcasting during the late 1960s and early 1970s also led to significant regulatory revisions. Renewed government interest in broadcasting was signaled by the reopening of the Education Ministry's radio education project in 1967 with station XEEP. After much wrangling between the government and the industry, a 1969 agreement gave 12.5 percent of the broadcasting day to the state, but did not allow that time to accrue. Regulatory adjustments continued over the course of the 1970s as both the state and commercial interests jockeyed for privileged access to the broadcast media. By the late 1970s, "right to information" debates succeeded in breaking the state's moratorium against political broadcasting: for the first time all political parties were guaranteed access to the mass media.

Crisis and Consolidation: The 1980s and 1990s

The last two decades of the 20th century were characterized by technological innovation, new program formats, and the rise of a significant non-commercial radio sector. Many changes during this period were motivated by crisis conditions in the Mexican economy in the 1980s and early 1990s. Economic pressures forced broadcasters to seek new means of competing with television, which gobbled up almost 75 percent of the media advertising pie by the early 1990s. Beginning in 1986, radio chains began to use satellite technology as a means of increasing market share and reducing costs. Satellites not only improved networks' abilities to reach targeted markets nationwide, they also helped Mexican broadcasters reach international markets, including the lucrative U.S. Latino market. Centralization and consolidation continued to characterize the radio industry during the 1980s and 1990s, as fewer than a dozen groups controlled the majority of radio stations.

Political and social upheaval stimulated significant changes in radio program forms and content. As a range of political and civic voices began to call for democratic change in Mexico, radio became a ready outlet for political dissent. For commercial broadcasters, the decision to give voice to political opposition was, in part, a strategic decision. By airing oppositional voices, radio was able to provide a competitive information product that television broadcasters would be unable to offer until the mid-1990s. Radio's currency was also increased by the 1985 Mexico City earthquake. During the disaster, radio became a central means of coordinating relief efforts, disseminating information, and bringing the concerns of community and civic groups to the attention of government officials. All of these events contributed to the rise of news and talk-radio formats in the late 1980s and early 1990s and promoted social, cultural, and political openness on the air. Radio Red's *Monitor*, for example, became a prominent national news program. Overall, commercial radio news and information shows continued to reflect the centralized nature of the radio industry by focusing on Mexico City–based politics and culture.

Mexico experienced considerable growth in noncommercial broadcasting during this period. The number of noncommercial, "permissioned" stations doubled between 1981 and 1991 (from 47 to 100) and doubled again by 1999 (reaching 223). Growth in noncommercial broadcasting included two state-sponsored networks, Grupo IMER and Indigenous Cultural Radio (RCI), independent community radio, and university radio. Grupo IMER constitutes a unique hybrid in Mexican broadcasting, combining both state and nongovernmental funding and receiving special permission to supplement its budget with advertising. Unable to sell advertising, independents and university stations were hard hit by economic crises during this period. Despite calls for a new category of "social enterprise" radio that would allow nonprofit stations to sell advertising, community broadcasters remained "weak voices" on the Mexican airwaves.

The Future of Radio in Mexico

Mexican radio in the 21st century has entered a period of transition. Calls for the revision of the Federal Law of Radio and Television can be heard in a variety of circles, from civic and nongovernmental groups that would like to see new opportunities for community radio and low-power FM, to commercial broadcasters with interest in convergence and cross-media acquisitions. While the oligopolistic structure of commercial radio remains firmly in place, the government's anti-monopoly commission has so far prohibited the massive media mergers that have characterized U.S. radio. In sum, radio remains a lively medium of social communication that promises to play a central role in Mexico's changing economic, political, and cultural landscape.

JOY ELIZABETH HAYES

See also Border Radio; Hispanic Radio; South America

Further Reading

Alisky, Marvin, "Early Mexican Broadcasting," *Hispanic American Historical Review* 24, no. 4 (November 1954)

Barbour, Phillip L., "Commercial and Cultural Broadcasting in Mexico," *Annals of the American Academy of Political and Social Science* 108 (March 1940)

Bohmann, Karin, *Massenmedien und Nachrichtengebung in Mexiko: Eine empirische Analyse zum Spannungsverhältnis von staatlichen, privatwirtschaftlichen und transnationaler Einflussnahme*, Saarbrücken, Germany, and Fort Lauderdale, Florida: Breitenbach, 1986

Emery, Walter B., "Mexican Broadcasting," in *National and International Systems of Broadcasting: Their History, Operation, and Control*, by Emery, East Lansing: Michigan State University Press, 1969

Fernández Christlieb, Fátima, *La radio mexicana: Centro y regiones*, Mexico City: Pablos, 1991; 3rd edition, 1997

Hayes, Joy Elizabeth, *Radio Nation: Communication, Popular Culture, and Nationalism in Mexico, 1920–1950*, Tucson: University of Arizona Press, 2000

Hayes, Joy Elizabeth, and Corynne McSherry, "Radio," in *Encyclopedia of Mexico: History, Society, and Culture*, edited by Michael S. Werner, 2 vols., Chicago and London: Fitzroy Dearborn, 1997

Leyva, Juan, *Política educativa y comunicación social: La Radio en México, 1940–1946*, Mexico City: Universidad Nacional Autónoma de México, 1992

Mejía Barquera, Fernando, *La industria de la radio y la televisión y la política del estado mexicano*, Mexico City: Fundación Manuel Buendía, 1989

Noriega, Luis Antonio de, and Frances Leach, *Broadcasting in Mexico*, London and Boston: Routledge and Kegan Paul, 1979

Rebeil Corella, María Antonieta, Alma Rosa Alva de la Selva, and Ignacio Rodríguez Zárate, editors, *Perfiles del cuadrante: Experiencias de la radio,* Mexico City: Trillas, 1989

Romo, Cristina, *La otra radio: Voces débiles, voces de esperanza,* Mexico City: Fundación Manuel Buendía, and Instituto Mexicano de la Radio, 1990

Scharfeld, Arthur W., "The Mexican Broadcasting Situation," *Journal of Radio Law* 1, no. 2 (July 1931)

Microradio. *See* Low-Power Radio/Microradio

Middle East. *See* Arab World Radio; Israel

Middle East Radio Network. *See* Radio Sawa/Middle East Radio Network

Middle of the Road Format

Middle of the road (MOR) refers to a form of radio music programming that features popular standards and current hits, mainly adult contemporary in nature. MOR relies on broad-based music that appeals to adults 45 and older, and it serves as a "bridge" between the adult contemporary and easy listening formats. Other industry terms that describe the MOR approach include *full-service, variety, general appeal,* and *diversified* (Keith, 1997).

MOR serves as "one of the oldest and most durable types of programming within format radio" (Howard, Kievman, and Moore, 1994). It finds its origins in the 1940s, when radio offered a variety of program material and before rock and roll as a musical genre spurred the creation of specialized formats. Traditional MOR stations of this radio era appealed to adults by giving them "lots of news, sports, and safe, comfortable music" (Halper, 1991). As more and more stations sought to attract teen audiences, whom they saw as becoming more important as a demographic group, they began to air countdown shows of popular hits during nights and weekends. In this capacity, MOR serves as the predecessor of Top 40 radio.

During the 1950s, television began to displace radio as a source of entertainment programming, as embodied in serialized dramas and the like. Keith (1987) notes that as the networks left radio, stations found themselves having to fill their schedules with recorded music, news, and sports. When rock and roll arrived on the radio scene, marking the start of format specialization, MOR stations modified their playlists to secure the older adult audience. Thus, MOR established itself as a true radio format, characterized by broad-appeal music and a "full-service" function of providing music, news, and sports. By the mid-1950s, "MOR dominated the radio programming scene" (Keith, 1987).

Between the 1950s and 1970s, MOR enjoyed high popularity. But MOR as a programming powerhouse began to lose strength as the radio industry evolved during those decades. As radio became further fragmented, MOR had to contend with competition from new programming styles, such as beautiful music in the late 1950s and soft rock and oldies in the 1960s. Keith (1987) points out that these formats, plus the updating of easy listening station playlists and the rise of adult contemporary, took away some of MOR's audience. Because MOR was a mainstay of AM, its numbers fell further as FM grew in popularity in the 1970s, with mellow rock taking away the younger side of its demographic, 25- to 40-year-olds.

By the 1980s, the MOR audience consisted mainly of the 45 and older crowd, with a number-2 Arbitron rating in AM listenership and a number-11 ranking among the 12 formats listed for FM (Keith, 1987). Indeed, some believed that by the mid-1980s, MOR ceased to exist altogether, as other programming formats, especially adult contemporary, took its place. Fewer than 100 stations holding the label MOR remained by the mid-1990s (Keith, 1997).

Music-wise, the traditional MOR format through the years consistently centered on popular standards that emphasized melody more than a beat (Howard, Kievman, and Moore, 1994). Indeed, Hyatt (1999) considers the term *middle of the road* as synonymous to *adult contemporary* and *easy listening.* The term *middle of the road* accurately describes this type of music, which is similar to the more modern adult contemporary genre—neither too soft nor too raucous, music that walks the line musically, "avoiding anything too old, too new, too upbeat, or too solemn," as Keith (1987) describes it. Asserts Gregory (1998), "MOR was coined by broadcasters to describe a style of popular music that is high on melody, but short on substance."

Traditional MOR station playlists might include "traditional" pop vocalists such as Frank Sinatra, Tony Bennett, Rosemary Clooney, Ella Fitzgerald, Perry Como, and Peggy Lee; big band acts such as Benny Goodman and Glenn Miller; and relatively "contemporary" acts such as Helen Reddy, Olivia Newton-John, Barbra Streisand, Roger Whittaker, Ray Conniff, and Sergio Mendez (Howard, Kievman, and Moore, 1994; Keith, 1987, 1984). Crossover artists who found success in the MOR format during the 1970s included the Carpenters, Glen Campbell, and Anne Murray (Keith, 1984).

During the 1980s and 1990s, notes Gregory (1998), further updating of the MOR style came with the crossover success of artists with soul and rhythm and blues backgrounds, such as Whitney Houston, Toni Braxton, and Luther Vandross. The demarcation between MOR and adult contemporary formats eroded even further during this time, if one believes Gregory (1998) when he asserts that "the whole concept of what MOR actually represented was embodied by Canadian Celine Dion, Elton John and the modern musicals of Andrew Lloyd Webber and Tim Rice." In short, when considering the range of artists found on station playlists, MOR and adult contemporary mirror each other in terms of melodic style, but the MOR playlist includes older standards.

In addition to the inclusion of older tunes, MOR differentiates itself from other similar formats in its use of on-air personalities and its added emphasis on news. For example, whereas adult contemporary stresses music, MOR "has always been the home of the radio personality" (Keith, 1984). On-air announcers and disc jockeys enjoy considerably more freedom on MOR than on other music-based formats; they often choose individual selections to play and may have extensive programming experience (Howard, Kievman, and Moore, 1994). Indeed, "MOR personalities often serve as the cornerstone of their station's air product" (Keith, 1997).

Though fewer traditional MOR stations existed in the late 1990s, the format, encompassing heavy news and informational programming, still found success in the larger metropolitan markets. Just as the radio industry as a whole had experienced "frag-out" during the 1970s, the MOR label became delineated at the end of the 20th century with descriptors such as "nostalgia," "golden oldies," and "adult standard." Stations employing the MOR genre in the late 1990s reflected this emphasis on music favored by its older-adult audience through slogans such as "Unforgettable Favorites," "The Original Hits Station," "Station of the Stars," "The Greatest Music of All Time," "The Memory Station," and "Great Songs, Great Memories."

ERIKA ENGSTROM

See also Adult Contemporary Format; Easy Listening/Beautiful Music Format; Formats; Oldies Format

Further Reading

Gregory, Hugh, *A Century of Pop,* Chicago: A Capella, 1998
Halper, Donna L., *Radio Music Directing,* Boston and London: Focal Press, 1991
Howard, Herbert H., and Michael S. Kievman, *Radio and TV Programming,* Ames: Iowa State University Press, 1986; 2nd edition, as *Radio, TV, and Cable Programming,* by Howard, Kievman, and Barbara A. Moore, 1994
Hyatt, Wesley, *The Billboard Book of Number One Adult Contemporary Hits,* New York: Billboard Books, 1999
Keith, Michael C., *Production in Format Radio Handbook,* Lanham, Maryland: University Press of America, 1984
Keith, Michael C., and Joseph M. Krause, *The Radio Station,* Boston: Focal Press, 1986; 4th edition, by Michael C. Keith, 1997; 5th edition, Boston and Oxford: Focal Press, 2000
Keith, Michael C., *Radio Programming: Consultancy and Formatics,* Boston and London: Focal Press, 1987

Milam, Lorenzo 1933–

U.S. Community Radio Activist

Lorenzo Wilson Milam is a broadcast activist, teacher, and writer who founded or helped to get licensed more than 40 community-based FM radio stations between 1962 and 1976. Originally published in 1975, his book *Sex and Broadcasting: A Handbook on Starting a Radio Station for the Community* showed nonprofit groups how to get on the air, legally licensed by the Federal Communications Commission (FCC). Typically underfunded, most of these stations used donated and home-built equipment, all were programmed by volunteers, and most have not survived in their original forms. What Milam accomplished in the 1970s is similar to what the microradio proponents achieved for community groups in the late 1990s, but with one major difference: Milam's stations had government licenses, and microradio did not.

Many of Lorenzo Milam's social and political goals for radio were repeated 30 years later by Stephen Dunifer of Radio Free Berkeley. Dunifer believed, as Milam did, that radio was in the firm control of corporate entities and that community groups such as antiwar activists, tenants' rights groups, homeless advocates, the disabled, and all others denied a voice by the mainstream media were entitled to broadcast. Unlike Dunifer, Lorenzo Milam's 1970s timing allowed him access to open FM channels now no longer available. During the time that Milam was helping community groups get licensed, the dominant medium was AM radio. Most commercial FM stations were not profitable, and there were few educational licensees on the air, so a lack of interest in FM made it easier for Milam to obtain licenses.

The 1945 allocation of VHF channels set aside a portion of the then underused FM band for a license category called "educational, non-commercial." Channels between 88.1 and 91.9 megahertz were reserved for colleges, high schools, community nonprofit foundations, churches, and other institutions without a commercial purpose. A category known as 10-watt Class D allowed entry-level broadcasters, such as high schools, to purchase inexpensive transmitters. In 1978 Class D was eliminated, but in January 2000 the FCC created a special class of licenses called Low Power FM Radio (LPFM). The LPFM service is designed to create opportunities for new voices to be heard on the radio.

The LPFM service consists of two types of radio station: 100-watt stations that reach an area with a radius of approximately three and one-half miles; and 10-watt stations that generally reach an area with a radius of between one and two miles. By contrast, full-power FM radio stations generally operate at between 6,000 and 100,000 watts.

LPFM stations are available only to noncommercial educational entities and to non-profit public safety or transportation organizations. Licenses are not available to individuals or to commercial operations. In order to assure the greatest diversity of ownership, existing broadcasters and other media entities are prohibited from owning LPFM stations, and an entity may own only one LPFM station in the same area.

There are several informal categories of noncommercial FM stations. Most successful, as defined by funding success and audience numbers, are those affiliated with National Public Radio (NPR). A second category, college radio, is typically programmed by students, often as part of a radio-TV-film degree. Third, the religious category includes Christian music and talk. A fourth category, defined by the 1946 founding of the Pacifica Foundation, is community radio, featuring alternative forms of music and talk and commentary by and for communities of minorities, women, gays and lesbians, poor people, and others. If the microradio movement in the late 1990s can be traced back to Lorenzo Milam's work in the 1970s, Milam's work had as its basis Pacifica and KPFK-FM, Berkeley, California.

In 1958 Milam, then a graduate student at the University of California, Berkeley, began to volunteer at KPFA, where he studied the community programming philosophy of Lewis Hill. This philosophy encouraged Milam to introduce this unique concept to other cities. After his first station, KRAB in Seattle, was licensed in 1962, he traveled the country, writing and lecturing about community radio and helping at least 40 stations get on the air. He revealed his sense of humor in the call letters of some of these: KBOO, KPOO, WAIF, KCHU, KDNA, and KUSP. The stations typically suffered from organizational problems, philosophical conflicts, and lack of funding; because they were run by volunteers, the sound was uneven and the equipment insufficiently maintained. Many of these stations failed, or else the licenses were transferred to other nonprofit groups, which then reorganized, adequately funded, and upgraded them.

Milam's advice about dealing with the FCC can be found in *Sex and Broadcasting:*

Remember this about them: 1. They don't care about you; 2. They have heard your story before; 3. They don't care about you; 4. Influence means little to them; 5. You mean more work for them; 6. They don't care about you, at all. However, if you submit a clean, respectable application, and pray fervently to The Great Aether

God—you may well get a permit to go on the air. They aren't out to help you until you have a construction permit, but they do recognize that they have a job to do. And if you are right, and honorable, and persistent, then they'll get tired of saying can't-have-it can't-have-it can't-have-it like some miserable child and will grant you permission to do the thing that you wanted to do all along; that is, to broadcast, to transmit the sounds of generations across the halls of our ages.

Lorenzo Milam was an idealist at a time when using radio as a force for change seemed possible. He became proficient at FCC license applications, and he had enough technical expertise to find and install broadcast equipment. Originally influenced by Lewis Hill, he wanted his stations to be less encumbered by political infighting and to have less of a left-wing litmus test for programming. But after 15 years of station building, Milam and his allies fell prey to the major reality of broadcasting: one needed a great deal of money to continue operating.

In a 1996 email message in response to an invitation to speak at a radio conference, Milam wrote: "I'm totally out of radio. It's something I did, and I did well, for 20 years, and that was plenty. I did yeoman service to The Cause, and thank God I'm done with it. Which is not unlike entropy: we either grow, or we rot. I have several other reasons for being out of the picture now, more than being 63, and being mostly unwilling to travel in the U.S. The most compelling reason for me to be done with it is the things I have gone on to in the last 15 years." Those activities include editing an on-line publication called RALPH. Milam currently lives in Mexico, about which he says, "It's a wonderful new life, as compelling as radio was."

MICHAEL H. ADAMS

See also Community Radio; Educational Radio to 1967; Hill, Lewis; Localism in Radio; Low-Power Radio/Microradio; Public Radio Since 1967

Lorenzo Wilson Milam. Born in Jacksonville, Florida, 2 August 1933. Attended Yale University 1951–52, and Haverford College, B.A. 1957; graduate work at University of California, Berkeley, 1958. Programmer, WIVY Jacksonville, 1952; volunteer at Pacifica's KPFA, 1958; worked for FCC lawyer Michael Bader, Washington, D.C.; founded KRAB Seattle, 1962; editor (as "Lolita Lark") of *RALPH: The Review of Arts, Literature, Philosophy, and the Humanities,* 1995–present.

Publications
Myrkin Papers, 1969
Sex and Broadcasting: A Handbook on Starting a Radio Station for the Community, 1975
Cripple Liberation Front Marching Band Blues, 1984
The Radio Papers: From KRAB to KCHU: Essays on the Art and Practice of Radio Transmission, 1986

Further Reading
Free Radio Network Homepage, <www.frn.net/links>
Hill, Lewis, *Voluntary Listener Sponsorship: A Report to Educational Broadcasters on the Experiment at KPFA,* Berkeley, California: Pacifica Foundation, 1958
New York Free Media Alliance Website: Microradio Documents, <artcon.Rutgers.edu/papertiger/nyfma/str/links.html>
RALPH Online: The Review of Arts, Literature, Philosophy and the Humanities, <www.ralphmag.org>
Rogue Radio Research Website, <www.roguecom.com/rogueradio>

Minnesota Public Radio

One of the major trends in public radio during the 1990s has been the growth of "superstations," whose signals, relayed by repeater antennae and satellites, may blanket an entire region or reach halfway across the United States. The first, and leading, public radio superstation is Minnesota Public Radio (MPR), which extended into seven states and Canada by the late 1990s.

MPR originated with KSJR-FM, a classical music station licensed to St. Johns University, which went on the air in Collegeville, Minnesota—approximately 75 miles northwest of Minneapolis—on 22 January 1967. William Kling, a St. Johns graduate, served as the station's program director. In the fall of 1969, a student announcer from the University of Minnesota named Garrison Keillor took over hosting duties of KSJR's

Morning Program and began telling stories in addition to spinning records. By 1971 Keillor had changed the program's name to *A Prairie Home Morning Show* and enjoyed a wide following, ultimately leading to the wildly successful *A Prairie Home Companion*. Kling had left the station for a job at the Corporation for Public Broadcasting in 1969, but he returned two years later when St. Johns turned control of KSJR over to a nonprofit concern, Minnesota Educational Radio. Kling obtained federal funding and foundation grants to develop a St. Paul–based regional news service, and the group changed its name to Minnesota Public Radio in 1974. In addition to completing a network of its six licensees in 1975, Minnesota Public Radio also pioneered radio reading services for the blind through the use of FM subcarriers.

Under Kling's leadership, Minnesota Public Radio grew at a phenomenal pace in the 1980s. To capitalize on the success of *A Prairie Home Companion,* MPR founded the Rivertown Trading Company in 1981 to sell merchandise connected to the program. In April 1983 MPR launched American Public Radio (APR) as an independent corporation and rival to National Public Radio (NPR); MPR also initially provided the bulk of APR's programming. The statewide MPR network grew to include 12 stations by 1985. Two years later the Rivertown operation was reorganized as the Greenspring Company, a for-profit subsidiary of MPR. Kling's fund-raising and entrepreneurial skills were reflected in the fact that by 1988 MPR received nearly $5 million from listeners, more than $3 million in government funding, and close to $8 million in revenues from broadcasting and other activities, including *Minnesota Monthly* magazine and catalog sales. By the end of the 1980s, MPR was operating 17 licensees, with another station under construction and applications for four more stations on file with the FCC.

MPR President Kling claimed that MPR moved into an area only after a community requested that it do so, and he insisted that the community finance station construction and the first year of operation. In late 1989 residents of Sun Valley, Idaho, applied to the FCC for a permit to install a translator and a 100-watt station with MPR's assistance; soon, MPR's signal was bouncing off the mountains of Idaho. Not surprisingly, these expansionist policies led to direct conflicts with local stations. MPR established a transmitter near Grand Forks, North Dakota, in 1990, although the area already was served by AM and FM public stations licensed to the nearby University of North Dakota. Much of MPR's programming was the same as that of the local stations, who could not hope to match MPR's marketing and production resources and who watched helplessly as MPR skimmed off the cream of their subscriber base.

MPR's profits from Greenspring (which Kling termed an "experiment in 'social purpose' capitalism") also began to attract considerable attention from those outside the organization. Although MPR was ostensibly a separate entity, its ties to Greenspring represented a potential conflict of interest and led to an inquiry by the Minnesota attorney general's office. MPR ultimately was cleared of wrongdoing and sold its catalog business to Minneapolis retailer Dayton Hudson for $120 million in March 1998. Kling personally received $2.6 million from the deal. Minnesota Public Radio also began operating the Public Radio Music Source (PRMS) in conjunction with 66 other public radio stations in January 1993. Participating stations advertise a toll-free number for listeners to purchase the CDs on their station's playlist. In return, the station earns up to 10 percent of the gross from sales. However, critics argue that PRMS encourages stations to narrow their programming and aggressively promote particular releases, with the result that public radio increasingly resembles its commercial counterparts.

MPR spent much of the 1990s consolidating its sprawling operations, and it expanded into southern California in 1999 when it took over Pasadena's financially beleaguered KPCC. Its defenders (and many listeners) argue that Minnesota Public Radio is a paragon of professionalism and vision that will serve as a model for public radio in the 21st century, but its detractors claim that MPR is driven by little more than cutthroat competitive imperatives. Both would agree that MPR rejects the traditional model of public radio, in which stations serve small geographic areas with programming that is not considered commercially viable. In its embrace of professionalism, expansion, and entrepreneurship, Minnesota Public Radio has in many ways set the agenda for public radio in the United States.

TOM McCOURT

See also Keillor, Garrison; Kling, William; National Public Radio; Prairie Home Companion; Public Radio International; Public Radio Since 1967

Further Reading

Engelman, Ralph, *Public Radio and Television in America: A Political History,* Thousand Oaks, California, and London: Sage, 1996

Ledbetter, James, *Made Possible by . . . : The Death of Public Broadcasting in the United States,* New York and London: Verso, 1997

McCourt, Tom, *Conflicting Communication Interests in America: The Case of National Public Radio,* Westport, Connecticut, and London: Praeger, 1999

Witherspoon, John, Roselle Kovitz, Robert K. Avery, and Alan G. Stavitsky, *A History of Public Broadcasting,* Washington, D.C.: Current, 2000

Monitor

News and Features Program

A breakthrough in radio journalism formats, *Monitor* premiered on the NBC network in 1955. It was the first regular radio broadcast to employ the magazine format, offering a mix of late-breaking news, interviews, features, humor, and music. The weekend broadcasts continued for nearly 20 years.

The arrival of television in the United States after World War II prompted a dramatic shift in the habits of radio listeners. By the mid-1950s Americans owned more radios and chose from more radio stations than ever, but instead of being the center of attention in the living room, radios had been moved into the kitchen, the bedroom, and the automobile. Surveys suggested that listeners were tuning in more frequently and for shorter periods of time while performing other tasks around the home, at work, or while driving. This high rate of listener turnover made it difficult for soap operas, variety shows, and concert performances to maintain their audiences, and such shows began disappearing from network schedules. Programming began to emphasize news, music, and local personalities, or disc jockeys, reflecting radio's new role inside—and outside—the typical American home.

Symbolizing this trend was *Monitor*, which premiered on NBC radio on 12 June 1955 as a weekend feature for local affiliates to carry at their discretion, either in its full, 40-hour Friday night-through-Sunday package, or as selected portions to complement local schedules. Since *Monitor* did not employ actors or use complex production techniques, its budget was relatively modest. Its electronic theme, nicknamed the "*Monitor* beacon*," became a familiar sound to millions of listeners over the next 20 years. A multiple series of variably pitched and paced beeps, the theme allowed affiliates to leave or join the network at scheduled times and also identified the program to its audience.

With its novel potpourri of segments entailing sports, news, interviews, comedy, music, and commentary, *Monitor* became a commercial success. In 1956, Patrick D. Hazard described *Monitor*'s unique format:

> First of all, in a magazine-type broadcast, it is possible to mix levels of taste in the material presented—something for everyone, in the *Life* [magazine] tradition of photojournalism. And just as in one issue of that magazine, one may see "horror" photos as well as a brilliant color essay on a phase of American art history . . . so a listener dialed to *Monitor* [may] psychologically tune out, by degrees, program material not compelling to him. . . . There is flexibility of appeal (see Hazard, 1956).

This same flexibility in programming permitted greater numbers of advertisers to sponsor smaller blocks of time, a reflection of the new economic order of radio in the 1950s.

Broadcasting magazine had given a sense of *Monitor*'s flavor at the time the program was debuting:

> NBC said a typical hour on the weekend service might include the following: the first segment of a trip through Paris with *Monitor*'s roving European correspondent (succeeding segments would be positioned throughout the rest of the day); a dramatic highlight from a current hit Broadway play or movie; live or taped appearances by people at the top of the news that weekend; comedy of all types, including live and recorded routines by stars from all fields of show business, both jokes and stories; a *Monitor* exclusive—which might be a dive with the atomic-powered submarine, the *Nautilus*, firing a rocket at White Sands or visiting Birdland, New York's mecca of jazz; a behind-the-scenes visit with a top star of Broadway or Hollywood; plus, of course, *Monitor*'s basic news, time, weather, sports and local features (*Broadcasting*, 11 April 1955).

Monitor was the brainchild of Sylvester L. (Pat) Weaver, a former Young and Rubicam advertising executive who had joined NBC in 1949 as its vice president in charge of television. By the end of 1953, in a climate of tension and uncertainty, he was promoted to president of NBC. In its radio and television audience ratings, NBC was trailing rival CBS, and Weaver vowed to radically change his network's fortunes with new directions in programming. The networks, he said, "must gamble on shows, on talent, on projects; and we will lose in doing this all too often. But only a great network can afford the risk, and that is essentially why the great network service is so important to this country." In addition to *Monitor*, Weaver created *Today* and *The Tonight Show* for NBC television, and he also is credited with the programming strategy of offering occasional specials in lieu of regular shows.

Because of its success, *Monitor* was later imitated on CBS and ABC radio and is arguably a model for the style employed by National Public Radio's *All Things Considered*, beginning in 1971, and *Morning Edition* in 1979. The *Monitor* style also inspired the creation of television magazines, beginning in 1968 with CBS's *Sixty Minutes*, and later with NBC's *Dateline*, ABC's *20/20*, and many others.

Scores of well-known radio personalities hosted *Monitor* segments during its 20-year run, including Ben Grauer, Hugh

Downs, Gene Rayburn, Bert Parks, Hal March, Jim Backus, Ed McMahon, Henry Morgan, Joe Garagiola, Garry Moore, Bill Cullen, Cindy Adams, Wolfman Jack, Don Imus, and Robert W. Morgan. It began as a 40-hour weekend broadcast, airing almost continuously from Friday night to midnight Sunday, but was later shortened to 16 hours, from 1961 until 1974. In its final months of production, *Monitor* was offered for 12 live hours each weekend, with nine repeat hours. Its final broadcast was Sunday, 26 January 1975, hosted by John Bartholomew Tucker.

DAVID MCCARTNEY

See also National Broadcasting Company; Weaver, Sylvester

Creator
Pat Weaver

Producer
James Fleming

Programming History
NBC   June 1955–January 1975

Further Reading
Hazard, Patrick D., "Weaver's Magazine Concept: Notes on Auditioning Radio's New Sound," in *The Quarterly of Film, Radio and Television* 10, no. 4, Berkeley: University of California Press, 1956
"NBC Radio: Pioneer in New Programming," *Tide* (3 December 1955)
"NBC Radio Tells Plans for 'Monitor,' Its 40-Hour Weekend Program Service," *Broadcasting* (11 April 1955)

Morgan, Henry 1915–1994

U.S. Radio Humorist

Although Henry Morgan is chiefly remembered as radio's "bad boy"—because he openly criticized the products offered by his sponsors—this reputation has tended to divert attention from his considerable skills as a satirist and writer. At times in the post–World War II years, Morgan's barbs were as sharp as those delivered by his idol, Fred Allen, although Allen seemed more in control of both his gifts and his material.

Morgan's first job in radio as a page boy at WMCA in New York in 1931 did not last long because he had the congenital habit of saying what he felt, but his loud and clear delivery soon earned him a position at the station as announcer. In 1933, at Philadelphia's WCAU, Morgan could claim to be the youngest announcer in radio. His tenure there, however, did not last long. One evening, out of boredom or giving in to his love of mischief, he included the name of the man who owned the station in the missing person's report, and soon Morgan himself was missing from WCAU's payroll. After working for a year at WEBC in Duluth, Morgan joined WNAC in Boston as night-shift announcer, a job that lasted until he was dismissed for assigning other announcers to do his shift while he attended classes at Suffolk Law School.

Morgan finally found his niche in 1940, at WOR in New York, when he was given first a Saturday morning show and then a 15-minute evening show six times a week that was intended to get the devilishness out of his system. Instead, *Meet Mr. Morgan* and *Here's Morgan* found a willing audience eager to hear Morgan's odd mixture of novelty songs, ad-libs, invitations to tune in to other stations, and peculiar weather reports such as "falling barometer, followed by loud crash." But it was the baiting of sponsors that made *Here's Morgan* so refreshingly appealing to listeners, because here was Morgan saying exactly what they wanted to say, for example, that he wouldn't wear Adler's Elevator Shoes to a dog fight and that Life Savers were a gyp because the centers were missing. The outraged sponsors departed, but the delighted fans stayed.

After serving in the army, Morgan continued the 15-minute format on WJZ until September 1946, when *The Henry Morgan Show* debuted on the American Broadcasting Companies (ABC). The program began unconventionally, with the announcer asking instead of declaring the title of the program, a peculiar version of "For He's a Jolly Good Fellow," and Morgan casually mocking Kate Smith's sunny greeting by muttering, "Hello, anybody. Here's Morgan." What followed might be a parody of a soap opera or quiz show; an interview with Dr. Heinrich Von Morgan; a visit to an old jokes' home; or a strange commingling of odd pairs, such as baseball and opera or *Hamlet* and a detective show. Unlike many other comedians of the time, Morgan did not build his shows around a theme. It was the unpredictable nature of *The Henry*

Morgan Show that kept listeners wondering, "What's going to happen next?"

What they could expect, however, was Morgan's unmerciful ribbing of his sponsors. He introduced a spot for Schick by calling it "the world's worst commercial" and implied that the victor in an on-stage "shaveathon" won not because of a Schick razor but because he was only eight years old. He even carried his weekly lashing of Rayve Cream Shampoo over to Fred Allen's show, where he told Allen that his contract required him to throw dirt in men's hair to boost sales and to offer users "24 tubes of the same stuff to teach you a lesson." Both sponsors were unusually patient, with Eversharp Schick taking it on the chin from 1946 through 1947 and Rayve sticking with Morgan to the end of the 1948 run.

Chief among Morgan's supporting cast was Arnold Stang, who played recurring character Gerard opposite girlfriend Hortense and Morgan's "Hank." Stang, assuming less obnoxious roles than he did on *The Milton Berle Show*, ably assisted Morgan in skits with help from regulars Art Carney, Betty Garde, and Minerva Pious.

Morgan's desire to keep audiences off-balance with audacity made him the darling of the cognoscenti, but his scattershot approach of taking aim at every target in sight did not appeal to the masses, who preferred the gentler humor coming from the residents of Allen's Alley, Wistful Vista, and Pine Ridge. Morgan sometimes let his personal peeves supercede his function as entertainer, as occurred in his rebuttal to a U.S. senator who had criticized the way New Yorkers talk or in his defenses of jokes that laid eggs. On the radio, Morgan was always playing more to his iconoclastic soul than to any audience, and that independent streak contributed to his cancellations as much as his ambushing of sponsors did.

Although Morgan freely bashed people of all political stripes, his anarchic attitude and association with organizations allegedly tied to communism led to his name's appearance in *Red Channels* (1950) and his subsequent blacklisting. After a period of being considered unemployable, he landed a late-evening show on WMGM on which he interviewed diners at a Manhattan restaurant. One of those customers happened to be Mark Goodson, who hired Morgan to be a panelist on television's *I've Got a Secret*. After the popular game show ended its long run, Morgan had flings at delivering brief commentaries on WNEW and longer discourses on a talk show for WOR before entering a phase of what he called "full-time shabby employment" providing voice-overs for television commercials, which he continued to do until shortly before he died of lung cancer in 1994.

CLAIR SCHULZ

Henry Morgan. Born Henry Lerner von Ost, Jr., in New York City, 31 March 1915. Page boy, WMCA, 1931; changed name to Henry Morgan, 1932; announcer, WABC, WCAU, WNAC, WOR, 1933–40; host, *Here's Morgan*, 1940–43; served in U.S. Army, 1943–45; starred on *The Henry Morgan Show*, 1946–48 (ABC), 1949–50 (NBC); appeared on television game show *I've Got a Secret*, CBS, 1952–67, 1976. Died in New York City, 19 May 1994.

Radio Series

1940	*Meet Mr. Morgan*
1940–1943, 1945–1946	*Here's Morgan*
1946–1950	*The Henry Morgan Show*

Television Series

On the Corner, 1948; *Henry Morgan's Great Talent Hunt/The Henry Morgan Show*, 1951; *Draw to Win*, 1952; *I've Got a Secret*, 1952–1967, 1976; *That Was the Week That Was*, 1964; *My World and Welcome to It*, 1969–1970

Films

So This Is New York, 1948; *Murder, Inc.*, 1960

Selected Publications

O-Sono and the Magician's Nephew and the Elephant, 1965
Dogs, 1977
The Uncensored Letters of Loreeta Pernie, 1982
Here's Morgan, 1994

Further Reading

Schulz, Clair, "For He's a Jolly Bad Fellow," *Old Time Radio Digest* (January–February 1994)
Schulz, Clair, "Here's Morgan," *Nostalgia Digest* (August–September 1998)
Taylor, Robert Lewis, "Henry Morgan," *Life* (14 April 1947)
Wertheim, Arthur Frank, "'The Bad Boy of Radio': Henry Morgan and Censorship," *Journal of Popular Culture* (Fall 1979)

Morgan, Robert W. 1937–1998

U.S. Disc Jockey

Robert W. Morgan became one of the most influential disc jockeys of the rock era when he took a job in 1965 as one of the "Boss Jocks" at Los Angeles "Boss Radio," 93-KHJ. The station's format consisted of playing selected hits and placing strong emphasis on its disc jockeys. The format changed radio programming and made Morgan's style one of the most copied in U.S. radio.

Origins

Morgan was born in Mansfield, Ohio, in 1937 and was raised in the small town of Galion, Ohio. He attended Wooster College, where in 1955 he got his first job in broadcasting (earning a dollar an hour) working at stations WWST and WWST-FM. There, he became known as the "Rooster of Wooster."

Morgan left Wooster College to pursue a career in broadcasting, moving to Oxnard, California, where he took a job doing an all-night show called "Kegler's Spare Time with Bob Morgan," which he broadcast live from the Wagon Wheel Bowling Alley.

In 1959 Morgan entered the army and was stationed at Fort Ord, in Monterey, California. After completing his tour of duty, he moved down to Carmel, where he got a job working for the small 500-watt station KTEE-AM. There he was teamed with Marine Corps Heavyweight Boxing Champion Bob "K.O. Bailey" Elliott for a classical music program.

Morgan remained at KTEE for only six months, because he grew tired of working within the classical genre. He took a job working as the morning drive disc jockey for the larger KMBY-AM in Monterey. While there he also operated and ran the control board for the *Arthur Godfrey Time* program. In 1961, once again feeling dissatisfied, he moved to a job at KOMY-AM in nearby Watsonville. However, he was there for only one day, because instead of giving out the request number for KOMY, he gave out the number for his former station, KMBY. Soon, KMBY found itself flooded with phone calls from listeners asking for him. He was offered five times his salary to take his former job back, and he immediately went back to work at KMBY.

In 1962 Morgan moved to Fresno, California, where he took a job with KMAK-AM working with Ron Jacobs, a Top 40 format pioneer who was to become one of radio's most influential program directors. Morgan took over the afternoon drive time, and he and Jacobs began working on a series of jingles and promotions for his show. The professional quality of these promotions became the groundwork for the eventual design of "Boss Radio." It was also during his stint at KMAK

that he began occasionally using the name "Robert W" for his promotions. However, he still referred to himself as Bob on the air.

Morgan left KMAK after only one year and spent the next couple of years moving around northern California from station to station. In 1963 he took a job at KROY-AM in Sacramento, where he spent eight months. Then, in 1964, he took a job at San Francisco's KEWB-AM, a Top 40 station where he first met "The Real Don Steele," a fellow disc jockey who became one of his closest friends.

Boss Radio

In 1965, after a successful Top 40 show at KEWB, Morgan was offered a job on a new radio station in Los Angeles. The station was being developed by RKO consultants Bill Drake and Gene Chenault (a team later known simply as Drake-Chenault). They had the goal of simultaneously programming a chain of stations throughout the United States and were seeking a way to improve upon the Top 40 radio format to keep it fresh and exciting.

After developing stations in Fresno and San Diego, Drake-Chenault went to work on RKO's Los Angeles flagship station, 93 KHJ-AM. They hired Ron Jacobs, Morgan's former program director from Fresno, to be the program director for KHJ, and Jacobs immediately hired Morgan to be the morning man, working 6:00 A.M. to 9:00 A.M.

The new station's slogan was to be "Boss Radio." The Boss Radio format was simple: the station only broadcast selected hit records to make sure they maintained a loyal following, and they also created vivid imagery with their jingles and on-air promotions. Rather than using traditional jingles, the station shortened them, using brief phrases and slogans that were constantly repeated.

The most important component of the format, however, was the strong emphasis on the on-air personalities, who were called "The Boss Jocks." Morgan was one of seven original Boss Jocks, which included his coworker from San Francisco, The Real Don Steele.

Morgan went to work on the new Boss Radio in May 1965, and from that time on, he dominated Los Angeles radio. He developed his own signature statement for his daily sign-on— "Good Morgan!"—which he used for the rest of his broadcasting career. He and the other Boss Jocks were responsible for turning the Boss Radio format into a major success. Not only did Boss Radio become the number one radio station in Los Angeles within six months, but the format achieved national recognition and spread to stations throughout the United States and Canada.

Over the next five years on KHJ, Morgan earned unparalleled shares in the Arbitron radio ratings, with over 20 percent of Los Angeles listeners tuned to him each morning. He became the voice of Boss Radio and introduced a cast of characters, slogans, and routines that made him even more popular. His "Getting Morganized," a machine he created to give his listeners a zap of extra luck or energy, became so popular that he took it with him when he left KHJ.

During these years, Morgan did all of KHJ's promotions and images, and he began to take on work outside of Los Angeles. He became known as the quintessential boss jock, and his style was frequently copied by morning disc jockeys throughout the country. He was one of the best-known broadcasters in the country, and in 1967 he received *Billboard* magazine's "Air Personality of the Year Award."

In 1969 Morgan narrated and coproduced (with Ron Jacobs) the first ever "rockumentary," the 48-hour *KHJ History of Rock and Roll*. It aired worldwide, and when it was broadcast in the Los Angeles market, it received a 60 share in the ratings.

During this time, Morgan also began appearing on television, hosting and narrating for several shows, including *Boss City, Morgan's Alley*, the American Broadcasting Companies' (ABC) *In Concert*, the National Broadcasting Company's (NBC) *The Helen Reddy Show*, and the local KHJ-TV channel 9's *Groovy Show*.

Morgan left KHJ in 1970 to move to Chicago to work at WIND, but, not liking the cold climate, he returned to Los Angeles in 1972 to his morning drive slot at KHJ. He remained there until 1974, when he took a job at FM station K-100 (KIQQ) another Drake-Chenault programmed station. The team re-created their AM radio success on the FM dial, and soon it became the number-one morning program in Los Angeles.

In 1975, Morgan took a job at KMPC-AM as a staff announcer, working a split shift on the weekends and filling in for the weekday staff, including legendary Dick Whittinghill. In 1979 Morgan took over for Whittinghill when he retired. At KMPC Morgan formed his "Good Morgan Team," a group of radio professionals that specialized not only in music, but also in news, weather, sports, and traffic. He stayed at KMPC through the early 1980s despite several format changes and finally a transition to talk radio. Even this did not hurt his popularity: he had the best ratings on the station and became highly successful at the talk format as well.

During this time, Morgan also cohosted a local television show on KNBC-TV called *The Everywhere Show* and became the announcer on the nationally syndicated musical series *Solid Gold*. He also hosted several nationally syndicated radio shows, including *Record Report* and the ABC/Watermarks

The Robert W. Morgan Special of the Week, on which Morgan interviewed the most popular music personalities in the world. He even recorded a program for TWA's in-flight radio called *Morgan's Manor*. During this period, he also recorded thousands of radio and TV commercials, movie trailers, and documentaries.

In 1982 Morgan left KMPC to return to a music show and took a job at Emmis Broadcasting's KMGG Magic 106 FM. In 1985 he returned to KMPC when they returned to a music format, and in 1986 he gave the last broadcast of 93 KHJ when it signed off the air (the station was sold and subsequently became a Spanish format).

In August 1992 Morgan took over as the morning disc jockey at KRTH (K-Earth) 101-FM, oldies radio, and was reunited with The Real Don Steele. He remained there until 1998, when lung cancer forced him to retire. When K-Earth 101 held a retirement tribute for him at the Museum of Television and Radio in Beverly Hills, it was hosted by Dick Clark, who spoke at great length of Morgan's influence on Top 40 radio. In 1993 Morgan received a star on the Hollywood Walk of Fame, and he was inducted into the National Broadcasters Hall of Fame in 1994. He was also inducted into the Ohio Broadcaster's Hall of Fame. He died of lung cancer in 1998 and was posthumously inducted into the Radio Hall of Fame at Chicago's Museum of Broadcast Communications. Samples of his work are on permanent display at the Museums of Television and Radio in Beverly Hills and New York and at the International Broadcasting Congress Archives in Brussels.

JUDITH GERBER

See also Disk Jockeys; Drake, Bill; KHJ; Radio Hall of Fame

Robert W. Morgan. Born in Mansfield, Ohio, 23 July 1937. Oldest child of Arthur and Florence Morgan; attended Wooster College and worked at WWST, 1955; worked at several California radio stations, such as KMAK, Fresno, and KEWB, San Francisco; morning disc jokey at KHJ, Los Angeles, 1965–71 and 1972–73; disc jockey, various Los Angeles stations 1973–98; retired, 1998. Inducted into Broadcasters Hall of Fame, 1994, and Radio Hall of Fame, 1999. Died in Los Angeles, California, 22 May 1998.

Radio Series

1969	*KHJ'S History of Rock and Roll*
1976–81	*Robert W. Morgan Special of the Week*
1977	*Record Report*

Television Series

Morgan's Alley, 1968; *Boss City,* 1968; *Groovy Show,* late 1960s; *In Concert,* 1973–75; *Everywhere Show,* 1979

Further Reading

Barrett, Don, *Los Angeles Radio People: Volume 2, 1957–1997,* Valencia, California: db Marketing, 1997

Fong-Torres, Ben, *The Hits Just Keep on Coming: The History of Top 40 Radio,* San Francisco: Miller Freeman Books, 1998

MacFarland, David, *Development of the Top Forty Radio Format,* New York: Arno Press, 1979

Mormon Tabernacle Choir

U.S. Choral Group Featured in Radio Broadcasts

The Mormon Tabernacle Choir's broadcast program, *Music and the Spoken Word,* began soon after The Church of Jesus Christ of Latter-day Saints began broadcasting in 1922 on KZN (today's KSL) radio in Salt Lake City. Only rehearsals were broadcast occasionally at first, in part because the musicians were skeptical of the fidelity of radio. The first formal broadcast came on 26 June 1923, when President Warren G. Harding also spoke. The choir began its regular live performance schedule when KSL became an NBC affiliate, and on 15 July 1929 the first regular network Tabernacle Choir program was aired nationally. Today, it claims the title, "longest running continuous network radio program in America" with more than 3,600 broadcasts to its credit. The performance is delivered live when every Sunday morning more than 2,000 radio, television, and cable operations broadcast the program worldwide.

Choir History

The Mormon Choir first sang in Utah's Salt Lake Valley more than 150 years ago, coming into existence in 1847. There was no "Tabernacle" or organ at that time so the group sang in an improvised bower of trees where adobe blocks and poles supported the roof of leaves and branches. From this beginning it played a central part in the early church's commitment to celebrate culture—both sacred and secular events. The historic auditorium, the Tabernacle, is a dome-shaped building in Salt Lake's Temple Square, first used in 1867. The Tabernacle organ was installed that same year and it has become the most recognized symbol of the choir.

In 1849 John Perry, a Welshman, became the choir's first regular director. Perry was followed by others who brought formality and discipline to the choir organization. Evan Stephens, also from Wales, conducted the choir for 27 years. Under his leadership, the choir grew from 125 singers to over

300. Stephens directed the choir on its first major concert tour in 1893 and is credited with laying the foundation for the choir's growing international acclaim.

The choir program tradition consists of song, organ recitals, and a short non-denominational sermon dubbed the "Spoken Word." For more than 40 years, Richard L. Evans provided the latter—thought-provoking, inspirational messages usually two to three minutes in length, all eventually published in a series of books. Upon his death, Evans was replaced by J. Spencer Kinard, who worked for 19 years. He was replaced by the current voice, Lloyd Newell.

The Choir on the Air

The choir began its national broadcast history with the NBC network in 1929, when KSL became an affiliate. When KSL switched to the CBS network in 1933, the choir followed. The "Spoken Word" unit of the program was added in 1936.

It is no wonder that the fidelity of these first programs was questioned by the musicians. As the story goes, KZN/KSL apparently owned only one microphone in those early days. Thus, according to a prearranged plan, the station briefly went off the air as a courier dashed across the street from the station to the Tabernacle carrying that one microphone. There, a tall stepladder was installed near the organ console, and the announcer climbed to his precarious perch atop that ladder holding the microphone that was to pick up both the music and the announcer's words.

Coverage of the choir has grown with technology. In 1948, television broadcasts began in Salt Lake and the choir was among the station program lineup. In 1961, it became a part of the church's launch into international shortwave radio. In the 1970s, the choir took part in the first satellite broadcasts. Today, choir presentations use radio, television, cable, satellite, motion picture recording technology, and the internet in its world-wide distribution. The choir has made more than 150 recordings (some of them CDs), five of which have attained gold status with sales of over 500,000, and two have received platinum awards for sales of more than 1 million. Perhaps best known is their classic recording of "Battle Hymn of the Republic," recorded with the Philadelphia Orchestra, for which the choir was awarded a Grammy in 1959.

ELDEAN BENNETT

See also KSL

Further Reading

Evans, Richard L., *Unto the Hills*, New York: Harper, 1940
Evans, Richard L., *This Day and Always*, New York: Harper, 1942

Godfrey, Donald, Val E. Limburg, and Heber Wolsey, "KSL, Salt Lake City: At the Crossroads of the West," in *Television in America: Local Station History from Across the Nation*, edited by Michael D. Murray and Donald G. Godfrey, Ames: Iowa State University Press, 1997

Hicks, M., *Mormonism and Music: A History*, Urbana: University of Illinois Press, 1989

Jeffery, Charles, *The Mormon Tabernacle Choir*, New York: Harper and Row, 1979

Limburg, Val E., "Mormon Tabernacle Choir," in *Historical Dictionary of American Radio*, edited by Donald G. Godfrey and Frederic A. Leigh, Westport, Connecticut: Greenwood Press, 1998

Mormon Tabernacle Choir website, <www.musicandthespokenword.com>

Morning Edition

U.S. Newsmagazine Program

For millions of Americans, weekday consciousness begins with *Morning Edition*: the clock radio turns itself on to the razzle of B.J. Liederman's theme music or the resonant calm of host Bob Edwards.

The program began on 5 November 1979. After National Public Radio (NPR) scored a success with its afternoon newsmagazine, *All Things Considered*, the network's member stations wanted a morning service. They were not necessarily looking for a program. Most member stations at the time ran classical music in the morning, but they wanted news and feature elements they could drop into those programs. Unlike *All Things Considered*, which had evolved on the air, *Morning Edition* was to be a planned creation, conceived by a committee with input from stations and guidance from audience researchers. The format was to be a two-hour series of segments, with a mix of news, sports, arts, and features. None of the segments was to be longer than nine minutes, with fixed times so that stations could take what they wished and cover the rest with local news, weather, and traffic. But production of the pilot was handed over to two morning newsmen from the immensely popular Washington commercial station WMAL. As former producer Jay Kernis recalls, "they knew how to do *AM* drive-time radio, but they broke the promise of public radio. They ignored the audience we'd been building." The pilot failed. Host Bob Edwards remembers them as sounding "like a bad talk show in a small market."

NPR's news director, Barbara Cohen, fired the producers and the first two hosts. Kernis, the arts producer, was promoted to senior producer and "given ten days to re-invent the show and teach the staff how to produce it." Frank Fitzmaurice came in as executive producer to oversee the program's news content. Bob Edwards, who had spent five years as cohost of *All Things Considered* with Susan Stamberg, was recruited to fill in as host for 30 days, until the network could find someone to take over.

Jay Kernis recalls how he and Edwards thought through the role that began Edwards' more than two decades as the solo host of the program. "A host is not an announcer," Kernis says. "A host is the glue that holds the show together. There should be this vortex of information, and in the calm center, there should be the host, Bob, steady Bob, carrying it all back to you."

Kernis also preached to his staff that the show's strict format should be liberating rather than restricting, a concept he says he got from the late arts producer Fred Calland, who pointed out that *All Things Considered* had to create a new architecture in its relatively free-form 90 minutes every day. The program could succeed or fail, depending on whether that structure was successful. With *Morning Edition*, the architecture was a given. As Calland put it, "you know the perimeters of the canvas, now you can paint."

One example of working within the structure came when Kernis had to write a short piece of advance copy for Bob's interview with American haiku poet Nick Virgilio, to be read just before newscaster Jean Cochran delivered the top stories. He did it in classic, 17-syllable form:

Some words hit; some hurt.
Jersey poet writes *haiku*.
News from Jean Cochran:

Resources were stretched thin in the early days of the program. *All Things Considered* was not anxious to share its small pool of reporters, and some reporters preferred being heard on the established afternoon flagship. That meant that Edwards had to get at the news through live interviews, often a dozen or more in a day. Kernis credits three of NPR's most successful female reporters, Cokie Roberts, Nina Totenberg, and Linda Wertheimer, with seeing the audience potential in *Morning Edition* and doing extra work to make sure their reports got on its air.

Morning Edition's voracious format made more room for commentators, too, such as retired sportscaster Red Barber, whose weekly chats with Edwards were one of the program's most popular features for a dozen years.

Morning Edition's producers say the feel of the program is governed by two factors: it is the first thing many people hear each day, and the format is designed to be shared with local stations.

Executive producer Ellen McDonnell says that listeners need to be nudged into their day: "I tell our substitute hosts 'you're up; we're not. People don't want to be blown out of bed.'" Though the show has aired vivid personalities, including Susan Stamberg, Alex Chadwick, and Renee Montaigne as substitute hosts, senior producer Greg Allen says that focus groups consistently favor Bob Edwards' reassuring, understated style. "When Bob's on vacation, we get letters from listeners urging us to bring him back."

The fact that *Morning Edition* begins the day means that its news content is more anticipatory than that of *All Things Considered*. Producers look for items about what's coming up in the day, and what those events are likely to mean for the listener.

Producer Jay Kernis says he decided early on that if he could not know which 20 minutes of the show listeners were going to hear, he would try to make sure that any 20 minutes contained some news, some arts, and some feature. Although the program no longer has specific times dedicated to arts or sports, producers still try to maintain a mix that balances hard news with human emotion. Ellen McDonnell says, "you need a smile, music, a commentary. When the news is grim, we try to be cognizant of the time of day. We don't sugar-coat the news, but we don't have to report every graphic detail." Edwards and McDonnell say that *Morning Edition* aims for a certain civility. McDonnell keeps in mind that "we're a guest who's been invited into your home or your car." Edwards points out that, in the morning at least, "people want that familiar voice, the radio friend."

COREY FLINTOFF

See also All Things Considered; Edwards, Bob; National Public Radio; Totenberg, Nina; Wertheimer, Linda

Host	Bob Edwards
Contributors	Baxter Black, Frank Deford, Joe Davidson, John Feinstein, David Frum, Matt Miller, Patt Morrison, Judy Muller, Ruben Navarette, Kevin Phillips, John Ridley, Cokie Roberts, Amity Shlaes, Kenneth Turan

Programming History
National Public Radio   5 November 1979–present

Further Reading

Collins, Mary, *National Public Radio: The Cast of Characters*, Washington, D.C.: Seven Locks Press, 1993

Looker, Tom, *The Sound and the Story: NPR and the Art of Radio*, Boston: Houghton Mifflin, 1995

Siegel, Robert, editor, *The NPR Interviews, 1996*, Boston: Houghton Mifflin, 1996

Stamberg, Susan, *Every Night at Five: Susan Stamberg's All Things Considered Book*, New York: Pantheon, 1982

Stamberg, Susan, *Talk: NPR's Susan Stamberg Considers All Things*, New York: Turtle Bay Books, 1993

Wertheimer, Linda, editor, *Listening to America: Twenty-five Years in the Life of a Nation, As Heard on National Public Radio*, Boston: Houghton Mifflin, 1995

Morning Programs

Morning programming developed slowly in radio, an ironic fact given that morning or "drive time" would by the 1960s become the most valuable radio broadcast time to advertisers seeking the largest audiences available.

Origins

Radio stations were slow to program morning hours as there was seemingly little audience interest in listening so early. Radio began as an evening service, only gradually moving into daytime hours. Beginning in larger cities, however, by the mid-1920s many stations had expanded their schedules to program the entire day. Their schedules included early morning hours, sometimes beginning at 7 or 8 A.M., and usually offered some type of uplifting talk and/or music. Among the best known of the pioneers was Charles K. Field, who created the "Cheerio" personality for early morning KGO listeners in San Francisco starting in 1927. At the same time Anthony Snow was broadcasting homespun philosophy as "Tony Wons" to Chicago listeners over WLS. Both soon moved to the national scene for lengthy network runs into the 1930s. A few other stations offered a variety of music and talk. Baltimore's WCAU began its *Morning Musical Clock* in 1927 or perhaps earlier (station records are unclear), built around a theme of the passing early morning time. It was still on the air two decades later. The program title would in future years come to label a format on many radio stations.

With a growing audience of radio set owners by the late 1920s and slowly awakening advertiser interest in reaching those listeners, the new national networks began to expand their program offerings into earlier daytime hours as well. Programs took many forms, from informal talks and music to those aimed at children. Virtually all were upbeat in tone as befitted the start of the day. Among the first was Field's organ music and talk-filled *Cheerio*, moved from San Francisco and heard for a half hour daily on NBC at 8:30 A.M. beginning in 1927 and continuing for a decade. *Jolly Bill and Jane*, with music and chatter aimed at children, was also heard daily on NBC at various early morning hours and ran for a decade beginning in 1928. *Gene and Glen* provided early morning comedy (and a multitude of voices) for many years on NBC starting in 1930. *Tony Wons' Scrapbook* moved from Chicago to New York and was heard daily on CBS (and later NBC) during the 1930s. The host would begin each program asking "are yuh listenin'?" and millions of women were. Wons edited nearly a dozen published collections of the poetry and prose he had used on the air.

Golden Years

Network offerings broadened in the 1930s to include drama (*Vic and Sade* began in 1932 on NBC Blue and was first heard at 9:30 A.M.), comedy (*Laugh Club* on NBC-Blue), comedy household hints (*The Wife Saver*, on various morning slots on NBC and NBC-Blue from 1932 until 1943), news commentary (Ann Hard on weekday mornings on NBC), and health (*Health Talk* daily on CBS). In 1940 CBS offered early morning classes from the *American School of the Air*.

As happened with other radio programming, the developing world crisis and eventual outbreak of war in 1941 was reflected in morning programs. Many stations, especially those near military bases, offered morning "Reville" shows, a variation of the "musical clock" format already present in many markets. Early morning network newscasts became a staple on all the networks beginning in 1940. They were heard daily, typically for 15 minutes, and were soon filled with wartime news and information.

As soap operas filled most network daytime hours in the early 1940s, some of the series, such as the CBS drama *Woman of Courage* (1939–42), began as early as 9 A.M. Local stations (and sometimes the networks) took a different tack and offered many homemaking programs at various daytime hours. *Adelaide Hawley Homemaking* was heard most weekday mornings on CBS in 1940.

Networks increasingly focused on talk variety programs for morning hours. Arthur Godfrey's CBS show (so popular he had to give up his local morning program on Washington, D.C.'s WMAL in 1948) and Don McNeill's *Breakfast Club* on ABC had strong audience appeal during the 1940s and 1950s. Such network morning shows became a popular way to start the day along with regular newscasts, a pattern that had developed first during the war.

Postwar "Musical Clocks"

Music-based programming by local stations dramatically expanded daytime program offerings. These "musical clock" or "early bird" or "wake-up" programs had developed in some markets in the 1930s, grew during the war, and expanded greatly in the postwar years. Virtually all of them were based on a combination of music, news, weather, and talk items with constant references to the time and, in larger cities, to traffic conditions. As radio prime time remained the most important listening period (and thus expensive for advertisers), advertising in morning programs could be purchased for one-third to one-half the cost of advertising in the evening hours, and advertisers flocked to the proven ability of early morning radio to sell listeners.

By mid-decade, local station morning broadcast hours were rapidly becoming radio's prime time as network offerings faded away in the face of television competition. Costs to advertisers rose and morning hosts became the new stars of radio. One, Tom Joyner, was in such demand that for many years he hosted a morning show in Dallas and then flew to Chicago for an afternoon drive-time program. He stuck to this grueling schedule for years. The parallel rise of rock and roll music in the 1950s helped fuel a faster-paced morning show still based on a mixture of recorded music and live news, weather, and sports reports. Radio listening became a popular way to make increasingly congested traffic and long commutes more tolerable. In major markets regular traffic reports became an important part of the morning show format.

In the 1970s the morning period spawned the so-called "morning zoo" format, a fast-paced, high-energy approach that is known to disregard traditional programming rules. The concept behind this morning programming approach is to create a zany, often irreverent atmosphere designed to keep listeners fully engaged, awake, and on the edge of their car seats during the commute to work and school. Employing an ensemble cast of characters, its prevailing programming ingredient is comedy and pop-culture chatter usually revolving around hit movies and TV shows, celebrities, and sports. This morning daypart schematic has been refined (toned down in some cases) over the years and has become a mainstay at most larger market contemporary music outlets.

Non-commercial stations also got into the act. Local university and community stations had long provided a mixture of news, features, and, often, classical music. In 1981 National Public Radio developed *Morning Edition* as an expanded long-form news program designed to compete with the more concise commercial radio news programs.

Modern Mornings

Local radio stations seek to provide audiences with personalities who would build a "listener habit" and amass large and loyal followings. In most markets morning radio hosts became celebrities attracting huge rating numbers that advertisers found compelling and appealing. Among the myriad stars of the sunrise hours was WTIC-AM's Bob Steele, who began entertaining Hartford, Connecticut area listeners in the late 1930s and continued doing so into the 1990s. Steele's tenure on the air, while exceptional, was not atypical, as morning radio hosts around the country often enjoyed greater longevity than other on-air personnel. One indication of the enormous status of certain popular morning hosts is that on occasion radio facilities have actually been named or renamed in their

honor. One such example is WPRO's Brine Broadcast Center in Providence, Rhode Island, whose moniker pays tribute to morning radio giant Salty Brine for his nearly half century of service.

Modern morning disk jockeys tend to talk more than they do in other dayparts. They continue to provide a generally upbeat tone just as their forbears did eight decades ago. News and traffic reporters often are part of a "morning team" as a star disk jockey often has a regular sidekick, or co-anchor.

Morning or drive-time radio continues to be a radio staple. Increasingly dominated by the personalities heard daily, such programs have thus far thrived despite increased competition from local and national morning television shows. Fragmentation of audiences because of cable and the internet mean that morning programming is under intense competition. New York's Don Imus had his morning radio show rebroadcast on MSNBC, and Howard Stern's morning program, also from New York, is widely rebroadcast across the country. Syndication of popular national figures has surged as cost-cutting has diminished the quality of morning radio, particularly in small and medium markets.

MICHAEL C. KEITH AND CHRISTOPHER H. STERLING

See also Bob and Ray; Farm/Agricultural Radio; Gambling, John; Godfrey, Arthur; Imus, Don; Joyner, Tom; McNeill, Don; Morning Edition; Shock Jocks; Stern, Howard; Talk Radio; Vic and Sade

Further Reading

Eastman, Susan Tyler, and Douglas A. Ferguson, *Broadcast/Cable Programming: Strategies and Practices*, 5th edition, by Eastman and Ferguson, Belmont, California: Wadsworth, 1996 (see especially chapters 13 and 14)

Field, Charles Kellogg, *The Story of Cheerio*, New York: Garden City, 1936

Garver, Robert I., "The Musical Clock," in *Successful Radio Advertising with Sponsor Participation Programs*, New York: Prentice-Hall, 1949

Harden, Frank, Jackson Weaver, and Ed Meyer, *On the Radio with Harden and Weaver*, New York: Morrow, 1983

Joyner, Tom, Mary Flowers Boyce, and Muriel L. Sims, "*Go with the Bit*": The Tom Joyner Morning Show, Chicago: Johnson, 1999

Lieberman, Philip A., *Radio's Morning Show Personalities: Early Hour Broadcasters and DJs from the 1920s to the 1990s*, Jefferson, North Carolina: McFarland, 1996

Wons, Anthony, '*R' You Listenin'?* Chicago: Reilly and Lee, 1931

Wons, Anthony, compiler, *Tony's Scrap Book*, Cincinnati, Ohio: Wons, 1929; 1944–45 edition, Chicago: Reilly and Lee, 1944

Morrow, Bruce "Cousin Brucie" 1937–

U.S. Radio Personality

From early on, radio called to Bruce Meyerowitz. Radio was very real to him, whether it broadcast World War II, the death of President Franklin D. Roosevelt, Superman, the Bickersons, or the Shadow. Meyerowitz was so hooked by the time he was 16 that he and a friend created his first radio name of Bruce Morrow even before he landed a job.

After high school, Meyerowitz enrolled at Brooklyn College. Having no interest in a liberal education, he transferred to New York University's Communication Arts program in 1953. The better fit was immediately apparent to Meyerowitz, who was extremely interested in broadcast technology. Interestingly, television was the major catalyst for initiating Meyerowitz's broadcasting career. The Columbia Broadcasting System (CBS) was demonstrating its color TV system on campus, so he successfully convinced the National Broadcasting Company (NBC) to let him cover it as a stringer. Amazed by color TV, he saw the future and wanted to be a part of it.

Meyerowitz was tired of pretending to do radio in labs, so he single-handedly founded New York University's station. WCAG, for Communication Arts Group, was a primitive setup that sent its signal via wire from the lab to a lounge area. It became a carrier-current station serving the campus during the 1950s, an exciting time in the history of music. Meyerowitz programmed a classical format with some news, but rock and roll was garnering tremendous attention nationwide.

In 1957 Meyerowitz became a radio professional. A Hamilton, Bermuda, station manager wanted to develop a big-city sound and was seeking the next Alan "Moondog" Freed. Meyerowitz was offered a job, and, as "Bruce Morrow," he made his professional debut on ZBM. In Bermuda, Morrow encountered anti-Semitism and racism, so he did not stay long.

Morrow idolized Freed on New York's WINS and realized his dream in 1958 by taking a producer job there. Morrow recalled: "They wanted somebody young and eager (and cheap). I was all that, and I was one thing more. I was a WINS freak." WINS built its popularity on Top 40 music and on Freed, who left for WABC. Although he would not be on the air, Morrow was overjoyed to work for WINS. He said, "I was going to be a producer for the station that had brought Moondog to New York—Ten Ten WINS!"

Morrow got his big break when the American Federation of Television and Radio Artists (AFTRA) staged a strike. Morrow went on the air from 2 P.M. to 8 P.M., stumbling his way through news and record introductions. Although he later joined AFTRA, Morrow was maligned as a scab. He felt uncomfortable about crossing the picket line, but he landed a permanent 7 P.M. to 11 P.M. announcer position.

One evening in 1959, an elderly woman wandered into WINS and asked: "Well, cousin, can you give me fifty cents please? I want to get home to the Bronx." The encounter inspired the evolution of his name to Cousin Brucie. That year, Murray the K (Murray Kaufman) took the WINS night shift as heir apparent to Freed. Although impressed by Murray on the air, Cousin Brucie did not see eye to eye with him. Murray wanted Cousin Brucie's evening shift and convinced management to give it to him. Morrow would not switch and was out of a job. Cousin Brucie claimed that Murray bought the shift using payola money.

"Cousin Brucie" Morrow
Courtesy Radio Hall of Fame

In 1960 Miami's WINZ hired Cousin Brucie, who initiated the *Pepsi-Cola Cousin Brucie Saturday Night Party* from Kingston, Jamaica, every other Saturday. He also met and married Susan Stoloff in Miami. Cousin Brucie worked for WINZ less than a year before receiving a Christmastime telegram from WABC in New York inviting him to "come home." In 1961 he took the 10 P.M. to midnight shift at WABC before moving to the 7 P.M. to 11 P.M. evening time period, which he dominated in New York until 1974.

At WABC Cousin Brucie helped define a generation's music. For many summers his live music shows were fixtures at New Jersey's Palisades Amusement Park. In 1965 Cousin Brucie played a role in Beatlemania. Although Murray the K dubbed himself "the Fifth Beatle," Brucie was not impressed, calling the statement "a lapse of taste if not sense shared by many a jock in many a radio market." Brucie helped WABC become "W-A-Beatle-C," and he hosted the Beatles' legendary Shea Stadium performance in August 1965.

In 1973 WNBC hired Wolfman Jack to compete against Cousin Brucie. WNBC had already hired Don Imus to go against Dan Ingram. Both Cousin Brucie and Wolfman Jack claimed victory, but the truth seems to lie somewhere in between. When Wolfman Jack wanted his contract voided, he says he convinced WNBC to hire Cousin Brucie. Whether true or not, Cousin Brucie left WABC on 7 August 1974 to join WNBC-AM, which no longer had to worry about his competing against them.

Brucie resigned from WNBC in 1977 and became a partner in the Sillerman Morrow Broadcast Group. In 1979 the group launched WALL-AM-FM in Middletown, New York, and Cousin Brucie went back on the air. By 1981 he moved to another group station, WRAN-AM in Dover, New Jersey. Cousin Brucie joined WCBS-FM in New York in 1984, where he still hosts *Cousin Brucie's Yearbook* on Wednesdays from 7

P.M. to 10 P.M. and *Cousin Brucie's Saturday Night Oldies Party* from 7 P.M. to midnight.

W.A. KELLY HUFF

See also Freed, Alan; Murray the K; WABC; WINS; Wolfman Jack

"Cousin Brucie" Morrow. Born Bruce Meyerowitz in Brooklyn, New York, 13 October 1937. Founded WCAG at New York University, 1953; graduated New York University, 1957; worked at ZBM, Hamilton, Bermuda, 1957; producer, disc jockey, WINS, New York, 1958–60; disc jockey, WINZ, Miami, 1960; disc jockey, WABC, New York, 1961–74; disc jockey, WNBC, New York, 1974–77; became Sillerman Morrow Broadcast Group partner, 1977; on-air/owner WALL AM-FM, Middletown, New York, 1979–81, and WRAN-AM, Dover, New Jersey, 1981–84; host, *Cousin Brucie's Yearbook* and *Cousin Brucie's Saturday Night Oldies Party*, WCBS-FM, New York, 1984–present. Inducted into Radio Hall of Fame, 1988, and Broadcasting and Cable's Hall of Fame, 1990.

Publication

Cousin Brucie: My Life in Rock 'n' Roll Radio (with Laura Baudo), 1987

Further Reading

Hilliard, Robert L., and Michael C. Keith, *The Broadcast Century: A Biography of American Broadcasting*, Boston: Focal Press, 1992

Jack, Wolfman, and Byron Laursen, *Have Mercy! Confessions of the Original Rock 'n' Roll Animal*, New York: Warner Books, 1995

Smith, Wes, *The Pied Pipers of Rock 'n' Roll: Radio Deejays of the 50s and 60s*, Marietta, Georgia: Longstreet Press, 1989

Motorola

Radio Manufacturer

Motorola has been a leader in exploring and promoting new uses of radio technology. The Chicago-based company initially focused on radio receivers. Later, Motorola developed applications of the technology for government, military, and private use, helping radio to realize its potential as a two-way communication tool. In so doing, Motorola became a haven for engineering and high-quality technological innovation.

The Motorola story starts in the 1920s, with a business-savvy young man from north central Illinois. Paul Galvin quickly saw the potential of radio as the medium developed. Galvin and partners formed two companies to produce storage batteries and power converters for radios. Both were closed by 1928, but Galvin continued to believe in the potential of the business. After borrowing $1,000, Paul Galvin and his brother

Joseph formed the Galvin Manufacturing Corporation in September 1928.

Galvin Manufacturing quickly moved into the production of private label radios for wholesalers and retailers and experienced some moderate growth. But smaller firms like Galvin's were hit hard by the economic downturn that followed the stock market crash in late 1929. If Galvin Manufacturing was to remain in business, the company needed to develop a landmark product that would mark it as a vital player in radio. Paul Galvin found the cornerstone for his company with the automobile radio.

Although auto radios had been available in the 1920s, they were expensive, difficult to install, and sounded terrible because of static interference from electric devices within the car. Galvin and his associates developed a prototype that solved these problems and installed it in his car in time for the 1930 Radio Manufacturer's Association convention. Galvin drove to Atlantic City for the show and demonstrated his new product to conventioneers who marveled at the innovation.

Galvin Manufacturing's 5T71 was the first commercial radio designed to fit most automobiles and sold for about $120 including installation. In order to create a name that would associate sound with motion, Galvin coined the name Motorola for his radio by combining the word *motor* with *ola* from *Victrola*. Though Galvin Manufacturing retained its original moniker for years, it was the trademarked Motorola name that became famous. By 1936 Motorola was an industry leader and was among the first brands of car radio to include push buttons, fine tuning, and tone controls.

That same year, the Federal Communications Commission (FCC) took action that facilitated Galvin's move into other radio products. After the FCC allocated spectrum space for police communications, Galvin introduced its first AM mobile receiver, called the Police Cruiser, and the following year introduced accompanying transmission equipment. Soon, the need for two-way communications became apparent, so Galvin developed mobile AM transmitters for officers in the field. The cost of a complete system, including one base station and three mobile radios, was about $4,000.

Motorola introduced the first line of improved two-way FM equipment in 1941. This innovation marked the start of a 30-year period in which Motorola engineer Daniel Noble and the company became internationally known for research and development. Motorola later adapted this same FM technology for use in larger commercial and industrial markets as two-way radio communication became commonplace in the 1950s.

During this same era, Motorola became an important supplier to the American military. When World War II broke out in Europe, Galvin assembled an engineering team to develop a lightweight, portable, two-way radio that could be used on the battlefield. Eventually, the U.S. Army awarded Galvin Manufacturing a contract for the Handie-Talkie, a five-pound AM radio with a range of about one mile. Galvin manufactured more than 100,000 of the radios before the end of the war. The company also developed a 35-pound FM two-way radio in a backpack with a range of ten miles. This device, the Galvin SCR-300, became better known as the Walkie-Talkie and was hailed by military leaders as a pivotal communication device. Galvin produced 45,000 of the Walkie-Talkies along with jeep and tank radios to aid the war effort.

Galvin Manufacturing became a publicly traded stock in 1943. In 1947 the company formally changed its name to Motorola and prepared to reap the dividends of a booming postwar economy. It did so by continuing to expand on its radio business but also by continued research and development efforts and what company officials call "continuous self-renewal" into other areas of electronics. In the 1950s, Motorola became an important supplier of automobile radios to Ford, General Motors, and Chrysler. Almost one-third of the car radios on American highways had been made by Motorola as the decade concluded. It was also during this period that Motorola started to manufacture television sets, developed some of the first radio paging systems, and became involved in the semiconductor business. Motorola initially used transistors to miniaturize its own products, leading to a line of pocket-sized radios. Transistors were also crucial in the development of its advanced, two-way Motrac system that ultimately boasted a 50 percent global market share for mobile radios.

Over the years Motorola maintained a partnership with the American government on various projects, including the space program. Motorola systems have played a vital role in tracking and communications between earth and outer space since the company developed a system for an early satellite mission in 1958. Motorola endures as an important, diversified, global corporation in electronic communications. Despite some serious business problems in the 1990s, Motorola remains involved in wireless telephone and messaging, two-way radio communications, semiconductors, networking, and more. The Galvin legacy at Motorola also continues; a third generation of the family is now running the company.

STUART L. ESROCK

See also Automobile Radios; Receivers

Further Reading

Collins, James C., and Jerry I. Porras, *Built to Last: Successful Habits of Visionary Companies,* New York: HarperBusiness, 1994; London: Century, 1995; 3rd edition, London: Random House Business, 2000

Crockett, Roger, and Peter Elstrom, "How Motorola Lost Its Way," *Business Week* (4 May 1998)

Motorola website, <www.motorola.com/home/>

Motorola, Inc., *Managing Change: Positioning for the Future-Summary Annual Report*

Petrakis, Harry Mark, *The Founder's Touch: The Life of Paul Galvin of Motorola*, New York: McGraw-Hill, 1965; 3rd edition, Chicago: Motorola University Press/Ferguson, 1991

Tetzeli, Rick, "And Now for Motorola's Next Trick," *Fortune* (28 April 1997)

Weingartner, Fannia, editor, *Motorola: A Journey through Time and Technology,* Schaumburg, Illinois: Motorola, 1994

Movies. *See* Film Depictions of Radio; Hollywood and Radio

Murray, Lyn 1909–1989

U.S. (British-Born) Radio Composer and Conductor

Lyn Murray began his career in radio in the early 1930s. His life work included composing and conducting music for radio, television, and film for more than half a century.

Murray was born Lionel Breese in London in 1909. His father emigrated to Philadelphia in 1923 and the family followed in 1925. Murray entered radio by working for the Columbia Broadcasting System (CBS) at their station WCAU in Philadelphia as a staff conductor and arranger from 1931 to 1934. He then moved to CBS in New York as a staff conductor, composer, and arranger, remaining in New York until 1947.

During Murray's years with CBS radio, he worked on a wide variety of programs. These included *The Adventures of Ellery Queen,* 1939 to 1942; *Radio Reader's Digest,* 1942 to 1944; *Columbia Presents Corwin,* 1944 to 1945; *The Ford Theater,* 1947 to 1949; and *The Hallmark Playhouse,* 1948 to 1953. He also worked for the National Broadcasting Company (NBC), composing and conducting the music for *The Adventures of Philip Marlowe,* 1947. Other programs for which Murray composed or conducted episodes include: *Chrysler Airshow,* 1937; *An American in England,* 1942; *The March of Time, Your All-Time Hit Parade, Sunday Night Party, Rippling Rhythm Revue, The Danny Kaye Show, Watch the Fords Go By, Lucky Strike Hit Parade, Heinz Magazine of the Air,* and *Music from the House of Squibb.* Murray also directed *The Lyn Murray Singers,* a choral group that appeared regularly on the *Texaco Star Theater* and *Hit Parade.* Murray's excellence as a conductor, as well as his extensive knowledge of popular and classical music, led many in the industry to consider him one of the best directors.

In the summer of 1946, Murray taught a course in radio choral techniques at the Julliard School. Murray offered students an opportunity to appear on network commercial shows. In his publicity for the course, Murray noted that he was organizing a concert tour that would include qualified students. Pete Seeger, folk singer and banjoist, and Norman Cordon of the Metropolitan Opera were expected to be part of the tour.

In 1947 Murray moved to Hollywood to find work in television and movies. In his diary, Murray makes occasional reference to being listed in *Red Channels,* a factor that he felt limited his employability in his early days in Hollywood. In 1952 Paramount Studios held up a contract with Murray, which he later wrote was probably related to his listing. Then, when negotiating a contract with the American Broadcasting Companies (ABC) in 1954, the issue of *Red Channels* came up but was dismissed.

Murray was instrumental in founding the Composers Guild of America in 1953 and 1954. He co-wrote the organization's constitution and by-laws with Sandy Courage. The name was changed to Composers and Lyricists Guild of America in 1956. (It is currently known as the Society of Composers and Lyricists.) Murray also served as a board member for the National Academy of Music.

Murray won two Emmy Awards for musical scores. The first, in 1986, was for *National Geographic*'s television special "Miraculous Machines," and the second was in 1988 for *National Geographic*'s special "Treasures of the Past."

Murray's diary of his career from 1947 through 1987, published as *Musician,* chronicles his ups and downs in the radio, television, and film industries. Murray died at age 79 of cancer in Pacific Palisades, California.

MARGARET FINUCANE

See also Blacklisting; Red Channels

Lyn Murray. Born Lionel Breese in London, England, 6 December 1909. Worked as staff conductor and arranger, WCAU Radio, Philadelphia, 1931–34; staff conductor, composer, and arranger, CBS Radio, New York City, 1934–47; moved to Hollywood, 1947, and worked for Hallmark Playhouse, 1947–51; composer and conductor in television and film industry, 1951–89. Received Emmy awards, 1986, 1988, for scores for National Geographic television specials. Died in Pacific Palisades, California, 20 May 1989.

Radio Series

1939–42	*Adventures of Ellery Queen*
1942–44	*Radio Reader's Digest*
1944–45	*Columbia Presents Corwin*
1947–49	*Ford Theater*
1948–53	*Hallmark Playhouse*

Publication
Musician, 1987

Further Reading

Grams, Martin, Jr., *Radio Drama: A Comprehensive Chronicle of American Network Programs, 1932–1962,* Jefferson, North Carolina: McFarland, 2000

Murray the K (Murray Kaufman) 1922–1982

U.S. Radio Personality

Murray the K was a popular New York City radio personality in the 1950s and 1960s who gained national fame through the promotion of popular music and culture. He produced many package shows that featured now legendary American recording artists. Even the Beatles, before they were known in the United States, were encouraged by other international performers to work with Murray the K when they came to the United States.

Origins

Murray the K's real name was Murray Kaufman. He was born in Virginia to a show business mother, Jean Greenblatt, and a leather merchant father named Max. He entered show business as a child by appearing as a dancer and extra in several Hollywood films. He later dropped out of high school in the late 1930s to become a catcher in the New York Yankees' minor league baseball organization. World War II disrupted Kaufman's dream of playing for the major leagues, however, and he changed direction by preparing for a career in show business. While serving in the U.S. Army during the war, he produced entertainment shows for American soldiers. In the late 1940s he found his way into New York's Catskill mountains, where he began producing nightclub shows and working as an emcee. In the off season (November through April), Kaufman returned to New York City and worked in promo-

tion. Most notably he helped push Patti Page's recording of "How Much Is that Doggie in the Window?" to number one on the music charts in the early 1950s.

Radio Career

In 1953 Kaufman got his first radio job producing a remote interview show that was broadcast from a New York nightclub and hosted by various movie stars such as Lorraine Day, Eva Gabor, and Virginia Graham. After two years Kaufman moved behind the microphone at New York's WMCA and co-hosted the talk show with his wife in addition to taking on some general announcing for the station. He began working as a late-night disc jockey at WMGM in 1957, just as radio was beginning to cater to younger audiences and to play more recorded music. Kaufman joined the National Conference of Disk Jockeys, as did Dick Clark and others, to help advance the image of radio broadcasting's new professional generation.

WINS New York hired Kaufman in 1958 to produce a late night show he called *Swingin' Soiree* on their 50,000-watt station. He followed Bruce "Cousin Brucie" Morrow in their lineup; Morrow had moved into the 7:00 P.M. to 11:00 P.M. time period that had been occupied previously by Alan Freed, a casualty of the payola scandal. Murray the K developed a large, loyal audience at WINS, and in 1959 he succeeded Morrow, who moved to another station.

Murray the K in 1965
Courtesy AP/Wide World Photos

Kaufman parlayed his radio success into other successful business ventures. From his *Swingin' Soiree* popularity and visibility he was able to generate huge audience attendance for four annual live music shows that he produced at the Brooklyn Fox Theater. His pioneering lineups of recording artists were racially integrated and drew multi-racial audiences.

Kaufman worked obsessively and seemed to be omnipresent as he promoted or produced shows at venues throughout the city. He also floated among shows, acting as host or emcee, and took his disc jockey radio program to numerous remote sites at theaters, on the streets, in the subway, or in air force jets. He also produced a series of oldies albums, placed his picture on their covers, and sold Murray the K T-shirts. In 1965, Kaufman's estimated combined income was $150,000.

Murray the K's radio style has been called "hip." Some historians refer to him as "the king of hysterical disc jockeys." He used his vibrant vocal chords, accented with nasal tone, to voice plays on words, pig Latin expressions, and sound effects. Each of his sound effects was prerecorded and placed on a separately labeled cart. They were aired at strategic spots in his show and ranged from roaring freight trains, cavalry

bugle charges, and nutty macaw laughter to screaming men plunging down an abyss. He took great pride in studying popular culture and recognizing new trends. Some teens from his era, now older adults, can still repeat portions of his zany nonstop patter and retain a deep respect for his cleverly humorous style.

During one rating period, Murray the K was 20 points ahead of his nearest competitor. Subsequently it took two years of competition, from two rival New York radio stations (WABC and WMCA) that converted Kaufman's program style into full-time formats, to dethrone his show. Kaufman maintained that this was only possible because his show on WINS was preceded by a two-hour newscast and followed with talk and interview programming.

The Beatles already knew about Murray the K's reputation when they were welcomed to America in early 1964 by a huge media contingent and 4,000 screaming teens at New York's Kennedy Airport. Kaufman represented WINS radio at the news conference. To conduct a live remote, he drew upon his veteran radio interviewing experience and strategically positioned himself and his microphone in front of the Beatles' makeshift platform. Then, using his hip radio styled language ("Hey, George, baby!" "Ringo, over here, baby!"), Murray the K smoothly dominated the entire affair. The knowledge that he displayed about the Beatles' career, as well as his quick wit, convinced the singers that Kaufman held the key to their conquest of New York. So the Beatles made Murray the K a part of their entourage. He traveled with them in the United States and Europe, and served as master of ceremonies at their second Carnegie Hall performance. He also visited with them on their movie set, appeared in their film *Help!* and roomed with George Harrison. Harrison, in an effort to protect Kaufman from other reporters' jealousy, referred to him as "the fifth Beatle." Murray the K was catapulted to national and international fame.

Early in 1965 Murray the K came to the attention of some U.S. government officials who were endeavoring to locate the most appropriate national spokesperson for a youth program. The Office of Economic Opportunity, headed by Sargent Shriver, hired Kaufman to lead a national communication effort about a summer jobs initiative called "New Chance," which would be aimed primarily at urban youth. Kaufman, with typical high energy and vision, traveled throughout America to shoot a series of musical performances on location by leading black and white recording artists. He interspersed the music videos with informational announcements about New Chance and called the show *It's What's Happening, Baby*. The Columbia Broadcasting System (CBS) agreed to donate 90 minutes of national prime time to air the program in late June 1965, and it received high ratings. The recording artists accepted scale pay and CBS paid the bill. Kaufman, far from being commended for his brilliant work, was censured by some

U.S. Congressmen who criticized rock and roll as being repulsive African jungle music. Later in the year, WINS-AM, perhaps unable to compete with Murray the K's institutional imitators WABC and WMCA, was sold to Westinghouse, Inc., and its format was switched to all news. After eight years, Murray the K left WINS radio.

By early 1966 Kaufman had established "Murray the K's World" in Garden City on Long Island, New York—a multilevel and multimedia entertainment complex converted from an abandoned airplane hangar. Although short-lived, the nightspot is said to have influenced music venues such as the Plastic Inevitable, Manhattan's Cheetah, and the Fillmore Auditorium in San Francisco. Unfortunately, Kaufman suffered huge financial losses from his intended month-long run of rock shows, due to a subway workers strike. According to his lawyer, the strike prevented performers and audiences from coming to the theater after the first few performances. He sought $25 million in damages.

The determined Murray Kaufman then turned his efforts to another television concept for the Office of Economic Opportunity, this time at the local level, producing at least two highly rated television programs for New York's Channel 5. His first was a 90-minute combination of in-concert and on-location clips of popular recording artists, with drop-in talk segments by other noted celebrities. The first show drew an estimated 3 million viewers to two broadcasts. The second show was entitled *Murray the K's Special for the Year 2000*. It aired in May 1966 and sought to explain the vast differences in language, music tastes, and dress that would exist between youth and adults at the turn of the century.

Early in 1966 WOR Radio hired Kaufman as its program director. However, in July 1966 management shifted Kaufman and three other disc jockeys from WOR-AM to WOR-FM and cut their wages by 50 percent. FM radio was still developing its economic base, but the American Federation of Television and Radio Artists represented the four disc jockeys in their efforts to retain their AM salaries. Kaufman and the others went on strike until October 1966 when the matter was resolved, although they remained at lower salaries.

The low frequency of commercials on FM radio allowed Kaufman to initiate an indelible radio programming innovation by pioneering progressive radio. He emphasized the perspective that albums contained many good songs that were appropriate for airplay. He also encouraged exposing the full artistic expressions of recording artists by playing their extended-time productions. Nonetheless, a very proud Murray

the K cut short his tenure at WOR-FM in 1967 when program consultant Bill Drake was brought in by management to institute programming guidelines and policies. Before departing, Kaufman went on the air and blasted WOR's decision, just as he had done previously at WINS.

From 1967 to 1976 Kaufman worked short stints at various radio stations but never achieved the high points of his earlier career. He began with CHUM (Canada) from 1967 to 1968. Later in 1968 he took a weekend slot on his old WMCA station from 2:00 to 7:00 P.M. on Sundays. After several other brief stints, in the late 1970s he moved to California with his sixth wife, soap opera actress Jacklyn Zeeman. He had three sons from previous marriages. His last job in radio was hosting a syndicated radio program for Watermark.

Kaufman, a smoker, had battled cancer since 1973 and was finally forced to relinquish the job with Watermark in 1981 due to his failing health. After retirement he was financially strained but lived in comfortable surroundings. (Tony Orlando provided him with a 24-hour nurse and housekeeper.) Murray Kaufman died of cancer in Los Angeles on 21 February 1982.

LAWRENCE N. REDD

Murray the K. Born Murray Kaufman in New York City, 14 February 1922. Song plugger for Bob Merrill, 1950s; popularized Merrill's "How Much Is That Doggie in the Window," 1950s; president, National Council of Disc Jockeys, 1950s; spearheaded council's relief effort during Hungarian Revolution, 1956; late-night radio disc jockey, WMGM, 1957; hosted *Swingin' Soiree* for WINS, 1958; spokesperson for government youth program "New Chance," 1965; hosted "Murray the K's Special for the Year 2000" for television, 1966; worked short stints at various radio stations, 1967–76. Died in Los Angeles, California, 21 February 1982.

Publication
Murray the K Tells It Like It Is, Baby, 1966

Further Reading
"Dropout TV Show Irks Republicans," *New York Times* (30 June 1965)
"Jockeys Finally Catch up with WOR-FM," *New York Times* (7 October 1966)
Price, Richard, "Going Down with Murray the K," *Rolling Stone* (15 April 1982)
"Youth Wants to Uh Uh Uh," *New York Times* (15 May 1966)

Murrow, Edward R. 1908–1965

U.S. Radio Journalist

Journalists from broadcast and print media alike consider Edward R. Murrow one of the greats of his time. His legacy was to be among the first to put radio news into a league of respectable journalism. He later helped to launch serious television journalism and started the first TV newsmagazine program. Most important, he established traditions of courage and integrity in the profession of broadcast journalism at a time when radio was still developing the tone of its news function.

Murrow's work spanned from the onset of World War II until the Kennedy administration, from his radio reporter years to president of Columbia Broadcasting System (CBS) News, to director of the U.S. Information Agency. His on-air radio reports of events helped shaped the nation's ideas of what was occurring in the world. His dramatic language in radio formed aural word pictures that were rare and striking to his listeners, and he carried his style into the new medium of television. Murrow became a mentor to many in broadcast news, who carry his ethics and style into today's news efforts. His legacy can be found in the most prestigious journalism awards, in schools named after him, and in historical accounts of corporate and government integrity.

Origins

Murrow was born on 25 April 1908 in Polecat Creek, North Carolina, as Egbert Roscoe Murrow, the son of a farmer. He had two older brothers, Lacey and Dewey. When Egbert was six years old, the family migrated by train to the Northwest. They ended up near Blanchard, in the northwest corner of Washington State, where the family struggled to make ends meet.

As a teen, Egbert changed his name to Edward. He became active in sports, debate, and drama, and he even served as a bus driver for the scattered students of his small school. After his graduation from high school, he worked as a logger in the virgin woods of the Olympic Peninsula. It was in this setting that he learned both virtues and vices, appreciation for the rugged beauty of the Olympic Mountains, and the language and smoking habits of the rough brotherhood of lumberjacks, which tempered the Quaker traditions of his family.

After a year and two summers of working in the woods, Murrow enrolled in 1926 at Washington State College (WSC; now Washington State University) in Pullman, on the east side of the state. His intentions were to pursue a curriculum in prelaw and then go to law school. But circumstances led him to a public-speaking course taught by a dedicated and inspiring teacher, Ida Lou Anderson. She was demanding, but she recog-

nized a talent in Murrow and helped him to develop his potential. Eventually she became his mentor and instilled in him a love of the use of language, a somber introspection regarding his own values, a love of philosophy, and a flare for the dramatic. He went on to enroll in the first broadcasting course, "Radio Speaking."

After his first year of working for his room and board, he became involved in the Greek fraternity system at WSC. Through the political influence of his peers, Murrow was elected student body president for his senior year. He graduated in 1930. He then became an officer for the National Student Federation of America in 1932, traveling to New York City with a meager living expense to run the national office. Soon, Morrow became active in encouraging student exchange among various countries, working for the International Institute of Education.

Honing Radio Journalism

In 1935, Murrow was hired as director of talks at CBS. In this position, he traveled to Europe to line up speakers, and he was there in 1938 at the time of Hitler's invasion and annexation of Austria. The event was described by Murrow in a radio report from Vienna (the beginning of his journalistic career), in which he described the mood of the people, the political setting, and the street scenes in vivid details that made his verbal descriptions come to life. This was to be the first of many descriptions he would later give of the effects of World War II.

Murrow's observations from the European front often came from mere notes used when he dictated his descriptions from his mind's eye. His descriptions and dramatic use of language captured the ear of American listeners, who were compelled not only by the events but by Murrow's style as well.

As the war intensified, Murrow began to broadcast about war events from the basement of the British Broadcasting Corporation (BBC)'s Broadcast House. Murrow turned to shortwave radio for his 1940–41 London "Blitz" broadcasts. The broadcast quality was questionable, with fading and fidelity dependent on the earth's atmosphere. Yet it was those broadcasts, often sent late at night London time for the convenience of listeners on the U.S. East Coast, that led to his first real fame. They were timely, compelling, and immediate for a world breathlessly awaiting word about the quickly growing war. And each one began with his standard and quite dramatic signature opening: "This . . . is London." (In later years he said that Ida Anderson had suggested to him that he insert the pause after the first word.)

Edward R. Murrow
Courtesy CBS Photo Archive

His descriptions of the English people under siege carried the insights of a sociologist:

> This is a class conscious country. People live in the same small street or apartment building for years and never talk to each other. The man with a fine car, good clothes and perhaps an unearned income doesn't generally fraternize with the tradesmen, day laborers and truck drivers. His fences are always up. He doesn't meet them as equals. He's surrounded with certain evidences of worldly wealth calculated to keep others at a distance. But if he's caught in Piccadilly Circus when the sirens sound, he may have a waitress stepping on his heels and see before him the broad back of a day laborer as he goes underground. If the alarm sounds about four in the morning, as it did this morning, his dignity, reserve and authority may suffer when he arrives half-dressed and sleepy, minus his usual defenses and possessed of no more courage than those other who have arrived in similar state. . . . Maybe I'm wrong . . . but I can tell you this from personal experience, that sirens would improve your knowledge of even your most intimate friend (Broadcast, 4 September 1939).

Murrow reported not only on the war situation, but on the people. He spoke of girls in light dresses, boys sobbing, old toothless men, and women clutching their belongings as they left their bombed-out homes. His characterizations were vivid and insightful:

> I'm standing tonight on a rooftop looking out over London. . . . Out of one window there waves something that looks like a white bed sheet, a window curtain swinging free in this night breeze. It looks as though it were being shaken by a ghost. There are a great many ghosts around these buildings in London. . . . Down below in the streets I can see just that red and green wink of the traffic lights; one lone taxicab moving slowly down the street. Not a sound to be heard. As I look out across the miles and miles of rooftops and chimney pots, some of those dirty-gray fronts of the buildings look almost snow-white in this moonlight here tonight (Broadcast, 22 September 1940).

Sometimes Murrow's courage bordered on foolhardiness. On one notable occasion, and ignoring direct network orders that he not place himself in harms way, he accompanied a B-17 bomber crew on a bombing mission over Berlin. His descriptions became some of his most memorable writing:

> The clouds below us were white, and we were black. D-Dog [the plane] seemed like a black bug on a white sheet. The flack began coming up. . . . The small incendiaries [we dropped were] going down like a fistful of white rice thrown on a piece of black velvet. As Jock hauled the Dog up again, I was thrown to the other side of the cockpit, and there below were more incendiaries, glowing white and then turning red. The cookies—the four-thousand-pound high explosives—were bursting below like great sunflowers gone mad. And then, as we started down again, still held in the lights, I remembered that the Dog still had one of those cookies and a whole basket of incendiaries in his belly, and the lights still held us. And I was very frightened (Broadcast, 3 December 1943).

As the war ended, Murrow accompanied the troops into the concentration camps of Germany. He told his listeners:

> If you are at lunch, or if you have no appetite to hear what Germans have done, now is a good time to switch off the radio, for I propose to tell you of Buchenwald. . . . The prisoners crowded up behind the wire. We entered. . . . There surged around me an evil-smelling horde. Men and boys reached out to touch me; they were in rags and the remnants of uniform. Death had already marked many of them, but they were smiling with their eyes. . . . When I entered [one of the barracks] men crowded around, tried to lift me to their shoulders. They were too weak. Many of them could not get out of bed. I was told that this building had once stabled eighty horses. There were twelve hundred men in it, five to a bunk. The stink was beyond all description (Broadcast, 15 April 1945).

Postwar Broadcast Journalism

After the war, Murrow returned to the states and to CBS, which was now a much different organization than the one he had left in 1937. William Paley, head of CBS, persuaded Murrow to take over the network's news organization. His radio war broadcasts had become famous, and his fame would certainly help enhance the network's programs. In his new position, Murrow tried to reflect American life, with both its shortcomings and strengths. He created the radio programs *As Others See Us,* a report on how the foreign press viewed the United States, and *You Are There,* a recreation of historical events. And, since radio had been looked down upon by the print media, Murrow produced the program *CBS Reviews the Press,* in which he ensured that the criticism of radio would become a two-way street, and that "mutual criticism will benefit both."

Eventually Murrow was joined by a young producer, Fred Friendly, and together they produced *I Can Hear It Now,* a 45-minute record that was soon followed by others. The 1950–51 network program *Hear It Now* evolved from that project. It was a sound documentary, a kind of magazine on the air, covering several subjects each week in its hourly network format.

Murrow reluctantly entered into television with Friendly. They produced a 1952 TV counterpart to their radio series entitled *See It Now*. Early programs appear rough and unpolished compared to today's network magazine shows, but the focus was not on appearance but on substance.

Not all of Murrow's work was flattering to the news efforts of his day. In 1958, in an address to his colleagues at the meeting of Radio and Television News Directors Association, he told a startled audience:

> So far as radio—that most satisfying and rewarding instrument—is concerned, the diagnosis of its difficulties is rather easy. . . . In order to progress, it need only go backward. To the time when singing commercials were not allowed on news reports, when there was no middle commercial in a 15-minute news report, when radio was rather proud, alert and fast. . . . If radio news is to be regarded as a commodity, only acceptable when saleable, then I don't care what you call it—I say it isn't news.

The same speech was highly critical of television, which helped to further sour Murrow's already poor relations with CBS.

After the election of John F. Kennedy as president in 1960, Murrow was chosen to head the U.S. Information Agency. Once critical of government positions, he now found himself spokesperson for the Kennedy administration and its relay of news throughout the world.

In the fading days of his career, Murrow's contributions were recognized with the Medal of Freedom, the country's highest civilian honor. He was also knighted by Queen Elizabeth for his vital role to England during World War II. Ill health, likely brought on by his chain smoking, forced Murrow into early retirement. He died of cancer in 1965 at the age of 57, leaving his wife, Janet, and one son, Casey.

VAL E. LIMBURG

See also Columbia Broadcasting System; Friendly, Fred; Hear It Now; News

Edward R. Murrow. Born Egbert Roscoe Murrow in Polecat Creek, North Carolina, 25 April 1908. Attended Stanford University and the University of Washington; graduated from Washington State College (now Washington State University),

1930. Served as assistant director of the Institute of International Education, 1932–35; began career with CBS as director of talks and education, 1935; became director of CBS' European Bureau in London, 1937; during World War II, hired and trained distinguished corps of war correspondents, including Eric Sevareid, Howard K. Smith, Charles Collingwood, and Richard C. Hottelet; returned to U.S. as CBS vice-president and director of public affairs, 1946; resigned to return to radio broadcasting, 1947; narrated and produced *Hear It Now* radio series, 1950–51; brought series to television as *See It Now*, 1952–58; began *Person to Person* television program in 1953; moderated and produced *Small World*, television series featuring discussions among world figures, 1958–60; appointed by President John F. Kennedy to head U.S. Information Agency (USIA) in 1961, and remained in post until 1964. Recipient: nine Emmy Awards. Died in New York, 27 April 1965.

Radio Series
1950–51   *Hear It Now*

Television Series
See It Now (1952–58); *Person to Person* (1953–59); *Small World* (1958–60)

Selected Publications
This Is London, edited by Elmer Holmes Davis, 1941
In Search of Light: The Broadcasts of Edward R. Murrow, edited by Edward Bliss, Jr., 1967

Further Reading
Bernstein, Mark, and Alex Lubertozzi, editors, *World War II on the Air: Edward R. Murrow and the Broadcasts that Riveted a Nation*, Naperville, Illinois: Sourcebooks/MediaFusion, 2003
Cloud, Stanley, and Lynne Olson, *The Murrow Boys: Pioneers on the Front Lines of Broadcast Journalism*, Boston: Houghton Mifflin, 1996
Kendrick, Alexander, *Prime Time: The Life of Edward R. Murrow*, Boston: Little Brown, 1969
Persico, Joseph E., *Edward R. Murrow: An American Original*, New York: McGraw-Hill, 1988
Smith, Robert Franklin, *Edward R. Murrow: The War Years*, Kalamazoo, Michigan: New Issues Press, 1978
Sperber, Ann M., *Murrow: His Life and Times*, New York: Freundlich Books, 1986

Museums and Archives of Radio

Repositories of Radio History

There are many public, private, and academic archives and museums whose sole purpose is to preserve radio broadcast documents and programs. Most of them have audio and visual recordings, books, periodicals, pamphlets, oral histories, interviews, and other documents that trace the history of radio programming and radio broadcasting. In addition, several archives and museums are devoted to the history of radio technology itself and the development and advancement of this technology. Still others trace the important figures and individuals in radio broadcasting, radio technology, and radio history. There are also dozens of old-time-radio collector's clubs with less extensive collections of radio broadcasts.

Origins of Museums and Archives of Radio

The idea of establishing formal radio museums and archives began in the 1940s, and such institutions were actually developed in the 1970s. The Broadcast Pioneers Library was the first organized library of radio history; it was begun in the 1960s and formally opened in 1972. However, some less formal collections began much earlier. For example, in 1949 the Library of Congress began to collect and preserve some radio programming. At the same time, the National Archives started collecting and preserving programming from governmental sources and began receiving donated new programs and material from radio stations and networks throughout the U.S.

During World War II, the Armed Forces Radio Services began to produce discs in order to bring radio programs to U.S. troops during the war. These discs would later become the basis of privately traded material. During the same period, a few network and syndicated programs were distributed on discs as well.

In the 1950s the Broadcast Pioneers organization unsuccessfully attempted to establish a museum of broadcast history. During the same decade, individuals began seriously recording and collecting radio programs with the introduction of home-recording equipment and the demise of network radio. Reliable and affordable reel-to-reel recorders were first introduced into the consumer market during this time.

However, radio program collecting did not become truly popular until the 1960s, when classic radio programming began to change dramatically and, many felt, to disappear. As a result, many individuals began to realize that preserving such programs was essential for documenting the history of radio. Individuals began to organize for the purpose of exchanging radio programs, information, and resources. As expected, as radio formats rapidly changed, radio stations began to discard their old stored material and programs. These informal groups began collecting such materials, and a collectors movement started to grow. These groups also created newsletters on radio program collecting.

One of the earliest and most influential of the collectors groups was the Radio Historical Society of America, founded by Charles Ingersoll in the 1960s. Ingersoll also started one of the first newsletters for collectors of old-time radio programs, and *Radio Dial* set the standard for those to follow. One of these was *Hello Again*, started in 1970 by Jay Hickerson. It remains the most popular of old-time-radio collector group newsletters. This newsletter was also part of the formation of the Friends of Old Time Radio. *Hello Again* was successful because it brought together more than 100 of the most active program collectors. According to Professor Marvin R. Bensman of the University of Memphis Radio Archives, "Today, approximately 160-plus active collectors comprise the mass of privately collected broadcast material available."

Another factor that helped spawn the radio collector movement was the sale of radio programs to private individuals. J. David Goldin, a former Columbia Broadcasting System (CBS), National Broadcasting Company (NBC), and Mutual engineer, first mass-marketed and sold radio programs. In the late 1960s, Goldin formed Radio Yesteryear, a company that sells audio recordings of classic radio programs. He also started an album subsidiary of the company called Radiola.

A big boost came for the establishment of the first broadcast history library when William S. Hedges, a former NBC executive, began collecting items for the Broadcast Pioneers History Project between 1964 and 1971. This collection, which consists of nearly 13,000 items, including correspondence, articles, and speeches in 540 different subject categories, formed the core collection of the Broadcast Pioneers Library, which opened in 1972 and led to the establishment of the Library of American Broadcasting.

Public and Academic Museum and Archive Collections

Library of American Broadcasting (University of Maryland)

The first formally established institutional radio archive was the Broadcast Pioneers Library, begun in the 1960s and formally opened in 1972. It was housed in the headquarters of the National Association of Broadcasters (NAB) in Washington, D.C., until 1994. It then became part of the library system at the University of Maryland, College Park, and became known as the Library of American Broadcasting, one of the most extensive collections of the history of broadcasting. The collection consists of audio and video recordings, books, periodicals, pamphlets, oral histories, photographs, personal collections, and scripts that pertain to the history of broadcasting. The library features more than 8,000 volumes ranging from engineering manuals to programming histories. It is particularly strong in its book collection from the early part of the 1920s and 1930s, tracing the evolution of broadcasting.

The library's audio holdings include 1,000 interviews, speeches, news broadcasts, special events, and oral histories (with many accompanied by transcripts) of such important radio figures as Edgar Bergen, Norman Corwin, Leonard Goldenson, Lowell Thomas, and William Paley. There are also thousands of recordings in many formats, including more than 8,300 recorded disks, 25,000 photographs, and 10,000 CDs of commercials in its Radio Advertising Bureau Collection. Also housed here are many specialized collections from radio performers, executives, broadcast engineers, writers, producers, and magazine publishers. Highlights include political speeches from Franklin D. Roosevelt, Winston Churchill, and Harry S. Truman in the Donald H. Kirkley collection; more than 160 recordings of congressional hearings, political speeches, and other media events of the 1960s and 1970s in the Daniel Brechner Collection; and The Center for Media and Public Affairs Collection, which contains talk radio programs.

Some of its other holdings include some 7,000 pamphlets, ranging from 1920s Bell Laboratories radio engineering bulletins to promotional materials from broadcast networks; the Westinghouse News Collection (1958–82), which consists mainly of raw feeds from the Washington bureau; the Associated Press Radio Competition Collection (1967–68), which contains samples of radio journalism, almost exclusively from California.

There is also a collection of government documents that includes the Navigation Bureau List of Radio Stations (1913–27), Federal Radio Commission (FRC) and Federal Communications Commission (FCC) decisions, and congressional reports and hearings.

The museum acquired the Chester Coleman Collection of the NAB Library and Historical Archive in June 1998. This collection includes more than 4,000 books and periodicals. The NAB collection also includes historical meeting and convention minutes, newsletters, promotional materials, and scrapbooks.

National Public Broadcasting Archives (University of Maryland)

An additional archive housed at the University of Maryland is the National Public Broadcasting Archives (NPBA). The archives originated as a cooperative effort between both educational institutions and broadcasting organizations, including the Corporation for Public Broadcasting (CPB), Public Broadcasting Service (PBS), National Public Radio (NPR), the Academy for Educational Development, and the University of Maryland. The idea was spearheaded by Donald R. McNeil, a former PBS board member who was concerned that the history of public broadcasting was at risk.

The archives, which opened 1 June 1990, form part of the Archives and Manuscripts Department of the University of Maryland Libraries. They consist of historical materials from the major organizations of U.S. noncommercial broadcasting. These include PBS, Children's Television Workshop, CPB, NPR, Agency for Instructional Technology, America's Public Television Stations, Association for Educational Telecommunications and Technology, Public Service Satellite Consortium, and the Joint Council for Educational Telecommunications.

The NPBA also has personal papers from many influential public broadcasting figures and a reference library containing basic studies of the broadcasting industry, rare pamphlets, and journals on relevant topics. The archives also house a collection of audio and video programs from public broadcasting's national production and support centers and from local stations. There is also a collection of oral history tapes and transcripts from the NPR Oral History Project.

Museum of Broadcast Communications (Chicago)

The Museum of Broadcast Communications is devoted solely to radio and television broadcasting and is housed on two floors of the Chicago Cultural Center. (The Museum was scheduled to relocate to new premises in Chicago's River North area as of Spring 2004.) The museum's purpose is to educate the "public, teachers, and students about the profound influence of radio, television, and advertising in our world." It does this via hands-on exhibits, broadcasting memorabilia, a public archives collection, and educational outreach programs.

The Museum was founded in 1987 by Bruce DuMont, the nephew of television pioneer Allen B. DuMont, using private contributions. It consists of changing exhibits, radio and television archives, a Radio Hall of Fame, an Advertising Hall of Fame, the Lynne Harvey Radio Center, and a gift shop. The museum's public archive, the Arthur C. Nielsen Jr. Research Center, contains over 85,000 hours of television and radio broadcasts, commercials, and newscasts, with 13,000 television programs, 4,000 radio broadcasts, and 11,000 television commercials, all of which can be screened on site in one of 26 study suites. All programs in the archive's collection are cross-referenced and cataloged in a fully computerized retrieval system. The collection focuses on Chicago television news, talk/interview programs, documentaries, political broadcasts, programs of its Radio Hall of Fame inductees, sports programming, and "Golden Era" television dramas.

Included in its archives is an extensive historic radio program collection, the Chuck Schaden Radio Collection, which contains more than 50,000 programs and is considered to be the largest of its kind in the United States. The Lynne Harvey Radio Center features a live, weekly broadcast of *Those Were the Days,* by radio historian Chuck Schaden, complete with a live studio audience, as well as other live broadcasts. The museum also hosts many special events, including an annual induction ceremony into its Radio Hall of Fame, which pays tribute to the legends of radio. The Hall of Fame was founded by the Emerson Radio Corporation in 1988 and was taken over by the Museum of Broadcast Communication in 1991. There is also a collection of vintage radio and television sets from local donors.

Museum of Television and Radio (New York and Los Angeles)

The bicoastal Museum of Television and Radio (New York and Los Angeles) is devoted to radio and television broadcast history, particularly focusing on the individuals and programs that make up that history. The museum was founded in New York in 1975 by William S. Paley, chairman of CBS, as the Museum of Broadcasting. The museum changed its name and moved to a larger headquarters in September 1991. The New York museum's holdings include some 100,000 radio and television programs, as well as 10,000 commercials. It also includes two screening rooms, two theaters, a group listening room, 96 individual booths equipped with television and radio consoles, a research library, and a gift shop. In addition, there are three public galleries that display broadcast industry artifacts.

In March 1996 the Los Angeles branch of the museum opened in Beverly Hills. It has the same features as its East Coast predecessor. Because Los Angeles is the number-one radio market in the United States, the Los Angeles museum offers more of an emphasis on radio than the New York branch (which focuses more on television). In addition, when radio was in its heyday during the 1930s and 1940s, many shows were made in Los Angeles. According to Norm Pattiz, a trustee of the museum and chairman of Westwood One, "We're now in the No. 1 and No. 2 radio markets, with exactly the same material available at both museums."

Both locations offer seminars by critics, directors, producers, performers, journalists, and writers, including University Satellite Seminars, and both offer a wide variety of programs from the collection in two screening rooms and two main theaters, as well as constantly changing special exhibits. Programming from current series and exhibitions is shown throughout the day.

American Library of Radio and Television (Thousand Oaks, California)

The American Library of Radio and Television is part of the Special Collections Department of the Thousand Oaks Library System. Its holdings focus specifically on the history of radio rather than on the individuals in the profession. The library was founded in 1984 after the Thousand Oaks Library System broke away from the Ventura County System. The newly formed Library Foundation and the Friends of the Library decided that they wanted the library to focus on larger programs and a research collection. Specifically, they were anxious to fill a niche in the Los Angeles area by focusing on a special historical collection. They chose broadcasting because several of the library organizers had extensive contacts in the radio broadcasting industry.

Along with Maryland's Library of Broadcasting, the American Library of Radio and Television offers one of the largest collections of broadcasting documents in the United States, and it has an extensive reference collection of radio materials including 23,000 radio and television scripts, 10,000 photographs, 10,000 books on the history of radio and television broadcasting, pamphlets, sound recordings, periodicals, 200 maps and charts, manuscripts and personal papers, 5,000 audio recordings, and 50 oral history tapes.

In addition, the library contains archives of such notable individuals and stations as Norman Corwin, Bob Crosby, Monty Masters, Carlton E. Morse, Rudy Vallee, and KNX AM. Their Radio Series Scripts Collection contains scripts from 1930 through 1990, and their Radio Sound Recordings Collection contains recordings from 1932 to 1994.

The George Clark Radioana Collection at the Smithsonian Institution

The George H. Clark Radioana Collection is a part of the National Museum of American History of the Smithsonian Institution. The collection was assembled by George Clark of the Radio Corporation of America (RCA) and is one of the most extensive collections of documents and publications on the history of wireless and radio in the United States. It was transferred from the Massachusetts Institute of Technology to the National Museum of American History in 1959. The collection occupies more than 276 linear feet of shelf space, but it has not been fully indexed.

The collection is particularly strong from 1900 through 1935. There is extensive biographical information on the men who developed the technical aspects of radio and the industry; information on the inception, growth, and activities of radio companies, most notably the National Electric Signaling Company and RCA; and photographs of all aspects of radio.

The United States Library of Congress and the National Archives

Both the United States Library of Congress and the National Archives in Washington, D.C., have collections of voice recordings and radio programs. The Library of Congress has received donations of transcriptions of old radio shows. There are over 500,000 programs in their collection, including a large number of British Broadcasting Corporation (BBC) and Armed Forces Radio and Television Service (AFRTS) recordings. The library also has a large collection of radio-related items, such as early folk and regional programs, as well as a large selection of NBC Radio's broadcast discs from 1935 to 1970, which cover the Depression, World War II, postwar recovery, and radio comedy and drama programs. Other radio collections include the WOR-AM collection, United Nations recordings, Library of Congress concerts and literary recordings, and the Armed Forces Radio Collection. There is also an extensive collection from the U.S. Office of War Information (OWI), which, between 1944 and 1947, transferred thousands of items used to support the war effort to the Library of Congress. These items include OWI sound recordings, photographs, and a small number of research papers. In addition, the Motion Picture, Broadcasting, and Recorded Sound Division holds nearly 50,000 acetate disc recordings of foreign and domestic radio broadcasts.

The National Archives of the United States also features a broad collection of radio-related material. Most of these are housed at the Special Media Archives Services Division's Motion Picture, Sound, and Video unit at Archives II in College Park, Maryland. The holdings include 150,000 reels of film, 160,000 sound recordings, and 20,000 videotapes. These materials were obtained from both public and private sources. The sound recordings catalog includes radio broadcasts, speeches, interviews, documentaries, oral histories, and public information programs. The library indicates that the earliest recording they have dates from 1896, with the bulk of their recordings coming from between 1935 and the present.

Some of the specialized catalogs in the holdings include the NPR catalog, which contains NPR news and public-affairs broadcasts from 1971 to 1978, and the Milo Ryan Photoarchive Collection, which includes 5,000 recordings, primarily of CBS-KIRO radio broadcasts from 1931 to 1977. These materials were originally kept at the University of Washington and contain news and public-affairs programs, speeches, interviews, wartime dramas, and daily World War II news programs. The library also features the American Broadcasting Companies (ABC) radio collection, which consists of 27,000 radio broadcasts of news and public-affairs programs from 1943 to 1971.

Duke University Library Advertising History Archive

Duke University Library has a special Advertising History Archive that is part of the John W. Hartman Center for Sales, Advertising, and Marketing History. The advertising history collection located in the Hartman Center is the J. Walter Thompson Company Archives. The J. Walter Thompson Company is one of the world's oldest, largest, and most innovative advertising firms. The collection documents the history of the company and, as part of this, its role in radio broadcasting. The J. Walter Thompson Company's Radio Department produced some of the most popular radio shows on the air during the 1930s and 1940s. These include *Kraft Music Hall, Lux Radio Theater,* and *The Chase and Sanborn Hour.* These and other Thompson programs are housed in the collection.

In 1979 the J. Walter Thompson Company Archives were formally established in the company's New York Office. In 1987 Chief Executive Officer Burt Manning authorized the gift of the entire collection to Duke University. The archives contain over 2,000 linear feet of printed and manuscript materials, nearly 2 million items in all, half of which are advertisements. The archives house the Radio-Television Department files, which include microfilm of scripts of most of the agency-produced radio and television shows from 1930 to 1960, including *Kraft Music Hall, Lux Radio Theatre,* and *Lux Video Theatre.* Most of the holdings in the archives are open to researchers except for recent and unprocessed materials.

The Pavek Museum of Broadcasting (St. Louis Park, Minnesota)

The Pavek Museum of Broadcasting, located in St. Louis Park, Minnesota, a suburb of Minneapolis, houses a large collection of antique radios, televisions, and other broadcasting memorabilia and equipment, including an actual old-time radio studio. The mission of the museum is to provide a broader knowledge of how pioneers in electronic communications affected the evolution of society, to stimulate a new recognition of the practical and real contributions that exploring science and the communication arts can bring, and to provide a permanent and living repository for the preservation of these historic items.

The museum opened in 1988, and most of its collection comes from the original Joseph R. Pavek Collection. Pavek, an electronics instructor for Dunwoody Institute, started his collection in 1946. He also had his own electronics business, and he began storing his collection at his business. By the 1970s he began to look for someone to take over the collection, house it, staff if, and make it available to the public. In 1984, unable to find such a person, he was set to sell the collection, but Earl Bakken, the inventor of the pacemaker, stepped in and, with Paul Hedberg of the Minnesota Broadcasters Association, formed the nonprofit organization that became the umbrella for the museum.

The Pavek collection consists of over 1,000 radio receivers, transmitters, and televisions from the first half of the 20th century. Highlights of the collection include a working 1912 rotary spark-gap transmitter, crystal radios of the early 1920s, a collection of vacuum tubes (including several original de Forest Audions), and a large collection of radio literature. Additional donations from radio and television stations and from other collectors have greatly increased the size of the original collection.

Included at the museum is the Charles Bradley Collection, which has examples from over 60 Minnesota radio and television manufacturers from the 1920s and 1930s. There are also many examples of historic broadcast equipment on display, such as cameras, consoles, and microphones. The museum also houses the Jack Mullin Collection, which documents the history of recorded sound, with over 125 years of audio recording technology, starting with the earliest days of the phonograph. Mullin is credited as being the person who brought back two tape recorders from a German radio station while serving in the Signal Corps at the end of World War II. At the time, tape recording was an unknown technology in the United States, and Mullin was immediately hired by Bing Crosby to tape-record his popular radio program for broadcast, the first use of tape recording in American broadcasting.

Also featured in the archives is the Pioneer Broadcaster Series, which preserves videotaped interviews with radio pioneers. The museum also has an educational program with classes, workshops, and exhibits for both children and adults. There is also a library of technical and service information on electronics and electronic communication. Besides the permanent collection, the Pavek also displays items on loan from other private collections.

University of Memphis Radio Archive

The University of Memphis Radio Archive is a collection of broadcast programs that was started over 30 years ago by Dr. Marvin R. Bensman of the Department of Communication. Bensman began his radio collection from original transcriptions, private collectors, and other institutional collections. The collection is intended to be a representative sampling of most series and shows.

The collection is housed in the Microforms Department of the McWherter Library at the University of Memphis. Individuals may request audiocassettes of these radio programs. Programs have been selected because they give a sense of the history and development of broadcasting. They feature the key events that influenced the regulation of broadcasting and of broadcasting programming. Some highlights of the archive include Westinghouse's 50th Anniversary program; the history of broadcasting from the 1920s to the 1970s; 50th anniversary

shows about the development of the BBC, NBC, and CBS; early pioneer broadcasters and/or inventors; Aimee Semple McPherson's broadcasts; the American Society of Composers, Authors, and Publishers' (ASCAP) Cavalcade of Music concert in 1940 consisting of live performances by musical stars including Berlin, Handy, and others; *Year-end Reviews;* CBS Radio Workshops; World War II broadcasts; numerous movie dramatizations; and classic comedies.

Private/Personal Museum and Archive Collections

American Museum of Radio

The Bellingham Antique Radio Museum is a nonprofit museum located in Bellingham, Washington. It is a private collection gathered over the past 25 years by Jonathan Winter, who started collecting radios when he was a child. The collection spans the history of radio from the time it began through the early 1940s and features over 1,000 antique radios on display. The Bellingham Antique Radio Museum, as it was originally called, opened in 1988 in a small room and moved to larger quarters in downtown Bellingham in 1990. In 2001 the museum moved to a new, larger facility.

In addition to its collection of antique radios, there is other material on display highlighting the history of radio technology, including historical photographs; books and magazines from radio's early days; microphones, coils, tubes, speakers, and other parts; biographies of people involved in radio history; audio clips of some of the more historic broadcasts; and clips of radio entertainment shows from the early days of broadcasting.

U.S. National Marconi Museum (Bedford, New Hampshire)

The U.S. National Marconi Museum was created by the Guglielmo Marconi Foundation in 1995 to help publicize the name of Marconi, the "Father of Wireless." The museum is located in Bedford, New Hampshire, and the collection features equipment, historical literature, and audiovisual presentations on the development of radio communications. It features displays of early Marconi wireless equipment, along with the progression of radios up to a current cellular telephone exhibit. The museum also features a restoration room for repairing vintage radios, a machine shop, and a facility room for educational lectures to school groups and for meetings of electronic-oriented organizations.

The John Frey Technical Library contains thousands of radio communication periodicals, some in a series dating from 1920. All the publications are indexed and cataloged on CD-ROM and can be accessed by internet on the library computer. The library also features hundreds of engineering, text, and reference books.

Museum of Radio and Technology (Huntington, West Virginia)

The Museum of Radio and Technology is a small, private collection consisting of old radio and television sets, and it is staffed exclusively by volunteer museum members. It features several displays, including a radio shop of the 1920s and 1930s that has a variety of radios from that era, including battery radios; horn speakers; a wind-powered generator; a radio-television sale room featuring radios, television sets, and wire recorders; a Gilbert toy display; a vintage hi-fi room with tube-type audio equipment and related components such as amplifiers, tuners, tape recorders, receivers, microphones, and turntables. The highlight of the display is the Western Electric transmitter, a 1930s 5,000-watt AM transmitter complete with power supply components and studio equipment.

The Radio History Society's Radio-Television Museum (Bowie, Maryland)

The Radio History Society is a nonprofit organization dedicated to the preservation of radio and television history. In June 1999 the society opened its new Radio-Television Museum in Bowie, Maryland, housed in a fully restored turn-of-the-century building.

The Radio Historical Society owns a large collection of old literature and radio artifacts relating to the history of radio and television broadcasting. Some of their collection includes radio sets from the 1920s through the 1960s plus local broadcast memorabilia. Their permanent and changing exhibits include home receivers, novelty radios, broadcast microphones, and communication and ham radio equipment. They also maintain a display area at George Washington University's Media and Public Affairs Building in downtown Washington, D.C., with changing displays.

Society to Preserve and Encourage Radio Drama, Variety, and Comedy

The Society to Preserve and Encourage Radio Drama, Variety, and Comedy (SPERDVAC) is an organization of old-time radio enthusiasts that has assembled one of the most important and well-maintained radio program archives in the world. There are over 20,000 original transcription discs, as well as a large library of printed materials and scripts. In addition, there are over 2,000 reels of old-time radio available only to its members. SPERDVAC also produces a monthly newsletter and a catalog listing the thousands of shows in its collection, and it hosts monthly meetings and annual conventions in the Los Angeles area.

JUDITH GERBER

See also Nostalgia Radio; Peabody Awards; Radio Hall of Fame

Further Reading

Godfrey, Donald G., compiler, *Reruns on File: A Guide to Electronic Media Archives*, Hillside, New Jersey: Erlbaum, 1992

Hedges, William, and Edwin L. Dunham, compilers, *Broadcast Pioneers History Project; Third Progress Report and Historical Inventory*, New York: Broadcast Pioneers, 1967

Hickerson, Jay, *What You Always Wanted to Know about Circulating Old-Time Radio Shows (But Could Never Find Out)*, N.p.: 1986

Lichty, Lawrence W., Douglas Gomery, and Shirley L. Green, *Scholars' Guide to Washington, D.C., Media Collections*, Baltimore, Maryland: Johns Hopkins University Press, and Washington, D.C.: Woodrow Wilson Center Press, 1994

Pitts, Michael R., *Radio Soundtracks: A Reference Guide*, Metuchen, New Jersey: Scarecrow Press, 1976; 2nd edition, Metuchen, New Jersey, and London: Scarecrow Press, 1986

Sherman, Barry, et al., "The Peabody Archive and Other Resources," *Journal of Radio Studies* 1 (1992)

Smart, James Robert, compiler, *Radio Broadcasts in the Library of Congress, 1924–1941: A Catalog of Recordings*, Washington, D.C.: Library of Congress, 1982

Swartz, Jon David, and Robert C. Reinehr, *Handbook of Old-Time Radio: A Comprehensive Guide to Golden Age Radio Listening and Collecting*, Metuchen, New Jersey, and London: Scarecrow Press, 1993

Music on Radio

Music has been a staple of radio programming since the medium's creation in the early 1920s. Indeed, David Sarnoff's historically fabled memo—real or not—foresaw radio's potential future as a "music box." Before radio, to be able listen to music one had to play an instrument (most often a piano), purchase a poorly recorded disc, or pay to attend a live performance. Radio broadcasting changed that by offering frequent free musical performances for the simple purchase of a radio receiver.

Radio music history can be divided into two eras, divided by a short but confusing transition period. During the first (to 1950), most music was broadcast live as a part of a variety of radio formats, both network and local. The second era (since 1955) followed a brief and difficult transition but soon saw station programmers regularly playing music using specific short lists of recordings. This focus on specific formats has defined radio music, with only the conversion from various disc formats to audiotape and then back to digital discs and tapes changing the means of recording and playback. Indeed, technical change underlies any historical analysis of music on radio. The phonograph record as a means of listening to music preceded radio, but it was radio broadcasting that vastly expanded the musical recording industry—first on 78-rpm records, then, after the war, on 33 1/3-rpm long-playing records and 45-rpm records into the 1960s. Thereafter came a decade or so of analog audiocassettes, and finally, at the end of the 20th century, compact discs and other digital formats.

Network Tin Pan Alley Era (to 1950)

Music as a popular radio program genre started when many advocated the new medium as a means to bring high-art music such as opera and orchestral recitals to the mass public. But although European classical music never disappeared from radio's schedule as radio entered the network era during the late 1920s, its presence quickly gave way to popular music and in particular to variety shows starring musical talents such as Rudy Vallee and Al Jolson. New York City's Tin Pan Alley created the music that big bands and their singers offered radio listeners.

By the early 1930s, both the National Broadcasting Company (NBC) and the Columbia Broadcasting System (CBS) had discovered genres of musical programs that the public preferred. The networks tried classical music; varieties of popular music; and what might be called light or background music, which was designed for listeners involved in activities other than dedicated listening. But although broadcasting classical concert music suggested that radio was providing a "good" to the masses, comedy and variety shows created the mass audiences advertisers sought. Broadcasts of the Chicago Civic

Opera on NBC Blue (Saturday), the Cities Service Orchestra on NBC Red (Friday), the Edison Electric Orchestra on NBC Blue (Monday), and the Paramount Symphony Orchestra on CBS (Saturday) maximized prestige but drew small audiences.

Variety shows proved to be the most successful means of creating a profit with music programming. These shows varied depending on how pop music was emphasized—from a comic host with a musical guest to a musical host with a comic as guest. The latter—the musical variety program—became the most popular network radio genre during the 1930s. Top attractions centered more and more on name bands, including Guy Lombardo's Orchestra on CBS or the Paul Whiteman Orchestra on NBC, both broadcast on Monday nights.

Through the 1930s, so-called light music offered the second-largest musical category of radio shows; for example, Jesse Crawford played the pipe organ on CBS on Sunday nights, Lanny Ross (later of *Your Hit Parade* fame) soothed his audiences on NBC on Saturday nights, and—in a rare case of sponsor naming—The Wheaties Quartet performed as intended background music on CBS on Wednesday nights.

By the mid–1930s, NBC and CBS were offering some of the most popular free musical entertainment during those hard times. Indeed, sales of phonograph records plunged during the Great Depression as fans substituted listening to music on the radio for the relatively expensive purchasing of individual phonograph records. Radio became the place where new popular tunes were introduced, and their creators and players became musical stars.

Although during the day local stations still offered non–network live music from the community, prime time had become big time for radio listeners and programmers. Yet stations in large cities did maintain orchestras to play for the local programming. In reality the music that most fans sought came primarily from New York City and then in small doses from Los Angeles–based studios that used musical talent associated with movie making.

By 1940 classical concert music still offered prestige, but on fewer and fewer programs. A star system developed as NBC put together its own classical orchestra, led by Arturo Toscanini. At CBS, William S. Paley signaled that his star was Andre Kostelanetz, who by 1940 was on the air not one night, but two. NBC continued to hire a classical orchestra in order to identify itself as the higher-class network, and by the early 1940s they had scheduled the Boston Symphony, the Firestone Concert, the Minneapolis Symphony, and the Rochester Philharmonic Orchestra.

Judging by the number of shows offered in 1935, radio listeners seemed to prefer a named band with an identifiable sound to a group with the name of its sponsor—even if that was a full classical orchestra. Yet some names in the light music category could and did become pop music stars, such as Kate Smith, who had high ratings in 1935 despite being on the air for only 15 minutes on CBS on Saturday nights.

By 1935 variety shows—which had always had a popular music component—reigned as the most popular of radio's genres. No list can be complete, but the big bands of the day could be found throughout the schedules of NBC and CBS—including the Bob Crosby orchestra, Fred Waring, Horace Heidt, Paul Whiteman, and the "waltz king" Wayne King. Guy Lombardo's orchestra remained a fixture on CBS on Monday nights, symbolizing more and more that the name was in the band and its singers, not in some amalgamation fashioned directly by the sponsor.

In short, the popular mainstream music of the 1930s and 1940s was found primarily on network radio. Orchestras were hired to perform live to generate a studio-made "high-fidelity" sound before the innovation in the late 1940s of 33 1/3-rpm and 45-rpm records. In-house studio orchestras were formed to provide background music for dramatic shows as well.

Big bands played remotes for dances in such ballrooms as the Aragon in Chicago and the Pacific Square in San Diego, at beach or other waterside attractions (the Steel Pier in Atlantic City and the Glen Island Casino in New Rochelle, New York), at restaurants (the Blackhawk in Chicago, the Copacabana in New York City), and at major hotels in most big cities. Such remotes offered popular venues for radio broadcasting through the 1940s and symbolized the hot new sounds for dancers of the era.

The rise of "name" singers was another emerging trend. Through the 1930s singers, led by Bing Crosby, learned to use the microphone for effect, not simply as a means of broadcasting. Ratings spiked when Crosby and Frank Sinatra—as well as Rosemary Clooney, Ruth Etting, Helen Kane, Peggy Lee, and Doris Day—were scheduled. Soloists hardly represented the lone form of popular radio singing. There were duos, trios, and quartets—from the Ink Spots to the Mills Brothers, from the Andrews Sisters to the Boswell Sisters. Singing intimately and in a number of styles, all based on Tin Pan Alley arrangements, became a true art form through radio broadcasting.

The war years proved to be the final hurrah for the musical variety show. National defense bond rallies often functioned as all-star radio variety shows, meant to outdo all other radio extravaganzas. Programs such as *Music for Millions, Treasury Star Parade,* and *Millions for Defense* not only drew needed bond sales but also were beamed overseas or recorded for later playback for the troops fighting in Europe and the Pacific. The top stars of network radio toured for the United Service Organizations (USO) and went abroad to entertain soldiers near the fronts. Indeed, radio star and big band leader Glenn Miller was killed while traveling from one such show to another. The war years also proved the crest for big band singers on net-

work radio. Kate Smith and Dinah Shore, for example, starred in some of the most popular shows on radio.

This system of making live music came apart, however, because of the demands of its most famous star, Bing Crosby. Crosby hated the necessities of live broadcasting, which demanded a rigid schedule that included doing shows twice (once for the Eastern and Central time zones and then a second time for Mountain and Pacific time zones). In 1946 Cosby moved his top-rated show from NBC to ABC to obtain relief. ABC, desperate for ratings, allowed Crosby to prerecord his *Philco Radio Time* using newly developed audiotape technology. He did not have to be in the studio when his show debuted (on 16 October 1946), nor weekly as it ran on ABC until June 1949. At that point William S. Paley, head of CBS, also gave into recorded music programs and as a part of his famous "talent raids," offered Crosby more money than ABC could afford.

Even though Tin Pan Alley and its allies in Hollywood largely dominated music played on the radio through the 1940s, there were alternatives. In particular, hillbilly music shows were becoming hits on the networks and on many local stations, particularly on small-town outlets in the South and West.

NBC led the way on the network level with *The National Barn Dance* and *The Grand Ole Opry,* both on Saturday nights. Numerous Southern stations offered live music, particularly during early morning hours. The demand for hillbilly music exceeded the supply, and so border stations based in Mexico blasted at 1 million watts music by hillbilly favorites such as the Carter Family, Jimmie Rodgers, Cowboy Slim Rinehart, and Patsy Montana.

The Carter Family—a trio composed of A.P. Carter, Sara Carter, and Maybelle Carter—was the first family of country music, and their famed 1928 Bristol, Tennessee, recording sessions kicked off a new genre of popular music. Jimmie Rodgers was also at those Bristol sessions and should be counted among the creators of hillbilly music. Nolan "Cowboy Slim" Rinehart, "the king of border radio," was a singing cowboy who, because of border stations' power, was heard across the nation as much as his more popular rival, singing cowboy Gene Autry. Cowgirl Patsy Montana teamed up with Rinehart for a series of transcribed duets during the 1930s and became so popular that her 1935 recording "I Wanna Be a Cowboy's Sweetheart" became the first million-selling record by a female hillbilly artist.

Ethnic artists found it more difficult to gain access to even local radio. In particular, although African-Americans were developing rhythm and blues music, the genre could rarely be heard on the radio during the 1930s and 1940s. Race records and juke joints offered the sole outlets, but the music was there and rich in form and style for the great change that was about to happen to radio music broadcasting.

Transition (1948–55)

Beginning in the late 1940s, NBC and CBS committed themselves to network television. They transferred their big bands and pop singers—plus some symphonic music—to TV and used profits from network radio to fund their new, and in the future far more profitable, medium. This worked well for the networks, and Bing Crosby, Kate Smith, Tommy Dorsey, and particularly Dinah Shore became mainstays of network television programming of the 1950s.

Their departure—and that of most other network programming—left radio stations looking for something new. Stations would find their salvation and reinvention in rock, an amalgamation of country and race forms. As rock was developing through the early and middle 1950s, Todd Stortz and Gordon McLendon pioneered Top 40 radio. They developed a short list of top tunes and played them over and over again. Teenagers of the 1950s—not interested in the big band, Tin Pan Alley music of their parents—embraced Top 40 radio. AM radio stations—looking for something to fill their time as network programs migrated to television—looked to Top 40 as their salvation.

There were sizable vested interests in keeping the live musical variety show going. These included the performing music societies, the American Society of Composers, Authors, and Publishers (ASCAP) and Broadcast Music Incorporated (BMI). Even more concerned was the American Federation of Musicians, the performer's union which tried to slow adoption of the innovative recording techniques—tape and discs—which union leaders and members feared (correctly) would lessen the demand for their live services. These parties, in addition to many parents and religious leaders, found rock music subversive and threatening. Even NBC tried to keep the variety musical show alive on radio with *The Big Show* on Sunday nights in 1951, but with no success.

Format Radio (Since 1955)

The symbol of the Top 40 revolution in radio was singer Elvis Presley. Gone were the big bands, dominated by brass and woodwinds, with dozens of players; these had been replaced by combos of a drummer and a couple of guitars. The electric guitar gave the necessary amplified sound and beat. The singer, who had been just one part of the big band, was now moved to the forefront, and with Chuck Berry, the singer sang his or her own compositions (so the songwriters of Tin Pan Alley were no longer needed). And, most important, the music of the margins—hillbilly and race—moved to the forefront as the amalgam labeled rock and roll. Elvis was the "hillbilly cat." Chuck Berry grew up in St. Louis listening to both *The National Barn Dance* and *The Grand Ole Opry*. After more of a struggle, blues music, later dubbed rhythm and blues in its urban form,

came to mainstream rock in the form of Detroit's "Motown Sound."

Rock, country, and rhythm and blues formats spawned a myriad of newer sub-formats for radio stations that wanted to be more than just "the other" Top 40 station in town. Taking but a single example, the history of country symbolizes how one marginal form became mainstream in the last half of the 20th century—indeed the top format in all radio by century's turn.

As rock splintered into many subtypes, each with devoted audiences, country rose to become the music that many white Americans listened to, in part because during an era of civil rights unrest, country recognized and appreciated that its roots were not tinged by music with more direct African-American roots. Country had its origins in the folk and hillbilly music that was so marginal during the network radio era—save for the popular "barn dance" programs. For advertisers, country attracted white, middle-class, suburban America—the audience they most wanted to reach.

Entrepreneurs provided a new name, and "country and western" was used into the 1960s. With the rise of Nashville (Tennessee) as an important recording center, however, the "western" was dropped, and by the time country format radio took off, the name was simply "country." What would become known as the "Nashville sound" worked as Hank Williams made country songs popular as pop music—an approach also heralded by Jim Reeves and Patsy Cline. By the 1960s, country emerged as an alternative genre, with stars such as Johnny Cash, Jimmy Dean, Loretta Lynn, and Dolly Parton. As rock seemed to lose its roots in the 1970s, country became an even more popular radio format. By the 1980s many surveys found country to be the most popular format on radio. A once marginal music style had become a dominant form of pop music, all made from a central location in Nashville.

With the innovation of portable and automobile radios, radio listening moved out of the home and became ubiquitous, particularly with the advent of the Walkman. The average person listened more than three hours per week. Advertisers targeted ethnic groups (principally African-Americans and Latinos), different age groups, income classes, and genders with different types of music. Adult contemporary music worked best for those 25–34 years old, whereas album-oriented rock was aimed at teenagers; their college-aged cousins seemed to prefer classic rock and contemporary hits radio. Country generally appealed to an older audience.

By the middle 1990s, many argued that radio had become too formulaic. Virtually all radio sought female suburban adults 18–34 who listened to radio on their way to and from work. Artists (in any format) who did not fit that pattern of attraction were simply not played. In the 1990s, for example, Top 40 morphed into "contemporary hits radio" and largely abandoned those who had once helped to create it: teenagers.

Creating a complete listing of these format formulas is almost fruitless—the annual *Broadcasting and Cable Yearbook* by the late 1990s listed more than 75 formats—starting with adult album alternative or AAA, moving on to urban contemporary, variety (four or more formats), Vietnamese, and finally women.

In the 1990s country music was among the most popular formats on U.S. radio. In turn, country spun off the gospel music format, and later the Christian contemporary music format. Its composers and stars were influenced by rock stylings they grew up with; superstar Garth Brooks recalled the group Kiss as his key influence. Indeed, during the 1990s one could more easily find a Willie Nelson or Loretta Lynn "classic" tune covered and then played on an adult contemporary format, a beautiful music format, or an easy listening format station than on a country station.

Other formats enjoyed great popularity during this turn of the century period as well, among them what was termed Contemporary Rock, Rhythmic Oldies, Urban, and Hot AC. Perhaps the most tuned by young listeners was Hip Hop. It inspired the newest incarnation of the Top 40/CHR format because the Hip Hop sound dominated the best selling music charts nationally, if not globally.

DOUGLAS GOMERY

See also, in addition to individual formats discussed above, American Federation of Musicians; American Society of Composers, Authors and Publishers; Broadcast Music Incorporated; Canadian Radio and the Music Industry; Classical Music Format; Crosby, Bing; Formats; Grand Ole Opry; McClendon, Gordon; Metropolitan Opera; National Barn Dance; Recordings and the Radio Industry; Singers on Radio; Storz, Todd; Talent Raids; Vallee, Rudy; Walkman

Further Reading

DeLong, Thomas A., *The Mighty Music Box: The Golden Age of Musical Radio,* Los Angeles: Amber Crest Books, 1980

Eberly, Philip K., *Music in the Air: America's Changing Tastes in Popular Music, 1920–1980,* New York: Hastings House, 1982

Fornatale, Peter, and Joshua E. Mills, *Radio in the Television Age,* Woodstock, New York: Overlook Press, 1980

Fowler, Gene, and Bill Crawford, *Border Radio,* Austin: Texas Monthly Press, 1987

Hickerson, Jay, *The Ultimate History of Network Radio Programming and Guide to All Circulating Shows,* Hamden, Connecticut: Hickerson, 1992; 3rd edition, as *The New, Revised, Ultimate History of Network Radio Programming and Guide to All Circulating Shows,* 1996

Joyner, David Lee, *American Popular Music,* Madison, Wisconsin: Brown and Benchmark, 1993

Landry, Robert John, *This Fascinating Radio Business,* Indianapolis, Indiana: Bobbs-Merrill, 1946

MacDonald, J. Fred, *Don't Touch That Dial! Radio Programming in American Life, 1920–1960,* Chicago: Nelson-Hall, 1979

Malone, Bill C., *Country Music U.S.A.,* Austin: University of Texas Press, 1968; revised edition, 1985

Routt, Edd, James B. McGrath, and Frederic A. Weiss, *The Radio Format Conundrum,* New York: Hastings House, 1978

Sanjek, Russell, and David Sanjek, *American Popular Music Business in the 20th Century,* New York: Oxford University Press, 1991

Whetmore, Edward Jay, *The Magic Medium: An Introduction to Radio in America,* Belmont, California: Wadsworth, 1981

Music Testing

Determining Radio Audience Preferences

There has never been as great a need for accurate music research data in the radio industry as there is today. Not only are many more entertainment options available to potential listeners, but the expectations for ratings and profit performance continue to increase. As a result, programmers of music-oriented stations have adopted a variety of research methods to better understand their listeners' attitudes toward particular songs.

Requests

Perhaps the most easily overlooked source of music data is a station's request line. Many programmers recognize requests as an inexpensive and simple way to collect music information. Instructing disc jockeys to tally songs that people care enough about to request is an easy and cheap way to obtain a daily glimpse of titles that excite listeners. However, programmers should be careful not to place too much confidence in request data. Listeners with enough spare time to place requests may not best represent a station's audience. To better ensure that a station's entire audience range is represented, programmers rely on more scientific methods.

Callout

The primary method of music testing is callout research. Callout consists of trained interviewers telephoning randomly selected listeners of a particular station and having them use a pre-established scale to rate 15 or 20 "hooks" from songs the station plays. A hook is a brief lyrical segment, often the title or chorus, that captures the essential quality of the song.

According to Tony Novia of *Radio and Records* magazine, callout began in the 1970s when broadcasters believed they could predict which new songs would become popular by having listeners rate hooks from the very latest releases. Unfortunately, because the songs were so new and had not received any airplay, respondent unfamiliarity resulted in unreliable data. Beginning in the 1980s, programmers realized that callout was an effective tool for obtaining data about familiar music. The hook, in effect, was just long enough to "jog the memory about a song in question" (Novia, 2000). Today, most users of callout recommend that songs not be included in research until they reach a high level of familiarity through airplay. For example, radio consultant Guy Zapoleon reports that a general rule is to have a song play at least 100 times on a station before placing it into callout.

During callout, respondents provide data after each hook is heard over the phone line. First, they are asked if they recognize the song. If they do, a favorability-scale question is generally asked next. For example, listeners may rate the song on a scale of 1 to 10, where 1 means they dislike the song very much and 10 means they like the song very much. Another type of data often obtained during callout is a fatigue or burnout measurement. Listeners are asked, "Are you tired of hearing this song on the radio?" Especially in contemporary music formats, fatigue data is important for determining when to decrease airplay of a popular song title.

Perhaps the biggest benefit of callout research is the ability to gather music data quickly, easily, and inexpensively. These benefits result in the ability to generate weekly reports on current music. Drawbacks to callout include the reliance on hooks, the brevity of which sometimes fail to capture the essence of a song; the comparative low fidelity of telephone lines, which may negatively bias results; and the high refusal rates of respondents, which can be expected any time researchers make unscheduled telephone calls. Two newer and less prevalent music testing techniques, the personal music test and call-in research, have been developed to address these shortcomings.

Call-in and Personal Music Tests

As is implied by its name, call-in research consists of listeners telephoning a station's research department to complete music tests. This method allows listeners to provide information at their convenience. A similar method involves invitations to visit the station's website, where listeners can participate in a music test in which audio of hooks (or even of entire songs) is streamed. There are several drawbacks to these two methods that must be kept in mind. First, just as with those who request songs, listeners who have the time or interest to phone a station or visit its website to participate in a music survey may not be representative of listeners in general. Second, there is no way to adequately prevent one listener from providing opinions more than once, thereby biasing the results.

A personal music test attempts to combine the scheduling convenience of call-in with the representativeness and quality control of callout. Using this music testing method, telephone interviewers call a random selection of station listeners and schedule an appointment for them to visit a research facility at a convenient time. Upon their arrival, listeners are given a hook tape of current music and a personal cassette player with headphones. Listeners work through the hooks, providing ratings for each hook at their own pace. The personal music test ensures that respondents devote the undistracted time required to provide valid data. Furthermore, because telephone lines are not involved, the fidelity of the music being tested is much closer to what is actually heard over the air. A major drawback to the personal music test, however, is cost, because most stations employing the method have found that a financial incentive is necessary to increase participation.

Auditorium Music Tests

Although the methods mentioned above tend to be used to collect opinions of fewer than 30 current songs, auditorium music tests (AMTs) are generally employed to test between 350 and 700 older songs. Familiarity with the titles is assumed; the goal here is to determine the best-liked "gold" music among the station's target audience. For oldies formats, the method is often used to determine the entire playlist; therefore, oldies programmers conduct AMTs each quarter, whereas more contemporary music stations can afford to do them only once or twice a year. AMTs consist of inviting between 75 and 150 randomly selected listeners to an auditorium and playing a hook tape for them. The shared sense of purpose and controlled environment are key benefits to this method. One drawback is the cost of auditorium rental and respondent incentives. Another is the possibility of respondent fatigue, which can be lessened by scheduling breaks periodically during hook presentation.

ROBERT F. POTTER

See also Audience Research Methods; Auditorium Testing

Further Reading

Eastman, Susan T., Douglas A. Ferguson, and Timothy P. Meyer, "Program and Audience Research," in *Broadcast/ Cable Programming,* 5th edition, edited by Eastman and Ferguson, Belmont, California, and London: Wadsworth, 1997

Kelly, Tom, *Music Research: The Silver Bullet to Eternal Success,* Washington, D.C.: National Association of Broadcasters, 2000

Lynch, Joanna R., and Gillispie, Greg, "Creating an Image," in *Process and Practice of Radio Programming,* by Lynch and Gillispie, Lanham, Maryland: University Press of America, 1998

MacFarland, David T., *Contemporary Radio Programming Strategies,* Mahwah, New Jersey: Erlbaum, 1990; 2nd edition, as *Future Radio Programming Strategies: Cultivating Leadership in the Digital Age,* 1997

Norberg, Eric, G., "Promoting Your Station," in *Radio Programming: Tactics and Strategy,* by Norberg, Boston and Oxford: Focal Press, 1996

Novia, Tony, "Reach Out and Touch Some Listeners," *Radio and Records* (11 February 2000)

Porter, Chris, "Music Testing: Pros and Cons," *Radio and Records* (28 August 1998)

Zapoleon, Guy, "When to Put a Song into Callout," *Radio@Large* (15 July 1999)

Mutual Broadcasting System

U.S. National Radio Network

The Mutual Broadcasting System was unique among the four national radio networks. Whereas the other networks originated most of their programming from studios in New York City and Hollywood, Mutual was a cooperative program-sharing venture whose member stations around the country provided most of the programming. As the last major network to be established, Mutual's stations tended to be the ones the other networks did not want: low-powered rural stations with limited listening areas. Thus, although Mutual was eventually to proclaim itself the nation's largest radio network based on the number of affiliates it served, it was continually mired in last place in a four-way race.

Mutual and its affiliates created many memorable programs, such as *The Adventures of Bulldog Drummond, Buck Rogers, Double or Nothing, 20 Questions, The Falcon, The Green Hornet, The Shadow, Sherlock Holmes, The Lone Ranger, Dick Tracy, Queen for a Day,* and *Captain Midnight,* and featured personalities such as the controversial Father Charles E. Coughlin, Dick Clark, Merv Griffin, Mike Wallace, and, in later days, Larry King. But the network's fourth-place status and chronically weak financial position often resulted in its best programs being lured away to the deeper-pocketed competing networks.

Creating a Fourth Network

Because local radio listening areas, or markets, varied widely in both population and number of stations locally available, the three-network system (National Broadcasting Company [NBC] Red, NBC Blue, and the Columbia Broadcasting System [CBS]) worked well in some places and not as well in others. Markets with three local stations willing to affiliate with a network (despite the advantages, not all stations desired affiliation) were ideally suited to the status quo. Markets with fewer than three stations frequently saw a station affiliated with more than one network, with one network considered the station's primary affiliation and another network constituting a "secondary" affiliation. In markets with four or more stations desiring network affiliation, somebody, obviously, was going to be disappointed. In a competitive environment with four or more stations, the affiliation contracts usually went to the more powerful stations.

The early 1930s saw several attempts to start a fourth radio network, from the Amalgamated Broadcasting System (headed by popular radio comedian Ed Wynn, often billed as "the perfect fool": the network folded in five weeks) to an American Broadcasting Company (no relation to today's ABC) that lasted a few months. Among the many reasons for the high failure rate, two deserve special consideration, because they were to resurface continually as formidable challenges to anyone trying to compete with NBC or CBS. The first was the fact that the three major networks already had solid relationships with the best advertisers, and they still had much airtime to sell. In many ways, a sustaining program represented an unsold commercial slot. Ideally (for the network), the entire schedule would be commercial. Thus, the sales representatives at NBC and CBS aggressively went after advertisers to buy more time, often offering discounted rates to large advertising accounts. Any start-up radio network was going to have a tough time convincing advertisers to stray from the majors. A second problem was the ragtag nature of most of the stations not already signed with NBC or CBS. As much as these stations wanted network affiliation, this accumulation of largely low-powered and/or rural stations would not be very attractive to national advertisers.

Ironically, the company that was finally to establish a fourth network started life with no national network intentions. In 1934 four powerful independent (non-network) stations banded together to form the Quality Group. The purpose of the group, which consisted of WOR (New York), WGN (Chicago), WLW (Cincinnati), and WXYZ (Detroit), was twofold. First, they would share their better sustaining programs among themselves. Second, they would offer an alternative to the producers of commercial programs who wanted access to four major metropolitan markets without going through one of the established networks. As a Quality Group spokesman stated, "We will endeavor to make suitable time arrangements for advertisers seeking to broadcast in important markets through the use of a few stations having high power and a vast listening audience. . . . Each station will remain independent and make its own decision in accepting programs. . . . Several programs are now broadcast over this group of stations by mutual agreement." The "mutual" nature of the cooperative venture apparently struck a chord, because the organization was almost immediately renamed the Mutual Broadcasting System (MBS). By the time it celebrated its first anniversary in 1935, Mutual carried 20 hours of commercial broadcasts and 40 hours of sustaining broadcasts per week. The anniversary was bittersweet, however. The one non-stockholding partner in the venture, WXYZ, had just jumped ship to NBC Blue. Mutual was able to replace WXYZ in the Detroit market by signing CKLW, an across-the-border Canadian station that had served as the area's CBS affiliate. CBS had dumped CKLW in favor of yet another Detroit station, WJR, when it increased its power to 50,000 watts.

More significantly, a major schism regarding the future of the company was developing among the three owner stations. Desiring to increase the operation's revenue, WGN and WOR wanted to open Mutual up into a broader network serving more stations. WLW was opposed to this plan. Whereas the metropolitan locations of WGN and WOR (Chicago and New York City) gave them local access to millions of listeners, WLW got most of its audience through the far-flung reach of its nighttime 500,000-watt signal. If Mutual began to sign affiliates in the cities reached by WLW's signal, the station reasoned, WLW would lose much of its audience to these local stations. WLW wanted MBS programming to remain exclu-

sively available to the original four markets to preserve its own unique appeal to its geographically widespread audience.

WLW was outvoted. By early 1936 some individual Mutual programs (but not the complete network schedule) were being carried on a network of nine stations. By the fall of 1936, Mutual announced expansion to the West, signing affiliation agreements with the Don Lee regional network in California and with several Midwest stations along the American Telephone and Telegraph (AT&T) line, which was leased to carry the network's signal to the West Coast. At the same time, WLW announced that it was turning in its MBS stock. It remained an MBS affiliate for many years, even continuing to supply Mutual with some original programming. Its own schedule, however, became increasingly a mix of MBS and NBC. The Federal Communications Commission (FCC) eventually decided that the "superstation" experiment was a failure, placing WLW at too much of a competitive advantage over other stations, and WLW became a regular 50,000-watt clear channel station. The Don Lee network picked up WLW's stock, as well as one-third of the cost of the expanded network operations. Before the network hookup to California was in operation, Mutual signed a Washington, D.C., station and another regional network, Colonial, as a New England affiliate. Thus by the end of 1936, Mutual was a true transcontinental network, albeit one with huge gaps (most significantly, the southern half of the United States). Despite this expansion, MBS executives remained committed to the network's unique vision. Company President W.E. Macfarlane emphasized the independent nature of Mutual's affiliates by noting, "The Mutual Broadcasting System was organized with the purpose of presenting better programs, allowing stations to maintain their independence, and creating a network of stations which would serve the country's listening audience and still allow stations to fulfill obligations to their various local communities."

By 1937 Mutual was serving 51 affiliates. The complete network schedule consisted of 30-3/4 hours of commercial programs and 93-1/4 hours of sustaining programs per week. Within a year, the total number of affiliates was up to 51. Yet increasingly, Mutual was finding itself frustrated by the major networks. Many of its new affiliates were only secondary Mutual stations. These stations owed their primary allegiance (and best broadcasting hours) to one of the major networks. On these stations, Mutual only got the broadcast times the major networks did not want: the hours with the fewest listeners that were the most difficult to sell to national advertisers. Because of its weak position relative to the other networks, Mutual became an early practitioner of "counter-programming." If the most popular program on radio in a given time slot was a drama, Mutual would schedule a musical show opposite it.

The FCC Network Probe

Early in 1938, in part responding to growing complaints from Mutual about its difficulty in competing with the entrenched New York-based networks, the FCC initiated a probe of possible network monopolistic practices. Data soon confirmed some of Mutual's complaints—CBS and NBC, with three networks between them, dominated the strongest stations across the country. Mutual was having trouble getting a competitive foothold in the business.

Mutual's winning of the rights to provide the baseball World Series broadcasts in 1938 and 1939 brought other network practices into sharp contrast. CBS and NBC ordered their affiliates to stick with their own network programs, even when those stations wanted to carry the highly popular games (and Mutual was willing to provide them). The closed-door approach of the New York networks certainly helped to underline Mutual's anti-competitive arguments.

Based in part on information provided by Mutual, the FCC issued its final report on chain broadcasting in May 1941, calling for a host of changes in the relationship between networks and their affiliates. After a fierce legal battle, and several long congressional hearings, the rules were upheld in a landmark Supreme Court decision in 1943. NBC and CBS were forced to modify many of their affiliation contracts, somewhat evening the playing field for Mutual.

The Decline of Mutual and Network Radio

The MBS continued to expand through the 1940s, reaching 400 affiliates in 1947. It became the first network to include FM stations in its lineup, although these affiliations were plagued in the beginning by a dispute with the American Federation of Musicians that prohibited any musical programs from being carried over FM stations without an additional fee. The expanded Mutual network now reached 84 percent of the nation's radio homes, although only 60 percent of the network's programming was actually carried over the entire system.

Although the post–World War II structure of Mutual was basically the same as it had always been—a program-sharing cooperative owned by three major stockholders (WGN, WOR, Don Lee) and a few minor stockholders (including the New England–based Colonial regional network)—major changes in the broadcasting landscape and in Mutual's corporate structure loomed on the horizon.

After decades of development, television was finally ready for its commercial launch immediately following World War II. Although CBS, NBC, ABC, and an electronics firm named DuMont all announced plans for television networks, Mutual's stand on the matter was ambivalent. Although WGN, WOR,

Don Lee, and some Mutual affiliates were getting into television, MBS announced in 1948 that it would "leave actual video operations to its stockholder stations." The decision was made that these stockholder stations might provide programming to MBS affiliates, but that such programming, for the time being, would be outside of Mutual. Although he assumed that MBS would eventually become the fourth television network, MBS president Edgar Kobak stated, "I have a hunch that a few years from now survival may be difficult and one way to survive is to be careful now. That's what we at Mutual are doing." Survival for Mutual would indeed soon become difficult, and the decision not to actively develop a television arm would be one of the major contributing factors.

In 1943 General Tire and Rubber bought the Colonial network, giving it a small stake in MBS. In 1950 it expanded its broadcast holdings with the acquisition of the Don Lee network (giving the company 38 percent ownership of MBS), and its purchase of WOR the following year made it the controlling partner in Mutual, with 58 percent of the stock. Under the new corporate name of General Teleradio, the company acquired the remainder of Mutual's outstanding stock to become the sole owner of MBS. General Teleradio bought RKO-Radio Pictures in the mid-1950s. General's interest in the studio was solely to obtain its backlog of old theatrical movies as programming for General's growing roster of independent television stations. General had no intention of getting into the theatrical film business or of using RKO's studios as a production center for a possible MBS television network. Content to run its television outlets as independent stations, the newly renamed RKO-General immediately liquidated the film studio and, in 1957, sold MBS to oil tycoon Armand Hammer. The company would pass through the hands of five more owners in the next three years.

In the fall of 1958, Mutual was sold again, this time to Hal Roach Studios. A venerable producer of theatrical short comedies in the 1920s and 1930s, Roach had become a major television producer in the 1950s. By the late 1950s, however, the company was in the throes of serious financial reversals, compelling it to accept a buyout offer from a businessman named Alexander Guterma. Guterma immediately announced plans to combine the Roach operation and MBS into a broadcasting powerhouse of both radio and television networks, the latter of which would be supplied with programming from the Roach Studios. Within months, however, the Guterma empire collapsed under allegations of stock fraud.

In February 1959, MBS was sold by the Hal Roach Studios to recording executive Malcolm Smith. Smith sold MBS within months to a new set of owners, the McCarthy-Ferguson Group, who entered the network into bankruptcy reorganization.

During the transition from Smith to McCarthy-Ferguson, a final peculiar twist to the Roach-Guterma era emerged. In an effort to save his flagging business empire, Alexander Guterma had accepted $750,000 in January 1959 from the dictator of the Dominican Republic, Generalissimo Rafael Trujillo, in exchange for up to 425 minutes per month of favorable coverage of the Dominican Republic on Mutual radio news broadcasts. Negative reports on the Dominican Republic would not appear on MBS. The arrangement was reported to federal authorities by the new MBS management, who had found themselves accosted by agents of the Dominican Republic demanding performance on the deal or return of the money. In addition to his problems with the Securities and Exchange Commission, Guterma found himself tried and convicted of failing to register himself as an agent of a foreign principal.

In April 1960, McCarthy-Ferguson sold the network to the giant manufacturing company 3M, which was seeking to diversify into new fields. By the 1960s, however, network radio had become little more than a news-delivery service. As a corollary enterprise to the news division of a television network, a radio news service could return a profit. Despite the fact that it could boast the largest number of affiliates of any radio network, over 500 in 1967, with no television operation to share the costs of news gathering Mutual was locked in a terminal slide toward oblivion.

Despite the inevitability of its demise, MBS lasted considerably longer than most industry analysts expected (and longer than the pioneering NBC Radio Network). The end for Mutual came on 18 April 1999. Its final owner was the Westwood One radio group, which had bought Mutual from Amway in 1985. Shortly before Mutual's demise, Westwood One had turned most management decisions over to CBS Radio, which saw Mutual as redundant to other services offered by both Westwood One and CBS. The last Mutual sta-tions were offered affiliation with Westwood One's CNN Radio operation to replace the departed 65-year-old Mutual network.

RICHARD WARD

See also American Broadcasting Company; CKLW; Columbia Broadcasting System; National Broadcasting Company; Network Monopoly Probe; Westwood One; WGN; WLW; WOR

Further Reading

"After 50 Years the Feeling's Still Mutual," *Broadcasting* (10 September 1984)

Crater, Rufus, "What Happens to MBS?" *Broadcasting-Telecasting* (15 October 1951)

Federal Communications Commission, *Report on Chain Broadcasting,* Washington, D.C.: Government Printing Office, 1941; reprint, New York: Arno Press, 1974

"First 12 Years of Mutual Network: A Study in 'Operations Grass Roots'" *Variety* (23 October 1946)

"Grand Jury Indicts Guterma Trio: Charged with Selling MBS as Dominican Propaganda Vehicle," *Broadcasting* (7 September 1959)

The Money Faces of Mutual, New York: Mutual Radio Networks, 1974

"New Giant Growing in Radio-TV?" *Broadcasting* (15 September 1958)

Robertson, Bruce, "Mutual Reaches Its 20th Birthday," *Broadcasting-Telecasting* (27 September 1954)

Robinson, Thomas Porter, *Radio Networks and the Federal Government,* New York: Columbia University Press, 1943

N

Narrowcasting

Narrowcasting is the process of identifying or selecting a specific portion of the overall radio audience and designing a station's programming to attract and retain that audience. Other related terms include *audience fragmentation, target audience, listener segmentation, niche audience,* and *format-specific, cultural-specific,* or *audience-specific programming.*

Narrowcasting stands in contrast to the older word *broadcasting,* which was borrowed from the agricultural industry. To a farmer, broadcasting means to sow seeds as widely as possible throughout a field; in radio, stations transmit their signal widely throughout their coverage area. In the early decades of radio, stations designed their programming to meet the needs of the largest, widest possible audience. However, stations could not always meet everyone's needs adequately, and portions of the population were left underserved or neglected by programming intended for an aggregate audience.

During the 1930s and 1940s, some independent, non–network stations in larger U.S. markets sold air time to African-American or non English-language programmers. In addition, some country and folk listeners could find programs to meet their needs in the various barn dance and jamboree shows around the country, although few stations featured around-the-clock music for rural listeners.

After World War II, the number of radio stations on the air increased dramatically, increasing the pressure on each outlet to find programs that would appeal to at least some listeners. Managers of newer stations who were willing to forgo the "golden age" approach to programming focused their programs to attract specific audiences; as a result, African-American and country stations first appeared in the late 1940s and early 1950s. During the same period, Top 40 programmers reached out to teens, and Middle-of-the-Road stations attracted older audiences: thus the first true formats were born.

The practice of narrowcasting is of particular interest to advertisers, because even though audiences are typically divided by listening characteristics, listener segmentation also results in buyer segmentation. When special audiences are targeted for specific products, the result is a more efficient use of advertising dollars. Teens are more likely to buy acne medicine and soft drinks. Mature audiences are more prone to invest in luxury cars, health care products, or mutual funds. This improved efficiency can be illustrated by the question, "Would you rather stand on the street and try to sell hot dogs to all the people passing by or would you rather talk to ten hungry people?" On the street, a salesperson will meet many people, but not all will be prepared to purchase. On the other hand, ten hungry people may find themselves quite interested in the prospect of a hot dog, if the salesperson can only locate them.

Over time, the practice of narrowcasting has enhanced the partnership between stations and advertisers. *Broadcasting and Cable Yearbook* in 2000 recognized 70 different radio formats in use. These various narrowcast formats divide the total audience into listener groups according to the demographic characteristics of age, gender, culture, or income. The station programmer's job is to design a total package of program elements, including music, news, IDs, liners, and public service announcements, to attract and retain their specific audience. The advertiser's task is to match audiences with products. A successful link of programs, audiences, and advertisers results in a more efficient and, in the long run, more economical effort enabling stations to deliver audiences to advertisers.

CHARLES F. GANZERT

See also Formats; Programming Strategies and Processes

Further Reading

Fornatale, Peter, and Joshua E. Mills, *Radio in the Television Age,* Woodstock, New York: Overlook Press, 1980
Ganzert, Charles, "Platter Chatter and the Pancake Impresarios: The Re-Invention of Radio in the Age of Television, 1946–1959," Ph.D. diss., Ohio University, 1992

Hall, Claude, and Barbara Hall, *This Business of Radio Programming: A Comprehensive Look at Modern Programming Techniques Used throughout the Radio World,* New York: Billboard, 1977

MacFarland, David, *The Development of the Top 40 Radio Format,* New York: Arno Press, 1979

Routt, Edd, James McGrath, and Frederick Weiss, *The Radio Format Conundrum,* New York: Hastings House, 1978

National Association of Broadcasters

U.S. Broadcast Trade Organization

The National Association of Broadcasters (NAB) is the primary trade association of the American broadcasting industry. The NAB represents the industry before the Federal Communications Commission (FCC), Congress, and other government entities and takes a proactive role in acquainting the public with the importance of radio and television communications.

Members of the association set policies and make decisions on industry-wide matters through a board of directors composed of radio and television broadcasters elected by fellow members. This joint board is subdivided into a radio and a television board, each with its own chair. The joint board also has a chairman. NAB is overseen by a full-time president.

NAB has an extensive committee structure that enables it to draw on the specialized knowledge of its members in dealing with industry causes and in making recommendations to the board of directors. These committees are composed of representatives of individual stations, broadcast groups, and the networks. Active member support and participation are the basis for NAB decisions and activities.

According to its charter, NAB operates "to foster and promote the development of the arts of aural and visual broadcasting in all forms; to protect its members in every lawful and proper manner from injustices and unjust exactions; to do all things necessary and proper to encourage and promote customs and practices which will strengthen and maintain the broadcasting industry to the end that it may best serve the people."

Origins

The early history of NAB is closely tied to the issue of using recorded music in early radio broadcasts of the 1920s. At that time, broadcasters freely used phonograph records without compensating the artists involved, in spite of a 1917 court decision that upheld the right of creative artists to license their products under provisions of the 1909 copyright act. By early 1922, the declining sale of phonograph records in the face of radio broadcasting caused the American Society of Composers, Authors, and Publishers (ASCAP) to look for ways to recover lost royalties directly from broadcasters. ASCAP, founded in 1914, provided the means for artists to license and copyright their creative efforts.

In April 1922 ASCAP determined that the radio reproduction of copyrighted songs fell under the "public performance for profit" portion of the copyright law and that the copyright owners were entitled to compensation from the broadcasters. ASCAP notified all broadcast stations of their intention to collect royalties for their members, but the announcement was largely ignored by the fledgling industry.

After finding little success pursuing its aims within the broadcast industry as a whole, ASCAP decided specifically to move against Westinghouse, General Electric (GE), the Radio Corporation of America (RCA), and a few other giants of the new industry. ASCAP called for a conference to discuss the issue, but it was once again ignored. The broadcasters agreed to a meeting only after ASCAP threatened to sue them for copyright infringements if they did not meet.

At the meeting on 20 September 1922, ASCAP presented as its major concern artists' rights to royalty payments, while broadcasters expressed their desire not to pay royalties. Of major importance to the broadcasters was the payment of performers; at that time, many musicians performed on radio free for the exposure, and broadcasters felt that if they paid some, they would have to pay them all. The broadcasters told ASCAP that they would go on the air with "The Old Gray Mare, She Ain't What She Used to Be" rather then pay ASCAP for the privilege of broadcasting the latest ASCAP licensed hit, "My Bromo-Seltzer Bride." The meeting ended without resolution.

Organization by Zenith's McDonald

The second ASCAP-broadcaster conference occurred one month later, on 25 October 1922. At this meeting, broadcasters expressed sympathy for the artists' position but stated that they could not afford to pay for the music if it would lead to paying all composers, individual performers, and orchestras. ASCAP responded by filing a suit and notifying all broadcasters that it was revoking all temporary licenses for broadcast of ASCAP members' music. Additionally, ASCAP established a rate schedule that fixed fees for the use of music at $250 to $5,000 per year per station depending on the size of the station's audience (determined by location, wattage, and profits). The arbitrary nature of the ASCAP action caused a small group of broadcasters, organized by "Commander" Eugene F. McDonald, Jr., founder-president of Zenith Radio Corporation (and station WJAZ), to meet in Chicago in early 1923 to form an organization to oppose ASCAP; this organization would become the National Association of Broadcasters.

The group, all pioneer broadcasters, moved quickly from a discussion of ASCAP to the need for a regulatory body for radio similar to the Interstate Commerce Commission. At this initial meeting of concerned broadcasters, McDonald first used the name "Federal Communications Commission" for such a group. They also considered rules and regulations that they felt should apply to a free enterprise system for radio.

Shortly after this meeting, McDonald, who knew little of the music business, called on his friend and business colleague Thomas Pletcher, president of the QRS Music Company, for advice. He told Pletcher that his group of broadcasters believed that authors and composers should be paid directly for their contributions, rather then through ASCAP, but that they did not know how to proceed with the organization. Pletcher suggested that the group hire Paul B. Klugh (a knowledgeable, recently retired music roll manufacturer) as secretary of the new organization. McDonald successfully recruited Klugh, who assumed the position of executive chairman. McDonald embarked on a campaign to persuade RCA, GE, Westinghouse, and American Telephone and Telegraph (ATT) to join the fledgling group, but he was initially unsuccessful.

The actual organizational meeting for the NAB was held in the studios of WDAP (Chicago) on 25 and 26 April 1923, with 54 representatives of various radio constituencies. Representatives of ASCAP presented their positions and, after discussion, left the meeting. A committee was then formed to propose the structure for an organization that would carry out the aims of the broadcasters. The committee consisted of McDonald (WJAZ), T. Donnelley (WDAP), J.E. Jenkins (WDAP), W.S. Hedges (WMAQ), P.B. Klugh, R.M. Johnson (Alabama Power and Light Company), and George Lewis (Crosley Manufacturing Company). The group, known as "the Committee of Seven," reported on 26 April 1923, and their recommendations were accepted: the association was to be known as The National Association of Broadcasters, NAB's offices would be established in New York City, and they would employ a managing director. Paul Klugh was selected as the managing direc-

tor by a unanimous vote. Two other meetings were held in 1923 with the main subject of discussion being the development of an NAB "music bureau" of copyright-free music.

The first annual meeting of the National Association of Broadcasters was held in conjunction with the annual National Radio Show held in New York on 11 October 1923. This meeting, called to order by Chairman Klugh in the Commodore Hotel in New York City, resulted in the election of the first real officers of the NAB. McDonald was elected president. A number of addresses were presented, and the group received a list of holdings in the NAB Music Bureau. A discussion of legislation plans was also undertaken. The group wanted to accomplish two goals with their legislation: (1) music copyright revision and (2) modernization of the 1912 Radio Act. During the meeting, McDonald conducted a test of the size of the audience at WJAZ by asking listeners to send in paid telegrams acknowledging their reception. The audience was estimated to be 400,000, based on receiving 4,284 telegrams in four hours. The public relations coup resulted in considerable publicity for the young broadcasters group.

In conjunction with the 1923 Chicago Radio Show in November, McDonald and his good friend Thorne Donnelley of WDAP, both officers of the NAB, along with Chicago station KYW, conducted an audience census to determine music preference in the Chicago listening area. For 12 days the stations requested listeners to write in telling what they most desired to hear. The three stations received a total of 263,410 pieces of mail, with WJAZ receiving 170,699; WDAP, 54,811; and KYW, 37,900. It was estimated that not more than 1 in 50 listeners would respond, which suggested that the three stations were being heard by an audience of more than 13 million.

In 1924 ASCAP attempted to flex its muscle and thus created a situation that brought the music copyright problem before Congress. The Edgewater Beach Hotel (home of WJAZ) had always paid a fee to ASCAP for the music used in its dining room. Because at times this music had also been broadcast live over WJAZ, ASCAP refused to renew the performance license for the music unless a broadcast license was also secured, even though the hotel no longer allowed WJAZ to broadcast the music. The broadcasters determined that this situation was a good legal test case. The fact that McDonald's WJAZ was involved and that he was also president of the NAB undoubtedly was an important factor in choosing this incident for the test case.

On 22 February 1924, Senator C.C. Dill, at the urging of the NAB, introduced a bill to the Senate that amended the Copyright Act of 1909 to make radio performances of copyrighted material essentially legal and royalty-free. A nasty battle ensued, with ASCAP waging a publicity campaign encouraging all musicians to join the fight. NAB, small and new, had little money to fight back, and a plea to broadcasters for financial help brought nothing.

The NAB cause was represented by NAB President McDonald, Executive Secretary Klugh, and Counsel Charles Tuttle. In January 1925, the ASCAP-supported Perkins Bill (H.R. 11258) was introduced in the House. This bill called for massive changes in the copyright law in general and particularly in those portions concerned with radio broadcasting.

Years of debate followed. The NAB endorsed its stand at each succeeding annual conference. McDonald's involvement also continued. As NAB president, he was appointed one of ten members of the Copyright Committee of the Fourth National Radio Conference called by then Commerce Secretary Herbert Hoover in Washington on 9 November 1925. The fight to avoid paying royalties, however, was rapidly being lost, and the NAB and ASCAP entered secret negotiations. McDonald stepped down as president of the NAB in 1926 as he began a battle with Secretary Hoover over frequency allocations, but he continued his strong involvement with NAB for many years, holding a variety of offices.

NAB Radio and Television Codes

The NAB has been involved in voluntary compliance broadcast codes since 1929, when it produced its first "Code of Ethics" in an attempt to preempt the Federal Radio Commission from imposing such a code. In 1939, attempting to avoid FCC action regarding children's programs, the NAB issued a "Radio Code" dealing with profanity and limits on commercial time in children's programming. NAB issued a guide for broadcasters in 1942 covering security in wartime broadcasting. Although compliance with these codes was voluntary, many NAB members subscribed to them, and the various NAB radio and television codes existed until they were dropped in 1982 after a court case found a portion of the code unconstitutional. Today the NAB operates under a "Statement of Principles" dealing with program content.

The NAB expanded greatly in 1938 and has grown with the broadcasting industry, incorporating other groups in the industry. The FM Broadcaster Association became a department of NAB in 1945, and in 1951 the Television Broadcasters Association also merged with NAB. Springing from NAB membership in 1959, a new and independent National Association of FM Broadcasters met for the first time; by 1984, the 2000-member group, then named the National Radio Broadcasters Association, merged with NAB. NAB also accepts associate members in fields allied to broadcasting.

The Modern NAB

Although much of the association's focus since the 1950s has been on television, cable, and newer media, radio continues to occupy NAB lobbying and developmental efforts. NAB championed FM in the 1960s and 1970s, publishing a monthly newsletter tracing industry developments. In the early 1980s, NAB fought strenuously and eventually successfully to beat back an FCC proposal to reduce AM channels from 10 kilohertz to 9 kilohertz, parallel to much of the rest of the world. The association argued that such a move would increase interference and make many push-button radios obsolete. At the same time, NAB supported efforts to create AM stereo and to select a technical standard for the service.

In the late 1990s, NAB radio interests focused on digital radio and on developing a successful technical standard to allow digital audio broadcasting (DAB) service to begin. At the same time, NAB fought hard against allowing satellite digital services to develop, because they would threaten the local stations represented by the association. And NAB fought against the highly popular introduction of low-power FM stations (LPFM) in 2000, arguing that the potential for hundreds of new stations would greatly increase interference problems. NAB maintains an ongoing educational program on its agenda.

The huge annual four-day NAB conventions, which now attract more than 115,000 attendees, are held every spring (in Las Vegas since the early 1970s) and devote considerable conference time and exhibition space to radio and audio topics. A fall conference focused entirely on radio programming and operations is also held, and radio-related publications are issued regularly. With more than 100 full-time employees housed in its own modern building in Washington, D.C., the NAB has gained a reputation as one of the strongest and most effective lobbies in the nation's capital. Part of this strength comes from the clout inherent in member stations, which provide airtime for political candidates and which will readily call congresspersons to press their views.

HAROLD N. CONES AND JOHN H. BRYANT

See also American Society of Composers, Authors and Publishers; Broadcast Music Incorporated; FM Trade Associations; McDonald, Eugene F.; Trade Associations

Further Reading

Barnouw, Erik, *A History of Broadcasting in the United States*, 3 vols., New York: Oxford University Press, 1966–70; see especially vol. 1, *A Tower in Babel: To 1933*, 1966, and vol. 2, *The Golden Web, 1933 to 1953*, 1968
Cones, Harold, and John Bryant, *Eugene F. McDonald: Communications Pioneer Lost to History*, Record of Proceedings, 3rd International Symposium on Telecommunications History, Washington, D.C.: Independent Telephone Historical Foundation, 1995
Hilliard, Robert L., and Michael C. Keith, *The Broadcast Century: A Biography of American Broadcasting*, Boston: Focal Press, 1992; 2nd edition, Boston and Oxford, 1997

Mackey, David, "The Development of the National Association of Broadcasters," *Journal of Broadcasting* 1 (Fall 1957)

National Association of Broadcasters website, <www.nab.org>

Smith, Frederick, "Fees for Composers—None for Broadcasters," *Radio Age* (February 1923)

Smulyan, Susan, *Selling Radio: The Commercialization of American Broadcasting, 1920–1934*, Washington, D.C.: Smithsonian Institution Press, 1994

National Association of Educational Broadcasters

The National Association of Educational Broadcasters (NAEB) was the oldest professional educational broadcasting organization in the United States, founded as the Association of College and University Stations in 1925. Until its demise in 1981, the NAEB served as the nation's most influential force in the establishment and preservation of an alternative system of noncommercial educational (public) radio stations.

Origins

The historical roots of American public radio extend back at least as far as those of commercial radio broadcasters. Early in the 1900s experimental stations began appearing in electrical engineering departments of universities and colleges across the country, the first being station 9XM (now WHA) at the University of Wisconsin in Madison. Unfortunately, the primary motivation for building many of these stations was limited to the study of technical considerations, without much concern about the programming and service potential of this new electronic medium. By 1926, roughly half of these early stations had gone off the air, but among those remaining, there was a growing interest in exploring educational uses for radio.

Secretary of Commerce Herbert Hoover had already begun a series of annual National Radio Conferences in Washington, D.C., and it was at the fourth of these gatherings, on 12 November 1925, that a group of educational broadcasters created a new organization, the Association of College and University Broadcasting Stations. At first, this fledgling collective of broadcast pioneers was loosely knit and had no specific purpose other than to support and promote radio for educational use. Membership was open to all educational institutions that operated radio stations, but even with annual dues set at only $3.00, less than half of the qualified institutions joined the association during its first few years of existence. Documentation for this period is extremely limited, but it is clear that the members struggled against enormous odds to hold the organization together, as the Great Depression began to bring financial hardships to institutions of higher learning.

The first formal convention of the 25-member association was held on the Ohio State University campus in Columbus in July of 1930, convened in conjunction with the Institute for Education by Radio. Recent licensing actions by the Federal Radio Commission were seen as clearly favoring the commercial use of radio at the expense of educational development. Hence, there was a growing sense of urgency that something needed to be done to stem the tide of lost licenses for educational institutions. Association president Robert Higgy, Director of Ohio State's WOSU, launched a campaign to seek legislation that would reserve a portion of the radio spectrum exclusively for noncommercial educational use. Association members joined with other educational radio advocates, including the National Advisory Council on Radio in Education and the National Committee on Education by Radio, in that pursuit over the next several years. However, when the Communications Act was signed into law on 19 June 1934, the provision for which they had fought so hard had been deleted. Instead, Congress specified that the newly created Federal Communications Commission would study the matter of nonprofit allocations to educational institutions and report back on their findings.

Reorganization and Name Change

When the association members gathered on 10 September 1934, in Kansas City, Missouri, for their annual meeting, there was a renewed determination to influence the work of the FCC. A new constitution was adopted and the organization's name was changed to the National Association of Educational Broadcasters. This new label better reflected the interests of existing members, particularly those that were producing educational programs that were being broadcast over commercial radio stations. The NAEB members rededicated themselves to three goals: reserving channels for educational use, establishing a national headquarters, and creating a mechanism for program exchange. Toward this third goal, three committees were established, each to study a specific means of program exchange: shortwave transmission between stations, the establishment of a chain network, and the recording of programs.

The FCC hearings that stemmed from the congressional statute to study the matter failed to result in the desired educational reservations, though the NAEB continued to lobby both the FCC and members of Congress in the years to follow. When the NAEB assembled in Iowa City on 9 September 1935, each of the program exchange committees made their reports. The use of shortwave interconnection was judged impractical, but there was some optimism expressed that federal and state appropriations might enable the creation of a chain network at some future date. However, the only short-term means of program exchange seemed to be to record programs and exchange them among stations through the U.S. mail service. The goal of establishing a national office was still well beyond the members' reach.

The NAEB continued to meet annually through 1938 but suspended its regular meeting schedule during the years 1939–41. Throughout this period the association achieved modest accomplishments, including purchasing of sound transcription equipment, beginning the publication of a regular newsletter, creating of a radio script exchange, and successfully lobbying the FCC to reserve designated "curricular channels" in 1938, though the authorization of FM broadcasting would render this initial lobbying victory moot. The continued efforts by the NAEB culminated in the FCC's acceptance of the reservation principle when the Commission first authorized FM service in 1941, reserving the five lowest channels for noncommercial educational use. Four years later, the FCC shifted the placement of FM broadcasting to its present location, and set aside the lowest 20 channels (88–92 MHz) for educational use.

Although membership in the association during the early 1940s did not increase significantly, the organization gained greater cohesion and confidence as representatives from member stations worked cooperatively on a variety of association initiatives, including FM channel reservations. Efforts were stepped up to get educational institutions to apply for construction permits for FM stations, and discussions about establishing a national headquarters with paid personnel continued to gain momentum. In an attempt to encourage more stations into operation, the NAEB convinced the FCC to liberalize its FM rules by creating a new Class D license in 1948 that allowed stations to broadcast with as little power as 10 watts, thus greatly reducing the costs of transmitter equipment and ongoing operations for the many colleges and universities that wanted to mount student-operated radio stations.

In 1949, the long-envisioned program exchange was formally begun when station WNYC in New York City made five sets of recordings of the *Herald Tribune Forum* series that were mailed among 22 NAEB member stations in a distribution system that came to be known as the bicycle network. Prompted by the success of this bicycle tape network, University of Illinois Dean Wilbur Schramm offered a plan at the 1950 NAEB convention in Lexington, Kentucky, to house the network headquarters on his Urbana, Illinois, campus, with funding generated by a series of grants. The following year the NAEB received a major grant from the W.K. Kellogg Foundation to fund a permanent national headquarters and distribution center at the University of Illinois. A series of other major grants were soon forthcoming, and both the financial posture and the services provided by the NAEB improved significantly. Increases in NAEB membership quickly followed, and by January of 1954 there were 218 members and 78 stations participating in the tape network. The national headquarters staff had expanded to seven full-time employees. After nearly 30 years of struggling for its own survival, the NAEB had become the dominant force in U.S. educational broadcasting.

Organizational Transitions

During the 1950s, the NAEB greatly improved its stature within the educational community, both nationally and internationally. Increased human and financial resources enabled the association to exhibit expanded leadership and professional development for the educational broadcasting establishment. Workshops, seminars, and regional conferences soon complemented the annual convention. In 1956, a sister organization of individual members from a wide range of educational professions—the Association for Education by Radio-Television (AERT)—merged with the NAEB and brought with it a scholarly publication, the *AERT Journal*. The following year, the association began publication of the *NAEB Journal*, in addition to the monthly *NAEB Newsletter* and other occasional reports and monographs. By the 1959 convention in Detroit, Michigan, it was evident that the NAEB's ever-widening vision had outgrown its home in Urbana, Illinois.

From the inception of the national headquarters at the University of Illinois, the NAEB had operated with an elected president from one of the member stations and a full-time executive director located at the national office. It was time to move the national headquarters to Washington, D.C., and to hire a full-time president. On 1 September 1960, the NAEB's new offices opened in the DuPont Circle Office Building at 1346 Connecticut Avenue, NW. The new president who would lead the organization into a new era of educational broadcasting was William G. Harley, a former elected NAEB president and chairman of the board of directors who had gained national prominence as manager for the highly successful WHA-AM-FM-TV stations at the University of Wisconsin.

Harley moved quickly to establish the NAEB as a lobbying force on Capitol Hill while expanding the number of grants that enabled the NAEB to enhance its intellectual position. A new publication, the *Washington Report,* was created to help keep members posted of important developments in the capital city. The NAEB Radio Network took full advantage of the Washington connection by producing a new public affairs show, *Report from Washington,* that was sent by air mail to the Center in Urbana for distribution to member stations. Harley also secured letters pledging support from both presidential hopefuls, Richard M. Nixon and John F. Kennedy, as a way of building bridges with the new administration. And among the first academic projects to come out of this period was the commissioning of Marshall McLuhan to prepare a report on the new media's role in the future of education. The book resulting from that project, *Understanding Media,* remains one of the most influential mass communication publications of the 20th century.

NAEB leaders had long advocated that the association should be more of a professional organization than a trade association in the traditional sense. The influx of individual members brought about by the merger with AERT in 1956 and the growing ranks of members from closed-circuit instructional television facilities were causing growing dissatisfaction with the existing governance structure, which was controlled by radio and television station representatives. At the 1963 NAEB convention in Milwaukee, Wisconsin, the members voted unanimously to reorganize the association into four divisions: Radio Station Division, Television Station Division, Instruction Division, and Individual Member Division. Each was to elect its own board, with the four boards comprising the NAEB Board of Directors. Offices and support staff for each of the units would be established within the national headquarters.

For radio interests, the reorganization was a major step forward. Television representatives had been exercising more and more control over the NAEB since the mid-1950s. Growing numbers of radio representatives wanted a separate organization of their own but knew full well that they did not have the resources to go it alone. The reorganization gave radio the independence it needed to chart a new course, while allowing it to benefit from the largesse of the higher television station dues. The new configuration also afforded the opportunity for a new name—National Educational Radio (NER)—while remaining under the NAEB umbrella. In the spring of 1964, the radio board appointed WUOM (University of Michigan) production manager Jerrold Sandler to be NER's first executive director. The tape exchange network—now officially named the National Educational Radio Network—remained in Urbana.

Under Sandler's guidance, NER acquired the kind of representational and leadership presence in Washington, D.C., that the radio representatives had envisioned. In addition to continuing the program exchange system, the new division became far more active on Capitol Hill, raised major grants for program and research projects, built relationships in the international community, provided a unified voice in professional circles, offered consulting advice to member stations, and distributed grants-in-aid to support special projects. During

1966–67, Sandler contracted with Herbert W. Land Associates to conduct a national study of the status of educational radio in the United States. The resulting report, *The Hidden Medium: Educational Radio,* offered the documentation needed for Sandler to lobby Congress on behalf of radio during the drafting of what had been the Public Television Act of 1967. As a direct result of Sandler's efforts, radio was written into the language during the eleventh hour, and the final legislation was called the Public Broadcasting Act of 1967.

A Forecast of Demise

While passage of this historic legislation dramatically changed educational radio and television for the better, it signaled the beginning of a transformation that would eventually mean an end to the NAEB. The Act created the Corporation for Public Broadcasting (CPB), which was charged with strengthening the newly relabeled *public* radio and television stations in the United States. This mandate led to the creation of the Public Broadcasting Service (PBS) and National Public Radio (NPR). In 1971, NPR began live national network interconnection of member stations, and the National Educational Radio Network soon merged with NPR. For a number of months, NAEB continued to represent radio stations before Congress, but by 1973, the stations had created a new lobbying and public relations organization—the Association of Public Radio Stations (APRS)—and so NAEB ceased its radio representation function. (APTS would later merge with NPR in 1977.)

Just as NPR and APRS took over the functions of NAEB's Radio Division, PBS soon acquired the functions of the Television Division. By the mid-1970s, the NAEB was again forced to undergo a major reorganization and a redirection of its mission solely as a professional organization. When Harley retired in 1975, James A. Fellows became NAEB's last president. Fellows worked tirelessly to revitalize the association and to generate a solid funding base through individual member services. A variety of public telecommunication institutes on such topics as management skills, graphic arts, instructional design, and audience research methods were scheduled throughout the country. The publications program was expanded with the creation of *Public Telecommunications Review,* a research index and reprint series, and later with the *Current* newspaper. Members were served by various professional councils, ranging from broadcast education and research to engineering and management. The annual convention afforded additional professional training opportunities and a career placement center. In short, the NAEB attempted to become the professional standard bearer for the public broadcasting industry.

Despite a herculean effort by Fellows and his ever-shrinking staff, the NAEB could not sustain itself as an organization supported solely by individual members. At its final convention at the Hyatt Regency Hotel in New Orleans on 3 November

1981, NAEB board chairman Robert K. Avery recalled the association's important accomplishments over the preceding 56 years. With the vote taken to declare bankruptcy, he brought down the final gavel and dissolved the organization.

ROBERT K. AVERY

See also Educational Radio to 1967; National Public Radio; Public Broadcasting Act of 1967; Public Radio Since 1967

Further Reading

Avery, Robert K., Paul E. Burrows, and Clara J. Pincus, *Research Index for NAEB Journals: NAEB Journal,* *Educational Broadcasting Review, Public Telecommunications Review, 1957–1979,* Washington, D.C.: National Association of Educational Broadcasters, 1980

Blakely, Robert J., *To Serve the Public Interest: Educational Broadcasting in the United States,* Syracuse, New York: Syracuse University Press, 1979

Hill, Harold E., and W. Wayne Alford, *NAEB History,* 2 vols., Urbana, Illinois: National Association of Educational Broadcasters, 1966

Witherspoon, John, Roselle Kovitz, Robert K. Avery, and Alan G. Stavitsky, *A History of Public Broadcasting,* Washington, D.C.: Current, 2000

National Association of Educational Broadcasters Tape Network

Early Program Exchange for Educational Broadcasters

The National Association of Educational Broadcasters (NAEB) Tape Network was the first formal agreement among educational broadcasters to allow for the exchange of programs for rebroadcast. This system was important because it provided for the sharing of much-needed program materials between financially strapped broadcast stations across the United States.

Origins

In the 1930s a growing concept of educational broadcasting was developing at a few scattered stations, most of which were loosely affiliated with colleges and universities. Representatives held annual conventions, which led to formation of the Association of College and University Broadcasting Stations, predecessor to what became the NAEB. The group's primary purpose was to persuade the government to set aside radio channels for state, college, and university operated stations. Another goal was to develop a mechanism for program exchange.

These broadcasters watched the successful sharing of programming taking place in commercial radio through the National Broadcasting Company (NBC) Red and Blue networks and the Columbia Broadcasting System (CBS). A network for educational radio was discussed but was dismissed as too costly; an idea for a script exchange met with little enthusiasm. A few stations did exchange scripts, but few of these exchanges resulted in produced programs.

In 1932 NAEB secured a $500 grant from the National Advisory Council on Radio Education and purchased a wire recorder. The device was to be circulated among stations for recording programs for air. In 1949 the director of New York's municipal station WNYC, Seymour Siegel, made five sets of recordings of the *Herald Tribune Forum* and distributed them to 22 NAEB member stations throughout the year. This event marks the start of what was labeled a "bicycle" (mailed tape exchange) network.

Postwar Developments

In 1950 NAEB was able to secure more funding, this time from the Kellogg Foundation. The purpose of the grant was to support a systemized national noncommercial education and culture tape network to serve the growing demand for educational radio programming. The exchange system delivered programming from the British Broadcasting Corporation (BBC), the Canadian Broadcasting Corporation (CBC), and domestic stations and production centers. In its first year, what became the National Educational Radio (NER) network mailed over 500 hours of programming to 52 NAEB member stations coast to coast.

A network headquarters was established in Urbana, Illinois. Programs were duplicated on high-speed equipment. A fee was established for member stations, and within five years, the organization was modestly financed but self-sustaining. By 1967 it was estimated that the network distributed some

35,400 hours (more than 80 million feet of tape) of educational radio programming in the United States on a budget of less than $60,000.

Sample bulletins from the early years of the tape exchange demonstrate diverse program offerings. Program topics included physical sciences ("The Impact of Atomic Energy"), social sciences ("Woman's Role in Society"), mental and physical health ("The Effects of Smoking"), and arts and literature ("The Alabama String Quartet"). Children's programming was a category listed in early bulletins, but specific examples are difficult to find. Networks supplied their affiliates with tapes to be used in local schools as well. Subject matter for kindergarten through 12th grade included science, foreign languages, guidance, language arts, music and art, safety and health, and social studies.

Most of the programs distributed by the tape network in return for the regular affiliation fee consisted of offerings from individual affiliates. Production costs for these programs were generally covered by the local stations. Some stations enhanced programs with modest grants from organizations such as the National Home Library Foundation and the Johnson Foundation.

The network also delivered some special programming to affiliates at no additional cost. For instance, a 30-minute *Special of the Week* produced out of the University of Michigan featured addresses by national and world leaders on public affairs. In addition, an 11-program series by WGBH Boston (*A Chance to Grow*) examined how families dealt with critical changes in their lives. The series featured interviews with families and was produced with the aid of grants and contributions. The government also provided some "no-charge" programs, such as a panel discussion from a conference held by the Selective Service System at the University of Chicago. And finally, the Library of Congress had a special arrangement with the tape network to allow the network to distribute certain readings and lectures given by the library.

Programs were also provided to affiliates from a wide variety of international sources. Regular contributors to the network included the BBC (*Translantic Forum, The World Report,* and *Science Magazine*), Radio Netherlands, Berne, Italian Radio, UNESCO, and the CBC, among others.

While the tape exchange network was still in a growth mode, educational broadcasters were still pushing for a more permanent way to exchange programming—a real network. In September 1965 some 70 NER stations linked together for a historic live interconnection to broadcast three hours of German national election results coverage.

In 1966 at a NER conference (The Wingspread Conference), 70 leaders from the industry, government, the academic community, philanthropy, and the arts came up with a seven-point plan for developing educational radio that included a national production center and the use of communications satellites for transmitting noncommercial programming. A concrete step toward centralized programming was made in March 1967 when NER set up a Public Affairs Bureau in Washington. However, a centralized network was yet to come. During the Carnegie Commission's study of 1965–67, the need for an interconnected educational radio system was again stressed. The Public Broadcasting Act (1967) that followed set the stage for the development of that network. In the years following the passage of the act, educational broadcasters met to plan the network. Finally, on 3 May 1971, the goal of national programming distribution sources for noncommercial radio broadcasters was realized, when National Public Radio premiered its first live show—*All Things Considered*. Other programs and a satellite interconnect to allow members to share programming would follow. Educational broadcasters no longer had to duplicate and mail tapes to deliver shared programs to the public.

PAMELA K. DOYLE

See also Educational Radio to 1967; National Association of Educational Broadcasters; National Public Radio; Public Radio Since 1967

Further Reading

Blakely, Robert J., *To Serve the Public Interest: Educational Broadcasting in the United States,* Syracuse, New York: Syracuse University Press, 1979

Herman W. Land Associates, *The Hidden Medium: A Status Report on Educational Radio in the United States,* New York: Herman W. Land Associates, 1967

Saettler, L. Paul, *A History of Instructional Technology,* New York: McGraw Hill, 1968

Siegel, Seymour N., "Educational Broadcasting Comes of Age," in *Education on the Air: Twenty-First Yearbook of the Institute for Education by Radio,* Columbus: Ohio State University, 1951

Witherspoon, John, Roselle Kovitz, Robert K. Avery, and Alan G. Stavitsky, *A History of Public Broadcasting,* Washington, D.C.: Current, 2000

National Barn Dance

Country Music Variety Program

Although the *Grand Ole Opry* is best remembered because it survived far longer, the WLS *National Barn Dance* before World War II ranked as America's most popular country music program. After being picked up by the National Broadcasting Company (NBC) network in 1933, and sponsored and supported by Miles Laboratories' Alka-Selzer, the WLS *National Barn Dance* became a Saturday night radio network fixture.

The show's long time home was WLS-AM, a pioneering and important station in Chicago, named by owner Sears-Roe-

buck to herald itself as the "World's Largest Store." First under Sears, and then after 1928 with new owner *Prairie Farmer* magazine, the focus of this clear channel station was always the rural American. Clear channel status made WLS-AM a fixture in homes throughout the Midwestern farm belt.

Originally called the *WLS Barn Dance*, by 1930 the program had expanded to fill WLS's Saturday nights. When the NBC Blue network began on 30 September 1933 to run a portion, sponsored by Miles Laboratories' Alka-Seltzer, the pro-

WLS National Barn Dance Cast, 1944
Courtesy Radio Hall of Fame

gram was renamed the *National Barn Dance*. Though NBC varied the program's length (from 30 to 60 minutes and back, again and again), from 1936 to 1946, the network always penciled the *National Barn Dance* on the schedule starting at 9 P.M. on Saturday nights. Indeed, in 1940 when NBC picked up the *Grand Ole Opry*, the *National Barn Dance* was already a network fixture, signaling to all who paid attention to radio industry trends a growing interest in the "hillbilly" musical form.

The statistics were impressive. For example, on 25 October 1930 nearly 20,000 fans poured into Chicago's massive International Amphitheater for a special performance, and an estimated 10,000 had to be turned away. The popularity peak of the *National Barn Dance* came during World War II, but after the war the *Opry* surpassed its predecessor in ratings, and the shift to Nashville was underway. NBC dropped the *National Barn Dance* in 1946.

But in its heyday, beginning with a move in 1932 to the Loop's Eighth Street Theater, the success of the *National Barn Dance* could literally be seen as crowds lined up for precious Saturday night tickets and regularly filled the theater's 1,200 seats for two shows. Stars included those remembered by country music historians (Bradley Kincaid, Arkie the Arkansas Woodchopper, and Lulu Belle and Scotty) and those who would help define popular culture of the 20th century (Gene Autry).

Bradley Kincaid was one of country music's first popular sellers. He was a student in Chicago in 1926, having moved there from his native Kentucky, when a friend suggested he try out for the hillbilly show on the radio. Kincaid borrowed a guitar, practiced a few ballads he had learned from his family, and soon was a star. His name is usually lost in country music history, but Kincaid helped define the genre as it emerged during the 1920s and 1930s.

Missourian Luther Ossenbrink renamed himself "Arkie, the Arkansas Woodchopper" when he arrived at WLS in the middle of 1929 after some experience on the radio in Kansas City. While playing the fiddle, guitar, or banjo, he sang and told cornball jokes. Sears executives must have loved his favorite song, "A Dollar Down and a Dollar a Week."

Although the husband-and-wife singing duo, Lulu Belle and Scotty (Wiseman), who appeared from 1935 through 1958, may have been the *Barn Dance*'s most enduring act, to the world Gene Autry symbolized the star-making power of the National Barn Dance. Autry appeared during the early 1930s as the "Oklahoma Yodeling Cowboy," but when his "Silver Haired Daddy of Mine" became a hit, he was off to Hollywood and became part of radio legend.

Following NBC's dropping of the *National Barn Dance*, the program reverted to again being a local show until 1949, when the American Broadcasting Companies (ABC) radio network, sponsored by the Phillips Petroleum Company, picked up the show. The ratings on ABC were anemic, and so by the mid-1950s the *National Barn Dance* was a faded memory for everyone except the aging Chicagoans who continued to embrace its radio and television versions. The Eighth Street Theater closed on 31 August 1957, and WLS abandoned it.

In 1960, many of the former *National Barn Dance* regulars appeared on Chicago's WGN-AM under the name *WGN Barn Dance*. But after the Tribune Company, the owner of WGN, syndicated the show for television in the 1960s with limited success, Tribune executives closed the show for good in 1971.

DOUGLAS GOMERY

See also Autrey, Gene; Country Music Format; Grand Ole Opry; WGN; WLS

Cast

Hosts	Hal O'Halloran (pre-network), Joe Kelly (1933–50)
Announcer	Jack Holden
Performers (partial listing)	Bradley Kincaid, Gene Autry, George Gobel, Red Foley, Homer and Jethro, Lulu Belle and Scotty, Louise Massey Mabie and the Westerners, Arkie, the Arkansas Woodchopper, Wilson Sisters, Dolph Hewitt, Hoosier Hotshots, Pat Butrum

Producers
Walter Wade, Peter Lund, Jack Frost

Director
Bill Jones

Programming History

WLS	April 1924–September 1933
NBC-Blue	September 1933–June 1940
NBC-Red	June 1940–September 1946
ABC	March 1949–March 1950

Further Reading
Baker, John Chester, *Farm Broadcasting: The First Sixty Years*, Ames: Iowa State University Press, 1981

Evans, James F., *Prairie Farmer and WLS: The Burridge D. Butler Years*, Urbana: University of Illinois Press, 1969

Malone, Bill C., *Country Music U.S.A.*, Austin: University of Texas Press, 1968; revised edition, 1985

Summers, Harrison Boyd, *A Thirty-Year History of Programs Carried on National Radio Networks in the United States, 1926–1956*, Columbus: Ohio State University, 1958

WLS Magazine (12 April 1949) (special 25th anniversary issue entitled "Stand By")

National Broadcasting Company

While now focused on television, the National Broadcasting Company (NBC) was the first purpose-built national radio network, although it continues as such today in name only. Begun with an emphasis on public service program orientation, NBC became a very profitable commercial venture that helped to dominate—and define—radio's golden age.

Origins

The origins of NBC lie in the extensive political and legal maneuvering of its parent company, the Radio Corporation of America (RCA), in the 1920s. One member of the RCA group, AT&T, found its phone lines could be used not only for remote broadcasts but could also connect stations together in a "chain" or network. AT&T announced the formation of 38 "radio telephone" stations linked by telephone lines, the purpose of which was not to provide programming but rather to "provide the channels through which anyone with whom it makes a contract can send out their own programs," an arrangement that soon became known as "toll broadcasting."

But RCA was operating its own New York City station as well. WJZ began operations as a Westinghouse outlet in 1921 but was purchased by RCA two years later. Unlike AT&T, RCA's interest in the medium was based on its desire to sell more receivers, the assumption being that entertaining programs would result in the sale of more sets. Thus, by 1923 there were two factions battling for control of radio: the "Telephone Group" led by AT&T and Western Electric, and the "Radio Group" consisting of RCA, General Electric (GE), and Westinghouse. AT&T sold its interest in RCA when conflict became inevitable and refused to allow any station aligned with the Radio Group to use its telephone lines to establish a network.

With the threat of government intervention looming, it was left to RCA General Manager David Sarnoff to broker a compromise. He proposed that "all stations of all parties [be put] into a broadcasting company which can be made self-supporting and probably revenue-producing, the telephone company to furnish the wires as needed." This marked the creation of NBC, which began operation in November 1926 with Merlin H. Aylesworth, former managing director of the National Electric Light Association, as president. Although ownership of NBC was originally divided among RCA, GE, and Westinghouse, AT&T profited the most, since it controlled the wires that would eventually connect thousands of stations nationwide (a franchise that would be extended even further with the introduction of television). In short, AT&T got to keep the toll without having to worry about the broadcasting.

Consolidation and Growth

NBC immediately adopted the practice of toll broadcasting by selling studio space and a time slot—"four walls and air" in trade lingo—to interested advertising agencies and their sponsor-clients. RCA also decided to operate two NBC networks, with WEAF as the flagship station of NBC-Red and WJZ anchoring NBC-Blue (the colors apparently derived from either the company's color-coded program charts or the pencil lines AT&T engineers drew to map the wire paths for the two networks).

NBC grew rapidly in size and profitability. In 1927 the network had 48 affiliates, including both the Red and Blue networks, and lost almost $500,000 in net income; by 1932—when RCA assumed complete ownership of the network—it had 85 affiliates and pretax profits of $1.2 million.

As both networks grew, so did the interest of advertising agencies and sponsors, who saw network radio as an increasingly effective way to reach a national audience of consumers. Fortunately for advertisers, the ability to reach a mass audience with radio intersected with an expansion of the American economy in the 1920s. In 1929 Merlin Aylesworth proclaimed that radio was "an open gateway to national markets, to millions of consumers, and to thousands upon thousands of retailers."

Soon, major advertising agencies were enthusiastically embracing the new medium, a revolution that was not dampened by the Great Depression. The NBC schedule in the 1930s was dominated by shows named for their sponsors, such as *The Chase and Sanborn Hour, Cliquot Club Eskimos,* and *Maxwell House Showboat.* By the early 1930s, the economic structure that would dominate radio for the next 20 years had emerged. The networks learned to be the middleman, selling time to advertising agencies that produced the commercial shows on behalf of paying sponsors, while their affiliates were responsible for developing a rapport with local audiences.

Throughout the decade, NBC continued to flourish. A sharper distinction between the Red and Blue networks came into focus. NBC-Red was home to the most popular programs, including *Fibber McGee and Molly, One Man's Family,* and *Amos 'n' Andy,* as well as such stars as Bob Hope, Jack Benny, and Fred Allen. Not surprisingly, it accounted for most of NBC's profits. NBC-Blue, on the other hand, was somewhat schizophrenic in character, as it was the home of cultural programming of the highest quality—the *NBC Symphony* led by Arturo Toscanini chief among them—but also was the dumping ground of sustained (unsponsored) programming that as often as not placed fourth in the ratings behind NBC-Red, CBS, and the less successful (after 1934) Mutual Broadcasting System. Still, Blue served as something of a loss leader for

RCA, as it was frequently touted by the company as a prestigious public service. Blue also allowed NBC to cultivate a reputation superior to that of CBS, which was always a special consideration for David Sarnoff.

NBC's economic strength derived almost wholly from its affiliate relationships. In 1932 the network initiated a plan to pay its affiliates a fee for every network-originated, sponsored program that the affiliate carried on its schedule. In return, the affiliate agreed to purchase NBC's sustained programs at a rate lower than what the station might typically produce in-house. This a la carte system still allowed the affiliates some freedom to pick and choose among the various network offerings, and although many of the larger stations objected to what they considered an inadequate reimbursement for their time costs, the arrangement allowed NBC to provide nationwide coverage to paying advertisers. However, both NBC and CBS continued to extract more concessions from their affiliates throughout the 1930s, knowing there was no shortage of local stations eager to accept whatever demands the networks might place upon them. As a result, government intervention became almost inevitable.

Report on Chain Broadcasting: 1941

Although the economic structure of commercial broadcasting was consolidated in the early 1930s, its regulatory parameters were slightly more fluid. In March 1938 the Federal Communications Commission (FCC) initiated an investigation into all phases of the broadcast industry, primarily at the instigation of the Mutual Broadcasting System. Mutual complained to the FCC that it was unable to expand into a national operation because NBC and CBS had affiliation agreements with more than 80 percent of the largest radio stations in the country.

The result of that inquiry, the 1941 *Report on Chain Broadcasting,* was highly critical of the network-affiliate relationship, and the regulations derived therein signaled the beginning of an on-going battle between broadcasters and the government over monopoly practices. To NBC and CBS, the rules set by the *Report* threatened to undermine the very structure of the broadcasting industry.

Most crucial among these were the establishment of strict limits on the length of affiliation contracts; the loosening of affiliation ties by allowing stations to broadcast programs from other networks or sources; the power of affiliates to reject network programs if the stations felt the offering was not in the public interest; and, most dramatically, the abolition of the practice of "option time."

This provision struck directly at the heart of network operations, and NBC, CBS, and Madison Avenue howled in protest. Option time was a standard feature of every affiliation contract, giving the network the legal right to preempt a station's schedule for network programming. CBS affiliates

agreed to give up their entire broadcast day if the network demanded it; NBC was slightly less stringent, asking for options on eight and a half hours a day, including the profitable 8 to 11 P.M. evening block. The stations were compensated for all hours claimed by the networks at a rate adequate to cover the loss of potential sales to local advertisers (these local rates were set by the network as well, a procedure also abolished by the 1941 regulations). It was a profitable arrangement. The affiliates received popular national programming, relieving them of the chore of local production, and were compensated for their airtime—NBC took in three times more money from time sales than it dispensed in compensation and could guarantee advertisers a national audience.

The networks bitterly denounced the new regulations and brought suit in federal court to stop their implementation, but it was pressure from the business and advertising communities that caused the FCC to revise the chain broadcasting rules in an October 1941 supplemental report. The commission reasoned that while it remained unconvinced by the NBC and CBS contention that option time was indispensable to network operations, "it is clear that some optioning of time by networks in order to clear the same period of time over a number of stations for network programs will operate as a business convenience." As a result, the networks were permitted to maintain control over the 8 to 11 P.M. slot, the most heavily attended and profitable portion of the broadcast day. Thus, the prime-time schedule remained closed to independent and local producers on affiliate schedules.

Of more direct impact to NBC was the regulation that "no license shall be issued to a standard broadcasting station affiliated with a network organization which maintains more than one network." In other words, either Red or Blue had to go. Despite some public grumbling, RCA was not entirely unhappy with this ruling, having long considered the sale of Blue as a possible source of financing for television activities. Still, NBC filed suit in federal court challenging the Chain Broadcasting rules, but in May 1943, the Supreme Court ruled for the FCC in *NBC v the United States.* Five months later, RCA sold the Blue Network to Life Savers magnate Edward J. Noble for $8 million. The sale provided RCA with a cash infusion with which to prepare NBC-TV for an anticipated boom following World War II and led to the formation of the American Broadcasting Company (ABC) in 1945.

NBC Radio and the Emergence of Television

The immediate postwar era was enormously profitable for radio as pent-up consumer demand, combined with a shift from military to domestic manufacturing, unleashed a spectacular buying binge. However, television loomed on the horizon, and the new medium promised to have a dramatic impact on network radio. In 1945, 95 percent of all radio stations were network affiliates; in 1948—the year NBC, CBS, and ABC began seven-day-a-week television broadcasting—the figure was 68 percent and dropping fast.

Ironically, the end of network radio as a source of major entertainment was hastened by the CBS "talent raids" of 1948–49. In order to attract NBC's biggest radio stars, CBS designed a clever finance mechanism that had the practical effect of placing performers under long-term contract to the network. It was an elegant scheme: radio stars (who were otherwise taxed at personal income rates of up to 75 percent) would incorporate themselves and, in turn, license their company to CBS. The amount paid by CBS would be considered a capital gain and taxed at 25 percent. As a result, NBC performers left the network in droves for CBS, starting with *Amos 'n' Andy* creators Freeman Gosden and Charles Correll in September 1948, soon followed by Jack Benny, George Burns and Gracie Allen, Red Skelton, Bing Crosby, and Edgar Bergen.

The talent raids certainly paid off for CBS in terms of income (a profit increase of almost $7 million), more successful programming (12 of the top 15 radio shows in 1949), and tangential publicity. Most important, radio provided both the financial and programming foundation for the network's television operation. Every star brought over in the talent raids eventually appeared on CBS-TV, draining resources away from NBC.

As television continued to attract an increasingly larger audience, major advertisers rapidly left radio and moved their dollars into the new medium. By the early 1950s, the trend toward television was readily apparent. Fewer and fewer network-originated radio shows were made available to affiliates, while the number of programs that were simulcast (broadcast simultaneously on both radio and TV) increased. By the end of the decade, stations across the country began severing their network affiliations to produce their own programming, an action unthinkable during radio's heyday.

In 1960 NBC stopped production on its last remaining daytime radio serial, *True Story*, and thereafter existed almost solely as a news feed to subscribing stations. In 1986 RCA (including NBC) was purchased by GE (in a sense returning to its original owner), and that same year the network formally split its broadcasting divisions. NBC Radio was then sold to radio conglomerate Westwood One, which continues to maintain "NBC Radio Networks" as a separate brand, although in reality the network has no journalistic responsibility for newscasts labeled as "NBC."

MIKE MASHON

See also American Telephone and Telegraph; Blue Network; Network Monopoly Probe; Radio Corporation of America; Sarnoff, David; Talent Raids

Further Reading

Archer, Gleason Leonard, *History of Radio to 1926*, New York: American Historical Society, 1938; reprint, New York: Arno Press, 1971

Archer, Gleason Leonard, *Big Business and Radio*, New York: American Historical Company, 1939; reprint, New York: Arno Press, 1971

Bilby, Kenneth W., *The General: David Sarnoff and the Rise of the Communications Industry*, New York: Harper and Row, 1986

Campbell, Robert, *The Golden Years of Broadcasting: A Celebration of the First 50 Years of Radio and TV on NBC*, New York: Scribner, 1976

Cook, David, "The Birth of the Network: How Westinghouse, GE, AT&T, and RCA Invented the Concept of Advertiser-Supported Broadcasting," *Quarterly Review of Film Studies* 8, no. 3 (Summer 1983)

Federal Communications Commission, *Report on Chain Broadcasting*, Washington, D.C.: GPO, 1941

Federal Communications Commission, *Supplemental Report on Chain Broadcasting*, Washington, D.C.: GPO, 1941

Fifty Years with the NBC Radio Network, New York: NBC, 1976

"The First 50 Years of NBC," *Broadcasting* (21 June 1976)

Hilmes, Michele, *Hollywood and Broadcasting: From Radio to Cable*, Urbana: University of Illinois Press, 1990

National Broadcasting Company, *NBC and You: An Account of the Organization, Operation, and Employee-Company Policies of the N.B.C.: Designed As a Handbook to Aid You in Your Daily Work*, New York: NBC, 1944

National Broadcasting Company, *NBC Program Policies and Working Manual*, New York: NBC, 1944

"NBC 60th Anniversary Issue," *Television/Radio Age* 33 (May 1986)

"NBC: A Documentary," *Sponsor* 20, no. 10 (May 1966)

Sarnoff, David, *Looking Ahead: The Papers of David Sarnoff*, New York: McGraw-Hill, 1968

Smulyan, Susan, *Selling Radio: The Commercialization of American Broadcasting, 1920–1934*, Washington, D.C., Smithsonian Institution Press, 1994

"A Study of the National Broadcasting Company," *The Advertiser* 14, no. 9 (1943)

National Federation of Community Broadcasters

Member Organization of Community Radio Stations and Producers

The National Federation of Community Broadcasters (NFCB) is a membership organization representing more than 200 radio stations in the United States; it provides legal, technical, and logistical support for community-oriented, educational, and noncommercial broadcasters. Under its leadership, the community radio sector of U.S. broadcasting has emerged as a viable service in major urban centers and rural communities across the country.

In 1973 a group of dedicated community broadcasters met in Seattle to consider the possibilities of coordinating their efforts and promoting community radio throughout the United States. Two years later, in the summer of 1975, the National Alternative Radio Konference (NARK) convened in Madison, Wisconsin. The conference participants—an assortment of radio enthusiasts, artists, musicians, and community activists from across the country—resolved to form a national organization that would represent the interests of community broadcasters before the U.S. Congress and federal regulators. Within a matter of months, the newly formed NFCB located its headquarters in the Washington, D.C. apartment of two of the conference organizers, Tom Thomas and Terry Clifford. From these humble beginnings, the NFCB began its lobbying efforts in support of community-oriented radio. From the outset, the NFCB had two goals: to influence national broadcast policy-making and to secure federal grant money to support this new, locally oriented radio service.

Central to the NFCB's mission is enhancing and increasing diversity in radio broadcasting. Throughout its history, the NCFB has placed special emphasis on opening up the airwaves to women, people of color, and other cultural minorities whose voices are largely absent from mainstream media. In this way, the NFCB promotes volunteerism, supports localism, and encourages the development of programs and services specifically designed to address the needs and interests of underserved audiences. For example, community volunteers program music and public-affairs programming on WFHB in Bloomington, Indiana; WVMR is the only broadcast service for people living in the isolated region of Pocahontas County, West Virginia; and member station KBRW provides multilingual programming for native peoples in Alaska's North Slope region.

In addition, the NFCB provides all manner of technical and logistical support for community broadcasters. To that end, the NFCB has developed training materials that outline the procedures for license applications, describe the use of broadcasting equipment, and offer practical suggestions for enlisting local community support. Some of these publications include *The Public Radio Legal Handbook*, a reference guide to broadcast regulations; *Audiocraft*, a textbook on audio production techniques; and the *Volunteer Management Handbook*, which provides useful strategies for securing and maintaining an enthusiastic volunteer base. Crucially, the NFCB also provides the legal and engineering expertise necessary to successfully secure a broadcasting license from the Federal Communications Commission (FCC). Moreover, through its monthly newsletter, *Community Radio News*, and its annual conventions, the NFCB continues to keep its member stations abreast of ongoing policy debates, new funding initiatives, and the latest technological innovations. Finally, the NFCB established the Program Exchange service in recognition of the need for new and existing stations to round out their broadcast schedules. This scheme encouraged community broadcasters across the country to trade tapes produced by member stations as well as programming developed by independent producers. Not only did this service help offset the costs associated with program production, it had the added benefits of creating an informal network between community stations and helping to define community radio's national identity.

Under the auspices of the NFCB, the community radio movement of the late 1970s challenged the conventions of commercial radio, forever changing the landscape of U.S. broadcasting. The NFCB successfully lobbied the U.S. Congress, regulatory bodies, and government funding agencies to support noncommercial broadcasting in general and community broadcasting in particular. Most important, perhaps, in its commitment to community access, control, and participation, the NFCB popularized listener-supported radio. This model, first championed by Lewis Hill and the Pacifica stations, encourages community residents to become involved in every aspect of the local radio station: management, governance, finance, promotion, and production. Like the Pacifica stations and those associated with Lorenzo Milam's KRAB nebula, NFCB member stations seek to enhance radio's role in the civic, cultural, and social life of the community. Unlike commercial radio, which shies away from innovative and controversial programming, NFCB member stations encourage local cultural expression and support community activism.

Over time, as the organization's influence with industry leaders and policy makers grew, the NFCB became firmly entrenched in the Washington establishment. As a result, the NFCB's fortunes became linked to those of National Public Radio (NPR) and the Corporation for Public Broadcasting (CPB). For a time, this relationship proved beneficial to both parties. For example, in 1982 the NFCB organized the first Minority Producers Conference, which was instrumental in diversifying the staff at public and community radio stations across the country. However, the NFCB's relationship with the CPB has been a source of controversy among some community radio advocates. For instance, the NFCB and NPR supported the FCC's 1978 termination of 10-watt Class D stations, a prohibition that has fundamentally altered the character of community radio in the United States and that has, more recently, prompted the rise of the so-called microradio movement.

Over the past decade, community radio stations have grown increasingly dependent upon CPB funds, such as the Community Service Grant, to support their efforts and improve their services. However, the eligibility requirements for these funds were far beyond the means of small stations with modest resources. As a result, these stations were confronted with the unpleasant choice between shutting down or hiring professional staff to generate income, produce or acquire more "polished" programming, and oversee the station's daily operation. This condition seriously undermines community participation and has led to the "professionalization" of community radio. In recent years, some community stations have become little more than supplemental outlets for the nationally produced programming of NPR, effectively consolidating the public radio sector and eliminating community radio's greatest strength: its localism. Furthermore, the NFCB's Healthy Station Project, with its emphasis on attracting upscale demographics to community stations, has been sharply criticized for its chilling effect on community radio's news and public-affairs programming and the attendant homogenization of music and cultural fare.

Following a period of considerable internal unrest and organizational restructuring, the NFCB moved its headquarters to San Francisco in 1995 and began sharing its operation with Western Public Radio, a not-for-profit radio training and production center. In 2002, NFCB relocated again, this time across the bay to Oakland. With new offices, facilities, and staff, NFCB launched exciting new initiatives, most notably the National Youth in Radio Training Project.

KEVIN HOWLEY

See also Community Radio; Corporation for Public Broadcasting; Low-Power Radio/Microradio; Milam, Lorenzo; National Public Radio; Pacifica Foundation; Public Radio Since 1967; Ten-Watt Stations; Trade Associations

Further Reading

Barlow, William, "Community Radio in the U.S.: The Struggle for a Democratic Medium," *Media, Culture, and Society* 10 (1988)

Bekken, Jon, "Community Radio at the Crossroads: Federal Policy and the Professionalization of a Grassroots Medium," in *Seizing the Airwaves: A Free Radio Handbook*, edited by Ronald B. Sakolsky and Steven Dunifer, Edinburgh and San Francisco: AK Press, 1998

Hochheimer, John L., "Organizing Democratic Radio: Issues in Praxis," *Media, Culture, and Society* 15 (1993)

Lewis, Peter M., and Jerry Booth, *The Invisible Medium: Public, Commercial, and Community Radio*, London: Macmillan, 1989; Washington, D.C.: Howard University Press, 1990

Milam, Lorenzo W., *Sex and Broadcasting: A Handbook on Starting a Radio Station for the Community*, 2nd edition, Saratoga, California: Dildo Press, 1972; 4th edition, as *The Original Sex and Broadcasting*, San Diego, California: MHO and MHO, 1988

National Public Radio

U.S. Noncommercial Radio Network

National Public Radio (NPR) is the U.S.'s largest public radio producer and distributor, providing more than 100 hours of news and cultural programming each week to more than 600 member stations. The network is probably best known for its drive-time newsmagazines, *Morning Edition* and *All Things Considered*, but it produces a wide range of radio fare, including music and cultural programs, such as *Performance Today* and *Jazz Profiles*, and the nationwide call-in program *Talk of the Nation*. In the course of its 30-year history, the network has won virtually every major broadcast award and has figured prominently in the nation's political and artistic life.

Origins

Public radio in the United States had its origins in the 1920s, when low-budget community and college stations sprang up around the country. Hundreds of such stations took hold in the early, unregulated days of radio, but not many of these "educational stations" survived the Depression, especially as commercial broadcasters saw radio's potential as a vehicle for mass-market entertainment and lucrative advertising.

The National Association of Educational Broadcasters (NAEB) argued that educational stations could not compete for spectrum space with commercial giants such as the National Broadcasting Company (NBC) and the Columbia Broadcasting System (CBS). In 1945 the NAEB convinced the Federal Communications Commission (FCC) to allot the low end of the radio dial to educational broadcasters, winning 20 FM channels, from 88 to 92 megahertz. The allotment gave educational radio the stability to build up a small but hardy core of stations.

The Public Broadcasting Act

By the early 1960s, educational broadcasters were exploring the possibility of networking to help fill their program days. Don Quayle, the first president of NPR, recalls "there was a general feeling, both in television and in radio, that no single station had the resources to do the quality of programming we wanted." Quayle helped link up educational radio and television networks in the northeastern United States that were among the precursors of NPR.

Those networks lacked the resources to do much more than instructional broadcasting until the mid-1960s, when President Lyndon Johnson called on the Carnegie Foundation to look into the possibility of a federally funded broadcasting system. After a two-year study, the Carnegie Commission firmly backed the idea of federal funding, but it envisioned a far wider focus, distinguishing between educational and *public* broadcasting.

The commission offered 12 recommendations for the new service, including public-affairs programming that sought insights into controversial issues, diversified programming in which minorities were represented, and coverage of contemporary arts and culture. The commission's recommendations dealt only with television, but President Johnson, a successful radio station owner himself, was sympathetic to radio advocates who fought to be included. Critics argued that adding hundreds of weak and needy radio stations to the measure would dilute the federal funding and drag the whole project down. Supporters pointed out that radio could offer more services than television at a far cheaper cost.

Congress passed the Public Broadcasting Act in October 1967 and included radio, but the funding available to the newly formed Corporation for Public Broadcasting (CPB) quickly dwindled from a proposed $20 million to $5 million. Without financial support from the Carnegie Commission, CBS, the Communications Workers of America, and the Ford Foundation, CPB would not have been able to fund much programming.

In 1969 CPB sponsored a conference in San Diego that laid the foundation for National Public Radio, an entity that, unlike its television counterpart, the Public Broadcasting Service, would produce as well as distribute programs. The corporation invited Bill Siemering, then the station manager of WBFO in Buffalo, New York, to help conduct the discussion. Siemering had already articulated a vision for the service in an essay called "Public Radio: Some Essential Ingredients," in which he argued that public radio should be "on the frontier of the contemporary and help create new tastes," but that it also had to meet the information needs of the public.

Don Quayle was chosen as the organization's first president, not long after he had made a presentation to the Ford Foundation showing that he could interconnect all the qualified public radio stations "for less than [New York public station] WNET spent on television." Quayle hired Bill Siemering as the network's first program director and set him to work on what was to be its first regular program, *All Things Considered*.

National Public Radio Goes On the Air

National Public Radio was incorporated on 26 February 1970 with 90 charter stations. The network set up offices and studios in Washington, D.C., closer to the heart of the nation's politics than the big commercial networks, which had long been based in New York. NPR officially went on the air in April 1971, offering live coverage of the Senate hearings on Vietnam. Less than a month later, on 3 May 1971, the network aired its first edition of *All Things Considered*. Siemering, who directed the first program himself, recalls that it got off to a "rocky and exhilarating" start, with host Robert Conley unable to hear the cues in his headphones. But as to content, it fulfilled practically all the elements that Siemering had outlined. The program went on the air as thousands of antiwar demonstrators filled the streets of Washington in what was to be the last major protest of the Vietnam War. Reporter Jeff Kamin brought back tape of the chanting and the sirens as police waded into the crowds of demonstrators and made more than 7,000 arrests. The same program featured a young black woman speaking dreamily about her heroin addiction. As Siemering had promised, the program transmitted "the experience of people and institutions from as widely varying backgrounds and areas as are feasible." It spoke "with many voices and dialects." Siemering says that it also illustrated many of the network's goals: "using sound to tell the story; and presentation of multiple perspectives rather than a single truth."

Over the next few months, the program took shape. Siemering found a distinctive voice and sensibility for the program and the network in Susan Stamberg, who became the first woman to host a daily national newsmagazine. Stamberg was paired with Mike Waters and later with Bob Edwards. The network offset its limited resources and relatively inexperienced staff with a creative, conversational approach that began to gather fans. Producers at the network tried to explore the possibilities of the medium, emulating the sound-rich work of the Canadian Broadcasting Corporation (CBC) in Canada and the German producer Peter Leonhard Braun at *Sender Freies Berlin.*

During the first decade, cultural programming was a strong component of the network's output. Bob Malesky, now the executive producer of NPR's weekend programming, puts it this way: "*All Things Considered* was experimental, while concert programs gave stations the solid base to build a day's programming around, for what was still a largely conservative audience." NPR's first arts program was *Voices in the Wind,* and during its five-year life span (1974–1979), it was second only to *All Things Considered* in station usage." NPR also provided stations with *Folk Festival USA* (1974–79) and *Jazz Alive* (1977–83), both the work of producer Steve Rathe. In 1982 the network launched the *Sunday Show,* a five-hour cultural newsmagazine that won a Peabody Award for its first year but, like *Jazz Alive,* fell victim to the NPR financial crisis in 1983.

Expanding Role

For its first five years, NPR functioned primarily as a production and distribution center for its member stations, which had grown over the years to 190. The network took on a bigger role in 1977, after a merger with the stations' lobbying organization, the Association of Public Radio Stations. Don Quayle had left the network in 1973 to become a senior vice president at CPB, and the merger took place under President Lee Frischnecht. NPR offered member services, including training, management assistance, and help with program promotion. The network also began representing the member stations' interests before Congress and the FCC.

The network gained a great deal more national visibility under its third president, Frank Mankiewicz, who was hired in 1977. Mankiewicz came to the job from a background in freelance journalism and politics. He had been Robert Kennedy's press secretary during the presidential campaign that ended with the senator's assassination in Los Angeles, and he had managed the presidential campaign of Senator George McGovern. He had barely heard of NPR. He recalls that he got the job after promising the board that he "would do whatever was necessary so that people like me will know what NPR is."

Mankiewicz's first coup was getting permission for NPR to do live coverage of the Panama Canal debate in the Senate in 1978. It was the first live broadcast ever from the Senate floor.

He chose NPR's Senate reporter, Linda Wertheimer, to anchor the coverage, despite complaints from station managers who worried that a woman would sound "too shrill."

Mankiewicz also fostered the network's longtime goal of offering a morning program service. When *All Things Considered* was first conceived, many public radio stations were not even on the air in the mornings. Bill Siemering says he felt that a new staff creating a new kind of program needed to work together on the day's news, without having to contend with the problems of preparing a program overnight, so the network's flagship program was designed for afternoon drive time. But the network was well aware that radio's biggest audience was in the morning, and NPR was eager to reach it. Mankiewicz also believed that if listeners tuned to an NPR program in the morning, there was a good chance the dial would remain there the rest of the day.

Mankiewicz says he saw his chance to start a morning program when CPB President Henry Loomis offered him a big chunk of money. Loomis pointed out one day that CPB, unlike most federally funded agencies, received its appropriation in a lump sum at the beginning of the fiscal year. That meant that the money accrued a lot of interest in the course of the year, about $4 million. Loomis, a radio fan, asked Mankiewicz what he would do with that money if he got it. "I'd use it to start a morning radio program." Loomis liked the idea and put up the money to start *Morning Edition,* which went on the air in November 1979. After the member stations roundly rejected a pilot version of the program, Bob Edwards was lured from his position as *All Things Considered* cohost with Susan Stamberg to take over *Morning Edition* on a temporary basis. Edwards stayed on, and the program became a hit.

Morning Edition marked an important departure in program style for the network. Whereas *All Things Considered* flowed relatively freely through its 90 minutes, from beginning to middle to end, *Morning Edition* was conceived as a *program service,* structured into rigid segments that member stations could either use or replace with their own local news, weather, and traffic reporting. The success of the *Morning Edition* format led many station managers to lobby for similar changes in the afternoon program, changes that the producers resisted until the mid-1990s.

The demands of providing material for two major programs each day also forced a significant change in the structure of the organization. In the early years, all reporters and producers worked directly for *All Things Considered,* tailoring their work to the eclectic and free-flowing style of that program. The advent of *Morning Edition* meant that the same reporters had to write and produce for the more rigid time constraints of the program service as well. To avoid having reporters pulled by the conflicting demands of the two shows, the news department adopted a "desk" system like those at major newspapers. Editors with specific expertise and experience set up a national desk, a foreign desk, a science desk, and so on. Reporters now worked for NPR news, rather than for a particular show.

In 1980 the network made a striking improvement in its sound quality with the launch of the nation's first satellite-delivered radio distribution system. Overnight, the programs went from the tinny, telephone quality of a 5 kilohertz phone line to the clarity and intimacy of the studio. Mankiewicz likes to joke that he told the technicians to add a bit of static to the broadcast for the first few days, "to lend an air of verisimilitude" to the otherwise too-perfect sound. The satellite also expanded the network's delivery capacity from a single channel to four, allowing stations to choose alternative programs without having to wait for the tapes to arrive in the mail.

The satellite meant that listeners could hear complex, skillfully layered sound without the degradation of telephone lines, and it cleared the way for the golden period of NPR documentaries. In 1980 the network broadcast a 13-part series by former *Voices in the Wind* producer Robert Montiegal called *A Question of Place*. The series used sound to bring to life the work of writers and thinkers such as James Joyce, Michel Foucault, Simone de Beauvoir, and Bertrand Russell. The following year, writer James Reston, Jr., producer Deborah Amos, and host Noah Adams used tape from the last days of the Jonestown religious cult to show how a leader's egomania led to the mass suicides of more than 900 people in Guyana. The network even branched into radio theater, with the series *Earplay, Masterpiece Radio Theater,* and a radio version of the George Lucas hit film *Star Wars.*

Financial Crisis

NPR was riding high and spending freely in 1983. Under Frank Mankiewicz, the network's membership had grown to more than 250 stations, and as he had promised, it was familiar to people like him, people in politics, the arts, and business. When Mankiewicz took over in 1977, the network was dependent on the federal government for 90 percent of its funding. By 1983 corporate underwriting, foundation grants, and other income had brought that figure down to around 50 percent. But the network was not in good financial shape. The network's chief operating officer, Tom Warnock, came to Mankiewicz with the news that NPR might be as much as $2 million in debt. As Warnock delved deeper, the estimate of the debt grew, finally reaching $9 million, a third of the network's budget. Subsequent audits revealed that NPR's accounting was so sloppy that some of the spending could not be tracked. As an example, the network had issued more than 100 American Express cards to its administrators, who ran up hundreds of thousands of dollars in bills for entertainment and travel. Teetering on the edge of bankruptcy, the network slashed department budgets and ultimately had to lay off about 100 people.

The staff of the cultural programs department shrank from 33 to 8. Mankiewicz says he could have saved the situation with an ordinary bank loan, but political differences with the CPB's leadership made that impossible. In the end, Mankiewicz resigned.

Ronald Bornstein, the director of telecommunications at the University of Wisconsin, took over as acting president, leading a rescue team of lawyers and accountants from some of the top firms in Washington. For the first and only time in its history, the network went directly to its listeners to help pay off the debt, by including a fund-raising segment in *All Things Considered.* The member stations were wary of allowing the network to raise money from among their contributors, and only about a third of them chose to carry the segments. Even so, the "Drive to Survive" brought in $2.25 million in just three days. The balance of NPR's debt was to be paid off over a three-year period, under the terms of a loan agreement that was hammered out in often-rancorous negotiations with the CPB.

Messy and embarrassing as it was, NPR reported the story of its near-disaster as it happened. That, too, was part of Mankiewicz's legacy. "By that time, NPR had cast itself unambiguously as a news organization, so the standards of news applied to it," recalls Doug Bennet, who took over as president in 1983. Bennet says that what Mankiewicz "really did was to establish NPR in the news niche, and that was genius. Before, there was some news, but nowhere near the scale of investment or the staff." Scott Simon, then the network's Chicago bureau chief, was brought in to report on the financial crisis, interviewing beleaguered staffers and disgusted members of Congress. Bennet found himself taking over at an organization that was tense and distrustful.

Return to Stability

Bennet recalls that during his first one and a half years, he had to cut the budget eight more times, as new deficits were discovered, but he says, "I never believed that NPR would disappear." Bennet's first task was to develop a plan that would reassure the stations and Congress that NPR could be turned around.

The feud with the CPB eventually led the CPB to open up its funding process so that NPR would not be the only recipient. CPB created a Radio Fund, permitting any radio organization to apply for the money. The new funding system was approved without NPR's knowledge, to the fury of station managers. NPR had lost its funding monopoly and faced the prospect of presiding over an ever-diminishing cut of the pie. Doug Bennet recalls sitting in a bar with then-Board Chairman Don Mullally, charting out a radical and risky new funding plan on a bar napkin. The business plan, announced in February 1985, proposed giving all the CPB money to the member stations and letting them use it to acquire programming wherever they wished. "We were saying to the stations, you can take this money and run, if you want to," Bennet says, "and for about five years, it was a much more market-like relationship." NPR's biggest competitor in that market was American Public Radio (APR).

APR was formed by a group of stations led by William Kling, the president of Minnesota Public Radio. The group had long been critical of NPR's cultural offerings and established its own network to acquire and distribute programs. APR's strongest offering was Garrison Keillor's *Prairie Home Companion,* once rejected by NPR's Mankiewicz as elitist and patronizing to middle-American values. *Prairie Home Companion* quickly became the most popular program on public radio.

Bennet says that, despite the funding pinch, he felt NPR had to prove that it could go forward. "We had to show we weren't locked in a zero-sum game, that we could invent and invest." Bennet backed the development of new programs, such as *Weekend Sunday* and *Performance Today.* The new funding scheme meant that new programs "had to be viable from a market standpoint," Bennet says. "The concept behind *Performance Today* was to showcase contemporary American performances—last night's, if possible—and to give stations a show that funders would support." The network also picked up new programs for distribution, including *Car Talk; Fresh Air with Terry Gross;* and *Afropop,* a review of African popular music that Bennet says "was always my proof that the NPR audience was willing to consider all kinds of music, and not just Brahms."

The new programs exemplified the deep change in NPR's mission that took place in the aftermath of the funding crisis, a change from offering listeners an alternative to being a force in the marketplace. Bennet says that NPR formally established that building its audience was an important goal, something that had been debatable in the past. Along with the funding control, stations had assumed more power over programming by refusing to buy any program that seemed unlikely to draw a significant audience in their area. The result was a gradual strengthening of the hard-news content of the magazine programs, leaving much of the network's arts and cultural programming struggling.

News took an even stronger hold as NPR's foreign desk reached out to report more and more ambitious stories. In 1986 NPR's coverage of the overthrow of Philippine President Ferdinand Marcos was more comprehensive than any of its previous reports. Cadi Simon, then the foreign editor, described the change in Mary Collins' (1993) book *National Public Radio: The Cast of Characters,* saying NPR "treated the story like an ongoing news event rather than just coming back and gathering tape." The network applied the same technique to later stories, including the Tiananmen Square uprising in China and the fall of the Berlin Wall, preparing the ground for full-scale reporting on the Persian Gulf War. Simon told Col-

lins, "The coverage of the Gulf War did not happen in a void. It came out of a network that was established, a mind-set that we had come into."

The network fielded some of its top reporters during the 1991 war, including Deborah Amos, Deborah Wang, Scott Simon, John Hockenberry, John Ydstie, and Neal Conan. Conan was among a group of correspondents who were captured and held for several days by Iraqi forces. Their reporting on the war and its aftermath—the oil-field environmental disaster in Kuwait and the Kurdish refugee crisis in northern Iraq—showed that NPR could compete with the television networks and with 24-hour cable news. It was a pattern that would be repeated throughout the decade in places such as Ethiopia, Bosnia, and Kosovo. The network's round-the-clock coverage of the war strengthened NPR's weekend programs and led to the creation of a nationwide call-in show, *Talk of the Nation.*

NPR was also establishing itself as a strong source of political news, with coverage of the presidential campaigns and political conventions. The network's top political correspondents included Linda Wertheimer, Cokie Roberts, Mara Liasson, Brian Naylor, Elizabeth Arnold, and Peter Kenyon. NPR's legal affairs correspondent, Nina Totenberg, enhanced the network's reputation with her coverage of the Supreme Court. In 1987 Totenberg broke the story that Supreme Court nominee Douglas Ginsburg had smoked marijuana while he was a professor at Harvard Law School in the 1970s. The story led to Ginsburg's withdrawal. In 1991 Totenberg reported Anita Hill's allegations of sexual harassment against another Supreme Court nominee, Clarence Thomas. Both stories put NPR squarely in the media spotlight.

Expansion

By the time it celebrated its 20th anniversary in 1991, NPR had grown to nearly 400 member stations nationwide. When Doug Bennet stepped down as president in 1993, the network had begun extending its reach around the world, with the establishment of an international service, beamed by satellite to Europe through the World Radio network in London. Over the next five years, that network evolved into NPR Worldwide, reaching more than 50 countries and territories, from Antarctica to Finland.

NPR's new president, Delano Lewis, oversaw the establishment of the NPR Foundation, designed to help insulate the network against financial crises like the one that had nearly destroyed it ten years earlier. Lewis, the first African-American to head the network, was a former telephone company executive with broad connections to the business and political communities in Washington. He expanded the network's fundraising base and strengthened relations with the member stations. In 1994 the network moved into its own building, at 635

Massachusetts Avenue in Washington, D.C. The move allowed NPR to bring all its news, production, and administrative operations under one roof and provided state-of-the-art facilities for production.

The expansion of production facilities came as NPR was returning to the creation of sound-rich, highly textured documentaries. In 1992 the network had begun *Radio Expeditions* as a joint venture with the National Geographic Society. In 1994 it premiered the 26-part series *Wade in the Water: African-American Sacred Music Traditions.*

NPR also began exploring the possibilities of the internet. The network launched its website in 1994, and the following year it teamed with the Progressive network, using RealAudio technology that allows users to hear prerecorded audio files of the programs on-line.

After a long struggle, *All Things Considered* moved to capture a bigger segment of the national drive-time audience by advancing its East Coast start time to 4:00 P.M. and expanding from 90 minutes to two hours. Although not as rigidly segmented as *Morning Edition*, the new *All Things Considered* format provided more fixed points at which member stations could insert local programming. Two years later, in 1997, *Morning Edition* also stretched its airtime, moving to a 5:00 A.M. start.

The network expanded its own programming and its program distribution in the late 1990s. NPR's *Performance Today* grew from five to seven days a week in 1996. The following year, the network introduced *Sounds Like Science* and began distributing more programs produced by member stations, including the talk shows the *Diane Rehm Show* and *Public Interest* and the sports program *Only a Game*. In 1998 NPR premiered its cross-country news quiz *Wait, Wait . . . Don't Tell Me* and a short-lived music and popular culture program, *Anthem*.

The network expanded its presence on the worldwide web in 1998, making an agreement with Yahoo!, the internet media company, to provide selected audio content to *Yahoo! News*. When new president Kevin Klose took over in 1999, the company was entering an agreement with Minnesota Public Radio to create an on-line network supplying interactive news, information, arts, and entertainment.

Klose, a former head of the government's Radio Liberty and Radio Free Europe, says he wants to bring NPR to its fulfillment as a major player in the world of news and information. He is pressing to move the network into new technologies, including satellite radio, which would allow NPR to provide some programming directly to its listeners for the first time ever, without going through its member stations. Klose says a major challenge for NPR's future will be how to become a multimedia enterprise without compromising its values.

Former President Doug Bennet sees other challenges, including the danger of commercialization at NPR, in which underwriting credits come to sound more and more like advertising. "I think it's a terrible mistake," he says, "to give up the niche of a non-advertising entity to compete ineffectively for advertising." Kevin Klose says he wants to make sure that NPR's "content is not penetrated by commerce."

Governance and Funding

Unlike most commercial networks, NPR does not own or operate any of its member stations. The private, nonprofit corporation is a membership organization, a structure that Klose says is "at the heart of its dynamism." It is governed by a 17-member board composed of the NPR president, ten station managers elected by the membership, and six public members chosen by the board and confirmed by the member stations. The member stations are autonomous entities, most often licensed to colleges and universities or community groups. In exchange for their dues and program-licensing fees, NPR stations receive programming, professional training for staff members, help in promoting programs, and representation in Washington on issues affecting public broadcasting.

On average, member stations take about 27 percent of their programming from NPR. Local staff members produce about 48 percent of the station's program content, and another 25 percent comes from other public radio producers and distributors, such as Public Radio International.

More than 92 percent of the U.S. population now lives within reach of an NPR member station. The stations have a combined audience of some 19 million people, of whom more than 13 million listen to programming provided by the network.

The typical member station gets about a quarter of its funding from its listeners, soliciting donations with on-air and direct-mail appeals. Stations that are licensed to educational institutions generally get around 19 percent of their revenues from their colleges or universities. Corporate donors provide around 17 percent of station support, and about 14 percent comes from CPB. The remainder comes from foundations and other sources.

Although it was created with an infusion of federal money, NPR no longer receives any direct federal funding for general support. Slightly more than half of its funding comes from dues and program fees paid by the member stations. Most of the rest of its $80 million budget is contributed by private foundations and corporations.

COREY FLINTOFF

See also All Things Considered; Car Talk; Edwards, Bob; Fresh Air; Keillor, Garrison; Mankiewicz, Frank; Morning Edition; National Association of Educational Broadcasters; Prairie Home Companion; Public Broadcasting Act; Public Radio

International; Public Radio Since 1967; Siemering, William; Simon, Scott; Stamberg, Susan; Star Wars; Totenberg, Nina; Wertheimer, Linda

Further Reading
Adams, Noah, *Noah Adams on "All Things Considered": A Radio Journal*, New York: Norton, 1992
Collins, Mary, *National Public Radio: The Cast of Characters*, Washington, D.C.: Seven Locks Press, 1993
Edwards, Bob, *Fridays with Red: A Radio Friendship*, New York: Simon and Schuster, 1993
Engelman, Ralph, *Public Radio and Television in America: A Political History*, Thousand Oaks, California: Sage, 1996
Looker, Thomas, *The Sound and the Story: NPR and the Art of Radio*, Boston: Houghton Mifflin, 1995
McCourt, Tom, *Conflicting Communications Interests in America: The Case of National Public Radio*, Westport, Connecticut: Praeger, 1999
Siegel, Robert, editor, *The NPR Interviews, 1996*, Boston: Houghton Mifflin, 1996
Stamberg, Susan, *Every Night at Five: Susan Stamberg's All Things Considered Book*, New York: Pantheon, 1982
Stamberg, Susan, *Talk: NPR's Susan Stamberg Considers All Things*, New York: Turtle Bay Books, 1993
Wertheimer, Linda, editor, *Listening to America: Twenty-five Years in the Life of a Nation, As Heard on National Public Radio*, Boston, Houghton Mifflin, 1995
Witherspoon, John, Roselle Kovitz, Robert K. Avery, and Alan G. Stavitsky, *A History of Public Broadcasting*, Washington, D.C.: Current, 2000

National Radio Systems Committee

Recommending New Technical Standards for Radio

A cooperative entity of the broadcast and consumer electronics industry, the National Radio Systems Committee (NRSC) recommends technical standards relating to radio broadcasting in the United States. It is particularly concerned with development of standards for both digital audio broadcasting and the radio broadcast data system. The NRSC was originally established in 1985 and initially investigated aspects of AM radio transmission. It has since taken on several other projects.

NRSC members are generally engineers, scientists, or technicians with in-depth knowledge of the subject being studied. They may be from companies, nonprofit organizations, or government entities. Anyone who has a business interest in the technology being investigated by the NRSC is welcome to join and participate. Meetings are held on an as-needed basis. Member organizations fund the participation of NRSC committee participants.

The NRSC receives information from a variety of sources—the companies interested in manufacturing new devices, the International Telecommunication Union (ITU) and other bodies that deal with worldwide standards, and the Federal Communications Commission (FCC). In turn, it monitors and assists with technical testing of proposed new systems.

The NRSC accomplishes its work by establishing subcommittees to focus discussion and development efforts. Two were active as the new century began—one concerning digital audio broadcasting (DAB) and the other concerning radio broadcast data systems (RBDS, or simply RDS). In April 1998 the NRSC suspended activities of a third subcommittee (concerned with high-speed FM subcarriers) because the group had reached an impasse in its deliberations to develop a voluntary standard.

As recommendations emerge from the subcommittees, they are considered and voted upon by the full NRSC membership. These final agreements are in the form of recommendations to both industries (electronic media and consumer electronics) and to the FCC, which must issue any formal standards decisions.

The DAB subcommittee worked for several years to agree upon a final technical standard for in-band, on-channel ("IBOC") digital radio for the United States. The subcommittee also established working groups to compare and contrast two potential DAB systems (one developed by USA Digital Radio and the other by Lucent Digital Radio). By late 2002, there were two operating satellite-delivered digital radio services in the U.S., and the FCC had issued an NRSC-recommended standard for terrestrial digital radio service.

The RBDS subcommittee originally approved RBDS standards in 1993 and last revised and updated them in 1998. Largely based on the European system, the RBDS signal is a low-bit rate data stream transmitted on the 57-kilohertz subcarrier of an FM radio signal. Radio listeners know RBDS mostly through its ability to permit RBDS-equipped radio receivers to display station call letters and search for stations based on their program format. In addition, special traffic announcements can be transmitted to RBDS radios as well as weather or other emergency alerts.

CHRISTOPHER H. STERLING

See also Digital Audio Broadcasting; Digital Satellite Radio; Radio Data System

Further Reading

National Association of Broadcasters: The National Radio
    Systems Committee, <www.nab.org/SciTech/nrsc.asp>

National Religious Broadcasters

Trade Association

The National Religious Broadcasters (NRB) is a trade association of more than 1,200 Christian radio and television stations, most of which broadcast from an evangelical Protestant perspective. Full membership in the NRB is granted to those who meet financial accountability standards and sign a seven-point "Statement of Faith." The organization has grown from a small group of separatist broadcasters in the 1940s to a professionally staffed organization with both political and spiritual influence.

Origins

By the 1940s, radio airtime had become so valuable that commercial non-religious stations began placing preachers in Sunday morning time slots. Networks preferred to offer organized religious groups "sustaining," or free, airtime to meet government requirements for religious or public affairs programming. Time was offered to organizations representing Roman Catholics, Jews, and mainline Protestants through the Federal Council of Churches (later know as the National Council of Churches). However, evangelical churches, such as the Southern Baptists and the Assemblies of God, were not members of the mainline Protestant organization and were not allowed to share in the free air time.

Disgruntled evangelical broadcasters joined churches, parachurch ministries, and educators in the 1942 formation of the National Association of Evangelicals (NAE). Two years later the NAE chartered the formation of the National Religious Broadcasters to address more specifically the concerns of evangelical radio stations and programs. The NRB grew to become independent of the NAE, although the two groups remained affiliated until 2001, when the NRB voted to formally end the relationship after the NAE began accepting members who were part of the National Council of Churches. The National Association of Evangelicals today represents over 50 denominations and 250 parachurch ministries.

The National Religious Broadcasters set up headquarters near Washington, D.C., since a major function of the organization was lobbying the Federal Communications Commission. The NRB also created a code of ethics for broadcast ministries and has provided legal advice to members. The group, however, was mostly unsuccessful in securing free broadcast time for evangelical ministries, so in the late 1940s members began to buy airtime and start their own Christian radio stations. The success of Billy Graham, Oral Roberts, Rex Humbard, and others led to an explosion of Christian programming in the 1960s and 1970s.

The NRB began holding its annual convention in Washington, D.C., in 1956, attempting to influence politicians and FCC commissioners. For more than 30 years, the annual D.C. meetings attracted thousands of increasingly vocal Christian communicators, who took credit for helping to elect born-again President Jimmy Carter and conservative Ronald Reagan (who addressed the NRB delegates). The NRB was also instrumental in influencing the government to redefine equal employment laws to allow Christian radio stations to use faith-based criteria when hiring new employees.

NRB Executive Director Ben Armstrong led the organization's growth from 1966 to 1989; over that period, the NRB quadrupled in size to include almost 100 syndicated television preachers and three major religious TV networks. The religious broadcasting audience grew from around 5 million in the mid-1960s to more than 25 million two decades later. The most successful radio member has been *Focus on the Family* with Dr. James Dobson, which started in 1977 and currently airs on more than 3,000 radio stations in 95 countries.

By the early 1980s, the NRB had become the spiritual and political voice for the estimated $2 billion religious radio and television industry, but the end of that decade saw a dramatic decline in the religious broadcasting industry. In 1987 former NRB member Jim Bakker, who hosted the daily *PTL Club*, resigned his radio and television ministry after it was revealed that his organization had been paying a woman to keep quiet about her sexual encounter with him. The following year brought more scandal and controversy: Oral Roberts was chastised by the media for stating that God would "call him home" if he did not raise $8 million; Pat Robertson of the Christian Broadcasting Network briefly ran for president of the United States; and evangelist Jimmy Swaggart was accused of soliciting a prostitute. Nationally, Christian broadcasters experienced a dramatic decline in their audiences, and some lost up to three fourths of their contributions.

The NRB, accused of not properly monitoring the ethical standards of its members, responded to the crisis by strengthening financial accountability procedures and tightening membership requirements. By the 1990s, leader E. Brandt Gustavson moved the annual convention to other cities, trading the politically oriented meetings of Washington, D.C., for a more spiritual emphasis outside the beltway. By the end of the decade, religious broadcasters had stopped the decline in audience and contributions and saw a slow growth in the trust of those looking for spiritual programming. In 2002 the group ousted new president Wayne Pederson after only one month in office for his criticisms of members who were better known for their politics than their ministries. New leader Frank Wright attempted to keep NRB's spiritual focus while increasing its political influence, and President George W. Bush addressed the group's 2003 convention.

Today some major evangelical religious broadcasters are not members of the NRB because they wish to avoid the full financial disclosure required by the organization. Ministers who receive more than $500,000 annually in donations must meet the strict standards of the Evangelical Council for Financial Accountability. Smaller ministries must still meet the NRB in-house standards, but denominational and church-sponsored broadcasters are exempt from the financial accountability requirements. Associate, non-voting memberships that do not require signing the NRB's "Statement of Faith" are available to secular organizations or mainline churches.

Religious Radio Today

"Sustaining" or free radio time is no longer given to the three major religious bodies, and mainline churches are generally unwilling to compete with the big dollars spent by evangelicals. But the current environment can be traced to the unwillingness of mainline churches to share their free time in the 1940s, forcing NRB members to buy airtime in order to get their gospel message over the airwaves. Some non-evangelical denominations are gradually budgeting for media time, and a network of Roman Catholic radio stations was started in the United States in 1999. Most Catholic broadcasters are not members of the NRB but are part of the Catholic Academy for Communication Arts Professionals.

With the fourth-largest format among commercial stations and a directory that lists over 1,600 radio stations playing religious programming at some point during the broadcast week, the National Religious Broadcasters has grown to become a significant political, economic, and spiritual organization for the evangelical Christians who use radio to spread their gospel.

STEPHEN M. WINZENBURG

See also Christian Contemporary Music Format; Evangelists/ Evangelical Radio; Gospel Music Format; Jewish Radio Programs in the United States; Religion on Radio

Further Reading
Armstrong, Ben, and William F. Fore, *The Electric Church*, Nashville, Tennessee: Nelson, 1979
Barnhart, Joe E., and Steven Winzenburg, *Jim and Tammy: Charismatic Intrigue Inside PTL*, Buffalo, New York: Prometheus Books, 1988
Ellens, J. Harold, *Models of Religious Broadcasting*, Grand Rapids, Michigan: Eerdmans, 1974
Melton, J. Gordon, Phillip Charles Lucas, and Jon R. Stone, editors, *Prime Time Religion: An Encyclopedia of Religious Broadcasting*, Phoenix, Arizona: Oryx Press, 1997
Ward, Mark, *Air of Salvation: The Story of Christian Broadcasting*, Grand Rapids, Michigan: Baker Books, 1994

National Telecommunications and Information Administration

U.S. Telecommunications Policy Agency

The National Telecommunications and Information Administration (NTIA) is a Department of Commerce agency responsible for advising the Executive Branch on matters of domestic and international telecommunications and information policy. This includes managing federal government uses of the radio spectrum, which is used for wireless microwave or satellite-based broadcasting and telecommunications.

Background

The NTIA's role today carries the legacy of the Commerce Department's radio activity, which began in the early 1900s. The cabinet-level Department of Commerce and Labor was established on 14 February 1903. Because the earliest uses of radio were both commerce and navigation based, the Department of Commerce and Labor was involved with establishing radio standards, procedures, and equipment requirements in conjunction with national navigation, ship outfitting, and lighthouse communications. The April 1912 *Titanic* disaster highlighted the need for greater commercial, government, and amateur radio standardization and regulation procedures. These were included in the Radio Act of 1912, which required radio apparatus on all passenger steamers and established a system of allocating and assigning both frequencies and licenses to commercial, government, and amateur radio operators. These administrative duties fell primarily to the Commerce Department's Bureau of Navigation.

On 4 March 1913, ten years after the creation of the Department of Commerce and Labor, President Taft signed legislation dividing the unit into separate Labor and Commerce Departments. Increasingly, the Commerce Department was called upon for research and development of radio's commercial and defense applications, including "the investigation and standardization of methods and instruments employed in radio communication," which fell primarily to the Bureau of Standards. In 1916 it developed a radio laboratory—the predecessor of the current Institute of Telecommunication Services (ITS). The Commerce Department's early radio development efforts also extended to the general public. For example, the Bureau of Standards determined standards for homemade crystal detector sets and distributed instructions for constructing them in 1922.

The second secretary of commerce, Herbert Hoover, served from 1921 to 1929. Intent on harnessing the commercial power of radio advances, Hoover convened four national radio conferences to discuss how new radio technologies and capabilities should be regulated in light of increasingly diverse and complex demand. In 1927 a new Radio Act created a Radio Division in the Department of Commerce and an independent Federal Radio Commission (FRC). The FRC relieved the Bureau of Navigation's licensing, frequency allocation and assignment, and transmitter power output regulation duties. Enforcement oversight and technical research duties fell to the Department of Commerce's Radio Division. With creation of the Federal Communications Commission (FCC) in 1934, the Department of Commerce retained oversight of government radio spectrum allocation and technical research.

NTIA Origins

It was Executive Branch activity in the late 1960s and early 1970s, however—particularly in the Nixon administration—that resulted in the current configuration of the NTIA. An Office of Telecommunications Policy (OTP) was created within the Executive Office of the President in 1970. Under its first director, Dr. Clay Whitehead, OTP worked to coordinate federal agency concerns about telecommunication. (In one administrative response, the Federal Communications Commission formed its own Office of Plans and Policies to deal with longer-range studies, so as not to let OTP completely control that role.) OTP became involved in both electronic media questions as well as telephone industry concerns. After Nixon resigned from office in August 1974, OTP was guided by an acting director. When President Jimmy Carter took office in 1977, officials initiated a planning process to decide how to deal with OTP. Henry Geller, former FCC general counsel, headed up a team to assess what was needed and how best to accomplish that need. The result was to shift OTP out of the Executive Office of the President and to the Department of Commerce.

The NTIA was created in 1978 by merging the Executive Branch's Office of Technology Policy and the Department of Commerce's Office of Telecommunications. This merger was effected through Reorganization Plan No. 1 of 1977 and Executive Order 12046 of 27 March 1978.

Responsibilities

The NTIA's radio-related policy, technical, research, and spectrum-management functions are overseen through five offices and three staff groups.

Domestically, the Office of Policy Analysis and Development (OPAD) develops policy recommendations for the Executive Branch regarding common-carrier, broadcast, cable, digital, radio spectrum, wireless, and information technologies. It focuses on promoting universal, affordable radio, television, and telecommunications in the public and commercial sectors and works alongside the FCC. OPAD was instrumental in developing legislation and a computerized system for auctioning excess government radio spectrum for nongovernmental use. It also gathers data and makes recommendations to encourage minority radio and television station ownership through its Minority Telecommunications Development Program. The Office of Telecommunication and Information Applications undertakes funding for new technology demonstration projects, with a specific focus on underserved public-sector areas.

The Office of Spectrum Management (OSM) oversees planning and policy strategy and implementation of federal government radio spectrum use in conjunction with its advisory Interdepartmental Radio Advisory Committee. This includes spectrum for federal government radio transmitters such as those used by the Department of Defense, the National Aeronautics and Space Administration (NASA), the National Park Service, airport communication, and public safety and emergency services. The OSM also offers technical and policy courses to interested international parties on spectrum makeup and management. The OSM deals specifically with federal government radio spectrum use, whereas the FCC deals with nongovernmental uses of spectrum; the two coordinate their activities closely.

Government spectrum applications overseen by the NTIA include defense; Voice of America facilities; radar and voice communications necessary for weather radio and flood warning services, commercial and pleasure aeronautical and maritime traffic, and weather satellite systems; and floodwater management systems and time signals. Government spectrum ranges throughout the 0- to 300-gigahertz range; at this writing, the government has more than a quarter million assignments: 43 percent for defense, 19 percent for resource management, 18 percent for public safety, 13 percent for transportation, and 8 percent for other purposes.

The Office of International Affairs provides policy and technical counsel regarding international radio frequency spectrum allocation, the Global Information Infrastructure initiative, and other issues of legal and technical standards to advance U.S. commercial interests. In this capacity, it works closely with the State Department and with such international bodies as the International Telecommunication Union, the Organization for Economic Cooperation and Development,

the World Trade Organization, the International Telecommunications Satellite Organization, the International Mobile Satellite Organization, the Organization of American States Inter-American Telecommunications Commission, the Asia Pacific Economic Cooperation Telecommunications Working Group, and the Southern African Regional Telecommunications Restructuring Program.

ITS undertakes engineering research for the NTIA. From its laboratory in Boulder, Colorado, ITS generates knowledge about domestic and international infrastructure development and enhancement, more effective use of radio spectrum, and resolving various technical concerns of federal, state, and local governments and of commercial and nonprofit industries and organizations. The Federal Technology Transfer Act of 1986 is the legal basis for any of these activities that require sharing government facilities or resources, including radio spectrum.

NTIA is a relatively small agency—about 300 people, compared to the FCC's 2,000 or more. The former concentrates on mid- and long-range policy, while the latter focuses on day-to-day licensing and related decisions. They must and do work closely together on spectrum matters. In its near quarter-century of operation, NTIA has waxed and waned in importance, often depending on the political trends and personalities of the times. Although Critics have claimed NTIA should stand for "not terribly important agency," the NTIA has performed significant duties related to radio and radio spectrum management.

Sousan Arafeh

See also Federal Communications Commission; Frequency Allocation; Hoover, Herbert; World Radiocommunication Conference

Further Reading

Bowers, Helen, editor, *From Lighthouses to Laserbeams: A History of the U.S. Department of Commerce, 1913–1988*, Washington, D.C.: U.S. Department of Commerce, 1988

Cabinets and Counselors: The President and the Executive Branch, Washington, D.C.: Congressional Quarterly, 1989; 2nd edition, 1997

National Telecommunications and Information Administration,

National Telecommunications and Information Administration: Office of Spectrum Management, <www.ntia.doc.gov/osmhome/osmhome.html>

Native American Radio

Native Owned and Operated Stations

Native American radio is perceived as a way to help retain the languages and traditions of the tribes as well as a method for communicating to Native Americans who speak a Native tongue exclusively. Many older Native Americans use English as a second language, if they use it at all, and are unserved by "Anglo" broadcasting stations. Native-operated stations are also seen as potential tools to help combat the negative images and false impressions of Native Americans often prevalent in mainstream society.

Origins

Hundreds of years of exploitation and oppression by non-Native Americans, mainly whites, served as the primary impetus behind the establishment of Native-controlled broadcast media. In the 1960s Native Americans resoundingly rejected the paternal rule of the "Great White Father" in Washington in favor of playing a greater role in their own affairs and destiny. In the eyes of many, an historic Native American action at Alcatraz in 1969 was another catalyst for the creation of Native-controlled radio outlets in the United States. Dozens of statements (by those occupying the island in San Francisco Bay) concerning the plight of Natives were broadcast via Pacifica's KPFA-FM. The station loaned the Native Americans on the island a Marti transmitter to relay their messages to its studios in Berkeley, which it then broadcast live. Radio Free Alcatraz, as it was called, focused on the impoverished state of Native American affairs, demanding that attention be paid to Native American health, education, and cultural issues. From the perspective of those who occupied the tiny island, radio was the medium whereby the truth could be conveyed. It could leap barriers and roadblocks and reach the ears and hearts of the public.

The Red Power Movement was born against a backdrop of civil unrest stemming from a call by African-Americans and other minorities for equal rights. Out of this crusade came the American Indian Movement (AIM) in the late 1960s. Driving AIM was the restoration of Native pride and identity through the preservation of Native American culture and language. AIM's primary function was to call attention to the human rights violations against Native Americans and to ensure that the Native American culture would not be exterminated. AIM's seizure of Wounded Knee, South Dakota, in 1973, and its use of the media to dramatize the situation, raised Native awareness of the potency of electronic media, which were an integral part of the organization's strategy to expose to the world what it perceived as gross injustices against its people.

This particular incident would be a key factor in the development of Native-controlled and operated broadcast stations.

Ray Cook, executive director of what was formerly the Indigenous Communications Association in the early 1990s, holds that AIM helped plant the seed that led to the creation of Native electronic media. In interviews with the author of this entry, he also cites the 1934 Native American Restoration Act as providing the initial interest among Native Americans in the potential use of radio to achieve a voice of their own. The Economic Opportunity Act of 1965 also helped set the stage for the creation of tribally licensed radio stations, since it permitted Native American organizations and tribes to work independent of the Bureau of Indian Affairs (BIA) while developing social, economic, and educational agendas.

The construction of the first Native-owned radio stations began in 1971 at the height of the Native American rights movement and today number over two dozen. With but one exception (CKON on the border of Canada and New York state) all Native American broadcast facilities operate under the auspices of the Federal Communications Commission. Tribal governments or local school boards typically are the principal licensees. KILI-FM in Porcupine, South Dakota, is, however, licensed to a corporation.

Patterns of Operation

Support for Native-operated stations comes from a variety of sources, chief among them the Corporation for Public Broadcasting and the National Telecommunications and Information Administration (NTIA). While the former was instrumental in launching the now defunct Indigenous Communications Association, NTIA breathed life into several Native broadcast projects through its Public Telecommunications Program. Of the 28 (figure varies due to frequent start-ups and occasional shut-downs) Native stations in the United States, only four are commercially licensed. As such they have little to do with the funding sources so vital to the existence of their broadcast brethren. The public broadcasting initiatives of the 1970s and 1980s (which made funds widely available for Native radio projects), coupled with the lack of a sufficient economic base for advertiser-supported stations in most Indigenous communities, has resulted in a predominantly noncommercial medium.

The majority of Native stations broadcast west of the Mississippi, while Alaska and New Mexico boast the largest number of Indigenous outlets. All but three Native stations have ethnically diverse or mixed staffs, while KDLG, KABR, and KCIE limit their hiring to Native Americans exclusively. However, at this writing, only four have staffs that are less than 50 percent Native American. Most Native stations serve rural audiences with a mixture of diverse and often eclectic programming. Music is the primary programming ingredient with a host of genres, among them country, rock, jazz, and rap. Most Native stations air traditional tribal music and language programs and receive additional programming in English and Native American from American Indian Radio on Satellite (AIROS).

The future of Native American radio appears at once both bright and uncertain at the start of the new millennium. Although the continuation of government funding remains in question, the Indigenous broadcasting community is building (and plans to build) dozens of additional radio stations on reservations throughout the country, especially in the midwest and Alaska.

MICHAEL C. KEITH

See also Australian Aboriginal Radio; Canadian Radio and Multiculturalism; Stereotypes on Radio

Further Reading
Eiselein, Eddie Bill, *Indian Issues*, Browning, Montana: Spirit Talk Press, 1993
Grame, Theodore, *Ethnic Broadcasting in the United States*, Washington, D.C.: American Folklife Center, 1980
Keith, Michael C., *Signals in the Air: Native Broadcasting in America*, Westport, Connecticut: Praeger, 1995
Murphy, James E., "Alaska Native Communications Media: An Over-View," *Gazette* (Fairbanks, Alaska, 1982)
Smith, Bruce L., and M.L. Cornette, "*Eyapaha* for Today: American Indian Radio in the Dakotas," *Journal of Radio Studies* (Summer 1998)

Netherlands

Birthplace of Broadcasting in Europe

Radio in the Netherlands began in November 1919 when an engineer named Idzerda broadcast from the Hague laboratory of his company, the Netherlands Radio Industry. He paid for the broadcast himself and with funds he raised through on-air appeals to listeners throughout Western Europe. For several years thereafter, new broadcast services proliferated, causing the minister of public works to require joint franchise applications from current and would-be broadcasters. Idzerda was almost bankrupt, and the only company to obtain government permission to lease airtime to organizations was the Netherlands Transmitter Industry. The first to do so was the Netherlands Christian Radio Association in 1924. By 1928 there were four others: Workers Radio Amateurs Association (1925), Catholic Radio Broadcasting Foundation (1925), Liberal Protestant Radio Broadcasting Association (1926), and General Radio Broadcasting Association (1928). These five services (networks) had to share time on two transmitters.

The government's position was not to operate broadcast services but to require the diverse organizations that did operate such services to air a broad range of programming for all Dutch citizens. Given the biases of the five organizations, as indicated by their names, it is understandable that a great deal of bickering and politicking went on about how each should meet its government mandate. Each organization was responsible for funding its own operations. Most did this with listener donations and funding from parent organizations (e.g., the Catholic Radio Broadcasting Foundation received support from the Catholic Church). There were no license fees, a common funding practice in other European countries. Although there was a small amount of advertising early on, all on-air advertising ceased by 1935.

The influence of religion on Dutch society is significant, even though almost half of the Dutch population is not affiliated with any organized religion. The principal religions are Roman Catholicism, Liberal Protestantism, and Calvinism, although there are many others. The central role of these three dominant religions, along with the influence of political parties, is referred to as the "pillar" concept, with each organization serving as a pillar that supports the nation's structure.

Nazi Germany occupied the Netherlands from 1940 to 1945, during which time it controlled all broadcasting facilities and instituted a license fee, which the postwar government retained. In 1947 the five prewar organizations agreed to pool resources and form the Netherlands Radio Union (NRU). Each organization retained its autonomy but worked cooperatively with the others under the jurisdiction of the minister of education, arts, and sciences.

Experiments with television in the Netherlands began prior to World War II, ceased during the Nazi occupation, and began again in 1948. The NRU organizations agreed to finance television from their radio revenues and from regular television service in 1951. License fees for television-set ownership were established, and television grew, creating changes in radio similar to those occurring in the United States.

Dutch society became very liberal in the 1960s, and popular music (e.g., the Beatles, the Who) spawned a proliferation of illegal (unlicensed) pirate radio stations that aired primarily rock and roll music. These stations became so rampant that the Dutch military was called in to take them off the air. All this illegal broadcasting resulted in the Dutch Parliament's giving consideration to a new form of broadcasting system that might eliminate the pillar organizations. The Broadcasting Act of 1967 retained the pillars but allowed additional groups to apply for airtime. It also created the Netherlands Broadcasting Foundation, which combined the functions of the old NRU and the Netherlands Television Foundation, the overseer for Dutch television.

Two more broadcasting organizations were created in the early 1970s: the Evangelical Organization (EO) and the Veronica Omroep Organisatie (VOO). The EO was similar to the traditional pillars, whereas VOO grew out of an outlawed pirate radio station.

Another law, the Media Act of 1987, provided for independent local radio stations to transmit at low power via cable systems and set up a regional radio system. The government maintained its involvement in regulating broadcasting. Since then, however, it has been reluctant to get involved in program matters, beyond occasional warnings.

Today, radio at the national level is facing a loss of listeners to the popular formats of local, regional, and some foreign stations delivered via satellite such as U.K.-based Sky Radio. At the national level, there are now 5 public service radio channels (Hilversum 1–5), 10 domestic commercial channels that play mostly music, and 6 commercial imported services. The regional stations include 13 public and 6 commercial radio services. There are also 356 local radio stations.

Programming on the national public service radio channels includes news and music, but each channel has a particular focus. Hilversum 1 is family oriented in addition to carrying a lot of sports. Hilversum 2 provides light entertainment and discussion shows. Hilversum 3 airs primarily popular music and commands the largest audience share (up to 15 percent). Hilversum 4 broadcasts primarily classical music and is similar to the Third Programme services in England and Germany. Hilversum 5 provides programming in several languages for cul-

tural and ethnic minorities (e.g., Turkish, Arabic, Chinese, etc.). All five are disparaged for their formality by younger listeners, most of whom prefer the commercial channels.

Most commercial competition at the national level comes from foreign pop music satellite channels (e.g., Sky Radio, Kink-FM, Radio 10 Gold) and domestic music satellite channels (e.g., Jazzradio, Radio 21, Concertradio). Similar competition occurs between public service and commercial stations at the regional level. Most local stations operate at low power with volunteer staffs and limited revenue. Many provide information and music programming for narrowly targeted local audiences.

New developments in technology and politics, including the European Union, have steered the Dutch toward a dual system combining its well-established public service radio system with a more recent but growing commercial business. The public service has a bright future, because both politicians and pillars are cooperating in cautiously adopting new technology. Thus, radio in the Netherlands, which has provided an unusual diversity of original programming for such a small country, is likely to continue to do so.

ROBERT G. FINNEY

Further Reading

Browne, Donald R., "The Netherlands," in *Electronic Media and Industrialized Nations: A Comparative Study*, by Browne, Ames: Iowa State University Press, 1999

Emery, Walter B., "The Netherlands: Pluralism with Freedom," in *National and International Systems of Broadcasting: Their History, Operation and Control*, East Lansing: Michigan State University Press, 1969

Gross, Lynne Schafer, editor, *The International World of Electronic Media*, New York and London: McGraw-Hill, 1995

Haak, Kees van der, and Joanna Spicer, *Broadcasting in the Netherlands*, London and Boston: Routledge and Kegan Paul, 1977

Hiemstra, John Lucas, *Worldviews on the Air: The Struggle to Create a Pluralist Broadcasting System in The Netherlands*, Lanham, Maryland: University Press of America, 1997

Hilliard, Robert L., and Michael C. Keith, *Global Broadcasting Systems*, Boston and Oxford: Focal Press, 1996

Swipstra, N.Ij., "The Birth of Broadcasting," *EBU Review* 114B (March 1969)

Network Monopoly Probe

Landmark Policy Decision

Under pressure from many political figures and a fledgling network having trouble competing, the Federal Communications Commission (FCC) launched an investigation of potential radio network monopoly practices early in 1938. The probe lasted until 1941 and became the subject of a landmark Supreme Court case.

Origins

The radio industry had already been the subject of one investigation into possible monopoly practices. On the order of the House of Representatives, in 1923 the Federal Trade Commission (FTC) had examined the radio manufacturing industry's patent sharing and marketing agreements and determined they amounted to an illegal cartel.

The national radio broadcasting networks began operation as the National Broadcasting Company (NBC) in 1926 and the Columbia Broadcasting System (CBS) in 1927; the Mutual Broadcasting System (MBS) had initiated its very different approach in 1934. But very quickly it became apparent the newest network was having a hard time breaking into major radio markets already served by affiliates of the existing networks. Making competition harder, NBC in the 1930s operated a "Red" and "Blue" network that gave it two affiliate stations in larger markets. Between the two of them, sometimes in "competitive cooperation" with a CBS affiliate, these powerful network-affiliated stations could lower prices to the point that a potential newcomer could not break even. By the late 1930s the pattern of network dominance was hard to miss.

Of the 49 most powerful stations (the 50,000-watt clear channel outlets) in the United States, 21 were affiliated with NBC Red, 20 were affiliated with CBS, 6 were affiliated with NBC Blue, and only 2 had signed with Mutual. On the other hand, of the least desirable (lowest-powered) stations, Mutual led the pack with 111 affiliates, followed by 44 on NBC Blue, 34 connected to NBC Red, and only 18 affiliated with CBS. Of the nearly 200 Mutual stations in 1942, 26 in important cities had contracts with another network which had first call on their best hours. Examined another way, NBC and CBS controlled more than 85 percent of total broadcasting nighttime wattage.

To network critics the problem went even deeper. Networks totally dominated their affiliates. Contracts favored the networks at every turn because it was obvious that network affiliation was vital to true financial success in the radio business. Networks were tied to their stations for only a year while stations were often contracted for three to five years. Networks

could "option" chunks of affiliate time for network programs. Networks dictated many operational aspects of their supposedly independently owned affiliate stations.

CBS and NBC made a major blunder as the FCC proceedings got under way. The baseball World Series had been carried on all four networks from 1935 to 1938. In 1939 a new sponsor (Gillette) paid the baseball leagues for the rights to broadcast the series exclusively over Mutual. To better distribute the series nationwide, Mutual entered into temporary affiliation agreements with several NBC and CBS affiliates in communities with no regular MBS affiliate in order to permit the stations to broadcast the games. NBC and CBS informed their wayward affiliates that they would not be released from their contractual obligation to run their regular network programming while the games were being played even though in some cases the requested program preemptions amounted to little more than an hour of the daytime schedule. Although a few stations defied their networks and carried the series games anyway, most capitulated. The same drama played out the following year, when Mutual again got exclusive rights to broadcast the series and signed up a large temporary network, only to lose much of it under threats from NBC and CBS.

FCC Decision

After extensive 1938–39 hearings and an initial staff report in 1940, the FCC issued its final chain (network) broadcasting report in May 1941, a 153-page analysis that reviewed past network development and practices. The commission found that NBC and CBS were engaged in a number of anti-competitive practices, and it issued new rules to curtail these practices. The report was one thing; its conclusions and proposed order for rule changes was quite another.

In its most controversial finding, the commission concluded (in the seventh of its eight rule changes) that NBC would have to sell one of its two networks. As the FCC had no direct regulatory role over networks, the wording of the proposed rule was clever: "No license shall be granted to a standard broadcast [AM] station affiliated with a network organization which maintains more than one network." As the FCC licensed all broadcast stations, network structure could be controlled in this indirect fashion. The order made clear the rule would not be applied if the networks were not operated simultaneously or if there was no overlap in the areas served by the network (such as the many operating regional networks).

Using the same approach, the commission further decreed that stations could not be forced to sign exclusive network contracts that forbade them from preempting network programming. Licensees, the commission continued, had the absolute right to accept or reject network programs on a show-by-show basis. Contracts could only bind networks and stations for the same period of time. The effect of the rule changes was to increase the power of the licensee over what it broadcast. Given that the FCC held licensees responsible for what they put over the air, this made eminent sense to the commissioners.

Aftermath

Infuriated and concerned, however, both NBC and CBS mounted a strong attack on the chain broadcasting order. Amidst considerable publicity and press releases, they sued the FCC while also persuading sympathetic members of Congress to investigate the agency. In the end both the commission and its new network regulations emerged largely intact.

The networks' lawsuit was eventually (January 1942) dismissed by the Federal District Court for the Southern District of New York, the judge arguing that the court had no jurisdiction. At nearly the same time, however, the U.S. Justice Department brought an antitrust suit against the networks, using the FCC report and data as support. In June 1942 the Supreme Court agreed to review the FCC rules. On 10 May 1943, by a vote of 5 to 2, the court held in favor of the commission, concluding that the rules in no way violated the First Amendment rights of the networks. The court noted the World Series fiasco, commenting that "restraints having this effect are to be condemned as contrary to the public interest irrespective of whether it be assumed that Mutual programs are of equal, superior, or inferior quality." Following the decision, NBC sold its Blue network in 1943, which in 1945 was renamed the American Broadcasting Company (ABC).

The FCC did have to suffer through months of intense congressional scrutiny, in part for the network rules, but also for congressional dislike of activist FCC chairman James Lawrence Fly. The U.S. Senate held hearings on the network rules before which both the CBS and NBC leadership testified. A bit later Representative Eugene E. Cox (Democrat-Georgia) undertook an 18-month investigation of all aspects of the FCC that led to a number of published hearings but little real change. The pressure of all these investigations on the commission, however, clearly took its toll on the personnel and on other regulatory activities.

The chain broadcasting proceeding was only the first of three FCC probes of the networks, although the later investigations (1955–57 and 1978–81) focused almost entirely on television. The 1957 report did include one chapter reviewing radio networks, but noted their decline in the face of television expansion, and thus proposed no further action. Some FCC rules limiting television networks continued for decades, but most were abandoned by the 1990s. The commission had qui-

etly dropped virtually all of its radio chain broadcasting rules decades earlier. The decline of radio networks had made them unnecessary.

CHRISTOPHER H. STERLING

See also Columbia Broadcasting System; Federal Communications Commission; Mutual Broadcasting System; National Broadcasting Company; United States Congress and Radio; United States Supreme Court and Radio

Further Reading

Bergreen, Laurence, *Look Now, Pay Later: The Rise of Network Broadcasting*, Garden City, New York: Doubleday, 1980

Columbia Broadcasting System, *What the New Radio Rules Mean*, New York: CBS, 1941

Federal Communications Commission, *Report on Chain Broadcasting*, Washington, D.C.: Government Printing Office, 1941; reprint, New York: Arno Press, 1974

Federal Trade Commission, *Report of the Federal Trade Commission on the Radio Industry*, Washington, D.C.: Government Printing Office, 1924

National Broadcasting Company Inc. v United States 319 US 190 (10 May 1943)

"Nets Prepare to Operate Under New Rules," *Broadcasting* (17 May 1943)

"The Radio Industry," in *Network Broadcasting: Report of the Network Study Staff*, U.S. House of Representatives, 85th Cong., 2nd Sess., House Report 1297 (27 January 1958)

Robinson, Thomas Porter, *Radio Networks and the Federal Government*, New York: Columbia University Press, 1943; reprint, New York: Arno Press, 1979

Sarnoff, David, *Principles and Practices of Network Radio Broadcasting*, New York: RCA Institutes Technical Press, 1939

Statement by Niles Trammell, President, National Broadcasting Company, Before Senate Interstate Commerce Committee, June 17-18, 1941, New York: NBC, 1941

U.S. House of Representatives, Select Committee to Investigate the Federal Communications Commission, *Study and Investigation of the Federal Communications Commission: Hearings*, 78th Cong., 1st and 2nd Sess., July 1943–December 1944

U.S. Senate Committee on Interstate Commerce, *To Authorize a Study of the Radio Rules and Regulations of Federal Communications Commission: Hearings*. 77th Cong., 1st Sess., June 1941

Why We Need A New Radio Law: Statement by William S. Paley, President of the Columbia Broadcasting System, Delivered Before the United States Senate Committee on Interstate Commerce, June 16, 1941, New York: CBS, 1941

New Zealand

An early adopter of radio technology, New Zealand saw considerable variation in its radio system over the years, thanks to both political changes and social pressure. For decades the system was dominated by a state-controlled network of stations.

Origins

New Zealand stations began transmitting in the early 1920s, and by 1925 there was at least one service in all the major population centers. In 1926 the state began a process that would lead to politics and politicians dominating radio for more than 60 years. That year, the government established the Radio Broadcasting Company (RBC) to provide a national broadcasting service. Its revenue came from a licensing fee paid annually by every owner of a radio receiver. Existing stations not absorbed by the new company were permitted to continue broadcasting, but with heavy restrictions. They became known as "B" stations, in contrast to the RBC's "A" stations.

During these early years, in deference to newspaper proprietors, advertising was prohibited on radio. The state not only controlled the allocation of transmission frequencies but also licensed the right to receive. There was also an informal set of conditions in place based on broadcasters' knowledge that the government frowned upon any form of vulgarity, controversial political or social topics, and direct or indirect criticism of the state. Significant visitors to New Zealand in the early days of broadcasting, including philosopher Krishnamurti and the Canadian politician Major Douglas, were prohibited from broadcasting.

However, the peculiar shape of radio broadcasting in New Zealand was forged in the 1930s. In 1932 the RBC was replaced by a direct government agency, the New Zealand Broadcasting Board. The board's stations were conservative, and many listeners preferred the more lively and still independent B stations, although these stations were subject to strict government inspection and had no rights to generate revenue from commercial activities. Many of them were able to stay on the air only because they were subsidiary activities of radio and record retailers or were sustained by voluntary work and donations.

The first "personalities" in New Zealand radio were on the B stations. One, a Methodist minister, Colin Scrimgeour, used his religious program to attack the Depression policies of the government, which, in turn, tried to prevent his broadcasting by jamming the station's frequency.

State Control

Ironically, the election in 1935 of the socialist Labour Party to government saw the end of the B stations that had helped Labour to victory. The New Zealand Broadcasting Service (NZBS) was established as a department of state, and it immediately absorbed or closed down all remaining independent radio stations, establishing direct state control of all broadcasting.

Negative experiences with the nation's overwhelmingly conservative newspapers encouraged the government to create something unique in the world of broadcasting: a state-owned commercial radio organization. In 1937 the NZBS was split into two divisions, with the A stations remaining noncommercial and somewhat elitist and the B stations forming a popular state-run commercial radio division. The combination of advertising revenue and annual receiver license fees made broadcasting a significant income generator for the government. Broadcasting also became the country's most significant patron of the arts, publishing the country's leading journal of culture, operating the only symphony orchestra, and providing valuable employment for New Zealanders with creative ability.

Postwar Change

A change of government in 1960 saw the first of many attempts to reduce the role of government in broadcasting. Given responsibility for the development of a television service, the NZBS was changed from a state department to a public corporation, although radio remained much as it had been, with bureaucrats remaining in control. The only significant change was the development of a local radio news service, some 40 years after radio began!

However, changes in social taste were not being reflected in radio, and there was strong resistance to the popular music of the 1960s and to other "foreign" influences. This led to the launch in 1967 of a "pirate" radio ship broadcasting from international waters. The success of the pirate Radio Hauraki in capturing the younger radio audience began a process of change that eventually led to the licensing of private radio stations and a reduction of state influence and control.

These changes were not without resistance. During the 1970s there was a rash of legislative changes to broadcasting structures, as first one government and then another tried to maintain control of the airwaves. It was a period of change and tension between broadcasters and politicians. New broadcasting legislation appeared almost annually. Gradually, however, the influence of state broadcasting waned.

Over these years, the number of private radio broadcasters rose steadily, from three in 1972, to nine by 1976, and 22 by 1984.

Modern Radio

Then a new government ushered in a period of radical change. In 1988 New Zealand radio broadcasting was completely deregulated. Frequencies were auctioned, and frequency owners were given trading rights. Deregulation led to a dramatic increase in the number of radio stations, up from 69 in 1988 to 164 in 1993, to nearly 300 in 1999, serving a population of less than 3.5 million.

The government sold its commercial radio stations to a consortium of overseas broadcasters in 1994. In 2000 commercial radio in New Zealand consisted of three major ownership groups and a large number of small private operators. However, by 2002 consolidation had reduced the major groups to just two, both controlled by overseas interests. Other radio included two public radio networks, 25 stations dedicated to the indigenous Maori language, and 11 community-access radio stations wholly or partially funded by the state.

At the beginning of the century New Zealand's unique and intense relationship with radio is reflected in a number of facts, not the least of which are the large number of radio stations servicing a relatively small population (arguably the greatest number of stations per capita in the world), the time spent listening to radio (with youth time-spent-listening bucking the worldwide trend and actually increasing), and the consequent amount of revenue generated (at times rising close to 14 percent of the total national advertising expenditure).

BRIAN T. PAULING

Further Reading

Blackburn, Adrian, *The Shoestring Pirates: Radio Hauraki*, Auckland: Hodder and Stoughton, 1974

Day, Patrick, *The Radio Years: A History of Broadcasting in New Zealand*, 2 vols., Auckland: Auckland University Press, 1994

Downes, Peter, and Peter Harcourt, *Voices in the Air: Radio Broadcasting in New Zealand: A Documentary*, Wellington: Methuen, 1976

Edwards, Les, *Scrim: Radio Rebel in Retrospect*, Auckland: Hodder and Stoughton, 1971

Gregory, Robert John, *Politics and Broadcasting: Before and Beyond the NZBC*, Palmerston North, New Zealand: Dunmore Press, 1985

Hall, John Herbert, *The History of Broadcasting in New Zealand: 1920–1954*, N.p.: Broadcasting Corporation of New Zealand, 1980

Mackay, Ian, *Broadcasting in New Zealand*, Wellington: Reed, 1953

New Zealand Committee on Broadcasting, *The Broadcasting Future for New Zealand: Report of the Committee on Broadcasting*, Wellington: Shearer, 1973

Wilson, Helen, editor, *The Radio Book, 1994*, Christchurch: Christchurch Polytechnic, 1994

News

News did not become a regular feature of radio programming until the early 1930s, although some stations offered occasional news programs as early as the late 1920s. Radio news remains a fundamental albeit reduced segment in the program schedule of most radio stations today. For many stations, the genre of "news" has been redefined to include entertainment information as well as hard news. The style of writing and announcing radio news in its early years differs significantly from the writing and announcing style that is now known as broadcast journalism.

Origins (1920–35)

Radio news in the early 1920s was essentially an oral version of national newspaper news. Radio broadcasters took to reading newspaper stories on the air because newspapers were the main source of news and because many radio stations were owned by newspaper companies. In addition, some big-city stations initiated the practice of interrupting regular programming to carry election results or other breaking news events. Radio news reports were a relatively small part of the overall program content for most stations, which followed an "all things to all people" programming strategy by broadcasting a variety of programs, primarily music and variety and various forms of talk, only slowly including regularly-scheduled newscasts.

At first, there were no daily newscasts. Newspaper-owned stations provided sporadic news bulletins as teasers to increase newspaper sales. At other stations, hosts read news as a filler, often without identifying the source of information. A few major-market stations broadcast once-a-week commentaries on current news events, such as those aired in New York by H.V. Kaltenborn, an assistant editor of the *Brooklyn Eagle* newspaper. A few stations carried news of shipwrecks (early operators were required to tune marine emergency bands) or special news events. For example, in 1925 the infamous Scopes "monkey" trial in Tennessee was covered using long-distance telephone lines by WGN radio in Chicago.

With the advent of national network programming, radio newscasts slowly became a feature of the evening schedule. Gathering information primarily from press association news-wires, radio networks distributed national news to their affiliate stations through phone lines. However, regular network news did not begin until a 15-minute newscast was inaugurated by NBC's Lowell Thomas in 1930. Two years later, the Lindbergh baby kidnapping became a major network news event, for which networks often preempted their regular schedules.

By this time, however, a number of newspapers, fearing radio's growing competition, began to impose limits on radio use of their stories, as well as those supplied by the newspaper-controlled wire services, the Associated Press (AP) United Press (UP), and the International News Service (INS). In response, CBS formed its own newsgathering organization in 1933 by putting together a nationwide corps of correspondents made up primarily of freelance "stringers." Both NBC and CBS used newly founded independent news services such as Transradio to assist in gathering news during the press embargo.

Eventually realizing that radio stations would continue to find a way to gather and deliver news, newspaper owners proposed a compromise in 1933 called the Biltmore Agreement, after the New York City hotel where it was hammered out. According to the terms of the agreement, CBS was to halt its own newsgathering and both CBS and NBC were to restrict their newscasts to two 5-minute news summaries obtained from a newly created Press-Radio bureau. The news summaries were to be aired only after morning or evening newspapers had been published. And radio reporters were limited to providing background information as opposed to detailed news.

However, the Biltmore Agreement was hardly effective. Only a third of radio stations—the network affiliate stations—were bound by it. In addition, the agreement had loopholes that radio stations took advantage of by offering news "commentaries," which the agreement allowed.

Realizing the ineffectiveness of the Biltmore Agreement, two newswire services—UP and INS—broke the news embargo in 1935. Finally, in 1940, AP agreed once again to sell its news services to radio, thus effectively ending the blackout. Re-establishment of radio news wire services coupled with network and local stations' own newsgathering resources provided the necessary preconditions for placing news firmly in the broadcast program schedule.

Golden Age (1935–50)

By the late 1930s, news had become an expected function of radio and it constituted an average of more than ten percent of the radio programming. Individual stations broadcast news that varied in length and depth. Local news gained greater prominence in the average station's program schedule, though it often amounted to just the headlines. By 1938 many radio stations were subscribing to more than one news wire service, and the services were carrying information written especially for radio delivery as opposed to newspaper publication. Several news wire services allowed their news to be sponsored during radio newscasts. Network news reporting was expanded as political crises in Europe and the Pacific deepened. Yet both NBC and CBS also covered many world-wide sporting events and human interest stories in addition to the often grim news of the day.

In 1937 one of the most dramatic news reports ever broadcast was on WLS in Chicago the morning after the German airship *Hindenburg* burned at Lakehurst, New Jersey. Reporter Herb Morrison had intended to record his report on the flight of this airship for archival purposes, but the networks viewed the disaster and Morrison's memorable eyewitness account as so significant that they aired portions of it despite policies allowing only live broadcasts.

Events leading to World War II proved a catalyst for radio news because of a growing public desire for the latest information. To meet the increasing demand for news from abroad, NBC developed a European news operation in 1937, which ushered in a new kind of news reporting that included on-the-spot reports and interviews, commentaries, and actual sounds of people and events being covered "in the field." Both NBC and CBS established foreign news bureaus and developed their first live overseas news reports, which were relayed by short-wave radio to New York City and then by telephone lines to affiliate stations.

CBS expanded news coverage to a half-hour segment for the first time with its *Foreign News Roundup*, which focused on the 1938 German occupation of Austria. *Roundup* originated from key European cities including London, Paris, Rome, Berlin, and Vienna. Reporters in these cities would stand by microphones recounting and assessing events of the day. They could also hear and react to their colleagues' reports.

Roundup was anchored by Edward R. Murrow in London. Murrow and CBS are largely credited with helping radio to mature into a full-fledged news medium. One notable legacy of Murrow and his team would prove to be the development of "broadcast journalism" as a distinctive syntax of writing and reporting news—conversational and brief writing that incorporates sound from the field, or *actualities,* into the news story. Murrow's actualities often included exploding bombs and screaming sirens.

Some war correspondents were limited to recording their reports before airtime because of government restrictions. But most reporters managed to broadcast their reports live, proving over time that they could do so without breaching military secrets. CBS introduced the term "news analyst" as a replacement for the term "commentator" specifically to avoid the impression that its radio news improperly shaped public opinion.

While the BBC and other European services widely reported the expanding war after 1939, entry of the United States into the war in late 1941 dramatically increased American radio news reporting. From 1940 to 1944, scheduled network news increased by more than 50 percent. By 1944, NBC-Red was offering 1,726 hours of news annually, while CBS was a close second with 1,497 hours. Despite a postwar decline in overall news hours, news still occupied more than 12 percent of network evening airtime.

Improving technology, such as portable recorders and smaller transmitters, provided the means for such dramatic broadcasts as Edward R. Murrow's recording of a bomber's run over Germany, George Hicks' live coverage of the June 1944 D-Day landings in Normandy, and pick-ups of news from distant Pacific island battlefields. Listeners heard the war begin by radio in 1939 (or in the U.S. on an otherwise quiet Sunday in December 1941)—and heard world leaders announce the end of the war in Europe in May 1945 and in the Pacific just three months later. Millions tuned to the Japanese surrender as it was broadcast from the deck of the battleship *Missouri* in Tokyo Bay in September 1945. And radio carried the resulting celebrations in cities around the world.

Adjustment (1950–70)

Despite the growing diffusion of television into American households in the late 1940s and into the 1950s, radio networks continued providing an extensive schedule of news and commentary for years after World War II. Only after the mid-1950s did network news schedules begin to dip sharply, soon to decline to hourly summaries of top stories. News continued to be an important element of most local station schedules.

Networks attempted to redesign their radio news. Network executives decided that the five-minute news summaries supplied on the hour should now be delivered by experienced reporters with recognizable names, rather than by staff announcers. In addition, the networks tried rolling out "variety news programs" that offered a greater emphasis on feature stories. In 1955, NBC began airing *Monitor,* a mixture of news, music, interviews, dramatic sketches, and sports. *Monitor* was hosted by Frank Blair and Hugh Downs; Gene Shalit did occasional film reviews. ABC began *New Sounds,* a weekday evening series patterned after *Monitor.* In 1960, CBS began *Dimension,* a series consisting of five-minute informational inserts on the half hour. For all the network's efforts, however, their audience and network radio news continued to decline in the face of television's increasing viewership.

As radio stations increasingly programmed according to some music format by the mid-1950s, news was made a part of the schedule. Only major-market stations provided more than a news headline service.

In the 1960s, news finally became its own radio format. KFAX in San Francisco adopted the first "All News" format in 1960 with each hour containing 25 minutes of hard news, updated throughout the day. The remaining minutes were filled with sports, business news, and feature stories. But KFAX failed after four months because of a lack of advertising support. The first commercially successful all-news radio station was founded by Gordon McLendon in 1961. McLendon took a rock-and roll radio station in Tijuana, Mexico, changed its format to hard news, and targeted it at listeners in Los Angeles. News was recycled every half hour to coincide with the commuting times of drivers going into and out of Los Angeles. No reporters were used—just hard news from the newswires AP, UPI and the Los Angeles City News Service. In 1965, WINS in New York City became an all-news station and began airing the promotional advertisement that has now become standard to Westinghouse (Group W) news stations: "All news, all the time." WINS used its own reporters and focused heavily on local news, as did KYW in Philadelphia, Pennsylvania, and other stations in cities large enough to support the expensive format.

Radio News Formats

Most aspects of modern radio news vary widely among stations, including the number, scheduling, and length of newscasts, the content of stories broadcast, and their order of presentation. Each of these, in turn, may depend on market size, station format, and any news policy of the owners, especially of multiple outlets. Overall, less news is offered on radio today than was the case a decade or two ago.

While some stations still retain regular newscasts, many music and all-talk outlets focus on feature material. Contemporary Hit Radio (CHR) and Adult Contemporary (AC) stations often still provide brief newscasts, for example; others, such as Country, Easy Listening, and Album-Oriented Rock (AOR), more often run features or have eliminated news, reasoning that not every station in a multi-station market has to provide it. If stations affiliate with a network at all, it is most often to carry their brief national newscasts. Some networks are designed to serve up news to fit within specific radio formats.

Through the 1980s the typical pattern for small- and medium-market music stations was to offer five minutes of news on the hour, usually combining world, national, and local stories with a growing emphasis on the latter. World and national news is most often received as an audio feed from a network or syndicated satellite service or as text from the Associated Press, and may be recast to include a local angle.

On stations still offering news, newscasts range from a minute of headlines to three or four minutes long. Most "stories" are now limited to a sentence or two totaling 10 to 20 seconds—a 60 second story would be very unusual. Stories may contain a sound bite or sound actuality, perhaps bits of an interview. Short newscasts are often devoted to but one or two stories, especially with breaking news. While major-market AM radio stations once offered up to a half hour of news in morning or afternoon drive time, that model has all but disappeared as most stations trim or even eliminate news staffs.

The largest markets typically include an all-news AM station. These often utilize a "news wheel" to format their newscasts. This displays the length, order, and content-type of stories to be broadcast over a half hour or hour cycle, after which the wheel repeats itself. Ideally, each time the news wheel begins again, stories have been refreshed with new information or have been replaced with new stories. The news wheel is especially convenient for listeners who like to know that they can hear a specific type of information (e.g. the weather forecast) by tuning in at exactly :20 and :50 minutes past the hour. As radio news is easier to prepare than reports for TV or newspapers, radio is often quicker at getting breaking news on the air, though internet-based services can be the fastest of all.

Information Sources

Radio stations gather news from a number of sources, including the local newspaper, the telephone, and the field interview. The local newspaper is especially important to smaller stations with a limited budget and news staff. Reporters will rarely admit to using the local newspaper as a primary source of news, instead describing the newspaper as source for obtaining leads to develop news stories. However, reporters at smaller radio stations often do not have the time to gather their own news, so they end up rewriting newspaper stories for their own newscasts.

The telephone is used for conducting interviews with officials and experts—such as politicians, police officers, and cor-

oners—to acquire actualities to be edited later into sound bites. The radio reporter often initiates a phone call from the studio and then records the conversation on tape or computer. FCC regulations specify that reporters must identify themselves as such and name the station they work for and that they must indicate that the station plans to broadcast portions of the interview. All of this has to be done before the reporter begins recording the interview. The telephone is also used to receive live or pre-recorded traffic and weather reports from companies that sell these services to radio stations. *Accuweather* is widely subscribed to for weather information, while *Cellular 1* and *Shadow Traffic* are widely subscribed to for traffic information.

Hand-held cassette and minidisk recorders are used by radio reporters to gather actualities from the field. Hand-held recorders are used to record actualities and then to play them back over a telephone line to the studio.

To gather national news, radio stations use newswires, satellite feeds, and the internet. The main newswire subscribed to by both small-market and major-market radio stations is AP; what is left of the UPI agency is used by a small and dwindling number of stations. Typically only the very largest stations in the U.S. subscribe to the other three big international newswire services—Reuters from England, the French Agency Press (AFP) from France, and ITAR-Tass from Russia. Major-market radio stations normally subscribe to regional and city newswire services as well. Newswire services deliver information mainly through satellite downlinks or conventional phone lines connected to a radio station's computer.

Radio stations also use satellite dishes to receive audio news from satellite news feeds. These feeds can be re-broadcast as self-contained newscasts, or they can be used as actualities to be edited into sound bites. Satellite feeds come down at specific times determined by the satellite service. Satellite feeds are provided by the networks CBS, NPR, and CNN, as well as the news wire service AP. They are normally provided free of charge to radio stations in exchange for pre-selected advertising spots in the radio station's program schedule, which will generate revenue for the satellite service. The remaining available spots will be made available for the local stations to fill with news sponsorships. Television is also used to gather information for radio newscasts. The advent of all-news channels and mostly news channels (e.g., CNN, Fox, MSNBC, ESPN, Weather Channel) has allowed radio reporters to monitor nationally developing news stories constantly.

Increasingly, radio stations are relying on the internet to gather national and international news. Many traditional media organizations such as CNN and NBC as well as non-traditional news organizations provide websites with news and information that can be downloaded as text or audio. The internet provides a cheaper alternative to subscribing to a newswire or satellite, but the boundaries for copyright infringement and source credibility are less clear than for newswire or satellite news information.

Regulation and Deregulation of News

For many years, the FCC's licensing renewal guidelines strongly encouraged stations to provide from 6 to 8 percent of total airtime to news and public affairs. Those rules disappeared in the early 1980s, leaving stations to determine their own journalistic role—if any. As a result, in the past two decades many stations have opted out of any news programming at all. However, most small-market Top 40/Contemporary Hit Radio stations have retained news programming because of a traditional listener base that has expectations for local, community-oriented news with a practical quality, such as local events, traffic reports, and high school and college sports.

Industry consolidation in the 1990s has led to further reductions in radio news programming as part of corporate cost-cutting strategies. Multiple stations with common corporate ownership now routinely obtain news by purchasing national news feeds from independent "outsourcing" companies, such as Metro Network's *MetroSource*.

Significantly, the marketplace guideline of deregulation has led many radio stations to air a new kind of news in their program schedules. Today news has come to be defined not strictly as hard news but also as entertainment-oriented information. Medium-market and major-market radio stations have reinforced this redefinition through the news covered in syndicated talk shows they program. National hosts such as Rush Limbaugh, Don Imus, G. Gordon Liddy, Laura Schlessinger, Howard Stern, as well as many local talk-show hosts now feature political, sexual, or celebrity news in their shows. These and other talk-show hosts routinely deliver news stories and then offer their own opinionated comments, after which listeners are invited to engage in the discussion by calling, faxing, or emailing the program.

ROBERT MCKENZIE

See also All News Format; British Radio Journalism; Canadian Radio News; Commentators; Documentary Programs; Editorializing; Election Coverage; Fairness Doctrine; Fireside Chats; News Agencies; Politics and Radio; Press-Radio War; Public Affairs Programming; United States Presidency and Radio; World War II and U.S. Radio

Further Reading

Bliss, Edward Jr., *Now the News: The Story of Broadcast Journalism,* New York: Columbia University Press, 1991

Charnley, Mitchell V., *News By Radio,* New York: Macmillan, 1948

Greenfield, Thomas Allen, *Radio: A Reference Guide,* New York: Greenwood Press, 1989

Hausman, Carl, *Crafting the News for Electronic Media: Writing, Reporting and Producing,* Belmont, California: Wadsworth, 1992

Mayeux, Peter E., *Broadcast News: Writing and Reporting,* Dubuque, Iowa: Wm. C. Brown, 1991; 2nd edition, Prospect Heights, Illinois: Waveland Press, 2000

McKenzie, Robert, *How Selected Pennsylvania Radio Stations Use Technology to Gather Information for News Programs: A Field Study,* PhD. diss., Pennsylvania State University, August 1990

Sterling, Christopher H., and John M. Kittross, *Stay Tuned: A History of American Broadcasting,* 3rd edition, Mahwah, New Jersey: Lawrence Erlbaum, 2002

White, Paul W., *News on the Air,* New York: Harcourt Brace, 1947

News Agencies

For most of their history, radio stations have relied on national sources for much of their news. Other than the radio network news divisions, the prime source for national and international news has usually been one or more of the news agencies (also called news or wire services or press associations) such as the Associated Press (AP), United Press International (UPI), or Reuters. In recent years, the news agencies have provided considerable regional and local news as well. As more radio stations reduce their news staffs (or eliminate them entirely), "rip 'n' read" newscasts based entirely on news agency copy have once again become common.

Cooperative news gathering began in the United States with the formation of the Associated Press by a number of New York daily newspapers in 1848. Although reorganized several times, the AP has always been a cooperative rather than a profit-seeking venture. The United Press (UP) was begun as a profit-seeking affiliate of the Scripps newspaper chain in 1907, and the International News Service (INS) appeared as another commercial venture in 1909, controlled by the Hearst newspapers. Each of the three was based on service to newspapers, and newspaper-based board members controlled their operation. Radio's arrival and demand for service created big questions for the agencies.

Associated Press

The oldest and largest news agency had the most trouble deciding how to handle the new medium. As early as 1922, when few stations offered news, the AP warned its member newspapers not to allow use of AP news reports on their own radio stations. But in 1924 and 1928, AP did allow election returns to be broadcast. Starting in 1933, AP adopted a policy of allowing radio use of AP news stories only for events of "transcendent importance," and this continued until 1941, long after its competitors were serving broadcasters.

In 1941 AP initiated a radio wire—a news service written for use on the air, as opposed to the traditional service for newspapers designed to be read. Dubbed "Circuit 7760," it operated 24 hours a day under the direction of Oliver Gramling. Within a year AP was serving 200 (of about 750 total) stations in 120 cities, with 110 stations on its broadcast wire payroll. After the war, some 450 stations were elected to associate membership (an important status within the AP cooperative organization, as radio now had more of a voice in management decisions). By the early 1950s, AP was providing some 75,000 words every 24 hours, written for audio reading, and usually condensed and rephrased from the main newspaper service.

AP news for radio was usually provided in the shape of ready-to-use newscasts of different lengths. This led many smaller stations, lacking their own news staffs, to simply have an announcer assemble a news program from the news agency wire stories ("rip 'n' read"). As more stations developed popular music formats, many relied on this practice for their entire news operation. Now dubbed the AP Radio Network, the agency launched an audio service with actualities (sound recordings from the field) for stations to use in their own newscasts in 1974. Just five years later, the AP Broadcast Wire was said to be the longest leased telecommunication circuit in the world.

In 1980 the AP broadcast service became the first radio network in the world to use a communications satellite. Just four years later, AP owned its own satellite transponder, making it the first news organization to do so. In the meantime, AP had shifted its broadcast operations from New York to Washington, D.C. A decade later, AP was serving just over half the commercial radio stations in the nation with four focused services designed to better serve varied radio formats: AP NewsPower, AP DriveTime, AP NewsTalk, and AP Specialty Wires. To these was added AP All-News Radio in 1994, a 24-hour

service of "full packed" radio newscasts that served more than 70 stations by 2000, with another 750 taking news feeds.

United Press and International News Service

The story of UPI and radio is more complex and begins with its two commercial predecessors: the United Press and the International News Service.

The United Press provided a 1924 general election hook-up using WEAF in New York as the base station. UP's president Karl Bickel argued strongly in favor of serving radio in the 1920s and saw the new medium as an exciting development. But his newspaper-dominated board of directors prevented such a service until 1935 when he resigned owing to ill-health at age 53, leaving his successor Hugh Baillie to bring UP service to radio station subscribers. In the meantime, a number of radio stations owned by UP client newspapers had been using UP reports on the air, despite news agency policy banning such practices. In 1943, UP published a *United Press Radio News Style Book,* an indicator of the growing importance of radio to the commercial news agency. By the early 1950s, UP was providing about 70,000 words per day to its radio subscribers.

The smaller and weaker International News Service began a "radio-script" service providing radio material 40 times a week in addition to its regular print service. In the face of AP expansion and success in luring away newspaper clients, however, the weaker INS and UP agreed to merge to form UPI in 1958.

United Press International

With the merger, UPI, under Scripps control, began to provide its client radio stations with audio reports to use in their own news programs. By 1965 clients were receiving about 65 voice stories a day from the UPI radio center in Chicago. Nine years later they were also receiving 20 full newscasts a day with inputs from London and Hong Kong. In 1977 UPI was serving about 900 client stations (almost twice the number reached by the AP). UPI also moved to distribute its radio news service by satellite in the early 1980s.

But UPI was in deep financial trouble. Although intended from the start as a commercial affiliate of a for-profit newspaper company, the agency had fairly consistently lost money. By the 1970s it was rapidly losing newspaper clients to the larger and better-financed AP and began to focus more on its radio station business.

In 1982, after a two year effort, Scripps sold the company it had founded nearly three-quarters of a century earlier. The sale led to two decades of drastic decline under several successive owners and two separate declarations of bankruptcy. UPI declined from about 1,800 employees at the time of the Scripps sale to less than 200 in mid-2000 when a Unification Church affiliate took control of the remains of the Washington-based news agency.

The UPI radio network was now the central part of the now much smaller news service. It offered 24 hours of fully produced programs for use at the top of each hour plus an actuality service for stations to use in their own newscasts (called "Selectnews," it began in 1992). While UPI reached some 2,000 stations in 1994 and radio accounted for half of the agency's income three years later, UPI had to end its radio service on 19 August 1999 for lack of funds, competition from newer news sources, and a drastic drop-off in the number of client stations (to just 400). Its final words:

This is the final broadcast from UPI Radio. United Press International is getting out of the broadcast news business and has sold its contracts to Associated Press Radio. For those of us suddenly out of work, it's been fun. We feel UPI Radio has done its job well overall, even as we struggled with fewer and fewer resources. So we sign off now with smiles, memories, a few tears . . . but no regrets.

Other Services

Although most stations relied upon their network affiliation (if any), a specialized news service, or AP for world and national news, competing news sources had existed even in the early years of radio. Several entities, for example, had developed to serve radio in the wake of the brief 1930s "war" that limited availability of AP, UP, and INS news feeds. The agencies created the Press-Radio Bureau to combine service from the three in special radio reports, and it lasted until 1938. The Yankee News Service served the New England regional network's affiliates, the Continental Radio News Service based in Washington, and the Radio News Association from Los Angeles also began operation in 1934. Transradio Press Service began at the same time, largely built with former Columbia Broadcasting System (CBS) news people, aimed at serving non-network radio stations. Transradio survived beyond the 1930s (to December 1951, when it closed for lack of sufficient station clients) because stations could again obtain their news from the traditional news agencies.

London-based Reuters made its first radio agreement with the then-commercial BBC in 1922, although with provisions that no news would be broadcast before 7 P.M. in the evening, thus protecting the circulation of evening London dailies. Continuing negotiations in the mid-1920s allowed the BBC to cover current events as they were happening, and by 1929 the now government-chartered BBC received the full Reuters news wire for use in its news programs. Only in 1972 did Reuters begin its first voice news service for local stations in Britain and the United States. By the 1990s the firm had refocused on financial reporting and information and no longer served radio stations.

The expansion (and by the late 1990s, the consolidation) of the radio business contributed to a variety of other radio news services including Unistar (which carried CNN Radio), Capnews, the Business Radio Network, and the USA Radio Network. This expansion of syndicated news sources paralleled the decline of individual local station news efforts; instead of supporting local station news, these services were increasingly replacing local efforts.

CHRISTOPHER H. STERLING

See also News; Press-Radio War; Yankee Network

Further Reading

Bickel, Karl August, *New Empires: The Newspaper and the Radio,* Philadelphia, Pennsylvania: Lippincott, 1930

Bliss, Edward, Jr., *Now the News: The Story of Broadcast Journalism,* New York: Columbia University Press, 1991

Boyd-Barrett, Oliver, *The International News Agencies,* London: Constable, and Beverly Hills: Sage, 1980

Jackaway, Gwenyth L., *Media at War: Radio's Challenge to the Newspapers, 1924–1939,* Westport, Connecticut: Praeger, 1995

Moore, Herbert, et al., *"More News—After This . . . ": The Untold Story of Transradio Press,* Warrenton, Virginia: Sun Dial, 1983

Morris, Joe Alex, *Deadline Every Minute: The Story of the United Press,* Garden City, New York: Doubleday, 1957

"News Agencies and Radio Broadcasting," in *News Agencies, Their Structure and Operation,* Paris: Unesco, 1953

Nielsen. *See* A.C. Nielsen Company

Nightingale, Earl 1921–1989

U.S. Radio Commentator and Actor

With a sonorous voice characteristic of his English surname, combined with his writing and verbal styling, Earl Nightingale led a distinguished career as a radio inspirational speaker and actor. He was the voice of radio serial hero *Sky King*, and with his five-minute daily program *Our Changing World* lasting for almost 30 years, Nightingale created one of the longest-running syndicated programs in the history of radio. The innovative talk show he wrote and hosted for WGN was one of the most heavily sponsored shows in radio. Venturing beyond traditional broadcasting, Nightingale took his radio writing and speaking skills into new media, producing history's best-selling non-entertainment recording, *The Strangest Secret*. In addition, the Nightingale-Conant audio publishing and syndication corporation he co-founded pioneered motivational recordings.

Origins

Nightingale was born in March 1921 in Los Angeles, California. Encouraged by his mother, he became a good reader by the time he entered kindergarten. His passion for reading became the foundation of his writing and gave him the ideas he was later to broadcast. Seeing his family in the depth of the Depression in 1933, 12-year-old Nightingale became intensely curious about what separated the "haves" from the "have-nots." He began looking for answers in his local library. Vowing to find a way to become financially independent by the age of 35, his search for answers became the defining quest of his life and career. It also contributed to his personal library of over 6,000 books.

Nightingale joined the U.S. Marines in 1938 and was one of only 12 Marines to survive the Japanese bombing of the battleship *U.S.S. Arizona* at Pearl Harbor in 1941. While he was a Marine instructor at Jacksonville, North Carolina, in 1945, Nightingale worked part-time at a local radio station and quickly discovered his gift for broadcasting. After leaving the service, he became a broadcaster for KTAR in Phoenix, Arizona. Three years later, he was an announcer and news commentator with the Columbia Broadcasting System (CBS) in Chicago. Having been with CBS for only a year, Nightingale joined the staff of WGN in Chicago as a writer-producer in 1950. From 1950 until 1954, his radio role as the dashing radio adventurer *Sky King* was broadcast nationally.

Inspirational Radio

While portraying *Sky King*, Nightingale created and hosted a 90-minute daily talk show at WGN that soon became, in his words, "one of the most heavily-sponsored programs in the industry"—due in large measure to Nightingale's remarkable ability to sell advertisers. His guest-interview "talk" format, according to some, served as a prototype for talk show formats popular today. The success of the radio talk show that Nightingale wrote, hosted, and sold led to a television version on WGN-TV.

In 1956 the *Chicago Daily Tribune* reported that Nightingale's childhood dream had been realized:

> An intense young radio commentator will retire tomorrow at the age of 35, on a life income he estimates will be from $30,000 to $50,000 a year. He is Earl Nightingale, who heads three corporations built up out of his radio work, and who will say farewell tomorrow night to his WGN listeners who have heard him ten times a week since 1950 (Hughes, 1956).

While meeting the demands of his daily radio and television programs at WGN, Nightingale's entrepreneurial drive had enabled him to develop several sales firms, one of which was a nationally ranked life insurance agency. He also had formed his own firm, Earl Nightingale, Incorporated, through which he bought radio time from WGN. He once estimated that he had worked 12 to 14 hours a day from 1944 until 1956 to achieve his determined childhood goal of early retirement.

Nightingale had also been in demand as a public speaker while he was at WGN. One of his platform messages, "The Strangest Secret," was a compilation of key ideas from his reading about success, wealth, and achievement. On hearing Nightingale's talk, the president of the Pure Oil Company urged him to record it; during the same month he retired from WGN, Nightingale made the recording.

In 1959, Nightingale returned to work to write and record his own daily syndicated radio program, *Our Changing World*. In five years the program was syndicated to the largest number of stations in the history of broadcasting to that time. As Nightingale described his approach, "[W]e take the refined knowledge that has been promulgated by the great thinkers of our time . . . and winnow from it that which we feel is vital to the average person and then put it into language that he can easily understand." With 7,000 radio commentaries recorded, *Our Changing World* lasted for almost 30 years, making it one of the longest-running syndicated radio programs in history.

In 1960, Nightingale and Lloyd Conant formed the Nightingale-Conant Corporation around the success of *The Strangest Secret* and the syndicated *Our Changing World*. *Standard and Poor's Register of Corporations, Directors, and Execu-*

Earl Nightingale
Courtesy Nightingale-Conant Corporation

tives described the Nightingale-Conant Corporation in January 2000 as having 250 employees, having annual sales of over $30 million, and producing "motivational, educational and communication programs, cassette tapes, recordings and films, radio and television programs, graphic arts." Fellow radio commentator Paul Harvey described Nightingale as "the dean of self-development."

In 1986 Earl Nightingale was inducted into the National Association of Broadcasting Hall of Fame. This radio personality, with an extraordinary genius for touching an audience through a microphone, died in early 1989.

EDGAR B. WYCOFF

See also WGN

Earl Clifford Nightingale. Born in Los Angeles, California, 12 March 1921. Son of Albert Victor and Gladys Fae (Hamer) Nightingale; served in U.S. Marine Corps, 1938–46; broadcaster, KTAR, Phoenix, Arizona, 1946–49; announcer, CBS, Chicago, Illinois 1949–50; formed Earl Nightingale, Inc., 1950; wrote, produced, and hosted *The Earl Nightingale Show* on WGN-Chicago, 1950–56; host, *Our Changing World,* 1959–89; voice of *Sky King* in series from WGN, 1950–54; co-founded radio syndication and motivational firm Nightingale-Conant, 1960. Inducted into National Association of Broadcasters Radio Hall of Fame, 1986; received Napoleon Hill Foundation Gold Medal Award for Literary Excellence, Gold Record from Columbia Records, and Golden Gavel Award from Toastmasters International. Died in Scottsdale, Arizona, 25 March 1989.

Radio Series

1950–54	*Sky King*
1950–56	*The Earl Nightingale Show*
1959–89	*Our Changing World*

Publications

This Is Earl Nightingale, 1969
Earl Nightingale's Greatest Discovery: The Strangest Secret Revisited, 1987

Further Reading

Broadcasting: The Businessweekly of Television and Radio (21 February 1972)
Cruz, Georgina, "Nightingales Migrate to Broward," *Fort Lauderdale News and Sun-Sentinel* (29 March 1956)
Harmon, Jim, *The Great Radio Heroes,* Garden City, New York: Doubleday, 1967
Hughes, Frank, "Success at 35: Retirement at $30,000 a Year," *Chicago Daily Tribune* (29 March 1956)
"He Hit Pay Dirt by 35," *Parade Magazine* (11 January 1959)
Wycoff, Edgar Byron, "An Analysis of Earl Nightingale's Audio Cassette Counseling Programs: A Case Study in the Rhetoric of Success Motivation," Ph.D. diss., Florida State University, 1974

Non-English-Language Radio in the United States

In the United States, the radio boom of 1923 coincided roughly with the legislated end of the largest wave of international immigration in modern history. Some 20 million immigrants arrived on the shores of the United States between 1871 and 1920, some settling permanently, some returning home, and others traveling that route a number of times. The result was a proliferation of people and communities who spoke German, Polish, Spanish, Yiddish, Italian, and other languages. At the end of the 19th century, newspapers were the primary vehicle for the dissemination of information, with countless daily papers from every ethnic and political angle being published every day. As cities grew and the networks of newspaper distribution had not yet expanded, radio became a vital alternative to the printed word.

As early as 1926, foreign-language markets were being identified as potential profit centers. Despite indications by the advertising industry, major networks such as the National Broadcasting Company (NBC) and soon the Columbia Broadcasting System (CBS) were loath to incorporate foreign-language programming into their schedules. (However, for two years beginning in 1928, NBC briefly broadcast *Der Tog*, a Yiddish-language program.) Yet by 1964 more than 340 radio and television stations broadcast non-English-language programs in everything from Italian to Navajo. The majority of these stations were local, low-wattage stations without access to national networks. More recently the number of non-English broadcasts has increased exponentially with the popularization of web-based broadcasting. The development of non-English programming through alternative formats (local versus network and web versus traditional radio) is not coincidental but speaks of a particular power relationship between language and radio.

Throughout radio's history, the number of non-English stations in the United States has been quite significant, which suggests a considerable listening audience despite its traditional exclusion from market studies. As NBC and CBS rapidly grew to dominate the national networked radio dial, numerous local radio stations, generally with a broadcast power between 100 and 500 watts, began to spring up in urban areas. Almost always, these stations rented portions of their broadcast day to different community groups who wished to broadcast. Two of the most prominent examples are New York's WEVD and Chicago's WCFL. Founded in 1927, WEVD was owned by the Debs Radio Trust and broadcast programs in at least four languages, while WCFL hosted broadcasting in no fewer than 11. In 1924 WOAI in San Antonio, Texas, aired its first Spanish language broadcast, and Cleveland's WJAY initiated a weekly Polish-language program beginning in 1926.

Following the Federal Radio Commission's reorganization of the radio dial in November 1928, the majority of the stations that carried non-English-language programming found themselves relegated to the low and high frequency margins of the broadcast spectrum. Additionally, the FRC forced many of these stations to share frequencies and therefore also divide up the broadcast day. Broadcasting from the margin and on power that typically ranged from 250 to 1,000 watts, these stations cobbled together whatever broadcasting they could, usually comprised of a loose coalition of multi-lingual programs, performers, advertising agents, and sponsors. Few if any of these stations could choose to broadcast in only one language. The only significant exception to this rule was organized during the late 1930s, when New York-based station WOV organized 15 east-coast stations into the International Broadcasting Corporation which served as an Italian-only network, serving an audience of nearly 3 million listeners.

With the organization of the Federal Radio Commission in 1927 and amid the growing concern about the "decency" of radio programs, Section 29 of the Radio Act of 1927 sought to regulate U.S. airwaves by providing that "whoever utters any obscene, indecent, or profane language by means of radio communication shall be fined not more than $10,000 or imprisoned not more than two years." As it was impossible to listen to every broadcast nationwide, the FRC mandated that broadcasts be recorded if a listener had filed a complaint against that program. In the beginning, these recordings were made on glass plates (78-rpm records could not hold long enough segments, and magnetic recording tape had not yet been invented). This concern about the "decency" of language contributed to a general suspicion about non-English broadcasts and led to additional federal policing and harassment of such programs. Of course, it was also true that non-English broadcasts could elude the surveying ear of the FRC because often FRC monitors could not understand their content.

If non-English-language programs were considered a marginal segment of radio broadcasting in the United States, the incorporation of non-standard English speakers into English-language programs fueled the popular imagination. During the Depression years, the networks established themselves nationally via the appeal of ethno-comedies such as *The Goldbergs* and *Amos 'n' Andy*. These two programs, as some of the first to reach national audiences, drew significantly on cultural, linguistic, and dialectical differences for their humor. In the case of *The Goldbergs*, the common problems of language acquisition (mispronunciation, spoonerisms, malapropisms, etc.) and accent were the source of a great deal of the humor that Molly Berg wrote into the program. *Amos 'n' Andy* drew on a much older tradition of minstrelsy (and played on its racial stereotypes), but the particular challenge of putting blackface on radio turned the emphasis from appearance to dialect as the primary signifier of difference. Even though the Goldbergs were clearly on the path toward becoming ordinary Americans, whereas Amos and Andy were depicted as unassimilable, in both cases mastery of English was highlighted as the key determinant of mainstream acceptance. These programs clearly appealed to English-speaking audiences as they poked fun at members of non-traditional-English-speaking population groups.

Although culturally and linguistically marginal, non-English-language programs occupied a substantial amount of the radio dial. Statistics for non-English broadcasts during the Depression era are scant, but one source reports that nearly 200 stations out of a total of 850 broadcast non-English-language programs for some part of the day.

In a 1941 anthology entitled *Radio Research* (edited by Paul Lazarsfeld and Frank Stanton), sociologists Arnheim and Bayne published a survey of non-English-language broadcasts. They reported the presence of German, Italian, Yiddish, Polish, Lithuanian, and Spanish broadcasts. However, there were almost certainly Greek, Croatian, Russian, Hungarian, Bulgarian, Romanian, Chinese, Japanese, and Gaelic broadcasts at the time, as well. Although Arnheim and Bayne were primarily interested in the content of a typical broadcast day, their study is the first organized examination of ethnic radio in the United States, representing an early effort to include non-English-speaking audiences in radio market research.

Limitations

As soon as the United States entered World War II, the Federal Communications Commission (FCC) and the Foreign Language Division of the Office of Facts and Figures began investigations of all major East Coast stations (as well as others farther west) that broadcast foreign-language programs. Stations in New York, Philadelphia, Boston, and Chicago were targeted, and Alan Cranston, then chief of the foreign language division, recommended that certain broadcasters be "barred from the air immediately." Following the removal of a handful of German and Italian broadcasters and a general decline of foreign-language broadcasts, in March 1942 Cranston initiated new programs in German and Italian. The programs, entitled *Uncle Sam Speaks*, were designed to encourage ethnic listeners to join the war effort through volunteering or taking jobs in the defense industry.

Despite this overall reduction in U.S. foreign-language broadcasting, the World War II era also marked the emergence of substantial Spanish-language broadcasting, which has grown exponentially since that time, with about 500 stations including Spanish-language programming by 1980. In the

postwar years, broadcasters in Yiddish actively involved themselves in reuniting Jewish refugees with their families by broadcasting names of people who were looking for family members. Despite these brief highlights, the 1940s were devastating to non-English-language broadcasting, with the exception of Spanish broadcasts, which managed steady growth. Not coincidentally, the postwar years also witnessed the near-total domination of radio by the networks.

With the rise of McCarthyism in the 1950s, radio stations that previously housed foreign-language programs began dropping them from their rosters, fearing that broadcasters from Eastern Europe might use their airtime to spread communist propaganda. These station owners were responding to demographic changes, as well; first-generation groups began to give way to their English-speaking children. As language and residence patterns changed, so did cultural tastes, and programming once valued for its cultural specificity began to sound old-fashioned. However, this era should not be seen as the end of foreign-language radio, but rather as a reflection of changing immigration and settlement patterns and changes in the cultural preferences of many European immigrants. Thus, as European-language broadcasts decreased, a sizable immigration from Asia (most significantly from the Philippines, India, and Korea) gave birth to new broadcast options. And Spanish-language broadcasting continued its growth.

Since the late 1960s, non-English-language radio in the United States has seen a massive growth in both the overall number of stations, as well as the size and impact of audiences. Stations broadcasting primarily in Spanish, Korean, and Chinese have multiplied in conjunction with the growth of immigrant populations in primarily urban areas. What distinguishes the growth of non-English-language radio programming in the second half of the century from that of the first half is the development of single-language stations that are able to compete in larger metropolitan markets. Whereas network interests choked off the development of single-language radio stations during radio's golden age, the virtual dominance of radio by local interests has opened the door for radio stations that target a particular ethno-linguistic population in a particular area.

Online Radio

Recently, with the popularity of the internet and the increasing availability of web-based broadcasts, non-English "radio" broadcasts are flourishing. For example, www.live-radio.net contains a listing of online broadcasts from radio stations all over the globe in virtually every language imaginable. The two primary interfaces from accessing online media also include simple ways of locating and accessing online broadcasts of all kinds. No longer restricted by the narrow spectrum of radio frequencies, broadcasters can reach audiences of size and scope never before imaginable. At the same time, audiences can tune in to a wider variety of programs originating from more locations, and broadcasting in more languages than has ever before been possible.

With the spread of online broadcast technology and an FCC ruling in 2000 to create a class of low-wattage stations, the future of non-English-language broadcasting is bright, if not in traditional broadcasting. Insofar as non-English-language programs have long been on the margin of mainstream broadcasting, they have also often been in the vanguard of broadcast practices, conventions, and styles. Thus the sheer number of non-English web-based broadcasts should come as no surprise. Their proliferation indicates that the future of radio is wide open, a form of expression that cannot be limited by traditional broadcast practices or geographical location. It also heralds a return to the origins of non-English-language broadcasting in the United States, which were rooted in the needs and preferences of immigrants from other countries.

ARI KELMAN

See also Canadian Radio and Multiculturalism; Hispanic Radio; Internet Radio; Jewish Radio; Native American Radio; Stereotypes on Radio; WCFL; WEVD

Further Reading

Arnheim, R., and M. Bayme, "Foreign Language Broadcasts over Local American Stations," in *Radio Research,* edited by Paul Felix Lazarsfeld and Fred Stanton, New York: Duell, Sloan, and Pearce, 1941; reprint, New York: Arno Press, 1971

Grame, Theodore C., *Ethnic Broadcasting in the United States,* Washington, D.C.: American Folklife Center, Library of Congress, 1980

Gutiérrez, Felix F., and Jorge Reina Schement, *Spanish Language Radio in the Southwestern United States,* Austin: Center for Mexican American Studies, University of Texas, 1979

Hilmes, Michele, *Radio Voices: American Broadcasting, 1922–1952,* Minneapolis: University of Minnesota Press, 1997

Horton, Gerd, "Unity on the Air? Fifth Columnists and Foreign Language Broadcasting in the United States during World War II," *Ethnic Forum* 13, no. 1 (1993)

Keith, Michael C., *Signals in the Air: Native Broadcasting in America,* Westport, Connecticut: Praeger, 1995

Klopf, Donald, and John Highlander, "Foreign Language Broadcasting in the Western States" *Western Speech* 29, no. 4 (Fall 1965)

Migala, Józef, *Polish Radio Broadcasting in the United States,* Boulder, Colorado: East European Monographs, 1987

North American Regional Broadcasting Agreement

Sharing Frequencies among the U.S., Canada, Mexico, and the Caribbean

First placed into effect early in 1941, the North American Regional Broadcasting Agreement (NARBA) treaty doled out radio channels to Canada, Cuba, Mexico, and the United States. Renewed after extensive negotiations in 1960, it remained for years the basis for cooperative regulation and interference reduction among these countries until it was replaced by bilateral agreements and treaties affecting all of the Western Hemisphere.

As the number of radio stations in North America grew, countries neighboring the United States felt increasingly squeezed out of valuable medium wave frequencies used for AM radio broadcasting. Naturally the potential for trouble was greatest along the northern and southern borders of the United States, where American stations could—and did—cause interference to outlets in other countries, and vice versa. Given the larger U.S. population and expanding radio industry, American broadcasters sought the lion's share of available frequencies, leaving little to be shared by Canada, Mexico, and Cuba.

In 1937 representatives of the four nations met in Havana and hammered out the gist of a proposed frequency-sharing treaty. The task was not easy: given the great distances covered by AM signals, the work was complex and occasionally contentious. Nevertheless, the treaty was ratified by each nation and entered force on 29 March 1941. At the time, there were about 750 broadcast stations on the air in the United States, most of which had to shift their frequency (some only slightly), primarily to clear some radio channels for expanded use in Mexico. But for the remainder of the decade, the four nations were able to license stations in accordance with NARBA, thus greatly reducing potential interference problems.

The treaty expired in March 1949 after initial attempts to renew it failed. The demise of NARBA occurred despite considerable effort and controversy. The key problem was the dramatic expansion of American broadcasting—to 2,127 stations when NARBA expired—and thus the greater (and steadily expanding) use of spectrum by the U.S. radio industry. At the same time, driven in part by understandable nationalism, governments in the neighboring countries felt they were (again) getting the short end of the frequency stick, because the number of their stations had increased as well.

Cuba was the loudest complainer, even in the late 1940s. It demanded use of more frequencies and threatened to not ratify a NARBA renewal if it did not get them. Likewise, Mexico moved to protect some of the border stations serving American audiences. Complicating matters was the addition of new negotiating players: Haiti, the Dominican Republic, and Britain (on behalf of the Bahamas and Jamaica). Still, after several rounds of engineering work and diplomatic negotiation, a draft of a second NARBA treaty was initialed in 1950. But because of continuing negotiation problems—and rising pressure from big clear channel broadcasters fearful of losing some of their coverage as well as from small daytime-only stations hoping for longer broadcast hours (both groups felt they had given up enough already)—American ratification was delayed.

Between 1953 and 1962, a second NARBA was ratified by Cuba, Canada, the Dominican Republic, and the Bahamas. In 1960 the U.S. Congress ratified it as well, placing the treaty into force despite the lack of agreement from Mexico, Jamaica, and Haiti. Bilateral agreements with Mexico in 1969–70 and again in 1986 (as well as with Canada in 1984), served to keep the lid on potential interference problems and allowed many American daytime-only stations operating on Mexican or Canadian clear channels to begin operations before local sunrise and sometimes to extend operating hours into the evening with greater power. These agreements remain in force as long as the three nations agree.

Politics, always potent in international agreements, became central in dealing with the island nation of Cuba. By the late 1960s, the Castro regime in Cuba was informally ignoring the 1960 NARBA treaty. In 1981 Cuba formally abrogated the agreement and began to build stations that went well beyond the agreement in terms of power and frequencies used. When the United States began propaganda broadcasts into Cuba over Radio Martí, the Castro government retaliated by building high-power transmitters that caused considerable interference, especially with stations in the American South and Midwest. The Federal Communications Commission began to make case-by-case decisions allowing the affected stations to increase their own power—in essence recognizing exactly the kind of "radio war" the original NARBA treaty was designed to prevent.

As for the other nations in the region, the second NARBA treaty was eventually superseded by various Region II (Western Hemisphere) radio broadcasting agreements established under the auspices of the International Telecommunication Union in a series of regional radio conferences.

CHRISTOPHER H. STERLING

See also Border Radio; Canada; Cuba; Frequency Allocation; International Telecommunication Union; Licensing; Mexico; Radio Martí

Further Reading

North American Regional Broadcasting Agreement: Final Protocol to the Agreement, Resolutions, and Recommendations, Washington, D.C.: International Telecommunication Union, 1950
Rankin, Forney Anderson, Who Gets the Air? The U.S. Broadcaster in World Affairs, Washington, D.C.: National Association of Broadcasters, 1949

Nostalgia Radio

Broadcast audio programming has been collected by both institutions and interested individuals and most recently has become a battleground of interests. Central to the ability to collect such programs, of course, was the development of a means to make permanent recordings. Broadcasters from the beginning of radio needed some way to record. Initially the only means for recording was cutting a disc. Western Electric had developed the 16-inch, 33 1/3-rpm recording disc for use as the sound tracks for early 1920 "talkies." Sound-on-Film (SOF) optical tracks did not follow until later. The same medium was used in radio to record programs, usually for archiving, but sometimes for program syndication to multiple markets. Those Electrical Transcriptions (ETs) that survived were preserved by sponsors, their advertising agencies, the talent on the shows, and some broadcast engineers.

Beginnings of Programming Collecting

The Library of Congress began to collect and preserve some programming in 1949 in its role as the U.S. copyright depository. The National Archives also collected and preserved programming from governmental sources and increasingly received donated event and news materials from stations and networks. Institutional archives are as variable as the institutions preserving the available material. Funding difficulties led the UCLA Film and Television Archive to concentrate on their film collection and discontinue the development of its radio archive, which consisted of 50,000 ETs and 10,000 tapes of radio dating from 1933 to 1983 (which the Archive still retains). The Milo Ryan Phonoarchive at the University of Washington, obtained from radio station KIRO, consisted of CBS programming from 1938 to 1962. These ETs were subsequently transferred to the National Archives. Material became available as people gained access to more ETs as radio stations began disposing of their stored material and donations were made to institutions. A large source of material was recordings that had been made for Armed Forces Radio to bring radio programs to U.S. troops during World War II. Those ETs that survived and a few network and syndicated discs comprised the basis for collectors in the sixties, when radio as it had been was almost gone. From these and other sources ETs were transferred to audiotape.

Serious collecting of radio programs by individuals was the result of the introduction of home reel-to-reel tape recording decks to the consumer market around 1950. Small groups formed to exchange material, information, and sources on both the East and West coasts. A number of clubs began to trade tapes, the earliest being the Radio Collectors of America. Some of these grew into large organizations of members who gathered and traded from their shared collections, such as the North American Radio Archive (NARA) and the Society to Preserve and Encourage Radio Drama, Variety and Comedy (SPERDVAC).

In 1954 Charles Michelson developed a rebroadcast market by obtaining an umbrella agreement to license *The Shadow* to individual radio stations, long-playing record manufacturers, and producers of home-enjoyment tapes. The first aggressively marketed private dealer was J. David Goldin, a former engineer at CBS, NBC, and Mutual, who formed "Radio Yesteryear" and an album subsidiary, "Radiola," in the late 1960s. Michelson began to send "cease and desist" letters to collectors selling any of the series he had licensed.

Newsletters about radio program collecting began to circulate in the late 1960s. The most influential, which set the standard, was "Radio Dial" by the *Radio Historical Society of America* founded by Charles Ingersoll. Carrying on the tradition, the leading newsletter today is "Hello Again" by Jay Hickerson, which began publication in 1970 and tied together more than 100 of the most active collectors at that time. Today, more than 160 active collectors comprise the mass of privately collected broadcast material available, but thousands of other collectors maintain some program recordings. No one knows how many shows survive, but 150,000 or more are documented as existing in Jay Hickerson's *Ultimate History of Network Radio Programming*, which is an attempt to catalog every radio program currently circulating. The publications of *Radio's Golden Age* in 1966 and its updated revision as *The Big Broadcast 1920–1950* in 1973 by Frank Buxton and Gary Owen also increased interest in old radio programs.

Despite the interest of individual private collectors and the growth of institutional archives, the preservation of radio programming faces a crisis stemming from a combination of concerns. The most basic problem is the increasing rate of disposal and destruction of material. The way programs have been recorded—electrical transcription to tape formats—poses problems for preservationists. As transcription turntables disappear and reel-to-reel tape recorders are replaced with cassette recorders (and cassette recorders replaced with CD players), the means for playing the available material is lost or exists only in museums. The need to transfer the older formats into new formats is a time consuming and costly process. Many radio programs have been made available over the worldwide web in the downloadable MP3 format, free to anyone with a computer and an internet connection. Some collectors sell home-recorded CDs on their own websites, with as many as 50 or more shows on a single disk. There are numerous sites on the internet dealing with Old Time Radio (OTR).

Copyrighting and Collecting

Another problem is one of copyright ownership and control. As the nostalgia market for old radio programming has developed, copyright owners became more interested in protecting their copyrights. Ownership of many programs is very complex and depends upon contracts with directors, writers, performers, and rights holders of music and other materials used in the broadcasts. Private collectors who charge for duplication or sell programs are more susceptible to copyright problems than are institutions. Under certain conditions specified in the copyright law, libraries and other archives are authorized to photocopy or make other reproductions for research and teaching. However, Congress, through changes in the current copyright law, has placed most old radio programs under copyright even though they aired 75 years ago. Although sound recordings could not be copyrighted until 1972, the underlying script could be copyrighted as an "unpublished work." If producers registered copyrights and then failed to renew them, the script and the show are in the public domain.

Marketing Old Radio Programs

There are a number of people who broadcast OTR, such as Chuck Shaden in Chicago and the country's biggest seller of old-time radio programs, Carl Amari, founder of "Radio Spirits." In 1990 Amari began syndicating his own old-time radio compilation program, "When Radio Was," hosted by Stan Freberg and heard nationwide in some 300 markets. Another program is "Radio Hall of Fame," licensed through "Radio Spirits." "Radio Spirits" has been estimated to be a $14-million-a-year business, selling lavishly packaged tapes and CDs through its own catalog, bookstores, and discount outlets such as Costco. Amari purchased "Radio Yesteryear" and another rival "Adventures in Cassettes." He then sold "Radio Spirits" to Media Bay. "Radio Spirits" has threatened litigation against website operators, tape dealers, and CD distributors. It claims to have exclusive agreements with radio-show creators and their heirs. The threat of litigation has done little to slow the internet activity but website owners face the prospect of having to pay a fee for each download. A major difficulty is that Amari will not reveal the full list of programs he claims to control, calling it proprietary information.

MARVIN BENSMAN

See also Copyright; Museums and Archives of Radio; Recording and Studio Equipment

Further Reading

Bensman, Marvin, "Radio Broadcast Programming for Research and Teaching," *Journal of Radio Studies* 1, no. 1 (1992)

Dunning, John, *Tune in Yesterday: The Ultimate Encyclopedia of Old-Time Radio, 1925–1976,* Englewood Cliffs, New Jersey: Prentice-Hall, 1976; revised edition, as *On the Air: The Encyclopedia of Old-Time Radio,* New York: Oxford University Press, 1998

Godfrey, Donald, editor, *Re-Runs on File: A Directory of Broadcast Archives,* Hillsdale, New Jersey: Erlbaum, 1992

Hickerson, Jay, *The Ultimate History of Network Radio Programming and Guide to All Circulating Shows,* 2nd edition, Hamden, Connecticut: J. Hickerson, 1992

Ryan, Milo, *History of Sound: A Descriptive Listing of the KIRO-CBS Collection of Broadcasts of the World War II Years,* Seattle: University of Washington Press, 1963

Swartz, Jon D., and Robert Reinehr, *Handbook of Old-Time Radio: A Comprehensive Guide to Golden Age Radio Listening and Collecting,* Metuchen, New Jersey: Scarecrow Press, 1993